Introduction to
LITERATURE

British · American · Canadian

ROBERT LECKER

McGILL UNIVERSITY

JACK DAVID

CENTENNIAL COLLEGE

PETER O'BRIEN

HARPER & ROW, PUBLISHERS, New York

Cambridge, Philadelphia, San Francisco, Washington,
London, Mexico City, São Paulo, Singapore, Sydney

1817

Acknowledgments can be found at the back of the text on page 1049.

Sponsoring Editor: *Phillip Leininger*
Project Editor: *Ellen Meek Tweedy*
Text Design: *Mina Greenstein*
Cover Design: *Nancy Sugihara*
Cover Painting: FITZGERALD, Lionel Le Moine, Canadian (1890–1956). *At Silver Heights,* 1931. Oil on canvas board, 35.8 × 40.8 cm (14 1/8 × 15 13/16 in.), ART GALLERY OF ONTARIO, Toronto
Production Manager: *Jeanie Berke*
Production Assistant: *Brenda DeMartini*
Compositor: *ComCom Division of Haddon Craftsmen, Inc.*
Printer and Binder: R. R. Donnelly & Sons Company

Introduction to Literature: British, American, Canadian

Library of Congress Cataloging in Publication Data

Introduction to literature.

   1. English literature. 2. American literature.
3. Canadian literature. I. Lecker, Robert, 1951–
II. David, Jack, 1946–   . III. O'Brien, Peter,
1957– .
PR9194.4.I58 1987   820'.8   86-19366
ISBN 0-06-043891-6

87 88 89 90 9 8 7 6 5 4 3 2 1

61,358

Introduction to Literature

Contents

PART ONE
POETRY

PART TWO
DRAMA

PART THREE
SHORT STORIES

Preface

Introduction to Literature: British, American, Canadian has been designed for use in introductory university courses in literature. The intent of this anthology is to present a substantial amount of Canadian material together with representative British and American writing. In many international anthologies Canadian literature is little more than an appendage; in this anthology Canadian literature is integral. We have sought to present a selection of works that are most frequently used in introductory literature courses, including, at the same time, many other items we feel might be taught more often. We are grateful to the early reviewers of our manuscript for their helpful suggestions concerning our choice of this material.

The anthology has been arranged chronologically: the three sections themselves—poetry, drama, short stories—and the work within each section. This allows for a discussion of the historical development of each genre. Glosses and footnotes have been included to assist the student's understanding of words or proper names not generally found in a good dictionary. The notes for each author provide brief biographical, interpretive, and bibliographic information to further the student's interests and research.

We thank the many professors who have suggested improvements in the anthology at various points in its planning. Thanks are also due to Michael Darling, Barbara Leckie, and David Manicom for their excellent technical assistance.

ROBERT LECKER
JACK DAVID
PETER O'BRIEN

POETRY

Caedmon's Hymn

Caedmon was an uneducated Northumbrian herdsman who entered the monastery of Streaneschalch in the late seventh century, when he was already an old man. According to Bede, the eighth-century historian and scholar, Caedmon, who had always avoided invitations to sing because he was ashamed of his incompetence, was told in a dream to compose and sing a song about the glory of the creation of all things. After he awoke, Caedmon remembered the verses, which survive as "Caedmon's Hymn." The hymn, one of the oldest poems in English to have been preserved, was written in the West Saxon dialect of Old English in the common verse form of the period, distinguished by alliteration and the midline caesura. The song was probably sung with accompaniment by a harp. Many Old English religious poems have been ascribed by various sources to Caedmon, but this hymn is the only work that can be credited to him with any certainty.

Caedmon's Hymn

Nū scylun hergan hefænrīcæs Uard,
Metudæs mæcti end His mōdgidanc,
uerc Uuldurfadur, suē Hē uundra gihuæs,[1]
ēci Dryctin, ōr āstelidæ.
5 Hē ǣrist scōp ælda barnum
heben til hrōfe, hāleg Scepen.
Thā middungeard moncynnæs Uard,[2]
ēci Dryctin, æfter tīadæ
fīrum foldu, Frēa allmectig.

Now must we praise the Guardian of heaven,
The power and conception of the Lord,
And all His works, as He, eternal Lord,
Father of glory, started every wonder.

[1] lines 3–4. Literally "the works of the Father of glory, as He, eternal Lord, made the beginning of every wonder."
[2] "eternal" added in translation.

5   First He created heaven as a roof,
     The holy Maker, for the sons of men.
     Then the eternal Keeper of mankind
     Furnished the earth below, the land for men,
     Almighty God and everlasting Lord.

                                        (ca. 670)

TRANSLATION BY RICHARD HAMER

Beowulf

The epic *Beowulf* is one of the greatest poetic remnants of pre-Christian European civilization and the finest surviving poem written in Old English. The poem was probably first written down by an unknown composer in the early eighth century in the West Midlands of England. The oldest surviving manuscript dates from the tenth century. The poem is the product of migrant Germanic tribes that originated in Denmark and Sweden, and overran Britain in the sixth century. *Beowulf* was put into its present form by a Christian poet who was probably working from an older, more pagan version; the Christian touches the poet grafted onto the work do little to alter the somber and ferocious grandeur of a world fascinatingly remote from our own.

 Beowulf is the tale of a warrior society whose heroic king works to rid his ravaged country of the monster Grendel and Grendel's even more ferocious mother. The poem has an overwhelming atmosphere of doom, of societies that live precariously but defiantly in a dark, foreboding universe bordered by night. In undertaking his campaign against Grendel, Beowulf courageously pits himself against the malignant forces of fate and hopes to defeat inevitable doom with acts that will transcend his own lifetime. The poem contains earlier oral versions and is a work of considerable artistic accomplishment: it is written in vivid, ringing language that utilizes the powerful pulsing rhythm of Anglo-Saxon alliterative verse.

Beowulf

PROLOGUE

Attend!
We have heard of the thriving of the throne of Denmark,
how the folk-kings flourished in former days,
how those royal athelings° earned that glory.   princes

5 Was it not *Scyld Shefing*[1] that shook the halls,
took mead-benches, taught encroaching
foes to fear him—who, found in childhood,

---

[1] Son of Sceaf.

lacked clothing? Yet he lived and prospered,
grew in strength and stature under the heavens
10   until the clans settled in the sea-coasts neighbouring
over the whale-road all must obey him
and give tribute. That was a king!

A boy child was afterwards born to Scyld,
a young child in hall-yard, a hope for the people,
15   sent them by God; the griefs long endured
were not unknown to Him, the harshness of years
without a lord. Therefore the Life-bestowing
Wielder of Glory granted them this blessing.
Through the northern lands the name of Beow,
20   the son of Scyld, sprang widely.
For in youth an atheling should so use his virtue,
give with a free hand while in his father's house,
that in old age, when enemies gather,
established friends shall stand by him
25   and serve him gladly. It is by glorious action
that a man comes by honour in any people.

At the hour shaped for him Scyld departed,
the hero crossed into the keeping of his Lord.
They carried him out to the edge of the sea,
30   his sworn arms-fellows, as he had himself desired them
while he wielded his words, Warden of the Scyldings,[2]
beloved folk-founder; long had he ruled.

A boat with a ringed neck rode in the haven,
icy, out-eager, the atheling's vessel,
35   and there they laid out their lord and master,
dealer of wound gold, in the waist of the ship,
in majesty by the mast. A mound of treasures
from far countries was fetched aboard her,
and it is said that no boat was ever more bravely fitted out
40   with the weapons of a warrior, war accoutrement,
swords and body-armour; on his breast were set
treasures and trappings to travel with him
on his far faring into the flood's sway.

This hoard was not less great than the gifts he had had
45   from those who at the outset had adventured him
over seas, alone, a small child.

---

[2] I.e., the Danes.

High over head they hoisted and fixed
a gold *signum;*° gave him to the flood,   sign
let the seas take him, with sour hearts
50   and mourning mood. Men under heaven's
shifting skies, though skilled in counsel,
cannot say surely who unshipped that cargo.

Then for a long space there lodged in the stronghold
Beowulf the Dane, dear king of his people,
55   famed among nations—his father had taken
leave of the land—when late was born to him
the lord Healfdene, lifelong the ruler
and war-feared patriarch of the proud Scyldings.
He next fathered four children
60   that leaped into the world, this leader of armies,
Heorogar and *Hrothgar* and Halga the Good;
and Ursula, I have heard, who was Onela's queen,
knew the bed's embrace of the Battle-Scylfing.

excerpt from THE FIGHT WITH GRENDEL

Thus did the King of Glory,
to oppose this Grendel, appoint a hall-guard
—as the tale went abroad—who took on himself a special
task at the court—to cope with the monster.
670   The Geat prince placed all his trust
in his mighty strength, his Maker's favour.

He now uncased himself of his coat of mail,
unhelmed his head, handed his attendant
his embellished sword, best of weapons,
675   and bade him take care of these trappings of war.
Beowulf then made a boasting speech,
the Geat man, before mounting his bed:
'I fancy my fighting-strength, my performance in combat,
at least as greatly as Grendel does his;
680   and therefore I shall not cut short his life
with a slashing sword, too simple a matter;
he has not the art to answer me in kind,
hew at my shield, shrewd though he be
at his nasty catches. No, we'll at night play
685   without any weapons—if unweaponed he dare
to face me in fight. The Father in His wisdom

shall apportion the honours then, the All-holy Lord,
to whichever side shall seem to him fit.'

Then the hero lay down, leant his head
690 on the bolster there; about him many
brave sea-warriors bowed to their hall-rest.
Not one of them thought he would thence be departing
ever to set eyes on his own country,
the home that nourished him, or its noble people;
695 tor they had heard how many men of the Danes
death had dragged from that drinking-hall.
But God was to grant to the Geat people
the clue to war-success in the web of fate—
His help and support; so that they all did
700 overcome the foe—through the force of one
unweaponed man. The Almighty Lord
has ruled the affairs of the race of men
thus from the beginning.
                      Gliding through the shadows came
the walker in the night; the warriors slept
705 whose task was to hold the horned building,
all except one. It was well-known to men
that the demon could not drag them to the shades
without God's willing it; yet the one man kept
unblinking watch. He awaited, heart swelling
710 with anger against his foe, the ordeal of battle.
Down off the moorlands' misting fells came
Grendel stalking; God's brand was on him.
The spoiler meant to snatch away
from the high hall some of human race.
715 He came on under the clouds, clearly saw at last
the gold-hall of men, the mead-drinking place
nailed with gold plates. That was not the first visit
he had paid to the hall of Hrothgar the Dane:
he never before and never after
720 harder luck nor hall-guards found.

Walking to the hall came this warlike creature
condemned to agony. The door gave way,
toughtened with iron, at the touch of those hands.
Rage-inflamed, wreckage-bent, he ripped open
725 the jaws of the hall. Hastening on,
the foe then stepped onto the unstained floor,
angrily advanced: out of his eyes stood
an unlovely light like that of fire.
He saw then in the hall a host of young soldiers,

730   a company of kinsmen caught away in sleep,
      a whole warrior-band. In his heart he laughed then,
      horrible monster, his hopes swelling
      to a gluttonous meal. He meant to wrench
      the life from each body that lay in the place
735   before night was done. It was not to be;
      he was no longer to feast on the flesh of mankind
      after that night.
                          Narrowly the powerful
      kinsman of Hygelac kept watch how the ravager
      set to work with his sudden catches;
740   nor did the monster mean to hang back.
      As a first step he set his hands on
      a sleeping soldier, savagely tore at him,
      gnashed at his bone-joints, bolted huge gobbets,
      sucked at his veins, and had soon eaten
745   all of the dead man, even down to his
      hands and feet.
                          Forward he stepped,
      stretched out his hands to attach the warrior
      calmly at rest there, reached out for him with his
      unfriendly fingers: but the faster man
750   forestalling, sat up, sent back his arm.
      The upholder of evils at once knew
      he had not met, on middle earth's
      extremest acres, with any man
      of harder hand-grip: his heart panicked.
755   He was quit of the place no more quickly for that.

      Eager to be away, he ailed for his darkness
      and the company of devils; the dealings he had there
      were like nothing he had come across in his lifetime.
      Then Hygelac's brave kinsman called to mind
760   that evening's utterance, upright he stood,
      fastened his hold till fingers were bursting.
      The monster strained away: the man stepped closer.
      The monster's desire was for darkness between them,
      direction regardless, to get out and run
765   for his fen-bordered lair; he felt his grip's strength
      crushed by his enemy. It was an ill journey
      the rough marauder had made to Heorot.

      The crash in the banqueting-hall came to the Danes,
      the men of the guard that remained in the building,
770   with the taste of death. The deepening rage
      of the claimants to Heorot caused it to resound.

It was indeed wonderful that the wine-supper-hall
withstood the wrestling pair, that the world's palace
fell not to the ground. But it was girt firmly,
775 both inside and out, by iron braces
of skilled manufacture. Many a figured
gold-worked wine-bench, as we heard it,
started from the floor at the struggles of that pair.
The men of the Danes had not imagined that
780 any of mankind by what method soever
might undo that intricate, antlered hall,
sunder it by strength—unless it were swallowed up in
the embraces of fire.
                          Fear entered into
the listening North Danes, as that noise rose up again
785 strange and strident. It shrilled terror
to the ears that heard it through the hall's side-wall,
the grisly plaint of God's enemy,
his song of ill-success, the sobs of the damned one
bewailing his pain. He was pinioned there
790 by the man of all mankind living
in this world's estate the strongest of his hands.

Not for anything would the earls' guardian
let his deadly guest go living:
he did not count his continued existence
795 of the least use to anyone. The earls ran
to defend the person of their famous prince;
they drew their ancestral swords to bring
what aid they could to their captain, Beowulf.
They were ignorant of this, when they entered the fight,
800 boldly-intentioned battle-friends,
to hew at Grendel, hunt his life
on every side—that no sword on earth,
not the truest steel, could touch their assailant;
for by a spell he had dispossessed all
blades of their bite on him.
805   A bitter parting
from life was that day destined for him;
the eldritch spirit was sent off on his
far faring into the fiends' domain.

It was then that this monster, who, moved by spite
810 against human kind, had caused so much harm
—so feuding with God—found at last
that flesh and bone were to fail him in the end;
for Hygelac's great-hearted kinsman

had him by the hand; and hateful to each
was the breath of the other.
815   A breach in the giant
flesh-frame showed then, shoulder-muscles
sprang apart, there was a snapping of tendons,
bone-locks burst. To Beowulf the glory
of this fight was granted; Grendel's lot
820   to flee the slopes fen-ward with flagging heart,
to a den where he knew there could be no relief,
no refuge for a life at its very last stage,
whose surrender-day had dawned. The Danish hopes
in this fatal fight had found their answer.

825   He had cleansed Hcorot. He who had come from afar,
deep-minded, strong-hearted, had saved the hall
from persecution. He was pleased with his night's work,
the deed he had done. Before the Danish people
the Geat captain had made good his boast,
830   had taken away all their unhappiness,
the evil menace under which they had lived,
enduring it by dire constraint,
no slight affliction. As a signal to all
the hero hung up the hand, the arm
835   and torn-off shoulder, the entire limb,
Grendel's whole grip, below the gable of the roof.
                                        (ca. 700)

The Wanderer

The Wanderer is a poem by an unknown author. It is preserved in the Exeter Book, a famous manuscript collection of Old English poems copied in the late tenth century at Exeter Cathedral, where it remains. The poem is an elegiac lament, a common genre in Old English poetry. *The Wanderer* describes the loss of home, the alienation of an exile in a strange land that lacks the stabilizing elements of Germanic heroic societies: companions-in-arms, the mead-hall, the liege-lord, and the family. Pathetic fallacy is prominent in the poem. To the isolated roamer, the world of nature is cold and barren, a reflection of the wanderer's inner state. The poem's somewhat tangled structure describes the thoughts of the wanderer as he searches for a new home. In the end, his predicament is made universal. He speaks of the ultimate homelessness of mortal beings while on earth and implies that life is a form of exile from a permanent, truly fulfilling home in God. As the poem closes, the speaker resolves to find comfort in a stoicism apart from the councils of men and to find comfort in heaven.

The Wanderer

'Often the solitary man enjoys
The grace and mercy of the Lord, though he
Careworn has long been forced to stir by hand
The ice-cold sea on many waterways,
5   Travel the exile's path; fate is relentless.'
So spoke a wanderer who called to mind
Hardships and cruel wars and deaths of lords.
Frequently have I had to mourn alone
My cares each morning; now no living man
10   Exists to whom I dare reveal my heart
Openly; and I know it for a truth
That in a man it is a noble virtue
To hide his thoughts, lock up his private feelings,
However he may feel. A weary heart
15   Cannot oppose inexorable fate,
And anxious thoughts can bring no remedy.
And so those jealous of their reputation
Often bind fast their sadness in their breasts.
So I, careworn, deprived of fatherland,

20 Far from my noble kin, have often had
   To tie in fetters my own troubled spirit,
   Since long ago I wrapped my lord's remains
   In darkness of the earth, and sadly thence
   Journeyed by winter over icy waves,
25 And suffering sought the hall of a new patron,
   If I in any land might find one willing
   To show me recognition in his mead-hall,
   Comfort my loneliness, tempt me with pleasures.
   He knows who has experienced it how bitter
30 Is sorrow as a comrade to the man
   Who lacks dear human friends; fair twisted gold
   Is not for him, but rather paths of exile,
   Coldness of heart for the gay countryside.
   He calls to mind receiving gifts of treasure
35 And former hall-retainers, and remembers
   How in his younger years his lordly patron
   Was wont to entertain him at the feast.
   Now all that joy has gone. He understands
   Who long must do without the kind advice
40 Of his beloved lord, while sleep and sorrow
   Together often bind him, sad and lonely,
   How in his mind it seems that he embraces
   And kisses his liege lord, and on his knee
   Lays hand and head, as when he formerly
45 Received as a retainer in the hall
   Gifts from the throne; but then the joyless man
   Wakes up and sees instead the yellow waves,
   The sea-birds bathing, stretching out their wings,
   While snow and hail and frost fall all together.
50 The heart's wounds seem by that yet heavier,
   Grief for the dear one gone: care is renewed,
   When memories of kinsmen fill the mind,
   He greets them gladly, contemplates them keenly,
   But his old friends swim frequently away;
55 The floating spirits bring him all too few
   Of the old well-known songs; care is renewed
   For him who must continually send
   His weary spirit over icy waves.
   Therefore I see no reason in the world
60 Why my heart grows not dark, when I consider
   The lives of warriors, how they suddenly
   Have left their hall, the bold and noble thanes,
   Just as this earth and everything thereon
   Declines and weakens each and every day.
65 Certainly no man may be wise before

He's lived his share of winters in the world.
A wise man must be patient, not too hasty
In speech, or passionate, impetuous
Or timid as a fighter, nor too anxious
70 Or carefree or too covetous of wealth;
Nor ever must he be too quick to boast
Before he's gained experience of himself.
A man should wait, before he makes a vow,
Until in pride he truly can assess
75 How, when a crisis comes, he will re-act.
The wise must know how awesome it will be
When all the wealth of earth stands desolate,
As now in various parts throughout the world
Stand wind-blown walls, frost-covered, ruined buildings.
80 The wine-halls crumble; monarchs lifeless lie,
Deprived of pleasures, all the doughty troop
Dead by the wall; some battle carried off,
Took from this world; one the dire bird removed
Over the ocean deep; one the grey wolf
85 Consigned to death; and one a tear-stained hero
Concealed from daylight in an earthy cave.
Just so in days long past mankind's Creator
Destroyed this earth, till lacking the gay sounds
Of citizens the ancient works of giants
90 Stood desolate. He who has wisely thought
And carefully considered this creation
And this dark life, experienced in spirit
Has often pondered many massacres
In far off ages, and might say these words:
95 'Where is the horse now, where the hero gone?
Where is the bounteous lord, and where the benches
For feasting? Where are all the joys of hall?
Alas for the bright cup, the armoured warrior,
The glory of the prince. That time is over,
100 Passed into night as it had never been.
Stands now memorial to that dear band
The splendid lofty wall, adorned with shapes
Of serpents; but the strong blood-greedy spear
And mighty destiny removed the heroes,
105 And storms now strike against these stony slopes.
The falling tempest binds in winter's vice
The earth, and darkness comes with shades of night,
And from the north fierce hail is felt to fall
In malice against men. And all is hardship
110 On earth, the immutable decree of fate
Alters the world which lies beneath the heavens.

Here property and friendship pass away,
Here man himself and kinsmen pass away,
And all this earthly structure comes to nought.'
115 Thus spoke the thoughtful sage, he sat apart.
Blessed is he who keeps his faith; a man
Must never be too eager to reveal
His cares, unless he knows already how
To bring about a cure by his own zeal.
120 Well shall it be for him who looks for grace
And comfort from our father in the heavens,
Where is ordained all our security.

(ca. 900)

Geoffrey Chaucer

(ca. 1 3 4 0 – 1 4 0 0)

One of the greatest figures in English literature, Geoffrey Chaucer was born at a time when the middle class was first rising into prominence. Chaucer's social position (he was the son of a wine merchant) gave him acquaintance with all classes of English society and contributed to his ability to portray "God's plenty" (as Dryden described Chaucer's characters) with such sympathetic understanding. Chaucer spent most of his life in the service of the crown, working in close association with the powerful John of Gaunt, son of Edward III. His wife, Philippa, was a member of the household of the Queen. Chaucer undertook diplomatic missions for the courts to Italy, Flanders, and France, journeys where he learned about the work of Dante, Petrarch, and Boccaccio. Chaucer also served as controller of customs, justice of the peace, and knight of the shire. He was the first poet to be buried in Westminster Abbey.

Despite his many public roles, Chaucer found time to produce a large body of work that established him as the first great English poet. At a time when French was still considered the language of polite society in England, Chaucer's genius played a significant part in establishing English as a literary language. His early work, including the beautiful *The Book of the Duchess* (1369), shows the French influence most strongly, especially in its use of the French octosyllabic couplet. After a diplomatic journey to Italy in 1372, Chaucer began an "Italian" period, where he used the seven-line stanza and the heroic couplet. During this period he produced two shorter poems, "The House of Fame" and "The Parliament of Fowls," and his masterpiece *Troilus and Criseyde,* a complex novel in verse that tells a love story by turns romantic and ironic. The capstone of Chaucer's career was *The Canterbury Tales,* an unfinished work of massive design that ranges from the pious to the bawdy, from the peasantry to the nobility. The poem's prologue is a superb portrait in miniature of medieval society.

Chaucer also wrote "The Legend of Good Women," some short lyrics, and a prose piece called "Treatise on the Astrolabe." He also translated Boethius, a sixth-century Latin philosopher whose influence can be seen in Chaucer's long allegorical poem, *The Romaunt of the Rose.*

GEOFFREY CHAUCER

The Canterbury Tales

from GENERAL PROLOGUE

Whan that Aprill with his shoures soote°	sweet
The droghte of March hath perced to the roote,	
And bathed every veyne in swich° licour°	such / juice
Of which vertu° engendred is the flour;	power
5 Whan Zephirus° eek° with his sweete breeth	the West Wind / also
Inspired hath in every holt° and heeth°	grove / moor
The tendre croppes,° and the yonge sonne	sprouts
Hath in the Ram[1] his halve cours yronne,	
And smale foweles maken melodye,	
10 That slepen al the nyght with open ye	
(So priketh hem° nature in hir corages°);	them / hearts
Thanne longen folk to goon on pilgrimages,	
And palmeres[2] for to seken straunge strondes,°	shores
To ferne° halwes,° kowthe° in sondry londes;	distant / shrines / known
15 And specially from every shires ende	
Of Engelond to Caunterbury they wende,	
The hooly blisful martir[3] for to seke,	
That hem hath holpen° whan that they were seeke.°	helped / sick
Bilfil° that in that seson on a day,	It happened
20 In Southwerk at the Tabard[4] as I lay	
Redy to wenden on my pilgrymage	
To Caunterbury with ful devout corage,	
At nyght was come into that hostelrye	
Wel nyne and twenty in a compaignye,	
25 Of sondry folk, by aventure yfalle	
In felaweshipe, and pilgrimes were they alle,	
That toward Caunterbury wolden ryde.	
The chambres and the stables weren wyde,	
And wel we weren esed° atte beste.	accommodated

[1] Aries, the first sign of the zodiac.
[2] Pilgrims, especially those who carried a palm leaf to show they had been to the Holy Land.
[3] St. Thomas à Becket, murdered in the Canterbury Cathedral in 1170.
[4] The Tabard Inn, in Southwark, which was then a suburb of London.

30 And shortly, whan the sonne was to reste,
   So hadde I spoken with hem everichon°   every one
   That I was of hir felaweshipe anon,
   And made forward erly for to ryse,
   To take oure wey ther as I yow devyse.°   describe
     But nathelees, whil I have tyme and space,
35 Er that I ferther in this tale pace,°   pass
   Me thynketh it acordaunt to resoun°   reason
   To telle yow al the condicioun
   Of ech of hem, so as it semed me,
   And whiche they weren, and of what degree,
40 And eek in what array that they were inne;
   And at a knyght than wol I first bigynne.
     A KNYGHT ther was, and that a worthy man,
   That fro the tyme that he first bigan
45 To riden out, he loved chivalrie,
   Trouthe and honour, fredom and curteisie.
   Ful worthy was he in his lordes werre,°   war
   And therto hadde he riden, no man ferre,°   farther
   As wel in cristendom as in hethenesse,°   heathendom
50 And evere honoured for his worthynesse.
   At Alisaundre[5] he was whan it was wonne.
   Ful ofte tyme he hadde the bord bigonne[6]
   Aboven alle nacions in Pruce;
   In Lettow hadde he reysed° and in Ruce,   campaigned
55 No Cristen man so ofte of his degree.
   In Gernade at the seege eek hadde he be
   Of Algezir, and riden in Belmarye.
   At Lyeys was he and at Satalye,
   Whan they were wonne; and in the Grete See[7]
60 At many a noble armee hadde he be.
   At mortal batailles hadde he been fiftene,
   And foughten for oure feith at Tramyssene
   In lystes° thries,° and ay slayn his foo.   tournament lists / thrice
   This ilke° worthy knyght hadde been also   same
65 Somtyme with the lord of Palatye[8]
   Agayn° another hethen in Turkye.   against
   And everemoore he hadde a sovereyn prys;°   reputation
   And though that he were worthy, he was wys,
   And of his port° as meeke as is a mayde.   behavior

---

[5] The place names in the following lines refer to battlegrounds where Christians and pagans
   fought.
[6] The seat of honor.
[7] The Mediterranean.
[8] The "lord of Palatye" was a pagan.

70 He nevere yet no vileynye ne sayde	
In al his lyf unto no maner wight.	
He was a verray,° parfit gentil knyght.	true
But, for to tellen yow of his array,	
His hors° were goode, but he was nat gay.	horses
75 Of fustian° he wered a gypon⁹	thick cotton cloth
Al bismotered° with his habergeon,°	stained / mail plates
For he was late ycome from his viage,°	voyage
And wente for to doon his pilgrymage.	
With hym ther was his sone, a yong SQUIER,¹⁰	
80 A lovyere and a lusty bacheler,	
With lokkes crulle° as they were leyd in presse.	curly
Of twenty yeer of age he was, I gesse.	
Of his stature he was of evene° lengthe,	moderate
And wonderly delyvere,° and of greet strengthe.	agile
85 And he hadde been somtyme in chyvachie°	cavalry expeditions
In Flaundres, in Artoys, and Pycardie,¹¹	
And born hym weel, as of so litel space,°	space of time
In hope to stonden in his lady grace.	
Embrouded° was he, as it were a meede°	embroidered / meadow
90 Al ful of fresshe floures, whyte and reede.	
Syngynge he was, or floytynge,° al the day;	whistling
He was as fressh as is the month of May	
Short was his gowne, with sleves longe and wyde.	
Wel koude he sitte on hors and faire ryde.	
95 He koude songes make and wel endite,°	recite
Juste° and eek daunce, and weel purtreye° and	joust / draw
write.	
So hoote° he lovede that by nyghtertale°	voraciously / night-time
He sleep namoore than dooth a nyghtyngale.	
Curteis he was, lowely,° and servysable,	humble
100 And carf° biforn° his fader at the table.	carve / before
A YEMAN hadde he and servantz namo°	no more
At that tyme, for hym liste° ride so,	it pleases to
And he was clad in cote and hood of grene.	
A sheef of pecok arwes,° bright and kene,	arrows
105 Under his belt he bar ful thriftily,°	sensibly
(Wel koude he dresse his takel° yemanly:¹²	gear
His arwes drouped noght with fetheres lowe)	
And in his hand he baar a myghty bowe.	
A not heed° hadde he, with a broun visage.	short haircut

⁹ A tunic, worn under armour.
¹⁰ A knight's attendant.
¹¹ Sites of skirmishes between the English and French.
¹² In yeomanlike fashion.

110   Of wodecraft wel koude he al the usage.
       Upon his arm he baar a gay bracer,[13]
       And by his syde a swerd and a bokeler,°   small shield
       And on that oother syde a gay daggere
       Harneised wel and sharp as point of spere;
115   A Cristopher[14] on his brest of silver sheene.
       An horn he bar, the bawdryk° was of grene;   belt
       A forster° was he, soothly, as I gesse.   forester
          Ther was also a Nonne, a PRIORESSE,
       That of hir smylyng was ful symple and coy;°   modest
120   Hire gretteste ooth was but by Seinte Loy;[15]
       And she was cleped° madame Eglentyne.   named
       Ful weel she soong the service dyvyne,
       Entuned° in hir nose ful semely,   intoned
       And Frenssh she spak ful faire and fetisly,°   gracefully
125   After the scole of Stratford atte Bowe,[16]
       For Frenssh of Parys was to hire unknowe.
       At mete° wel ytaught was she with alle: meals
       She leet no morsel from hir lippes falle,
       Ne wette hir fyngres in hir sauce depe;
130   Wel koude she carie a morsel and wel kepe
       That no drope ne fille° upon hire brest.   fall
       In curteisie was set ful muchel hir lest.°   pleasure
       Hir over-lippe wyped she so clene
       That in hir coppe° ther was no ferthyng° sene   cup / bit
135   Of grece,° whan she dronken hadde hir draughte.   grease
       Ful semely after hir mete she raughte.°   reached
       And sikerly° she was of greet desport,°   surely / merriment
       And ful plesaunt, and amyable of port,°   manner
       And peyned° hire to countrefete cheere   strove
140   Of court, and to been estatlich° of manere,   dignified
       And to ben holden digne° of reverence.   worthy
       But, for to speken of hire conscience,
       She was so charitable and so pitous°   merciful
       She wolde wepe, if that she saugh° a mous   saw
145   Kaught in a trappe, if it were deed or bledde.
       Of smale houndes hadde she that she fedde
       With rosted flessh, or milk and wastel-breed.°   fine white bread
       But soore wepte she if oon of hem were deed,
       Or if men smoot it with a yerde° smerte;   stick
150   And al was conscience and tendre herte.
       Ful semyly hir wympul° pynched° was,   head garment / pleated

[13] Arm guard (for archery).
[14] St. Christopher medal.
[15] St. Eloi, patron saint of goldsmiths.
[16] Stratford at Bow, a British convent school.

Hir nose tretys,° hir eyen greye as glas,   well-formed
Hir mouth ful smal, and therto softe and reed;
But sikerly she hadde a fair forheed;
155 It was almoost a spanne brood,° I trowe;°   handsbreadth wide /
For, hardily, she was nat undergrowe.   think
Ful fetys° was hir cloke, as I was war.°   well-made / aware
Of smal coral aboute hire arm she bar
A peire of bedes, gauded al with grene,
160 And theron heng a brooch of gold ful sheene,
On which ther was first write a crowned A,
And after *Amor vincit omnia.* [17]
     Another NONNE with hire hadde she,
That was hir chapeleyne,° and preestes thre.   secretary
165 A MONK ther was, a fair for the maistrie,°   extremely fine
An outridere, that lovede venerie,°   hunting
A manly man, to been an abbot able.
Ful many a deyntee° hors hadde he in stable,   superior
And whan he rood, men myghte his brydel heere
170 Gynglen° in a whistlynge wynd als cleere   jingle
And eek as loude as dooth the chapel belle.
Ther as this lord was kepere of the celle,[18]
The reule of seint Maure or of seint Beneit,[19]
By cause that it was old and somdel° streit°   somewhat / strict
175 This ilke Monk leet olde thynges pace,°   pass
And heeld after the newe world the space.
He yaf nat of that text a pulled hen,[20]
That seith that hunters ben nat hooly men,
Ne that a monk, whan he is recchelees,°   reckless
180 Is likned til a fissh that is waterlees,—
This is to seyn, a monk out of his cloystre.
But thilke text heeld he nat worth an oystre;
And I seyde his opinion was good.
What sholde he studie and make hymselven wood,° mad
185 Upon a book in cloystre alwey to poure,
Or swynken° with his handes, and laboure,   labor
As Austyn bit?[21] How shal the world be served?
Lat Austyn have his swynk to hym reserved!
Therfore he was a prikasour° aright: hunter on horseback
190 Grehoundes he hadde as swift as fowel in flight;
Of prikyng° and of huntyng for the hare   riding
Was al his lust, for no cost wolde he spare.

[17] Love conquers all.
[18] Branch of the monastery.
[19] St. Benedict, the father of western monasticism, and his disciple, St. Maurus.
[20] He did not give a plucked hen for the text.
[21] As St. Augustine demands.

I seigh his sleves purfiled° at the hond   lined
With grys,° and that the fyneste of a lond;   expensive grey fur
195 And, for to festne his hood under his chyn,
He hadde of gold ywroght a ful curious° pyn;   skillfully made
A love-knotte in the gretter ende ther was.
His heed was balled, that shoon as any glas,
And eek his face, as he hadde been enoynt.
200 He was a lord ful fat and in good poynt;°   condition
His eyen stepe,° and rollynge in his heed,   prominent
That stemed as a forneys of a leed;²²
His bootes souple, his hors in greet estaat.
Now certeinly he was a fair prelaat;²³
205 He was nat pale as a forpyned° goost.   tormented
A fat swan loved he best of any roost.
His palfrey° was as broun as is a berye.   riding-horse

THE NUN'S PRIEST'S TALE

A povre wydwe, somdeel stape° in age   advanced
Was whilom° dwellyng in a narwe cotage,   once
Biside a grove, stondynge in a dale.
This wydwe, of which I telle yow my tale,
5 Syn thilke° day that she was last a wyf,   that same
In pacience laddc a ful symple lyf,
For litel was hir catel° and hir rente.   property
By housbondrie° of swich as God hire sente   economy
Shc foond° hirself and eek hir doghtren two.   supported
10 Thre large sowes hadde she, and namo,
Three keen,° and eek a sheep that highte° Malle.   cows / named
Ful sooty was hire bour° and eek hir halle,   bedchamber
In which she eet ful many a sklendre meel.
Of poynaunt° sauce hir neded never a deel.   spicy
15 No deyntee morsel passed thurgh hir throte;
Hir diete was accordant to hir cote.
Repleccioun° ne made hire nevere sik;   overeating
Attempree° diete was al hir phisik,°   modest / medicine
And exercise, and hertes suffisaunce.
20 The goute lette° hire nothyng for to daunce,   prevented
N'apoplexie shente° nat hir heed.°   hurt / head
No wyn ne drank she, neither whit ne reed;

²² That glowed like a furnace under a pot.
²³ High-ranking churchman.

Hir bord was served moost with whit and blak,—
Milk and broun breed, in which she foond no lak,
25 Seynd° bacoun, and somtyme an ey° or tweye;   cooked / egg
For she was, as it were, a maner deye.°   dairy-woman
    A yeerd she hadde, enclosed al aboute
With stikkes, and a drye dych withoute,
In which she hadde a cok, hight Chauntecleer.
30 In al the land, of crowyng nas his peer.
His voys was murier than the murie orgon
On messe-dayes that in the chirche gon.
Wel sikerer° was his crowyng in his logge°   reliable / house
Than is a clokke or an abbey orlogge.°   clock
35 By nature he knew ech ascencioun
Of the equynoxial in thilke toun;
For whan degrees fiftene weren ascended,
Thanne crew he, that it myghte nat been amended.[1]
His coomb was redder than the fyn coral,
40 And batailled[2] as it were a castel wal;
His byle° was blak, and as the jeet it shoon;   bill
Lyk asure° were his legges and his toon;°   azure / toes
His nayles whitter than the lylye flour,
And lyk the burned gold was his colour.
45 This gentil cok hadde in his governaunce
Sevene hennes for to doon al his plesaunce,
Whiche were his sustres° and his paramours,°   sisters / mistresses
And wonder lyk to hym, as of colours;
Of whiche the faireste hewed° on hir throte   colored
50 Was cleped faire damoysele Pertelote.
Curteys she was, discreet, and debonaire,°   calm
And compaignable, and bar° hyrself so faire,   bore
Syn thilke day that she was seven nyght oold,
That trewely she hath the herte in hoold
55 Of Chauntecleer, loken° in every lith;°   locked / limb
He loved hire so that wel was hym therwith.
But swich a joye was it to here hem synge,
Whan that the brighte sonne gan to sprynge,
In sweete accord, "My lief is faren in londe!"
60 For thilke tyme, as I have understonde,
Beestes and briddes koude speke and synge.
    And so bifel that in a dawenynge,°   dawn
As Chauntecleer among his wyves alle

[1] According to early astronomy, the celestial equator was thought to make a 360-degree rotation around the earth every 24 hours. Hence, the passing of 15 degrees would amount to the passing of one hour; that is, he crowed every hour, on the hour.
[2] Pockmarked with dents.

Sat on his perche, that was in the halle,
65 And next hym sat this faire Pertelote,
This Chauntecleer gan gronen in his throte,
As man that in his dreem is drecched° soore.   annoyed
And whan that Pertelote thus herde hym roore,
She was agast, and seyde, "Herte deere,
70 What eyleth° yow, to grone in this manere?   ails
Ye been a verray° sleper; fy, for shame!"   sound
      And he answerde, and seyde thus: "Madame,
I pray yow that ye take it nat agrief.
By God, me mette I was in swich meschief
75 Right now, that yet myn herte is soore afright.
Now God," quod he, "my swevene recche aright,³
And kepe my body out of foul prisoun!
Me mette how that I romed up and doun
Withinne our yeerd, wheer as I saugh a beest
80 Was lyk an hound, and wolde han maad areest°   taken hold
Upon my body, and wolde han had me deed.
His colour was bitwixe yelow and reed,
And tipped was his tayl and bothe his eeris
With blak, unlyk the remenant° of his heeris;°   rest / hair
85 His snowte smal, with glowynge eyen tweye.
Yet of his look for feere almoost I deye;
This caused me my gronyng, doutelees."
      "Avoy!" quod she, "fy on yow, hertelees!°   coward
Allas!" quod she, "for, by that God above,
90 Now han ye lost myn herte and al my love.
I kan nat love a coward, by my feith!
For certes, what so any womman seith,
We alle desiren, if it myghte bee,
To han housbondes hardy, wise, and free,°   noble
95 And secree,° and no nygard, ne no fool,   trustworthy
Ne hym that is agast of every tool,°   weapon
Ne noon avauntour,° by that God above!   boaster
How dorste ye seyn, for shame, unto youre love
That any thyng myghte make yow aferd?
100 Have ye no mannes herte, and han a berd?°   beard
Allas! and konne ye been agast of swevenys?°   dreams
Nothyng, God woot, but vanitee in sweven is.
Swevenes engendren° of replecciouns,°   come / overeating
And ofte of fume° and of complecciouns,°   gas / humors in the
105 Whan humours been to habundant in a wight.°   body / person
Certes this dreem, which ye han met to-nyght,

---

³ Interpret my dream for me properly.

Cometh of the greete superfluytee
Of youre rede colera,° pardee,   bile
Which causeth folk to dreden° in hir dremes   dread
110 Of arwes,° and of fyr with rede lemes,°   arrows / flames
Of rede beestes, that they wol hem byte,
Of contek,° and of whelpes,° grete and lyte;   strife / dogs
Right as the humour of malencolie
Causeth ful many a man in sleep to crie
115 For feere of blake beres,° or boles° blake,   bears / bulls
Or elles blake develes wole hem take.
Of othere humours koude I telle also
That werken many a man sleep ful wo;
But I wol passe as lightly as I kan.
120   Lo Catoun,⁴ which that was so wys a man,
Seyde he nat thus, 'Ne do no fors of dremes?'⁵
    Now sire," quod she, "whan we flee fro the bemes,
For Goddes love, as taak som laxatyf.
Up° peril of my soule and of my lyf,   Upon
125 I conseille yow the beste, I wol nat lye,
That bothe of colere and of malencolye
Ye purge yow; and for ye shal nat tarie,
Though in this toun is noon apothecarie,
I shal myself to herbes techen yow
130 That shul been for youre hele° and for youre prow;° health / advantage
And in oure yeerd tho herbes shal I fynde
The whiche han of hire propretee by kynde
To purge yow bynethe° and eek above.   below
Foryet nat this, for Goddes owene love!
135 Ye been ful coleryk° of compleccioun;   hot-tempered
Ware° the sonne in his ascencioun   Avoid
Ne fynde yow nat repleet° of humours hoote.°   filled / hot
And if it do, I dar wel leye° a grote,°   bet / coin
That ye shul have a fevere terciane,⁶
140 Or an agu,° that may be youre bane.°   fever / destruction
A day or two ye shul have digestyves
Of wormes, er ye take youre laxatyves
Of lawriol,⁷ centaure, and fumetere,
Or elles of ellebor, that groweth there,
145 Of katapuce, or of gaitrys beryis,
Of herbe yve, growyng in oure yeerd, ther mery is;
Pekke° hem up right as they growe and ete hem yn.   Pick

---

⁴ Dionysius Cato, author of a book of rules used in schools.
⁵ Give no thought to dreams.
⁶ Recurring every third day.
⁷ This herb, and the next few mentioned, were common medieval medicines.

Be myrie, housbonde, for youre fader kyn!
Dredeth no dreem, I kan sey yow namoore."
150   "Madame," quod he, "graunt mercy of youre loore.
But nathelees, as touchyng daun° Catoun,   lord
That hath of wysdom swich a greet renoun,
Though that he bad no dremes for to drede,
By God, men may in olde bookes rede
155 Of many a man moore of auctorite°   authority
Than evere Caton was, so moot I thee,°   prosper
That al the revers seyn of this sentence,
And han wel founden by experience
That dremes been significaciouns
160 As wel of joye as of tribulaciouns
That folk enduren in this lif present.
Ther nedeth make of this noon argument;
The verray preeve° sheweth it in dede.   proof
    Oon of the gretteste auctour° that men rede   authors
165 Seith thus: that whilom two felawes wente
On pilgrimage, in a ful good entente;
And happed so, they coomen in a toun
Wher as ther was swich congregacioun
Of peple, and eek so streit° of herbergage,°   short / lodging
170 That they ne founde as muche as o cotage
In which they bothe myghte ylogged bee.
Wherfore they mosten° of necessitee,   must
As for that nyght, departen compaignye;
And ech of hem gooth to his hostelrye,
175 And took his loggyng as it wolde falle.
That oon of hem was logged in a stalle,
Fer in a yeerd, with oxen of the plough;
That oother man was logged wel ynough,
As was his aventure or his fortune,
180 That us governeth alle as in commune.
    And so bifel that, longe er it were day,
This man mette° in his bed, ther as he lay,   dreamed
How that his felawe gan upon hym calle,
And seyde, 'Allas! for in an oxes stalle
185 This nyght I shal be mordred ther I lye.
Now help me, deere brother, or I dye.
In alle haste com to me!' he sayde.
This man out of his sleep for feere abrayde;°   awoke
But whan that he was wakened of his sleep,
190 He turned hym, and took of this no keep.°   notice
Hym thoughte his dreem nas but a vanitee.

Thus twies in his slepyng dremed hee;
And atte thridde tyme yet his felawe
Cam, as hym thoughte, and seide, 'I am now slawe.°   slain
195 Bihoold my bloody woundes depe and wyde!
Arys up erly in the morwe tyde,°   morning time
And at the west gate of the toun,' quod he,
'A carte ful of dong ther shaltow se,
In which my body is hid ful prively;
200 Do thilke° carte arresten° boldely.   that / stop
My gold caused my mordre, sooth to sayn.'
And tolde hym every point how he was slayn,
With a ful pitous face, pale of hewe.
And truste wel, his dreem he foond ful trewe,
205 For on the morwe, as soone as it was day,
To his fclawes in° he took the way;   lodging
And whan that he cam to this oxes stalle,
After his felawe he bigan to calle.
   The hostiler° answerede hym anon,   innkeeper
210 And seyde, 'Sire, your felawe is agon.
As soone as day he wente out of the toun.'
   This man gan fallen in suspecioun,
Remembrynge on his dremes that he mette,
And forth he gooth—no lenger wolde he lette°—   delay
215 Unto the west gate ot the toun, and fond
A dong-carte, wente as it were to donge° lond,   fertilize with
That was arrayed in that same wise   dung
As ye han herd the dede° man devyse.   dead
And with an hardy herte he gan to crye
220 Vengeance and justice of this felonye.
'My felawe mordred is this same nyght,
And in this carte he lith° gapyng upright.   lives
I crye out on the ministres,' quod he,
'That sholden kepe and reulen° this citee.   rule
225 Harrow!° allas! heere lith my felawe slayn!'   Help!
What sholde I moore unto this tale sayn?
The peple out sterte and caste the cart to grounde,
And in the myddel of the dong they founde
The dede man, that mordred was al newe.°   recently
230   O blisful God, that art so just and trewe,
Lo, how that thou biwreyest° mordre alway!   reveals
Mordre wol out, that se we day by day.
Mordre is so wlatsom° and abhomynable   disgusting
To God, that is so just and resonable,
235 That he ne wol nat suffre it heled° be,   hidden

Though it abyde a yeer, or two, or thre.
Mordre wol out, this my conclusioun.
And right anon, ministres of that toun
Han hent° the carter and so soore hym pyned,°   seized / tortured
240 And eek the hostiler so soore engyned,°   concerned
That they biknewe° hire wikkednesse anon,   confessed
And were anhanged by the nekke-bon.
    Heere may men seen that dremes been to drede.
And certes in the same book I rede,
245 Right in the nexte chapitre after this—
I gabbe° nat, so have I joye or blis—   lie
Two men that wolde han passed over see,
For certeyn cause, into a fer contree,
If that the wynd ne hadde been contrarie,
250 That made hem in a citee for to tarie
That stood ful myrie upon an haven-syde;°   harbour
But on a day, agayn° the even-tyde,   before
The wynd gan chaunge, and blew right as hem
        leste.°   wished
Jolif° and glad they wente unto hir reste,   Jolly
255 And casten hem ful erly for to saille.
But to that o man fil° a greet mervaille: came
That oon of hem, in slepyng as he lay,
Hym mette° a wonder dreem agayn the day.   dreamed
Hym thoughte a man stood by his beddes syde,
260 And hym comanded that he sholde abyde,
And seyde hym thus: 'If thou tomorwe wende,
Thow shalt be dreynt;° my tale is at an ende.'   drowned
He wook, and tolde his felawe what he mette,
And preyde hym his viage° for to lette;°   voyage / delay
265 As for that day, he preyde hym to byde.
His felawe, that lay by his beddes syde,
Can for to laughe, and scorned him ful faste.
'No dreem,' quod he, 'may so myn herte agaste
That I wol lette for to do my thynges.
270 I sette nat a straw by thy dremynges,
For swevenes° been but vanytees and japes.°   dreams / jokes
Men dreme alday of owles and of apes,
And eek of many a maze therwithal;
Men dreme of thyng that nevere was ne shal.°   nor shall be
275 But sith I see that thou wolt heere abyde,
And thus forslewthen° wilfully thy tyde,°   waste / time
God woot, it reweth me;° and have good day!'   I pity it
And thus he took his leve, and wente his way.
But er that he hadde half his cours yseyled,

280 Noot I nat why, ne what myschaunce it eyled,
But casuelly the shippes botme° rente,   bottom
And ship and man under the water wente
In sighte of othere shippes it bisyde,
That with hem seyled at the same tyde.
285 And therfore, faire Pertelote so deere,
By swiche ensamples olde maistow leere°   learn
That no man sholde been to recchelees°   careless
Of dremes; for I seye thee, doutelees,
That many a dreem ful soore is for to drede.
290   Lo, in the lyf of Seint Kenelm I rede,
That was Kenulphus sone, the noble kyng
Of Mercenrike, how Kenelm mette a thyng.
A lite er he was mordred, on a day,
His mordre in his avysioun° he say.°   dream / saw
295 His norice° hym expowned every deel°   nurse / bit
His sweven, and bad hym for to kepe hym weel
For traisoun; but he nas but seven yeer oold,
And therfore litel tale hath he toold
Of any dreem, so hooly was his herte.
300 By God! I hadde levere than my sherte[8]
That ye hadde rad° his legende, as have I.   read
      Dame Pertelote, I sey yow trewely,
Macrobeus,[9] that writ the avisioun
In Affrike of the worthy Cipioun,
305 Affermeth° dremes, and seith that they been   Confirms
Warnynge of thynges that men after seen.
And forthermoore, I pray yow, looketh wel
In the olde testament, of Daniel,
If he heeld dremes any vanitee.[10]
310 Reed eek of Joseph, and ther shul ye see
Wher dremes be somtyme—I sey nat alle—
Warnynge of thynges that shul after falle.[11]
Looke of Egipte the kyng, daun Pharao,
His bakere and his butiller° also,   butler
315 Wher they ne felte noon effect in dremes.[12]
Whoso wol seken actes of sondry remes°   lands
May rede of dremes many a wonder thyng.
Lo Cresus, which that was of Lyde kyng,
Mette° he nat that he sat upon a tree,   Dreamed

[8] I'd rather give my shirt.
[9] Macrobius, an early author on dreams.
[10] Cf. Daniel vii.
[11] Cf. Genesis xxxvii.
[12] Cf. Genesis xxxiv.

320 Which signified he sholde anhanged bee?
  Lo heere Andromacha, Ectores° wyf,   Hector's
  That day that Ector sholde lese° his lyf,   lose
  She dremed on the same nyght biforn
  How that the lyf of Ector sholde be lorn,°   lost
325 If thilke° day he wente into bataille.   that
  She warned hym, but it myghte nat availle;
  He wente for to fighte natheles,°   nevertheless
  But he was slayn anon° of Achilles.   at once
  But thilke tale is al to longe to telle,
330 And eek it is ny day, I may nat dwelle.
  Shortly I seye, as for conclusioun,
  That I shal han of this avisioun
  Adversitee; and I seye forthermoor,
  That I ne telle° of laxatyves no stoor,°   hold / stock
335 For they been venymous, I woot it weel;
  I hem diffye, I love hem never a deel!°   not a bit!
   Now let us speke of myrthe, and stynte° al this. stop
  Madame Pertelote, so have I blis,
  Of o thyng God hath sent me large grace;
340 For whan I se the beautee of youre face,
  Ye been so scarlet reed aboute youre yen,°   eyes
  It maketh al my drede for to dyen;
  For al so siker as *In principio,*
  Mulier est hominis confusio,—[13]
345 Madame, the sentence of this Latyn is,
  'Womman is mannes joye and al his blis.'
  For whan I feele a-nyght your softe syde,
  Al be it that I may nat on yow ryde,
  For that oure perche is maad so narwe, allas!
350 I am so ful of joye and of solas,°   comfort
  That I diffye bothe sweven and dreem."[14]
  And with that word he fley doun fro the beem,
  For it was day, and eke his hennes alle,
  And with a chuk he gan hem for to calle,
355 For he hadde founde a corn, lay in the yerd.
  Real he was, he was namoore aferd.
  He fethered° Pertelote twenty tyme,   embraced
  And trad° hire eke as ofte, er it was pryme.   copulated with
  He looketh as it were a grym leoun,°   lion
360 And on his toos° he rometh up and doun;   toes

---

[13] For as certain as "In the beginning [was the word]," "Woman is man's damnation."
[14] Vision and dream.

Hym deigned nat to sette his foot to grounde.
He chukketh whan he hath a corn yfounde,
And to hym rennen° thanne his wyves alle.   run
Thus roial, as a prince is in his halle,
365 Leve I this Chauntecleer in his pasture,
And after wol I telle his aventure.
      Whan that the month in which the world bigan,
That highte March, whan God first maked man,
Was compleet, and passed were also,
370 Syn March bigan, thritty dayes and two,
Bifel that Chauntecleer in al his pryde,
His sevene wyves walkynge by his syde,
Caste up his eyen to the brighte sonne,
That in the signe of Taurus hadde yronne
375 Twenty degrees and oon, and somwhat moore,
And knew by kynde,° and by noon oother loore,   nature
That it was pryme, and crew with blisful stevene.°   voice
"The sonne," he seyde, "is clomben up on hevene
Fourty degrees and oon, and moore ywis.°   certainly
380 Madame Pertelote, my worldes blis,
Herkneth thise blisful briddes how they synge,
And se the fresshe floures how they sprynge;
Ful is myn herte of revel and solas!"
But sodeynly hym fil a sorweful cas,°   case
385 For evere the latter ende of joye is wo.
God woot that worldly joye is soone ago;
And if a rethor° koude faire endite,   orator
He in a cronycle saufly° myghte it write   safely
As for a sovereyn notabilitee.°   notable fact
390 Now every wys man, lat him herkne me;
This storie is also trewe, I undertake,
As is the book of Launcelot de Lake,[15]
That wommen holde in ful greet reverence.
Now wol I torne agayn to my sentence.°   meaning
395   A col-fox,[16] ful of sly iniquitee,
That in the grove hadde woned° yeres three,   lived
By heigh ymaginacioun forncast,°   forecast
The same nyght thurghout the hegges° brast°   hedges / burst
Into the yerd ther Chauntecleer the faire
400 Was wont, and eek his wyves, to repaire;
And in a bed of wortes° stille he lay,   herbs

[15] Lancelot of the Lake.
[16] Fox with black tips.

Til it was passed undren° of the day,   midmorning
Waitynge his tyme on Chauntecleer to falle,
As gladly doon thise homycides alle
405 That in await liggen° to mordre men.   lie
O false mordrour, lurkynge in thy den!
O newe Scariot,[17] newe Genylon,
False dissymulour, o Greek Synon,
That broghtest Troye al outrely to sorwe!
410 O Chauntecleer, acursed be that morwe
That thou into that yerd flaugh° fro the bemes!   flew
Thou were ful wel ywarned by thy dremes
That thilke day was perilous to thee;
But what that God forwoot° moot° nedes bee,   foreknows / must
415 After° the opinioun of certein clerkis.   According to
Witnesse on hym that any parfit clerk is,
That in scole is greet altercacioun
In this mateere, and greet disputisoun,°   disputation
And hath been of an hundred thousand men.
420 But I ne kan nat bulte° it to the bren°   sift / bran
As kan the hooly doctour Augustyn,[18]
Or Boece, or the Bisshop Bradwardyn,
Wheither that Goddes worthy forwityng°   foreknowledge
Streyneth° me nedely° for to doon a thyng,—   Prevents / of necessity
425 "Nedely" clepe I symple necessitee;
Or elles, if free choys be graunted me
To do that same thyng, or do it noght,
Though God forwoot it er that was wroght;
Or if his wityng° streyneth never a deel   knowledge
430 But by necessitee condicioneel.
I wol nat han to do of swich mateere;
My tale is of a cok, as ye may heere,
That tok his conseil of his wyf, with sorwe,
To walken in the yerd upon that morwe
435 That he hadde met° that dreem that I yow tolde.   dreamed
Wommennes conseils been ful ofte colde;
Wommannes conseil broghte us first to wo,
And made Adam fro Paradys to go,
Ther as he was ful myrie and wel at ese.
440 But for I noot° to whom it myght displese,   don't know
If I conseil of wommen wolde blame,

---

[17] Judas Iscariot, betrayer of Christ; Ganelon betrayed Roland to the Saracens (in *The Song of Roland*); Sinon persuaded the Trojans to take the wooden horse of the Greeks into their city, and the city as a result was sacked.

[18] St. Augustine, Boethius, and Bishop Bradwardine (who lived during Chaucer's time) were all concerned with man's free will in the face of God's all-knowing intelligence.

Passe over, for I seyde it in my game.
Rede auctours, where they trete of swich° mateere,   such
And what they seyn of wommen ye may heere.
445   Thise been the cokkes wordes, and nat myne;
I kan noon harm of no womman divyne.°   declare
   Faire in the soond,° to bathe hire myrily,   sand
Lith° Pertelote, and alle hire sustres by,   Lies
Agayn the sonne, and Chauntecleer so free
450   Soong° murier than the mermayde in the see;   Sang
For Phisiologus[19] seith sikerly
How that they syngen wel and myrily.
And so bifel that, as he caste his ye
Among the wortes on a boterflye,
455   He was war° of this fox, that lay ful lowe.   aware
Nothyng ne liste hym thanne for to crowe,[20]
But cride anon, "Cok! cok!" and up he sterte
As man that was affrayed in his herte.
For natureelly a beest desireth flee
460   Fro his contrarie,° if he may it see,   enemy
Though he never erst° hadde seyn it with his ye.   before
   This Chauntecleer, whan he gan hym espye,
He wolde han fled, but that the fox anon
Seyde, "Gentil sire, allas! wher wol ye gon?
465   Be ye affrayed of me that am youre freend?
Now, certes, I were worse than a feend,
If I to yow wolde harm or vileynye!
I am nat come youre conseil° for t'espye,   secrets
But trewely, the cause of my comynge
470   Was oonly for to herkne how that ye synge.
For trewely, ye have as myrie a stevene°   voice
As any aungel hath that is in hevene.
Therwith ye han in musyk moore feelynge
Than hadde Boece, or any that kan synge.
475   My lord youre fader—God his soule blesse!—
And eek youre mooder, of hire gentillesse,
Han in myn hous ybeen to my greet ese;
And certes, sire, ful fayn° wolde I yow plese.   happily
But, for men speke of syngyng, I wol seye,—
480   So moote I brouke° wel myne eyen tweye,—   enjoy
Save yow, I herde nevere man so synge
As dide youre fader in the morwenynge.
Certes, it was of herte,° al that he song.   of the heart

---

[19] A Latin bestiary, which contains a section on mermaids.
[20] He wished only to crow.

And for to make his voys the moore strong,
485 He wolde so peyne hym that with bothe his yen
He moste wynke,° so loude he wolde cryen,   close his eyes
And stonden on his tiptoon therwithal,
And strecche forth his nekke long and smal.
And eek he was of swich discrecioun
490 That ther nas no man in no regioun
That hym in song or wisedom myghte passe.
I have wel rad° in 'Daun Burnel the Asse,'[21]   read
Among his vers, how that ther was a cok,
For that a preestes sone yaf hym a knok
495 Upon his leg whil he was yong and nyce,°   foolish
He made hym for to lese his benefice.
But certeyn, ther nys no comparisoun
Bitwixe the wisedom and discrecioun
Of youre fader and of his subtiltee.
500 Now syngeth, sire, for seinte° charitee;   holy
Lat se, konne° ye youre fader countrefete?"°   can / imitate
    This Chauntecleer his wynges gan to bete,
As man that koude his traysoun nat espie,
So was he ravysshed with his flaterie.
505   Allas! ye lordes, many a fals flatour°   flatterer
Is in youre courtes, and many a losengeour,°   false praiser
That plesen yow wel moore, by my feith,
Than he that soothfastnesse° unto yow seith.   truth
Redeth Ecclesiaste[22] of flaterye;
510 Beth war, ye lordes, of hir trecherye.
    This Chauntecleer stood hye upon his toos,
Strecchynge his nekke, and heeld his eyen cloos,
And gan to crowe loude for the nones.°   occasion
And daun Russell the fox stirte up atones,°   at once
515 And by the gargat° hente° Chauntecleer,   throat / seized
And on his bak toward the wode hym beer,°   took
For yet ne was ther no man that hym sewed.°   followed
    O destinee, that mayst nat been eschewed!
Allas, that Chauntecleer fleigh° fro the bemes!   flew
520 Allas, his wyf ne roghte° nat of dremes!   heed
And on a Friday fil° al this meschaunce.   fell
    O Venus, that art goddesse of plesaunce,
Syn that thy servant was this Chauntecleer,
And in thy servyce dide al his poweer,

---

21 A twelfth-century poem by Nigellus Wireker about a cock that had its leg broken by a young
man; in return the cock's crowing disturbed the young man's sleep, who overslept and lost
his job ("benefice").
22 Ecclesiasticus.

525 Moore for delit than world to multiplye,
Why woldestow suffre hym on thy day to dye?
    O Gaufred,[23] deere maister soverayn,
That whan thy worthy kyng Richard was slayn
With shot,° compleynedest his deeth so soore,   arrow
530 Why ne hadde I now thy sentence° and thy loore,°   wisdom / learning
The Friday for to chide, as diden ye?
For on a Friday, soothly, slayn was he.
Thanne wolde I shewe yow how that I koude pleyne°   lament
For Chauntecleres drede and for his peyne.
535   Certes, swich cry ne lamentacion,
Was nevere of ladyes maad whan Ylion[24]
Was wonne, and Pirrus[25] with his streite swerd,
Whan he hadde hent° kyng Priam by the berd,   seized
And slayn hym, as seith us *Eneydos,*[26]
540 As maden alle the hennes in the clos,°   yard
Whan they had seyn of Chauntecleer the sighte.
But sovereynly dame Pertelote shrighte°   shrieked
Ful louder than dide Hasdrubales[27] wyf,
Whan that hir housbonde hadde lost his lyf,
545 And that the Romayns hadde brend° Cartage.   burned
She was so ful of torment and of rage
That wilfully into the fyr she sterte,°   leaped
And brende hirselven with a stedefast herte.
    O woful hennes, right so criden ye,
550 As, whan that Nero brende the citee
Of Rome, cryden senatoures wyves
For that hir husbondes losten alle hir lyves,—
Withouten gilt this Nero hath hem slayn.
Now wole I turne to my tale agayn.
555   This sely° wydwe and eek hir doghtres two   blessed
Herden thise hennes crie and maken wo,
And out at dores stirten° they anon,   jumped
And syen° the fox toward the grove gon,   saw
And bar upon his bak the cok away,
560 And cryden, "Out! harrow!° and weylaway   help!
Ha! ha! the fox!" and after hym they ran,
And eek with staves many another man.
Ran Colle oure dogge, and Talbot and Gerland,
And Malkyn, with a dystaf in hir hand;
565 Ran cow and calf, and eek the verray hogges,

---

[23] Geoffrey on Vinsauf, who wrote a poem on the death of Richard I, who died on a Friday.
[24] I.e., Troy.
[25] The Greek who slew the King of Troy, Priam.
[26] I.e., *The Aeneid.*
[27] King of Carthage, when it was sacked by the Romans.

So fered° for the berkyng of the dogges ——— frightened
And shoutyng of the men and wommen eeke,
They ronne so hem thoughte hir herte breeke.
They yolleden as feendes doon in helle;
570 The dokes° cryden as men wolde hem quelle;° ——— ducks / kill
The gees for feere flowen over the trees;
Out of the hyve cam the swarm of bees.
So hydous was the noyse, a, *benedicitee!*° ——— bless the Lord!
Certes, he Jakke Straw²⁸ and his meynee
575 Ne made nevere shoutes half so shrille
Whan that they wolden any Flemyng kille,
As thilke day was maad upon the fox.
Of bras they broghten bemes,° and of box,° ——— trumpets / box-tree
Of horn, of boon,° in whiche they blewe and ——— bone /
        powped,° ——— puffed
580 And therwithal they skriked and they howped.° ——— whooped
It semed as that hevene sholde falle.
    Now, goode men, I prey yow herkneth alle:
Lo, how Fortune turneth sodeynly
The hope and pryde eek of hir enemy!
585 This cok, that lay upon the foxes bak,
In al his drede unto the fox he spak,
And seyde, "Sire, if that I were as ye,
Yet sholde I seyn, as wys° God helpe me, ——— wise
'Turneth agayn, ye proude cherles° alle! ——— churls
590 A verray pestilence upon yow falle!
Now am I come unto the wodes syde;
Maugree° youre heed, the cok shal heere abyde. ——— In spite of
I wol hym ete, in feith, and that anon!' "
    The fox answerde, "In feith, it shal be don."
595 And as he spak that word, al sodeynly
This cok brak from his mouth delyverly,° ——— delicately
And heighe upon a tree he fleigh anon.
And whan the fox saugh that the cok was gon,
    "Allas!" quod he, "O Chauntecleer, allas!
600 I have to yow," quod he, "ydoon trespas,
In as muche as I maked yow aferd
Whan I yow hente° and broghte out of the yerd. ——— seized
But, sire, I dide it in no wikke° entente. ——— wicked
Com doun, and I shal telle yow what I mente;
605 I shal seye sooth to yow, God help me so!"
    "Nay thanne," quod he, "I shrewe° us bothe two. ——— curse
And first I shrewe myself, bothe blood and bones,
If thou bigyle me ofter than ones.° ——— once

²⁸ A leader of the Peasants' Revolt of 1381.

Thou shalt namoore, thurgh thy flaterye,
610 Do me to synge and wynke with myn ye;
For he that wynketh, whan he sholde see,
Al wilfully, God lat him nevere thee!"°   thrive
    "Nay," quod the fox, "but God yeve hym
        meschaunce,
That is so undiscreet of governaunce°   self-control
615 That jangleth whan he sholde holde his pees."°   peace
    Lo, swich it is for to be recchelees°   careless
And necligent, and truste on flaterye.
    But ye that holden this tale a folye,
As of a fox, or of a cok and hen,
620 Taketh the moralite, goode men.
For seint Paul seith that al that writen is,
To oure doctrine it is ywrite, ywis;
Taketh the fruyt, and lat the chaf be stille.
Now, goode God, if that it be thy wille,
625 As seith my lord, so make us alle goode men,
And brynge us to his heighe blisse! Amen.

Middle English Lyrics

The themes of the finest Middle English songs and lyrics are convention-al—the Virgin Mary, the Crucifixion, the lover, and so on. The forms were developed in France. But the pure musicality of the lyrics and the universality of their concerns make them seem eternally new. A lyric such as "Ubi Sunt" describes human transience and our perpetual sense of loss. "Sunset on Calvary" evokes, with remarkable vividness, the feeling of standing with the Virgin at the foot of the cross. The medieval English lyricist translated biblical themes into the terms of his own times. The song "The Corpus Christi Carol" describes the pagan myth of the Fisher King, in which the desire of the king poisons the countryside, but the song also teaches about the grace of Christ. Although the lyrics cannot be precisely dated, they range in time from the "Cuckoo Song," from the twelfth century, to "I Sing of a Maiden," probably from the fifteenth. No authors are known because most of the songs have gradually evolved from a multitude of early oral versions.

MIDDLE ENGLISH LYRICS

The Irish Dancer

Ich° am of Irlande,   I
And of the holy lande
  Of Irlande.
Goode sire, pray ich thee,
5 Of° saintė charité,   For the sake of
Come and daunce with me
  In Irlande.

Sumer is y-cumen in

Sumer is y-cumen in,
Ludė° sing, cuccu!   Loudly
Groweth sed° and bloweth med°   seed / meadow
And springth the wudė° nu.°   wood / now

5   Sing, cuccu!
   Awė° bleteth after lamb,   Ewe
   Lowth after calvė cu;
   Bulluc sterteth,° buckė ferteth.° jumps / farts
   Meriė sing, cuccu!
10   Cuccu, cuccu,
   Wel singės thu, cuccu;
   Ne swik° thu never nu!   stop

   Sing, cuccu, nu! Sing, cuccu!
   Sing, cuccu! Sing, cuccu, nu!

Ubi Sunt?[1]

Where beeth they biforen us weren,
Houndės ladden and havekės beren,[2]
 And hadden feeld and wode?
The richė levedies° in here bour,   ladies
5 That werėden° gold in here tressour, wore
 With here brightė rode,°   skin

Eten and drunken and maden hem glad;
Here lif was al with gamen° y-lad;° fun / led
 Men knelėden hem biforen.
10 They beren hem wel swithė heye,° with much pride
And in a twinkling of an eye
 Here soulės weren forloren.

Where is that lawing° and that song, laughing
That trailing and that proudė yong,° walk
15 Tho° havekes and tho houndes? Those
Al that joy is went away;
That wele° is comen to waylaway,° joy / sadness
 To manye hardė stoundes.°   times

Here paradis hy nomen° here,   they took
20 And now they lien in helle y-fere;° together
 That fire it brennės° evere.   burns
Long is ay° and long is o,°   always / forever
Long is way and long is wo;
 Thennes ne cometh they nevere.

---

[1] The full title is *Ubi Sunt Qui Ante Nos Fuerunt?*, the translation of which is in the first line of the poem: Where are they who were before us?
[2] Who led hounds and carried hawks.

25 Dreghy° here, man, then, if thou wilt,   Endure
     A litel pine° that me thee bit;   suffering
        Withdraw thine eises° ofte.   comforts
     Thegh° thy pinĕ° be unrede,°   Though / sorrow /
     And thou thenke on thy mede,   hard
30   It shal thee thinken° softe.   seem

     If that feend, that foulĕ thing,
     Through wikkĕ roun,° through fals egging,   counsel
        Nethere° thee haveth y-cast,   Down
     Up! and be good chaunpioun;
35   Stand, ne fall na more adown
        For a litel blast.³

     Thou tak the roodĕ to thy staf,°   staff
     And thenk on Him that there-on yaf°   gave
        His lif that was so leef.°   dear
40   He it yaf for thee; thou yeeld° it Him;   repay
     Ayein His fo that staf thou nim,
        And wrek° Him of that theef. . . .   avenge

     Maiden moder,° hevene-queen,   mother
     Thou might and canst and owest° to been   ought
45   Oure sheeld ayein° the fende.°   against / fiend
     Help us sinnĕ for to fleen,°   flee
     That we moten thy Sone y-seen
        In joye withouten ende.

I Sing of a Maiden

        I sing of a maiden
           That is makĕles;°   matchless
        King of alle kingĕs
           To her son she ches.°   chose
5   He cam also stillĕ°   quietly
           Ther° His moder was,   Where
        As dew in Aprìlle
           That falleth on the gras.
        He cam also stillĕ
10   To His moderes bowr,
        As dew in Aprìlle

³ Because of a little blast of wind.

That falleth on the flowr.
He cam also stillè
   Ther His moder lay,
15 As dew in Aprìlle
   That falleth on the spray.
Moder and maiden
   Was never none but she;
Wel may swich° a lady   such
20   Godès moder be.

Medieval Ballads

These ballads are anonymous narrative compositions that were preserved by oral transmission. Older theories that the poems were cooperatively or communally composed now tend to be discounted, but it is true that the ballads generally tell stories that were probably part of popular culture long before they were incorporated into song; as well, they have been revised many times by many hands and tongues. Most of the English ballads included here originated between 1300 and 1600. Many of them have survived because of Bishop Thomas Percy (1729–1811), who collected ballads written in Middle English and published them in his *Reliques of Ancient English Poetry.* Some of the basic features common to most ballads include a concentration on event rather than on description, repetitions and refrains, a tragic story line (often involving murder or supernatural events), and emphatic rhyme. Many have four-line stanzas whose second and fourth lines—which are shorter (usually iambic trimeter) than the first and third lines—rhyme. A majority of the ballads originated in northern England and Scotland.

MEDIEVAL BALLADS

Lord Randal

O where ha' you been, Lord Randal my son?
And where ha' you been, my handsome young man?
I ha' been at the greenwood; mother, mak my bed soon,
For I'm wearied wi' hunting and fain wad° lie down.   would

5 An' wha met ye there, Lord Randal my son?
An' wha met you there, my handsome young man?
O I met wi my true-love; mother, mak my bed soon,
For I'm wearied wi' huntin' an' fain wad lie down.

And what did she give you, Lord Randal my son?
10 And what did she give you, my handsome young man?

Eels fried in a pan; mother, mak my bed soon,
For I'm wearied wi' huntin' and fain wad lie down.

And wha gat your leavins, Lord Randal my son?
And wha gat your leavins, my handsom young man?
15   My hawks and my hounds; mother, mak my bed soon,
For I'm wearied wi' hunting and fain wad lie down.

And what becam of them, Lord Randal my son?
And what becam of them, my handsome young man?
They stretched their legs out an' died; mother, mak my bed soon,
20   For I'm wearied wi' huntin' and fain wad lie down.

O I fear you are poisoned, Lord Randal my son,
I fear you are poisoned, my handsome young man.
O yes, I am poisoned; mother, mak my bed soon,
For I'm sick at the heart and I fain wad lie down.

25   What d'ye leave to your mother, Lord Randal my son?
What d'ye leave to your mother, my handsome young man?
Four and twenty milk kye;° mother, mak my bed soon,   cattle
For I'm sick at the heart and I fain wad lie down.

What d'ye leave to your sister, Lord Randal my son?
30   What d'ye leave to your sister, my handsome young man?
My gold and my silver; mother, mak my bed soon,
For I'm sick at the heart an' I fain wad lie down.

What d'ye leave to your brother, Lord Randal my son?
What d'ye leave to your brother, my handsome young man?
35   My houses and my lands; mother, mak my bed soon,
For I'm sick at the heart and I fain wad lie down.

What d'ye leave to your true-love, Lord Randal my son?
What d'ye leave to your true-love, my handsome young man?
I leave her hell and fire; mother, mak my bed soon,
40   For I'm sick at the heart and I fain wad lie down.

Bonnie George Campbell

Hie upon Hielands and laigh° upon Tay   low
Bonnie George Campbell rode out on a day;
He saddled, he bridled, and gallant rode he,
And hame cam his guid horse, but never cam he.

5 Out cam his mother dear greeting° fu' sair,°   weeping / loudly
And out cam his bonnie bryde riving° her hair;   tearing
My meadow lies green and my corn is unshorn,
My barn is to build and my baby's unborn.

Saddled and bridled and booted rode he,
10 A plume in his helmet, a sword at his knee;
But toom° cam his saddle all bloody to see;   empty
Oh hame cam his guid horse, but never cam he.

Sir Patrick Spence

The king sits in Dumferling toune,°   town
    Drinking the blude-reid wine:
O quhar° will I get [a] guid sailor,   where
    To sail this schip of mine?

5 Up and spak an eldern knicht,
    Sat at the kings richt kne:
Sir Patrick Spence is the best sailor,
    That sails upon the se.

The king has written a braid° letter,   broad
10   And sign'd it wi' his hand;
And sent it to Sir Patrick Spence,
    Was walking on the sand.

The first line that Sir Patrick red,
    A loud lauch° lauched he: laugh
15 The next line that Sir Patrick red,
    The teir blinded his e'e.

O quha° is this has don this deid,   who
    This ill deid don to me;

To send me out this time o' the yeir,
20   To sail upon the se?

Mak haste, mak haste, my mirry men all,
    Our guid schip sails the morne.
O say na sae,° my master deir,   so
    For I feir a deadlie storme.

25 Late, late yestreen I saw the new moone
    Wi' the auld moone in hir arme;
And I feir, I feir, my deir master,
    That we will com to harme.

O our Scots nobles wer richt laith°   loath
30   To weet° their cork-heil'd schoone;°   wet / shoes
Bot lang owre° a' the play wer play'd,   before
    Thair hats they swam aboone.°   above

O lang, lang may thair ladies sit
    Wi' thair fans into their hand,
35 Or eir they se Sir Patrick Spence
    Cum sailing to the land.

O lang, lang may the ladies stand
    Wi' thair gold kems° in their hair,   combs
Waiting for thair ain deir lords,
40   For they'll se thame na mair.

Haf owre,° haf owre to Aberdour,   over
    It's fiftie fadom deip:
And thair lies guid Sir Patrick Spence,
    Wi' the Scots lords at his feit.

Edmund Spenser

(1 5 5 2 – 1 5 9 9)

Edmund Spenser, a nondramatic poet of the Elizabethan period, was born in London. He was educated at the Merchant Taylors' School (his father was a clothmaker) and at Cambridge, where the anti-Catholic, Puritan environment had a lasting effect on his outlook. He obtained a place in the house of the Earl of Leicester, Queen Elizabeth's favorite, and there he met Sir Philip Sidney and helped form the "Areopagus" literary club. In 1580 Spenser obtained a post that took him to Ireland. In 1594 he married Elizabeth Boyle, the inspiration for his *Amoretti* sonnet sequence. Despite his desire to return to London, Spenser remained in Ireland until an Irish revolt forced him to flee to England, where he died at the age of 47. He was buried in Westminster Abbey.

Spenser's first work, *The Shepheardes Calender,* used the classical eclogue form to make a veiled didactic and satiric analysis of contemporary society. The work shows Spenser's talent for technical innovation, a penchant he continued in his vast allegorical masterpiece, *The Faerie Queene,* where he developed the nine-line stanza later used by Keats, Shelley, and Byron. Spenser used intentionally archaic language, both to pay tribute to Chaucer and to create rustic and exotic effects. Before his death, Spenser completed six of the projected twelve books of *The Faerie Queene.* (If finished according to the original plan, the poem would have been almost two thousand pages long.) The poem is a complex allegory operating on religious, political, and philosophical planes as well as the traditional "romance" plane. It represents the Faerie Queene as Glory and Truth in the abstract and Queen Elizabeth in the particular. Each book was to describe the adventure of one of the Queen's twelve knights, or "patrons," the most important being Arthur. In Book One, the Red Cross Knight (symbolically, Holiness and the Anglican Church) protects the Virgin Una (Truth) against the wiles of Archimago and Duessa (falseness, Catholicism). Strongly nationalistic, Spenser was both a Renaissance humanist and a medieval writer. He was influenced by Italian Renaissance Neoplatonism; yet he was also profoundly and sternly religious. His poetry celebrates the world of the flesh (the real world) and the world of a Renaissance man's visionary spirit (the ideal world).

Spenser's main works were *The Shepheardes Calender* (1579), *Amoretti* (1595), the marriage poems *Epithalamion* (1595), and *Prothalamion* (1596), the *Cantos of Mutabilitie,* and *The Faerie Queene* (both published in 1609).

EDMUND SPENSER

The Faerie Queene

from *Book I, Canto I*

1

	A Gentle Knight was pricking° on the plaine,	riding
	Y cladd in mightie armes and silver shielde,	
	Wherein old dints of deepe wounds did remaine,	
	The cruell markes of many a bloudy fielde;	
5	Yet armes till that time did he never wield:	
	His angry steede did chide his foming bitt,	
	As much disdayning to the curbe to yield:	
	Full jolly° knight he seemd, and faire did sitt,	brave
	As one for knightly giusts° and fierce encounters fitt.	jousts

2

10	But on his brest a bloudie Crosse he bore,	
	The deare remembrance of his dying Lord,	
	For whose sweete sake that glorious badge he wore,	
	And dead as living ever him adored:	
	Upon his shield the like was also scored,	
15	For soveraine hope, which in his helpe he had:	
	Right faithfull true he was in deede and word,	
	But of his cheere did seeme too solemne sad;°	serious
	Yet nothing did he dread, but ever was ydrad.°	dreaded

3

	Upon a great adventure he was bond,	
20	That greatest Gloriana to him gave,	
	That greatest Glorious Queene of Faerie lond,	
	To winne him worship, and her grace to have,	
	Which of all earthly things he most did crave;	
	And ever as he rode, his hart did earne°	yearn
25	To prove his puissance° in battell brave	strength
	Upon his foe, and his new force to learne;	
	Upon his foe, a Dragon horrible and stearne.	

4

A lovely Ladie rode him faire beside,
  Upon a lowly Asse more white then snow,
30   Yet she much whiter, but the same did hide
  Under a vele, that wimpled° was full low,   folded
  And over all a blacke stole she did throw,
  As one that inly mournd: so was she sad,
  And heavie sat upon her palfrey slow;
35   Seeméd in heart some hidden care she had,
And by her in a line° a milke white lambe she lad.°   leash / led

5

So pure an innocent, as that same lambe,
  She was in life and every vertuous lore,
  And by descent from Royall lynage came
40   Of ancient Kings and Queenes, that had of yore
  Their scepters stretcht from East to Westerne
        shore,
  And all the world in their subjection held;
  Till that infernall feend with foule uprore
  Forwasted all their land, and them expeld:
45 Whom to avenge, she had this Knight from far
      compeld.°   summoned

6

Behind her farre away a Dwarfe did lag,
  That lasie seemd in being ever last,
  Or weariéd with bearing of her bag
  Of needments at his backe. Thus as they past,
50   The day with cloudes was suddeine overcast,
  And angry Jove an hideous storme of raine
  Did poure into his Lemans lap° so fast,   his lover (earth)
  That every wight° to shrowd° it did constrain,   creature / cover
And this faire couple eke to shroud themselves were
    fain.°   eager

7

55 Enforst to seeke some covert nigh at hand,
  A shadie grove not far away they spide,
  That promist ayde the tempest to withstand:
  Whose loftie trees yclad with sommers pride,
  Did spred so broad, that heavens light did hide,
60   Not perceable with power of any starre:
  And all within were pathes and alleies wide,

With footing worne, and leading inward farre:
Faire harbour that them seemes; so in they entred arre.

8

And foorth they passe, with pleasure forward led,
65   Joying to heare the birdes sweete harmony,
Which therein shrouded from the tempest dred,
Seemd in their song to scorne the cruell sky.
Much can° they prayse the trees so straight and hy,   *did*
The sayling Pine, the Cedar proud and tall,
70   The vine-prop Elme, the Poplar never dry,
The builder Oake, sole king of forrests all,
The Aspine good for staves, the Cypresse funerall.

9

The Laurell, meed° of mightie Conquerours   *reward*
And Poets sage, the Firre that weepeth still,
75   The Willow worne of forlorne Paramours,
The Eugh° obedient to the benders will,   *yew*
The Birch for shaftes, the Sallow for the mill,
The Mirrhe sweete bleeding in the bitter wound,
The warlike Beech, the Ash for nothing ill,
80   The fruitfull Olive, and the Platane° round,   *plane-tree*
The carver Holme,° the Maple sceldom inward sound.   *oak*

10

Led with delight, they thus beguile the way,
Untill the blustring storme is overblowne;
When weening° to returne, whence they did stray,   *thinking*
85   They cannot finde that path, which first was showne,
But wander too and fro in wayes unknowne,
Furthest from end then, when they neerest weene,
That makes them doubt, their wits be not their owne:
So many pathes, so many turnings seene,
90   That which of them to take, in diverse doubt they been.

11

At last resolving forward still to fare,
Till that some end they finde or° in or out,   *either*
That path they take, that beaten seemd most bare,
And like to lead the labyrinth about;°   *out of*
95   Which when by tract they hunted had throughout,
At length it brought them to a hollow cave,
Amid the thickest woods. The Champion stout

Eftsoones° dismounted from his courser brave,   soon
And to the Dwarfe a while his needlesse spere he gave.

12

100 "Be well aware," quoth then that Ladie milde,
"Least suddaine mischiefe ye too rash provoke:
The danger hid, the place unknowne and wilde,
Breedes dreadfull doubts: Oft fire is without smoke,
And perill without show: therefore your stroke
105 Sir knight with-hold, till further triall made."
"Ah Ladie," said he, "shame were to revoke
The forward footing for° an hidden shade: because of
Vertue gives her selfe light, through darkenesse for to
    wade."

13

"Yea but," quoth she, "the perill of this place
110 I better wot° then you, though now too late   know
To wish you backe returne with foule disgrace,
Yet wisedome warnes, whilest foot is in the gate,
To stay the steppe, ere forcéd to retrate.
This is the wandring wood, this Errours den,
115 A monster vile, whom God and man does hate:
Therefore I read° beware." "Fly fly," quoth then   advise
The fearefull Dwarfe: "this is no place for living men."

14

But full of fire and greedy hardiment,
The youthful knight could not for ought be staide,
120 But forth unto the darksome hole he went,
And lookéd in: his glistring armor made
A little glooming light, much like a shade,
By which he saw the ugly monster plaine,
Halfe like a serpent horribly displaide,
125 But th'other halfe did womans shape retaine,
Most lothsom, filthie, foule, and full of vile disdaine.

15

And as she lay upon the durtie ground,
Her huge long taile her den all overspred,
Yet was in knots and many boughtes° upwound,   coils
130 Pointed with mortall sting. Of her there bred
A thousand yong ones, which she dayly fed,
Sucking upon her poisonous dugs, cachone
Of sundry shapes, yet all ill favoréd:
Soone as that uncouth° light upon them shone,   unfamiliar
135 Into her mouth they crept, and suddain all were gone.

16

Their dam upstart, out of her den effraide,
  And rushéd forth, hurling her hideous taile
  About her curséd head, whose folds displaid
  Were stretcht now forth at length without entraile.°   winding
140 She lookt about, and seeing one in mayle
  Arméd to point,° sought backe to turne againe;   completely
  For light she hated as the deadly bale,°   harm
  Ay wont in desert darknesse to remaine,
Where plaine none might her see, nor she see any plaine.

17

145 Which when the valiant Elfe perceived, he lept
  As Lyon fierce upon the flying pray,
  And with his trenchand° blade her boldly kept   sharp
  From turning backe, and forcéd her to stay:
  Therewith enraged she loudly gan to bray,
150 And turning fierce, her speckled taile advaunst,
  Threatning her angry sting, him to dismay:
  Who nought aghast, his mightie hand enhaunst:°   raised up
The stroke down from her head unto her shoulder
    glauinst.

18

Much daunted with that dint, her sence was dazd,
155 Yet kindling rage, her selfe she gathered round,
  And all attonce her beastly body raizd
  With doubled forces high above the ground:
  Tho° wrapping up her wrethéd sterne arownd,   then
  Lept fierce upon his shield, and her huge traine°   tail
160 All suddenly about his body wound,
  That hand or foot to stirre he strove in vaine:
God helpe the man so wrapt in Errours endlesse traine.

19

His Lady sad to see his sore constraint,
  Cride out, "Now now Sir knight, shew what ye bee,
165 Add faith unto your force, and be not faint:
  Strangle her, else she sure will strangle thee."
  That when he heard, in great perplexitie,
  His gall did grate for griefe° and high disdaine,   anger
  And knitting all his force got one hand free,
170 Wherewith he grypt her gorge° with so great paine,   neck
That soone to loose her wicked bands did her constraine.

20

Therewith she spewd out of her filthy maw
  A floud of poyson horrible and blacke,
  Full of great lumpes of flesh and gobbets° raw,   pieces
175 Which stunck so vildly, that it forst him slacke
  His grasping hold, and from her turne him backe:
  Her vomit full of bookes and papers was,
  With loathly frogs and toades, which eyes did lacke,
  And creeping sought way in the weedy gras:
180 Her filthy parbreake° all the place defiléd has.   vomit

21

As when old father Nilus gins to swell
  With timely pride above the Aegyptian vale,
  His fattie° waves do fertile slime outwell,   rich
  And overflow each plaine and lowly dale:
185 But when his later spring gins to avale,°   subside
  Huge heapes of mudd he leaves, wherein there breed
  Ten thousand kindes of creatures, partly male
  And partly female of his fruitfull seed;
Such ugly monstrous shapes elsewhere may no man reed.° see

22

190 The same so sore annoyéd has the knight,
  That welnigh chokéd with the deadly stinke,
  His forces faile, ne can no longer fight.
  Whose corage when the feend perceived to shrinke,
  She pouréd forth out of her hellish sinke
195 Her fruitfull curséd spawne of serpents small,
  Deforméd monsters, fowle, and blacke as inke,
  Which swarming all about his legs did crall,
And him encombred sore, but could not hurt at all.

23

As gentle Shepheard in sweete even-tide,
200 When ruddy Phoebus gins to welke° in west,   sink
  High on an hill, his flocke to vewen wide,
  Markes which do byte their hasty supper best;
  A cloud of combrous gnattes do him molest,
  All striving to infixe their feeble stings,
205 That from their noyance he no where can rest,

But with his clownish° hands their tender wings   rustic
He brusheth oft, and oft doth mar their murmurings.

24

Thus ill bestedd,° and fearefull more of shame,   situated
  Then of the certaine perill he stood in,
210   Halfe furious unto his foe he came,
  Resolved in minde all suddenly to win,
  Or soone to lose, before he once would lin;°   cease
  And strooke at her with more then manly force,
  That from her body full of filthie sin
215   He raft° her hatefull head without remorse;   cut off
A streame of cole black bloud forth gushéd from her corse.

25

Her scattred brood, soone as their Parent deare
  They saw so rudely falling to the ground,
  Groning full deadly, all with troublous feare,
220   Gathred themselves about her body round,
  Weening their wonted entrance to have found
  At her wide mouth: but being there withstood
  They flockéd all about her bleeding wound,
  And suckéd up their dying mothers blood,
225 Making her death their life, and eke her hurt their good.

26

That detestable sight him much amazde,
  To see th'unkindly Impes of heaven accurst,
  Devoure their dam; on whom while so he gazd,
  Having all satisfide their bloudy thurst,
230   Their bellies swolne he saw with fulnesse burst,
  And bowels gushing forth: well worthy end
  Of such as drunke her life, the which them nurst;
  Now needeth him no lenger labour spend,
His foes have slaine themselves, with whom he should contend.

27

235 His Ladie seeing all, that chaunst, from farre
  Approcht in hast to greet his victorie,
  And said, "Faire knight, borne under happy starre,
  Who see your vanquisht foes before you lye:

Well worthy be you of that Armorie,°   armor
240 Wherein ye have great glory wonne this day,
And prooved your strength on a strong enimie,
Your first adventure: many such I pray,
And henceforth ever wish, that like succeed it may."

(1590)

Sir Philip Sidney

(1 5 5 4 – 1 5 8 6)

Although he died young, Sir Philip Sidney rose to great prominence as a politician and a writer in Elizabethan England. The son of Sir Henry Sidney and the nephew of Dudley, Earl of Leicester, Sidney attended Oxford briefly before traveling to the Continent. In 1586 he became acquainted with the Earl of Essex and his daughter Penelope, to whom he addressed his famous sonnet sequence, *Astrophil and Stella.* An archetypal Renaissance man, Sidney was a courtier, a diplomat, a scholar, an essayist, a soldier, a poet, and a patron of the arts. He died in an attack against the Spanish forces in the Low Countries.

Sidney influenced the poets of his generation. A friend of Spenser, Gabriel Harvey, and Fulke Greville, he devoted much energy to adapting English poetry to classical tastes. His sonnets, imitative of Petrarch, helped to spur the outpouring of English sonnet sequences in the late Elizabethan period. Traditionally, the Elizabethan sonnet writer displays the frantic, often contradictory emotions of the lover through a series of elaborate conceits addressed to an idealized loved one. Sidney's special achievement in *Astrophil and Stella* was the incorporation of dialogue and other dramatic devices into the 14-line framework. Sidney was also the author of two exceptional prose works. *The Arcadia* is a pastoral romance; its technically innovative poems were woven into the narrative. It is a pastoral work that, like Spenser's *Shepheardes Calender,* contains contemporary political references as well as rustic romance and melodrama. *An Apology for Poetry,* also known as *The Defence of Poesie,* is a long essay that defends literature against the attacks of the Puritans. It emphasizes poetry's antiquity, its universality, its twin functions of teaching and giving pleasure, and its ability to imitate what is, while also suggesting what might be. Sidney's rigorous yet graceful verse mirrored one of the most extraordinary minds of the period. He helped to bring English literature into the Renaissance.

SIR PHILIP SIDNEY

Sonnets from *Astrophil and Stella*

I

Loving in truth, and faine° in verse my love to show,   wanting
That the deare She might take some pleasure of my paine:
Pleasure might cause her reade, reading might make her know,
Knowledge might pitie winne, and pitie grace obtaine,
5   I sought fit words to paint the blackest face of woe,
Studying inventions fine, her wits to entertaine:
Oft turning others' leaves, to see if thence would flow
Some fresh and fruitfull showers upon my sunne-burn'd braine.
   But words came halting forth, wanting Invention's stay,
10   Invention, Nature's child, fled step-dame Studie's blowes,
And others' feete still seem'd but strangers in my way.
   Thus great with child to speake, and helplesse in my throwes,
      Biting my trewand pen, beating my selfe for spite,
      'Foole,' said my Muse to me, 'looke in thy heart and write.'

5

It is most true, that eyes are form'd to serve
The inward light: and that the heavenly part
Ought to be king, from whose rules who do swerve,
Rebels to Nature, strive for their owne smart.
5   It is most true, what we call *Cupid's* dart,
   An image is, which for our selves we carve;
And, fooles, adore in temple of our hart,
Till that good God make Church and Churchman starve.
   True, that true Beautie Vertue is indeed,
10   Whereof this Beautie can be but a shade,
Which elements with mortall mixture breed:[1]
True, that on earth we are but pilgrims made,
   And should in soule up to our countrey move:
   True, and yet true that I must *Stella* love.

6

Some Lovers speake when they their Muses entertaine,
Of hopes begot by feare, of wot° not what desires: know

[1] The four mortal elements are earth, air, fire, and water.

Of force of heav'nly beames, infusing hellish paine:
Of living deaths, deare wounds, faire stormes and freesing fires:
5   Some one his song in *Jove,* and *Jove's* strange tales attires,
Broadred with buls and swans, powdred with golden raine:
Another humbler wit to shepheard's pipe retires,
Yet hiding royall bloud full oft in rurall vaine.
To some a sweetest plaint, a sweetest stile affords,
10   While teares powre out his inke, and sighs breathe out his words:
His paper, pale dispaire, and paine his pen doth move.
I can speake what I feele, and feele as much as they,
But thinke that all the Map of my state I display,
When trembling voice brings forth that I do *Stella* love.

14

Alas have I not paine enough my friend,
    Upon whose breast a fiercer Gripe doth tire
    Then did on him who first stale downe the fire,
While *Love* on me doth all his quiver spend,
5   But with your Rubarb° words yow must contend   bitter
    To grieve me worse, in saying that Desire
    Doth plunge my wel-form'd soule even in the mire
Of sinfull thoughts, which do in ruine end?
    If that be sinne which doth the maners frame,
10   Well staid with truth in word and faith of deed,
Readie of wit and fearing nought but shame:
If that be sinne which in fixt hearts doth breed
    A loathing of all loose unchastitie,
    Then Love is sinne, and let me sinfull be.

31

With how sad steps, ô Moone, thou climb'st the skies,
    How silently, and with how wanne a face,
    What, may it be that even in heav'nly place
That busie archer[2] his sharpe arrowes tries?
5   Sure, if that long with *Love* acquainted eyes
    Can judge of *Love,* thou feel'st a Lover's case;
    I reade it in thy lookes, thy languisht grace,
To me that feele the like, thy state descries.
    Then ev'n of fellowship, ô Moone, tell me
10   Is constant *Love* deem'd there but want of wit?
Are Beauties there as proud as here they be?
Do they above love to be lov'd, and yet
    Those Lovers scorne whom that *Love* doth possesse?
    Do they call *Vertue* there ungratefulnesse?

[2] I.e., Cupid, the god of love.

39

Come sleepe, ô sleepe, the certaine knot of peace,
The baiting place of wit, the balme of woe,
The poore man's wealth, the prisoner's release,
Th'indifferent Judge betweene the high and low;
5   With shield of proofe shield me from out the prease°   press
Of those fierce darts, dispaire at me doth throw:
O make in me those civill warres to cease;
I will good tribute pay if thou do so.
   Take thou of me smooth pillowes, sweetest bed,
10 A chamber deafe to noise, and blind to light:
A rosie garland, and a wearie hed:
And if these things, as being thine by right,
   Move not thy heavy grace, thou shalt in me,
   Livelier than else-where, *Stella's* image see.

64

No more, my deare, no more these counsels trie,
   O give my passions leave to run their race:
   Let Fortune lay on me her worst disgrace,
Let folke orecharg'd with braine against me crie,
5 Let clouds bedimme my face, breake in mine eye,
   Let me no steps but of lost labour trace,
   Let all the earth with scorne recount my case,
But do not will me from my *Love* to flie.
   I do not envie *Aristotle's* wit,
10 Nor do aspire to *Cæsar's* bleeding fame,
Nor ought do care, though some above me sit,
Nor hope, nor wishe another course to frame,
   But that which once may win thy cruell hart:
   Thou art my Wit, and thou my Vertue art.

71

Who will in fairest booke of Nature know,
   How Vertue may best lodg'd in beautie be,
   Let him but learne of *Love* to reade in thee,
Stella, those faire lines, which true goodnesse show.
5 There shall he find all vices' overthrow,
   Not by rude force, but sweetest soveraigntie
   Of reason, from whose light those night-birds flie;
That inward sunne in thine eyes shineth so.
   And not content to be Perfection's heire
10 Thy selfe, doest strive all minds that way to move,
Who marke in thee what is in thee most faire.
So while thy beautie drawes the heart to love,

As fast thy Vertue bends that love to good:
"But ah," Desire still cries, "give me some food."

107

Stella since thou so right a Princesse art
  Of all the powers which life bestowes on me,
  That ere by them ought undertaken be,
They first resort unto that soueraigne part;
5 Sweete, for a while give respite to my hart,
  Which pants as though it still should leape to thee:
  And on my thoughts give thy Lieftenancy
To this great cause, which needs both use and art,
  And as a Queene, who from her presence sends
10 Whom she imployes, dismisse from thee my wit,
Till it have wrought what thy owne will attends.
On servants' shame oft Maister's blame doth sit;
  O let not fooles in me thy workes reprove,
  And scorning say, "See what it is to love."

(1591)

William Shakespeare

(1 5 6 4 – 1 6 1 6)

Frustratingly little is known of Shakespeare's life. Shakespeare was probably educated at the Stratford grammar school, but nothing is known of his youth and it seems that he did not have any higher education. At age 18 he married 26-year-old Anne Hathaway; a first daughter was born six months later. About 1585, Shakespeare moved to London and eventually became chief playwright and occasional actor for the Lord Chamberlain's company of players. Shakespeare's first plays began to appear in 1590. In the next 23 years he produced 37 of the greatest plays in any language. His "sugared sonnets" were published in 1609, apparently without his authorization. Little is known of the biographical background to the sonnets, and we will probably never know the order in which Shakespeare wrote them. Shakespeare retired to Stratford and died there on April 23, 1616.

Shakespeare was a rich and complex playwright, whose plays include a vast range of character, genre, atmosphere, and situation. He produced work in many modes: insightful meditations on the nature of leadership and its relation to society in historical plays such as *Richard II* and the *Henry IV* trilogy; delightful and hilarious comedy, often with dark veins of serious intent, in *A Midsummer Night's Dream, Twelfth Night,* and *As You Like It;* and intricate portrayals of melancholy, ambition, love, old age, jealousy, and pride in the great tragedies, *Hamlet, Macbeth, Antony and Cleopatra, Romeo and Juliet, King Lear, Othello,* and *Coriolanus.* The "problem plays," such as *Troilus and Cressida* and *Measure for Measure,* tend to deal with hypocrisy and deceit. At the end of his career, Shakespeare described fantasy and imagination, the conjunction of romance and realism, magic and the mundane, in *The Tempest* and *The Winter's Tale.* His themes are too numerous to catalog, but two central ones might be mentioned: the consequences of the breakdown of societal and natural hierarchies and the implications of such a breakdown to questions of chance and fate; and man's wearing of masks, the disjunction of appearance and reality, of word and intent, and the intricate, often symbiotic relationship between what we are and what we pretend to be. But perhaps the key to the lasting popularity and relevance of Shakespeare's writing is his delight in language, his inexhaustible creation of living characters, and his unwavering fascination with the poetry of the imagination.

Shakespeare wrote 12 comedies, 10 histories, 11 tragedies, and 4 romances, although the distinctions between these categories are not watertight. He also wrote 154 sonnets and the long dramatic poems *Venus and Adonis, The Rape of Lucrece,* and *The Phoenix and the Turtle.* Many of his works survived due to the *First Folio,* produced by his colleagues after his death; they are read and performed in almost every country and in many languages.

WILLIAM SHAKESPEARE

from *Sonnets*

3

Look in thy glass, and tell the face thou viewest
Now is the time that face should form another,
Whose fresh repair if now thou not renewest,
Thou dost beguile the world, unbless some mother.
5 For where is she so fair whose uneared womb
Disdains the tillage of thy husbandry?
Or who is he so fond will be the tomb
Of his self-love, to stop posterity?
Thou art thy mother's glass, and she in thee
10 Calls back the lovely April of her prime;
So thou through windows of thine age shalt see,
Despite of wrinkles, this thy golden time.
   But if thou live rememb'red not to be,
   Die single, and thine image dies with thee.

12

When I do count the clock that tells the time
And see the brave day sunk in hideous night,
When I behold the violet past prime
And sable curls all silvered o'er with white,
5 When lofty trees I see barren of leaves,
Which erst from heat did canopy the herd,
And summer's green all girded up in sheaves
Borne on the bier with white and bristly beard;
Then of thy beauty do I question make
10 That thou among the wastes of time must go,
Since sweets and beauties do themselves forsake
And die as fast as they see others grow;
   And nothing 'gainst Time's scythe can make defense
   Save breed, to brave him when he takes thee hence.

3: 3 *fresh repair* youthful state   4 *unbless some mother* fail to bless some woman with motherhood
5 *uneared* untilled   7 *fond* foolish; *tomb* monument   8 *to stop posterity* thus bringing an end to
his line   11 *windows . . . age* apertures in the enclosure of old age   13 *rememb'red . . . be* to be
forgotten
12: 2 *brave* splendid   4 *sable* black   6 *erst* formerly   7 *summer's green* i.e., wheat   8 *bier* i.e., the
harvest cart   9 *question make* speculate   14 *breed* offspring; *brave* defy

18

Shall I compare thee to a summer's day?
Thou art more lovely and more temperate.
Rough winds do shake the darling buds of May,
And summer's lease hath all too short a date.
5   Sometime too hot the eye of heaven shines,
And often is his gold complexion dimmed;
And every fair from fair sometime declines,
By chance, or nature's changing course, untrimmed:
But thy eternal summer shall not fade
10   Nor lose possession of that fair thou ow'st,
Nor shall Death brag thou wand'rest in his shade
When in eternal lines to time thou grow'st.
      So long as men can breathe or eyes can see,
      So long lives this, and this gives life to thee.

29

When, in disgrace with Fortune and men's eyes,
I all alone beweep my outcast state,
And trouble deaf heaven with my bootless cries,
And look upon myself and curse my fate,
5   Wishing me like to one more rich in hope,
Featured like him, like him with friends possessed,
Desiring this man's art, and that man's scope,
With what I most enjoy contented least;
Yet in these thoughts myself almost despising,
10   Haply I think on thee, and then my state,
Like to the lark at break of day arising
From sullen earth, sings hymns at heaven's gate;
      For thy sweet love rememb'red such wealth brings
      That then I scorn to change my state with kings.

30

When to the sessions of sweet silent thought
I summon up remembrance of things past,
I sigh the lack of many a thing I sought,
And with old woes new wail my dear time's waste:
5   Then can I drown an eye, unused to flow,

18: 4 *lease* allotted time; *date* duration **5** *eye* sun **6** *dimmed* clouded over **7** *fair from fair*
beautiful thing from beauty **8** *untrimmed* stripped of adornment **10** *thou ow'st* you own
11 *shade* i.e., oblivion **12** *lines* poetry; *thou grow'st* you are grafted
29: 1 *disgrace* disfavor; *eyes* regard **3** *bootless* useless **6** *like him, like him* i.e., like another, like
still another **7** *art* literary skill; *scope* intellectual power **10** *Haply* perchance; *state* i.e., mood,
state of mind **12** *sullen* gloomy **14** *state* lot
30: 1 *sessions* sittings, as of a court **3** *sigh* lament **4** *new wail* newly bewail; *dear time's waste*
time's destruction of precious things (?), the wasteful passing of precious time (?)

For precious friends hid in death's dateless night,
And weep afresh love's long since cancelled woe,
And moan th' expense of many a vanished sight.
Then can I grieve at grievances foregone,
10   And heavily from woe to woe tell o'er
The sad account of fore-bemoanèd moan,
Which I new pay as if not paid before.
      But if the while I think on thee, dear friend,
      All losses are restored and sorrows end.

55

Not marble nor the gilded monuments
Of princes shall outlive this pow'rful rime,
But you shall shine more bright in these contents
Than unswept stone, besmeared with sluttish time.
5   When wasteful war shall statues overturn,
And broils root out the work of masonry,
Nor Mars his sword nor war's quick fire shall burn
The living record of your memory.
'Gainst death and all oblivious enmity
10   Shall you pace forth; your praise shall still find room
Even in the eyes of all posterity
That wear this world out to the ending doom.
      So, till the judgment that yourself arise,
      You live in this, and dwell in lovers' eyes.

60

Like as the waves make towards the pebbled shore,
So do our minutes hasten to their end;
Each changing place with that which goes before,
In sequent toil all forwards do contend.
5   Nativity, once in the main of light,
Crawls to maturity, wherewith being crowned,
Crooked eclipses 'gainst his glory fight,
And Time that gave doth now his gift confound.
Time doth transfix the flourish set on youth
10   And delves the parallels in beauty's brow,
Feeds on the rarities of nature's truth,
And nothing stands but for his scythe to mow:

---

6 *dateless* endless   7 *cancelled* fully paid   8 *expense* loss   9 *foregone* former   10 *tell* count
55: 2 *rime* poem   3 *these contents* what is here contained   4 *Than* than in; *stone* memorial tablet;
sluttish untidy   6 *broils* battles   7 *Nor* neither; *Mars his sword* i.e., the sword of Mars shall
destroy   9 *all oblivious enmity* i.e., oblivion the enemy of all   12 *That wear* who last   13 *judgment
that* judgment day when
60: 4 *sequent* successive; *contend* struggle   5 *Nativity* the newborn; *the . . . light* orbit   7 *Crooked*
adverse, malignant   8 *confound* destroy   10 *delves the parallels* digs the lines

And yet to times in hope my verse shall stand,
Praising thy worth, despite his cruel hand.

71

No longer mourn for me when I am dead
Than you shall hear the surly sullen bell
Give warning to the world that I am fled
From this vile world, with vilest worms to dwell.
5 Nay, if you read this line, remember not
The hand that writ it, for I love you so
That I in your sweet thoughts would be forgot
If thinking on me then should make you woe.
O, if, I say, you look upon this verse
10 When I, perhaps, compounded am with clay,
Do not so much as my poor name rehearse,
But let your love even with my life decay,
    Lest the wise world should look into your moan
    And mock you with me after I am gone.

73

That time of year thou mayst in me behold
When yellow leaves, or none, or few, do hang
Upon those boughs which shake against the cold,
Bare ruined choirs where late the sweet birds sang.
5 In me thou seest the twilight of such day
As after sunset fadeth in the west,
Which by and by black night doth take away,
Death's second self that seals up all in rest.
In me thou seest the glowing of such fire
10 That on the ashes of his youth doth lie,
As the deathbed whereon it must expire,
Consumed with that which it was nourished by.
    This thou perceiv'st, which makes thy love more strong,
    To love that well which thou must leave ere long.

106

When in the chronicle of wasted time
I see descriptions of the fairest wights,
And beauty making beautiful old rime

---

13 *times in hope* hoped-for times; *stand* endure
71: 8 *make you woe* make woe for you   **10** *compounded* blended   **13** *wise* i.e., disdainful of foolish sentiment   **14** *with* because of
73: 4 *choirs* i.e., the part of a church or monastery where services were sung   **7** *by and by* shortly
8 *seals up* encloses   **10** *That* as   **12** *with . . . by* i.e., by life
106: 1 *wasted* past   **2** *wights* persons

In praise of ladies dead and lovely knights;
5 Then, in the blazon of sweet beauty's best,
Of hand, of foot, of lip, of eye, of brow,
I see their antique pen would have expressed
Even such a beauty as you master now.
So all their praises are but prophecies
10 Of this our time, all you prefiguring;
And, for they looked but with divining eyes,
They had not skill enough your worth to sing:
    For we, which now behold these present days,
    Have eyes to wonder, but lack tongues to praise.

116

Let me not to the marriage of true minds
Admit impediments; love is not love
Which alters when it alteration finds
Or bends with the remover to remove.
5 O, no, it is an ever-fixèd mark
That looks on tempests and is never shaken;
It is the star to every wand'ring bark,
Whose worth's unknown, although his height be taken.
Love's not Time's fool, though rosy lips and cheeks
10 Within his bending sickle's compass come;
Love alters not with his brief hours and weeks,
But bears it out even to the edge of doom.
    If this be error, and upon me proved,
    I never writ, nor no man ever loved.

129

Th' expense of spirit in a waste of shame
Is lust in action; and, till action, lust
Is perjured, murd'rous, bloody, full of blame,
Savage, extreme, rude, cruel, not to trust;
5 Enjoyed no sooner but despisèd straight;
Past reason hunted, and no sooner had,
Past reason hated as a swallowed bait
On purpose laid to make the taker mad:
Mad in pursuit, and in possession so;

---

5 *blazon* commemorative record 8 *master* command 10 *prefiguring* picturing in advance
11 *for* because; *divining* guessing 13 *we* i.e., even we
116: 2 *impediments* (an echo of the marriage service) 4 *bends . . . remove* i.e., agrees with the
withdrawer to withdraw 5 *mark* sea-mark 8 *worth's unknown* i.e., value is incalculable; *his
height* the star's altitude 9 *fool* plaything 10 *Within . . . compass* i.e., within the range of Time's
curving sickle 11 *his* Time's 12 *bears it out* persists 13 *upon* against
129: 1 *Th' expense . . . shame* i.e., the expenditure of vital power in shameful waste 2 *action*
consummation 4 *rude* brutal; *to trust* to be trusted 6 *Past reason hunted* i.e., madly sought

10   Had, having, and in quest to have, extreme;
A bliss in proof, and proved, a very woe;
Before, a joy proposed; behind, a dream.
    All this the world well knows; yet none knows well
    To shun the heaven that leads men to this hell.

130

My mistress' eyes are nothing like the sun;
Coral is far more red than her lips' red;
If snow be white, why then her breasts are dun;
If hairs be wires, black wires grow on her head.
5   I have seen roses damasked, red and white,
But no such roses see I in her cheeks;
And in some perfumes is there more delight
Than in the breath that from my mistress reeks.
I love to hear her speak; yet well I know
10   That music hath a far more pleasing sound:
I grant I never saw a goddess go;
My mistress, when she walks, treads on the ground.
    And yet, by heaven, I think my love as rare
    As any she belied with false compare.

138

When my love swears that she is made of truth
I do believe her, though I know she lies,
That she might think me some untutored youth,
Unlearnèd in the world's false subtilties.
5   Thus vainly thinking that she thinks me young,
Although she knows my days are past the best,
Simply I credit her false-speaking tongue;
On both sides thus is simple truth suppressed.
But wherefore says she not she is unjust?
10   And wherefore say not I that I am old?
O, love's best habit is in seeming trust,
And age in love loves not to have years told.
    Therefore I lie with her and she with me,
    And in our faults by lies we flattered be.

10 *quest* pursuit; *extreme* excessive, given to extremes   11 *in proof* in testing; *proved* tested
12 *dream* delusion   14 *heaven* i.e., promise of bliss
130: 5 *damasked* mingled red and white   8 *reeks* breathes forth   11 *go* walk   14 *compare* comparison (with sun, coral, snow, etc.)
138: 1 *truth* fidelity   2 *believe* seem to believe   5 *vainly thinking* i.e., acting as if I thought
7 *Simply* pretending to be simple; *credit* give credence to   9 *unjust* unfaithful   11 *habit* dress,
guise; *seeming trust* apparent fidelity   12 *told* counted   13 *lie with* i.e., lie to (with *double entendre*)

140

Be wise as thou art cruel: do not press
My tongue-tied patience with too much disdain,
Lest sorrow lend me words, and words express
The manner of my pity-wanting pain.
5 If I might teach thee wit, better it were,
Though not to love, yet, love, to tell me so;
As testy sick men, when their deaths be near,
No news but health from their physicians know.
For if I should despair, I should grow mad,
10 And in my madness might speak ill of thee:
Now this ill-wresting world is grown so bad
Mad slanderers by mad ears believèd be.
 That I may not be so, nor thou belied,
 Bear thine eyes straight, though thy proud heart go wide.

        (1609)

140: 1 *press* oppress   4 *manner* nature; *pity-wanting* unpitied   5 *wit* wisdom   6 *so* i.e., that you do love me   7 *testy* peevish   8 *know* i.e., hear   11 *ill-wresting* i.e., that wrests things to an evil sense   13 *so* i.e., a "mad slanderer"   14 *wide* astray

Thomas Campion

(1 5 6 7 - 1 6 2 0)

Thomas Campion was a law student, a Cambridge scholar, a doctor of medicine, a composer, a prose writer, and a poet. He was also a devoted enthusiast of the poetry of the Roman lyricists Catullus and Horace, and an advocate of the quantitative meter (where syllables are patterned according to duration rather than stress) in which they wrote. Much of Campion's best poetry was composed in Latin.

Campion published his theories on quantitative verse and its application to English poetry in *Observations in the Art of English Poesy.* He also published a treatise on music, then combined his talents to produce a large body of songs for which he composed both lyrics and music. His songs and poems have an attractively classical, even pagan, tone and display freshness and inventiveness. Many of Campion's best poems, such as "My Sweetest Lesbia," are imitations of or translations from Catullus and Horace. His "Rose-cheeked Laura" is a skillfully executed example of the use of quantitative meter in English.

Campion published a volume of Latin verse, "Poemata," in 1592, and his *Observations in the Art of English Poesy* in 1602. He wrote a volume of songs on the death of Prince Henry. The bulk of his lyric verse appeared in four "Books of Ayres," from 1610 to 1612.

THOMAS CAMPION

My Sweetest Lesbia

>   My sweetest Lesbia, let us live and love,
>   And, though the sager sort our deedes reprove,
>   Let us not way them: heav'ns great lampes doe dive
>   Into their west, and strait againe revive,
> 5 But, soone as once set is our little light,
>   Then must we sleepe one ever-during night.
>
>   If all would lead their lives in love like mee,
>   Then bloudie swords and armour should not be,
>   No drum nor trumpet peaceful sleepes should move,

10   Unles alar'me came from the campe of love:
    But fooles do live, and wast their little light,
    And seeke with paine their ever-during night.

    When timely death my life and fortune ends,
    Let not my hearse be vext with mourning friends,
15   But let all lovers, rich in triumph, come,
    And with sweet pastimes grace my happie tombe;
    And, Lesbia, close up thou my little light,
    And crowne with love my ever-during night.

                                  (1601)

There Is a Garden in Her Face

    There is a Garden in her face,
  Where Roses and white Lillies grow;
    A heav'nly paradice is that place,
  Wherein all pleasant fruits doe flow.
5   There Cherries grow, which none may buy
    Till Cherry ripe[1] themselves doe cry.

    Those Cherries fayrely doe enclose
  Of Orient Pearle a double row,
    Which when her lovely laughter showes,
10   They looke like Rose-buds fill'd with snow.
    Yet them nor Peere nor Prince can buy,
    Till Cherry ripe themselves doe cry.

    Her Eyes like Angels watch them still;
  Her Browes like bended bowes doe stand,
15   Threatning with piercing frownes to kill
  All that attempt with eye or hand
    Those sacred Cherries to come nigh,
    Till Cherry ripe themselves doe cry.

                                    (1617)

---

[1] A common phrase used by London street vendors.

Think'st Thou to Seduce Me Then

Think'st thou to seduce me then with words that
    have no meaning?
Parats° so can learne to prate, our speech by pieces   Parrots
    gleaning:
Nurces teach their children so about the time of
    weaning.

Learne to speake first, then to wooe: to wooing much
    pertayneth:
5 Hee that courts us, wanting Arte, soone falters when
    he fayneth,
Lookes a-squint on his discourse,[1] and smiles when
    hee complaineth.

Skilfull Anglers hide their hookes, fit baytes for every
    season;
But with crooked pins fish thou, as babes doe that
    want reason;
Gogians[2] onely can be caught with such poore trickes
    of treason.

10 Ruth° forgive me, if I err'd from humane hearts   Pity
    compassion
When I laught sometimes too much to see thy
    foolish fashion:
But, alas, who lesse could doe that found so good
    occasion?

                        (1617)

---

[1] Takes a look at his (lover's) notes.
[2] A small fish easily caught; one who is easily entrapped or deceived.

John Donne

(1 5 7 2 – 1 6 3 1)

The son of a Catholic ironmonger who lived in London, John Donne was educated at Oxford, Cambridge, and Lincoln's Inn, but obtained no degrees. His religion barred him from many professions. Donne secretly married Anne More, thus alienating his patron, her uncle. He lost his seat in Parliament and spent time in prison. By age 35 he was sick and poor and had to struggle to support a growing family. He began to compose a treatise on the legality of suicide. After a period of inner turmoil, Donne took Anglican orders in 1615. By 1621 he was Dean of St. Paul's and the most famous preacher in London. Shortly before his death he gave what was considered his own funeral sermon—a powerful, terrifying analysis of human decay.

Donne was best known in his own day as a writer of great sermons and as the author of the brilliant series of prayers and meditations, *Devotions upon Emergent Occasions,* composed in 1623. In dense, rhythmical, energetic prose, Donne's *Devotions* stands as a profound investigation of man's moral relation to himself, his society, and his God. The sermons, like much of Donne's religious poetry, take a tortured, even confrontational, stance before the deity. They describe the activity of being both mortal and immortal, both soul and flesh, both joyous and despairing. His religious verse uses much the same technique as the great love poetry from his "Jake the Rake" days, and is filled with the erotic metaphors of a passionate, turbulent relationship. The best known of the "metaphysical" poets (the term was first applied to Donne in the eighteenth century), Donne wrote in a new form that was unlike the sugared, musical lyrics of Campion or Sidney. His work is characterized by jagged but kinetic rhythms, complex rhetorical constructions, and the use of elaborate "conceits," sustained metaphors such as the compass symbol that describes the relationship of lovers in "A Valediction: Forbidding Mourning." Donne's conceits are always striking and sometimes outrageous, but they are never boring. As Thomas Carew wrote, Donne was a "king who ruled as he thought fit / The universal monarchy of wit." Donne's poetry, written as Renaissance ideas took hold in England, is a searching study of humanity's place in the new, more chaotic cosmos.

Donne was the author of many early love poems, few published in his own lifetime, and a body of sacred poems, including the superb "Holy Sonnets." *Songs and Sonnets* appeared in 1633. His most important long poem is *An Anatomy of the World.* A series of satires and elegies is also highly regarded. One hundred sixty of his sermons survive, as well as the famous *Devotions.*

JOHN DONNE

The Good Morrow

I wonder by my troth, what thou, and I
   Did, till we loved? were we not weaned till then,
But sucked on country pleasures, childishly?
   Or snorted we in the seven sleepers' den?[1]
5   'Twas so; but this, all pleasures fancies be.
If ever any beauty I did see,
Which I desired, and got, 'twas but a dream of thee.

And now good morrow to our waking souls,
   Which watch not one another out of fear;
10   For love, all love of other sights controls,
   And makes one little room, an every where.
Let sea-discoverers to new worlds have gone,
Let maps to others, worlds on worlds have shown,
Let us possess one world, each hath one, and is one.

15   My face in thine eye, thine in mine appears,
   And true plain hearts do in the faces rest,
Where can we find two better hemispheres
   Without sharp north, without declining west?
What ever dies, was not mixed equally;[2]
20   If our two loves be one, or, thou and I
Love so alike, that none do slacken, none can die.

(1633)

Song

Go, and catch a falling star,
   Get with child a mandrake root,[1]

---

[1] A reference to the seven youths who, according to legend, slept in a cave for 187 years to avoid persecution from the Roman emperor Decius.
[2] According to Medieval philosophy, if the elements were imperfectly mixed, the matter was mortal; when they were perfectly balanced, immortality would be possible.
[1] The root of the mandrake is shaped like a human torso and legs and was thought to have magical powers.

Tell me, where all past years are,
  Or who cleft the Devil's foot,
5 Teach me to hear mermaids singing,
  Or to keep off envy's stinging,
      And find
      What wind
Serves to advance an honest mind.

10 If thou be'est born to strange sights,
  Things invisible to see,
Ride ten thousand days and nights,
  Till age snow white hairs on thee,
Thou, when thou return'st, wilt tell me
15 All strange wonders that befell thee,
      And swear
      No where
Lives a woman true, and fair.

If thou find'st one, let me know,
20   Such a pilgrimage were sweet;
Yet do not, I would not go,
  Though at next door we might meet;
Though she were true when you met her,
And last till you write your letter,
25   Yet she
      Will be
False, ere I come, to two, or three.

             (1633)

The Canonization

For God's sake hold your tongue, and let me love,
  Or chide my palsy, or my gout,
My five grey hairs, or ruined fortune flout,
  With wealth your state, your mind with arts improve,
5   Take you a course, get you a place,[1]
    Observe his Honour, or his Grace,
Or the King's real, or his stamped face[2]
    Contemplate; what you will, approve,°   experience
  So you will let me love.

[1] Get a direction in life; get an appointment.
[2] On coins.

10 Alas, alas, who's injured by my love?
        What merchant's ships have my sighs drowned?
    Who says my tears have overflowed his ground?
        When did my colds a forward spring remove?
            When did the heats which my veins fill
15   Add one more to the plaguy bill?[3]
    Soldiers find wars, and lawyers find out still
        Litigious men, which quarrels move,
        Though she and I do love.

    Call us what you will, we are made such by love;
20   Call her one, me another fly,
    We are tapers too, and at our own cost die,
        And we in us find the eagle and the dove,
            The phoenix riddle hath more wit
            By us; we two being one, are it.
25 So to one neutral thing both sexes fit
        We die and rise the same, and prove
        Mysterious by this love.

    We can die by it, if not live by love,
        And if unfit for tombs and hearse
30 Our legend be, it will be fit for verse;
        And if no piece of chronicle we prove,
            We'll build in sonnets pretty rooms;
            As well a well-wrought urn becomes
    The greatest ashes, as half-acre tombs,
35   And by these hymns, all shall approve
        Us canonized for love:

    And thus invoke us: You whom reverend love
        Made one another's hermitage;
    You, to whom love was peace, that now is rage;
40   Who did the whole world's soul contract, and drove
            Into the glasses of your eyes
            (So made such mirrors, and such spies,
    That they did all to you epitomize)
        Countries, towns, courts: Beg from above
45   A pattern of your love![4]

                                    (1633)

---

[3] Deaths from the plague were recorded on a weekly bill or list.
[4] The poet and his mistress are implored to ask the heavens to send to earth a pattern of their love so that all people may learn from it.

The Flea

Mark but this flea, and mark in this,
How little that which thou deny'st me is;
Me it sucked first, and now sucks thee,
And in this flea, our two bloods mingled be;
5 Confess it, this cannot be said
A sin, or shame, or loss of maidenhead,
   Yet this enjoys before it woo,
   And pampered swells with one blood made of two,
   And this, alas, is more than we would do.

10 Oh stay, three lives in one flea spare,
Where we almost, nay more than married are.
This flea is you and I, and this
Our marriage bed, and marriage temple is;
Though parents grudge, and you, we'are met,
15 And cloistered in these living walls of jet.
   Though use° make you apt to kill me,   custom
   Let not to this, self murder added be,
   And sacrilege, three sins in killing three.

Cruel and sudden, hast thou since
20 Purpled thy nail, in blood of innocence?
In what could this flea guilty be,
Except in that drop which it sucked from thee?
Yet thou triumph'st, and say'st that thou
Find'st not thyself, nor me the weaker now;
25   'Tis true, then learn how false, fears be;
   Just so much honour, when thou yield'st to me,
   Will waste, as this flea's death took life from thee.
                         (1633)

The Bait

Come live with me, and be my love,
And we will some new pleasures prove
Of golden sands, and crystal brooks,
With silken lines, and silver hooks.

5 There will the river whispering run
   Warmed by thy eyes, more than the sun.
   And there the'enamoured fish will stay,
   Begging themselves they may betray.

   When thou wilt swim in that live bath,
10 Each fish, which every channel hath,
   Will amorously to thee swim,
   Gladder to catch thee, than thou him.

   If thou, to be so seen, be'st loth,
   By sun, or moon, thou darkenest both,
15 And if myself have leave to see,
   I need not their light, having thee.

   Let others freeze with angling reeds,
   And cut their legs, with shells and weeds,
   Or treacherously poor fish beset,
20 With strangling snare, or windowy net:

   Let coarse bold hands, from slimy nest
   The bedded fish in banks out-wrest,
   Or curious traitors, sleavesilk flies
   Bewitch poor fishes' wandering eyes.

25 For thee, thou need'st no such deceit,
   For thou thyself art thine own bait,
   That fish, that is not catched thereby,
   Alas, is wiser far than I.

                                    (1633)

A Valediction: Forbidding Mourning

   As virtuous men pass mildly away,
      And whisper to their souls, to go,
   Whilst some of their sad friends do say,
      The breath goes now, and some say, no:

5 So let us melt, and make no noise,
      No tear-floods, nor sigh-tempests move,
   'Twere profanation of our joys
      To tell the laity our love.

Moving of th' earth brings harms and fears,
10   Men reckon what it did and meant,
But trepidation of the spheres,
        Though greater far, is innocent.

Dull sublunary lovers' love
        (Whose soul is sense) cannot admit
15   Absence, because it doth remove
        Those things which elemented it.°   composed it

But we by a love, so much refined,
        That our selves know not what it is,
Inter-assured of the mind,
20   Care less, eyes, lips, and hands to miss.

Our two souls therefore, which are one,
        Though I must go, endure not yet
A breach, but an expansion,
        Like gold to aery thinness beat.

25   If they be two, they are two so
        As stiff twin compasses are two,
'Thy soul the fixed foot, makes no show
        To move, but doth, if th'other do.

And though it in the centre sit,
30   Yet when the other far doth roam,
It leans, and hearkens after it,
        And grows erect, as that comes home.

Such wilt thou be to me, who must
        Like th' other foot, obliquely run;
35   Thy firmness makes my circle just,
        And makes me end, where I begun.

                                      (1633)

The Ecstasy

Where, like a pillow on a bed,
        A pregnant bank swelled up, to rest
The violet's reclining head,
        Sat we two, one another's best;

5   Our hands were firmly cemented
    With a fast balm, which thence did spring,
Our eye-beams twisted, and did thread
    Our eyes, upon one double string;

So to' intergraft our hands, as yet
10   Was all our means to make us one,
And pictures in our eyes to get
    Was all our propagation.

As 'twixt two equal armies, Fate
    Suspends uncertain victory,
15   Our souls, (which to advance their state,
    Were gone out), hung 'twixt her, and me.

And whilst our souls negotiate there,
    We like sepulchral statues lay;
All day, the same our postures were,
20   And we said nothing, all the day.

If any, so by love refined,
    That he soul's language understood,
And by good love were grown all mind,
    Within convenient distance stood,

25   He (though he knew not which soul spake
    Because both meant, both spake the same)
Might thence a new concoction take,
    And part far purer than he came.

This ecstasy doth unperplex
30   (We said) and tell us what we love,
We see by this, it was not sex,
    We see, we saw not what did move:[1]

But as all several souls contain
    Mixture of things, they know not what,
35   Love, these mixed souls doth mix again,
    And makes both one, each this and that.

A single violet transplant,
    The strength, the colour, and the size,

[1] We see *now* that we did not see *before* what motivated us.

(All which before was poor, and scant,)
40   Redoubles still, and multiplies.

When love, with one another so
    Interinanimates two souls,
That abler soul, which thence doth flow,
    Defects of loneliness controls.

45 We then, who are this new soul, know,
    Of what we are composed, and made,
For, th' atomies of which we grow,
    Are souls, whom no change can invade.

But O alas, so long, so far
50   Our bodies why do we forbear?
They are ours, though they are not we, we are
    The intelligences, they the sphere.[2]

We owe them thanks, because they thus,
    Did us, to us, at first convey,
55 Yielded their forces, sense, to us,
    Nor are dross to us, but allay,°   alloy

On man heaven's influence works not so,
    But that it first imprints the air,
So soul into the soul may flow,
60   Though it to body first repair.

As our blood labours to beget
    Spirits, as like souls as it can,
Because such fingers need to knit
    That subtle knot, which makes us man:

65 So must pure lovers' souls descend
    T' affections, and to faculties,
Which sense may reach and apprehend,
    Else a great prince in prison lies.

To our bodies turn we then, that so
70   Weak men on love revealed may look;
Love's mysteries in souls do grow,
    But yet the body is his book.

---

[2] Medieval astronomers thought that the planets were set in spheres that were inhabited by
"intelligences" that controlled them.

And if some lover, such as we,
 Have heard this dialogue of one,
75 Let him still mark us, he shall see
 Small change, when we'are to bodies gone.

        (1633)

from *Holy Sonnets*

5

I am a little world made cunningly
Of elements, and an angelic sprite,
But black sin hath betrayed to endless night
My world's both parts, and, oh, both parts must die.
5 You which beyond that heaven which was most high
Have found new spheres, and of new lands can write,
Pour new seas in mine eyes, that so I might
Drown my world with my weeping earnestly,
Or wash it if it must be drowned no more:
10 But oh it must be burnt; alas the fire
Of lust and envy have burnt it heretofore,
And made it fouler; let their flames retire,
And burn me O Lord, with a fiery zeal
Of thee and thy house, which doth in eating heal.

        (1633)

7

At the round earth's imagined corners, blow
Your trumpets, angels, and arise, arise
From death, you numberless infinities
Of souls, and to your scattered bodies go,
5 All whom the flood did, and fire shall o'erthrow,
All whom war, dearth, age, agues, tyrannies,
Despair, law, chance, hath slain, and you whose eyes,
Shall behold God, and never taste death's woe.
But let them sleep, Lord, and me mourn a space,
10 For, if above all these, my sins abound,
'Tis late to ask abundance of thy grace,
When we are there; here on this lowly ground,
Teach me how to repent; for that's as good
As if thou hadst sealed my pardon, with thy blood.

        (1633)

10

Death be not proud, though some have called thee
Mighty and dreadful, for, thou art not so,
For, those, whom thou think'st, thou dost overthrow,
Die not, poor death, nor yet canst thou kill me;
5 From rest and sleep, which but thy pictures be,
Much pleasure, then from thee, much more must flow,
And soonest our best men with thee do go,
Rest of° their bones, and soul's delivery.   for
Thou art slave to fate, chance, kings, and desperate men,
10 And dost with poison, war, and sickness dwell,
And poppy, or charms can make us sleep as well,
And better than thy stroke; why swell'st thou then?
One short sleep past, we wake eternally,
And death shall be no more, Death thou shalt die.

(1633)

14

Batter my heart, three-personed God; for, you
As yet but knock, breathe, shine, and seek to mend;
That I may rise, and stand, o'erthrow me, and bend
Your force, to break, blow, burn, and make me new.
5 I, like an usurped town, to another due,
Labour to admit you, but oh, to no end,
Reason your viceroy in me, me should defend,
But is captived, and proves weak or untrue,
Yet dearly' I love you, and would be loved fain,
10 But am betrothed unto your enemy,
Divorce me, untie, or break that knot again,
Take me to you, imprison me, for I
Except you enthral me, never shall be free,
Nor ever chaste, except you ravish me.

(1633)

18

Show me dear Christ, thy spouse, so bright and clear.
What, is it she, which on the other shore
Goes richly painted?[1] or which robbed and tore
Laments and mourns in Germany and here?
5 Sleeps she a thousand, then peeps up one year?
Is she self truth and errs? now new, now outwore?
Doth she, and did she, and shall she evermore
On one, on seven, or on no hill appear?
Dwells she with us, or like adventuring knights

[1] The Church.

10   First travail we to seek and then make love?
Betray kind husband thy spouse to our sights,
And let mine amorous soul court thy mild dove,
Who is most true, and pleasing to thee, then
When she' is embraced and open to most men.

(1633)

Hymn to God My God, in My Sickness

Since I am coming to that holy room,
    Where, with thy choir of saints for evermore,
I shall be made thy music; as I come
    I tune the instrument here at the door,
5   And what I must do then, think here before.

Whilst my physicians by their love are grown
    Cosmographers, and I their map, who lie
Flat on this bed, that by them may be shown
    That this is my south-west discovery[1]
10   *Per fretum febris,*[2] by these straits to die,

I joy, that in these straits, I see my west;
    For, though their currents yield return to none,
What shall my west hurt me? As west and east
    In all flat maps (and I am one) are one,
15   So death doth touch the resurrection.

Is the Pacific Sea my home? Or are
    The eastern riches? Is Jerusalem?
Anyan,[3] and Magellan, and Gibraltar,
    All straits, and none but straits, are ways to them,
20   Whether where Japhet dwelt, or Cham, or Shem.[4]

We think that Paradise and Calvary,
    Christ's Cross, and Adam's tree, stood in one place;
Look Lord, and find both Adams met in me;
    As the first Adam's sweat surrounds my face,
25   May the last Adam's blood my soul embrace.

---

[1] The Straits of Magellan, at the southern tip of South America.
[2] By way of the straits of fever.
[3] The Bering Strait, the stretch of water between Alaska and Siberia.
[4] The three sons of Noah.

So, in his purple wrapped receive me Lord,
  By these his thorns give me his other crown;
And as to others' souls I preached thy word,
  Be this my text, my sermon to mine own,
30   Therefore that he may raise the Lord throws down.

                      (1635)

Ben Jonson

(1 5 7 2 – 1 6 3 7)

Ben Jonson led a brilliant but turbulent life. After his father's early death, he was adopted by a bricklayer, who secured him a classical education from the scholar William Camden. Financial necessity caused him to enlist in the army, where he gained fame by fighting in single combat before the massed armies in Flanders and killing his opponent. In 1597 he began to work as an actor and playwright. After spending time in prison for killing a fellow actor in a duel, he produced his first major play, *Every Man in His Humour.* (Actor William Shakespeare played a lead role.) A flurry of plays, poems, and masques followed; his masques were coproduced with Inigo Jones and won him approval at court. In 1616 he was appointed the first poet laureate and published a large volume called *Works.* A friend of most of the famous writers of his day from Shakespeare to John Donne, the arrogant, quarrelsome, fearless, and warm-hearted Jonson was rewarded with the epitaph "O rare Ben Jonson," inscribed on his tomb in Westminster Abbey by his admirers.

Jonson's accomplishments as an artist are varied. He introduced the "comedy of humors," where various predominating passions of men are cleverly deflated, to the English stage. His plays *Volpone* and *The Alchemist* are two of the greatest satires in the language. A restless innovator, Jonson also wrote many unsuccessful plays; for example, the static, classical tragedy *Sejanus.* His poetry includes verse of festive delight, opulent imitations of classical authors, brief, classically crafted elegies, and epitaphs of cold but brilliant austerity, songs, and a large collection of lewd, vicious, and funny epigrams in the manner of Martial. The central thrust of much of his best work is satiric. His keen eye for the foibles of individuals and society made his writing a scathing but healthy insult to all of his open-minded readers.

Jonson wrote many plays. The best known are *Every Man in His Humour* (1598), *Every Man Out of His Humour* (1599), *The Poetaster* (1601), *Sejanus* (1603), *Volpone* (1606), *The Alchemist* (1610), *Bartholomew Fair* (1614), and *The Staple of the News* (1625). He was involved in the production of several masques, including *Pleasure Reconciled to Virtue* (1618), which inspired Milton's "Comus." His poems fill volumes. A collection of notes and essays in prose, *Timber: or Discoveries Made Upon Men and Matter,* appeared after his death.

BEN JONSON

Inviting a Friend to Supper

Tonight, grave sir, both my poor house, and I
Do equally desire your company:
Not that we think us worthy such a guest,
But that your worth will dignify our feast,
5   With those that come; whose grace may make that seem
Something, which, else, could hope for no esteem.
It is the fair acceptance, sir, creates
The entertainment perfect: not the cates.°   *delicious food*
Yet shall you have, to rectify your palate,
10   An olive, capers, or some better salad
Ush'ring the mutton; with a short-legged hen,
If we can get her, full of eggs, and then,
Lemons, and wine for sauce: to these, a cony°   *rabbit*
Is not to be despaired of, for our money;
15   And, though fowl, now, be scarce, yet there are clerks,
The sky not falling, think we may have larks.
I'll tell you of more, and lie, so you will come:
Of partridge, pheasant, woodcock, of which some
May yet be there; and godwit, if we can:
20   Knat, rail, and ruff too.[1] Howsoe'er, my man
Shall read a piece of Virgil, Tacitus,
Livy, or of some better book to us,
Of which we'll speak our minds, amidst our meat;
And I'll profess no verses to repeat:
25   To this, if aught appear, which I not know of,
That will the pastry, not my paper, show of.
Digestive cheese, and fruit there sure will be;
But that, which most doth take my muse, and me,
Is a pure cup of rich canary wine,
30   Which is the Mermaid's,[2] now, but shall be mine:
Of which had Horace, or Anacreon tasted,
Their lives, as do their lines, till now had lasted.
Tobacco, nectar, or the Thespian spring,
Are all but Luther's beer,[3] to this I sing.

[1] Curlew, snipe, marsh-hen, and sandpiper.
[2] Mermaid Tavern, well known among poets.
[3] Watered-down beer.

35 Of this we will sup free, but moderately,
And we will have no Pooly, or Parrot[4] by;
Nor shall our cups make any guilty men:
But, at our parting, we will be, as when
We innocently met. No simple word,
40 That shall be uttered at our mirthful board,
Shall make us sad next morning: or affright
The liberty, that we'll enjoy tonight.

(1616)

Song: To Celia

Drink to me, only, with thine eyes,
    And I will pledge with mine;
Or leave a kiss but in the cup,
    And I'll not look for wine.
5 The thirst, that from the soul doth rise,
    Doth ask a drink divine:
But might I of Jove's nectar sup,
    I would not change for thine.
I sent thee, late, a rosy wreath,
10   Not so much honouring thee,
As giving it a hope, that there
    It could not withered be.
But thou thereon didst only breathe,
    And send'st it back to me:
15 Since when it grows, and smells, I swear,
    Not of itself, but thee.

(1616)

To the Memory of My Beloved, the Author Mr William Shakespeare: And What He Hath Left Us

To draw no envy (Shakespeare) on thy name,
Am I thus ample to thy book, and fame:
While I confess thy writings to be such,
As neither man, nor muse, can praise too much.

---

4 Two government spies.

5 'Tis true, and all men's suffrage.° But these ways   agreement
 Were not the paths I meant unto thy praise:
 For seeliest ignorance on these may light,
 Which, when it sounds at best, but echoes right;
 Or blind affection, which doth ne'er advance
10 The truth, but gropes, and urgeth all by chance;
 Or crafty malice, might pretend this praise,
 And think to ruin, where it seemed to raise.
 These are, as some infamous bawd, or whore,
 Should praise a matron. What could hurt her more?
15 But thou art proof against them, and indeed
 Above the ill fortune of them, or the need.
 I therefore will begin. Soul of the age!
 The applause, delight, the wonder of our stage!
 My Shakespeare, rise; I will not lodge thee by
20 Chaucer, or Spenser, or bid Beaumont lie
 A little further, to make thee a room:[1]
 Thou art a monument, without a tomb,
 And art alive still, while thy book doth live,
 And we have wits to read, and praise to give.
25 That I not mix thee so, my brain excuses;
 I mean with great, but disproportioned muses:
 For, if I thought my judgement were of years,
 I should commit thee surely with thy peers,
 And tell, how far thou didst our Lyly outshine,
30 Or sporting Kyd, or Marlowe's mighty line.[2]
 And though thou hadst small Latin, and less Greek,
 From thence to honour thee, I would not seek
 For names; but call forth thundering Aeschylus,
 Euripides, and Sophocles to us,
35 Pacuvius, Accius, him of Cordova dead,[3]
 To life again, to hear thy buskin tread,
 And shake a stage: or, when thy socks were on,[4]
 Leave thee alone, for the comparison
 Of all that insolent Greece, or haughty Rome
40 Sent forth, or since did from their ashes come.
 Triumph, my Britain, thou hast one to show,
 To whom all scenes of Europe homage owe.
 He was not of an age, but for all time!
 And all the muses still were in their prime,
45 When like Apollo he came forth to warm

---

[1] Geoffrey Chaucer, Edmund Spenser, and Francis Beaumont were buried in Westminster Abbey, Shakespeare at Stratford.
[2] John Lyly, Thomas Kyd, and Christopher Marlowe, three Elizabethan dramatists.
[3] Marcus Pacuvius, Lucius Accius, and Seneca the Younger ("him of Cordova"), three Latin tragedians.
[4] Buskin: a laced boot, symbol of tragedy; socks: symbol of comedy.

Our ears, or like a Mercury to charm!
Nature herself was proud of his designs,
And joyed to wear the dressing of his lines!
Which were so richly spun, and woven so fit,
50   As, since, she will vouchsafe no other wit.
The merry Greek, tart Aristophanes,
Neat Terence, witty Plautus, now not please;[5]
But antiquated, and deserted lie
As they were not of nature's family.
55   Yet must I not give nature all: thy art,
My gentle Shakespeare, must enjoy a part.
For though the poet's matter, nature be,
His art doth give the fashion. And, that he,
Who casts to write a living line, must sweat,
60   (Such as thine are) and strike the second heat
Upon the muses' anvil: turn the same,
(And himself with it) that he thinks to frame;
Or for the laurel, he may gain a scorn,
For a good poet's made, as well as born.
65   And such wert thou. Look how the father's face
Lives in his issue, even so, the race
Of Shakespeare's mind, and manners brightly shines
In his well-turnéd, and true-filéd lines:
In each of which, he seems to shake a lance,
70   As brandished at the eyes of ignorance.
Sweet swan of Avon, what a sight it were
To see thee in our waters yet appear,
And make those flights upon the banks of Thames,
That so did take Eliza, and our James![6]
75   But stay, I see thee in the hemisphere
Advanced, and made a constellation there!
Shine forth, thou star of poets, and with rage,
Or influence, chide, or cheer the drooping stage;
Which, since thy flight from hence, hath mourned like night.
80   And despairs day, but for thy volume's light.

(1623)

[5] Aristophanes, Terence, and Plautus, three Roman writers of comedies.
[6] Queen Elizabeth and King James.

Robert Herrick

(1 5 9 1 – 1 6 7 4)

The son of a wealthy London goldsmith, Robert Herrick spent ten years as a goldsmith's apprentice. After a leisurely visit to Cambridge, he took a degree when he was 26. A lover of leisure, drink, and the verse of "Saint" Ben Jonson, he reluctantly took up a belated career in the church in 1629. His collection of 1200 lyrics, *Hesperides,* did not appear until he was 57. He died, still a bachelor, at his longtime parish at Dean Prior in Devonshire.

Herrick wrote imitations of Horace and Catullus, eclogues, epistles, epigrams, love poems, and folk songs. He had a bright, buoyant, polished style and his poems are about reconciliation, deism, and romantic love affairs. Despite his position in the church, Herrick practiced a half-serious personal paganism; he described rituals and sacrifices to minor nature gods and alluded to ancient incantations in his writing. The poems are filled with brooks, birds, blossoms, and bosoms of rustic maidens. (Herrick utilized a series of imaginary mistresses for the purposes of poetry.) His style owes more to the work of the courtly Cavalier poets, such as Carew and Suckling, than to the metaphysical intricacies of Donne and Herbert. Although much of his poetry is trivial, Herrick's pretty surfaces conceal a careful structure and a powerful evocation of nature and man in sympathetic union. He is a prime example of the good "minor" poet.

Hesperides appeared in 1648 and was Herrick's only significant publication. A collection of poems on sacred subjects, "Noble Numbers," was published in the same volume, but with a separate title page dated 1647. Many of his poems have been set to music.

ROBERT HERRICK

To the Virgins, to Make Much of Time

Gather ye Rose-buds while ye may,
    Old Time is still a flying:
And this same flower that smiles to day,
    To morrow will be dying.

5   The glorious Lamp of Heaven, the Sun,
        The higher he's a getting;
    The sooner will his Race be run,
        And neerer he's to Setting.

    That Age is best, which is the first,
10   When Youth and Blood are warmer;
    But being spent, the worse, and worst
        Times, still succeed the former.

    Then be not coy, but use your time;
        And while ye may, goe marry:
15   For having lost but once your prime,
        You may for ever tarry.
                                            (1648)

Delight in Disorder

    A sweet disorder in the dresse
    Kindles in cloathes a wantonnesse:
    A Lawne[1] about the shoulders thrown
    Into a fine distraction:
5   An erring Lace, which here and there
    Enthralls the Crimson Stomacher:[2]
    A Cuffe neglectfull, and thereby
    Ribbands° to flow confusedly: ribbons
    A winning wave (deserving Note)
10   In the tempestuous petticote:
    A carelesse shooe-string, in whose tye
    I see a wilde civility:
    Doe more bewitch me, then when Art
    Is too precise in every part.
                                            (1648)

[1] A shawl of fine linen.
[2] A piece of cloth held by laces and covering a woman's chest and abdomen.

Upon Julia's Clothes

When as in silks my *Julia* goes,
Then, then (me thinks) how sweetly flowes
That liquefaction of her clothes.

Next, when I cast mine eyes and see
5   That brave Vibration each way free;
O how that glittering taketh me!

                                        (1648)

George Herbert

(1 5 9 3 – 1 6 3 3)

In contrast to many of his contemporaries who took livings in the church for financial and social convenience, George Herbert was devoted to his mission as a pastor. His devotion is reflected in his poetry. After graduating from Cambridge with distinction, Herbert gave up a prestigious post—public orator of the university—to enter the church. He married and in 1630 settled in Bemerton, near Salisbury, and began to preach, pray, and rebuild the church with his own funds. He visited the sick and poor and became known generally as "Holy Mr. Herbert." He died only three years later.

Herbert's volume of religious lyrics, *The Temple*, was published shortly after his death. The intricacy and variety of technique exhibited in the volume is perhaps unparalleled: His 169 poems employ 140 different stanzaic patterns. Herbert attempted to develop a different form to suit each of the many moods he wished to evoke. His "shaped verse," poems in the typographical outline of their subject, show ingenuity and influenced Dylan Thomas and Mallarmé; they can be seen as forerunners of the experimentation in "concrete poetry" that flowered in the 1960s and 1970s. Although his poetry includes elaborate images (or "conceits"), the poems generally tend to more subtle mood painting. Herbert used simple language to convey emotional intensity. The poetry is religious, but, unlike Donne's work, is not about doubt and anxiety. Herbert's verse is like his life and his faith: simple, muted, subtle, and accepting, but deeply felt. His best work belies the notion that pious art need be intellectually shallow or emotionally simplistic.

The Temple, Sacred Poems and Private Ejaculations appeared in 1633. It contains almost all of Herbert's English verse and was immediately popular: it went through five editions in five years. Herbert also wrote Latin poems and a prose account of clerical life entitled *A Priest to the Temple* (1652), a work that provides insights into the world out of which his poetry grew.

GEORGE HERBERT

The Altar

A broken A L T A R, Lord, thy servant reares,
Made of a heart, and cemented with teares:
  Whose parts are as thy hand did frame;
  No workmans tool hath touch'd the same.
5   A H E A R T alone
       Is   such   a   stone,
       As   nothing   but
       Thy pow'r doth cut.
       Wherefore each part
10   Of my hard heart
       Meets in this frame,
       To praise thy Name:
  That, if I chance to hold my peace,
  These stones to praise thee may not cease.
15 O let thy blessed S A C R I F I C E be mine,
  And sanctifie this A L T A R to be thine.

                   (1633)

The Pulley

    When God at first made man,
    Having a glasse of blessings standing by;
Let us (said he) poure on him all we can:
Let the worlds riches, which dispersed lie,
5   Contract into a span.

    So strength first made a way;
Then beautie flow'd, then wisdome, honour, pleasure:
When almost all was out, God made a stay,
Perceiving that alone of all his treasure
10   Rest in the bottome lay.

    For if I should (said he)
Bestow this jewell also on my creature,
He would adore my gifts in stead of me,

And rest in Nature, not the God of Nature:
15   So both should losers be.

Yet let him keep the rest,
But keep them with repining restlesnesse:
Let him be rich and wearie, that at least,
If goodnesse leade him not, yet wearinesse
20   May tosse him to my breast.

(1633)

Easter-wings

Lord, who createdst man in wealth and store,
Though foolishly he lost the same,
Decaying more and more,
Till he became
5   Most poore:
With   thee
O let me rise
As larks, harmoniously,
And sing this day thy victories:
10 Then shall the fall further the flight in me.

My   tender   age   in   sorrow   did   beginne:
And still with sicknesses and shame
Thou didst so punish sinne,
That I became
15   Most thinne.
With   thee
Let me combine
And feel this day thy victorie:
For, if I imp° my wing on thine,   graft
20 Affliction   shall   advance   the   flight   in   me.

(1633)

The Collar

I Struck the board, and cry'd, No more.
I will abroad.
What? shall I ever sigh and pine?
My lines and life are free, free as the rode,

5   Loose as the winde, as large as store.
              Shall I be still in suit?
       Have I no harvest but a thorn
       To let me bloud,° and not restore   bleed
       What I have lost with cordiall° fruit?   restorative
10   Sure there was wine
    Before my sighs did drie it: there was corn
                    Before my tears did drown it.
         Is the yeare onely lost to me?
                    Have I no bayes to crown it?
15 No flowers, no garlands gay? all blasted?
                    All wasted?
         Not so, my heart: but there is fruit,
                    And thou hast hands.
         Recover all thy sigh-blown age
20 On double pleasures: leave thy cold dispute
    Of what is fit, and not. Forsake thy cage,
                    Thy rope of sands,
    Which pettie thoughts have made, and made to
         thee
         Good cable, to enforce and draw,
25   And be thy law,
       While thou didst wink and wouldst not see.
                    Away; take heed:
                    I will abroad.
    Call in thy deaths head there: tie up thy fears.
30   He that forbears
              To suit and serve his need,
                    Deserves his load.
    But as I rav'd and grew more fierce and wilde
                    At every word,
35 Me thoughts I heard one calling, *Child!*
              And I reply'd, *My Lord.*

                    (1633)

John Milton

(1 6 0 8 – 1 6 7 4)

John Milton was the dominant literary figure of mid-seventeenth-century England. A brilliant student, Milton refused to take religious orders after he earned his M.A. at Cambridge. Instead, he spent the next five years reading according to a study plan of his own devising. Milton read Latin and Greek with ease and was adept at French, German, Italian, and Hebrew. A tour of Europe in 1638 and 1639 completed his splendid education. From 1640 to 1660 he was already known as a poet for the masque *Comus* and the elegy to Edward King, *Lycidas,* but Milton dedicated himself to the "pamphlet wars." He produced a flurry of tracts against the current form of church government, on divorce (his first wife left him temporarily after six weeks of marriage), and in defense of the execution of Charles I. Although he was going blind, he worked in Cromwell's government. His first wife, Mary Powell, bore him three children before her death in 1652. His second wife, Katherine Woodcock, died in 1658. When Cromwell was ousted, Milton was imprisoned and nearly died. By the time of his third marriage, to Elizabeth Minshull in 1663, he was blind, poor, and isolated. In the last period of his life, Milton turned to the vast artistic projects that have been his most enduring legacy: *Paradise Lost* (1667), *Paradise Regained* (1671), and *Samson Agonistes* (1671).

Milton wrote some brilliant minor poems—"L'Allegro," "Il Penseroso," *Lycidas*—and many outstanding sonnets. But *Paradise Lost* is his supreme creation. The poem, an attempt to "justify the ways of God to men," is, like Homer's *Iliad,* the biblical *Psalms,* Virgil's *Aeneid,* and Dante's *Divine Comedy,* a large-scale expression of Western civilization. It is written in throbbing blank verse, which harnesses Milton's complex periodic sentences. *Paradise Lost* attempts to contain the whole of human imagination and experience, from creation to damnation; from the summits of Paradise to Satan's lightless, infernal lake; from the majestic wars in Heaven to the petty but irrevocably significant actions of humanity's fall from grace. It contains the greatest portrait of Satan in English nondramatic verse. All of Milton's poetry is charged with his Christian humanism and with a post-Reformation sense of individual responsibility for one's fate. As an epic poet, Milton deals with the subtler heroism involved when one faces a moral choice. Humankind's greatest wars are fought not on a battlefield but within ourselves. The post-Milton hero is a Leopold Bloom rather than an Achilles.

Milton's literary output was prodigious. His most important shorter poems are the ode "On the Morning of Christ's Nativity" (1629), "On Shakespeare" (1630), "L'Allegro" and "Il Penseroso" (1632), *Comus* (1637), *Lycidas* (1637), and the Latin poem "Epitaphium Damonis" (1639). He wrote many prose essays and tracts, including a *History of Britain* (1670), and a brilliant defense of the liberty of the press, *Areopagitica* (1644).

JOHN MILTON

L'Allegro

Hence loathed Melancholy
  Of *Cerberus* and blackest midnight born,
In *Stygian* Cave forlorn
  'Mongst horrid shapes, and shrieks, and sights
    unholy,
5 Find out some uncouth° cell,   unknown
    Where brooding darkness spreads his jealous
      wings,
And the night-Raven sings;
    There under *Ebon* shades, and low-brow'd Rocks,
As ragged as thy Locks,
10   In dark *Cimmerian* desert ever dwell.
But come thou Goddess fair and free,
In Heav'n yclep'd° *Euphrosyne,*   called
And by men, heart-easing Mirth,
Whom lovely *Venus* at a birth
15 With two sister Graces more
To Ivy-crowned *Bacchus* bore;
Or whether (as some Sager sing)
The frolic Wind that breathes the Spring,
Zephyr with *Aurora* playing,
20 As he met her once a-Maying,
There on Beds of Violets blue,
And fresh-blown Roses washt in dew,
Fill'd her with thee a daughter fair,
So buxom, blithe, and debonair.
25 Haste thee nymph, and bring with thee
Jest and youthful Jollity,
Quips and Cranks,° and wanton Wiles,   jokes
Nods, and Becks, and Wreathed Smiles,
Such as hang on *Hebe's* cheek,
30 And love to live in dimple sleek;
Sport that wrinkled Care derides,
And Laughter holding both his sides.
Come, and trip it as ye go
On the light fantastic toe,
35 And in thy right hand lead with thee,
The Mountain Nymph, sweet Liberty;
And if I give thee honor due,

Mirth, admit me of thy crew
To live with her, and live with thee,
40   In unreproved pleasures free;
To hear the Lark begin his flight,
And singing startle the dull night,
From his watch-tow'r in the skies,
Till the dappled dawn doth rise;
45   Then to come in spite of sorrow,
And at my window bid good-morrow,
Through the Sweet-Briar, or the Vine,
Or the twisted Eglantine;
While the Cock with lively din,
50   Scatters the rear of darkness thin,
And to the stack, or the Barn door,
Stoutly struts his Dames before;
Oft list'ning how the Hounds and horn
Cheerly rouse the slumb'ring morn,
55   From the side of some Hoar Hill,
Through the high wood echoing shrill;
Some time walking not unseen
By Hedgerow Elms, on Hillocks green,
Right against the Eastern gate,
60   Where the great Sun begins his state,
Rob'd in flames, and Amber light,
The clouds in thousand Liveries dight;°   dressed
While the Plowman near at hand,
Whistles o'er the Furrow'd Land,
65   And the Milkmaid singeth blithe,
And the Mower whets his scythe,
And every Shepherd tells his tale
Under the Hawthorn in the dale.
Straight mine eye hath caught new pleasures
70   Whilst the Landscape round it measures,
Russet Lawns and Fallows Gray,
Where the nibbling flocks do stray;
Mountains on whose barren breast
The laboring clouds do often rest;
75   Meadows trim with Daisies pied,
Shallow Brooks, and Rivers wide.
Towers and Battlements it sees
Bosom'd high in tufted Trees,
Where perhaps some beauty lies,
80   The Cynosure of neighboring eyes.
Hard by, a Cottage chimney smokes,
From betwixt two aged Oaks,

Where *Corydon*[1] and *Thyrsis* met,
Are at their savory dinner set
85 Of Herbs, and other Country Messes,
Which the neat-handed *Phillis* dresses;
And then in haste her Bow'r she leaves,
With *Thestylis* to bind the Sheaves;
Or if the earlier season lead
90 To the tann'd Haycock in the Mead.
Sometimes with secure delight
The upland Hamlets will invite,
When the merry Bells ring round,
And the jocund rebecs sound
95 To many a youth, and many a maid,
Dancing in the Checker'd shade;
And young and old come forth to play
On a Sunshine Holiday,
Till the livelong daylight fail;
100 Then to the Spicy Nut-brown Ale,
With stories told of many a feat,
How *Faery Mab*[2] the junkets eat;
She was pincht and pull'd, she said,
And he, by Friar's Lantern led,
105 Tells how the drudging Goblin sweat[3]
To earn his Cream-bowl duly set,
When in one night, ere glimpse of morn,
His shadowy Flail hath thresh'd the Corn
That ten day-laborers could not end;
110 Then lies him down the Lubber Fiend,°   loutish spirit
And, stretch'd out all the Chimney's length,
Basks at the fire his hairy strength;
And Crop-full out of doors he flings,
Ere the first Cock his Matin rings.
115 Thus done the Tales, to bed they creep,
By whispering Winds soon lull'd asleep.
Tow'red Cities please us then,
And the busy hum of men,
Where throngs of Knights and Barons bold,
120 In weeds° of Peace high triumphs hold,   clothes
With store of Ladies, whose bright eyes
Rain influence, and judge the prize
Of Wit, or Arms, while both contend

---

[1] This name, and the following three names, are traditionally given to shepherds.
[2] Queen of the fairies.
[3] Robin Goodfellow, or Puck.

To win her Grace, whom all commend.
125 There let *Hymen* oft appear
In Saffron robe, with Taper clear,
And pomp, and feast, and revelry,
With mask, and antique Pageantry—
Such sights as youthful Poets dream
130 On Summer eves by haunted stream.
Then to the well-trod stage anon,
If *Jonson's* learned Sock[4] be on,
Or sweetest *Shakespeare,* fancy's child,
Warble his native Wood-notes wild.
135 And ever against eating Cares,
Lap me in soft *Lydian* Airs,[5]
Married to immortal verse,
Such as the meeting soul may pierce
In notes, with many a winding bout°   passage
140 Of linked sweetness long drawn out,
With wanton heed, and giddy cunning,
The melting voice through mazes running;
Untwisting all the chains that tie
The hidden soul of harmony;
145 That *Orpheus'* self may heave his head
From golden slumber on a bed
Of heapt *Elysian* flow'rs, and hear
Such strains as would have won the ear
Of *Pluto,* to have quite set free
150 His half-regain'd *Eurydice.*
These delights if thou canst give,
Mirth, with thee I mean to live.

(1645)

Il Penseroso

Hence vain deluding joys,
    The brood of folly without father bred,
How little you bested,°   help
    Or fill the fixed mind with all your toys;° trifles
5 Dwell in some idle brain,
    And fancies fond° with gaudy shapes possess, foolish
As thick and numberless

---

4 Symbol of comedy.
5 Noted for its sensuality.

As the gay motes that people the Sunbeams,
Or likest hovering dreams,
10   The fickle Pensioners° of *Morpheus'* train.   adherents
But hail thou Goddess, sage and holy,
Hail divinest Melancholy,
Whose Saintly visage is too bright
To hit the Sense of human sight;
15 And therefore to our weaker view,
O'erlaid with black, staid Wisdom's hue.
Black, but such as in esteem,
Prince *Memnon's* sister might beseem,
Or that Starr'd *Ethiop* Queen° that strove   Cassiopeia
20 To set her beauty's praise above
The Sea Nymphs, and their powers offended.
Yet thou art higher far descended;
Thee bright-hair'd *Vesta* long of yore,
To solitary *Saturn* bore;
25 His daughter she (in *Saturn's* reign,
Such mixture was not held a stain).
Oft in glimmering Bow'rs and glades
He met her, and in secret shades
Of woody *Ida's* inmost grove,
30 While yet there was no fear of *Jove.*
Come pensive Nun, devout and pure,
Sober, steadfast, and demure,
All in a robe of darkest grain,°   color
Flowing with majestic train,
35 And sable stole of *Cypress* Lawn,°   thin, gauze-like cloth
Over thy decent shoulders drawn.
Come, but keep thy wonted state,
With ev'n step, and musing gait,
And looks commercing with the skies,
40 Thy rapt soul sitting in thine eyes:
There held in holy passion still,
Forget thyself to Marble, till
With a sad Leaden downward cast,
Thou fix them on the earth as fast.
45 And join with thee calm Peace and Quiet,
Spare Fast, that oft with gods doth diet,
And hears the Muses in a ring
Aye round about *Jove's* Altar sing.
And add to these retired Leisure,
50 That in trim Gardens takes his pleasure;
But first, and chiefest, with thee bring
Him that yon soars on golden wing,
Guiding the fiery-wheeled throne,
The Cherub Contemplation;

55 And the mute Silence hist° along,   summons
   'Less *Philomel* will deign a Song,
   In her sweetest, saddest plight,
   Smoothing the rugged brow of night.
   While *Cynthia* checks her Dragon yoke,
60 Gently o'er th' accustom'd Oak;
   Sweet Bird that shunn'st the noise of folly,
   Most musical, most melancholy!
   Thee Chantress oft the Woods among,
   I woo to hear thy Even-Song;
65 And missing thee, I walk unseen
   On the dry smooth-shaven Green,
   To behold the wand'ring Moon,
   Riding near her highest noon,
   Like one that had been led astray
70 Through the Heav'n's wide pathless way;
   And oft, as if her head she bow'd,
   Stooping through a fleecy cloud.
   Oft on a Plat° of rising ground,   plot
   I hear the far-off *Curfew* sound,
75 Over some wide-water'd shore,
   Swinging slow with sullen roar;
   Or if the Air will not permit,
   Some still removed place will fit,
   Where glowing Embers through the room
80 Teach light to counterfeit a gloom,
   Far from all resort of mirth,
   Save the Cricket on the hearth,
   Or the Bellman's° drowsy charm,   night watchman
   To bless the doors from nightly harm:
85 Or let my Lamp at midnight hour,
   Be seen in some high lonely Tow'r,
   Where I may oft outwatch the *Bear*,
   With thrice great *Hermes,* or unsphere
   The spirit of *Plato* to unfold
90 What Worlds, or what vast Regions hold
   The immortal mind that hath forsook
   Her mansion in this fleshly nook:
   And of those *Dæmons* that are found
   In fire, air, flood, or underground,
95 Whose power hath a true consent
   With Planet, or with Element.
   Sometime let Gorgeous Tragedy
   In Scepter'd Pall° come sweeping by,   robe
   Presenting *Thebes,* or *Pelops'* line,
100 Or the tale of *Troy* divine,

Or what (though rare) of later age,
Ennobled hath the Buskin'd[1] stage.
But, O sad Virgin, that thy power
Might raise *Musaeus* from his bower,
105 Or bid the soul of *Orpheus* sing
Such notes as, warbled to the string,
Drew Iron tears down *Pluto's* cheek,
And made Hell grant what Love did seek.
Or call up him[2] that left half told
110 The story of *Cambuscan* bold,
Of *Camball,* and of *Algarsife,*
And who had *Canace* to wife,
That own'd the virtuous° Ring and Glass,   special
And of the wondrous Horse of Brass,
115 On which the *Tartar* King did ride;
And if aught else great Bards beside
In sage and solemn tunes have sung,
Of Tourneys and of Trophies hung,
Of Forests, and enchantments drear,
120 Where more is meant than meets the ear.
Thus night oft see me in thy pale career,
Till civil-suited Morn appear,
Not trickt and frounc't as she was wont
With the Attic Boy to hunt,
125 But kerchieft in a comely Cloud,
While rocking Winds are Piping loud,
Or usher'd with a shower still,
When the gust hath blown his fill,
Ending on the rustling Leaves,
130 With minute-drops from off the Eaves.
And when the Sun begins to fling
His flaring beams, me Goddess bring
To arched walks of twilight groves,
And shadows brown that *Sylvan* loves
135 Of Pine or monumental Oak,
Where the rude Axe with heaved stroke
Was never heard the Nymphs to daunt,
Or fright them from their hallow'd haunt.
There in close covert by some Brook,
140 Where no profaner eye may look,
Hide me from Day's garish eye,
While the Bee with Honied thigh,
That at her flow'ry work doth sing,

[1] Buskin: symbol of tragedy.
[2] I.e., Chaucer (see pp. 16–37).

And the Waters murmuring
145 With such consort° as they keep,   company
Entice the dewy-feather'd Sleep;
And let some strange mysterious dream
Wave at his Wings in Airy stream,
Of lively portraiture display'd,
150 Softly on my eyelids laid.
And as I wake, sweet music breathe
Above, about, or underneath,
Sent by some spirit to mortals good,
Or th'unseen Genius° of the Wood.   spirit
155 But let my due feet never fail
To walk the studious Cloister's pale,°   enclosure
And love the high embowed Roof,
With antic Pillars massy proof,
And storied Windows richly dight,°   decorated
160 Casting a dim religious light.
There let the pealing Organ blow
To the full voic'd Choir below,
In Service high and Anthems clear,
As may with sweetness, through mine ear,
165 Dissolve me into ecstasies,
And bring all Heav'n before mine eyes.
And may at last my weary age
Find out the peaceful hermitage,
The Hairy Gown and Mossy Cell,
170 Where I may sit and rightly spell°   consider
Of every Star that Heav'n doth shew,
And every Herb that sips the dew;
Till old experience do attain
To something like Prophetic strain.
175 These pleasures *Melancholy* give,
And I with thee will choose to live.

(1645)

How Soon Hath Time

How soon hath Time, the subtle thief of youth,
  Stol'n on his wing my three and twentieth year!
  My hasting days fly on with full career,
  But my late spring no bud or blossom show'th.
5 Perhaps my semblance might deceive the truth,
  That I to manhood am arriv'd so near,

And inward ripeness doth much less appear,
   That some more timely-happy spirits endu'th.°   endoweth
Yet be it less or more, or soon or slow,
10   It shall be still in strictest measure ev'n°   equal
   To that same lot, however mean or high,
Toward which Time leads me, and the will of Heav'n;
   All is, if I have grace to use it so,
   As ever in my great task-Master's eye.

(1645)

When I Consider How My Light Is Spent[1]

When I consider how my light is spent,
   Ere half my days, in this dark world and wide,
   And that one Talent which is death to hide,
   Lodg'd with me useless, though my Soul more bent
5 To serve therewith my Maker, and present
   My true account, lest he returning chide;
   "Doth God exact day-labor, light denied,"
   I fondly° ask; But patience to prevent   foolishly
That murmur, soon replies, "God doth not need
10   Either man's work or his own gifts; who best
   Bear his mild yoke, they serve him best; his State
Is Kingly. Thousands at his bidding speed
   And post o'er Land and Ocean without rest:
   They also serve who only stand and wait."

(1673)

from *Paradise Lost*

from Book I

THE ARGUMENT

This first Book proposes, first in brief, the whole Subject, *Man's disobedience, and the loss thereupon of Paradise wherein he was plac't:* Then touches *the prime cause of his fall, the Serpent, or rather* Satan *in the Serpent; who revolting from God, and drawing to his side many Legions of Angels, was by the command of God driven out of Heaven with all his Crew into the great Deep.* Which action past over, the Poem hastes into the midst of things, presenting *Satan with his Angels now fallen into Hell,* describ'd here, *not in the Centre* (for Heaven and Earth may be suppos'd as yet not made, certainly not yet accurst) *but in a place*

[1] Milton was totally blind when he wrote this poem.

of utter darkness, fitliest call'd Chaos: *Here* Satan *with his Angels lying on the burning Lake, thunder-struck and astonisht, after a certain space recovers, as from confusion, calls up him who next in Order and Dignity lay by him; they confer of thir miserable fall.* Satan *awakens all his Legions, who lay till then in the same manner confounded; They rise, thir Numbers, array of Battle, thir chief Leaders nam'd, according to the Idols known afterwards in* Canaan *and the Countries adjoining. To these* Satan *directs his Speech, comforts them with hope yet of regaining Heaven, but tells them lastly of a new World and new kind of Creature to be created, according to an ancient Prophecy or report in Heaven;* for that Angels were long before this visible Creation, was the opinion of many ancient Fathers. *To find out the truth of this Prophecy, and what to determine thereon he refers to a full Council. What his Associates thence attempt.* Pandemonium *the Palace of* Satan *rises, suddenly built out of the Deep: The infernal Peers there sit in Council.*

      Of Man's First Disobedience, and the Fruit
      Of that Forbidden Tree, whose mortal taste
      Brought Death into the World, and all our woe,
      With loss of *Eden,* till one greater Man°   Jesus Christ
5   Restore us, and regain the blissful Seat,
      Sing Heav'nly Muse, that on the secret top
      Of *Oreb,* or of *Sinai,* didst inspire
      That Shepherd, who first taught the chosen Seed,
      In the Beginning how the Heav'ns and Earth
10   Rose out of *Chaos:* Or if *Sion* Hill
      Delight thee more, and *Siloa's* Brook that flow'd
      Fast by the Oracle of God; I thence
      Invoke thy aid to my advent'rous Song,
      That with no middle flight intends to soar
15   Above th' *Aonian* Mount, while it pursues
      Things unattempted yet in Prose or Rhyme.
      And chiefly Thou O Spirit, that dost prefer
      Before all Temples th' upright heart and pure,
      Instruct me, for Thou know'st; Thou from the first
20   Wast present, and with mighty wings outspread
      Dove-like satst brooding on the vast Abyss
      And mad'st it pregnant: What in me is dark
      Illumine, what is low raise and support;
      That to the highth of this great Argument°   theme
25   I may assert Eternal Providence,
      And justify the ways of God to men.

      All these and more came flocking; but with looks
      Downcast and damp, yet such wherein appear'd
      Obscure some glimpse of joy, to have found thir chief[1]

---

[1] I.e., Satan.

525 Not in despair, to have found themselves not lost
    In loss itself; which on his count'nance cast
    Like doubtful hue: but he his wonted pride
    Soon recollecting, with high words, that bore
    Semblance of worth, not substance, gently rais'd
530 Thir fainting courage, and dispell'd thir fears.
    Then straight commands that at the warlike sound
    Of Trumpets loud and Clarions be uprear'd
    His mighty Standard; that proud honor claim'd
    Azazel as his right, a Cherub tall:
535 Who forthwith from the glittering Staff unfurl'd
    Th' Imperial Ensign, which full high advanc't
    Shone like a Meteor streaming to the Wind
    With Gems and Golden lustre rich imblaz'd,
    Seraphic arms and Trophies: all the while
540 Sonorous metal blowing Martial sounds:
    At which the universal Host upsent
    A shout that tore Hell's Concave, and beyond
    Frighted the Reign of *Chaos* and old Night.
    All in a moment through the gloom were seen
545 Ten thousand Banners rise into the Air
    With Orient° Colors waving: with them rose   lustrous
    A Forest huge of Spears: and thronging Helms
    Appear'd, and serried° Shields in thick array   closely packed
    Of depth immeasurable: Anon they move
550 In perfect *Phalanx* to the *Dorian* mood
    Of Flutes and soft Recorders; such as rais'd
    To highth of noblest temper Heroes old
    Arming to Battle, and instead of rage
    Deliberate valor breath'd, firm and unmov'd
555 With dread of death to flight or foul retreat,
    Nor wanting power to mitigate and swage
    With solemn touches, troubl'd thoughts, and chase
    Anguish and doubt and fear and sorrow and pain
    From mortal or immortal minds. Thus they
560 Breathing united force with fixed thought
    Mov'd on in silence to soft Pipes that charm'd
    Thir painful steps o'er the burnt soil; and now
    Advanc't in view they stand, a horrid Front
    Of dreadful length and dazzling Arms, in guise
565 Of Warriors old with order'd Spear and Shield,
    Awaiting what command thir mighty Chief
    Had to impose: He through the armed Files
    Darts his experienc't eye, and soon traverse
    The whole Battalion views, thir order due,
570 Thir visages and stature as of Gods;

Thir number last he sums. And now his heart
Distends with pride, and hard'ning in his strength
Glories: For never since created man,
Met such imbodied force, as nam'd with these
575   Could merit more than that small infantry
Warr'd on by Cranes: though all the Giant brood
Of *Phlegra*² with th' Heroic Race were join'd
That fought at *Thebes* and *Ilium,* on each side
Mixt with auxiliar Gods; and what resounds
580   In Fable or *Romance* of *Uther's* Son
Begirt with *British* and *Armoric* Knights;
And all who since, Baptiz'd or Infidel
Jousted in *Aspramont* or *Montalban,*
Damasco, or *Marocco,* or *Trebisond,*
585   Or whom *Biserta* sent from *Afric* shore
When *Charlemain* with all his Peerage fell
By *Fontarabbia.* Thus far these beyond
Compare of mortal prowess, yet observ'd
Thir dread commander: he above the rest
590   In shape and gesture proudly eminent
Stood like a Tow'r; his form had yet not lost
All her Original brightness, nor appear'd
Less than Arch-Angel ruin'd, and th' excess
Of Glory obscur'd: As when the Sun new ris'n
595   Looks through the Horizontal misty Air
Shorn of his Beams, or from behind the Moon
In dim Eclipse disastrous twilight sheds
On half the Nations, and with fear of change
Perplexes Monarchs. Dark'n'd so, yet shone
600   Above them all th' Arch-Angel: but his face
Deep scars of Thunder had intrencht, and care
Sat on his faded cheek, but under Brows
Of dauntless courage, and considerate Pride
Waiting revenge: cruel his eye, but cast
605   Signs of remorse and passion° to behold   *compassion*
The fellows of his crime, the followers rather
(Far other once beheld in bliss) condemn'd
For ever now to have thir lot in pain,
Millions of Spirits for his fault amerc't°   *deprived*
610   Of Heav'n, and from Eternal Splendors flung
For his revolt, yet faithful how they stood,

---

² Where the giants of Greek mythology were born. The following names are taken from various Greek myths.

Thir Glory wither'd. As when Heaven's Fire
Hath scath'd the Forest Oaks, or Mountain Pines,
With singed top thir stately growth though bare
615 Stands on the blasted Heath. He now prepar'd
To speak; whereat thir doubl'd Ranks they bend
From wing to wing, and half enclose him round
With all his Peers: attention held them mute.
Thrice he assay'd, and thrice in spite of scorn,
620 Tears such as Angels weep, burst forth: at last
Words interwove with sighs found out thir way.
   O Myriads of immortal Spirits, O Powers
Matchless, but with th' Almighty, and that strife
Was not inglorious, though th' event was dire,
625 As this place testifies, and this dire change
Hateful to utter: but what power of mind
Foreseeing or presaging, from the Depth
Of knowledge past or present, could have fear'd
How such united force of Gods, how such
630 As stood like these, could ever know repulse?
For who can yet believe, though after loss,
That all these puissant° Legions, whose exíle   powerful
Hath emptied Heav'n, shall fail to re-ascend
Self-rais'd, and repossess thir native seat?
635 For mee be witness all the Host of Heav'n,
If counsels different, or danger shunn'd
By me, have lost our hopes. But he who reigns
Monarch in Heav'n, till then as one secure
Sat on his Throne, upheld by old repute,
640 Consent or custom, and his Regal State
Put forth at full, but still his strength conceal'd,
Which tempted our attempt, and wrought our fall.
Henceforth his might we know, and know our own
So as not either to provoke, or dread
645 New War, provok't; our better part remains
To work in close design, by fraud or guile
What force effected not: that he no less
At length from us may find, who overcomes
By force, hath overcome but half his foe.
650 Space may produce new Worlds; whereof so rife
There went a fame° in Heav'n that he ere long   rumor
Intended to create, and therein plant
A generation, whom his choice regard
Should favor equal to the Sons of Heaven:
655 Thither, if but to pry, shall be perhaps

Our first eruption, thither or elsewhere:
For this Infernal Pit shall never hold
Celestial Spirits in Bondage, nor th' Abyss
Long under darkness cover. But these thoughts
660 Full Counsel must mature: Peace is despair'd,
For who can think Submission? War then, War
Open or understood, must be resolv'd.

(1667)

Richard Lovelace

(1 6 1 8 – 1 6 5 7)

With Sir John Suckling, Richard Lovelace led the courtly "Cavalier" poets. He was born of an aristocratic family and was heir to his family's extensive estates in Kent. He was educated at Charterhouse School and at Oxford, where he cut a dashing figure as a model Renaissance courtier. He impressed King Charles and Queen Henrietta on a royal visit to the university, and they made him an M.A. on the spot. Wealthy, handsome, witty, and graceful, Lovelace led a romantic life. His career was destroyed in the crossfire of the English Civil War. In 1642 he was imprisoned by Parliament. In prison, he composed "To Althea, from Prison," perhaps his best-known lyric. He was released from prison and exiled, and he joined Charles I on the Continent. Lovelace also spent time in the military service of the French crown. His betrothed, Lucy Sacheverall, heard that he was killed in battle and married another man. Lovelace was again imprisoned in England in 1648, where he prepared a collection of his verse for publication. Eventually he was released. He died, unemployed and penniless, three years before the Restoration.

Lovelace is mostly remembered for two fine lyrics, "To Althea, from Prison," and "To Lucasta, Going to the Warres." His lines, "Stone walls do not a prison make / Nor iron bars a cage" are often quoted. A longer pastoral, *Amarantha,* is obscure and excessive; his other poetry is generally of uneven quality. His songs were much admired in his own time, and many were set to music. Other poems include a series of gentle philosophical pieces on grasshoppers, flies, ants, snails, and other small creatures, and a pretty sonnet called "Elinda's Glove."

Lovelace's volume of verse, *Lucasta: Epodes, Odes, Sonnets, Songs,* appeared in 1649. His brother gathered the remaining poems into *Lucasta: Posthumous Poems* (1659). Lovelace also wrote two plays, which have not survived.

RICHARD LOVELACE

To Lucasta, Going to the Warres

I

Tell me not (Sweet) I am unkinde,
    That from the Nunnerie
Of thy chaste breast, and quiet minde,
    To Warre and Armes I flie.

II

5 True; a new Mistresse now I chase,
    The first Foe in the Field;
And with a stronger Faith imbrace
    A Sword, a Horse, a Shield.

III

Yet this Inconstancy is such,
10   As you too shall adore;
I could not love thee (Deare) so much,
    Lov'd I not Honour more.

                 (1649)

To Althea, from Prison

I

When Love with unconfined wings
    Hovers within my Gates;
And my divine *Althea* brings
    To whisper at the Grates;
5 When I lye tangled in her haire,
    And fettered to her eye;
The *Gods* that wanton in the Aire,
    Know no such Liberty.

II

When flowing Cups run swiftly round
10   With no allaying *Thames,* [1]

---

[1] Undiluted by water.

Our carelesse heads with Roses bound,
   Our hearts with Loyall Flames;
When thirsty griefe in Wine we steepe,
   When Healths and draughts go free,
15 Fishes that tipple in the Deepe,
   Know no such Libertie.

III

When (like committed Linnets)° I   caged songbirds
   With shriller throat shall sing
The sweetness, Mercy, Majesty,
20   And glories of my KING;
When I shall voyce aloud, how Good
   He is, how Great should be;
      Inlarged Winds that curle the Flood,
      Know no such Liberty.

IV

25 Stone Walls doe not a Prison make,
   Nor I'ron bars a Cage;
Mindes innocent and quiet take
   That for an Hermitage;
If I have freedome in my Love,
30   And in my soule am free;
Angels alone that sore above,
   Injoy such Liberty.

                              (1649)

Andrew Marvell

(1 6 2 1 – 1 6 7 8)

The son of a moderate Puritan clergyman, Andrew Marvell took the side of Parliament during the Cromwellian period. He avoided the post-Restoration purges and served as a Member of Parliament for his hometown of Hull for the last 20 years of his life. We know nothing of his life between his Cambridge B.A. in 1638 and his appointment as tutor to the daughter of a leader of the parliamentary forces in 1650, except that he spent time traveling on the Continent. While he was a tutor, Marvell composed much of his poetry. In 1657 he served as an assistant to the blind John Milton. In his customary quiet manner, he helped save Milton from execution after the Restoration. Marvell died at the age of 57 from an accidental overdose of opiates.

In many ways, Andrew Marvell serves as a transition figure between the metaphysical poets of the previous generation and the rhyming-couplet satirists—Dryden and Pope—who followed. In his charming bucolic, pastoral, and romantic verses, Marvell perfected the conceit; he used it beautifully to evoke the human pleasures of nature. He combined his emblematic talents with a lighthearted but polished rhythm, a casual, witty tone, and precise diction to create "To His Coy Mistress," a genuine masterpiece of the *carpe diem* ("seize the day") tradition. The poem displays a surprisingly complex blend of intellect and imagination, and contains subtle shadows of darker themes. At his best, Marvell raised his simple subjects to a level of almost mythic intensity. He was also a politician, however, and in his lifetime was best known for his biting political satires. A significant part of his work deals with Cromwell. The "Horatian Ode upon Cromwell's Return from Ireland" is narrow in its sympathies, but it is a technical triumph of meter and tone.

Most of Marvell's nonpolitical verse was published in 1681; his satires appeared in 1689. His most important verse satire, *Last Instructions to a Painter,* is about the Dutch war. Marvell also wrote many political pamphlets and prose satires; a series of newsletters to his constituents in Hull also has historical value. Marvell's lines in praise of *Paradise Lost* appeared in the poem's second edition.

ANDREW MARVELL

To His Coy Mistress

Had we but World enough, and Time,
This coyness Lady were no crime.
We would sit down, and think which way
To walk, and pass our long Loves Day.
5 Thou by the *Indian Ganges* side
Should'st Rubies find: I by the Tide
Of *Humber*[1] would complain. I would
Love you ten years before the Flood:
And you should if you please refuse
10 Till the Conversion of the *Jews.*
My vegetable Love should grow
Vaster then Empires, and more slow.
An hundred years should go to praise
Thine Eyes, and on thy Forehead Gaze.
15 Two hundred to adore each Breast:
But thirty thousand to the rest.
An Age at least to every part,
And the last Age should show your Heart.
For Lady you deserve this State;°   dignity
20 Nor would I love at lower rate.
    But at my back I alwaies hear
Times winged Charriot hurrying near:
And yonder all before us lye
Desarts of vast Eternity.
25 Thy Beauty shall no more be found;
Nor, in thy marble Vault, shall sound
My ecchoing Song: then Worms shall try
That long preserv'd Virginity:
And your quaint Honour turn to dust;
30 And into ashes all my Lust.
The Grave's a fine and private place,
But none I think do there embrace.
    Now therefore, while the youthful hew
Sits on thy skin like morning dew,
35 And while thy willing Soul transpires
At every pore with instant Fires,

---

[1] The Humber River flows through Marvell's hometown of Hull, in the north of England.

Now let us sport us while we may;
And now, like am'rous birds of prey,
Rather at once our Time devour,
40   Than languish in his slow-chapt² pow'r.
Let us roll all our Strength, and all
Our sweetness, up into one Ball:
And tear our Pleasures with rough strife,
Thorough the Iron gates of Life.
45   Thus, though we cannot make our Sun
Stand still, yet we will make him run.

(1681)

The Garden

I

How vainly men themselves amaze
To win the Palm, the Oke, or Bayes;
And their uncessant Labours see
Crown'd from some single Herb or Tree.
5   Whose short and narrow verged Shade
Does prudently their Toyles upbraid;
While all Flow'rs and all Trees do close°   come together
To weave the Garlands of repose.

II

Fair quiet, have I found thee here,
10   And Innocence thy Sister dear!
Mistaken long, I sought you then
In busie Companies of Men.
Your sacred Plants, if here below,
Only among the Plants will grow.
15   Society is all but rude,
To this delicious Solitude.

III

No white nor red was ever seen
So am'rous as this lovely green.
Fond Lovers, cruel as their Flame,
20   Cut in these Trees their Mistress name.
Little, Alas, they know, or heed,
How far these Beauties Hers exceed!

² Slow-jawed; therefore, slowly eating or destroying.

Fair Trees! where s'eer your barkes I wound,
No Name shall but your own be found.

IV

25 When we have run our Passions heat,
Love hither makes his best retreat.
The *Gods,* that mortal Beauty chase,
Still in a Tree did end their race.
Apollo hunted *Daphne* so,
30 Only that She might Laurel grow.
And *Pan* did after *Syrinx* speed,
Not as a Nymph, but for a Reed.

V

What wond'rous Life in this I lead!
Ripe Apples drop about my head;
35 The Luscious Clusters of the Vine
Upon my Mouth do crush their Wine;
The Nectaren, and curious Peach,
Into my hands themselves do reach;
Stumbling on Melons, as I pass,
40 Insnar'd with Flow'rs, I fall on Grass.

VI

Mean while the Mind, from pleasure less,
Withdraws into its happiness:
The Mind, that Ocean where each kind
Does streight its own resemblance find;
45 Yet it creates, transcending these,
Far other Worlds, and other Seas;
Annihilating all that's made
To a green Thought in a green Shade.

VII

Here at the Fountains sliding foot,
50 Or at some Fruit-trees mossy root,
Casting the Bodies Vest aside,
My Soul into the boughs does glide:
There like a Bird it sits, and sings,
Then whets,° and combs its silver Wings;   preens
55 And, till prepar'd for longer flight,
Waves in its Plumes the various Light.

VIII

Such was that happy Garden-state,
While Man there walk'd without a Mate:

After a Place so pure, and sweet,
60   What other Help could yet be meet!
But 'twas beyond a Mortal's share
To wander solitary there:
Two Paradises 'twere in one
To live in Paradise alone.

IX

65   How well the skillful Gardner drew
Of flow'rs and herbes this Dial° new;   clock
Where from above the milder Sun
Does through a fragrant Zodiack run;
And, as it works, th' industrious Bee
70   Computes its time as well as we.
How could such sweet and wholsome Hours
Be reckon'd but with herbs and flow'rs!

                                        (1681)

John Dryden

(1 6 3 1 – 1 7 0 0)

John Dryden was the leading literary figure of the Restoration period and one of England's best satirical poets. Dryden had a modest inheritance from his father. After leaving Cambridge, he seems to have held a minor post in Cromwell's government. (He wrote a poem lamenting Cromwell's death.) Politically flexible, like many of his compatriots, he wrote *Astraea Redux* in honor of the returning monarch. For the rest of his life Dryden was a loyal royalist; he was made poet laureate in 1668. He converted to Catholicism in 1686, when the Catholic James II took the throne; his conversion led to the loss of his official posts in 1689, when William and Mary came to the throne. Dryden spent his last years writing in the mornings and whiling away leisurely afternoons in an honored seat in Will's Coffee House, where he chatted with friends such as William Wycherley and William Congreve. Dryden was buried next to Chaucer in Westminster Abbey.

With Dryden, poetry moves decisively away from the personal, "expressive" function and becomes a vehicle for commentary on and satire of social and political events; poetry would remain predominantly social and political for the next century. Many of Dryden's nondramatic works are occasional poems that deal with specific contemporary events of public importance, but he also wrote prose essays and drama. In keeping with the increasing esteem for "reason" in his era, Dryden disparaged the emotional elements of poetry in favor of control. He established the heroic couplet (rhyming pentameter couplets, which are normally end-stopped to form a discrete, balanced unit of thought) as the dominant verse form of the period. Dryden is read today for two witty political satires: *Absalom and Achitophel* (1681), which deals with the 1678 accession crisis, and *Mac Flecknoe* (1682), which is concerned with political and artistic questions. Dryden gained much fame and fortune as the author of a score of plays. The most famous are the melodramatic tragedy *The Conquest of Grenada* (1672), the burlesque comedy *Marriage-à-la-Mode* (1673), and *All for Love* (1678), a work written in emulation of Shakespeare's *Antony and Cleopatra*.

Dryden's major poems include *Annus Mirabilis* (1667), his religious poems, *Religio Laici* (1682), and *The Hind and the Panther* (1687), "Ode to the Memory of Mrs. Anne Killigrew" (1685), and his famous ode to St. Cecilia's Day (1687). Dryden translated Virgil's works, the satires of Juvenal, and some Horace, Ovid, Homer, Lucretius, and other classical authors, and wrote many prose works.

JOHN DRYDEN

Mac Flecknoe

Or a Satire upon the True-Blue-Protestant Poet, T. S.[1]

All humane things are subject to decay,
And, when Fate summons, Monarchs must obey:
This *Fleckno* found, who, like *Augustus,* young
Was call'd to Empire, and had govern'd long:
5   In Prose and Verse, was own'd, without dispute
Through all the Realms of *Non-sense,* absolute.
This aged Prince now flourishing in Peace,
And blest with issue of a large increase,
Worn out with business, did at length debate
10   To settle the succession of the State:
And pond'ring which of all his Sons was fit
To Reign, and wage immortal War with Wit;
Cry'd, 'tis resolv'd; for Nature pleads that He
Should onely rule, who most resembles me:
15   *Sh* —————— alone my perfect image bears,
Mature in dullness from his tender years.
Sh —————— alone, all of my Sons, is he
Who stands confirm'd in full stupidity.
The rest to some faint meaning make pretence,
20   But *Sh* —————— never deviates into sense.
Some Beams of Wit on other souls may fall,
Strike through and make a lucid intervall;
But *Sh* —————— 's genuine night admits no ray,
His rising Fogs prevail upon the Day:
25   Besides his goodly Fabrick° fills the eye,   body
And seems design'd for thoughtless Majesty:
Thoughtless as Monarch Oakes, that shade the plain,
And, spread in solemn state, supinely reign.
Heywood and Shirley[2] were but Types of thee,
30   Thou last great Prophet of Tautology:

---

[1] The poem is a satire on Thomas Shadwell (1640–1692), a playwright who thought himself the literary heir of Ben Jonson (see pp. 84–88). Dryden calls him "Mac Flecknoe," or the son of Flecknoe—Richard Flecknoe was an insignificant Irish poet and playwright who died in 1678.

[2] Thomas Heywood (ca. 1570–1641) and James Shirley (1596–1666), two playwrights out of fashion by the time Dryden wrote his poem.

Even I, a dunce of more renown than they,
Was sent before but to prepare thy way;
And coursly clad in *Norwich* Drugget° came   coarse cloth
To teach the Nations in thy greater name.
35   My warbling Lute, the Lute I whilom° strung   formerly
When to King *John* of *Portugal* I sung,[3]
Was but the prelude to that glorious day,
When thou on silver *Thames* did'st cut thy way,
With well tim'd Oars before the Royal Barge,
40   Swell'd with the Pride of thy Celestial charge;
And big with Hymn, Commander of an Host,
The like was ne'er in *Epsom*[4] Blankets tost.
Methinks I see the new *Arion* Sail,
The Lute still trembling underneath thy nail.
45   At thy well sharpened thumb from Shore to Shore
The Treble squeaks for fear, the Bases roar:
Echoes from *Pissing-Ally, Sh*——— call,
And *Sh*——— they resound from *A*——— *Hall.*
About thy boat the little Fishes throng,
50   As at the Morning Toast,[5] that Floats along.
Sometimes as Prince of thy Harmonious band
Thou weild'st thy Papers in thy threshing hand.
St. *Andre's*[6] feet ne'er kept more equal time,
Not ev'n the feet of thy own *Psyche*'s rhime:
55   Though they in number as in sense excell;
So just, so like tautology they fell,
That, pale with envy, *Singleton*[7] foreswore
The Lute and Sword which he in Triumph bore,
And vow'd he ne'er would act *Villerius*[8] more.
60   Here stopt the good old *Syre;* and wept for joy
In silent raptures of the hopefull boy.
All arguments, but most his Plays, perswade,
That for anointed dullness he was made.
      Close to the Walls which fair *Augusta*[9] bind,
65   (The fair *Augusta* much to fears inclin'd)
An ancient fabrick,° rais'd t' inform the sight,   building
There stood of yore, and *Barbican* it hight:
A watch Tower once; but now, so Fate ordains,
Of all the Pile an empty name remains.
70   From its old Ruins Brothel-houses rise,

[3] Flecknoe boasted that he had the patronage of the King of Portugal.
[4] *Epsom Wells* was one of Shadwell's plays.
[5] I.e., sewage.
[6] Choreographer of one of Shadwell's operas.
[7] John Singleton was a musician at the Theatre Royal.
[8] A character in Sir William Davenport's opera *The Siege of Rhodes.*
[9] I.e., London.

Scenes of lewd loves, and of polluted joys;
Where their vast Courts the Mother-Strumpets keep,
And, undisturb'd by Watch, in silence sleep.
Near these a Nursery[10] erects its head,
75   Where Queens are form'd, and future Hero's bred; –
Where unfledg'd Actors learn to laugh and cry, ⎤
Where infant Punks° their tender Voices try,   ⎬   prostitutes
And little *Maximins*[11] the Gods defy.   ⎦
Great *Fletcher*[12] never treads in Buskins here,
80   Nor greater *Johnson*[13] dares in Socks appear.
But gentle *Simkin*° just reception finds   a clown
Amidst this Monument of vanisht minds:
Pure Clinches,° the suburbian Muse affords;   puns
And *Panton*[14] waging harmless War with words.
85   Here *Fleckno,* as a place to Fame well known,
Ambitiously design'd his *Sh* ——— 's Throne.
For ancient *Decker*[15] prophesi'd long since,   ⎤
That in this Pile should Reign a mighty Prince, ⎬
Born for a scourge of Wit, and flayle of Sense: ⎦
90   To whom true dulness should some *Psyches* owe,
But Worlds of *Misers*[16] from his pen should flow;
Humorists and *Hypocrites* it should produce,
Whole *Raymond* families, and Tribes of *Bruce.*
    Now Empress *Fame* had publisht the renown,
95   Of *Sh* ——— 's Coronation through the Town.
Rows'd by report of Fame, the Nations meet,
From near *Bun-Hill,* and distant *Watling-street.*
No *Persian* Carpets spread th' Imperial way,
But scatter'd Limbs of mangled Poets lay:
100   From dusty shops neglected Authors come,
Martyrs of Pies, and Reliques of the Bum.[17]
Much *Heywood, Shirly, Ogleby*[18] there lay,
But loads of *Sh* ——— almost choakt the way.
Bilk't *Stationers*° for Yeomen stood prepar'd,   publishers
105   And *H* ——— was Captain of the Guard.
The hoary Prince in Majesty appear'd,
High on a Throne of his own Labours rear'd.
At his right hand our young *Ascanius*[19] sate,

[10] Training school for actors.
[11] The bombastic emperor in Dryden's *Tyrranic Love.*
[12] John Fletcher (1579–1625), an English playwright.
[13] I.e., Ben Jonson; buskins are a symbol of tragedy, socks of comedy.
[14] A well-known punster.
[15] Thomas Dekker (ca. 1572–1632), an English playwright satirized by Jonson.
[16] In the following three lines Dryden mentions plays and characters of Shadwell.
[17] Unused books were used by bakers and for toilet paper.
[18] John Ogilby, a translator of Homer and Virgil, was made fun of by Dryden.
[19] The son of Aeneas.

Rome's other hope, and pillar of the State.
110 His Brows thick fogs, instead of glories, grace,
And lambent dullness plaid around his face.
As *Hannibal* did to the Altars come,
Sworn by his *Syre* a mortal Foe to *Rome;*
So *Sh*——swore, nor should his Vow bee vain,
115 That he till Death true dullness would maintain;
And in his father's Right, and Realms defence,
Ne'er to have peace with Wit, nor truce with Sense.
The King himself the sacred Unction made,
As King by Office, and as Priest by Trade:
120 In his sinister[20] hand, instead of Ball,
He plac'd a mighty Mug of potent Ale;
Love's Kingdom[21] to his right he did convey,
At once his Sceptre and his rule of Sway;
Whose righteous Lore the Prince had practis'd young,
125 And from whose Loyns recorded *Psyche* sprung.
His Temples last with Poppies were o'erspread,
That nodding seem'd to consecrate his head:
Just at that point of time, if Fame not lye,
On his left hand twelve reverend *Owls* did fly.
130 So *Romulus*, 'tis sung, by *Tyber*'s Brook,
Presage of Sway from twice six Vultures took.[22]
Th' admiring throng loud acclamations make,
And Omens of his future Empire take.
The *Syre* then shook the honours° of his head,   locks
135 And from his brows damps° of oblivion shed   vapors
Full on the filial dullness: long he stood,
Repelling from his Breast the raging God;
At length burst out in this prophetick mood:
    Heavens bless my Son, from *Ireland* let him reign
140 To farr *Barbadoes* on the Western main;
Of his Dominion may no end be known,
And greater than his Father's be his Throne.
Beyond loves Kingdom let him stretch his Pen;
He paus'd, and all the people cry'd *Amen.*
145 Then thus, continu'd he, my Son advance
Still in new Impudence, new Ignorance.
Success let others teach, learn thou from me
Pangs without birth, and fruitless Industry.
Let *Virtuoso's* in five years be Writ;
150 Yet not one thought accuse thy toyl of wit.

[20] I.e., his left hand.
[21] A play by Flecknoe.
[22] According to legend, the site Romulus picked for Rome was visited by 12 vultures, the site
   Remus picked was visited by 6. Romulus therefore became the first king of Rome.

Let gentle *George*[23] in triumph tread the Stage,
Make *Dorimant* betray, and *Loveit* rage;
Let *Cully, Cockwood, Fopling,* charm the Pit,
And in their folly shew the Writers wit.
155   Yet still thy fools shall stand in thy defence,
And justifie their Author's want of sense.
Let 'em be all by thy own model made
Of dullness, and desire no foreign aid:
That they to future ages may be known,
160   Not Copies drawn, but Issue of thy own.
Nay let thy men of wit too be the same,
All full of thee, and differing but in name;
But let no alien *S——— dl———y*[24] interpose
To lard with wit thy hungry *Epsom* prose.
165   And when false flowers of *Rhetorick* thou would'st cull,
Trust Nature, do not labour to be dull;
But write thy best, and top; and in each line,
Sir *Formal's*[25] oratory will be thine.
Sir *Formal,* though unsought, attends thy quill,
170   And does thy *Northern Dedications*[26] fill.
Nor let false friends seduce thy mind to fame,
By arrogating *Johnson's* Hostile name.
Let Father *Fleckno* fire thy mind with praise,
And Uncle *Ogleby* thy envy raise.
175   Thou art my blood, where *Johnson* has no part;
What share have we in Nature or in Art?
Where did his wit on learning fix a brand,
And rail at Arts he did not understand?
Where made he love in Prince *Nicander's*[27] vein,
180   Or swept the dust in *Psyche's* humble strain?
Where sold he Bargains,[28] Whip-stitch, kiss my Arse,
Promis'd a Play and dwindled to a Farce?
When did his Muse from *Fletcher* scenes purloin,
As thou whole *Eth'ridg* dost transfuse to thine?
185   But so transfus'd as Oyl on Waters flow,
His always floats above, thine sinks below.
This is thy Province, this thy wondrous way,
New Humours to invent for each new Play:
This is that boasted Byas of thy mind,

---

[23] Sir George Etherege (1635–1691), British dramatist. The next five names are all characters from his plays.
[24] Sir Charles Sedley (1638–1701), who contributed a prologue (and perhaps more) to Shadwell's play *Epsom Wells.*
[25] A character in *The Virtuoso.*
[26] Shadwell dedicated many of his plays to his patron, the Duke of Newcastle.
[27] A character in Shadwell's *Psyche.*
[28] A "bargain" is a coarse response to an innocent question.

190 By which one way, to dullness, 'tis inclin'd;
Which makes thy writings lean on one side still,
And in all changes that way bends thy will.
Nor let thy mountain belly make pretence
Of likeness; thine's a tympany[29] of sense.
195 A Tun° of Man in thy Large bulk is writ,   large cask
But sure thou 'rt but a Kilderkin° of wit.   small cask
Like mine thy gentle numbers feebly creep,
Thy Tragick Muse gives smiles, thy Comick sleep.
With whate'er gall thou sett'st thy self to write,
200 Thy in offensive Satyrs never bite.
In thy fellonious heart, though Venom lies,
It does but touch thy *Irish* pen, and dyes.
Thy Genius calls thee not to purchase fame
In keen Iambicks,[30] but mild Anagram:
205 Leave writing Plays, and chuse for thy command
Some peacefull Province in Acrostick Land.
There thou maist wings display and Altars raise,
And torture one poor word Ten thousand ways.
Or if thou would'st thy diff'rent talents suit,
210 Set thy own Songs, and sing them to thy lute.
He said, but his last words were scarcely heard,
For *Bruce* and *Longvil* had a *Trap* prepar'd,
And down they sent the yet declaiming Bard.[31]
Sinking he left his Drugget robe behind,
215 Born upwards by a subterranean wind.
The Mantle fell to the young Prophet's part,[32]
With double portion of his Father's Art.

          (1682)

---

[29] A swelling in the body caused by air.
[30] I.e., satire.
[31] A scene from *The Virtuoso*.
[32] See II Kings ii, where Elijah's mantle falls on Elisha.

Alexander Pope

(1 6 8 8 – 1 7 4 4)

Alexander Pope was the major poet of the eighteenth century, the successor to John Dryden, and perhaps the greatest satiric and didactic English poet. Plagued by ill health, Pope grew up in the rural surroundings of a small estate owned by his father, a retired London merchant. He was to be hampered throughout his life by severe headaches, delicate nerves, and deformities caused by tuberculosis of the spine. Because he was a Catholic, Pope was unable to attend university or take up a profession. He earned a living from his writing. By the age of 30 he acquired a large villa on the Thames in Twickenham, where he spent the remainder of his life perfecting the landscapes of the gardens he loved so well and making frequent forays, primarily in verse, into the lively literary wars of London. From the precocious *An Essay on Criticism,* written when he was 20, to his late ethical and philosophical poetry, Pope was in the center of English literary life at a time when Jonathan Swift, Steele, Addison, and William Congreve were in mid-career.

Pope represents the height of the Augustan (or "neo-Classical") impulse in English literature, a period when wit, satire, reason, and "proper" classical forms were the highest virtues of art. His *An Essay on Criticism* and *An Essay on Man* became the Bible of Augustan literary and social values. Pope perfected the closed-couplet form and subjected it to standards of regularity even more rigid than Dryden's. He relied on subtle shifts in meter and variations in caesurae placement for variety. A glittering witty surface and a condensed, epigrammatic economy of expression make Pope one of the most quotable of writers: *Bartlett's* lists nearly 300 citations under his name. Pope achieved fame as a translator, editor, and philosophical poet, but his greatest achievement was as a brilliant satirist. *The Rape of the Lock,* the greatest mock-heroic poem in the language, is his masterpiece. The poem operates on many levels: it burlesques epic conventions, analyzes a contemporary social scandal, and satirizes—even travesties—the social customs and mores of an age. *The Dunciad,* a savage but hilarious attack on Pope's literary opponents (he had many) and on all pedants, is only slightly less brilliant. Pope made much of his sizable fortune by translating the Homeric epics. The translations are marred by Pope's editing and amending, and by his affected phrasing ("finny prey" for "fish"). But they are lively and readable, certainly the finest translations of the century.

Pope's major poems, in the order of their publication, include *Pastorals* (1709); *An Essay on Criticism* (1711); *The Rape of the Lock* (1712; revised 1714); *Windsor-Forest* (1713); *Eloisa to Abelard* (1717); "Elegy to the Memory of an Unfortunate Lady" (1717); *The Dunciad* (1728; revised 1742–1743); *An Essay* on Man (1733–1734); *Imitations of Horace* (1733–1739); and *An Epistle to Dr. Arbuthnot* (1735). Pope also published prose essays, letters, and a popular if eccentric edition of Shakespeare, much revised to suit the era's tastes.

ALEXANDER POPE

from *An Essay on Criticism*

Of all the Causes which conspire to blind
Man's erring Judgment, and misguide the Mind,
What the weak Head with strongest Byass rules,
Is *Pride,* the *never-failing Vice of Fools.*
205 Whatever Nature has in *Worth* deny'd,
She gives in large Recruits of *needful Pride;*
For as in *Bodies,* thus in *Souls,* we find
What wants in *Blood* and *Spirits,* swell'd with *Wind;*
Pride, where Wit fails, steps in to our Defence,
210 And fills up all the *mighty Void* of *Sense!*
If once right Reason drives *that Cloud* away,
Truth breaks upon us with *resistless Day;*
Trust not your self; but your Defects to know,
Make use of ev'ry *Friend*—and ev'ry *Foe.*
215   A *little Learning* is a dang'rous Thing;
Drink deep, or taste not the *Pierian* Spring:
There *shallow Draughts* intoxicate the Brain,
And drinking *largely* sobers us again.
Fir'd at first Sight with what the *Muse* imparts,
220 In *fearless Youth* we tempt the Heights of Arts,
While from the bounded *Level* of our Mind,
Short Views we take, nor see the *Lengths behind,*
But *more advanc'd,* behold with strange Surprize
New, distant Scenes of *endless* Science rise!
225 So pleas'd at first, the towring *Alps* we try,
Mount o'er the Vales, and seem to tread the Sky;
Th' Eternal Snows appear already past,
And the first *Clouds* and *Mountains* seem the last:
But *those attain'd,* we tremble to survey
230 The growing Labours of the lengthen'd Way,
Th' *increasing* Prospect *tires* our wandring Eyes,
Hills peep o'er Hills, and *Alps* on *Alps* arise!
  A perfect Judge will *read* each Work of Wit

With the same Spirit that its Author *writ,*
235 Survey the *Whole,* nor seek slight Faults to find,
Where *Nature moves,* and *Rapture warms* the Mind;
Nor lose, for that malignant dull Delight,
The *gen'rous Pleasure* to be charm'd with Wit.
But in such Lays as neither *ebb,* nor *flow,*
240 *Correctly cold,* and *regularly low,*
That shunning Faults, one quiet *Tenour* keep;
We cannot *blame* indeed—but we may *sleep.*
In Wit, as Nature, what affects our Hearts
Is not th' Exactness of peculiar Parts;
245 'Tis not a *Lip,* or *Eye,* we Beauty call,
But the joint Force and full *Result* of *all.*
Thus when we view some well-proportion'd Dome,
(The *World*'s just Wonder, and ev'n *thine* O *Rome!*)
No single Parts unequally surprize;
250 All comes *united* to th' admiring Eyes;
No monstrous Height, or Breadth, or Length appear;
The *Whole* at once is *Bold,* and *Regular.*
    Whoever thinks a faultless Piece to see,
Thinks what ne'er was, nor is, nor e'er shall be.
255 In ev'ry Work regard the *Writer's End,*
Since none can compass more than they *Intend;*
And if the *Means* be just, the *Conduct* true,
Applause, in spite of trivial Faults, is due.
As Men of Breeding, sometimes Men of Wit,
260 T' avoid *great Errors,* must the *less* commit,
Neglect the Rules each *Verbal Critick* lays,
For *not* to know some Trifles, is a Praise.
Most Criticks, fond of some subservient Art,
Still make the *Whole* depend upon a *Part,*
265 They talk of *Principles,* but Notions prize,
And All to one lov'd Folly Sacrifice.
    Once on a time, *La Mancha*'s Knight,[1] they say,
A certain *Bard* encountring on the Way,
Discours'd in Terms as just, with Looks as Sage,
270 As e'er cou'd *Dennis,*[2] of the *Grecian* Stage;
Concluding all were desp'rate Sots and Fools,
Who durst depart from *Aristotle*'s Rules.
Our Author, happy in a Judge so nice,
Produc'd his Play, and beg'd the Knight's Advice,
275 Made him observe the *Subject* and the *Plot,*
The *Manners, Passions, Unities,* what not?

[1] Don Quixote.
[2] John Dennis (1657–1734), a British critic, whose work Pope knew.

All which, exact to *Rule* were brought about,
Were but a *Combate in the Lists* left out.
What! Leave the Combate out? Exclaims the Knight;
280 Yes, or we must renounce the *Stagyrite.*
Not so by Heav'n (he answers in a Rage)
Knights, Squires, and Steeds, must enter on the Stage.
So vast a Throng the Stage can ne'er contain.
Then build a New, or act it in a Plain.
285   Thus Criticks, of less *Judgment* than *Caprice,*
Curious, not *Knowing,* not *exact,* but *nice,*
Form *short Ideas;* and offend in *Arts*
(As most in *Manners*) by a *Love to Parts.*
    Some to *Conceit* alone their Taste confine,
290 And glitt'ring Thoughts struck out at ev'ry Line;
Pleas'd with a Work where nothing's just or fit;
One *glaring Chaos* and *wild Heap* of *Wit:*
Poets like Painters, thus, unskill'd to trace
The *naked Nature* and the *living Grace,*
295 With *Gold* and *Jewels* cover ev'ry Part,
And hide with *Ornaments* their *Want of Art.*
True Wit is *Nature* to Advantage drest,
What oft was *Thought,* but ne'er so well *Exprest,*
Something, whose Truth convinc'd at Sight we find,
300 That gives us back the Image of our Mind:
As Shades more sweetly recommend the Light,
So modest Plainness sets off sprightly Wit:
For *Works* may have more *Wit* than does 'em good,
As *Bodies* perish through Excess of *Blood.*

(1711)

from *The Rape of the Lock*[1]

What dire Offence from am'rous Causes springs,
What mighty Contests rise from trivial Things,
I sing—This Verse to *Caryll,* Muse! is due;
This, ev'n *Belinda* may vouchsafe to view:
5 Slight is the Subject, but not so the Praise,
If She inspire, and He approve my Lays.
    Say what strange Motive, Goddess! cou'd compel

[1] The poem is based on an actual incident—Lord Petre cutting off a lock of Arabella Fermor's hair. Her family was angered and John Caryll (mentioned in line 3), a friend of Pope's, asked Pope to write a comic poem about the incident.

A well-bred *Lord* t'assault a gentle *Belle*?
Oh say what stranger Cause, yet unexplor'd,
10 Cou'd make a gentle *Belle* reject a *Lord*?
In Tasks so bold, can Little Men engage,
And in soft Bosoms dwells such mighty Rage?
    Sol thro' white Curtains shot a tim'rous Ray,
And op'd those Eyes that must eclipse the Day;
15 Now Lapdogs give themselves the rowzing Shake,
And sleepless Lovers, just at Twelve, awake:
Thrice rung the Bell, the Slipper knock'd the Ground,[2]
And the press'd Watch return'd a silver Sound.
Belinda still her downy Pillow prest,
20 Her Guardian *Sylph* prolong'd the balmy Rest.
'Twas he had summon'd to her silent Bed
The Morning-Dream that hover'd o'er her Head.
A Youth more glitt'ring than a *Birth-night Beau*,
(That ev'n in Slumber caus'd her Cheek to glow)
25 Seem'd to her Ear his winning Lips to lay,
And thus in Whispers said, or seem'd to say.
    Fairest of Mortals, thou distinguish'd Care
Of thousand bright Inhabitants of Air!
If e'er one Vision touch'd thy infant Thought,
30 Of all the Nurse and all the Priest have taught,
Of airy Elves by Moonlight Shadows seen,
The silver Token, and the circled Green,[3]
Or Virgins visited by Angel-Pow'rs,
With Golden Crowns and Wreaths of heavn'ly Flow'rs,
35 Hear and believe! thy own Importance know,
Nor bound thy narrow Views to Things below.
Some secret Truths from Learned Pride conceal'd,
To Maids alone and Children are reveal'd:
What tho' no Credit doubting Wits may give?
40 The Fair and Innocent shall still believe.
Know then, unnumber'd Spirits round thee fly,
The light *Militia* of the lower Sky;
These, tho' unseen, are ever on the Wing,
Hang o'er the *Box*, and hover round the *Ring*.[4]
45 Think what an Equipage thou hast in Air,
And view with scorn *Two Pages* and a *Chair*.
As now your own, our Beings were of old,
And once inclos'd in Woman's beauteous Mold;
Thence, by a soft Transition, we repair

2 Belinda summoning her maids.
3 The silver token is the payment fairies leave for stealing cream; the circled green is the worn path that fairies leave after dancing.
4 The theater box; the ring is the circular driveway in Hyde Park, London.

50 From earthly Vehicles to these of Air.
    Think not, when Woman's transient Breath is fled,
    That all her Vanities at once are dead:
    Succeeding Vanities she still regards,
    And tho' she plays no more, o'erlooks the Cards.
55 Her Joy in gilded Chariots, when alive,
    And Love of *Ombre,*⁵ after Death survive.
    For when the Fair in all their Pride expire,
    To their first Elements⁶ their Souls retire:
    The Sprights of fiery Termagants in Flame
60 Mount up, and take a *Salamander*'s Name.⁷
    Soft yielding Minds to Water glide away,
    And sip with *Nymphs,* their Elemental Tea.
    The graver Prude sinks downward to a *Gnome,*
    In search of Mischief still on Earth to roam.
65 The light Coquettes in *Sylphs* aloft repair,
    And sport and flutter in the Fields of Air.
        Know farther yet; Whoever fair and chaste
    Rejects Mankind, is by some *Sylph* embrac'd:
    For Spirits, freed from mortal Laws, with ease
70 Assume what Sexes and what Shapes they please.
    What guards the Purity of melting Maids,
    In Courtly Balls, and Midnight Masquerades,
    Safe from the treach'rous Friend, the daring Spark,
    The Glance by Day, the Whisper in the Dark;
75 When kind Occasion prompts their warm Desires,
    When Musick softens, and when Dancing fires?
    'Tis but their *Sylph,* the wise Celestials know,
    Tho 'Honour is the Word with Men below.
        Some Nymphs there are, too conscious of their Face,
80 For Life predestin'd to the *Gnomes'* Embrace.
    These swell their Prospects and exalt their Pride,
    When Offers are disdain'd, and Love deny'd.
    Then gay Ideas crowd the vacant Brain;
    While Peers and Dukes, and all their sweeping Train,
85 And Garters, Stars and Coronets appear,
    And in soft Sounds, *Your Grace* salutes their Ear.
    'Tis these that early taint the Female Soul,
    Instruct the Eyes of young *Coquettes* to roll,
    Teach Infant-Cheeks a bidden Blush to know,
90 And little Hearts to flutter at a *Beau.*
        Oft when the World imagine Women stray,

---

⁵ Popular card game.
⁶ I.e., earth, air, fire, and water.
⁷ Salamanders were believed to live in fire; Pope has changed termagants (quarrelsome women)
into salamanders.

The *Sylphs* thro' mystick Mazes guide their Way,
Thro' all the giddy Circle they pursue,
And old Impertinence expel by new.
95   What tender Maid but must a Victim fall
To one Man's Treat, but for another's Ball?
When *Florio* speaks, what Virgin could withstand,
If gentle *Damon* did not squeeze her Hand?
With varying Vanities, from ev'ry Part,
100   They shift the moving Toyshop of their Heart;
Where Wigs with Wigs, with Sword-knots
        Sword-knots strive,
Beaus banish Beaus, and Coaches Coaches drive.
This erring Mortals Levity may call,
Oh blind to Truth! the *Sylphs* contrive it all.
105   Of these am I, who thy Protection claim,
A watchful Sprite, and *Ariel* is my Name.
Late, as I rang'd the Crystal Wilds of Air,
In the clear Mirror of thy ruling *Star*
I saw, alas! some dread Event impend,
110   Ere to the Main this Morning Sun descend.
But Heav'n reveals not what, or how, or where:
Warn'd by thy *Sylph,* oh Pious Maid beware!
This to disclose is all thy Guardian can.
Beware of all, but most beware of Man!
115   He said; when *Shock,*[8] who thought she slept too
        long,
Leapt up, and wak'd his Mistress with his Tongue.
'Twas then *Belinda*! if Report say true,
Thy Eyes first open'd on a *Billet-doux;*°   love letter
Wounds, Charms, and *Ardors,* were no sooner read,
120   But all the Vision vanish'd from thy Head.
    And now, unveil'd, the *Toilet* stands display'd,
Each Silver Vase in mystic Order laid.
First, rob'd in White, the Nymph intent adores
With Head uncover'd, the *Cosmetic* Pow'rs.
125   A heav'nly Image in the Glass appears,
To that she bends, to that her Eyes she rears;
Th'inferior Priestess, at her Altar's side,
Trembling, begins the sacred Rites of Pride.
Unnumber'd Treasures ope at once, and here
130   The various Off'rings of the World appear;
From each she nicely culls with curious Toil,
And decks the Goddess with the glitt'ring Spoil.
This Casket *India*'s glowing Gems unlocks,

[8] Belinda's lapdog.

And all *Arabia* breathes from yonder Box.
135 The Tortoise here and Elephant unite,
Transform'd to *Combs,* the speckled and the white.
Here Files of Pins extend their shining Rows,
Puffs, Powders, Patches, Bibles, Billet-doux.
Now awful Beauty puts on all its Arms;
140 The Fair each moment rises in her Charms,
Repairs her Smiles, awakens ev'ry Grace,
And calls forth all the Wonders of her Face;
Sees by Degrees a purer Blush arise,
And keener Lightnings quicken in her Eyes.
145 The busy *Sylphs* surround their darling Care;
These set the Head, and those divide the Hair,
Some fold the Sleeve, whilst others plait the Gown;
And *Betty's*[9] prais'd for Labours not her own.

                                        (1714)

from *An Essay on Man*

From Epistle II. Of the Nature and State of Man with Respect to Himself,
as an Individual

Know then thyself, presume not God to scan;
The proper study of Mankind is Man.
Plac'd on this isthmus of a middle state,
A being darkly wise, and rudely great:
5 With too much knowledge for the Sceptic side,
With too much weakness for the Stoic's pride,
He hangs between; in doubt to act, or rest,
In doubt to deem himself a God, or Beast;
In doubt his Mind or Body to prefer,
10 Born but to die, and reas'ning but to err;
Alike in ignorance, his reason such,
Whether he thinks too little, or too much:
Chaos of Thought and Passion, all confus'd;
Still by himself abus'd, or disabus'd;
15 Created half to rise, and half to fall;
Great lord of all things, yet a prey to all;
Sole judge of Truth, in endless Error hurl'd:
The glory, jest, and riddle of the world!

                                        (1733)

9 Belinda's maid.

Thomas Gray

(1 7 1 6 – 1 7 7 1)

Thomas Gray provides a link between the public, rational poetry of the eighteenth century and the private, emotional outpourings of the great Romantics. After his education at Eton and Cambridge, he took a long tour of the Continent with Horace Walpole, son of the prime minister, from 1739 to 1741. Walpole later helped to make Gray's poetry public. Gray began to make a mark as a poet in 1742; in 1757 he was offered the poet laureateship. A scholar more than a poet, Gray did not accept the honor; in 1768 he became a professor of history at Cambridge. One of the most widely learned of the English poets, Gray was expert in classical and English literature and history. He was also interested in Old Norse and Welsh literature.

Gray's reputation rests almost entirely on one poem, "Elegy Written in a Country Church Yard," perhaps the most anthologized poem in the language. Although it is only 128 lines long, Gray apparently composed, recomposed, and polished the poem for more than six years. The elegy is a classic, a lament for all those doomed to obscurity and for humanity itself, doomed to the dust of history. The poem's melancholy mood and rural setting foreshadow the Romantic era, but its precise, controlled diction; its quiet, understated themes; and its decorous nobility root it securely in the eighteenth century. In Gray's Pindaric odes, in his translations from Welsh and Norse poetry, and in his love of wild landscapes, his "romantic" tendencies are most clear. Gray's poems are public utterances tinged with personal feeling, muted reflections on sorrow and human transience. His output was extremely small, but his fastidious approach is in part responsible for the durability and universality of his best work.

Gray's best-known poems include "Ode on the Spring," "Ode on a Distant Prospect of Eton College," "Hymn to Adversity," "Sonnet on the Death of West" (all written in 1742); "Elegy Written in a Country Church Yard" (1751); "Ode on the Death of a Favorite Cat" (1748); two Pindaric odes, "The Progress of Poesy" (1757) and "The Bard" (1757); and two late poems inspired by Icelandic and Celtic poetry, "The Fatal Sisters" and "The Descent of Odin" (1761). His best-known prose work is his *Journal* (written after a trip to the Lake District). Gray's letters are considered among the finest of his time.

THOMAS GRAY

Ode on a Distant Prospect of Eton College[1]

Ye distant spires, ye antique towers,
That crown the watry glade,
Where grateful Science° still adores   learning
Her HENRY'S[2] holy Shade;
5 And ye, that from the stately brow
Of WINDSOR's heights th' expanse below
Of grove, of lawn, of mead survey,
Whose turf, whose shade, whose flowers among
Wanders the hoary Thames along
10 His silver-winding way.

    Ah happy hills, ah pleasing shade,
Ah fields belov'd in vain,
Where once my careless childhood stray'd,
A stranger yet to pain!
15 I feel the gales, that from ye blow,
A momentary bliss bestow,
As waving fresh their gladsome wing,
My weary soul they seem to sooth[e],
And, redolent of joy and youth,
20 To breathe a second spring.

    Say, Father THAMES, for thou hast seen
Full many a sprightly race
Disporting on thy margent green
The paths of pleasure trace,
25 Who foremost now delight to cleave
With pliant arm thy glassy wave?
The captive linnet which enthrall?
What idle progeny succeed
To chase the rolling circle's speed,
30 Or urge the flying ball?

    While some on earnest business bent
Their murm'ring labours ply

---

[1] One of the manuscript versions of the poem has a Greek epigraph from Menander following
the title: ἄνθρωπος ἱκανὴ πρόφασις εἰς τὸ δυστυχεῖν (I am a man—a sufficient excuse for
being miserable).
[2] Henry VI founded Eton College in 1440.

'Gainst graver hours, that bring constraint
To sweeten liberty:
35 Some bold adventurers disdain
The limits of their little reign,
And unknown regions dare descry:
Still as they run they look behind,
They hear a voice in every wind,
40 And snatch a fearful joy.

Gay hope is theirs by fancy fed,
Less pleasing when possest;
The tear forgot as soon as shed,
The sunshine of the breast:
45 Theirs buxom health of rosy hue,
Wild wit, invention ever-new,
And lively chear of vigour born;
The thoughtless day, the easy night,
The spirits pure, the slumbers light,
50 That fly th' approach of morn.

Alas, regardless of their doom,
The little victims play!
No sense have they of ills to come,
Nor care beyond to-day:
55 Yet see how all around 'em wait
The Ministers of human fate,
And black Misfortune's baleful train!
Ah, shew them where in ambush stand
To seize their prey the murth'rous band!
60 Ah, tell them, they are men!

These shall the fury Passions tear,
The vultur[e]s of the mind,
Disdainful Anger, pallid Fear,
And Shame that sculks behind;
65 Or pineing Love shall waste their youth,
Or Jealousy with rankling tooth,
That inly gnaws the secret heart,
And Envy wan, and faded Care,
Grim-visag'd comfortless Despair,
70 And Sorrow's piercing dart.

Ambition this shall tempt to rise,
Then whirl the wretch from high,
To bitter Scorn a sacrifice,
And grinning Infamy.

75 The stings of Falshood those shall try,
And hard Unkindness' alter'd eye,
That mocks the tear it forc'd to flow;
And keen Remorse with blood defil'd,
And moody Madness laughing wild
80 Amid severest woe.

Lo, in the vale of years beneath
A griesly troop are seen,
The painful family of Death,
More hideous than their Queen:
85 This racks the joints, this fires the veins,
That every labouring sinew strains,
Those in the deeper vitals rage:
Lo, Poverty, to fill the band,
That numbs the soul with icy hand,
90 And slow-consuming Age.

To each his suff'rings: all are men,
Condemn'd alike to groan,
The tender for another's pain;
Th' unfeeling for his own.
95 Yet ah! why should they know their fate?
Since sorrow never comes too late,
And happiness too swiftly flies.
Thought would destroy their paradise.
No more; where ignorance is bliss,
100 'Tis folly to be wise.

(1747)

Elegy Written in a Country Church Yard

The Curfew tolls the knell of parting day,
The lowing herd wind slowly o'er the lea,
The plowman homeward plods his weary way,
And leaves the world to darkness and to me.

5 Now fades the glimmering landscape on the sight,
And all the air a solemn stillness holds,
Save where the beetle wheels his droning flight,
And drowsy tinklings lull the distant folds;

Save that from yonder ivy-mantled tow'r
10 The mopeing owl does to the moon complain

Of such, as wand'ring near her secret bow'r,
Molest her ancient solitary reign.

Beneath those rugged elms, that yew-tree's shade,
Where heaves the turf in many a mould'ring heap,
15   Each in his narrow cell for ever laid,
The rude° Forefathers of the hamlet sleep.   unschooled

The breezy call of incense-breathing Morn,
The swallow twitt'ring from the straw-built shed,
The cock's shrill clarion, or the ecchoing horn,
20   No more shall rouse them from their lowly bed.

For them no more the blazing hearth shall burn,
Or busy housewife ply her evening care:
No children run to lisp their sire's return,
Or climb his knees the envied kiss to share.

25   Oft did the harvest to their sickle yield,
Their furrow oft the stubborn glebe° has broke;   field
How jocund did they drive their team afield!
How bow'd the woods beneath their sturdy stroke!

Let not Ambition mock their useful toil,
30   Their homely joys, and destiny obscure;
Nor Grandeur hear with a disdainful smile,
The short and simple annals of the poor.

The boast of heraldry, the pomp of pow'r,
And all that beauty, all that wealth e'cr gave,
35   Awaits alike th' inevitable hour.
The paths of glory lead but to the grave.

Nor you, ye Proud, impute to These the fault,
If Mem'ry o'er their Tomb no Trophies° raise,   monuments
Where thro' the long-drawn isle and fretted°vault   decorated
40   The pealing anthem swells the note of praise.

Can storied urn or animated bust
Back to its mansion call the fleeting breath?
Can Honour's voice provoke° the silent dust,   enliven
Or Flatt'ry sooth the dull cold ear of Death?

45   Perhaps in this neglected spot is laid
Some heart once pregnant with celestial fire,
Hands, that the rod of empire might have sway'd,
Or wak'd to extasy the living lyre.

But Knowledge to their eyes her ample page
50   Rich with the spoils of time did ne'er unroll;
Chill Penury repress'd their noble rage,
And froze the genial current of the soul.

Full many a gem of purest ray serene,
The dark unfathom'd caves of ocean bear:
55   Full many a flower is born to blush unseen,
And waste its sweetness on the desert air.

Some village-Hampden,[1] that with dauntless breast
The little Tyrant of his fields withstood;
Some mute inglorious Milton here may rest,
60   Some Cromwell guiltless of his country's blood.

Th' applause of list'ning senates to command,
The threats of pain and ruin to despise,
To scatter plenty o'er a smiling land,
And read their hist'ry in a nation's eyes

65   Their lot forbad: nor circumscrib'd alone
Their growing virtues, but their crimes confin'd;
Forbad to wade through slaughter to a throne,
And shut the gates of mercy on mankind,

The struggling pangs of conscious truth to hide,
70   To quench the blushes of ingenuous shame,
Or heap the shrine of Luxury and Pride
With incense kindled at the Muse's flame.

Far from the madding crowd's ignoble strife,
Their sober wishes never learn'd to stray;
75   Along the cool sequester'd vale of life
They kept the noiseless tenor of their way.

Yet ev'n these bones from insult to protect
Some frail memorial still erected nigh,
With uncouth rhimes and shapeless sculpture deck'd,°   adorned
80   Implores the passing tribute of a sigh.

Their name, their years, spelt by th' unletter'd muse,
The place of fame and elegy supply:
And many a holy text around she strews,
That teach the rustic moralist to die.

---

[1] John Hampden (1594–1643), a Member of Parliament, opposed the autocratic rule of
Charles I.

85   For who to dumb Forgetfulness a prey,
      This pleasing anxious being e'er resign'd,
      Left the warm precincts of the chearful day,
      Nor cast one longing ling'ring look behind?

      On some fond breast the parting soul relies,
90   Some pious drops the closing eye requires;
      Ev'n from the tomb the voice of Nature cries,
      Ev'n in our Ashes live their wonted Fires.

      For thee, who mindful of th' unhonour'd Dead
      Dost in these lines their artless tale relate;
95   If chance, by lonely contemplation led,
      Some kindred Spirit shall inquire thy fate,

      Haply some hoary-headed Swain may say,
      "Oft have we seen him at the peep of dawn
      "Brushing with hasty steps the dews away
100   "To meet the sun upon the upland lawn.

      "There at the foot of yonder nodding beech
      "That wreathes its old fantastic roots so high,
      "His listless length at noontide wou'd he stretch,
      "And pore upon the brook that babbles by.

105   "Hard by yon wood, now smiling as in scorn,
      "Mutt'ring his wayward fancies he wou'd rove,
      "Now drooping, woeful wan, like one forlorn,
      "Or craz'd with care, or cross'd in hopeless love.

      "One morn I miss'd him on the custom'd hill,
110   "Along the heath and near his fav'rite tree;
      "Another came; nor yet beside the rill,
      "Nor up the lawn, nor at the wood was he,

      "The next with dirges due in sad array
      "Slow thro' the church-way path we saw him born[e].
115   "Approach and read (for thou can'st read) the lay,
      "Grav'd on the stone beneath yon aged thorn."

THE EPITAPH

Here rests his head upon the lap of Earth
A Youth to Fortune and to Fame unknown,

Fair Science° frown'd not on his humble birth,　　　　learning
120　*And Melancholy mark'd him for her own.*

Large was his bounty, and his soul sincere,
Heav'n did a recompence as largely send:
He gave to Mis'ry all he had, a tear,
He gain'd from Heav'n ('twas all he wish'd) a friend.

125　*No farther seek his merits to disclose,*
Or draw his frailties from their dread abode,
(There they alike in trembling hope repose)
The bosom of his Father and his God.

(1751)

William Blake

(1 7 5 7 – 1 8 2 7)

Mystic, artist, engraver, prophet, and poet, William Blake is one of the most fascinating, eccentric, and profound figures in English literature. The son of a London haberdasher, Blake had no formal schooling. As a teenager he was apprenticed for seven years to an engraver. He married Catherine Boucher, who was illiterate, when he was 24, and taught her to read and to help him with his engraving and printing. As a child Blake had a vision of a tree full of angels; as a youth he had a vision of ancient kings in Westminster Abbey. Throughout his life his mystical experiences were an integral part of his art and his unique philosophy. Blake labored for much of his life in total obscurity, printing a few editions of his poems accompanied by his magnificent and breathtakingly original engravings and watercolors. A one-man art exhibit in 1809 was a total failure. Although Blake attracted a small group of followers in his old age, he was a man too much of another era: in this century, his genius has become widely appreciated.

Blake was the first Romantic poet, although he had much more in common with later Romantics, such as Shelley, than with Wordsworth, his near contemporary. Samuel Johnson ruled literary London when Blake was growing up, but Blake had nothing of the eighteenth-century poet about him. His poetry is filled with the energy of human spirituality, sexuality, and imagination. In his world, authority must be resisted in favor of the individual's vision; the categories of good and evil are too simple to explain reality; the Fall of Man and the Gospels of Christ are transformed from rigidly interpreted historical events to challenging myths of psychic disintegration and an ultimate renewal of a human community of vision. In the words of his character Los, Blake felt that the artist "must Create a System or be enslaved by another Man's." Influenced by the Bible, Swedenborg, and other esoteric philosophies, Blake created a system entirely his own, a complex and sometimes obscure mythology of revolution, purification, and ecstasy, a renunciation of the fetters he felt humankind had created for itself (our "mind-forged manacles"). In stark contrast to the rocking-horse couplets of his contemporaries, Blake developed, in his later work, a long, pulsing, irregular line. He produced pure hard lyrics such as "The Tyger" and "The Sick Rose," among the finest ever written, and great, sprawling, apocalyptic epics like *Milton* and *Jerusalem*.

Blake's major works are the lyrics from *Poetical Sketches* (1783) and from the brilliant *Songs of Innocence and Experience* (1789, 1794); and the prophetic works, *The Book of Thel* (1789), *Visions of the Daughters of Albion* (1793), *The Marriage of Heaven and Hell* (1792), *America: A Prophecy* (1793), *Europe: A Prophecy* (1794), *The First Book of Urizen* (1794), *Milton* (1804), *The Four Zoas* (ca. 1805), *Jerusalem* (1820), and *The Everlasting Gospel* (date unknown). Some lyrics also survive from Blake's notebooks. Blake produced hundreds of paintings and engravings of a stature near that of his poetry. Many were used to illustrate his own books; he also did an engraving of Chaucer's Canterbury pilgrims, a set of designs for *Job,* and a series of illustrations of Dante.

WILLIAM BLAKE

Song

Memory, hither come,
   And tune your merry notes;
And, while upon the wind,
   Your music floats,
5 I'll pore upon the stream,
Where sighing lovers dream,
And fish for fancies as they pass
Within the watery glass.

I'll drink of the clear stream,
10   And hear the linnet's song;
And there I'll lie and dream
   The day along:
And, when night comes, I'll go
   To places fit for woe;
15 Walking along the darken'd valley,
   With silent Melancholy.

(1783)

Mad Song

The wild winds weep,
   And the night is a-cold;
Come hither, Sleep,
   And my griefs infold:
5 But lo! the morning peeps
   Over the eastern steeps,

And the rustling birds of dawn
The earth do scorn.

Lo! to the vault
10   Of paved heaven,
With sorrow fraught
    My notes are driven:
They strike the ear of night,
    Make weep the eyes of day;
15 They make mad the roaring winds,
    And with tempests play.

Like a fiend in a cloud
    With howling woe,
After night I do croud,
20   And with night will go;
I turn my back to the east,
From whence comforts have increas'd;
For light doth seize my brain
With frantic pain.

(1783)

from *Songs of Innocence*

INTRODUCTION

Piping down the valleys wild
Piping songs of pleasant glee
On a cloud I saw a child.
And he laughing said to me.

5 Pipe a song about a Lamb;
So I piped with merry chear,
Piper pipe that song again—
So I piped, he wept to hear.

Drop thy pipe thy happy pipe
10 Sing thy songs of happy chear,
So I sung the same again
While he wept with joy to hear

Piper sit thee down and write
In a book that all may read—

15 So he vanish'd from my sight.
And I pluck'd a hollow reed.

And I made a rural pen,
And I stain'd the water clear,
And I wrote my happy songs
20 Every child may joy to hear
(1789)

THE LAMB

Little Lamb who made thee
Dost thou know who made thee
Gave thee life & bid thee feed.
By the stream & o'er the mead;
5 Gave thee clothing of delight,
Softest clothing wooly bright;
Gave thee such a tender voice,
Making all the vales rejoice!
Little Lamb who made thee
10 Dost thou know who made thee
Little Lamb I'll tell thee,
Little Lamb I'll tell thee!
He is called by thy name,
For he calls himself a Lamb:
15 He is meek & he is mild,
He became a little child:
I a child & thou a lamb,
We are called by his name.
Little Lamb God bless thee.
20 Little Lamb God bless thee.
(1789)

THE CHIMNEY SWEEPER

When my mother died I was very young,
And my father sold me while yet my tongue,
Could scarcely cry weep weep weep weep.
So your chimneys I sweep & in soot I sleep.

5 Theres little Tom Dacre, who cried when his head
That curl'd like a lambs back, was shav'd, so I said.
Hush Tom never mind it, for when your head's bare,
You know that the soot cannot spoil your white hair.

And so he was quiet, & that very night,
10   As Tom was a sleeping he had such a sight,
That thousands of sweepers Dick, Joe Ned & Jack
Were all of them lock'd up in coffins of black

And by came an Angel who had a bright key,
And he open'd the coffins & set them all free.
15   Then down a green plain leaping laughing they run
And wash in a river and shine in the Sun.

Then naked & white, all their bags left behind,
They rise upon clouds, and sport in the wind.
And the Angel told Tom if he'd be a good boy,
20   He'd have God for his father & never want joy.

And so Tom awoke and we rose in the dark
And got with our bags & our brushes to work.
Tho' the morning was cold, Tom was happy & warm,
So if all do their duty, they need not fear harm.

(1789)

THE DIVINE IMAGE

To Mercy Pity Peace and Love,
All pray in their distress:
And to these virtues of delight
Return their thankfulness.

5   For Mercy Pity Peace and Love,
Is God our father dear:
And Mercy Pity Peace and Love,
Is Man his child and care.

For Mercy has a human heart
10   Pity, a human face:
And Love, the human form divine,
And Peace, the human dress.

Then every man of every clime,
That prays in his distress,
15   Prays to the human form divine
Love Mercy Pity Peace.

And all must love the human form,
In heathen, turk or jew.
Where Mercy, Love & Pity dwell
20   There God is dwelling too.

(1789)

HOLY THURSDAY

Twas on a Holy Thursday their innocent faces clean
The children walking two & two in red & blue & green
Grey headed beadles[1] walkd before with wands as white as snow
Till into the high dome of Pauls they like Thames waters flow

5   O what a multitude they seemd these flowers of London town
Seated in companies they sit with radiance all their own
The hum of multitudes was there but multitudes of lambs
Thousands of little boys & girls raising their innocent hands

Now like a mighty wind they raise to heaven the voice of song
10   Or like harmonious thunderings the seats of heaven among
Beneath them sit the aged men wise guardians of the poor
Then cherish pity, lest you drive an angel from your door

(1789)

from *Songs of Experience*

INTRODUCTION

Hear the voice of the Bard!
Who Present, Past, & Future sees
Whose ears have heard,
The Holy Word,
5   That walk'd among the ancient trees.

Calling the lapsed Soul
And weeping in the evening dew;
That might controll,

---

[1] Minor parish officers who kept order in the church.

The starry pole;
10 And fallen fallen light renew!

O Earth O Earth return!
Arise from out the dewy grass;
Night is worn,
And the morn
15 Rises from the slumberous mass.

Turn away no more:
Why wilt thou turn away
The starry floor
The watry shore
20 Is giv'n thee till the break of day.

(1794)

EARTH'S ANSWER

Earth rais'd up her head,
From the darkness dread & drear.
Her light fled:
Stony dread!
5 And her locks cover'd with grey despair.

Prison'd on watry shore
Starry Jealousy does keep my den
Cold and hoar
Weeping o'er
10 I hear the Father of the ancient men

Selfish father of men
Cruel jealous selfish fear
Can delight
Chain'd in night
15 The virgins of youth and morning bear.

Does spring hide its joy
When buds and blossoms grow?
Does the sower?
Sow by night?
20 Or the plowman in darkness plow?

Break this heavy chain,
That does freeze my bones around

Selfish! vain,
Eternal bane!
25 That free Love with bondage bound.

(1794)

HOLY THURSDAY

Is this a holy thing to see,
In a rich and fruitful land,
Babes reduced to misery,
Fed with cold and usurous hand?

5 Is that trembling cry a song?
Can it be a song of joy?
And so many children poor?
It is a land of poverty!

And their sun does never shine.
10 And their fields are bleak & bare.
And their ways are fill'd with thorns.
It is eternal winter there.

For where-e'er the sun does shine,
And where-e'er the rain does fall:
15 Babe can never hunger there,
Nor poverty the mind appall.

(1794)

THE CHIMNEY SWEEPER

A little black thing among the snow:
Crying weep, weep, in notes of woe!
Where are thy father & mother? say?
They are both gone up to the church to pray.

5 Because I was happy upon the heath,
And smil'd among the winters snow:
They clothed me in the clothes of death,
And taught me to sing the notes of woe.

And because I am happy, & dance & sing,
10 They think they have done me no injury:
And are gone to praise God & his Priest & King
Who make up a heaven of our misery.

(1794)

THE SICK ROSE

O Rose thou art sick.
The invisible worm,
That flies in the night
In the howling storm:

5 Has found out thy bed
Of crimson joy:
And his dark secret love
Does thy life destroy.

(1794)

THE TYGER

Tyger Tyger, burning bright,
In the forests of the night;
What immortal hand or eye,
Could frame thy fearful symmetry?

5 In what distant deeps or skies
Burnt the fire of thine eyes!
On what wings dare he aspire?
What the hand, dare sieze the fire?

And what shoulder, & what art,
10 Could twist the sinews of thy heart?
And when thy heart began to beat,
What dread hand? & what dread feet?

What the hammer? what the chain,
In what furnace was thy brain?
15 What the anvil? what dread grasp,
Dare its deadly terrors clasp?

When the stars threw down their spears
And water'd heaven with their tears:
Did he smile his work to see?
20 Did he who made the Lamb make thee?

Tyger, Tyger burning bright,
In the forests of the night:
What immortal hand or eye,
Dare frame thy fearful symmetry?

(1794)

THE GARDEN OF LOVE

I went to the Garden of Love,
And saw what I never had seen:
A Chapel was built in the midst,
Where I used to play on the green.

5   And the gates of this Chapel were shut,
And Thou shalt not. writ over the door;
So I turn'd to the Garden of Love,
That so many sweet flowers bore,

And I saw it was filled with graves,
10   And tomb-stones where flowers should be:
And Priests in black gowns, were walking their rounds,
And binding with briars, my joys & desires.

(1794)

LONDON

I wander thro' each charter'd street,
Near where the charter'd Thames does flow.
And mark in every face I meet
Marks of weakness, marks of woe.

5   In every cry of every Man,
In every Infants cry of fear,
In every voice: in every ban,
The mind-forg'd manacles I hear

How the Chimney-sweepers cry
10   Every blackning Church appalls,
And the hapless Soldiers sigh,
Runs in blood down Palace walls

But most thro' midnight streets I hear
How the youthful Harlots curse
15   Blasts the new-born Infants tear
And blights with plagues the Marriage hearse

(1794)

INFANT SORROW

My mother groand! my father wept.
Into the dangerous world I leapt:

Helpless, naked, piping loud;
Like a fiend hid in a cloud.

5   Struggling in my fathers hands:
Striving against my swadling bands:
Bound and weary I thought best
To sulk upon my mothers breast.

(1794)

"Mock on, Mock on, Voltaire, Rousseau"

Mock on, mock on, Voltaire, Rousseau;
Mock on, mock on; 'tis all in vain!
You throw the sand against the wind,
And the wind blows it back again.

5   And every sand becomes a gem
Reflected in the beams divine;
Blown back they blind the mocking eye,
But still in Israel's paths they shine.

The Atoms of Democritus
10   And Newton's Particles of Light[1]
Are sands upon the Red Sea shore,
Where Israel's tents do shine so bright.

(1863)

---

[1] Democritus (460–362 B.C.) hypothesized that atoms were the ultimate building blocks of the universe; Sir Isaac Newton (1642–1727) hypothesized that light was composed of minute particles.

Robert Burns

(1 7 5 9 – 1 7 9 6)

"Robbie" Burns, an accomplished and popular Scottish poet, was born at Alloway in Ayrshire, the son of a pious and hard-working farmer. Burns received little formal education but was encouraged by his father to read literature, theology, and politics. From 1784 until 1788, after his father's death, he helped his brother farm; he wrote much of his best poetry in this period. Burns early acquired an aversion to the Calvinist bent of much of Scottish thought; he had an instinctive belief in the freedom and natural goodness of humanity. As a young man he developed a propensity for "Love and Poesy" and he produced a steady stream of verses and illegitimate children. In 1786 he published the "Kilmarnock" edition of his poetry and was immediately lionized by Edinburgh intellectuals and by the common folk of Scotland. He was a brilliant conversationalist and a fierce democrat (he fervently argued on behalf of the American and French revolutions). He married Jean Armour in 1788 and settled on a farm, which failed. Famous for his hard drinking and living, he died, short of money, at the age of 37. He devoted many of his last years to a labor of love: collecting traditional Scottish airs.

In the late eighteenth century, people wanted to believe in "natural" poetry and Burns was a favorite. They saw his poetry as a spontaneous overflow of natural feeling. In fact, Burns was both well read and a meticulous reviser. He made extensive use of folk traditions, superstitions, and legends. He generally rejected the couplet in favor of ballad meter and wrote about the basic human emotions—love, melancholy, joy, desire. Burns's narrative masterpiece, the mock-heroic "Tam o'Shanter," demonstrates his use of vivid description, local color, and rural mythology. Burns also wrote 300 songs, pure and fervid evocations of the powerful emotion of a moment. The poetry is filled with the love of liquor, romance, labor, fellowship, and sexuality, and above all with the swinging rhythms and patterns of Scottish speech. Appropriately, Burns's best-known song, "Auld Lang Syne," is today accompanied by song, dance, and drink.

The "Kilmarnock edition" of 1786 was entitled *Poems, Chiefly in the Scottish Dialect.* A second edition, with some additions, was published in 1787. Burns contributed 200 songs, original or adapted, to James Johnson's *Scots Musical Museum,* including "Auld Lang Syne" and "A Red, Red Rose." In 1792 he supplied songs for *Scottish Airs with Poetry,* among which were the beautiful lyrics "Comin' thro' the Rye" and "The Banks of Doon."

ROBERT BURNS

To a Mouse, On Turning Her Up in Her Nest, with the Plough, November, *1785*

Wee, sleeket,° cowran, tim'rous *beastie*,	sleek
O, what a panic's in thy breastie!	
Thou need na start awa sae hasty,	
Wi' bickering° brattle!°	hurried / scamper
5 I wad be laith to rin an' chase thee,	
Wi' murd'ring *pattle*!°	plowstaff
I'm truly sorry Man's dominion	
Has broken Nature's social union,	
An' justifies that ill opinion,	
10 Which makes thee startle,	
At me, thy poor, earth-born companion,	
An' *fellow-mortal*!	
I doubt na, whyles,° but thou may *thieve;*	sometimes
What then? poor beastie, thou maun° live!	must
15 A *daimen-icker* in a *thrave*[1]	
'S a sma' request:	
I'll get a blessin wi' the lave,°	remainder
An' never miss't!	
Thy wee-bit *housie,* too, in ruin!	
20 It's silly° wa's the win's are strewin!	weak
An' naething, now, to big° a new ane,	build
O' foggage° green!	moss
An' bleak *December's winds* ensuin,	
Baith snell° an' keen!	bitter
25 Thou saw the fields laid bare an' wast,	
An' weary *Winter* comin fast,	
An' cozie here, beneath the blast,	
Thou thought to dwell,	
Till crash! the cruel *coulter*° past	plow-blade
30 Out thro' thy cell.	

[1] A random ear of corn in a sheaf.

That wee-bit heap o' leaves an' stibble,°   stubble
Has cost thee monie a weary nibble!
Now thou's turn'd out, for a' thy trouble,
      But° house or hald,°   without / **home**
35 To thole° the Winter's *sleety dribble,*   endure
      An' *cranreuch°* cauld!   hoarfrost
But Mousie, thou art no thy-lane,
In proving *foresight* may be vain:
The best laid schemes o' *Mice* an' *Men,*
40   Gang aft agley,[2]
An' lea'e us nought but grief an' pain,
      For promis'd joy!

Still, thou art blest, compar'd wi' *me*!
The *present* only toucheth thee:
45 But Och! I *backward* cast my e'e,
      On prospects drear!
An' *forward,* tho' I canna *see,*
      I *guess* an' *fear*!

      (1786)

Song—For a' That and a' That—

    Is there, for honest Poverty
      That hings his head, and a' that;
  The coward-slave, we pass him by,
      We dare be poor for a' that!
5   For a' that, and a' that,
      Our toils obscure, and a' that,
  The rank is but the guinea's stamp,
      The Man's the gowd° for a' that.—   gold

  What though on hamely fare we dine,
10   Wear hoddin grey,° and a' that.   coarse cloth
  Gie fools their silks, and knaves their wine,
      A Man's a Man for a' that.
    For a' that, and a' that,
      Their tinsel show, and a' that;
15   The honest man, though e'er sae poor,
      Is king o' men for a' that.—

[2] Go off astray.

Ye see yon birkie° ca'd, a lord,   young man
    Wha struts, and stares, and a' that,
Though hundreds worship at his word,
20   He's but a coof° for a' that.   fool
    For a' that, and a' that,
      His ribband, star and a' that,
The man of independant mind,
    He looks and laughs at a' that.—

25 A prince can mak a belted knight,
    A marquis, duke, and a' that;
But an honest man's aboon° his might,   above
    Gude faith he mauna fa' that!
    For a' that, and a' that,
30   Their dignities, and a' that,
The pith o' Sense, and pride o' Worth,
    Are higher rank that a' that.—

Then let us pray that come it may,
    As come it will for a' that,
35 That Sense and Worth, o'er a' the earth
    Shall bear° the gree,° and a' that.   gain / prize
    For a' that, and a' that,
      Its comin yet for a' that,
That Man to Man the warld o'er,
40   Shall brothers be for a' that.—

(1795)

A Red, Red Rose

O my Luve's like a red, red rose,
    That's newly sprung in June;
O my Luve's like the melodie
    That's sweetly play'd in tune.—

5 As fair art thou, my bonie lass,
    So deep in luve am I;
And I will love thee still, my Dear,
    Till a' the seas gang dry.—

Till a' the seas gang dry, my Dear,
10   And the rocks melt wi' the sun:

I will love thee still, my Dear,
  While the sands o' life shall run.—

And fare thee weel, my only Luve!
  And fare thee weel, a while!
15 And I will come again, my Luve,
  Tho' it were ten thousand mile!

(1796)

Auld Lang Syne[1]

Should auld acquaintance be forgot
  And never brought to mind?
Should auld acquaintance be forgot,
  And auld lang syne!

Chorus

5 For auld lang syne, my jo,°   dear
  For auld lang syne,
We'll tak a cup o' kindness yet
  For auld lang syne.

And surely ye'll be° your pint stowp!°   pay for / glass
10 And surely I'll be mine!
And we'll tak a cup o' kindness yet,
  For auld lang syne.
    For auld, &c.

We twa hae run about the braes,°   hills
  And pou'd the gowans° fine;   daisies
15 But we've wander'd mony a weary fitt,°   foot
  Sin auld lang syne.
    For auld, &c.

We twa hae paidl'd in the burn,°   stream
  Frae morning sun till dine;
But seas between us braid° hae roar'd,   broad
20 Sin auld lang syne.
    For auld, &c.

[1] Of Long Ago.

And there's a hand, my trusty fiere!°   friend
    And gie's a hand o' thine!
And we'll tak a right gude-willie-waught,[2]
    For auld lang syne.
        For auld, &c.

                                    (1796)

[2] Big drink.

William Wordsworth

(1 7 7 0 – 1 8 5 0)

William Wordsworth, one of the major poets of the nineteenth century, helped to change English poetry from the neo-Classical to the Romantic mode. The son of an attorney, Wordsworth was born near the Lake District, whose landscape had a profound influence on his work. He left Cambridge and took a walking tour through Europe, where he was for a time entranced by French revolutionary fervor. While he was in Europe, Annette Vallon bore his illegitimate daughter. In 1795 he met Samuel Taylor Coleridge, with whom he published his second book, *Lyrical Ballads,* in 1798. Despite its initially hostile reception, the slender volume helped to spread new ideas about what poetry could and should do. Wordsworth moved back to the Lake District with his sister, married, and began to enjoy increased reputation and prosperity. He eventually became poet laureate, and continued to write and publish until his death, at the age of 80.

In the late 1790s Coleridge and Wordsworth developed the principle that poetry should be composed of "a selection from the real language of men in a state of vivid sensation." This theory, together with Wordsworth's conviction that the mind was not merely a passive receiver of the sensory world but, like a lamp, the illuminator and half-creator of that world, provided the basis for a body of work that was influential throughout the next century. Wordsworth composed poems on "ordinary" people, often in rural settings, and he used nature in a new way: to evoke the experience of the poet, thus shifting poetry's function decisively from the didactic to the expressive. The nature of Wordsworth's particular genius is most clear in *Tintern Abbey,* in short lyrics such as "I Wandered Lonely as a Cloud," and in *The Prelude,* a poetic autobiography and one of the greatest works of psychology in English poetry. Wordsworth mastered many forms, as evidenced by the superb blank verse of *The Prelude,* his sonnets, and his "Ode: Intimations of Immortality," a masterpiece that contains most of the poet's pervasive themes. Wordsworth's poetry is weakened by a flatness of diction and by obsessive introspection; yet these two traits helped him to turn English poetry in a new and fruitful direction.

Wordsworth published his first book, *Descriptive Sketches,* in 1793. A ponderous drama, *The Borderers,* followed in 1796, and the poems of *Lyrical Ballads* appeared in three editions, in 1798, 1800 (with the famous preface), and 1802. The beautiful poem *Michael* appeared in 1800. By 1805 *The Prelude* was substantially complete, although it was revised continually during the next 50 years. A volume published in 1807 included "Ode: Intimations of Immortality" and most of the best sonnets. His last volume was *Poems Chiefly of Early and Late Years* (1842).

WILLIAM WORDSWORTH

My Heart Leaps Up

My heart leaps up when I behold
   A rainbow in the sky:
So was it when my life began;
So is it now I am a man;
5 So be it when I shall grow old,
   Or let me die!
The Child is father of the Man;
And I could wish my days to be
Bound each to each by natural piety.

                         (1807)

Strange Fits of Passion Have I Known

Strange fits of passion have I known:
And I will dare to tell,
But in the Lover's ear alone,
What once to me befell.

5 When she I loved looked every day
Fresh as a rose in June,
I to her cottage bent my way,
 Beneath an evening-moon.

Upon the moon I fixed my eye,
10 All over the wide lea;
With quickening pace my horse drew nigh
Those paths so dear to me.

And now we reached the orchard-plot;
And, as we climbed the hill,
15 The sinking moon to Lucy's cot
Came near, and nearer still.

In one of those sweet dreams I slept,
Kind Nature's gentlest boon!
And all the while my eyes I kept
20 On the descending moon.

My horse moved on; hoof after hoof
He raised, and never stopped:
When down behind the cottage roof,
At once, the bright moon dropped.

25 What fond and wayward thoughts will slide
Into a Lover's head!
'O mercy!' to myself I cried,
'If Lucy should be dead!'

                                        (1800)

She Dwelt Among the Untrodden Ways

She dwelt among the untrodden ways
    Beside the springs of Dove,
A Maid whom there were none to praise
    And very few to love:

5 A violet by a mossy stone
    Half hidden from the eye!
—Fair as a star, when only one
    Is shining in the sky.

She lived unknown, and few could know
10   When Lucy ceased to be;
But she is in her grave, and, oh,
    The difference to me!

                                        (1800)

A Slumber Did My Spirit Seal

A slumber did my spirit seal;
    I had no human fears:
She seemed a thing that could not feel
    The touch of earthly years.

5 No motion has she now, no force;
    She neither hears nor sees;
Rolled round in earth's diurnal course,
    With rocks, and stones, and trees.

                                        (1800)

I Wandered Lonely as a Cloud

I wandered lonely as a cloud
That floats on high o'er vales and hills,
When all at once I saw a crowd,
A host, of golden daffodils;
5   Beside the lake, beneath the trees,
Fluttering and dancing in the breeze.

Continuous as the stars that shine
And twinkle on the milky way,
They stretched in never-ending line
10   Along the margin of a bay:
Ten thousand saw I at a glance,
Tossing their heads in sprightly dance.

The waves beside them danced; but they
Out-did the sparkling waves in glee:
15   A poet could not but be gay,
In such a jocund company:
I gazed—and gazed—but little thought
What wealth the show to me had brought:

For oft, when on my couch I lie
20   In vacant or in pensive mood,
They flash upon that inward eye
Which is the bliss of solitude;
And then my heart with pleasure fills,
And dances with the daffodils.

(1807)

Lines

COMPOSED A FEW MILES ABOVE TINTERN ABBEY, ON REVISITING THE BANKS OF THE WYE DURING A TOUR. JULY 13, 1798

Five years have past; five summers, with the length
Of five long winters! and again I hear
These waters, rolling from their mountain-springs
With a soft inland murmur Once again
5   Do I behold these steep and lofty cliffs,

That on a wild secluded scene impress
Thoughts of more deep seclusion; and connect
The landscape with the quiet of the sky.
The day is come when I again repose
10   Here, under this dark sycamore, and view
These plots of cottage-ground, these orchard-tufts,
Which at this season, with their unripe fruits,
Are clad in one green hue, and lose themselves
'Mid groves and copses. Once again I see
15   These hedge-rows, hardly hedge-rows, little lines
Of sportive wood run wild: these pastoral farms,
Green to the very door; and wreaths of smoke
Sent up, in silence, from among the trees!
With some uncertain notice, as might seem
20   Of vagrant dwellers in the houseless woods,
Or of some Hermit's cave, where by his fire
The Hermit sits alone.

                              These beauteous forms,
Through a long absence, have not been to me
As is a landscape to a blind man's eye:
25   But oft, in lonely rooms, and 'mid the din
Of towns and cities, I have owed to them,
In hours of weariness, sensations sweet,
Felt in the blood, and felt along the heart;
And passing even into my purer mind,
30   With tranquil restoration:—feelings too
Of unremembered pleasure: such, perhaps,
As have no slight or trivial influence
On that best portion of a good man's life,
His little, nameless, unremembered, acts
35   Of kindness and of love. Nor less, I trust,
To them I may have owed another gift,
Of aspect more sublime; that blessed mood,
In which the burthen of the mystery,
In which the heavy and the weary weight
40   Of all this unintelligible world,
Is lightened:—that serene and blessed mood,
In which the affections gently lead us on,—
Until, the breath of this corporeal frame
And even the motion of our human blood
45   Almost suspended, we are laid asleep
In body, and become a living soul:
While with an eye made quiet by the power
Of harmony, and the deep power of joy,
We see into the life of things.

                                  If this
50   Be but a vain belief, yet, oh! how oft—
     In darkness and amid the many shapes
     Of joyless daylight; when the fretful stir
     Unprofitable, and the fever of the world,
     Have hung upon the beatings of my heart—
55   How oft, in spirit, have I turned to thee,
     O sylvan Wye! thou wanderer thro' the woods,
     How often has my spirit turned to thee!

        And now, with gleams of half-extinguished thought,
     With many recognitions dim and faint,
60   And somewhat of a sad perplexity,
     The picture of the mind revives again:
     While here I stand, not only with the sense
     Of present pleasure, but with pleasing thoughts
     That in this moment there is life and food
65   For future years. And so I dare to hope,
     Though changed, no doubt, from what I was when first
     I came among these hills; when like a roe
     I bounded o'er the mountains, by the sides
     Of the deep rivers, and the lonely streams,
70   Wherever nature led: more like a man
     Flying from something that he dreads than one
     Who sought the thing he loved. For nature then
     (The coarser pleasures of my boyish days,
     And their glad animal movements all gone by)
75   To me was all in all.—I cannot paint
     What then I was. The sounding cataract
     Haunted me like a passion: the tall rock,
     The mountain, and the deep and gloomy wood,
     Their colours and their forms, were then to me
80   An appetite; a feeling and a love,
     That had no need of a remoter charm,
     By thought supplied, nor any interest
     Unborrowed from the eye.—That time is past,
     And all its aching joys are now no more,
85   And all its dizzy raptures. Not for this
     Faint I, nor mourn nor murmur; other gifts
     Have followed; for such loss, I would believe,
     Abundant recompense. For I have learned
     To look on nature, not as in the hour
90   Of thoughtless youth; but hearing oftentimes
     The still, sad music of humanity,
     Nor harsh nor grating, though of ample power
     To chasten and subdue. And I have felt

A presence that disturbs me with the joy
95 Of elevated thoughts; a sense sublime
Of something far more deeply interfused,
Whose dwelling is the light of setting suns,
And the round ocean and the living air,
And the blue sky, and in the mind of man:
100 A motion and a spirit, that impels
All thinking things, all objects of all thought,
And rolls through all things. Therefore am I still
A lover of the meadows and the woods,
And mountains; and of all that we behold
105 From this green earth; of all the mighty world
Of eye, and ear,—both what they half create,
And what perceive; well pleased to recognise
In nature and the language of the sense
The anchor of my purest thoughts, the nurse,
110 The guide, the guardian of my heart, and soul
Of all my moral being.

                       Nor perchance,
If I were not thus taught, should I the more
Suffer my genial spirits to decay:
For thou art with me here upon the banks
115 Of this fair river; thou my dearest Friend,
My dear, dear Friend; and in thy voice I catch
The language of my former heart, and read
My former pleasures in the shooting lights
Of thy wild eyes. Oh! yet a little while
120 May I behold in thee what I was once,
My dear, dear Sister! and this prayer I make,
Knowing that Nature never did betray
The heart that loved her; 'tis her privilege,
Through all the years of this our life, to lead
125 From joy to joy: for she can so inform
The mind that is within us, so impress
With quietness and beauty, and so feed
With lofty thoughts, that neither evil tongues,
Rash judgments, nor the sneers of selfish men,
130 Nor greetings where no kindness is, nor all
The dreary intercourse of daily life,
Shall e'er prevail against us, or disturb
Our cheerful faith, that all which we behold
Is full of blessings. Therefore let the moon
135 Shine on thee in thy solitary walk;
And let the misty mountain-winds be free
To blow against thee: and, in after years,

When these wild ecstasies shall be matured
Into a sober pleasure; when thy mind
140   Shall be a mansion for all lovely forms,
Thy memory be as a dwelling-place
For all sweet sounds and harmonies; oh! then,
If solitude, or fear, or pain, or grief,
Should be thy portion, with what healing thoughts
145   Of tender joy wilt thou remember me,
And these my exhortations! Nor, perchance—
If I should be where I no more can hear
Thy voice, nor catch from thy wild eyes these gleams
Of past existence—wilt thou then forget
150   That on the banks of this delightful stream
We stood together; and that I, so long
A worshipper of Nature, hither came
Unwearied in that service: rather say
With warmer love—oh! with far deeper zeal
155   Of holier love. Nor wilt thou then forget
That after many wanderings, many years
Of absence, these steep woods and lofty cliffs,
And this green pastoral landscape, were to me
More dear, both for themselves and for thy sake!

(1798)

The World Is Too Much with Us

The world is too much with us; late and soon,
Getting and spending, we lay waste our powers:
Little we see in Nature that is ours;
We have given our hearts away, a sordid boon!
5   This Sea that bares her bosom to the moon;
The winds that will be howling at all hours,
And are up-gathered now like sleeping flowers;
For this, for everything, we are out of tune;
It moves us not.—Great God! I'd rather be
10   A Pagan suckled in a creed outworn;
So might I, standing on this pleasant lea,
Have glimpses that would make me less forlorn;
Have sight of Proteus rising from the sea;
Or hear old Triton blow his wreathed horn.

(1807)

Composed upon Westminster Bridge, September 3, 1802

Earth has not anything to show more fair:
Dull would he be of soul who could pass by
A sight so touching in its majesty:
This City now doth, like a garment, wear
5 The beauty of the morning; silent, bare,
Ships, towers, domes, theatres, and temples lie
Open unto the fields, and to the sky;
All bright and glittering in the smokeless air.
Never did sun more beautifully steep
10 In his first splendour, valley, rock, or hill;
Ne'er saw I, never felt, a calm so deep!
The river glideth at his own sweet will:
Dear God! the very houses seem asleep;
And all that mighty heart is lying still!

(1807)

Ode

INTIMATIONS OF IMMORTALITY FROM RECOLLECTIONS OF EARLY CHILDHOOD

The Child is father of the Man;
And I could wish my days to be
Bound each to each by natural piety.[1]

I

There was a time when meadow, grove, and stream,
The earth, and every common sight,
To me did seem
Apparelled in celestial light,
5 The glory and the freshness of a dream.
It is not now as it hath been of yore;—
Turn wheresoe'er I may,
By night or day,
The things which I have seen I now can see no more.

II

10 The Rainbow comes and goes,
And lovely is the Rose,

---

[1] The concluding lines of Wordsworth's "My Heart Leaps Up."

The Moon doth with delight
Look round her when the heavens are bare,
Waters on a starry night
15   Are beautiful and fair;
The sunshine is a glorious birth;
But yet I know, where'er I go,
That there hath past away a glory from the earth.

III

Now, while the birds thus sing a joyous song,
20   And while the young lambs bound
As to the tabor's sound,
To me alone there came a thought of grief:
A timely utterance gave that thought relief,
And I again am strong:
25   The cataracts blow their trumpets from the steep;
No more shall grief of mine the season wrong;
I hear the Echoes through the mountains throng,
The Winds come to me from the fields of sleep,
And all the earth is gay;
30   Land and sea
Give themselves up to jollity,
And with the heart of May
Doth every Beast keep holiday;—
Thou Child of Joy,
35   Shout round me, let me hear thy shouts, thou happy
Shepherd-boy!

IV

Ye blessed Creatures, I have heard the call
Ye to each other make; I see
The heavens laugh with you in your jubilee;
My heart is at your festival,
40   My head hath its coronal,
The fulness of your bliss, I feel—I feel it all.
Oh evil day! if I were sullen
While Earth herself is adorning,
This sweet May-morning,
45   And the Children are culling
On every side,
In a thousand valleys far and wide,
Fresh flowers; while the sun shines warm,
And the Babe leaps up on his Mother's arm:—
50   I hear, I hear, with joy I hear!
—But there's a Tree, of many, one,

A single Field which I have looked upon,
Both of them speak of something that is gone:
  The Pansy at my feet
55   Doth the same tale repeat:
Whither is fled the visionary gleam?
Where is it now, the glory and the dream?

     V

Our birth is but a sleep and a forgetting:
The Soul that rises with us, our life's Star,
60   Hath had elsewhere its setting,
   And cometh from afar:
  Not in entire forgetfulness,
  And not in utter nakedness,
But trailing clouds of glory do we come
65   From God, who is our home:
Heaven lies about us in our infancy!
Shades of the prison-house begin to close
  Upon the growing Boy
But He beholds the light, and whence it flows,
70   He sees it in his joy;
The Youth, who daily farther from the east
  Must travel, still is Nature's Priest,
  And by the vision splendid
  Is on his way attended;
75 At length the Man perceives it die away,
And fade into the light of common day.

     VI

Earth fills her lap with pleasures of her own;
Yearnings she hath in her own natural kind,
And, even with something of a Mother's mind,
80   And no unworthy aim,
  The homely Nurse doth all she can
To make her Foster-child, her Inmate
  Man,
  Forget the glories he hath known,
And that imperial palace whence he came.

     VII

85 Behold the Child among his new-born blisses,
A six years' Darling of a pigmy size!
See, where 'mid work of his own hand he lies,
Fretted by sallies of his mother's kisses,

With light upon him from his father's eyes!
90   See, at his feet, some little plan or chart,
Some fragment from his dream of human life,
Shaped by himself with newly-learned art;
        A wedding or a festival,
        A mourning or a funeral;
95   And this hath now his heart,
        And unto this he frames his song:
            Then will he fit his tongue
To dialogues of business, love, or strife;
        But it will not be long
100   Ere this be thrown aside,
        And with new joy and pride
The little Actor cons another part;
Filling from time to time his 'humorous stage'
With all the Persons, down to palsied
            Age,
105 That Life brings with her in her equipage;
        As if his whole vocation
        Were endless imitation.

VIII

Thou, whose exterior semblance doth belie
        Thy Soul's immensity;
110 Thou best Philosopher, who yet dost keep
Thy heritage, thou Eye among the blind,
That, deaf and silent, read'st the eternal deep,
Haunted for ever by the eternal mind,—
        Mighty Prophet! Seer blest!
115   On whom those truths do rest,
Which we are toiling all our lives to find,
In darkness lost, the darkness of the grave;
Thou, over whom thy Immortality
Broods like the Day, a Master o'er a Slave,
120 A Presence which is not to be put by;
        To whom the grave
Is but a lonely bed without the sense or sight
        Of day or the warm light,
A place of thought where we in waiting lie;
125 Thou little Child, yet glorious in the might
Of heaven-born freedom on thy being's height,
Why with such earnest pains dost thou provoke
The years to bring the inevitable yoke,
Thus blindly with thy blessedness at strife?
130 Full soon thy Soul shall have her earthly freight,
And custom lie upon thee with a weight,
Heavy as frost, and deep almost as life!

IX

O joy! that in our embers
Is something that doth live,
135   That nature yet remembers
What was so fugitive!
The thought of our past years in me doth breed
Perpetual benediction: not indeed
For that which is most worthy to be blest;
140 Delight and liberty, the simple creed
Of Childhood, whether busy or at rest,
With new-fledged hope still fluttering in his breast:—
    Not for these I raise
    The song of thanks and praise;
145   But for those obstinate questionings
    Of sense and outward things,
    Fallings from us, vanishings;
    Blank misgivings of a Creature
Moving about in worlds not realised,
150 High instincts before which our mortal
        Nature
Did tremble like a guilty Thing surprised:
    But for those first affections,
    Those shadowy recollections,
    Which, be they what they may,
155 Are yet the fountain-light of all our day,
Are yet a master-light of all our seeing;
    Uphold us, cherish, and have power to make
Our noisy years seem moments in the being
Of the eternal Silence: truths that wake,
160   To perish never:
Which neither listlessness, nor mad endeavour,
    Nor Man nor Boy,
Nor all that is at enmity with joy,
Can utterly abolish or destroy!
165   Hence in a season of calm weather
    Though inland far we be,
Our Souls have sight of that immortal sea
    Which brought us hither,
    Can in a moment travel thither,
170 And see the Children sport upon the shore,
And hear the mighty waters rolling evermore.

X

Then sing, ye Birds, sing, sing a joyous song!
    And let the young Lambs bound
    As to the tabor's sound!
175 We in thought will join your throng,

Ye that pipe and ye that play,
Ye that through your hearts today
Feel the gladness of the May!
What though the radiance which was once so bright
180 Be now for ever taken from my sight,
   Though nothing can bring back the hour
Of splendour in the grass, of glory in the flower;
   We will grieve not, rather find
   Strength in what remains behind;
185   In the primal sympathy
   Which having been must ever be;
   In the soothing thoughts that spring
   Out of human suffering;
   In the faith that looks through death,
190 In years that bring the philosophic mind.

XI

And O, ye Fountains, Meadows, Hills, and Groves,
Forebode not any severing of our loves!
Yet in my heart of hearts I feel your might;
I only have relinquished one delight
195 To live beneath your more habitual sway.
I love the Brooks which down their channels fret,
Even more than when I tripped lightly as they;
The innocent brightness of a new-born
   Day
     Is lovely yet;
200 The Clouds that gather round the setting sun
Do take a sober colouring from an eye
That hath kept watch o'er man's mortality;
Another race hath been, and other palms are won.
Thanks to the human heart by which we live,
205 Thanks to its tenderness, its joys, and fears,
To me the meanest flower that blows can give
Thoughts that do often lie too deep for tears.

(1807)

Samuel Taylor Coleridge

(1 7 7 2 – 1 8 3 4)

Author of a small but brilliant body of poetry and literary criticism, Samuel Taylor Coleridge was the son of a clergyman. From youth he was ambitious, an isolated but eloquent student. After attending Cambridge and a brief stint in the army, Coleridge and the poet Southey planned an ideal community in America. To help the community, Coleridge agreed to marry the sister of Southey's fiancée. The ideal community fell through, but Coleridge went ahead with the marriage, "resolved but wretched." He met William Wordsworth in 1795 and immediately idolized him, a situation that seemed to damage Coleridge's precarious self-confidence. He contributed poems, including *Rime of the Ancient Mariner,* to the *Lyrical Ballads* volume in 1798. Miserable in his marriage, he fell hopelessly in love with Sara Hutchinson, sister of Wordsworth's wife. Heavy dosages of opium in 1800 and 1801, taken to combat rheumatism, damaged his health, and after 1802 Coleridge's writing declined. But despite drug addiction, estrangement from his wife and from Wordsworth, and horrible bouts of guilt and despair, Coleridge accomplished a great deal: He gave lectures, published a journal, and wrote a popular tragedy, essays, reviews, and the *Biographia Literaria.* His fame grew. In his last years he lived with Dr. and Mrs. Gillman and was reconciled with Wordsworth. Those years were relatively peaceful, despite his own conviction, only partially true, that he had failed to fulfill his great promise.

Coleridge's poetry is of major status. Coleridge looked upon the mind as a creative rather than merely a perceptive faculty, able to intuit the premises of metaphysics and to rework the sensory world into a new universe of the "secondary imagination." "Kubla Khan" (1797), *The Rime of the Ancient Mariner* (1798), and the unfinished *Christabel* (1797–1801) show Coleridge transforming the nightmarish and ecstatic fancies of his own mind into vividly realized supernatural landscapes. He also produced verse in a "psychological" medium, blank verse meditations comparable to Wordsworth's work. These "conversation" poems include the early and idyllic "The Eolian Harp" (written in a moment of enthusiasm about his marriage), "This Lime-Tree Bower My Prison," which expresses the core of Coleridge's poetic theory, the moving "Frost at Midnight," and "Dejection: An Ode," a powerful description of the loss of youth and poetic power, a poem belying its own message through its eloquence. At its best, as in "Kubla Khan," Coleridge's poetry has a musicality that only Keats, among the Romantics, could rival.

Coleridge also wrote "France: An Ode" (1798), "The Pains of Sleep" (1803), "To William Wordsworth" (1807), "Recollections of Love" (ca. 1807), "Work Without Hope" (1825), and "Constancy to an Ideal Object"

(1825). The fragmentary but insightful *Biographia Literaria* appeared in 1817; *Aids to Reflection* (on German philosophy) was published in 1825. Coleridge also wrote a critical work about Shakespeare.

SAMUEL TAYLOR COLERIDGE

The Rime of the Ancient Mariner

In Seven Parts

Facile credo, plures esse Naturas invisibiles quam visibiles in rerum universitate. Sed horum omnium familiam quis nobis enarrabit? et gradus et cognationes et discrimina et singulorum munera? Quid agunt? quae loca habitant? Harum rerum notitiam semper ambivit ingenium humanum, nunquam attigit. Juvat, interea, non diffiteor, quandoque in animo, tanquam in tabulâ, majoris et melioris mundi imaginem contemplari: ne mens assuefacta hodiernae vitae minutiis se contrahat nimis, et tota subsidat in pusillas cogitationes. Sed veritati interea invigilandum est, modusque servandus, ut certa ab incertis, diem a nocte, distinguamus.—T. Burnet, *Archaeol. Phil.* p. 68.[1]

ARGUMENT

How a Ship having passed the Line was driven by storms to the cold Country towards the South Pole; and how from thence she made her course to the tropical Latitude of the Great Pacific Ocean; and of the strange things that befell; and in what manner the Ancyent Marinere came back to his own Country.

PART I

An ancient Mariner meeteth three Gallants bidden to a wedding-feast, and detaineth one.

It is an ancient Mariner,
And he stoppeth one of three.
'By thy long grey beard and glittering eye,
Now wherefore stopp'st thou me?

5 The Bridegroom's doors are opened wide,
And I am next of kin;

---

[1] "I willingly believe that there are more invisible Natures than visible ones in the universe. But who can explain the family of these beings, and the grades and relations and features and functions of each? What is it they do, and where are they located? The mind has always attempted to understand these things, but has never been successful. At the same time, I don't deny that it is sometimes a help to contemplate in the mind, as on a tablet, the picture of a better and greater world, to prevent the intellect, so weighted down by ephemeral concerns, from becoming narrow and sinking into trivial thoughts. Yet we must be attentive to the truth and retain a sense of proportion, so that we can distinguish the certain from the uncertain, and the day from night."

The guests are met, the feast is set:
May'st hear the merry din.'

He holds him with his skinny hand,
10 "There was a ship," quoth he.
"Hold off! unhand me, grey-beard
          loon!"
Eftsoons° his hand dropt he.   immediately

The
Wedding-Guest
is spellbound by   He holds him with his glittering eye—
the eye of the   The Wedding-Guest stood still,
old seafaring   15 And listens like a three years' child:
man, and   The Mariner hath his will.
constrained to
hear his tale.
                         The Wedding-Guest sat on a stone:
                         He cannot choose but hear;
                         And thus spake on that ancient man,
20 The bright-eyed Mariner.

                         "The ship was cheered, the harbour
                               cleared,
                         Merrily did we drop
                         Below the kirk,° below the hill,   church
                         Below the lighthouse top.

The Mariner   25 The Sun came up upon the left,
tells how the   Out of the sea came he!
ship sailed   And he shone bright, and on the right
southward with   Went down into the sea.
a good wind
and fair
weather, till it   Higher and higher every day,
reached the   30 Till over the mast at noon—"
line.   The Wedding-Guest here beat his breast,
                         For he heard the loud bassoon.

The Wedding-
Guest heareth   The bride hath paced into the hall,
the bridal   Red as a rose is she;
music; but the   35 Nodding their heads before her goes
Mariner contin-   The merry minstrelsy.
ueth his tale.

                         The Wedding-Guest he beat his breast,
                         Yet he cannot choose but hear;
                         And thus spake on that ancient man,
40 The bright-eyed Mariner.

<table>
<tr><td>

The ship driven
by a storm
toward the
south pole.

</td><td>

'And now the STORM-BLAST came, and he
Was tyrannous and strong:
He struck with his o'ertaking wings,
And chased us south along.

</td></tr>
</table>

45 With sloping masts and dipping prow,
As who pursued with yell and blow
Still treads the shadow of his foe,
And forward bends his head,
The ship drove fast, loud roared the blast,
50 And southward aye we fled.

And now there came both mist and snow,
And it grew wondrous cold:
And ice, mast-high, came floating by,
As green as emerald.

The land of ice,   55 And through the drifts the snowy clifts
and of fearful   Did send a dismal sheen:
sounds where   Nor shapes of men nor beasts we ken—
no living thing   The ice was all between.
was to be seen

The ice was here, the ice was there,
60 The ice was all around:
It cracked and growled, and roared
            and howled,
Like noises in a swound!°   swoon

Till a great   At length did cross an Albatross,
sea bird, called   Thorough the fog it came;
the Albatross,   65 As if it had been a Christian soul,
came through   We hailed it in God's name.
the snow-fog,
and was
received with   It ate the food it ne'er had eat,
great joy and   And round and round it flew.
hospitality.   The ice did split with a thunder-fit;
                  70 The helmsman steered us through!

And lo! the   And a good south wind sprung up behind;
Albatross   The Albatross did follow,
proveth a bird   And every day, for food or play,
of good omen,   Came to the mariner's hollo!
and followeth
the ship as it
returned   75 In mist or cloud, on mast or shroud,
northward   It perched for vespers nine;
through fog and   Whiles all the night, through fog-smoke white,
floating ice.   Glimmered the white Moon-shine.''

The ancient
Mariner
inhospitably
killeth the pious
bird of good
omen.

"God save thee, ancient Mariner!
80 From the fiends, that plague thee thus!—
Why look'st thou so?"—With my cross-bow
I shot the ALBATROSS.

PART II

The Sun now rose upon the right:
Out of the sea came he,
85 Still hid in mist, and on the left
Went down into the sea.

And the good south wind still blew behind,
But no sweet bird did follow,
Nor any day for food or play
90 Came to the mariners' hollo!

His shipmates
cry out against
the ancient
Mariner, for
killing the bird
of good luck.

And I had done a hellish thing,
And it would work 'em woe:
For all averred, I had killed the bird
That made the breeze to blow.
95 Ah wretch! said they, the bird to slay,
That made the breeze to blow!

But when the
fog cleared off,
they justify the
same, and thus
make
themselves
accomplices in
the crime.

Nor dim nor red, like God's own head,
The glorious Sun uprist:
Then all averred, I had killed the bird
100 That brought the fog and mist.
'Twas right, said they, such birds to slay,
That bring the fog and mist.

The fair breeze
continues; the
ship enters the
Pacific Ocean,
and sails
northward, even
till it reaches
the Line. The
ship hath been
suddenly
becalmed.

The fair breeze blew, the white foam flew,
The furrow followed free;
105 We were the first that ever burst
Into that silent sea.

Down dropt the breeze, the sails dropt down,
'Twas sad as sad could be;
And we did speak only to break
110 The silence of the sea!

All in a hot and copper sky,
The bloody Sun, at noon,
Right up above the mast did stand,
No bigger than the Moon.

115 Day after day, day after day,
We stuck, nor breath nor motion;
As idle as a painted ship
Upon a painted ocean.

And the
Albatross
begins to be
avenged.

Water, water, every where,
120 And all the boards did shrink;
Water, water, every where,
Nor any drop to drink.

The very deep did rot: O Christ!
That ever this should be!
125 Yea, slimy things did crawl with legs
Upon the slimy sea.

About, about, in reel and rout
The death-fires danced at night;
The water, like a witch's oils,
130 Burnt green, and blue and white.

A Spirit had
followed them;
one of the
invisible
inhabitants of
this planet,

And some in dreams assuréd were
Of the Spirit that plagued us so;
Nine fathom deep he had followed us
From the land of mist and snow.

neither departed souls nor angels; concerning whom the learned Jew,
Josephus, and the Platonic Constantinopolitan, Michael Psellus, may be
consulted. They are very numerous, and there is no climate or element
without one or more.

135 And every tongue, through utter drought,
Was withered at the root;
We could not speak, no more than if
We had been choked with soot.

The shipmates,
in their sore
distress, would
fain throw the
whole guilt on
the ancient
Mariner: in sign
whereof they
hang the dead
sea-bird round
his neck.

Ah! well a-day! what evil looks
140 Had I from old and young!
Instead of the cross, the Albatross
About my neck was hung.

PART III

There passed a weary time. Each throat
Was parched, and glazed each eye.
145 A weary time! a weary time!
How glazed each weary eye,
When looking westward, I beheld
A something in the sky.

The ancient
Mariner
150 beholdeth a
sign in the
element afar
off.

At first it seemed a little speck,
And then it seemed a mist;
It moved and moved, and took at last
A certain shape, I wist.°   knew

A speck, a mist, a shape, I wist!
And still it neared and neared:
155 As if it dodged a water-sprite,
It plunged and tacked and veered.

As its nearer
approach, it
seemeth him to
be a ship; and
at a dear
160 ransom he
freeth his speech
from the bonds of thirst.

With throats unslaked, with black lips baked,
We could nor laugh nor wail;
Through utter drought all dumb we stood!
I bit my arm, I sucked the blood,
And cried, A sail! a sail!

A flash of joy;

With throats unslaked, with black lips baked,
Agape they heard me call:
Gramercy!° they for joy did grin,   great thanks
165 And all at once their breath drew in,
As they were drinking all.

And horror
follows. For can
it be a ship that
comes onward
without wind or
170 tide?

See! see! (I cried) she tacks no more!
Hither to work us weal;°   good
Without a breeze, without a tide,
She steadies with upright keel!

The western wave was all a-flame.
The day was well nigh done!
Almost upon the western wave
Rested the broad bright Sun;
175 When that strange shape drove suddenly
Betwixt us and the Sun.

It seemeth him
but the skeleton
of a ship.

And straight the Sun was flecked with bars,
(Heaven's Mother send us grace!)
As if through a dungeon-grate he peered
180 With broad and burning face.

And its ribs are
seen as bars on
the face of the
setting Sun.

Alas! (thought I, and my heart beat loud)
How fast she nears and nears!
Are those *her* sails that glance in the Sun,
Like restless gossameres?

185 Are those *her* ribs through which the Sun
Did peer, as through a grate?
And is that Woman all her crew?
Is that a DEATH? and are there two?
Is DEATH that woman's mate?

190 *Her* lips were red, *her* looks were free,
Her locks were yellow as gold:
Her skin was as white as leprosy,
The Night-mare LIFE-IN-DEATH was she,
Who thicks man's blood with cold.

195 The naked hulk alongside came,
And the twain were casting dice;
"The game is done! I've won! I've won!"
Quoth she, and whistles thrice.

The Sun's rim dips; the stars rush out:
200 At one stride comes the dark;
With far-heard whisper, o'er the sea,
Off shot the spectre-bark.

We listened and looked sideways up!
Fear at my heart, as at a cup,
205 My life-blood seemed to sip!
The stars were dim, and thick the night,
The steersman's face by his lamp gleamed white;
From the sails the dew did drip—
Till clomb above the eastern bar
210 The hornéd Moon, with one bright star
Within the nether tip.

One after one, by the star-dogged Moon,
Too quick for groan or sigh,
Each turned his face with a ghastly pang,
215 And cursed me with his eye.

Four times fifty living men,
(And I heard nor sigh nor groan)
With heavy thump, a lifeless lump,
They dropped down one by one.

220 The souls did from their bodies fly,—
They fled to bliss or woe!
And every soul, it passed me by,
Like the whizz of my cross-bow!

The
Spectre-Woman
and her
Deathmate, and
no other on
board the
skeleton ship.

Like vessel, like
crew! Death
and Life-in-
Death have
diced for the
ship's crew, and
she (the latter)
winneth the
ancient Mariner.

No twilight
within the
courts of the
Sun.

At the rising of
the Moon,

One after
another,

His shipmates
drop down
dead.

But
Life-in-Death
begins her work
on the ancient
Mariner.

PART IV

The
Wedding-Guest
feareth that a
Spirit is talking
to him;

225

"I fear thee, ancient Mariner!
I fear thy skinny hand!
And thou art long, and lank, and brown,
As is the ribbed sea-sand.

But the ancient
Mariner
assureth him of
his bodily life,
and proceedeth
to relate his
horrible
penance.

230

I fear thee and thy glittering eye,
And thy skinny hand, so brown."—
Fear not, fear not, thou Wedding-Guest!
This body dropt not down.

235

Alone, alone, all, all alone,
Alone on a wide wide sea!
And never a saint took pity on
My soul in agony.

He despiseth
the creatures of
the calm.

The many men, so beautiful!
And they all dead did lie:
And a thousand thousand slimy things
Lived on; and so did I.

And envieth
that *they* should
live, and so
many lie dead.

240

I looked upon the rotting sea,
And drew my eyes away;
I looked upon the rotting deck,
And there the dead men lay.

245

I looked to heaven, and tried to pray;
But or ever a prayer had gusht,
A wicked whisper came, and made
My heart as dry as dust.

250

I closed my lids, and kept them close,
And the balls like pulses beat;
For the sky and the sea, and the sea and the sky
Lay like a load on my weary eye,
And the dead were at my feet.

But the curse
liveth for him in
the eye of the
dead men.

255

The cold sweat melted from their limbs,
Nor rot nor reek did they:
The look with which they looked on me
Had never passed away.

An orphan's curse would drag to hell
A spirit from on high;
But oh! more horrible than that

260 Is the curse in a dead man's eye!
Seven days, seven nights, I saw that curse,
And yet I could not die.

In his loneliness
and fixedness
he yearneth
towards the
journeying
Moon, and the
stars that still
sojourn, yet still
move onward;
and every
where the blue
sky belongs to
them, and is
their appointed rest, and their native country and their
own natural homes, which they enter unannounced, as
lords that are certainly expected and yet there is a silent
joy at their arrival. By the light of the Moon he beholdeth
God's creatures of the great calm.

The moving Moon went up the sky,
And no where did abide:
265 Softly she was going up,
And a star or two beside—

Her beams bemocked the sultry main,
Like April hoar-frost spread;
But where the ship's huge shadow lay,
270 The charmèd water burnt alway
A still and awful red.

Beyond the shadow of the ship,
I watched the water-snakes:
They moved in tracks of shining white,
275 And when they reared, the elfish light
Fell off in hoary flakes.

Within the shadow of the ship
I watched their rich attire:
Blue, glossy green, and velvet black,
280 They coiled and swam; and every track
Was a flash of golden fire.

Their beauty
and their
happiness. He
blesseth them
in his heart.

O happy living things! no tongue
Their beauty might declare:
A spring of love gushed from my heart,
285 And I blessed them unaware:
Sure my kind saint took pity on me,
And I blessed them unaware.

The spell
begins to break.

The self-same moment I could pray;
And from my neck so free
290 The Albatross fell off, and sank
Like lead into the sea.

PART V

Oh sleep! it is a gentle thing,
Beloved from pole to pole!

To Mary Queen the praise be given!
295 She sent the gentle sleep from Heaven,
That slid into my soul.

By grace of the
holy Mother,
the ancient
Mariner is
refreshed with
rain.

The silly buckets on the deck,
That had so long remained,
I dreamt that they were filled with dew;
300 And when I awoke, it rained.

My lips were wet, my throat was cold,
My garments all were dank;
Sure I had drunken in my dreams,
And still my body drank.

305 I moved, and could not feel my limbs:
I was so light—almost
I thought that I had died in sleep,
And was a blessèd ghost.

He heareth
sounds and
seeth strange
sights and
commotions in
the sky and the
element.

And soon I heard a roaring wind:
310 It did not come anear;
But with its sound it shook the sails,
That were so thin and sere.

The upper air burst into life!
And a hundred fire-flags sheen,
315 To and fro they were hurried about!
And to and fro, and in and out,
The wan stars danced between.

And the coming wind did roar more loud,
And the sails did sigh like sedge;
320 And the rain poured down from one black cloud;
The Moon was at its edge.

The thick black cloud was cleft, and still
The Moon was at its side:
Like waters shot from some high crag,
325 The lightning fell with never a jag,
A river steep and wide.

The bodies of
the ship's crew
are inspired and
the ship moves
on;

The loud wind never reached the ship,
Yet now the ship moved on!
Beneath the lightning and the Moon
330 The dead men gave a groan.

They groaned, they stirred, they all uprose,
Nor spake, nor moved their eyes;

It had been strange, even in a dream,
To have seen those dead men rise.

335 The helmsman steered, the ship moved on;
Yet never a breeze up-blew;
The mariners all 'gan work the ropes,
Where they were wont to do;
They raised their limbs like lifeless tools—
340 We were a ghastly crew.

The body of my brother's son
Stood by me, knee to knee:
The body and I pulled at one rope,
But he said nought to me.

345 "I fear thee, ancient Mariner!"
Be calm, thou Wedding-Guest!
'Twas not those souls that fled in pain,
Which to their corses° came again,   corpses
But a troop of spirits blest:

350 For when it dawned—they dropped their arms,
And clustered round the mast;
Sweet sounds rose slowly through their mouths,
And from their bodies passed.

Around, around, flew each sweet sound,
355 Then darted to the Sun;
Slowly the sounds came back again,
Now mixed, now one by one.

Sometimes a-dropping from the sky
I heard the sky-lark sing;
360 Sometimes all little birds that are,
How they seemed to fill the sea and air
With their sweet jargoning!

And now 'twas like all instruments,
Now like a lonely flute;
365 And now it is an angel's song,
That makes the heavens be mute.

It ceased; yet still the sails made on
A pleasant noise till noon,
A noise like of a hidden brook

Marginal gloss (lines 345–349): But not by the souls of the men, nor by dæmons of earth or middle air, but by a blessed troop of angelic spirits, sent down by the invocation of the guardian saint.

370 In the leafy month of June,
That to the sleeping woods all night
Singeth a quiet tune.

Till noon we quietly sailed on,
Yet never a breeze did breathe:
375 Slowly and smoothly went the ship,
Moved onward from beneath.

The lonesome
Spirit from the
south-pole
carries on the
ship as far as
the Line, in
obedience to
the angelic
troop, but still
requireth
vengeance.

Under the keel nine fathom deep,
From the land of mist and snow,
The spirit slid: and it was he
380 That made the ship to go.
The sails at noon left off their tune,
And the ship stood still also.

The Sun, right up above the mast,
Had fixed her to the ocean:
385 But in a minute she 'gan stir,
With a short uneasy motion—
Backwards and forwards half her length
With a short uneasy motion.

Then like a pawing horse let go,
390 She made a sudden bound:
It flung the blood into my head,
And I fell down in a swound.

The Polar
Spirit's fellow-
dæmons, the
invisible
inhabitants of
the element,
take part in his
wrong; and two
of them relate,
one to the
other, that
penance long
and heavy for
the ancient
Mariner hath
been accorded
to the Polar
Spirit, who
returneth
southward.

How long in that same fit I lay,
I have not to declare;
395 But ere my living life returned,
I heard and in my soul discerned
Two voices in the air.

"Is it he?" quoth one, "Is this the man?
By him who died on cross,
400 With his cruel bow he laid full low
The harmless Albatross.

The spirit who bideth by himself
In the land of mist and snow,
He loved the bird that loved the man
405 Who shot him with his bow."

The other was a softer voice,
As soft as honey-dew:

Quoth he, "The man hath penance done,
And penance more will do."

PART VI

FIRST VOICE

410 "But tell me, tell me! speak again,
Thy soft response renewing—
What makes that ship drive on so fast?
What is the ocean doing?"

SECOND VOICE

"Still as a slave before his lord,
415 The ocean hath no blast;
His great bright eye most silently
Up to the Moon is cast—

If he may know which way to go;
For she guides him smooth or grim.
420 See, brother, see! how graciously
She looketh down on him."

FIRST VOICE

The Mariner   "But why drives on that ship so fast,
hath been cast   Without or wave or wind?"
into a trance;
for the angelic
power causeth
the vessel to
drive northward
faster than   SECOND VOICE
human life
could endure.   "The air is cut away before,
425 And closes from behind.

Fly, brother, fly! more high, more high!
Or we shall be belated:
For slow and slow that ship will go,
When the Mariner's trance is abated."

The   430 I woke, and we were sailing on
supernatural   As in a gentle weather:

motion is
retarded; the
Mariner awakes,
and his penance
begins anew.

'Twas night, calm night, the moon was high;
The dead men stood together.

All stood together on the deck,
435 For a charnel-dungeon fitter:
All fixed on me their stony eyes,
That in the Moon did glitter.

The pang, the curse, with which they died,
Had never passed away:
440 I could not draw my eyes from theirs,
Nor turn them up to pray.

The curse is
finally expiated.

And now this spell was snapt: once more
I viewed the ocean green,
And looked far forth, yet little saw
445 Of what had else been seen—

Like one, that on a lonesome road
Doth walk in fear and dread,
And having once turned round walks on,
And turns no more his head;
450 Because he knows, a frightful fiend
Doth close behind him tread.

But soon there breathed a wind on me,
Nor sound nor motion made:
Its path was not upon the sea,
455 In ripple or in shade.

It raised my hair, it fanned my cheek
Like a meadow-gale of spring—
It mingled strangely with my fears,
Yet it felt like a welcoming.

460 Swiftly, swiftly flew the ship,
Yet she sailed softly too:
Sweetly, sweetly blew the breeze—
On me alone it blew.

And the ancient
Mariner
beholdeth his
native country.

Oh! dream of joy! is this indeed
465 The light-house top I see?
Is this the hill? is this the kirk?
Is this mine own countree?

We drifted o'er the harbour-bar,
And I with sobs did pray—
470   O let me be awake, my God!
Or let me sleep alway.

The harbour-bay was clear as glass,
So smoothly it was strewn!
And on the bay the moonlight lay,
475   And the shadow of the Moon.

The rock shone bright, the kirk no less,
That stands above the rock:
The moonlight steeped in silentness
The steady weathercock.

The angelic
spirits leave the
dead bodies,
480   And the bay was white with silent light,
Till rising from the same,
Full many shapes, that shadows were,
In crimson colours came.

And appear in
their own forms
of light.
A little distance from the prow
485   Those crimson shadows were:
I turned my eyes upon the deck—
Oh, Christ! what saw I there!

Each corse lay flat, lifeless and flat,
And, by the holy rood!
490   A man all light, a seraph-man,
On every corse there stood.

This seraph-band, each waved his hand:
It was a heavenly sight!
They stood as signals to the land,
495   Each one a lovely light;

This seraph-band, each waved his hand.
No voice did they impart—
No voice; but oh! the silence sank
Like music on my heart.

500   But soon I heard the dash of oars,
I heard the Pilot's cheer;
My head was turned perforce away,
And I saw a boat appear.

The Pilot and the Pilot's boy,
505   I heard them coming fast:

Dear Lord in Heaven! it was a joy
The dead men could not blast.

I saw a third—I heard his voice:
It is the Hermit good!
510 He singeth loud his godly hymns
That he makes in the wood.
He'll shrieve my soul, he'll wash away
The Albatross's blood.

PART VII

The Hermit of
the Wood,

515 This Hermit good lives in that wood
Which slopes down to the sea.
How loudly his sweet voice he rears!
He loves to talk with marineres
That come from a far countree.

He kneels at morn, and noon, and eve—
520 He hath a cushion plump:
It is the moss that wholly hides
The rotted old oak-stump.

The skiff-boat neared: I heard them talk,
"Why, this is strange, I trow!
525 Where are those lights so many and fair,
That signal made but now?"

Approacheth
the ship with
wonder.

"Strange, by my faith!" the Hermit said—
"And they answered not our cheer!
The planks looked warped! and see
            those sails,
530 How thin they are and sere!
I never saw aught like to them,
Unless perchance it were

Brown skeletons of leaves that lag
My forest-brook along;
535 When the ivy-tod° is heavy with snow,   clump of ivy
And the owlet whoops to the wolf below,
That eats the she-wolf's young."

"Dear Lord! it hath a fiendish look—
(The Pilot made reply)

540   I am a-feared"—"Push on, push on!"
    Said the Hermit cheerily.

The boat came closer to the ship,
    But I nor spake nor stirred;
The boat came close beneath the ship,
545   And straight a sound was heard.

*The ship
suddenly
sinketh.*

Under the water it rumbled on,
    Still louder and more dread:
It reached the ship, it split the bay;
    The ship went down like lead.

*The ancient
Mariner is
saved in the
Pilot's boat.*

550   Stunned by that loud and dreadful sound,
    Which sky and ocean smote,
Like one that hath been seven days drowned
    My body lay afloat;
But swift as dreams, myself I found
555   Within the Pilot's boat.

Upon the whirl, where sank the ship,
    The boat spun round and round;
And all was still, save that the hill
    Was telling of the sound.

560   I moved my lips—the Pilot shrieked
    And fell down in a fit;
The holy Hermit raised his eyes,
    And prayed where he did sit.

I took the oars: the Pilot's boy,
565   Who now doth crazy go,
Laughed loud and long, and all the while
    His eyes went to and fro.
"Ha! ha!" quoth he, "full plain I see,
    The Devil knows how to row."

570   And now, all in my own countree,
    I stood on the firm land!
The Hermit stepped forth from the boat,
    And scarcely he could stand.

*The ancient
Mariner*

"O shrieve° me, shrieve me, holy man!"   *absolve*
575   The Hermit crossed his brow.

earnestly
entreateth the
Hermit to
shrieve him;
and the
penance of life
falls on him.

"Say quick," quoth he, "I bid thee say—
What manner of man art thou?"

Forthwith this frame of mine was wrenched
With a woful agony,
580 Which forced me to begin my tale;
And then it left me free.

And ever and
anon
throughout his
future life an
agony
constraineth
him to travel
from land to
land;

Since then, at an uncertain hour,
That agony returns:
And till my ghastly tale is told,
585 This heart within me burns.

I pass, like night, from land to land;
I have strange power of speech;
That moment that his face I see,
I know the man that must hear me:
590 To him my tale I teach.

What loud uproar bursts from that door!
The wedding-guests are there:
But in the garden-bower the bride
And bride-maids singing are:
595 And hark the little vesper bell,
Which biddeth me to prayer!

O Wedding-Guest! this soul hath been
Alone on a wide wide sea:
So lonely 'twas, that God himself
600 Scarce seeméd there to be.

O sweeter than the marriage-feast,
'Tis sweeter far to me,
To walk together to the kirk
With a goodly company!—

605 To walk together to the kirk,
And all together pray,
While each to his great Father bends,
Old men, and babes, and loving friends
And youths and maidens gay!

And to teach,
by his own

610 Farewell, farewell! but this I tell
To thee, thou Wedding-Guest!

example, love
and reverence
to all things
that God made
and loveth.

He prayeth well, who loveth well
Both man and bird and beast.

He prayeth best, who loveth best
615   All things both great and small;
For the dear God who loveth us,
He made and loveth all.

The Mariner, whose eye is bright,
Whose beard with age is hoar,
620   Is gone: and now the Wedding-Guest
Turned from the bridegroom's door.

He went like one that hath been stunned,
And is of sense forlorn:
A sadder and a wiser man,
625   He rose the morrow morn.

(1798)

Kubla Khan

In Xanadu did Kubla Khan
A stately pleasure-dome decree:
Where Alph, the sacred river, ran
Through caverns measureless to man
5   Down to a sunless sea.
So twice five miles of fertile ground
With walls and towers were girdled round:
And there were gardens bright with sinuous rills,
Where blossomed many an incense-bearing tree;
10   And here were forests ancient as the hills,
Enfolding sunny spots of greenery.

But oh! that deep romantic chasm which slanted
Down the green hill athwart a cedarn cover!
A savage place! as holy and enchanted
15   As e'er beneath a waning moon was haunted
By woman wailing for her demon-lover!
And from this chasm, with ceaseless turmoil seething,
As if this earth in fast thick pants were breathing,
A mighty fountain momently was forced:
20   Amid whose swift half-intermitted burst
Huge fragments vaulted like rebounding hail,

Or chaffy grain beneath the thresher's flail:
And 'mid these dancing rocks at once and ever
It flung up momently the sacred river.
25 Five miles meandering with a mazy motion
Through wood and dale the sacred river ran,
Then reached the caverns measureless to man,
And sank in tumult to a lifeless ocean:
And 'mid this tumult Kubla heard from far
30 Ancestral voices prophesying war!
   The shadow of the dome of pleasure
   Floated midway on the waves;
   Where was heard the mingled measure
   From the fountain and the caves.
35 It was a miracle of rare device,
A sunny pleasure-dome with caves of ice!

   A damsel with a dulcimer
   In a vision once I saw:
   It was an Abyssinian maid,
40   And on her dulcimer she played,
   Singing of Mount Abora.
   Could I revive within me
   Her symphony and song,
   To such a deep delight 'twould win me,
45 That with music loud and long,
I would build that dome in air,
That sunny dome! those caves of ice!
And all who heard should see them there,
And all should cry, Beware! Beware!
50 His flashing eyes, his floating hair!
Weave a circle round him thrice,
And close your eyes with holy dread,
For he on honey-dew hath fed,
And drunk the milk of Paradise.

(1816)

George Gordon, Lord Byron

(1 7 8 8 – 1 8 2 4)

Lord Byron came from a family with a history of emotional instability. Once he came into his inheritance at the age of 10, Byron lived a turbulent and spectacular life. His instability was perhaps exacerbated by his extreme sensitivity about the clubfoot with which he was born, a sensitivity he tried to fight by becoming an outstanding athlete and a powerful swimmer. The pedantic, negative reviews of his first slim volume spurred Byron's first important poem, the satiric *English Bards and Scotch Reviewers*. A tour of Europe helped provide materials for the "epic" *Childe Harold,* a poem that made Byron famous overnight. Sitting in the House of Lords, Byron began to espouse the liberal causes that he would advocate all his life. He was extremely handsome and was besieged by women; he besieged them in turn. A marriage to Annabella Milbanke led to increasingly erratic behavior. (He had an incestuous affair with his half-sister and several homosexual relationships.) By 1816, Byron's star was obscured by scandal and he left England. He spent some time with Percy Bysshe Shelley in Geneva, then went to Venice, where he became the lover of Countess Teresa Guiccioli. Then Byron, Shelley, and others formed the flamboyant "Pisan Circle." Shelley drowned in 1822, and Byron swam far out to sea to watch as Shelley's funeral pyre burned on the beach. While he was in Europe he was working on *Don Juan.* When he was 36 Byron went to Greece to help in the fight for independence. While in Greece he died of a fever.

More than any other writer of his time, Byron set the tone for the age. His reputation in England has gradually declined, but "Byronic" stances were adopted by Goethe, Balzac, Pushkin, Dostoevsky, Melville, Delacroix, and Beethoven. The "Byronic hero" is a misanthropic, melancholy figure, superior in intellect and emotion, disdainful of the common man, and burdened by an obscure and unspeakable guilt. Byron's ideas influenced Nietzsche's portrait of the titanic amoral "Superman." We should not assume that the Byronic hero is autobiographical in any simplistic way, and it is important to remember that Byron's poetry is in many ways very "un-Romantic." Much of his work is neo-Classical in structure and type: satires such as *Don Juan* have more in common with Pope (whom Byron admired) than with the meditative nature verse of Wordsworth. Byron could, when he chose, write lyrics of great beauty, but this is not his dominant mode. On the whole he was, like the Augustans, a social poet (although in a more radical vein), persistently attacking cant and orthodoxy of all kinds and advocating means of freeing the human spirit from social constrictions. The grand scale of his ideas, his curious mixture of cynicism and idealism, and his brilliant wit make Byron's life and poetry a fascinating study.

Hours of Idleness appeared in 1807, when Byron was 19. *English Bards and Scotch Reviewers* (1809) and *Childe Harold* (1812) are also early poems. Additional cantos of *Childe Harold* were published in 1816 and 1818. The first five cantos of *Don Juan,* a *bildüngsroman* satire, appeared in 1818; Byron finished a total of 16 cantos in *ottava rima* before his death. Other important works are the dramas *Manfred* (1816) and *Cain* (1821), and *The Vision of Judgment* (1822). The best shorter poems are "Written After Swimming from Sestos to Abydos" (1810), "When We Two Parted" (1813), "She Walks in Beauty" (1814), and "Stanzas Written on the Road Between Florence and Pisa" (1821).

GEORGE GORDON, LORD BYRON

She Walks in Beauty

    She walks in beauty, like the night
      Of cloudless climes and starry skies;
    And all that's best of dark and bright
      Meet in her aspect and her eyes:
5 Thus mellow'd to that tender light
      Which heaven to gaudy day denies.

    One shade the more, one ray the less,
      Had half impair'd the nameless grace
    Which waves in every raven tress,
10   Or softly lightens o'er her face;
    Where thoughts serenely sweet express
      How pure, how dear their dwelling-place.

    And on that cheek, and o'er that brow,
      So soft, so calm, yet eloquent,
15 The smiles that win, the tints that glow,
      But tell of days in goodness spent,
    A mind at peace with all below,
      A heart whose love is innocent!
      June 12, 1814.

                (1815)

from *Childe Harold's Pilgrimage*

I

Oh, thou! in Hellas deem'd of heavenly birth,
Muse! form'd or fabled at the minstrel's will!
Since shamed full oft by later lyres on earth,
Mine dares not call thee from thy sacred hill:
5   Yet there I've wander'd by thy vaunted rill;
Yes! sigh'd o'er Delphi's long-deserted shrine,
Where, save that feeble fountain, all is still;
Nor mote my shell awake the weary Nine[1]
To grace so plain a tale, this lowly lay of mine.

II

10   Whilome[2] in Albion's isle there dwelt a youth,
Who ne in virtue's ways did take delight;
But spent his days in riot most uncouth,
And vex'd with mirth the drowsy ear of Night.
Ah me! in sooth he was a shameless wight,
15   Sore given to revel and ungodly glee;
Few earthly things found favour in his sight
Save concubines and carnal companie,
And flaunting wassailers of high and low degree.

III

Childe Harold was he hight:—but whence his name
20   And lineage long, it suits me not to say;
Suffice it, that perchance they were of fame,
And had been glorious in another day:
But one sad losel° soils a name for aye,   scoundrel
However mighty in the olden time;
25   Nor all that heralds rake from coffin'd clay,
Nor florid prose, nor honey'd lies of rhyme,
Can blazon evil deeds or consecrate a crime.

IV

Childe Harold basked him in the noon-tide sun,
Disporting there like any other fly,
30   Nor deem'd before his little day was done
One blast might chill him into misery.

---

[1] Nor may my lyre awake the nine Muses.
[2] Once upon a time.

But long ere scarce a third of his pass'd by,
Worse than adversity the Childe befell,—
He felt the fulness of satiety;
35 Then loathed he in his native land to dwell,
Which seem'd to him more lone than Eremite's³ sad cell.

V

For he through Sin's long labyrinth had run,
Nor made atonement when he did amiss;
Had sigh'd to many though he loved but one,
40 And that loved one, alas! could ne'er be his.
Ah, happy she! to 'scape from him whose kiss
Had been pollution unto aught so chaste;
Who soon had left her charms for vulgar bliss,
And spoil'd her goodly lands to gild his waste,
45 Nor calm domestic peace had ever deign'd to taste.

VI

And now Childe Harold was sore sick at heart,
And from his fellow bacchanals would flee;
'T is said, at times the sullen tear would start,
But Pride congeal'd the drop within his ee.°   eye
50 Apart he stalk'd in joyless reverie,
And from his native land resolved to go,
And visit scorching climes beyond the sea;
With pleasure drugg'd, he almost long'd for woe,
And e'en for change of scene would seek the shades below.

                                        (1812)

from *Don Juan*¹

from Canto 1

I

I want a hero: an uncommon want,
    When every year and month sends forth a new one,
Till, after cloying the gazettes with cant,
    The age discovers he is not the true one;

---

³ Religious hermit.
¹ According to Spanish legend, a nobleman and infamous seducer of women.

5   Of such as these I should not care to vaunt,
       I'll therefore take our ancient friend Don Juan—
     We all have seen him, in the pantomime,
     Sent to the devil somewhat ere his time.

                              V
     Brave men were living before Agamemnon
       And since, exceeding valorous and sage,
35   A good deal like him too, though quite the same none;
       But then they shone not on the poet's page,
     And so have been forgotten:—I condemn none,
       But can't find any in the present age
     Fit for my poem (that is, for my new one);
40   So, as I said, I'll take my friend Don Juan.

                             VI
     Most epic poets plunge "in medias res"[2]
       (Horace makes this the heroic turnpike road),
     And then your hero tells, whene'er you please,
       What went before—by way of episode,
45   While seated after dinner at his ease,
       Beside his mistress in some soft abode,
     Palace, or garden, paradise, or cavern,
     Which serves the happy couple for a tavern.

                            VII
     That is the usual method, but not mine—
50   My way is to begin with the beginning;
     The regularity of my design
       Forbids all wandering as the worst of sinning,
     And therefore I shall open with a line
       (Although it cost me half an hour in spinning)
55   Narrating somewhat of Don Juan's father,
     And also of his mother, if you'd rather.

                            VIII
     In Seville was he born, a pleasant city,
       Famous for oranges and women—he
     Who has not seen it will be much to pity,
60   So says the proverb—and I quite agree;
     Of all the Spanish towns is none more pretty,
       Cadiz perhaps—but that you soon may see;
     Don Juan's parents lived beside the river,
     A noble stream, and call'd the Guadalquivir.

---

[2] In the middle of things.

IX

65 His father's name was José—*Don,* of course,—
　　A true Hidalgo,[3] free from every stain
　　Of Moor or Hebrew blood, he traced his source
　　　Through the most Gothic gentlemen of Spain;
　　A better cavalier ne'er mounted horse,
70 　Or, being mounted, e'er got down again,
　　Than José, who begot our hero, who
　　Begot—but that's to come—Well, to renew:

X

　　His mother was a learned lady, famed
　　　For every branch of every science known
75 In every Christian language ever named,
　　　With virtues equall'd by her wit alone,
　　She made the cleverest people quite ashamed,
　　　And even the good with inward envy groan,
　　Finding themselves so very much exceeded
80 In their own way by all the things that she did.

XI

　　Her memory was a mine: she knew by heart
　　　All Calderon and greater part of Lopé,[4]
　　So that if any actor miss'd his part
　　　She could have served him for the prompter's copy;
85 For her Feinagle's[5] were an useless art,
　　　And he himself obliged to shut up shop—he
　　Could never make a memory so fine as
　　That which adorn'd the brain of Donna Inez.

XXII

　　'T is pity learned virgins ever wed
170 　With persons of no sort of education,
　　Or gentlemen, who, though well born and bred,
　　　Grow tired of scientific conversation:
　　I don't choose to say much upon this head,
　　　I'm a plain man, and in a single station,
175 But—Oh! ye lords of ladies intellectual,
　　Inform us truly, have they not hen-peck'd you all?

XXIII

　　Don José and his lady quarrell'd—*why,*
　　　Not any of the many could divine,

---

[3] Minor Spanish nobleman.
[4] Calderón de la Barca (1600–1681) and Lopé de Vega (1562–1635), two of the greatest Spanish dramatists.
[5] Gregor von Feinagle, an expert on the art of memorization; he lectured in England in 1811.

Though several thousand people chose to try,
180   'T was surely no concern of theirs nor mine;
I loathe that low vice—curiosity;
    But if there's anything in which I shine,
'T is in arranging all my friends' affairs,
Not having of my own domestic cares.

XXIV

185   And so I interfered, and with the best
    Intentions, but their treatment was not kind;
I think the foolish people were possess'd,
    For neither of them could I ever find,
Although their porter afterwards confess'd—
190   But that's no matter, and the worst's behind,
For little Juan o'er me threw, down stairs,
A pail of housemaid's water unawares.

XXV

A little curly-headed, good-for-nothing,
    And mischief-making monkey from his birth;
195   His parents ne'er agreed except in doting
    Upon the most unquiet imp on earth;
Instead of quarrelling, had they been but both in
    Their senses, they'd have sent young master forth
To school, or had him soundly whipp'd at home,
200   To teach him manners for the time to come.

XXVI

Don José and the Donna Inez led
    For some time an unhappy sort of life,
Wishing each other, not divorced, but dead;
    They lived respectably as man and wife,
205   Their conduct was exceedingly well-bred,
    And gave no outward signs of inward strife,
Until at length the smother'd fire broke out,
And put the business past all kind of doubt.

XXVII

For Inez call'd some druggists and physicians,
210   And tried to prove her loving lord was *mad;*
But as he had some lucid intermissions,
    She next decided he was only *bad;*
Yet when they ask'd her for her depositions,
    No sort of explanation could be had,
215   Save that her duty both to man and God
Required this conduct—which seem'd very odd.

XXVIII

She kept a journal, where his faults were noted,
  And open'd certain trunks of books and letters,
All which might, if occasion served, be quoted;
220   And then she had all Seville for abettors,
Besides her good old grandmother (who doted);
  The hearers of her case became repeaters,
Then advocates, inquisitors, and judges,
Some for amusement, others for old grudges.

XXIX

225 And then this best and weakest woman bore
  With such serenity her husband's woes,
Just as the Spartan ladies did of yore,
  Who saw their spouses kill'd, and nobly chose
Never to say a word about them more—
230   Calmly she heard each calumny that rose,
And saw *his* agonies with such sublimity,
That all the world exclaim'd, 'What magnanimity!'

XXXII

Their friends had tried at reconciliation,
250   Then their relations, who made matters worse.
('T were hard to tell upon a like occasion
  To whom it may be best to have recourse—
I can't say much for friend or yet relation):
  The lawyers did their utmost for divorce,
255 But scarce a fee was paid on either side
Before, unluckily, Don José died.

XXXIII

He died: and most unluckily, because,
  According to all hints I could collect
From counsel learned in those kinds of laws
260   (Although their talk's obscure and circumspect),
His death contrived to spoil a charming cause;
  A thousand pities also with respect
To public feeling, which on this occasion
Was manifested in a great sensation.

                              (1819)

Percy Bysshe Shelley

(1 7 9 2 – 1 8 2 2)

The son of a conservative parliamentarian, Percy Bysshe Shelley spent his life battling orthodoxy and conformity. In 1810 he was expelled from Oxford for coauthoring a pamphlet advocating atheism. Soon after, he eloped with Harriet Westbrook, a 16-year-old girl Shelley thought was tyrannized by her father. He continued to work for the emancipation of all oppressed groups, and in 1813 became a disciple of William Godwin's radical social philosophy, which prompted him to see institutions as an artificial source of most human evil. He abandoned Harriet for Godwin's daughter, Mary Wollstonecraft Godwin, was ostracized, and eventually left England. When Harriet committed suicide two years later, Shelley was denied custody of their two children. He and Mary moved around Italy dogged by tragedy: their young son and daughter both died in the same year. In 1820 the Shelleys found some stability with a circle of English artists—one of them Lord Byron—in Pisa, but the contentment was cut short when Shelley drowned in a violent storm. (He had predicted his death in *Adonais.*) Despite Shelley's reputation for immorality, Byron called him "the *best* and least selfish man" he had ever known.

Shelley's poetry has a complex and carefully organized structure. The range of his poetic voice, his command of tone, and different rhythms (a musicality best exemplified in "Ode to the West Wind") and the breadth of his ideas have few peers. In his mature work Shelley discussed the bursting of all bonds on the human imagination and a neo-Platonic vision of the universe that consisted of two parts: the mundane world of transitory suffering and a perfect poetic sphere of unchanging beauty. This latter theme is powerfully evident in *Adonais,* his moving elegy on the death of Keats, and in *Prometheus Unbound,* a visionary verse drama that attempts to unite political radicalism, Platonism, Christian ethics, and contemporary science. In *Alastor* Shelley approaches Byronic isolation, but in general his was a world of the mind that pierced, rather than fled, the veil-like physical world. Shelley's *Defence of Poetry* is an articulate advocacy of the imagination as central to all human activity. A poet, to Shelley, helps give birth to the future by breaking free from the assumptions of his or her own era, thus becoming "the unacknowledged legislator of the world."

Shelley's major poems are *Queen Mab* (1813), *Alastor* (1815), "Mont Blanc" (1816), "Hymn to Intellectual Beauty" (1817), *The Revolt of Islam* (1817), "Stanzas Written in Dejection" (1818), the great lyrics "Ode to the West Wind," "The Cloud," and "To a Skylark" (1819–1820), *Prometheus Unbound* (1820), *Adonais* (1821), and the unfinished *The Triumph of Life* (1822).

PERCY BYSSHE SHELLEY

Hymn to Intellectual Beauty

The awful shadow of some unseen Power
  Floats tho' unseen among us; visiting
  This various world with as inconstant wing
As summer winds that creep from flower to flower;
5 Like moonbeams that behind some piny mountain shower,
    It visits with inconstant glance
    Each human heart and countenance;
Like hues and harmonies of evening,
    Like clouds in starlight widely spread,
10   Like memory of music fled,
    Like aught that for its grace may be
Dear, and yet dearer for its mystery.

Spirit of BEAUTY, that dost consecrate
  With thine own hues all thou dost shine upon
15   Of human thought or form, where art thou gone?
Why dost thou pass away and leave our state,
This dim vast vale of tears, vacant and desolate?
    Ask why the sunlight not forever
    Weaves rainbows o'er yon mountain river
20 Why aught should fail and fade that once is shown;
    Why fear and dream and death and birth
    Cast on the daylight of this earth
    Such gloom, why man has such a scope
For love and hate, despondency and hope?

25 No voice from some sublimer world hath ever
    To sage or poet these responses given:
    Therefore the names of Demon, Ghost, and Heaven,
Remain the records of their vain endeavour:
Frail spells, whose uttered charm might not avail to sever,
30   From all we hear and all we see,
    Doubt, chance, and mutability.
Thy light alone, like mist o'er mountains driven,
    Or music by the night wind sent
    Thro' strings of some still instrument,
35   Or moonlight on a midnight stream,
Gives grace and truth to life's unquiet dream.

Love, Hope, and Self-esteem, like clouds, depart
    And come, for some uncertain moments lent.
    Man were immortal and omnipotent,
40 Didst thou, unknown and awful as thou art,
Keep with thy glorious train firm state within his heart.
    Thou messenger of sympathies
    That wax and wane in lovers' eyes;
Thou, that to human thought art nourishment,
45   Like darkness to a dying flame!
    Depart not as thy shadow came:
    Depart not, lest the grave should be,
Like life and fear, a dark reality.

While yet a boy I sought for ghosts, and sped
50   Thro' many a listening chamber, cave, and ruin,
    And starlight wood, with fearful steps pursuing
Hopes of high talk with the departed dead.
I called on poisonous names with which our youth is fed:
    I was not heard: I saw them not:
55   When musing deeply on the lot
Of life, at that sweet time when winds are wooing
    All vital things that wake to bring
    News of birds and blossoming,
    Sudden, thy shadow fell on me;
60 I shrieked, and clasped my hands in extacy!

I vowed that I would dedicate my powers
    To thee and thine: have I not kept the vow?
    With beating heart and streaming eyes, even now
I call the phantoms of a thousand hours
65 Each from his voiceless grave: they have in visioned bowers
    Of studious zeal or love's delight
    Outwatched with me the envious night:
They know that never joy illumed my brow,
    Unlinked with hope that thou wouldst free
70   This world from its dark slavery,
    That thou, O awful LOVELINESS,
Wouldst give whate'er these words cannot express.

The day becomes more solemn and serene
    When noon is past: there is a harmony
75   In autumn, and a lustre in its sky,
Which thro' the summer is not heard or seen,
As if it could not be, as if it had not been!
    Thus let thy power, which like the truth
    Of nature on my passive youth

80 Descended, to my onward life supply
       Its calm, to one who worships thee,
       And every form containing thee,
       Whom, SPIRIT fair, thy spells did bind
    To fear himself, and love all human kind.

(1817)

Ozymandias[1]

'I met a traveller from an antique land
Who said: Two vast and trunkless legs of stone
Stand in the desert. Near them, on the sand,
Half sunk, a shattered visage lies, whose frown,
5 And wrinkled lip, and sneer of cold command,
Tell that its sculptor well those passions read
Which yet survive, stamped on these lifeless things,
The hand that mocked them and the heart that fed;
And on the pedestal these words appear:
10 "My name is Ozymandias, king of kings:
Look on my works, ye Mighty, and despair!"
Nothing beside remains. Round the decay
Of that colossal wreck, boundless and bare,
The lone and level sands stretch far away.

(1818)

Visage - face

Ode to the West Wind[2]

I

O Wild West Wind, thou breath of Autumn's being,
Thou, from whose unseen presence the leaves dead
Are driven, like ghosts from an enchanter fleeing,

[1] Ozymandias is the Greek name for Ramses II, the Egyptian ruler of the thirteenth century B.C.
[2] This poem was conceived and chiefly written in a wood that skirts the Arno, near Florence, and on a day when that tempestuous wind, whose temperature is at once mild and animating, was collecting the vapours which pour down the autumnal rains. They began, as I foresaw, at sunset with a violent tempest of hail and rain, attended by that magnificent thunder and lightning peculiar to the Cisalpine regions.
   The phenomenon alluded to at the conclusion of the third stanza is well known to naturalists. The vegetation at the bottom of the sea, of rivers, and of lakes, sympathises with that of the land in the change of seasons, and is consequently influenced by the winds which announce it. (Shelley's Note.)

Yellow, and black, and pale, and hectic red,
5 Pestilence-stricken multitudes: O thou,
Who chariotest to their dark wintry bed

The winged seeds, where they lie cold and low,
Each like a corpse within its grave, until
Thine azure sister of the spring shall blow

10 Her clarion o'er the dreaming earth, and fill
(Driving sweet buds like flocks to feed in air)
With living hues and odours plain and hill:

Wild Spirit, which art moving every where;
Destroyer and preserver; hear, O, hear!

II

15 Thou on whose stream, 'mid the steep sky's commotion,
Loose clouds like earth's decaying leaves are shed,
Shook from the tangled boughs of Heaven and Ocean,

Angels of rain and lightning: there are spread
On the blue surface of thine airy surge,
20 Like the bright hair uplifted from the head

Of some fierce Mænad,[3] even from the dim verge
Of the horizon to the zenith's height
The locks of the approaching storm. Thou dirge

Of the dying year, to which this closing night
25 Will be the dome of a vast sepulchre,
Vaulted with all thy congregated might

Of vapours, from whose solid atmosphere
Black rain, and fire, and hail will burst: O, hear!

III

Thou who didst waken from his summer dreams
30 The blue Mediterranean, where he lay,
Lulled by the coil of his crystalline streams,

Beside a pumice isle in Baiæ's bay,[4]
And saw in sleep dim palaces and towers
Quivering within the wave's intenser day,

[3] A frenzied dancer who worshipped Dionysus, the god of wine and fertility.
[4] Near Naples, Italy.

35 All overgrown with azure moss and flowers
    So sweet, the sense faints picturing them! Thou
    For whose path the Atlantic's level powers

    Cleave themselves into chasms, while far below
    The sea-blooms and the oozy woods which wear
40 The sapless foliage of the ocean, know

    Thy voice, and suddenly grow grey with fear,
    And tremble and despoil themselves: O, hear!

                    IV

    If I were a dead leaf thou mightest bear;
    If I were a swift cloud to fly with thee;
45 A wave to pant beneath thy power, and share

    The impulse of thy strength, only less free
    Than thou, O uncontroulable! If even
    I were as in my boyhood, and could be

    The comrade of thy wanderings over heaven,
50 As then, when to outstrip thy skiey speed
    Scarce seemed a vision, I would ne'er have striven

    As thus with thee in prayer in my sore need.
    Oh! lift me as a wave, a leaf, a cloud!
    I fall upon the thorns of life! I bleed!

55 A heavy weight of hours has chained and bowed
    One too like thee: tameless, and swift, and proud.

                    V

    Make me thy lyre, even as the forest is:
    What if my leaves are falling like its own!
    The tumult of thy mighty harmonies

60 Will take from both a deep, autumnal tone,
    Sweet though in sadness. Be thou, spirit fierce,
    My spirit! Be thou me, impetuous one!

    Drive my dead thoughts over the universe
    Like withered leaves to quicken a new birth!
65 And, by the incantation of this verse,

Scatter, as from an unextinguished hearth
Ashes and sparks, my words among mankind!
Be through my lips to unawakened earth

The trumpet of a prophecy! O, wind,
70 If Winter comes, can Spring be far behind?

(1820)

John Keats

(1 7 9 5 – 1 8 2 1)

John Keats, the son of a livery stablekeeper who died when Keats was young, was in continual financial trouble. After briefly studying medicine, he devoted himself to poetry in 1815. In the next five years he progressed with amazing speed from diffuse, sentimental verse to the densely textured subtlety of the great odes. In 1818 Keats's *Endymion* was condemned by the critics (an event Shelley incorrectly saw as contributing to his death), his brother George emigrated to America, he fell in love with Fanny Brawne and was forced to watch his younger brother die slowly and painfully of tuberculosis. Tragedy gave Keats a sharp sense of mortality and perhaps spurred the rapid maturing of his poetry, which culminated in an amazing string of masterpieces written in six months in 1819. In February 1820 Keats coughed up blood and recognized his fate, which he had half suspected since his younger brother's death. The warmer climate of Italy did little to slow the tuberculosis that killed Keats when he was 25. Keats sensed that he had failed to gain recognition from his contemporaries. This sense is reflected in the epitaph he chose for his tombstone in Rome: "Here lies one whose name was writ in water."

Keats consciously moved away from Wordsworthian subjective landscapes toward what he saw as a Shakespearean objectivity, a "Negative Capability," the art of living amidst mystery and doubt without grasping after artificial certainty. Among the Romantics, Keats was unusually attached to the sensual surface of the world. In his best work the physical reality of existence is examined with a trancelike concentration until mind and object, feeling and sensation, word and mood seem to blend. His ode "To Autumn" is the finest example of this feature of Keats's genius. Another major theme is the continual redefinition of the art-nature dichotomy. In 1815 Keats was writing almost purely escapist verse; he began to write poetry, determined to create a world for the mind entirely predicated on the concrete world, a poetry in some ways as organic as nature but forced to blossom from within by the force of the human mind. His concerns are most fully worked out in concert with the preoccupation with mortality in "Ode on Melancholy," "Ode on a Grecian Urn," and "Ode to a Nightingale." In the odes and in other poems Keats achieves a complex yet graceful music, striking imagery, and a beauty of expression. To have achieved this in a career of five years is miraculous and tragic.

Keats also wrote *Endymion* (1817), "On First Looking into Chapman's Homer" (1816), *Sleep and Poetry* (1816), "On Sitting Down to Read *King Lear*," "When I Have Fears," and "To Homer" (all 1818), *The Eve of St. Agnes* (1819), "Bright Star" (1819–1820), "La Belle Dame Sans Merci" (1819),

"Sonnet to Sleep" (1819), "Ode to Psyche" (1819), *Lamia* (1819), and the fragmentary but powerful *Hyperion* (1818) and *The Fall of Hyperion* (1819). Keats's letters are moving and intelligent and serve better than any of the biographies to define the man.

JOHN KEATS

On First Looking into Chapman's Homer[1]

Much have I travell'd in the realms of gold,
  And many goodly states and kingdoms seen;
  Round many western islands have I been
Which bards in fealty to Apollo hold.
5 Oft of one wide expanse had I been told
  That deep-brow'd Homer ruled as his demesne;°   domain
  Yet did I never breathe its pure serene°   air
Till I heard Chapman speak out loud and bold:
  Then felt I like some watcher of the skies
10 When a new planet swims into his ken;
  Or like stout Cortez when with eagle eyes
  He star'd at the Pacific—and all his men
Look'd at each other with a wild surmise—
  Silent, upon a peak in Darien.   (1816)

When I Have Fears

When I have fears that I may cease to be
  Before my pen has glean'd my teeming brain,
Before high-piled books, in charact'ry,°   letters, writing
  Hold like rich garners the full-ripen'd grain;
5 When I behold, upon the night's starr'd face,
  Huge cloudy symbols of a high romance,
And think that I may never live to trace
  Their shadows, with the magic hand of chance;

[1] George Chapman (ca. 1559–1634), poet and translator of Homer.

And when I feel, fair creature of an hour!
10   That I shall never look upon thee more,
Never have relish in the faery power
    Of unreflecting love!—then on the shore
Of the wide world I stand alone, and think
Till love and fame to nothingness do sink.

(1848)

La Belle Dame sans Merci[1]

I

O what can ail thee, knight-at-arms,
    Alone and palely loitering?
The sedge has wither'd from the lake,
    And no birds sing.

II

5 O what can ail thee, knight-at-arms!
    So haggard and so woe-begone?
The squirrel's granary is full,
    And the harvest's done.

III

I see a lilly on thy brow,
10   With anguish moist and fever dew,
And on thy cheeks a fading rose
    Fast withereth too.

IV

I met a lady in the meads,°   meadows
    Full beautiful—a faery's child,
15 Her hair was long, her foot was light,
    And her eyes were wild.

V

I made a garland for her head,
    And bracelets too, and fragrant zone;°   girdle
She look'd at me as she did love,
20   And made sweet moan.

[1] The beautiful lady without pity.

VI

I set her on my pacing steed,
   And nothing else saw all day long,
For sidelong would she bend, and sing
   A faery's song.

VII

25 She found me roots of relish sweet,
   And honey wild, and manna dew,
And sure in language strange she said—
   "I love thee true".

VIII

She took me to her elfin grot,
30   And there she wept, and sigh'd full sore,
And there I shut her wild wild eyes
   With kisses four.

IX

And there she lulled me asleep,
   And there I dream'd—Ah! woe betide!
35 The latest dream I ever dream'd
   On the cold hill side.

X

I saw pale kings and princes too,
   Pale warriors, death-pale were they all;
They cried—'La Belle Dame sans Merci
40   Hath thee in thrall!'

XI

I saw their starved lips in the gloam,
   With horrid warning gaped wide,
And I awoke and found me here,
   On the cold hill's side.

XII

45 And this is why I sojourn here,
   Alone and palely loitering,
Though the sedge has wither'd from the lake,
   And no birds sing.

                        (1820)

Ode on a Grecian Urn

1

Thou still unravish'd bride of quietness,
   Thou foster-child of silence and slow time,
Sylvan historian, who canst thus express
   A flowery tale more sweetly than our rhyme:
5 What leaf-fring'd legend haunts about thy shape
   Of deities or mortals, or of both,
     In Tempe or the dales of Arcady?[1]
What men or gods are these? What maidens loth?
What mad pursuit? What struggle to escape?
10   What pipes and timbrels? What wild ecstasy?

2

Heard melodies are sweet, but those unheard
   Are sweeter; therefore, ye soft pipes, play on;
Not to the sensual ear, but, more endear'd,
   Pipe to the spirit ditties of no tone:
15 Fair youth, beneath the trees, thou canst not leave
   Thy song, nor ever can those trees be bare;
     Bold Lover, never, never canst thou kiss,
Though winning near the goal—yet, do not grieve;
   She cannot fade, though thou hast not thy bliss,
20   For ever wilt thou love, and she be fair!

3

Ah, happy, happy boughs! that cannot shed
   Your leaves, nor ever bid the Spring adieu;
And, happy melodist, unwearied,
   For ever piping songs for ever new;
25 More happy love! more happy, happy love!
   For ever warm and still to be enjoy'd,
     For ever panting, and for ever young;
All breathing human passion far above,
   That leaves a heart high-sorrowful and cloy'd,
30   A burning forehead, and a parching tongue.

4

Who are these coming to the sacrifice?
   To what green altar, O mysterious priest,

---

[1] Tempe and Arcady represent ideal pastoral beauty.

Lead'st thou that heifer lowing at the skies,
    And all her silken flanks with garlands drest?
35 What little town by river or sea shore,
    Or mountain-built with peaceful citadel,
        Is emptied of this folk, this pious morn?
And, little town, thy streets for evermore
    Will silent be; and not a soul to tell
40   Why thou art desolate, can e'er return.

5

O Attic shape! Fair attitude! with brede[2]
    Of marble men and maidens overwrought,
With forest branches and the trodden weed;
    Thou, silent form, dost tease us out of thought
45 As doth eternity: Cold Pastoral!
    When old age shall this generation waste,
        Thou shalt remain, in midst of other woe
Than ours, a friend to man, to whom thou say'st,
    Beauty is truth, truth beauty,—that is all
50   Ye know on earth, and all ye need to know.

                                        (1820)

Ode to a Nightingale

1

My heart aches, and a drowsy numbness pains
    My sense, as though of hemlock I had drunk,
Or emptied some dull opiate to the drains
    One minute past, and Lethe-wards[1] had sunk:
5 'Tis not through envy of thy happy lot,
    But being too happy in thine happiness,—
        That thou, light-winged Dryad of the trees,
            In some melodious plot
Of beechen green, and shadows numberless,
10   Singest of summer in full-throated ease.

2

O, for a draught of vintage! that hath been
    Cool'd a long age in the deep-delved earth,
Tasting of Flora and the country green,

---

[2] Braided ornamentation.
[1] Toward Lethe, the river of forgetfulness in the underworld.

Dance, and Provençal song,² and sunburnt mirth!
15 O for a beaker full of the warm South,
   Full of the true, the blushful Hippocrene,³
     With beaded bubbles winking at the brim,
      And purple-stained mouth;
    That I might drink, and leave the world unseen,
20   And with thee fade away into the forest dim:

3

Fade far away, dissolve, and quite forget
   What thou among the leaves hast never known,
The weariness, the fever, and the fret
   Here, where men sit and hear each other groan;
25 Where palsy shakes a few, sad, last gray hairs,
   Where youth grows pale, and spectre-thin, and
       dies;
     Where but to think is to be full of sorrow
      And leaden-eyed despairs,
   Where Beauty cannot keep her lustrous eyes,
30   Or new Love pine at them beyond to-morrow.

4

Away! away! for I will fly to thee,
   Not charioted by Bacchus and his pards,⁴
But on the viewless wings of Poesy,
   Though the dull brain perplexes and retards:
35 Already with thee! tender is the night,
   And haply the Queen-Moon is on her throne,
     Cluster'd around by all her starry Fays;°   fairies
      But here there is no light,
   Save what from heaven is with the breezes blown
40   Through verdurous glooms and winding mossy ways.

5

I cannot see what flowers are at my feet,
   Nor what soft incense hangs upon the boughs,
But, in embalmed darkness, guess each sweet
   Wherewith the seasonable month endows
45 The grass, the thicket, and the fruit-tree wild;
   White hawthorn, and the pastoral eglantine;
     Fast fading violets cover'd up in leaves;
     And mid-May's eldest child,

---

² Provence, in France, was well known for its troubadors.
³ The fountain of the muses.
⁴ Bacchus, the god of wine, was often represented in a chariot drawn by leopards.

The coming musk-rose, full of dewy wine,
50   The murmurous haunt of flies on summer eves.

6

Darkling° I listen; and, for many a time   in the dark
  I have been half in love with easeful Death,
Call'd him soft names in many a mused rhyme,
  To take into the air my quiet breath;
55 Now more than ever seems it rich to die,
  To cease upon the midnight with no pain,
    While thou art pouring forth thy soul abroad
      In such an ecstasy!
  Still wouldst thou sing, and I have ears in vain—
60   To thy high requiem become a sod.

7

Thou wast not born for death, immortal Bird!
  No hungry generations tread thee down;
The voice I hear this passing night was heard
  In ancient days by emperor and clown:
65 Perhaps the self-same song that found a path
  Through the sad heart of Ruth, when, sick for
      home,
    She stood in tears amid the alien corn;
      The same that oft-times hath
  Charm'd magic casements, opening on the foam
70   Of perilous seas, in faery lands forlorn.

8

Forlorn! the very word is like a bell
  To toll me back from thee to my sole self!
Adieu! the fancy cannot cheat so well
  As she is fam'd to do, deceiving elf.
75 Adieu! adieu! thy plaintive anthem fades
  Past the near meadows, over the still stream,
    Up the hill-side; and now 'tis buried deep
      In the next valley-glades:
  Was it a vision, or a waking dream?
80   Fled is that music:—Do I wake or sleep?

                                        (1819)

Ode on Melancholy

I

No, no, go not to Lethe, neither twist
  Wolf's-bane, tight-rooted, for its poisonous wine;

Nor suffer thy pale forehead to be kiss'd
   By nightshade, ruby grape of Proserpine;
5 Make not your rosary of yew-berries,
   Nor let the beetle, nor the death-moth be
     Your mournful Psyche, nor the downy owl
A partner in your sorrow's mysteries;
   For shade to shade will come too drowsily,
10   And drown the wakeful anguish of the soul.

2

But when the melancholy fit shall fall
   Sudden from heaven like a weeping cloud,
That fosters the droop-headed flowers all,
   And hides the green hill in an April shroud;
15 Then glut thy sorrow on a morning rose,
   Or on the rainbow of the salt sand-wave,
     Or on the wealth of globed peonies;
Or if thy mistress some rich anger shows,
   Emprison her soft hand, and let her rave,
20   And feed deep, deep upon her peerless eyes.

3

She dwells with Beauty—Beauty that must die;
   And Joy, whose hand is ever at his lips
Bidding adieu; and aching Pleasure nigh,
   Turning to poison while the bee-mouth sips:
25 Ay, in the very temple of Delight
   Veil'd Melancholy has her sovran shrine,
     Though seen of none save him whose strenuous tongue
Can burst Joy's grape against his palate fine;
   His soul shall taste the sadness of her might,
30   And be among her cloudy trophies hung.

(1820)

To Autumn

I

Season of mists and mellow fruitfulness,
   Close bosom-friend of the maturing sun;
Conspiring with him how to load and bless
   With fruit the vines that round the thatch-eves run;
5 To bend with apples the moss'd cottage-trees,
   And fill all fruit with ripeness to the core;

To swell the gourd, and plump the hazel shells
With a sweet kernel; to set budding more,
   And still more, later flowers for the bees,
10   Until they think warm days will never cease,
         For Summer has o'er-brimm'd their clammy
            cells.

2

Who hath not seen thee oft amid thy store?
   Sometimes whoever seeks abroad may find
Thee sitting careless on a granary floor,
15   Thy hair soft-lifted by the winnowing wind;
Or on a half-reap'd furrow sound asleep,
   Drows'd with the fume of poppies, while thy hook
   Spares the next swath and all its twined flowers:
And sometimes like a gleaner thou dost keep
20   Steady thy laden head across a brook;
   Or by a cyder-press, with patient look,   To pick
      Thou watchest the last oozings hours by hours.   up whats
                                                        left after
                                                        harvesting

3

Where are the songs of Spring? Ay, where are they?
   Think not of them, thou hast thy music too,—
25 While barred clouds bloom the soft-dying day,
   And touch the stubble-plains with rosy hue;
Then in a wailful choir the small gnats mourn
      Among the river shallows,° borne aloft   willow trees
         Or sinking as the light wind lives or dies;
30 And full-grown lambs loud bleat from hilly bourn;°   land
      Hedge-crickets sing; and now with treble soft
   The red-breast whistles from a garden-croft;°   garden-plot
      And gathering swallows twitter in the skies.

                                       (1820)

Alfred, Lord Tennyson

(1 8 0 9 – 1 8 9 2)

Although he was the son of a clergyman, Tennyson did not grow up in a sheltered environment: one brother went insane, another was an opium addict, and his father became a drunkard. At Cambridge, Tennyson met A. H. Hallam, who became a close friend. Early volumes of verse were mediocre and poorly received, but the sudden death of Hallam spurred Tennyson to write *In Memoriam,* a long meditation on faith, doubt, and loss. When it was published in 1850, Tennyson became famous and was chosen as poet laureate. Also in 1850, he married Emily Sellwood after a 14-year betrothal, which had been lengthened by the poet's uncertain finances. He was England's most celebrated poet at the time, and he began to amass considerable wealth. He moved to a large estate in the country, to the seclusion he loved. Tennyson was a tall, striking man; in his old age, in a wide-brimmed hat and black cloak, he walked on the moors. When he died, in 1892, Tennyson was the most widely read poet in the English-speaking world.

Tennyson's reputation plummeted drastically after his death, and critics of the early twentieth century thought his poetry was all surface without emotion or intellect. They thought Tennyson had merely popularized the received ideas of Imperial England. Both this view and the adulation of the 1850s and 1860s are extreme. Tennyson's work does not have the analytical precision of Browning's or the complexity and originality of metaphor and theme found in Keats's poetry. But he had, as Auden suggested, "the finest ear, perhaps, of any English poet," and his best work is hardly intellectually vacant. He dealt with the impact of the new science on religious and societal beliefs in "Locksley Hall" (1838), with the personal struggle for faith and peace (in passages of great feeling and an ethereal, haunting beauty) in his masterpiece, *In Memoriam* (1850), and with the cycles of civilizations in his Arthurian epic, *Idylls of the King* (1888). The monologue "Maud" (1855) shows considerable talent. "Ulysses" (written in 1833), although perhaps conventional in thought, is undeniably grand in expression, and many of the shorter lyrics, poems such as "Crossing the Bar" (1889), "Tears, Idle Tears" (1847), "Break, Break, Break" (1834), and "Flower in the Crannied Wall" (1869) are true classics. Tennyson might best be regarded as a fine minor poet of unrivaled craftsmanship.

Tennyson also wrote "Mariana" (1830), "The Lady of Shalott" (1832), "The Lotos-Eaters" (1832), "Tithonus" (1833, 1859), an ever-popular song of Empire, "The Charge of the Light Brigade" (1854), and "The Revenge" (1878).

ALFRED, LORD TENNYSON

The Lady of Shalott

PART I

On either side the river lie
Long fields of barley and of rye,
That clothe the wold° and meet the sky;   treeless, rolling plain
And through the field the road runs by
5   To many-towered Camelot;
And up and down the people go,
Gazing where the lilies blow
Round an island there below,
        The island of Shalott.

10 Willows whiten, aspens quiver,
Little breezes dusk and shiver
Through the wave that runs for ever
By the island in the river
        Flowing down to Camelot.
15 Four gray walls, and four gray towers,
Overlook a space of flowers,
And the silent isle imbowers
        The Lady of Shalott.

By the margin, willow-veiled,
20 Slide the heavy barges trailed
By slow horses; and unhailed
The shallop flitteth silken-sailed
        Skimming down to Camelot:
But who hath seen her wave her hand?
25 Or at the casement seen her stand?
Or is she known in all the land,
        The Lady of Shalott?

Only reapers, reaping early
In among the bearded barley,
30 Hear a song that echoes cheerly
From the river winding clearly,
        Down to towered Camelot.

And by the moon the reaper weary,
Piling sheaves in uplands airy,
35   Listening, whispers "'Tis the fairy
        Lady of Shalott."

PART II

There she weaves by night and day
A magic web with colours gay.
She has heard a whisper say,
40   A curse is on her if she stay
        To look down to Camelot.
She knows not what the curse may be,
And so she weaveth steadily,
And little other care hath she,
45   The Lady of Shalott.

And moving through a mirror clear
That hangs before her all the year,
Shadows of the world appear.
There she sees the highway near
50   Winding down to Camelot:
There the river eddy whirls,
And there the surly village-churls,
And the red cloaks of market girls,
        Pass onward from Shalott.

55   Sometimes a troop of damsels glad,
An abbot on an ambling pad,[1]
Sometimes a curly shepherd-lad,
Or long-haired page in crimson clad,
        Goes by to towered Camelot;
60   And sometimes through the mirror blue
The knights come riding two and two:
She hath no loyal knight and true,
        The Lady of Shalott.

But in her web she still delights
65   To weave the mirror's magic sights,
For often through the silent nights
A funeral, with plumes and lights
        And music, went to Camelot:
Or when the moon was overhead,

[1] Horse with an easy, slow pace.

70   Came two young lovers lately wed;
        "I am half sick of shadows," said
            The Lady of Shalott.

PART III

        A bow-shot from her bower-eaves,
        He rode between the barley-sheaves,
75   The sun came dazzling through the leaves,
        And flamed upon the brazen greaves[2]
            Of bold Sir Lancelot.
        A red-cross knight for ever kneeled
        To a lady in his shield,
80   That sparkled on the yellow field,
            Beside remote Shalott.

        The gemmy bridle glittered free,
        Like to some branch of stars we see
        Hung in the golden Galaxy.
85   The bridle bells rang merrily
            As he rode down to Camelot:
        And from his blazoned baldric slung
        A mighty silver bugle hung,
        And as he rode his armour rung,
90   Beside remote Shalott.

        All in the blue unclouded weather
        Thick-jewelled shone the saddle-leather,
        The helmet and the helmet-feather
        Burned like one burning flame together,
95   As he rode down to Camelot.
        As often through the purple night,
        Below the starry clusters bright,
        Some bearded meteor, trailing light,
            Moves over still Shalott.

100   His broad clear brow in sunlight glowed;
        On burnished hooves his war-horse trode;
        From underneath his helmet flowed
        His coal-black curls as on he rode,
            As he rode down to Camelot.
105   From the bank and from the river
        He flashed into the crystal mirror,

─────────────
[2] Armor for the shin.

"Tirra lirra," by the river
  Sang Sir Lancelot.

She left the web, she left the loom,
110   She made three paces through the room,
She saw the water-lily bloom,
She saw the helmet and the plume,
    She looked down to Camelot.
Out flew the web and floated wide;
115   The mirror cracked from side to side;
"The curse is come upon me," cried
  The Lady of Shalott.

PART IV

In the stormy east-wind straining,
The pale yellow woods were waning,
120   The broad stream in his banks complaining.
Heavily the low sky raining
    Over towered Camelot;
Down she came and found a boat
Beneath a willow left afloat,
125   And round about the prow she wrote
  The Lady of Shalott.

And down the river's dim expanse
Like some bold seër in a trance,
Seeing all his own mischance—
130   With a glassy countenance
    Did she look to Camelot.
And at the closing of the day
She loosed the chain, and down she lay;
The broad stream bore her far away,
135   The Lady of Shalott.

Lying, robed in snowy white
That loosely flew to left and right—
The leaves upon her falling light—
Through the noises of the night
140   She floated down to Camelot:
And as the boat-head wound along
The willowy hills and fields among,
They heard her singing her last song,
    The Lady of Shalott.

145 Heard a carol, mournful, holy,
Chanted loudly, chanted lowly,
Till her blood was frozen slowly,
And her eyes were darkened wholly,
　　Turned to towered Camelot.
150 For ere she reached upon the tide
The first house by the water-side,
Singing in her song she died,
　　The Lady of Shalott.

Under tower and balcony,
155 By garden-wall and gallery,
A gleaming shape she floated by,
Dead-pale between the houses high,
　　Silent into Camelot.
Out upon the wharfs they came,
160 Knight and burgher, lord and dame,
And round the prow they read her name,
　　The Lady of Shalott.

Who is this? and what is here?
And in the lighted palace near
165 Died the sound of royal cheer;
And they crossed themselves for fear,
　　All the knights at Camelot:
But Lancelot mused a little space;
He said, "She has a lovely face;
170 God in his mercy lend her grace,
　　The Lady of Shalott."

　　　　　　　　　　　　　　(1832)

Ulysses

It little profits that an idle king,
By this still hearth, among these barren crags,
Matched with an agèd wife, I mete and dole
Unequal laws unto a savage race,
5 That hoard, and sleep, and feed, and know not me.

I cannot rest from travel: I will drink
Life to the lees: all times I have enjoyed
Greatly, have suffered greatly, both with those
That loved me, and alone; on shore, and when

10   Through scudding drifts the rainy Hyades
     Vext the dim sea: I am become a name;
     For always roaming with a hungry heart
     Much have I seen and known; cities of men
     And manners, climates, councils, governments,
15   Myself not least, but honoured of them all;
     And drunk delight of battle with my peers,
     Far on the ringing plains of windy Troy.
     I am a part of all that I have met;
     Yet all experience is an arch wherethrough
20   Gleams that untravelled world, whose margin fades
     For ever and for ever when I move.
     How dull it is to pause, to make an end,
     To rust unburnished, not to shine in use!
     As though to breathe were life. Life piled on life
25   Were all too little, and of one to me
     Little remains: but every hour is saved
     From that eternal silence, something more,
     A bringer of new things; and vile it were
     For some three suns° to store and hoard myself,   years
30   And this gray spirit yearning in desire
     To follow knowledge like a sinking star,
     Beyond the utmost bound of human thought.

        This is my son, mine own Telemachus,
     To whom I leave the sceptre and the isle—
35   Well-loved of me, discerning to fulfill
     This labour, by slow prudence to make mild
     A rugged people, and through soft degrees
     Subdue them to the useful and the good.
     Most blameless is he, centred in the sphere
40   Of common duties, decent not to fail
     In offices of tenderness, and pay
     Meet adoration to my household gods,
     When I am gone. He works his work, I mine.

        There lies the port; the vessel puffs her sail:
45   There gloom the dark broad seas. My mariners,
     Souls that have toiled, and wrought, and thought
              with me—
     That ever with a frolic welcome took
     The thunder and the sunshine, and opposed
     Free hearts, free foreheads—you and I are old;
50   Old age hath yet his honour and his toil;
     Death closes all: but something ere the end,
     Some work of noble note, may yet be done,

Not unbecoming men that strove with Gods.
The lights begin to twinkle from the rocks:
55 The long day wanes: the slow moon climbs: the deep
Moans round with many voices. Come, my friends,
'Tis not too late to seek a newer world.
Push off, and sitting well in order smite
The sounding furrows; for my purpose holds
60 To sail beyond the sunset, and the baths
Of all the western stars, until I die.
It may be that the gulfs will wash us down:
It may be we shall touch the Happy Isles,[1]
And see the great Achilles, whom we knew.
65 Though much is taken, much abides; and though
We are not now that strength which in old days
Moved earth and heaven; that which we are, we are;
One equal temper of heroic hearts,
Made weak by time and fate, but strong in will
70 To strive, to seek, to find, and not to yield.

                                                    (1842)

The Eagle: Fragment

He clasps the crag with crookèd hands;
Close to the sun in lonely lands,
Ringed with the azure world, he stands.

The wrinkled sea beneath him crawls;
5 He watches from his mountain walls,
And like a thunderbolt he falls.

                                                    (1851)

Flower in the Crannied Wall

Flower in the crannied wall,
I pluck you out of the crannies,
I hold you here, root and all, in my hand,
Little flower—but *if* I could understand
5 What you are, root and all, and all in all,
I should know what God and man is.

                                                    (1869)

---

[1] The Isles of the Blessed, where heroes were supposed to go after their death.

Crossing the Bar

Sunset and evening star,
   And one clear call for me!
And may there be no moaning of the bar,
   When I put out to sea,

5 But such a tide as moving seems asleep,
   Too full for sound and foam,
When that which drew from out the boundless deep
   Turns again home.

Twilight and evening bell,
10   And after that the dark!
And may there be no sadness of farewell,
   When I embark;

For though from out our bourne of Time and Place
   The flood may bear me far,
15 I hope to see my Pilot face to face
   When I have crost the bar.

                              (1889)

Robert Browning

(1 8 1 2 – 1 8 8 9)

Robert Browning was born in the same year as Dickens. Most of his education was gained in his parents' large library. He published a poem in 1833 but it was not successful, and he struggled to survive as a playwright. All productions of his plays were failures, but he learned to write dialogue. When Browning was 34, his idealistic romanticism found an outlet: he met Elizabeth Barrett, a 40-year-old semi-invalid, who was a well-known poet. He helped Elizabeth to escape from her tyrannically protective father, and the couple spent 15 idyllic years in Italy before Elizabeth's death. Browning returned to England, and finally gained public recognition in the 1860s. His reputation, second only to Tennyson's, was bolstered by the publication of *The Ring and the Book,* a murder "novel" told from various refracting perspectives. The poet led a cheerful and voluble social life, which masked a more complicated, doubt-ridden inner life. He was buried in Westminster Abbey.

Browning's poetry is in many respects the precursor of modern poetry. His concern with perspective in the dramatic monologues and in *The Ring and the Book* anticipates an era that sees "truth" as increasingly subjective. Browning allowed a character in his narrative to tell the story, thereby revealing the narrative and the narrator simultaneously. The poems adopt a position far removed from that of the author or the audience, and tone becomes important in interpretation. If we base our judgment entirely on the "facts" in such poems as "My Last Duchess," we are apt to side with the Duke. The poet's "message" necessarily becomes oblique and the poem becomes an object to interpret in somewhat the same way we must interpret appearance, motive, and reality in the words of a real-life person.

Browning anticipated novelists like Henry James, Ford Madox Ford, and Joseph Conrad in their narratives about the relationships among perspective, narration, and truth. Through his technique, Browning was able to evoke the very real evil he saw in the world while admitting the possibility of a God who worked above this evil and could see through the façade of words. In his handling of the psychology of desire and virtue, revelation and deception, hatred and love, Browning was at his best. His second innovation was in style. He generally ignored the lure of the fluid, Tennysonian surface in favor of a jarring, discordant energy reminiscent of Donne, Shakespeare, and Chaucer. His style is Gothic and sometimes baroque, in keeping with Browning's restless, digressive mind. Wilde's comment that George Meredith was a prose Browning and "so is Browning" indicates the reservations many felt about Browning's style.

His canon is large. Many of the best-known dramatic monologues were published in *Dramatic Lyrics* (1842); others, such as "Fra Lippo Lippi" (1855), "Andrea del Sarto" (1855), and "Rabbi Ben Ezra" (1864) followed in later volumes. Other poems include "The Lost Leader" (1845), "How They Brought the Good News from Ghent to Aix" (1845), "Home-Thoughts, from Abroad" (1845), "Love Among the Ruins" (1855), "Childe Roland to the Dark Tower Came" (1855), *Caliban Upon Setebos* (1864), "Prospice" (1864), and *The Ring and the Book* (1868–1869).

ROBERT BROWNING

My Last Duchess

FERRAR

That's my last Duchess painted on the wall,
Looking as if she were alive. I call
That piece a wonder, now: Frà Pandolf's[1] hands
Worked busily a day, and there she stands.
5   Will't please you sit and look at her? I said
"Frà Pandolf" by design, for never read
Strangers like you that pictured countenance,
The depth and passion of its earnest glance,
But to myself they turned (since none puts by
10   The curtain I have drawn for you, but I)
And seemed as they would ask me, if they durst,
How such a glance came there; so, not the first
Are you to turn and ask thus. Sir, 'twas not
Her husband's presence only, called that spot
15   Of joy into the Duchess' cheek: perhaps
Frà Pandolf chanced to say "Her mantle laps
Over my lady's wrist too much," or "Paint
Must never hope to reproduce the faint
Half-flush that dies along her throat": such stuff
20   Was courtesy, she thought, and cause enough
For calling up that spot of joy. She had
A heart—how shall I say?—too soon made glad,
Too easily impressed; she liked whate'er
She looked on, and her looks went everywhere.
25   Sir, 'twas all one! My favour at her breast,

---

[1] Fra Pandolf and Claus of Innsbruck (line 56) are fictional persons.

The dropping of the daylight in the West,
The bough of cherries some officious fool
Broke in the orchard for her, the white mule
She rode with round the terrace—all and each
30   Would draw from her alike the approving speech,
Or blush, at least. She thanked men,—good! but thanked
Somehow—I know not how—as if she ranked
My gift of a nine-hundred-years-old name
With anybody's gift. Who'd stoop to blame
35   This sort of trifling? Even had you skill
In speech—(which I have not)—to make your will
Quite clear to such an one, and say, 'Just this
Or that in you disgusts me; here you miss,
Or there exceed the mark'—and if she let
40   Herself be lessoned so, nor plainly set
Her wits to yours, forsooth, and made excuse,
—E'en then would be some stooping; and I choose
Never to stoop. Oh sir, she smiled, no doubt,
Whene'er I passed her; but who passed without
45   Much the same smile? This grew; I gave commands;
Then all smiles stopped together. There she stands
As if alive. Will't please you rise? We'll meet
The company below, then. I repeat,
The Count your master's known munificence
50   Is ample warrant that no just pretence
Of mine for dowry will be disallowed;
Though his fair daughter's self, as I avowed
At starting, is my object. Nay, we'll go
Together down, sir. Notice Neptune, though,
55   Taming a sea-horse, thought a rarity,
Which Claus of Innsbruck cast in bronze for me!

(1842)

Soliloquy of the Spanish Cloister

I

Gr-r-r—there go, my heart's abhorrence!
    Water your damned flower-pots, do!
If hate killed men, Brother Lawrence,
    God's blood, would not mine kill you!
5   What? your myrtle-bush wants trimming?
    Oh; that rose has prior claims—

Needs its leaden vase filled brimming?
   Hell dry you up with its flames!

II

At the meal we sit together:
10   *Salve tibi!*[1] I must hear
Wise talk of the kind of weather,
   Sort of season, time of year:
Not a plenteous cork-crop: scarcely
   Dare we hope oak-galls,[2] *I doubt:*
15   *What's the Latin name for "parsley"?*
   What's the Greek name for Swine's Snout?

III

Whew! We'll have our platter burnished,
   Laid with care on our own shelf!
With a fire-new spoon we're furnished,
20   And a goblet for ourself,
Rinsed like something sacrificial
   Ere 'tis fit to touch our chaps—
Marked with L. for our initial!
   (He-he! There his lily snaps!)

IV

25 *Saint,* forsooth! While brown Dolores
   Squats outside the Convent bank
With Sanchicha, telling stories,
   Steeping tresses in the tank,
Blue-black, lustrous, thick like horsehairs,
30   —Can't I see his dead eye glow,
Bright as 'twere a Barbary corsair's?[3]
   (That is, if he'd let it show!)

V

When he finishes refection,°   dinner
   Knife and fork he never lays
35 Cross-wise, to my recollection,
   As do I, in Jesu's praise.
I the Trinity illustrate,
   Drinking watered orange-pulp—
In three sips the Arian[4] frustrate;
40   While he drains his at one gulp.

[1] Hail to thee!
[2] Abnormal growths on oak leaves.
[3] Pirate from the Barbary Coast of northern Africa.
[4] Arius (AD 256–336) was a heretic who denied the doctrine of the Trinity.

VI

Oh, those melons? If he's able
  We're to have a feast! so nice!
One goes to the Abbot's table,
  All of us get each a slice.
45 How go on your flowers? None double?
  Not one fruit-sort can you spy?
Strange!—And I, too, at such trouble,
  Keep them close-nipped on the sly!

VII

There's a great text in Galatians,[5]
50 Once you trip on it, entails
Twenty-nine distinct damnations,
  One sure, if another fails:
If I trip him just a-dying,
  Sure of heaven as sure can be,
55 Spin him round and send him flying
  Off to hell, a Manichee?[6]

VIII

Or, my scrofulous French novel
  On grey paper with blunt type!
Simply glance at it, you grovel
60 Hand and foot in Belial's[7] gripe:
If I double down its pages
  At the woeful sixteenth print,
When he gathers his greengages,
  Ope a sieve and slip it in't?

IX

65 Or, there's Satan!—one might venture
  Pledge one's soul to him, yet leave
Such a flaw in the indenture
  As he'd miss till, past retrieve,
Blasted lay that rose-acacia
70 We're so proud of! *Hy, Zy, Hine* . . .[8]
'St, there's Vespers! *Plena gratiâ*
  Ave, Virgo![9] Gr-r-r—you swine!

(1842)

---

5 See Galatians V. 14–23.
6 Another heretic, who claimed that the world was divided between the forces of good and the forces of evil.
7 I.e., the devil.
8 Perhaps a curse or incantation against Brother Lawrence.
9 Full of grace, Hail, Mary!, a reversal of the opening words of the *Hail Mary*.

The Bishop Orders His Tomb
at Saint Praxed's Church[1]

ROME, 15—

Vanity, saith the preacher, vanity!
Draw round my bed: is Anselm keeping back?
Nephews—sons mine . . . ah God, I know not! Well—
She, men would have to be your mother once,
5 Old Gandolf envied me, so fair she was!
What's done is done, and she is dead beside,
Dead long ago, and I am Bishop since,
And as she died so much we die ourselves,
And thence ye may perceive the world's a dream.
10 Life, how and what is it? As here I lie
In this state-chamber, dying by degrees,
Hours and long hours in the dead night, I ask
"Do I live, am I dead?" Peace, peace seems all.
Saint Praxed's ever was the church for peace;
15 And so, about this tomb of mine. I fought
With tooth and nail to save my niche, ye know:
—Old Gandolf cozened° me, despite my care;   tricked
Shrewd was that snatch from out the corner South
He graced his carrion with, God curse the same!
20 Yet still my niche is not so cramped but thence
One sees the pulpit o' the epistle-side,[2]
And somewhat of the choir, those silent seats,
And up into the airy dome where live
The angels, and a sunbeam's sure to lurk:
25 And I shall fill my slab of basalt there,
And 'neath my tabernacle[3] take my rest,
With those nine columns round me, two and two,
The odd one at my feet where Anselm stands:
Peach-blossom marble all, the rare, the ripe
30 As fresh-poured red wine of a mighty pulse.
—Old Gandolf with his paltry onion-stone,
Put me where I may look at him! True peach,
Rosy and flawless: how I earned the prize!
Draw close: that conflagration of my church

---

[1] Both the Bishop and Gandolf, his predecessor, are fictional persons. Saint Praxed's Church is in Rome.
[2] I.e., the right side, when facing the altar—the side from which the epistle is read.
[3] Stone canopy over a tomb.

35 —What then? So much was saved if aught were missed!
My sons, ye would not be my death? Go dig
The white-grape vineyard where the oil-press stood,
Drop water gently till the surface sink,
And if ye find . . . Ah God, I know not, I! . . .
40 Bedded in store of rotten fig-leaves soft,
And corded up in a tight olive-frail,°   olive basket
Some lump, ah God, of *lapis lazuli,*
Big as a Jew's head cut off at the nape,
Blue as a vein o'er the Madonna's breast . . .
45 Sons, all have I bequeathed you, villas, all,
That brave Frascati⁴ villa with its bath,
So, let the blue lump poise between my knees,
Like God the Father's globe on both his hands
Ye worship in the Jesu Church⁵ so gay,
50 For Gandolf shall not choose but see and burst!
Swift as a weaver's shuttle fleet our years:
Man goeth to the grave, and where is he?
Did I say basalt for my slab, sons? Black—
'Twas ever antique-black I meant! How else
55 Shall ye contrast my frieze to come beneath?
The bas-relief in bronze ye promised me,
Those Pans and Nymphs ye wot of, and perchance
Some tripod, thyrsus, with a vase or so,
The Saviour at his sermon on the mount,
60 Saint Praxed in a glory,° and one Pan   halo
Ready to twitch the Nymph's last garment off,
And Moses with the tables . . . but I know
Ye mark me not! What do they whisper thee,
Child of my bowels, Anselm? Ah, ye hope
65 To revel down my villas while I gasp
Bricked o'er with beggar's mouldy travertine°   limestone
Which Gandolf from his tomb-top chuckles at!
Nay, boys, ye love me—all of jasper, then!
'Tis jasper ye stand pledged to, lest I grieve
70 My bath must needs be left behind, alas!
One block, pure green as a pistachio-nut,
There's plenty jasper somewhere in the world—
And have I not Saint Praxed's ear to pray
Horses for ye, and brown Greek manuscripts,
75 And mistresses with great smooth marbly limbs?
—That's if ye carve my epitaph aright,

---

⁴ Frascati is an affluent resort town near Rome.
⁵ A grand baroque church in Rome.

Choice Latin, picked phrase, Tully's every word,[6]
No gaudy ware like Gandolf's second line—
Tully, my masters? Ulpian serves his need!
80 And then how I shall lie through centuries,
And hear the blessed mutter of the mass,
And see God made and eaten all day long,
And feel the steady candle-flame, and taste
Good strong thick stupefying incense-smoke!
85 For as I lie here, hours of the dead night,
Dying in state and by such slow degrees,
I fold my arms as if they clasped a crook,[7]
And stretch my feet forth straight as stone can point,
And let the bedclothes, for a mortcloth,[8] drop
90 Into great laps and folds of sculptor's-work:
And as yon tapers dwindle, and strange thoughts
Grow, with a certain humming in my ears,
About the life before I lived this life,
And this life too, popes, cardinals and priests,
95 Saint Praxed at his sermon on the mount,
Your tall pale mother with her talking eyes,
And new-found agate urns as fresh as day,
And marble's language, Latin pure, discreet,
—Aha, ELUCESCEBAT[9] quoth our friend?
100 No Tully, said I, Ulpian at the best!
Evil and brief hath been my pilgrimage.
All *lapis,* all, sons! Else I give the Pope
My villas! Will ye ever eat my heart?
Ever your eyes were as a lizard's quick,
105 They glitter like your mother's for my soul,
Or ye would heighten my impoverished frieze,
Piece out its starved design, and fill my vase
With grapes, and add a vizor and a Term,[10]
And to the tripod ye would tie a lynx
110 That in his struggle throws the thyrsus down,
To comfort me on my entablature
Whereon I am to lie till I must ask
"Do I live, am I dead?" There, leave me, there!
For ye have stabbed me with ingratitude
115 To death—ye wish it—God, ye wish it! Stone—

---

[6] Tully is another name for Cicero; Ulpian's writing is not considered as well crafted as Tully's.
[7] The bishop's staff.
[8] The cloth that drapes over the coffin.
[9] A word from Gandolf's epitaph that means "he shone forth"; the bishop thinks that this form is inferior to the one Cicero would have used: *elucebat.*
[10] *Vizor* is a mask, *Term* is a bust: both are traditional parts of church sculptures.

Gritstone, a-crumble! Clammy squares which sweat
As if the corpse they keep were oozing through—
And no more *lapis* to delight the world!
Well go! I bless ye. Fewer tapers there,
120 But in a row: and, going, turn your backs
—Ay, like departing altar-ministrants,
And leave me in my church, the church for peace,
That I may watch at leisure if he leers—
Old Gandolf, at me, from his onion-stone,
125 As still he envied me, so fair she was!

(1845)

Walt Whitman

(1 8 1 9 – 1 8 9 2)

Walt Whitman was the most important American poet of the nineteenth century and a central influence on the direction of modern poetry. The son of a politically radical Long Island farmer and carpenter, Whitman grew up in Brooklyn. He left school at the age of 12 and worked his way from office boy to editor at a New York newspaper. In 1848 a political disagreement with his publisher led him to leave the Brooklyn *Eagle* and to travel to New Orleans. Despite his pose as an unlettered, untutored "natural" poet, Whitman had read the classics of Western culture—the Bible, Shakespeare, Homer, Aeschylus, Sophocles, Dante—as well as contemporaries such as Carlyle and Emerson. In 1851 he abandoned journalism to work as a carpenter and to write poetry. In 1855 *Leaves of Grass* was published anonymously; it attracted little public notice, but garnered the support of Emerson and Thoreau. During the Civil War, Whitman worked with the wounded in camp hospitals. He lived his final decades in increasingly poor health but with growing fame as he produced larger and larger versions of his one great book.

The poems of *Leaves of Grass* were revolutionary, and the public was suitably shocked. In poetics and philosophy, Whitman was an original. He wrote extremely long lines that flowed with a pulsing energy in no regular meter. His diction was frank, sensuous, and sibilant. He wrote about a deified democracy, which has made him something like the national bard of a nation strongly tied to a vision of itself as the genuine cradle and guardian of the democratic impulse. He expressed an ecstatic vision of the fullness of physical and emotional existence, and saw each individual as symbolically unifying all of the organic world, absorbing and containing all experience. *Leaves of Grass* belongs to a group of poems called "Subjective epics"— libidinous, exultant poetry lying halfway between Wordsworth's *Prelude* and Blake's apocalyptic prophecies. Whitman's free-form verse and his desire for a community that would not restrict individuality influenced such modern poets as Allen Ginsberg, John Berryman, Ezra Pound, Stephen Crane, and William Carlos Williams. The great Chilean poet Pablo Neruda saw Whitman as the founder of a New World poetic: "We continue to live in a Whitmanesque age seeing how new men and new societies rise and grow, despite their birth pangs." Some of Whitman's poetry is marred by a diffuseness and randomness, but at its finest it is sheer energy strung on a taut line of song.

Leaves of Grass (1855) had its second edition in 1856 and its third in 1860, when 124 poems were added. The 1865 edition included the famous Civil War poem "Drum Taps," and the 1871 version "Sequel to Drum Taps."

New editions appeared until Whitman's death. Critics generally consider "Song of Myself," "Out of the Cradle Endlessly Rocking," and "When Lilacs Last in the Dooryard Bloom'd," an elegy for Lincoln, the most important sections of the work.

WALT WHITMAN

from *Song of Myself*

1

I celebrate myself, and sing myself,
And what I assume you shall assume,
For every atom belonging to me as good belongs to you.

I loafe and invite my soul,
5 I lean and loafe at my ease observing a spear of summer grass.

My tongue, every atom of my blood, form'd from this soil, this air,
Born here of parents born here from parents the same, and their
    parents the same,
I, now thirty-seven years old in perfect health begin,
Hoping to cease not till death.

10 Creeds and schools in abeyance,
Retiring back a while sufficed at what they are, but never forgotten,
I harbor for good or bad, I permit to speak at every hazard,
Nature without check with original energy.

2

Houses and rooms are full of perfumes, the shelves are crowded
    with perfumes,
15 I breathe the fragrance myself and know it and like it,
The distillation would intoxicate me also, but I shall not let it.

The atmosphere is not a perfume, it has no taste of the distillation,
    it is odorless,
It is for my mouth forever, I am in love with it,
I will go to the bank by the wood and become undisguised and
    naked,
20 I am mad for it to be in contact with me.

The smoke of my own breath,
Echoes, ripples, buzz'd whispers, love-root, silk-thread, crotch and
    vine,
My respiration and inspiration, the beating of my heart, the passing
    of blood and air through my lungs,
The sniff of green leaves and dry leaves, and of the shore and
    dark-color'd sea-rocks, and of hay in the barn,
25 The sound of the belch'd words of my voice loos'd to the eddies of
    the wind,
A few light kisses, a few embraces, a reaching around of arms,
The play of shine and shade on the trees as the supple boughs wag,
The delight alone or in the rush of the streets, or along the fields
    and hill-sides,
The feeling of health, the full-noon trill, the song of me rising from
    bed and meeting the sun.

30 Have you reckon'd a thousand acres much? have you reckon'd the
    earth much?
Have you practis'd so long to learn to read?
Have you felt so proud to get at the meaning of poems?

Stop this day and night with me and you shall possess the origin of
    all poems,
You shall possess the good of the earth and sun, (there are millions
    of suns left,)
35 You shall no longer take things at second or third hand, nor look
    through the eyes of the dead, nor feed on the spectres in
    books,
You shall not look through my eyes either, nor take things from
    me,
You shall listen to all sides and filter them from your self.

3

I have heard what the talkers were talking, the talk of the beginning
    and the end,
But I do not talk of the beginning or the end.

40 There was never any more inception than there is now,
Nor any more youth or age than there is now,
And will never be any more perfection than there is now,
Nor any more heaven or hell than there is now.

Urge and urge and urge,
45 Always the procreant urge of the world.

Out of the dimness opposite equals advance, always substance and
  increase, always sex,
Always a knit of identity, always distinction, always a breed of life.

To elaborate is no avail, learn'd and unlearn'd feel that it is so.

Sure as the most certain sure, plumb in the uprights, well entretied,
  braced in the beams,
50 Stout as a horse, affectionate, haughty, electrical,
I and this mystery here we stand.

Clear and sweet is my soul, and clear and sweet is all that is not my
  soul.

Lack one lacks both, and the unseen is proved by the seen,
Till that becomes unseen and receives proof in its turn.

55 Showing the best and dividing it from the worst age vexes age,
Knowing the perfect fitness and equanimity of things, while they
  discuss I am silent, and go bathe and admire myself.

Welcome is every organ and attribute of me, and of any man hearty
  and clean,
Not an inch nor a particle of an inch is vile, and none shall be less
  familiar than the rest.

I am satisfied—I see, dance, laugh, sing;
60 As the hugging and loving bed-fellow sleeps at my side through the
  night, and withdraws at the peep of the day with stealthy
  tread,
Leaving me baskets cover'd with white towels swelling the house
  with their plenty,
Shall I postpone my acceptation and realization and scream at my
  eyes,
That they turn from gazing after and down the road,
And forthwith cipher and show me to a cent,
65 Exactly the value of one and exactly the value of two, and which is
  ahead?

4

Trippers and askers surround me,
People I meet, the effect upon me of my early life or the ward and
  city I live in, or the nation,
The latest dates, discoveries, inventions, societies, authors old and
  new,
My dinner, dress, associates, looks, compliments, dues,

70 The real or fancied indifference of some man or woman I love,
The sickness of one of my folks or of myself, or ill-doing or loss
        or lack of money, or depressions or exaltations,
Battles, the horrors of fratricidal war, the fever of doubtful news,
        the fitful events;
These come to me days and nights and go from me again,
But they are not the Me myself.

75 Apart from the pulling and hauling stands what I am,
Stands amused, complacement, compassionating, idle, unitary,
Looks down, is erect, or bends an arm on an impalpable certain
        rest,
Looking with side-curved head curious what will come next,
Both in and out of the game and watching and wondering at it.

80 Backward I see in my own days where I sweated through fog with
        linguists and contenders,
I have no mockings or arguments, I witness and wait.

(1855)

Out of the Cradle Endlessly Rocking

Out of the cradle endlessly rocking,
Out of the mocking-bird's throat, the musical shuttle,
Out of the Ninth-month midnight,
Over the sterile sands and the fields beyond, where the child
        leaving his bed wander'd alone, bareheaded, barefoot,
5 Down from the shower'd halo,
Up from the mystic play of shadows twining and twisting as if they
        were alive,
Out from the patches of briers and blackberries,
From the memories of the bird that chanted to me,
From your memories sad brother, from the fitful risings and fallings
        I heard,
10 From under that yellow half-moon late-risen and swollen as if with
        tears,
From those beginning notes of yearning and love there in the mist,
From the thousand responses of my heart never to cease,
From the myriad thence-arous'd words,
From the word stronger and more delicious than any,
15 From such as now they start the scene revisiting,
As a flock, twittering, rising, or overhead passing,
Borne hither, ere all eludes me, hurriedly,

A man, yet by these tears a little boy again,
Throwing myself on the sand, confronting the waves,
20   I, chanter of pains and joys, uniter of here and hereafter,
Taking all hints to use them, but swiftly leaping beyond them,
A reminiscence sing.

Once Paumanok,[1]
When the lilac-scent was in the air and Fifth-month grass was
        growing,
25   Up this seashore in some briers,
Two feather'd guests from Alabama, two together,
And their nest, and four light-green eggs spotted with brown,
And every day the he-bird to and fro near at hand,
And every day the she-bird crouch'd on her nest, silent, with bright
        eyes,
30   And every day I, a curious boy, never too close, never disturbing
        them,
Cautiously peering, absorbing, translating.

Shine! shine! shine!
Pour down your warmth, great sun!
While we bask, we two together.
35   *Two together!*
Winds blow south, or winds blow north,
Day come white, or night come black,
Home, or rivers and mountains from home,
Singing all time, minding no time,
40   *While we two keep together.*

Till of a sudden,
May-be kill'd, unknown to her mate,
One forenoon the she-bird crouch'd not on the nest,
Nor return'd that afternoon, nor the next,
45   Nor ever appear'd again.

And thenceforward all summer in the sound of the sea,
And at night under the full of the moon in calmer weather,
Over the hoarse surging of the sea,
Or flitting from brier to brier by day,
50   I saw, I heard at intervals the remaining one, the he-bird,
The solitary guest from Alabama.

Blow! blow! blow!
Blow up sea-winds along Paumanok's shore;
I wait and I wait till you blow my mate to me.

[1] The Indian name for Long Island.

55 Yes, when the stars glisten'd,
All night long on the prong of a moss-scallop'd stake,
Down almost amid the slapping waves,
Sat the lone singer wonderful causing tears.

He call'd on his mate,
60 He pour'd forth the meanings which I of all men know.

Yes my brother I know,
The rest might not, but I have treasur'd every note,
For more than once dimly down to the beach gliding,
Silent, avoiding the moonbeams, blending myself with the
        shadows,
65 Recalling now the obscure shapes, the echoes, the sounds and
        sights after their sorts,
The white arms out in the breakers tirelessly tossing,
I, with bare feet, a child, the wind wafting my hair,
Listen'd long and long.

Listen'd to keep, to sing, now translating the notes,
70 Following you my brother.

Soothe! soothe! soothe!
Close on its wave soothes the wave behind,
And again another behind embracing and lapping, every one close,
But my love soothes not me, not me.

75 *Low hangs the moon, it rose late,*
It is lagging—O I think it is heavy with love, with love.

O madly the sea pushes upon the land,
With love, with love.

O night! do I not see my love fluttering out among the breakers?
80 *What is that little black thing I see there in the white?*

Loud! loud! loud!
Loud I call to you, my love!
High and clear I shoot my voice over the waves,
Surely you must know who is here, is here,
85 *You must know who I am, my love.*

Low-hanging moon!
What is that dusky spot in your brown yellow?
O it is the shape, the shape of my mate!
O moon do not keep her from me any longer.

90   *Land! land! O land!*
Whichever way I turn, O I think you could give me my mate back again if
      you only would,
For I am almost sure I see her dimly whichever way I look.

O rising stars!
Perhaps the one I want so much will rise, will rise with some of you.

95   *O throat! O trembling throat!*
Sound clearer through the atmosphere!
Pierce the woods, the earth,
Somewhere listening to catch you must be the one I want.

Shake out carols!
100 *Solitary here, the night's carols!*
Carols of lonesome love! death's carols!
Carols under that lagging, yellow, waning moon!
O under that moon where she droops almost down into the sea!
O reckless despairing carols.

105 *But soft! sink low!*
Soft! let me just murmur,
And do you wait a moment you husky-nois'd sea,
For somewhere I believe I heard my mate responding to me,
So faint, I must be still, be still to listen,
110 *But not altogether still, for then she might not come immediately to me.*

Hither my love!
Here I am! here!
With this just-sustain'd note I announce myself to you,
This gentle call is for you my love, for you.

115 *Do not be decoy'd elsewhere,*
That is the whistle of the wind, it is not my voice,
That is the fluttering, the fluttering of the spray,
Those are the shadows of leaves.

O darkness! O in vain!
120 *O I am very sick and sorrowful.*

O brown halo in the sky near the moon, drooping upon the sea!
O troubled reflection in the sea!
O throat! O throbbing heart!
And I singing uselessly, uselessly all the night.

125 *O past! O happy life! O songs of joy!*
In the air, in the woods, over fields,

Loved! loved! loved! loved! loved!
But my mate no more, no more with me!
We two together no more.

130 The aria sinking,
      All else continuing, the stars shining,
      The winds blowing, the notes of the bird continuous echoing,
      With angry moans the fierce old mother incessantly moaning,
      On the sands of Paumanok's shore gray and rustling,
135 The yellow half-moon enlarged, sagging down, drooping, the face
         of the sea almost touching,
      The boy ecstatic, with his bare feet the waves, with his hair the
         atmosphere dallying,
      The love in the heart long pent, now loose, now at last
         tumultuously bursting,
      The aria's meaning, the ears, the soul, swiftly depositing,
      The strange tears down the cheeks coursing,
140 The colloquy there, the trio, each uttering,
      The undertone, the savage old mother incessantly crying,
      To the boy's soul's questions sullenly timing, some drown'd secret
         hissing,
      To the outsetting bard.

      Demon or bird! (said the boy's soul,)
145 Is it indeed toward your mate you sing? or is it really to me?
      For I, that was a child, my tongue's use sleeping, now I have heard
         you,
      Now in a moment I know what I am for, I awake,
      And already a thousand singers, a thousand songs, clearer, louder
         and more sorrowful than yours,
      A thousand warbling echoes have started to life within me, never to
         die.

150 O you singer solitary, singing by yourself, projecting me,
      O solitary me listening, never more shall I cease perpetuating you,
      Never more shall I escape, never more the reverberations,
      Never more the cries of unsatisfied love be absent from me,
      Never again leave me to be the peaceful child I was before what
         there in the night,
155 By the sea under the yellow and sagging moon,
      The messenger there arous'd, the fire, the sweet hell within,
      The unknown want, the destiny of me.
      O give me the clew! (it lurks in the night here somewhere,)
      O if I am to have so much, let me have more!

160 A word then, (for I will conquer it,)
      The word final, superior to all,

Subtle, sent up—what is it?—I listen;
Are you whispering it, and have been all the time, you sea-waves?
Is that it from your liquid rims and wet sands?

165   Whereto answering, the sea,
Delaying not, hurrying not,
Whisper'd me through the night, and very plainly before daybreak,
Lisp'd to me the low and delicious word death,
And again death, death, death, death,
170   Hissing melodious, neither like the bird nor like my arous'd child's
heart,
But edging near as privately for me rustling at my feet,
Creeping thence steadily up to my ears and laving me softly all
over,
Death, death, death, death, death.

Which I do not forget,
175   But fuse the song of my dusky demon and brother,
That he sang to me in the moonlight on Paumanok's gray beach,
With the thousand responsive songs at random,
My own songs awaked from that hour,
And with them the key, the word up from the waves,
180   The word of the sweetest song and all songs,
That strong and delicious word which, creeping to my feet,
(Or like some old crone rocking the cradle, swathed in sweet
garments, bending aside,)
The sea whisper'd me.

(1859)

The Dalliance of the Eagles

Skirting the river road, (my forenoon walk, my rest,)
Skyward in air a sudden muffled sound, the dalliance of the eagles,
The rushing amorous contact high in space together,
The clinching interlocking claws, a living, fierce, gyrating wheel,
5   Four beating wings, two beaks, a swirling mass tight grappling,
In tumbling turning clustering loops, straight downward falling,
Till o'er the river pois'd, the twain yet one, a moment's lull,
A motionless still balance in the air, then parting, talons loosing,
Upward again on slow-firm pinions slanting, their separate diverse
flight,
10   She hers, he his, pursuing.

(1880)

Matthew Arnold

(1 8 2 2 - 1 8 8 8)

Matthew Arnold, a critic of culture and literature in the Victorian period, was the son of a headmaster at Rugby whose views on religion, education, and society had wide influence. While visiting Switzerland, Arnold fell in love with a Swiss girl and wrote the "Marguerite" poems, but in 1851 he married an English woman, Frances Wightman. He left Oxford and briefly held a post as secretary to Lord Landsdowne, then became an inspector of schools, a job he kept for 35 years. By the time he was 40, Arnold turned from poetry to essays in literary and social criticism and writings on education and religion. He was appointed Professor of Poetry at Oxford, and toured America as a lecturer.

Arnold's reputation rests on his prose as well as on his verse. Only some of the poetry has lasting merit; for example, "Dover Beach," a powerful lyric that seems to prophesy the great cataclysms of the next century. Arnold felt he had less poetic talent than Tennyson and less intellectual vigor than Browning, but he hoped that his balance would win his poetry a lasting audience. Much of the poetry is weakened by forced imagery and Arnold's poor ear; he is at his best when describing nature or his feelings of isolation from God and men.

His prose is probably more important than his poetry. He believed that religion was important, but he failed to find personal faith. This feeling was shared by many. His *Essays in Criticism* state that the study of literature should never be narrowly aesthetic; criticism should connect with human society. His most important work on culture, *Culture and Anarchy,* defines the civilized mind as "sweetness and light" and rails against the dull, narrow world of the Puritan impulse, which Arnold thought was rampant in the English middle class. He distinguished between Hellenic (aesthetic, intellectual) and Hebraic (moral, ordered, energetic) impulses and stressed the balancing role of each in a healthy civilization.

Arnold's poems were published in five small volumes. The best-known poems are a sonnet to Shakespeare (1844), "The Forsaken Merman" (1849), "Isolation. To Marguerite" (1857), "To Marguerite—Continued" (ca. 1849), "The Buried Life" (1852), *The Scholar Gypsy* (1853), "Dover Beach" (ca. 1851), "Stanzas from the Grande Chartreuse" (ca. 1852), his elegy "Thyrsis," about Arthur Clough (1866), and *Empedocles on Etna* (1852). The prose works include *Essays in Criticism* (1865, 1888), *Culture and Anarchy* (1869), and *Literature and Dogma* (1873).

MATTHEW ARNOLD

Dover Beach

The sea is calm to-night.
The tide is full, the moon lies fair
Upon the straits; on the French coast the light
Gleams and is gone; the cliffs of England stand,
5   Glimmering and vast, out in the tranquil bay.
Come to the window, sweet is the night-air!
Only, from the long line of spray
Where the sea meets the moon-blanched land,
Listen! you hear the grating roar
10   Of pebbles which the waves draw back, and fling,
At their return, up the high strand,
Begin, and cease, and then again begin,
With tremulous cadence slow, and bring
The eternal note of sadness in.

15   Sophocles long ago
Heard it on the Ægæan, and it brought
Into his mind the turbid ebb and flow
Of human misery; we
Find also in the sound a thought,
20   Hearing it by this distant northern sea.

The Sea of Faith
Was once, too, at the full, and round earth's shore
Lay like the folds of a bright girdle furled.
But now I only hear
25   Its melancholy, long, withdrawing roar,
Retreating, to the breath
Of the night-wind, down the vast edges drear
And naked shingles° of the world.   pebble-covered beaches

Ah, love, let us be true
30   To one another! for the world, which seems
To lie before us like a land of dreams,
So various, so beautiful, so new,
Hath really neither joy, nor love, nor light,
Nor certitude, nor peace, nor help for pain;

35 And we are here as on a darkling plain
   Swept with confused alarms of struggle and flight,
   Where ignorant armies clash by night.

(1867)

Lines Written in Kensington Gardens

In this lone, open glade I lie,
Screened by deep boughs on either hand;
And at its end, to stay the eye,
Those black-crowned, red-boled pine-trees stand!

5 Birds here make song, each bird has his,
  Across the girdling city's hum.
  How green under the boughs it is!
  How thick the tremulous sheep-cries come!

Sometimes a child will cross the glade
10 To take his nurse his broken toy;
   Sometimes a thrush flit overhead
   Deep in her unknown day's employ.

Here at my feet what wonders pass,
What endless, active life is here!
15 What blowing daisies, fragrant grass!
   An air-stirred forest, fresh and clear.

Scarce fresher is the mountain-sod
Where the tired angler lies, stretched out,
And, eased of basket and of rod,
20 Counts his day's spoil, the spotted trout.

In the huge world, which roars hard by,
Be others happy if they can!
But in my helpless cradle I
Was breathed on by the rural Pan.

25 I, on men's impious uproar hurled,
   Think often, as I hear them rave,
   That peace has left the upper world
   And now keeps only in the grave.

Yet here is peace for ever new!
30 When I who watch them am away,
Still all things in this glade go through
The changes of their quiet day.

Then to their happy rest they pass!
The flowers upclose, the birds are fed,
35 The night comes down upon the grass,
The child sleeps warmly in his bed.

Calm soul of all things! make it mine
To feel, amid the city's jar,
That there abides a peace of thine,
40 Man did not make, and cannot mar.

The will to neither strive nor cry,
The power to feel with others give!
Calm, calm me more! nor let me die
Before I have begun to live.

(1852)

The Last Word

Creep into thy narrow bed,
Creep, and let no more be said!
Vain thy onset! all stands fast.
Thou thyself must break at last.

5 Let the long contention cease!
Geese are swans, and swans are geese.
Let them have it how they will!
Thou art tired; best be still.

They out-talked thee, hissed thee, tore thee?
10 Better men fared thus before thee;
Fired their ringing shot and passed,
Hotly charged—and sank at last.

Charge once more, then, and be dumb!
Let the victors, when they come,
15 When the forts of folly fall,
Find thy body by the wall!

(1867)

Dante Gabriel Rossetti

(1 8 2 8 – 1 8 8 2)

The son of an Italian expatriate who loved above all Dante and the opera, Rossetti attended King's College, then studied painting. He was influenced by Dante, Keats, Browning, Blake, and Poe. In 1848 he and a circle of friends formed the pre-Raphaelite Brotherhood, a group devoted to reviving the simple outlines and pure color tones of Renaissance painting. In the 1850s, Rossetti produced his finest paintings and gained a substantial reputation. He influenced the aesthetics of Morris and Swinburne. His wife, Elizabeth Siddal, committed suicide in 1862, after two years of marriage. Rossetti's *Poems* appeared in 1870. Many of the verses functioned as commentaries on his paintings. In the final decade of his life, Rossetti, whose powerful personality had dominated his contemporaries, retreated into melancholy isolation, his health broken by drug addiction.

Rossetti's view of art veered toward the purely aesthetic. He insisted that art must be concerned only with the beautiful, that it had no "useful" or didactic function. Rossetti's painting soon departed from the relatively simple style of the other pre-Raphaelites as he began to paint ornate, elaborate compositions that often approached the Gothic. His poetry also contains Gothic elements. Religion and literature were sources for Rossetti's paintings and poetry. Some of his writing conveys a feeling of belonging to a self-enclosed universe, with little contact with the "mundane" world. Rossetti's best poetry describes a world of silent waters and shadowy passions evoked in precious metaphors and a carefully controlled, often intentionally artificial meter. He made many technical innovations: He rhymed unaccented syllables and utilized half-rhymes. Rossetti's tendency toward abstract, sentimental "romanticism" was rejected by the modernists of the next generation.

Poems (1870) was followed by *Ballads and Sonnets* (1881). Rossetti also published many fine translations from Italian, French, and German poets.

DANTE GABRIEL ROSSETTI

The Blessed Damozel

The blessed damozel leaned out
  From the gold bar of Heaven;
Her eyes were deeper than the depth
  Of waters stilled at even;
5 She had three lillies in her hand,
  And the stars in her hair were seven.

Her robe, ungirt from clasp to hem,
  No wrought flowers did adorn,
But a white rose of Mary's gift,
10   For service meetly worn;
Her hair that lay along her back
  Was yellow like ripe corn.

Herseemed[1] she scarce had been a day
  One of God's choristers;
15 The wonder was not yet quite gone
  From that still look of hers;
Albeit, to them she left, her day
  Had counted as ten years.

(To one, it is ten years of years.
20   ... Yet now, and in this place,
Surely she leaned o'er me—her hair
  Fell all about my face. ...
Nothing: the autumn-fall of leaves.
  The whole year sets apace.)

25 It was the rampart of God's house
  That she was standing on;
By God built over the sheer depth
  The which is Space begun;
So high, that looking downward thence
30   She scarce could see the sun.

It lies in Heaven, across the flood
  Of ether, as a bridge.

---

[1] It seemed to her.

Beneath, the tides of day and night
   With flame and darkness ridge
35 The void, as low as where this earth
   Spins like a fretful midge.

Around her, lovers, newly met
   'Mid deathless love's acclaims,
Spoke evermore among themselves
40   Their heart-remembered names;
And the souls mounting up to God
   Went by her like thin flames.

And still she bowed herself and stooped
   Out of the circling charm;
45 Until her bosom must have made
   The bar she leaned on warm,
And the lilies lay as if asleep
   Along her bended arm.

From the fixed place of Heaven she saw
50   Time like a pulse shake fierce
Through all the worlds. Her gaze still strove
   Within the gulf to pierce
Its path; and now she spoke as when
   The stars sang in their spheres

55 The sun was gone now; the curled moon
   Was like a little feather
Fluttering far down the gulf; and now
   She spoke through the still weather,
Her voice was like the voice the stars
60   Had when they sang together.

(Ah sweet! Even now, in that bird's song,
   Strove not her accents there,
Fain to be hearkened? When those bells
   Possessed the mid-day air,
65 Strove not her steps to reach my side
   Down all the echoing stair?)

"I wish that he were come to me,
   For he will come," she said.
"Have I not prayed in Heaven?—on earth,
70   Lord, Lord, has he not pray'd?
Are not two prayers a perfect strength?
   And shall I feel afraid?

"When round his head the aureole clings,
    And he is clothed in white,
75 I'll take his hand and go with him
    To the deep wells of light;
As unto a stream we will step down,
    And bathe there in God's sight.

"We two will stand beside that shrine,
80   Occult, withheld, untrod,
Whose lamps are stirred continually
    With prayer sent up to God;
And see our old prayers, granted, melt
    Each like a little cloud.

85 "We two will lie i' the shadow of
    That living mystic tree
Within whose secret growth the Dove
    Is sometimes felt to be,
While every leaf that His plumes touch
90   Saith His Name audibly.

"And I myself will teach to him,
    I myself, lying so,
The songs I sing here; which his voice
    Shall pause in, hushed and slow,
95 And find some knowledge at each pause,
    Or some new thing to know."

(Alas! we two, we two, thou say'st!
    Yea, one wast thou with me
That once of old. But shall God lift
100   To endless unity
The soul whose likeness with thy soul
    Was but its love for thee?)

"We two," she said, "will seek the groves
    Where the lady Mary is,
105 With her five handmaidens, whose names
    Are five sweet symphonies,
Cecily, Gertrude, Magdalen,
    Margaret and Rosalys.

"Circlewise sit they, with bound locks
110   And foreheads garlanded;
Into the fine cloth white like flame
    Weaving the golden thread,

To fashion the birth-robes for them
  Who are just born, being dead.

115 "He shall fear, haply, and be dumb:
  Then will I lay my cheek
To his, and tell about our love,
  Not once abashed or weak:
And the dear Mother will approve
120   My pride, and let me speak.

"Herself shall bring us, hand in hand,
  To Him round whom all souls
Kneel, the clear-ranged unnumbered heads
  Bowed with their aureoles:
125 And angels meeting us shall sing
  To their citherns and citoles.

"There will I ask of Christ the Lord
  Thus much for him and me:—
Only to live as once on earth
130   With Love,—only to be,
As then awhile, for ever now
  Together, I and he."

She gazed and listened and then said,
  Less sad of speech than mild,—
135 "All this is when he comes." She ceased.
  The light thrilled towards her, fill'd
With angels in strong level flight.
  Her eyes prayed, and she smil'd.

(I saw her smile.) But soon their path
140   Was vague in distant spheres:
And then she cast her arms along
  The golden barriers,
And laid her face between her hands,
  And wept. (I heard her tears.)

                              (1850)

The Woodspurge

The wind flapped loose, the wind was still,
Shaken out dead from tree and hill:

I had walked on at the wind's will,—
I sat now, for the wind was still.

5   Between my knees my forehead was,—
My lips, drawn in, said not Alas!
My hair was over in the grass,
My naked ears heard the day pass.

My eyes, wide open, had the run
10   Of some ten weeds to fix upon;
Among those few, out of the sun,
The woodspurge flowered, three cups in one.

From perfect grief there need not be
Wisdom or even memory:
15   One thing then learnt remains to me,—
The woodspurge has a cup of three.

(1870)

Sudden Light

I have been here before,
But when or how I cannot tell:
I know the grass beyond the door,
The sweet keen smell,
5   The sighing sound, the lights around the shore.

You have been mine before,—
How long ago I may not know:
But just when at that swallow's soar
Your neck turned so,
10   Some veil did fall,—I knew it all of yore.

Has this been thus before?
And shall not thus time's eddying flight
Still with our lives our love restore
In death's despite,
15   And day and night yield one delight once more?

(1870)

Emily Dickinson

(1 8 3 0 – 1 8 8 6)

Emily Dickinson was born in Amherst, Massachusetts, and led a seemingly uneventful life; she died in the house in which she was born. The daughter of a Calvinist lawyer and congressman, her natural inclination toward reticence was strengthened by a Puritan upbringing. She graduated from Amherst Academy, then entered Mount Holyoke Female Seminary, but homesickness drove her back to Amherst in a year. She never married and it seems she had no lovers; instead, she was infatuated first with one of her father's law apprentices, then with Reverend Charles Wadsworth. Her emotional turmoils led to some of her finest poems. She became increasingly reclusive in the 1860s, and spent her time writing unpublished lyrics. Only 8 of her almost 1800 poems were published in her lifetime. It was not until after World War I that her genius was acknowledged.

Dickinson read the literature and philosophy of her time, but her inspiration came from the rhythms and themes of the King James Bible and Protestant hymns. Her poems, which are written in a remarkably intense, idiosyncratic style, dwell on the revealed wonders of ordinary nature and common village happenings. Dickinson transfuses these subjects into a dialogue on the relationship between man and God. She was obsessed with the rich profusion of life and the terrifying, half-alluring shadow of death. Her poetry is condensed, yet alive and even sprightly, with a charged diction and cadence, and with imagery startling in its originality. Her tight quatrains draw a focusing circle that is capable of containing central philosophical ideas and grand metaphors. The poems are by no means Puritan: They are full of a sensuous enthusiasm for life and are often addressed to a God she finds by turns ridiculous, awesome, and gently paternal. Although some poems falter, the poetry is on the whole some of the most remarkable of the later nineteenth century.

Two of Dickinson's friends, Mabel Loomis Todd and Thomas Higginson, produced a considerably edited volume of her poems in 1890. The volume was popular for a time. More poems were printed in 1891 and 1896, and an edition of her letters appeared in 1894. For 30 years her reputation languished, but a 1924 biography and *Complete Poems* (a misnomer) established her as a major writer. In 1929, 176 unpublished poems were "found." Finally, in 1955, Thomas Johnson published an edition that did much to restore the original texts and order of the poems.

EMILY DICKINSON

67

Success is counted sweetest
By those who ne'er succeed.
To comprehend a nectar
Requires sorest need.

5   Not one of all the purple Host
Who took the Flag today
Can tell the definition
So clear of Victory

As he defeated—dying—
10   On whose forbidden ear
The distant strains of triumph
Burst agonized and clear!

(1878)

214

I taste a liquor never brewed—
From Tankards scooped in Pearl—
Not all the Vats upon the Rhine
Yield such an Alcohol!

5   Inebriate of Air—am I—
And Debauchee of Dew—
Reeling—thro endless summer days—
From inns of Molten Blue—

When "Landlords" turn the drunken Bee
10   Out of the Foxglove's door—
When Butterflies—renounce their "drams"—
I shall but drink the more!

Till Seraphs swing their snowy Hats—
And Saints—to windows run—
15   To see the little Tippler
Leaning against the—Sun—

(1861)

258

There's a certain Slant of light,
Winter Afternoons—
That oppresses, like the Heft
Of Cathedral Tunes—

5 Heavenly Hurt, it gives us—
We can find no scar,
But internal difference,
Where the Meanings, are—

None may teach it—Any—
10 'Tis the Seal Despair—
An imperial affliction
Sent us of the Air—

When it comes, the Landscape listens—
Shadows—hold their breath—
15 When it goes, 'tis like the Distance
On the look of Death—

(1890)

328

A Bird came down the Walk—
He did not know I saw—
He bit an Angleworm in halves
And ate the fellow, raw,

5 And then he drank a Dew
From a convenient Grass—
And then hopped sidewise to the Wall
To let a Beetle pass—

He glanced with rapid eyes
10 That hurried all around—
They looked like frightened Beads, I thought—
He stirred his Velvet Head

Like one in danger, Cautious,
I offered him a Crumb
15 And he unrolled his feathers
And rowed him softer home—

Than Oars divide the Ocean,
Too silver for a seam—

Or Butterflies, off Banks of Noon
20 Leap, plashless as they swim.

(1891)

435
Much Madness is divinest Sense—
To a discerning Eye—
Much Sense—the starkest Madness—
'Tis the Majority
5 In this, as All, prevail—
Assent—and you are sane—
Demur—you're straightway dangerous—
And handled with a Chain—

(1890)

465
I heard a Fly buzz—when I died—
The Stillness in the Room
Was like the Stillness in the Air—
Between the Heaves of Storm—

5 The Eyes around—had wrung them dry—
And Breaths were gathering firm
For that last Onset—when the King
Be witnessed—in the Room—

I willed my Keepsakes—Signed away
10 What portion of me be
Assignable—and then it was
There interposed a Fly—

With Blue—uncertain stumbling Buzz—
Between the light—and me—
15 And then the Windows failed—and then
I could not see to see—

(1896)

712
Because I could not stop for Death—
He kindly stopped for me—
The Carriage held but just Ourselves—
And Immortality.

5 We slowly drove—He knew no haste
And I had put away

My labor and my leisure too,
For His Civility—

We passed the School, where Children strove
10   At Recess—in the Ring—
We passed the Fields of Gazing Grain—
We passed the Setting Sun—

Or rather—He passed Us—
The Dews drew quivering and chill—
15   For only Gossamer, my Gown—
My Tippet°—only Tulle—°   scarf / silk

We paused before a House that seemed
A Swelling of the Ground—
The Roof was scarcely visible—
20   The Cornice—in the Ground—

Since then—'tis Centuries—and yet
Feels shorter than the Day
I first surmised the Horses' Heads
Were toward Eternity—

                                (1890)

986

A narrow Fellow in the Grass
Occasionally rides—
You may have met Him—did you not
His notice sudden is—

5   The Grass divides as with a Comb—
A spotted shaft is seen—
And then it closes at your feet
And opens further on—

He likes a Boggy Acre
10   A Floor too cool for Corn—
Yet when a Boy, and Barefoot—
I more than once at Noon
Have passed, I thought, a Whip lash
Unbraiding in the Sun
15   When stooping to secure it
It wrinkled, and was gone—

Several of Nature's People
I know, and they know me—
I feel for them a transport
20   Of cordiality—

But never met this Fellow
Attended, or alone
Without a tighter breathing
And Zero at the Bone—

(1866)

1263

There is no Frigate like a Book
To take us Lands away
Nor any Coursers like a Page
Of prancing Poetry—
5   This Traverse may the poorest take
Without oppress of Toll—
How frugal is the Chariot
That bears the Human soul.

(1894)

1732

My life closed twice before its close—
It yet remains to see
If Immortality unveil
A third event to me

5   So huge, so hopeless to conceive
As these that twice befell.
Parting is all we know of heaven,
And all we need of hell.

(1896)

Gerard Manley Hopkins

(1 8 4 4 – 1 8 8 9)

The most technically innovative of the nineteenth-century English poets, Gerard Manley Hopkins was born in Essex and studied classics at Oxford. At the age of 22, he converted to Catholicism, entered the Jesuit order, and burned all his early "worldly" poetry. He received final ordination in 1877, then served as a priest and teacher before he was appointed to University College, Dublin, in 1884. He wrote his first "adult" poem at the encouragement of his superior in 1875. From the beginning, he experimented with forms of sound and rhythm antithetical to much of the century's poetry and in disagreement with the theory that poetry should use the same language as the language of prose. Hopkins began to correspond with his friend Robert Bridges about verse and gradually convinced Bridges of the possibilities of his unique style. Hopkins experienced periods of severe depression and spiritual failure, feelings he expressed in the "terrible sonnets" written between 1885 and 1889, but he was also capable of ecstatic love for the physical glories of God's creation. At the age of 44 Hopkins contracted typhus and died.

None of Hopkins's poems was published in his lifetime. Almost 30 years after his death, Robert Bridges published a book that brought his poetry into sudden prominence. Hopkins was enthusiastically adopted as a spiritual forefather by W. H. Auden and Dylan Thomas. Although some critics think Hopkins was a mere dabbler who mistook clumsy experimentation for accomplishment, most find him to be a superb, if limited, poet, capable of moments of great beauty and insight.

His verse is highly eccentric in form. Hopkins employed highly charged, sometimes esoteric diction and a leaping and surging meter that he described as "sprung rhythm," which concerned itself with the number of strong beats per line rather than the number of syllables and worked as a flexible, musical pattern with predominantly rising or falling feet. He also used strong alliteration and frequent internal rhyme. In many ways his poetry looks back to the Anglo-Saxon verse forms; in its striking juxtapositions of harsh sounds, it imitates Germanic poetry. The diction is dialectic and colorful and contains clever puns; the imagery is highly sensuous and attempts to invoke the individual mind's response to the empirical world, a response Hopkins called "inscape." Hopkins's themes are mostly religious and ecstatic. He wanted to capture the prodigal bounties of a lavish and terrible God.

Many of the poems appeared in Bridges's edition of 1918. An enlarged version, prepared by W. H. Gardner and N. Mackenzie, appeared in 1967.

Hopkins's letters were published in 1935 and 1955 and his *Notebooks and Papers* in 1937 and 1959.

GERARD MANLEY HOPKINS

God's Grandeur

The world is charged with the grandeur of God.
    It will flame out, like shining from shook foil;
    It gathers to a greatness, like the ooze of oil
Crushed. Why do men then now not reck his rod?
5 Generations have trod, have trod, have trod;
    And all is seared with trade; bleared, smeared with toil;
    And wears man's smudge and shares man's smell: the soil
Is bare now, nor can foot feel, being shod.

And for all this, nature is never spent;
10   There lives the dearest freshness deep down things;
And though the last lights off the black West went
    Oh, morning, at the brown brink eastward, springs—
Because the Holy Ghost over the bent
    World broods with warm breast and with ah! bright wings.
                           (1918)

Pied Beauty

Glory be to God for dappled things—
    For skies of couple-colour as a brinded cow;
      For rose-moles in all stipple upon trout that swim;
Fresh-firecoal chestnut-falls; finches' wings;
5   Landscape plotted and pieced—fold, fallow, and plough;
    And áll trádes, their gear and tackle and trim.
All things counter, original, spare, strange;
    Whatever is fickle, freckled (who knows how?)
      With swift, slow; sweet, sour; adazzle, dim;
10 He fathers-forth whose beauty is past change:
          Praise him.
                           (1918)

Hurrahing in Harvest

Summer ends now; now, barbarous in beauty, the stooks rise
    Around; up above, what wind-walks! what lovely behaviour
Of silk-sack clouds! has wilder, wilful-wavier
Meal-drift moulded ever and melted across skies?

5 I walk, I lift up, I lift up heart, eyes,
    Down all that glory in the heavens to glean our Saviour;
And, éyes, heárt, what looks, what lips yet gave you a
Rapturous love's greeting of realer, of rounder replies?

And the azurous hung hills are his world-wielding shoulder
10   Majestic—as a stallion stalwart, very-violet-sweet!—
These things, these things were here and but the beholder
    Wanting; which two when they once meet,
The heart réars wíngs bold and bolder
    And hurls for him, O half curls earth for him off under his
        feet.

(1918)

Thou Art Indeed Just, Lord

Justus quidem tu es, Domine, is disputem tecum;
verumtamen justa loquar ad te: Quare via impiorum prosperatur? &c. [1]

Thou art indeed just, Lord, if I contend
With thee; but, sir, so what I plead is just.
Why do sinners' ways prosper? and why must
Disappointment all I endeavour end?
5   Wert thou my enemy, O thou my friend,
How wouldst thou worse, I wonder, than thou dost
Defeat, thwart me? Oh, the sots and thralls of lust
Do in spare hours more thrive than I that spend,
Sir, life upon thy cause. See, banks and brakes
10 Now, leavèd how thick! lacèd they are again
With fretty chervil, look, and fresh wind shakes
Them; birds build—but not I build; no, but strain,
Time's eunuch, and not breed one work that wakes.
Mine, O thou lord of life, send my roots rain.

(1918)

---

[1] "Righteous art thou, O Lord, when I plead with thee: yet let me talk of thy judgements:
Wherefore doth the way of the wicked prosper? . . ."—Jeremiah xii.1 (King James Version)

A. E. Housman

(1 8 5 9 - 1 9 3 6)

Alfred Edward Housman was born in Worcestershire, near the hills of Shropshire he would make famous in his poetry. A devoted classical scholar at Oxford, Housman gradually built a reputation through textual studies published in learned journals; eventually he won a post at University College, London, in 1892, and a professorship at Cambridge in 1911, which he held to his death. In 1896 he published *A Shropshire Lad.* The book was received coolly but became popular during World War I. A second slender volume appeared in 1922. Housman lived a solitary life in Cambridge until his death.

The mood of Housman's poetry is pessimistic, but the poems contain beautiful, lilting measures that seem to lift the melancholy to an attractive, stolid wisdom. The poetry forcefully supports Housman's view that verse cannot be logically explicated but must achieve its purpose through an almost physical effect on the reader. Nature is never sympathetic to man, and humans compound their problems by betraying each other. The only value that can be praised in a hopeless world is a stoic courage. Housman's favorite figure is the Shropshire lad, an emblem of youth doomed to a brief and tragic existence. His tones and themes are limited. But Housman's best poetry, influenced by the compact lyric forms of classical poetry and the work of the German poet Heine, has an almost haunting purity.

A Shropshire Lad (1896) was followed by *Last Poems* (1922). After Housman's death his brother edited *More Poems* (1936). Housman's textual work was brilliant but bitter, legendary for its scathing, satiric condemnations of previous editors.

A. E. HOUSMAN

Loveliest of Trees

Loveliest of trees, the cherry now
Is hung with bloom along the bough,
And stands about the woodland ride
Wearing white for Eastertide.

5 Now, of my threescore years and ten,
  Twenty will not come again,
  And take from seventy springs a score,
  It only leaves me fifty more.

  And since to look at things in bloom
10 Fifty springs are little room,
  About the woodlands I will go
  To see the cherry hung with snow.

  (1896)

When I Was One-and-Twenty

  When I was one-and-twenty
    I heard a wise man say,
  "Give crowns and pounds and guineas
    But not your heart away;
5 Give pearls away and rubies
    But keep your fancy free."
  But I was one-and-twenty,
    No use to talk to me.

  When I was one-and-twenty
10 I heard him say again,
    "The heart out of the bosom
    Was never given in vain;
  'Tis paid with sighs a plenty
    And sold for endless rue."
15 And I am two-and-twenty,
    And oh, 'tis true, 'tis true.

  (1896)

To An Athlete Dying Young

The time you won your town the race
We chaired you through the market-place;
Man and boy stood cheering by,
And home we brought you shoulder-high.

5   To-day, the road all runners come,
    Shoulder-high we bring you home,
    And set you at your threshold down,
    Townsman of a stiller town.

    Smart lad, to slip betimes away
10 From fields where glory does not stay
    And early though the laurel grows
    It withers quicker than the rose.

    Eyes the shady night has shut
    Cannot see the record cut,
15 And silence sounds no worse than cheers
    After earth has stopped the ears:

    Now you will not swell the rout
    Of lads that wore their honours out,
    Runners whom renown outran
20 And the name died before the man.

    So set, before its echoes fade,
    The fleet foot on the sill of shade,
    And hold to the low lintel up
    The still-defended challenge-cup.

25 And round that early-laurelled head
    Will flock to gaze the strengthless dead,
    And find unwithered on its curls
    The garland briefer than a girl's.

                                    (1896)

Bliss Carman

(1 8 6 1 – 1 9 2 9)

Perhaps the most widely known nineteenth-century Canadian poet, Bliss Carman was born in Fredericton, New Brunswick, in 1861. He was a first cousin of the poet Charles G. D. Roberts and was distantly related to Ralph Waldo Emerson. After graduating from the University of New Brunswick, he pursued sporadic studies at Oxford, Edinburgh, London, and Harvard. Following the death of his parents in the mid-1880s, Carman settled in New York, although he traveled continually. He tried many professions, then worked as a literary journalist in New York. The publication of *Low Tide on Grande Pré* in 1893 gained him fame in Canada, the United States, and England. In the next 30 years, he made a living primarily as a poet. He turned out more than 50 books and chapbooks and toured widely, especially in Canada, where he was something of an unofficial poet laureate. A lifelong bachelor, Carman avoided expenses by living for long periods of time with friends. He was awarded the Lorne Pierce Medal in Canada and the medal of the Poetry Society of America. He died in Connecticut in 1929, and his ashes were buried in Fredericton.

Carman's work is as varied in quality as it is voluminous. His poetry ranges from the lyric to the dramatic to the meditative. Many of his books contain light verse that evokes a nostalgic world of pastoral values; his best writing explores landscape as perception and depicts the world as it relates to the psyche of the melancholy, yearning, occasionally ecstatic observer. Basically a Romantic nature poet, Carman wrote poems that reflected the extremes of his moody personality. Unlike many poets of his time, Carman knew about modernist poetry. Although he rejected most tenets of modernist theory, he experimented with traditional forms and adopted many poetic personae—mystic, elegist, bohemian traveler, philosopher—to express the various facets of what he called his "cheerful pessimism."

Bliss Carman's books include *Low Tide on Grande Pré* (1893), *Behind the Arras: A Book of the Unseen* (1895), *Pipes of Pan* (1906), *Later Poems* (1921), and *Ballads and Lyrics* (1923). His most popular poetry was from the four-volume Vagabond series (1894 to 1912).

BLISS CARMAN

Low Tide on Grand Pré

The sun goes down, and over all
   These barren reaches by the tide
Such unelusive glories fall,
   I almost dream they yet will bide
5   Until the coming of the tide.

And yet I know that not for us,
   By any ecstasy of dream,
He lingers to keep luminous
   A little while the grievous stream,
10   Which frets, uncomforted of dream—

A grievous stream, that to and fro
   Although the fields of Acadie
Goes wandering, as if to know
   Why one beloved face should be
15   So long from home and Acadie.

Was it a year or lives ago
   We took the grasses in our hands,
And caught the summer flying low
   Over the waving meadow lands,
20   And held it there between our hands?

The while the river at our feet—
   A drowsy inland meadow stream—
At set of sun the after-heat
   Made running gold, and in the gleam
25   We freed our birch upon the stream.

There down along the elms at dusk
   We lifted dripping blade to drift,
Through twilight scented fine like musk,
   Where night and gloom awhile uplift,
30   Nor sunder soul and soul adrift.

And that we took into our hands
   Spirit of life or subtler thing—

Breathed on us there, and loosed the bands
  Of death, and taught us, whispering,
35   The secret of some wonder-thing.

Then all your face grew light, and seemed
  To hold the shadow of the sun;
The evening faltered, and I deemed
  That time was ripe, and years had done
40   Their wheeling underneath the sun.

So all desire and all regret,
  And fear and memory, were naught;
One to remember or forget
  The keen delight our hands had caught;
45   Morrow and yesterday were naught.

The night has fallen, and the tide . . .
  Now and again comes drifting home,
Across these aching barrens wide,
  A sigh like driven wind or foam:
50   In grief the flood is bursting home.

                (1893)

Archibald Lampman

(1 8 6 1 – 1 8 9 9)

Although he did not gain widespread recognition in his lifetime, Archibald Lampman is now considered by some critics to be the finest poet of nineteenth-century Canada. The son of an Anglican clergyman, Lampman was born in the village of Morpeth, in what is now southwestern Ontario. He graduated from Trinity College, University of Toronto, taught for a while, then settled into a civil service job in Ottawa, where he remained for the rest of his life. He became close friends with the poet D. C. Scott, and together they cultivated a love of poetry and the Canadian wilderness. From his university days on, Lampman published poetry in journals across North America. He produced his first volume privately, his second with an American publisher. Lampman died at the age of 37, just before his third volume of poetry was published.

Like the other Confederation Poets—Charles G. D. Roberts, Bliss Carman, and D. C. Scott—Lampman was influenced by English romanticism (he considered himself a follower of Keats). He was also determined to capture the unique characteristics of the Canadian landscape and to write in an indigenous Canadian voice. He saw the return to nature as a rejuvenating and spiritually cleansing activity, and attempted to recreate this experience through the use of vivid yet simple sensory images that captured the sounds, colors, and contours of wilderness landscapes. Lampman was an uneven craftsman, by turns monotonously regular and daringly experimental in his prosody. Many of his poems describe a dream where the poet is transformed and is replenished after the draining effects of urban life. Unlike most Romantics, however, Lampman confronted a nature that could be terrifying, malevolent, and incomprehensible. His perception creates a rich tension and sense of mystery in many of the poems. In his later work, Lampman turned to questions of human society. His finest poems are hypnotically intense studies of the human mind in the presence of a powerful and ambiguous nature force.

Lampman's three volumes of poetry were *Among the Millet and Other Poems* (1888), *Lyrics of Earth* (1895), and *Alcyone* (1899). Some of his unpublished poems were collected in *At the Long Sault and Other New Poems* (1943); a volume of prose writings appeared in 1975.

ARCHIBALD LAMPMAN

Heat

From plains that reel to southward, dim,
   The road runs by me white and bare;
Up the steep hill it seems to swim
   Beyond, and melt into the glare.
5 Upward half-way, or it may be
   Nearer the summit, slowly steals
A hay-cart, moving dustily
   With idly clacking wheels.

By his cart's side the wagoner
10   Is slouching slowly at his ease,
Half-hidden in the windless blur
   Of white dust puffing to his knees.
This wagon on the height above,
   From sky to sky on either hand,
15 Is the sole thing that seems to move
   In all the heat-held land.

Beyond me in the fields the sun
   Soaks in the grass and hath his will;
I count the marguerites one by one;
20   Even the buttercups are still.
On the brook yonder not a breath
   Disturbs the spider or the midge.
The water-bugs draw close beneath
   The cool gloom of the bridge.

25 Where the far elm-tree shadows flood
   Dark patches in the burning grass,
The cows, each with her peaceful cud,
   Lie waiting for the heat to pass.
From somewhere on the slope near by
30   Into the pale depth of the noon
A wandering thrush slides leisurely
   His thin revolving tune.

In intervals of dreams I hear
   The cricket from the droughty ground;

35 The grasshoppers spin into mine ear
      A small innumerable sound.
    I lift mine eyes sometimes to gaze:
      The burning sky-line blinds my sight:
    The woods far off are blue with haze:
40   The hills are drenched in light.

    And yet to me not this or that
      Is always sharp or always sweet;
    In the sloped shadow of my hat
      I lean at rest, and drain the heat;
45 Nay more, I think some blessèd power
      Hath brought me wandering idly here:
    In the full furnace of this hour
      My thoughts grow keen and clear.

                                    (1888)

The City of the End of Things

    Beside the pounding cataracts
    Of midnight streams unknown to us
    'Tis builded in the leafless tracts
    And valleys huge of Tartarus.
5   Lurid and lofty and vast it seems;
    It hath no rounded name that rings,
    But I have heard it called in dreams
    The City of the End of Things.

    Its roofs and iron towers have grown
10 None knoweth how high within the night,
    But in its murky streets far down
    A flaming terrible and bright
    Shakes all the stalking shadows there,
    Across the walls, across the floors,
15 And shifts upon the upper air
    From out a thousand furnace doors;
    And all the while an awful sound
    Keeps roaring on continually,
    And crashes in the ceaseless round
20 Of a gigantic harmony.
    Through its grim depths re-echoing
    And all its weary height of walls,
    With measured roar and iron ring,

The inhuman music lifts and falls.
25 Where no thing rests and no man is,
And only fire and night hold sway;
The beat, the thunder and the hiss
Cease not, and change not, night nor day.
And moving at unheard commands,
30 The abysses and vast fires between,
Flit figures that with clanking hands
Obey a hideous routine;
They are not flesh, they are not bone,
They see not with the human eye,
35 And from their iron lips is blown
A dreadful and monotonous cry;
And whoso of our mortal race
Should find that city unaware,
Lean Death would smite him face to face,
40 And blanch him with its venomed air:
Or caught by the terrific spell,
Each thread of memory snapt and cut,
His soul would shrivel and its shell
Go rattling like an empty nut.

45 It was not always so, but once,
In days that no man thinks upon,
Fair voices echoed from its stones,
The light above it leaped and shone:
Once there were multitudes of men,
50 That built that city in their pride,
Until its might was made, and then
They withered age by age and died.
But now of that prodigious race,
Three only in an iron tower,
55 Set like carved idols face to face,
Remain the masters of its power;
And at the city gate a fourth,
Gigantic and with dreadful eyes,
Sits looking toward the lightless north,
60 Beyond the reach of memories;
Fast rooted to the lurid floor,
A bulk that never moves a jot,
In his pale body dwells no more,
Or mind or soul,—an idiot!
65 But sometime in the end those three
Shall perish and their hands be still,
And with the master's touch shall flee
Their incommunicable skill.

A stillness absolute as death
70   Along the slacking wheels shall lie,
And, flagging at a single breath,
The fires that moulder out and die.
The roar shall vanish at its height,
And over that tremendous town
75   The silence of eternal night
Shall gather close and settle down.
All its grim grandeur, tower and hall,
Shall be abandoned utterly,
And into rust and dust shall fall
80   From century to century;
Nor ever living thing shall grow,
Nor trunk of tree, nor blade of grass;
No drop shall fall, no wind shall blow,
Nor sound of any foot shall pass:
85   Alone of its accursèd state,
One thing the hand of Time shall spare,
For the grim Idiot at the gate
Is deathless and eternal there.

(1895)

In November

With loitering step and quiet eye,
Beneath the low November sky,
I wandered in the woods, and found
A clearing, where the broken ground
5   Was scattered with black stumps and briers,
And the old wreck of forest fires.
It was a bleak and sandy spot,
And, all about, the vacant plot,
Was peopled and inhabited
10   By scores of mulleins long since dead.
A silent and forsaken brood
In that mute opening of the wood,
So shrivelled and so thin they were,
So gray, so haggard, and austere,
15   Not plants at all they seemed to me,
But rather some spare company
Of hermit folk, who long ago,
Wandering in bodies to and fro,
Had chanced upon this lonely way,

20   And rested thus, till death one day
     Surprised them at their compline prayer,
     And left them standing lifeless there.

     There was no sound about the wood
     Save the wind's secret stir. I stood
25   Among the mullein-stalks as still
     As if myself had grown to be
     One of their sombre company,
     A body without wish or will.
     And as I stood, quite suddenly,
30   Down from a furrow in the sky
     The sun shone out a little space
     Across that silent sober place,
     Over the sand heaps and brown sod,
     The mulleins and dead goldenrod,
35   And passed beyond the thickets gray,
     And lit the fallen leaves that lay,
     Level and deep within the wood,
     A rustling yellow multitude.

     And all around me the thin light,
40   So sere, so melancholy bright,
     Fell like the half-reflected gleam
     Or shadow of some former dream;
     A moment's golden reverie
     Poured out on every plant and tree
45   A semblance of weird joy, or less,
     A sort of spectral happiness;
     And I, too, standing idly there,
     With muffled hands in the chill air,
     Felt the warm glow about my feet,
50   And shuddering betwixt cold and heat,
     Drew my thoughts closer, like a cloak,
     While something in my blood awoke,
     A nameless and unnatural cheer,
     A pleasure secret and austere.

                              (1895)

William Butler Yeats

(1 8 6 5 - 1 9 3 9)

William Butler Yeats, the son of the painter John B. Yeats, was born at Sandymount, near Dublin. During his childhood he lived in London, Dublin, and Sligo, a starkly beautiful county in the west of Ireland that left a permanent mark on his landscapes and fueled the mystic turn of his imagination. Yeats studied art briefly, then turned decisively to poetry. In London in the 1890s he cofounded the Rhymers Club and adopted the pre-Raphaelite poetics of the time, which were characterized by vague, dreamy diction and ethereal "landscapes." His first volume of poetry was published in 1889.

Yeats spent much of his time in Dublin, where he tried to create a distinctively Irish poetry. With the help of Lady Gregory, he formed the Irish National Theatre in 1899; the company eventually settled at the Abbey Theatre, and Yeats wrote many plays for them. An encounter with the young Ezra Pound reinforced Yeats's movement toward a sharper, more concrete imagery and less ornamental diction, a change that became clear in *Responsibilities* (1914). Yeats wrote most of his greatest lyrics in his fifties and sixties—"The Second Coming," "Sailing to Byzantium," "The Circus Animals' Desertion," "Among School Children," and others. The symbolic patterns for these poems derived partly from the "automatic" writing of Yeats's wife, Georgie Hyde-Lees, who cured Yeats (at least partly) of his long, tormented passion for Maud Gonne and brought to fruition his lifelong interest in the occult. Yeats was awarded the Nobel Prize in 1924. He died in Nice, France, and was buried near Sligo.

When Yeats was young, his father impressed upon him the belief that all great art must contain the clear "lineaments of some desireable, familiar life." The thought was to remain with the poet all his life. Yeats was a great mythologizer and created superb lyric verse from the themes of Irish, Greek, and Christian legend. He was also a great creator of symbol—the Tower, the gyre, Byzantium—but he utilized his material in such a way that it expressed a human life of the mind, a life rooted in the localities and incidents of actual experience. Yeats is the great poet of antithesis. He donned various poetic masks to explore the tensions within himself, between nature and art, body and soul, action and passivity, society and poetry, youth and age. In his late poetry, Yeats was realistic and metaphysical, naturalistic and symbolical. His last, turbulent verses contain lines of stunning power and near-brutality, lines that exult in and damn the "foul rag-and-bone shop of the heart." Throughout his career, Yeats's mastery of language was unrivaled. He showed an ability to give even abstractions a startling new precision of thought ("the ceremony of innocence"), and to remake common words to suit his own ends ("cold and passionate as the dawn"). He was also a playwright of considerable accomplishment.

Yeats's many volumes of verse include *Crossways* (1889), *The Wind Among the Reeds* (1899), *The Wild Swans at Coole* (1919), *Michael Robartes and the Dancer* (1921), *The Tower* (1928), and *The Winding Stair and Other Poems* (1933). He wrote more than 25 plays, including *The Countess Cathleen* (1892), *Deirdre* (1907), *At the Hawk's Well* (1917), *The Cat and the Moon* (1926), and *The Death of Cuchulain* (1939). He also edited volumes of Irish folklore and the first *Oxford Book of Modern Poetry;* he published his *Autobiography* (1924) and *A Vision* (1925, 1937), as well as various volumes of essays.

WILLIAM BUTLER YEATS

The Lake Isle of Innisfree

I will arise and go now, and go to Innisfree,
And a small cabin build there, of clay and wattles made:
Nine bean-rows will I have there, a hive for the honey bee,
And live alone in the bee-loud glade.

5   And I shall have some peace there, for peace comes dropping
        slow,
Dropping from the veils of the morning to where the cricket
        sings;
There midnight's all a glimmer, and noon a purple glow,
And evening full of the linnet's wings.

I will arise and go now, for always night and day
10 I hear lake water lapping with low sounds by the shore;
While I stand on the roadway, or on the pavements grey,
I hear it in the deep heart's core.

                                                            (1892)

When You Are Old

When you are old and grey and full of sleep,
And nodding by the fire, take down this book,
And slowly read, and dream of the soft look
Your eyes had once, and of their shadows deep;

5   How many loved your moments of glad grace,
And loved your beauty with love false or true,
But one man loved the pilgrim soul in you,
And loved the sorrows of your changing face;

And bending down beside the glowing bars,
10   Murmur, a little sadly, how Love fled
And paced upon the mountains overhead
And hid his face amid a crowd of stars.

(1892)

The Fascination of What's Difficult

The fascination of what's difficult
Has dried the sap out of my veins, and rent
Spontaneous joy and natural content
Out of my heart. There's something ails our colt
5   That must, as if it had not holy blood
Nor on Olympus leaped from cloud to cloud,
Shiver under the lash, strain, sweat and jolt
As though it dragged road-metal. My curse on plays
That have to be set up in fifty ways,
10   On the day's war with every knave and dolt,
Theatre business, management of men.
I swear before the dawn comes round again
I'll find the stable and pull out the bolt.

(1910)

Easter 1916[1]

I have met them at close of day
Coming with vivid faces
From counter or desk among grey
Eighteenth-century houses.
5   I have passed with a nod of the head
Or polite meaningless words,
Or have lingered awhile and said

[1] On April 23, 1916, Easter Sunday, Irish nationalists launched an attempt to establish an Irish Republic free from Britain's rule. The British forces suppressed the rebellion six days later.

Polite meaningless words,
And thought before I had done
10   Of a mocking tale or a gibe
To please a companion
Around the fire at the club,
Being certain that they and I
But lived where motley is worn:
15   All changed, changed utterly:
A terrible beauty is born.

That woman's days were spent
In ignorant good-will,
Her nights in argument
20   Until her voice grew shrill.
What voice more sweet than hers
When, young and beautiful,
She rode to harriers?
This man had kept a school
25   And rode our wingèd horse;[2]
This other his helper and friend
Was coming into his force;
He might have won fame in the end,
So sensitive his nature seemed,
30   So daring and sweet his thought.
This other man I had dreamed
A drunken, vainglorious lout.
He had done most bitter wrong
To some who are near my heart,
35   Yet I number him in the song;
He, too, has resigned his part
In the casual comedy;
He, too, has been changed in his turn,
Transformed utterly:
40   A terrible beauty is born.

Hearts with one purpose alone
Through summer and winter seem
Enchanted to a stone
To trouble the living stream.
45   The horse that comes from the road,
The rider, the birds that range
From cloud to tumbling cloud,
Minute by minute they change;
A shadow of cloud on the stream

---

[2] Pegasus, the winged horse of the Muses.

50 Changes minute by minute;
A horse-hoof slides on the brim,
And a horse plashes within it;
The long-legged moor-hens dive,
And hens to moor-cocks call;
55 Minute by minute they live:
The stone's in the midst of all.

Too long a sacrifice
Can make a stone of the heart.
O when may it suffice?
60 That is Heaven's part, our part
To murmur name upon name,
As a mother names her child
When sleep at last has come
On limbs that had run wild.
65 What is it but nightfall?
No, no, not night but death;
Was it needless death after all?
For England may keep faith
For all that is done and said.
70 We know their dream; enough
To know they dreamed and are dead;
And what if excess of love
Bewildered them till they died?
I write it out in a verse—
75 MacDonagh and MacBride
And Connolly and Pearse[3]
Now and in time to be,
Wherever green is worn,
Are changed, changed utterly:
80 A terrible beauty is born.

                                        (1916)

The Second Coming

Turning and turning in the widening gyre[1]
The falcon cannot hear the falconer;
Things fall apart; the centre cannot hold;

[3] Four of the 16 Irish nationalists who were executed by the British for their role in the Easter uprising.
[1] A spiral, for Yeats also an emblem of the cyclical rise and fall of civilizations.

Mere anarchy is loosed upon the world,
5 The blood-dimmed tide is loosed, and everywhere
The ceremony of innocence is drowned;
The best lack all conviction, while the worst
Are full of passionate intensity.

Surely some revelation is at hand;
10 Surely the Second Coming is at hand.
The Second Coming! Hardly are those words out
When a vast image out of *Spiritus Mundi*[2]
Troubles my sight: somewhere in sands of the desert
A shape with lion body and the head of a man,
15 A gaze blank and pitiless as the sun,
Is moving its slow thighs, while all about it
Reel shadows of the indignant desert birds.
The darkness drops again; but now I know
That twenty centuries of stony sleep
20 Were vexed to nightmare by a rocking cradle,
And what rough beast, its hour come round at last,
Slouches towards Bethlehem to be born?

(1921)

Sailing to Byzantium[1]

I

That is no country for old men. The young
In one another's arms, birds in the trees
—Those dying generations—at their song,
The salmon-falls, the mackerel-crowded seas,
5 Fish, flesh, or fowl, commend all summer long
Whatever is begotten, born, and dies.
Caught in that sensual music all neglect
Monuments of unageing intellect.

II

An aged man is but a paltry thing,
10 A tattered coat upon a stick, unless
Soul clap its hands and sing, and louder sing
For every tatter in its mortal dress,

---

[2] Yeats refers to the *Spiritus Mundi* as a "general storehouse of images" or universal sub-conscious.
[1] "I have read somewhere that in the Emperor's palace at Byzantium was a tree made of gold and silver, and artificial birds that sang." (Yeats's note.)

Nor is there singing school but studying
Monuments of its own magnificence;
15   And therefore I have sailed the seas and come
To the holy city of Byzantium.

III

O sages standing in God's holy fire
As in the gold mosaic of a wall,
Come from the holy fire, perne in a gyre,[2]
20   And be the singing-masters of my soul.
Consume my heart away; sick with desire
And fastened to a dying animal
It knows not what it is; and gather me
Into the artifice of eternity.

IV

25   Once out of nature I shall never take
My bodily form from any natural thing,
But such a form as Grecian goldsmiths make
Of hammered gold and gold enamelling
To keep a drowsy Emperor awake;
30   Or set upon a golden bough to sing
To lords and ladies of Byzantium
Of what is past, or passing, or to come.

(1927)

Among School Children

I

I walk through the long schoolroom questioning;
A kind old nun in a white hood replies;
The children learn to cipher and to sing,
To study reading-books and history,
5   To cut and sew, be neat in everything
In the best modern way—the children's eyes
In momentary wonder stare upon
A sixty-year-old smiling public man.

II

I dream of a Ledaean[1] body, bent
10   Above a sinking fire, a tale that she

---

[2] A downward spiral.
[1] In classical mythology, Zeus, in the form of a swan, seduces the mortal Leda. As a result, Leda gives birth to Helen of Troy.

Told of a harsh reproof, or trivial event
That changed some childish day to tragedy—
Told, and it seemed that our two natures blent
Into a sphere from youthful sympathy,
15 Or else, to alter Plato's parable,
Into the yolk and white of the one shell.[2]

III

And thinking of that fit of grief or rage
I look upon one child or t'other there
And wonder if she stood so at that age—
20 For even daughters of the swan can share
Something of every paddler's heritage—
And had that colour upon cheek or hair,
And thereupon my heart is driven wild:
She stands before me as a living child.

IV

25 Her present image floats into the mind—
Did Quattrocento[3] finger fashion it
Hollow of cheek as though it drank the wind
And took a mess of shadows for its meat?
And I though never of Ledaean kind
30 Had pretty plumage once—enough of that,
Better to smile on all that smile, and show
There is a comfortable kind of old scarecrow.

V

What youthful mother, a shape upon her lap
Honey of generation had betrayed,
35 And that must sleep, shriek, struggle to escape
As recollection or the drug decide,[4]
Would think her son, did she but see that shape
With sixty or more winters on its head,
A compensation for the pang of his birth,
40 Or the uncertainty of his setting forth?

VI

Plato thought nature but a spume that plays
Upon a ghostly paradigm of things;

[2] In Plato's *Symposium* the Greek playwright Aristophanes explains that primeval man was double, until Zeus divided him in two.
[3] A fifteenth-century Italian artist.
[4] "I have taken the 'honey of generation' from Porphyry's essay on 'The Cave of the Nymphs,' but find no warrant in Porphyry for considering it the 'drug' that destroys the 'recollection' of pre-natal freedom. He blamed a cup of oblivion given in the zodiacal sign of Cancer." Here a contrast is set up between pre-natal freedom and the struggles and uncertainties of life.

Solider Aristotle played the taws
Upon the bottom of a king of kings;
45 World-famous golden-thighed Pythagoras
Fingered upon a fiddle-stick or strings
What a star sang and careless Muses heard:
Old clothes upon old sticks to scare a bird.

VII

Both nuns and mothers worship images,
50 But those the candles light are not as those
That animate a mother's reveries,
But keep a marble or a bronze repose.
And yet they too break hearts—O Presences
That passion, piety or affection knows,
55 And that all heavenly glory symbolise—
O self-born mockers of man's enterprise;

VIII

Labour is blossoming or dancing where
The body is not bruised to pleasure soul,
Nor beauty born out of its own despair,
60 Nor blear-eyed wisdom out of midnight oil.
O chestnut-tree, great-rooted blossomer,
Are you the leaf, the blossom or the bole?
O body swayed to music, O brightening glance,
How can we know the dancer from the dance?

(1927)

Crazy Jane Talks with the Bishop

I met the Bishop on the road
And much said he and I.
"Those breasts are flat and fallen now,
Those veins must soon be dry;
5 Live in a heavenly mansion,
Not in some foul sty."

"Fair and foul are near of kin,
And fair needs foul," I cried.
"My friends are gone, but that's a truth
10 Nor grave nor bed denied,
Learned in bodily lowliness
And in the heart's pride.

"A woman can be proud and stiff
When on love intent;
15 But Love has pitched his mansion in
The place of excrement;
For nothing can be sole or whole
That has not been rent."

(1932)

Robert Frost

(1 8 7 4 - 1 9 6 3)

Robert Frost was born in San Francisco. When he was 10, his father, a native of New England, died and his mother returned east with the family. After a few months at Dartmouth, Frost dropped out to work in the mills in Lawrence, Massachusetts, and to write poems, which were consistently rejected by the magazines he sent them to. In 1895 he married Elinor White, and in 1899, after a brief period at Harvard, he moved to a farm in Derry, New Hampshire. For a decade, as his family grew and his bouts of depression mounted, Frost farmed a bit and labored on his idiosyncratic poetry in total obscurity. In 1911 he took his family to England, where he met Ezra Pound, William Butler Yeats, and Edward Thomas. *A Boy's Will* was accepted by a London publisher in 1913 and was followed by *North of Boston* in 1914. The outbreak of war forced Frost to return to New England, and his fame gradually climbed. He won four Pulitzer prizes and was invited to read at John Kennedy's inauguration. But the years were also marred by tragedy: Frost's wife died in 1938, and in 1940 a son committed suicide. At his death, Frost was an unofficial poet laureate, and he remains one of the few poets of this century with a wide public audience.

Frost's poems offer deceptively simple surfaces that, upon close reading, give way to a surprisingly complex structure and a darker mood. He was a symbolic poet, who tried to arrive at basic truths of human experience through the study of the thoughts and feelings involved in the simple, often bucolic events he described. Many of his best poems are almost parables. Technically, his work is important for his attempt to integrate natural speech rhythms and common diction into formal verse patterns. He rejected free verse, feeling it was akin to "playing tennis with the net down." In many poems, he managed to develop a sense of rhythm that is both a natural imitation of speech and intensely poetic. His poems explore the tension between love and hatred, kindness and cruelty, which he found within himself and within a natural world that seemed to him both the feeder of the human spirit and an indifferent adversary to human survival. Frost always insisted that a true poem was partly the result of fortunate accident, that a poem must be given enough free rein to, with luck, "begin in delight and end in wisdom." In spite of the dark shadows that inhabit much of his work, Frost's delight in the New England earth, woods, mountains, and people should not be overlooked.

Frost also published *Mountain Interval* (1916), *New Hampshire* (1923), *West-Running Brook* (1928), *A Further Range* (1936), *A Witness Tree* (1942), *Steeple Bush* (1947), *A Masque of Reason* (1945), *A Masque of Mercy* (1947), and *In the Clearing* (1962).

ROBERT FROST

After Apple-Picking

My long two-pointed ladder's sticking through a tree
Toward heaven still,
And there's a barrel that I didn't fill
Beside it, and there may be two or three
5   Apples I didn't pick upon some bough.
But I am done with apple-picking now.
Essence of winter sleep is on the night,
The scent of apples: I am drowsing off.
I cannot rub the strangeness from my sight
10   I got from looking through a pane of glass
I skimmed this morning from the drinking trough
And held against the world of hoary grass.
It melted, and I let it fall and break.
But I was well
15   Upon my way to sleep before it fell,
And I could tell
What form my dreaming was about to take.
Magnified apples appear and disappear,
Stem end and blossom end,
20   And every fleck of russet showing clear.
My instep arch not only keeps the ache,
It keeps the pressure of a ladder-round.
I feel the ladder sway as the boughs bend.
And I keep hearing from the cellar bin
25   The rumbling sound
Of load on load of apples coming in.
For I have had too much
Of apple-picking: I am overtired
Of the great harvest I myself desired.
30   There were ten thousand thousand fruit to touch,
Cherish in hand, lift down, and not let fall.
For all
That struck the earth,
No matter if not bruised or spiked with stubble,
35   Went surely to the cider-apple heap
As of no worth.
One can see what will trouble
This sleep of mine, whatever sleep it is.

Were he not gone,
40   The woodchuck could say whether it's like his
Long sleep, as I describe its coming on,
Or just some human sleep.

(1914)

Fire and Ice

Some say the world will end in fire,
Some say in ice.
From what I've tasted of desire
I hold with those who favor fire.
5   But if it had to perish twice,
I think I know enough of hate
To say that for destruction ice
Is also great
And would suffice.

(1920)

Stopping by Woods on a Snowy Evening

Whose woods these are I think I know.
His house is in the village, though;
He will not see me stopping here
To watch his woods fill up with snow.

5   My little horse must think it queer
To stop without a farmhouse near
Between the woods and frozen lake
The darkest evening of the year.

He gives his harness bells a shake
10   To ask if there is some mistake.
The only other sound's the sweep
Of easy wind and downy flake.

The woods are lovely, dark, and deep,
But I have promises to keep,
15   And miles to go before I sleep,
And miles to go before I sleep.

(1923)

Directive

Back out of all this now too much for us,
Back in a time made simple by the loss
Of detail, burned, dissolved, and broken off
Like graveyard marble sculpture in the weather,
5   There is a house that is no more a house
Upon a farm that is no more a farm
And in a town that is no more a town.
The road there, if you'll let a guide direct you
Who only has at heart your getting lost,
10 May seem as if it should have been a quarry—
Great monolithic knees the former town
Long since gave up pretense of keeping covered.
And there's a story in a book about it:
Besides the wear of iron wagon wheels
15 The ledges show lines ruled southeast-northwest,
The chisel work of an enormous Glacier
That braced his feet against the Arctic Pole.
You must not mind a certain coolness from him
Still said to haunt this side of Panther Mountain.
20 Nor need you mind the serial ordeal
Of being watched from forty cellar holes
As if by eye pairs out of forty firkins.
As for the woods' excitement over you
That sends light rustle rushes to their leaves,
25 Charge that to upstart inexperience.
Where were they all not twenty years ago?
They think too much of having shaded out
A few old pecker-fretted apple trees.
Make yourself up a cheering song of how
30 Someone's road home from work this once was,
Who may be just ahead of you on foot
Or creaking with a buggy load of grain.
The height of the adventure is the height
Of country where two village cultures faded
35 Into each other. Both of them are lost.
And if you're lost enough to find yourself
By now, pull in your ladder road behind you
And put a sign up CLOSED to all but me.
Then make yourself at home. The only field
40 Now left's no bigger than a harness gall.
First there's the children's house of make-believe,
Some shattered dishes underneath a pine,

The playthings in the playhouse of the children.
Weep for what little things could make them glad.
45   Then for the house that is no more a house,
But only a belilaced cellar hole,
Now slowly closing like a dent in dough.
This was no playhouse but a house in earnest.
Your destination and your destiny's
50   A brook that was the water of the house,
Cold as a spring as yet so near its source,
Too lofty and original to rage.
(We know the valley streams that when aroused
Will leave their tatters hung on barb and thorn.)
55   I have kept hidden in the instep arch
Of an old cedar at the waterside
A broken drinking goblet like the Grail
Under a spell so the wrong ones can't find it,
So can't get saved, as Saint Mark says they mustn't.[1]
60   (I stole the goblet from the children's playhouse.)
Here are your waters and your watering place.
Drink and be whole again beyond confusion.

(1947)

---

[1] Frost's reference is to Mark 4:11–12, in which Jesus says to his disciples: "Unto you it is given to know the mystery of the kingdom of God: but unto them that are without, all *these* things are done in parables: That seeing they may see, and not perceive; and hearing they may hear, and not understand; lest at any time they should be converted, and *their* sins should be forgiven them."

Wallace Stevens

(1 8 7 9 – 1 9 5 5)

Wallace Stevens is slowly coming to be seen as a major twentieth-century American poet. He was born in Reading, Pennsylvania, and studied at Harvard and the New York Law School. He practiced law in New York City, then joined a Hartford insurance company, where he became vice-president in 1934. In 1909 he married Elsie Moll; a daughter, Holly, was born in 1924. Stevens wrote his poetry in the evenings after his routine labors at the office, where, he told his wife, "I certainly do not exist between nine and six." Self-critical, Stevens did not publish a volume of his poetry until 1923, when he was 44; the volume, *Harmonium,* was overshadowed by the publication of Eliot's *The Waste Land.* Not an outgoing man, Stevens had little contact with other writers. He was still working as a life-insurance executive when he won the Pulitzer Prize for his *Collected Poems* in 1955, the year of his death.

Stevens is perhaps the most philosophical of modern poets. His work addresses questions of perception, epistemology, the relationship between object and subject, and the nature of the poetic imagination. His poems tend to analyze the process of seeing objects rather than the objects themselves. Yet his poems are also celebrations of the senses and pleasurable extravaganzas of wit and sound. Stevens is, in the tradition of Coleridge, a celebrator of the power of the imagination to create a "supreme fiction" that is more real than objective, "historical" life. He always saw poetry as something in itself, a process of living. A poem was not *about* something: "The poem is the cry of its occasion." His later poems are perhaps his best—these sparer, meditative long poems examine the relationship between the poet and his world. Nature itself and, in an oblique way, humanity begin to play larger roles. In the great poems ("Credences of Summer," "The Auroras of Autumn," "The Idea of Order at Key West," "An Ordinary Evening in New Haven," and others), Stevens rejects visions of the world as either chaotic or ordered. He asserts instead the *idea* of order. The notion of "festival" is central to his work; it is a structured freedom, a celebration with freely chosen restrictions. Stevens's poems are festivals for the mind, worlds of verbal grace constructed of tantalizing, dissolving metaphors that never quite freeze into reality.

Stevens published *Harmonium* in 1923. His second volume, *Ideas of Order,* did not appear until 1935. He also wrote *Owl's Clover* (1936), *The Man with the Blue Guitar* (1937), *Parts of a World* (1939), and the long poem *Notes Toward a Supreme Fiction* (1942), *Esthetique du Mal* (1944), *Transport to Summer* (1947), and *The Auroras of Autumn* (1950). *The Necessary Angel: Essays on Reality and the Imagination* was published in 1951.

WALLACE STEVENS

The Snow Man

One must have a mind of winter
To regard the frost and the boughs
Of the pine-trees crusted with snow;

And have been cold a long time
5   To behold the junipers shagged with ice,
The spruces rough in the distant glitter

Of the January sun; and not to think
Of any misery in the sound of the wind,
In the sound of a few leaves,

10   Which is the sound of the land
Full of the same wind
That is blowing in the same bare place

For the listener, who listens in the snow,
And, nothing himself, beholds
15   Nothing that is not there and the nothing that is.

(1923)

The Emperor of Ice-Cream

Call the roller of big cigars,
The muscular one, and bid him whip
In kitchen cups concupiscent curds.
Let the wenches dawdle in such dress
5   As they are used to wear, and let the boys
Bring flowers in last month's newspapers.
Let be be finale of seem.
The only emperor is the emperor of ice-cream.

Take from the dresser of deal,°   pine
10   Lacking the three glass knobs, that sheet
On which she embroidered fantails once

And spread it so as to cover her face.
If her horny feet protrude, they come
To show how cold she is, and dumb.
15 Let the lamp affix its beam.
The only emperor is the emperor of ice-cream.

(1923)

Thirteen Ways of Looking at a Blackbird

I

Among twenty snowy mountains,
The only moving thing
Was the eye of the blackbird.

II

I was of three minds,
5 Like a tree
In which there are three blackbirds.

III

The blackbird whirled in the autumn winds.
It was a small part of the pantomime.

IV

A man and a woman
10 Are one.
A man and a woman and a blackbird
Are one.

V

I do not know which to prefer,
The beauty of inflections
15 Or the beauty of innuendoes,
The blackbird whistling
Or just after.

VI

Icicles filled the long window
With barbaric glass.
20 The shadow of the blackbird
Crossed it, to and fro.
The mood
Traced in the shadow
An indecipherable cause.

VII

25 O thin men of Haddam,[1]
Why do you imagine golden birds?
Do you not see how the blackbird
Walks around the feet
Of the women about you?

VIII

30 I know noble accents
And lucid, inescapable rhythms;
But I know, too,
That the blackbird is involved
In what I know.

IX

35 When the blackbird flew out of sight,
It marked the edge
Of one of many circles.

X

At the sight of blackbirds
Flying in a green light,
40 Even the bawds of euphony
Would cry out sharply.

XI

He rode over Connecticut
In a glass coach.
Once, a fear pierced him,
45 In that he mistook
The shadow of his equipage
For blackbirds.

XII

The river is moving.
The blackbird must be flying.

XIII

50 It was evening all afternoon.
It was snowing
And it was going to snow.
The blackbird sat
In the cedar-limbs.

(1923)

[1] A town in Connecticut. Stevens explains in his *Letters* (p. 340) that "the thin men of Haddam are entirely fictitious. . . . I just like the name. It is an old whaling town, I believe. In any case, it has a completely Yankee sound."

E. J. Pratt

(1 8 8 3 – 1 9 6 4)

Edwin John Pratt was born in the small fishing village of Western Bay, Newfoundland. Pratt at first planned to emulate his father, who was a Methodist minister. After graduating from St. John's Methodist College, Pratt taught and preached for 4 years in rural Newfoundland. He entered Victoria College at the University of Toronto and gained his Ph.D. in Theology in 1917. He decided that teaching was his true vocation and joined the English faculty at Victoria College, where he taught for more than 30 years. A witty and enthusiastic teacher, Pratt was interested in science, the occult, philosophy, and popular tales. His first book was *Newfoundland Verse* (1923). He won the Governor-General's award three times.

Pratt felt that poetry should be, above all, energetic and exciting, "the expression of a grand binge, making for healthy psychological releases where . . . the poet becomes gloriously emancipated from the thralldom of day-to-day routine." Somewhat at odds with the experimental modernist era in which he wrote, Pratt usually worked within formal constraints, generally in octosyllabic couplets or blank verse. But the extravagant "epics" in which he celebrated Canada's history and landscape, and for which he is most famous (*The Titanic*, 1935, *Dunkirk*, 1941, *Brebeuf and His Brethren*, 1940, *Towards the Last Spike*, 1952) are frequently infused with sudden twists of grotesque detail that give them a flavor more modern than their traditional narrative forms might suggest. Pratt was excited by the potential for poetry in a country whose history and geography were still largely untouched by good poetry. Pratt's concern for intricate symbolic patterning and the moral implications of his subject matter have made the modern response to his work equivocal. Yet, even for those poets who consciously work against Pratt's example, his work remains important for its demonstration of the possibility of large-scale poetic creations on Canadian themes and elegant, insightfully original, and entertaining poetry.

Pratt also published *The Witches' Brew* (1926), *Titans* (1926), *The Fable of the Goats and Other Poems* (1943), and *Collected Poems* (1958, 1962).

E. J. PRATT

Newfoundland

Here the tides flow,
And here they ebb;
Not with that dull, unsinewed tread of waters
Held under bonds to move
5   Around unpeopled shores—
Moon-driven through a timeless circuit
Of invasion and retreat;
But with a lusty stroke of life
Pounding at stubborn gates,
10 That they might run
Within the sluices of men's hearts,
Leap under throb of pulse and nerve,
And teach the sea's strong voice
To learn the harmonies of new floods,
15 The peal of cataract,
And the soft wash of currents
Against resilient banks,
Or the broken rhythms from old chords
Along dark passages
20 That once were pathways of authentic fires.

Red is the sea-kelp on the beach,
Red as the heart's blood,
Nor is there power in tide or sun
To bleach its stain.
25 *It lies there piled thick*
Above the gulch-line.
It is rooted in the joints of rocks,
It is tangled around a spar,
It covers a broken rudder,
30 *It is red as the heart's blood,*
And salt as tears.

Here the winds blow,
And here they die,
Not with that wild, exotic rage
35 That vainly sweeps untrodden shores,
But with familiar breath

Holding a partnership with life,
Resonant with the hopes of spring,
Pungent with the airs of harvest.
40 They call with the silver fifes of the sea,
They breathe with the lungs of men,
They are one with the tides of the sea,
They are one with the tides of the heart,
They blow with the rising octaves of dawn,
45 They die with the largo of dusk,
Their hands are full to the overflow,
In their right is the bread of life,
In their left are the waters of death.

Scattered on boom
50 *And rudder and weed*
Are tangles of shells;
Some with backs of crusted bronze,
And faces of porcelain blue,
Some crushed by the beach stones
55 *To chips of jade;*
And some are spiral-cleft
Spreading their tracery on the sand
In the rich veining of an agate's heart;
And others remain unscarred,
60 *To babble of the passing of the winds.*

Here the crags
Meet with winds and tides—
Not with that blind interchange
Of blow for blow
65 That spills the thunder of insentient seas;
But with the mind that reads assault
In crouch and leap and the quick stealth,
Stiffening the muscles of the waves.
Here they flank the harbours,
70 Keeping watch
On thresholds, altars and the fires of home,
Or, like mastiffs,
Over-zealous,
Guard too well.

75 *Tide and wind and crag,*
Sea-weed and sea-shell
And broken rudder—
And the story is told
Of human veins and pulses,

80   *Of eternal pathways of fire,*
Of dreams that survive the night,
Of doors held ajar in storms.

(1923)

The Shark

He seemed to know the harbour,
So leisurely he swam;
His fin,
Like a piece of sheet-iron,
5   Three-cornered,
And with knife-edge,
Stirred not a bubble
As it moved
With its base-line on the water.

10   His body was tubular
And tapered
And smoke-blue,
And as he passed the wharf
He turned,
15   And snapped at a flat-fish
That was dead and floating.
And I saw the flash of a white throat,
And a double row of white teeth,
And eyes of metallic grey,
20   Hard and narrow and slit.

Then out of the harbour,
With that three-cornered fin
Shearing without a bubble the water
Lithely,
25   Leisurely,
He swam—
That strange fish,
Tubular, tapered, smoke-blue,
Part vulture, part wolf,
30   Part neither—for his blood was cold.

(1923)

From Stone to Steel

From stone to bronze, from bronze to steel
Along the road-dust of the sun,
Two revolutions of the wheel
From Java to Geneva run.

5 The snarl Neanderthal is worn
Close to the smiling Aryan lips,
The civil polish of the horn
Gleams from our praying finger tips.

The evolution of desire
10 Has but matured a toxic wine,
Drunk long before its heady fire
Reddened Euphrates or the Rhine.

Between the temple and the cave
The boundary lies tissue-thin:
15 The yearlings still the altars crave
As satisfaction for a sin.

The road goes up, the road goes down—
Let Java or Geneva be—
But whether to the cross or crown,
20 The path lies through Gethsemane.

(1932)

The Lee-Shore

Her heart cried out,—"Come home, come home,"
When the storm beat in at the door,
When the window showed a spatter of foam,
And her ear rang with the roar
5 Of the reef; and she called again, "Come home,"
To the ship in reach of the shore.

"But not to-night," flashed the signal light
From the Cape that guarded the bay,

"No, not to-night," rang the foam where the white
10 Hard edge of the breakers lay;
"Keep away from the crash of the storm at its height,
Keep away from the land, keep away."

"Come home," her heart cried out again,
"For the edge of the reef is white."
15 But she pressed her face to the window-pane,
And read the flash of the signal light;
Then her voice called out when her heart was slain,
"Keep away, my love, to-night."

(1932)

Come Away, Death

Willy-nilly, he comes or goes, with the clown's logic,
Comic in epitaph, tragic in epithalamium,
And unseduced by any mused rhyme.
However blow the winds over the pollen,
5 Whatever the course of the garden variables,
He remains the constant,
Ever flowering from the poppy seeds.

There was a time he came in formal dress,
Announced by Silence tapping at the panels
10 In deep apology.
A touch of chivalry in his approach,
He offered sacramental wine,
And with acanthus leaf
And petals of the hyacinth
15 He took the fever from the temples
And closed the eyelids,
Then led the way to his cool longitudes
In the dignity of the candles.

His mediaeval grace is gone—
20 Gone with the flame of the capitals
And the leisured turn of the thumb
Leafing the manuscripts,
Gone with the marbles
And the Venetian mosaics,
25 With the bend of the knee
Before the rose-strewn feet of the Virgin.

The *paternosters*[1] of his priests,
Committing clay to clay,
Have rattled in their throats
30   Under the gride of his traction tread.

One night we heard his footfall—one September night—
In the outskirts of a village near the sea.
There was a moment when the storm
Delayed its fist, when the surf fell
35   Like velvet on the rocks—a moment only;
The strangest lull we ever knew!
A sudden truce among the oaks
Released their fratricidal arms;
The poplars straightened to attention
40   As the winds stopped to listen
To the sound of a motor drone—
And then the drone was still.
We heard the tick-tock on the shelf,
And the leak of valves in our hearts.
45   A calm condensed and lidded
As at the core of a cyclone ended breathing
This was the monologue of Silence
Grave and unequivocal.

What followed was a bolt
50   Outside the range and target of the thunder,
And human speech curved back upon itself
Through Druid runways and the Piltdown scarps,[2]
Beyond the stammers of the Java caves,
To find its origins in hieroglyphs
55   On mouths and eyes and cheeks
Etched by a foreign stylus never used
On the outmoded page of the Apocalypse.

                                    (1943)

---

[1] The Lord's Prayer, commonly called The Our Father.
[2] Druid runways are the pathways around monuments erected by the Druids, an ancient Celtic order of priests, soothsayers, and poets; Piltdown scarps are steep cliffs that protected the supposed dwelling places of Piltdown man, a supposed species of primitive man that was proven a hoax in 1953.

William Carlos Williams

(1 8 8 3 – 1 9 6 3)

Like Wallace Stevens, William Carlos Williams worked at a profession far removed from literature: he was the most famous literary doctor since Chekhov. Williams knew most of the leading poets of his time—William Butler Yeats, Ezra Pound, H.D. (Hilda Doolittle), Wallace Stevens, and Reznikoff and Zukofsky. Born in Rutherford, New Jersey, Williams, who came to be seen as one of the most characteristically "American" poets, had a "melting-pot" ancestry: his father was English, his mother a Puerto Rican of French, Basque, and Jewish descent. Williams attended schools in Switzerland, Paris, and New York before he studied medicine in Pennsylvania. For a short while he was a consultant to the Library of Congress, but lost the job because he was deemed a "leftist." After that, Williams practiced medicine and lived with his wife and two sons in New Jersey until his death. He published his first book, *Poems,* in 1909, and achieved his first decisive success with *Spring and All* in 1923. Williams was given the National Book Award in 1950 and the Pulitzer Prize, for *Pictures from Breughel,* in 1963.

Williams's ideas about poetry have had a profound influence on modern poetry, particularly in America, where the "objectivist" group, and later Charles Olson, Robert Creeley, and the Black Mountain Poets were indebted to Williams's insistence on the centrality of human emotion in a physical environment, the abandonment of formal structures, the use of ordinary language, and the need for poetry to reflect the "flux of modern life." Williams's poetry follows his insistence, in his great epic *Paterson,* that there must be for poetry "No ideas but in things," that thought must not go beyond the specific context that gives rise to it. The poet must "think with his poem." Williams insisted on a poetry rooted in American experience, not out of patriotism but from a sense that real insight must arise out of a living place, a sense of the locale. His verse is spare, almost chiseled, purposefully unadorned and "antipoetic." Yet the poems are rarely prosaic. Williams achieves a nervous tension of rhythm that is always reaching toward a suspended fulfillment. His luminous perception of objects continually courts, but refuses to embrace, the symbolic. In his long poem *Paterson* (1946–1958), Williams attempted to discover new forms, to be local yet universal, to inculcate the particular detail into a large, anthropomorphizing epic that has some strategic similarities to *Finnegans Wake.*

Williams's publications include *The Tempers* (1913), *Al Que Quiere!* (1917), and the prose poems *Kora in Hell* (1920), *Collected Earlier Poems* (1951), *Collected Later Poems* (1950), *Journey to Love* (1955). His prose works include

In the American Grain (1925), *Make Light of It: Collected Stories* (1950), *Autobiography* (1951), and *Selected Essays* (1954).

WILLIAM CARLOS WILLIAMS

Spring and All

By the road to the contagious hospital
under the surge of the blue
mottled clouds driven from the
northeast—a cold wind. Beyond, the
5 waste of broad, muddy fields
brown with dried weeds, standing and fallen

patches of standing water
the scattering of tall trees

All along the road the reddish
10 purplish, forked, upstanding, twiggy
stuff of bushes and small trees
with dead, brown leaves under them
leafless vines—

Lifeless in appearance, sluggish
15 dazed spring approaches—

They enter the new world naked,
cold, uncertain of all
save that they enter. All about them
the cold, familiar wind—

20 Now the grass, tomorrow
the stiff curl of wildcarrot leaf
One by one objects are defined—
It quickens: clarity, outline of leaf

But now the stark dignity of
25 entrance—Still, the profound change
has come upon them: rooted, they
grip down and begin to awaken

(1923)

The Red Wheelbarrow

so much depends
upon

a red wheel
barrow

5   glazed with rain
water

beside the white
chickens.

(1923)

This Is Just to Say

I have eaten
the plums
that were in
the icebox

5   and which
you were probably
saving
for breakfast

Forgive me
10   they were delicious
so sweet
and so cold

(1934)

The Poor

It's the anarchy of poverty
delights me, the old
yellow wooden house indented
among the new brick tenements

5 Or a cast-iron balcony
with panels showing oak branches
in full leaf. It fits
the dress of the children

reflecting every stage and
10 custom of necessity—
Chimneys, roofs, fences of
wood and metal in an unfenced

age and enclosing next to
nothing at all: the old man
15 in a sweater and soft black
hat who sweeps the sidewalk—

his own ten feet of it
in a wind that fitfully
turning his corner has
20 overwhelmed the entire city

(1938)

The Dance

In Breughel's great picture, The Kermess,[1]
the dancers go round, they go round and
around, the squeal and the blare and the
tweedle of bagpipes, a bugle and fiddles
5 tipping their bellies (round as the thick-
sided glasses whose wash they impound)
their hips and their bellies off balance
to turn them. Kicking and rolling about
the Fair Grounds, swinging their butts, those
10 shanks must be sound to bear up under such
rollicking measures, prance as they dance
in Breughel's great picture, The Kermess.

(1944)

[1] Peter Breughel (ca. 1525–1569) was a Flemish painter. A kermess is an outdoor carnival.

Ezra Pound

(1 8 8 5 – 1 9 7 2)

The life of Ezra Pound is inextricably linked to the story of modern literature. Born in Idaho, Pound studied Romance languages and began translating verse at the University of Pennsylvania; then he moved to Italy. In 1908 he published his first volume, *A lume spento,* in Venice. In 1909 he was in London, where he set out to revolutionize modern writing. With T. E. Hulme, he founded an Imagist movement, operated as a correspondent for the American journal *Poetry,* and studied Provençal ballads, Anglo-Saxon poetry, and Chinese. Sometime before 1914 he began to plan the *Cantos,* an endeavor that would still be occupying him in his final, silent years, more than half a century later. In the 1920s Pound set up shop in Paris with a whole new circle of writers who worked tirelessly and selflessly on behalf of a host of authors. Despairing of the current economic and political order, he moved to Italy in 1924 and fell gradually under the sway of Mussolini's fascism. After World War II he was charged with treason for wartime radio broadcasts to American troops and was briefly imprisoned under harsh conditions in Pisa, where he wrote the magnificent "Pisan Cantos." Pound was eventually declared insane and incarcerated at St. Elizabeth's, in Washington, D.C. In 1958, pressure from writers, including Robert Frost and Ernest Hemingway, succeeded in securing Pound's release. Pound returned to Italy, where he lived with his daughter and his longtime companion, Olga Rudge. He died in Venice.

Ezra Pound helped to effect the change from the tired, sentimental vagueness of late Victorian poetry and fiction to the charged experimentation of modernism. He influenced or helped the careers of many of the century's greatest writers: William Carlos Williams, T. S. Eliot, William Butler Yeats, Robert Frost, D. H. Lawrence, James Joyce, Ernest Hemingway, Marianne Moore, H. D., Wyndham Lewis, and many others. Like T. S. Eliot and James Joyce, he believed that new life could be breathed into ancient myths through freely "translating" the essence of those myths into the terms of modern culture. He rejected the effusive lushness of Swinburne and insisted on the "direct treatment of the thing," on eliminating every word not essential to the presentation and on a rhythm that would utilize "the sequence of the musical phrase . . . not the sequence of the metronome." He defined the image as "an intellectual and emotional complex in an instant of time." Most of all he urged his followers to "go in fear of abstractions." Pound's own work is immensely varied and ranges from the superbly condensed knot of the two-line "In a Station of the Metro" to beautiful adaptations from the Chinese to the gigantic *Cantos,* a poem on which—despite undeniably classic sections—critical opinion is deeply divided. Pound's body of lasting verse is perhaps not large, but the shadow of his mind and his energy looms over all modern writers.

Pound's publications include *Personae* (1909), *Cathay* (1915), *Lustra* (1916), *Hugh Selwyn Mauberley* (1920), and *Homage to Sextus Propertius* (1939). His essays were collected in *The Literary Essays of Ezra Pound* (1954). Various drafts of parts of the *Cantos* began to appear as early as 1925. Cantos 1–84 were published in 1948 and the final, still uncompleted manuscript appeared in 1972.

EZRA POUND

The Return

See, they return; ah, see the tentative
Movements, and the slow feet,
The trouble in the pace and the uncertain
Wavering!

5 See, they return, one, and by one,
With fear, as half-awakened;
As if the snow should hesitate
And murmur in the wind,
          and half turn back;
10 These were the "Wing'd-with-Awe,"
    Inviolable,

Gods of the wingèd shoe!
With them the silver hounds,
        sniffing the trace of air!

15 Haie! Haie!
    These were the swift to harry;
These the keen-scented;
These were the souls of blood.

Slow on the leash,
20   pallid the leash-men!

(1912)

In a Station of the Metro

The apparition of these faces in the crowd;
Petals on a wet, black bough.

(1916)

Canto I[1]

AND then went down to the ship,
Set keel to breakers, forth on the godly sea, and
We set up mast and sail on that swart ship,
Bore sheep aboard her, and our bodies also
5 Heavy with weeping, and winds from sternward
Bore us out onward with bellying canvas,
Circe's this craft, the trim-coifed goddess.
Then sat we amidships, wind jamming the tiller,
Thus with stretched sail, we went over sea till day's end.
10 Sun to his slumber, shadows o'er all the ocean,
Came we then to the bounds of deepest water,
To the Kimmerian lands,[2] and peopled cities
Covered with close-webbed mist, unpierced ever
With glitter of sun-rays
15 Nor with stars stretched, nor looking back from heaven
Swartest night stretched over wretched men there.
The ocean flowing backward, came we then to the place
Aforesaid by Circe.
Here did they rites, Perimedes and Eurylochus,[3]
20 And drawing sword from my hip
I dug the ell-square pitkin;[4]
Poured we libations unto each the dead,
First mead and then sweet wine, water mixed with white flour.
Then prayed I many a prayer to the sickly death's-heads;
25 As set in Ithaca, sterile bulls of the best
For sacrifice, heaping the pyre with goods,
A sheep to Tiresias only, black and a bell-sheep.
Dark blood flowed in the fosse,°   ditch

---

[1] The first 68 lines of this canto is Pound's loose translation of an episode from Book XI of
Homer's *Odyssey,* which describes Odysseus's trip to the underworld.
[2] The Cimmerians were a mythical people living on the edge of the world.
[3] Two of Odysseus's men.
[4] Small hole in the earth.

Souls out of Erebus,° cadaverous dead, of brides   the underworld
30 Of youths and of the old who had borne much;
Souls stained with recent tears, girls tender,
Men many, mauled with bronze lance heads,
Battle spoil, bearing yet dreory° arms,   bloody
These many crowded about me; with shouting,
35 Pallor upon me, cried to my men for more beasts;
Slaughtered the herds, sheep slain of bronze;
Poured ointment, cried to the gods,
To Pluto the strong, and praised Proserpine;
Unsheathed the narrow sword,
40 I sat to keep off the impetuous impotent dead,
Till I should hear Tiresias.
But first Elpenor⁵ came, our friend Elpenor,
Unburied, cast on the wide earth,
Limbs that we left in the house of Circe,
45 Unwept, unwrapped in sepulchre, since toils urged other.
Pitiful spirit. And I cried in hurried speech:
"Elpenor, how art thou come to this dark coast?
"Cam'st thou afoot, outstripping seamen?"
            And he in heavy speech:
50 "Ill fate and abundant wine. I slept in Circe's ingle.
"Going down the long ladder unguarded,
"I fell against the buttress,
"Shattered the nape-nerve, the soul sought Avernus.⁶
"But thou, O King, I bid remember me, unwept, unburied,
55 "Heap up mine arms, be tomb by sea-bord, and inscribed:
"A man of no fortune, and with a name to come.
"And set my oar up, that I swung mid fellows."

And Anticlea⁷ came, whom I beat off, and then
            Tiresias Theban,
Holding his golden wand, knew me, and spoke first:
60 "A second time? why? man of ill star,
"Facing the sunless dead and this joyless region?
"Stand from the fosse, leave me my bloody bever°   drink
"For soothsay."
            And I stepped back,
65 And he strong with the blood, said then: "Odysseus
"Shalt return through spiteful Neptune, over dark seas,
"Lose all companions." And then Anticlea came.
Lie quiet Divus. I mean, that is Andreas Divus,

⁵ One of Odysseus's men.
⁶ A lake believed to be the entrance to the underworld; also a name for the underworld itself.
⁷ Odysseus's mother.

In officina Wecheli, 1538, out of Homer.[8]
70 And he sailed, by Sirens and thence outward and away
And unto Circe.
                    Venerandam,[9]
In the Cretan's phrase, with the golden crown, Aphrodite,
Cypri munimenta sortita est, mirthful, orichalchi,[10] with golden
75 Girdles and breast bands, thou with dark eyelids
Bearing the golden bough of Argicida.[11] So that:

                                        (1925)

---

[8] Andreas Divus is a sixteenth-century Italian translator of the *Odyssey;* his translation was
published at the printing shop of Wechel in Paris, in 1538.
[9] Worthy of reverence.
[10] *"Cypri munimenta sortita est":* "The citadels of Cyprus were her home"; "orichalchi": brass.
[11] An epithet for Hermes, messenger of the gods. The first of Pound's cantos ends with a colon.

T. S. Eliot

(1 8 8 8 – 1 9 6 5)

A poet and literary critic, Thomas Stearns Eliot was born and raised in St. Louis, Missouri. His family was wealthy. He received a classical education at home, then went to Harvard where he earned an M.A., and to the Sorbonne and Oxford. In 1910 he wrote his first major poem, "The Love Song of J. Alfred Prufrock." In 1914 he met Ezra Pound in London. Pound declared Eliot a "modern" poet and arranged to have "Prufrock" published in *Poetry*. In 1915 Eliot married Vivien Haigh-Wood. The marriage was disastrous. Much of the tortured sterility of *The Waste Land* mirrors Eliot's private life. To make money, he worked as a bank clerk. A nervous breakdown was followed by treatment in Lausanne, where he wrote the drafts of *The Waste Land* that Pound brilliantly edited into the poem published in 1922. The poem made Eliot famous and controversial. From 1922 to 1939 Eliot edited a journal called *The Criterion*. He also worked as an editor at Faber and Faber, and was a preeminent literary figure. His poetry became influential throughout the world. He separated from his wife in 1932 and his second marriage was a happy one. He converted to Anglo Catholicism, which spurred the more optimistic religious poetry of his late period. Eliot was awarded the Nobel Prize for literature in 1948.

Two ideas are central to an appreciation of Eliot's complex work: the notion of the "objective correlative" and his sense of "tradition and the individual talent." Eliot was influenced by the work of French symbolist poets, from whom he learned the possibility of the "objective" image of extreme symbolic condensation and great intellectual intricacy. The objective correlative, most clearly used in "Prufrock," was Eliot's term for an image that corresponded to an emotional state without symbolizing it in any conventional way. The technique was related to Eliot's conviction that poetry is "not a turning loose of an emotion, but an escape from emotion." The conviction has dubious validity, but it was a necessary reaction against the total expressionism of late-Victorian verse. Eliot also felt that each writer worked from within the entire literary tradition, and that that tradition altered a poet's work and the work altered the tradition in a subtle way. An interplay of allusion makes *The Waste Land* obscure; like James Joyce and Ezra Pound, Eliot attempted to use the vast resources of past literary genius to express his sense of the fragmented modern world. In his Christian period, particularly in the *Four Quartets,* Eliot dealt with the archetypal themes of pain and recovery, remorse and salvation. His verse is musical: The "free" verse of "Prufrock" is far more "poetic" than the formal verse of many other poets.

Prufrock and Other Observations appeared in 1917. *Poems* (1920) included

"Gerontion." *The Waste Land* (1922) and "The Hollow Men" (1925) consti-
tute the middle period and precede the first outwardly religious work, *Ash
Wednesday* (1930). *Four Quartets* was published in 1943. Eliot was also well
known as a playwright. His first and best play was *Murder in the Cathedral*
(1935). Later plays included *The Cocktail Party* (1950) and *The Confidential
Clerk* (1948). Eliot's enormously influential essays were gathered in *Selected
Essays* (1932, 1951), *The Use of Poetry and the Use of Criticism* (1933), and *On
Poetry and Poets* (1957).

T. S. ELIOT

The Love Song of J. Alfred Prufrock

*S'io credessi che mia risposta fosse
a persona che mai tornasse al mondo,
questa fiamma staria senza più scosse.
Ma per ciò che giammai di questo fondo
non tornò vivo alcun, s'i'odo il vero,
senza tema d'infamia ti rispondo.* [1]

　　Let us go then, you and I,
When the evening is spread out against the sky
Like a patient etherised upon a table;
Let us go, through certain half-deserted streets,
5　The muttering retreats
Of restless nights in one-night cheap hotels
And sawdust restaurants with oyster-shells:
Streets that follow like a tedious argument
Of insidious intent
10　To lead you to an overwhelming question . . .
Oh, do not ask, "What is it?"
Let us go and make our visit.

　　In the room the women come and go
Talking of Michelangelo.

[1] From Dante's *Inferno*, XXVII. 61–66. These words are spoken by Guido de Montefeltro, who
speaks from a flame in the chasm where false counselors are kept: "If I thought I was
answering one who would return to the world, this flame would cease to move any further.
But since no one has ever returned alive from this abyss, if what I hear is true, I answer you
without fear of infamy."

15 The yellow fog that rubs its back upon the window-panes,
The yellow smoke that rubs its muzzle on the window-panes,
Licked its tongue into the corners of the evening,
Lingered upon the pools that stand in drains,
Let fall upon its back the soot that falls from chimneys,
20 Slipped by the terrace, made a sudden leap,
And seeing that it was a soft October night,
Curled once about the house, and fell asleep.

And indeed there will be time
For the yellow smoke that slides along the street
25 Rubbing its back upon the window-panes;
There will be time, there will be time
To prepare a face to meet the faces that you meet;
There will be time to murder and create,
And time for all the works and days of hands
30 That lift and drop a question on your plate;
Time for you and time for me,
And time yet for a hundred indecisions,
And for a hundred visions and revisions,
Before the taking of a toast and tea.

35 In the room the women come and go
Talking of Michelangelo.

And indeed there will be time
To wonder, "Do I dare?" and, "Do I dare?"
Time to turn back and descend the stair,
40 With a bald spot in the middle of my hair—
(They will say: "How his hair is growing thin!")
My morning coat, my collar mounting firmly to the chin,
My necktie rich and modest, but asserted by a simple pin—
(They will say: "But how his arms and legs are thin!")
45 Do I dare
Disturb the universe?
In a minute there is time
For decisions and revisions which a minute will reverse.

For I have known them all already, known them all—
50 Have known the evenings, mornings, afternoons,
I have measured out my life with coffee spoons;
I know the voices dying with a dying fall
Beneath the music from a farther room.
So how should I presume?

55 And I have known the eyes already, known them all—
The eyes that fix you in a formulated phrase,

And when I am formulated, sprawling on a pin,
When I am pinned and wriggling on the wall,
Then how should I begin
60 To spit out all the butt-ends of my days and ways?
     And how should I presume?

     And I have known the arms already, known them all—
Arms that are braceleted and white and bare
(But in the lamplight, downed with light brown hair!)
65 Is it perfume from a dress
That makes me so digress?
Arms that lie along a table, or wrap about a shawl.
     And should I then presume?
     And how should I begin?

                    .   .   .   .   .

70   Shall I say, I have gone at dusk through narrow streets
And watched the smoke that rises from the pipes
Of lonely men in shirt-sleeves, leaning out of windows? . . .
     I should have been a pair of ragged claws
Scuttling across the floors of silent seas.

                    .   .   .   .   .

75   And the afternoon, the evening, sleeps so peacefully!
Smoothed by long fingers,
Asleep . . . tired . . . or it malingers,
Stretched on the floor, here beside you and me.
Should I, after tea and cakes and ices,
80 Have the strength to force the moment to its crisis?
But though I have wept and fasted, wept and prayed,
Though I have seen my head (grown slightly bald)
          brought in upon a platter,
I am no prophet—and here's no great matter;
I have seen the moment of my greatness flicker,
85 And I have seen the eternal Footman hold my coat, and snicker,
And in short, I was afraid.

     And would it have been worth it, after all,
After the cups, the marmalade, the tea,
Among the porcelain, among some talk of you and me,
90 Would it have been worth while,
To have bitten off the matter with a smile,
To have squeezed the universe into a ball
To roll it towards some overwhelming question,
To say: "I am Lazarus, come from the dead,
95 Come back to tell you all, I shall tell you all"—
If one, settling a pillow by her head,

Should say: "That is not what I meant at all.
That is not it, at all."

    And would it have been worth it, after all,
100 Would it have been worth while,
After the sunsets and the dooryards and the sprinkled streets,
After the novels, after the teacups, after the skirts that trail along
       the floor—
And this, and so much more?—
It is impossible to say just what I mean!
105 But as if a magic lantern threw the nerves in patterns on a screen:
Would it have been worth while
If one, settling a pillow or throwing off a shawl,
And turning toward the window, should say:
    "That is not it at all,
110 That is not what I meant, at all."

      .   .   .   .   .

    —No! I am not Prince Hamlet, nor was meant to be;
Am an attendant lord, one that will do
To swell a progress, start a scene or two,
Advise the prince; no doubt, an easy tool,
115 Deferential, glad to be of use,
Politic, cautious, and meticulous;
Full of high sentence, but a bit obtuse;
At times, indeed, almost ridiculous—
Almost, at times, the Fool.

120   I grow old . . . I grow old . . .
I shall wear the bottoms of my trousers rolled.

    Shall I part my hair behind? Do I dare to eat a peach?
I shall wear white flannel trousers, and walk upon the beach.
I have heard the mermaids singing, each to each.

125 I do not think that they will sing to me.

I have seen them riding seaward on the waves
Combing the white hair of the waves blown back
When the wind blows the water white and black.

We have lingered in the chambers of the sea
130 By sea-girls wreathed with seaweed red and brown
Till human voices wake us, and we drown.

                      (1917)

The Waste Land[1]

"Nam Sibyllam quidem Cumis ego ipse oculis meis
vidi in ampulla pendere, et cum illi pueri dicerent:
Σίβυλλα τί θέλεις; respondebat illa: ἀποθανεῖν θέλω."[2]

For Ezra Pound
il miglior fabbro.[3]

I. THE BURIAL OF THE DEAD

April is the cruellest month, breeding
Lilacs out of the dead land, mixing
Memory and desire, stirring
Dull roots with spring rain.
5   Winter kept us warm, covering
Earth in forgetful snow, feeding
A little life with dried tubers.
Summer surprised us, coming over the Starnbergersee[4]
With a shower of rain; we stopped in the colonnade,
10   And went on in sunlight, into the Hofgarten,[5]
And drank coffee, and talked for an hour.
Bin gar keine Russin, stamm' aus Litauen, echt deutsch.[6]
And when we were children, staying at the arch-duke's,
My cousin's, he took me out on a sled,
15   And I was frightened. He said, Marie,
Marie, hold on tight. And down we went.
In the mountains, there you feel free.
I read, much of the night, and go south in the winter.

---

[1] Not only the title, but the plan and a good deal of the incidental symbolism of the poem were suggested by Miss Jessie L. Weston's book on the Grail legend: *From Ritual to Romance* (Cambridge). Indeed, so deeply am I indebted, Miss Weston's book will elucidate the difficulties of the poem much better than my notes can do; and I recommend it (apart from the great interest of the book itself) to any who think such elucidation of the poem worth the trouble. To another work of anthropology I am indebted in general, one which has influenced our generation profoundly; I mean *The Golden Bough* [by Sir James Fraser]; I have used especially the two volumes *Adonis, Attis, Osiris.* Anyone who is acquainted with these works will immediately recognise in the poem certain references to vegetation ceremonies (Eliot's note).

[2] "For once, I saw with my own eyes the Sibyl at Cumae hanging in a cage, and when the boys said to her 'Sibyl, what do you want?' she answered 'I want to die.'" (From *Satyricon*, by Petronius, a first century A.D. Roman satirist.)

[3] The better craftsman.

[4] A lake near Munich, West Germany.

[5] A small park in Munich.

[6] "I am not Russian, I come from Lithuania, a real German."

What are the roots that clutch, what branches grow
20 Out of this stony rubbish? Son of man,[7]
You cannot say, or guess, for you know only
A heap of broken images, where the sun beats,
And the dead tree gives no shelter, the cricket no relief,[8]
And the dry stone no sound of water. Only
25 There is shadow under this red rock,
(Come in under the shadow of this red rock),
And I will show you something different from either
Your shadow at morning striding behind you
Or your shadow at evening rising to meet you;
30 I will show you fear in a handful of dust.

Frisch weht der Wind
Der Heimat zu
Mein Irisch Kind,
Wo weilest du?[9]

35 "You gave me hyacinths first a year ago;
"They called me the hyacinth girl."
—Yet when we came back, late, from the hyacinth garden,
Your arms full, and your hair wet, I could not
Speak, and my eyes failed, I was neither
40 Living nor dead, and I knew nothing,
Looking into the heart of light, the silence.
Oed' und leer das Meer.[10]

Madame Sosostris, famous clairvoyante,
Had a bad cold, nevertheless
45 Is known to be the wisest woman in Europe,
With a wicked pack of cards.[11] Here, said she,
Is your card, the drowned Phoenician Sailor,

---

[7] Cf. Ezekiel II, i (Eliot's note). "And he said unto me, Son of man, stand upon thy feet, and I will speak unto thee."

[8] Cf. Ecclesiastes XII, v (Eliot's note). "Also *when* they shall be afraid of *that which is* high, and fears *shall be* in the way, and the almond tree shall flourish, and the grasshopper shall be a burden, and desire shall fail: because man goeth to his long home, and the mourners go about the streets:"

[9] V. Tristan and Isolde, I, verses 5–8 (Eliot's note). "Fresh blows the wind to the homeland. My Irish child, where are you waiting?"

[10] Id. III, verse 24 (Eliot's note). "The sea is barren and empty."

[11] I am not familiar with the exact constitution of the Tarot pack of cards, from which I have obviously departed to suit my own convenience. The Hanged Man, a member of the traditional pack, fits my purpose in two ways: because he is associated in my mind with the Hanged God of Frazer, and because I associate him with the hooded figure in the passage of the disciples to Emmaus in Part V. The Phoenician Sailor and the Merchant appear later; also the "crowds of people", and Death by Water is executed in Part IV. The Man with Three Staves (an authentic member of the Tarot pack) I associate, quite arbitrarily, with the Fisher King himself (Eliot's note).

(Those are pearls that were his eyes. Look!)
Here is Belladonna, the Lady of the Rocks,
50 The lady of situations.
Here is the man with three staves, and here the Wheel,
And here is the one-eyed merchant, and this card,
Which is blank, is something he carries on his back,
Which I am forbidden to see. I do not find
55 The Hanged Man. Fear death by water.
I see crowds of people, walking round in a ring.
Thank you. If you see dear Mrs. Equitone,
Tell her I bring the horoscope myself:
One must be so careful these days.

60   Unreal City,[12]
Under the brown fog of a winter dawn,
A crowd flowed over London Bridge, so many,
I had not thought death had undone so many.[13]
Sighs, short and infrequent, were exhaled,[14]
65 And each man fixed his eyes before his feet.
Flowed up the hill and down King William Street,
To where Saint Mary Woolnoth kept the hours
With a dead sound on the final stroke of nine.[15]
There I saw one I knew, and stopped him, crying: 'Stetson!
70 "You who were with me in the ships at Mylae!
"'That corpse you planted last year in your garden,
"'Has it begun to sprout? Will it bloom this year?

[12] Cf. Baudelaire:

> "Fourmillante cité, cité pleine de rêves,
> "Où le spectre en plein jour raccroche le passant." (Eliot's note).

> "Teeming city, city full of dreams,
> Where spectres in broad daylight confront the passer-by."

[13] Cf. Inferno III, 55–57:

>   si lunga tratta
> di gente, ch'io non averei creduto
>   che morte tanta n'avesse disfatta. (Eliot's note.)

> "Such an endless train of people / That I never would have
> thought / That death had done away with so many."

[14] Cf. Inferno IV, 25–27:

> Quivi, secondo che per ascoltare,
> non avea pianto mai che di sospiri
> che l'aura eterna facevan tremare. (Eliot's note.)

> "We heard no complaints or crying there, / No lamentation
> except the sound of sighing / That floated through the
> eternal air."

[15] A phenomenon which I have often noticed (Eliot's note).

"Or has the sudden frost disturbed its bed?
"O keep the Dog far hence, that's friend to men,[16]
75 "Or with his nails he'll dig it up again!
"You! hypocrite lecteur!—mon semblable,—mon frère!"[17]

II. A GAME OF CHESS

The Chair she sat in, like a burnished throne,[18]
Glowed on the marble, where the glass
Held up by standards wrought with fruited vines
80 From which a golden Cupidon peeped out
(Another hid his eyes behind his wing)
Doubled the flames of sevenbranched candelabra
Reflecting light upon the table as
The glitter of her jewels rose to meet it,
85 From satin cases poured in rich profusion.
In vials of ivory and coloured glass
Unstoppered, lurked her strange synthetic perfumes,
Unguent, powdered, or liquid—troubled, confused
And drowned the sense in odours; stirred by the air
90 That freshened from the window, these ascended
In fattening the prolonged candle-flames,
Flung their smoke into the laquearia,[19]
Stirring the pattern on the coffered ceiling.
Huge sea-wood fed with copper
95 Burned green and orange, framed by the coloured stone,
In which sad light a carvèd dolphin swam.
Above the antique mantel was displayed
As though a window gave upon the sylvan scene[20]
The change of Philomel, by the barbarous king[21]
100 So rudely forced; yet there the nightingale[22]
Filled all the desert with inviolable voice

[16] Cf. the Dirge in Webster's *White Devil* (Eliot's note). The dirge includes the lines: "But keep the wolf far thence, that's foe to men, / For with his nails he'll dig them up again."

[17] V. Baudelaire, Preface to *Fleurs du Mal* (Eliot's note). Eliot borrows a line from Baudelaire's *Fleurs du Mal (The Flowers of Evil):* "Hypocrite reader!—my mirror,—my brother!"

[18] Cf. *Antony and Cleopatra,* II ii, 1. 190 (Eliot's note). "I will tell you. The barge she sat in, like a burnish'd throne, / Burn'd on the water . . ."

[19] Laquearia. V. *Aeneid,* I, 726:

> dependent lychni laquearibus aureis
> incensi, et noctem flammis funalia vincunt. (Eliot's note.)

A passage from Virgil's *Aeneid:* "Burning torches hang from the golden ceilings, and flames disperse the night with their brightness."

[20] Sylvan scene. V. Milton, *Paradise Lost,* IV, 140 (Eliot's note).

[21] V. Ovid, *Metamorphoses,* VI, Philomela (Eliot's note). In Ovid's version of the myth of the rape of Philomela by Tereus ("the barbarous king"), Philomela was transformed into a nightingale.

[22] Cf. Part III, 1. 204 (Eliot's note).

And still she cried, and still the world pursues,
"Jug Jug"[23] to dirty ears.
And other withered stumps of time
105 Were told upon the walls; staring forms
Leaned out, leaning, hushing the room enclosed.
Footsteps shuffled on the stair.
Under the firelight, under the brush, her hair
Spread out in fiery points
110 Glowed into words, then would be savagely still.

  "My nerves are bad to-night. Yes, bad. Stay with me.
"Speak to me. Why do you never speak. Speak.
  "What are you thinking of? What thinking? What?
"I never know what you are thinking. Think."

115   I think we are in rats' alley[24]
Where the dead men lost their bones.

  "What is that noise?"
      The wind under the door.[25]
"What is that noise now? What is the wind doing?"
120   Nothing again nothing.
            "Do
"You know nothing? Do you see nothing? Do you remember
"Nothing?"

    I remember
125 Those are pearls that were his eyes.
"Are you alive, or not? Is there nothing in your head?"[26]
           But
O O O O that Shakespeherian Rag—
It's so elegant
130 So intelligent
"What shall I do now? What shall I do?"
"I shall rush out as I am, and walk the street
"With my hair down, so. What shall we do tomorrow?
"What shall we ever do?"
135   The hot water at ten.
And if it rains, a closed car at four.
And we shall play a game of chess,
Pressing lidless eyes and waiting for a knock upon the door.[27]

[23] The song of the nightingale in Elizabethan poetry and drama.
[24] Cf. Part III, l. 195 (Eliot's note).
[25] Cf. Webster: "Is the wind in that door still?" (Eliot's note.) This line comes from Webster's *The Devil Law's Case,* the source of the next of Eliot's glosses as well.
[26] Cf. Part I, l. 37, 48 (Eliot's note).
[27] Cf. the game of chess in (Thomas) Middleton's *Women beware Women* (Eliot's note). In the play a woman is seduced while her mother-in-law is distracted by a game of chess.

When Lil's husband got demobbed,[28] I said—
140 I didn't mince my words, I said to her myself,
HURRY UP PLEASE ITS TIME
Now Albert's coming back, make yourself a bit smart.
He'll want to know what you done with that money he gave you
To get yourself some teeth. He did, I was there.
145 You have them all out, Lil, and get a nice set,
He said, I swear, I can't bear to look at you.
And no more can't I, I said, and think of poor Albert,
He's been in the army four years, he wants a good time,
And if you don't give it him, there's others will, I said.
150 Oh is there, she said. Something o' that, I said.
Then I'll know who to thank, she said, and give me a straight look.
HURRY UP PLEASE ITS TIME
If you don't like it you can get on with it, I said.
Others can pick and choose if you can't.
155 But if Albert makes off, it won't be for lack of telling.
You ought to be ashamed, I said, to look so antique.
(And her only thirty-one.)
I can't help it, she said, pulling a long face,
It's them pills I took, to bring it off, she said.
160 (She's had five already, and nearly died of young George.)
The chemist said it would be all right, but I've never been the
    same.
You *are* a proper fool, I said.
Well, if Albert won't leave you alone, there it is, I said,
What you get married for if you don't want children?
165 HURRY UP PLEASE ITS TIME
Well, that Sunday Albert was home, they had a hot gammon,
And they asked me in to dinner, to get the beauty of it hot—
HURRY UP PLEASE ITS TIME
HURRY UP PLEASE ITS TIME
170 Goonight Bill. Goonight Lou. Goonight May. Goonight.
Ta ta. Goonight. Goonight.
Good night, ladies, good night, sweet ladies, good night, good
    night.

III. THE FIRE SERMON

The river's tent is broken; the last fingers of leaf
Clutch and sink into the wet bank. The wind
175 Crosses the brown land, unheard. The nymphs are departed.
Sweet Thames, run softly, till I end my song.[29]

---

[28] I.e., demobilized from active military service.
[29] V. Spenser, *Prothalamion* (Eliot's note). Eliot uses the refrain from Spenser's poem.

The river bears no empty bottles, sandwich papers,
Silk handkerchiefs, cardboard boxes, cigarette ends
Or other testimony of summer nights. The nymphs are
        departed.
180 And their friends, the loitering heirs of City directors;
Departed, have left no addresses.
By the waters of Leman I sat down and wept . . .[30]
Sweet Thames, run softly till I end my song,
Sweet Thames, run softly, for I speak not loud or long.
185 But at my back in a cold blast I hear
The rattle of the bones, and chuckle spread from ear to ear.

A rat crept softly through the vegetation
Dragging its slimy belly on the bank
While I was fishing in the dull canal
190 On a winter evening round behind the gashouse
Musing upon the king my brother's wreck
And on the king my father's death before him.[31]
White bodies naked on the low damp ground
And bones cast in a little low dry garret,
195 Rattled by the rat's foot only, year to year.
But at my back from time to time I hear[32]
The sound of horns and motors, which shall bring
Sweeney to Mrs. Porter in the spring.[33]
O the moon shone bright on Mrs. Porter
200 And on her daughter
They wash their feet in soda water[34]
Et O ces voix d'enfants, chantant dans la coupole![35]

Twit twit twit
Jug jug jug jug jug jug
205 So rudely forc'd.
Tereu[36]

    Unreal City
    Under the brown fog of a winter noon

[30] Cf. Psalm 137. Lake Geneva is also known as Lake Leman.
[31] Cf. *The Tempest,* I, ii (Eliot's note).
[32] Cf. Marvell, *To His Coy Mistress* (Eliot's note), especially lines 21–24. See p. 115.
[33] Cf. Day, *Parliament of Bees:*

> "When of the sudden, listening, you shall hear,
> "A noise of horns and hunting, which shall bring
> "Actaeon to Diana in the spring,
> "Where all shall see her naked skin . . ." (Eliot's note.)

[34] I do not know the origin of the ballad from which these lines are taken: it was reported to
me from Sydney, Australia (Eliot's note).
[35] V. Verlaine, *Parsifal* (Eliot's note). "And O these children's voices, singing in the dome!"
[36] I.e., Tereus.

Mr. Eugenides, the Smyrna merchant
210 Unshaven, with a pocket full of currants[37]
C.i.f. London: documents at sight,
Asked me in demotic French
To luncheon at the Cannon Street Hotel
Followed by a weekend at the Metropole.

215   At the violet hour, when the eyes and back
Turn upward from the desk, when the human engine waits
Like a taxi throbbing waiting,
I Tiresias,[38] though blind, throbbing between two lives,
Old man with wrinkled female breasts, can see
220 At the violet hour, the evening hour that strives
Homeward, and brings the sailor home from sea,[39]
The typist home at teatime, clears her breakfast, lights
Her stove, and lays out food in tins.
Out of the window perilously spread
225 Her drying combinations touched by the sun's last rays,
On the divan are piled (at night her bed)
Stockings, slippers, camisoles, and stays.
I Tiresias, old man with wrinkled dugs
Perceived the scene, and foretold the rest—
230 I too awaited the expected guest.
He, the young man carbuncular, arrives,
A small house agent's clerk, with one bold stare,
One of the low on whom assurance sits
As a silk hat on a Bradford millionaire.[40]
235 The time is now propitious, as he guesses,

---

[37] The currants were quoted at a price "cost insurance and freight to London"; and the Bill of Lading, etc., were to be handed to the buyer upon payment of the sight draft (Eliot's note).

[38] Tiresias, although a mere spectator and not indeed a "character," is yet the most important personage in the poem, uniting all the rest. Just as the one-eyed merchant, seller of currants, melts into the Phoenician Sailor, and the latter is not wholly distinct from Ferdinand Prince of Naples, so all the women are one woman, and the two sexes meet in Tiresias. What Tiresias *sees*, in fact, is the substance of the poem. The whole passage from Ovid is of great anthropological interest: . . . (Eliot's note.) Eliot quotes a long passage in Latin from Ovid's *Metamorphoses*: "After drinking a great deal, Jupiter teased Juno, who shared in the game, by saying: 'You women enjoy love more than men, and your pleasure is greater.' Juno denied this, so they decided to ask the opinion of wise Tiresias, since he had experienced love as both a man and a woman. Once, he saw two snakes copulating in a green forest, and hit them with his staff. He was miraculously changed into a woman and stayed that way for seven years. In the eighth year he saw the snakes again and said: 'If hitting you is so magical that it changes the sex of the hitter, then I will hit you again.' He struck the snakes again and was changed back to his original shape, the one that he was born with. Because of this, he was chosen to arbitrate this playful argument, and supported what Jupiter had said. It is said that Juno was more upset than she really should have been, and she condemned Tiresias to eternal blindness. Although no god can undo what another god has done, the almighty father gave Tiresias the power to know the future, and thereby lightened the punishment by this honor."

[39] This may not appear as exact as Sappho's lines, but I had in mind the "longshore" or "dory" fisherman, who returns at nightfall (Eliot's note).

[40] Bradford is a manufacturing town in Yorkshire, England, where many people made quick fortunes during World War I.

The meal is ended, she is bored and tired,
Endeavours to engage her in caresses
Which still are unreproved, if undesired.
Flushed and decided, he assaults at once;
240   Exploring hands encounter no defence;
His vanity requires no response,
And makes a welcome of indifference.
(And I Tiresias have foresuffered all
Enacted on this same divan or bed;
245   I who have sat by Thebes below the wall
And walked among the lowest of the dead.)
Bestows one final patronising kiss,
And gropes his way, finding the stairs unlit . . .

She turns and looks a moment in the glass,
250   Hardly aware of her departed lover;
Her brain allows one half-formed thought to pass:
'Well now that's done: and I'm glad it's over.'
When lovely woman stoops to folly and
Paces about her room again, alone,
255   She smoothes her hair with automatic hand,
And puts a record on the gramophone.[41]

"This music crept by me upon the waters"[42]
And along the Strand, up Queen Victoria Street.
O City city, I can sometimes hear
260   Beside a public bar in Lower Thames Street,
The pleasant whining of a mandoline
And a clatter and a chatter from within
Where fishmen lounge at noon: where the walls
Of Magnus Martyr hold
265   Inexplicable splendour of Ionian white and gold.[43]

The river sweats[44]
Oil and tar
The barges drift

[41] V. Goldsmith, the song in *The Vicar of Wakefield* (Eliot's note). In Oliver Goldsmith's novel is the following song: "When lovely woman stoops to folly / And finds too late that men betray / What charm can soothe her melancholy, / What art can wash her guilt away? / The only art her guilt to cover, / To hide her shame from every eye, / To give repentence to her lover / And wring his bosom—is to die."

[42] V. *The Tempest,* as above (Eliot's note).

[43] The interior of St. Magnus Martyr is to my mind one of the finest among (Christopher) Wren's interiors. See *The Proposed Demolition of Nineteen City Churches* (P. S. King & Son, Ltd.) (Eliot's note).

[44] The song of the (three) Thames-daughters begins here. From line 392 to 306 inclusive they speak in turn. V. *Götterdämmerung,* III, i: the Rhine-daughters (Eliot's note). Eliot here directs the reader to Wagner's opera *Die Götterdämmerung.*

With the turning tide
270   Red sails
Wide
To leeward, swing on the heavy spar.
The barges wash
Drifting logs
275   Down Greenwich reach
Past the Isle of Dogs.
                Weialala leia
                Wallala leialala

Elizabeth and Leicester[45]
280   Beating oars
The stern was formed
A gilded shell
Red and gold
The brisk swell
285   Rippled both shores
Southwest wind
Carried down stream
The peal of bells
White towers
290   Weialala leia
                Wallala leialala

'Trams and dusty trees.
Highbury bore me. Richmond and Kew
Undid me.[46] By Richmond I raised my knees
295   Supine on the floor of a narrow canoe.'

'My feet are at Moorgate, and my heart
Under my feet. After the event
He wept. He promised "a new start."
I made no comment. What should I resent?'

300   'On Margate Sands.
I can connect
Nothing with nothing.

---

[45] V. Froude, *Elizabeth*, Vol. I, ch. iv, letter of De Quadra to Philip of Spain: "In the afternoon we were in a barge, watching the games on the river. (The Queen) was alone with Lord Robert and myself on the poop, when they began to talk nonsense, and went so far that Lord Robert at last said, as I was on the spot there was no reason why they should not be married if the queen pleased." (Eliot's note.)

[46] Cf. *Purgatorio*, V. 133:

> "Ricorditi di me, che son la Pia;
> "Siena mi fe', disfecemi Maremma." (Eliot's note.)

"Remember me, I am La Pia; / Siena made me, Maremma broke me."

The broken fingernails of dirty hands.
My people humble people who expect
305 Nothing."
                    la la

To Carthage then I came[47]

Burning burning burning burning[48]
O Lord Thou pluckest me out[49]
310 O Lord Thou pluckest

burning

IV. DEATH BY WATER

Phlebas the Phoenician, a fortnight dead,
Forgot the cry of gulls, and the deep sea swell
And the profit and loss.
315   A current under sea
Picked his bones in whispers. As he rose and fell
He passed the stages of his age and youth
Entering the whirlpool.
                        Gentile or Jew
320 O you who turn the wheel and look to windward,
Consider Phlebas, who was once handsome and tall as you.

V. WHAT THE THUNDER SAID[50]

After the torchlight red on sweaty faces
After the frosty silence in the gardens
After the agony in stony places
325 The shouting and the crying
Prison and palace and reverberation

[47] V. St. Augustine's *Confessions:* "to Carthage then I came, where a cauldron of unholy loves sang all about mine ears" (Eliot's note).
[48] The complete text of the Buddha's Fire Sermon (which corresponds in importance to the Sermon on the Mount) from which these words are taken, will be found translated in the late Henry Clarke Warren's *Buddhism in Translation* (Harvard Oriental Series). Mr. Warren was one of the great pioneers of Buddhist studies in the Occident (Eliot's note).
[49] From St. Augustine's *Confessions* again. The collocation of these two representatives of eastern and western asceticism, as the culmination of this part of the poem, is not an accident (Eliot's note).
[50] In the first part of Part V three themes are employed: the journey to Emmaus, the approach to the Chapel Perilous (see Miss Weston's book) and the present decay of eastern Europe (Eliot's note).

Of thunder of spring over distant mountains
He who was living is now dead
We who were living are now dying
330   With a little patience

Here is no water but only rock
Rock and no water and the sandy road
The road winding above among the mountains
Which are mountains of rock without water
335   If there were water we should stop and drink
Amongst the rock one cannot stop or think
Sweat is dry and feet are in the sand
If there were only water amongst the rock
Dead mountain mouth of carious teeth that cannot spit
340   Here one can neither stand nor lie nor sit
There is not even silence in the mountains
But dry sterile thunder without rain
There is not even solitude in the mountains
But red sullen faces sneer and snarl
345   From doors of mudcracked houses
                      If there were water

And no rock
If there were rock
And also water
350   And water
A spring
A pool among the rock
If there were the sound of water only
Not the cicada
355   And dry grass singing
But sound of water over a rock
Where the hermit-thrush sings in the pine trees[51]
Drip drop drip drop drop drop drop
But there is no water

360   Who is the third who walks always beside you?[52]
When I count, there are only you and I together

[51] This is *Turdus aonalaschkae pallasii,* the hermit-thrush which I have heard in Quebec Province. Chapman says *(Handbook of Birds of Eastern North America)* "it is most at home in secluded woodland and thickety retreats. . . . Its notes are not remarkable for variety or volume, but in purity and sweetness of tone and exquisite modulation they are unequalled." Its "water-dripping song" is justly celebrated (Eliot's note).

[52] The following lines were stimulated by the account of one of the Antarctic expeditions (I forget which, but I think one of Shackleton's): it was related that the party of explorers, at the extremity of their strength, had the constant delusion that there was *one more member* than could actually be counted (Eliot's note).

But when I look ahead up the white road
There is always another one walking beside you
Gliding wrapt in a brown mantle, hooded
365 I do not know whether a man or a woman
    —But who is that on the other side of you?

    What is that sound high in the air[53]
    Murmur of maternal lamentation
    Who are those hooded hordes swarming
370 Over endless plains, stumbling in cracked earth
    Ringed by the flat horizon only
    What is the city over the mountains
    Cracks and reforms and bursts in the violet air
    Falling towers
375 Jerusalem Athens Alexandria
    Vienna London
    Unreal

    A woman drew her long black hair out tight
    And fiddled whisper music on those strings
380 And bats with baby faces in the violet light
    Whistled, and beat their wings
    And crawled head downward down a blackened wall
    And upside down in air were towers
    Tolling reminiscent bells, that kept the hours
385 And voices singing out of empty cisterns and exhausted
        wells.

    In this decayed hole among the mountains
    In the faint moonlight, the grass is singing
    Over the tumbled graves, about the chapel
    There is the empty chapel, only the wind's home.
390 It has no windows, and the door swings,
    Dry bones can harm no one.
    Only a cock stood on the rooftree
    Co co rico co co rico
    In a flash of lightning. Then a damp gust
395 Bringing rain

[53] 366–376. Cf. Hermann Hesse, *Blick ins Chaos:* "Schon ist halb Europa, schon ist zumindest der halbe Osten Europas auf dem Wege zum Chaos, fährt betrunken im heiligen Wahn am Abgrund entlang und singt dazu, singt betrunken und hymnisch wie Dmitri Karamasoff sang. Ueber diese Lieder lacht der Bürger beleidigt, der Heilige und Seher hört sie mit Tränen" (Eliot's note). "Already half Europe, already half of Eastern Europe, is on the way to chaos, and drives drunkenly along the edge of the cliff, and sings drunkenly, like Dmitri Karamasoff singing hymns. The offended bourgeois laughs at the songs, the saint and the mystic listen to them with tears."

Ganga[54] was sunken, and the limp leaves
Waited for rain, while the black clouds
Gathered far distant, over Himavant.
The jungle crouched, humped in silence.
400   Then spoke the thunder
DA[55]
Datta: what have we given?
My friend, blood shaking my heart
The awful daring of a moment's surrender
405   Which an age of prudence can never retract
By this, and this only, we have existed
Which is not to be found in our obituaries
Or in memories draped by the beneficent spider[56]
Or under seals broken by the lean solicitor
410   In our empty rooms

DA
Dayadhvam: I have heard the key[57]
Turn in the door once and turn once only
We think of the key, each in his prison
415   Thinking of the key, each confirms a prison
Only at nightfall, aethereal rumours
Revive for a moment a broken Coriolanus
DA
Damyata: The boat responded
420   Gaily, to the hand expert with sail and oar
The sea was calm, your heart would have responded
Gaily, when invited, beating obedient
To controlling hands

---

[54] The River Ganges, in India.
[55] "Datta, dayadhvam, damyata" (Give, sympathise, control). The fable of the meaning of the Thunder is found in the *Brihadaranyaka—Upanishad*, 5, 1. A translation is found in Deussen's *Sechzig Upanishads des Veda*, p. 489 (Eliot's note).
[56] Cf. Webster, *The White Devil*, V, vi:

> ". . . they'll remarry
> Ere the worm pierce your winding-sheet, ere the spider
> Make a thin curtain for your epitaphs" (Eliot's note).

[57] Cf. *Inferno*, XXXIII, 46:

> "ed io senti chiavar l'uscio di sotto
> all' orribile torre." ("Then I heard, from the base
> of the tower, the gates being locked up.")

Also F. H. Bradley, *Appearance and Reality*, p. 306. "My external sensations are no less private to my self than are my thoughts or my feelings. In either case my experience falls within my own circle, a circle closed on the outside; and, with all its elements alike, every sphere is opaque to the others which surround it . . . In brief, regarded as an existence which appears in a soul, the whole world for each is peculiar and private to that soul" (Eliot's note).

I sat upon the shore

425 Fishing,[58] with the arid plain behind me

Shall I at least set my lands in order?

London Bridge is falling down falling down falling down

Poi s'ascose nel foco che gli affina[59]

Quando fiam uti chelidon[60]—O swallow swallow

430 *Le Prince d' Aquitaine à la tour abolie*[61]

These fragments I have shored against my ruins

Why then Ile fit you. Hieronymo's mad againe.[62]

Datta. Dayadhvam. Damyata.

Shantih shantih shantih[63]

(1922)

---

[58] V. Weston: *From Ritual to Romance;* chapter on the Fisher King (Eliot's note).

[59] V *Purgatorio,* XXVI, 148.

> ' "Ara vos prec per aquella valor
> "que vos condus al som de l'escalina,
> "sovenha vos a temps de ma dolor."
> "Poi s'ascose nel foco che li affina."

(Eliot's note.) "Now I ask you, because of that grace which guides you to the top of the stairway, think of me and my pain in your own time." The line that Eliot quotes (line 428) can be translated: "Then he hid himself back in the consuming flames."

[60] V. *Pervigilium Veneris.* Cf. Philomela in Parts II and III (Eliot's note). The line that Eliot quotes (line 429) can be translated: "When will I be like the swallow?"

[61] V. Gerard de Nerval, Sonnet *El Desdichado* (Eliot's note). The line that Eliot quotes (line 430) can be translated: "The Prince of Aquitane in the abolished tower."

[62] V. Kyd's *Spanish Tragedy* (Eliot's note).

[63] Shantih. Repeated as here, a formal ending to an Upanishad. "The Peace which passeth understanding" is our equivalent to this word (Eliot's note).

e. e. cummings

(1 8 9 4 – 1 9 6 2)

Edward Estlin Cummings was born in Cambridge, Massachusetts; his father was a minister and a lecturer at Harvard. Cummings went to Harvard where he earned a B.A. and an M.A.; then he volunteered for service with the Norton Harjes Ambulance Service in France. Because of a bureaucratic mistake, Cummings was imprisoned in a French detention camp for three months. The experience, described in his autobiographical novel, *The Enormous Room* (1922), fueled his defense of the individual against social structures. After the war Cummings settled in Europe and became a poet and painter. His first collection of poetry, *Tulips and Chimneys,* appeared in 1923. His typographical idiosyncracies caused considerable controversy, but he gained acceptance and won the *Dial* award in 1925 and an invitation to give the Norton lectures at Harvard in 1953. Cummings died in New York City.

Cummings is less radical than his lowercase, spatially organized poems suggest. His poetry is in many ways a throwback to the Romantic era when poetry championed nature over the brutalizing works of man and the individual over society. More original are his colloquial transformations of poetic language, his alteration of parts of speech (verbs become nouns, nouns become adjectives, and so on), and his explosion of syntax into a free emotive structure of his own creation. His use of the resources of the typewriter is often only superficial, but in some poems he cleverly uses spacing to add to the emotional experience of the reader-viewer, thereby opening up a whole new resource for poets. Cummings's poetry sets itself against all forms of abstraction and empty generalization—entities used, in Cummings's opinion, mainly as tools of oppression. His poems are filled with a sentimental delight in the simple pleasures of nature, sexuality, and love. Cummings was one of the few poets who was capable of combining romanticism and satire in the same poem.

After *Tulips and Chimneys* (1923), Cummings published *&* (1925), *XLI Poems* (1925), and several other small books. *Collected Poems* (1938) and *Poems 1923–1954* (1954) followed. *Six Non-Lectures* (1953), his travel book about Russia, *Tom* (1935), and *The Enormous Room* (1922) are his best-known prose works.

e. e. cummings

(in Just-)

in Just-
spring   when the world is mud-
luscious the little
lame balloonman

5   whistles   far   and wee

and eddieandbill come
running from marbles and
piracies and it's
spring

10   when the world is puddle-wonderful

the queer
old balloonman whistles
far   and   wee
and bettyandisbel come dancing

15   from hop-scotch and jump-rope and

it's
spring
and
        the

20   goat-footed

balloonMan   whistles
far
and
wee

                              (1923)

(O sweet spontaneous)

O sweet spontaneous
earth how often have
the
doting

5   fingers of
prurient philosophers pinched
and
poked

thee
10 ,has the naughty thumb
of science prodded
thy

beauty   .how
often have religions taken
15 thee upon their scraggy knees
squeezing and

buffeting thee that thou mightest conceive
gods
      (but
20 true

to the incomparable
couch of death thy
rhythmic
lover

25   thou answerest

them only with

         spring)

(1923)

(Buffalo Bill's)

Buffalo Bill's
defunct
      who used to
      ride a watersmooth-silver
5   stallion
and break onetwothreefourfive pigeonsjustlikethat
                                         Jesus

he was a handsome man
                  and what i want to know is
10 how do you like your blueeyed boy
Mister Death

                              (1923)

("next to of course god america i")

   "next to of course god america i
   love you land of the pilgrims' and so forth oh
   say can you see by the dawn's early my
   country 'tis of centuries come and go
5   and are no more what of it we should worry
   in every language even deafanddumb
   thy sons acclaim your glorious name by gorry
   by jingo by gee by gosh by gum
   why talk of beauty what could be more beaut-
10 iful than these heroic happy dead
   who rushed like lions to the roaring slaughter
   they did not stop to think they died instead
   then shall the voice of liberty be mute?"

He spoke. And drank rapidly a glass of water
                        (1926)

(since feeling is first)

since feeling is first
who pays any attention

to the syntax of things
will never wholly kiss you;

5 wholly to be a fool
while Spring is in the world

my blood approves,
and kisses are a better fate
than wisdom
10 lady i swear by all flowers. Don't cry
—the best gesture of my brain is less than
your eyelids' flutter which says

we are for each other:then
laugh,leaning back in my arms
15 for life's not a paragraph

And death i think is no parenthesis

(1926)

F. R. Scott

(1 8 9 9 - 1 9 8 5)

The two careers of Francis Reginald Scott flourished during his long life. He was almost equally well known in Canada as a constitutional and civil-rights lawyer and as a poet. The son of a poet (and archdeacon), Scott was born in Quebec City and studied at Bishop's College, at Oxford, where he was a Rhodes scholar, and at McGill University, where he taught at the law school for more than four decades and served as dean from 1961 to 1964. An ardent believer in social justice, Scott was a central participant in the drafting of the CCF socialist manifesto and the foundation of the New Democratic party. In court, he fought against censorship, once pleading on behalf of *Lady Chatterley's Lover.* He was a cofounder of the *McGill Fortnightly Review* (1925 to 1927), the first important Canadian literary journal. Scott's *Collected Poems* won the Governor-General's award for poetry in 1981.

Scott often wrote satirically from within the Christian and socialist traditions in which he was raised. He commented that poetry and legal constitutions are similar in that they attempt to capture the essence of the human spirit. But Scott was also a poet of landscape and searched for epiphanic beauty. Like his contemporaries A. J. M. Smith and A. M. Klein, he helped to usher in modern Canadian poetry. He insisted on hard, fresh diction and images. Yet there is a romantic facet to Scott's work. A great deal of his poetry is concerned with human love and desire, with man's dream of beauty and the realities of his imaginative and physical hunger, his spiritual and material poverty. Influenced by Ezra Pound, T. S. Eliot, W. H. Auden, e. e. cummings, Robert Frost, and William Carlos Williams, Scott gave the Canadian literary scene of the 1930s and 1940s a voice cosmopolitan, yet devoted to the peculiar concerns of his country and his city.

Scott's works include *Overture* (1945), *Events and Signals* (1954), *The Eye of the Needle* (1957), *Signature* (1964), *The Dance Is One* (1973), and *Collected Poems* (1981). A volume of his translations, *Poems of French Canada,* was published in 1977.

F. R. SCOTT

March Field

Now the old folded snow
Shrinks from black earth.
Now is thrust forth
Heavy and still
5 The field's dark furrow.

Not yet the flowing
The mound-stirring
Not yet the inevitable flow.

There is a warm wind, stealing
10 From blunt brown hills, loosening
Sod and cold loam
Round rigid root and stem.

But no seed stirs
In this bare prison
15 Under the hollow sky.

The stone is not yet rolled away
Nor the body risen.

(1945)

Trans Canada

Pulled from our ruts by the made-to-order gale
We sprang upward into a wider prairie
And dropped Regina below like a pile of bones.

Sky tumbled upon us in waterfalls,
5 But we were smarter than a Skeena salmon
And shot our silver body over the lip of air
To rest in a pool of space
On the top storey of our adventure.

A solar peace
10   And a six-way choice.

Clouds, now, are the solid substance,
A floor of wood roughed by the wind
Standing in waves that halt in their fall.
A still of troughs.

15   The plane, our planet,
Travels on roads that are not seen or laid
But sound in instruments on pilots' ears,
While underneath
The sure wings
20   Are the everlasting arms of science.

Man, the lofty worm, tunnels his latest clay,
And bores his new career.

This frontier, too, is ours.
This everywhere whose life can only be led
25   At the pace of a rocket
Is common to man and man.
And every country below is an I land.

The sun sets on its top shelf,
And stars seem farther from our nearer grasp.

30   I have sat by night beside a cold lake
And touched things smoother than moonlight on still water,
But the moon on this cloud sea is not human,
And here is no shore, no intimacy,
Only the start of space, the road to suns.

(1945)

On the Terrace, Quebec

Northward, the ice-carved land,
les pays d'en haut. [1]

South, the softer continent,
river-split.

---

[1] The north country.

5 By Valcartier, three Laurentian hills.
Many years ago, as children,
looking north from the Rectory window
on the longest day of each year
we saw the sun set
10 in the second dip.

I walk these boards under the citadel,
see the narrow streets below,
the basin, l'Ile d'Orléans,
the gateway.

15 I think of the English troops
imprisoned in the broken city
in the spring of 1760
waiting the first ship.

Whose flag would it fly?

20 And that other army, under de Lévis,
victorious at Ste. Foy,
still strong,
watching too,

Suddenly, round the bend,
25 masts and sails
begin to finger the sky.

The first question was answered.

(1973)

A. J. M. Smith

(1 9 0 2 – 1 9 8 0)

Arthur James Marshall Smith was born in Montreal. He attended McGill University, where he obtained a B.S. and an M.A. and helped F. R. Scott found the influential journal, *The McGill Fortnightly Review*. In 1931 he received his Ph.D. from Edinburgh University. From 1936 to 1972 Smith taught at Michigan State University and frequently taught summer terms at the University of Toronto, at McGill, or at Queen's. His poetry was published in leading literary magazines—*The Dial, Poetry, New Verse*—when Smith was young, but his first book did not appear until 1943. His poetry, essays, and anthologies led to many awards, including a Governor-General's award in 1943 and the Medal of the Royal Society of Canada in 1966.

Smith helped to transmit modernist ideas of poetry into Canada. He edited two landmark anthologies of Canadian poetry, *The Book of Canadian Poetry* (1943) and the *Oxford Book of Canadian Verse* (1960). His essays and reviews of Canadian literature left Smith's mark clearly on our conception of modern poetry in Canada. Although his own poetry was small in volume, it was of consistently high quality. Smith was preoccupied with suffering and pain, but his poetry is tightly controlled, austere, precise, and graceful. His outstanding poem "The Lonely Land" is an incantatory evocation of the harsh Canadian landscape. Smith had many interests and wrote in a wide range of forms on a great number of themes. In the thirties, like his friend F. R. Scott, he wrote many satirical poems on social issues. Later, Smith's work became increasingly metaphysical.

Smith published five books of poetry: *News of the Phoenix* (1943), *A Sort of Ecstasy* (1954), *Collected Poems* (1962), *Poems New and Collected* (1967), and *The Classic Shade* (1978). Two well-known collections of essays are *Towards a View of Canadian Letters* (1973) and *On Poetry and Poets* (1977).

A. J. M. SMITH

The Lonely Land

Cedar and jagged fir
uplift sharp barbs
against the gray
and cloud-piled sky;
5 and in the bay
blown spume and windrift
and thin, bitter spray
snap
at the whirling sky;
10 and the pine trees
lean one way.

A wild duck calls
to her mate,
and the ragged
15 and passionate tones
stagger and fall,
and recover,
and stagger and fall,
on these stones—
20 are lost
in the lapping of water
on smooth, flat stones.
This is a beauty
of dissonance,
25 this resonance
of stony strand,
this smoky cry
curled over a black pine
like a broken
30 and wind-battered branch
when the wind
bends the tops of the pines
and curdles the sky
from the north.

35 This is the beauty
of strength

broken by strength
and still strong.
(1943)

Swift Current

This is a visible
and crystal wind:
no ragged edge,
no splash of foam,
5   no whirlpool's scar;
only
—in the narrows,
sharpness cutting sharpness,
arrows of direction,
10   spears of speed.
(1943)

News of the Phoenix

They say the Phoenix is dying, some say dead.
Dead without issue is what one message said,
But that has been suppressed, officially denied.

I think myself the man who sent it lied.
5   In any case, I'm told, he has been shot,
As a precautionary measure, whether he did or not.
(1943)

Noctambule

Under the flag of this pneumatic moon,
—Blown up to bursting, whitewashed white,
And painted like the moon—the piracies of day
Scuttle the crank hulk of witless night.
5   The great black innocent Othello of a thing
Is undone by the nice clean pockethandkerchief
Of 6 a.m., and though the moon is only an old
Wetwash snotrag—horsemeat for good rosbif—

Perhaps to utilize substitutes is what
10 The age has to teach us,
                                    wherefore let the loud
Unmeaning warcry of treacherous daytime
Issue like whispers of love in the moonlight,
—Poxy old cheat!
15   So mewed the lion,
Until mouse roared once and after lashed
His tail: Shellshock came on again, his skin
Twitched in the rancid margarine, his eye
Like a lake isle in a florist's window:
20 Reality at two removes, and mouse and moon
Successful.

                                              (1943)

The Archer

Bend back thy bow, O Archer, till the string
Is level with thine ear, they body taut,
Its nature art, thyself thy statue wrought
Of marble blood, they weapon the poised wing
5   Of coiled and aquiline Fate. Then, loosening, fling
The hissing arrow like a burning thought
Into the empty sky that smokes as the hot
Shaft plunges to the bullseye's quenching ring.

So for a moment, motionless, serene,
10 Fixed between time and time, I aim and wait;
Nothing remains for breath now but to waive
His prior claim and let the barb fly clean
Into the heart of what I know and hate—
That central black, the ringed and targeted grave.

                                              (1943)

The Wisdom of Old Jelly Roll[1]

How all men wrongly death to dignify
Conspire, I tell. Parson, poetaster, pimp,
Each acts or acquiesces. They prettify,
Dress up, deodorize, embellish, primp,

---

[1] "Jelly Roll" Morton (1885–1941), an American jazz musician.

5   And make a show of Nothing. Ah, but met-
aphysics laughs: she touches, tastes, and smells
—Hence knows—the diamond holes that make a net.
Silence resettled testifies to bells.
"Nothing" depends on "Thing", which is or was:
10   So death makes life or makes life's worth, a worth
Beyond all highfalutin' woes or shows
To publish and confess. "Cry at the birth,
Rejoice at the death," old Jelly Roll said,
Being on whisky, ragtime, chicken, and the scriptures fed.

(1962)

Earle Birney

(b. 1 9 0 4)

Earle Birney was born in Calgary, Alberta, and grew up on farms and ranches in Alberta and British Columbia. As a youth he was a surveyor, road construction laborer, and mountain guide. He graduated from the University of British Columbia, then studied in California, taught in Utah, and worked for the *Trotskyite* in New York. He completed a Ph.D. on Chaucer in London and Toronto. Birney taught at University College, in Toronto, while serving as literary editor of the *Canadian Forum*. After World War II, Birney taught at the University of British Columbia, where he established Canada's first department of creative writing. Throughout his life Birney has worked actively for social causes; he was a Trotskyist in the 1930s and a supporter of peace and disarmament in the 1960s and 1970s. His first poetry appeared in the 1940s, but his career again flowered in the 1960s, when he wrote "The Bear on the Delhi Road." In recent years he has been writer-in-residence at several Canadian universities. Birney received the Governor-General's award in 1942 and 1945. A frequent traveler, he has read his work throughout the world.

Birney writes in a wide variety of styles. He is the master of traditional forms—the narrative poem, the meditative lyric, verse satire, and Anglo-Saxon alliterative verse—as well as an innovator with the concrete poem and the sound poem. He is one of the first Canadian poets to emphasize a meter based on speech and to accomplish this without sacrificing musicality. His mature poetry combines the mythical allusiveness of his early work with a leaner, more starkly crafted verse form in which the poetic persona speaks more directly. He has written a great deal of angry, bitterly satiric poetry on behalf of the causes he has championed. In his later years, however, Birney has tended to write more from the perspective of a sensitive "tourist" who records what he has seen, allowing the reader's sense of injustice to arise inevitably from the material. His many "travel poems" demonstrate Birney's conviction, emblematic of much of the best of Canadian poetry, that poetry must have a particular geography and be closely rooted in a specific time and place. Birney is Canada's most varied and complex poetic voice and the composer of some of its most moving lyrics.

Birney made his mark with *David and Other Poems* (1942) and *Now Is Time* (1945). Later books include *Ice Cod Bell or Stone* (1962), *Near False Creek Mouth* (1964), *Rag and Bone Shop* (1971), *Collected Poems* (1975), *Ghost in the Wheels: Selected Poems* (1977), and *Fall by Fury and Other Makings* (1978). Birney's novel *Turvey* (1949) won the Stephen Leacock medal for humor.

EARLE BIRNEY

Vancouver Lights

About me the night   moonless   wimples the mountains
wraps ocean   land   air   and mounting
sucks at the stars   The city   throbbing below
webs the sable peninsula   The golden
5 strands overleap the seajet   by bridge and buoy
vault the shears of the inlet   climb the woods
toward me   falter   and halt   Across to the firefly
haze of a ship on the gulf's erased horizon
roll the lambent spokes of a lighthouse

10 Through the feckless years we have come to the time
when to look on this quilt of lamps is a troubling delight
Welling from Europe's bog   through Africa flowing
and Asia   drowning the lonely lumes on the oceans
tiding up over Halifax   now to this winking
15 outpost comes flooding the primal ink

On this mountain's brutish forehead with terror of space
I stir   of the changeless night and the stark ranges
of nothing   pulsing down from beyond and between
the fragile planets   We are a spark beleaguered
20 by darkness   this twinkle we make in a corner of emptiness
how shall we utter our fear that the black Experimentress
will never in the range of her microscope find it?   Our Phoebus
himself is a bubble that dries on Her slide   while the Nubian
wears for an evening's whim a necklace of nebulae

25 Yet we must speak   we the unique glowworms
Out of the waters and rocks of our little world
we conjured these flames   hooped these sparks
by our will   From blankness and cold we fashioned stars
to our size   and signalled Aldebaran
30 This must we say   whoever may be to hear us
if murk devour   and none weave again in gossamer:

                            These rays were ours
we made and unmade them   Not the shudder of continents

doused us   the moon's passion   nor crash of comets
35 In the fathomless heat of our dwarfdom   our dream's combustion
we contrived the power   the blast that snuffed us
No one bound Prometheus   Himself he chained
and consumed his own bright liver   O stranger
Plutonian   descendant   or beast in the stretching night—
40 there was light

(1941)

Bushed

He invented a rainbow but lightning struck it
shattered it into the lake-lap of a mountain
so big his mind slowed when he looked at it

Yet he built a shack on the shore
5   learned to roast porcupine belly and
wore the quills on his hatband

At first he was out with the dawn
whether it yellowed bright as wood-columbine
or was only a fuzzed moth in a flannel of storm
10   But he found the mountain was clearly alive
sent messages whizzing down every hot morning
boomed proclamations at noon and spread out
a white guard of goat
before falling asleep on its feet at sundown

15   When he tried his eyes on the lake   ospreys
would fall like valkyries
choosing the cut-throat
He took then to waiting
till the night smoke rose from the boil of the sunset

20   But the moon carved unknown totems
out of the lakeshore
owls in the beardusky woods derided him
moosehorned cedars circled his swamps and tossed
their antlers up to the stars
25   then he knew   though the mountain slept   the winds
were shaping its peak to an arrowhead
poised

And now he could only
bar himself in and wait
30 for the great flint to come singing into his heart

(Wreck Beach 1951)

The Bear on the Delhi Road

Unreal   tall as a myth
by the road the Himalayan bear
is beating the brilliant air
with his crooked arms
5 About him two men   bare
spindly as locusts   leap

One pulls on a ring
in the great soft nose   His mate
flicks   flicks with a stick
10 up at the rolling eyes

They have not led him here
down from the fabulous hills
to this bald alien plain
and the clamorous world   to kill
15 but simply to teach him to dance

They are peaceful both   these spare
men of Kashmir   and the bear
alive is their living   too
If   far on the Delhi way
20 around him galvanic they dance
it is merely to wear   wear
from his shaggy body the tranced
wish forever to stay
only an ambling bear
25 four-footed in berries

It is no more joyous for them
in this hot dust to prance
out of reach of the praying claws
sharpened to paw for ants
30 in the shadows of deodars
It is not easy to free
myth from reality

or rear this fellow up
to lurch   lurch with them
35   in the tranced dancing of men
(Srinagar 1958/Île des
Porquerolles 1959)

ka pass age alaska passage ALASKA PASSAGE alaska passage alas

our ship seems reefed
and only the land comes swimming past alaska pass

the firs through gr e e n cresc enDOe fOR E/
tramp downwards the fogin

SHore'S pIeD coMmotion of bristled ROC K S

and blanching   d r i f t

uP from a spew of sp & BaRK A Logchutews
lniters

(one mark of few that men have scribbled
on this lucky palimpsest of ranges)

at times a shake-built shack exchanges
passive stares with Come & Gone
or eyeless waits with stoven side

to slide its bones in a   gr e e n tide

age alaska passage alaska passage alaska passage alas-ka pass

(Alberni Canal 1934/1947/1960)

W. H. Auden

(1 9 0 7 – 1 9 7 3)

Wystan Hugh Auden was born in York, England. At Oxford, he began to write poetry and published it in *Poems* (1928), a slim volume produced by his friend Stephen Spender on a hand press. After graduation, Auden visited Germany, then returned to England. In the 1930s he became the country's major poet and was the center of a group that included Louis MacNeice, Cecil Day Lewis, and Spender. Like many other writers at the time, Auden was on the political left. During the Depression he wrote many poems about the "antiquated" economic system. Auden supported himself by teaching and writing. He visited Iceland, Spain, and China, then moved to the United States in 1939 and became an American citizen. Later he lived in New York and Austria. He served as Oxford Professor of Poetry from 1956 to 1960. In 1972 he returned to England. He won the Pulitzer Prize in 1948.

Auden's restless search for an intellectual "home" led him from Marxism to Freudianism to existentialism to Anglo-Catholicism. In the beginning Auden was a topical public poet, in the vein of John Dryden, and wrote about contemporary situations with analytical and didactic intent. His urbane, ironic style owed much to T. S. Eliot; his poetic experiments in meter and diction show the influence of Gerard Manley Hopkins and Wilfred Owen. Always witty, exuberant, and flexible, Auden's early revolt against contemporary society gradually gave way to the meditative, cautiously optimistic poetry that was prominent in his later volumes. His greatest technical achievement was perhaps his ability to combine elements of formal craft with a colloquial tone. Auden has been called the poet of the Age of the Refugee. He had a strong sense of the individual in exile from his own culture, from a culture that, in its increasing mechanization, was becoming progressively depersonalized. Auden was the voice of a particular era, but in many of his finest lyrics ("Musée des Beaux Arts," "In Memory of W. B. Yeats," "The Shield of Achilles"), and in the best of his satiric pieces ("The Unknown Citizen"), he captured the universal particular.

Auden's many volumes of poetry include *On This Island* (1937), *The Double Man* (1941), *For the Time Being* (1945), *The Age of Anxiety* (1947), *Nones* (1951), *The Shield of Achilles* (1955), *Homage to Clio* (1960), and volumes of selected and collected poems. He also wrote several plays, two travel books, and two collections of essays, *The Enchafèd Flood: The Romantic Iconography of the Sea* (1951) and *The Dyer's Hand* (1962).

W. H. AUDEN

This Lunar Beauty

This lunar beauty
Has no history,
Is complete and early;
If beauty later
5 Bear any feature,
It had a lover
And is another.

This like a dream
Keeps other time,
10 And daytime is
The loss of this;
For time is inches
And the heart's changes,
Where ghost has haunted
15 Lost and wanted.

But this was never
A ghost's endeavour
Nor, finished this,
Was ghost at ease;
20 And till it pass
Love shall not near
The sweetness here,
Nor sorrow take
His endless look.

(1930)

Partition

Unbiassed at least he was when he arrived on his mission,
Having never set eyes on this land he was called to partition
Between two peoples fanatically at odds,
With their different diets and incompatible gods.
5 "Time," they had briefed him in London, "is short. It's too late

For mutual reconciliation or rational debate:
The only solution now lies in separation.
The Viceroy thinks, as you will see from his letter,
That the less you are seen in his company the better,
10 So we've arranged to provide you with other accommodation.
We can give you four judges, two Moslem and two Hindu,
To consult with, but the final decision must rest with you."

Shut up in a lonely mansion, with police night and day
Patrolling the gardens to keep assassins away,
15 He got down to work, to the task of settling the fate
Of millions. The maps at his disposal were out of date
And the Census Returns almost certainly incorrect,
But there was no time to check them, no time to inspect
Contested areas. The weather was frightfully hot,
20 And a bout of dysentery kept him constantly on the trot,
But in seven weeks it was done, the frontiers decided,
A continent for better or worse divided.

The next day he sailed for England, where he quickly forgot
The case, as a good lawyer must. Return he would not,
25 Afraid, as he told his Club, that he might get shot.

(1966)

Musée des Beaux Arts [1]

About suffering they were never wrong,
The Old Masters: how well they understood
Its human position; how it takes place
While someone else is eating or opening a window or just walking
     dully along;
5 How, when the aged are reverently, passionately waiting
For the miraculous birth, there always must be
Children who did not specially want it to happen, skating
On a pond at the edge of the wood:
They never forgot
10 That even the dreadful martyrdom must run its course
Anyhow in a corner, some untidy spot
Where the dogs go on with their doggy life and the torturer's horse

---

[1] Museum of Fine Arts.

Scratches its innocent behind on a tree.
In Breughel's *Icarus,* [2] for instance: how everything turns away

15 Quite leisurely from the disaster; the ploughman may
Have heard the splash, the forsaken cry,
But for him it was not an important failure; the sun shone
As it had to on the white legs disappearing into the green
Water; and the expensive delicate ship that must have seen
20 Something amazing, a boy falling out of the sky,
Had somewhere to get to and sailed calmly on.

(1940)

In Memory of W. B. Yeats
[d. Jan. 1939]

I

He disappeared in the dead of winter:
The brooks were frozen, the airports almost deserted,
And snow disfigured the public statues;
The mercury sank in the mouth of the dying day.
5 What instruments we have agree
The day of his death was a dark cold day.

Far from his illness
The wolves ran on through the evergreen forests,
The peasant river was untempted by the fashionable quays;
10 By mourning tongues
The death of the poet was kept from his poems.

But for him it was his last afternoon as himself,
An afternoon of nurses and rumours;
The provinces of his body revolted,
15 The squares of his mind were empty,
Silence invaded the suburbs,
The current of his feeling failed; he became his admirers.

Now he is scattered among a hundred cities
And wholly given over to unfamiliar affections,
20 To find his happiness in another kind of wood

---

[2] *Icarus,* a painting by the Flemish painter Peter Breughel (ca. 1520–1569) depicts the falling Icarus, a character from Greek mythology who fashioned hand-made wings of wax and feathers; when he flew too close to the sun the wax melted and he fell into the sea.

And be punished under a foreign code of conscience.
The words of a dead man
Are modified in the guts of the living.

But in the importance of noise of to-morrow
25 When the brokers are roaring like beasts on the floor of the Bourse,
And the poor have the sufferings to which they are fairly accustomed,
And each in the cell of himself is almost convinced of his freedom,
A few thousand will think of this day
As one thinks of a day when one did something slightly unusual.
30 What instruments we have agree
The day of his death was a dark cold day.

II

You were silly like us; your gift survived it all:
The parish of rich women, physical decay,
Yourself. Mad Ireland hurt you into poetry.
35 Now Ireland has her madness and her weather still,
For poetry makes nothing happen: it survives
In the valley of its making where executives
Would never want to tamper, flows on south
From ranches of isolation and the busy griefs,
40 Raw towns that we believe and die in; it survives,
A way of happening, a mouth.

III

Earth, receive an honoured guest:
William Yeats is laid to rest.
Let the Irish vessel lie
45 Emptied of its poetry.

In the nightmare of the dark
All the dogs of Europe bark,
And the living nations wait,
Each sequestered in its hate;

50 Intellectual disgrace
Stares from every human face,
And the seas of pity lie
Locked and frozen in each eye.

Follow, poet, follow right
55 To the bottom of the night,
With your unconstraining voice
Still persuade us to rejoice;

With the farming of a verse
Make a vineyard of the curse,
60 Sing of human unsuccess
In a rapture of distress;

In the deserts of the heart
Let the healing fountain start,
In the prison of his days
65 Teach the free man how to praise.

(1940)

Theodore Roethke

(1 9 0 8 – 1 9 6 3)

Theodore Roethke was born in Saginaw, Michigan, and attended the University of Michigan and Harvard University. He taught at Pennsylvania State and Washington State. He lived in the American Northwest, the setting for much of his poetry. His first book appeared in 1941 and gained immediate recognition, but a desire for greater attention and skill as a poet fueled deep depressions that were compounded by alcoholism. Although his output was small, Roethke won many honors, including Guggenheim fellowships, the 1953 Pulitzer Prize, and the National Book Award.

Roethke's poetry details his mental breakdown, depression, loss, love, and his tortured pilgrimage toward the elusive ideals of self-knowledge and permanence. His work is unusual for its time in its preoccupation with spiritual order and the power of nature and in his concern for rhythm and rhyme. Roethke felt that free verse was a "denial in terms." In his greatest poetry, Roethke's nature world was both a landscape that reflected the poet's psyche and a palpable, living force that enabled him to rise above his own personality. The desire for transcendence of the self is a recurring theme in Roethke's work. He mastered many styles, including nonsensical, childlike rhymes and long, introspective soliloquies. Always, his startling imagination rose above the tightly controlled forms to inject his poems with a sense of energetic, almost mystical searching. Roethke considered himself a visionary poet in the tradition of Ralph Waldo Emerson, Walt Whitman, and William Blake. His visionary qualities combine with his rigorous yet innovative craftsmanship to ensure his small canon a lasting reputation.

Open House (1941), *The Lost Son* (1948), and *Praise to the End!* (1951) were followed by the collected volume *The Waking: Poems, 1933–1953* (1953) and *Words for the Wind* (1958). *The Far Field* appeared in 1964, after the poet's death. Roethke's prose was collected in *On the Poet and His Craft* (1965).

THEODORE ROETHKE

Old Florist

That hump of a man bunching chrysanthemums
Or pinching-back asters, or planting azaleas,
Tamping and stamping dirt into pots,—
How he could flick and pick
5   Rotten leaves or yellowy petals,
Or scoop out a weed close to flourishing roots,
Or make the dust buzz with a light spray,
Or drown a bug in one spit of tobacco juice,
Or fan life into wilted sweet-peas with his hat,
10 Or stand all night watering roses, his feet blue in rubber boots.

(1948)

My Papa's Waltz

The whiskey on your breath
Could make a small boy dizzy;
But I hung on like death:
Such waltzing was not easy.

5   We romped until the pans
Slid from the kitchen shelf;
My mother's countenance
Could not unfrown itself.

The hand that held my wrist
10 Was battered on one knuckle;
At every step you missed
My right ear scraped a buckle.

You beat time on my head
With a palm caked hard by dirt,
15 Then waltzed me off to bed
Still clinging to your shirt.

(1948)

I Knew a Woman

I knew a woman, lovely in her bones,
When small birds sighed, she would sigh back at them;
Ah, when she moved, she moved more ways than one:
The shapes a bright container can contain!
5   Of her choice virtues only gods should speak,
Or English poets who grew up on Greek
(I'd have them sing in chorus, cheek to cheek).

How well her wishes went! She stroked my chin,
She taught me Turn, and Counter-turn, and Stand;
10   She taught me Touch, that undulant white skin;
I nibbled meekly from her proffered hand;
She was the sickle; I, poor I, the rake,
Coming behind her for her pretty sake
(But what prodigious mowing we did make).

15   Love likes a gander, and adores a goose:
Her full lips pursed, the errant note to seize;
She played it quick, she played it light and loose;
My eyes, they dazzled at her flowing knees;
Her several parts could keep a pure repose,
20   Or one hip quiver with a mobile nose
(She moved in circles, and those circles moved).

Let seed be grass, and grass turn into hay:
I'm martyr to a motion not my own;
What's freedom for? To know eternity.
25   I swear she cast a shadow white as stone.
But who would count eternity in days?
These old bones live to learn her wanton ways:
(I measure time by how a body sways).

                                                    (1958)

In a Dark Time

In a dark time, the eye begins to see,
I meet my shadow in the deepening shade;
I hear my echo in the echoing wood—
A lord of nature weeping to a tree.

5   I live between the heron and the wren,
    Beasts of the hill and serpents of the den.

    What's madness but nobility of soul
    At odds with circumstance? The day's on fire!
    I know the purity of pure despair,
10 My shadow pinned against a sweating wall.
    That place among the rocks—is it a cave,
    Or winding path? The edge is what I have.

    A steady storm of correspondences!
    A night flowing with birds, a ragged moon,
15 And in broad day the midnight come again!
    A man goes far to find out what he is—
    Death of the self in a long, tearless night,
    All natural shapes blazing unnatural light.

    Dark, dark my light, and darker my desire.
20 My soul, like some heat-maddened summer fly,
    Keeps buzzing at the sill. Which I is *I*?
    A fallen man, I climb out of my fear.
    The mind enters itself, and God the mind,
    And one is One, free in the tearing wind.

                      (1964)

A. M. Klein

(1 9 0 9 – 1 9 7 2)

Abraham Moses Klein was born in the Ukraine. The son of Orthodox Jews, Klein grew up in the east end of Montreal. He entered McGill University on a Classics scholarship and later earned a law degree from the University of Montreal. He married Bessie Kozlov in 1935 and practiced law briefly in Noranda, Quebec, then returned to Montreal, where he worked in the law firm of Chart and Klein until 1954, when emotional stress forced him to withdraw from the profession—and from poetry as well. Klein also edited the weekly *Canadian Jewish Chronicle* and ıan as CCF candidate in the 1949 election. (He was not elected.) Klein published his first poems in the McGill *Daily* in 1927 and his first volume of verse in 1940. In 1949 *The Rocking Chair and Other Poems* received the Governor-General's award.

Klein was proficient in five languages—Latin, French, Yiddish, Hebrew, and English—and his poetry illustrates the richness of his ethnic and religious heritage. His themes are almost always informed by his Jewish-Canadian experience and his strong sense of loyalty to tradition. Klein was also familiar with and influenced by the work of the modernists, especially James Joyce. The combination of historical consciousness and modernist influence produced Klein's central concern: multiplicity and surface fragmentation as manifestations of an unseen unity. A humanist, Klein expressed his concern regarding humankind's responsibility for past wrongs, particularly anti-Semitism. His poetry is by turns lyrical, rhapsodic, religious, humorous, and satiric. He uses lengthy lists and elaborate metaphors that suggest a world dancing around an implied center of unity. His diction is frequently arcane: he uses puns and archaisms from many languages. The famous "Portrait of the Poet as Landscape" captures a concern particular to the Canadian artist yet also common to the modern individual: the attempt to achieve integration and communication in a community without destroying the individuality of the self.

Klein's volumes of poetry were *Hath Not a Jew . . .* (1940), *The Hitleriad* (1944), *Poems* (1944), *The Rocking Chair and Other Poems* (1948), and his *Collected Poems* (1974). A novel, *The Second Scroll,* was published in 1951.

A. M. KLEIN

Psalm XXVII: A Psalm to Teach Humility

O sign and wonder of the barnyard, more
beautiful than the pheasant, more melodious
than nightingale! O creature marvellous!

Prophet of sunrise, and foreteller of times!
5 Vizier of the constellations! Sage,
red-bearded, scarlet-turbaned, in whose brain
the stars lie scattered like well-scattered grain!

Calligraphist upon the barnyard page!
Five-noted balladist! Crower of rhymes!

10 O morning-glory mouth, O throat of dew,
announcing the out-faring of the blue,
the greying and the going of the night,
the coming on,
the imminent coming of the dawn,
15 the coming of the kinsman, the brightly-plumaged sun!

O creature marvellous—and O blessed Creator,
Who givest to the rooster wit
to know the movements of the turning day,
to understand, to herald it,
20 better than I, who neither sing nor crow
and of the sun's goings and comings nothing know.

(1944)

The Rocking Chair

It seconds the crickets of the province. Heard
in the clean lamplit farmhouses of Quebec,—
wooden,—it is no less a national bird;
and rivals, in its cage, the mere stuttering clock.
5 To its time, the evenings are rolled away;
and in its peace the pensive mother knits

contentment to be worn by her family,
grown-up, but still cradled by the chair in which she sits.

It is also the old man's pet, pair to his pipe,
10 the two aids of his arithmetic and plans,
plans rocking and puffing into market-shape;
and it is the toddler's game and dangerous dance.
Moved to the verandah, on summer Sundays, it is,
among the hanging plants, the girls, the boy-friends,
15 sabbatical and clumsy, like the white haloes
dangling above the blue serge suits of the young men.

It has a personality of its own;
is a character (like that old drunk Lacoste,
exhaling amber, and toppling on his pins);
20 it is alive; individual; and no less
an identity than those about it. And
it is tradition. Centuries have been flicked
from its arcs, alternately flicked and pinned.
It rolls with the gait of St. Malo. It is act

25 and symbol, symbol of this static folk
which moves in segments, and returns to base,—
a sunken pendulum: *invoke, revoke;*
loosed yon, leashed hither, motion on no space.
O, like some Anjou ballad, all refrain,
30 which turns about its longing, and seems to move
to make a pleasure out of repeated pain,
its music moves, as if always back to a first love.

(1948)

Portrait of the Poet as Landscape

i

Not an editorial-writer, bereaved with bartlett,[1]
mourns him, the shelved Lycidas.[2]
No actress squeezes a glycerine tear for him.
The radio broadcast lets his passing pass.
5 And with the police, no record. Nobody, it appears,

---

[1] The reference is to Bartlett's well-known book *Familiar Quotations.*
[2] John Milton (see p. 96) wrote a poem entitled "Lycidas" on the death of his friend Edward King.

either under his real name or his alias,
missed him enough to report.

It is possible that he is dead, and not discovered.
It is possible that he can be found some place
10 in a narrow closet, like the corpse in a detective story,
standing, his eyes staring, and ready to fall on his face.
It is also possible that he is alive
and amnesiac, or mad, or in retired disgrace,
or beyond recognition lost in love.

15 We are sure only that from our real society
he has disappeared; he simply does not count,
except in the pullulation of vital statistics—
somebody's vote, perhaps, an anonymous taunt
of the Gallup poll, a dot in a government table—
20 but not felt, and certainly far from eminent—
in a shouting mob, somebody's sigh.

O, he who unrolled our culture from his scroll—
the prince's quote, the rostrum-rounding roar—
who under one name made articulate
25 heaven, and under another the seven-circled air,
is, if he is at all, a number, an x,
a Mr. Smith in a hotel register,—
incognito, lost, lacunal.

ii

The truth is he's not dead, but only ignored—
30 like the mirroring lenses forgotten on a brow
that shine with the guilt of their unnoticed world.
The truth is he lives among neighbours, who, though they will
        allow
him a passable fellow, think him eccentric, not solid,
a type that one can forgive, and for that matter, forgo.

35 Himself he has his moods, just like a poet.
Sometimes, depressed to nadir, he will think all lost,
will see himself as throwback, relict, freak,
his mother's miscarriage, his great-grandfather's ghost,
and he will curse his quintuplet senses, and their tutors
40 in whom he put, as he should not have put, his trust.

Then he will remember his travels over that body—
the torso verb, the beautiful face of the noun,
and all those shaped and warm auxiliaries!

A first love it was, the recognition of his own.
45 Dear limbs adverbial, complexion of adjective,
    dimple and dip of conjugation!

And then remember how this made a change in him
affecting for always the glow and growth of his being;
how suddenly was aware of the air, like shaken tinfoil,
50 of the patents of nature, the shock of belated seeing,
    the lonelinesses peering from the eyes of crowds;
    the integers of thought; the cube-roots of feeling.

Thus, zoomed to zenith, sometimes he hopes again,
and sees himself as a character, with a rehearsed role:
55 the Count of Monte Cristo, come for his revenges;
    the unsuspected heir, with papers; the risen soul;
    or the chloroformed prince awaking from his flowers;
    or—deflated again—the convict on parole.

iii

He is alone; yet not completely alone.
60 Pins on a map of a colour similar to his,
    each city has one, sometimes more than one;
    here, caretakers of art, in colleges;
    in offices, there, with arm-bands, and green-shaded;
    and there, pounding their catalogued beats in libraries,—

65 everywhere menial, a shadow's shadow.
    And always for their egos—their outmoded art.
    Thus, having lost the bevel in the ear,
    they know neither up nor down, mistake the part
    for the whole, curl themselves in a comma,
70 talk technics, make a colon their eyes. They distort—
    such is the pain of their frustration—truth
    to something convolute and cerebral.
    How they do fear the slap of the flat of the platitude!
    Now Pavlov's victims, their mouths water at bell,
75 the platter empty.
                    See they set twenty-one jewels
    into their watches; the time they do not tell!

Some, patagonian in their own esteem,
and longing for the multiplying word,
80 join party and wear pins, now have a message,
    an ear, and the convention-hall's regard.
    Upon the knees of ventriloquists, they own,
    of their dandled brightness, only the paint and board.

And some go mystical, and some go mad.
85 One stares at a mirror all day long, as if
to recognize himself; another courts
angels,—for here he does not fear rebuff;
and a third, alone, and sick with sex, and rapt,
doodles him symbols convex and concave.

90 O schizoid solitudes! O purities
curdling upon themselves! Who live for themselves,
or for each other, but for nobody else;
desire affection, private and public loves;
are friendly, and then quarrel and surmise
95 the secret perversions of each other's lives.

iv

He suspects that something has happened, a law
been passed, a nightmare ordered. Set apart,
he finds himself, with special haircut and dress,
as on a reservation. Introvert.
100 He does not understand this; sad conjecture
muscles and palls thrombotic on his heart.

He thinks an impostor, having studied his personal biography,
his gestures, his moods, now has come forward to pose
in the shivering vacuums his absence leaves.
105 Wigged with his laurel, that other, and faked with his face,
he pats the heads of his children, pecks his wife,
and is at home, and slippered, in his house.

So he guesses at the impertinent silhouette
that talks to his phone-piece and slits open his mail.
110 Is it the local tycoon who for a hobby
plays poet, he so epical in steel?
The orator, making a pause? Or is that man
he who blows his flash of brass in the jittering hall?

Or is he cuckolded by the troubadour
115 rich and successful out of celluloid?
Or by the don who unrhymes atoms? Or
the chemist death built up? Pride, lost impostor'd pride,
it is another, another, whoever he is,
who rides where he should ride.

v

120 *Fame,* the adrenalin: to be talked about;
to be a verb; to be introduced as *The:*

to smile with endorsement from slick paper; make
caprices anecdotal; to nod to the world; to see
one's name like a song upon the marquees played;
125   to be forgotten with embarrassment; to be—
to be.

It has its attractions, but is not the thing;
nor is it the ape mimesis who speaks from the tree
ancestral; nor the merkin joy . . .
130   Rather it is stark infelicity
which stirs him from his sleep, undressed, asleep
to walk upon roofs and window-sills and defy
the gape of gravity.

vi

Therefore he seeds illusions. Look, he is
135   the nth Adam taking a green inventory
in world but scarcely uttered, naming, praising,
the flowering fiats in the meadow, the
syllabled fur, stars aspirate, the pollen
whose sweet collision sounds eternally.
140   For to praise

the world—he, solitary man—is breath
to him. Until it has been praised, that part
has not been. Item by exciting item—
air to his lungs, and pressured blood to his heart.—
145   they are pulsated, and breathed, until they map,
not the world's, but his own body's chart!

And now in imagination he has climbed
another planet, the better to look
with single camera view upon this earth—
150   its total scope, and each afflated tick,
its talk, its trick, its tracklessness—and this
this, he would like to write down in a book!

To find a new function for the *déclassé*° craft   unclassed;
archaic like the fletcher's; to make a new thing;   obsolete
155   to say the word that will become sixth sense;
perhaps by necessity and indirection bring
new forms to life, anonymously, new creeds—
O, somehow pay back the daily larcenies of the lung!

These are not mean ambitions. It is already something
160   merely to entertain them. Meanwhile, he
makes of his status as zero a rich garland,
a halo of his anonymity,
and lives alone, and in his secret shines
like phosphorus. At the bottom of the sea.

(1948)

Dorothy Livesay

(b. 1 9 0 9)

Dorothy Livesay was born in Winnipeg, Manitoba, and received her education at the University of Toronto and the Sorbonne, in Paris. Her first book appeared in 1928, when Livesay was 19. Like many of her contemporaries in Canadian poetry, Livesay became involved in social and political issues in the 1930s, and as a social worker in Toronto during the Depression she worked for the left-wing political movement. In 1936 she moved to the west coast and settled in Vancouver, where she married and worked as a teacher and a journalist. Two volumes of her poetry won the Governor-General's award: *Day and Night* (1944) and *Poems for People* (1947). In 1960 Livesay moved to Northern Rhodesia (now Zambia) to teach English. She returned to Canada in 1963 and has taught at various universities. Livesay now lives on Galiano Island, in British Columbia.

Livesay was one of the first Canadian poets to explore the long "documentary" poem, a genre that enabled her to explore her political concerns within a "factual" social context. An example is "Day and Night," which appeared in 1944. Livesay substituted a cinematic technique, cut and collage, for the sustained narrative thread usually found in long poems. The technique has become central to modern Canadian writing, used by poets and novelists like Michael Ondaatje and Daphne Marlatt. Many of Livesay's poems are implicitly political: They deal with the alienation of the mass-production laborer and the mass-production consumer. In her work she often advocates feminist views, for which she was one of the earliest and most eloquent voices in Canada. Many of Livesay's finest lyrics are personal visions, which she has rendered in a delicate, moving play of carefully observed images.

In addition to the preceding works, Livesay's books of poetry include *Green Pitcher* (1928), *Signpost* (1932), *The Unquiet Bed* (1967), *The Documentaries* (1968), *Ice Age* (1972), and *The Phases of Love* (1983). Her *Collected Poems* was published in 1972; a memoir, *A Winnipeg Childhood,* appeared in 1973.

DOROTHY LIVESAY

Green Rain

I remember long veils of green rain
Feathered like the shawl of my grandmother—
Green from the half-green of the spring trees
Waving in the valley.

5   I remember the road
Like the one which leads to my grandmother's house,
A warm house, with green carpets,
Geraniums, a trilling canary
And shining horse-hair chairs;
10   And the silence, full of the rain's falling
Was like my grandmother's parlour
Alive with herself and her voice, rising and falling—
Rain and wind intermingled.

I remember on that day
15   I was thinking only of my love
And of my love's house.
But now I remember the day
As I remember my grandmother.
I remember the rain as the feathery fringe of her shawl.

(1932)

Autumn: 1939

In our time the great ones fade
We hear the whisper of their falling
Words on a radio announce
How Yeats and Freud within a year
5   Heard the insistent silence calling.

In our time torpedoes score
In thunder-foam the ships go under
Blood is spurted from the sky

Ashes smoke where children played—
10   Gardens, pavements, split in plunder.

In our time no great ones live
For ears are censored from their singing—
No surgeon of the mind can touch
Pillar of salt, idiot stare,
15   Bell-tongues meaninglessly swinging.

(1944)

The Three Emily's [1]

These women crying in my head
Walk alone, uncomforted:
The Emily's, these three
Cry to be set free—
5   And others whom I will not name
Each different, each the same.

Yet they had liberty!
Their kingdom was the sky:
They batted clouds with easy hand,
10   Found a mountain for their stand;
From wandering lonely they could catch
The inner magic of a heath—
A lake their palette, any tree
Their brush could be.

15   And still they cry to me
As in reproach—
I, born to hear their inner storm
Of separate man in woman's form,
I yet possess another kingdom, barred
20   To them, these three, this Emily.
I move as mother in a frame,
My arteries
Flow the immemorial way
Towards the child, the man;
25   And only for brief span
Am I an Emily on mountain snows
And one of these.

[1] Emily Brontë, Emily Dickinson, and Emily Carr (Livesay's note).

And so the whole that I possess
Is still much less—
30 They move triumphant through my head:
I am the one
Uncomforted.

(1955)

Irving Layton

(b. 1 9 1 2)

The best-known poet of the post-World War II period in Canada, Irving Layton was born in Rumania in 1912 and came to Montreal as a small child. He studied agriculture at Macdonald College and economics and political science at McGill. Layton helped John Sutherland and Louis Dudek with the influential Montreal journals *First Statement* and *Northern Review* in the 1940s. His first book of poetry appeared in 1945. Layton taught in Montreal high schools and at Sir George Williams College and traveled in Europe. He helped to bring the work of Charles Olson and the Black Mountain School to the notice of Canadian writers and was once invited to teach at Black Mountain College. Layton served as writer-in-residence at Sir George Williams in 1965 and at the University of Guelph in 1969. From 1969 to 1979 he was professor of English at York University in Toronto. He won the Governor-General's award for *A Red Carpet for the Sun* in 1959.

Layton is an enormously prolific poet: since 1950 he has published about one volume per year. It is fair to say that he has published too much, but overexposure is a necessary evil for a poet who takes his vocation as prophet, satirist, and lyricist as seriously as Layton does. Layton's body of verse is unique. It is violent, outrageous, graphic and acute, analytical, tender, and sometimes sentimental. Layton's prominent public role as Nietzschean prophet bombastically damning the prudes, the intellectuals, and the philistines has obscured the true power of his poetic imagination, the richness of his language and imagery, and the careful craftsmanship that makes such poems as "The Cold Green Element," "A Tall Man Executes a Jig," and "The Birth of Tragedy" lasting achievements. The energetic vision of his best poetry also makes reams of mediocre verse inevitable. Layton champions excess over restraint, passion over reason, poetry over "literature," the individual over the state, vulgarity over decorum.

Layton's numerous books include *Here and Now* (1945), *The Cold Green Element* (1955), *The Improved Binoculars* (1956), *A Red Carpet for the Sun* (1959), *Balls for a One-Armed Juggler* (1963), *The Unwavering Eye: Selected Poems 1968–1975* (1975), and *A Wild Peculiar Joy* (1982). Layton's *Collected Poems* appeared in 1965 and 1971; a collection of his prose, *Engagements,* was published in 1972.

IRVING LAYTON

The Cold Green Element

At the end of the garden walk
the wind and its satellite wait for me;
their meaning I will not know
    until I go there,
5 but the black-hatted undertaker

who, passing, saw my heart beating in the grass,
is also going there. Hi, I tell him,
a great squall in the Pacific blew a dead poet
    out of the water,
10 who now hangs from the city's gates.

Crowds depart daily to see it, and return
with grimaces and incomprehension;
if its limbs twitched in the air
    they would sit at its feet
15 peeling their oranges.

And turning over I embrace like a lover
the trunk of a tree, one of those
for whom the lightning was too much
    and grew a brilliant
20 hunchback with a crown of leaves.

The ailments escaped from the labels
of medicine bottles are all fled to the wind;
I've seen myself lately in the eyes
    of old women,
25 spent streams mourning my manhood,

in whose old pupils the sun became
a bloodsmear on broad catalpa leaves
and hanging from ancient twigs,
    my murdered selves
30 sparked the air like the muted collisions

of fruit. A black dog howls down my blood,
a black dog with yellow eyes;

he too by someone's inadvertence
   saw the bloodsmear
35 on the broad catalpa leaves.

But the furies clear a path for me to the worm
who sang for an hour in the throat of a robin,
and misled by the cries of young boys
   I am again
40 a breathless swimmer in that cold green element.

           (1955)

Whatever Else Poetry Is Freedom

Whatever else poetry is freedom.
Forget the rhetoric, the trick of lying
All poets pick up sooner or later. From the river,
Rising like the thin voice of grey castratos—the mist;
5 Poplars and pines grow straight but oaks are gnarled;
Old codgers must speak of death, boys break windows;
Women lie honestly by their men at last.

And I who gave my Kate a blackened eye
Did to its vivid changing colours
10 Make up an incredible musical scale;
And now I balance on wooden stilts and dance
And thereby sing to the loftiest casements.
See how with polish I bow from the waist.
Space for these stilts! More space or I fail!

15 And a crown I say for my buffoon's head.
Yet no more fool am I than King Canute,
Lord of our tribe, who scanned and scorned;
Who half-deceived, believed; and, poet, missed
The first white waves come nuzzling at his feet;
20 Then damned the courtiers and the foolish trial
With a most bewildering and unkingly jest.

It was the mist. It lies inside one like a destiny.
A real Jonah it lies rotting like a lung.
And I know myself undone who am a clown
25 And wear a wreath of mist for a crown;
Mist with the scent of dead apples,

Mist swirling from black oily waters at evening,
Mist from the fraternal graves of cemeteries.

It shall drive me to beg my food and at last
30 Hurl me broken I know and prostrate on the road;
Like a huge toad I saw, entire but dead,
That Time mordantly had blacked; O pressed
To the moist earth it pled for entry.
I shall be I say that stiff toad for sick with mist
35 And crazed I smell the odour of mortality.

And Time flames like a paraffin stove
And what it burns are the minutes I live.
At certain middays I have watched the cars
Bring me from afar their windshield suns;
40 What lay to my hand were blue fenders,
The suns extinguished, the drivers wearing sunglasses.
And it made me think I had touched a hearse.

So whatever else poetry is freedom. Let
Far off the impatient cadences reveal
45 A padding for my breathless stilts. Swivel,
O hero, in the fleshy groves, skin and glycerine,
And sing of lust, the sun's accompanying shadow
Like a vampire's wing, the stillness in dead feet—
Your stave brings resurrection, O aggrievèd king.

                                      (1958)

A Tall Man Executes a Jig

I

So the man spread his blanket on the field
And watched the shafts of light between the tufts
And felt the sun push the grass towards him;
The noise he heard was that of whizzing flies,
5   The whistlings of some small imprudent birds,
And the ambiguous rumbles of cars
That made him look up at the sky, aware
Of the gnats that tilted against the wind
And in the sunlight turned to jigging motes.
10 Fruitflies he'd call them except there was no fruit
About, spoiling to hatch these glitterings,

These nervous dots for which the mind supplied
The closing sentences from Thucydides,
Or from Euclid having a savage nightmare.

II

15 Jig jig, jig jig. Like minuscule black links
Of a chain played with by some playful
Unapparent hand or the palpitant
Summer haze bored with the hour's stillness.
He felt the sting and tingle afterwards
20 Of those leaving their orthodox unrest,
Leaving their undulant excitation
To drop upon his sleeveless arm. The grass,
Even the wildflowers became black hairs
And himself a maddened speck among them.
25 Still the assaults of the small flies made him
Glad at last, until he saw purest joy
In their frantic jiggings under a hair,
So changed from those in the unrestraining air.

III

He stood up and felt himself enormous.
30 Felt as might Donatello over stone,
Or Plato, or as a man who has held
A loved and lovely woman in his arms
And feels his forehead touch the emptied sky
Where all antinomies flood into light.
35 Yet jig jig jig, the haloing black jots
Meshed with the wheeling fire of the sun:
Motion without meaning, disquietude
Without sense or purpose, ephermerides
That mottled the resting summer air till
40 Gusts swept them from his sight like wisps of smoke.
Yet they returned, bring a bee who, seeing
But a tall man, left him for a marigold.

IV

He doffed his aureole of gnats and moved
Out of the field as the sun sank down,
45 A dying god upon the blood-red hills.
Ambition, pride, the ecstasy of sex,
And all circumstance of delight and grief,
That blood upon the mountain's side, that flood
Washed into a clear incredible pool
50 Below the ruddied peaks that pierced the sun.
He stood still and waited. If ever

The hour of revelation was come
It was now, here on the transfigured steep.
The sky darkened. Some birds chirped. Nothing else.
55 He thought the dying god had gone to sleep:
An Indian fakir on his mat of nails.

V

And on the summit of the asphalt road
Which stretched towards the fiery town, the man
Saw one hill raised like a hairy arm, dark
60 With pines and cedars against the stricken sun
—The arm of Moses or of Joshua.
He dropped his head and let fall the halo
Of mountains, purpling and silent as time,
To see temptation coiled before his feet:
65 A violated grass snake that lugged
Its intestine like a small red valise.
A cold-eyed skinflint it now was, and not
The manifest of that joyful wisdom,
The mirth and arrogant green flame of life;
70 Or earth's vivid tongue that flicked in praise of earth.

VI

And the man wept because pity was useless.
"Your jig's up; the flies come like kites," he said
And watched the grass snake crawl towards the hedge,
Convulsing and dragging into the dark
75 The satchel filled with curses for the earth,
For the odours of warm sedge, and the sun,
A blood-red organ in the dying sky.
Backwards it fell into a grassy ditch
Exposing its underside, white as milk,
80 And mocked by wisps of hay between its jaws;
And then it stiffened to its final length.
But though it opened its thin mouth to scream
A last silent scream that shook the black sky,
Adamant and fierce, the tall man did not curse.

VII

85 Beside the rigid snake the man stretched out
In fellowship of death; he lay silent
And stiff in the heavy grass with eyes shut,
Inhaling the moist odours of the night
Through which his mind tunnelled with flicking tongue
90 Backwards to caves, mounds, and sunken ledges
And desolate cliffs where come only kites,

And where of perished badgers and racoons
The claws alone remain, gripping the earth.
Meanwhile the green snake crept upon the sky,
95   Huge, his mailed coat glittering with stars that made
The night bright, and blowing thin wreaths of cloud
Athwart the moon; and as the weary man
Stood up, coiled above his head, transforming all.

(1963)

Butterfly on Rock

The large yellow wings, black-fringed,
were motionless

They say the soul of a dead person
will settle like that on the still face

5   But I thought: the rock has borne this;
this butterfly is the rock's grace,
its most obstinate and secret desire
to be a thing alive made manifest

Forgot were the two shattered porcupines
10   I had seen die in the bleak forest.
Pain is unreal; death, an illusion:
There is no death in all the land,
I heard my voice cry;
And brought my hand down on the butterfly
15   And felt the rock move beneath my hand.

(1963)

Dylan Thomas

(1 9 1 4 – 1 9 5 3)

The purest, most musical lyrics of the twentieth century were written by Dylan Thomas. The son of a schoolteacher, Thomas was born in the town of Swansea, Wales, and attended Swansea Grammar School. He found his vocation early and resisted his father's pressure to attend university; instead, he devoted himself to poetry. At the age of 19 he won a newspaper poetry contest; when he was 20, his small volume, *18 Poems,* received critical acclaim. In 1936 Thomas moved to London, where he met and married Caitlin Macnamara. The couple had three children. Between the drinking bouts, which he thought necessary to play the role of "Poet," Thomas wrote poetry, plays, filmscripts, and material for the BBC. He was probably the most famous poet of his time in the English-speaking world. A magnificent reader, he earned large amounts of money (which he promptly squandered) on spectacularly successful reading tours of North America. On the third of these tours a prolonged drinking spree led to his death in New York City. He was 39.

Thomas was a master of the music of language. His talent effected his belief that poetry must be read aloud to be complete. Thomas was a meticulous craftsman. He wrote extremely slowly and revised endlessly, a habit that made some of his poetry so symbolically dense that it seems obscure. But the density unpacks itself with repeated readings. Thomas's poems are tightly controlled metaphorical structures that operate on primary, archetypal symbols drawn from nature and Christian legend and ritual. Thomas's compressed metaphors and juxtaposed, clotted constructions owe something to the influence of Hopkins. The poems are a lavish, rhetorical celebration of the life process, "the force that through the green fuse drives the flower," which often rebels against the death that is an integral part of it. Thomas was obsessed with this essential contradiction: To live is to run headlong toward death. He described his image clusters in a similar way: "each image holds within it the seed of its own destruction." In essence, Thomas was a religious poet, if an unconventional one, as he made clear in the preface to his collected poems: "These poems . . . are written for the love of Man and in praise of God, and I'd be a damn fool if they weren't."

His first volume, *18 Poems* (1934), was followed by *25 Poems* (1936), *The Map of Love* (1939), *Deaths and Entrances* (1946), and *Collected Poems* (1952). A prose work, *Portrait of the Artist as a Young Dog,* was published in 1940; his beautiful radio play, *Under Milk Wood,* appeared in 1954. Thomas also wrote a classic children's story, *A Child's Christmas in Wales.*

DYLAN THOMAS

The Force That Through the Green Fuse Drives the Flower

The force that through the green fuse drives the flower
Drives my green age; that blasts the roots of trees
Is my destroyer.
And I am dumb to tell the crooked rose
5   My youth is bent by the same wintry fever.

The force that drives the water through the rocks
Drives my red blood; that dries the mouthing streams
Turns mine to wax.
And I am dumb to mouth unto my veins
10   How at the mountain spring the same mouth sucks.

The hand that whirls the water in the pool
Stirs the quicksand; that ropes the blowing wind
Hauls my shroud sail.
And I am dumb to tell the hanging man
15   How of my clay is made the hangman's lime.

The lips of time leech to the fountain head;
Love drips and gathers, but the fallen blood
Shall calm her sores.
And I am dumb to tell a weather's wind
20   How time has ticked a heaven round the stars.

And I am dumb to tell the lover's tomb
How at my sheet goes the same crooked worm.

(1933)

And Death Shall Have No Dominion

And death shall have no dominion.
Dead men naked they shall be one
With the man in the wind and the west moon;

When their bones are picked clean and the clean bones gone,
5   They shall have stars at elbow and foot;
Though they go mad they shall be sane,
Though they sink through the sea they shall rise again;
Though lovers be lost love shall not;
And death shall have no dominion.

10   And death shall have no dominion.
Under the windings of the sea
They lying long shall not die windily;
Twisting on racks when sinews give way,
Strapped to a wheel, yet they shall not break;
15   Faith in their hands shall snap in two,
And the unicorn evils run them through;
Split all ends up they shan't crack;
And death shall have no dominion.

And death shall have no dominion.
20   No more may gulls cry at their ears
Or waves break loud on the seashores;
Where blew a flower may a flower no more
Lift its head to the blows of the rain;
Though they be mad and dead as nails,
25   Heads of the characters hammer through daisies;
Break in the sun till the sun breaks down,
And death shall have no dominion.

                                              (1936)

After the Funeral

(In memory of Ann Jones)[1]

After the funeral, mule praises, brays,
Windshake of sailshaped ears, muffle-toed tap
Tap happily of one peg in the thick
Grave's foot, blinds down the lids, the teeth in black,
5   The spittled eyes, the salt ponds in the sleeves,
Morning smack of the spade that wakes up sleep,
Shakes a desolate boy who slits his throat
In the dark of the coffin and sheds dry leaves,
That breaks one bone to light with a judgment clout,

[1] Ann Jones was Dylan Thomas's aunt; she died in 1933.

10 After the feast of tear-stuffed time and thistles
    In a room with a stuffed fox and a stale fern,
    I stand, for this memorial's sake, alone
    In the snivelling hours with dead, humped Ann
    Whose hooded, fountain heart once fell in puddles
15 Round the parched worlds of Wales and drowned each sun
    (Though this for her is a monstrous image blindly
    Magnified out of praise; her death was a still drop;
    She would not have me sinking in the holy
    Flood of her heart's fame; she would lie dumb and deep
20 And need no druid[2] of her broken body).
    But I, Ann's bard on a raised hearth, call all
    The seas to service that her wood-tongued virtue
    Babble like a bellbuoy over the hymning heads,
    Bow down the walls of the ferned and foxy woods
25 That her love sing and swing through a brown chapel,
    Bless her bent spirit with four, crossing birds.
    Her flesh was meek as milk, but this skyward statue
    With the wild breast and blessed and giant skull
    Is carved from her in a room with a wet window
30 In a fiercely mourning house in a crooked year.
    I know her scrubbed and sour humble hands
    Lie with religion in their cramp, her threadbare
    Whisper in a damp word, her wits drilled hollow,
    Her fist of a face died clenched on a round pain;
35 And sculptured Ann is seventy years of stone.
    These cloud-sopped, marble hands, this monumental
    Argument of the hewn voice, gesture and psalm,
    Storm me forever over her grave until
    The stuffed lung of the fox twitch and cry Love
40 And the strutting fern lay seeds on the black sill.

                                                        (1939)

Fern Hill

    Now as I was young and easy under the apple boughs
    About the lilting house and happy as the grass was green,
        The night above the dingle starry,
            Time let me hail and climb

[2] A member of the ancient Celtic religious order of priests, soothsayers, and poets.

5   Golden in the heydays of his eyes,
And honoured among wagons I was prince of the apple towns
And once below a time I lordly had the trees and leaves
      Trail with daisies and barley
     Down the rivers of the windfall light.

10   And as I was green and carefree, famous among the barns
About the happy yard and singing as the farm was home,
     In the sun that is young once only,
      Time let me play and be
     Golden in the mercy of his means,
15   And green and golden I was huntsman and herdsman, the calves
Sang to my horn, the foxes on the hills barked clear and cold,
      And the sabbath rang slowly
     In the pebbles of the holy streams.

All the sun long it was running, it was lovely, the hay
20 Fields high as the house, the tunes from the chimneys, it was air
      And playing, lovely and watery
        And fire green as grass.
        And nightly under the simple stars
As I rode to sleep the owls were bearing the farm away,
25 All the moon long I heard, blessed among stables, the nightjars
      Flying with the ricks, and the horses
       Flashing into the dark.

And then to awake, and the farm, like a wanderer white
With the dew, come back, the cock on his shoulder: it was all
30   Shining, it was Adam and maiden,
       The sky gathered again
      And the sun grew round that very day.
So it must have been after the birth of the simple light
In the first, spinning place, the spellbound horses walking warm
35   Out of the whinnying green stable
       On to the fields of praise.

And honoured among foxes and pheasants by the gay house
Under the new made clouds and happy as the heart was long,
      In the sun born over and over,
40   I ran my heedless ways,
       My wishes raced through the house high hay
And nothing I cared, at my sky blue trades, that time allows
In all his tuneful turning so few and such morning songs

Before the children green and golden
45   Follow him out of grace,

Nothing I cared, in the lamb white days, that time would take me
Up to the swallow thronged loft by the shadow of my hand,
    In the moon that is always rising,
        Nor that riding to sleep
50   I should hear him fly with the high fields
And wake to the farm forever fled from the childless land.
Oh as I was young and easy in the mercy of his means,
    Time held me green and dying
    Though I sang in my chains like the sea.

(1946)

Do Not Go Gentle into That Good Night

Do not go gentle into that good night,
Old age should burn and rave at close of day;
Rage, rage against the dying of the light.

Though wise men at their end know dark is right,
5   Because their words had forked no lightning they
Do not go gentle into that good night.

Good men, the last wave by, crying how bright
Their frail deeds might have danced in a green bay,
Rage, rage against the dying of the light.

10 Wild men who caught and sang the sun in flight,
And learn, too late, they grieved it on its way,
Do not go gentle into that good night.

Grave men, near death, who see with blinding sight
Blind eyes could blaze like meteors and be gay,
15 Rage, rage against the dying of the light.

And you, my father, there on the sad height,
Curse, bless, me now with your fierce tears, I pray.
Do not go gentle into that good night.
Rage, rage against the dying of the light.

(1952)

A Refusal to Mourn the Death,
by Fire, of a Child in London

Never until the mankind making
Bird beast and flower
Fathering and all humbling darkness
Tells with silence the last light breaking
5　And the still hour
Is come of the sea tumbling in harness

And I must enter again the round
Zion of the water bead
And the synagogue of the ear of corn
10　Shall I let pray the shadow of a sound
Or sow my salt seed
In the least valley of sackcloth to mourn

The majesty and burning of the child's death.
I shall not murder
15　The mankind of her going with a grave truth
Nor blaspheme down the stations of the breath
With any further
Elegy of inocence and youth.

Deep with the first dead lies London's daughter,
20　Robed in the long friends,
The grains beyond age, the dark veins of her mother,
Secret by the unmourning water
Of the riding Thames.
After the first death, there is no other.

(1946)

Al Purdy

(b. 1 9 1 8)

Al Purdy was born in the village of Wooler, Ontario. He dropped out of Albert College in Belleville when he was 16 and moved to British Columbia, where he worked at odd jobs. He joined the Canadian air force during World War II and published his first volume of poetry in 1944. After the war, Purdy worked at a variety of jobs: factory laborer, taxi driver, bootlegger, and many others "too numerous to mention," in Purdy's words. From 1949 to 1955 he and his wife lived in Vancouver. Purdy moved to Montreal in 1955, then to Roblin Lake at Ameliasburg, the rugged Loyalist country of eastern Ontario that provides the setting for some of his finest poems. But Purdy has never stopped traveling. He has visited Greece, northern British Columbia, and the Canadian high arctic, where he spent the summer of 1965 among the Inuit of Baffin Island, an experience reflected in the outstanding collection *North of Summer* (1967). His volume *The Cariboo Horses* (1965) won the Governor-General's award.

In his poetry, Purdy is a traveler in both space and time. He is a mythologizer of Canadian landscape and history. In poems such as "Roblin Lake" and "The Country North of Belleville," he shows an intense passion for the rugged landscape near his home, and he gives his poems a keen sense of history and of the battle between man and a nature that is less than accommodating. Man's struggle with nature is not a negative thing. The hard, resisting Canadian landscape is a world in which a man can test himself and find a sense of beauty and true accomplishment when a place within that nature is finally achieved. Man's place is always temporary, though, and his victories Pyrrhic. Poems such as "Lament for the Dorsets" and "The Runners" are meditations on the transience of man's accomplishments, the fragility of our structures in the face of patient time. Despite Purdy's wide learning, his poetry is consciously antiacademic, written in an open, anecdotal form. Purdy can be an energetic, boisterous, and witty poet (as in *Poems for All the Annettes*, 1962), or a restrained, sensitive lyricist (as in poems like "Eskimo Graveyard," "Arctic Rhododendrons," and "Poem"). His verse is often sprawling and incompletely realized, but at his best he is a poet of great power.

In addition to the books mentioned, Purdy's volumes include *The Enchanted Echo* (1944), *Pressed on Sand* (1955), *Wild Grape Wine* (1968), *Sex and Death* (1973), *Sundance at Dusk* (1976), *Being Alive: Poems 1958–1978* (1978), *The Stone Bird* (1981), and *Piling Blood* (1984).

AL PURDY

The Country North of Belleville

Bush land scrub land—
       Cashel Township and Wollaston
Elzevir McClure and Dungannon
green lands of Weslemkoon Lake
5 where a man might have some
        opinion of what beauty
is and none deny him
            for miles—

Yet this is the country of defeat
10 where Sisyphus rolls a big stone
year after year up the ancient hills
picnicking glaciers have left strewn
with centuries' rubble
                backbreaking days
15   in the sun and rain
when realization seeps slow in the mind
without grandeur or self deception in
             noble struggle
of being a fool—

20 A country of quiescence and still distance
a lean land
        not like the fat south
with inches of black soil on
        earth's round belly—
25 And where the farms are
        it's as if a man stuck
both thumbs in the stony earth and pulled

           it apart
           to make room
30 enough between the trees
for a wife
        and maybe some cows and
        room for some
of the more easily kept illusions—

35   And where the farms have gone back
     to forest
                    are only soft outlines
                    shadowy differences—

     Old fences drift vaguely among the trees
40   a pile of moss-covered stones
     gathered for some ghost purpose
     has lost meaning under the meaningless sky
                    —they are like cities under water
     and the undulating green waves of time
45   are laid on them—

     This is the country of our defeat
                    and yet
     during the fall plowing a man
     might stop and stand in a brown valley of the furrows
50   and shade his eyes to watch for the same
                    red patch mixed with gold
                    that appears on the same
                    spot in the hills
                    year after year
55   and grow old
     plowing and plowing a ten-acre field until
     the convolutions run parallel with his own brain—

     And this is a country where the young
                    leave quickly
60   unwilling to know what their fathers know
     or think the words their mothers do not say—

     Herschel Monteagle and Faraday
     lakeland rockland and hill country
     a little adjacent to where the world is
65   a little north of where the cities are and
     sometime
     we may go back there
                         to the country of our defeat
     Wollaston Elzevir and Dungannon
70   and Weslemkoon lake land
     where the high townships of Cashel
                         McClure and Marmora once were—
     But it's been a long time since
     and we must enquire the way
75   of strangers—

                                              (1972)

Song of the Impermanent Husband

Oh I would
I would in a minute
if the cusswords and bitter anger couldn't—
if the either / or quarrel didn't—
5 and the fat around my middle wasn't—
if I was young if
                I wasn't so damn sure
I couldn't find another maddening bitch
like you holding on for dear life to
10 all the different parts of me for
twenty or twenty
                thousand years
I'd leave in the night like
a disgraced caviar salesman
15   descend the moonlight
stairs to Halifax
               (uh-no-not Halifax)
well then Toronto
            ah
20 I guess not Toronto either / or
rain-soaked Vancouver down
                     down
                       down
the dark stairs to
25 the South Seas' sunlit milky reefs and
          the jungle's green
              unending bank account with
all the brown girls being brown
          as they can be and all
30 the one piece behinds stretched tight tonight
in small sarongs gawd not to be touched tho Oh
beautiful as an angel's ass
—without the genitals
And me
35   in Paris like a smudged Canadian postcard and
(dear me)
       all the importuning white and lily girls
of Rue Pigalle
          and stroll
40 the sodden London streets and
             find a sullen foggy woman who
enjoyed my odd colonial ways and send

a postcard back to you about my faithfulness and
talk about the lovely beastly English weather
45 I'd be the slimiest most uxorious wife deserter
                    my shrunk amoeba self absurd inside
a saffron girl's geography and
hating me between magnetic nipples
but
50   fooling no one
in all the sad and much emancipated world
Why then I'll stay
                    at least for tea for
all the brownness is too brown and
55 all the whiteness too damned white
and I'm afraid
                    afraid of being
any other woman's man
who might be me
60   afraid
the unctuous and uneasy self I glimpse
sometimes might lose my faint and yapping cry
for being anything
                    was never quite what I intended
65 And you you
                    bitch no irritating
questions re love and permanence only
                    an unrolling lifetime here
between your rocking thighs

70   and the semblance of motion

                                        (1967)

Piling Blood

It was powdered blood
in heavy brown paper bags
supposed to be strong enough
to prevent the stuff from escaping
5 but didn't

We piled it ten feet high
right to the shed roof
working at Arrow Transfer
on Granville Island

10 The bags weighed 75 pounds
and you had to stand on two
of the bags to pile the top rows
I was six feet three inches
and needed all of it

15 I forgot to say
the blood was cattle blood
horses sheep and cows
to be used for fertilizer
the foreman said

20 It was a matter of some delicacy
to plop the bags down softly
as if you were piling dynamite
if you weren't gentle
the stuff would belly out
25 from bags in brown clouds
settle on your sweating face
cover hands and arms
enter ears and nose
seep inside pants and shirt
30 reverting back to liquid blood
and you looked like
you'd been scalped
by a tribe of
particularly unfriendly
35 Indians and forgot to die

We piled glass as well
it came in wooden crates
two of us hoicking them
off trucks into warehouses
40 every crate
weighing 200 pounds
By late afternoon
my muscles would twitch and throb
in a death-like rhythm
45 from hundreds of bags of blood
and hundreds of crates of glass

Then at Burns' slaughterhouse
on East Hastings Street
I got a job part time
50 shouldering sides of frozen beef
hoisting it from steel hooks

staggering to and from
the refrigerated trucks
and eerie freezing rooms
55 with breath a white vapour
among the dangling corpses
and the sound of bawling animals
screeched down from an upper floor
with their throats cut
60 and blood gurgling into special drains
for later retrieval

And the blood smell clung to me
clung to clothes and body
sickly and sweet
65 and I heard the screams
of dying cattle
and I wrote no poems
there were no poems
to exclude the screams
70 which boarded the streetcar
and travelled with me
till I reached home
turned on the record player
and faintly
75 in the last century
heard Beethoven weeping

(1984)

Lawrence Ferlinghetti

(b. 1 9 1 9)

Born in New York, Ferlinghetti had a troubled childhood. His father died when Ferlinghetti was an infant, and his mother was committed to an insane asylum. He was rescued from an orphanage by a relative who took him to France for several years. The relative found a job as a governess with an American family named Lawrence. When the relative also went insane, Ferlinghetti was raised by the Lawrences. He attended the University of North Carolina, Columbia University, and the Sorbonne, where he earned a doctorate in fine arts in 1951. During the war he worked for the French and Norwegian resistance movements. He moved to San Francisco, the center of the Beat poetry movement, founded the country's first paperback bookstore, City Lights, and began to publish poetry under the City Lights imprint. Unlike many Beat poets, Ferlinghetti rejected the idea that poetry should be disengaged from society; he wrote many satiric poems on political subjects and on the American "throwaway" society. Ferlinghetti's second book, *A Coney Island of the Mind* (1958), brought him public recognition.

Ferlinghetti is a great lover-critic of American cultural values. He has articulated American aspirations and denounced its policies (Korea, Vietnam), its presidents (Eisenhower, Johnson, Nixon), and its public clichés. He stressed the oral aspect of poetry, as had Dylan Thomas a few years earlier. Ferlinghetti's work is euphonic, hilarious, colorful, and endlessly inventive in both sound and image. A highly allusive poet, Ferlinghetti translates the metaphors and ideas of poets like Keats, Yeats, and Eliot into strikingly new and revelatory contexts. Like the other Beat poets, he cultivates jazz rhythms, drugs, Eastern religions (though with a good deal of self-satire), and the Kerouacian anarchy of the restless wanderer. He also has insisted that poetry has a popular role, that it must be marketed, advocated, and endorsed and, most of all, it must be wrested from the grasp of academia.

Ferlinghetti's first book, *Pictures of the Gone World* (1955), was followed by *A Coney Island of the Mind* (1958) and many other volumes and broadsides, including *Starting from San Francisco* (1961), *The Secret Meaning of Things* (1969), *Open Eye, Open Heart* (1973), *Who Are We Now?* (1976), *Landscapes of Living and Dying* (1979), and *Endless Life: The Selected Poems* (1981). He has also published a novel, *Her* (1960), and two volumes of short plays.

LAWRENCE FERLINGHETTI

from *A Coney Island of the Mind*

The title of this book is taken from Henry Miller's *Into the Night Life.* It is used out of context but expresses the way I felt about these poems when I wrote them—as if they were, taken together, a kind of Coney Island of the mind, a kind of circus of the soul.

1

In Goya's greatest scenes we seem to see
                        the people of the world
      exactly at the moment when
        they first attained the title of
                  "suffering humanity"
5   They writhe upon the page
           in a veritable rage
               of adversity
     Heaped up
10   groaning with babies and bayonets
            under cement skies
    in an abstract landscape of blasted trees
     bent statues bats wings and beaks
        slippery gibbets
15   cadavers and carnivorous cocks
    and all the final hollering monsters
      of the
        "imagination of disaster"
    they are so bloody real
20   it is as if they really still existed

    And they do

    Only the landscape is changed

They still are ranged along the roads
     plagued by legionaires
25   false windmills and demented
roosters

They are the same people
        only further from home

on freeways fifty lanes wide
30   on a concrete continent
                                    spaced with bland billboards
                            illustrating imbecile illusions of happiness
The scene shows fewer tumbrils
                            but more maimed citizens
35   in painted cars
            and they have strange license plates
and engines
            that devour America

2
                Sailing thru the straits of Demos
40   we saw symbolic birds
                                    shrieking over us
                while eager eagles hovered
                                and elephants in bathtubs
                floated past us out to sea
45   strumming bent mandolins
            and bailing for old glory with their ears
                                    while patriotic maidens
                wearing paper poppies
                        and eating bonbons
50   ran along the shores
                                    wailing after us
and while we lashed ourselves to masts
                            and stopt our ears with chewing gum
                dying donkeys on high hills
55   sang low songs
                and gay cows flew away
                                chanting Athenian anthems
            as their pods turned to tulips
                                and heliocopters from Helios
60   flew over us
                                    dropping free railway tickets
                from Los Angeles to Heaven
                                and promising Free Elections
                        So that
65   we set up mast and sail
on that swart ship once more
                            and so set forth once more
            forth upon the gobbly sea
                                loaded with liberated vestal virgins
70   and discus throwers reading Walden
                but
                        shortly after reaching
                                    the strange suburban shores

of that great American
75   demi-democracy
                           looked at each other
                                       with a mild surprise
                   silent upon a peak
                                       in Darien
                                                 (1958)

from *Pictures of the Gone World*

II
The world is a beautiful place
                                       to be born into
        if you don't mind happiness
                                 not always being
5   so very much fun
                if you don't mind a touch of hell
                                       now and then
                   just when everything is fine
                                       because even in heaven
10   they don't sing
                                       all the time

        The world is a beautiful place
                                       to be born into
        if you don't mind some people dying
15   all the time
                   or maybe only starving
                                       some of the time
                   which isn't half so bad
                                       if it isn't you

20   Oh the world is a beautiful place
                                       to be born into
                if you don't much mind
                                       a few dead minds
                   in the higher places
25   or a bomb or two
                           now and then
                                       in your upturned faces
                or such other improprieties
                                       as our Name Brand society

30   is prey to
                                    with its men of distinction
                    and its men of extinction
                                        and its priests
                    and other patrolmen
35   and its various segregations
                and congressional investigations
                                        and other constipations
                    that our fool flesh
                                    is heir to

40   Yes the world is the best place of all
                                        for a lot of such things as
                    making the fun scene
                                    and making the love scene
            and making the sad scene
45   and singing low songs and having inspirations
                and walking around
                            looking at everything
                                        and smelling flowers
                and goosing statues
50   and even thinking
                                        and kissing people and
                    making babies and wearing pants
                                        and waving hats and
                            dancing
55   and going swimming in rivers
                    on picnics
                        in the middle of the summer
                and just generally
                        "living it up"

60   Yes
            but then right in the middle of it
                                        comes the smiling

                        mortician
                                            (1958)

Denise Levertov

(b. 1 9 2 3)

Denise Levertov has always emphasized her mystic heritage: she is descended on her mother's side from a Welsh tailor and mystic named Angel Jones and on her father's side from Scheour Zaimon, a renowned member of a Jewish mystical movement that found glory, as Levertov does, in commonplace occurrences. Her father was Jewish, but he became an Anglican priest. Levertov was born at Ilford, Essex, and was educated in the literary and artistic household of her parents. During the war she served as an army nurse. Shortly after the war she published her first book of poetry, *The Double Image* (1946). In 1947 she met the American writer Mitchell Goodman in Geneva; they married and moved to New York. Residence in the United States strengthened the influence of William Carlos Williams and the "Projective Verse" ideas of Charles Olson. Her interest in the Hasidic ideas of Martin Buber and in the concepts of Carl Jung have also influenced her work. Her first American volume, *Here and Now,* was published in 1956; by the early 1960s, Levertov was recognized as one of the country's finest poets.

Levertov is an ecstatic poet who plumbs the depths of ordinary objects and experiences to find hidden beauties. Her poems are paced carefully, to maximize the effect of their final, explosive images. She carefully breaks lines to suspend clarity and to generate tension. She is much more focused than the Beat poets, and she attempts to create a harmony within fully realized chaos, rather than merely imitating the chaos. Following somewhat from the Imagists, Levertov's work has a vivid, incantatory quality and a precision and restraint of metaphor and diction. She frequently employs traditional sound techniques—assonance, rhyme, alliteration—without actually writing within a formal structure. Her poems cast a strong light on human experience and the physical world, but they never evade the mysteriousness of final essences.

Levertov's books include *Here and Now* (1956), *Overland to the Islands* (1958), *Jacob's Ladder* (1961), *O Taste and See* (1964), *To Stay Alive* (1971), *Footprints* (1972), *The Freeing of the Dust* (1975), *Life in the Forest* (1975), *Collected Earlier Poems* (1979), and *Light Up the Cave* (1981). A collection of essays, *The Poet in the World,* appeared in 1973.

DENISE LEVERTOV

The Way It Is

More real than ever, as I move
in the world, and never out of it,
Solitude.

Typewriter, telephone, ugly names
5   of things we use, I use. Among them, though,
float milkweed silks.

Like a mollusk's, my hermitage
is built of my own cells.
Burned faces, stretched horribly,

10 eyes and mouths forever open,
weight the papers down on my desk.
No day for years I have not thought of them.

And more true than ever the familiar image
placing love on a border
15 where, solitary, it paces, exchanging
across the line a deep attentive gaze
with another solitude pacing there.

Yet almost no day, too, with no
happiness, no
20 exaltation of larks uprising from the heart's
peat-bog darkness.

(1964)

O Taste and See

The world is
not with us enough.
O taste and see

the subway Bible poster said,
5   meaning **The Lord,** meaning

if anything all that lives
to the imagination's tongue,

grief, mercy, language,
tangerine, weather, to
10   breathe them, bite,
savor, chew, swallow, transform

into our flesh our
deaths, crossing the street, plum, quince,
living in the orchard and being

15   hungry, and plucking
the fruit.

(1964)

Prayer for Revolutionary Love

That a woman not ask a man to leave meaningful work to follow her.
That a man not ask a woman to leave meaningful work to follow him.

That no one try to put Eros in bondage.
But that no one put a cudgel in the hands of Eros.

5   That our loyalty to one another and our loyalty to our work
not be set in false conflict.

That our love for each other give us love for each other's work.
That our love for each other's work give us love for one another.

That our love for each other's work give us love for one another.
10   *That our love for each other give us love for each other's work.*

That our love for each other, if need be,
give way to absence. And the unknown.

That we endure absence, if need be,
without losing our love for each other.
15   Without closing our doors to the unknown.

(1975)

James Reaney

(b. 1 9 2 6)

James Reaney was born on a farm near Stratford, in southwestern Ontario, where he has lived most of his life. The area has provided the setting and history for much of his writing. He attended the University of Toronto and received a Ph.D. in 1958. His first volume of poetry, *The Red Heart,* was published in 1949; it won the Governor-General's award, the first of four he was to win. In the 1950s Reaney taught English at the University of Manitoba; since 1960 he has served on the faculty of the University of Western Ontario in London. Reaney has also written award-winning plays and directed an experimental drama center. He edited the literary magazine *Alphabet* from 1960 until 1971. In recent years he has been combining poetry with film, painting, and photographs. He is married to poet Colleen Thibaudeau.

In his poetry and drama, Reaney explores the geography and history of the rural Ontario countryside and infuses them with the mythic structures he found in the criticism of Northrop Frye. He has, for example, written a trilogy of plays, *The Donnellys,* which examines the interplay of history, rumor, and myth surrounding the semilegendary Donnelly family, murdered near London in the nineteenth century. Reaney uses rural landscapes and natural cycles to combine particular local events and places with larger archetypal structures. To Reaney, the poet, like the child, is a force of creative energy and inverts given social forms. Reaney's later work has become increasingly complex and encyclopedic and more explicitly concerned with the fusion of opposites, which he sees as one of the great challenges of the poet. His lyric poetry is perhaps best exemplified by the fine poems in *A Suit of Nettles.*

Reaney's work includes *The Red Heart* (1949), *A Suit of Nettles* (1958), *The Killdeer and Other Plays* (1962), *Colours in the Dark* (1969), *Listen to the Wind* (1972), *Poems* (1972), and *The Donnellys* (1975–1977).

JAMES REANEY

Antichrist as a Child

When Antichrist was a child
He caught himself tracing
The capital letter A
On a window sill
5 And wondered why
Because his name contained no A.
And as he crookedly stood
In his mother's flower-garden
He wondered why she looked so sadly
10 Out of an upstairs window at him.
He wondered why his father stared so
Whenever he saw his little son
Walking in his soot-coloured suit.
He wondered why the flowers
15 And even the ugliest weeds
Avoided his fingers and his touch.
And when his shoes began to hurt
Because his feet were becoming hooves
He did not let on to anyone
20 For fear they would shoot him for a monster.
He wondered why he more and more
Dreamed of eclipses of the sun,
Of sunsets, ruined towns and zeppelins,
And especially inverted, upside down churches.

(1949)

The Red Heart

The only leaf upon its tree of blood,
My red heart hangs heavily
And will never fall loose,
But grow so heavy
5 After only a certain number of seasons
(Sixty winters, and fifty-nine falls,
Fifty-eight summers, and fifty-seven springs)

That it will bring bough
Tree and the fences of my bones
10 Down to a grave in the forest
Of my still upright fellows.

So does the sun hang now
From a branch of Time
In this wild fall sunset.
15 Who shall pick the sun
From the tree of Eternity?
Who shall thresh the ripe sun?
What midwife shall deliver
The Sun's great heir?
20 It seems that no one can,
And so the sun shall drag
Gods, goddesses and parliament buildings,
Time, Fate, gramaphones and Man
To a gray grave
25 Where all shall be trampled
Beneath the dancing feet of crowds
Of other still-living suns and stars.

(1949)

The Alphabet

Where are the fields of dew?
I cannot keep them.
They quip and pun
The rising sun
5 Who plucks them out of view:
But lay down fire-veined jasper!

For out of my cloudy head
Come Ay Ee I Oh and U,
Five thunders shouted;
10   *Drive in sardonyx!*

And Ull Mm Nn Rr and hisSsings
Proclaim huge wings;
Pour in sea blue sapphires!

Through my bristling hair
15   Blows Wuh and Yuh

Puh, Buh, Phuh and Vuh,
The humorous air:
Lift up skies of chalcedony!

Huh, Cuh, Guh and Chuh
20   Grunt like pigs in my acorn mind:
Arrange these emeralds in a meadow!

Come down Tuh, Duh and Thuh!
Consonantly rain
On the windowpane
25   Of the shrunken house of the heart;
Lift up blood red sardius!

Lift up golden chrysolite!
Juh, Quuh, Zuh and X
Scribble heavens with light,
30   Steeples take fright.

In my mouth like bread
Stands the shape of this glory;
Consonants and vowels
Repeat the story:
35   *And sea-green beryl is carried up!*

The candle tongue in my dark mouth
Is anguished with its sloth
And stung with self-scoff
As my eyes behold this treasure.
40   *Let them bring up topaz now!*

Dazzling chrysoprase!
Dewdrops tempt dark wick to sparkle.
Growl Spark! you whelp and cur,
Leap out of tongue kennel
45   And candle sepulchre.

I faint in the hyacinthine quarries!
My words pursue
Through the forest of time
The fading antlers of this dew.

50   A B C D E F G H I J K L M
Take captive the sun
Slay the dew quarry
Adam's Eve is morning rib

Bride and bridegroom marry
55   Still coffin is rocking crib
Tower and well are one
The stone is the wind, the wind is the stone
New Jerusalem
N O P Q R S T U V W X Y Z !

(1960)

Robert Creeley

(b. 1 9 2 6)

Robert Creeley was born in Arlington, Massachusetts, and grew up in Massachusetts and New Hampshire. He went to Harvard but never took a degree. In the early 1940s he worked with the American Field Service in India and Burma. He was married in 1946 and lived on Cape Cod, in New Hampshire, in France, and in Spain, where he started Divers Press. In the mid-fifties, after publishing three books of poetry, Creeley taught briefly at Black Mountain College at the invitation of Charles Olson, then founded the *Black Mountain Review.* He left the college when his marriage broke down in 1956 and moved to New Mexico. He taught for a time in Guatemala, then joined the faculty of State University of New York, in Buffalo, in 1966. He continues to spend part of each year in New Mexico.

Creeley's poems are focused and minimal. They are intent on reporting brief emotional transitions as accurately and as concisely as possible. Creeley rejected Olson's idea that projective verse was an "open field," and instead has emphasized the fact that one's perceptions are momentarily focused and continually slipping into another node or center; to express this, poetry must be continually qualifying, rigorously receptive to revision. The poet lets a theme play upon his consciousness, rather than attempting to mold the theme to fit a preconception. Creeley's poetic stance is passive, a carefully studied shifting mirror rather than a transforming lamp. What must be captured is immediate sensation. Creeley's attempts to do so are generally brief, written in simple, lucid language devoid of striking imagery. Poetry, he asserts, can be small and quiet without being inferior. Creeley focuses on the way emotions are affected by personal relationships. It is only in relationships, he has said, "that men live at all."

More than 30 volumes have been published by Creeley since *Le Fou* in 1952, including some 20 books of poetry. These include *The Immoral Proposition* (1953), *For Love: Poems 1950–60* (1962), *Selected Poems* (1976), and *Later* (1979). He has also published a volume of stories, *The Gold Diggers* (1954, 1965), a novel, *The Island* (1963), and two volumes of essays.

ROBERT CREELEY

I Know a Man

As I sd to my
friend, because I am
always talking,—John, I

sd, which was not his
5   name, the darkness sur-
rounds us, what

can we do against
it, or else, shall we &
why not, buy a goddamn big car,

10   drive, he sd, for
christ's sake, look
out where yr going.

(1962)

La Noche[1]

In the court-
yard at midnight, at

midnight. The moon is
locked in itself, to

5   a man a
familiar thing.

(1962)

For W.C.W.[2]

The pleasure of the wit sustains
a vague aroma

[1] The night.
[2] William Carlos Williams.

The fox-glove (unseen) the
wild flower

5   To the hands come
many things. In time of trouble

a wild exultation.

(1962)

Robert Kroetsch

(b. 1 9 2 7)

Robert Kroetsch was born in Heisler, Alberta. He received a B.A. from the University of Alberta in 1948, then worked on riverboats in the Northwest Territories. In 1954 he studied with Hugh MacLennan at McGill University. He received an M.A. from Middlebury College in 1956 and a Ph.D. from the University of Iowa in 1961. He taught at the State University of New York, in Binghamton; in 1978 he returned to Canada to teach at the University of Manitoba.

Kroetsch is Canada's most eloquent spokesman for postmodernism. In his poems, many of which are collected in *Field Notes,* he displays his continuing fascination with "doubling," with form (and the disintegration of form), with the notions of beginning and ending, and with the relationship of a poem's voice to the poem and to the audience. His poems are full of dialectical tensions: past and present fuse, love and loss are inextricable, and death embraces life. Kroetsch has also produced seven novels, among them *The Studhorse Man,* for which he won a Governor-General's award, and *Badlands,* which is set in the Alberta badlands and explores the constantly metamorphosing present and the search for both "real" and invented history. His work is colloquial and anecdotal yet formally complex. Kroetsch has had a considerable impact on younger writers. He cofounded and edits *Boundary 2: A Journal of Post-Modern Literature.*

Among Kroetsch's books of poetry are *The Stone Hammer Poems: 1960–1975* (1975), *Seed Catalogue* (1977), and *Field Notes* (1981); his novels include *But We Are Exiles* (1965), *The Studhorse Man* (1969), *Badlands* (1975), *What the Crow Said* (1978), and *Alibi* (1983). His essays have been collected in the journal *Open Letter,* 5th Series, No. 4 (Spring 1983).

ROBERT KROETSCH

Stone Hammer Poem

1

This stone
become a hammer
of stone, this maul

is the colour
5 of bone (no,
bone is the colour
of this stone maul).

The rawhide loops
are gone, the
10 hand is gone, the
buffalo's skull
is gone;

the stone is
shaped like the skull
15 of a child.

2

This paperweight on my desk

where I begin
this poem   was

found in a wheatfield
20 lost (this hammer,
this poem).

Cut to a function,
this stone was
(the hand is   gone—

3

25 Grey, two-headed,
the pemmican maul

fell from the travois or
a boy playing   lost it in
the prairie wool or
30 a squaw   left it in
the brain of a buffalo or

It is a million
years older than
the hand that
35 chipped stone or
raised slough
water (or blood) or

4

This stone maul
was found.

40 In the field
my grandfather
thought
was his

my father
45 thought was his

5

It is a stone
old as the last
Ice Age, the
retreating / the
50 recreating ice,
the retreating
buffalo, the
retreating Indians

(the saskatoons bloom
55 white (infrequently
the chokecherries the
highbush cranberries the
pincherries bloom
white along the barbed
60 wire fence (the
pemmican   winter

6

This stone maul
stopped a plow
long enough for one
65 *Gott im Himmel.* [1]

The Blackfoot (the
Cree?) not

finding the maul
cursed.

[1] God in Heaven.

70   ?did he curse
     ?did he try to
     go back
     ?what happened
     I have to / I want
75   to know (not know)
     ?WHAT HAPPENED

                    7
     The poem
     is the stone
     chipped and hammered
80   until it is shaped
     like the stone
     hammer, the maul.

                    8
     Now the field is
     mine because
85   I gave it
     (for a price)

     to a young man
     (with a growing son)
     who did not

90   notice that the land
     did not belong

     to the Indian who
     gave it to the Queen
     (for a price) who
95   gave it to the CPR
     (for a price) which
     gave it to my grandfather
     (for a price) who
     gave it to my father
100 (50 bucks an acre
     Gott im Himmel I cut
     down all the trees I
     picked up all the stones) who

     gave it to his son
105 (who sold it)

9

This won't
surprise you.

My grandfather
lost the stone maul.

10

110 My father (retired)
grew raspberries.
He dug in his potato patch.
He drank one glass of wine
each morning.
115 He was lonesome
for death.

He was lonesome for the
hot wind on his face, the smell
of horses, the distant
120 hum of a threshing machine,
the oilcan he carried, the weight
of a crescent wrench in his hind pocket.

He was lonesome for his absent
son and his daughters,
125 for his wife, for his own
brothers and sisters and
his own mother and father.

He found the stone maul
on a rockpile in the
130 north-west corner of what
he thought of
as his wheatfield.

He kept it (the
stone maul) on the railing
135 of the back porch in
a raspberry basket.

11

I keep it
on my desk
(the stone).

140 Sometimes I use it
in the (hot) wind
(to hold down paper)

smelling a little of cut
grass or maybe even of
145 ripening wheat or of
buffalo blood hot
in the dying sun.

Sometimes I write
my poems for that

150 stone hammer.

(1975)

from *Seed Catalogue*

I

No. 176—*Copenhagen Market Cabbage:* 'This *new introduction,
strictly speaking,* is in every respect a *thoroughbred,* a *cabbage*
of *highest pedigree,* and is *creating considerable flurry* among
professional gardeners all *over the world!'*

5 We took the storm windows / off
the south side of the house
and put them on the hotbed.
Then it was spring. Or, no:
then winter was ending.

10   "I wish to say we had lovely success
this summer with the seed purchased
of you. We had the finest Sweet
Corn in the country, and Cabbage
were dandy."
15   —W.W. Lyon, South Junction, Man.

My mother said:
Did you wash your ears?
You could grow cabbages
in those ears.

20 Winter was ending.
This is what happened:

we were harrowing the garden.
You've got to understand this:
I was sitting on the horse.
25   The horse was standing still.
I fell off.

The hired man laughed: how
in hell did you manage to
fall off a horse that was
30   *standing still?*

Bring me the radish seeds,
my mother whispered.

Into the dark of January
the seed catalogue bloomed

35   a winter proposition, if
spring should come, then,

with illustrations:

No. 25—*McKenzie's Improved Golden Wax Bean:* "THE MOST
PRIZED OF ALL BEANS. *Virtue* is its own reward. We have had
many expressions from *keen discriminating gardeners extolling
our seed* and *this variety.*"

Beans, beans,
the musical fruit;
the more you eat,
45   the more you virtue.

My mother was marking the first row
with a piece of binder twine, stretched
between two pegs.

The hired man laughed: just
50   about planted the little bugger.
Cover him up and see what grows.
My father didn't laugh. He was puzzled
by any garden that was smaller than a
quarter-section of wheat and summerfallow.

55   the home place: N.E. 17-42-16-w4th

the home place: one and a half miles west of Heisler, Alberta,
                    on the correction line road
                    and three miles south.

   No trees
60 around the house.
   Only the wind.
   Only the January snow.
   Only the summer sun.
   The home place:
65 a terrible symmetry.

   How do you grow a gardener?

               Telephone Peas
               Garden Gem Carrots
               Early Snowcap Cauliflower
70   Perfection Globe Onions
               Hubbard Squash
               Early Ohio Potatoes

   This is what happened—at my mother's wake. This
   is a fact—the World Series was in progress. The
75 Cincinnati Reds were playing the Detroit Tigers.
   It was raining. The road to the graveyard was barely
   passable. The horse was standing still. Bring me
   the radish seeds, my mother whispered.

                                                        (1977)

Phyllis Webb

(b. 1 9 2 7)

Phyllis Webb was born in Victoria, British Columbia. She attended the University of British Columbia, where she received her B.A. in English and philosophy in 1949. In the same year she ran as a candidate for the CCF in the provincial election. At the university Webb became involved in a writing group led by Earle Birney. After a year of graduate work at McGill University, Webb lived in Montreal for five years. Some of her poems, along with those of Eli Mandel and Gael Turnbull, appeared in *Trio,* published by Contact Press in 1954. She lived for a time in France, then took a position at the University of British Columbia in 1961. In 1964 she moved to Toronto and became the executive producer of "Ideas," a CBC radio program. In 1967 Webb retired from the program; after a short stay in the Soviet Union, she settled on Saltspring Island, off the coast of British Columbia. In the late seventies, Webb taught creative writing in Victoria, Vancouver, and Alberta. Her volume *The Vision Tree* won a Governor-General's award in 1983.

Webb's early poetry experiments with vivid metaphors and diction; her later work (as in *Wilson's Bowl*) is marked by a clear, stark, elegant tone and short, minimalist forms. She is interested in both the large cycles of time and space and in the constricting boundaries of individual existence. Her poetic world is bleak, but Webb is, intellectually and emotionally, a challenging and complex thinker. Her intricate, refined verse blends sound and idea. The voice is calm yet visionary, ironically accepting the darkest facets of reality and bravely confronting despair. There are brief moments of joy, but the moments are overwhelmed by the poet's refusal to ignore joy's dark underside.

After the *Trio* poems, Webb wrote *Even Your Right Eye* (1956), *The Sea Is Also a Garden* (1962), *Naked Poems* (1965), *Selected Poems 1954–1965* (1971), *Wilson's Bowl* (1980), *Talking* (1982), *Sunday Water: Thirteen Anti-Ghazals* (1982), and *Selected Poems: A Vision Tree* (1982).

PHYLLIS WEBB

Marvell's Garden [1]

Marvell's garden, that place of solitude,
is not where I'd choose to live
yet is the fixed sundial
that turns me round
5   unwillingly
in a hot glade
as closer, closer I come to contradiction,
to the shade green within the green shade.

The garden where Marvell scorned love's solicitude—
10   that dream—and played instead an arcane solitaire,
shuffling his thoughts like shadowy chance
across the shrubs of ecstasy,
and cast the myths away to flowering hours
as yes, his mind, that sea, caught at green
15   thoughts shadowing a green infinity.

And yet Marvell's garden was not Plato's
garden—and yet—he *did* care more for the form
of things than for the thing itself—
ideas and visions,
20   resemblances and echoes,
things seeming and being
not quite what they were.

That was his garden, a kind of attitude
struck out of an earth too carefully attended,
25   wanting to be left alone.
And I don't blame him for that.
God knows, too many fences fence us out
and his garden closed in on Paradise.

On Paradise! When I think of his hymning
30   Puritans in the Bermudas, the bright oranges
lighting up that night! When I recall
his rustling tinsel hopes

[1] See Andrew Marvell's poem "The Garden," on pp. 116–118.

beneath the cold decree of steel,
Oh, I have wept for some new convulsion
35   to tear together this world and his.

But then I saw his luminous plumèd Wings
prepared for flight,
and then I heard him singing glory
in a green tree,
40   and then I caught the vest he'd laid aside
all blest with fire.

And I have gone walking slowly in
his garden of necessity
leaving brothers, lovers, Christ
45   outside my walls
where they have wept without
and I within.

(1956)

Breaking

Give us wholeness, for we are broken.
But who are we asking, and why do we ask?
Destructive element heaves close to home,
our years of work broken against a breakwater.

5   Shattered gods, self-iconoclasts,
it is with Lazarus unattended we belong
(the fall of the sparrow is unbroken song).
The crucifix has clattered to the ground,
the living Christ has spent a year in Paris,
10   travelled on the Métro, fallen in the Seine.
We would not raise our silly gods again.
Stigmata sting, they suddenly appear
on every blessed person everywhere.
If there is agitation there is cause.

15   Ophelia, Hamlet, Othello, Lear,
Kit Smart, William Blake, John Clare,
Van Gogh, Henry IV of Pirandello,
Gerard de Nerval, Antonin Artaud
bear a crown of darkness.
20   It is better so.

Responsible now each to his own attack,
we are bequeathed their ethos and our death.
Greek marble white and whiter grows
breaking into history of a west.
25   If we could stand so virtuously white
crumbling in the terrible Grecian light.

There is a justice in destruction.
It isn't "isn't fair"
A madhouse is designed for the insane,
30   a hospital for wounds that will re-open,
a war is architecture for aggression,
and Christ's stigmata body-minted token.
What are we whole or beautiful or good for but to be absolutely
        broken?

(1971)

from *A Question of Questions*

I

question
query
hook
        of the soul
5   a question of
questions
                    why / how
                        oh God
                    has it come to this

10   hook
sickle
scythe
        to cut us down this
mark?
15   who—how many years
        to shape the mind to make
        its turn toward this?
        the where / when of the type
        the proper fall of lead
20   in the printer's font?
        and who are you in this

school
room
torture chamber?
25   whose are you?
and what of your
trials and errors?
the judge
in his echo chamber
30   cannot know
and nor can you
you cannot answer

IV

Extracted toenails.
I have nothing to say.

Burns on the breasts.
I have nothing to say.

5   Electric shock.
I have nothing to say.

Beatings.
I have nothing to say.

Refinements of an old skill.
10   Make the inner outer.

I am what I am.
All one.

Done. Take it away.

V

for R.D.L. [1]
The error lies in
the state of desire
in wanting the answers

[1] "If the dominant phantasy in this particular group was that the therapist had 'the answer' and that if they could get 'the answer' they would not be suffering. The therapist's task, like a Zen Master's, is to point out that their suffering is not due to their getting 'the answer' from him, but is in the state of desire they are in, whereby they posit the existence of 'an answer' and are frustrated because they do not seem to be getting it." I am indebted to R.D. Laing (*The Self and Others*, Tavistock Publications, London, 1961, p. 114) for the inspiration for this poem —as well as the red-crested woodpecker. The description of *dryocopus pileatus* comes from Roger Tory Peterson's *Field Guide to Western Birds* (Houghton-Mifflin Co., Boston, 1961). (Webb's note.)

wanting the red-crested
5   woodpecker to pose
among red berries
of the ash tree
wanting its names
its habitations
10   the instinct
of its ways for
my head-travelling
wanting its colours
its red, white, its black
15   pressed behind my eyes
a triptych
three-fold
and over
and wanting the bird
20   to be still and
wanting it moving
whiteflash of underwings
dazzling all questions
out of me, amazement
25   and outbreathing
become a form
of my knowing.

I move and it moves
into a cedar tree.
30   I walk and I walk.
My deceiving angel's
in-shadow joins me
paces my steps and threatens
to take my head
35   between its hands.
I keep walking.
Trying to think.
Here on the island
there is time
40   on the Isabella
Point Road.
We pass a dead
deer on the beach.
Bloated. It stinks.
45   The angel insists, 'Keep
walking. It has all the time
in the world. Is sufficient.
Is alone. Keep walking.'

it says and flies off
50 with my head.

What's left of me
remembers a funny song
also a headless
man on rockface
55 painted in red
by Indian finger spirits.

The red-crested woodpecker swoops down
and sits on my trunk. Posing.
Dryocopus pileatus. 'Spectacular, black,
60 *Crow-sized* woodpecker with a red *crest,*
great size, sweeping wingbeats, flashing
white underwing.' Pileated woodpecker.
Posing. Many questions.
'The diggings, large *oval* or *oblong* holes,
65 indicate its presence.'

Zen Master.

(1980)

Anne Sexton

(1 9 2 8 – 1 9 7 4)

Anne Sexton was born in Newton, Massachusetts, and lived most of her life in New England. She was a direct descendant of one of the Mayflower Pilgrims, and described her upbringing as "puritanical and stifled." At the age of 19 she eloped with Alfred Sexton and worked as a salesgirl, a fashion model, and a librarian. She lived briefly in upstate New York, Baltimore, and San Francisco. After the birth of her second child, Sexton suffered a nervous breakdown. She began writing poetry, which was accepted by prestigious magazines. She published her first book, *To Bedlam and Part Way Back,* in 1960. In 1961 she was appointed to the Radcliffe Institute, then went to Europe on a traveling fellowship. In 1965 she was elected to the British Royal Society of Literature. She also taught at Boston College and at Colgate. Sexton won the Pulitzer Prize in 1966. She committed suicide at the age of 46.

Like Sylvia Plath, Sexton was influenced by the "confessional" poetry of Robert Lowell and W. D. Snodgrass. Her poetry is a painfully explicit analysis of her own psychology and details the causes, the tortures, and the agonizing, partial recoveries of her severe depressions and breakdowns. She sets her poems in the context of familial, everyday occurrences, and demonstrates a strong belief in the power of ordinary objects and situations in poetic composition. Although some critics have dismissed Sexton's work as melodramatic ("terribly serious soap opera," in the words of James Dickey), her best work is an extraordinary experience. The reader is plunged into startling spheres of revelation that teach as much about the reader's own life as that of the poetic persona. Sexton has quoted favorably Kafka's dictum that "A book should serve as an axe for the frozen sea within us," and the line serves as a succinct appraisal of her work. Sexton's poetic success seems to rely on personal suffering.

Sexton's volumes of poetry were *To Bedlam and Part Way Back* (1960), *All My Pretty Ones* (1962), *Love Poems* (1969), *The Book of Folly* (1972), *The Death Notebooks* (1974), and the posthumous volumes *The Awful Rowing Toward God* (1975), *45 Mercy Street* (1976), *Words for Dr. Y.* (1978), and *The Complete Poems* (1981).

ANNE SEXTON

The Children

The children are all crying in their pens
and the surf carries their cries away.
They are old men who have seen too much,
their mouths are full of dirty clothes,
5   the tongues poverty, tears like pus.
The surf pushes their cries back.
Listen.
They are bewitched.
They are writing down their life
10   on the wings of an elf
who then dissolves.
They are writing down their life
on a century fallen to ruin.
They are writing down their life
15   on the bomb of an alien God.
I am too.

We must get help.
The children are dying in their pens.
Their bodies are crumbling.
20   Their tongues are twisting backwards.
There is a certain ritual to it.
There is a dance they do in their pens.
Their mouths are immense.
They are swallowing monster hearts.
25   So is my mouth.

Listen.
We must all stop dying in the little ways,
in the craters of hate,
in the potholes of indifference—
30   a murder in the temple.
The place I live in
is a kind of maze
and I keep seeking
the exit or the home.
35   Yet if I could listen
to the bulldog courage of those children

and turn inward into the plague of my soul
with more eyes than the stars
I could melt the darkness—
40   as suddenly as that time
when an awful headache goes away
or someone puts out the fire—
and stop the darkness and its amputations
and find the real McCoy
45   in the private holiness
of my hands.

(1975)

Riding the Elevator into the Sky

As the fireman said:
Don't book a room over the fifth floor
in any hotel in New York.
They have ladders that will reach further
5   but no one will climb them.
As the New York *Times* said:
The elevator always seeks out
the floor of the fire
and automatically opens
10   and won't shut.
These are the warnings
that you must forget
if you're climbing out of yourself.
If you're going to smash into the sky.

15   Many times I've gone past
the fifth floor,
cranking upward,
but only once
have I gone all the way up.
20   Sixtieth floor:
small plants and swans bending
into their grave.
Floor two hundred:
mountains with the patience of a cat,
25   silence wearing its sneakers.
Floor five hundred:
messages and letters centuries old,
birds to drink,

a kitchen of clouds.
30 Floor six thousand:
the stars,
skeletons on fire,
their arms singing.
And a key,
35 a very large key,
that opens something—
some useful door—
somewhere—
up there.

(1975)

The Rowing Endeth

I'm mooring my rowboat
at the dock of the island called God.
This dock is made in the shape of a fish
and there are many boats moored
5 at many different docks.
"It's okay," I say to myself,
with blisters that broke and healed
and broke and healed—
saving themselves over and over.
10 And salt sticking to my face and arms like
a glue-skin pocked with grains of tapioca.
I empty myself from my wooden boat
and onto the flesh of The Island.

"On with it!" He says and thus
15 we squat on the rocks by the sea
and play—can it be true—
a game of poker.
He calls me.
I win because I hold a royal straight flush.
20 He wins because He holds five aces.
A wild card had been announced
but I had not heard it
being in such a state of awe
when He took out the cards and dealt.
25 As he plunks down His five aces
and I sit grinning at my royal flush,
He starts to laugh,

the laughter rolling like a hoop out of His mouth
and into mine,
30   and such laughter that He doubles right over me
laughing a Rejoice-Chorus at our two triumphs.
Then I laugh, the fishy dock laughs
the sea laughs. The Island laughs.
The Absurd laughs.

35   Dearest dealer,
I with my royal straight flush,
love you so for your wild card,
that untamable, eternal, gut-driven *ha-ha*
and lucky love.

(1975)

Ted Hughes

(b. 1 9 3 0)

Ted Hughes was born in Mytholmroyd, Yorkshire, and was brought up in the West Country of England. He worked as a ground wireless mechanic in the Royal Air Force, then entered Cambridge and earned a B.A. At Cambridge Hughes met and married the brilliant but troubled young American poet, Sylvia Plath. They moved to the United States and Hughes's first volume of poetry, *Hawk in the Rain,* appeared in 1957. The book won the first-publication award at the New York City Poetry Center. Hughes and Plath returned to England and had two children. They separated in 1962, shortly before Plath's death. Hughes has won several awards, including the 1961 Hawthorndon Prize. In 1984 he was named England's Poet Laureate.

Hughes's poetry is most striking for its dramatic reenactments of man's interaction with animals. His subject matter is frequently violent, and he writes from the perspective of the predator rather than the victim. Threatening birds of prey, especially hawks and crows, have symbolized this theme, although Hughes has also used the horse to represent gracefulness and a power that approaches ferocity. The implication lying behind much of the poetry is that the distinction between animal and human is suspect, that the strangeness in man's violent, relentless predators is only the strangeness of those parts of ourselves we refuse to know. Hughes is a consistently exciting poet, a master of dense symbolic suggestiveness, daring diction, and unique, jarring yet musical rhythms. In the muscular physicality of his language and in his love of the sensuous life of the English countryside, he bears some resemblance to his Irish contemporary Seamus Heaney, although Hughes's natural world is more consistently threatening.

Hawk in the Rain (1957) was followed by, among others, *Lupercal* (1960), *Wodwo* (1967), *Crow* (1970), *Cave Birds: An Alchemical Cave Drama* (1978), *Gaudete* (1977), *Moortown* (1979), *Selected Poems 1957–67* (1972), and *Selected Poems 1957–81* (1982). Hughes has also written eight books for children.

TED HUGHES

View of a Pig

The pig lay on a barrow dead.
It weighed, they said, as much as three men.
Its eyes closed, pink white eyelashes.
Its trotters stuck straight out.

5   Such weight and thick pink bulk
Set in death seemed not just dead.
It was less than lifeless, further off.
It was like a sack of wheat.

I thumped it without feeling remorse.
10 One feels guilty insulting the dead,
Walking on graves. But this pig
Did not seem able to accuse.

It was too dead. Just so much
A poundage of lard and pork.
15 Its last dignity had entirely gone.
It was not a figure of fun.

Too dead now to pity.
To remember its life, din, stronghold
Of earthly pleasure as it had been,
20 Seemed a false effort, and off the point.

Too deadly factual. Its weight
Oppressed me—how could it be moved?
And the trouble of cutting it up!
The gash in its throat was shocking, but not pathetic.

25 Once I ran at a fair in the noise
To catch a greased piglet
That was faster and nimbler than a cat,
Its squeal was the rending of metal.

Pigs must have hot blood, they feel like ovens.
30 Their bite is worse than a horse's—
They chop a half-moon clean out.
They eat cinders, dead cats.

Distinctions and admirations such
As this one was long finished with.
35   I stared at it a long time. They were going to scald it,
Scald it and scour it like a doorstep.

(1960)

Examination at the Womb-Door

Who owns these scrawny little feet?   *Death.*
Who owns this bristly scorched-looking face?   *Death.*
Who owns these still-working lungs?   *Death.*
Who owns this utility coat of muscles?   *Death.*
5   Who owns these unspeakable guts?   *Death.*
Who owns these questionable brains?   *Death.*
All this messy blood?   *Death.*
These minimum-efficiency eyes?   *Death.*
This wicked little tongue?   *Death.*
10   This occasional wakefulness?   *Death.*

Given, stolen, or held pending trial?
Held.

Who owns the whole rainy, stony earth?   *Death.*
Who owns all of space?   *Death.*

15   Who is stronger than hope?   *Death.*
Who is stronger than the will?   *Death.*
Stronger than love?   *Death.*
Stronger than life?   *Death.*

But who is stronger than death?
20   *Me, evidently.*

Pass, Crow.

(1970)

Jay Macpherson

(b. 1 9 3 1)

Jay Macpherson was born in England and emigrated to Canada with her family, settling in Newfoundland. Four years later, she moved to Ottawa, Ontario, where she received a B.A. from Carleton University. Macpherson continued her studies in English literature at Victoria College, University of Toronto, and began teaching there after receiving her M.A. for a thesis on John Milton. In 1952 she published her first small book of poems, *Nineteen Poems.* In 1964 she received her Ph.D. from the University of Toronto, where she still teaches. Macpherson's first major book of poems, *The Boatman,* won the Governor-General's award in 1957.

Macpherson works within the constraints of traditional verse forms and explores the technical innovations to be made within these forms and their applicability to modern themes. Many of her best poems are written in tight, four-line rhyming stanzas. Macpherson expresses her original, personal vision of the human situation in the context of the great themes from mythology. She alludes to biblical, classical, and eastern mythologies and to the poetry of the Romantic period. She uses these contexts to find a voice or perspective through which to express her own ideas in a larger, universalized frame of reference, and to set them within the great cycles of fall, exile, and redemption. In her poetry, Macpherson suggests that we must confront the ghosts and beasts within us to escape from an unending pattern of self-hatred and isolation.

Macpherson's volumes of poetry are *Nineteen Poems* (1952), *O Earth Return* (1954), *The Boatman* (1957, 1968), *Welcoming Disaster* (1974), and *Poems Twice Told* (1982). In 1982 she published a study of the Romance genre, *The Spirit of Solitude.*

JAY MACPHERSON

The Boatman

You might suppose it easy
For a maker not too lazy
To convert the gentle reader to an Ark:
But it takes a willing pupil

5   To admit both gnat and camel
     —Quite an eyeful, all the crew that must embark.

     After me when comes the deluge
     And you're looking around for refuge
     From God's anger pouring down in gush and spout,
10   Then you take the tender creature
     —You remember, that's the reader—
     And you pull him through his navel inside out.

     That's to get his beasts outside him,
     For they've got to come aboard him,
15   As the best directions have it, two by two.
     When you've taken all their tickets
     And you've marched them through his sockets,
     Let the tempest bust Creation: heed not you.

     For you're riding high and mighty
20   In a gale that's pushing ninety
     With a solid bottom under you—that's his.
     Fellow flesh affords a rampart,
     And you've got along for comfort
     All the world there ever shall be, was, and is.

                                        (1957)

Absence, Havoc

     Absence, havoc—well, I missed you—
     Near and dear turned far and strange,
     Dayshine came disguised as midnight:
     One thing altered made all change.

5   Fallen? stolen? trapped? entangled?
     To a lower world betrayed?
     Endless error held your footsteps,
     On your brow a deepening shade.

     Long I sought you, late I found you,
10   Straying on the farther shore:
     You indeed? a swaying phantom
     Fades, that flickered on before.
     Lost, no rescue: only dreams our
     Wandered, wandered loves restore.
                              (1974)

Words Failing

When we were young, they filched and harried for us,
Scoured on our errands lands and seas untiring,
Laboured in mines, brought treasure from the mountains,
 Eager, obedient.

5 Can spirits age like us? I found them weary—
Sick—hard to rouse, old spells near failing—then, like
Ghosts of the dead their faces, hands, were empty,
 Hollow their answers.

Worst is the last: their wilful, vengeful absence.
10 Can you forget, ungrateful, how you need me,
Now more than ever? mine the word that drags you
 Into existing.

Strangers they haunt, are drawn to others' windows.
I, drooping here, search for the word to free you,
15 Me too release, as—was it in a story?—
 Sins are forgiven.

         (1974)

Sylvia Plath

(1 9 3 2 – 1 9 6 3)

Sylvia Plath was born in Boston, Massachusetts, of Austrian and German parents. Her father died in 1940 and was "elegized" in the brutally critical poem "Daddy." Plath graduated from Smith College, where she won election to Phi Beta Kappa; she was awarded a Fulbright Scholarship to Cambridge, where she met and married the British poet Ted Hughes. After a year of teaching at Smith, Plath and her husband returned to England and settled in Devon. Plath had two children, one in 1960 and another in 1962; in 1960, she published her first book, *The Colossus,* to widespread praise. In late 1962, Plath left Hughes and moved to London with the children. The poems collected in her second book document her increasing depression and desperation. She committed suicide at the age of 30.

An enthusiast of Robert Lowell's "intense breakthrough into very serious, very personal, emotional experience which . . . has been partly taboo," Plath's own intense poetry is a searing odyssey into a personal landscape of despair, morbidity, suffering, and occasional defiant ecstasy. The poetry is filled with powerful imagery and concentrates on the painful and the macabre, on suicide, the Holocaust, the burning skin of the victims of Hiroshima. Plath blends poetry with madness; she stares forward and risks the downhill, suicidal flight inward. Occasionally her poetry is masochistic or solipsistic, but the power of expression and the carefully carved images make her work eye-wrenching and original.

The Colossus (1960) was followed by an autobiographical novel, *The Bell Jar* (1963), and a posthumous volume of poems, *Ariel* (1965). Ted Hughes edited the *Collected Poems* (1981).

SYLVIA PLATH

The Applicant

First, are you our sort of a person?
Do you wear
A glass eye, false teeth or a crutch,

A brace or a hook,
5   Rubber breasts or a rubber crotch,

Stitches to show something's missing? No, no? Then
How can we give you a thing?
Stop crying.
Open your hand.
10 Empty? Empty. Here is a hand

To fill it and willing
To bring teacups and roll away headaches
And do whatever you tell it.
Will you marry it?
15 It is guaranteed

To thumb shut your eyes at the end
And dissolve of sorrow.
We make new stock from the salt.
I notice you are stark naked.
20 How about this suit——

Black and stiff, but not a bad fit.
Will you marry it?
It is waterproof, shatterproof, proof
Against fire and bombs through the roof.
25 Believe me, they'll bury you in it.

Now your head, excuse me, is empty.
I have the ticket for that.
Come here, sweetie, out of the closet.
Well, what do you think of *that*?
30 Naked as paper to start

But in twenty-five years she'll be silver,
In fifty, gold.
A living doll, everywhere you look.
It can sew, it can cook,
35 It can talk, talk, talk.

It works, there is nothing wrong with it.
You have a hole, it's a poultice.
You have an eye, it's an image.
My boy, it's your last resort.
40 Will you marry it, marry it, marry it.

(1963)

Daddy

You do not do, you do not do
Any more, black shoe
In which I have lived like a foot
For thirty years, poor and white,
5   Barely daring to breathe or Achoo.

Daddy, I have had to kill you.
You died before I had time—
Marble-heavy, a bag full of God,
Ghastly statue with one gray toe
10   Big as a Frisco seal

And a head in the freakish Atlantic
Where it pours bean green over blue
In the waters off beautiful Nauset.
I used to pray to recover you.
15   Ach, du.[1]

In the German tongue, in the Polish town
Scraped flat by the roller
Of wars, wars, wars.
But the name of the town is common.
20   My Polack friend

Says there are a dozen or two.
So I never could tell where you
Put your foot, your root,
I never could talk to you.
25   The tongue stuck in my jaw.

It stuck in a barb wire snare.
Ich, ich, ich, ich,[2]
I could hardly speak.
I thought every German was you.
30   And the language obscene

An engine, an engine
Chuffing me off like a Jew.
A Jew to Dachau, Auschwitz, Belsen.[3]

[1] Ah, you.
[2] I, I, I, I,
[3] Nazi concentration camps.

I began to talk like a Jew.
35   I think I may well be a Jew.

The snows of the Tyrol, the clear beer of Vienna
Are not very pure or true.
With my gipsy ancestress and my weird luck
And my Taroc pack and my Taroc pack
40   I may be a bit of a Jew.

I have always been scared of *you*,
With your Luftwaffe,° your gobbledygoo.   German Air
And your neat mustache   Force
And your Aryan eye, bright blue.
45   Panzer-man, panzer-man,⁴ O You—

Not God but a swastika
So black no sky could squeak through.
Every woman adores a Fascist,
The boot in the face, the brute
50   Brute heart of a brute like you.

You stand at the blackboard, daddy,
In the picture I have of you,
A cleft in your chin instead of your foot
But no less a devil for that, no not
55   Any less the black man who

Bit my pretty red heart in two.
I was ten when they buried you.
At twenty I tried to die
And get back, back, back to you.
60   I thought even the bones would do.

But they pulled me out of the sack,
And they stuck me together with glue.
And then I knew what to do.
I made a model of you,
65   A man in black with a Meinkampf⁵ look

And a love of the rack and the screw.
And I said I do, I do.
So daddy, I'm finally through.

---

⁴ A member of the German armored tank troops.
⁵ *Mein Kampf* (My Fight) is the title of Adolf Hitler's (1889–1945) autobiography.

The black telephone's off at the root,
70 The voices just can't worm through.

If I've killed one man, I've killed two—
The vampire who said he was you
And drank my blood for a year,
Seven years, if you want to know.
75 Daddy, you can lie back now.

There's a stake in your fat black heart
And the villagers never liked you.
They are dancing and stamping on you.
They always *knew* it was you.
80 Daddy, daddy, you bastard, I'm through.

(1963)

Margaret Atwood

(b. 1 9 3 9)

Margaret Atwood, poet, novelist, short-story writer, critic, and anthologist, is a dominant figure in contemporary Canadian literature. She was born in Ottawa and spent much of her childhood with her parents in the bush country of northern Ontario and Quebec. She published her first small collection of poems in 1961, the year she received her B.A. from Victoria College, University of Toronto. After an M.A. from Harvard in 1962, Atwood lectured at the University of British Columbia and Sir George Williams College in Montreal, and was writer-in-residence at the University of Toronto. She has worked as an editor for House of Anansi press and was president of the Writers' Union of Canada. She lived for a number of years on a farm near Alliston, Ontario, then moved to Toronto. Her first full-length collection of poems, *The Circle Game* (1966), was awarded the Governor-General's award. Her first novel, *The Edible Woman*, appeared in 1969.

Atwood has extraordinarily lucid insights into human predicaments, into the subtle causal substructures of human motivation and behavior. She is a sociological and political writer: she analyzes the forces and preconceptions that influence us, torture us, constrain us, liberate us. In her work, humans, particularly women, are always in danger of being consumed by a predominantly masculine consumer society. Atwood is keenly aware of a modern sense of alienation, the loneliness at the center of our daily lives. She has insisted that poetry "does not express emotion. What poetry does is to evoke emotion from the reader, and that is a very different thing. As someone once said, if you want to express emotion, scream. If you want to evoke emotion, it's more complicated." She writes reflective lyrics with a finely modulated ironic wit, compressed syntax, pared-down forms, and an affection for the striking, often grotesque image. Her prose, always sparkling, exhibits a fine eye for the minor yet suggestive details of characterization and a preoccupation with the position of women in a transitional yet still male-dominated society.

Atwood's books of poetry are: *Double Persephone* (1961), *The Circle Game* (1966), *The Animals in That Country* (1968), *The Journals of Susanna Moodie* (1970), *Procedures for Underground* (1970), *Power Politics* (1971), *You Are Happy* (1974), *Selected Poems* (1976), *Two-Headed Poems* (1978), *True Stories* (1981), and *Interlunar* (1984). She has written six novels: *The Edible Woman* (1969), *Surfacing* (1972), *Lady Oracle* (1976), *Life Before Man* (1979), *Bodily Harm* (1981), and *The Handmaid's Tale* (1985); and three volumes of short fiction: *Dancing Girls* (1977), *Murder in the Dark* (1983), and *Bluebeard's Egg* (1984).

Atwood also wrote *Survival: A Thematic Guide to Canadian Literature* (1972) and edited *The New Oxford Book of Canadian Verse in English* (1982).

❧

MARGARET ATWOOD

This Is a Photograph of Me

It was taken some time ago.
At first it seems to be
a smeared
print: blurred lines and grey flecks
5   blended with the paper;

then, as you scan
it, you see in the left-hand corner
a thing that is like a branch: part of a tree
(balsam or spruce) emerging
10   and, to the right, halfway up
what ought to be a gentle
slope, a small frame house.

In the background there is a lake,
and beyond that, some low hills.

15   (The photograph was taken
the day after I drowned.

I am in the lake, in the center
of the picture, just under the surface.

It is difficult to say where
20   precisely, or to say
how large or small I am:
the effect of water
on light is a distortion

but if you look long enough,
25   eventually
you will be able to see me.)

(1976)

Progressive Insanities of a Pioneer

i

He stood, a point
on a sheet of green paper
proclaiming himself the centre,

with no walls, no borders
5 anywhere; the sky no height
above him, totally un-
enclosed
and shouted:

Let me out!

ii

10 He dug the soil in rows,
imposed himself with shovels
He asserted
into the furrows, I
am not random.

15 The ground
replied with aphorisms:

a tree-sprout, a nameless
weed, words
he couldn't understand.

iii

20 The house pitched
the plot staked
in the middle of nowhere.

At night the mind
inside, in the middle
25 of nowhere.

The idea of an animal
patters across the roof.

In the darkness the fields
defend themselves with fences
30 in vain:

everything
is getting in.

iv

By daylight he resisted.
He said, disgusted
35 with the swamp's clamourings and the outbursts
of rocks,
    This is not order
    but the absence
    of order.

40 He was wrong, the unanswering
forest implied:

    It was
    an ordered absence

v

For many years
45 he fished for a great vision,
dangling the hooks of sown
roots under the surface
of the shallow earth.

It was like
50 enticing whales with a bent
pin. Besides he thought

in that country
only the worms were biting.

vi

If he had known unstructured
55 space is a deluge
and stocked his log house-
boat with all the animals

even the wolves,

he might have floated.

60 But obstinate he
stated, The land is solid
and stamped,

watching his foot sink
down through stone
65   up to the knee.

vii

Things
refused to name themselves; refused
to let him name them.

The wolves hunted
70   outside.

On his beaches, his clearings,
by the surf of under-
growth breaking
at his feet, he foresaw
75   disintegration
                and in the end
through eyes
made ragged by his
effort, the tension
80   between subject and object,

the green
vision, the unnamed
whale invaded.

(1976)

You Begin

You begin this way:
this is your hand,
this is your eye,
that is a fish, blue and flat
5   on the paper, almost
the shape of an eye.
This is your mouth, this is an O
or a moon, whichever
you like. This is yellow.

10   Outside the window
is the rain, green
because it is summer, and beyond that

the trees and then the world,
which is round and has only
15 the colours of these nine crayons.

This is the world, which is fuller
and more difficult to learn than I have said.
You are right to smudge it that way
with the red and then
20 the orange: the world burns.

Once you have learned these words
you will learn that there are more
words than you can ever learn.
The word *hand* floats above your hand
25 like a small cloud over a lake.
The word *hand* anchors
your hand to this table,
your hand is a warm stone
I hold between two words.

30 This is your hand, these are my hands, this is the world,
which is round but not flat and has more colours
than we can see.

It begins, it has an end,
this is what you will
35 come back to, this is your hand.

(1978)

Burned Space

What comes in after a burn?
You could say nothing,

but there are flowers like dampened embers
that burst in cool white smoke

5 and after that, blue lights
among the leaves

that grow at the bases
of these blackened monoliths.

Before the burn, this was a forest.
10   Now it is something else:

a burn twists the green
eternal into singed grey

history: these discarded
stag-heads and small charred bones.

15   In a burn you kneel among the
reddish flowers and glowing seeds,

you give thanks as after a disaster
you were not part of,

though any burn
20   might have been your skin:

despite these liquid petals
against smoked rock, after a burn

your hands are never the same.
(1978)

Interlunar

Darkness waits apart from any occasion for it;
like sorrow it is always available.
This is only one kind,

the kind in which there are stars
5   above the leaves, brilliant as steel nails
and countless and without regard.

We are walking together
on dead wet leaves in the intermoon
among the looming nocturnal rocks
10   which would be pinkish grey
in daylight, gnawed and softened
by moss and ferns, which would be green,
in the musty fresh yeast smell
of trees rotting, earth returning
15   itself to itself

and I take your hand, which is the shape a hand
would be if you existed truly.
I wish to show you the darkness
you are so afraid of.

20 Trust me. This darkness
is a place you can enter and be
as safe in as you are anywhere;
you can put one foot in front of the other
and believe the sides of your eyes.
25 Memorize it. You will know it
again in your own time.
When the appearances of things have left you,
you will still have this darkness.
Something of your own you can carry with you.

30 We have come to the edge:
the lake gives off its hush;
in the outer night there is a barred owl
calling, like a moth
against the ear, from the far shore
35 which is invisible.
The lake, vast and dimensionless,
doubles everything, the stars,
the boulders, itself, even the darkness
that you can walk so long in
40 it becomes light.

(1984)

Seamus Heaney

(b. 1 9 3 9)

Seamus Heaney was born in Country Derry, Northern Ireland. He attended St. Columb's College, then took a B.A. in English from Queen's University in Belfast. There he met Henry Chambers, the editor of the journal *Phoenix*, which professed, as Heaney did in his poetry, "a faith in words and all that reflected ordinary human activity." Heaney taught high school for a year, then became a lecturer at Queen's University in 1966, the year his first volume, *Death of a Naturalist*, appeared. The book won many awards and made Heaney famous. Subsequent volumes increased his reputation in England and North America. Heaney divides his time between Massachusetts, where he teaches at Harvard, and Dublin.

Heaney's poetry is rooted in the Irish landscape and in the shapes, colors, and textures of agricultural life and rural crafts. His poems have an assertive physicality and are rich in sound and rhythm. Heaney explores the possibilities of formal verse patterns and exploits assonance, consonance, and half-rhymes to develop a poetry that has a feeling of historical continuity and contemporaneity. In the Irish tradition, Heaney is not interested in the obscure posturing or random incoherence in vogue during the years he was developing as a poet. Heaney is dedicated to a clarity of thought and to a simple yet richly poetic mode of expression designed to "rend the veil of the usual." Like Robert Frost, a poet Heaney resembles, Heaney's best work is more subtle than its accessible surfaces suggest. In *North*, his third volume, Heaney moved to a shorter, sparer line to explore the poet's relationship to what might be called the geography of history, the way in which identity is tied to a place rich in historical associations. Heaney's work has grown progressively wider in scope. A recent volume, *Station Island*, continues Heaney's love of the physical objects of existence and the wisdom to be drawn from them, but also explores the poet's uneasy relationship to the political strife that is never far from the Irish mind. It is becoming increasingly clear that the sharpness of Heaney's vision, the complexity of his response, and his craftsmanship give him a stature equal to any poet writing today anywhere in the world.

Heaney has published seven volumes of poetry: *Death of a Naturalist* (1966), *Door into the Dark* (1969), *Wintering Out* (1972), *North* (1975), *Field Work* (1979), *Selected Poems 1965–1975* (1980), and *Station Island* (1984). A translation from the Irish, *Sweeney Astray*, appeared in 1984, and *Preoccupations: Selected Prose 1968–78*, in 1980.

SEAMUS HEANEY

Death of a Naturalist

All year the flax-dam festered in the heart
Of the townland; green and heavy headed
Flax had rotted there, weighted down by huge sods.
Daily it sweltered in the punishing sun.
5   Bubbles gargled delicately, bluebottles
Wove a strong gauze of sound around the smell.
There were dragon-flies, spotted butterflies,
But best of all was the warm thick slobber
Of frogspawn that grew like clotted water
10   In the shade of the banks. Here, every spring
I would fill jampotfuls of the jellied
Specks to range on window-sills at home,
On shelves at school, and wait and watch until
The fattening dots burst into nimble-
15   Swimming tadpoles. Miss Walls would tell us how
The daddy frog was called a bullfrog
And how he croaked and how the mammy frog
Laid hundreds of little eggs and this was
Frogspawn. You could tell the weather by frogs too
20   For they were yellow in the sun and brown
In rain.

Then one hot day when fields were rank
With cowdung in the grass the angry frogs
Invaded the flax-dam; I ducked through hedges
25   To a coarse croaking that I had not heard
Before. The air was thick with a bass chorus.
Right down the dam gross-bellied frogs were cocked
On sods; their loose necks pulsed like sails. Some hopped:
The slap and plop were obscene threats. Some sat
30   Poised like mud grenades, their blunt heads farting.
I sickened, turned, and ran. The great slime kings
Were gathered there for vengeance and I knew
That if I dipped my hand the spawn would clutch it.

(1966)

Churning Day

A thick crust, coarse-grained as limestone rough-cast,
hardened gradually on top of the four crocks
that stood, large pottery bombs, in the small pantry.
After the hot brewery of gland, cud and udder
5   cool porous earthenware fermented the buttermilk
for churning day, when the hooped churn was scoured
with plumping kettles and the busy scrubber
echoed daintily on the seasoned wood.
It stood then, purified, on the flagged kitchen floor.

10   Out came the four crocks, spilled their heavy lip
of cream, their white insides, into the sterile churn.
The staff, like a great whisky muddler fashioned
in deal wood, was plunged in, the lid fitted.
My mother took first turn, set up rhythms
15   that slugged and thumped for hours. Arms ached.
Hands blistered. Cheeks and clothes were spattered
with flabby milk.

            Where finally gold flecks
began to dance. They poured hot water then,
20   sterilized a birchwood-bowl
and little corrugated butter-spades.
Their short stroke quickened, suddenly
a yellow curd was weighting the churned up white,
heavy and rich, coagulated sunlight
25   that they fished, dripping, in a wide tin strainer,
heaped up like gilded gravel in the bowl.

The house would stink long after churning day,
acrid as a sulphur mine. The empty crocks
were ranged along the wall again, the butter
30   in soft printed slabs was piled on pantry shelves.
And in the house we moved with gravid ease,
our brains turned crystals full of clean deal churns,
the plash and gurgle of the sour-breathed milk,
the pat and slap of small spades on wet lumps.

(1966)

North

I returned to a long strand,
the hammered shod of a bay,
and found only the secular
powers of the Atlantic thundering.

5   I faced the unmagical
invitations of Iceland,
the pathetic colonies
of Greenland, and suddenly

those fabulous raiders,
10 those lying in Orkney and Dublin
measured against
their long swords rusting,

those in the solid
belly of stone ships,
15 those hacked and glinting
in the gravel of thawed streams

were ocean-deafened voices
warning me, lifted again
in violence and epiphany.
20 The longship's swimming tongue

was buoyant with hindsight—
it said Thor's hammer swung
to geography and trade,
thick-witted couplings and revenges,

25 the hatreds and behind backs
of the althing, lies and women,
exhaustions nominated peace,
memory incubating the spilled blood.

It said, "Lie down
30 in the word-hoard, burrow
the coil and gleam
of your furrowed brain.

Compose in darkness.
Expect aurora borealis
35 in the long foray
but no cascade of light.

Keep your eye clear
as the bleb of the icicle,
trust the feel of what nubbed treasure
40 your hands have known."

(1975)

An Ulster Twilight

The bare bulb, a scatter of nails,
Shelved timber, glinting chisels:
In a shed of corrugated iron
Eric Dawson stoops to his plane

5   At five o'clock on a Christmas Eve.
Carpenter's pencil next, the spoke-shave,
Fretsaw, auger, rasp and awl,
A rub with a rag of linseed oil.

A mile away it was taking shape,
10 The hulk of a toy battleship,
As waterbuckets iced and frost
Hardened the quiet on roof and post.

Where is he now?
There were fifteen years between us two
15 That night I strained to hear the bells
Of a sleigh of the mind and heard him pedal

Into our lane, get off at the gable,
Steady his Raleigh bicycle
Against the whitewash, stand to make sure
20 The house was quiet, knock at the door

And hand his parcel to a peering woman:
'I suppose you thought I was never coming.'
Eric, tonight I saw it all
Like shadows on your workshop wall,

25 Smelled wood shavings under the bench,
Weighed the cold steel monkey-wrench
In my soft hand, then stood at the road
To watch your wavering tail-light fade

And knew that if we met again
30 In an Ulster twilight we would begin
And end whatever we might say
In a speech all toys and carpentry,

A doorstep courtesy to shun
Your father's uniform and gun,
35 But—now that I have said it out—
Maybe none the worse for that.

(1984)

Michael Ondaatje

(b. 1 9 4 3)

Michael Ondaatje was born in Ceylon (now Sri Lanka), where he spent his early years, lived in England for nine years, then came to Canada in 1962. He earned a B.A. from the University of Toronto in 1965 and an M.A. from Queen's University in 1967. He taught at the University of Western Ontario and now teaches at Glendon College, York University.

In his writing, Ondaatje explores a variety of formal and narrative techniques. His poetry is often concerned with the relationship between the normal and the abnormal and with the way history needs constantly to be retold and reinvented. His most important collection of poems, *There's a Trick with a Knife I'm Learning to Do: Poems 1963–1978,* won a Governor-General's award; it includes work from two earlier collections, *The Dainty Monsters* and *Rat Jelly.* In the poem " 'The Gate in His Head,' " Ondaatje talks about "The beautiful formed things caught at the wrong moment / so they are shapeless, awkward / moving to the clear." His fascination with movement and with the attempt to capture movement gives Ondaatje's writing a sense of immediacy and passion that is rare in contemporary poetry. *The Collected Works of Billy the Kid: Left Handed Poems,* which also won a Governor-General's award, combines prose, poetry, and photographs. His book *Coming Through Slaughter* invents and documents the story of American jazz musician Buddy Bolden. *Running in the Family* is an engaging and idiosyncratic book about Ondaatje's exotic family background.

Works by Ondaatje include *The Dainty Monsters* (1967), *The Man with Seven Toes* (1969), *The Collected Works of Billy the Kid* (1970), *Rat Jelly* (1973), *Coming Through Slaughter* (1976), *There's a Trick with a Knife I'm Learning to Do* (1979), *Running in the Family* (1982), and *Secular Love* (1984). He has made several films and edited *The Long Poem Anthology,* a collection of contemporary Canadian long poems.

๛

MICHAEL ONDAATJE

Letters & Other Worlds

*"for there was no more darkness for him and, no doubt
like Adam before the fall, he could see in the dark"*

My father's body was a globe of fear
His body was a town we never knew
He hid that he had been where we were going
His letters were a room he seldom lived in
5   In them the logic of his love could grow

My father's body was a town of fear
He was the only witness to its fear dance
He hid where he had been that we might lose
      him
His letters were a room his body scared

10   He came to death with his mind drowning.
On the last day he enclosed himself
in a room with two bottles of gin, later
fell the length of his body
so that brain blood moved
15   to new compartments
that never knew the wash of fluid
and he died in minutes of a new equilibrium.

His early life was a terrifying comedy
and my mother divorced him again and again.
20   He would rush into tunnels magnetized
by the white eye of trains
and once, gaining instant fame,
managed to stop a Perahara[1] in Ceylon
—the whole procession of elephants dancers
25   local dignitaries—by falling
dead drunk onto the street.
As a semi-official, and semi-white at that,
the act was seen as a crucial
turning point in the Home Rule Movement
30   and led to Ceylon's independence in 1948.

[1] Religious parade.

(My mother had done her share too—
her driving so bad
she was stoned by villagers
whenever her car was recognized)

35 For 14 years of marriage
each of them claimed he or she
was the injured party.
Once on the Colombo docks
saying goodbye to a recently married couple
40 my father, jealous
at my mother's articulate emotion,
dove into the waters of the harbour
and swam after the ship waving farewell.
My mother pretending no affiliation
45 mingled with the crowd back to the hotel.

Once again he made the papers
though this time my mother
with a note to the editor
corrected the report—saying he was drunk
50 rather than broken hearted at the parting of friends.
The married couple received both editions
of *The Ceylon Times* when their ship reached Aden.

And then in his last years
he was the silent drinker,
55 the man who once a week
disappeared into his room with bottles
and stayed there until he was drunk
and until he was sober.

There speeches, head dreams, apologies,
60 the gentle letters, were composed.
With the clarity of architects
he would write of the row of blue flowers
his new wife had planted,
the plans for electricity in the house,
65 how my half-sister fell near a snake
and it had awakened and not touched her.
Letters in a clear hand of the most complete empathy
his heart widening and widening and widening
to all manner of change in his children and friends
70 while he himself edged
into the terrible acute hatred
of his own privacy

till he balanced and fell
the length of his body
75   the blood screaming in
the empty reservoir of bones
the blood searching in his head without metaphor

(1973)

King Kong meets Wallace Stevens

Take two photographs—
Wallace Stevens and King Kong
(Is it significant that I eat bananas as I write this?)

Stevens is portly, benign, a white brush cut
5   striped tie. Businessman but
for the dark thick hands, the naked brain
the thought in him.

Kong is staggering
lost in New York streets again
10   a spawn of annoyed cars at his toes.
The mind is nowhere.
Fingers are plastic, electric under the skin.
He's at the call of Metro-Goldwyn-Mayer.

Meanwhile W. S. in his suit
15   is thinking chaos is thinking fences.
In his head the seeds of fresh pain
his exorcising,
the bellow of locked blood.

The hands drain from his jacket,
20   pose in the murderer's shadow.

(1973)

"The gate in his head"

for Victor Coleman

Victor, the shy mind
revealing the faint scars

coloured strata of the brain,
not clarity but the sense of shift

5   a few lines, the tracks of thought

Landscape of busted trees
the melted tires in the sun
Stan's fishbowl
with a book inside
10   turning its pages
like some sea animal
camouflaging itself
the typeface clarity
going slow blonde in the sun full water

15   My mind is pouring chaos
in nets onto the page.
A blind lover, dont know
what I love till I write it out.
And then from Gibson's your letter
20   with a blurred photograph of a gull.
Caught vision. The stunning white bird
an unclear stir.

And that is all this writing should be then.
The beautiful formed things caught at the wrong moment
25   so they are shapeless, awkward
moving to the clear.

(1973)

White Dwarfs

This is for people who disappear
for those who descend into the code
and make their room a fridge for Superman
—who exhaust costume and bones that could perform flight,
5   who shave their moral so raw
they can tear themselves through the eye of a needle
this is for those people
that hover and hover
and die in the ether peripheries

10   There is my fear
of no words   of

falling without words
over and over   of
mouthing the silence
15 Why do I love most
among my heroes those
who sail to that perfect edge
where there is no social fuel
Release of sandbags
20 to understand their altitude—

that silence of the third cross
3rd man hung so high and lonely
we dont hear him say
say his pain, say his unbrotherhood
25 What has he to do with the smell of ladies
can they eat off his skeleton of pain?

The Gurkhas in Malaya
cut the tongues of mules
so they were silent beasts of burden
30 in enemy territories
after such cruelty what could they speak of anyway
And Dashiell Hammett in success
suffered conversation and moved
to the perfect white between the words

35 This white that can grow
is fridge, bed,
is an egg—most beautiful
when unbroken, where
what we cannot see is growing
40 in all the colours we cannot see

there are those burned out stars
who implode into silence
after parading in the sky
after such choreography what would they wish to speak of
anyway

(1973)

Christopher Dewdney

(b. 1 9 5 1)

Christopher Dewdney was born in London, Ontario. His father was the well-known archeologist, historian, and writer Selwyn Dewdney. Dewdney spent a good portion of his youth on expeditions with his father and brothers, recording pictographs, investigating the geological and imaginative qualities of limestone, and talking with shamans and storytellers. He has published his writing and exhibited his art internationally. He lives in Toronto and teaches literature at York University.

Dewdney is one of the most complex and fascinating contemporary poets. His poetry transcribes the mysteries of the mind and the physical world in language that is dense, often labyrinthine, and always rich and magical. In the preface to his selected poems, *Predators of the Adoration,* he speaks of the indigenous limestone deposits of his home territory as condensing "exotic tropical landscapes and fabulous creatures," and of how the book "is the voice of the land and the creatures themselves." Dewdney's respect for the environment and his restless intellect are everywhere present in his poems. He reaches back into prehistory, examines the ever-present convolutions of the brain, and expostulates on the possibilities of the future. His language is religious, scientific, and playful. For Dewdney, science is truly magical; nature is the divine technology. Dewdney is interested in the similarities of heart, brain, and body, and how these three are symbiotically connected.

His work includes *Golders Green* (1972), *A Paleozoic Geology of London, Ontario* (1973), *Fovea Centralis* (1975), *Spring Trances in the Control Emerald Night* (1978), *Alter Sublime* (1980), and *Predators of the Adoration: Selected Poems 1972–82* (1983).

CHRISTOPHER DEWDNEY

In the Critical Half Light

In the critical half light
a remote personal operation
is performed with mirrors.
"Ground zero" of the poem.

5 Love's surrogate
the absolute invokes pain.
Even THIS
locked into
an impossible monotheistic language
10 and Olson's[1] baited breath.

What we evidence to be
                     circumstantial
is singularity, within, and not out of
a word's jurisdiction.

15 Comprehensile folk edition
mine heir apparently self evident
Kant[2] hell you how it feels
deliver us of
the deliberate.

20 In the critical half light
a man is looking at you.
Describe the bullets.

                           (1973)

The Drawing Out of Colour

In the silent radar forest
iridescent scarabs bear coiled trilobites
in slow procession
                  up the meridian of symmetry.
5 A canopy of precision optical instruments
eidetically dissolves in the rain of sensorium.

The voice of cicada in this forest
is the long sustained note
of an indeterminate philosophy
10 in a court where the evidence
neither confirms nor denies
its testimony.

[1] Charles Olson (1910–1970), American poet.
[2] Immanuel Kant (1724–1804), German philosopher.

We are informed.

Motion within time's arena
15 is repealed here with the proceeds
of all our invisible centres.
Each act in the scene of its occurrence
etches an observation gallery
into the rich and mute loam
20 of the forest floor.

The forest translates itself
into each perception generated
by the meeting of heaven and earth.
At twilight the bat's synaptic flight
25 darkly traces the foliage processional
while the leaves
                cast in water
become as violins or cryptogam.
                      Witness
30 the drawing out of colour.

                      (1975)

The Song of Remote Control

Give yourselves up to Remote Control.
There is no choice, either you come knowing
or not knowing. You come.

Grovel like newborn in total submission
5 throwing away jewels and watches in
profusion to our sweet robbers.
Give up totally.
Step down from the control tower &
marvel at the jets colliding in brilliant explosions
10 over the airstrip. Grimace
piss with fear if you like,
then give up.
Give up like a joyful suicide
gracefully from a high building.
15 Give up like the never-to-be-born are giving up.
Give yourselves over to Remote Control.
We will take care of everything.

Give up.

                      (1975)

PART TWO

DRAMA

WILLIAM SHAKESPEARE*
[1564–1616]

Hamlet Prince of Denmark

NAMES OF THE ACTORS

Claudius, *King of Denmark*
Hamlet, *son to the late, and nephew to the present, King*
Polonius, *Lord Chamberlain*
Horatio, *friend to Hamlet*
Laertes, *son to Polonius*
Voltemand ⎫
Cornelius ⎪
Rosencrantz ⎪
Guildenstern ⎬ *courtiers*
Osric ⎪
A Gentleman ⎭
A Priest
Marcellus ⎫ *officers*
Bernardo ⎭
Francisco, *a soldier*
Reynaldo, *servant to Polonius*
Players
Two Clowns, *gravediggers*
Fortinbras, *Prince of Norway*
A Norwegian Captain
English Ambassadors
Gertrude, *Queen of Denmark, mother to Hamlet*
Ophelia, *daughter to Polonius*
Ghost of Hamlet's Father
Lords, Ladies, Officers, Soldiers, Sailors, Messengers,
   Attendants

*For biographical information, see page 60.

NOTE: The text of *Hamlet* presented here is based on the "good" quarto of 1604–05. It includes few emendations but does account for problems in the quarto text by referring to the folio text, and to the 1603 quarto. Additions to the quarto stage directions are enclosed in brackets, as are full lines of dialogue from the folio.

[SCENE: *Elsinore*]

I, i   *Enter Bernardo and Francisco, two sentinels.*

BERNARDO: Who's there?
FRANCISCO: Nay, answer me. Stand and unfold yourself.
BERNARDO: Long live the king!
FRANCISCO: Bernardo?
BERNARDO: He.
FRANCISCO: You come most carefully upon your hour.
BERNARDO: 'Tis now struck twelve. Get thee to bed, Francisco.
FRANCISCO: For this relief much thanks. 'Tis bitter cold,
   And I am sick at heart.
BERNARDO: Have you had quiet guard?
FRANCISCO: Not a mouse stirring.
BERNARDO: Well, good night.
   If you do meet Horatio and Marcellus,
13   The rivals of my watch, bid them make haste.

Enter Horatio and Marcellus.

FRANCISCO: I think I hear them. Stand, ho! Who is there?
HORATIO: Friends to this ground.
15   MARCELLUS: And liegemen to the Dane.
FRANCISCO: Give you good night.
MARCELLUS: O, farewell, honest soldier.
   Who hath relieved you?
FRANCISCO: Bernardo hath my place.
   Give you good night.

                                                   Exit Francisco.

MARCELLUS: Holla, Bernardo!
BERNARDO: Say—
   What, is Horatio there?
HORATIO: A piece of him.
BERNARDO: Welcome, Horatio. Welcome, good Marcellus.
HORATIO: What, has this thing appeared again to-night?
BERNARDO: I have seen nothing.
MARCELLUS: Horatio says 'tis but our fantasy,
   And will not let belief take hold of him
   Touching this dreaded sight twice seen of us.
   Therefore I have entreated him along

I, i Elsinore Castle: a sentry-post   **13** *rivals* shares   **15** *Dane* King of Denmark

With us to watch the minutes of this night,
That, if again this apparition come,
29   He may approve our eyes and speak to it.
HORATIO: Tush, tush, 'twill not appear.
BERNARDO: Sit down a while,
And let us once again assail your ears,
That are so fortified against our story,
What we two nights have seen.
HORATIO: Well, sit we down,
And let us hear Bernardo speak of this.
BERNARDO: Last night of all,
36   When yond same star that's westward from the pole
Had made his course t' illume that part of heaven
Where now it burns, Marcellus and myself,
The bell then beating one—

Enter Ghost.

MARCELLUS: Peace, break thee off. Look where it comes again.
BERNARDO: In the same figure like the king that's dead.
MARCELLUS: Thou art a scholar; speak to it, Horatio.
BERNARDO: Looks 'a not like the king? Mark it, Horatio.
HORATIO: Most like. It harrows me with fear and wonder.
BERNARDO: It would be spoke to.
MARCELLUS: Speak to it, Horatio.
HORATIO: What are thou that usurp'st this time of night
Together with that fair and warlike form
48   In which the majesty of buried Denmark
49   Did sometimes march? By heaven I charge thee, speak.
MARCELLUS: It is offended.
BERNARDO: See, it stalks away.
HORATIO: Stay. Speak, speak. I charge thee, speak.

Exit Ghost.

MARCELLUS: 'Tis gone and will not answer.
BERNARDO: How now, Horatio? You tremble and look pale.
Is not this something more than fantasy?
What think you on't?
HORATIO: Before my God, I might not this believe
Without the sensible and true avouch
Of mine own eyes.
MARCELLUS: Is it not like the king?

29 *approve* confirm **36** *pole* polestar **48** *buried Denmark* the buried King of Denmark
49 *sometimes* formerly

HORATIO: As thou art to thyself.
　　　　Such was the very armor he had on
61　　When he th' ambitious Norway combated.
62　　So frowned he once when, in an angry parle,
　　　　He smote the sledded Polacks on the ice.
　　　　'Tis strange.
65　MARCELLUS: Thus twice before, and jump at this dead hour,
　　　　With martial stalk hath he gone by our watch.
　　　HORATIO: In what particular thought to work I know not;
68　　But, in the gross and scope of my opinion,
　　　　This bodes some strange eruption to our state.
　　　MARCELLUS: Good now, sit down, and tell me he that knows,
　　　　Why this same strict and most observant watch
72　　So nightly toils the subject of the land,
　　　　And why such daily cast of brazen cannon
74　　And foreign mart for implements of war,
75　　Why such impress of shipwrights, whose sore task
　　　　Does not divide the Sunday from the week.
77　　What might be toward that this sweaty haste
　　　　Doth make the night joint-laborer with the day?
　　　　Who is't that can inform me?
　　　HORATIO:　　　　　　　　　　That can I.
　　　　At least the whisper goes so. Our last king,
　　　　Whose image even but now appeared to us,
　　　　Was as you know by Fortinbras of Norway,
83　　Thereto pricked on by a most emulate pride,
　　　　Dared to the combat; in which our valiant Hamlet
　　　　(For so this side of our known world esteemed him)
　　　　Did slay this Fortinbras; who, by a sealed compact
87　　Well ratified by law and heraldry,
　　　　Did forfeit, with his life, all those his lands
89　　Which he stood seized of to the conqueror;
90　　Against the which a moiety competent
91　　Was gagèd by our king, which had returned
　　　　To the inheritance of Fortinbras
93　　Had he been vanquisher, as, by the same comart
94　　And carriage of the article designed,
　　　　His fell to Hamlet. Now, sir, young Fortinbras,
96　　Of unimprovèd mettle hot and full,
　　　　Hath in the skirts of Norway here and there
98　　Sharked up a list of lawless resolutes

61 *Norway* King of Norway   **62** *parle* parley   **65** *jump* just, exactly   **68** *gross and scope* gross scope, general view   **72** *toils* makes toil; *subject* subjects   **74** *mart* trading   **75** *impress* conscription   **77** *toward* in preparation   **83** *emulate* jealously rivalling   **87** *law and heraldry* law of heralds regulating combat   **89** *seized* possessed   **90** *moiety competent* sufficient portion   **91** *gagèd* engaged, staked   **93** *comart* joint bargain   **94** *carriage* purport   **96** *unimprovèd* unused   **98** *Sharked* snatched indiscriminately as the shark takes prey; *resolutes* desperadoes

For food and diet to some enterprise
100   That hath a stomach in't; which is no other,
As it doth well appear unto our state,
But to recover of us by strong hand
And terms compulsatory those foresaid lands
So by his father lost; and this, I take it,
Is the main motive of our preparations,
106   The source of this our watch, and the chief head
107   Of this posthaste and romage in the land.
    BERNARDO: I think it be no other but e'en so.
109   Well may it sort that this portentous figure
Comes armèd through our watch so like the king
That was and is the question of these wars.
112   HORATIO: A mote it is to trouble the mind's eye.
In the most high and palmy state of Rome,
A little ere the mightiest Julius fell,
115   The graves stood tenantless and the sheeted dead
Did squeak and gibber in the Roman streets;
As stars with trains of fire and dews of blood,
118   Disasters in the sun; and the moist star
Upon whose influence Neptune's empire stands
Was sick almost to doomsday with eclipse.
121   And even the like precurse of feared events,
122   As harbingers preceding still the fates
123   And prologue to the omen coming on,
Have heaven and earth together demonstrated
125   Unto our climatures and countrymen.

    Enter Ghost.

But soft, behold, lo where it comes again!
127   I'll cross it, though it blast me.—Stay, illusion.

    He spreads his arms.

If thou hast any sound or use of voice,
Speak to me.
If there be any good thing to be done
That may to thee do ease and grace to me,
Speak to me.
If thou art privy to thy country's fate,
134   Which happily foreknowing may avoid,

---

100 *stomach* show of venturesomeness   **106** *head* fountainhead, source   **107** *romage* intense activity   **109** *sort* suit   **112** *mote* speck of dust   **115** *sheeted* in shrouds   **118** *Disasters* ominous signs; *moist star* moon   **121** *precurse* foreshadowing   **122** *harbingers* forerunners; *still* constantly   **123** *omen* calamity   **125** *climatures* regions   **127** *cross it* cross its path   **134** *happily* haply, perchance

O, speak!
Or if thou hast uphoarded in thy life
Extorted treasure in the womb of earth,
For which, they say, you spirits oft walk in death,

The cock crows.

      Speak of it. Stay and speak. Stop it, Marcellus.
140 MARCELLUS: Shall I strike at it with my partisan?
     HORATIO: Do, if it will not stand.
     BERNARDO: 'Tis here.
     HORATIO: 'Tis here.
     MARCELLUS: 'Tis gone.   *[Exit Ghost.]*
      We do it wrong, being so majestical,
      To offer it the show of violence,
      For it is as the air invulnerable,
      And our vain blows malicious mockery.
     BERNARDO: It was about to speak when the cock crew.
     HORATIO: And then it started, like a guilty thing
      Upon a fearful summons. I have heard
      The cock, that is the trumpet to the morn,
      Doth with his lofty and shrill-sounding throat
      Awake the god of day, and at his warning,
      Whether in sea or fire, in earth or air,
154   Th' extravagant and erring spirit hies
      To his confine; and of the truth herein
156   This present object made probation.
     MARCELLUS: It faded on the crowing of the cock.
158   Some say that ever 'gainst that season comes
      Wherein our Saviour's birth is celebrated,
      This bird of dawning singeth all night long,
      And then, they say, no spirit dare stir abroad,
162   The nights are wholesome, then no planets strike,
163   No fairy takes, nor witch hath power to charm.
      So hallowed and so gracious is that time.
     HORATIO: So have I heard and do in part believe it.
      But look, the morn in russet mantle clad
      Walks o'er the dew of yon high eastward hill.
      Break we our watch up, and by my advice
      Let us impart what we have seen to-night
      Unto young Hamlet, for upon my life
      This spirit, dumb to us, will speak to him.
      Do you consent we shall acquaint him with it,

140 *partisan* pike   **154** *extravagant* wandering beyond bounds; *erring* wandering   **156** *probation* proof   **158** *'gainst* just before   **162** *strike* work evil by influence   **163** *takes* bewitches

As needful in our loves, fitting our duty?
MARCELLUS: Let's do't, I pray, and I this morning know
Where we shall find him most conveniently.

Exeunt.

I, ii   *Flourish. Enter Claudius, King of Denmark, Gertrude the Queen, Councillors,
Polonius and his son Laertes, Hamlet, cum aliis [including Voltemand and
Cornelius]*

KING: Though yet of Hamlet our dear brother's death
The memory be green, and that it us befitted
To bear our hearts in grief, and our whole kingdom
To be contracted in one brow of woe,
Yet so far hath discretion fought with nature
That we with wisest sorrow think on him
Together with remembrance of ourselves.
Therefore our sometime sister, now our queen,
9   Th' imperial jointress to this warlike state,
Have we, as 'twere with a defeated joy,
With an auspicious and a dropping eye,
With mirth in funeral and with dirge in marriage,
In equal scale weighing delight and dole,
14   Taken to wife. Nor have we herein barred
Your better wisdoms, which have freely gone
With this affair along. For all, our thanks.
Now follows, that you know, young Fortinbras,
Holding a weak supposal of our worth,
Or thinking by our late dear brother's death
Our state to be disjoint and out of frame,
21   Colleaguèd with this dream of his advantage,
He hath not failed to pester us with message
Importing the surrender of those lands
Lost by his father, with all bands of law,
To our most valiant brother. So much for him.
Now for ourself and for this time of meeting.
Thus much the business is: we have here writ
To Norway, uncle of young Fortinbras—
Who, impotent and bedrid, scarcely hears
Of this his nephew's purpose—to suppress
31   His further gait herein, in that the levies,

I, ii Elsinore Castle: a room of state; **s.d.** *cum aliis* with others   **9** *jointress* a woman who has
a jointure, or joint tenancy of an estate   **14** *barred* excluded   **21** *Colleaguèd* united
31 *gait* going

32   The lists, and full proportions are all made
       Out of his subject; and we here dispatch
       You, good Cornelius, and you, Voltemand,
       For bearers of this greeting to old Norway,
       Giving to you no further personal power
       To business with the king, more than the scope
38   Of these delated articles allow.
       Farewell, and let your haste commend your duty.
CORNELIUS, VOLTEMAND: In that, and all things, will we show our
       duty.
KING: We doubt it nothing. Heartily farewell.

[Exeunt Voltemand and Cornelius.]

       And now, Laertes, what's the news with you?
       You told us of some suit. What is't, Laertes?
44   You cannot speak of reason to the Dane
45   And lose your voice. What wouldst thou beg, Laertes,
       That shall not be my offer, not thy asking?
47   The head is not more native to the heart,
48   The hand more instrumental to the mouth,
       Than is the throne of Denmark to thy father.
       What wouldst thou have, Laertes?
LAERTES: My dread lord,
       Your leave and favor to return to France,
       From whence though willingly I came to Denmark
       To show my duty in your coronation,
       Yet now I must confess, that duty done,
       My thoughts and wishes bend again toward France
       And bow them to your gracious leave and pardon.
KING: Have you your father's leave? What says Polonius?
POLONIUS: He hath, my lord, wrung from me my slow leave
       By laborsome petition, and at last
       Upon his will I sealed my hard consent.
       I do beseech you give him leave to go.
KING: Take thy fair hour, Laertes. Time be thine,
       And thy best graces spend it at thy will.
64   But now, my cousin Hamlet, and my son—
65   HAMLET*[aside]*:   A little more than kin, and less than kind!
KING: How is it that the clouds still hang on you?
67   HAMLET: Not so, my lord. I am too much in the sun.

---

32 *proportions* amounts of forces and supplies   **38** *delated* detailed   **44** *Dane* King of Denmark
45 *lose your voice* speak in vain   **47** *native* joined by nature   **48** *instrumental* serviceable
64 *cousin* kinsman more distant than parent, child, brother, or sister   **65** *kin* related as nephew;
kind kindly in feeling, as by kind, or nature, a son would be to his father   **67** *sun* sunshine of
the king's undesired favor (with the punning additional meaning of "place of a son")

QUEEN: Good Hamlet, cast thy nighted color off,
And let thine eye look like a friend on Denmark.
70   Do not for ever with thy vailèd lids
Seek for thy noble father in the dust.
Thou know'st 'tis common. All that lives must die,
Passing through nature to eternity.

HAMLET: Ay, madam, it is common.

QUEEN: If it be,
Why seems it so particular with thee?

HAMLET: Seems, madam? Nay, it is. I know not 'seems.'
'Tis not alone my inky cloak, good mother,
Nor customary suits of solemn black,
Nor windy suspiration of forced breath,
No, nor the fruitful river in the eye,
Nor the dejected havior of the visage,
Together with all forms, moods, shapes of grief,
That can denote me truly. These indeed seem,
For they are actions that a man might play,
But I have that within which passeth show—
These but the trappings and the suits of woe.

KING: 'Tis sweet and commendable in your nature, Hamlet,
To give these mourning duties to your father,
But you must know your father lost a father,
That father lost, lost his, and the survivor bound
In filial obligation for some term
92   To do obsequious sorrow. But to persever
In obstinate condolement is a course
Of impious stubbornness. 'Tis unmanly grief.
It shows a will most incorrect to heaven,
A heart unfortified, a mind impatient,
An understanding simple and unschooled.
For what we know must be and is as common
As any the most vulgar thing to sense,
Why should we in our peevish opposition
Take it to heart? Fie, 'tis a fault to heaven,
A fault against the dead, a fault to nature,
To reason most absurd, whose common theme
Is death of fathers, and who still hath cried,
From the first corse till he that died to-day,
'This must be so.' We pray you throw to earth
This unprevailing woe, and think of us
As of a father, for let the world take note
You are the most immediate to our throne,

---

70 *vailèd* downcast   **92** *obsequious* proper to obsequies or funerals; *persever* persevere (accented on the second syllable, as always in Shakespeare)

And with no less nobility of love
Than that which dearest father bears his son
Do I impart toward you. For your intent
In going back to school in Wittenberg,
114   It is most retrograde to our desire,
And we beseech you, bend you to remain
Here in the cheer and comfort of our eye,
Our chiefest courtier, cousin, and our son.
QUEEN: Let not thy mother lose her prayers, Hamlet.
I pray thee stay with us, go not to Wittenberg.
HAMLET: I shall in all my best obey you, madam.
KING: Why, 'tis a loving and a fair reply.
Be as ourself in Denmark. Madam, come.
This gentle and unforced accord of Hamlet
Sits smiling to my heart, in grace whereof
No jocund health that Denmark drinks to-day
But the great cannon to the clouds shall tell,
127   And the king's rouse the heaven shall bruit again,
Respeaking earthly thunder. Come away.

Flourish. Exeunt all but Hamlet.

HAMLET: O that this too too sullied flesh would melt,
Thaw, and resolve itself into a dew,
Or that the Everlasting had not fixed
132   His canon 'gainst self-slaughter. O God, God,
How weary, stale, flat, and unprofitable
Seem to me all the uses of this world!
Fie on't, ah, fie, 'tis an unweeded garden
That grows to seed. Things rank and gross in nature
137   Possess it merely. That it should come to this,
But two months dead, nay, not so much, not two,
So excellent a king, that was to this
140   Hyperion to a satyr, so loving to my mother
141   That he might not beteem the winds of heaven
Visit her face too roughly. Heaven and earth,
Must I remember? Why, she would hang on him
As if increase of appetite had grown
By what it fed on, and yet within a month—
Let me not think on't; frailty, thy name is woman—
A little month, or ere those shoes were old
With which she followed my poor father's body
149   Like Niobe, all tears, why she, even she—

114 *retrograde* contrary 127 *rouse* toast drunk in wine; *bruit* echo 132 *canon* law
137 *merely* completely 140 *Hyperion* the sun god 141 *beteem* allow 149 *Niobe* the proud
mother who boasted of having more children than Leto and was punished when they were slain
by Apollo and Artemis, children of Leto; the grieving Niobe was changed by Zeus into a stone,
which continually dropped tears

150   O God, a beast that wants discourse of reason
           Would have mourned longer—married with my uncle,
           My father's brother, but no more like my father
           Than I to Hercules. Within a month,
           Ere yet the salt of most unrighteous tears
155   Had left the flushing in her gallèd eyes,
           She married. O, most wicked speed, to post
           With such dexterity to incestuous sheets!
           It is not nor it cannot come to good.
           But break my heart, for I must hold my tongue.

Enter Horatio, Marcellus, and Bernardo.

HORATIO: Hail to your lordship!
HAMLET: I am glad to see you well.
   Horatio—or I do forget myself.
HORATIO: The same, my lord, and your poor servant ever.
163 HAMLET: Sir, my good friend, I'll change that name with you.
164   And what make you from Wittenberg, Horatio?
   Marcellus?
MARCELLUS: My good lord!
HAMLET: I am very glad to see you. *[to Bernardo]* Good even, sir.
   But what, in faith, make you from Wittenberg?
HORATIO: A truant disposition, good my lord.
HAMLET: I would not hear your enemy say so,
   Nor shall you do my ear that violence
   To make it truster of your own report
   Against yourself. I know you are no truant.
   But what is your affair in Elsinore?
   We'll teach you to drink deep ere you depart.
HORATIO: My lord, I came to see your father's funeral.
HAMLET: I prithee do not mock me, fellow student.
   I think it was to see my mother's wedding.
HORATIO: Indeed, my lord, it followed hard upon.
HAMLET: Thrift, thrift, Horatio. The funeral baked meats
   Did coldly furnish forth the marriage tables.
182   Would I had met my dearest foe in heaven
   Or ever I had seen that day, Horatio!
   My father—methinks I see my father.
HORATIO: Where, my lord?
HAMLET: In my mind's eye, Horatio.
HORATIO: I saw him once. 'A was a goodly king.
HAMLET: 'A was a man, take him for all in all,
   I shall not look upon his like again.

150 *discourse* logical power or process   **155** *gallèd* irritated   **163** *change* exchange
164 *make* do   **182** *dearest* direst, bitterest

HORATIO: My lord, I think I saw him yesternight.

HAMLET: Saw? who?

HORATIO: My lord, the king your father.

HAMLET: The king my father?

192 HORATIO: Season your admiration for a while

With an attent ear till I may deliver

Upon the witness of these gentlemen

This marvel to you.

HAMLET: For God's love let me hear!

HORATIO: Two nights together had these gentlemen,

Marcellus and Bernardo, on their watch

In the dead waste and middle of the night

Been thus encountered. A figure like your father,

200 Armèd at point exactly, cap-a-pe,

Appears before them and with solemn march

Goes slow and stately by them. Thrice he walked

By their oppressed and fear-surprisèd eyes

204 Within his truncheon's length, whilst they, distilled

Almost to jelly with the act of fear,

Stand dumb and speak not to him. This to me

In dreadful secrecy impart they did,

And I with them the third night kept the watch,

Where, as they had delivered, both in time,

Form of the thing, each word made true and good,

The apparition comes. I knew your father.

These hands are not more like.

HAMLET: But where was this?

MARCELLUS: My lord, upon the platform where we watched.

HAMLET: Did you not speak to it?

HORATIO: My lord, I did,

But answer made it none. Yet once methought

216 It lifted up it head and did address

Itself to motion like as it would speak.

But even then the morning cock crew loud,

And at the sound it shrunk in haste away

And vanished from our sight.

HAMLET: 'Tis very strange.

HORATIO: As I do live, my honored lord, 'tis true,

And we did think it writ down in our duty

To let you know of it.

HAMLET: Indeed, indeed, sirs, but this troubles me.

Hold you the watch to-night?

ALL: We do, my lord.

HAMLET: Armed, say you?

---

192 *Season your admiration* control your wonder   **200** *at point* completely; *cap-a-pe* from head to
foot   **204** *truncheon* military commander's baton   **216** *it* its

ALL: Armed, my lord.

HAMLET: From top to toe?

ALL: My lord, from head to foot.

HAMLET: Then saw you not his face?

230   HORATIO: O, yes, my lord. He wore his beaver up.

HAMLET: What, looked he frowningly?

HORATIO: A countenance more in sorrow than in anger.

HAMLET: Pale or red?

HORATIO: Nay, very pale.

HAMLET: And fixed his eyes upon you?

HORATIO: Most constantly.

HAMLET: I would I had been there.

HORATIO: It would have much amazed you.

HAMLET: Very like, very like. Stayed it long?

238   HORATIO: While one with moderate haste might tell a hundred.

BOTH: Longer, longer.

HORATIO: Not when I saw't.

240   HAMLET: His beard was grizzled, no?

HORATIO: It was as I have seen it in his life,

242   A sable silvered.

HAMLET: I will watch to-night.

Perchance 'twill walk again.

HORATIO: I warr'nt it will.

HAMLET: If it assume my noble father's person,

I'll speak to it though hell itself should gape

And bid me hold my peace. I pray you all,

If you have hitherto concealed this sight,

248   Let it be tenable in your silence still,

And whatsomever else shall hap to-night,

Give it an understanding but no tongue.

I will requite your loves. So fare you well.

Upon the platform, 'twixt eleven and twelve

I'll visit you.

ALL: Our duty to your honor.

HAMLET: Your loves, as mine to you. Farewell.

Exeunt [all but Hamlet].

My father's spirit—in arms? All is not well.

256   I doubt some foul play. Would the night were come!

Till then sit still, my soul. Foul deeds will rise,

Though all the earth o'erwhelm them, to men's eyes.

Exit.

---

230 *beaver* visor or movable face-guard of the helmet   **238** *tell* count   **240** *grizzled* grey
242 *sable silvered* black mixed with white   **248** *tenable* held firmly   **256** *doubt* suspect, fear

I, iii   *Enter Laertes and Ophelia, his sister.*

LAERTES: My necessaries are embarked. Farewell.
    And, sister, as the winds give benefit
3   And convoy is assistant, do not sleep,
    But let me hear from you.
OPHELIA: Do you doubt that?
LAERTES: For Hamlet, and the trifling of his favor,
    Hold it a fashion and a toy in blood,
7   A violet in the youth of primy nature,
    Forward, not permanent, sweet, not lasting,
9   The perfume and suppliance of a minute,
    No more.
OPHELIA: No more but so?
LAERTES: Think it no more.
11   For nature crescent does not grow alone
12   In thews and bulk, but as this temple waxes
    The inward service of the mind and soul
    Grows wide withal. Perhaps he loves you now,
15   And now no soil nor cautel doth besmirch
16   The virtue of his will, but you must fear,
17   His greatness weighed, his will is not his own.
    [For he himself is subject to his birth.]
    He may not, as unvalued persons do,
    Carve for himself, for on his choice depends
    The safety and health of this whole state,
    And therefore must his choice be circumscribed
23   Unto the voice and yielding of that body
    Whereof he is the head. Then if he says he loves you,
    It fits your wisdom so far to believe it
    As he in his particular act and place
    May give his saying deed, which is no further
    Than the main voice of Denmark goes withal.
    Then weigh what loss your honor may sustain
30   If with too credent ear you list his songs,
    Or lose your heart, or your chaste treasure open
    To his unmastered importunity.
    Fear it, Ophelia, fear it, my dear sister,
34   And keep you in the rear of your affection,
    Out of the shot and danger of desire.
    The chariest maid is prodigal enough

I, iii Elsinore Castle: the chambers of Polonius   **3** *convoy* means of transport   **7** *primy* of the springtime   **9** *perfume and suppliance* filling sweetness   **11** *crescent* growing   **12** *this temple* the body   **15** *cautel* deceit   **16** *will* desire   **17** *greatness weighed* high position considered   **23** *yielding* assent   **30** *credent* credulous   **34** *affection* feelings, which rashly lead forward into dangers

If she unmask her beauty to the moon.
Virtue itself scapes not calumnious strokes.
39   The canker galls the infants of the spring
40   Too oft before their buttons be disclosed,
And in the morn and liquid dew of youth
42   Contagious blastments are most imminent.
Be wary then; best safety lies in fear.
Youth to itself rebels, though none else near.
OPHELIA: I shall the effect of this good lesson keep
As watchman to my heart, but, good my brother,
Do not as some ungracious pastors do,
Show me the steep and thorny way to heaven,
Whiles like a puffed and reckless libertine
Himself the primrose path of dalliance treads
51   And recks not his own rede.

Enter Polonius.

LAERTES: O, fear me not.
I stay too long. But here my father comes.
A double blessing is a double grace;
Occasion smiles upon a second leave.
POLONIUS: Yet here, Laertes? Aboard, aboard, for shame!
The wind sits in the shoulder of your sail,
And you are stayed for. There—my blessing with thee,
And these few precepts in thy memory
59   Look thou character. Give thy thoughts no tongue,
60   Nor any unproportioned thought his act.
Be thou familiar, but by no means vulgar.
Those friends thou hast, and their adoption tried,
Grapple them unto thy soul with hoops of steel,
But do not dull thy palm with entertainment
65   Of each new-hatched, unfledged courage. Beware
Of entrance to a quarrel; but being in,
Bear't that th' opposèd may beware of thee.
Give every man thine ear, but few thy voice;
69   Take each man's censure, but reserve thy judgment.
Costly thy habit as thy purse can buy,
But not expressed in fancy; rich, not gaudy,
For the apparel oft proclaims the man,
And they in France of the best rank and station
74   Are of a most select and generous chief in that.

---

39 *canker* rose worm; *galls* injures   **40** *buttons* buds   **42** *blastments* blights   **51** *recks* regards;
rede counsel   **59** *character* inscribe   **60** *unproportioned* unadjusted to what is right   **65** *courage*
man of spirit, young blood   **69** *censure* judgment   **74** *chief* eminence

Neither a borrower nor a lender be,
For loan oft loses both itself and friend,
77   And borrowing dulleth edge of husbandry.
This above all, to thine own self be true,
And it must follow as the night the day
Thou canst not then be false to any man.
81   Farewell. My blessing season this in thee!
LAERTES: Most humbly do I take my leave, my lord.
83   POLONIUS: The time invites you. Go, your servants tend.
LAERTES: Farewell, Ophelia, and remember well
What I have said to you.
OPHELIA: 'Tis in my memory locked,
And you yourself shall keep the key of it.
LAERTES: Farewell.

Exit Laertes.

POLONIUS: What is't, Ophelia, he hath said to you?
OPHELIA: So please you, something touching the Lord Hamlet.
90   POLONIUS: Marry, well bethought.
'Tis told me he hath very oft of late
Given private time to you, and you yourself
Have of your audience been most free and bounteous.
If it be so—as so 'tis put on me,
And that in way of caution—I must tell you
You do not understand yourself so clearly
As it behooves my daughter and your honor.
What is between you? Give me up the truth.
99   OPHELIA: He hath, my lord, of late made many tenders
Of his affection to me.
POLONIUS: Affection? Pooh! You speak like a green girl,
102   Unsifted in such perilous circumstance.
Do you believe his tenders, as you call them?
OPHELIA: I do not know, my lord, what I should think.
POLONIUS: Marry, I will teach you. Think yourself a baby
106   That you have ta'en these tenders for true pay
Which are not sterling. Tender yourself more dearly,
108   Or (not to crack the wind of the poor phrase,
Running it thus) you'll tender me a fool.

---

77 *husbandry* thriftiness   **81** *season* ripen and make fruitful   **83** *tend* wait   **90** *Marry* by Mary
99 *tenders* offers   **102** *Unsifted* untested   **106–09** *tenders . . . Tender . . . tender* offers . . . hold
in regard . . . present (a word play going through three meanings, the last use of the word
yielding further complexity with its valid implications that she will show herself to him as a fool,
will show him to the world as a fool, and may go so far as to present him with a baby, which
would be a fool because "fool" was an Elizabethan term of endearment especially applicable
to an infant as a "little innocent")   **108** *crack . . . of* make wheeze like a horse driven too hard

OPHELIA: My lord, he hath importuned me with love
In honorable fashion.
112 POLONIUS: Ay, fashion you may call it. Go to, go to.
OPHELIA: And hath given countenance to his speech, my lord,
With almost all the holy vows of heaven.
115 POLONIUS: Ay, springes to catch woodcocks. I do know,
When the blood burns, how prodigal the soul
Lends the tongue vows. These blazes, daughter,
Giving more light than heat, extinct in both
Even in their promise, as it is a-making,
You must not take for fire. From this time
Be something scanter of your maiden presence.
122 Set your entreatments at a higher rate
123 Than a command to parley. For Lord Hamlet,
Believe so much in him that he is young,
And with a larger tether may he walk
Than may be given you. In few, Ophelia,
127 Do not believe his vows, for they are brokers,
128 Not of that dye which their investments show,
But mere implorators of unholy suits,
Breathing like sanctified and pious bawds,
The better to beguile. This is for all:
I would not, in plain terms, from this time forth
133 Have you so slander any moment leisure
As to give words or talk with the Lord Hamlet.
Look to't, I charge you. Come your ways.
OPHELIA: I shall obey, my lord.

Exeunt.

I, iv   *Enter Hamlet, Horatio, and Marcellus.*

1 HAMLET: The air bites shrewdly; it is very cold.
2 HORATIO: It is a nipping and an eager air.
HAMLET: What hour now?
HORATIO: I think it lacks of twelve.
MARCELLUS: No, it is struck.
HORATIO: Indeed? I heard it not. It then draws near the season
Wherein the spirit held his wont to walk.

A flourish of trumpets, and two pieces goes off.

---

112 *Go to* go away, go on (expressing impatience)   115 *springes* snares; *woodcocks* birds believed
foolish   122 *entreatments* military negotiations for surrender   123 *parley* confer with a besieger
127 *brokers* middlemen, panders   128 *investments* clothes   133 *slander* use disgracefully; *moment*
momentary   **I, iv** The sentry-post   1 *shrewdly* wickedly   2 *eager* sharp

What does this mean, my lord?

8 HAMLET: The king doth wake to-night and takes his rouse,
9   Keeps wassail, and the swaggering upspring reels,
10   And as he drains his draughts of Rhenish down
           The kettledrum and trumpet thus bray out
12   The triumph of his pledge.
   HORATIO: Is it a custom?
   HAMLET: Ay, marry, is't,
           But to my mind, though I am native here
           And to the manner born, it is a custom
16   More honored in the breach than the observance.
           This heavy-headed revel east and west
18   Makes us traduced and taxed of other nations.
19   They clepe us drunkards and with swinish phrase
20   Soil our addition, and indeed it takes
           From our achievements, though performed at height,
22   The pith and marrow of our attribute.
           So oft it chances in particular men
24   That (for some vicious mole of nature in them,
           As in their birth, wherein they are not guilty,
26   Since nature cannot choose his origin)
27   By the o'ergrowth of some complexion,
28   Oft breaking down the pales and forts of reason,
29   Or by some habit that too much o'erleavens
30   The form of plausive manners—that (these men
           Carrying, I say, the stamp of one defect,
32   Being nature's livery, or fortune's star)
           Their virtues else, be they as pure as grace,
           As infinite as man may undergo,
           Shall in the general censure take corruption
           From that particular fault. The dram of evil
           Doth all the noble substance of a doubt,
           To his own scandal.

   Enter Ghost.

   HORATIO: Look, my lord, it comes.
   HAMLET: Angels and ministers of grace defend us!
40   Be thou a spirit of health or goblin damned,

---

8 *rouse* carousal   **9** *upspring* a German dance   **10** *Rhenish* Rhine wine   **12** *triumph* achievement, feat (in downing a cup of wine at one draught)   **16** *More . . . observance* better broken than observed   **18** *taxed of* censured by   **19** *clepe* call   **20** *addition* reputation, title added as a distinction   **22** *attribute* reputation, what is attributed   **24** *mole* blemish, flaw   **26** *his* its   **27** *complexion* part of the makeup, combination of humors   **28** *pales* barriers, fences   **29** *o'erleavens* works change throughout, as yeast ferments dough   **30** *plausive* pleasing   **32** *livery* characteristic equipment or provision; *star* makeup as formed by stellar influence   **40** *of health* sound, good; *goblin* fiend

Bring with thee airs from heaven or blasts from hell,
Be thy intents wicked or charitable,
Thou com'st in such a questionable shape
That I will speak to thee. I'll call thee Hamlet,
King, father, royal Dane. O, answer me!
Let me not burst in ignorance, but tell
47   Why thy canonized bones, hearsèd in death,
48   Have burst their cerements, why the sepulchre
Wherein we saw thee quietly interred
Hath oped his ponderous and marble jaws
To cast thee up again. What may this mean
That thou, dead corse, again in complete steel,
Revisits thus the glimpses of the moon,
54   Making night hideous, and we fools of nature
So horridly to shake our disposition
With thoughts beyond the reaches of our souls?
Say, why is this? wherefore? what should we do?

[Ghost] beckons.

HORATIO: It beckons you to go away with it,
   As if it some impartment did desire
   To you alone.
MARCELLUS: Look with what courteous action
   It waves you to a more removèd ground.
   But do not go with it.
HORATIO: No, by no means.
HAMLET: It will not speak. Then will I follow it.
HORATIO: Do not, my lord.
HAMLET: Why, what should be the fear?
   I do not set my life at a pin's fee,
   And for my soul, what can it do to that,
   Being a thing immortal as itself?
   It waves me forth again. I'll follow it.
HORATIO: What if it tempt you toward the flood, my lord,
   Or to the dreadful summit of the cliff
71   That beetles o'er his base into the sea,
   And there assume some other horrible form,
73   Which might deprive your sovereignty of reason
   And draw you into madness? Think of it.
75   The very place puts toys of desperation,
   Without more motive, into every brain

---

47 *canonized* buried with the established rites of the Church   **48** *cerements* waxed grave-cloths
54 *fools of nature* men made conscious of natural limitations by a supernatural manifestation
71 *beetles* juts out   **73** *deprive* take away; *sovereignty of reason* state of being ruled by reason
75 *toys* fancies

that looks so many fathoms to the sea
And hears it roar beneath.

HAMLET: It waves me still.
Go on. I'll follow thee.

MARCELLUS: You shall not go, my lord.

HAMLET: Hold off your hands.

HORATIO: Be ruled. You shall not go.

HAMLET: My fate cries out

82   And makes each petty artere in this body
83   As hardy as the Nemean lion's nerve.
Still am I called. Unhand me, gentlemen.

85   By heaven, I'll make a ghost of him that lets me!
I say, away! Go on. I'll follow thee.

Exit Ghost, and Hamlet.

HORATIO: He waxes desperate with imagination.
MARCELLUS: Let's follow. 'Tis not fit thus to obey him.
HORATIO: Have after. To what issue will this come?
MARCELLUS: Something is rotten in the state of Denmark.
HORATIO: Heaven will direct it.
MARCELLUS: Nay, let's follow him.

Exeunt.

I, v   *Enter Ghost and Hamlet.*

HAMLET: Whither wilt thou lead me? Speak. I'll go no further.
GHOST: Mark me.
HAMLET: I will.
GHOST: My hour is almost come,

3   When I to sulph'rous and tormenting flames
Must render up myself.

HAMLET: Alas, poor ghost!

GHOST: Pity me not, but lend thy serious hearing
To what I shall unfold.

HAMLET: Speak. I am bound to hear.

GHOST: So art thou to revenge, when thou shalt hear.

HAMLET: What?

GHOST: I am thy father's spirit,
Doomed for a certain term to walk the night,

11   And for the day confined to fast in fires,

---

82 *artere* artery   **83** *Nemean lion* a lion slain by Hercules in the performance of one of his twelve labors; *nerve* sinew   **85** *lets* hinders   **I, v** Another part of the fortifications   **3** *flames* sufferings in purgatory (not hell)   **11** *fast* do penance

Till the foul crimes done in my days of nature
Are burnt and purged away. But that I am forbid
To tell the secrets of my prison house,
I could a tale unfold whose lightest word
Would harrow up thy soul, freeze thy young blood,

17   Make thy two eyes like stars start from their spheres,
Thy knotted and combinèd locks to part,

19   And each particular hair to stand an end
20   Like quills upon the fretful porpentine.
21   But this eternal blazon must not be
To ears of flesh and blood. List, list, O, list!
If thou didst ever thy dear father love—
HAMLET: O God!
GHOST: Revenge his foul and most unnatural murder.
HAMLET: Murder?
GHOST: Murder most foul, as in the best it is,
But this most foul, strange, and unnatural.
HAMLET: Haste me to know't, that I, with wings as swift

30   As meditation or the thoughts of love,
May sweep to my revenge.
GHOST: I find thee apt,
And duller shouldst thou be than the fat weed

33   That roots itself in ease on Lethe wharf,
Wouldst thou not stir in this. Now, Hamlet, hear.
'Tis given out that, sleeping in my orchard,
A serpent stung me. So the whole ear of Denmark

37   Is by a forgèd process of my death
Rankly abused. But know, thou noble youth,
The serpent that did sting thy father's life
Now wears his crown.
HAMLET: O my prophetic soul!
My uncle?

42   GHOST: Ay, that incestuous, that adulterate beast,
With witchcraft of his wit, with traitorous gifts—
O wicked wit and gifts, that have the power
So to seduce!—won to his shameful lust
The will of my most seeming-virtuous queen.
O Hamlet, what a falling-off was there,
From me, whose love was of that dignity
That it went hand in hand even with the vow
I made to her in marriage, and to decline
Upon a wretch whose natural gifts were poor

---

17 *spheres* transparent revolving shells in each of which, according to the Ptolemaic astronomy, a planet or other heavenly body was placed   **19** *an* on   **20** *porpentine* porcupine   **21** *eternal blazon* revelation of eternity   **30** *meditation* thought   **33** *Lethe* the river in Hades which brings forgetfulness of past life to a spirit who drinks of it   **37** *forgèd process* falsified official report **42** *adulterate* adulterous

To those of mine!
But virtue, as it never will be moved,
54   Though lewdness court it in a shape of heaven,
So lust, though to a radiant angel linked,
Will sate itself in a celestial bed
And prey on garbage.
But soft, methinks I scent the morning air.
Brief let me be. Sleeping within my orchard,
My custom always of the afternoon,
61   Upon my secure hour thy uncle stole
62   With juice of cursed hebona in a vial,
And in the porches of my ears did pour
The leperous distilment, whose effect
Holds such an enmity with blood of man
That swift as quicksilver it courses through
The natural gates and alleys of the body,
68   And with a sudden vigor it doth posset
69   And curd, like eager droppings into milk,
The thin and wholesome blood. So did it mine,
71   And a most instant tetter barked about
72   Most lazar-like with vile and loathsome crust
All my smooth body.
Thus was I sleeping by a brother's hand
Of life, of crown, of queen at once dispatched,
Cut off even in the blossoms of my sin,
77   Unhouseled, disappointed, unaneled,
No reck'ning made, but sent to my account
With all my imperfections on my head.
O, horrible! O, horrible! most horrible!
If thou hast nature in thee, bear it not.
Let not the royal bed of Denmark be
83   A couch for luxury and damnèd incest.
But howsomever thou pursues this act,
Taint not thy mind, nor let thy soul contrive
Against thy mother aught. Leave her to heaven
And to those thorns that in her bosom lodge
To prick and sting her. Fare thee well at once.
89   The glowworm shows the matin to be near
And gins to pale his uneffectual fire.
Adieu, adieu, adieu. Remember me.

[Exit.]

---

54 *shape of heaven* angelic disguise   **61** *secure* carefree, unsuspecting   **62** *hebona* some poisonous plant   **68** *posset* curdle   **69** *eager* sour   **71** *tetter* eruption; *barked* covered as with a bark   **72** *lazar-like* leper-like   **77** *Unhouseled* without the Sacrament; *disappointed* unprepared spiritually; *unaneled* without extreme unction   **83** *luxury* lust   **89** *matin* morning

HAMLET: O all you host of heaven! O earth! What else?
And shall I couple hell? O fie! Hold, hold, my heart,
And you, my sinews, grow not instant old,
But bear me stiffly up. Remember thee?
Ay, thou poor ghost, while memory holds a seat
97   In this distracted globe. Remember thee?
98   Yea, from the table of my memory
I'll wipe away all trivial fond records,
100   All saws of books, all forms, all pressures past
That youth and observation copied there,
And thy commandment all alone shall live
Within the book and volume of my brain,
Unmixed with baser matter. Yes, by heaven!
O most pernicious woman!
O villain, villain, smiling, damnèd villain!
My tables—meet it is I set it down
That one may smile, and smile, and be a villain.
At least I am sure it may be so in Denmark.

[Writes.]

So, uncle, there you are. Now to my word:
It is 'Adieu, adieu, remember me.'
I have sworn't.

Enter Horatio and Marcellus.

HORATIO: My lord, my lord!
MARCELLUS: Lord Hamlet!
HORATIO: Heavens secure him!
HAMLET: So be it!
MARCELLUS: Illo, ho, ho, my lord!
115   HAMLET: Illo, ho, ho, boy! Come, bird, come.
MARCELLUS: How is't, my noble lord?
HORATIO: What news, my lord?
HAMLET: O, wonderful!
HORATIO: Good my lord, tell it.
HAMLET: No, you will reveal it.
HORATIO: Not I, my lord, by heaven.
MARCELLUS: Nor I, my lord.
HAMLET: How say you then? Would heart of man once think it?
But you'll be secret?
BOTH: Ay, by heaven, my lord.

97 *globe* head   **98** *table* writing tablet, record book   **100** *saws* wise sayings; *forms* mental images,
concepts; *pressures* impressions   **115** *Illo, ho, ho* cry of the falconer to summon his hawk

HAMLET: There's never a villain dwelling in all Denmark
But he's an arrant knave.

HORATIO: There needs no ghost, my lord, come from the grave
To tell us this.

HAMLET: Why, right, you are in the right,

127   And so, without more circumstance at all,
I hold it fit that we shake hands and part:
You, as your business and desires shall point you,
For every man hath business and desire
Such as it is, and for my own poor part,
Look you, I'll go pray.

HORATIO: These are but wild and whirling words, my lord.

HAMLET: I am sorry they offend you, heartily;
Yes, faith, heartily.

HORATIO: There's no offense, my lord.

HAMLET: Yes, by Saint Patrick, but there is, Horatio,
And much offense too. Touching this vision here,

138   It is an honest ghost, that let me tell you.
For your desire to know what is between us,
O'ermaster't as you may. And now, good friends,
As you are friends, scholars, and soldiers,
Give me one poor request.

HORATIO: What is't, my lord? We will.

HAMLET: Never make known what you have seen to-night.

BOTH: My lord, we will not.

HAMLET: Nay, but swear't.

HORATIO: In faith,
My lord, not I.

MARCELLUS: Nor I, my lord—in faith.

147   HAMLET: Upon my sword.

MARCELLUS: We have sworn, my lord, already.

HAMLET: Indeed, upon my sword, indeed.

Ghost cries under the stage.

GHOST: Swear.

150   HAMLET: Ha, ha, boy, say'st thou so? Art thou there, truepenny?
Come on. You hear this fellow in the cellarage.
Consent to swear.

HORATIO: Propose the oath, my lord.

HAMLET: Never to speak of this that you have seen,
Swear by my sword.

GHOST *[beneath]*:   Swear.

156   HAMLET: Hic et ubique? Then we'll shift our ground.

---

127 *circumstance* ceremony   **138** *honest* genuine (not a disguised demon)   **147** *sword* i.e., upon
the cross formed by the sword hilt   **150** *truepenny* honest old fellow   **156** *Hic et ubique* here and
everywhere

Come hither, gentlemen,
And lay your hands again upon my sword.
Swear by my sword
Never to speak of this that you have heard.
GHOST *[beneath]*:   Swear by his sword.
HAMLET: Well said, old mole! Canst work i' th' earth so fast?
163   A worthy pioner! Once more remove, good friends.
HORATIO: O day and night, but this is wondrous strange!
HAMLET: And therefore as a stranger give it welcome.
There are more things in heaven and earth, Horatio,
167   Than are dreamt of in your philosophy.
But come:
Here as before, never, so help you mercy,
How strange or odd some'er I bear myself
(As I perchance hereafter shall think meet
172   To put an antic disposition on),
That you, at such times seeing me, never shall,
174   With arms encumb'red thus, or this head-shake,
Or by pronouncing of some doubtful phrase,
176   As 'Well, well, we know,' or 'We could, an if we would,'
Or 'If we list to speak,' or 'There be, an if they might,'
Or such ambiguous giving out, to note
That you know aught of me—this do swear,
So grace and mercy at your most need help you.
GHOST *[beneath]*:   Swear.

[They swear.]

HAMLET: Rest, rest, perturbèd spirit! So, gentlemen,
183   With all my love I do commend me to you,
And what so poor a man as Hamlet is
May do t' express his love and friending to you,
God willing, shall not lack. Let us go in together,
187   And still your fingers on your lips, I pray.
The time is out of joint. O cursèd spite
That ever I was born to set it right!
Nay, come, let's go together.

                                                                Exeunt.

II, i   *Enter old Polonius, with his man [Reynaldo].*

POLONIUS: Give him this money and these notes, Reynaldo.
REYNALDO: I will, my lord.

---

163 *pioner* pioneer, miner   167 *your philosophy* this philosophy one hears about   172 *antic* grotesque, mad   174 *encumb'red* folded   176 *an if* if   183 *commend* entrust   187 *still* always II, i The chambers of Polonius

POLONIUS: You shall do marvellous wisely, good Reynaldo,
Before you visit him, to make inquire
Of his behavior.
REYNALDO: My lord, I did intend it.
POLONIUS: Marry, well said, very well said. Look you, sir,
7   Enquire me first what Danskers are in Paris,
8   And how, and who, what means, and where they keep,
What company, at what expense; and finding
10   By this encompassment and drift of question
That they do know my son, come you more nearer
12   Than your particular demands will touch it.
Take you as 'twere some distant knowledge of him,
As thus, 'I know his father and his friends,
And in part him'—do you mark this, Reynaldo?
REYNALDO: Ay, very well, my lord.
POLONIUS: 'And in part him, but,' you may say, 'not well,
But if't be he I mean, he's very wild
Addicted so and so.' And there put on him
20   What forgeries you please; marry, none so rank
As may dishonor him—take heed of that—
But, sir, such wanton, wild, and usual slips
As are companions noted and most known
To youth and liberty.
REYNALDO: As gaming, my lord.
POLONIUS: Ay, or drinking, fencing, swearing, quarrelling,
26   Drabbing. You may go so far.
REYNALDO: My lord, that would dishonor him.
28   POLONIUS: Faith, no, as you may season it in the charge.
You must not put another scandal on him,
30   That he is open to incontinency.
31   That's not my meaning. But breathe his faults so quaintly
That they may seem the taints of liberty,
The flash and outbreak of a fiery mind,
34   A savageness in unreclaimèd blood,
35   Of general assault.
REYNALDO: But, my good lord—
POLONIUS: Wherefore should you do this?
REYNALDO: Ay, my lord,
I would know that.
POLONIUS: Marry, sir, here's my drift,
38   And I believe it is a fetch of warrant.

7 *Danskers* Danes   8 *what means* what their wealth; *keep* dwell   10 *encompassment* circling about
12 *particular demands* definite questions   20 *forgeries* invented wrongdoings   26 *Drabbing* whoring   28 *season* soften   30 *incontinency* extreme sensuality   31 *quaintly* expertly, gracefully
34 *unreclaimèd* untamed   35 *Of general assault* assailing all young men   38 *fetch of warrant*
allowable trick

You laying these slight sullies on my son
As 'twere a thing a little soiled i' th' working,
Mark you,
Your party in converse, him you would sound,

43 Having ever seen in the prenominate crimes
The youth you breathe of guilty, be assured

45 He closes with you in this consequence.
'Good sir,' or so, or 'friend,' or 'gentleman'—

47 According to the phrase or the addition
Of man and country—

REYNALDO: Very good, my lord.

POLONIUS: And then, sir, does 'a this—'a does—
What was I about to say? By the mass, I was about to
say something! Where did I leave?

REYNALDO: At 'closes in the consequence,' at 'friend or
so,' and 'gentleman.'

POLONIUS: At 'closes in the consequence'—Ay, marry!
He closes thus: 'I know the gentleman;
I saw him yesterday, or t' other day,
Or then, or then, with such or such, and, as you say,

58 There was 'a gaming, there o'ertook in's rouse,

59 There falling out at tennis'; or perchance,
'I saw him enter such a house of sale,'

61 Videlicet, a brothel, or so forth.
See you now—
Your bait of falsehood takes this carp of truth,

64 And thus do we of wisdom and of reach,

65 With windlasses and with assays of bias,

66 By indirections find directions out.
So, by my former lecture and advice,
Shall you my son. You have me, have you not?

REYNALDO: My lord, I have.

69 POLONIUS: God bye ye, fare ye well.

REYNALDO: Good my lord.

POLONIUS: Observe his inclination in yourself.

REYNALDO: I shall, my lord.

POLONIUS: And let him ply his music.

REYNALDO: Well, my lord.

POLONIUS: Farewell.

Exit Reynaldo.

---

43 *Having ever* if he has ever; *prenominate* aforementioned   **45** *closes with you* follows your lead
to a conclusion; *consequence* following way   **47** *addition* title   **58** *o'ertook* overcome with drunkenness; *rouse* carousal   **59** *falling out* quarrelling   **61** *Videlicet* namely   **64** *reach* far-reaching
comprehension   **65** *windlasses* roundabout courses; *assays of bias* devious attacks   **66** *directions*
ways of procedure   **69** *God bye ye* God be with you, good-bye

Enter Ophelia.

How now, Ophelia, what's the matter?
OPHELIA: O my lord, my lord, I have been so affrighted!
POLONIUS: With what, i' th' name of God?
77 OPHELIA: My lord, as I was sewing in my closet,
78 Lord Hamlet, with his doublet all unbraced,
No hat upon his head, his stockings fouled,
80 Ungartered, and down-gyvèd to his ankle,
Pale as his shirt, his knees knocking each other,
And with a look so piteous in purport
As if he had been loosèd out of hell
To speak of horrors—he comes before me.
POLONIUS: Mad for thy love?
OPHELIA: My lord, I do not know,
But truly I do fear it.
POLONIUS: What said he?
OPHELIA: He took me by the wrist and held me hard.
Then goes he to the length of all his arm,
And with his other hand thus o'er his brow
He falls to such perusal of my face
As 'a would draw it. Long stayed he so.
At last, a little shaking of mine arm
And thrice his head thus waving up and down,
He raised a sigh so piteous and profound
As it did seem to shatter all his bulk
And end his being. That done, he lets me go,
And with his head over his shoulder turned
He seemed to find his way without his eyes,
For out o' doors he went without their helps
And to the last bended their light on me.
POLONIUS: Come, go with me. I will go seek the king.
102 This is the very ecstasy of love,
103 Whose violent property fordoes itself
And leads the will to desperate undertakings
As oft as any passion under heaven
That does afflict our natures. I am sorry.
What, have you given him any hard words of late?
OPHELIA: No, my good lord; but as you did command
I did repel his letters and denied
His access to me.
POLONIUS: That hath made him mad.

77 *closet* private living-room   78 *doublet* jacket; *unbraced* unlaced   80 *down-gyvèd* fallen down
like gyves or fetters on a prisoner's legs   102 *ecstasy* madness   103 *property* quality; *fordoes*
destroys

I am sorry that with better heed and judgment
112 I had not quoted him. I feared he did but trifle
113 And meant to wrack thee; but beshrew my jealousy.
By heaven, it is as proper to our age
115 To cast beyond ourselves in our opinions
As it is common for the younger sort
To lack discretion. Come, go we to the king.
118 This must be known, which, being kept close, might move
119 More grief to hide than hate to utter love.
Come.

Exeunt.

II, ii   *Flourish. Enter King and Queen, Rosencrantz, and Guildenstern [with others].*

KING: Welcome, dear Rosencrantz and Guildenstern.
2 Moreover that we much did long to see you,
The need we have to use you did provoke
Our hasty sending. Something have you heard
Of Hamlet's transformation—so call it,
6 Sith nor th' exterior nor the inward man
Resembles that it was. What it should be,
More than his father's death, that thus hath put him
So much from th' understanding of himself,
I cannot dream of. I entreat you both
That, being of so young days brought up with him,
12 And sith so neighbored to his youth and havior,
That you vouchsafe your rest here in our court
Some little time, so by your companies
To draw him on to pleasures, and to gather
So much as from occasion you may glean,
Whether aught to us unknown afflicts him thus,
18 That opened lies within our remedy.
QUEEN: Good gentlemen, he hath much talked of you
And sure I am two men there are not living
21 To whom he more adheres. If it will please you
22 To show us so much gentry and good will
As to expend your time with us awhile

---

112 *quoted* observed   **113** *beshrew* curse   **115** *cast beyond ourselves* find by calculation more significance in something than we ought to   **118** *close* secret; *move* cause   **119** *to hide . . . love* by such hiding of love than there would be hate moved by a revelation of it (a violently condensed putting of the case which is a triumph of special statement for Polonius) **II, ii** A chamber in the Castle   **2** *Moreover that* besides the fact that   **6** *Sith* since **12** *youth and havior* youthful ways of life   **18** *opened* revealed   **21** *more adheres* is more attached **22** *gentry* courtesy

For the supply and profit of our hope,
Your visitation shall receive such thanks
As fits a king's remembrance.
ROSENCRANTZ: Both your majesties
Might, by the sovereign power you have of us,
Put your dread pleasures more into command
Than to entreaty.
GUILDENSTERN: But we both obey,
30   And here give up ourselves in the full bent
To lay our service freely at your feet,
To be commanded.
KING: Thanks, Rosencrantz and gentle Guildenstern.
QUEEN: Thanks, Guildenstern and gentle Rosencrantz.
And I beseech you instantly to visit
My too much changèd son.—Go, some of you,
And bring these gentlemen where Hamlet is.
GUILDENSTERN: Heavens make our presence and our practices
Pleasant and helpful to him!
QUEEN: Ay, amen!

Exeunt Rosencrantz and Guildenstern
[with some Attendants].

Enter Polonius.

POLONIUS: Th' ambassadors from Norway, my good lord,
Are joyfully returned.
42   KING: Thou still hast been the father of good news.
POLONIUS: Have I, my lord? Assure you, my good liege,
I hold my duty as I hold my soul,
Both to my God and to my gracious king,
And I do think—or else this brain of mine
Hunts not the trail of policy so sure
As it hath used to do—that I have found
The very cause of Hamlet's lunacy.
KING: O, speak of that! That do I long to hear.
POLONIUS: Give first admittance to th' ambassadors.
52   My news shall be the fruit to that great feast.
53   KING: Thyself do grace to them and bring them in.

[Exit Polonius.]

He tells me, my dear Gertrude, he hath found
The head and source of all your son's distemper.

---

30 *in the full bent* at the limit of bending (of a bow), to full capacity   **42** *still* always
52 *fruit* dessert   **53** *grace* honor

56 QUEEN: I doubt it is no other but the main,
　　　His father's death and our o'er hasty marriage.
　　KING: Well, we shall sift him.

　　　　　　　Enter Ambassadors [Voltemand and Cornelius, with Polonius].

　　　　　　　　　　　　　　　Welcome, my good friends.
　　　Say, Voltemand, what from our brother Norway?
　　VOLTEMAND: Most fair return of greetings and desires.
61 Upon our first, he sent out to suppress
　　　His nephew's levies, which to him appeared
　　　To be a preparation 'gainst the Polack,
　　　But better looked into, he truly found
　　　It was against your highness, whereat grieved,
　　　That so his sickness, age, and impotence
67 Was falsely borne in hand, send out arrests
　　　On Fortinbras; which he in brief obeys,
69 Receives rebuke from Norway, and in fine
　　　Makes vow before his uncle never more
71 To give th' assay of arms against your majesty.
　　　Whereon old Norway, overcome with joy,
　　　Gives him threescore thousand crowns in annual fee
　　　And his commission to employ those soldiers,
　　　So levied as before, against the Polack,
　　　With an entreaty, herein further shown,

　　[Gives a paper.]

　　　That it might please you to give quiet pass
　　　Through your dominions for this enterprise,
79 On such regards of safety and allowance
　　　As therein are set down.
　　KING:　　　　　　　　　　　It likes us well;
81 And at our more considered time we'll read,
　　　Answer, and think upon this business.
　　　Meantime we thank you for your well-took labor.
　　　Go to your rest; at night we'll feast together.
　　　Most welcome home!

　　　　　　　　　　　　　　　　　　Exeunt Ambassadors.

　　POLONIUS:　　　　　　　　This business is well ended.
86 My liege and madam, to expostulate

---

56 *doubt* suspect   **61** *our first* our first words about the matter   **67** *borne in hand* deceived
69 *in fine* in the end   **71** *assay* trial   **79** *regards* terms   **81** *considered time* convenient time for
consideration   **86** *expostulate* discuss

What majesty should be, what duty is,
Why day is day, night night, and time is time,
Were nothing but to waste night, day, and time.
90   Therefore, since brevity is the soul of wit,
And tediousness the limbs and outward flourishes,
I will be brief. Your noble son is mad.
Mad call I it, for, to define true madness,
What is't but to be nothing else but mad?
But let that go.
QUEEN: More matter, with less art.
POLONIUS: Madam, I swear I use no art at all.
That he is mad, 'tis true: 'tis true 'tis pity,
98   And pity 'tis 'tis true—a foolish figure.
But farewell it, for I will use no art.
Mad let us grant him then, and now remains
That we find out the cause of this effect—
Or rather say, the cause of this defect,
For this effect defective comes by cause.
Thus it remains, and the remainder thus.
105   Perpend.
I have a daughter (have while she is mine),
Who in her duty and obedience, mark,
Hath given me this. Now gather, and surmise.

[Reads the] letter.

'To the celestial, and my soul's idol, the most beautified
Ophelia,'—
That's an ill phrase, a vile phrase; 'beautified' is a vile
phrase. But you shall hear. Thus:

[Reads.]

'In her excellent white bosom, these, &c.'
QUEEN: Came this from Hamlet to her?
POLONIUS: Good madam, stay awhile. I will be faithful.

[Reads.]

                    'Doubt thou the stars are fire;
                    Doubt that the sun doth move;
118   Doubt truth to be a liar;
                    But never doubt I love.

90 *wit* understanding   98 *figure* figure in rhetoric   105 *Perpend* ponder   118 *Doubt* suspect

120   'O dear Ophelia, I am ill at these numbers. I have not
art to reckon my groans, but that I love thee best, O
most best, believe it. Adieu.

                  'Thine evermore, most dear lady,
124   whilst this machine is to him, Hamlet.'

This in obedience hath my daughter shown me,
126 And more above hath his solicitings,
As they fell out by time, by means, and place,
All given to mine ear.

KING: But how hath she
Received his love?

POLONIUS: What do you think of me?

KING: As of a man faithful and honorable.

POLONIUS: I would fain prove so. But what might you think,
When I had seen this hot love on the wing
(As I perceived it, I must tell you that,
Before my daughter told me), what might you,
Or my dear majesty your queen here, think,
136 If I had played the desk or table book,
137 Or given my heart a winking, mute and dumb,
Or looked upon this love with idle sight?
139 What might you think? No, I went round to work
And my young mistress thus I did bespeak:
141 'Lord Hamlet is a prince, out of thy star.
142 This must not be.' And then I prescripts gave her,
That she should lock herself from his resort,
Admit no messengers, receive no tokens.
Which done, she took the fruits of my advice,
And he, repellèd, a short tale to make,
Fell into a sadness, then into a fast,
148 Thence to a watch, thence into a weakness,
149 Thence to a lightness, and, by this declension,
Into the madness wherein now he raves,
And all we mourn for.

KING: Do you think 'tis this?

QUEEN: It may be, very like.

POLONIUS: Hath there been such a time—I would fain know that—
That I have positively said ''Tis so,'
When it proved otherwise?

KING: Not that I know.

120 *numbers* verses   124 *machine* body; *to* attached to   126 *above* besides   136 *desk or table book*
i.e., silent receiver   137 *winking* closing of the eyes   139 *round* roundly, plainly   141 *star*
condition determined by stellar influence   142 *prescripts* instructions   148 *watch* sleepless
state   149 *lightness* lightheadedness

POLONIUS *[pointing to his head and shoulder]:*
Take this from this, if this be otherwise.
If circumstances lead me, I will find
Where truth is hid, though it were hid indeed
159   Within the center.
KING: How may we try it further?
POLONIUS: You know sometimes he walks four hours together
Here in the lobby.
QUEEN: So he does indeed.
POLONIUS: At such a time I'll loose my daughter to him.
163   Be you and I behind an arras then.
Mark the encounter. If he love her not,
165   And be not from his reason fallen thereon,
Let me be no assistant for a state
But keep a farm and carters.
KING: We will try it.

Enter Hamlet [reading on a book].

QUEEN: But look where sadly the poor wretch comes reading.
POLONIUS: Away, I do beseech you both, away.

Exit King and Queen [with Attendants].

170   I'll board him presently. O, give me leave.
How does my good Lord Hamlet?
172   HAMLET: Well, God-a-mercy.
POLONIUS: Do you know me, my lord?
174   HAMLET: Excellent well. You are a fishmonger.
POLONIUS: Not I, my lord.
HAMLET: Then I would you were so honest a man.
POLONIUS: Honest, my lord?
HAMLET: Ay, sir. To be honest, as this world goes, is to be one man
picked out of ten thousand.
POLONIUS: That's very true, my lord.
182   HAMLET: For if the sun breed maggots in a dead dog, being a good
kissing carrion—Have you a daughter?
POLONIUS: I have, my lord.
HAMLET: Let her not walk i' th' sun. Conception is a blessing, but as
your daughter may conceive, friend, look to 't.
POLONIUS *[aside]:*   How say you by that? Still harping on my daughter.

159 *center* center of the earth and also of the Ptolemaic universe   163 *arras* hanging tapestry
165 *thereon* on that account   170 *board* accost; *presently* at once   172 *God-a-mercy* thank you
(literally, "God have mercy!")   174 *fishmonger* seller of harlots, procurer (a cant term used here
with a glance at the fishing Polonius is doing when he offers Ophelia as bait)   182 *good kissing
carrion* good bit of flesh for kissing

Yet he knew me not at first. 'A said I was a fishmonger. 'A is far gone,
far gone. And truly in my youth I suffered much extremity for love,
very near this. I'll speak to him again.—What do you read, my lord?

HAMLET: Words, words, words.

POLONIUS: What is the matter, my lord?

193 HAMLET: Between who?

POLONIUS: I mean the matter that you read, my lord.

HAMLET: Slanders, sir, for the satirical rogue says here that old men
have grey beards, that their faces are wrinkled, their eyes purging
thick amber and plum-tree gum, and that they have a plentiful lack
of wit, together with most weak hams. All which, sir, though I most
powerfully and potently believe, yet I hold it not honesty to have it
thus set down, for you yourself, sir, should be old as I am if, like a
crab, you could go backward.

POLONIUS *[aside]*:   Though this be madness, yet there is method in't.
—Will you walk out of the air, my lord?

HAMLET: Into my grave?

205 POLONIUS: Indeed, that's out of the air. *[aside]* How pregnant some-
206 times his replies are! a happiness that often madness hits on, which
reason and sanity could not so prosperously be delivered of. I will
leave him and suddenly contrive the means of meeting between him
and my daughter.—My honorable lord, I will most humbly take my
leave of you.

HAMLET: You cannot, sir, take from me anything that I will more
212 willingly part withal—except my life, except my life, except my life.

Enter Guildenstern and Rosencrantz.

POLONIUS: Fare you well, my lord.

HAMLET: These tedious old fools!

POLONIUS: You go to seek the Lord Hamlet. There he is.

ROSENCRANTZ *[to Polonius]*:   God save you, sir!

[Exit Polonius.]

GUILDENSTERN: My honored lord!

ROSENCRANTZ: My most dear lord!

HAMLET: My excellent good friends! How dost thou, Guildenstern?
Ah, Rosencrantz! Good lads, how do ye both?

221 ROSENCRANTZ: As the indifferent children of the earth.

GUILDENSTERN: Happy in that we are not over-happy.
On Fortune's cap we are not the very button.

HAMLET: Nor the soles of her shoe?

193 *Between who* matter for a quarrel between what persons (Hamlet's willful misunderstanding)
205 *pregnant* full of meaning **206** *happiness* aptness of expression **212** *withal* with
221 *indifferent* average

ROSENCRANTZ: Neither, my lord.

HAMLET: Then you live about her waist, or in the middle of her favors?

228 GUILDENSTERN: Faith, her privates we.

HAMLET: In the secret parts of Fortune? O, most true! she is a strum-
pet. What news?

ROSENCRANTZ: None, my lord, but that the world's grown honest.

HAMLET: Then is doomsday near. But your news is not true. [Let me
question more in particular. What have you, my good friends, deserved at the hands of Fortune that she sends you to prison hither?

GUILDENSTERN: Prison, my lord?

HAMLET: Denmark's a prison.

ROSENCRANTZ: Then is the world one.

238 HAMLET: A goodly one; in which there are many confines, wards, and
dungeons, Denmark being one o' th' worst.

ROSENCRANTZ: We think not so, my lord.

HAMLET: Why, then 'tis none to you, for there is nothing either good
or bad but thinking makes it so. To me it is a prison.

ROSENCRANTZ: Why, then your ambition makes it one. 'Tis too narrow
for your mind.

HAMLET: O God, I could be bounded in a nutshell and count myself
a king of infinite space, were it not that I have bad dreams.

GUILDENSTERN: Which dreams indeed are ambition, for the very substance of the ambitious is merely the shadow of a dream.

HAMLET: A dream itself is but a shadow.

ROSENCRANTZ: Truly, and I hold ambition of so airy and light a quality
that it is but a shadow's shadow.

252 HAMLET: Then are our beggars bodies, and our monarchs and out-
253   stretched heroes the beggars' shadows. Shall we to th' court? for, by
254   my fay, I cannot reason.

255 BOTH: We'll wait upon you.

HAMLET: No such matter. I will not sort you with the rest of my
servants, for, to speak to you like an honest man, I am most dread-
258   fully attended.] But in the beaten way of friendship, what make you
at Elsinore?

ROSENCRANTZ: To visit you, my lord; no other occasion.

HAMLET: Beggar that I am, I am even poor in thanks, but I thank you;
262   and sure, dear friends, my thanks are too dear a halfpenny. Were you
not sent for? Is it your own inclining? Is it a free visitation? Come,
come, deal justly with me. Come, come. Nay, speak.

---

228 *privates* ordinary men in private, not public, life (with obvious play upon the sexual term
"private parts")   **238** *confines* places of imprisonment; *wards* cells   **252** *bodies* solid substances,
not shadows (because beggars lack ambition)   **253** *outstretched* elongated as shadows (with a
corollary implication of far-reaching with respect to the ambitions that make both heroes and
monarchs into shadows)   **254** *fay* faith   **255** *wait upon* attend   **258** *make* do   **262** *a halfpenny*
at a halfpenny

GUILDENSTERN: What should we say, my lord?

HAMLET: Why, anything—but to th' purpose. You were sent for, and there is a kind of confession in your looks, which your modesties have not craft enough to color. I know the good king and queen have sent for you.

ROSENCRANTZ: To what end, my lord?

HAMLET: That you must teach me. But let me conjure you by the
272   rights of our fellowship, by the consonancy of our youth, by the obligation of our ever-preserved love, and by what more dear a
274   better proposer can charge you withal, be even and direct with me whether you were sent for or no.

ROSENCRANTZ *[aside to Guildenstern]*:   What say you?

HAMLET *[aside]*:   Nay then, I have an eye of you.—If you love me, hold not off.

GUILDENSTERN: My lord, we were sent for.

280   HAMLET: I will tell you why. So shall my anticipation prevent your
281   discovery, and your secrecy to the king and queen moult no feather. I have of late—but wherefore I know not—lost all my mirth, forgone all custom of exercises; and indeed, it goes so heavily with my disposition that this goodly frame the earth seems to me a sterile promontory; this most excellent canopy, the air, look you, this brave o'er-
286   hanging firmament, this majestical roof fretted with golden fire— why, it appeareth nothing to me but a foul and pestilent congregation of vapors. What a piece of work is a man, how noble in reason,
289   how infinite in faculties; in form and moving how express and admirable, in action how like an angel, in apprehension how like a god: the beauty of the world, the paragon of animals! And yet to me what
292   is this quintessence of dust? Man delights not me—nor woman neither, though by your smiling you seem to say so.

ROSENCRANTZ: My lord, there was no such stuff in my thoughts.

HAMLET: Why did ye laugh then, when I said 'Man delights not me'?

ROSENCRANTZ: To think, my lord, if you delight not in man, what
297   lenten entertainment the players shall receive from you. We coted them on the way, and hither are they coming to offer you service.

HAMLET: He that plays the king shall be welcome—his majesty shall
300   have tribute of me—, the adventurous knight shall use his foil and target, the lover shall not sigh gratis, the humorous man shall end his part in peace, the clown shall make those laugh whose lungs are
303   tickle o' th' sere, and the lady shall say her mind freely, or the blank
304   verse shall halt for 't. What players are they?

---

272 *consonancy* accord (in sameness of age)   **274** *proposer* propounder; *withal* with; *even* straight   **280** *prevent* forestall   **281** *discovery* disclosure; *moult no feather* be left whole   **286** *firmament* sky; *fretted* decorated with fretwork   **289** *express* well framed   **292** *quintessence* fifth or last and finest essence (an alchemical term)   **297** *lenten* scanty; *coted* overtook   **300-301** *foil and target* sword and shield; *humorous man* eccentric character dominated by one of the humours   **303** *tickle o' th' sere* hair-triggered for the discharge of laughter ("sere": part of a gunlock)   **304** *halt* go lame

ROSENCRANTZ: Even those you were wont to take such delight in, the
tragedians of the city.

307 HAMLET: How chances it they travel? Their residence, both in reputation and profit, was better both ways.

309 ROSENCRANTZ: I think their inhibition comes by the means of the late
310 innovation.

HAMLET: Do they hold the same estimation they did when I was in the
city? Are they so followed?

ROSENCRANTZ: No indeed, are they not.

HAMLET: How comes it? Do they grow rusty?

ROSENCRANTZ: Nay, their endeavor keeps in the wonted pace, but
316 there is, sir, an eyrie of children, little eyases, that cry out on the top
of question and are most tyrannically clapped for't. These are now
318 the fashion, and so berattle the common stages (so they call them)
319 that many wearing rapiers are afraid of goosequills and dare scarce
come thither.

HAMLET: What, are they children? Who maintains 'em? How are they
322 escoted? Will they pursue the quality no longer than they can sing?
Will they not say afterwards, if they should grow themselves to
common players (as it is most like, if their means are no better), their
writers do them wrong to make them exclaim against their own
succession?

ROSENCRANTZ: Faith, there has been much to do on both sides, and
328 the nation holds it no sin to tarre them to controversy. There was,
329 for a while, no money bid for argument unless the poet and the
player went to cuffs in the question.

HAMLET: Is't possible?

GUILDENSTERN: O, there has been much throwing about of brains.

HAMLET: Do the boys carry it away?

331 ROSENCRANTZ: Ay, that they do, my lord—Hercules and his load too.]

HAMLET: It is not very strange, for my uncle is King of Denmark, and
336 those that would make mows at him while my father lived give
twenty, forty, fifty, a hundred ducats apiece for his picture in little.
338 'Sblood, there is something in this more than natural, if philosophy
could find it out.

A flourish.

307 *residence* residing at the capital   **309** *inhibition* impediment to acting in residence (formal
prohibition?)   **310** *innovation* new fashion of having companies of boy actors play on the
"private" stage (?), political upheaval (?)   **316-317** *eyrie* nest; *eyases* nestling hawks; *on the top
of question* above others on matter of dispute   **318** *berattle* berate; *common stages* "public"
theatres of the "common" players, who were organized in companies mainly composed of adult
actors (allusion being made to the "War of the Theatres" in Shakespeare's London)
319 *goosequills* pens (of satirists who made out that the London public stage showed low taste)
322 *escoted* supported; *quality* profession of acting; *sing* i.e., with unchanged voices
328 *tarre* incite   **329** *argument* matter of a play   **334** *load* i.e., the whole world (with a topical
reference to the sign of the Globe Theatre, a representation of Hercules bearing the world on
his shoulders)   **336** *mows* grimaces   **338** *'Sblood* by God's blood

GUILDENSTERN: There are the players.

HAMLET: Gentlemen, you are welcome to Elsinore. Your hands, come
then. Th' appurtenance of welcome is fashion and ceremony. Let me
343   comply with you in this garb, lest my extent to the players (which I
tell you must show fairly outwards) should more appear like entertainment than yours. You are welcome. But my uncle-father and
aunt-mother are deceived.

GUILDENSTERN: In what, my dear lord?

HAMLET: I am but mad north-north-west. When the wind is southerly
349   I know a hawk from a handsaw.

Enter Polonius.

POLONIUS: Well be with you, gentlemen.

HAMLET: Hark you, Guildenstern—and you too—at each ear a hearer.
352   That great baby you see there is not yet out of his swaddling clouts.

353   ROSENCRANTZ: Happily he is the second time come to them, for they
say an old man is twice a child.

HAMLET: I will prophesy he comes to tell me of the players. Mark it.
—You say right, sir; a Monday morning, 'twas then indeed.

POLONIUS: My lord, I have news to tell you.

358   HAMLET: My lord, I have news to tell you. When Roscius was an actor
in Rome—

POLONIUS: The actors are come hither, my lord.

HAMLET: Buzz, buzz.

POLONIUS: Upon my honor—

HAMLET: Then came each actor on his ass—

POLONIUS: The best actors in the world, either for tragedy, comedy,
history, pastoral, pastoral-comical, historical-pastoral, tragical-his-
366   torical, tragical-comical-historical-pastoral; scene individable, or
367   poem unlimited. Seneca cannot be too heavy, nor Plautus too light.
368   For the law of writ and the liberty, these are the only men.

369   HAMLET: O Jephthah, judge of Israel, what a treasure hadst thou!

POLONIUS: What treasure had he, my lord?

HAMLET: Why,
'One fair daughter, and no more,
373   The which he lovèd passing well.'

POLONIUS *[aside]*:   Still on my daughter.

---

343 *garb* fashion; *extent* showing of welcome   **349** *hawk* mattock or pickaxe (also called "hack";
here used apparently with a play on "hawk": a bird); *handsaw* carpenter's tool (apparently with
a play on some corrupt form of "hernshaw"; heron, a bird often hunted with the hawk)
352 *clouts* clothes   **353** *Happily* haply, perhaps   **358** *Roscius* the greatest of Roman comic
actors   **366** *scene individable* drama observing the unities   **367** *poem unlimited* drama not observing the unities; *Seneca* Roman writer of tragedies; *Plautus* Roman writer of comedies
368 *law of writ* orthodoxy determined by critical rules of the drama; *liberty* freedom from such
orthodoxy   **369** *Jephthah* the compelled sacrificer of a dearly beloved daughter (Judges xi)
373 *passing* surpassingly (verses are from a ballad on Jephthah)

HAMLET: Am I not i' th' right, old Jephthah?

POLONIUS: If you call me Jephthah, my lord, I have a daughter that I
love passing well.

HAMLET: Nay, that follows not.

POLONIUS: What follows then, my lord?

HAMLET: Why,

'As by lot, God wot,'

and then, you know,

'It came to pass, as most like it was.'

385 The first row of the pious chanson will show you more, for look
386 where my abridgment comes.

Enter the Players.

You are welcome, masters, welcome, all.—I am glad to see thee well.
388 —Welcome, good friends.—O, old friend, why, thy face is valanced
since I saw thee last. Com'st thou to beard me in Denmark?—What,
390 my young lady and mistress? By'r Lady, your ladyship is nearer to
391 heaven than when I saw you last by the altitude of a chopine. Pray
392 God your voice, like a piece of uncurrent gold, be not cracked with-
393 in the ring.—Masters, you are all welcome. We'll e'en to't like French
falconers, fly at anything we see. We'll have a speech straight. Come,
give us a taste of your quality. Come, a passionate speech.

PLAYER: What speech, my good lord?

HAMLET: I heard thee speak me a speech once, but it was never acted,
or if it was, not above once, for the play, I remember, pleased not
399 the million; 'twas caviary to the general, but it was (as I received it,
400 and others, whose judgments in such matters cried in the top of
mine) an excellent play, well digested in the scenes, set down with
as much modesty as cunning. I remember one said there were no
403 sallets in the lines to make the matter savory, nor no matter in the
phrase that might indict the author of affectation, but called it an
honest method, as wholesome as sweet, and by very much more
handsome than fine. One speech in't I chiefly loved. 'Twas Aeneas'
tale to Dido, and thereabout of it especially where he speaks of
408 Priam's slaughter. If it live in your memory, begin at this line—let
me see, let me see:
410 'The rugged Pyrrhus, like th' Hyrcanian beast—'
'Tis not so; it begins with Pyrrhus:

385 *row* stanza; *chanson* song   **386** *my abridgment* that which shortens my talk   **388** *valanced*
fringed (with a beard)   **390** *young lady* boy who plays women's parts   **391** *chopine* women's
thick-soled shoe   **392** *uncurrent* not legal tender   **393** *within the ring* from the edge through the
line circling the design on the coin (with a play on "ring": a sound)   **399** *caviary* caviare; *general*
multitude   **400** *in the top of* more authoritatively than   **403** *sallets* salads, highly seasoned
passages   **408** *Priam's slaughter* i.e., at the fall of Troy (Aeneid II, 506 ff.)   **410** *Hyrcanian beast*
tiger

412   'The rugged Pyrrhus, he whose sable arms,
        Black as his purpose, did the night resemble
414   When he lay couchèd in the ominous horse,
        Hath now this dread and black complexion smeared
416   With heraldry more dismal. Head to foot
417   Now is he total gules, horridly tricked
        With blood of fathers, mothers, daughters, sons,
419   Baked and impasted with the parching streets,
        That lend a tyrannous and a damnèd light
        To their lord's murder. Roasted in wrath and fire,
422   And thus o'ersizèd with coagulate gore,
        With eyes like carbuncles, the hellish Pyrrhus
        Old grandsire Priam seeks.'
    So, proceed you.

POLONIUS: Fore God, my lord, well spoken, with good accent and
good discretion.

PLAYER: 'Anon he finds him,
        Striking too short at Greeks. His antique sword,
        Rebellious to his arms, lies where it falls,
        Repugnant to command. Unequal matched,
        Pyrrhus at Priam drives, in rage strikes wide,
433   But with the whiff and wind of his fell sword
434   Th' unnervèd father falls. Then senseless Ilium,
        Seeming to feel this blow, with flaming top
436   Stoops to his base, and with a hideous crash
        Takes prisoner Pyrrhus' ear. For lo! his sword,
        Which was declining on the milky head
        Of reverend Priam, seemed i' th' air to stick.
440   So as a painted tyrant Pyrrhus stood,
441   And like a neutral to his will and matter
        Did nothing.
443   But as we often see, against some storm,
444   A silence in the heavens, the rack stand still,
        The bold winds speechless, and the orb below
        As hush as death, anon the dreadful thunder
447   Doth rend the region, so after Pyrrhus' pause,
        Arousèd vengeance sets him new awork,
449   And never did the Cyclops' hammers fall
450   On Mars' armor, forged for proof eterne,

---

412 *sable* black   **414** *ominous* fateful; *horse* the wooden horse by which the Greeks gained entrance to Troy   **416** *dismal* ill-omened   **417** *gules* red (heraldic term); *tricked* decorated in color (heraldic term)   **419** *parching* i.e., because Troy was burning   **422** *o'ersizèd* covered as with size, a glutinous material used for filling pores of plaster, etc.; *coagulate* clotted **433** *fell* cruel   **434** *senseless* without feeling   **436** *his* its   **440** *painted* pictured   **441** *will and matter* purpose and its realization (between which he stands motionless)   **443** *against* just before   **444** *rack* clouds   **447** *region* sky   **449** *Cyclops* giant workmen who made armor in the smithy of Vulcan   **450** *proof eterne* eternal protection

        With less remorse than Pyrrhus' bleeding sword
        Now falls on Priam.
        Out, out, thou strumpet Fortune! All you gods,
        In general synod take away her power,
455   Break all the spokes and fellies from her wheel,
456   And bowl the round nave down the hill of heaven,
        As low as to the fiends.'
   POLONIUS: This is too long.
   HAMLET: It shall to the barber's, with your beard.—
460   Prithee say on. He's for a jig or a tale of bawdry, or he sleeps. Say
        on; come to Hecuba.
462   PLAYER: 'But who (ah woe!) had seen the mobled queen—'
   HAMLET: 'The mobled queen'?
   POLONIUS: That's good. 'Mobled queen' is good.
   PLAYER: 'Run barefoot up and down, threat'ning the flames
466   With bisson rheum; a clout upon that head
        Where late the diadem stood, and for a robe,
468   About her lank and all o'erteemèd loins,
        A blanket in the alarm of fear caught up—
        Who this had seen, with tongue in venom steeped
471   'Gainst Fortune's state would treason have pronounced.
        But if the gods themselves did see her then,
        When she saw Pyrrhus make malicious sport
        In mincing with his sword her husband's limbs,
        The instant burst of clamor that she made
        (Unless things mortal move them not at all)
477   Would have made milch the burning eyes of heaven
        And passion in the gods.'
479   POLONIUS: Look, whe'r he has not turned his color, and has tears in's
        eyes. Prithee no more.
   HAMLET: 'Tis well. I'll have thee speak out the rest of this soon.—
482   Good my lord, will you see the players well bestowed? Do you hear?
        Let them be well used, for they are the abstract and brief chronicles
        of the time. After your death you were better have a bad epitaph than
        their ill report while you live.
   POLONIUS: My lord, I will use them according to their desert.
487   HAMLET: God's bodkin, man, much better! Use every man after his
        desert, and who shall scape whipping? Use them after your own
        honor and dignity. The less they deserve, the more merit is in your
        bounty. Take them in.
   POLONIUS: Come, sirs.

---

455 *fellies* segments of the rim **456** *nave* hub **460** *jig* short comic piece with singing and
dancing often presented after a play **462** *mobled* muffled **466** *bisson rheum* blinding tears; *clout*
cloth **468** *o'erteemèd* overproductive of children **471** *state* government of worldly events
477 *milch* tearful (milk-giving); *eyes* i.e., stars **479** *whe'r* whether **482** *bestowed* lodged
487 *God's bodkin* by God's little body

HAMLET: Follow him, friends. We'll hear a play tomorrow. *[aside to Player]* Dost thou hear me, old friend? Can you play 'The Murder of Gonzago'?

PLAYER: Ay, my lord.

HAMLET: We'll ha't to-morrow night. You could for a need study a speech of some dozen or sixteen lines which I would set down and insert in't, could you not?

PLAYER: Ay, my lord.

HAMLET: Very well. Follow that lord, and look you mock him not.— My good friends, I'll leave you till night. You are welcome to Elsinore.

Exeunt Polonius and Players.

ROSENCRANTZ: Good my lord.

Exeunt [Rosencrantz and Guildenstern].

HAMLET: Ay, so, God bye to you.—Now I am alone.
  O, what a rogue and peasant slave am I!
  Is it not monstrous that this player here,
  But in a fiction, in a dream of passion,
508 Could force his soul so to his own conceit
  That from her working all his visage wanned,
  Tears in his eyes, distraction in his aspect,
511 A broken voice, and his whole function suiting
  With forms to his conceit? And all for nothing,
  For Hecuba!
  What's Hecuba to him, or he to Hecuba,
  That he should weep for her? What would he do
  Had he the motive and the cue for passion
  That I have? He would drown the stage with tears
  And cleave the general ear with horrid speech,
  Make mad the guilty and appal the free,
  Confound the ignorant, and amaze indeed
  The very faculties of eyes and ears.
  Yet I,
523 A dull and muddy-mettled rascal, peak
524 Like John-a-dreams, unpregnant of my cause,
  And can say nothing. No, not for a king,
  Upon whose property and most dear life
  A damned defeat was made. Am I a coward?
  Who calls me villain? breaks my pate across?

508 *conceit* conception, idea **511** *function* action of bodily powers **523** *muddy-mettled* dull-spirited; *peak* mope **524** *John-a-dreams* a sleepy dawdler; *unpregnant* barren of realization

Plucks off my beard and blows it in my face?
Tweaks me by the nose? gives me the lie i' th' throat
As deep as to the lungs? Who does me this?

532   Ha, 'swounds, I should take it, for it cannot be
533   But I am pigeon-livered and lack gall
To make oppression bitter, or ere this
535   I should ha' fatted all the region kites
536   With this slave's offal. Bloody, bawdy villain!
537   Remorseless, treacherous, lecherous, kindless villain!
O, vengeance!
Why, what an ass am I! This is most brave,
That I, the son of a dear father murdered,
Prompted to my revenge by heaven and hell,
Must like a whore unpack my heart with words
And fall a-cursing like a very drab,
544   A stallion! Fie upon't, foh! About, my brains.
Hum—
I have heard that guilty creatures sitting at a play
Have by the very cunning of the scene
548   Been struck so to the soul that presently
They have proclaimed their malefactions.
For murder, though it have no tongue, will speak
With most miraculous organ. I'll have these players
Play something like the murder of my father
Before mine uncle. I'll observe his looks.
554   I'll tent him to the quick. If' a do blench,
I know my course. The spirit that I have seen
May be a devil, and the devil hath power
T' assume a pleasing shape, yea, and perhaps
Out of my weakness and my melancholy,
As he is very potent with such spirits,
560   Abuses me to damn me. I'll have grounds
561   More relative than this. The play's the thing
Wherein I'll catch the conscience of the king.

Exit.

III, i   *Enter King, Queen, Polonius, Ophelia, Rosencrantz, Guildenstern, Lords.*

1   KING: And can you by no drift of conference
Get from him why he puts on this confusion,

---

532 *'swounds* by God's wounds   **533** *pigeon-livered* of dove-like gentleness   **535** *region kites* kites of the air   **536** *offal* guts   **537** *kindless* unnatural   **544** *stallion* prostitute (male or female) **548** *presently* immediately   **554** *tent* probe; *blench* flinch   **560** *Abuses* deludes   **561** *relative* pertinent   **III, i** A chamber in the Castle   **1** *drift of conference* direction of conversation

Grating so harshly all his days of quiet
With turbulent and dangerous lunacy?
ROSENCRANTZ: He does confess he feels himself distracted,
But from what cause 'a will by no means speak.
GUILDENSTERN: Nor do we find him forward to be sounded,
But with a crafty madness keeps aloof
When we would bring him on to some confession
Of his true state.
QUEEN: Did he receive you well?
ROSENCRANTZ: Most like a gentleman.
GUILDENSTERN: But with much forcing of his disposition.
ROSENCRANTZ: Niggard of question, but of our demands
Most free in his reply.
14 QUEEN: Did you assay him
To any pastime?
ROSENCRANTZ: Madam, it so fell out that certain players
17 We o'erraught on the way. Of these we told him,
And there did seem in him a kind of joy
To hear of it. They are here about the court,
And, as I think, they have already order
This night to play before him.
POLONIUS: 'Tis most true,
And he beseeched me to entreat your majesties
To hear and see the matter.
KING: With all my heart, and it doth much content me
To hear him so inclined.
26 Good gentlemen, give him a further edge
And drive his purpose into these delights.
ROSENCRANTZ: We shall, my lord.

Exeunt Rosencrantz and Guildenstern.

KING: Sweet Gertrude, leave us too,
29 For we have closely sent for Hamlet hither,
That he, as 'twere by accident, may here
31 Affront Ophelia.
32 Her father and myself (lawful espials)
Will so bestow ourselves that, seeing unseen,
We may of their encounter frankly judge
And gather by him, as he is behaved,
If't be th' affliction of his love or no
That thus he suffers for.
QUEEN: I shall obey you.—

14 *assay* try to win   17 *o'erraught* overtook   26 *edge* keenness of desire   29 *closely* privately
31 *Affront* come face to face with   32 *espials* spies

And for your part, Ophelia, I do wish
That your good beauties be the happy cause
Of Hamlet's wildness. So shall I hope your virtues
Will bring him to his wonted way again,
To both your honors.

OPHELIA: Madam, I wish it may.

                              [Exit Queen.]

POLONIUS: Ophelia, walk you here.—Gracious, so please you,
We will bestow ourselves.—

[To Ophelia]

                              Read on this book,
45   That show of such an exercise may color
Your loneliness. We are oft to blame in this,
'Tis too much proved, that with devotion's visage
And pious action we do sugar o'er
The devil himself.

KING *[aside]*:   O, 'tis too true.
How smart a lash that speech doth give my conscience!
The harlot's cheek, beautied with plast'ring art,
52   Is not more ugly to the thing that helps it
Than is my deed to my most painted word.
O heavy burthen!

POLONIUS: I hear him coming. Let's withdraw, my lord.

                         [Exeunt King and Polonius.]

Enter Hamlet.

HAMLET: To be, or not to be—that is the question:
Whether 'tis nobler in the mind to suffer
The slings and arrows of outrageous fortune
Or to take arms against a sea of troubles
And by opposing end them. To die, to sleep—
No more—and by a sleep to say we end
The heartache, and the thousand natural shocks
That flesh is heir to. 'Tis a consummation
Devoutly to be wished. To die, to sleep—
65   To sleep—perchance to dream: ay, there's the rub,

---

45 *exercise* religious exercise (the book being obviously one of devotion); *color* give an appearance of naturalness to   **52** *to* compared to   **65** *rub* obstacle (literally, obstruction encountered by a bowler's ball)

For in that sleep of death what dreams may come
67 When we have shuffled off this mortal coil,
68 Must give us pause. There's the respect
69 That makes calamity of so long life.
For who would bear the whips and scorns of time,
Th' oppressor's wrong, the proud man's contumely
The pangs of despised love, the law's delay,
The insolence of office, and the spurns
That patient merit of th' unworthy takes,
75 When he himself might his quietus make
76 With a bare bodkin? Who would fardels bear,
To grunt and sweat under a weary life,
But that the dread of something after death,
79 The undiscovered country, from whose bourn
No traveller returns, puzzles the will,
And makes us rather bear those ills we have
Than fly to others that we know not of?
Thus conscience does make cowards of us all,
And thus the native hue of resolution
Is sicklied o'er with the pale cast of thought,
86 And enterprises of great pitch and moment
87 With this regard their currents turn awry
And lose the name of action.   Soft you now,
89 The fair Ophelia!—Nymph, in thy orisons
Be all my sins remembered.
OPHELIA: Good my lord,
How does your honor for this many a day?
HAMLET: I humbly thank you, well, well, well.
OPHELIA: My lord, I have remembrances of yours
That I have longèd long to re-deliver.
I pray you, now receive them.
HAMLET: No, not I,
I never gave you aught.
OPHELIA: My honored lord, you know right well you did,
And with them words of so sweet breath composed
As made the things more rich. Their perfume lost,
Take these again, for to the noble mind
Rich gifts wax poor when givers prove unkind.
There, my lord.
103 HAMLET: Ha, ha! Are you honest?
OPHELIA: My lord?

---

67 *shuffled off* cast off as an encumbrance; *coil* to-do, turmoil   **68** *respect* consideration
69 *of so long life* so long-lived   **75** *quietus* settlement (literally, release from debt)   **76** *bodkin*
dagger; *fardels* burdens   **79** *bourn* confine, region   **86** *pitch* height (of a soaring falcon's flight)
87 *regard* consideration   **89** *orisons* prayers (because of the book of devotion she reads)
103 *honest* chaste

HAMLET: Are you fair?

OPHELIA: What means your lordship?

HAMLET: That if you be honest and fair, your honesty should admit no discourse to your beauty.

109   OPHELIA: Could beauty, my lord, have better commerce than with honesty?

HAMLET: Ay, truly; for the power of beauty will sooner transform honesty from what it is to a bawd than the force of honesty can
113   translate beauty into his likeness. This was sometime a paradox, but now the time gives it proof. I did love you once.

OPHELIA: Indeed, my lord, you made me believe so.

HAMLET: You should not have believed me, for virtue cannot so inoc-
117   ulate our old stock but we shall relish of it. I loved you not.

OPHELIA: I was the more deceived.

HAMLET: Get thee to a nunnery. Why wouldst thou be a breeder of
120   sinners? I am myself indifferent honest, but yet I could accuse me of such things that it were better my mother had not borne me: I am very proud, revengeful, ambitious, with more offenses at my beck than I have thoughts to put them in, imagination to give them shape, or time to act them in. What should such fellows as I do crawling between earth and heaven? We are arrant knaves all; believe none of us. Go thy ways to a nunnery. Where's your father?

OPHELIA: At home, my lord.

HAMLET: Let the doors be shut upon him, that he may play the fool nowhere but in's own house. Farewell.

OPHELIA: O, help him, you sweet heavens!

HAMLET: If thou dost marry, I'll give thee this plague for thy dowry: be thou as chaste as ice, as pure as snow, thou shalt not escape calumny. Get thee to a nunnery. Go, farewell. Or if thou wilt needs
134   marry, marry a fool, for wise men know well enough what monsters you make of them. To a nunnery, go, and quickly too. Farewell.

OPHELIA: O heavenly powers, restore him!

HAMLET: I have heard of your paintings too, well enough. God hath given you one face, and you make yourselves another. You jig, you amble, and you lisp; you nickname God's creatures and make your
140   wantonness your ignorance. Go to, I'll no more on't; it hath made me mad. I say we will have no more marriage. Those that are married already—all but one—shall live. The rest shall keep as they are. To a nunnery, go.

Exit.

---

109 *commerce* intercourse   **113** *paradox* idea contrary to common opinion   **117** *inoculate* graft; *relish* have a flavor (because of original sin)   **120** *indifferent honest* moderately respectable **134** *monsters* i.e., unnatural combinations of wisdom and uxorious folly   **140** *wantonness* affecta-tion; *your ignorance* a matter for which you offer the excuse that you don't know any better

OPHELIA: O, what a noble mind is here o'erthrown!
The courtier's, soldier's, scholar's, eye, tongue, sword,
146   Th' expectancy and rose of the fair state,
147   The glass of fashion and the mould of form,
Th' observed of all observers, quite, quite down!
And I, of ladies most deject and wretched,
That sucked the honey of his music vows,
Now see that noble and most sovereign reason
Like sweet bells jangled, out of time and harsh,
That unmatched form and feature of blown youth
154   Blasted with ecstasy. O, woe is me
T' have seen what I have seen, see what I see!

Enter King and Polonius.

156   KING: Love? his affections do not that way tend,
Nor what he spake, though it lacked form a little,
Was not like madness. There's something in his soul
O'er which his melancholy sits on brood,
160   And I do doubt the hatch and the disclose
Will be some danger; which for to prevent,
I have in quick determination
Thus set it down: he shall with speed to England
For the demand of our neglected tribute.
Haply the seas, and countries different,
With variable objects, shall expel
167   This something-settled matter in his heart,
Whereon his brains still beating puts him thus
From fashion of himself. What think you on't?
POLONIUS: It shall do well. But yet do I believe
The origin and commencement of his grief
Sprung from neglected love.—How now, Ophelia?
You need not tell us what Lord Hamlet said.
We heard it all.—My lord, do as you please,
But if you hold it fit, after the play
Let his queen mother all alone entreat him
177   To show his grief. Let her be round with him,
And I'll be placed, so please you, in the ear
Of all their conference. If she find him not,
To England send him, or confine him where
Your wisdom best shall think.

---

146 *expectancy and rose* fair hope   **147** *glass* mirror   **154** *ecstasy* madness   **156** *affections* emotions   **160** *doubt* fear   **167** *something-settled* somewhat settled   **177** *round* plain-spoken

KING: It shall be so.
Madness in great ones must not unwatched go.

Exeunt.

III, ii   *Enter Hamlet and three of the Players.*

HAMLET: Speak the speech, I pray you, as I pronounced it to you,
2   trippingly on the tongue. But if you mouth it, as many of our players
do, I had as lief the town crier spoke my lines. Nor do not saw the
air too much with your hand, thus, but use all gently, for in the very
torrent, tempest, and (as I may say) whirlwind of your passion, you
must acquire and beget a temperance that may give it smoothness.
7   O, it offends me to the soul to hear a robustious periwig-pated fellow
8   tear a passion to tatters, to very rags, to split the ears of the groundlings, who for the most part are capable of nothing but inexplicable
10   dumb shows and noise. I would have such a fellow whipped for
11   o'erdoing Termagant. It out-herods Herod. Pray you avoid it.
PLAYER: I warrant your honor.
HAMLET: Be not too tame neither, but let your own discretion be your
tutor. Suit the action to the word, the word to the action, with this
special observance, that you o'erstep not the modesty of nature. For
16   anything so overdone is from the purpose of playing, whose end,
both at the first and now, was and is, to hold, as 'twere, the mirror
up to nature, to show virtue her own feature, scorn her own image,
19   and the very age and body of the time his form and pressure. Now
20   this overdone, or come tardy off, though it make the unskillful laugh,
21   cannot but make the judicious grieve, the censure of the which one
must in your allowance o'erweigh a whole theatre of others. O, there
be players that I have seen play, and heard others praise, and that
highly (not to speak it profanely), that neither having th' accent of
Christians, nor the gait of Christian, pagan, nor man, have so strut-
26   ted and bellowed that I have thought some of Nature's journeymen
had made men, and not made them well, they imitated humanity so
abominably.
29   PLAYER: I hope we have reformed that indifferently with us, sir.
HAMLET: O, reform it altogether! And let those that play your clowns
31   speak no more than is set down for them, for there be of them that

---

III, ii The hall of the Castle   **2** *trippingly* easily   **7** *robustious* boisterous; *periwig-pated* wig-
wearing (after the custom of actors)   **8** *groundlings* spectators who paid least and stood on the
ground in the pit or yard of the theatre   **10** *dumb shows* brief actions without words, forecasting
dramatic matter to follow (the play presented later in this scene giving an old-fashioned
example)   **11** *Termagant* a Saracen "god" in medieval romance and drama; *Herod* the raging
tyrant of old biblical plays   **16** *from* apart from   **19** *pressure* impressed or printed character
20 *come tardy off* brought off slowly and badly   **21** *the censure of the which one* the judgment of
even one of whom   **26** *journeymen* workmen not yet masters of their trade   **29** *indifferently* fairly
well   **31** *of them* some of them

will themselves laugh, to set on some quantity of barren spectators to laugh too, though in the mean time some necessary question of the play be then to be considered. That's villainous and shows a most pitiful ambition in the fool that uses it. Go make you ready.

[Exeunt Players.]

Enter Polonius, Guildenstern, and Rosencrantz.

How now, my lord? Will the king hear this piece of work?
37   POLONIUS: And the queen too, and that presently.
HAMLET: Bid the players make haste.

[Exit Polonius.]

Will you two help to hasten them?
ROSENCRANTZ: Ay, my lord.

Exeunt they two.

HAMLET: What, ho, Horatio!

Enter Horatio.

HORATIO: Here, sweet lord, at your service.
HAMLET: Horatio, thou art e'en as just a man
44   As e'er my conversation coped withal.
HORATIO: O, my dear lord—
HAMLET: Nay, do not think I flatter.
For what advancement may I hope from thee,
That no revenue hast but thy good spirits
To feed and clothe thee? Why should the poor be flattered?
No, let the candied tongue lick absurd pomp,
50   And crook the pregnant hinges of the knee
51   Where thrift may follow fawning. Dost thou hear?
Since my dear soul was mistress of her choice
And could of men distinguish her election,
54   S' hath sealed thee for herself, for thou hast been
As one in suff'ring all that suffers nothing,
A man that Fortune's buffets and rewards
Hast ta'en with equal thanks; and blest are those
58   Whose blood and judgment are so well commeddled

---

37 *presently* at once   **44** *conversation coped withal* intercourse with men encountered
50 *pregnant* quick to move   **51** *thrift* profit   **54** *sealed* marked   **58** *blood* passion; *commeddled* mixed together

That they are not a pipe for Fortune's finger
To sound what stop she please. Give me that man
That is not passion's slave, and I will wear him
In my heart's core, ay, in my heart of heart,
As I do thee. Something too much of this—
There is a play to-night before the king.
One scene of it comes near the circumstance
Which I have told thee, of my father's death.
I prithee, when thou seest that act afoot,
68   Even with the very comment of thy soul
69   Observe my uncle. If his occulted guilt
Do not itself unkennel in one speech,
71   It is a damnèd ghost that we have seen,
And my imaginations are as foul
73   As Vulcan's stithy. Give him heedful note,
For I mine eyes will rivet to his face,
And after we will both our judgments join
76   In censure of his seeming.

HORATIO: Well, my lord.
If'a steal aught the while this play is playing,
And scape detecting, I will pay the theft.

> *Enter Trumpets and Kettledrums, King, Queen, Polonius, Ophelia*
> *[, Rosencrantz, Guildenstern, and other Lords attendant].*

79   HAMLET: They are coming to the play. I must be idle.
Get you a place.
81   KING: How fares our cousin Hamlet?
82   HAMLET: Excellent, i'faith, of the chameleon's dish. I eat the air, prom-
ise-crammed. You cannot feed capons so.
KING: I have nothing with this answer, Hamlet. These words are not
mine.
86   HAMLET: No, nor mine now. *[to Polonius]* My lord, you played once i'
th' university, you say?
POLONIUS: That did I, my lord, and was accounted a good actor.
HAMLET: What did you enact?
POLONIUS: I did enact Julius Caesar. I was killed i' th' Capitol; Brutus
killed me.
HAMLET: It was a brute part of him to kill so capital a calf there. Be
the players ready?
94   ROSENCRANTZ: Ay, my lord. They stay upon your patience.

---

68 *the very . . . soul* thy deepest sagacity   **69** *occulted* hidden   **71** *damnèd ghost* evil spirit, devil
(as thought of in II, ii, 555 ff.)   **73** *stithy* smithy   **76** *censure of* sentence upon   **79** *be idle* be
foolish, act the madman   **81** *cousin* nephew   **82** *chameleon's dish* i.e., air (which was believed the
chameleon's food, Hamlet willfully takes *fares* in the sense of "feeds")   **86** *not mine* not for me
as the asker of my question   **94** *stay upon your patience* await your indulgence

QUEEN: Come hither, my dear Hamlet, sit by me.
HAMLET: No, good mother. Here's metal more attractive.
POLONIUS *[to the King]*:   O ho! do you mark that?
HAMLET: Lady, shall I lie in your lap?

[He lies at Ophelia's feet.]

OPHELIA: No, my lord.
HAMLET: I mean, my head upon your lap?
OPHELIA: Ay, my lord.
102   HAMLET: Do you think I meant country matters?
OPHELIA: I think nothing, my lord.
HAMLET: That's a fair thought to lie between maids' legs.
OPHELIA: What is, my lord?
HAMLET: Nothing.
OPHELIA: You are merry, my lord.
HAMLET: Who, I?
OPHELIA: Ay, my lord.
110   HAMLET: O God, your only jig-maker! What should a man do but be
merry? For look you how cheerfully my mother looks, and my father
died within's two hours.
OPHELIA: Nay, 'tis twice two months, my lord.
HAMLET: So long? Nay then, let the devil wear black, for I'll have a suit
115   of sables. O heavens! die two months ago, and not forgotten yet?
Then there's hope a great man's memory may outlive his life half a
year. But, by'r Lady, 'a must build churches then, or else shall 'a
118   suffer not thinking on, with the hobby-horse, whose epitaph is 'For
O, for O, the hobby-horse is forgot!'

The trumpets sound. Dumbshow follows:
Enter a King and a Queen [very lovingly], the Queen embracing him, and he her.
[She kneels; and makes show of protestation unto him.] He takes her up, and declines
his head upon her neck. He lies him down upon a bank of flowers. She, seeing him asleep,
leaves him. Anon come in another man: takes off his crown, kisses it, pours poison in
the sleeper's ears, and leaves him. The Queen returns, finds the King dead, makes
passionate action. The poisoner, with some three or four, come in again, seem to condole
with her. The dead body is carried away. The poisoner woos the Queen with gifts; she
seems harsh awhile, but in the end accepts love.

[Exeunt.]

102 *country matters* rustic goings-on, barnyard mating (with a play upon a sexual term)
110 *jig-maker* writer of jigs (see II, ii, 460)   115 *sables* black furs (luxurious garb, not for
mourning)   118 *hobby-horse* traditional figure strapped round the waist of a performer in May
games and morris dances

OPHELIA: What means this, my lord?

121   HAMLET: Marry, this is miching mallecho; it means mischief.

OPHELIA: Belike this show imports the argument of the play.

Enter Prologue.

HAMLET: We shall know by this fellow. The players cannot keep counsel; they'll tell all.

OPHELIA: Will 'a tell us what this show meant?

HAMLET: Ay, or any show that you'll show him. Be not you ashamed
to show, he'll not shame to tell you what it means.

128   OPHELIA: You are naught, you are naught. I'll mark the play.

PROLOGUE:

> For us and for our tragedy,
> Here stooping to your clemency,
> We beg your hearing patiently.

[Exit.]

132   HAMLET: Is this a prologue, or the posy of a ring?

OPHELIA: 'Tis brief, my lord.

HAMLET: As woman's love.

Enter [two Players as] King and Queen.

135   KING: Full thirty times hath Phoebus' cart gone round

136   Neptune's salt wash and Tellus' orbèd ground,

137   And thirty dozen moons with borrowed sheen

          About the world have times twelve thirties been,

139   Since love our hearts, and Hymen did our hands,

140   Unite commutual in most sacred bands.

QUEEN: So many journeys may the sun and moon

          Make us again count o'er ere love be done!

          But woe is me, you are so sick of late,

          So far from cheer and from your former state,

145   That I distrust you. Yet, though I distrust,

          Discomfort you, my lord, it nothing must.

          For women fear too much, even as they love,

148   And women's fear and love hold quantity,

          In neither aught, or in extremity.

          Now what my love is, proof hath made you know,

121 *miching mallecho* sneaking iniquity   128 *naught* indecent   132 *posy* brief motto in rhyme
("poesy"); *ring* finger ring   135 *Phoebus' cart* the sun's chariot   136 *Tellus* Roman goddess of
the earth   137 *borrowed* i.e., taken from the sun   139 *Hymen* Greek god of marriage
140 *commutual* mutually   145 *distrust you* fear for you   148 *quantity* proportion

And as my love is sized, my fear is so.
Where love is great, the littlest doubts are fear;
Where little fears grow great, great love grows there.
KING: Faith, I must leave thee, love, and shortly too;
155   My operant powers their functions leave to do.
And thou shalt live in this fair world behind,
Honored, beloved, and haply one as kind
For husband shalt thou—
QUEEN: O, confound the rest!
Such love must needs be treason in my breast.
In second husband let me be accurst!
None wed the second but who killed the first.
162   HAMLET *[aside]*:   That's wormwood.
163   QUEEN: The instances that second marriage move
Are base respects of thrift, but none of love.
A second time I kill my husband dead
When second husband kisses me in bed.
KING: I do believe you think what now you speak,
But what we do determine oft we break.
169   Purpose is but the slave to memory,
170   Of violent birth, but poor validity,
Which now like fruit unripe sticks on the tree,
But fall unshaken when they mellow be.
Most necessary 'tis that we forget
To pay ourselves what to ourselves is debt.
What to ourselves in passion we propose,
The passion ending, doth the purpose lose.
The violence of either grief or joy
178   Their own enactures with themselves destroy.
Where joy most revels, grief doth most lament;
Grief joys, joy grieves, on slender accident.
This world is not for aye, nor 'tis not strange
That even our loves should with our fortunes change,
For 'tis a question left us yet to prove,
Whether love lead fortune, or else fortune love.
The great man down, you mark his favorite flies,
The poor advanced makes friends of enemies;
And hitherto doth love on fortune tend,
For who not needs shall never lack a friend,
And who in want a hollow friend doth try,
190   Directly seasons him his enemy.
But, orderly to end where I begun,

---

155 *operant powers* active bodily forces   **162** *wormwood* a bitter herb   **163** *instances* motives
169 *slave to* i.e., dependent upon for life   **170** *validity* strength   **178** *enactures* fulfillments
190 *seasons him* ripens him into

Our wills and fates do so contrary run

193   That our devices still are overthrown;

Our thoughts are ours, their ends none of our own.

So think thou wilt no second husband wed,

But die thy thoughts when thy first lord is dead.

QUEEN: Nor earth to me give food, nor heaven light,

Sport and repose lock from me day and night,

To desperation turn my trust and hope,

200   An anchor's cheer in prison be my scope,

201   Each opposite that blanks the face of joy

Meet what I would have well, and it destroy,

203   Both here and hence pursue me lasting strife,

If, once a widow, ever I be wife!

HAMLET: If she should break it now!

KING: 'Tis deeply sworn. Sweet, leave me here awhile.

My spirits grow dull, and fain I would beguile

The tedious day with sleep.

QUEEN: Sleep rock thy brain,   *[He sleeps.]*

And never come mischance between us twain!

Exit.

HAMLET: Madam, how like you this play?

QUEEN: The lady doth protest too much, methinks.

HAMLET: O, but she'll keep her word

213   KING: Have you heard the argument? Is there no offense in't?

HAMLET: No, no, they do but jest, poison in jest; no offense i' th'
world.

KING: What do you call the play?

217   HAMLET: 'The Mousetrap.' Marry, how? Tropically. This play is the
image of a murder done in Vienna. Gonzago is the duke's name; his
wife, Baptista. You shall see anon. 'Tis a knavish piece of work, but

220   what o' that? Your majesty, and we that have free souls, it touches

221   us not. Let the galled jade winch; our withers are unwrung.

Enter Lucianus.

This is one Lucianus, nephew to the king.

223   OPHELIA: You are as good as a chorus, my lord.

HAMLET: I could interpret between you and your love, if I could see

225   the puppets dallying.

---

193 *still* always   **200** *anchor's* hermit's   **201** *blanks* blanches, makes pale   **203** *hence* in the next
world   **213** *argument* plot summary   **217** *Tropically* in the way of a trope or figure (with a play
on "trapically")   **220** *free* guiltless   **221** *galled* sore-backed; *jade* horse; *winch* wince; *withers*
shoulders   **223** *chorus* one in a play who explains the action   **225** *puppets* i.e., you and your
lover as in a puppet show

OPHELIA: You are keen, my lord, you are keen.

HAMLET: It would cost you a groaning to take off my edge.

OPHELIA: Still better, and worse.

HAMLET: So you must take your husbands.—Begin, murderer. Leave thy damnable faces and begin. Come, the croaking raven doth bellow for revenge.

LUCIANUS: Thoughts black, hands apt, drugs fit, and time agreeing,

233   Confederate season, else no creature seeing,
Thou mixture rank, of midnight weeds collected,

235   With Hecate's ban thrice blasted, thrice infected,
Thy natural magic and dire property
On wholesome life usurps immediately.

[Pours the poison in his ears.]

HAMLET: 'A poisons him i' th' garden for his estate. His name's Gonzago. The story is extant, and written in very choice Italian. You shall see anon how the murderer gets the love of Gonzago's wife.

OPHELIA: The king rises.

242 HAMLET: What, frighted with false fire?

QUEEN: How fares my lord?

POLONIUS: Give o'er the play.

KING;   Give me some light. Away!

POLONIUS: Lights, lights, lights!

Exeunt all but Hamlet and Horatio.

HAMLET: Why, let the strucken deer go weep,
The hart ungallèd play.
For some must watch, while some must sleep;
Thus runs the world away.

251   Would not this, sir, and a forest of feathers—if the rest of my for-
252   tunes turn Turk with me—with two Provincial roses on my razed
253   shoes, get me a fellowship in a cry of players, sir?

HORATIO: Half a share.

HAMLET: A whole one, I.
For thou dost know, O Damon dear,
This realm dismantled was
Of Jove himself; and now reigns here
A very, very—peacock.

HORATIO: You might have rhymed.

---

233 *Confederate season* the occasion being my ally   **235** *Hecate* goddess of witchcraft and black magic; *ban* curse   **242** *false fire* a firing of a gun charged with powder but no shot, a blank-discharge   **251** *feathers* plumes for actors' costumes   **252** *turn Turk* turn renegade, like a Christian turning Mohammedan; *Provincial roses* ribbon rosettes; *razed* decorated with cut patterns   **253** *cry* pack

HAMLET: O good Horatio, I'll take the ghost's word for a thousand
pound. Didst perceive?

HORATIO: Very well, my lord.

HAMLET: Upon the talk of the poisoning?

HORATIO: I did very well note him.

266 HAMLET: Aha! Come, some music! Come, the recorders!
For if the king like not the comedy,

268   Why then, belike he likes it not, perdy.
Come, some music!

Enter Rosencrantz and Guildenstern.

GUILDENSTERN: Good my lord, vouchsafe me a word with you.

HAMLET: Sir, a whole history.

GUILDENSTERN: The king, sir—

HAMLET: Ay, sir, what of him?

274 GUILDENSTERN: Is in his retirement marvellous distempered.

HAMLET: With drink, sir?

276 GUILDENSTERN: No, my lord, with choler.

HAMLET: Your wisdom should show itself more richer to signify this
to the doctor, for for me to put him to his purgation would perhaps
plunge him into more choler.

280 GUILDENSTERN: Good my lord, put your discourse into some frame,
and start not so wildly from my affair.

HAMLET: I am tame, sir; pronounce.

GUILDENSTERN: The queen, your mother, in most great affliction of
spirit hath sent me to you.

HAMLET: You are welcome.

GUILDENSTERN: Nay, good my lord, this courtesy is not of the right
breed. If it shall please you to make me a wholesome answer, I will
do your mother's commandment. If not, your pardon and my return
shall be the end of my business.

HAMLET: Sir, I cannot.

ROSENCRANTZ: What, my lord?

HAMLET: Make you a wholesome answer; my wit's diseased. But, sir,
such answer as I can make, you shall command, or rather, as you say,
my mother. Therefore no more, but to the matter. My mother, you
say—

ROSENCRANTZ: Then thus she says: your behavior hath struck her into

297 amazement and admiration.

---

266 *recorders* musical instruments of the flute class   **268** *perdy* by God (*"par dieu"*)
274 *distempered* out of temper, vexed (twisted by Hamlet into "deranged")   **276** *choler* anger
(twisted by Hamlet into "biliousness")   **280** *frame* logical order   **297** *admiration* wonder

HAMLET: O wonderful son, that can so stonish a mother! But is there no sequel at the heels of this mother's admiration? Impart.

300   ROSENCRANTZ: She desires to speak with you in her closet ere you go to bed.

HAMLET: We shall obey, were she ten times our mother. Have you any further trade with us?

ROSENCRANTZ: My lord, you once did love me.

305   HAMLET: And do still, by these pickers and stealers.

ROSENCRANTZ: Good my lord, what is your cause of distemper? You do surely bar the door upon your own liberty, if you deny your griefs to your friend.

HAMLET: Sir, I lack advancement.

ROSENCRANTZ: How can that be, when you have the voice of the king himself for your succession in Denmark?

312   HAMLET: Ay, sir, but 'while the grass grows'—the proverb is something musty.

Enter the Player with recorders.

314   O, the recorders. Let me see one. To withdraw with you—why do
315   you go about to recover the wind of me, as if you would drive me
316   into a toil?
317   GUILDENSTERN: O my lord, if my duty be too bold, my love is too unmannerly.

HAMLET: I do not well understand that. Will you play upon this pipe?

GUILDENSTERN: My lord, I cannot.

HAMLET: I pray you.

GUILDENSTERN: Believe me, I cannot.

HAMLET: I do beseech you.

GUILDENSTERN: I know no touch of it, my lord.

325   HAMLET: It is as easy as lying. Govern these ventages with your fingers and thumb, give it breath with your mouth, and it will discourse most eloquent music. Look you, these are the stops.

GUILDENSTERN: But these cannot I command to any utt'rance of harmony. I have not the skill.

HAMLET: Why, look you now, how unworthy a thing you make of me! You would play upon me, you would seem to know my stops, you would pluck out the heart of my mystery, you would sound me from my lowest note to the top of my compass; and there is much music, excellent voice, in this little organ, yet cannot you make it speak.

300 *closet* private room   **305** *pickers and stealers* i.e., hands   **312** *while the grass grows* (a proverb, ending: "the horse starves")   **314** *recorders* (see III, ii, 266n.); *withdraw* step aside   **315** *recover the wind* come up to windward like a hunter   **316** *toil* snare   **317-318** *is too unmannerly* leads me beyond the restraint of good manners   **325** *ventages* holes, vents

'Sblood, do you think I am easier to be played on than a pipe? Call
336   me what instrument you will, though you can fret me, you cannot
play upon me.

Enter Polonius.

God bless you, sir!
339   POLONIUS: My lord, the queen would speak with you, and presently.
HAMLET: Do you see yonder cloud that's almost in shape of a camel?
POLONIUS: By th' mass and 'tis, like a camel indeed.
HAMLET: Methinks it is like a weasel.
POLONIUS: It is backed like a weasel.
HAMLET: Or like a whale.
POLONIUS: Very like a whale.
346   HAMLET: Then I will come to my mother by and by. *[aside]* They fool
347   me to the top of my bent.—I will come by and by.
POLONIUS: I will say so.

[Exit.]

HAMLET: 'By and by' is easily said. Leave me, friends.

[Exeunt all but Hamlet.]

'Tis now the very witching time of night,
When churchyards yawn, and hell itself breathes out
Contagion to this world. Now could I drink hot blood
And do such bitter business as the day
Would quake to look on. Soft, now to my mother.
O heart, lose not thy nature; let not ever
356   The soul of Nero enter this firm bosom.
Let me be cruel, not unnatural;
I will speak daggers to her, but use none.
My tongue and soul in this be hypocrites:
360   How in my words somever she be shent,
361   To give them seals never, my soul, consent!

Exit.

III, iii   *Enter King, Rosencrantz, and Guildenstern.*

KING: I like him not, nor stands it safe with us
To let his madness range. Therefore prepare you.

---

336 *fret* irritate (with a play on the fret-fingering of certain stringed musical instruments)
339 *presently* at once   **346** *by and by* immediately   **347** *bent* (see II, ii, 30n.)   **356** *Nero* murderer
of his mother   **360** *shent* reproved   **361** *seals* authentications in actions   **III, iii** A chamber in
the Castle

I your commission will forthwith dispatch,
And he to England shall along with you.
5 The terms of our estate may not endure
Hazard so near's as doth hourly grow
7 Out of his brows.
GUILDENSTERN: We will ourselves provide.
Most holy and religious fear it is
To keep those many many bodies safe
That live and feed upon your majesty.
11 ROSENCRANTZ: The single and peculiar life is bound
With all the strength and armor of the mind
13 To keep itself from noyance, but much more
That spirit upon whose weal depends and rests
15 The lives of many. The cess of majesty
16 Dies not alone, but like a gulf doth draw
What's near it with it; or 'tis a massy wheel
Fixed on the summit of the highest mount,
To whose huge spokes ten thousand lesser things
Are mortised and adjoined, which when it falls,
Each small annexment, petty consequence,
22 Attends the boist'rous ruin. Never alone
Did the king sigh, but with a general groan.
24 KING: Arm you, I pray you, to this speedy voyage,
For we will fetters put upon this fear,
Which now goes too free-footed.
ROSENCRANTZ: We will haste us.

Exeunt Gentlemen.

Enter Polonius.

POLONIUS: My lord, he's going to his mother's closet.
Behind the arras I'll convey myself
29 To hear the process. I'll warrant she'll tax him home,
And, as you said, and wisely was it said,
'Tis meet that some more audience than a mother,
Since nature makes them partial, should o'erhear
33 The speech, of vantage. Fare you well, my liege.
I'll call upon you ere you go to bed
And tell you what I know.
KING: Thanks, dear my lord.

Exit [Polonius].

---

5 *terms* circumstances; *estate* royal position   **7** *brows* effronteries (apparently with an implication of knitted brows)   **11** *peculiar* individual   **13** *noyance* harm   **15** *cess* cessation, decease   **16** *gulf* whirlpool   **22** *Attends* joins in (like a royal attendant)   **24** *Arm* prepare   **29** *process* proceedings; *tax him home* thrust home in reprimanding him   **33** *of vantage* from an advantageous position

O, my offense is rank, it smells to heaven;

37 It hath the primal eldest curse upon't,
A brother's murder. Pray can I not,
Though inclination be as sharp as will.
My stronger guilt defeats my strong intent,
And like a man to double business bound
I stand in pause where I shall first begin,
And both neglect. What if this cursèd hand
Were thicker than itself with brother's blood,
Is there not rain enough in the sweet heavens
To wash it white as snow? Whereto serves mercy

47 But to confront the visage of offense?
And what's in prayer but this twofold force,
To be forestallèd ere we come to fall,
Or pardoned being down? Then I'll look up.
My fault is past. But, O, what form of prayer
Can serve my turn? 'Forgive me my foul murder'?
That cannot be, since I am still possessed

54 Of those effects for which I did the murder,
My crown, mine own ambition, and my queen.
May one be pardoned and retain th' offense?
In the corrupted currents of this world

58 Offense's gilded hand may shove by justice,
And oft 'tis seen the wicked prize itself
Buys out the law. But 'tis not so above.

61 There is no shuffling; there the action lies
In his true nature, and we ourselves compelled,

63 Even to the teeth and forehead of our faults,
To give in evidence. What then? What rests?
Try what repentance can. What can it not?
Yet what can it when one cannot repent?
O wretched state! O bosom black as death!

68 O limèd soul, that struggling to be free

69 Art more engaged! Help, angels! Make assay.
Bow, stubborn knees, and, heart with strings of steel,
Be soft as sinews of the new-born babe.
All may be well.

[He kneels.]

Enter Hamlet.

37 *primal eldest curse* that of Cain, who also murdered a brother   47 *offense* sin   54 *effects* things acquired   58 *gilded* gold-laden   61 *shuffling* sharp practice, double-dealing; *action* legal proceeding (in heaven's court)   63 *teeth and forehead* face-to-face recognition   68 *limèd* caught in birdlime, a gluey material spread as a bird-snare   69 *engaged* embedded; *assay* an attempt

73 HAMLET: Now might I do it pat, now 'a is a-praying,
And now I'll do't. And so 'a goes to heaven,
And so am I revenged. That would be scanned.
A villain kills my father, and for that
I, his sole son, do this same villain send
To heaven.
Why, this is hire and salary, not revenge.
80 'A took my father grossly, full of bread,
81 With all his crimes broad blown, as flush as May;
82 And how his audit stands, who knows save heaven?
But in our circumstance and course of thought,
'Tis heavy with him; and am I then revenged,
To take him in the purging of his soul,
When he is fit and seasoned for his passage?
No.
88 Up, sword, and know thou a more horrid hent.
When he is drunk asleep, or in his rage,
Or in th' incestuous pleasure of his bed,
At game a-swearing, or about some act
92 That has no relish of salvation in't—
Then trip him, that his heels may kick at heaven,
And that his soul may be as damned and black
As hell, whereto it goes. My mother stays.
This physic but prolongs thy sickly days.

Exit.

KING *[rises]*:   My words fly up, my thoughts remain below.
Words without thoughts never to heaven go.

Exit.

III, iv   *Enter [Queen] Gertrude and Polonius.*

1 POLONIUS: 'A will come straight. Look you lay home to him.
2 Tell him his pranks have been too broad to bear with,
And that your grace hath screened and stood between
Much heat and him. I'll silence me even here.
5 Pray you be round with him.

---

73 *pat* opportunely   **80** *grossly* in a state of gross unpreparedness; *bread* i.e., worldly sense
gratification   **81** *broad blown* fully blossomed; *flush* vigorous   **82** *audit* account   **88** *more horrid
hent* grasping by me on a more horrid occasion   **92** *relish* flavor   **III, iv** The private chamber
of the Queen   **1** *lay* thrust   **2** *broad* unrestrained   **5** *round* plain-spoken

[HAMLET *(within)*:   Mother, mother, mother!]
QUEEN: I'll warrant you; fear me not. Withdraw; I hear him coming.

> *[Polonius hides behind the arras.]*

Enter Hamlet.

HAMLET: Now, mother, what's the matter?
QUEEN: Hamlet, thou hast thy father much offended.
HAMLET: Mother, you have my father much offended.
12 QUEEN: Come, come, you answer with an idle tongue.
HAMLET: Go, go, you question with a wicked tongue.
QUEEN: Why, how now, Hamlet?
HAMLET: What's the matter now?
QUEEN: Have you forgot me?
15 HAMLET: No, by the rood, not so!
   You are the queen, your husband's brother's wife,
   And (would it were not so) you are my mother.
QUEEN: Nay, then I'll set those to you that can speak.
HAMLET: Come, come, and sit you down. You shall not budge.
   You go not till I set you up a glass
   Where you may see the inmost part of you.
QUEEN: What wilt thou do? Thou wilt not murder me?
   Help, ho!
POLONIUS *[behind]*:   What, ho! help!
HAMLET *[draws]*:   How now? a rat? Dead for a ducat, dead!

> *[Makes a pass through the arras and kills Polonius.]*

POLONIUS *[behind]*:   O, I am slain!
QUEEN: O me, what hast thou done?
HAMLET: Nay, I know not. Is it the king?
QUEEN: O, what a rash and bloody deed is this!
HAMLET: A bloody deed—almost as bad, good mother,
   As kill a king, and marry with his brother.
QUEEN: As kill a king?
HAMLET: Ay, lady, it was my word.

[Lifts up the arras and sees Polonius.]

   Thou wretched, rash, intruding fool, farewell!
   I took thee for thy better. Take thy fortune.
   Thou find'st to be too busy is some danger.—
   Leave wringing of your hands. Peace, sit you down

12 *idle* foolish   **15** *rood* cross

And let me wring your heart, for so I shall
If it be made of penetrable stuff,
38 If damnèd custom have not brazed it so
39 That it is proof and bulwark against sense.
QUEEN: What have I done that thou dar'st wag thy tongue
In noise so rude against me?
HAMLET: Such an act
That blurs the grace and blush of modesty,
Calls virtue hypocrite, takes off the rose
From the fair forehead of an innocent love,
45 And sets a blister there, makes marriage vows
As false as dicers' oaths. O, such a deed
47 As from the body of contraction plucks
48 The very soul, and sweet religion makes
A rhapsody of words! Heaven's face does glow,
50 And this solidity and compound mass,
51 With heated visage, as against the doom,
Is thought-sick at the act.
QUEEN: Ay me, what act,
53 That roars so loud and thunders in the index?
HAMLET: Look here upon this picture, and on this,
55 The counterfeit presentment of two brothers.
See what a grace was seated on this brow:
57 Hyperion's curls, the front of Jove himself,
An eye like Mars, to threaten and command,
59 A station like the herald Mercury
New lighted on a heaven-kissing hill—
A combination and a form indeed
Where every god did seem to set his seal
To give the world assurance of a man.
This was your husband. Look you now what follows.
Here is your husband, like a mildewed ear
Blasting his wholesome brother. Have you eyes?
Could you on this fair mountain leave to feed,
68 And batten on this moor? Ha! have you eyes?
You cannot call it love, for at your age
70 The heyday in the blood is tame, it's humble,
71 And waits upon the judgment, and what judgment
72 Would step from this to this? Sense sure you have,

38 *custom* habit; *brazed* hardened like brass   39 *proof* armor; *sense* feeling   45 *blister* brand (of degradation)   47 *contraction* the marriage contract   48 *religion* i.e., sacred marriage vows   50 *compound mass* the earth as compounded of the four elements   51 *against* in expectation of; *doom* Day of Judgment   53 *index* table of contents preceding the body of a book   55 *counterfeit presentment* portrayed representation   57 *Hyperion* the sun god; *front* forehead   59 *station* attitude in standing   68 *batten* feed greedily   70 *heyday* excitement of passion   71 *waits upon* yields to   72 *Sense* feeling

73   Else could you not have motion, but sure that sense
74   Is apoplexed, for madness would not err,
75   Nor sense to ecstasy was ne'er so thralled
      But it reserved some quantity of choice
      To serve in such a difference. What devil was't
78   That thus hath cozened you at hoodman-blind?
      Eyes without feeling, feeling without sight,
80   Ears without hands or eyes, smelling sans all,
      Or but a sickly part of one true sense
82   Could not so mope.
                        O shame, where is thy blush? Rebellious hell,
84   If thou canst mutine in a matron's bones,
      To flaming youth let virtue be as wax
      And melt in her own fire. Proclaim no shame
87   When the compulsive ardor gives the charge,
      Since frost itself as actively doth burn,
89   And reason panders will.
QUEEN: O Hamlet, speak no more.
      Thou turn'st mine eyes into my very soul,
91   And there I see such black and grainèd spots
92   As will not leave their tinct.
HAMLET: Nay, but to live
93   In the rank sweat of an enseamèd bed,
      Stewed in corruption, honeying and making love
      Over the nasty sty—
QUEEN: O, speak to me no more.
      These words like daggers enter in mine ears.
      No more, sweet Hamlet.
HAMLET: A murderer and a villain,
98   A slave that is not twentieth part the tithe
99   Of your precedent lord, a vice of kings,
100   A cutpurse of the empire and the rule,
      That from a shelf the precious diadem stole
      And put it in his pocket—
102 QUEEN: No more.

Enter [the] Ghost [in his nightgown].

HAMLET: A king of shreds and patches—
      Save me and hover o'er me with your wings,
      You heavenly guards? What would your gracious figure?

---

73 *motion* desire, impulse   **74** *apoplexed* paralyzed   **75** *ecstasy* madness   **78** *cozened* cheated;
hoodman-blind blindman's buff   **80** *sans* without   **82** *mope* be stupid   **84** *mutine* mutiny
87 *compulsive* compelling; *gives the charge* delivers the attack   **89** *panders will* acts as procurer for
desire   **91** *grainèd* dyed in grain   **92** *tinct* color   **93** *enseamèd* grease-laden   **98** *tithe* tenth part
99 *vice* clownish rogue (like the Vice of the morality plays)   **100** *cutpurse* skulking thief
102 s.d. *nightgown* dressing gown

QUEEN: Alas, he's mad.

HAMLET: Do you not come your tardy son to chide,
108   That, lapsed in time and passion, lets go by
Th' important acting of your dread command?
O, say!

GHOST: Do not forget. This visitation
Is but to whet thy almost blunted purpose.
But look, amazement on thy mother sits.
O, step between her and her fighting soul!
115   Conceit in weakest bodies strongest works.
Speak to her, Hamlet.

HAMLET: How is it with you, lady?

QUEEN: Alas, how is't with you,
That you do bend your eye on vacancy,
119   And with th' incorporal air do hold discourse?
Forth at your eyes your spirits wildly peep,
And as the sleeping soldiers in th' alarm
122   Your bedded hairs like life in excrements
123   Start up and stand an end. O gentle son,
124   Upon the heat and flame of thy distemper
Sprinkle cool patience. Whereon do you look?

HAMLET: On him, on him! Look you, how pale he glares!
His form and cause conjoined, preaching to stones,
128   Would make them capable.—Do not look upon me,
Lest with this piteous action you convert
130   My stern effects. Then what I have to do
Will want true color—tears perchance for blood.

QUEEN: To whom do you speak this?

HAMLET: Do you see nothing there?

QUEEN: Nothing at all; yet all that is I see.

HAMLET: Nor did you nothing hear?

QUEEN: No, nothing but ourselves.

HAMLET: Why, look you there! Look how it steals away!
My father, in his habit as he lived!
Look where he goes even now out at the portal!

Exit Ghost.

QUEEN: This is the very coinage of your brain.
139   This bodiless creation ecstasy
Is very cunning in.

HAMLET: Ecstasy?

---

108 *lapsed . . . passion* having let the moment slip and passion cool   **115** *Conceit* imagination
119 *incorporal* bodiless   **122** *excrements* outgrowths   **123** *an* on   **124** *distemper* mental disorder
128 *capable* susceptible   **130** *effects* manifestations of emotion and purpose   **139** *ecstasy* madness

My pulse as yours doth temperately keep time
And makes as healthful music. It is not madness
That I have uttered. Bring me to the test,
And I the matter will reword, which madness

145   Would gambol from. Mother, for love of grace,
146   Lay not that flattering unction to your soul,
That not your trespass but my madness speaks.
It will but skin and film the ulcerous place

149   Whiles rank corruption, mining all within,
Infects unseen. Confess yourself to heaven,
Repent what's past, avoid what is to come,

152   And do not spread the compost on the weeds
To make them ranker. Forgive me this my virtue.

154   For in the fatness of these pursy times
Virtue itself of vice must pardon beg,

156   Yea, curb and woo for leave to do him good.
QUEEN: O Hamlet, thou hast cleft my heart in twain.
HAMLET: O, throw away the worser part of it,
And live the purer with the other half
Good night—but go not to my uncle's bed.
Assume a virtue, if you have it not.
That monster custom, who all sense doth eat,
Of habits devil, is angel yet in this,
That to the use of actions fair and good

165   He likewise gives a frock or livery
That aptly is put on. Refrain to-night,
And that shall lend a kind of easiness
To the next abstinence; the next more easy;

169   For use almost can change the stamp of nature,
And either . . . the devil, or throw him out
With wondrous potency. Once more, good night,
And when you are desirous to be blest,
I'll blessing beg of you.—For this same lord,
I do repent; but heaven hath pleased it so,
To punish me with this, and this with me,
That I must be their scourge and minister.

177   I will bestow him and will answer well
The death I gave him. So again, good night.
I must be cruel only to be kind.

180   Thus bad begins, and worse remains behind.
One word more, good lady.
QUEEN: What shall I do?
HAMLET: Not this, by no means, that I bid you do:

---

145 *gambol* shy (like a startled horse)   **146** *unction* ointment   **149** *mining* undermining
152 *compost* fertilizing mixture   **154** *fatness* gross slackness; *pursy* corpulent   **156** *curb* bow to
165 *livery* characteristic dress (accompanying the suggestion of "garb" in *habits*)   **169** *use* habit;
stamp impression, form   **177** *bestow* stow, hide   **180** *behind* to come

183   Let the bloat king tempt you again to bed,
    Pinch wanton on your cheek, call you his mouse,
185   And let him, for a pair of reechy kisses,
    Or paddling in your neck with his damned fingers,
187   Make you to ravel all this matter out,
    That I essentially am not in madness,
    But mad in craft. 'Twere good you let him know,
    For who that's but a queen, fair, sober, wise,
191   Would from a paddock, from a bat, a gib,
192   Such dear concernings hide? Who would do so?
    No, in despite of sense and secrecy,
    Unpeg the basket on the house's top,
195   Let the birds fly, and like the famous ape,
196   To try conclusions, in the basket creep
    And break your own neck down.
QUEEN: Be thou assured, if words be made of breath,
    And breath of life, I have no life to breathe
    What thou hast said to me.
HAMLET: I must to England; you know that?
QUEEN: Alack,
    I had forgot. 'Tis so concluded on.
HAMLET: There's letters sealed, and my two schoolfellows,
    Whom I will trust as I will adders fanged,
205   They bear the mandate; they must sweep my way
    And marshal me to knavery. Let it work.
207   For 'tis the sport to have the enginer
208   Hoist with his own petar, and 't shall go hard
    But I will delve one yard below their mines
    And blow them at the moon. O, 'tis most sweet
    When in one line two crafts directly meet.
212   This man shall set me packing.
    I'll lug the guts into the neighbor room.
    Mother, good night. Indeed, this counsellor
    Is now most still, most secret, and most grave,
    Who was in life a foolish prating knave.
    Come, sir, to draw toward an end with you.
    Good night, mother.

[Exit the Queen. Then] exit [Hamlet,
tugging in Polonius].

183 *bloat* bloated with sense gratification   185 *reechy* filthy   187 *ravel . . . out* disentangle 191 *paddock* toad; *gib* tomcat   192 *dear concernings* matters of great personal significance 195 *famous ape* (one in a story now unknown)   196 *conclusions* experiments   205 *mandate* order 207 *enginer* engineer, constructor of military engines or works   208 *Hoist* blown up; *petar* petard, bomb or mine   212 *packing* travelling in a hurry (with a play upon his "packing" or shouldering of Polonius' body and also upon his "packing" in the sense of "plotting" or "contriving")

IV, i *Enter King and Queen, with Rosencrantz and Guildenstern.*

KING: There's matter in these sighs. These profound heaves
You must translate; 'tis fit we understand them.
Where is your son?
QUEEN: Bestow this place on us a little while.

[Exeunt Rosencrantz and Guildenstern.]

Ah, mine own lord, what have I seen to-night!
KING: What, Gertrude? How does Hamlet?
QUEEN: Mad as the sea and wind when both contend
Which is the mightier. In his lawless fit,
Behind the arras hearing something stir,
Whips out his rapier, cries, 'A rat, a rat!'
11   And in this brainish apprehension kills
The unseen good old man.
KING: O heavy deed!
It had been so with us, had we been there.
His liberty is full of threats to all,
To you yourself, to us, to every one.
Alas, how shall this bloody deed be answered?
17   It will be laid to us, whose providence
18   Should have kept short, restrained, and out of haunt
This mad young man. But so much was our love
We would not understand what was most fit,
But, like the owner of a foul disease,
22   To keep it from divulging, let it feed
Even on the pith of life. Where is he gone?
QUEEN: To draw apart the body he hath killed;
25   O'er whom his very madness, like some ore
26   Among a mineral of metals base,
Shows itself pure. 'A weeps for what is done.
KING: O Gertrude, come away!
The sun no sooner shall the mountains touch
But we will ship him hence, and this vile deed
We must with all our majesty and skill
Both countenance and excuse. Ho, Guildenstern!

Enter Rosencrantz and Guildenstern.

Friends both, go join you with some further aid.
Hamlet in madness hath Polonius slain,

IV, i A chamber in the Castle   **11** *brainish apprehension* headstrong conception   **17** *providence*
foresight   **18** *haunt* association with others   **22** *divulging* becoming known   **25** *ore* vein of gold
26 *mineral* mine

And from his mother's closet hath he dragged him.
Go seek him out; speak fair, and bring the body
Into the chapel. I pray you haste in this.

[Exeunt Rosencrantz and Guildenstern.]

Come, Gertrude, we'll call up our wisest friends
And let them know both what we mean to do
And what's untimely done . . .
Whose whisper o'er the world's diameter,
42   As level as the cannon to his blank
Transports his poisoned shot, may miss our name
And hit the woundless air. O, come away!
My soul is full of discord and dismay.

Exeunt.

IV, ii   *Enter Hamlet.*

HAMLET: Safely stowed.
GENTLEMEN *[within]*:   Hamlet! Lord Hamlet!
HAMLET: But soft, what noise? Who calls on Hamlet? O, here they
come.

[Enter] Rosencrantz, [Guildenstern,] and others.

ROSENCRANTZ: What have you done, my lord, with the dead body?
HAMLET: Compounded it with dust, whereto 'tis kin.
ROSENCRANTZ: Tell us where 'tis, that we may take it thence
And bear it to the chapel.
HAMLET: Do not believe it.
ROSENCRANTZ: Believe what?
HAMLET: That I can keep your counsel and not mine own. Besides, to
12   be demanded of a sponge, what replication should be made by the
son of a king?
ROSENCRANTZ: Take you me for a sponge, my lord?
15   HAMLET: Ay, sir, that soaks up the king's countenance, his rewards,
his authorities. But such officers do the king best service in the end.
He keeps them, like an ape, in the corner of his jaw, first mouthed,
to be last swallowed. When he needs what you have gleaned, it is but
squeezing you and, sponge, you shall be dry again.
ROSENCRANTZ: I understand you not, my lord.

42 *As level* with as direct aim; *blank* mark, central white spot on a target   **IV, ii** A passage in
the Castle   **12** *replication* reply   **15** *countenance* favor

21   HAMLET: I am glad of it. A knavish speech sleeps in a foolish ear.
      ROSENCRANTZ: My lord, you must tell us where the body is and go with
      us to the king.
      HAMLET: The body is with the king, but the king is not with the body.
      The king is a thing—
      GUILDENSTERN: A thing, my lord?
27   HAMLET: Of nothing. Bring me to him. Hide fox, and all after.

Exeunt.

IV, iii   *Enter King, and two or three.*

      KING: I have sent to seek him and to find the body.
      How dangerous is it that this man goes loose!
      Yet must not we put the strong law on him;
4   He's loved of the distracted multitude,
      Who like not in their judgment, but their eyes,
6   And where 'tis so, th' offender's scourge is weighed,
      But never the offense. To bear all smooth and even,
      This sudden sending him away must seem
9   Deliberate pause. Diseases desperate grown
      By desperate appliance are relieved,
      Or not at all.

Enter Rosencrantz, [Guildenstern,] and all the rest.

                  How now? What hath befallen?
      ROSENCRANTZ: Where the dead body is bestowed, my lord,
      We cannot get from him.
      KING: But where is he?
      ROSENCRANTZ: Without, my lord; guarded, to know your pleasure.
      KING: Bring him before us.
      ROSENCRANTZ: Ho! Bring in the lord.

They enter [with Hamlet].

      KING: Now, Hamlet, where's Polonius?
      HAMLET: At supper.
      KING: At supper? Where?

---

21 *sleeps in* means nothing to   27 *Of nothing* (cf. Prayer Book, Psalm cxliv, 4, 'Man is like a thing
of naught: his time passeth away like a shadow'); *Hide . . . after* (apparently well-known words
from some game of hide-and-seek)   **IV, iii** A chamber in the Castle   4 *distracted* confused
6 *scourge* punishment   9 *Deliberate pause* something done with much deliberation

HAMLET: Not where he eats, but where 'a is eaten. A certain convoca-
20   tion of politic worms are e'en at him. Your worm is your only em-
21   peror for diet. We fat all creatures else to fat us, and we fat ourselves
22   for maggots. Your fat king and your lean beggar is but variable
      service—two dishes, but to one table. That's the end.
KING: Alas, alas!
HAMLET: A man may fish with the worm that hath eat of a king, and
      eat of the fish that hath fed of that worm.
KING: What dost thou mean by this?
28   HAMLET: Nothing but to show you how a king may go a progress
      through the guts of a beggar.
KING: Where is Polonius?
HAMLET: In heaven. Send thither to see. If your messenger find him
      not there, seek him i' th' other place yourself. But if indeed you find
      him not within this month, you shall nose him as you go up the stairs
      into the lobby.
KING *[to Attendants]*:   Go seek him there.
HAMLET: 'A will stay till you come.

                                                    [Exeunt Attendants.]

KING: Hamlet, this deed, for thine especial safety,
38   Which we do tender as we dearly grieve
      For that which thou hast done, must send thee hence
      With fiery quickness. Therefore prepare thyself.
      The bark is ready and the wind at help,
42   Th' associates tend, and everything is bent
      For England.
HAMLET: For England?
KING: Ay, Hamlet.
HAMLET: Good.
KING: So is it, if thou knew'st our purposes.
45   HAMLET: I see a cherub that sees them. But come, for England! Fare-
      well, dear mother.
KING: Thy loving father, Hamlet.
HAMLET: My mother—father and mother is man and wife, man and
      wife is one flesh, and so, my mother. Come, for England!

                                                            Exit.

20 *politic worms* political and craftily scheming worms (such as Polonius might well attract)
21 *diet* food and drink (perhaps with a play upon a famous "convocation," the Diet of Worms
opened by the Emperor Charles V on January 28, 1521, before which Luther appeared)
22 *variable service* different servings of one food   **28** *progress* royal journey of state
38 *tender* hold dear; *dearly* intensely   **42** *tend* wait; *bent* set in readiness (like a bent bow)
45 *cherub* one of the cherubim (angels with a distinctive quality of knowledge)

50 KING: Follow him at foot; tempt him with speed aboard.
     Delay it not; I'll have him hence to-night.
     Away! for everything is sealed and done
53 That else leans on th' affair. Pray you make haste.

[Exeunt all but the King.]

54 And, England, if my love thou hold'st at aught—
     As my great power thereof may give thee sense,
     Since yet thy cicatrice looks raw and red
57 After the Danish sword, and thy free awe
58 Pays homage to us—thou mayst not coldly set
59 Our sovereign process, which imports at full
60 By letters congruing to that effect
61 The present death of Hamlet. Do it, England,
62 For like the hectic in my blood he rages,
     And thou must cure me. Till I know 'tis done,
64 Howe'er my haps, my joys were ne'er begun.

Exit.

IV, iv   *Enter Fortinbras with his Army over the stage.*

FORTINBRAS: Go, captain, from me greet the Danish king.
     Tell him that by his license Fortinbras
3   Craves the conveyance of a promised march
     Over his kingdom. You know the rendezvous.
     If that his majesty would aught with us,
6   We shall express our duty in his eye;
     And let him know so.
CAPTAIN: I will do't, my lord.
8   FORTINBRAS: Go softly on.

[Exeunt all but the Captain.]

Enter Hamlet, Rosencrantz, [Guildenstern,] and others.

9   HAMLET: Good sir, whose powers are these?
CAPTAIN: They are of Norway, sir.
HAMLET: How purposed, sir, I pray you?
CAPTAIN: Against some part of Poland.

50 *at foot* at heel, close 53 *leans on* is connected with 54 *England* King of England
57 *free awe* voluntary show of respect 58 *set* esteem 59 *process* formal command
60 *congruing* agreeing 61 *present* instant 62 *hectic* a continuous fever 64 *haps* fortunes
IV, iv A coastal highway 3 *conveyance* escort 6 *eye* presence 8 *softly* slowly 9 *powers* forces

HAMLET: Who commands them, sir?

CAPTAIN: The nephew to old Norway, Fortinbras.

15 HAMLET: Goes it against the main of Poland, sir,
Or for some frontier?

17 CAPTAIN: Truly to speak, and with no addition,
We go to gain a little patch of ground
That hath in it no profit but the name.

20 To pay five ducats, five, I would not farm it,
Nor will it yield to Norway or the Pole

22 A ranker rate, should it be sold in fee.

HAMLET: Why, then the Polack never will defend it.

CAPTAIN: Yes, it is already garrisoned.

HAMLET: Two thousand souls and twenty thousand ducats
Will not debate the question of this straw.

27 This is th' imposthume of much wealth and peace,
That inward breaks, and shows no cause without
Why the man dies. I humbly thank you, sir.

CAPTAIN: God bye you, sir.

[Exit.]

ROSENCRANTZ: Will't please you go, my lord?

HAMLET: I'll be with you straight. Go a little before.

[Exeunt all but Hamlet.]

32 How all occasions do inform against me
And spur my dull revenge! What is a man,

34 If his chief good and market of his time
Be but to sleep and feed? A beast, no more.

36 Sure he that made us with such large discourse,
Looking before and after, gave us not
That capability and godlike reason

39 To fust in us unused. Now, whether it be

40 Bestial oblivion, or some craven scruple

41 Of thinking too precisely on th' event—
A thought which, quartered, hath but one part wisdom
And ever three parts coward—I do not know
Why yet I live to say, 'This thing's to do,'
Sith I have cause, and will, and strength, and means

46 To do't. Examples gross as earth exhort me.

47 Witness this army of such mass and charge,

---

15 *main* main body **17** *addition* exaggeration **20** *To pay* i.e., for a yearly rental of
22 *ranker* more abundant; *in fee* outright **27** *imposthume* abscess **32** *inform* take shape
34 *market of* compensation for **36** *discourse* power of thought **39** *fust* grow mouldy
40 *oblivion* forgetfulness **41** *event* outcome (as also in l. 50) **46** *gross* large and evident
47 *charge* expense

Led by a delicate and tender prince,
Whose spirit, with divine ambition puffed,
50   Makes mouths at the invisible event,
Exposing what is mortal and unsure
To all that fortune, death, and danger dare,
Even for an eggshell. Rightly to be great
Is not to stir without great argument,
55   But greatly to find quarrel in a straw
When honor's at the stake. How stand I then,
That have a father killed, a mother stained,
Excitements of my reason and my blood,
And let all sleep, while to my shame I see
The imminent death of twenty thousand men
61   That for a fantasy and trick of fame
Go to their graves like beds, fight for a plot
63   Whereon the numbers cannot try the cause,
64   Which is not tomb enough and continent
To hide the slain? O, from this time forth,
My thoughts be bloody, or be nothing worth!

Exit.

IV, v   *Enter Horatio, [Queen] Gertrude, and a Gentleman.*

QUEEN: I will not speak with her.
2   GENTLEMAN: She is importunate, indeed distract.
Her mood will needs be pitied.
QUEEN: What would she have?
GENTLEMAN: She speaks much of her father, says she hears
5   There's tricks i' th' world, and hems, and beats her heart,
6   Spurns enviously at straws, speaks things in doubt
That carry but half sense. Her speech is nothing,
8   Yet the unshapèd use of it doth move
9   The hearers to collection; they aim at it,
10   And botch the words up fit to their own thoughts,
Which, as her winks and nods and gestures yield them,
Indeed would make one think there might be thought,
Though nothing sure, yet much unhappily.

---

50 *Makes mouths* makes faces scornfully   **55** *greatly . . . straw* to recognize the great argument even in some small matter   **61** *fantasy* fanciful image; *trick* toy   **63** *try the cause* find space in which to settle the issue by battle   **64** *continent* receptacle   **IV, v** A chamber in the Castle **2** *distract* insane   **5** *tricks* deceits   **6** *Spurns enviously* kicks spitefully, takes offense; *straws* trifles **8** *unshapèd use* disordered manner   **9** *collection* attempts at shaping meaning; *aim* guess **10** *botch* patch

HORATIO: 'Twere good she were spoken with, for she may strew
  Dangerous conjectures in ill-breeding minds.
QUEEN: Let her come in.

[Exit Gentleman.]

[Aside]

    To my sick soul (as sin's true nature is)
18   Each toy seems prologue to some great amiss.
19   So full of artless jealousy is guilt
20   It spills itself in fearing to be spilt.

Enter Ophelia [distracted].

OPHELIA: Where is the beauteous majesty of Denmark?
QUEEN: How now, Ophelia?
OPHELIA *[She sings]*:

        How should I your true-love know
          From another one?
25   By his cockle hat and staff
26   And his sandal shoon.

QUEEN: Alas, sweet lady, what imports this song?
OPHELIA: Say you? Nay, pray you mark.

              Song.
        He is dead and gone, lady,
          He is dead and gone;
        At his head a grass-green turf,
          At his heels a stone.

  O, ho!
QUEEN: Nay, but Ophelia—
OPHELIA: Pray you mark.

[Sings]

    White his shroud as the mountain snow—

Enter King.

18 *toy* trifle; *amiss* calamity   **19** *artless* unskillfully managed; *jealousy* suspicion   **20** *spills* destroys   **25** *cockle hat* hat bearing a cockle shell, worn by a pilgrim who had been to the shrine of St James of Compostela   **26** *shoon* shoes

QUEEN: Alas, look here, my lord.
OPHELIA:

Song.

38   Larded all with sweet flowers;
                 Which bewept to the grave did not go
                     With true-love showers.

KING: How do you, pretty lady?
42   OPHELIA: Well, God dild you! They say the owl was a baker's daugh-
        ter. Lord, we know what we are, but know not what we may be. God
        be at your table!
45   KING: Conceit upon her father.
     OPHELIA: Pray let's have no words of this, but when they ask you what
        it means, say you this:

Song.

                 To-morrow is Saint Valentine's day.
49   All in the morning betime,
                 And I a maid at your window,
                     To be your Valentine.
                 Then up he rose and donned his clo'es
53   And dupped the chamber door,
                 Let in the maid, that out a maid
                     Never departed more.

KING: Pretty Ophelia!
OPHELIA: Indeed, la, without an oath, I'll make an end on't:

[Sings]

58   By Gis and by Saint Charity,
                     Alack, and fie for shame!
                 Young men will do't if they come to't.
61   By Cock, they are to blame.
                 Quoth she, 'Before you tumbled me,
                     You promised me to wed.'

   He answers:

                 'So would I 'a' done, by yonder sun,
                     And thou hadst not come to my bed.'

KING: How long hath she been thus?
OPHELIA: I hope all will be well. We must be patient, but I cannot

---

38 *Larded* garnished   **42** *dild* yield, repay; *the owl* an owl into which, according to a folktale,
a baker's daughter was transformed because of her failure to show wholehearted generosity
when Christ asked for bread in the baker's shop   **45** *Conceit* thought   **49** *betime* early
53 *dupped* opened   **58** *Gis* Jesus   **61** *Cock* God (with a perversion of the name not uncommon
in oaths)

choose but weep to think they would lay him i' th' cold ground. My brother shall know of it; and so I thank you for your good counsel. Come, my coach! Good night, ladies, good night. Sweet ladies, good night, good night.

[Exit.]

KING: Follow her close; give her good watch, I pray you.

[Exit Horatio.]

O, this is the poison of deep grief; it springs
All from her father's death—and now behold!
O Gertrude, Gertrude,
When sorrows come, they come not single spies,
But in battalions: first, her father slain;
Next, your son gone, and he most violent author
81   Of his own just remove; the people muddied,
Thick and unwholesome in their thoughts and whispers
83   For good Polonius' death, and we have done but greenly
84   In hugger-mugger to inter him; poor Ophelia
Divided from herself and her fair judgment,
Without the which we are pictures or mere beasts;
Last, and as much containing as all these,
Her brother is in secret come from France,
89   Feeds on his wonder, keeps himself in clouds,
90   And wants not buzzers to infect his ear
With pestilent speeches of his father's death,
92   Wherein necessity, of matter beggared,
93   Will nothing stick our person to arraign
In ear and ear. O my dear Gertrude, this,
95   Like to a murd'ring piece, in many places
Gives me superfluous death.

A noise within.

Enter a Messenger.

QUEEN: Alack, what noise is this?
97   KING: Attend, where are my Switzers? Let them guard the door.
What is the matter?
MESSENGER: Save yourself, my lord.

81 *muddied* stirred up and confused   **83** *greenly* foolishly   **84** *hugger-mugger* secrecy and disorder
89 *clouds* obscurity   **90** *wants* lacks; *buzzers* whispering tale-bearers   **92** *of matter beggared* unprovided with facts   **93** *nothing stick* in no way hesitate; *arraign* accuse   **95** *murd'ring piece* cannon loaded with shot meant to scatter   **97** *Switzers* hired Swiss guards

99   The ocean, overpeering of his list,
100   Eats not the flats with more impiteous haste
101   Than young Laertes, in a riotous head,
      O'erbears your officers. The rabble call him lord,
      And, as the world were now but to begin,
      Antiquity forgot, custom not known,
105   The ratifiers and props of every word,
      They cry, 'Choose we! Laertes shall be king!'
      Caps, hands, and tongues applaud it to the clouds,
      'Laertes shall be king! Laertes king!'

A noise within.

QUEEN: How cheerfully on the false trail they cry!
110   O, this is counter, you false Danish dogs!
      KING: The doors are broke.

Enter Laertes with others.

LAERTES: Where is this king?—Sirs, stand you all without.
ALL: No, let's come in.
LAERTES: I pray you give me leave.
ALL: We will, we will.
LAERTES: I thank you. Keep the door.

                          [Exeunt his Followers.]

                                  O thou vile king,
      Give me my father.
      QUEEN: Calmly, good Laertes.
LAERTES: That drop of blood that's calm proclaims me bastard,
      Cries cuckold to my father, brands the harlot
      Even here between the chaste unsmirchèd brows
      Of my true mother.
      KING: What is the cause, Laertes,
      That thy rebellion looks so giant-like?
122   Let him go, Gertrude. Do not fear our person.
      There's such divinity doth hedge a king
124   That treason can but peep to what it would,
      Acts little of his will. Tell me, Laertes,
      Why thou art thus incensed. Let him go, Gertrude.
      Speak, man.

---

99 *overpeering of* rising to look over and pass beyond; *list* boundary   **100** *impiteous* pitiless
101 *head* armed force   **105** *word* promise   **110** *counter* hunting backward on the trail
122 *fear* fear for   **124** *peep to* i.e., through the barrier

LAERTES: Where is my father?

KING: Dead.

QUEEN: But not by him.

KING: Let him demand his fill.

LAERTES: How came he dead? I'll not be juggled with.
    To hell allegiance, vows to the blackest devil,
    Conscience and grace to the profoundest pit!
    I dare damnation. To this point I stand,

134   That both the worlds I give to negligence,
    Let come what comes, only I'll be revenged

136   Most throughly for my father.

KING: Who shall stay you?

LAERTES: My will, not all the world's.
    And for my means, I'll husband them so well
    They shall go far with little.

KING: Good Laertes,
    If you desire to know the certainty
    Of your dear father, is't writ in your revenge

142   That swoopstake you will draw both friend and foe,
    Winner and loser?

LAERTES: None but his enemies.

KING: Will you know them then?

LAERTES: To his good friends thus wide I'll ope my arms

146   And like the kind life-rend'ring pelican
    Repast them with my blood.

KING: Why, now you speak
    Like a good child and a true gentleman.
    That I am guiltless of your father's death,

150   And am most sensibly in grief for it,

151   It shall as level to your judgment 'pear
    As day does to your eye.

A noise within: 'Let her come in.'

LAERTES: How now? What noise is that?

Enter Ophelia.

    O heat, dry up my brains; tears seven times salt
    Burn out the sense and virtue of mine eye!
    By heaven, thy madness shall be paid by weight

134 *both the worlds* whatever may result in this world or the next; *give to negligence* disregard
136 *throughly* thoroughly   **142** *swoopstake* sweepstake, taking all stakes on the gambling table
146 *life-rend'ring* life-yielding (because the mother pelican supposedly took blood from her breast with her bill to feed her young)   **150** *sensibly* feelingly   **151** *level* plain

157   Till our scale turn the beam. O rose of May,
       Dear maid, kind sister, sweet Ophelia!
       O heavens, is't possible a young maid's wits
       Should be as mortal as an old man's life?
161   [Nature is fine in love, and where 'tis fine,
162   It sends some precious instance of itself
       After the thing it loves.]

OPHELIA:

Song.
They bore him barefaced on the bier
[Hey non nony, nony, hey nony]
And in his grave rained many a tear—

Fare you well, my dove!

LAERTES: Hadst thou thy wits, and didst persuade revenge,
       It could not move thus.

OPHELIA: You must sing 'A-down a-down, and you call him a-down-a.'
171   O, how the wheel becomes it! It is the false steward, that stole his
       master's daughter.
173   LAERTES: This nothing's more than matter.

OPHELIA: There's rosemary, that's for remembrance. Pray you, love,
       remember. And there is pansies, that's for thoughts.
176   LAERTES: A document in madness, thoughts and remembrance fitted.
177   OPHELIA: There's fennel for you, and columbines. There's rue for
       you, and here's some for me. We may call it herb of grace o'Sundays.
179   O, you must wear your rue with a difference. There's a daisy. I would
180   give you some violets, but they withered all when my father died.
       They say 'a made a good end.

[Sings]

For bonny sweet Robin is all my joy.

LAERTES: Thought and affliction, passion, hell itself,
184   She turns to favor and to prettiness.

OPHELIA:
Song.
And will'a not come again?
And will'a not come again?
    No, no, he is dead;
    Go to thy deathbed;
He never will come again.

157 *beam* bar of a balance   161 *fine* refined to purity   162 *instance* token   171 *wheel* burden,
refrain   173 *more than matter* more meaningful than sane speech   176 *document* lesson
177 *fennel* symbol of flattery; *columbines* symbol of thanklessness (?); *rue* symbol of repentance
179 *daisy* symbol of dissembling   180 *violets* symbol of faithfulness   184 *favor* charm

His beard was as white as snow,
191   All flaxen was his poll.
He is gone, he is gone,
And we cast away moan.
God 'a' mercy on his soul!

195   And of all Christian souls, I pray God. God bye you.

[Exit.]

LAERTES: Do you see this, O God?
KING: Laertes, I must commune with your grief,
Or you deny me right. Go but apart,
Make choice of whom your wisest friends you will,
And they shall hear and judge 'twixt you and me.
201   If by direct or by collateral hand
202   They find us touched, we will our kingdom give,
Our crown, our life, and all that we call ours,
To you in satisfaction; but if not,
Be you content to lend your patience to us,
And we shall jointly labor with your soul
To give it due content.
LAERTES: Let this be so.
His means of death, his obscure funeral—
209   No trophy, sword, nor hatchment o'er his bones,
210   No noble rite nor formal ostentation—
Cry to be heard, as 'twere from heaven to earth,
212   That I must call't in question.
KING: So you shall;
And where th' offense is, let the great axe fall.
I pray you go with me.

Exeunt.

IV, vi   *Enter Horatio and others.*

HORATIO: What are they that would speak with me?
GENTLEMAN: Seafaring men, sir. They say they have letters for you.
HORATIO: Let them come in.

[Exit Attendant.]

---

191 *poll* head **195** *of* on **201** *collateral* indirect **202** *touched* i.e., with the crime **209** *trophy* memorial; *hatchment* coat of arms **210** *ostentation* ceremony **212** *that* so that
IV, vi A chamber in the Castle

I do not know from what part of the world
I should be greeted, if not from Lord Hamlet.

Enter Sailors.

SAILOR: God bless you, sir.
HORATIO: Let him bless thee too.
SAILOR: 'A shall, sir, an't please him. There's a letter for you, sir—it
came from th' ambassador that was bound for England—if your
name be Horatio, as I am let to know it is.
11 HORATIO *[reads the letter]*: 'Horatio, when thou shalt have overlooked
this, give these fellows some means to the king. They have letters for
13 him. Ere we were two days old at sea, a pirate of very warlike appointment gave us chase. Finding ourselves too slow of sail, we put on a
compelled valor, and in the grapple I boarded them. On the instant
they got clear of our ship; so I alone became their prisoner. They
17 have dealt with me like thieves of mercy, but they knew what they did:
I am to do a good turn for them. Let the king have the letters I have
sent, and repair thou to me with as much speed as thou wouldest fly
death. I have words to speak in thine ear will make thee dumb; yet
21 are they much too light for the bore of the matter. These good
fellows will bring thee where I am. Rosencrantz and Guildenstern
hold their course for England. Of them I have much to tell thee.
Farewell.
          'He that thou knowest thine, Hamlet.'

Come, I will give you way for these your letters,
And do't the speedier that you may direct me
To him from whom you brought them.

                                        Exeunt.

IV, vii *Enter King and Laertes.*

KING: Now must your conscience my acquittance seal,
And you must put me in your heart for friend,
Sith you have heard, and with a knowing ear,
That he which hath your noble father slain
Pursued my life.
LAERTES: It well appears. But tell me

11-12 *overlooked* surveyed, scanned; *means* i.e., of access 13 *appointment* equipment
17 *thieves of mercy* merciful thieves 21 *bore* caliber (as of a gun) **IV, vii** A chamber in the Castle

6   Why you proceeded not against these feats
7   So crimeful and so capital in nature,
    As by your safety, wisdom, all things else,
9   You mainly were stirred up.

KING: O, for two special reasons,
    Which may to you perhaps seem much unsinewed,
    But yet to me they're strong. The queen his mother
    Lives almost by his looks, and for myself—
    My virtue or my plague, be it either which—
14   She is so conjunctive to my life and soul
    That, as the star moves not but in his sphere,
    I could not but by her. The other motive
17   Why to a public count I might not go
18   Is the great love the general gender bear him,
    Who, dipping all his faults in their affection,
    Would, like the spring that turneth wood to stone,
21   Convert his gyves to graces; so that my arrows,
    Too slightly timbered for so loud a wind,
    Would have reverted to my bow again,
    And not where I had aimed them.

LAERTES: And so have I a noble father lost,
26   A sister driven into desp'rate terms,
27   Whose worth, if praises may go back again,
28   Stood challenger on mount of all the age
    For her perfections. But my revenge will come.

KING: Break not your sleeps for that. You must not think
    That we are made of stuff so flat and dull
    That we can let our beard be shook with danger,
    And think it pastime. You shortly shall hear more.
    I loved your father, and we love ourself,
    And that, I hope, will teach you to imagine—

Enter a Messenger with letters.

[How now? What news?]
MESSENGER: [Letters, my lord, from Hamlet:]
    These to your majesty, this to the queen.
KING: From Hamlet? Who brought them?
MESSENGER: Sailors, my lord, they say; I saw them not.
    They were given me by Claudio; he received them
    Of him that brought them.

---

6 *feats* deeds   **7** *capital* punishable by death   **9** *mainly* powerfully   **14** *conjunctive* closely united
17 *count* trial, accounting   **18** *general gender* common people   **21** *gyves* fetters   **26** *terms* circumstances   **27** *back again* i.e., to her better circumstances   **28** *on mount* on a height

KING: Laertes, you shall hear them.—
   Leave us.

[*Exit Messenger.*]

[*Reads*]

43   'High and mighty, you shall know I am set naked on your kingdom.
To-morrow shall I beg leave to see your kingly eyes; when I shall
(first asking your pardon thereunto) recount the occasion of my
sudden and more strange return.   Hamlet.'
What should this mean? Are all the rest come back?
49   Or is it some abuse, and no such thing?
LAERTES: Know you the hand?
50 KING: 'Tis Hamlet's character. 'Naked'!
And in a postscript here, he says 'alone.'
52   Can you devise me?
LAERTES: I am lost in it, my lord. But let him come.
It warms the very sickness in my heart
That I shall live and tell him to his teeth,
'Thus diddest thou.'
KING: If it be so, Laertes,
(As how should it be so? how otherwise?)
Will you be ruled by me?
LAERTES: Ay, my lord,
So you will not o'errule me to a peace.
KING: To thine own peace. If he be now returned,
61   As checking at his voyage, and that he means
No more to undertake it, I will work him
To an exploit now ripe in my device,
Under the which he shall not choose but fall;
And for his death no wind of blame shall breathe,
66   But even his mother shall uncharge the practice
And call it accident.
LAERTES: My lord, I will be ruled;
The rather if you could devise it so
69   That I might be the organ.
KING: It falls right.
You have been talked of since your travel much,
And that in Hamlet's hearing, for a quality
Wherein they say you shine. Your sum of parts
Did not together pluck such envy from him

43 *naked* destitute   **49** *abuse* imposture   **50** *character* handwriting   **52** *devise* explain to
61 *checking at* turning aside from (like a falcon turning from its quarry for other prey)
66 *uncharge the practice* acquit the stratagem of being a plot   **69** *organ* instrument

As did that one, and that, in my regard,
75 Of the unworthiest siege.
LAERTES: What part is that, my lord?
76 KING: A very riband in the cap of youth,
Yet needful too, for youth no less becomes
78 The light and careless livery that it wears
79 Than settled age his sables and his weeds,
80 Importing health and graveness. Two months since
Here was a gentleman of Normandy.
I have seen myself, and served against, the French,
83 And they can well on horseback, but this gallant
Had witchcraft in't. He grew unto his seat,
And to such wondrous doing brought his horse
86 As had he been incorpsed and demi-natured
87 With the brave beast. So far he topped my thought
88 That I, in forgery of shapes and tricks,
Come short of what he did.
LAERTES: A Norman was't?
KING: A Norman.
LAERTES: Upon my life, Lamord.
KING: The very same.
92 LAERTES: I know him well. He is the brooch indeed
And gem of all the nation.
94 KING: He made confession of you,
And gave you such a masterly report
For art and exercise in your defense,
And for your rapier most especial,
That he cried out 'twould be a sight indeed
99 If one could match you. The scrimers of their nation
He swore had neither motion, guard, nor eye,
If you opposed them. Sir, this report of his
Did Hamlet so envenom with his envy
That he could nothing do but wish and beg
Your sudden coming o'er to play with you.
Now, out of this—
LAERTES: What out of this, my lord?
KING: Laertes, was your father dear to you?
Or are you like the painting of a sorrow,
A face without a heart?
LAERTES: Why ask you this?

---

75 *siege* seat, rank   **76** *riband* decoration   **78** *livery* distinctive attire   **79** *sables* dignified robes richly furred with sable; *weeds* distinctive garments   **80** *health* welfare, prosperity   **83** *can well* can perform well   **86** *incorpsed* made one body; *demi-natured* made sharer of nature half and half (as man shares with horse in the centaur)   **87** *topped* excelled; *thought* imagination of possibilities   **88** *forgery* invention   **92** *brooch* ornament   **94** *made confession* admitted the rival accomplishments   **99** *scrimers* fencers

KING: Not that I think you did not love your father,
But that I know love is begun by time,

111   And that I see, in passages of proof,

112   Time qualifies the spark and fire of it.
There lives within the very flame of love

114   A kind of wick or snuff that will abate it,

115   And nothing is at a like goodness still,

116   For goodness, growing to a plurisy,
Dies in his own too-much. That we would do
We should do when we would, for this 'would' changes,
And hath abatements and delays as many
As there are tongues, are hands, are accidents,
And then this 'should' is like a spendthrift sigh,

122   That hurts by easing. But to the quick o' th' ulcer—
Hamlet comes back; what would you undertake
To show yourself your father's son in deed
More than in words?

LAERTES: To cut his throat i' th' church!

126   KING: No place indeed should murder sanctuarize;
Revenge should have no bounds. But, good Laertes,
Will you do this? Keep close within your chamber.
Hamlet returned shall know you are come home.

130   We'll put on those shall praise your excellence
And set a double varnish on the fame

132   The Frenchman gave you, bring you in fine together

133   And wager on your heads. He, being remiss,
Most generous, and free from all contriving,

135   Will not peruse the foils, so that with ease,
Or with a little shuffling, you may choose

137   A sword unbated, and, in a pass of practice,
Requite him for your father.

LAERTES: I will do't,
And for that purpose I'll anoint my sword.

140   I bought an unction of a mountebank,
So mortal that, but dip a knife in it,

142   Where it draws blood no cataplasm so rare,

143   Collected from all simples that have virtue
Under the moon, can save the thing from death

145   That is but scratched withal. I'll touch my point

---

111 *passages of proof* incidents of experience   **112** *qualifies* weakens   **114** *snuff* unconsumed portion of the burned wick   **115** *still* always   **116** *plurisy* excess   **122** *hurts* i.e., shortens life by drawing blood from the heart (as was believed); *quick* sensitive flesh   **126** *sanctuarize* protect from punishment, give sanctuary to   **130** *put on* instigate   **132** *in fine* finally   **133** *remiss* negligent   **135** *peruse* scan   **137** *unbated* not blunted; *pass of practice* thrust made effective by trickery   **140** *unction* ointment; *mountebank* quack-doctor   **142** *cataplasm* poultice   **143** *simples* herbs   **145** *withal* with it

146   With this contagion, that, if I gall him slightly,
      It may be death.
      KING: Let's further think of this,
      Weigh what convenience both of time and means
149   May fit us to our shape. If this should fail,
150   And that our drift look through our bad performance,
      'Twere better not assayed. Therefore this project
      Should have a back or second, that might hold
153   If this did blast in proof. Soft, let me see.
      We'll make a solemn wager on your cunnings—
      I ha't!
      When in your motion you are hot and dry—
      As make your bouts more violent to that end—
158   And that he calls for drink, I'll have preferred him
159   A chalice for the nonce, whereon but sipping,
160   If he by chance escape your venomed stuck,
      Our purpose may hold there.—But stay, what noise?

Enter Queen.

      QUEEN: One woe doth tread upon another's heel,
      So fast they follow. Your sister's drowned, Laertes.
      LAERTES: Drowned! O, where?
165   QUEEN: There is a willow grows askant the brook,
166   That shows his hoar leaves in the glassy stream.
      Therewith fantastic garlands did she make
      Of crowflowers, nettles, daisies, and long purples,
169   That liberal shepherds give a grosser name,
      But our cold maids do dead men's fingers call them.
171   There on the pendent boughs her crownet weeds
      Clamb'ring to hang, an envious sliver broke,
      When down her weedy trophies and herself
      Fell in the weeping brook. Her clothes spread wide,
      And mermaid-like a while they bore her up,
176   Which time she chanted snatches of old lauds,
177   As one incapable of her own distress,
178   Or like a creature native and indued
      Unto that element. But long it could not be
      Till that her garments, heavy with their drink,
      Pulled the poor wretch from her melodious lay
      To muddy death.
      LAERTES: Alas, then she is drowned?

146 *gall* scratch   **149** *shape* plan   **150** *drift* intention; *look* show   **153** *blast in proof* burst during trial (like a faulty cannon)   **158** *preferred* offered   **159** *nonce* occasion   **160** *stuck* thrust **165** *askant* alongside   **166** *hoar* grey   **169** *liberal* free-spoken, licentious   **171** *crownet* coronet **176** *lauds* hymns   **177** *incapable of* insensible to   **178** *indued* endowed

QUEEN: Drowned, drowned.

LAERTES: Too much of water hast thou, poor Ophelia,
And therefore I forbid my tears; but yet
186   It is our trick; nature her custom holds,
Let shame say what it will. When these are gone,
188   The woman will be out. Adieu, my lord.
I have a speech o'fire, that fain would blaze
But that this folly drowns it.

Exit.

KING: Let's follow, Gertrude.
How much I had to do to calm his rage!
Now fear I this will give it start again;
Therefore let's follow.

Exeunt.

V, i   *Enter two Clowns.*

1   CLOWN: Is she to be buried in Christian burial when she willfully seeks
her own salvation?
3   OTHER: I tell thee she is. Therefore make her grave straight. The
4   crowner hath sate on her, and finds it Christian burial.
CLOWN: How can that be, unless she drowned herself in her own
defense?
OTHER: Why, 'tis found so.
8   CLOWN: It must be *se offendendo;* it cannot be else. For here lies the
point: if I drown myself wittingly, it argues an act, and an act hath
10   three branches—it is to act, to do, and to perform. Argal, she
drowned herself wittingly.
12   OTHER: Nay, but hear you, Goodman Delver.
CLOWN: Give me leave. Here lies the water—good. Here stands the
man—good. If the man go to this water and drown himself, it is, will
15   he nill he, he goes, mark you that. But if the water come to him and
drown him, he drowns not himself. Argal, he that is not guilty of his
own death shortens not his own life.
OTHER: But is this law?
19   CLOWN: Ay marry, is't—crowner's quest law.

---

186 *trick* way (i.e., to shed tears when sorrowful)   **188** *woman* unmanly part of nature.
V, i A churchyard; **s.d.** *Clowns* rustics   **1** *in Christian burial* in consecrated ground with the
prescribed service of the Church (a burial denied to suicides)   **3** *straight* straightway, at once
4 *crowner* coroner   **8** *se offendendo* a clownish transformation of *"se defendendo,"* "in self-defense"
10 *Argal* for *"ergo,"* "therefore"   **12** *Delver* Digger   **15** *will he nill he* willy-nilly   **19** *quest*
inquest

OTHER: Will you ha' the truth on't? If this had not been a gentle-woman, she should have been buried out o' Christian burial.

22 CLOWN: Why, there thou say'st. And the more pity that great folk
23 should have count'nance in this world to drown or hang themselves
24 more than their even-Christen. Come, my spade. There is no ancient gentlemen but gard'ners, ditchers, and grave-makers. They hold up Adam's profession.

OTHER: Was he a gentleman?

CLOWN: 'A was the first that ever bore arms.

29 [OTHER: Why, he had none.

CLOWN: What, art a heathen? How dost thou understand the Scripture? The Scripture says Adam digged. Could he dig without arms?] I'll put another question to thee. If thou answerest me not to the purpose, confess thyself—

OTHER: Go to.

CLOWN: What is he that builds stronger than either the mason, the shipwright, or the carpenter?

OTHER: The gallows-maker, for that frame outlives a thousand tenants.

CLOWN: I like thy wit well, in good faith. The gallows does well. But how does it well? It does well to those that do ill. Now thou dost ill to say the gallows is built stronger than the church. Argal, the gallows may do well to thee. To't again, come.

OTHER: Who builds stronger than a mason, a shipwright, or a carpenter?

45 CLOWN: Ay, tell me that, and unyoke.

OTHER: Marry, now I can tell.

CLOWN: To't.

48 OTHER: Mass, I cannot tell.

CLOWN: Cudgel thy brains no more about it, for your dull ass will not mend his pace with beating. And when you are asked this question next, say 'a grave-maker.' The houses he makes last till doomsday.
52 Go, get thee in, and fetch me a stoup of liquor.

[Exit Other Clown.].

Enter Hamlet and Horatio [as Clown digs and sings].

Song.
In youth when I did love, did love,
   Methought it was very sweet
55 To contract—O—the time for—a—my behove,
   O, methought there—a—was nothing—a—meet.

---

22 *thou say'st* you have it right **23** *count'nance* privilege **24** *even-Christen* fellow Christian
29 *had none* i.e., had no gentleman's coat of arms **45** *unyoke* i.e., unharness your powers of thought after a good day's work **48** *Mass* by the Mass **52** *stoup* large mug **55** *behove* behoof, benefit

HAMLET: Has this fellow no feeling of his business, that 'a sings at
grave-making?

59   HORATIO: Custom hath made it in him a property of easiness.

60   HAMLET: 'Tis e'en so. The hand of little employment hath the daintier
sense.

CLOWN:

Song.
But age with his stealing steps
Hath clawed me in his clutch,
64   And hath shipped me intil the land,
As if I had never been such.

[Throws up a skull.]

HAMLET: That skull had a tongue in it, and could sing once. How the
67   knave jowls it to the ground, as if 'twere Cain's jawbone, that did the
68   first murder! This might be the pate of a politician, which this ass
69   now o'erreaches; one that would circumvent God, might it not?

HORATIO: It might, my lord.

HAMLET: Or of a courtier, which could say 'Good morrow, sweet lord!
How dost thou, sweet lord? This might be my Lord Such-a-one, that
praised my Lord Such-a-one's horse when 'a meant to beg it, might
it not?

HORATIO: Ay, my lord.

76   HAMLET: Why, e'en so, and now my Lady Worm's, chapless, and
77   knocked about the mazzard with a sexton's spade. Here's fine revolution, an we had the trick to see't. Did these bones cost no more the
79   breeding but to play at loggets with 'em? Mine ache to think on't.

CLOWN:

Song.
A pickaxe and a spade, a spade,
81   For and a shrouding sheet;
O, a pit of clay for to be made
For such a guest is meet.

[Throws up another skull.]

HAMLET: There's another. Why may not that be the skull of a lawyer?
85   Where be his quiddities now, his quillities, his cases, his tenures, and

---

59 *property* peculiarity; *easiness* easy acceptability   **60-61** *daintier sense* more delicate feeling
(because the hand is less calloused)   **64** *intil* into   **67** *jowls* hurls   **68** *politician* crafty schemer
69 *o'erreaches* gets the better of (with a play upon the literal meaning)   **76** *chapless* lacking the
lower chap or jaw   **77** *mazzard* head   **79** *loggets* small pieces of wood thrown in a game
81 *For and* and   **85** *quiddities* subtleties (from scholastic *"quidditas,"* meaning the distinctive
nature of anything); *quillities* nice distinctions; *tenures* holdings of property

87 his tricks? Why does he suffer this mad knave now to knock him
about the sconce with a dirty shovel, and will not tell him of his action
of battery? Hum! This fellow might be in's time a great buyer of land,
89 with his statutes, his recognizances, his fines, his double vouchers, his
recoveries. [Is this the fine of his fines, and the recovery of his
recoveries,] to have his fine pate full of fine dirt? Will his vouchers
vouch him no more of his purchases, and double ones too, than the
93 length and breadth of a pair of indentures? The very conveyances
of his lands will scarcely lie in this box, and must th' inheritor himself
have no more, ha?

HORATIO: Not a jot more, my lord.

HAMLET: Is not parchment made of sheepskins?

HORATIO: Ay, my lord, and of calveskins too.

HAMLET: They are sheep and calves which seek out assurance in that.
I will speak to this fellow. Whose grave's this, sirrah?

CLOWN: Mine, sir.

[Sings]

> O, a pit of clay for to be made
> For such a guest is meet.

HAMLET: I think it be thine indeed, for thou liest in't.

CLOWN: You lie out on't, sir, and therefore 'tis not yours. For my part,
I do not lie in't, yet it is mine.

HAMLET: Thou dost lie in't, to be in't and say it is thine. 'Tis for the
108 dead, not for the quick; therefore thou liest.

CLOWN: 'Tis a quick lie, sir; 'twill away again from me to you.

HAMLET: What man dost thou dig it for?

CLOWN: For no man, sir.

HAMLET: What woman then?

CLOWN: For none neither.

HAMLET: Who is to be buried in't?

CLOWN: One that was a woman, sir; but, rest her soul, she's dead.

116 HAMLET: How absolute the knave is! We must speak by the card, or
117 equivocation will undo us. By the Lord, Horatio, this three years I
118 have taken note of it, the age is grown so picked that the toe of the
119 peasant comes so near the heel of the courtier he galls his kibe.—
How long hast thou been a grave-maker?

CLOWN: Of all the days i' th' year, I came to't that day that our last
king Hamlet overcame Fortinbras.

---

87 *sconce* head   **89-91** *statutes, recognizances* legal documents or bonds acknowledging debt; *fines, recoveries* modes of converting estate tail into fee simple; *vouchers* persons vouched or called on to warrant a title; *fine* end (introducing a word play involving four meanings of "fine") **93** *pair of indentures* deed or legal agreement in duplicate; *conveyances* deeds   **108** *quick* living **116** *absolute* positive; *by the card* by the card on which the points of the mariner's compass are marked, absolutely to the point   **117** *equivocation* ambiguity   **118** *picked* refined, spruce **119** *galls* chafes; *kibe* chilblain

HAMLET: How long is that since?

CLOWN: Cannot you tell that? Every fool can tell that. It was the very day that young Hamlet was born—he that is mad, and sent into England.

HAMLET: Ay, marry, why was he sent into England?

CLOWN: Why, because 'a was mad. 'A shall recover his wits there; or, if 'a do not, 'tis no great matter there.

HAMLET: Why?

CLOWN: 'Twill not be seen in him there. There the men are as mad as he.

HAMLET: How came he mad?

CLOWN: Very strangely, they say.

HAMLET: How strangely?

CLOWN: Faith, e'en with losing his wits.

HAMLET: Upon what ground?

CLOWN: Why, here in Denmark. I have been sexton here, man and boy, thirty years.

HAMLET: How long will a man lie i' th' earth ere he rot?

141 CLOWN: Faith, if 'a be not rotten before 'a die (as we have many pocky corses now-a-days that will scarce hold the laying in), 'a will last you some eight year or nine year. A tanner will last you nine year.

HAMLET: Why he more than another?

CLOWN: Why, sir, his hide is so tanned with his trade that 'a will keep out water a great while, and your water is a sore decayer of your whoreson dead body. Here's a skull now hath lien you i' th' earth three-and-twenty years.

HAMLET: Whose was it?

CLOWN: A whoreson mad fellow's it was. Whose do you think it was?

HAMLET: Nay, I know not.

CLOWN: A pestilence on him for a mad rogue! 'A poured a flagon of
153   Rhenish on my head once. This same skull, sir, was—sir—Yorick's skull, the king's jester.

HAMLET: This?

CLOWN: E'en that.

HAMLET: Let me see. *[Takes the skull.]*:   Alas, poor Yorick! I knew him, Horatio, a fellow of infinite jest, of most excellent fancy. He hath borne me on his back a thousand times. And now how abhorred in my imagination it is! My gorge rises at it. Here hung those lips that I have kissed I know not how oft. Where be your gibes now? Your gambols, your songs, your flashes of merriment that were wont to set the table on a roar? Not one now to mock your own grinning?
164   Quite chapfall'n? Now get you to my lady's chamber, and tell her,

---

141 *pocky* rotten (literally, corrupted by pox, or syphilis)   **153** *Rhenish* Rhine wine
164 *chapfall'n* lacking the lower chap, or jaw (with a play on the sense "down in the mouth," "dejected")

165   let her paint an inch thick, to his favor she must come. Make her
        laugh at that. Prithee, Horatio, tell me one thing.
HORATIO: What's that, my lord?
HAMLET: Dost thou think Alexander looked o' this fashion i' th' earth?
HORATIO: E'en so.
HAMLET: And smelt so? Pah!

[Puts down the skull.]

HORATIO: E'en so, my lord.
HAMLET: To what base uses we may return, Horatio! Why may not
        imagination trace the noble dust of Alexander till 'a find it stopping
        a bunghole?
175 HORATIO: 'Twere to consider too curiously, to consider so.
176 HAMLET: No, faith, not a jot, but to follow him thither with modesty
        enough, and likelihood to lead it; as thus: Alexander died, Alexander
        was buried, Alexander returneth to dust; the dust is earth; of earth
        we make loam; and why of that loam whereto he was converted might
        they not stop a beer barrel?
181 Imperious Caesar, dead and turned to clay,
        Might stop a hole to keep the wind away.
        O, that that earth which kept the world in awe
184 Should patch a wall t' expel the winter's flaw!
        But soft, but soft awhile! Here comes the king—

> *Enter King, Queen, Laertes, and the Corse [with*
> *Lords attendant and a Doctor of Divinity as Priest].*

        The queen, the courtiers. Who is this they follow?
        And with such maimèd rites? This doth betoken
        The corse they follow did with desp'rate hand
189 Fordo it own life. 'Twas of some estate.
190 Couch we awhile, and mark.

[Retires with Horatio.]

LAERTES: What ceremony else?
HAMLET: That is Laertes,
        A very noble youth. Mark.
LAERTES: What ceremony else?
DOCTOR: Her obsequies have been as far enlarged
        As we have warranty. Her death was doubtful,
        And, but that great command o'ersways the order,

---

165 *favor* countenance, aspect   **175** *curiously* minutely   **176** *modesty* moderation   **181** *Imperious*
imperial   **184** *flaw* gust of wind   **189** *Fordo* destroy; *it* its; *estate* rank   **190** *Couch* hide

She should in ground unsanctified have lodged
Till the last trumpet. For charitable prayers,
199   Shards, flints, and pebbles should be thrown on her.
200   Yet here she is allowed her virgin crants,
201   Her maiden strewments, and the bringing home
Of bell and burial.
LAERTES: Must there no more be done?
DOCTOR: No more be done.
We should profane the service of the dead
To sing a requiem and such rest to her
As to peace-parted souls.
LAERTES: Lay her i' th' earth,
And from her fair and unpolluted flesh
May violets spring! I tell thee, churlish priest,
A minist'ring angel shall my sister be
When thou liest howling.
HAMLET: What, the fair Ophelia?
QUEEN: Sweets to the sweet! Farewell.

[Scatters flowers.]

I hoped thou shouldst have been my Hamlet's wife.
I thought thy bride-bed to have decked, sweet maid,
And not have strewed thy grave.
LAERTES: O, treble woe
Fall ten times treble on that cursèd head
216   Whose wicked deed thy most ingenious sense
Deprived thee of! Hold off the earth awhile,
Till I have caught her once more in mine arms.

[Leaps in the grave.]

Now pile your dust upon the quick and dead
Till of this flat a mountain you have made
221   T' o'ertop old Pelion or the skyish head
Of blue Olympus.
HAMLET *[coming forward]*:   What is he whose grief
Bears such an emphasis? whose phrase of sorrow
225   Conjures the wand'ring stars, and makes them stand

199 *Shards* broken pieces of pottery   **200** *crants* garland   **201** *strewments* strewings of the grave with flowers; *bringing home* laying to rest   **216** *most ingenious* of quickest apprehension **221** *Pelion* a mountain in Thessaly, like Olympus and also Ossa (the allusion being to the war in which the Titans fought the gods and attempted to heap Ossa and Olympus on Pelion, or Pelion and Ossa on Olympus, in order to scale heaven)   **225** *Conjures* charms, puts a spell upon; *wand'ring stars* planets

Like wonder-wounded hearers? This is I,
Hamlet the Dane.

[Leaps in after Laertes.]

LAERTES   The devil take thy soul!

[Grapples with him.]

HAMLET: Thou pray'st not well.
　　I prithee take thy fingers from my throat,
230　For, though I am not splenitive and rash,
　　Yet have I in me something dangerous,
　　Which let thy wisdom fear. Hold off thy hand.
KING: Pluck them asunder.
QUEEN: Hamlet, Hamlet!
ALL: Gentlemen!
HORATIO: Good my lord, be quiet.

[Attendants part them, and they come out of the grave.]

HAMLET: Why, I will fight with him upon this theme
　　Until my eyelids will no longer wag.
QUEEN: O my son, what theme?
HAMLET: I loved Ophelia. Forty thousand brothers
　　Could not with all their quantity of love
　　Make up my sum. What wilt thou do for her?
KING: O, he is mad, Laertes.
QUEEN: For love of God, forbear him.
HAMLET: 'Swounds, show me what thou't do.
244　Woo't weep? woo't fight? woo't fast? woo't tear thyself?
245　Woo't drink up esill? eat a crocodile?
　　I'll do't. Dost thou come here to whine?
　　To outface me with leaping in her grave?
248　Be buried quick with her, and so will I.
　　And if thou prate of mountains, let them throw
　　Millions of acres on us, till our ground,
　　Singeing his pate against the burning zone,
　　Make Ossa like a wart! Nay, an thou'lt mouth,
　　I'll rant as well as thou.
253　QUEEN: This is mere madness;
　　And thus a while the fit will work on him.

230 *splenitive* of fiery temper (the spleen being considered the seat of anger)   **244** *Woo't* wilt
(thou)   **245** *esill* vinegar   **248** *quick* alive   **253** *mere* absolute

Anon, as patient as the female dove
256   When that her golden couplets are disclosed,
His silence will sit drooping.
HAMLET: Hear you, sir.
What is the reason that you use me thus?
I loved you ever. But it is no matter.
Let Hercules himself do what he may,
The cat will mew, and dog will have his day.
KING: I pray thee, good Horatio, wait upon him.

Exit Hamlet and Horatio.

[To Laertes]

263   Strengthen your patience in our last night's speech.
264   We'll put the matter to the present push.—
Good Gertrude, set some watch over your son.—
This grave shall have a living monument.
An hour of quiet shortly shall we see;
Till then in patience our proceeding be.

Exeunt.

V, ii   *Enter Hamlet and Horatio.*

HAMLET: So much for this, sir; now shall you see the other.
You do remember all the circumstance?
HORATIO: Remember it, my lord!
HAMLET: Sir, in my heart there was a kind of fighting
That would not let me sleep. Methought I lay
6   Worse than the mutines in the bilboes. Rashly,
And praised be rashness for it—let us know,
Our indiscretion sometime serves us well
9   When our deep plots do pall, and that should learn us
There's a divinity that shapes our ends,
11   Rough-hew them how we will—
HORATIO: That is most certain.
HAMLET: Up from my cabin,
My sea-gown scarfed about me, in the dark
Groped I to find out them, had my desire,
15   Fingered their packet, and in fine withdrew

256 *couplets* pair of fledglings; *disclosed* hatched   263 *in* by calling to mind   264 *present push*
immediate trial   **V, ii** The hall of the Castle   6 *mutines* mutineers; *bilboes* fetters   9 *pall* fail
11 *Rough-hew* shape roughly in trial form   15 *Fingered* filched; *in fine* finally

To mine own room again, making so bold,
My fears forgetting manners, to unseal
Their grand commission; where I found, Horatio—
Ah, royal knavery!—an exact command,
20 Larded with many several sorts of reasons,
21 Importing Denmark's health, and England's too,
22 With, ho! such bugs and goblins in my life,
23 That on the supervise, no leisure bated,
No, not to stay the grinding of the axe,
My head should be struck off.
HORATIO: Is't possible?
HAMLET: Here's the commission; read it at more leisure.
  But wilt thou hear me how I did proceed?
HORATIO: I beseech you.
HAMLET: Being thus benetted round with villainies,
30 Or I could make a prologue to my brains,
They had begun the play. I sat me down,
Devised a new commission, wrote it fair.
33 I once did hold it, as our statists do,
34 A baseness to write fair, and labored much
How to forget that learning, but, sir, now
36 It did me yeoman's service. Wilt thou know
37 Th' effect of what I wrote?
HORATIO: Ay, good my lord.
HAMLET: An earnest conjuration from the king,
As England was his faithful tributary,
As love between them like the palm might flourish,
41 As peace should still her wheaten garland wear
42 And stand a comma 'tween their amities,
43 And many such-like as's of great charge,
That on the view and knowing of these contents,
Without debatement further, more or less,
He should the bearers put to sudden death,
47 Not shriving time allowed.
HORATIO: How was this sealed?
48 HAMLET: Why, even in that was heaven ordinant.
I had my father's signet in my purse,
50 Which was the model of that Danish seal,
Folded the writ up in the form of th' other,

---

20 *Larded* enriched   **21** *Importing* relating to   **22** *bugs* bugbears; *in my life* to be encountered as dangers if I should be allowed to live   **23** *supervise* perusal; *bated* deducted, allowed   **30** *Or* ere   **33** *statists* statesmen   **34** *fair* with professional clarity (like a clerk or a scrivener, not like a gentleman)   **36** *yeoman's service* stout service such as yeomen foot soldiers gave as archers   **37** *effect* purport   **41** *wheaten garland* adornment of fruitful agriculture   **42** *comma* connective (because it indicates continuity of thought in a sentence)   **43** *charge* burden (with a double meaning to fit a play that makes *as's* into "asses")   **47** *shriving time* time for confession and absolution   **48** *ordinant* controlling   **50** *model* counterpart

52   Subscribed it, gave't th' impression, placed it safely,
      The changeling never known. Now, the next day
54   Was our sea-fight, and what to this was sequent
      Thou know'st already.
      HORATIO: So Guildenstern and Rosencrantz go to't.
      HAMLET: [Why, man, they did make love to this employment.]
      They are not near my conscience; their defeat
59   Does by their own insinuation grow.
      'Tis dangerous when the baser nature comes
61   Between the pass and fell incensèd points
      Of mighty opposites.
      HORATIO: Why, what a king is this!
63   HAMLET: Does it not, think thee, stand me now upon—
      He that hath killed my king, and whored my mother,
65   Popped in between th' election and my hopes,
66   Thrown out his angle for my proper life,
67   And with such coz'nage—is't not perfect conscience
68   [To quit him with this arm? And is't not to be damned
69   To let this canker of our nature come
      In further evil?
      HORATIO: It must be shortly known to him from England
      What is the issue of the business there.
      HAMLET: It will be short; the interim is mine,
      And a man's life's no more than to say 'one.'
      But I am very sorry, good Horatio,
      That to Laertes I forgot myself,
      For by the image of my cause I see
      The portraiture of his. I'll court his favors.
79   But sure the bravery of his grief did put me
      Into a tow'ring passion.
      HORATIO: Peace, who comes here?]

Enter [Osric,] a courtier.

      OSRIC: Your lordship is right welcome back to Denmark.
      HAMLET: I humbly thank you, sir. *[aside to Horatio]* Dost know this
      waterfly?
      HORATIO: *[aside to Hamlet]* No, my good lord.
      HAMLET: *[aside to Horatio]* Thy state is the more gracious, for 'tis a vice
      to know him. He hath much land, and fertile. Let a beast be lord of
87   beasts, and his crib shall stand at the king's mess. 'Tis a chough, but,
      as I say, spacious in the possession of dirt.

52 *impression* i.e., of the signet   **54** *sequent* subsequent   **59** *insinuation* intrusion   **61** *pass* thrust;
fell fierce   **63** *stand* rest incumbent   **65** *election* i.e., to the kingship (the Danish kingship being
elective)   **66** *angle* fishing line; *proper* own   **67** *coz'nage* cozenage, trickery   **68** *quit* repay
69 *canker* cancer, ulcer   **79** *bravery* ostentatious display   **87** *mess* table; *chough* jackdaw, chat-
terer

OSRIC: Sweet lord, if your lordship were at leisure, I should impart a thing to you from his majesty.

HAMLET: I will receive it, sir, with all diligence of spirit. Put your bonnet to his right use. 'Tis for the head.

OSRIC: I thank your lordship, it is very hot.

HAMLET: No, believe me, 'tis very cold; the wind is northerly.

95 OSRIC: It is indifferent cold, my lord, indeed.

96 HAMLET: But yet methinks it is very sultry and hot for my complexion.

OSRIC: Exceedingly, my lord; it is very sultry, as 'twere—I cannot tell how. But, my lord, his majesty bade me signify to you that 'a has laid a great wager on your head. Sir, this is the matter—

100 HAMLET: I beseech you remember.

[Hamlet moves him to put on his hat.]

101 OSRIC: Nay, good my lord; for mine ease, in good faith. Sir, here is newly come to court Laertes—believe me, an absolute gentleman,

103 full of most excellent differences, of very soft society and great

104 showing. Indeed, to speak feelingly of him, he is the card or calendar

105 of gentry; for you shall find in him the continent of what part a gentleman would see.

107 HAMLET: Sir, his definement suffers no perdition in you, though, I

108 know, to divide him inventorially would dozy th' arithmetic of mem-

109 ory, and yet but yaw neither in respect of his quick sail. But, in the

110 verity of extolment, I take him to be a soul of great article, and his

111 infusion of such dearth and rareness as, to make true diction of him,

112 his semblable is his mirror, and who else would trace him, his um-

113 brage, nothing more.

OSRIC: Your lordship speaks most infallibly of him.

115 HAMLET: The concernancy, sir? Why do we wrap the gentleman in our

116 more rawer breath?

OSRIC: Sir?

HORATIO: Is't not possible to understand in another tongue? You will

119 to't, sir, really.

120 HAMLET: What imports the nomination of this gentleman?

OSRIC: Of Laertes?

HORATIO *[aside to Hamlet]*:   His purse is empty already. All's golden words are spent.

---

95 *indifferent* somewhat   **96** *complexion* temperament   **100** *remember* i.e., remember you have done all that courtesy demands   **101** *for mine ease* i.e., I keep my hat off just for comfort (a conventional polite phrase)   **103** *differences* differentiating characteristics, special qualities; *soft society* gentle manners; *great showing* noble appearance   **104** *feelingly* appropriately; *card* map; *calendar* guide   **105** *gentry* gentlemanliness; *continent* all-containing embodiment (with an implication of geographical continent to go with *card*)   **107** *definement* definition; *perdition* loss **108** *dozy* dizzy, stagger   **109** *yaw* hold to a course unsteadily like a ship that steers wild; *neither* for all that; *in respect of* in comparison with   **110** *article* scope, importance;   **111** *infusion* essence; *dearth* scarcity   **112** *semblable* likeness (i.e., only true likeness); *trace* follow   **113** *umbrage* shadow   **115** *concernancy* relevance   **116** *rawer breath* cruder speech   **119** *to't* i.e., get to an understanding   **120** *nomination* mention

HAMLET: Of him, sir.

OSRIC: I know you are not ignorant—

HAMLET: I would you did, sir; yet, in faith, if you did, it would not
127   much approve me. Well, sir?

OSRIC: You are not ignorant of what excellence Laertes is—

129   HAMLET: I dare not confess that, lest I should compare with him in
excellence; but to know a man well were to know himself.

OSRIC: I mean, sir, for his weapon; but in the imputation laid on him
132   by them, in his meed he's unfellowed.

HAMLET: What's his weapon?

OSRIC: Rapier and dagger.

HAMLET: That's two of his weapons—but well.

OSRIC: The king, sir, hath wagered with him six Barbary horses,
137   against the which he has impawned, as I take it, six French rapiers
138   and poniards, with their assigns, as girdle, hangers, and so. Three
139   of the carriages, in faith, are very dear to fancy, very responsive to
140   to the hilts, most delicate carriages, and of very liberal conceit.

HAMLET: What call you the carriages?

142   HORATIO *[aside to Hamlet]*:   I knew you must be edified by the margent
ere you had done.

OSRIC: The carriages, sir, are the hangers.

HAMLET: The phrase would be more germane to the matter if we
could carry a cannon by our sides. I would it might be hangers till
then. But on! Six Barbary horses against six French swords, their
assigns, and three liberal-conceited carriages—that's the French bet
against the Danish. Why is this all impawned, as you call it?

OSRIC: The king, sir, hath laid, sir, that in a dozen passes between
yourself and him he shall not exceed you three hits; he hath laid on
twelve for nine, and it would come to immediate trial if your lordship
would vouchsafe the answer.

HAMLET: How if I answer no?

OSRIC: I mean, my lord, the opposition of your person in trial.

HAMLET: Sir, I will walk here in the hall. If it please his majesty, it is
157   the breathing time of day with me. Let the foils be brought, the
gentleman willing, and the king hold his purpose, I will win for
159   him an I can; if not, I will gain nothing but my shame and the odd
hits.

OSRIC: Shall I redeliver you e'en so?

HAMLET: To this effect, sir, after what flourish your nature will.

OSRIC: I commend my duty to your lordship.

---

127 *approve me* be to my credit   **129** *compare* compete   **132** *meed* worth   **137** *impawned* staked
138 *assigns* appurtenances; *hangers* straps by which the sword hangs from the belt
139 *dear to fancy* finely designed; *responsive* corresponding closely   **140** *liberal conceit* tasteful
design, refined conception   **142** *margent* margin (i.e., explanatory notes there printed)
157 *breathing time* exercise hour   **159** *an* if

HAMLET: Yours, yours. *[Exit Osric.]* He does well to commend it himself; there are no tongues else for's turn.

166   HORATIO: This lapwing runs away with the shell on his head.

167   HAMLET: 'A did comply, sir, with his dug before 'a sucked it. Thus has
168   he, and many more of the same bevy that I know the drossy age dotes
on, only got the tune of the time and, out of an habit of encounter,
a kind of yeasty collection, which carries them through and through
171   the most fanned and winnowed opinions; and do but blow them to
their trial, the bubbles are out.

Enter a Lord.

LORD: My lord, his majesty commended him to you by young Osric,
who brings back to him that you attend him in the hall. He sends to
know if your pleasure hold to play with Laertes, or that you will take
longer time.

HAMLET: I am constant to my purposes; they follow the king's pleasure. If his fitness speaks, mine is ready; now or whensoever, provided
I be so able as now.

LORD: The king and queen and all are coming down.

181   HAMLET: In happy time.

182   LORD: The queen desires you to use some gentle entertainment to
Laertes before you fall to play.

HAMLET: She well instructs me.

[Exit Lord.]

HORATIO: You will lose this wager, my lord.

HAMLET: I do not think so. Since he went into France I have been in
continual practice. I shall win at the odds. But thou wouldst not think
how ill all's here about my heart. But it is no matter.

HORATIO: Nay, good my lord—

190   HAMLET: It is but foolery, but it is such a kind of gaingiving as would
perhaps trouble a woman.

HORATIO: If your mind dislike anything, obey it. I will forestall their
repair hither and say you are not fit.

HAMLET: Not a whit, we defy augury. There is special providence in
the fall of a sparrow. If it be now, 'tis not to come; if it be not to come,
196   it will be now; if it be not now, yet it will come. The readiness is all.
Since no man of aught he leaves knows, what is't to leave betimes?
Let be.

---

166 *lapwing* a bird reputed to be so precocious as to run as soon as hatched   **167** *comply* observe
formalities of courtesy; *dug* mother's nipple   **168** *bevy* company; *drossy* frivolous   **171** *fanned
and winnowed* select and refined   **181** *In happy time* I am happy (a polite response)
182 *entertainment* words of reception or greeting   **190** *gaingiving* misgiving   **196** *all* all that
matters

A table prepared. [Enter] Trumpets, Drums, and Officers with cushions; King, Queen, [Osric,] and all the State, [with] foils, daggers, [and stoups of wine borne in;] and Laertes.

KING: Come, Hamlet, come, and take this hand from me.

[The King puts Laertes' hand into Hamlet's.]

HAMLET: Give me your pardon, sir. I have done you wrong,
But pardon't, as you are a gentleman.
202   This presence knows, and you must needs have heard,
How I am punished with a sore distraction.
What I have done
205   That might your nature, honor, and exception
Roughly awake, I here proclaim was madness.
Was't Hamlet wronged Laertes? Never Hamlet.
If Hamlet from himself be ta'en away,
And when he's not himself does wrong Laertes,
Then Hamlet does it not, Hamlet denies it.
Who does it then? His madness. If't be so,
212   Hamlet is of the faction that is wronged;
His madness is poor Hamlet's enemy.
Sir, in this audience,
Let my disclaiming from a purposed evil
Free me so far in your most generous thoughts
That I have shot my arrow o'er the house
And hurt my brother.
218   LAERTES: I am satisfied in nature,
Whose motive in this case should stir me most
220   To my revenge. But in my terms of honor
I stand aloof, and will no reconcilement
Till by some elder masters of known honor
223   I have a voice and precedent of peace
224   To keep my name ungored. But till that time
I do receive your offered love like love,
And will not wrong it.
HAMLET: I embrace it freely,
And will this brother's wager frankly play.
Give us the foils. Come on.
LAERTES: Come, one for me.
229   HAMLET: I'll be your foil, Laertes. In mine ignorance

202 *presence* assembly   **205** *exception* disapproval   **212** *faction* body of persons taking a side in a contention   **218** *nature* natural feeling as a person   **220** *terms of honor* position as a man of honor   **223** *voice* authoritative statement   **224** *ungored* uninjured   **229** *foil* setting that displays a jewel advantageously (with a play upon the meaning "weapon")

Your skill shall, like a star i' th' darkest night,
231   Stick fiery off indeed.
LAERTES: You mock me, sir.
HAMLET: No, by this hand.
KING: Give them the foils, young Osric. Cousin Hamlet,
   You know the wager?
HAMLET: Very well, my lord.
   Your grace has laid the odds o' th' weaker side.
KING: I do not fear it, I have seen you both;
   But since he is bettered, we have therefore odds.
LAERTES: This is too heavy; let me see another.
HAMLET: This likes me well. These foils have all a length?

[Prepare to play.]

OSRIC: Ay, my good lord.
KING: Set me the stoups of wine upon that table.
   If Hamlet give the first or second hit,
243   Or quit in answer of the third exchange,
   Let all the battlements their ordnance fire.
   The king shall drink to Hamlet's better breath,
246   And in the cup an union shall he throw
   Richer than that which four successive kings
   In Denmark's crown have worn. Give me the cups,
249   And let the kettle to the trumpet speak,
   The trumpet to the cannoneer without,
   The cannons to the heavens, the heaven to earth,
   "Now the king drinks to Hamlet." Come, begin.

Trumpets the while.

And you, the judges, bear a wary eye.
HAMLET: Come on, sir.
LAERTES: Come, my lord.

[They play.]

HAMLET: One.
LAERTES: No.
HAMLET: Judgment?
OSRIC: A hit, a very palpable hit.

Drum, trumpets, and shot. Flourish; a piece goes off.

231 *Stick fiery off* show in brilliant relief   **243** *quit* repay by a hit   **246** *union* pearl
249 *kettle* kettledrum

LAERTES: Well, again.

KING: Stay, give me drink. Hamlet, this pearl is thine.
   Here's to thy health. Give him the cup.

HAMLET: I'll play this bout first; set it by awhile.
   Come. *[They play.]* Another hit. What say you?

LAERTES: A touch, a touch; I do confess't.

KING: Our son shall win.

261   QUEEN: He's fat, and scant of breath.

262   Here, Hamlet, take my napkin, rub thy brows.

263   The queen carouses to thy fortune, Hamlet.

HAMLET: Good madam!

KING: Gertrude, do not drink.

QUEEN: I will, my lord; I pray you pardon me.

[Drinks.]

KING *[aside]*:   It is the poisoned cup; it is too late.

HAMLET: I dare not drink yet, madam—by and by.

QUEEN: Come, let me wipe thy face.

LAERTES: My lord, I'll hit him now.

KING: I do not think't.

LAERTES *[aside]*:   And yet it is almost against my conscience.

HAMLET: Come for the third, Laertes. You but dally.
   I pray you pass with your best violence;

273   I am afeard you make a wanton of me.

LAERTES: Say you so? Come on.

[They play.]

OSRIC: Nothing neither way.

LAERTES: Have at you now!

*[In scuffling they change rapiers, and both are wounded with the poisoned
   weapon.]*

KING: Part them. They are incensed.

HAMLET: Nay, come—again!

[The Queen falls.]

OSRIC: Look to the queen there, ho!

HORATIO: They bleed on both sides. How is it, my lord?

OSRIC: How is't, Laertes?

---

261 *fat* not physically fit, out of training   **262** *napkin* handkerchief   **263** *carouses* drinks a toast
273 *wanton* pampered child

280 LAERTES: Why, as a woodcock to mine own springe, Osric.
    I am justly killed with mine own treachery.
    HAMLET: How does the queen?
282 KING: She sounds to see them bleed.
    QUEEN: No, no, the drink, the drink! O my dear Hamlet!
    The drink, the drink! I am poisoned.

[Dies.]

    HAMLET: O villainy! Ho! let the door be locked.
    Treachery! Seek it out.

[Laertes falls.]

    LAERTES: It is here, Hamlet. Hamlet, thou art slain;
    No med'cine in the world can do thee good.
    In thee there is not half an hour's life.
    The treacherous instrument is in thy hand,
291 Unbated and envenomed. The foul practice
    Hath turned itself on me. Lo, here I lie,
    Never to rise again. Thy mother's poisoned.
    I can no more. The king, the king's to blame.
    HAMLET: The point envenomed too?
    Then venom, to thy work.

[Hurts the King.]

    ALL: Treason! treason!
    KING: O, yet defend me, friends. I am but hurt.
    HAMLET: Here, thou incestuous, murd'rous, damnèd Dane,
    Drink off this potion. Is thy union here?
    Follow my mother.

[King dies.]

    LAERTES: He is justly served.
302 It is a poison tempered by himself.
    Exchange forgiveness with me, noble Hamlet.
    Mine and my father's death come not upon thee,
    Nor thine on me!

[Dies.]

---

280 *woodcock* a bird reputed to be stupid and easily trapped; *springe* trap   **282** *sounds* swoons
291 *Unbated* unblunted; *practice* stratagem   **302** *tempered* mixed

HAMLET: Heaven make thee free of it! I follow thee.
I am dead, Horatio. Wretched queen, adieu!
You that look pale and tremble at this chance,
309   That are but mutes or audience to this act,
310   Had I but time—as this fell sergeant, Death,
Is strict in his arrest—O, I could tell you—
But let it be. Horatio, I am dead;
Thou livest; report me and my cause aright
To the unsatisfied.
HORATIO: Never believe it.
I am more an antique Roman than a Dane.
Here's yet some liquor left.
HAMLET: As th' art a man,
Give me the cup. Let go. By heaven, I'll ha't!
O God, Horatio, what a wounded name,
Things standing thus unknown, shall live behind me!
If thou didst ever hold me in thy heart,
Absent thee from felicity awhile,
And in this harsh world draw thy breath in pain,
To tell my story.

A march afar off.

                        What warlike noise is this?
OSRIC: Young Fortinbras, with conquest come from Poland,
To the ambassadors of England gives
This warlike volley.
HAMLET: O, I die, Horatio!
327   The potent poison quite o'ercrows my spirit.
I cannot live to hear the news from England,
329   But I do prophesy th' election lights
330   On Fortinbras. He has my dying voice.
331   So tell him, with th' occurrents, more and less,
332   Which have solicited—the rest is silence.

Dies.

HORATIO: Now cracks a noble heart. Good night, sweet prince,
And flights of angels sing thee to thy rest!

[March within.]

---

309 *mutes* actors in a play who speak no lines   **310** *sergeant* sheriff's officer   **327** *o'ercrows* triumphs over (like a victor in a cockfight)   **329** *election* i.e., to the throne   **330** *voice* vote   **331** *occurrents* occurrences   **332** *solicited* incited, provoked

Why does the drum come hither?

*Enter Fortinbras, with the Ambassadors [and with
his train of Drum, Colors, and Attendants].*

FORTINBRAS: Where is this sight?
HORATIO: What is it you would see?
If aught of woe or wonder, cease your search.
338 FORTINBRAS: This quarry cries on havoc. O proud Death,
339   What feast is toward in thine eternal cell
That thou so many princes at a shot
So bloodily hast struck?
AMBASSADOR: The sight is dismal;
And our affairs from England come too late.
The ears are senseless that should give us hearing
To tell him his commandment is fulfilled,
That Rosencrantz and Guildenstern are dead.
Where should we have our thanks?
HORATIO: Not from his mouth,
Had it th' ability of life to thank you.
He never gave commandment for their death.
349   But since, so jump upon this bloody question,
You from the Polack wars, and you from England,
Are here arrived, give order that these bodies
352   High on a stage be placèd to the view,
And let me speak to th' yet unknowing world
How these things came about. So shall you hear
Of carnal, bloody, and unnatural acts,
356   Of accidental judgments, casual slaughters,
357   Of deaths put on by cunning and forced cause,
And, in this upshot, purposes mistook
Fall'n on th' inventors' heads. All this can I
Truly deliver.
FORTINBRAS: Let us haste to hear it,
And call the noblest to the audience.
For me, with sorrow I embrace my fortune.
364   I have some rights of memory in this kingdom,
365   Which now to claim my vantage doth invite me.
HORATIO: Of that I shall have also cause to speak,
367   And from his mouth whose voice will draw on more.

---

338 *quarry* pile of dead (literally, of dead deer gathered after the hunt); *cries on* proclaims loudly; *havoc* indiscriminate killing and destruction such as would follow the order "havoc," or "pillage," given to an army   **339** *toward* forthcoming   **349** *jump* precisely   **352** *stage* platform   **356** *judgments* retributions; *casual* not humanly planned (reinforcing *accidental*)   **357** *put on* instigated   **364** *of memory* traditional and kept in mind   **365** *vantage* advantageous opportunity   **367** *more* i.e., more voices, or votes, for the kingship

368   But let this same be presently performed,
        Even while men's minds are wild, lest more mischance
370   On plots and errors happen.
        FORTINBRAS: Let four captains
        Bear Hamlet like a soldier to the stage,
372   For he was likely, had he been put on,
373   To have proved most royal; and for his passage
        The soldiers' music and the rites of war
        Speak loudly for him.
        Take up the bodies. Such a sight as this
        Becomes the field, but here shows much amiss.
        Go, bid the soldiers shoot.

                              *Exeunt [marching; after the which
                              a peal of ordinance are shot off].*

                                              (1604)

368 *presently* immediately **370** *On* on the basis of **372** *put on* set to perform in office
373 *passage* death

Arthur Miller

(b. 1 9 1 5)

One of the most distinguished modern American dramatists is Arthur Miller, who was born in New York City. After obtaining a B.A. in journalism at the University of Michigan in 1938, he wrote scripts and radio plays for CBS and NBC for the next five years. His first play, *The Man Who Had All the Luck,* was followed by the successful *All My Sons* (1947), which established Miller as one of the country's finest young dramatists. In 1956, the year he married actress Marilyn Monroe, Miller refused to betray his left-wing friends to Joseph McCarthy's congressional committee; he was convicted for contempt of Congress, but the conviction was overturned by the court of appeals. Miller and Monroe were divorced in 1961. Miller has won two Pulitzer prizes, for *Death of a Salesman* and for *A View from the Bridge.*

Miller writes well-made plays in the tradition of playwrights such as Henrik Ibsen and George Bernard Shaw, although the experimental techniques of Bertolt Brecht and Luigi Pirandello are evident in his work. Within this traditional framework Miller has written innovative plays. He has evolved a dramatic construction that allows the extensive exploration of ideas among his characters but does not cause the play to be moralizing or didactic. His dialogue captures the idioms and rhythms of middle-American speech patterns. *Death of a Salesman* is a fine modern tragedy that describes the experiences of the common man. The dialogue is rooted in realism yet powerfully poetic. At the center of Miller's dramas are individuals caught by society's standards in situations that are intolerable to their integrity.

Miller's major plays include *All My Sons* (1947), *Death of a Salesman* (1949), *The Crucible* (1953), *A View from the Bridge* (1955), *After the Fall* (1964), *The Price* (1968), and *The American Clock* (1979). He also wrote a filmscript, *The Misfits* (1961), and has published a collection of stories, a novel, a collection of essays, and, with his wife Inge Martin, three travel books.

ARTHUR MILLER

Death of a Salesman

Certain private conversations in two acts and a requiem

CAST
(in order of appearance)
Willy Loman
Linda
Biff
Happy
Bernard
The Woman
Charley
Uncle Ben
Howard Wagner
Jenny
Stanley
Miss Forsythe
Letta

The action takes place in Willy Loman's house and yard and in various places he visits in the New York and Boston of today.

Throughout the play, in the stage directions, left and right mean stage left and stage right.

ACT ONE

A melody is heard, played upon a flute. It is small and fine, telling of grass and trees and the horizon. The curtain rises.

Before us is the Salesman's house. We are aware of towering, angular shapes behind it, surrounding it on all sides. Only the blue light of the sky falls upon the house and forestage; the surrounding area shows an angry glow of orange. As more light appears, we see a solid vault of apartment houses around the small, fragile-seeming home. An air of the dream clings to the place, a dream rising out of reality. The kitchen at center seems actual enough, for there is a kitchen table with three chairs, and a refrigerator. But no other fixtures are seen. At the back of the kitchen there is a draped entrance, which leads to the living-room. To the right of the kitchen, on a level raised two feet, is a bedroom furnished only with a brass bedstead and a straight chair. On a shelf over the bed a silver athletic trophy stands. A window opens onto the apartment house at the side.

Behind the kitchen, on a level raised six and a half feet, is the boys' bedroom, at present barely visible. Two beds are dimly seen, and at the back of the room a dormer window. (This bedroom is above the unseen living-room.) At the left a stairway curves up to it from the kitchen.

The entire setting is wholly or, in some places, partially transparent. The roof-line of the house is one-dimensional; under and over it we see the apartment buildings. Before the house lies an apron, curving beyond the forestage into the orchestra. This forward area serves as the back yard as well as the locale of all Willy's imaginings and of his city scenes. Whenever the action is in the present the actors observe the imaginary wall-lines, entering the house only through its door at the left. But in the scenes of the past these boundaries are broken, and characters enter or leave a room by stepping "through" a wall onto the forestage.

From the right, Willy Loman, the Salesman, enters, carrying two large sample cases. The flute plays on. He hears but is not aware of it. He is past sixty years of age, dressed quietly. Even as he crosses the stage to the doorway of the house, his exhaustion is apparent. He unlocks the door, comes into the kitchen, and thankfully lets his burden down, feeling the soreness of his palms. A word-sigh escapes his lips—it might be "Oh, boy, oh, boy." He closes the door, then carries his cases out into the living-room, through the draped kitchen doorway.

Linda, his wife, has stirred in her bed at the right. She gets out and puts on a robe, listening. Most often jovial, she has developed an iron repression of her exceptions to Willy's behavior—she more than loves him, she admires him, as though his mercurial nature, his temper, his massive dreams and little cruelties, served her only as sharp reminders of the turbulent longings within him, longings which she shares but lacks the temperament to utter and follow to their end.

LINDA (*Hearing Willy outside the bedroom, calls with some trepidation*):   Willy!

WILLY: It's all right. I came back.

LINDA: Why? What happened? (*Slight pause.*) Did something happen, Willy?

WILLY: No, nothing happened.

LINDA: You didn't smash the car, did you?

WILLY (*With casual irritation*):   I said nothing happened. Didn't you hear me?

LINDA: Don't you feel well?

WILLY: I'm tired to the death. (*The flute has faded away. He sits on the bed beside her, a little numb.*) I couldn't make it. I just couldn't make it, Linda.

LINDA (*Very carefully, delicately*):   Where were you all day? You look terrible.

WILLY: I got as far as a little above Yonkers. I stopped for a cup of coffee. Maybe it was the coffee.

LINDA: What?

WILLY (*After a pause*):   I suddenly couldn't drive any more. The car kept going off onto the shoulder, y'know?

LINDA (*Helpfully*):   Oh. Maybe it was the steering again. I don't think Angelo knows the Studebaker.

WILLY: No, it's me, it's me. Suddenly I realize I'm goin' sixty miles an hour and I don't remember the last five minutes. I'm—I can't seem to—keep my mind to it.

LINDA: Maybe it's your glasses. You never went for your new glasses.

WILLY: No, I see everything. I came back ten miles an hour. It took me nearly four hours from Yonkers.

LINDA *(Resigned):*   Well, you'll just have to take a rest, Willy, you can't continue this way.

WILLY: I just got back from Florida.

LINDA: But you didn't rest your mind. Your mind is overactive, and the mind is what counts, dear.

WILLY: I'll start out in the morning. Maybe I'll feel better in the morning. *(She is taking off his shoes.)* These goddam arch supports are killing me.

LINDA: Take an aspirin. Should I get you an aspirin? It'll soothe you.

WILLY *(With wonder):*   I was driving along, you understand? And I was fine. I was even observing the scenery. You can imagine, me looking at scenery, on the road every week of my life. But it's so beautiful up there, Linda, the trees are so thick, and the sun is warm. I opened the windshield and just let the warm air bathe over me. And then all of a sudden I'm goin' off the road! I'm tellin' ya, I absolutely forgot I was driving. If I'd've gone the other way over the white line I might've killed somebody. So I went on again—and five minutes later I'm dreamin' again, and I nearly—*(He presses two fingers against his eyes.)* I have such thoughts, I have such strange thoughts.

LINDA: Willy, dear. Talk to them again. There's no reason why you can't work in New York.

WILLY: They don't need me in New York. I'm the New England man. I'm vital in New England.

LINDA: But you're sixty years old. They can't expect you to keep traveling every week.

WILLY: I'll have to send a wire to Portland. I'm supposed to see Brown and Morrison tomorrow morning at ten o'clock to show the line. Goddammit, I could sell them! *(He starts putting on his jacket.)*

LINDA *(Taking the jacket from him):*   Why don't you go down to the place tomorrow and tell Howard you've simply got to work in New York? You're too accommodating, dear.

WILLY: If old man Wagner was alive I'd a been in charge of New York now! That man was a prince, he was a masterful man. But that boy of his, that Howard, he don't appreciate. When I went north the first time, the Wagner Company didn't know where New England was!

LINDA: Why don't you tell those things to Howard, dear?

WILLY *(Encouraged):*   I will, I definitely will. Is there any cheese?

LINDA: I'll make you a sandwich.

WILLY: No, go to sleep. I'll take some milk. I'll be up right away. The boys in?

LINDA: They're sleeping. Happy took Biff on a date tonight.

WILLY *(Interested):*   That so?

LINDA: It was so nice to see them shaving together, one behind the other, in the bathroom. And going out together. You notice? The whole house smells of shaving lotion.

WILLY: Figure it out. Work a lifetime to pay off a house. You finally own it, and there's nobody to live in it.

LINDA: Well, dear, life is a casting off. It's always that way.

WILLY: No, no, some people—some people accomplish something. Did Biff say anything after I went this morning?

LINDA: You shouldn't have criticized him, Willy, especially after he just got off the train. You mustn't lose your temper with him.

WILLY: When the hell did I lose my temper? I simply asked him if he was making any money. Is that a criticism?

LINDA: But, dear, how could he make any money?

WILLY *(Worried and angered):*   There's such an undercurrent in him. He became a moody man. Did he apologize when I left this morning?

LINDA: He was crestfallen, Willy. You know how he admires you. I think if he finds himself, then you'll both be happier and not fight any more.

WILLY: How can he find himself on a farm? Is that a life? A farmhand? In the beginning, when he was young, I thought, well, a young man, it's good for him to tramp around, take a lot of different jobs. But it's more than ten years now and he has yet to make thirty-five dollars a week!

LINDA: He's finding himself, Willy.

WILLY: Not finding yourself at the age of thirty-four is a disgrace!

LINDA: Shh!

WILLY: The trouble is he's lazy, goddammit!

LINDA: Willy, please!

WILLY: Biff is a lazy bum!

LINDA: They're sleeping. Get something to eat. Go on down.

WILLY: Why did he come home? I would like to know what brought him home.

LINDA: I don't know. I think he's still lost, Willy. I think he's very lost.

WILLY: Biff Loman is lost. In the greatest country in the world a young man with such—personal attractiveness, gets lost. And such a hard worker. There's one thing about Biff—he's not lazy.

LINDA: Never.

WILLY *(With pity and resolve):*   I'll see him in the morning; I'll have a nice talk with him. I'll get him a job selling. He could be big in no time. My God! Remember how they used to follow him around in high school? When he smiled at one of them their faces lit up. When he walked down the street . . .

(He loses himself in reminiscences.)

LINDA *(Trying to bring him out of it):*   Willy, dear, I got a new kind of American-type cheese today. It's whipped.

WILLY: Why do you get American when I like Swiss?

LINDA: I just thought you'd like a change—

WILLY: I don't want a change! I want Swiss cheese. Why am I always being contradicted?

LINDA *(With a covering laugh):*   I thought it would be a surprise.

WILLY: Why don't you open a window in here, for God's sake?

LINDA *(With infinite patience):*   They're all open, dear.

WILLY: The way they boxed us in here. Bricks and windows, windows and bricks.

LINDA: We should've bought the land next door.

WILLY: The street is lined with cars. There's not a breath of fresh air in the neighborhood. The grass don't grow any more, you can't raise a carrot in the back yard. They should've had a law against apartment houses. Remember those two beautiful elm trees out there? When I and Biff hung the swing between them?

LINDA: Yeah, like being a million miles from the city.

WILLY: They should've arrested the builder for cutting those down. They massacred the neighborhood. *(Lost):* More and more I think of those days, Linda. This time of year it was lilac and wisteria. And then the peonies would come out, and the daffodils. What fragrance in this room!

LINDA: Well, after all, people had to move somewhere.

WILLY: No, there's more people now.

LINDA: I don't think there's more people. I think—

WILLY: There's more people! That's what's ruining this country! Population is getting out of control. The competition is maddening! Smell the stink from that apartment house! And another one on the other side . . . How can they whip cheese?

On Willy's last line, Biff and Happy raise themselves up in their beds, listening.

LINDA: Go down, try it. And be quiet.

WILLY *(Turning to Linda, guiltily):*   You're not worried about me, are you, sweetheart?

BIFF: What's the matter?

HAPPY: Listen!

LINDA: You've got too much on the ball to worry about.

WILLY: You're my foundation and my support, Linda.

LINDA: Just try to relax, dear. You make mountains out of molehills.

WILLY: I won't fight with him any more. If he wants to go back to Texas, let him go.

LINDA: He'll find his way.

WILLY: Sure. Certain men just don't get started till later in life. Like Thomas Edison, I think. Or B. F. Goodrich. One of them was deaf. *(He starts for the bedroom doorway.)* I'll put my money on Biff.

LINDA: And Willy—if it's warm Sunday we'll drive in the country. And we'll open the windshield, and take lunch.

WILLY: No, the windshields don't open on the new cars.

LINDA: But you opened it today.

WILLY: Me? I didn't. *(He stops.)* Now isn't that peculiar! Isn't that a re-markable—*(He breaks off in amazement and fright as the flute is heard distantly.)*

LINDA: What, darling?

WILLY: That is the most remarkable thing.

LINDA: What, dear?

WILLY: I was thinking of the Chevvy. *(Slight pause.)* Nineteen twenty-eight . . . when I had that red Chevvy—*(Breaks off.)* That funny? I coulda sworn I was driving that Chevvy today.

LINDA: Well, that's nothing. Something must've reminded you.

WILLY: Remarkable. Ts. Remember those days? The way Biff used to simo-nize that car? The dealer refused to believe there was eighty thousand miles on it. *(He shakes his head.)* Heh! *(To Linda):* Close your eyes, I'll be right up. *(He walks out of the bedroom.)*

HAPPY *(To Biff):*   Jesus, maybe he smashed up the car again!

LINDA *(Calling after Willy):*   Be careful on the stairs, dear! The cheese is on the middle shelf! *(She turns, goes over to the bed, takes his jacket, and goes out of the bedroom.)*

Light has risen on the boys' room. Unseen, Willy is heard talking to himself, "Eighty thousand miles," and a little laugh. Biff gets out of bed, comes downstage a bit, and stands attentively. Biff is two years older than his brother Happy, well built, but in these days bears a worn air and seems less self-assured. He has succeeded less, and his dreams are stronger and less acceptable than Happy's. Happy is tall, powerfully made. Sexuality is like a visible color on him, or a scent that many women have discovered. He, like his brother, is lost, but in a different way, for he has never allowed himself to turn his face toward defeat and is thus more confused and hard-skinned, although seemingly more content.

HAPPY *(Getting out of bed):*   He's going to get his license taken away if he keeps that up. I'm getting nervous about him, y'know, Biff?

BIFF: His eyes are going.

HAPPY: No, I've driven with him. He sees all right. He just doesn't keep his mind on it. I drove into the city with him last week. He stops at a green light and then it turns red and he goes. *(He laughs.)*

BIFF: Maybe he's color-blind.

HAPPY: Pop? Why he's got the finest eye for color in the business. You know that.

BIFF *(Sitting down on his bed):*   I'm going to sleep.

HAPPY: You're not still sour on Dad, are you, Biff?

BIFF: He's all right, I guess.

WILLY *(Underneath them, in the living-room):*   Yes, sir, eighty thousand miles —eighty-two thousand!

BIFF: You smoking?

HAPPY *(Holding out a pack of cigarettes):*   Want one?

BIFF *(Taking a cigarette):*   I can never sleep when I smell it.

WILLY: What a simonizing job, heh!

HAPPY *(With deep sentiment):*   Funny, Biff, y'know? Us sleeping in here again? The old beds. *(He pats his bed affectionately.)* All the talk that went across those two beds, huh? Our whole lives.

BIFF: Yeah. Lotta dreams and plans.

HAPPY *(With a deep and masculine laugh):*   About five hundred women would like to know what was said in this room.

They share a soft laugh.

BIFF: Remember that big Betsy something—what the hell was her name—over on Bushwick Avenue?

HAPPY *(Combing his hair):*   With the collie dog!

BIFF: That's the one. I got you in there, remember?

HAPPY: Yeah, that was my first time—I think. Boy, there was a pig! *(They laugh, almost crudely.)* You taught me everything I know about women. Don't forget that.

BIFF: I bet you forgot how bashful you used to be. Especially with girls.

HAPPY: Oh, I still am, Biff.

BIFF: Oh, go on.

HAPPY: I just control it, that's all. I think I got less bashful and you got more so. What happened, Biff? Where's the old humor, the old confidence? *(He shakes Biff's knee. Biff gets up and moves restlessly about the room.)* What's the matter?

BIFF: Why does Dad mock me all the time?

HAPPY: He's not mocking you, he—

BIFF: Everything I say there's a twist of mockery on his face. I can't get near him.

HAPPY: He just wants you to make good, that's all. I wanted to talk to you about Dad for a long time, Biff. Something's—happening to him. He—talks to himself.

BIFF: I noticed that this morning. But he always mumbled.

HAPPY: But not so noticeable. It got so embarrassing I sent him to Florida. And you know something? Most of the time he's talking to you.

BIFF: What's he say about me?

HAPPY: I can't make it out.

BIFF: What's he say about me?

HAPPY: I think the fact that you're not settled, that you're still kind of up in the air . . .

BIFF: There's one or two other things depressing him, Happy.

HAPPY: What do you mean?

BIFF: Never mind. Just don't lay it all to me.

HAPPY: But I think if you just got started—I mean—is there any future for you out there?

BIFF: I tell ya, Hap, I don't know what the future is. I don't know—what I'm supposed to want.

HAPPY: What do you mean?

BIFF: Well, I spent six or seven years after high school trying to work myself up. Shipping clerk, salesman, business of one kind or another. And it's a measly manner of existence. To get on that subway on the hot mornings in summer. To devote your whole life to keeping stock, or making phone calls, or selling or buying. To suffer fifty weeks of the year for the sake of a two-week vacation, when all you really desire is to be outdoors, with your shirt off. And always to have to get ahead of the next fella. And still—that's how you build a future.

HAPPY: Well, you really enjoy it on a farm? Are you content out there?

BIFF *(With rising agitation):*   Hap, I've had twenty or thirty different kinds of jobs since I left home before the war, and it always turns out the same. I just realized it lately. In Nebraska when I herded cattle, and the Dakotas, and Arizona, and now in Texas. It's why I came home now, I guess, because I realized it. This farm I work on, it's spring there now, see? And they've got about fifteen new colts. There's nothing more inspiring or—beautiful than the sight of a mare and a new colt. And it's cool there now, see? Texas is cool now, and it's spring. And whenever spring comes to where I am, I suddenly get the feeling, my God, I'm not gettin' anywhere! What the hell am I doing, playing around with horses, twenty-eight dollars a week! I'm thirty-four years old, I oughta be makin' my future. That's when I come running home. And now, I get here, and I don't know what to do with myself. *(After a pause):* I've always made a point of not wasting my life, and everytime I come back here I know that all I've done is to waste my life.

HAPPY: You're a poet, you know that, Biff? You're a—you're an idealist!

BIFF: No, I'm mixed up very bad. Maybe I oughta get married. Maybe I oughta get stuck into something. Maybe that's my trouble. I'm like a boy. I'm not married, I'm not in business, I just—I'm like a boy. Are you content, Hap? You're a success, aren't you? Are you content?

HAPPY: Hell, no!

BIFF: Why? You're making money, aren't you?

HAPPY *(Moving about with energy, expressiveness):*   All I can do now is wait for the merchandise manager to die. And suppose I get to be merchandise manager? He's a good friend of mine, and he just built a terrific estate on Long Island. And he lived there about two months and sold it, and now he's building another one. He can't enjoy it once it's finished. And I know that's just what I would do. I don't know what the hell I'm workin' for. Sometimes I sit in my apartment—all alone. And I think of the rent I'm paying. And it's crazy. But then, it's what I always wanted. My own apartment, a car, and plenty of women. And still, goddammit, I'm lonely.

BIFF *(With enthusiasm):*   Listen, why don't you come out West with me?

HAPPY: You and I, heh?

BIFF: Sure, maybe we could buy a ranch. Raise cattle, use our muscles. Men built like we are should be working out in the open.

HAPPY *(Avidly):*   The Loman Brothers, heh?

BIFF *(With vast affection):*   Sure, we'd be known all over the counties!

HAPPY *(Enthralled):*   That's what I dream about, Biff. Sometimes I want to just rip my clothes off in the middle of the store and outbox that goddam merchandise manager. I mean I can outbox, outrun, and outlift anybody in that store, and I have to take orders from those common, petty sons-of-bitches till I can't stand it any more.

BIFF: I'm tellin' you, kid, if you were with me I'd be happy out there.

HAPPY *(Enthused):*   See, Biff, everybody around me is so false that I'm constantly lowering my ideals . . .

BIFF: Baby, together we'd stand up for one another, we'd have someone to trust.

HAPPY: If I were around you—

BIFF: Hap, the trouble is we weren't brought up to grub for money. I don't know how to do it.

HAPPY: Neither can I!

BIFF: Then let's go!

HAPPY: The only thing is—what can you make out there?

BIFF: But look at your friend. Builds an estate and then hasn't the peace of mind to live in it.

HAPPY: Yeah, but when he walks into the store the waves part in front of him. That's fifty-two thousand dollars a year coming through the revolving door, and I got more in my pinky finger than he's got in his head.

BIFF: Yeah, but you just said—

HAPPY: I gotta show some of those pompous, self-important executives over there that Hap Loman can make the grade. I want to walk into the store the way he walks in. Then I'll go with you, Biff. We'll be together yet, I swear. But take those two we had tonight. Now weren't they gorgeous creatures?

BIFF: Yeah, yeah, most gorgeous I've had in years.

HAPPY: I get that any time I want, Biff. Whenever I feel disgusted. The only trouble is, it gets like bowling or something. I just keep knockin' them over and it doesn't mean anything. You still run around a lot?

BIFF: Naa. I'd like to find a girl—steady, somebody with substance.

HAPPY: That's what I long for.

BIFF: Go on! You'd never come home.

HAPPY: I would! Somebody with character, with resistance! Like Mom, y'know? You're gonna call me a bastard when I tell you this. That girl Charlotte I was with tonight is engaged to be married in five weeks. *(He tries on his new hat.)*

BIFF: No kiddin'!

HAPPY: Sure, the guy's in line for the vice-presidency of the store. I don't know what gets into me, maybe I just have an overdeveloped sense of competition or something, but I went and ruined her, and furthermore I can't get rid of her. And he's the third executive I've done that to. Isn't that a crummy characteristic? And to top it all, I go to their weddings! *(Indignantly, but laughing):* Like I'm not supposed to take bribes. Manufacturers offer me a hundred-dollar bill now and then to throw an order their way. You know how honest I am, but it's like this girl, see. I hate myself for it. Because I don't want the girl, and, still, I take it and—I love it!

BIFF: Let's go to sleep.

HAPPY: I guess we didn't settle anything, heh?

BIFF: I just got one idea that I think I'm going to try.

HAPPY: What's that?

BIFF: Remember Bill Oliver?

HAPPY: Sure, Oliver is very big now. You want to work for him again?

BIFF: No, but when I quit he said something to me. He put his arm on my shoulder, and he said, "Biff, if you ever need anything, come to me."

HAPPY: I remember that. That sounds good.

BIFF: I think I'll go to see him. If I could get ten thousand or even seven or eight thousand dollars I could buy a beautiful ranch.

HAPPY: I bet he'd back you. 'Cause he thought highly of you, Biff. I mean, they all do. You're well liked, Biff. That's why I say to come back here, and we both have the apartment. And I'm tellin' you, Biff, any babe you want . . .

BIFF: No, with a ranch I could do the work I like and still be something. I just wonder though. I wonder if Oliver still thinks I stole that carton of basketballs.

HAPPY: Oh, he probably forgot that long ago. It's almost ten years. You're too sensitive. Anyway, he didn't really fire you.

BIFF: Well, I think he was going to. I think that's why I quit. I was never sure whether he knew or not. I know he thought the world of me, though. I was the only one he'd let lock up the place.

WILLY *(Below):*   You gonna wash the engine, Biff?

HAPPY: Shh!

Biff looks at Happy, who is gazing down, listening. Willy is mumbling in the parlor.

HAPPY: You hear that?

They listen. Willy laughs warmly.

BIFF *(Growing angry):*   Doesn't he know Mom can hear that?

WILLY: Don't get your sweater dirty, Biff!

A look of pain crosses Biff's face.

HAPPY: Isn't that terrible? Don't leave again, will you? You'll find a job here. You gotta stick around. I don't know what to do about him, it's getting embarrassing.

WILLY: What a simonizing job!

BIFF: Mom's hearing that!

WILLY: No kiddin', Biff, you got a date? Wonderful!

HAPPY: Go on to sleep. But talk to him in the morning, will you?

BIFF *(Reluctantly getting into bed):*   With her in the house. Brother!

HAPPY *(Getting into bed):*   I wish you'd have a good talk with him.

The light on their room begins to fade.

BIFF *(To himself in bed):*   That selfish, stupid . . .
HAPPY: Sh . . . Sleep, Biff.

Their light is out. Well before they have finished speaking, Willy's form is dimly seen below in the darkened kitchen. He opens the refrigerator, searches in there, and takes out a bottle of milk. The apartment houses are fading out, and the entire house and surroundings become covered with leaves. Music insinuates itself as the leaves appear.

WILLY: Just wanna be careful with those girls, Biff, that's all. Don't make any promises. No promises of any kind. Because a girl, y'know, they always believe what you tell 'em, and you're very young, Biff, you're too young to be talking seriously to girls.

Light rises on the kitchen. Willy, talking, shuts the refrigerator door and comes downstage to the kitchen table. He pours milk into a glass. He is totally immersed in himself, smiling faintly.

WILLY: Too young entirely, Biff. You want to watch your schooling first. Then when you're all set, there'll be plenty of girls for a boy like you. *(He smiles broadly at a kitchen chair.)* That so? The girls pay for you? *(He laughs.)* Boy, you must really be makin' a hit.

Willy is gradually addressing—physically—a point offstage, speaking through the wall of the kitchen, and his voice has been rising in volume to that of a normal conversation.

WILLY: I been wondering why you polish the car so careful. Ha! Don't leave the hubcaps, boys. Get the chamois to the hubcaps. Happy, use newspaper on the windows, it's the easiest thing. Show him how to do it, Biff! You see, Happy? Pad it up, use it like a pad. That's it, that's it, good work. You're doin' all right, Hap. *(He pauses, then nods in approbation for a few seconds, then looks upward.)* Biff, first thing we gotta do when we get time is clip that big branch over the house. Afraid it's gonna fall in a storm and hit the roof. Tell you what. We get a rope and sling her around, and then we climb up there with a couple of saws and take her down. Soon as you finish the car, boys, I wanna see ya. I got a surprise for you, boys.
BIFF *(Offstage):*   Whatta ya got, Dad?
WILLY: No, you finish first. Never leave a job till you're finished—remember that. *(Looking toward the "big trees"):* Biff, up in Albany I saw a beautiful hammock. I think I'll buy it next trip, and we'll hang it right between those two elms. Wouldn't that be something? Just swingin' there under those branches. Boy, that would be . . .

Young Biff and Young Happy appear from the direction Willy was addressing. Happy carries rags and a pail of water. Biff, wearing a sweater with a block "S," carries a football.

BIFF *(Pointing in the direction of the car offstage):*   How's that, Pop, professional?

WILLY: Terrific. Terrific job, boys. Good work, Biff.

HAPPY: Where's the surprise, Pop?

WILLY: In the back seat of the car.

HAPPY: Boy! *(He runs off.)*

BIFF: What is it, Dad? Tell me, what'd you buy?

WILLY *(Laughing, cuffs him):*   Never mind, something I want you to have.

BIFF *(Turns and starts off):*   What is it, Hap?

HAPPY *(Offstage):*   It's a punching bag!

BIFF: Oh, Pop!

WILLY: It's got Gene Tunney's signature on it!

Happy runs onstage with a punching bag.

BIFF: Gee, how'd you know we wanted a punching bag?

WILLY: Well, it's the finest thing for the timing.

HAPPY *(Lies down on his back and pedals with his feet):*   I'm losing weight, you notice, Pop?

WILLY *(To Happy):*   Jumping rope is good too.

BIFF: Did you see the new football I got?

WILLY *(Examining the ball):*   Where'd you get a new ball?

BIFF: The coach told me to practice my passing.

WILLY: That so? And he gave you the ball, heh?

BIFF: Well, I borrowed it from the locker room. *(He laughs confidentially.)*

WILLY *(Laughing with him at the theft):*   I want you to return that.

HAPPY: I told you he wouldn't like it!

BIFF *(Angrily):*   Well, I'm bringing it back!

WILLY *(Stopping the incipient argument, to Happy):*   Sure, he's gotta practice with a regulation ball, doesn't he? *(To Biff):* Coach'll probably congratulate you on your initiative!

BIFF: Oh, he keeps congratulating my initiative all the time, Pop.

WILLY: That's because he likes you. If somebody else took that ball there'd be an uproar. So what's the report, boys, what's the report?

BIFF: Where'd you go this time, Dad? Gee we were lonesome for you.

WILLY *(Pleased, puts an arm around each boy and they come down to the apron):*   Lonesome, heh?

BIFF: Missed you every minute.

WILLY: Don't say? Tell you a secret, boys. Don't breathe it to a soul. Someday I'll have my own business, and I'll never have to leave home any more.

HAPPY: Like Uncle Charley, heh?

WILLY: Bigger than Uncle Charley! Because Charley is not—liked. He's liked, but he's not—well liked.

BIFF: Where'd you go this time, Dad?

WILLY: Well, I got on the road, and I went north to Providence. Met the Mayor.

BIFF: The Mayor of Providence!

WILLY: He was sitting in the hotel lobby.

BIFF: What'd he say?

WILLY: He said, "Morning!" And I said, "You got a fine city here, Mayor." And then he had coffee with me. And then I went to Waterbury. Waterbury is a fine city. Big clock city, the famous Waterbury clock. Sold a nice bill there. And then Boston—Boston is the cradle of the Revolution. A fine city. And a couple of other towns in Mass., and on to Portland and Bangor and straight home!

BIFF: Gee, I'd love to go with you sometime, Dad.

WILLY: Soon as summer comes.

HAPPY: Promise?

WILLY: You and Hap and I, and I'll show you all the towns. America is full of beautiful towns and fine, upstanding people. And they know me, boys, they know me up and down New England. The finest people. And when I bring you fellas up, there'll be open sesame for all of us, 'cause one thing, boys: I have friends. I can park my car in any street in New England, and the cops protect it like their own. This summer, heh?

BIFF and HAPPY *(Together):*   Yeah! You bet!

WILLY: We'll take our bathing suits.

HAPPY: We'll carry your bags, Pop!

WILLY: Oh, won't that be something! Me comin' into the Boston stores with you boys carryin' my bags. What a sensation!

Biff is prancing around, practicing passing the ball.

WILLY: You nervous, Biff, about the game?

BIFF: Not if you're gonna be there.

WILLY: What do they say about you in school, now that they made you captain?

HAPPY: There's a crowd of girls behind him everytime the classes change.

BIFF *(Taking Willy's hand):*   This Saturday, Pop, this Saturday—just for you, I'm going to break through for a touchdown.

HAPPY: You're supposed to pass.

BIFF: I'm takin' one play for Pop. You watch me, Pop, and when I take off my helmet, that means I'm breakin' out. Then you watch me crash through that line!

WILLY *(Kisses Biff):*   Oh, wait'll I tell this in Boston!

Bernard enters in knickers. He is younger than Biff, earnest and loyal, a worried boy.

BERNARD: Biff, where are you? You're supposed to study with me today.

WILLY: Hey, looka Bernard. What're you lookin' so anemic about, Bernard?

BERNARD: He's gotta study, Uncle Willy. He's got Regents next week.

HAPPY *(Tauntingly, spinning Bernard around):* Let's box, Bernard!

BERNARD: Biff! *(He gets away from Happy.)* Listen, Biff, I heard Mr. Birnbaum say that if you don't start studyin' math he's gonna flunk you, and you won't graduate. I heard him!

WILLY: You better study with him, Biff. Go ahead now.

BERNARD: I heard him!

BIFF: Oh, Pop, you didn't see my sneakers! *(He holds up a foot for Willy to look at.)*

WILLY: Hey, that's a beautiful job of printing!

BERNARD *(Wiping his glasses):* Just because he printed University of Virginia on his sneakers doesn't mean they've got to graduate him, Uncle Willy!

WILLY *(Angrily):* What're you talking about? With scholarships to three universities they're gonna flunk him?

BERNARD: But I heard Mr. Birnbaum say—

WILLY: Don't be a pest, Bernard! *(To his boys):* What an anemic!

BERNARD: Okay, I'm waiting for you in my house, Biff.

Bernard goes off. The Lomans laugh.

WILLY: Bernard is not well liked, is he?

BIFF: He's liked, but he's not well liked.

HAPPY: That's right, Pop.

WILLY: That's just what I mean. Bernard can get the best marks in school, y'understand, but when he gets out in the business world, y'understand, you are going to be five times ahead of him. That's why I thank Almighty God you're both built like Adonises. Because the man who makes an appearance in the business world, the man who creates personal interest, is the man who gets ahead. Be liked and you will never want. You take me, for instance. I never have to wait in line to see a buyer. "Willy Loman is here!" That's all they have to know, and I go right through.

BIFF: Did you knock them dead, Pop?

WILLY: Knocked 'em cold in Providence, slaughtered 'em in Boston.

HAPPY *(On his back, pedaling again):* I'm losing weight, you notice, Pop?

Linda enters, as of old, a ribbon in her hair, carrying a basket of washing.

LINDA *(With youthful energy):* Hello, dear!

WILLY: Sweetheart!

LINDA: How'd the Chevvy run?

WILLY: Chevrolet, Linda, is the greatest car ever built. *(To the boys):* Since when do you let your mother carry wash up the stairs?

BIFF: Grab hold there, boy!

HAPPY: Where to, Mom?

LINDA: Hang them up on the line. And you better go down to your friends, Biff. The cellar is full of boys. They don't know what to do with themselves.

BIFF: Ah, when Pop comes home they can wait!

WILLY *(Laughs appreciatively)*:   You better go down and tell them what to do, Biff.

BIFF: I think I'll have them sweep out the furnace room.

WILLY: Good work, Biff.

BIFF *(Goes through wall-line of kitchen to doorway at back and calls down)*:   Fellas! Everybody sweep out the furnace room! I'll be right down!

VOICES: All right! Okay, Biff.

BIFF: George and Sam and Frank, come out back! We're hangin' up the wash! Come on, Hap, on the double! *(He and Happy carry out the basket.)*

LINDA: The way they obey him!

WILLY: Well, that's training, the training. I'm tellin' you, I was sellin' thousands and thousands, but I had to come home.

LINDA: Oh, the whole block'll be at that game. Did you sell anything?

WILLY: I did five hundred gross in Providence and seven hundred gross in Boston.

LINDA: No! Wait a minute, I've got a pencil. *(She pulls pencil and paper out of her apron pocket.)* That makes your commission . . . Two hundred—my God! Two hundred and twelve dollars!

WILLY: Well, I didn't figure it yet, but . . .

LINDA: How much did you do?

WILLY: Well, I—I did—about a hundred and eighty gross in Providence. Well, no—it came to—roughly two hundred gross on the whole trip.

LINDA *(Without hesitation)*:   Two hundred gross. That's . . . *(She figures.)*

WILLY: The trouble was that three of the stores were half closed for inventory in Boston. Otherwise I woulda broke records.

LINDA: Well, it makes seventy dollars and some pennies. That's very good.

WILLY: What do we owe?

LINDA: Well, on the first there's sixteen dollars on the refrigerator—

WILLY: Why sixteen?

LINDA: Well, the fan belt broke, so it was a dollar eighty.

WILLY: But it's brand new.

LINDA: Well, the man said that's the way it is. Till they work themselves in, y'know.

They move through the wall-line into the kitchen.

WILLY: I hope we didn't get stuck on that machine.

LINDA: They got the biggest ads of any of them!

WILLY: I know, it's a fine machine. What else?

LINDA: Well, there's nine-sixty for the washing machine. And for the vacuum cleaner there's three and a half due on the fifteenth. Then the roof, you got twenty-one dollars remaining.

WILLY: It don't leak, does it?

LINDA: No, they did a wonderful job. Then you owe Frank for the carbu-retor.

WILLY: I'm not going to pay that man! That goddam Chevrolet, they ought to prohibit the manufacture of that car!

LINDA: Well, you owe him three and a half. And odds and ends, comes to around a hundred and twenty dollars by the fifteenth.

WILLY: A hundred and twenty dollars! My God, if business don't pick up I don't know what I'm gonna do!

LINDA: Well, next week you'll do better.

WILLY: Oh, I'll knock 'em dead next week. I'll go to Hartford. I'm very well liked in Hartford. You know, the trouble is, Linda, people don't seem to take to me.

The move onto the forestage.

LINDA: Oh, don't be foolish.

WILLY: I know it when I walk in. They seem to laugh at me.

LINDA: Why? Why would they laugh at you? Don't talk that way, Willy.

Willy moves to the edge of the stage. Linda goes into the kitchen and starts to darn stockings.

WILLY: I don't know the reason for it, but they just pass me by. I'm not noticed.

LINDA: But you're doing wonderful, dear. You're making seventy to a hun-dred dollars a week.

WILLY: But I gotta be at it ten, twelve hours a day. Other men—I don't know—they do it easier. I don't know why—I can't stop myself—I talk too much. A man oughta come in with a few words. One thing about Charley. He's a man of few words, and they respect him.

LINDA: You don't talk too much, you're just lively.

WILLY *(Smiling):*   Well, I figure, what the hell, life is short, a couple of jokes. *(To himself):* I joke too much! *The smile goes.*

LINDA: Why? You're—

WILLY: I'm fat. I'm very—foolish to look at, Linda. I didn't tell you, but Christmas time I happened to be calling on F. H. Stewarts, and a salesman I know, as I was going in to see the buyer I heard him say something about —walrus. And I—I cracked him right across the face. I won't take that. I simply will not take that. But they do laugh at me. I know that.

LINDA: Darling . . .

WILLY: I gotta overcome it. I know I gotta overcome it. I'm not dressing to advantage, maybe.

LINDA: Willy, darling, you're the handsomest man in the world—

WILLY: Oh, no, Linda.

LINDA: To me you are. *(Slight pause.)* The handsomest.

From the darkness is heard the laughter of a woman. Willy doesn't turn to it, but it continues through Linda's lines.

LINDA: And the boys, Willy. Few men are idolized by their children the way you are.

Music is heard as behind a scrim, to the left of the house, The Woman, dimly seen, is dressing.

WILLY *(With great feeling):*   You're the best there is, Linda, you're a pal, you know that? On the road—on the road I want to grab you sometimes and just kiss the life outa you.

The laughter is loud now, and he moves into a brightening area at the left, where The Woman has come from behind the scrim and is standing, putting on her hat, looking into a "mirror" and laughing.

WILLY: 'Cause I get so lonely—especially when business is bad and there's nobody to talk to. I get the feeling that I'll never sell anything again, that I won't make a living for you, or a business, a business for the boys. *(He talks through The Woman's subsiding laughter; The Woman primps at the "mirror.")* There's so much I want to make for—

THE WOMAN: Me? You didn't make me, Willy. I picked you.

WILLY *(Pleased):*   You picked me?

THE WOMAN *(Who is quite proper-looking, Willy's age):*   I did. I've been sitting at that desk watching all the salesmen go by, day in, day out. But you've got such a sense of humor, and we do have such a good time together, don't we?

WILLY: Sure, sure. *(He takes her in his arms.)* Why do you have to go now?

THE WOMAN: It's two o'clock . . .

WILLY: No, come on in! *(He pulls her.)*

THE WOMAN: . . . my sisters'll be scandalized. When'll you be back?

WILLY: Oh, two weeks about. Will you come up again?

THE WOMAN: Sure thing. You do make me laugh. It's good for me. *(She squeezes his arm, kisses him.)* And I think you're a wonderful man.

WILLY: You picked me, heh?

THE WOMAN: Sure. Because you're so sweet. And such a kidder.

WILLY: Well, I'll see you next time I'm in Boston.

THE WOMAN: I'll put you right through to the buyers.

WILLY *(Slapping her bottom):*   Right. Well, bottoms up!

THE WOMAN *(Slaps him gently and laughs):*   You just kill me, Willy. *(He suddenly*

grabs her and kisses her roughly.) You kill me. And thanks for the stockings.
   I love a lot of stockings. Well, good night.
WILLY: Good night. And keep your pores open!
THE WOMAN: Oh, Willy!

The Woman bursts out laughing, and Linda's laughter blends in. The Woman disappears into the dark. Now the area at the kitchen table brightens. Linda is sitting where she was at the kitchen table, but now is mending a pair of her silk stockings.

LINDA: You are, Willy. The handsomest man. You've got no reason to feel
   that—
WILLY (*Coming out of The Woman's dimming area and going over to Linda*):   I'll
   make it all up to you, Linda, I'll—
LINDA: There's nothing to make up, dear. You're doing fine, better
   than—
WILLY (*Noticing her mending*):   What's that?
LINDA: Just mending my stockings. They're so expensive—
WILLY (*Angrily, taking them from her*):   I won't have you mending stockings in
   this house! Now throw them out!

Linda puts the stockings in her pocket.

BERNARD (*Entering on the run*):   Where is he? If he doesn't study!
WILLY (*Moving to the forestage, with great agitation*):   You'll give him the answers!
BERNARD: I do, but I can't on a Regents! That's a state exam! They're liable
   to arrest me!
WILLY: Where is he? I'll whip him, I'll whip him!
LINDA: And he'd better give back that football, Willy, it's not nice.
WILLY: Biff! Where is he? Why is he taking everything?
LINDA: He's too rough with the girls, Willy. All the mothers are afraid of
   him!
WILLY: I'll whip him!
BERNARD: He's driving the car without a license!

The Woman's laugh is heard.

WILLY: Shut up!
LINDA: All the mothers—
WILLY: Shut up!
BERNARD (*Backing quietly away and out*):   Mr. Birnbaum says he's stuck up.
WILLY: Get outa here!
BERNARD: If he doesn't buckle down he'll flunk math! (*He goes off.*)
LINDA: He's right, Willy, you've gotta—
WILLY (*Exploding at her*):   There's nothing the matter with him! You want
   him to be a worm like Bernard? He's got spirit, personality . . .

As he speaks, Linda, almost in tears, exits into the living-room. Willy is alone in the kitchen, wilting and staring. The leaves are gone. It is night again, and the apartment houses look down from behing.

WILLY: Loaded with it. Loaded! What is he stealing? He's giving it back, isn't he? Why is he stealing? What did I tell him? I never in my life told him anything but decent things.

Happy in pajamas has come down the stairs; Willy suddenly becomes aware of Happy's presence.

HAPPY: Let's go now, come on.

WILLY *(Sitting down at the kitchen table):*   Huh! Why did she have to wax the floors herself? Everytime she waxes the floors she keels over. She knows that!

HAPPY: Shh! Take it easy. What brought you back tonight?

WILLY: I got an awful scare. Nearly hit a kid in Yonkers. God! Why didn't I go to Alaska with my brother Ben that time! Ben! That man was a genius, that man was success incarnate! What a mistake! He begged me to go.

HAPPY: Well, there's no use in—

WILLY: You guys! There was a man started with the clothes on his back and ended up with diamond mines!

HAPPY: Boy, someday I'd like to know how he did it.

WILLY: What's the mystery? The man knew what he wanted and went out and got it! Walked into a jungle, and comes out, the age of twenty-one, and he's rich! The world is an oyster, but you don't crack it open on a mattress!

HAPPY: Pop, I told you I'm gonna retire you for life.

WILLY: You'll retire me for life on seventy goddam dollars a week? And your women and your car and your apartment, and you'll retire me for life! Christ's sake, I couldn't get past Yonkers today! Where are you guys, where are you? The woods are burning! I can't drive a car!

Charley has appeared in the doorway. He is a large man, slow of speech, laconic, immovable. In all he says, despite what he says, there is pity, and, now, trepidation. He has a robe over pajamas, slippers on his feet. He enters the kitchen.

CHARLEY: Everything all right?

HAPPY: Yeah, Charley, everything's . . .

WILLY: What's the matter?

CHARLEY: I heard some noise. I thought something happened. Can't we do something about the walls? You sneeze in here, and in my house hats blow off.

HAPPY: Let's go to bed, Dad. Come on.

Charley signals to Happy to go.

WILLY: You go ahead, I'm not tired at the moment.

HAPPY *(To Willy):*   Take it easy, huh? *(He exits.)*

WILLY: What're you doin' up?

CHARLEY *(Sitting down at the kitchen table opposite Willy):*   Couldn't sleep good. I had a heartburn.

WILLY: Well, you don't know how to eat.

CHARLEY: I eat with my mouth.

WILLY: No, you're ignorant. You gotta know about vitamins and things like that.

CHARLEY: Come on, let's shoot. Tire you out a little.

WILLY *(Hesitantly):*   All right. You got cards?

CHARLEY *(Taking a deck from his pocket):*   Yeah, I got them. Someplace. What is it with those vitamins?

WILLY *(Dealing):*   They build up your bones. Chemistry.

CHARLEY: Yeah, but there's no bones in a heartburn.

WILLY: What are you talkin' about? Do you know the first thing about it?

CHARLEY: Don't get insulted.

WILLY: Don't talk about something you don't know anything about.

They are playing. Pause.

CHARLEY: What're you doin' home?

WILLY: A little trouble with the car.

CHARLEY: Oh. *(Pause.)* I'd like to take a trip to California.

WILLY: Don't say.

CHARLEY: You want a job?

WILLY: I got a job, I told you that. *(After a slight pause):* What the hell are you offering me a job for?

CHARLEY: Don't get insulted.

WILLY: Don't insult me.

CHARLEY: I don't see no sense in it. You don't have to go on this way.

WILLY: I got a good job. *(Slight pause.)* What do you keep comin' in here for?

CHARLEY: You want me to go?

WILLY *(After a pause, withering):*   I can't understand it. He's going back to Texas again. What the hell is that?

CHARLEY: Let him go.

WILLY: I got nothin' to give him, Charley, I'm clean, I'm clean.

CHARLEY: He won't starve. None a them starve. Forget about him.

WILLY: Then what have I got to remember?

CHARLEY: You take it too hard. To hell with it. When a deposit bottle is broken you don't get your nickel back.

WILLY: That's easy enough for you to say.

CHARLEY: That ain't easy for me to say.

WILLY: Did you see the ceiling I put up in the living-room?

CHARLEY: Yeah, that's a piece of work. To put up a ceiling is a mystery to me. How do you do it?

WILLY: What's the difference?
CHARLEY: Well, talk about it.
WILLY: You gonna put up a ceiling?
CHARLEY: How could I put up a ceiling?
WILLY: Then what the hell are you bothering me for?
CHARLEY: You're insulted again.
WILLY: A man who can't handle tools is not a man. You're disgusting.
CHARLEY: Don't call me disgusting, Willy.

Uncle Ben, carrying a valise and an umbrella, enters the forestage from around the right corner of the house. He is a stolid man, in his sixties, with a mustache and an authoritative air. He is utterly certain of his destiny, and there is an aura of far places about him. He enters exactly as Willy speaks.

WILLY: I'm getting awfully tired, Ben.

Ben's music is heard. Ben looks around at everything.

CHARLEY: Good, keep playing; you'll sleep better. Did you call me Ben?

Ben looks at his watch.

WILLY: That's funny. For a second there you reminded me of my brother Ben.
BEN: I only have a few minutes. *(He strolls, inspecting the place. Willy and Charley continue playing.)*
CHARLEY: You never heard from him again, heh? Since that time?
WILLY: Didn't Linda tell you? Couple of weeks ago we got a letter from his wife in Africa. He died.
CHARLEY: That so.
BEN *(Chuckling):*   So this is Brooklyn, eh?
CHARLEY: Maybe you're in for some of his money.
WILLY: Naa, he had seven sons. There's just one opportunity I had with that man . . .
BEN: I must make a train, William. There are several properties I'm looking at in Alaska.
WILLY: Sure, sure! If I'd gone with him to Alaska that time, everything would've been totally different.
CHARLEY: Go on, you'd froze to death up there.
WILLY: What're you talking about?
BEN: Opportunity is tremendous in Alaska, William. Surprised you're not up there.
WILLY: Sure, tremendous.
CHARLEY: Heh?
WILLY: There was the only man I ever met who knew the answers.
CHARLEY: Who?

BEN: How are you all?

WILLY *(Taking a pot, smiling)*:   Fine, fine.

CHARLEY: Pretty sharp tonight.

BEN: Is Mother living with you?

WILLY: No, she died a long time ago.

CHARLEY: Who?

BEN: That's too bad. Fine specimen of a lady, Mother.

WILLY *(To Charley)*:   Heh?

BEN: I'd hoped to see the old girl.

CHARLEY: Who died?

BEN: Heard anything from Father, have you?

WILLY *(Unnerved)*:   What do you mean, who died?

CHARLEY *(Taking a pot)*:   What're you talkin' about?

BEN *(Looking at his watch)*:   William, it's half-past eight!

WILLY *(As though to dispel his confusion he angrily stops Charley's hand)*:   That's my build!

CHARLEY: I put the ace—

WILLY: If you don't know how to play the game I'm not gonna throw my money away on you!

CHARLEY *(Rising)*:   It was my ace, for God's sake!

WILLY: I'm through, I'm through!

BEN: When did Mother die?

WILLY: Long ago. Since the beginning you never knew how to play cards.

CHARLEY *(Picks up the cards and goes to the door)*:   All right! Next time I'll bring a deck with five aces.

WILLY: I don't play that kind of game!

CHARLEY *(Turning to him)*:   You ought to be ashamed of yourself!

WILLY: Yeah?

CHARLEY: Yeah! *(He goes out.)*

WILLY *(Slamming the door after him)*:   Ignoramus!

BEN *(As Willy comes toward him through the wall-line of the kitchen)*:   So you're William.

WILLY *(Shaking Ben's hand)*:   Ben! I've been waiting for you so long! What's the answer? How did you do it?

BEN: Oh, there's a story in that.

Linda enters the forestage, as of old, carrying the wash basket.

LINDA: Is this Ben?

BEN *(Gallantly)*:   How do you do, my dear.

LINDA: Where've you been all these years? Willy's always wondered why you—

WILLY *(Pulling Ben away from her impatiently)*:   Where is Dad? Didn't you follow him? How did you get started?

BEN: Well, I don't know how much you remember.

WILLY: Well, I was just a baby, of course, only three or four years old—

BEN: Three years and eleven months.

WILLY: What a memory, Ben!

BEN: I have many enterprises, William, and I have never kept books.

WILLY: I remember I was sitting under the wagon in—was it Nebraska?

BEN: It was South Dakota, and I gave you a bunch of wild flowers.

WILLY: I remember you walking away down some open road.

BEN *(Laughing):*   I was going to find Father in Alaska.

WILLY: Where is he?

BEN: At that age I had a very faulty view of geography, William. I discovered after a few days that I was heading due south, so instead of Alaska, I ended up in Africa.

LINDA: Africa!

WILLY: The Gold Coast!

BEN: Principally diamond mines.

LINDA: Diamond mines!

BEN: Yes, my dear. But I've only a few minutes—

WILLY: No! Boys! Boys! *(Young Biff and Happy appear.)* Listen to this. This is your Uncle Ben, a great man! Tell my boys, Ben!

BEN: Why, boys, when I was seventeen I walked into the jungle, and when I was twenty-one I walked out. *(He laughs.)* And by God I was rich.

WILLY *(To the boys):*   You see what I been talking about? The greatest things can happen!

BEN *(Glancing at his watch):*   I have an appointment in Ketchikan Tuesday week.

WILLY: No, Ben! Please tell about Dad. I want my boys to hear. I want them to know the kind of stock they spring from. All I remember is a man with a big beard, and I was in Mamma's lap, sitting around a fire, and some kind of high music.

BEN: His flute. He played the flute.

WILLY: Sure, the flute, that's right!

New music is heard, a high, rollicking tune.

BEN: Father was a very great and a very wild-hearted man. We would start in Boston, and he'd toss the whole family into the wagon, and then he'd drive the team right across the country; through Ohio, and Indiana, Michigan, Illinois, and all the Western states. And we'd stop in the towns and sell the flutes that he'd made on the way. Great inventor, Father. With one gadget he made more in a week than a man like you could make in a lifetime.

WILLY: That's just the way I'm bringing them up, Ben—rugged, well liked, all-around.

BEN: Yeah? *(To Biff):* Hit that, boy—hard as you can. *(He pounds his stomach.)*

BIFF: Oh, no, sir!

BEN *(Taking boxing stance):*   Come on, get to me! *(He laughs.)*

WILLY: Go to it, Biff! Go ahead, show him!

BIFF: Okay! *(He cocks his fists and starts in.)*

LINDA *(To Willy):*   Why must he fight, dear?

BEN *(Sparring with Biff):*   Good boy! Good boy!

WILLY: How's that, Ben, heh?

HAPPY: Give him the left, Biff!

LINDA: Why are you fighting?

BEN: Good boy! *(Suddenly comes in, trips Biff, and stands over him, the point of his umbrella poised over Biff's eye.)*

LINDA: Look out, Biff!

BIFF: Gee!

BEN *(Patting Biff's knee):*   Never fight fair with a stranger, boy. You'll never get out of the jungle that way. *(Taking Linda's hand and bowing):* It was an honor and a pleasure to meet you, Linda.

LINDA *(Withdrawing her hand coldly, frightened):*   Have a nice—trip.

BEN *(To Willy):*   And good luck with your—what do you do?

WILLY: Selling.

BEN: Yes. Well . . . *(He raises his hand in farewell to all.)*

WILLY: No, Ben, I don't want you to think . . . *(He takes Ben's arm to show him.)* It's Brooklyn, I know, but we hunt too.

BEN: Really, now.

WILLY: Oh, sure, there's snakes and rabbits and—that's why I moved out here. Why, Biff can fell any one of these trees in no time! Boys! Go right over to where they're building the apartment house and get some sand. We're gonna rebuild the entire front stoop right now! Watch this, Ben!

BIFF: Yes, sir! On the double, Hap!

HAPPY *(As he and Biff run off):*   I lost weight, Pop, you notice?

Charley enters in knickers, even before the boys are gone.

CHARLEY: Listen, if they steal any more from that building the watchman'll put the cops on them!

LINDA *(To Willy):*   Don't let Biff . . .

Ben laughs lustily.

WILLY: You shoulda seen the lumber they brought home last week. At least a dozen six-by-tens worth all kinds a money.

CHARLEY: Listen, if that watchman—

WILLY: I gave them hell, understand. But I got a couple of fearless characters there.

CHARLEY: Willy, the jails are full of fearless characters.

BEN *(Clapping Willy on the back, with a laugh at Charley):*   And the stock exchange, friend!

WILLY *(Joining in Ben's laughter):*   Where are the rest of your pants?

CHARLEY: My wife bought them.

WILLY: Now all you need is a golf club and you can go upstairs and go to sleep. *(To Ben):* Great athlete! Between him and his son Bernard they can't hammer a nail!

BERNARD *(Rushing in):*   The watchman's chasing Biff!

WILLY *(Angrily):*   Shut up! He's not stealing anything!

LINDA *(Alarmed, hurrying off left):*   Where is he? Biff, dear! *(She exits.)*

WILLY *(Moving toward the left, away from Ben):*   There's nothing wrong. What's the matter with you?

BEN: Nervy boy. Good!

WILLY *(Laughing):*   Oh, nerves of iron, that Biff!

CHARLEY: Don't know what it is. My New England man comes back and he's bleedin', they murdered him up there.

WILLY: It's contacts, Charley, I got important contacts!

CHARLEY *(Sarcastically):*   Glad to hear it, Willy. Come in later, we'll shoot a little casino. I'll take some of your Portland money. *(He laughs at Willy and exits.)*

WILLY *(Turning to Ben):*   Business is bad, it's murderous. But not for me, of course.

BEN: I'll stop by on my way back to Africa.

WILLY *(Longingly):*   Can't you stay a few days? You're just what I need, Ben, because I—I have a fine position here, but I—well, Dad left when I was such a baby and I never had a chance to talk to him and I still feel—kind of temporary about myself.

BEN: I'll be late for my train.

They are at opposite ends of the stage.

WILLY: Ben, my boys—can't we talk? They'd go into the jaws of hell for me, see, but I—

BEN: William, you're being first-rate with your boys. Outstanding, manly chaps!

WILLY *(Hanging on to his words):*   Oh, Ben, that's good to hear! Because sometimes I'm afraid that I'm not teaching them the right kind of—Ben, how should I teach them?

BEN *(Giving great weight to each word, and with a certain vicious audacity):*   William, when I walked into the jungle, I was seventeen. When I walked out I was twenty-one. And, by God, I was rich! *(He goes off into darkness around the right corner of the house.)*

WILLY: . . . was rich! That's just the spirit I want to imbue them with! To walk into a jungle! I was right! I was right! I was right!

Ben is gone, but Willy is still speaking to him as Linda, in nightgown and robe, enters the kitchen, glances around for Willy, then goes to the door of the house, looks out and sees him. Comes down to his left. He looks at her.

LINDA: Willy, dear? Willy?

WILLY: I was right!

LINDA: Did you have some cheese? *(He can't answer)*. It's very late, darling. Come to bed, heh?

WILLY *(Looking straight up)*:   Gotta break your neck to see a star in this yard.

LINDA: You coming in?

WILLY: Whatever happened to that diamond watch fob? Remember? When Ben came from Africa that time? Didn't he give me a watch fob with a diamond in it?

LINDA: You pawned it, dear. Twelve, thirteen years ago. For Biff's radio correspondence course.

WILLY: Gee, that was a beautiful thing. I'll take a walk.

LINDA: But you're in your slippers.

WILLY *(Starting to go around the house at the left)*:   I was right! I was! *(Half to Linda, as he goes, shaking his head)*: What a man! There was a man worth talking to. I was right!

LINDA *(Calling after Willy)*:   But in your slippers, Willy!

Willy is almost gone when Biff, in his pajamas, comes down the stairs and enters the kitchen.

BIFF: What is he doing out there?

LINDA: Sh!

BIFF: God Almighty, Mom, how long has he been doing this?

LINDA: Don't, he'll hear you.

BIFF: What the hell is the matter with him?

LINDA: It'll pass by morning.

BIFF: Shouldn't we do anything?

LINDA: Oh, my dear, you should do a lot of things, but there's nothing to do, so go to sleep.

Happy comes down the stair and sits on the steps.

HAPPY: I never heard him so loud, Mom.

LINDA: Well, come around more often; you'll hear him. *(She sits down at the table and mends the lining of Willy's jacket.)*

BIFF: Why didn't you ever write me about this, Mom?

LINDA: How would I write to you? For over three months you had no address.

BIFF: I was on the move. But you know I thought of you all the time. You know that, don't you, pal?

LINDA: I know, dear, I know. But he likes to have a letter. Just to know that there's still a possibility for better things.

BIFF: He's not like this all the time, is he?

LINDA: It's when you come home he's always the worst.

BIFF: When I come home?

LINDA: When you write you're coming, he's all smiles, and talks about the future, and—he's just wonderful. And then the closer you seem to come, the more shaky he gets, and then, by the time you get here, he's arguing, and he seems angry at you. I think it's just that maybe he can't bring himself to—to open up to you. Why are you so hateful to each other? Why is that?

BIFF *(Evasively):*   I'm not hateful, Mom.

LINDA: But you no sooner come in the door than you're fighting!

BIFF: I don't know why. I mean to change. I'm tryin', Mom, you understand?

LINDA: Are you home to stay now?

BIFF: I don't know. I want to look around, see what's doin'.

LINDA: Biff, you can't look around all your life, can you?

BIFF: I just can't take hold, Mom. I can't take hold of some kind of a life.

LINDA: Biff, a man is not a bird, to come and go with the springtime.

BIFF: Your hair . . . *(He touches her hair.)* Your hair got so gray.

LINDA: Oh, it's been gray since you were in high school. I just stopped dyeing it, that's all.

BIFF: Dye it again, will ya? I don't want my pal looking old. *(He smiles.)*

LINDA: You're such a boy! You think you can go away for a year and . . . You've got to get it into your head now that one day you'll knock on this door and there'll be strange people here—

BIFF: What are you talking about? You're not even sixty, Mom.

LINDA: But what about your father?

BIFF *(Lamely):*   Well, I meant him too.

HAPPY: He admires Pop.

LINDA: Biff, dear, if you don't have any feeling for him, then you can't have any feeling for me.

BIFF: Sure I can, Mom.

LINDA: No. You can't just come to see me, because I love him. *(With a threat, but only a threat, of tears):* He's the dearest man in the world to me, and I won't have anyone making him feel unwanted and low and blue. You've got to make up your mind now, darling, there's no leeway any more. Either he's your father and you pay him that respect, or else you're not to come here. I know he's not easy to get along with—nobody knows that better than me—but . . .

WILLY *(From the left, with a laugh):*   Hey, hey, Biffo!

BIFF *(Starting to go out after Willy):*   What the hell is the matter with him? *(Happy stops him.)*

LINDA: Don't—don't go near him!

BIFF: Stop making excuses for him! He always, always wiped the floor with you. Never had an ounce of respect for you.

HAPPY: He's always had respect for—

BIFF: What the hell do you know about it?

HAPPY *(Surlily):*   Just don't call him crazy!

BIFF: He's got no character—Charley wouldn't do this. Not in his own house—spewing out that vomit from his mind.

HAPPY: Charley never had to cope with what he's got to.

BIFF: People are worse off than Willy Loman. Believe me, I've seen them!

LINDA: Then make Charley your father, Biff. You can't do that, can you? I don't say he's a great man. Willy Loman never made a lot of money. His name was never in the paper. He's not the finest character that ever lived. But he's a human being, and a terrible thing is happening to him. So attention must be paid. He's not to be allowed to fall into his grave like an old dog. Attention, attention must be finally paid to such a person. You called him crazy—

BIFF: I didn't mean—

LINDA: No, a lot of people think he's lost his—balance. But you don't have to be very smart to know what his trouble is. The man is exhausted.

HAPPY: Sure!

LINDA: A small man can be just as exhausted as a great man. He works for a company thirty-six years this March, opens up unheard-of territories to their trademark, and now in his old age they take his salary away.

HAPPY *(Indignantly):*   I didn't know that, Mom.

LINDA: You never asked, my dear! Now that you get your spending money someplace else you don't trouble your mind with him.

HAPPY: But I gave you money last—

LINDA: Christmas time, fifty dollars! To fix the hot water it cost ninety-seven fifty! For five weeks he's been on straight commission, like a beginner, an unknown!

BIFF: Those ungrateful bastards!

LINDA: Are they any worse than his sons? When he brought them business, when he was young, they were glad to see him. But now his old friends, the old buyers that loved him so and always found some order to hand him in a pinch—they're all dead, retired. He used to be able to make six, seven calls a day in Boston. Now he takes his valises out of the car and puts them back and takes them out again and he's exhausted. Instead of walking he talks now. He drives seven hundred miles, and when he gets there no one knows him any more, no one welcomes him. And what goes through a man's mind, driving seven hundred miles home without having earned a cent? Why shouldn't he talk to himself? Why? When he has to go to Charley and borrow fifty dollars a week and pretend to me that it's his pay? How long can that go on? How long? You see what I'm sitting here and waiting for? And you tell me he has no character? The man who never worked a day but for your benefit? When does he get the medal for that? Is this his reward—to turn around at the age of sixty-three and find his sons, who he loved better than his life, one a philandering bum—

HAPPY: Mom!

LINDA: That's all you are, my baby! *(To Biff):* And you! What happened to the love you had for him? You were such pals! How you used to talk to him on the phone every night! How lonely he was till he could come home to you!

BIFF: All right, Mom. I'll live here in my room, and I'll get a job. I'll keep away from him, that's all.

LINDA: No, Biff. You can't stay here and fight all the time.

BIFF: He threw me out of this house, remember that.

LINDA: Why did he do that? I never knew why.

BIFF: Because I know he's a fake and he doesn't like anybody around who knows!

LINDA: Why a fake? In what way? What do you mean?

BIFF: Just don't lay it all at my feet. It's between me and him—that's all I have to say. I'll chip in from now on. He'll settle for half my pay check. He'll be all right. I'm going to bed. (*He starts for the stairs.*)

LINDA: He won't be all right.

BIFF (*Turning on the stairs, furiously*):   I hate this city and I'll stay here. Now what do you want?

LINDA: He's dying, Biff.

Happy turns quickly to her, shocked.

BIFF (*After a pause*):   Why is he dying?

LINDA: He's been trying to kill himself.

BIFF (*With great horror*):   How?

LINDA: I live from day to day.

BIFF: What're you talking about?

LINDA: Remember I wrote you that he smashed up the car again? In February?

BIFF: Well?

LINDA: The insurance inspector came. He said that they have evidence. That all these accidents in the last year—weren't—weren't—accidents.

HAPPY: How can they tell that? That's a lie.

LINDA: It seems there's a woman . . . (*She takes a breath as*

BIFF (*Sharply but contained*):   What woman?

LINDA (*Simultaneously*):   . . . and this woman . . .

LINDA: What?

BIFF: Nothing. Go ahead.

LINDA: What did you say?

BIFF: Nothing. I just said what woman?

HAPPY: What about her?

LINDA: Well, it seems she was walking down the road and saw his car. She says that he wasn't driving fast at all, and that he didn't skid. She says he came to that little bridge, and then deliberately smashed into the railing, and it was only the shallowness of the water that saved him.

BIFF: Oh, no, he probably just fell asleep again.

LINDA: I don't think he fell asleep.

BIFF: Why not?

LINDA: Last month . . . (*With great difficulty*):   Oh, boys, it's so hard to say a thing like this! He's just a big stupid man to you, but I tell you there's more good in him than in many other people. (*She chokes, wipes her eyes.*) I was looking for a fuse. The lights blew out, and I went down the cellar.

And behind the fuse box—it happened to fall out—was a length of rubber pipe—just short.

HAPPY: No kidding?

LINDA: There's a little attachment on the end of it. I knew right away. And sure enough, on the bottom of the water heater there's a new little nipple on the gas pipe.

HAPPY *(Angrily)*:   That—jerk.

BIFF: Did you have it taken off?

LINDA: I'm—I'm ashamed to. How can I mention it to him? Every day I go down and take away that little rubber pipe. But, when he comes home, I put it back where it was. How can I insult him that way? I don't know what to do. I live from day to day, boys. I tell you, I know every thought in his mind. It sounds so old-fashioned and silly, but I tell you he put his whole life into you and you've turned your backs on him. *(She is bent over in the chair, weeping, her face in her hands.)* Biff, I swear to God! Biff, his life is in your hands!

HAPPY *(To Biff)*:   How do you like that damned fool!

BIFF *(Kissing her)*:   All right, pal, all right. It's all settled now. I've been remiss. I know that, Mom. But now I'll stay, and I swear to you, I'll apply myself. *(Kneeling in front of her, in a fever of self-reproach)*: It's just—you see, Mom, I don't fit in business. Not that I won't try. I'll try, and I'll make good.

HAPPY: Sure you will. The trouble with you in business was you never tried to please people.

BIFF: I know, I—

HAPPY: Like when you worked for Harrison's. Bob Harrison said you were tops, and then you go and do some damn fool thing like whistling whole songs in the elevator like a comedian.

BIFF *(Against Happy)*:   So what? I like to whistle sometimes.

HAPPY: You don't raise a guy to a responsible job who whistles in the elevator!

LINDA: Well, don't argue about it now.

HAPPY: Like when you'd go off and swim in the middle of the day instead of taking the line around.

BIFF *(His resentment rising)*:   Well, don't you run off? You take off sometimes, don't you? On a nice summer day?

HAPPY: Yeah, but I cover myself!

LINDA: Boys!

HAPPY: If I'm going to take a fade the boss can call any number where I'm supposed to be and they'll swear to him that I just left. I'll tell you something that I hate to say, Biff, but in the business world some of them think you're crazy.

BIFF *(Angered)*:   Screw the business world!

HAPPY: All right, screw it! Great, but cover yourself!

LINDA: Hap, Hap!

BIFF: I don't care what they think! They've laughed at Dad for years, and you know why? Because we don't belong in this nuthouse of a city! We should be mixing cement on some open plain, or—or carpenters. A carpenter is allowed to whistle!

Willy walks in from the entrance of the house, at left.

WILLY: Even your grandfather was better than a carpenter. *(Pause. They watch him.)* You never grew up. Bernard does not whistle in the elevator, I assure you.

BIFF *(As though to laugh Willy out of it):*   Yeah, but you do, Pop.

WILLY: I never in my life whistled in an elevator! And who in the business world thinks I'm crazy?

BIFF: I didn't mean it like that, Pop. Now don't make a whole thing out of it, will ya?

WILLY: Go back to the West! Be a carpenter, a cowboy, enjoy yourself!

LINDA: Willy, he was just saying—

WILLY: I heard what he said!

HAPPY *(Trying to quiet Willy):*   Hey, Pop, come on now . . .

WILLY *(Continuing over Happy's line):*   They laugh at me, heh? Go to Filene's, go to the Hub, go to Slattery's, Boston. Call out the name Willy Loman and see what happens! Big shot!

BIFF: All right, Pop.

WILLY: Big!

BIFF: All right!

WILLY: Why do you always insult me?

BIFF: I didn't say a word. *(To Linda):* Did I say a word?

LINDA: He didn't say anything, Willy.

WILLY *(Going to the doorway of the living-room):*   All right, good night, good night.

LINDA: Willy, dear, he just decided . . .

WILLY *(To Biff):*   If you get tired hanging around tomorrow, paint the ceiling I put up in the living-room.

BIFF: I'm leaving early tomorrow.

HAPPY: He's going to see Bill Oliver, Pop.

WILLY *(Interestedly):*   Oliver? For what?

BIFF *(With reserve, but trying, trying):*   He always said he'd stake me. I'd like to go into business, so maybe I can take him up on it.

LINDA: Isn't that wonderful?

WILLY: Don't interrupt. What's wonderful about it? There's fifty men in the City of New York who'd stake him. *(To Biff):* Sporting goods?

BIFF: I guess so. I know something about it and—

WILLY: He knows something about it! You know sporting goods better than Spalding, for God's sake! How much is he giving you?

BIFF: I don't know, I didn't even see him yet, but—

WILLY: Then what're you talkin' about?

BIFF *(Getting angry):*   Well, all I said was I'm gonna see him, that's all!

WILLY *(Turning away):*   Ah, you're counting your chickens again.

BIFF *(Starting left for the stairs):*   Oh, Jesus, I'm going to sleep!

WILLY *(Calling after him):*   Don't curse in this house!

BIFF *(Turning):*   Since when did you get so clean?

HAPPY *(Trying to stop them):*   Wait a . . .

WILLY: Don't use that language to me! I won't have it!

HAPPY *(Grabbing Biff, shouts):*   Wait a minute! I got an idea. I got a feasible idea. Come here, Biff, let's talk this over now, let's talk some sense here. When I was down in Florida last time, I thought of a great idea to sell sporting goods. It just came back to me. You and I, Biff—we have a line, the Loman Line. We train a couple of weeks, and put on a couple of exhibitions, see?

WILLY: That's an idea!

HAPPY: Wait! We form two basketball teams, see? Two water-polo teams. We play each other. It's a million dollars' worth of publicity. Two brothers, see? The Loman Brothers. Displays in the Royal Palms—all the hotels. And banners over the ring and the basketball court: "Loman Brothers." Baby, we could sell sporting goods!

WILLY: That is a one-million-dollar idea!

LINDA: Marvelous!

BIFF: I'm in great shape as far as that's concerned.

HAPPY: And the beauty of it is, Biff, it wouldn't be like a business. We'd be out playin' ball again . . .

BIFF *(Enthused):*   Yeah, that's . . .

WILLY: Million-dollar . . .

HAPPY: And you wouldn't get fed up with it, Biff. It'd be the family again. There'd be the old honor, and comradeship, and if you wanted to go off for a swim or somethin'—well, you'd do it! Without some smart cooky gettin' up ahead of you!

WILLY: Lick the world! You guys together could absolutely lick the civilized world.

BIFF: I'll see Oliver tomorrow. Hap, if we could work that out . . .

LINDA: Maybe things are beginning to—

WILLY *(Wildly enthused, to Linda):*   Stop interrupting! *(To Biff):* But don't wear sport jacket and slacks when you see Oliver.

BIFF: No, I'll—

WILLY: A business suit, and talk as little as possible, and don't crack any jokes.

BIFF: He did like me. Always liked me.

LINDA: He loved you!

WILLY *(To Linda):*   Will you stop! *(To Biff):* Walk in very serious. You are not applying for a boy's job. Money is to pass. Be quiet, fine, and serious. Everybody likes a kidder, but nobody lends him money.

HAPPY: I'll try to get some myself, Biff. I'm sure I can.

WILLY: I see great things for you kids, I think your troubles are over. But remember, start big and you'll end big. Ask for fifteen. How much you gonna ask for?

BIFF: Gee, I don't know—

WILLY: And don't say "Gee." "Gee" is a boy's word. A man walking in for fifteen thousand dollars does not say "Gee!"

BIFF: Ten, I think, would be top though.

WILLY: Don't be so modest. You always started too low. Walk in with a big laugh. Don't look worried. Start off with a couple of your good stories to lighten things up. It's not what you say, it's how you say it—because personality always wins the day.

LINDA: Oliver always thought the highest of him—

WILLY: Will you let me talk?

BIFF: Don't yell at her, Pop, will ya?

WILLY *(Angrily)*:   I was talking, wasn't I?

BIFF: I don't like you yelling at her all the time, and I'm tellin' you, that's all.

WILLY: What're you, takin' over this house?

LINDA: Willy—

WILLY *(Turning on her)*:   Don't take his side all the time, god-dammit!

BIFF *(Furiously)*:   Stop yelling at her!

WILLY *(Suddenly pulling on his cheek, beaten down, guilt ridden)*:   Give my best to Bill Oliver—he may remember me. *(He exits through the living-room doorway.)*

LINDA *(Her voice subdued)*:   What'd you have to start that for? *(Biff turns away.)* You see how sweet he was as soon as you talked hopefully? *(She goes over to Biff.)* Come up and say good night to him. Don't let him go to bed that way.

HAPPY: Come on, Biff, let's buck him up.

LINDA: Please, dear. Just say good night. It takes so little to make him happy. Come. *(She goes through the living-room doorway, calling upstairs from within the living-room)*: Your pajamas are hanging in the bathroom, Willy!

HAPPY *(Looking toward where Linda went out)*:   What a woman! They broke the mold when they made her. You know that, Biff?

BIFF: He's off salary. My God, working on commission!

HAPPY: Well, let's face it: he's no hot-shot selling man. Except that sometimes, you have to admit, he's a sweet personality.

BIFF *(Deciding)*:   Lend me ten bucks, will ya? I want to buy some new ties.

HAPPY: I'll take you to a place I know. Beautiful stuff. Wear one of my striped shirts tomorrow.

BIFF: She got gray. Mom got awful old. Gee, I'm gonna go in to Oliver tomorrow and knock him for a—

HAPPY: Come on up. Tell that to Dad. Let's give him a whirl. Come on.

BIFF *(Steamed up)*:   You know, with ten thousand bucks, boy!

HAPPY *(As they go into the living-room)*:   That's the talk, Biff, that's the first time I've heard the old confidence out of you! *(From within the living-room, fading off)*: You're gonna live with me, kid, and any babe you want just say the word . . . *(The last lines are hardly heard. They are mounting the stairs to their parents' bedroom.)*

LINDA *(Entering her bedroom and addressing Willy, who is in the bathroom. She is *straightening the bed for him):*   Can you do anything about the shower? It drips.

WILLY *(From the bathroom):*   All of a sudden everything falls to pieces! God-dam plumbing, oughta be sued, those people. I hardly finished putting it in and the thing . . . *(His words rumble off.)*

LINDA: I'm just wondering if Oliver will remember him. You think he might?

WILLY *(Coming out of the bathroom in his pajamas):*   Remember him? What's the matter with you, you crazy? If he'd've stayed with Oliver he'd be on top by now! Wait'll Oliver gets a look at him. You don't know the average caliber any more. The average young man today—*(He is getting into bed)*—is got a caliber of zero. Greatest thing in the world for him was to bum around.

Biff and Happy enter the bedroom. Slight pause.

WILLY *(Stops short, looking at Biff):*   Glad to hear it, boy.

HAPPY: He wanted to say good night to you, sport.

WILLY *(To Biff):*   Yeah. Knock him dead, boy. What'd you want to tell me?

BIFF: Just take it easy, Pop. Good night. *(He turns to go.)*

WILLY *(Unable to resist):*   And if anything falls off the desk while you're talking to him—like a package or something—don't you pick it up. They have office boys for that.

LINDA.   I'll make a big breakfast—

WILLY: Will you let me finish? *(To Biff):* Tell him you were in the business in the West. Not farm work.

BIFF: All right, Dad.

LINDA: I think everything—

WILLY *(Going right through her speech):*   And don't undersell yourself. No less than fifteen thousand dollars.

BIFF *(Unable to bear him):*   Okay. Good night, Mom. *(He starts moving.)*

WILLY: Because you got a greatness in you, Biff, remember that. You got all kinds a greatness . . . *(He lies back, exhausted. Biff walks out.)*

LINDA *(Calling after Biff):*   Sleep well, darling!

HAPPY: I'm gonna get married, Mom. I wanted to tell you.

LINDA: Go to sleep, dear.

HAPPY *(Going):*   I just wanted to tell you.

WILLY: Keep up the good work. *(Happy exits.)* God . . . remember that Ebbets Field game? The championship of the city?

LINDA: Just rest. Should I sing to you?

WILLY: Yeah. Sing to me. *(Linda hums a soft lullaby.)* When that team came out—he was the tallest, remember?

LINDA: Oh, yes. And in gold.

Biff enters the darkened kitchen, takes a cigarette, and leaves the house. He comes downstage into a golden pool of light. He smokes, staring at the night.

WILLY: Like a young god. Hercules—something like that. And the sun, the sun all around him. Remember how he waved to me? Right up from the field, with the representatives of three colleges standing by? And the buyers I brought, and the cheers when he came out—Loman, Loman, Loman! God Almighty, he'll be great yet. A star like that, magnificent, can never really fade away!

The light on Willy is fading. The gas heater begins to glow through the kitchen wall, near the stairs, a blue flame beneath red coils.

LINDA *(Timidly):*   Willy dear, what has he got against you?
WILLY: I'm so tired. Don't talk any more.

Biff slowly returns to the kitchen. He stops, stares toward the heater.

LINDA: Will you ask Howard to let you work in New York?
WILLY: First thing in the morning. Everything'll be all right.

Biff reaches behind the heater and draws out a length of rubber tubing. He is horrified and turns his head toward Willy's room, still dimly lit, from which the strains of Linda's desperate but monotonous humming rise.

WILLY *(Staring through the window into the moonlight):*   Gee, look at the moon moving between the buildings!

Biff wraps the tubing around his hand and quickly goes up the stairs.

Curtain

ACT TWO

Music is heard, gay and bright. The curtain rises as the music fades away. Willy, in shirt sleeves, is sitting at the kitchen table, sipping coffee, his hat in his lap. Linda is filling his cup when she can.

WILLY: Wonderful coffee. Meal in itself.
LINDA: Can I make you some eggs?
WILLY: No. Take a breath.
LINDA: You look so rested, dear.
WILLY: I slept like a dead one. First time in months. Imagine, sleeping till ten on a Tuesday morning. Boys left nice and early, heh?
LINDA: They were out of here by eight o'clock.
WILLY: Good work!
LINDA: It was so thrilling to see them leaving together. I can't get over the shaving lotion in this house!

WILLY *(Smiling):*   Mmm—

LINDA: Biff was very changed this morning. His whole attitude seemed to be hopeful. He couldn't wait to get downtown to see Oliver.

WILLY: He's heading for a change. There's no question, there simply are certain men that take longer to get—solidified. How did he dress?

LINDA: His blue suit. He's so handsome in that suit. He could be a—anything in that suit!

Willy gets up from the table. Linda holds his jacket for him.

WILLY: There's no question, no question at all. Gee, on the way home tonight I'd like to buy some seeds.

LINDA *(Laughing):*   That'd be wonderful. But not enough sun gets back there. Nothing'll grow any more.

WILLY: You wait, kid, before it's all over we're gonna get a little place out in the country, and I'll raise some vegetables, a couple of chickens . . .

LINDA: You'll do it yet, dear.

Willy walks out of his jacket. Linda follows him.

WILLY: And they'll get married, and come for a weekend. I'd build a little guest house. 'Cause I got so many fine tools, all I'd need would be a little lumber and some peace of mind.

LINDA *(Joyfully):*   I sewed the lining . . .

WILLY: I could build two guest houses, so they'd both come. Did he decide how much he's going to ask Oliver for?

LINDA *(Getting him into the jacket):*   He didn't mention it, but I imagine ten or fifteen thousand. You going to talk to Howard today?

WILLY: Yeah. I'll put it to him straight and simple. He'll just have to take me off the road.

LINDA: And Willy, don't forget to ask for a little advance, because we've got the insurance premium. It's the grace period now.

WILLY: That's a hundred . . . ?

LINDA: A hundred and eight, sixty-eight. Because we're a little short again.

WILLY: Why are we short?

LINDA: Well, you had the motor job on the car . . .

WILLY: That goddam Studebaker!

LINDA: And you got one more payment on the refrigerator . . .

WILLY: But it just broke again!

LINDA: Well, it's old, dear.

WILLY: I told you we should've bought a well-advertised machine. Charley bought a General Electric and it's twenty years old and it's still good, that son-of-a-bitch.

LINDA: But, Willy—

WILLY: Whoever heard of a Hastings refrigerator? Once in my life I would like to own something outright before it's broken! I'm always in a race with the junkyard! I just finished paying for the car and it's on its last legs. The refrigerator consumes belts like a goddam maniac. They time those things. They time them so when you finally paid for them, they're used up.

LINDA *(Buttoning up his jacket as he unbuttons it):*   All told, about two hundred dollars would carry us, dear. But that includes the last payment on the mortgage. After this payment, Willy, the house belongs to us.

WILLY: It's twenty-five years!

LINDA: Biff was nine years old when we bought it.

WILLY: Well, that's a great thing. To weather a twenty-five year mortgage is—

LINDA: It's an accomplishment.

WILLY: All the cement, the lumber, the reconstruction I put in this house! There ain't a crack to be found in it any more.

LINDA: Well, it served its purpose.

WILLY: What purpose? Some stranger'll come along, move in, and that's that. If only Biff would take this house, and raise a family . . . *(He starts to go.)* Good-by, I'm late.

LINDA *(Suddenly remembering):*   Oh, I forgot! You're supposed to meet them for dinner.

WILLY: Me?

LINDA: At Frank's Chop House on Forty-eighth near Sixth Avenue.

WILLY: Is that so! How about you?

LINDA: No, just the three of you. They're gonna blow you to a big meal!

WILLY: Don't say! Who thought of that?

LINDA: Biff came to me this morning, Willy, and he said, "Tell Dad, we want to blow him to a big meal." Be there six o'clock. You and your two boys are going to have dinner.

WILLY: Gee whiz! That's really somethin'. I'm gonna knock Howard for a loop, kid. I'll get an advance, and I'll come home with a New York job. Goddammit, now I'm gonna do it!

LINDA: Oh, that's the spirit, Willy!

WILLY: I will never get behind a wheel the rest of my life!

LINDA: It's changing, Willy, I can feel it changing!

WILLY: Beyond a question. G'by, I'm late. *(He starts to go again.)*

LINDA *(Calling after him as she runs to the kitchen table for a handkerchief):*   You got your glasses?

WILLY *(Feels for them, then comes back in):*   Yeah, yeah, got my glasses.

LINDA *(Giving him the handkerchief):*   And a handkerchief.

WILLY: Yeah, handkerchief.

LINDA: And your saccharine?

WILLY: Yeah, my saccharine.

LINDA: Be careful on the subway stairs.

She kisses him, and a silk stocking is seen hanging from her hand. Willy notices it.

WILLY: Will you stop mending stockings? At least while I'm in the house. It gets me nervous. I can't tell you. Please.

Linda hides the stocking in her hand as she follows Willy across the forestage in front of the house.

LINDA: Remember, Frank's Chop House.
WILLY *(Passing the apron):*   Maybe beets would grow out there.
LINDA *(Laughing):*   But you tried so many times.
WILLY: Yeah. Well, don't work hard today. *(He disappears around the right corner of the house.)*
LINDA: Be careful!

As Willy vanishes, Linda waves to him. Suddenly the phone rings. She runs across the stage and into the kitchen and lifts it.

LINDA: Hello? Oh, Biff! I'm so glad you called, I just . . . Yes, sure, I just told him. Yes, he'll be there for dinner at six o'clock, I didn't forget. Listen, I was just dying to tell you. You know that little rubber pipe I told you about? That he connected to the gas heater? I finally decided to go down the cellar this morning and take it away and destroy it. But it's gone! Imagine? He took it away himself, it isn't there! *(She listens.)* When? Oh, then you took it. Oh—nothing, it's just that I'd hoped he'd taken it away himself. Oh, I'm not worried, darling, because this morning he left in such high spirits, it was like the old days! I'm not afraid any more. Did Mr. Oliver see you? . . . Well, you wait there then. And make a nice impression on him, darling. Just don't perspire too much before you see him. And have a nice time with Dad. He may have big news too! . . . That's right, a New York job. And be sweet to him tonight, dear. Be loving to him. Because he's only a little boat looking for a harbor. *(She is trembling with sorrow and joy.)* Oh, that's wonderful, Biff, you'll save his life. Thanks, darling. Just put your arm around him when he comes into the restaurant. Give him a smile. That's the boy . . . Good-by, dear. . . . You got your comb? . . . That's fine. Good-by, Biff dear.

In the middle of her speech, Howard Wagner, thirty-six, wheels on a small typewriter table on which is a wire-recording machine and proceeds to plug it in. This is on the left forestage. Light slowly fades on Linda as it rises on Howard. Howard is intent on threading the machine and only glances over his shoulder as Willy appears.

WILLY: Pst! Pst!
HOWARD: Hello, Willy, come in.
WILLY: Like to have a little talk with you, Howard.
HOWARD: Sorry to keep you waiting. I'll be with you in a minute.
WILLY: What's that, Howard?

HOWARD: Didn't you ever see one of these? Wire recorder.

WILLY: Oh. Can we talk a minute?

HOWARD: Records things. Just got delivery yesterday. Been driving me
  crazy, the most terrific machine I ever saw in my life. I was up all night
  with it.

WILLY: What do you do with it?

HOWARD: I bought it for dictation, but you can do anything with it. Listen
  to this. I had it home last night. Listen to what I picked up. The first one
  is my daughter. Get this. *(He flicks the switch and "Roll out the Barrel" is heard
  being whistled.)* Listen to that kid whistle.

WILLY: That is lifelike, isn't it?

HOWARD: Seven years old. Get that tone.

WILLY: Ts, ts. Like to ask a little favor if you . . .

The whistling breaks off, and the voice of Howard's daughter is heard.

HIS DAUGHTER: "Now you, Daddy."

HOWARD: She's crazy for me! *(Again the same song is whistled.)* That's me! Ha!
  (He winks.)

WILLY: You're very good!

The whistling breaks off again. The machine runs silent for a moment.

HOWARD: Sh! Get this now, this is my son.

HIS SON: "The capital of Alabama is Montgomery; the capital of Arizona
  is Phoenix; the capital of Arkansas is Little Rock; the capital of California
  is Sacramento . . ." *and on, and on.*

HOWARD *(Holding up five fingers):*   Five years old, Willy!

WILLY: He'll make an announcer some day!

HIS SON *(Continuing):*   "The capital . . ."

HOWARD: Get that—alphabetical order! *(The machine breaks off suddenly.)*
  Wait a minute. The maid kicked the plug out.

WILLY: It certainly is a—

HOWARD: Sh, for God's sake!

HIS SON: "It's nine o'clock, Bulova watch time. So I have to go to sleep."

WILLY: That really is—

HOWARD: Wait a minute! The next is my wife.

They wait.

HOWARD'S VOICE: "Go on, say something." *(Pause.)* "Well, you gonna
  talk?"

HIS WIFE: "I can't think of anything."

HOWARD'S VOICE: "Well, talk—it's turning."

HIS WIFE *(Shyly, beaten):*   "Hello." *(Silence.)* "Oh, Howard, I can't talk into
  this . . ."

HOWARD *(Snapping the machine off):*   That was my wife.

WILLY: That is a wonderful machine. Can we—

HOWARD: I tell you, Willy, I'm gonna take my camera, and my bandsaw, and all my hobbies, and out they go. This is the most fascinating relaxation I ever found.

WILLY: I think I'll get one myself.

HOWARD: Sure, they're only a hundred and a half. You can't do without it. Supposing you wanna hear Jack Benny, see? But you can't be at home at that hour. So you tell the maid to turn the radio on when Jack Benny comes on, and this automatically goes on with the radio . . .

WILLY: And when you come home you . . .

HOWARD: You can come home twelve o'clock, one o'clock, any time you like, and you get yourself a Coke and sit yourself down, throw the switch, and there's Jack Benny's program in the middle of the night!

WILLY: I'm definitely going to get one. Because lots of time I'm on the road, and I think to myself, what I must be missing on the radio!

HOWARD: Don't you have a radio in the car?

WILLY: Well, yeah, but who ever thinks of turning it on?

HOWARD: Say, aren't you supposed to be in Boston?

WILLY: That's what I want to talk to you about, Howard. You got a minute? *(He draws a chair in from the wing.)*

HOWARD: What happened? What're you doing here?

WILLY: Well . . .

HOWARD: You didn't crack up again, did you?

WILLY: Oh, no. No . . .

HOWARD: Geez, you had me worried there for a minute. What's the trouble?

WILLY: Well, tell you the truth, Howard. I've come to the decision that I'd rather not travel any more.

HOWARD: Not travel! Well, what'll you do?

WILLY: Remember, Christmas time, when you had the party here? You said you'd try to think of some spot for me here in town.

HOWARD: With us?

WILLY: Well, sure.

HOWARD: Oh, yeah, yeah. I remember. Well, I couldn't think of anything for you, Willy.

WILLY: I tell ya, Howard. The kids are all grown up, y'know. I don't need much any more. If I could take home—well, sixty-five dollars a week, I could swing it.

HOWARD: Yeah, but Willy, see I—

WILLY: I tell ya why, Howard. Speaking frankly and between the two of us, y'know—I'm just a little tired.

HOWARD: Oh, I could understand that, Willy. But you're a road man, Willy, and we do a road business. We've only got a half-dozen salesmen on the floor here.

WILLY: God knows, Howard, I never asked a favor of any man. But I was with the firm when your father used to carry you in here in his arms.

HOWARD: I know that, Willy, but—

WILLY: Your father came to me the day you were born and asked me what
   I thought of the name of Howard, may he rest in peace.
HOWARD: I appreciate that, Willy, but there just is no spot here for you. If
   I had a spot I'd slam you right in, but I just don't have a single solitary
   spot.

He looks for his lighter. Willy has picked it up and gives it to him. Pause.

WILLY *(With increasing anger):*   Howard, all I need to set my table is fifty
   dollars a week.
HOWARD: But where am I going to put you, kid?
WILLY: Look, it isn't a question of whether I can sell merchandise, is it?
HOWARD: No, but it's a business, kid, and everybody's gotta pull his own
   weight.
WILLY *(Desperately):*   Just let me tell you a story, Howard—
HOWARD: 'Cause you gotta admit, business is business.
WILLY *(Angrily):*   Business is definitely business, but just listen for a minute.
   You don't understand this. When I was a boy—eighteen, nineteen—I was
   already on the road. And there was a question in my mind as to whether
   selling had a future for me. Because in those days I had a yearning to go
   to Alaska. See, there were three gold strikes in one month in Alaska, and
   I felt like going out. Just for the ride, you might say.
HOWARD *(Barely interested):*   Don't say.
WILLY: Oh, yeah, my father lived many years in Alaska. He was an adventurous man. We've got quite a little streak of self-reliance in our family.
   I thought I'd go out with my older brother and try to locate him, and
   maybe settle in the North with the old man. And I was almost decided to
   go, when I met a salesman in the Parker House. His name was Dave
   Singleman. And he was eighty-four years old, and he'd drummed merchandise in thirty-one states. And old Dave, he'd go up to his room,
   y'understand, put on his green velvet slippers—I'll never forget—and
   pick up his phone and call the buyers, and without ever leaving his room,
   at the age of eighty-four, he made his living. And when I saw that, I
   realized that selling was the greatest career a man could want. 'Cause what
   could be more satisfying than to be able to go, at the age of eighty-four,
   into twenty or thirty different cities, and pick up a phone, and be remembered and loved and helped by so many different people? Do you know?
   when he died—and by the way he died the death of a salesman, in his
   green velvet slippers in the smoker of the New York, New Haven and
   Hartford, going into Boston—when he died, hundreds of salesmen and
   buyers were at his funeral. Things were sad on a lotta trains for months
   after that. *(He stands up. Howard has not looked at him.)* In those days there
   was personality in it, Howard. There was respect, and comradeship, and
   gratitude in it. Today, it's all cut and dried, and there's no chance for
   bringing friendship to bear—or personality. You see what I mean? They
   don't know me any more.

HOWARD (*Moving away, to the right*):   That's just the thing, Willy.

WILLY: If I had forty dollars a week—that's all I'd need. Forty dollars, Howard.

HOWARD: Kid, I can't take blood from a stone, I—

WILLY (*Desperation is on him now*):   Howard, the year Al Smith was nominated, your father came to me and—

HOWARD (*Starting to go off*):   I've got to see some people, kid.

WILLY (*Stopping him*):   I'm talking about your father! There were promises made across this desk! You mustn't tell me you've got people to see—I put thirty-four years into this firm, Howard, and now I can't pay my insurance! You can't eat the orange and throw the peel away—a man is not a piece of fruit! (*After a pause*): Now pay attention. Your father—in 1928 I had a big year. I averaged a hundred and seventy dollars a week in commissions.

HOWARD (*Impatiently*):   Now, Willy, you never averaged—

WILLY (*Banging his hand on the desk*):   I averaged a hundred and seventy dollars a week in the year of 1928! And your father came to me—or rather, I was in the office here—it was right over this desk—and he put his hand on my shoulder—

HOWARD (*Getting up*):   You'll have to excuse me, Willy, I gotta see some people. Pull yourself together. (*Going out*): I'll be back in a little while.

On Howard's exit, the light on his chairs grows very bright and strange.

WILLY: Pull myself together! What the hell did I say to him? My God, I was yelling at him! How could I! (*Willy breaks off, staring at the light, which occupies the chair, animating it. He approaches this chair, standing across the desk from it.*) Frank, Frank, don't you remember what you told me that time? How you put your hand on my shoulder, and Frank . . . (*He leans on the desk and as he speaks the dead man's name he accidentally switches on the recorder, and instantly*)

HOWARD'S SON: ". . . of New York is Albany. The capital of Ohio is Cincinnati, the capital of Rhode Island is . . ." (*The recitation continues.*)

WILLY (*Leaping away with fright, shouting*):   Ha! Howard! Howard! Howard!

HOWARD (*Rushing in*):   What happened?

WILLY (*Pointing at the machine, which continues nasally, childishly, with the capital cities*):   Shut it off! Shut it off!

HOWARD (*Pulling the plug out*):   Look, Willy . . .

WILLY (*Pressing his hands to his eyes*):   I gotta get myself some coffee. I'll get some coffee . . .

Willy starts to walk out. Howard stops him.

HOWARD (*Rolling up the cord*):   Willy, look . . .

WILLY: I'll go to Boston.

HOWARD: Willy, you can't go to Boston for us.

WILLY: Why can't I go?

HOWARD: I don't want you to represent us. I've been meaning to tell you for a long time now.

WILLY: Howard, are you firing me?

HOWARD: I think you need a good long rest, Willy.

WILLY: Howard—

HOWARD: And when you feel better, come back, and we'll see if we can work something out.

WILLY: But I gotta earn money, Howard. I'm in no position to—

HOWARD: Where are your sons? Why don't your sons give you a hand?

WILLY: They're working on a very big deal.

HOWARD: This is no time for false pride, Willy. You go to your sons and you tell them that you're tired. You've got two great boys, haven't you?

WILLY: Oh, no question, no question, but in the meantime . . .

HOWARD: Then that's that, heh?

WILLY: All right, I'll go to Boston tomorrow.

HOWARD: No, no.

WILLY: I can't throw myself on my sons. I'm not a cripple!

HOWARD: Look, kid, I'm busy this morning.

WILLY *(Grasping Howard's arm):*   Howard, you've got to let me go to Boston!

HOWARD *(Hard, keeping himself under control):*   I've got a line of people to see this morning. Sit down, take five minutes, and pull yourself together, and then go home, will ya? I need the office, Willy. *(He starts to go; turns, remembering the recorder, starts to push off the table holding the recorder.)* Oh, yeah. Whenever you can this week, stop by and drop off the samples. You'll feel better, Willy, and then come back and we'll talk. Pull yourself together, kid, there's people outside.

Howard exits, pushing the table off left. Willy stares into space, exhausted. Now the music is heard—Ben's music—first distantly, then closer, closer. As Willy speaks, Ben enters from the right. He carries valise and umbrella.

WILLY: Oh, Ben, how did you do it? What is the answer? Did you wind up the Alaska deal already?

BEN: Doesn't take much time if you know what you're doing. Just a short business trip. Boarding ship in an hour. Wanted to say good-by.

WILLY: Ben, I've got to talk to you.

BEN *(Glancing at his watch):*   Haven't the time, William.

WILLY *(Crossing the apron to Ben):*   Ben, nothing's working out. I don't know what to do.

BEN: Now, look here, William. I've bought timberland in Alaska and I need a man to look after things for me.

WILLY: God, timberland! Me and my boys in those grand outdoors!

BEN: You've a new continent at your doorstep, William. Get out of these cities, they're full of talk and time payments and courts of law. Screw on your fists and you can fight for a fortune up there.

WILLY: Yes, yes! Linda, Linda!

Linda enters as of old, with the wash.

LINDA: Oh, you're back?

BEN: I haven't much time.

WILLY: No, wait! Linda, he's got a proposition for me in Alaska.

LINDA: But you've got—*(To Ben):* He's got a beautiful job here.

WILLY: But in Alaska, kid, I could—

LINDA: You're doing well enough, Willy!

BEN *(To Linda):*   Enough for what, my dear?

LINDA *(Frightened of Ben and angry at him):*   Don't say those things to him! Enough to be happy right here, right now. *(To Willy, while Ben laughs):* Why must everybody conquer the world? You're well liked, and the boys love you, and someday—*(To Ben)*—why, old man Wagner told him just the other day that if he keeps it up he'll be a member of the firm, didn't he, Willy?

WILLY: Sure, sure. I am building something with this firm, Ben, and if a man is building something he must be on the right track, mustn't he?

BEN: What are you building? Lay your hand on it. Where is it?

WILLY *(Hesitantly):*   That's true, Linda, there's nothing.

LINDA: Why? *(To Ben):* There's a man eighty-four years old—

WILLY: That's right, Ben, that's right. When I look at that man I say, what is there to worry about?

BEN: Bah!

WILLY: It's true, Ben. All he has to do is go into any city, pick up the phone, and he's making his living and you know why?

BEN *(Picking up his valise):*   I've got to go.

WILLY *(Holding Ben back):*   Look at this boy!

Biff, in his high school sweater, enters carrying suitcase. Happy carries Biff's shoulder guards, gold helmet, and football pants.

WILLY: Without a penny to his name, three great universities are begging for him, and from there the sky's the limit, because it's not what you do, Ben. It's who you know and the smile on your face! It's contacts, Ben, contacts! The whole wealth of Alaska passes over the lunch table at the Commodore Hotel, and that's the wonder, the wonder of this country, that a man can end with diamonds here on the basis of being liked! *(He turns to Biff.)* And that's why when you get out on that field today it's important. Because thousands of people will be rooting for you and loving you. *(To Ben, who has again begun to leave):* And Ben! when he walks into a business office his name will sound out like a bell and all the doors will open to him! I've seen it, Ben, I've seen it a thousand times! You can't feel it with your hand like timber, but it's there!

BEN: Good-by, William.

WILLY: Ben, am I right? Don't you think I'm right? I value your advice.

BEN: There's a new continent at your doorstep, William. You could walk out rich. Rich! *(He is gone.)*

WILLY: We'll do it here, Ben! You hear me? We're gonna do it here!

Young Bernard rushes in. The gay music of the Boys is heard.

BERNARD: Oh, gee, I was afraid you left already!

WILLY: Why? What time is it?

BERNARD: It's half-past one!

WILLY: Well, come on, everybody! Ebbets Field next stop! Where's the pennants? *(He rushes through the wall-line of the kitchen and out into the living-room.)*

LINDA *(To Biff):*   Did you pack fresh underwear?

BIFF *(Who has been limbering up):*   I want to go!

BERNARD: Biff, I'm carrying your helmet, ain't I?

HAPPY: No, I'm carrying the helmet.

BERNARD: Oh, Biff, you promised me.

HAPPY: I'm carrying the helmet.

BERNARD: How am I going to get in the locker room?

LINDA: Let him carry the shoulder guards. *(She puts her coat and hat on in the kitchen.)*

BERNARD: Can I, Biff? 'Cause I told everybody I'm going to be in the locker room.

HAPPY: In Ebbets Field it's the clubhouse.

BERNARD: I meant the clubhouse. Biff!

HAPPY: Biff!

BIFF *(Grandly, after a slight pause):*   Let him carry the shoulder guards.

HAPPY *(As he gives Bernard the shoulder guards):*   Stay close to us now.

Willy rushes in with the pennants.

WILLY *(Handing them out):*   Everybody wave when Biff comes out on the field. *(Happy and Bernard run off.)* You set now, boy?

The music has died away.

BIFF: Ready to go, Pop. Every muscle is ready.

WILLY *(At the edge of the apron):*   You realize what this means?

BIFF: That's right, Pop.

WILLY *(Feeling Biff's muscles):*   You're comin' home this afternoon captain of the All-Scholastic Championship Team of the City of New York.

BIFF: I got it, Pop. And remember, pal, when I take off my helmet, that touchdown is for you.

WILLY: Let's go! *(He is starting out, with his arm around Biff, when Charley enters, as of old, in knickers.)* I got no room for you, Charley.

CHARLEY: Room? For what?

WILLY: In the car.

CHARLEY: You goin' for a ride? I wanted to shoot some casino.

WILLY *(Furiously):*   Casino! *(Incredulously):* Don't you realize what today is?

LINDA: Oh, he knows, Willy. He's just kidding you.

WILLY: That's nothing to kid about!

CHARLEY: No, Linda, what's goin' on?

LINDA: He's playing in Ebbets Field.

CHARLEY: Baseball in this weather?

WILLY: Don't talk to him. Come on, come on! *(He is pushing them out.)*

CHARLEY: Wait a minute, didn't you hear the news?

WILLY: What?

CHARLEY: Don't you listen to the radio? Ebbets Field just blew up.

WILLY: You go to hell! *(Charley laughs. Pushing them out):* Come on, come on! We're late.

CHARLEY *(As they go):*   Knock a homer, Biff, knock a homer!

WILLY *(The last to leave, turning to Charley):*   I don't think that was funny, Charley. This is the greatest day of his life.

CHARLEY: Willy, when are you going to grow up?

WILLY: Yeah, heh? When this game is over, Charley, you'll be laughing out of the other side of your face. They'll be calling him another Red Grange. Twenty-five thousand a year.

CHARLEY *(Kidding):*   Is that so?

WILLY: Yeah, that's so.

CHARLEY: Well, then, I'm sorry, Willy. But tell me something.

WILLY: What?

CHARLEY: Who is Red Grange?

WILLY: Put up your hands. Goddam you, put up your hands!

Charley, chuckling, shakes his head and walks away, around the left corner of the stage. Willy follows him. The music rises to a mocking frenzy.

WILLY: Who the hell do you think you are, better than everybody else? You don't know everything, you big, ignorant, stupid . . . Put up your hands!

Light rises, on the right side of the forestage, on a small table in the reception room of Charley's office. Traffic sounds are heard. Bernard, now mature, sits whistling to himself. A pair of tennis rackets and an overnight bag are on the floor beside him.

WILLY *(Offstage):*   What are you walking away for? Don't walk away! If you're going to say something say it to my face! I know you laugh at me behind my back. You'll laugh out of the other side of your goddam face after this game. Touchdown! Touchdown! Eighty thousand people! Touchdown! Right between the goal posts.

Bernard is a quiet, earnest, but self-assured young man. Willy's voice is coming from right upstage now. Bernard lowers his feet off the table and listens. Jenny, his father's secretary, enters.

JENNY *(Distressed):*   Say, Bernard, will you go out in the hall?

BERNARD: What is that noise? Who is it?

JENNY: Mr. Loman. He just got off the elevator.

BERNARD *(Getting up)*:   Who's he arguing with?

JENNY: Nobody. There's nobody with him. I can't deal with him any more, and your father gets all upset everytime he comes. I've got a lot of typing to do, and your father's waiting to sign it. Will you see him?

WILLY *(Entering)*:   Touchdown! Touch—*(He sees Jenny.)* Jenny, Jenny, good to see you. How're ya? Workin'? Or still honest?

JENNY: Fine. How've you been feeling?

WILLY: Not much any more, Jenny. Ha, ha! *(He is surprised to see the rackets.)*

BERNARD: Hello, Uncle Willy.

WILLY *(Almost shocked)*:   Bernard! Well, look who's here! *(He comes quickly, guiltily, to Bernard and warmly shakes his hand.)*

BERNARD: How are you? Good to see you.

WILLY: What are you doing here?

BERNARD: Oh, just stopped by to see Pop. Get off my feet till my train leaves. I'm going to Washington in a few minutes.

WILLY: Is he in?

BERNARD: Yes, he's in his office with the accountant. Sit down.

WILLY *(Sitting down)*:   What're you going to do in Washington?

BERNARD: Oh, just a case I've got there, Willy.

WILLY: That so? *(Indicating the rackets)*:   You going to play tennis there?

BERNARD: I'm staying with a friend who's got a court.

WILLY: Don't say. His own tennis court. Must be fine people, I bet.

BERNARD: They are, very nice. Dad tells me Biff's in town.

WILLY *(With a big smile)*:   Yeah, Biff's in. Working on a very big deal, Bernard.

BERNARD: What's Biff doing?

WILLY: Well, he's been doing very big things in the West. But he decided to establish himself here. Very big. We're having dinner. Did I hear your wife had a boy?

BERNARD: That's right. Our second.

WILLY: Two boys! What do you know!

BERNARD: What kind of a deal has Biff got?

WILLY: Well, Bill Oliver—very big sporting-goods man—he wants Biff very badly. Called him in from the West. Long distance, carte blanche, special deliveries. Your friends have their own private tennis court?

BERNARD: You still with the old firm, Willy?

WILLY *(After a pause)*:   I'm—I'm overjoyed to see how you made the grade, Bernard, overjoyed. It's an encouraging thing to see a young man really —really—Looks very good for Biff—very—*(He breaks off, then)*: Bernard— *(He is so full of emotion, he breaks off again.)*

BERNARD: What is it, Willy?

WILLY *(Small and alone)*:   What—what's the secret?

BERNARD: What secret?

WILLY: How—how did you? Why didn't he ever catch on?

BERNARD: I wouldn't know that, Willy.

WILLY (*Confidentially, desperately*):   You were his friend, his boyhood friend. There's something I don't understand about it. His life ended after that Ebbets Field game. From the age of seventeen nothing good ever happened to him.

BERNARD: He never trained himself for anything.

WILLY: But he did, he did. After high school he took so many correspondence courses. Radio mechanics; television; God knows what, and never made the slightest mark.

BERNARD (*Taking off his glasses*):   Willy, do you want to talk candidly?

WILLY (*Rising, faces Bernard*):   I regard you as a very brilliant man, Bernard. I value your advice.

BERNARD: Oh, the hell with the advice, Willy. I couldn't advise you. There's just one thing I've always wanted to ask you. When he was supposed to graduate, and the math teacher flunked him—

WILLY: Oh, that son-of-a-bitch ruined his life.

BERNARD: Yeah, but, Willy, all he had to do was go to summer school and make up that subject.

WILLY: That's right, that's right.

BERNARD: Did you tell him not to go to summer school?

WILLY: Me? I begged him to go. I ordered him to go!

BERNARD: Then why wouldn't he go?

WILLY: Why? Why! Bernard, that question has been trailing me like a ghost for the last fifteen years. He flunked the subject, and laid down and died like a hammer hit him!

BERNARD: Take it easy, kid.

WILLY: Let me talk to you—I got nobody to talk to. Bernard, Bernard, was it my fault? Y'see? It keeps going around in my mind, maybe I did something to him. I got nothing to give him.

BERNARD: Don't take it so hard.

WILLY: Why did he lay down? What is the story there? You were his friend!

BERNARD: Willy, I remember, it was June, and our grades came out. And he'd flunked math.

WILLY: That son-of-a-bitch!

BERNARD: No, it wasn't right then. Biff just got very angry, I remember, and he was ready to enroll in summer school.

WILLY (*Surprised*):   He was?

BERNARD: He wasn't beaten by it at all. But then, Willy, he disappeared from the block for almost a month. And I got the idea that he'd gone up to New England to see you. Did he have a talk with you then?

Willy stares in silence.

BERNARD: Willy?

WILLY (*With a strong edge of resentment in his voice*):   Yeah, he came to Boston. What about it?

BERNARD: Well, just that when he came back—I'll never forget this, it always mystifies me. Because I'd thought so well of Biff, even though he'd always taken advantage of me. I loved him, Willy, y'know? And he came back after that month and took his sneakers—remember those sneakers with "University of Virginia" printed on them? He was so proud of those, wore them every day. And he took them down in the cellar, and burned them up in the furnace. We had a fist fight. It lasted at least half an hour. Just the two of us, punching each other down the cellar, and crying right through it. I've often thought of how strange it was that I knew he'd given up his life. What happened in Boston, Willy?

Willy looks at him as at an intruder.

BERNARD: I just bring it up because you asked me.
WILLY *(Angrily)*:   Nothing. What do you mean, "What happened?" What's that got to do with anything?
BERNARD: Well, don't get sore.
WILLY: What are you trying to do, blame it on me? If a boy lays down is that my fault?
BERNARD: Now, Willy, don't get—
WILLY: Well, don't—don't talk to me that way! What does that mean, "What happened?"

Charley enters. He is in his vest, and he carries a bottle of bourbon.

CHARLEY: Hey, you're going to miss that train. *(He waves the bottle.)*
BERNARD: Yeah, I'm going. *(He takes the bottle.)* Thanks, Pop. *(He picks up his rackets and bag.)* Good-by, Willy, and don't worry about it. You know, "If at first you don't succeed . . ."
WILLY: Yes, I believe in that.
BERNARD: But sometimes, Willy, it's better for a man just to walk away.
WILLY: Walk away?
BERNARD: That's right.
WILLY: But if you can't walk away?
BERNARD *(After a slight pause)*:   I guess that's when it's tough. *(Extending his hand)*: Good-by, Willy.
WILLY *(Shaking Bernard's hand)*:   Good-by, boy.
CHARLEY *(An arm on Bernard's shoulder)*:   How do you like this kid? Gonna argue a case in front of the Supreme Court.
BERNARD *(Protesting)*:   Pop!
WILLY *(Genuinely shocked, pained, and happy)*:   No! The Supreme Court!
BERNARD: I gotta run. 'By, Dad!
CHARLEY: Knock 'em dead, Bernard!

Bernard goes off.

WILLY *(As Charley takes out his wallet):*   The Supreme Court! And he didn't even mention it!

CHARLEY *(Counting out money on the desk):*   He don't have to—he's gonna do it.

WILLY: And you never told him what to do, did you? You never took any interest in him.

CHARLEY: My salvation is that I never took any interest in anything. There's some money—fifty dollars. I got an accountant inside.

WILLY: Charley, look . . . *(With difficulty):* I got my insurance to pay. If you can manage it—I need a hundred and ten dollars.

Charley doesn't reply for a moment; merely stops moving.

WILLY: I'd draw it from my bank but Linda would know, and I . . .

CHARLEY: Sit down, Willy.

WILLY *(Moving toward the chair):*   I'm keeping an account of everything, remember. I'll pay every penny back. *(He sits.)*

CHARLEY: Now listen to me, Willy.

WILLY: I want you to know I appreciate . . .

CHARLEY *(Sitting down on the table):*   Willy, what're you doin'? What the hell is goin' on in your head?

WILLY: Why? I'm simply . . .

CHARLEY: I offered you a job. You can make fifty dollars a week. And I won't send you on the road.

WILLY: I've got a job.

CHARLEY: Without pay? What kind of a job is a job without pay? *(He rises.)* Now, look, kid, enough is enough. I'm no genius but I know when I'm being insulted.

WILLY: Insulted!

CHARLEY: Why don't you want to work for me?

WILLY: What's the matter with you? I've got a job.

CHARLEY: Then what're you walkin' in here every week for?

WILLY *(Getting up):*   Well, if you don't want me to walk in here—

CHARLEY: I am offering you a job.

WILLY: I don't want your goddam job!

CHARLEY: When the hell are you going to grow up?

WILLY *(Furiously):*   You big ignoramus, if you say that to me again I'll rap you one! I don't care how big you are! *(He's ready to fight.)*

Pause.

CHARLEY *(Kindly, going to him):*   How much do you need, Willy?

WILLY: Charley, I'm strapped. I'm strapped. I don't know what to do. I was just fired.

CHARLEY: Howard fired you?

WILLY: That snotnose. Imagine that? I named him. I named him Howard.

CHARLEY: Willy, when're you gonna realize that them things don't mean anything? You named him Howard, but you can't sell that. The only thing you got in this world is what you can sell. And the funny thing is that you're a salesman, and you don't know that.

WILLY: I've always tried to think otherwise, I guess. I always felt that if a man was impressive, and well liked, that nothing—

CHARLEY: Why must everybody like you? Who liked J. P. Morgan? Was he impressive? In a Turkish bath he'd look like a butcher. But with his pockets on he was very well liked. Now listen, Willy, I know you don't like me, and nobody can say I'm in love with you, but I'll give you a job because—just for the hell of it, put it that way. Now what do you say?

WILLY: I—I just can't work for you, Charley.

CHARLEY: What're you, jealous of me?

WILLY: I can't work for you, that's all, don't ask me why.

CHARLEY *(Angered, takes out more bills):*   You been jealous of me all your life, you damned fool! Here, pay your insurance. *(He puts the money in Willy's hand.)*

WILLY: I'm keeping strict accounts.

CHARLEY: I've got some work to do. Take care of yourself. And pay your insurance.

WILLY *(Moving to the right):*   Funny, y'know? After all the highways, and the trains, and the appointments, and the years, you end up worth more dead than alive.

CHARLEY: Willy, nobody's worth nothin' dead. *(After a slight pause):* Did you hear what I said?

Willy stands still, dreaming.

CHARLEY: Willy!

WILLY: Apologize to Bernard for me when you see him. I didn't mean to argue with him. He's a fine boy. They're all fine boys, and they'll end up big—all of them. Someday they'll all play tennis together. Wish me luck, Charley. He saw Bill Oliver today.

CHARLEY: Good luck.

WILLY *(On the verge of tears):*   Charley, you're the only friend I got. Isn't that a remarkable thing? *(He goes out.)*

CHARLEY: Jesus!

Charley stares after him a moment and follows. All light blacks out. Suddenly raucous music is heard, and a red glow rises behind the screen at right. Stanley, a young waiter, appears, carrying a table, followed by Happy, who is carrying two chairs.

STANLEY *(Putting the table down):*   That's all right, Mr. Loman, I can handle it myself. *(He turns and takes the chairs from Happy and places them at the table.)*

HAPPY *(Glancing around):*   Oh, this is better.

STANLEY.   Sure, in the front there you're in the middle of all kinds a noise. Whenever you got a party, Mr. Loman, you just tell me and I'll put you back here. Y'know, there's a lotta people they don't like it private, because when they go out they like to see a lotta action around them because they're sick and tired to stay in the house by theirself. But I know you, you ain't from Hackensack. You know what I mean?

HAPPY *(Sitting down):*   So how's it coming, Stanley?

STANLEY: Ah, it's a dog's life. I only wish during the war they'd a took me in the Army. I coulda been dead by now.

HAPPY: My brother's back, Stanley.

STANLEY: Oh, he come back, heh? From the Far West.

HAPPY: Yeah, big cattle man, my brother, so treat him right. And my father's coming too.

STANLEY: Oh, your father too!

HAPPY: You got a couple of nice lobsters?

STANLEY: Hundred per cent, big.

HAPPY: I want them with the claws.

STANLEY: Don't worry, I don't give you no mice. *(Happy laughs.)* How about some wine? It'll put a head on the meal.

HAPPY: No. You remember, Stanley, that recipe I brought you from overseas? With the champagne in it?

STANLEY: Oh, yeah, sure. I still got it tacked up yet in the kitchen. But that'll have to cost a buck apiece anyways.

HAPPY: That's all right.

STANLEY: What'd you, hit a number or somethin'?

HAPPY: No, it's a little celebration. My brother is—I think he pulled off a big deal today. I think we're going into business together.

STANLEY: Great! That's the best for you. Because a family business, you know what I mean?—that's the best.

HAPPY: That's what I think.

STANLEY: 'Cause what's the difference? Somebody steals? It's in the family. Know what I mean? *(Sotto voce):* Like this bartender here. The boss is goin' crazy what kinda leak he's got in the cash register. You put it in but it don't come out.

HAPPY *(Raising his head):*   Sh!

STANLEY: What?

HAPPY: You notice I wasn't lookin' right or left, was I?

STANLEY: No.

HAPPY: And my eyes are closed.

STANLEY: So what's the—?

HAPPY: Strudel's comin'.

STANLEY *(Catching on, looks around):*   Ah, no, there's no—

He breaks off as a furred, lavishly dressed girl enters and sits at the next table. Both follow her with their eyes.

STANLEY: Geez, how'd ya know?

HAPPY: I got radar or something. *(Staring directly at her profile):* Oooooooo . . . Stanley.

STANLEY: I think that's for you, Mr. Loman.

HAPPY: Look at that mouth. Oh, God. And the binoculars.

STANLEY: Geez, you got a life, Mr. Loman.

HAPPY: Wait on her.

STANLEY *(Going to the girl's table):*   Would you like a menu, ma'am?

GIRL: I'm expecting someone, but I'd like a—

HAPPY: Why don't you bring her—excuse me, miss, do you mind? I sell champagne, and I'd like you to try my brand. Bring her a champagne, Stanley.

GIRL: That's awfully nice of you.

HAPPY: Don't mention it. It's all company money. *(He laughs.)*

GIRL: That's a charming product to be selling, isn't it?

HAPPY: Oh, gets to be like everything else. Selling is selling, y'know.

GIRL: I suppose.

HAPPY: You don't happen to sell, do you?

GIRL: No, I don't sell.

HAPPY: Would you object to a compliment from a stranger? You ought to be on a magazine cover.

GIRL *(Looking at him a little archly):*   I have been.

Stanley comes in with a glass of champagne.

HAPPY: What'd I say before, Stanley? You see? She's a cover girl.

STANLEY: Oh, I could see, I could see.

HAPPY *(To the Girl):*   What magazine?

GIRL: Oh, a lot of them. *(She takes the drink.)* Thank you.

HAPPY: You know what they say in France, don't you? "Champagne is the drink of the complexion"—Hya, Biff!

Biff has entered and sits with Happy.

BIFF: Hello, kid. Sorry I'm late.

HAPPY: I just got here. Uh, Miss—?

GIRL: Forsythe.

HAPPY: Miss Forsythe, this is my brother.

BIFF: Is Dad here?

HAPPY: His name is Biff. You might've heard of him. Great football player.

GIRL: Really? What team?

HAPPY: Are you familiar with football?

GIRL: No, I'm afraid I'm not.

HAPPY: Biff is quarterback with the New York Giants.

GIRL: Well, that is nice, isn't it? *(She drinks.)*

HAPPY: Good health.

GIRL: I'm happy to meet you.

HAPPY: That's my name. Hap. It's really Harold, but at West Point they called me Happy.

GIRL *(Now really impressed):*   Oh, I see. How do you do? *(She turns her profile.)*

BIFF: Isn't Dad coming?

HAPPY: You want her?

BIFF: Oh, I could never make that.

HAPPY: I remember the time that idea would never come into your head. Where's the old confidence, Biff?

BIFF: I just saw Oliver—

HAPPY: Wait a minute. I've got to see that old confidence again. Do you want her? She's on call.

BIFF: Oh, no. *(He turns to look at the Girl.)*

HAPPY: I'm telling you. Watch this. *(Turning to the Girl):* Honey? *(She turns to him.)* Are you busy?

GIRL: Well, I am . . . but I could make a phone call.

HAPPY: Do that, will you, honey? And see if you can get a friend. We'll be here for a while. Biff is one of the greatest football players in the country.

GIRL *(Standing up):*   Well, I'm certainly happy to meet you.

HAPPY: Come back soon.

GIRL: I'll try.

HAPPY: Don't try, honey, try hard.

The Girl exits. Stanley follows, shaking his head in bewildered admiration.

HAPPY: Isn't that a shame now? A beautiful girl like that? That's why I can't get married. There's not a good woman in a thousand. New York is loaded with them, kid!

BIFF: Hap, look—

HAPPY: I told you she was on call!

BIFF *(Strangely unnerved):*   Cut it out, will ya? I want to say something to you.

HAPPY: Did you see Oliver?

BIFF: I saw him all right. Now look, I want to tell Dad a couple of things and I want you to help me.

HAPPY: What? Is he going to back you?

BIFF: Are you crazy? You're out of your goddam head, you know that?

HAPPY: Why? What happened?

BIFF *(Breathlessly):*   I did a terrible thing today, Hap. It's been the strangest day I ever went through. I'm all numb, I swear.

HAPPY: You mean he wouldn't see you?

BIFF: Well, I waited six hours for him, see? All day. Kept sending my name in. Even tried to date his secretary so she'd get me to him, but no soap.

HAPPY: Because you're not showin' the old confidence, Biff. He remembered you, didn't he?

BIFF *(Stopping Happy with a gesture):*   Finally, about five o'clock, he comes out. Didn't remember who I was or anything. I felt like such an idiot, Hap.

HAPPY: Did you tell him my Florida idea?

BIFF: He walked away. I saw him for one minute. I got so mad I could've torn the walls down! How the hell did I ever get the idea I was a salesman there? I even believed myself that I'd been a salesman for him! And then he gave me one look and—I realized what a ridiculous lie my whole life has been! We've been talking in a dream for fifteen years. I was a shipping clerk.

HAPPY: What'd you do?

BIFF *(With great tension and wonder):*   Well, he left, see. And the secretary went out. I was all alone in the waiting-room. I don't know what came over me, Hap. The next thing I know I'm in his office—paneled walls, everything. I can't explain it. I—Hap, I took his fountain pen.

HAPPY: Geez, did he catch you?

BIFF: I ran out. I ran down all eleven flights. I ran and ran and ran.

HAPPY: That was an awful dumb—what'd you do that for?

BIFF *(Agonized):*   I don't know, I just—wanted to take something, I don't know. You gotta help me, Hap, I'm gonna tell Pop.

HAPPY: You crazy? What for?

BIFF: Hap, he's got to understand that I'm not the man somebody lends that kind of money to. He thinks I've been spiting him all these years and it's eating him up.

HAPPY: That's just it. You tell him something nice.

BIFF: I can't.

HAPPY: Say you got a lunch date with Oliver tomorrow.

BIFF: So what do I do tomorrow?

HAPPY: You leave the house tomorrow and come back at night and say Oliver is thinking it over. And he thinks it over for a couple of weeks, and gradually it fades away and nobody's the worse.

BIFF: But it'll go on forever!

HAPPY: Dad is never so happy as when he's looking forward to something!

Willy enters.

HAPPY: Hello, scout!

WILLY: Gee, I haven't been here in years!

Stanley has followed Willy in and sets a chair for him. Stanley starts off but Happy stops him.

HAPPY: Stanley!

Stanley stands by, waiting for an order.

BIFF *(Going to Willy with guilt, as to an invalid):*   Sit down, Pop. You want a drink?

WILLY: Sure, I don't mind.

BIFF: Let's get a load on.

WILLY: You look worried.

BIFF: N-no. *(To Stanley):* Scotch all around. Make it doubles.

STANLEY: Doubles, right. *(He goes.)*

WILLY: You had a couple already, didn't you?

BIFF: Just a couple, yeah.

WILLY: Well, what happened, boy? *(Nodding affirmatively, with a smile):* Everything go all right?

BIFF *(Takes a breath, then reaches out and grasps Willy's hand):*   Pal . . . *(He is smiling bravely, and Willy is smiling too.)* I had an experience today.

HAPPY: Terrific, Pop.

WILLY: That so? What happened?

BIFF *(High, slightly alcoholic, above the earth):*   I'm going to tell you everything from first to last. It's been a strange day. *(Silence. He looks around, composes himself as best he can, but his breath keeps breaking the rhythm of his voice.)* I had to wait quite a while for him, and—

WILLY: Oliver?

BIFF: Yeah, Oliver. All day, as a matter of cold fact. And a lot of—instances—facts, Pop, facts about my life came back to me. Who was it, Pop? Who ever said I was a salesman with Oliver?

WILLY: Well, you were.

BIFF: No, Dad, I was a shipping clerk.

WILLY: But you were practically—

BIFF *(With determination):*   Dad, I don't know who said it first, but I was never a salesman for Bill Oliver.

WILLY: What're you talking about?

BIFF: Let's hold on to the facts tonight, Pop. We're not going to get anywhere bullin' around. I was a shipping clerk.

WILLY *(Angrily):*   All right, now listen to me—

BIFF: Why don't you let me finish?

WILLY: I'm not interested in stories about the past or any crap of that kind because the woods are burning, boys, you understand? There's a big blaze going on all around. I was fired today.

BIFF *(Shocked):*   How could you be?

WILLY: I was fired, and I'm looking for a little good news to tell your mother, because the woman has waited and the woman has suffered. The gist of it is that I haven't got a story left in my head, Biff. So don't give me a lecture about facts and aspects. I am not interested. Now what've you got to say to me?

Stanley enters with three drinks. They wait until he leaves.

WILLY: Did you see Oliver?

BIFF: Jesus, Dad!

WILLY: You mean you didn't go up there?

HAPPY: Sure he went up there.

BIFF: I did. I—saw him. How could they fire you?

WILLY *(On the edge of his chair):*   What kind of a welcome did he give you?

BIFF: He won't even let you work on commission?

WILLY: I'm out! *(Driving):* So tell me, he gave you a warm welcome?

HAPPY: Sure, Pop, sure!

BIFF *(Driven):*   Well, it was kind of—

WILLY: I was wondering if he'd remember you. *(To Happy):* Imagine, man doesn't see him for ten, twelve years and gives him that kind of a welcome!

HAPPY: Damn right!

BIFF *(Trying to return to the offensive):*   Pop, look—

WILLY: You know why he remembered you, don't you? Because you impressed him in those days.

BIFF: Let's talk quietly and get this down to the facts, huh?

WILLY *(As though Biff had been interrupting):*   Well, what happened? It's great news, Biff. Did he take you into his office or'd you talk in the waiting-room?

BIFF: Well, he came in, see, and—

WILLY *(With a big smile):*   What'd he say? Betcha he threw his arm around you.

BIFF: Well, he kinda—

WILLY: He's a fine man. *(To Happy):* Very hard man to see, y'know.

HAPPY *(Agreeing):*   Oh, I know.

WILLY *(To Biff):*   Is that where you had the drinks?

BIFF: Yeah, he gave me a couple of—no, no!

HAPPY *(Cutting in):*   He told him my Florida idea.

WILLY: Don't interrupt. *(To Biff):* How'd he react to the Florida idea?

BIFF: Dad, will you give me a minute to explain?

WILLY: I've been waiting for you to explain since I sat down here! What happened? He took you into his office and what?

BIFF: Well—I talked. And—and he listened, see.

WILLY: Famous for the way he listens, y'know. What was his answer?

BIFF: His answer was—*(He breaks off, suddenly angry.)* Dad, you're not letting me tell you what I want to tell you!

WILLY *(Accusing, angered):*   You didn't see him, did you?

BIFF: I did see him!

WILLY: What'd you insult him or something? You insulted him, didn't you?

BIFF: Listen, will you let me out of it, will you just let me out of it!

HAPPY: What the hell!

WILLY: Tell me what happened!

BIFF *(To Happy):*   I can't talk to him!

A single trumpet note jars the ear. The light of green leaves stains the house, which holds the air of night and a dream. Young Bernard enters and knocks on the door of the house.

YOUNG BERNARD *(Frantically):*   Mrs. Loman, Mrs. Loman!

HAPPY: Tell him what happened!

BIFF *(To Happy):*   Shut up and leave me alone!

WILLY: No, no! You had to go and flunk math!

BIFF: What math? What're you talking about?

YOUNG BERNARD: Mrs. Loman, Mrs. Loman!

Linda appears in the house, as of old.

WILLY *(Wildly)*:   Math, math, math!

BIFF: Take it easy, Pop!

YOUNG BERNARD: Mrs. Loman!

WILLY *(Furiously)*:   If you hadn't flunked you'd've been set by now!

BIFF: Now, look, I'm gonna tell you what happened, and you're going to listen to me.

YOUNG BERNARD: Mrs. Loman!

BIFF: I waited six hours—

HAPPY: What the hell are you saying?

BIFF: I kept sending in my name but he wouldn't see me. So finally he . . . *(He continues unheard as light fades low on the restaurant.)*

YOUNG BERNARD: Biff flunked math!

LINDA: No!

YOUNG BERNARD: Birnbaum flunked him! They won't graduate him!

LINDA: But they have to. He's gotta go to the university. Where is he? Biff! Biff!

YOUNG BERNARD: No, he left. He went to Grand Central.

LINDA: Grand—You mean he went to Boston!

YOUNG BERNARD: Is Uncle Willy in Boston?

LINDA: Oh, maybe Willy can talk to the teacher. Oh, the poor, poor boy!

Light on house area snaps out.

BIFF *(At the table, now audible, holding up a gold fountain pen)*:   . . . so I'm washed up with Oliver, you understand? Are you listening to me?

WILLY *(At a loss)*:   Yeah, sure. If you hadn't flunked—

BIFF: Flunked what? What're you talking about?

WILLY: Don't blame everything on me! I didn't flunk math—you did! What pen?

HAPPY: That was awful dumb, Biff, a pen like that is worth—

WILLY *(Seeing the pen for the first time)*:   You took Oliver's pen?

BIFF *(Weakening)*:   Dad, I just explained it to you.

WILLY: You stole Bill Oliver's fountain pen!

BIFF: I didn't exactly steal it! That's just what I've been explaining to you!

HAPPY: He had it in his hand and just then Oliver walked in, so he got nervous and stuck it in his pocket!

WILLY: My God, Biff!

BIFF: I never intended to do it, Dad!

OPERATOR'S VOICE: Standish Arms, good evening!

WILLY *(Shouting)*:   I'm not in my room!

BIFF *(Frightened):*   Dad, what's the matter? *(He and Happy stand up.)*

OPERATOR: Ringing Mr. Loman for you!

WILLY: I'm not there, stop it!

BIFF *(Horrified, gets down on one knee before Willy):*   Dad, I'll make good, I'll make good. *(Willy tries to get to his feet. Biff holds him down.)* Sit down now.

WILLY: No, you're no good, you're no good for anything.

BIFF: I am, Dad, I'll find something else, you understand? Now don't worry about anything. *(He holds up Willy's face):* Talk to me, Dad.

OPERATOR: Mr. Loman does not answer. Shall I page him?

WILLY *(Attempting to stand, as though to rush and silence the Operator):*   No, no, no!

HAPPY: He'll strike something, Pop

WILLY: No, no . . .

BIFF *(Desperately, standing over Willy):*   Pop, listen! Listen to me! I'm telling you something good. Oliver talked to his partner about the Florida idea. You listening? He—he talked to his partner, and he came to me . . . I'm going to be all right, you hear? Dad, listen to me, he said it was just a question of the amount!

WILLY: Then you . . . got it?

HAPPY: He's gonna be terrific, Pop!

WILLY *(Trying to stand):*   Then you got it, haven't you? You got it! You got it!

BIFF *(Agonized, holds Willy down):*   No, no. Look, Pop. I'm supposed to have lunch with them tomorrow. I'm just telling you this so you'll know that I can still make an impression, Pop. And I'll make good somewhere, but I can't go tomorrow, see?

WILLY: Why not? You simply—

BIFF: But the pen, Pop!

WILLY: You give it to him and tell him it was an oversight!

HAPPY: Sure, have lunch tomorrow!

BIFF: I can't say that—

WILLY: You were doing a crossword puzzle and accidentally used his pen!

BIFF: Listen, kid, I took those balls years ago, now I walk in with his fountain pen? That clinches it, don't you see? I can't face him like that! I'll try elsewhere.

PAGE'S VOICE: Paging Mr. Loman!

WILLY: Don't you want to be anything?

BIFF: Pop, how can I go back?

WILLY: You don't want to be anything, is that what's behind it?

BIFF *(Now angry at Willy for not crediting his sympathy):*   Don't take it that way! You think it was easy walking into that office after what I'd done to him? A team of horses couldn't have dragged me back to Bill Oliver!

WILLY: Then why'd you go?

BIFF: Why did I go? Why did I go! Look at you! Look at what's become of you!

Off left, The Woman laughs.

WILLY: Biff, you're going to go to that lunch tomorrow, or—

BIFF: I can't go. I've got no appointment!

HAPPY: Biff, for . . .!

WILLY: Are you spiting me?

BIFF: Don't take it that way! Goddammit!

WILLY *(Strikes Biff and falters away from the table):*   You rotten little louse! Are you spiting me?

THE WOMAN: Someone's at the door, Willy!

BIFF: I'm no good, can't you see what I am?

HAPPY *(Separating them):*   Hey, you're in a restaurant! Now cut it out, both of you! *(The girls enter.)* Hello, girls, sit down.

The Woman laughs, off left.

MISS FORSYTHE: I guess we might as well. This is Letta.

THE WOMAN: Willy, are you going to wake up?

BIFF *(Ignoring Willy):*   How're ya, miss, sit down. What do you drink?

MISS FORSYTHE: Letta might not be able to stay long.

LETTA: I gotta get up very early tomorrow. I got jury duty. I'm so excited! Were you fellows ever on a jury?

BIFF: No, but I been in front of them! *(The girls laugh.)* This is my father.

LETTA: Isn't he cute? Sit down with us, Pop.

HAPPY: Sit him down, Biff!

BIFF *(Going to him):*   Come on, slugger, drink us under the table. To hell with it! Come on, sit down, pal.

On Biff's last insistence, Willy is about to sit.

THE WOMAN *(Now urgently):*   Willy, are you going to answer the door!

The Woman's call pulls Willy back. He starts right, befuddled.

BIFF: Hey, where are you going?

WILLY: Open the door.

BIFF: The door?

WILLY: The washroom . . . the door . . . where's the door?

BIFF *(Leading Willy to the left):*   Just go straight down.

Willy moves left.

THE WOMAN: Willy, Willy, are you going to get up, get up, get up, get up?

Willy exits left.

LETTA: I think it's sweet you bring your daddy along.

MISS FORSYTHE: Oh, he isn't really your father!

BIFF *(At left, turning to her resentfully):*   Miss Forsythe, you've just seen a prince walk by. A fine, troubled prince. A hard-working, unappreciated prince. A pal, you understand? A good companion. Always for his boys.

LETTA: That's so sweet.

HAPPY: Well, girls, what's the program? We're wasting time. Come on, Biff. Gather round. Where would you like to go?

BIFF: Why don't you do something for him?

HAPPY: Me!

BIFF: Don't you give a damn for him, Hap?

HAPPY: What're you talking about? I'm the one who—

BIFF: I sense it, you don't give a good goddam about him. (*He takes the rolled-up hose from his pocket and puts it on the table in front of Happy.*) Look what I found in the cellar, for Christ's sake. How can you bear to let it go on?

HAPPY: Me? Who goes away? Who runs off and—

BIFF: Yeah, but he doesn't mean anything to you. You could help him— I can't! Don't you understand what I'm talking about? He's going to kill himself, don't you know that?

HAPPY: Don't I know it! Me!

BIFF: Hap, help him! Jesus . . . help him . . . Help me, help me, I can't bear to look at his face! (*Ready to weep, he hurries out, up right.*)

HAPPY (*Starting after him*):   Where are you going?

MISS FORSYTHE: What's he so mad about?

HAPPY: Come on, girls, we'll catch up with him.

MISS FORSYTHE (*As Happy pushes her out*):   Say, I don't like that temper of his!

HAPPY: He's just a little overstrung, he'll be all right!

WILLY (*Off left, as The Woman laughs*):   Don't answer! Don't answer!

LETTA: Don't you want to tell your father—

HAPPY: No, that's not my father. He's just a guy. Come on, we'll catch Biff, and, honey, we're going to paint this town! Stanley, where's the check! Hey, Stanley!

They exit. Stanley looks toward left.

STANLEY (*Calling to Happy indignantly*):   Mr. Loman! Mr. Loman!

Stanley picks up a chair and follows them off. Knocking is heard off left. The Woman enters, laughing. Willy follows her. She is in a black slip; he is buttoning his shirt. Raw, sensuous music accompanies their speech.

WILLY: Will you stop laughing? Will you stop?

THE WOMAN: Aren't you going to answer the door? He'll wake the whole hotel.

WILLY: I'm not expecting anybody.

THE WOMAN: Whyn't you have another drink, honey, and stop being so damn self-centered?

WILLY: I'm so lonely.

THE WOMAN: You know you ruined me, Willy? From now on, whenever you come to the office, I'll see that you go right through to the buyers. No waiting at my desk any more, Willy. You ruined me.

WILLY: That's nice of you to say that.

THE WOMAN: Gee, you are self-centered! Why so sad? You are the saddest, self-centeredest soul I ever did see-saw. (*She laughs. He kisses her.*) Come on inside, drummer boy. It's silly to be dressing in the middle of the night. (*As knocking is heard*): Aren't you going to answer the door?

WILLY: They're knocking on the wrong door.

THE WOMAN: But I felt the knocking. And he heard us talking in here. Maybe the hotel's on fire!

WILLY (*His terror rising*):   It's a mistake.

THE WOMAN: Then tell him to go away!

WILLY: There's nobody there.

THE WOMAN: It's getting on my nerves, Willy. There's somebody standing out there and it's getting on my nerves!

WILLY (*Pushing her away from him*):   All right, stay in the bathroom here, and don't come out. I think there's a law in Massachusetts about it, so don't come out. It may be that new room clerk. He looked very mean. So don't come out. It's a mistake, there's no fire.

The knocking is heard again. He takes a few steps away from her, and she vanishes into the wing. The light follows him, and now he is facing Young Biff, who carries a suitcase. Biff steps toward him. The music is gone.

BIFF: Why didn't you answer?

WILLY: Biff! What are you doing in Boston?

BIFF: Why didn't you answer? I've been knocking for five minutes, I called you on the phone—

WILLY: I just heard you. I was in the bathroom and had the door shut. Did anything happen home?

BIFF: Dad—I let you down.

WILLY: What do you mean?

BIFF: Dad . . .

WILLY: Biffo, what's this about? (*Putting his arm around Biff*): Come on, let's go downstairs and get you a malted.

BIFF: Dad, I flunked math.

WILLY: Not for the term?

BIFF: The term. I haven't got enough credits to graduate.

WILLY: You mean to say Bernard wouldn't give you the answers?

BIFF: He did, he tried, but I only got a sixty-one.

WILLY: And they wouldn't give you four points?

BIFF: Birnbaum refused absolutely. I begged him, Pop, but he won't give me those points. You gotta talk to him before they close the school. Because if he saw the kind of man you are, and you just talked to him in your way, I'm sure he'd come through for me. The class came right before practice, see, and I didn't go enough. Would you talk to him? He'd like you, Pop. You know the way you could talk.

WILLY: You're on. We'll drive right back.

BIFF: Oh, Dad, good work! I'm sure he'll change it for you!

WILLY: Go downstairs and tell the clerk I'm checkin' out. Go right down.

BIFF: Yes, sir! See, the reason he hates me, Pop—one day he was late for class so I got up at the blackboard and imitated him. I crossed my eyes and talked with a lithp.

WILLY *(Laughing):*   You did? The kids like it?

BIFF: They nearly died laughing!

WILLY: Yeah? What'd you do?

BIFF: The thquare root of thixthy twee is . . . *(Willy bursts out laughing; Biff joins him.)* And in the middle of it he walked in!

Willy laughs and The Woman joins in offstage.

WILLY *(Without hesitation):*   Hurry downstairs and—

BIFF: Somebody in there?

WILLY: No, that was next door.

The Woman laughs offstage.

BIFF: Somebody got in your bathroom!

WILLY: No, it's the next room, there's a party—

THE WOMAN *(Enters, laughing. She lisps this):*   Can I come in? There's something in the bathtub, Willy, and it's moving!

Willy looks at Biff, who is staring open-mouthed and horrified at The Woman.

WILLY: Ah—you better go back to your room. They must be finished painting by now. They're painting her room so I let her take a shower here. Go back, go back . . . *(He pushes her.)*

THE WOMAN *(Resisting):*   But I've got to get dressed, Willy, I can't—

WILLY: Get out of here! Go back, go back . . . *(Suddenly striving for the ordinary):* This is Miss Francis, Biff, she's a buyer. They're painting her room. Go back, Miss Francis, go back . . .

THE WOMAN: But my clothes, I can't go out naked in the hall!

WILLY *(Pushing her offstage):*   Get outa here! Go back, go back!

Biff slowly sits down on his suitcase as the argument continues offstage.

THE WOMAN: Where's my stockings? You promised me stockings, Willy!

WILLY: I have no stockings here!

THE WOMAN: You had two boxes of size nine sheers for me, and I want them!

WILLY: Here, for God's sake, will you get outa here!

THE WOMAN (*Enters holding a box of stockings*):   I just hope there's nobody in the hall. That's all I hope. (*To Biff*): Are you football or baseball?

BIFF: Football.

THE WOMAN (*Angry, humiliated*):   That's me too. G'night. (*She snatches her clothes from Willy, and walks out.*)

WILLY (*After a pause*):   Well, better get going. I want to get to the school first thing in the morning. Get my suits out of the closet. I'll get my valise. (*Biff doesn't move.*) What's the matter? (*Biff remains motionless, tears falling.*) She's a buyer. Buys for J. H. Simmons. She lives down the hall—they're painting. You don't imagine— (*He breaks off. After a pause*): Now listen, pal, she's just a buyer. She sees merchandise in her room and they have to keep it looking just so . . . (*Pause. Assuming command*): All right, get my suits. (*Biff doesn't move.*) Now stop crying and do as I say. I gave you an order. Biff, I gave you an order! Is that what you do when I give you an order? How dare you cry! (*Putting his arm around Biff*): Now look, Biff, when you grow up you'll understand about these things. You mustn't—you mustn't overemphasize a thing like this. I'll see Birnbaum first thing in the morning.

BIFF: Never mind.

WILLY (*Getting down beside Biff*):   Never mind! He's going to give you those points. I'll see to it.

BIFF: He wouldn't listen to you.

WILLY: He certainly will listen to me. You need those points for the U of Virginia.

BIFF: I'm not going there.

WILLY: Heh? If I can't get him to change that mark you'll make it up in summer school. You've got all summer to—

BIFF (*His weeping breaking from him*):   Dad . . .

WILLY (*Infected by it*):   Oh, my boy . . .

BIFF: Dad . . .

WILLY: She's nothing to me, Biff. I was lonely, I was terribly lonely.

BIFF: You—you gave her Mama's stockings! (*His tears break through and he rises to go.*)

WILLY (*Grabbing for Biff*):   I gave you an order!

BIFF: Don't touch me, you—liar!

WILLY: Apologize for that!

BIFF: You fake! You phony little fake! You fake! (*Overcome, he turns quickly and weeping fully goes out with his suitcase. Willy is left on the floor on his knees.*)

WILLY: I gave you an order! Biff, come back here or I'll beat you! Come back here! I'll whip you!

Stanley comes quickly in from the right and stands in front of Willy.

WILLY (*Shouts at Stanley*):   I gave you an order . . .

STANLEY: Hey, let's pick it up, pick it up, Mr. Loman. (*He helps Willy to his feet.*) Your boys left with the chippies. They said they'll see you home.

A second waiter watches some distance away.

WILLY: But we were supposed to have dinner together.

Music is heard, Willy's theme.

STANLEY: Can you make it?
WILLY: I'll—sure, I can make it. *(Suddenly concerned about his clothes):* Do I—
I look all right?
STANLEY: Sure, you look all right. *(He flicks a speck off Willy's lapel.)*
WILLY: Here—here's a dollar.
STANLEY: Oh, your son paid me. It's all right.
WILLY *(Putting it in Stanley's hand):*   No, take it. You're a good boy.
STANLEY: Oh, no, you don't have to . . .
WILLY: Here—here's some more, I don't need it any more. *(After a slight
pause):* Tell me—is there a seed store in the neighborhood?
STANLEY: Seeds? You mean like to plant?

As Willy turns, Stanley slips the money back into his jacket pocket.

WILLY: Yes. Carrots, peas . . .
STANLEY: Well, there's hardware stores on Sixth Avenue, but it may be too
late now.
WILLY *(Anxiously):*   Oh, I'd better hurry. I've got to get some seeds. *(He starts
off to the right.)* I've got to get some seeds, right away. Nothing's planted.
I don't have a thing in the ground.

*Willy hurries out as the light goes down. Stanley moves over to the right after him,
watches him off. The other waiter has been staring at Willy.*

STANLEY *(To the waiter):*   Well, whatta you looking at?

*The waiter picks up the chairs and moves off right. Stanley takes the table and follows
him. The light fades on this area. There is a long pause, the sound of the flute coming
over. The light gradually rises on the kitchen, which is empty. Happy appears at the
door of the house, followed by Biff. Happy is carrying a large bunch of long-stemmed
roses. He enters the kitchen, looks around for Linda. Not seeing her, he turns to Biff,
who is just outside the house door, and makes a gesture with his hands, indicating "Not
here, I guess." He looks into the living-room and freezes. Inside, Linda, unseen, is seated,
Willy's coat on her lap. She rises ominously and quietly and moves toward Happy, who
backs up into the kitchen, afraid.*

HAPPY: Hey, what're you doing up? *(Linda says nothing but moves toward him
implacably.)* Where's Pop? *(He keeps backing to the right, and now Linda is in
full view in the doorway to the living-room.)* Is he sleeping?
LINDA: Where were you?

HAPPY (*Trying to laugh it off*):   We met two girls, Mom, very fine types. Here, we brought you some flowers. (*Offering them to her*): Put them in your room, Ma.

She knocks them to the floor at Biff's feet. He has now come inside and closed the door behind him. She stares at Biff, silent.

HAPPY: Now what'd you do that for? Mom, I want you to have some flowers—

LINDA (*Cutting Happy off, violently to Biff*):   Don't you care whether he lives or dies?

HAPPY (*Going to the stairs*):   Come upstairs, Biff.

BIFF (*With a flare of disgust, to Happy*):   Go away from me! (*To Linda*): What do you mean, lives or dies? Nobody's dying around here, pal.

LINDA: Get out of my sight! Get out of here!

BIFF: I wanna see the boss.

LINDA: You're not going near him!

BIFF: Where is he? (*He moves into the living-room and Linda follows.*)

LINDA (*Shouting after Biff*):   You invite him for dinner. He looks forward to it all day—(*Biff appears in his parents' bedroom, looks around, and exits*)—and then you desert him there. There's no stranger you'd do that to!

HAPPY: Why? He had a swell time with us. Listen, when I—(*Linda comes back into the kitchen*)   desert him I hope I don't outlive the day!

LINDA: Get out of here!

HAPPY: Now look, Mom . . .

LINDA: Did you have to go to women tonight? You and your lousy rotten whores!

Biff re-enters the kitchen.

HAPPY: Mom, all we did was follow Biff around trying to cheer him up! (*To Biff*): Boy, what a night you gave me!

LINDA: Get out of here, both of you, and don't come back! I don't want you tormenting him any more. Go on now, get your things together! (*To Biff*): You can sleep in his apartment. (*She starts to pick up the flowers and stops herself.*) Pick up this stuff, I'm not your maid any more. Pick it up, you bum, you!

Happy turns his back to her in refusal. Biff slowly moves over and gets down on his knees, picking up the flowers.

LINDA: You're a pair of animals! Not one, not another living soul would have had the cruelty to walk out on that man in a restaurant!

BIFF (*Not looking at her*):   Is that what he said?

LINDA: He didn't have to say anything. He was so humiliated he nearly limped when he came in.

HAPPY: But, Mom, he had a great time with us—
BIFF *(Cutting him off violently):*   Shut up!

Without another word, Happy goes upstairs.

LINDA: You! You didn't even go in to see if he was all right!
BIFF *(Still on the floor in front of Linda, the flowers in his hand; with self-loathing):*   No. Didn't. Didn't do a damned thing. How do you like that, heh? Left him babbling in a toilet.
LINDA: You louse. You . . .
BIFF: Now you hit it on the nose! *(He gets up, throws the flowers in the wastebasket.)* The scum of the earth, and you're looking at him!
LINDA: Get out of here!
BIFF: I gotta talk to the boss, Mom. Where is he?
LINDA: You're not going near him. Get out of this house!
BIFF *(With absolute assurance, determination):*   No. We're gonna have an abrupt conversation, him and me.
LINDA: You're not talking to him!

Hammering is heard from outside the house, off right. Biff turns toward the noise.

LINDA *(Suddenly pleading):*   Will you please leave him alone?
BIFF: What's he doing out there?
LINDA: He's planting the garden!
BIFF *(Quietly):*   Now? Oh, my God!

Biff moves outside, Linda following. The light dies down on them and comes up on the center of the apron as Willy walks into it. He is carrying a flashlight, a hoe, and a handful of seed packets. He raps the top of the hoe sharply to fix it firmly, and then moves to the left, measuring off the distance with his foot. He holds the flashlight to look at the seed packets, reading off the instructions. He is in the blue of night.

WILLY: Carrots . . . quarter-inch apart. Rows . . . one-foot rows. *(He measures it off.)* One foot. *(He puts down a package and measures off.)* Beets. *(He puts down another package and measures again.)* Lettuce. *(He reads the package, puts it down.)* One foot—*(He breaks off as Ben appears at the right and moves slowly down to him.)* What a proposition, ts, ts. Terrific, terrific. 'Cause she's suffered, Ben, the woman has suffered. You understand me? A man can't go out the way he came in, Ben, a man has got to add up to something. You can't, you can't— *(Ben moves toward him as though to interrupt.)* You gotta consider, now. Don't answer so quick. Remember, it's a guaranteed twenty-thousand-dollar proposition. Now look, Ben, I want you to go through the ins and outs of this thing with me. I've got nobody to talk to, Ben, and the woman has suffered, you hear me?
BEN *(Standing still, considering):*   What's the proposition?

WILLY: It's twenty thousand dollars on the barrelhead. Guaranteed, gilt-edged, you understand?

BEN: You don't want to make a fool of yourself. They might not honor the policy.

WILLY: How can they dare refuse? Didn't I work like a coolie to meet every premium on the nose? And now they don't pay off? Impossible!

BEN: It's called a cowardly thing, William.

WILLY: Why? Does it take more guts to stand here the rest of my life ringing up a zero?

BEN *(Yielding):*   That's a point, William. *(He moves, thinking, turns.)* And twenty thousand—that *is* something one can feel with the hand, it is there.

WILLY *(Now assured, with rising power):*   Oh, Ben, that's the whole beauty of it! I see it like a diamond, shining in the dark, hard and rough, that I can pick up and touch in my hand. Not like—like an appointment! This would not be another damned-fool appointment, Ben, and it changes all the aspects. Because he thinks I'm nothing, see, and so he spites me. But the funeral—*(Straightening up):* Ben, that funeral will be massive! They'll come from Maine, Massachusetts, Vermont, New Hampshire! All the old-timers with the strange license plates—that boy will be thunder-struck, Ben, because he never realized—I am known! Rhode Island, New York, New Jersey—I am known, Ben, and he'll see it with his eyes once and for all. He'll see what I am, Ben! He's in for a shock, that boy!

BEN *(Coming down to the edge of the garden):*   He'll call you a coward.

WILLY *(Suddenly fearful):*   No, that would be terrible.

BEN: Yes. And a damned fool.

WILLY: No, no, he mustn't, I won't have that! *(He is broken and desperate.)*

BEN: He'll hate you, William.

The gay music of the Boys is heard.

WILLY: Oh, Ben, how do we get back to all the great times? Used to be so full of light, and comradeship, the sleigh-riding in winter, and the ruddiness on his cheeks. And always some kind of good news coming up, always something nice coming up ahead. And never even let me carry the valises in the house, and simonizing, simonizing that little red car! Why, why can't I give him something and not have him hate me?

BEN: Let me think about it. *(He glances at his watch.)* I still have a little time. Remarkable proposition, but you've got to be sure you're not making a fool of yourself.

Ben drifts off upstage and goes out of sight. Biff comes down from the left.

WILLY *(Suddenly conscious of Biff, turns and looks up at him, then begins picking up the packages of seeds in confusion):*   Where the hell is that seed? *(Indignantly):* You can't see nothing out here! They boxed in the whole goddam neighborhood!

BIFF: There are people all around here. Don't you realize that?

WILLY: I'm busy. Don't bother me.

BIFF *(Taking the hoe from Willy):*   I'm saying good-by to you, Pop. *(Willy looks at him, silent, unable to move.)* I'm not coming back any more.

WILLY: You're not going to see Oliver tomorrow?

BIFF: I've got no appointment, Dad.

WILLY: He put his arm around you, and you've got no appointment?

BIFF: Pop, get this now, will you? Everytime I've left it's been a fight that sent me out of here. Today I realized something about myself and I tried to explain it to you and I—I think I'm just not smart enough to make any sense out of it for you. To hell with whose fault it is or anything like that. *(He takes Willy's arm.)* Let's just wrap it up, heh? Come on in, we'll tell Mom. *(He gently tries to pull Willy to left.)*

WILLY *(Frozen, immobile, with guilt in his voice):*   No, I don't want to see her.

BIFF: Come on! *(He pulls again, and Willy tries to pull away.)*

WILLY *(Highly nervous):*   No, no, I don't want to see her.

BIFF *(Tries to look into Willy's face, as if to find the answer there):*   Why don't you want to see her?

WILLY *(More harshly now):*   Don't bother me, will you?

BIFF: What do you mean, you don't want to see her? You don't want them calling you yellow, do you? This isn't your fault; it's me, I'm a bum. Now come inside! *(Willy strains to get away.)* Did you hear what I said to you?

Willy pulls away and quickly goes by himself into the house. Biff follows.

LINDA *(To Willy):*   Did you plant, dear?

BIFF *(At the door, to Linda):*   All right, we had it out. I'm going and I'm not writing any more.

LINDA *(Going to Willy in the kitchen):*   I think that's the best way, dear. 'Cause there's no use drawing it out, you'll just never get along.

Willy doesn't respond.

BIFF: People ask where I am and what I'm doing, you don't know, and you don't care. That way it'll be off your mind and you can start brightening up again. All right? That clears it, doesn't it? *(Willy is silent, and Biff goes to him.)* You gonna wish me luck, scout? *(He extends his hand.)* What do you say?

LINDA: Shake his hand, Willy.

WILLY *(Turning to her, seething with hurt):*   There's no necessity to mention the pen at all, y'know.

BIFF *(Gently):*   I've got no appointment, Dad.

WILLY *(Erupting fiercely):*   He put his arm around . . . ?

BIFF: Dad, you're never going to see what I am, so what's the use of arguing? If I strike oil I'll send you a check. Meantime forget I'm alive.

WILLY *(To Linda):*   Spite, see?

BIFF: Shake hands, Dad.

WILLY: Not my hand.

BIFF: I was hoping not to go this way.

WILLY: Well, this is the way you're going. Good-by.

Biff looks at him a moment, then turns sharply and goes to the stairs.

WILLY *(Stops him with):*   May you rot in hell if you leave this house!

BIFF *(Turning):*   Exactly what is it that you want from me?

WILLY: I want you to know, on the train, in the mountains, in the valleys, wherever you go, that you cut down your life for spite!

BIFF: No, no.

WILLY: Spite, spite, is the word of your undoing! And when you're down and out, remember what did it. When you're rotting somewhere beside the railroad tracks, remember, and don't you dare blame it on me!

BIFF: I'm not blaming it on you!

WILLY: I won't take the rap for this, you hear?

Happy comes down the stairs and stands on the bottom step, watching.

BIFF: That's just what I'm telling you!

WILLY *(Sinking into a chair at the table, with full accusation):*   You're trying to put a knife in me—don't think I don't know what you're doing!

BIFF: All right, phony! Then let's lay it on the line. *(He whips the rubber tube out of his pocket and puts it on the table.)*

HAPPY: You crazy—

LINDA: Biff! *(She moves to grab the hose, but Biff holds it down with his hand.)*

BIFF: Leave it there! Don't move it!

WILLY *(Not looking at it):*   What is that?

BIFF: You know goddam well what that is.

WILLY *(Caged, wanting to escape):*   I never saw that.

BIFF: You saw it. The mice didn't bring it into the cellar! What is this supposed to do, make a hero out of you? This supposed to make me sorry for you?

WILLY: Never heard of it.

BIFF: There'll be no pity for you, you hear it? No pity!

WILLY *(To Linda):*   You hear the spite!

BIFF: No, you're going to hear the truth—what you are and what I am!

LINDA: Stop it!

WILLY: Spite!

HAPPY *(Coming down toward Biff):*   You cut it now!

BIFF *(To Happy):*   The man don't know who we are! The man is gonna know! *(To Willy):*   We never told the truth for ten minutes in this house!

HAPPY: We always told the truth!

BIFF *(Turning on him):*   You big blow, are you the assistant buyer? You're one of the two assistants to the assistant, aren't you?

HAPPY: Well, I'm practically—

BIFF: You're practically full of it! We all are! And I'm through with it. *(To Willy):* Now hear this, Willy, this is me.

WILLY: I know you!

BIFF: You know why I had no address for three months? I stole a suit in Kansas City and I was in jail. *(To Linda, who is sobbing):* Stop crying. I'm through with it.

Linda turns away from them, her hands covering her face.

WILLY: I suppose that's my fault!

BIFF: I stole myself out of every good job since high school!

WILLY: And whose fault is that?

BIFF: And I never got anywhere because you blew me so full of hot air I could never stand taking orders from anybody! That's whose fault it is!

WILLY: I hear that!

LINDA: Don't, Biff!

BIFF: It's goddam time you heard that! I had to be boss big shot in two weeks, and I'm through with it!

WILLY: Then hang yourself! For spite, hang yourself!

BIFF: No! Nobody's hanging himself, Willy! I ran down eleven flights with a pen in my hand today. And suddenly I stopped, you hear me? And in the middle of that office building, do you hear this? I stopped in the middle of that building and I saw—the sky. I saw the things that I love in this world. The work and the food and time to sit and smoke. And I looked at the pen and said to myself, what the hell am I grabbing this for? Why am I trying to become what I don't want to be? What am I doing in an office, making a contemptuous, begging fool of myself, when all I want is out there, waiting for me the minute I say I know who I am! Why can't I say that, Willy? *(He tries to make Willy face him, but Willy pulls away and moves to the left.)*

WILLY *(With hatred, threateningly):*   The door of your life is wide open!

BIFF: Pop! I'm a dime a dozen, and so are you!

WILLY *(Turning on him now in an uncontrolled outburst):*   I am not a dime a dozen! I am Willy Loman, and you are Biff Loman!

Biff starts for Willy, but is blocked by Happy. In his fury, Biff seems on the verge of attacking his father.

BIFF: I am not a leader of men, Willy, and neither are you. You were never anything but a hard-working drummer who landed in the ash can like all the rest of them! I'm one dollar an hour, Willy! I tried seven states and couldn't raise it. A buck an hour! Do you gather my meaning? I'm not bringing home any prizes any more, and you're going to stop waiting for me to bring them home!

WILLY *(Directly to Biff):*   You vengeful, spiteful mutt!

Biff breaks from Happy. Willy, in fright, starts up the stairs. Biff grabs him.

BIFF *(At the peak of his fury):*   Pop, I'm nothing! I'm nothing, Pop. Can't you understand that? There's no spite in it any more. I'm just what I am, that's all.

Biff's fury has spent itself, and he breaks down, sobbing, holding on to Willy, who dumbly fumbles for Biff's face.

WILLY *(Astonished):*   What're you doing? What're you doing? *(To Linda):* Why is he crying?

BIFF *(Crying, broken):*   Will you let me go, for Christ's sake? Will you take that phony dream and burn it before something happens? *(Struggling to contain himself, he pulls away and moves to the stairs.)* I'll go in the morning. Put him—put him to bed. *(Exhausted, Biff moves up the stairs to his room.)*

WILLY *(After a long pause, astonished, elevated):*   Isn't that—isn't that remarkable? Biff—he likes me!

LINDA: He loves you, Willy!

HAPPY *(Deeply moved):*   Always did, Pop.

WILLY: Oh, Biff! *(Staring wildly):*   He cried! Cried to me. *(He is choking with his love, and now cries out his promise):* That boy—that boy is going to be magnificent!

Ben appears in the light just outside the kitchen.

BEN: Yes, outstanding, with twenty thousand behind him.

LINDA *(Sensing the racing of his mind, fearfully, carefully):*   Now come to bed, Willy. It's all settled now.

WILLY *(Finding it difficult not to rush out of the house):*   Yes, we'll sleep. Come on. Go to sleep, Hap.

BEN: And it does take a great kind of a man to crack the jungle.

In accents of dread, Ben's idyllic music starts up.

HAPPY *(His arm around Linda):*   I'm getting married, Pop, don't forget it. I'm changing everything. I'm gonna run that department before the year is up. You'll see, Mom. *(He kisses her.)*

BEN: The jungle is dark but full of diamonds, Willy.

Willy turns, moves, listening to Ben.

LINDA: Be good. You're both good boys, just act that way, that's all.

HAPPY: 'Night, Pop. *(He goes upstairs.)*

LINDA *(To Willy):*   Come, dear.

BEN *(With greater force):*   One must go in to fetch a diamond out.

WILLY *(To Linda, as he moves slowly along the edge of the kitchen, toward the door):*   I just want to get settled down, Linda. Let me sit alone for a little.

LINDA *(Almost uttering her fear):*   I want you upstairs.

WILLY *(Taking her in his arms):*   In a few minutes, Linda. I couldn't sleep right now. Go on, you look awful tired. *(He kisses her.)*

BEN: Not like an appointment at all. A diamond is rough and hard to the touch.

WILLY: Go on now. I'll be right up.

LINDA: I think this is the only way, Willy.

WILLY: Sure, it's the best thing.

BEN: Best thing!

WILLY: The only way. Everything is gonna be—go on, kid, get to bed. You look so tired.

LINDA: Come right up.

WILLY: Two minutes.

Linda goes into the living-room, then reappears in her bedroom. Willy moves just outside the kitchen door.

WILLY: Loves me. *(Wonderingly):* Always loved me. Isn't that a remarkable thing? Ben, he'll worship me for it!

BEN *(With promise):*   It's dark there, but full of diamonds.

WILLY: Can you imagine that magnificence with twenty thousand dollars in his pocket?

LINDA *(Calling from her room):*   Willy! Come up!

WILLY *(Calling into the kitchen):*   Yes! Yes. Coming! It's very smart, you realize that, don't you, sweetheart? Even Ben sees it. I gotta go, baby. 'By! 'By! *(Going over to Ben, almost dancing):* Imagine? When the mail comes he'll be ahead of Bernard again!

BEN: A perfect proposition all around.

WILLY: Did you see how he cried to me? Oh, if I could kiss him, Ben!

BEN: Time, William, time!

WILLY: Oh, Ben, I always knew one way or another we were gonna make it, Biff and I!

BEN *(Looking at his watch):*   The boat. We'll be late. *(He moves slowly off into the darkness.)*

WILLY *(Elegiacally, turning to the house):*   Now when you kick off, boy, I want a seventy-yard boot, and get right down the field under the ball, and when you hit, hit low and hit hard, because it's important, boy. *(He swings around and faces the audience.)* There's all kinds of important people in the stands, and the first thing you know . . . *(Suddenly realizing he is alone):* Ben! Ben, where do I . . . ? *(He makes a sudden movement of search.)* Ben, how do I . . . ?

LINDA *(Calling):*   Willy, you coming up?

WILLY *(Uttering a gasp of fear, whirling about as if to quiet her):*   Sh! *(He turns around as if to find his way; sounds, faces, voices, seem to be swarming in upon him *and he flicks at them, crying.)* Sh! Sh! *(Suddenly music, faint and high, stops him. It rises in intensity, almost to an unbearable scream. He goes up and down on his toes, and rushes off around the house.)* Shhh!

LINDA: Willy?

There is no answer. Linda waits. Biff gets up off his bed. He is still in his clothes. Happy sits up. Biff stands listening.

LINDA *(With real fear):*   Willy, answer me! Willy!

There is the sound of a car starting and moving away at full speed.

LINDA: No!
BIFF *(Rushing down the stairs):*   Pop!

As the car speeds off, the music crashes down in a frenzy of sound, which becomes the soft pulsation of a single cello string. Biff slowly returns to his bedroom. He and Happy gravely don their jackets. Linda slowly walks out of her room. The music has developed into a dead march. The leaves of day are appearing over everything. Charley and Bernard, somberly dressed, appear and knock on the kitchen door. Biff and Happy slowly descend the stairs to the kitchen as Charley and Bernard enter. All stop a moment when Linda, in clothes of mourning, bearing a little bunch of roses, comes through the draped doorway into the kitchen. She goes to Charley and takes his arm. Now all move toward the audience, through the wall-line of the kitchen. At the limit of the apron, Linda lays down the flowers, kneels, and sits back on her heels. All stare down at the grave.

REQUIEM

CHARLEY: It's getting dark, Linda.

Linda doesn't react. She stares at the grave.

BIFF: How about it, Mom? Better get some rest, heh? They'll be closing the gate soon.

Linda makes no move. Pause.

HAPPY *(Deeply angered):*   He had no right to do that. There was no necessity for it. We would've helped him.
CHARLEY *(Grunting):*   Hmmm.
BIFF: Come along, Mom.
LINDA: Why didn't anybody come?
CHARLEY: It was a very nice funeral.
LINDA: But where are all the people he knew? Maybe they blame him.
CHARLEY: Naa. It's a rough world, Linda. They wouldn't blame him.

LINDA: I can't understand it. At this time especially. First time in thirty-five years we were just about free and clear. He only needed a little salary. He was even finished with the dentist.

CHARLEY: No man only needs a little salary.

LINDA: I can't understand it.

BIFF: There were a lot of nice days. When he'd come home from a trip; or on Sundays, making the stoop; finishing the cellar; putting on the new porch; when he built the extra bathroom; and put up the garage. You know something, Charley, there's more of him in that front stoop than in all the sales he ever made.

CHARLEY: Yeah. He was a happy man with a batch of cement.

LINDA: He was so wonderful with his hands.

BIFF: He had the wrong dreams. All, all, wrong.

HAPPY *(Almost ready to fight Biff)*:   Don't say that!

BIFF: He never knew who he was.

CHARLEY *(Stopping Happy's movement and reply. To Biff)*:   Nobody dast blame this man. You don't understand: Willy was a salesman. And for a salesman, there is no rock bottom to life. He don't put a bolt to a nut, he don't tell you the law or give you medicine. He's a man way out there in the blue, riding on a smile and a shoeshine. And when they start not smiling back—that's an earthquake. And then you get yourself a couple of spots on your hat, and you're finished. Nobody dast blame this man. A salesman is got to dream, boy. It comes with the territory.

BIFF: Charley, the man didn't know who he was.

HAPPY *(Infuriated)*:   Don't say that!

BIFF: Why don't you come with me, Happy?

HAPPY: I'm not licked that easily. I'm staying right in this city, and I'm gonna beat this racket! *(He looks at Biff, his chin set.)* The Loman Brothers!

BIFF: I know who I am, kid.

HAPPY: All right, boy. I'm gonna show you and everybody else that Willy Loman did not die in vain. He had a good dream. It's the only dream you can have—to come out number-one man. He fought it out here, and this is where I'm gonna win it for him.

BIFF *(With a hopeless glance at Happy, bends toward his mother)*:   Let's go, Mom.

LINDA: I'll be with you in a minute. Go on, Charley. *(He hesitates.)* I want to, just for a minute. I never had a chance to say good-by.

Charley moves away, followed by Happy. Biff remains a slight distance up and left of Linda. She sits there, summoning herself. The flute begins, not far away, playing behind her speech.

LINDA: Forgive me, dear. I can't cry. I don't know what it is, but I can't cry. I don't understand it. Why did you ever do that? Help me, Willy, I can't cry. It seems to me that you're just on another trip. I keep expecting you. Willy, dear, I can't cry. Why did you do it? I search and search and I search, and I can't understand it, Willy. I made the last payment on the house today. Today, dear. And there'll be nobody home. *(A sob rises in her throat.)* We're free and clear. *(Sobbing more fully, released):* We're free. *(Biff comes slowly toward her.)* We're free . . . We're free . . .

Biff lifts her to her feet and moves out up right with her in his arms. Linda sobs quietly. Bernard and Charley come together and follow them, followed by Happy. Only the music of the flute is left on the darkening stage as over the house the hard towers of the apartment buildings rise into sharp focus, and

The Curtain Falls

(1949)

George Ryga

(b. 1 9 3 2)

George Ryga was born in Deep Creek, Alberta, and grew up in the rural
Ukrainian farming culture of the area. He was educated for seven years in
a one-room schoolhouse, and attended the University of Texas for a short
time. Most of his early work arose out of the songs, stories, and folk myths
of his upbringing; he wrote short stories, a novel, and scripts for radio and
television. Ryga worked as a farm laborer and construction worker, then at
a radio station, before he began to earn a living as a writer in 1962. His *The
Ecstasy of Rita Joe* was the first English-language play performed at the new
National Arts Centre in Ottawa in 1969. Ryga lives with his wife and family
in Summerland, British Columbia.

Some argue that Ryga is the finest playwright Canada has produced. His
innovative dramatic technique combines dance, music, and poetry with realistic detail and dialogue. He is essentially a social playwright and depicts the
concerns of economically and culturally exploited Canadians. In *The Ecstasy
of Rita Joe,* Ryga combines biting and vitriolic expressionist and surrealist
techniques to mesh the past and future so that the present almost disappears. The play uses mime, song, dance, and other effects. In recent work
Ryga deals with the subject of Paracelsus, the eccentric Renaissance physi-
cian and scientist, and the Prometheus story. Still, Ryga's central preoccupation is with an individual struggling against a powerful establishment.

Ryga's plays include *Grass and Wild Strawberries* (1969), *The Ecstasy of Rita
Joe* (1970), *Indian* (1971), *Captives of the Faceless Drummer* (1971), *Sunrise on
Sarah* (1973), *Paracelsus* (1974), and *Prometheus Unbound* (1982). Plays that
have been performed but not published include *Nothing But a Man* and
Jeremiah's Place. Ryga has also published novels, short stories, and a book on
a trip to China, *Beyond the Crimson Morning* (1979).

GEORGE RYGA

The Ecstasy of Rita Joe

CAST

Rita Joe
Jaimie Paul
Father, David Joe
Magistrate
Mr. Homer
Priest, Father Andrew
Eileen Joe
Old Indian Woman
Teacher, Miss Donohue
Policeman
Witness: Murderer
Witness: Murderer
Witness: Murderer
Young Indian Men

Guitarist-Singer

ACT ONE

A circular ramp beginning at floor level stage left and continuing downward below floor level at stage front, then rising and sweeping along stage back at two-foot elevation to disappear in the wings of stage left. This ramp dominates the stage by wrapping the central and forward playing area. A short approach ramp, meeting with the main ramp at stage right, expedites entrances from the wings of stage right.

The Magistrate's chair and representation of court desk are situated at stage right, enclosed within the sweep of the ramp. At the foot of the desk is a lip on stage right side. The Singer sits here, turned away from the focus of the play. Her songs and accompaniment appear almost accidental. She has all the reactions of a white liberal folklorist with a limited concern and understanding of an ethnic dilemma which she touches in the course of her research and work in compiling and writing folk songs. She serves too as an alter ego to Rita Joe.

No curtain is used during the play. At the opening, intermission and conclusion of the play, the curtain remains up. The onus for isolating scenes from the past and present in Rita Joe's life falls on highlight lighting.

Backstage, there is a mountain cyclorama. In front of the cyclorama there is a darker maze curtain to suggest gloom and confusion, and a cityscape.

The house lights and stage work lights remain on. Backstage, cyclorama, and maze curtains are up, revealing wall back of stage, exit doors, etc.

Cast, Singer enter offstage singly and in pairs from the wings, the exit doors at the back of the theatre, and from the auditorium side doors. The entrances are workmanlike and untheatrical. When all the Cast is on stage, they turn to face the audience momentarily. The house lights dim.

The cyclorama is lowered into place. The maze curtain follows. This creates a sense of compression of stage into the auditorium. Recorded voices are heard in a jumble of mutterings and throat clearings. The Magistrate enters as the Clerk begins.

CLERK *(Recorded):*   This court is in session. All present will rise . . .

The shuffling and scraping of furniture is heard.

The cast repeat "Rita Joe, Rita Joe." A policeman brings on Rita Joe.

MAGISTRATE: Who is she? Can she speak English?
POLICEMAN: Yes.
MAGISTRATE: Then let her speak for herself!

He speaks to the audience firmly and with reason.

To understand life in a given society, one must understand laws of that society. All relationships . . .
CLERK *(Recorded):*   Man to man . . . man to woman . . . man to property . . . man to the state . . .
MAGISTRATE: . . . are determined and enriched by laws that have grown out of social realities. The quality of the law under which you live and function determines the real quality of the freedom that was yours today.

The rest of the cast slowly move out.

Your home and your well-being were protected. The roads of the city are open to us. So are the galleries, libraries, the administrative and public buildings. There are buses, trains . . . going in and coming out. Nobody is a prisoner here.
RITA *(With humour, almost a sad sigh):*   The first time I tried to go home I was picked up by some men who gave me five dollars. An' then they arrested me.

The policeman retreats into the shadows. The singer crosses down.

MAGISTRATE: Thousands leave and enter the city everyday . . .
RITA: It wasn't true what they said, but nobody'd believe me . . .
SINGER *(Singing a recitativo searching for a melody):*

> Will the winds not blow
> My words to her
> Like the seeds
> Of the dandelion?

MAGISTRATE *(Smiles, as at a private joke):*   Once . . . I saw a little girl in the Cariboo country. It was summer then and she wore only a blouse and skirt. I wondered what she wore in winter?

The murderers hover in background on the upper ramp. One whistles and one lights a cigarette—an action which will be repeated at the end of the play.

RITA *(Moving to him, but hesitating):*   You look like a good man. Tell them to let me go, please!

The magistrate goes to his podium.

MAGISTRATE: Our nation is on an economic par with the state of Arkansas . . . We are a developing country, but a buoyant one. Still . . . the summer report of the Economic Council of Canada predicts a reduction in the gross national product unless we utilize our manpower for greater efficiency. Employed, happy people make for a prosperous, happy nation . . .

RITA *(Exultantly):*   I worked at some jobs, mister!

The magistrate turns to face Rita Joe. The murderers have gone.

MAGISTRATE: Gainful employment. Obedience to the law . . .

RITA *(To the magistrate):*   Once I had a job . . .

He does not relate to her. She is troubled. She talks to the audience.

Once I had a job in a tire store . . . an' I'd worry about what time my boss would come . . . He was always late . . . and so was everybody. Sometimes I got to thinkin' what would happen if he'd not come. And nobody else would come. And I'd be all day in this big room with no lights on an' the telephone ringing an' people asking for other people that weren't there . . . What would happen?

As she relates her concern, she laughs. Towards the end of her dialogue she is so amused by the absurdity of it all that she can hardly contain herself.

Lights fade on the magistrate who broods in his chair as he examines his court papers.

Lights up on Jaimie Paul approaching on the backstage ramp from stage left. He is jubilant, his laughter blending with her laughter. At the sound of his voice, Rita Joe runs to him, to the memory of him.

JAIMIE: I seen the city today and I seen things today I never knew was there, Rita Joe!

RITA *(Happily):*   I seen them too, Jaimie Paul!

He pauses above her, his mood light and childlike.

JAIMIE: I see a guy on top of a bridge, talkin' to himself . . . an' lots of people on the beach watchin' harbour seals . . . Kids feed popcorn to seagulls . . . an' I think to myself . . . Boy! Pigeons eat pretty good here!

RITA: In the morning, Jaimie Paul . . . very early in the morning . . . the air is cold like at home . . .

JAIMIE: Pretty soon I seen a little woman walkin' a big black dog on a rope . . . Dog is mad . . . Dog wants a man!

Jaimie Paul moves to Rita Joe. They embrace.

RITA: Clouds are red over the city in the morning. Clara Hill says to me if you're real happy . . . the clouds make you forget you're not home . . .

They laugh together. Jaimie Paul breaks from her. He punctuates his story with wide, sweeping gestures.

JAIMIE: I start singin' and some hotel windows open. I wave to them, but nobody waves back! They're watchin' me, like I was a harbour seal!

He laughs.

So I stopped singin'!

RITA: I remember colours, but I've forgot faces already . . .

Jaimie Paul looks at her as her mood changes. Faint light on the magistrate brightens.

A train whistle is white, with black lines . . . A sick man talkin' is brown like an overcoat with pockets torn an' string showin' . . . A sad woman is a room with the curtains shut . . .

MAGISTRATE: Rita Joe?

She becomes sobered, but Jaimie Paul continues laughing. She nods to the magistrate, then turns to Jaimie Paul.

RITA: Them bastards put me in jail. They're gonna do it again, they said . . . Them bastards!

JAIMIE: Guys who sell newspapers don't see nothin' . . .

RITA: They drive by me, lookin' . . .

JAIMIE: I'm gonna be a carpenter!

RITA: I walk like a stick, tryin' to keep my ass from showin' because I know what they're thinkin' . . . Them bastards!

JAIMIE: I got myself boots an' a new shirt . . . See!

RITA *(Worried now):*   I thought their jail was on fire . . . I thought it was burning.

JAIMIE: Room I got costs me seven bucks a week . . .

RITA: I can't leave town. Everytime I try, they put me in jail.

A policeman enters with a file folder.

JAIMIE: They say it's a pretty good room for seven bucks a week . . .

Jaimie Paul begins to retreat backwards from her, along the ramp to the wings of stage left. She is isolated in a pool of light away from the magistrate. The light isolation between her and Jaimie Paul deepens, as the scene turns into the courtroom again.

MAGISTRATE: Vagrancy . . . You are charged with vagrancy.

JAIMIE *(With enthusiasm, boyishly):*   First hundred bucks I make, Rita Joe . . . I'm gonna buy a car so I can take you everyplace!

RITA *(Moving after him):*   Jaimie!

He retreats, dreamlike, into the wings. The spell of memory between them is broken. Pools of light between her and the magistrate spread and fuse into a single light area. She turns to the magistrate, worried and confused.

MAGISTRATE *(Reading the documents in his hand):*   The charge against you this morning is vagrancy . . .

The magistrate continues studying the papers he holds. She looks up at him and shakes her head helplessly, then blurts out to him . . .

RITA: I had to spend last night in jail . . . Did you know?

MAGISTRATE: Yes. You were arrested.

RITA: I didn't know when morning came . . . There was no windows . . . The jail stinks! People in jail stink!

MAGISTRATE *(Indulgently):*   Are you surprised?

RITA: I didn't know anybody there . . . People in jail stink like paper that's been in the rain too long. But a jail stinks worse. It stinks of rust . . . an' old hair . . .

The magistrate looks down at her for the first time.

MAGISTRATE: You . . . are Rita Joe?

She nods quickly. A faint concern shows in his face. He watches her for a long moment.

I know your face . . . yet . . . it wasn't in this courtroom. Or was it?

RITA: I don't know . . .

MAGISTRATE *(Pondering):*   Have you appeared before me in the past year?

RITA *(Turning away from him, shrugging):*   I don't know. I can't remember . . .

The magistrate throws his head back and laughs. The policeman joins in.

MAGISTRATE: You can't remember? Come now . . .

RITA *(Laughing with him and looking to the policeman):*   I can't remember . . .

MAGISTRATE: Then I take it you haven't appeared before me. Certainly you and I would remember if you had.

RITA *(Smiling):*   I don't remember . . .

The magistrate makes some hurried notes, but he is watching Rita Joe, formulating his next thought.

She speaks naively . . .

My sister hitchhiked home an' she had no trouble like I . . .

MAGISTRATE: You'll need witnesses, Rita Joe. I'm only giving you eight hours to find witnesses for yourself . . .

RITA: Jaimie knows . . .

She turns to where Jaimie Paul had been, but the back of the stage is in darkness. The policeman exits suddenly.

Jaimie knew . . .

Her voice trails off pathetically. The magistrate shrugs and returns to studying his notes. Rita Joe chaffs during the silence which follows. She craves communion with people, with the magistrate.

My sister was a dressmaker, mister! But she only worked two weeks in the city . . . An' then she got sick and went back to the reserve to help my father catch fish an' cut pulpwood.

She smiles.

She's not coming back . . . that's for sure!

MAGISTRATE *(With interest):*   Should I know your sister? What was her name?

RITA: Eileen Joe.

Eileen Joe appears spotlit behind, a memory crowding in

MAGISTRATE: Eileen . . . that's a soft, undulating name.

RITA: Two weeks, and not one white woman came to her to leave an order or old clothes for her to fix. No work at all for two weeks, an' her money ran out . . . Isn't that funny?

The magistrate again studies Rita Joe, his mind elsewhere.

MAGISTRATE: Hmmmmm . . .

Eileen Joe disappears.

RITA: So she went back to the reserve to catch fish an' cut pulpwood!

MAGISTRATE: I do know your face . . . Yes! And yet . . .

RITA: Can I sit someplace?

MAGISTRATE *(Excited)*:   I remember now . . . Yes! I was on holidays three summers back in the Cariboo country . . . driving over this road with not a house or field in sight . . . just barren land, wild and windblown. And then I saw this child beside the road, dressed in a blouse and skirt, barefooted . . .

RITA *(Looking around)*:   I don't feel so good, mister.

MAGISTRATE: My God, she wasn't more than three or four years old . . . walking towards me beside the road. When I'd passed her, I stopped my car and then turned around and drove back to where I'd seen her, for I wondered what she could possibly be doing in such a lonely country at that age without her father or mother walking with her . . . Yet when I got back to where I'd seen her, she had disappeared. She was nowhere to be seen. Yet the land was flat for over a mile in every direction . . . I had to see her. But I couldn't . . .

He stares down at Rita Joe for a long moment.

You see, what I was going to say was that this child had your face! Isn't that strange?

RITA *(With disinterest)*:   Sure, if you think so, mister . . .

MAGISTRATE: Could she have been . . . your daughter?

RITA: What difference does it make?

MAGISTRATE: Children cannot be left like that . . . It takes money to raise children in the woods as in the cities . . . There are institutions and people with more money than you who could . . .

RITA: Nobody would get my child, mister!

She is distracted by Eileen Joe's voice in her memory. Eileen's voice begins in darkness, but as she speaks, a spotlight isolates her in front of the ramp, stage left. Eileen is on her hands and knees, two buckets beside her. She is picking berries in mime.

EILEEN: First was the strawberries an' then the blueberries. After the frost . . . we picked the cranberries . . .

She laughs with delight.

RITA *(Pleading with the magistrate, but her attention on Eileen):* Let me go, mister . . .

MAGISTRATE: I can't let you go. I don't think that would be of any use in the circumstances. Would you like a lawyer?

Even as he speaks, Rita Joe has entered the scene with Eileen picking berries.

The magistrate's light fades on his podium.

RITA: You ate the strawberries an' blueberries because you were always a hungry kid!

EILEEN: But not cranberries! They made my stomach hurt.

Rita Joe goes down on her knees with Eileen.

RITA: Let me pick . . . You rest.

She holds out the bucket to Eileen.

Mine's full aready . . . Let's change. You rest . . .

During the exchange of buckets, Eileen notices her hands are larger than Rita Joe's. She is both delighted and surprised by this.

EILEEN: My hands are bigger than yours, Rita . . . Look!

She takes Rita Joe's hands in hers.

When did my hands grow so big?

RITA *(Wisely and sadly):* You've worked so hard . . . I'm older than you, Leenie . . . I will always be older.

The two sisters are thoughtful for a moment, each watching the other in silence. Then Rita Joe becomes animated and resumes her mime of picking berries in the woods.

We picked lots of wild berries when we were kids, Leenie!

They turn away from their work and lie down alongside each other, facing the front of the stage.

The light on them becomes summery, warm.

In the summer, it was hot an' flies hummed so loud you'd go to sleep if you sat down an' just listened.

EILEEN: The leaves on the poplars used to turn black an' curl together with the heat . . .

RITA: One day you and I were pickin' blueberries and a big storm came . . .

A sudden crash of thunder and a lightning flash. The lights turn cold and blue. The three murderers stand in silhouette on a riser behind them. Eileen cringes in fear, afraid of the storm, aware of the presence of the murderers behind them.

Rita Joe springs to her feet, her being attuned to the wildness of the atmosphere. Lightning continues to flash and flicker.

EILEEN: Oh, no!

RITA *(Shouting):*   It got cold and the rain an' hail came . . . the sky falling!

EILEEN *(Crying in fear):*   Rita!

RITA *(Laughing, shouting):*   Stay there!

A high flash of lightning, silhouetting the murderers harshly. They take a step forward on the lightning flash. Eileen dashes into arms of Rita Joe. She screams and drags Rita Joe down with her.

Rita Joe struggles against Eileen.

RITA: Let me go! What in hell's wrong with you? Let me go!

MAGISTRATE: I can't let you go.

The lightning dies, but the thunder rumbles off into the distance. Eileen subsides and pressing herself into the arms of Rita Joe as a small child to her mother, she sobs quietly.

RITA: There, there . . .

With infinite tenderness.

You said to me, "What would happen if the storm hurt us an' we can't find our way home, but are lost together so far away in the bush?"

Eileen looks up, brushing away her tears and smiling at Rita Joe.

RITA & EILEEN *(In unison):*   Would you be my mother then?

RITA: Would I be your mother?

Rita Joe releases Eileen who looks back fearfully to where the murderers had stood. They are gone. She rises and, collecting the buckets, moves hesitantly to where they had been. Confident now, she laughs softly and nervously to herself and leaves the stage.

Rita Joe rises and talks to Eileen as she departs.

We walked home through the mud an' icy puddles among the trees. At first you cried, Leenie . . . and then you wanted to sleep. But I held you up an' when we got home you said you were sure you would've died in the bush if it hadn't been for us being together like that.

Eileen disappears from the stage. The magistrate's light comes up. Rita Joe shakes her head sadly at the memory, then comes forward to the apron of the stage. She is proud of her sister and her next speech reveals this pride.

She made a blouse for me that I wore everyday for one year, an' it never ripped at the armpits like the blouse I buy in the store does the first time I stretch . . .

She stretches languidly.

I like to stretch when I'm happy! It makes all the happiness go through me like warm water . . .

The priest, the teacher, and a young Indian man cross the stage directly behind her. The priest wears a Roman collar and a check bush-jacket of a worker-priest. He pauses before passing Rita Joe and goes to meet her.

PRIEST: Rita Joe? When did you get back? How's life?

Rita Joe shrugs noncommittally.

RITA: You know me, Father Andrew . . . Could be better, could be worse . . .
PRIEST: Are you still working?

Rita Joe is still noncommittal. She smiles at him. Her gestures are not definite.

RITA: I live.
PRIEST *(Serious and concerned):*   It's not easy, is it?
RITA: Not always.

The teacher and the young Indian man exit.

PRIEST: A lot of things are different in the city. It's easier here on the reserve . . . Life is simpler. You can be yourself. That's important to remember.
RITA: Yes, Father . . .

The priest wants to ask and say more, but he cannot. An awkward moment between them and he reaches out to touch her shoulder gently.

PRIEST: Well . . . be a good girl, Rita Joe . . .
RITA *(Without turning after him):*   Goodbye, Father.
MAGISTRATE *(More insistently):*   Do you want a lawyer?

The priest leaves stage right. As he leaves, cross light to where a happy Jaimie Paul enters from stage left. Jaimie Paul comes down to join Rita Joe.

JAIMIE: This guy asked me how much education I got, an' I says to him, "Grade six. How much education a man need for such a job?" . . . An' the bum, he says it's not enough! I should take night school. But I got the job, an' I start next Friday . . . Like this . . .

Jaimie Paul does a mock sweeping routine as if he was cleaning a vast office building. He and Rita Joe are both laughing.

Pretty good, eh?
RITA: Pretty good.
JAIMIE: Cleaning the floors an' desks in the building . . . But it's a government job, and that's good for life. Work hard, then the government give me a raise . . . I never had a job like that before . . .
RITA: When I sleep happy, I dream of blueberries an' sun an' all the nice things when I was a little kid, Jaimie Paul.

The sound of an airplane is heard. Jaimie Paul looks up. Rita Joe also stares into the sky of her memory. Jaimie Paul's face is touched with pain and recollection. The teacher, Rita Joe's father, an old woman, four young Indian men and Eileen Joe come into the background quietly, as if at a wharf watching the airplane leave the village. They stand looking up until the noise of the aircraft begins to diminish.

JAIMIE: That airplane . . . a Cessna . . .

He continues watching the aircraft and turns, following its flight path.

She said to me, maybe I never see you again, Jaimie Paul.

There is a faint light on the magistrate in his chair. He is thoughtful, looking down at his hands.

MAGISTRATE: Do you want a lawyer?
RITA (To Jaimie Paul):   Who?
JAIMIE: Your mother . . . I said to her, they'll fix you up good in the hospital. Better than before. . . . It was a Cessna that landed on the river an' took her away . . . Maybe I never see you again, Jaimie, she says to me. She knew she was gonna die, but I was a kid and so were you . . . What the hell did we know? I'll never forget . . .

Jaimie Paul joins the village group on the upper level.

SINGER (*Singing an indefinite melody developing into a square-dance tune*):

> There was a man in a beat-up hat
> Who runs a house in the middle of town,
> An' round his stove-pipe chimney house
> The magpies sat, just a-lookin' round.

The Indian village people remain in the back of the stage, still watching the airplane which has vanished.

Jaimie Paul, on his way, passes Mr. Homer, a white citizen who has the hurried but fulfilled appearance of the socially responsible man. Mr. Homer comes to front of the stage beside Rita Joe. He talks directly to the audience.

MR. HOMER: Sure, we do a lot of things for our Indians here in the city at the Centre . . . Bring 'em in from the cold an' give them food . . . The rest . . . Well, the rest kinda take care of itself.

Rita Joe lowers her head and looks away from him. Mr. Homer moves to her and places his hand on her shoulders possessively.

When your mother got sick we flew her out . . . You remember that, Rita Joe?
RITA (*Nodding, looking down*):   Yes, Mr. Homer . . . Thank you.
MR. HOMER: And we sent her body back for the funeral . . . Right, Rita Joe?

The people of the village leave except for the young Indian men who remain and mime drinking.

And then sometimes a man drinks it up an' leaves his wife an' kids and the poor dears come here for help. We give them food an' a place to sleep . . . Right, Rita?
RITA: Yes.
MR. HOMER: Clothes too . . . White people leave clothes here for the Indians to take if they need 'em. Used to have them all up on racks over there . . . just like in a store . . .

He points.

But now we got them all on a heap on a table in the basement.

He laughs and Rita Joe nods with him.

Indian people . . . 'specially the women . . . get more of a kick diggin' through stuff that's piled up like that . . .

Mr. Homer chuckles and shakes his head.

There is a pale light on the magistrate, who is still looking down at his hands.

MAGISTRATE: There are institutions to help you . . .

Mr. Homer again speaks to audience, but now he is angry over some personal beef.

MR. HOMER: So you see, the Centre serves a need that's real for Indians who come to the city . . .

He wags his finger at the audience angrily.

It's the do-gooders burn my ass, you know! They come in from television or the newspaper . . . hang around just long enough to see a drunken Indian . . . an' bingo!

JAIMIE: Bingo!

MR. HOMER: That's their story! Next thing, they're seeing some kind of Red Power . . .

The young Indian men laugh and Rita Joe gets up to join them.

. . . or beatin' the government over the head! Let them live an' work among the Indians for a few months . . . then they'd know what it's really like . . .

The music comes up sharply.

SINGER:

> Round and round the cenotaph,
> The clumsy seagulls play.
> Fed by funny men with hats
> Who watch them night and day.

The four young Indian men join with Rita Joe and dance. Leading the group is Jaimie Paul. He is drunk, disheveled.

Light spreads before them as they advance onstage. They are laughing rowdily.

Rita Joe moves to them.

RITA: Jaimie Paul?

Mr. Homer leaves. Jaimie Paul is overtaken by two of his companions who take him by the arms, but he pushes them roughly away.

JAIMIE: Get the hell outa my way! . . . I'm as good a man as him any time . . .

Jaimie Paul crosses downstage to confront a member of the audience.

You know me? . . . You think I'm a dirty Indian, eh? Get outa my way!

He puts his hands over his head and continues staggering away.

Goddamnit, I wanna sleep . . .

The young Indian men and Jaimie Paul exit. Rita Joe follows after Jaimie Paul, reaching out to touch him, but the singer stands in her way and drives her back, singing . . .

Music up tempo and volume.

SINGER:

> Oh, can't you see that train roll on,
> Its hot black wheels keep comin' on?
> A Kamloops Indian died today.
> Train didn't hit him, he just fell.
> Busy train with wheels on fire!

The music dies. A policeman enters.

POLICEMAN: Rita Joe!

He repeats her name many times.

The teacher enters ringing the school handbell and crosses through.

TEACHER *(Calling):*   Rita Joe! Rita Joe! Didn't you hear the bell ring? The class is waiting . . . The class is always waiting for you.

The teacher exits.

MAGISTRATE & POLICEMAN *(Sharply, in unison):*   Rita Joe!

The policeman grabs and shakes Rita Joe to snap her out of her reverie.

Light up on the magistrate who sits erect, with authority.

MAGISTRATE: I ask you for the last time, Rita Joe . . . Do you want a lawyer?
RITA *(Defiantly):*   What for? . . . I can take care of myself.

MAGISTRATE: The charge against you this morning is prostitution. Why did you not return to your people as you said you would?

The light on the backstage dies. Rita Joe stands before the magistrate and the policeman. She is contained in a pool of light before them.

RITA *(Nervous, with despair):*   I tried . . . I tried . . .

The magistrate settles back into his chair and takes a folder from his desk, which he opens and studies.

MAGISTRATE: Special Constable Eric Wilson has submitted a statement to the effect that on June 18th he and Special Constable Schneider approached you on Fourth Avenue at nine-forty in the evening . . .
POLICEMAN: We were impersonating two deck-hands newly arrived in the city . . .
MAGISTRATE: You were arrested an hour later on charges of prostitution.

The magistrate holds the folder threateningly and looks down at her. Rita Joe is defiant.

RITA: That's a goddamned lie!
MAGISTRATE *(Sternly, gesturing to the policeman):*   This is a police statement. Surely you don't think a mistake was made?
RITA *(Peering into the light above her, shuddering):*   Everything in this room is like ice . . . How can you stay alive working here? . . . I'm so hungry I want to throw up . . .
MAGISTRATE: You have heard the statement, Rita Joe . . . Do you deny it?
RITA: I was going home, trying to find the highway . . . I knew those two were cops the moment I saw them . . . I told them to go f . . . fly a kite! They got sore then an' started pushing me around . . .
MAGISTRATE *(Patiently now, waving down the objections of the policeman):*   Go on.
RITA: They followed me around until a third cop drove up. An' then they arrested me.
MAGISTRATE: Arrested you . . . Nothing else?
RITA: They stuffed five dollar bills in my pockets when they had me in the car . . . I ask you, mister, when are they gonna charge cops like that with contributing to . . .
POLICEMAN: Your Worship . . .
MAGISTRATE *(Irritably, indicating the folder on the table before him):*   Now it's your word against this! You need references . . . People who know you . . . who will come to court to substantiate what you say . . . today! That is the process of legal argument!
RITA: Can I bum a cigarette someplace?
MAGISTRATE: No. You can't smoke in court.

The policeman smiles and exits.

RITA: Then give me a bed to sleep on, or is the sun gonna rise an' rise until it burns a hole in my head?

Guitar music cues softly in the background.

MAGISTRATE: Tell me about the child.
RITA: What child?
MAGISTRATE: The little girl I once saw beside the road!
RITA: I don't know any girl, mister! When do I eat? Why does an Indian wait even when he's there first thing in the morning?

The pool of light tightens around magistrate and Rita Joe.

MAGISTRATE: I have children . . . two sons . . .
RITA *(Nodding):*   Sure. That's good.

The magistrate gropes for words to express a message that is very precious to him.

MAGISTRATE: My sons can go in any direction they wish . . . Into trades or university . . . But if I had a daughter, I would be more concerned . . .
RITA: What's so special about a girl?
MAGISTRATE: I would wish . . . Well, I'd be concerned about her choices . . . Her choices of living, school . . . friends . . . These things don't come as lightly for a girl. For boys it is different . . . But I would worry if I had a daughter . . . Don't hide your child! Someone else can be found to raise her if you can't!

Rita Joe shakes her head, a strange smile on her face.

Why not? There are people who would love to take care of it.
RITA: Nobody would get my child . . . I would sooner kill it an' bury it first! I am not a kind woman, mister judge!
MAGISTRATE *(At a loss):*   I see . . .
RITA *(A cry):*   I want to go home . . .

Quick up tempo music is heard. Suddenly, the lights change.

Jaimie Paul and the young Indian men sweep over the backstage ramp, the light widening for them. Rita Joe moves into this railway station crowd. She turns from one man to another until she sees Jaimie Paul.

Eileen Joe and an old woman enter.

RITA: Jaimie!
EILEEN *(Happily, running to him):*   Jaimie Paul! God's sakes . . . When did you get back from the north? . . . I thought you said you wasn't coming until breakup . . .

Jaimie Paul turns to Eileen.

JAIMIE: I was comin' home on the train . . . had a bit to drink and was feeling pretty good . . . Lots of women sleeping in their seats on the train . . . I'd lift their hats an' say, "Excuse me, lady . . . I'm lookin' for a wife!"

He turns to the old woman.

One fat lady got mad, an' I says to her, "That's alright, lady . . . You got no worries . . . You keep sleepin'!"

Laughter.

Jaimie Paul and the old woman move away.

Eileen sees Rita Joe who is standing watching.

EILEEN: Rita! . . . Tom an' I broke up . . . Did I tell you?
RITA: No, Leenie . . . You didn't tell me!
EILEEN: He was no good . . . He stopped comin' to see me when he said he would. I kept waiting, but he didn't come . . .
RITA: I sent you a pillow for your wedding!
EILEEN: I gave it away . . . I gave it to Clara Hill.
RITA (*Laughing bawdily and miming pregnancy*):   Clara Hill don't need no pillow now!
JAIMIE (*Smiling, crossing by her and exiting*):   I always came to see you, Rita Joe . . .

Rita Joe looks bewildered.

OLD WOMAN (*Exiting*):   I made two Saskatoon pies, Rita . . . You said next time you came home you wanted Saskatoon pie with lots of sugar . . .

Eileen and the old woman drift away.

Jaimie Paul moves on to the shadows.

The three murderers enter in silhouette; one whistles. Rita Joe rushes to the young Indian men in stagefront.

RITA: This is me, Rita Joe, God's sakes . . . We went to the same school together . . . Don't you know me now, Johnny? You remember how tough you was when you was a boy? . . . We tied you up in the Rainbow Creek and forgot you was there after recess . . . An' after school was out, somebody remembered . . .

She laughs.

> And you was blue when we got to you. Your clothes was wet to the chin, an' you said, "That's a pretty good knot . . . I almost give up trying to untie it!"

The music continues. Rita Joe steps among the young Indian men and they mime being piled in a car at a drive-in.

> Steve Laporte? . . . You remember us goin' to the drive-in and the cold rain comin' down the car windows so we couldn't see the picture show anyhow?

She sits beside Steve Laporte. They mime the windshield wipers.

A cold white light comes up on playing area directly in front of the magistrate's chair. A male witness of disheveled, dirty appearance steps into light and delivers testimony in a whining, defensive voice. He is one of the murderers, but apart from the other three, he is nervous.

WITNESS: I gave her three bucks . . . an' once I got her goin' she started yellin' like hell! Called me a dog, pig . . . some filthy kind of animal . . . So I slapped her around a bit . . . Guys said she was a funny kind of bim . . . would do it for them standing up, but not for me she wouldn't . . . So I slapped her around . . .

The magistrate nods and makes a notation. The light on the witness dies.

Rita Joe speaks with urgency and growing fear to Steve Laporte.

RITA: Then you shut the wipers off an' we were just sitting there, not knowing what to do . . . I wish . . . we could go back again there an' start livin' from that day on . . . Jaimie!

Rita Joe looks at Steve Laporte as at a stranger. She stands and draws away from him. Jaimie Paul enters behind Rita Joe.

There is a cold light before the magistrate again and another male witness moves into the light, replacing the first witness. He too is one of the murderers.

This witness testifies with full gusto.

WITNESS: Gave her a job in my tire store . . . took her over to my place after work once . . . She was scared when I tried a trick, but I'm easy on broads that get scared, providin' they keep their voices down . . . After that, I slipped her a fiver . . . Well, sir, she took the money, then she stood in front of the window, her head high an' her naked shoulders shakin' like she was cold. Well, sir, she cried a little an' then she says, "Goddamnit, but I wish I was a school teacher . . ."

He laughs and everyone onstage joins in the laughter.

The light dies out on the witness. Jaimie Paul enters and crosses to Rita Joe. They lie down and embrace.

RITA: You always came to see me, Jaimie Paul . . . The night we were in the cemetery . . . You remember Jaimie Paul? I turned my face from yours until I saw the ground . . . an' I knew that below us . . . they were like us once, and now they lie below the ground, their eyes gone, the bones showin' . . . They must've spoke and touched each other here . . . like you're touching me, Jaimie Paul . . . an' now there was nothing over them, except us . . . an' wind in the grass an' a barbwire fence creaking. An' behind that, a hundred acres of barley.

Jaimie Paul stands.

That's something to remember, when you're lovin', eh?

The sound of a train whistle is heard. Jaimie Paul goes and the lights onstage fade.

The music comes up and the singer sings. As Jaimie Paul passes her, the singer pursues him up the ramp, and Rita Joe runs after them.

SINGER:

> Oh, can't you see that train roll on,
> Gonna kill a man, before it's gone?
> Jaimie Paul fell and died.
> He had it comin', so it's alright.
> Silver train with wheels on fire!

The music dies instantly. Rita Joe's words come on the heels of music as a bitter extension of song.

She stands before the magistrate, again in the court, but looks back to where Jaimie Paul had been in the gloom. The policeman enters where Jaimie Paul has exited, replacing him, for the fourth trial scene.

RITA: Jaimie, why am I here? . . . Is it . . . because people are talkin' about me and all them men . . . Is that why? I never wanted to cut cordwood for a living . . .

With great bitterness.

Never once I thought . . . it'd be like this . . .

MAGISTRATE: What are we going to do about you, Rita Joe? This is the seventh charge against you in one year . . . Laws are not made to be violated in this way . . . Why did you steal?

RITA: I was hungry. I had no money.

MAGISTRATE: Yet you must have known you would be caught?

RITA: Yes.

MAGISTRATE: Are you not afraid of what is happening to you?

RITA: I am afraid of a lot of things. Put me in jail. I don't care . . .

MAGISTRATE *(With forced authority)*:   Law is a· procedure. The procedure must be respected. It took hundreds of years to develop this process of law.

RITA: I stole a sweater . . . They caught me in five minutes!

She smiles whimsically at this. The magistrate is leafing through the documents before him. The policeman stands to one side of him.

MAGISTRATE: The prosecutor's office has submitted some of the past history of Rita Joe . . .

POLICEMAN: She was born and raised on a reservation. Then came a brief period in a public school off the reservation . . . at which time Rita Joe established herself as something of a disruptive influence . . .

RITA: What's that mean?

MAGISTRATE *(Turning to her, smiling)*:   A trouble maker!

Rita Joe becomes animated, aware of the trap around her closing even at moments such as this.

RITA: Maybe it was about the horse, huh? . . .

She looks up at the magistrate who is still smiling, offering her no help.

There was this accident with a horse . . . It happened like this . . . I was riding a horse to school an' some of the boys shot a rifle an' my horse bucked an' I fell off. I fell in the bush an' got scratched . . . The boys caught the horse by the school and tried to ride him, but the horse bucked an' pinned a boy against a tree, breaking his leg in two places . . .

She indicates the place the leg got broken.

They said . . . an' he said I'd rode the horse over him on purpose!

MAGISTRATE: Well . . . Did you?

RITA: It wasn't that way at all, I tell you! They lied!

The policeman and the singer laugh.

MAGISTRATE: Why should they lie, and Rita Joe alone tell the truth? . . . Or are you a child enough to believe the civilization of which we are a part . . .

He indicates the audience as inclusive of civilization from his point of view.

    . . . does not understand Rita Joe?

RITA: I don't know what you're saying.

MAGISTRATE *(With a touch of compassion):*   Look at you, woman! Each time you come before me you are older. The lines in your face are those of . . .

RITA: I'm tired an' I want to eat, mister! I haven't had grub since day before yesterday . . . This room is like a boat on water . . . I'm so dizzy . . . What the hell kind of place is this won't let me go lie down on grass?

She doubles over to choke back her nausea.

MAGISTRATE: This is not the reservation, Rita Joe. This is another place, another time . . .

RITA *(Straining to remember, to herself):*   I was once in Whitecourt, Alberta. The cops are fatter there than here. I had to get out of Whitecourt, Alberta . . .

MAGISTRATE: Don't blame the police, Rita Joe! The obstacles to your life are here . . .

He touches his forefinger to his temples.

    . . . in your thoughts . . . possibly even in your culture . . .

Rita Joe turns away from him, searching the darkness behind her.

    What's the matter?

RITA: I want to go home!

MAGISTRATE: But you can't go now. You've broken a law for which you will have to pay a fine or go to prison . . .

RITA: I have no money.

MAGISTRATE *(With exasperation):*   Rita Joe . . . It is against the law to solicit men on the street. You have to wash . . .

Rita Joe begins to move away from him, crossing the front of the stage along the apron, her walk cocky.

The light spreads and follows her.

    You can't walk around in old clothes and running shoes made of canvas . . . You have to have some money in your pockets and an address where you live. You should fix your hair . . . perhaps even change your name. And try to tame that accent that sounds like you have a mouthful of sawdust . . . There is no peace in being extraordinary!

The light dies on the magistrate and the policeman.

Rita Joe is transported into another memory. Jaimie Paul enters and slides along the floor, left of centre stage. He is drunk, counting the fingers on his outstretched hands.

Mr. Homer has entered with a wagon carrying hot soup and mugs. Four young Indian men come in out of the cold. Mr. Homer speaks to audience in a matter-of-fact informative way.

MR. HOMER *(Dispensing soup to the young Indian men):*   The do-gooders make something special of the Indian . . . There's nothing special here . . . At the centre here the quick cure is a bowl of stew under the belt and a good night's sleep.

JAIMIE: Hey, Mister Homer! How come I got so many fingers? Heh?

He laughs.

Mr. Homer ignores Jaimie Paul and continues talking to the audience.

MR. HOMER: I wouldn't say they were brothers or sisters to me . . . No sir! But if you're . . .

Jaimie Paul gets up and embraces Rita Joe.

JAIMIE: I got two hands an' one neck . . . I can kill more than I can eat . . . If I had more fingers I would need mittens big as pie plates . . . Yeh?

MR. HOMER *(To Jaimie Paul):*   Lie down, Jaimie Paul, an' have some more sleep. When you feel better, I'll get you some soup.

Rita Joe laughs. Jaimie Paul weaves his way uncertainly to where Mr. Homer stands.

JAIMIE *(Laughing):*   I spit in your soup! You know what I say? . . . I say I spit in your soup, Mister Homer . . .

He comes to Mr. Homer and seems about to do just what he threatens.

MR. HOMER *(Pushing him away with good humour):*   I'll spit in your eyeball if you don't shut up!

JAIMIE *(Breaking away from Mr. Homer, taunting):*   You . . . are not Mister Homer!

MR. HOMER.   I'm not what?

JAIMIE: You're not Mister Homer . . . You're somebody wearing his pants an' shirt . . .

He stumbles away.

But you're not Mister Homer . . . Mister Homer never gets mad . . . No sir, not Mister Homer!

MR. HOMER: I'm not mad . . . What're you talkin' about?

Jaimie Paul turns and approaches the young Indian men. He threatens to fall off the apron of the stage.

JAIMIE: No . . . not Mister Homer! An' I got ten fingers . . . How's that?

MR. HOMER: For Chris' sake, Jaimie . . . Go to sleep.

Jaimie Paul stops and scowls, then grins knowingly. He begins to mime a clumsy paddler paddling a boat.

JAIMIE (*Laughing again*):   I know you . . . Hey? I know you! . . . I seen you up Rainbow Creek one time . . . I seen you paddling!

He breaks up with laughter.

MR. HOMER (*Amused, tolerant*):   Oh, come on . . . I've never been to Rainbow Creek.

Jaimie Paul controls his laughter.

JAIMIE: Sure you been to Rainbow Creek . . .

He begins to mime paddling again.

Next time you need a good paddler, you see me. I have a govermen' job, but screw that. I'm gonna paddle! I seen you paddle . . .

Again he breaks up in laughter as he once more demonstrates the quality of paddling he once saw.

Rita Joe is fully enjoying the spectacle. So are the young Indian men. Mr. Homer is also amused by the absurdity of the situation. Jaimie Paul turns, but chokes up with laughter after saying . . .

I have seen some paddlers . . . but you!

Jaimie Paul turns and waves his hand derisively, laughing.

MR. HOMER: It must've been somebody else . . . I've never been to Rainbow Creek.

JAIMIE: Like hell, you say!

Jaimie Paul paddles the soup wagon out. Guitar music comes in with an upbeat tempo. Rita Joe and the young Indian men dance to the beat. The young Indian men then drift after Mr. Homer.

The light fades slowly on centre stage and the music changes.

Rita Joe, happy in her memory, does a circling butch walk in the fading light to the song of the singer. At the conclusion of the song, she is on the apron, stage right, in a wash of light that includes the magistrate and the singer.

SINGER:

> I woke up at six o'clock
> Stumbled out of bed,
> Crash of cans an' diesel trucks
> Damned near killed me dead.
>
> Sleepless hours, heavy nights,
> Dream your dreams so pretty.
> God was gonna have a laugh
> An' gave me a job in the city!

Rita Joe is still elated at her memory of Jaimie Paul and his story. With unusual candour, she turns girlishly before the magistrate, and in mild imitation of her own moment of drunkenness, begins telling him a story.

Faint guitar music in the background continues.

RITA: One night I drank a little bit of wine, an' I was outside lookin' at the stars . . . thinking . . . when I was a little girl how much bigger the trees were . . . no clouds, but suddenly there was a light that made the whole sky look like day . . .

Guitar out.

. . . just for a moment . . . an' before I got used to the night . . . I saw animals, moving across the sky . . . two white horses . . . A man was takin' them by the halters, and I knew the man was my grandfather . . .

She stares at the magistrate, unsure of herself now.

MAGISTRATE: Yes! Is that all?

RITA: No . . . But I never seen my grandfather alive, and I got so sad thinkin' about it I wanted to cry. I wasn't sure it was him, even . . .

She begins to laugh.

I went an' telephoned the police and asked for the chief, but the chief was home and a guy asks what I want.

MAGISTRATE *(Mildly amused):*   You . . . called the police?

RITA: I told the guy I'd seen God, and he says, "Yeh? What would you like us to do about it?" An' I said, "Pray! Laugh! Shout!"

MAGISTRATE: Go on . . .

RITA: He . . . asked where I'd seen God, an' I told him in the sky. He says you better call this number . . . It's the Air Force. They'll take care of it!

She laughs and the magistrate smiles.

I called the number the guy gave me, but it was nighttime and there was no answer! If God was to come at night, after office hours, then . . .

A terrible awkwardness sets in. There is a harsh light on her. She turns away, aware that she is in captivity.

The magistrate stirs with discomfort.

RITA *(With great fear):*   How long will this be? Will I never be able to . . .

MAGISTRATE *(Annoyed at himself, at her):*   There is nothing here but a record of your convictions . . . Nothing to speak for you and provide me with any reason to moderate your sentence! What the hell am I supposed to do? Violate the law myself because I feel that somehow . . . I've known and felt . . . No!

He turns from her.

You give me no alternative . . . No alternative at all!

The magistrate packs up his books.

RITA: I'll go home . . . jus' let me go home. I can't get out of jail to find the highway . . . or some kind of job!

The magistrate stands.

MAGISTRATE: Prison and fines are not the only thing . . . Have you, for instance, considered that you might be an incurable carrier? There are people like that . . . They cannot come into contact with others without infecting them. They cannot eat from dishes others may use . . . They cannot prepare or touch food others will eat . . . The same with clothes, cars, hospital beds!

The magistrate exits.

Rita Joe shakes her head with disbelief. The idea of perpetual condemnation is beyond her comprehension. She falls to the floor.

Guitar music is heard in the background.

She turns away from the magistrate and the light comes up over the ramp at the back of the stage.

Another light comes up on centre stage left. Here, Eileen Joe and the old woman are miming clothes washing using a scrubbing board and placing the wash into woven baskets. The women and the girl are on their knees, facing each other.

On the ramp above them, Jaimie Paul is struggling with a policeman who is scolding him softly for being drunk, abusive and noisy. Jaimie Paul is jocular; the policeman, harassed and worried. They slowly cross the ramp from stage left.

SINGER:

> Four o'clock in the morning,
> The sailor rides the ship
> An' I ride the wind!
>
> Eight o'clock in the morning,
> My honey's scoldin' the sleepyheads
> An' I'm scoldin' him.

JAIMIE *(To the policeman):*   On the Smoky River . . . four o'clock in the morning . . . Hey? There was nobody . . . just me . . . You know that?
POLICEMAN: No, I don't. Come on. Let's get you home.

Jaimie Paul moves forward and embraces the policeman.

JAIMIE: You wanna see something?

Jaimie Paul takes out a coin to do a trick.

OLD WOMAN *(To Eileen):*   Your father's been very sick.
EILEEN: He won't eat nothing . . .
OLD WOMAN: Jus' sits and worries . . . That's no good.

Jaimie Paul finishes his coin trick.

JAIMIE: You like that one? Hey, we both work for the government, eh?

They exit laughing.

Watch the rough stuff . . . Just don't make me mad.

OLD WOMAN: If Rita Joe was to come and see him . . . maybe say good bye to him . . .

RITA *(Calling from her world to the world of her strongest fears):*   But he's not dying! I saw him not so long ago . . .

The women in her memory do not hear her. They continue discussing her father.

OLD WOMAN: He loved her an' always worried . . .

RITA: I didn't know he was sick!

OLD WOMAN: You were smart to come back, Eileen Joe.

RITA *(Again calling over the distance of her soul):*   Nobody told me!

SINGER:

> Nine o'clock in the evening,
> Moon is high in the blueberry sky
> An' I'm lovin' you.

JAIMIE *(Now passing along the apron beside Rita Joe, talking to the policeman):*   You seen where I live? Big house with a mongolia in front . . . Fancy place! You wanna see the room I got?

POLICEMAN *(Gruffly, aware that Jaimie Paul can become angry quickly):*   When I get holidays, we'll take a tour of everything you've got . . . but I don't get holidays until September!

From the apron they cross to the stage rear diagonally, between the old woman with Eileen, and Rita Joe.

JAIMIE: You're a good man . . . Good for a laugh. I'm a good man . . . You know me!

POLICEMAN: Sure, you're first class when you're sober!

JAIMIE: I got a cousin in the city. He got his wife a stove an' washing machine! He's a good man . . . You know my cousin maybe?

Fading off.

They leave the stage.

The old woman has risen from her knees and wearily collected one basket of clothes. She climbs the ramp and moves to the wings, stage right. Eileen is thoughtful and slower, but she also prepares her clothes wash and follows.

OLD WOMAN: Nothing in the city I can see . . . only if you're lucky. A good man who don't drink or play cards . . . that's all.

EILEEN: And if he's bad?

OLD WOMAN: Then leave him. I'm older than you, Eileen . . . I know what's best.

The old woman exits. The guitar music dies out. Jaimie Paul's laughter and voice is heard offstage.

JAIMIE *(Offstage, loud, boisterous):*   We both work for the gov'ment! We're buddies, no? . . . You think we're both the same?

Laughter.

The lights on the ramp and centre stage die.

RITA *(Following Jaimie Paul's laughter):*   Good or bad, what difference? So long as he's a livin' man!

Rita Joe and Eileen giggle.

The light spreads around her into pale infinity.

The teacher enters on the ramp. She rings a handbell and stops a short distance from wings to peer around. She is a shy, inadequate woman who moves and behaves jerkily, the product of incomplete education and poor job placement.

TEACHER *(In a scolding voice):*   Rita! Rita Joe!

The bell rings.

The class is waiting for you. The class is always waiting.

Rita Joe is startled to hear the bell and see the woman. She comes to her feet, now a child before the teacher, and runs to join Eileen. Jaimie Paul and the young Indian men have entered with the bell and sit cross-legged on the floor as school children.

RITA: The sun is in my skin, Miss Donohue. The leaves is red and orange, and the wind stopped blowin' an hour ago.

The teacher has stopped to listen to this. Rita Joe and Eileen, late again, slip into class and sit on the floor with the others.

TEACHER: Rita! What is a noun?

No answer. The kids poke Rita Joe to stand up.

Did you hear what I asked?
RITA *(Uncertain):*   No . . . Yes?
TEACHER: There's a lot you don't know . . . That kind of behaviour is exhibitionism! We are a melting pot!

RITA: A melting pot?

TEACHER: A melting pot! Do you know what a melting pot is?

RITA: It's . . .

She shrugs.

    . . . a melting pot!

The class laughs.

TEACHER: Precisely! You put copper and tin into a melting pot and out comes bronze . . . It's the same with people!

RITA: Yes, Miss Donohue . . . out comes bronze . . .

Laughter again.

The teacher calls Rita Joe over to her. The light fades on the other children.

TEACHER: Rita, what was it I said to you this morning?

RITA: You said . . . wash my neck, clean my fingernails . . .

TEACHER *(Cagey):*   No, it wasn't Rita!

RITA: I can't remember. It was long ago.

TEACHER: Try to remember, Rita.

RITA: I don't remember, Miss Donohue! I was thinkin' about you last night, thinkin' if you knew some . . .

TEACHER: You are straying off the topic! Never stray off the topic!

RITA: It was a dream, but now I'm scared, Miss Donohue. I've been a long time moving about . . . trying to find something! . . . I must've lost . . .

TEACHER: No, Rita. That is not important.

RITA: Not important?

TEACHER: No, Rita . . . Now you repeat after me like I said or I'm going to have to pass you by again. Say after me . . .

RITA: Sure. Say after you . . .

TEACHER: Say after me . . . "A book of verse underneath the spreading bough . . ."

RITA: "A book of verse underneath the spreading bough . . ."

TEACHER: "A jug of wine, a loaf of bread and thou beside me . . . singing in the wilderness."

RITA *(The child spell broken, she laughs bawdily):*   Jaimie said, "To heck with the wine an' loaf . . . Let's have some more of this here thou!"

Her laughter dies. She wipes her lips, as if trying to erase some stain there.

TEACHER *(Peevish):*   Alright, Rita . . . Alright, let's have none of that!

RITA *(Plaintively):*   I'm sorry, Miss Donohue . . . I'm sure sorry!

TEACHER: That's alright.

RITA: I'm sorry!

TEACHER: Alright . . .

RITA: Sorry . . .

TEACHER: You will never make bronze! Coming from nowhere and going no place! Who am I to change that?

Rita Joe grips the edge of the desk with both hands, holding on tightly.

RITA: No! They said for me to stay here, to learn something!

TEACHER *(With exasperation):*   I tried to teach you, but your head was in the clouds, and as for your body . . . Well! I wouldn't even think what I know you do!

The teacher crosses amongst the other children.

RITA: I'm sorry . . . please! Let me say it after you again . . .

Blurting it out . . .

"A book of verse underneath the spreading . . ."

TEACHER: Arguing . . . always trying to upset me . . . and in grade four . . . I saw it then . . . pawing the ground for men like a bitch in heat!

RITA *(Dismayed):*   It . . . isn't so!

TEACHER: You think I don't know? I'm not blind . . . I can see out of the windows.

The teacher marches off into wings and the class runs after her leaving Rita Joe alone onstage.

RITA: That's a lie! For God's sake, tell the judge I have a good character . . . I am clean an' honest . . . Everything you said is right, I'm never gonna argue again . . . I believe in God . . . an' I'm from the country and lost like hell! Tell him!

She shakes her head sadly, knowing the extent of her betrayal.

They only give me eight hours to find somebody who knows me . . . An' seven and a half hours is gone already!

The lights on the scene dies.

SINGER *(Recitativo):*

> Things that were . . .
> Life that might have been . . .

A pale backlight on the back of the ramp comes up.

Recorded sounds of crickets and the distant sound of a train whistle are heard.

Rita Joe's father and Jaimie Paul enter on the ramp from stage left. The father leads the way. Jaimie Paul is behind, rolling a cigarette. They walk slowly, thoughtfully, following the ramp across and downstage. Rita Joe stands separate, watching.

> The blue evening of the first
> Warm day
> Is the last evening.
> There'll not be another
> Like it.

JAIMIE: No more handouts, David Joe . . . We can pick an' can the berries ourselves.

FATHER: We need money to start a cooperative like that.

JAIMIE: Then some other way!

The old man listens, standing still, to the sounds of the train and night.

FATHER: You're a young man, Jaimie Paul . . . young an' angry. It's not good to be that angry.

JAIMIE: We're gonna work an' live like people . . . Not be afraid all the time . . . Stop listening to an old priest an' Indian department guys who're working for a pension!

FATHER: You're young man, Jaimie Paul . . .

JAIMIE: I say stop listening, David Joe! . . . In the city they never learned my name. It was "Hey, fella" . . . or "You, boy" . . . That kind of stuff.

Pause. The sound of the train whistle is heard.

FATHER: A beautiful night, Jaimie Paul.

JAIMIE: We can make some money. The berries are good this year!

Jaimie Paul is restless, edgy, particularly on the train whistle sound.

FATHER: Sometimes . . . children . . . You remember everyday with them . . . Never forget you are alive with children.

Jaimie Paul turns away and begins to retrace his steps.

JAIMIE: You want us all to leave an' go to the city? Is that what you want?

The father shakes his head. He does not wish for this, but the generation spread between them is great now. Jaimie Paul walks away with a gesture of contempt.

The sounds die.

The light dies and isolates the father and Rita Joe.

RITA: You were sick, an' now you're well.

FATHER *(In measured speech, turning away from Rita Joe, as if carefully recalling something of great importance):*   You left your father, Rita Joe . . . never wrote Eileen a letter that time . . . Your father was pretty sick man that time . . . pretty sick man . . . June ninth he got the cold, an' on June twenty he . . .

RITA: But you're alive! I had such crazy dreams I'd wake up laughing at myself!

FATHER: I have dreams too . . .

Rita Joe moves forward to him. She stops talking to him, as if communicating thoughts rather than words. He remains standing where he is, facing away from her.

RITA: I was in a big city . . . so many streets I'd get lost like nothin' . . . When you got sick I was on a job . . .

FATHER: June ninth I got the cold . . .

RITA: Good job in a tire store . . . Jaimie Paul's got a job with the government, you know?

FATHER: Pretty sick man, that time . . .

RITA: A good job in a tire store. They was gonna teach me how to file statements after I learned the telephone. Bus ticket home was twenty dollars . . . But I got drunk all the same when I heard an' I went in and tried to work that day . . .

She smiles and shakes her head.

Boy, I tried to work! Some day that was!

FATHER: I have dreams . . . Sometimes I'm scared . . .

They finally look at each other.

RITA *(Shuddering):*   I'm so cold . . .

FATHER: Long dreams . . . I dream about Rita Joe . . .

Sadly.

Have to get better. I've lived longer, but I know nothing . . . Nothing at all. Only the old stories.

Rita Joe moves sideways to him. She is smiling happily.

RITA: When I was little, a man came out of the bush to see you. Tell me why again!

The father hesitates, shaking his head, but he is also smiling.

The light of their separate yearnings fades out and the front of the stage is lit with the two of them together.

The father turns and comes forward to meet her.

FATHER: You don't want to hear that story again.

He sits on the slight elevation of the stage apron. Rita Joe sits down in front of him and snuggles between his knees. He leans forward over her.

RITA: It's the best story I ever heard!

FATHER: You were a little girl . . . four years old already . . . an' Eileen was getting big inside your mother. One day it was hot . . . sure was hot. Too hot to try an' fish in the lake, because the fish was down deep where the water was cold.

RITA: The dog started to bark . . .

FATHER: The dog started to bark . . . How!

FATHER & RITA *(In unison):*   How! How! How!

FATHER: Barking to beat hell an' I says to myself why . . . on such a hot day? Then I see the bushes moving . . . somebody was coming to see us. Your mother said from inside the house, "What's the matter with that dog?" An' I says to her, "Somebody coming to see me." It was big Sandy Collins, who ran the sawmill back of the reserve. Business was bad for big Sandy then . . . but he comes out of that bush like he was being chased . . . his clothes all wet an' stickin' to him . . . his cap in his hands, an' his face black with the heat and dirt from hard work . . . He says to me, "My little Millie got a cough last night an' today she's dead." . . . "She's dead," big Sandy says to me. I says to him, "I'm sorry to hear that, Sandy . . . Millie is the same age as my Rita." And he says to me, "David Joe . . . Look, you got another kid coming . . . Won't make much difference to you . . . Sell me Rita Joe like she is for a thousand dollars!"

Rita Joe giggles. The father raises his hand to silence her.

"A thousand dollars is a lot of money, Sandy," I says to him . . . "lots of money. You got to cut a lot of timber for a thousand dollars." Then he says to me, "Not a thousand cash at once, David Joe. First I give you two-hundred-fifty dollars . . . When Rita Joe comes ten years old and she's still alright, I give you the next two-hundred-fifty . . . An' if she don't die by fifteen, I guarantee you five-hundred dollars cash at once!"

Rita Joe and the father break into laughter. He reaches around her throat and draws her close.

So you see, Rita Joe, you lose me one thousand dollars from big Sandy Collins!

They continue laughing.

A harsh light on the magistrate, who enters and stands on his podium.

MAGISTRATE: Rita Joe, when was the last time you had dental treatment?

Rita Joe covers her ears, refusing to surrender this moment of security in the arms of her father.

RITA: I can't hear you!
MAGISTRATE *(Loudly)*:   You had your teeth fixed ever?

Rita Joe comes to her feet and turns on him.

RITA: Leave me alone!
MAGISTRATE: Have you had your lungs x-rayed recently?
RITA: I was hungry, that's all!
MAGISTRATE *(Becoming staccato, machine-like in his questions)*:   When was your last Wasserman taken?
RITA: What's that?

Rita Joe hears the teacher's voice. She turns to see the approaching teacher give the magistrate testimony.

The stage is lit in a cold blue light now.

TEACHER *(Crisply, to the magistrate as she approaches, her dialogue a reading)*:
  Dear Sir . . . In reply to your letter of the twelfth, I cannot in all sincerity provide a reference of good character for one Rita Joe . . .

The witnesses do not see her and the testimony takes on the air of a nightmare for Rita Joe. She is baffled and afraid. The teacher continues to quietly repeat her testimony.

Rita Joe appeals to the magistrate.

RITA: Why am I here? What've I done?
MAGISTRATE: You are charged with prostitution.

Her father stands and crosses upstage to the ramp to observe. He is joined by Eileen Joe, the old woman and the priest. Mr. Homer approaches briskly from stage left.

MR. HOMER: She'd been drinking when she comes into the centre . . .
  Nothing wrong in that I could see, 'specially on a Friday night. So I give
  her some soup an' a sandwich. Then all of a sudden in the middle of a

silly argument, she goes haywire . . . an' I see her comin' at me . . . I'll tell you, I was scared! I don't know Indian women that well!
MAGISTRATE: Assault!

Rita Joe retreats from him and the teacher and Mr. Homer now stand before the magistrate as if they were frozen. Mr. Homer repeats his testimony under the main dialogue. Jaimie Paul staggers in from stage right, over the ramp, heading to the wings of lower stage left.

JAIMIE *(To himself):*   What the hell are they doing?
RITA *(Running to him):*   Say a good word for me, Jaimie!
JAIMIE: They fired me yesterday . . . What the hell's the use of living?

Jaimie Paul leaves the stage as the school board clerk enters to offer further testimony to the magistrate.

SCHOOL BOARD CLERK: I recommended in a letter that she take school after grade five through correspondence courses from the Department of Education . . . but she never replied to the form letter the school division sent her . . .
RITA *(Defending herself to the magistrate):*   That drunken bastard Mahoney used it to light fire in his store . . . He'd never tell Indians when mail came for us!
SCHOOL BOARD CLERK: I repeat . . . I wish our position understood most clearly . . . No reply was ever received in this office to the letter we sent to Rita Joe!
RITA: One letter . . . one letter for a lifetime?
TEACHER: Say after me! "I wandered lonely as a cloud, that floats on high o'er vales and hills . . . when all at once I saw a crowd . . . a melting pot . . ."

A policeman and a male witness enter. The priest crosses downstage. The testimonies are becoming a nightmare babble.

Rita Joe is stung, stumbles backward from all of them as they face the magistrate with their condemnations.

POLICEMAN: We were impersonating two deckhands . . .

The priest is passing by Rita Joe. He makes the sign of the cross and offers comfort in a thin voice, lost in the noise.

PRIEST: Be patient, Rita . . . The young are always stormy, but in time, your understanding will deepen . . . There is an end to all things.
WITNESS: I gave her a job, but she was kind of slow . . . I can't wait around,

there's lots of white people goin' lookin' for work . . . so I figure, to hell with this noise . . .

MAGISTRATE *(Loudly over the other voices):*   Have your ears ached?

RITA: No!

MAGISTRATE: Have you any boils on your back? Any discharge? When did you bathe last?

The murderers appear and circle Rita Joe.

Answer me! Drunkenness! Shoplifting! Assault! Prostitution, prostitution, prostitution, prostitution!

RITA *(Her voice shrill, cutting over the babble):*   I don't know what happened . . . but you got to listen to me and believe me, mister!

The babble ceases abruptly.

Pleading with them as best she knows.

You got rules here that was made before I was born . . . I was hungry when I stole something . . . an' I was hollerin' I was so lonely when I started whoring . . .

The murderers come closer.

MAGISTRATE: Rita Joe . . . Has a doctor examined you? . . . I mean, really examined you? Rita Joe . . . You might be carrying and transmitting some disease and not aware of it!

RITA *(Breaking away from the murderers):*   Bastards!

To the magistrate.

Put me in jail . . . I don't care . . . I'll sign anything. I'm so goddamn hungry I'm sick . . . Whatever it is, I'm guilty!

She clutches her head and goes down in a squat of defeat.

MAGISTRATE: Are you free of venereal disease?

RITA: I don't know. I'm not sick that way.

MAGISTRATE: How can you tell?

RITA *(Lifting her face to him):*   I know . . . A woman knows them things . . .

Pause.

MAGISTRATE: Thirty days!

The policeman leads Rita Joe off and the house lights come up.

The actors and the singer walk off the stage, leaving emptiness as at opening of the act.

ACT TWO

The house lights dim.

A policeman brings Rita Joe in downstage centre. She curls up in her jail cell and sleeps.

Rita Joe's father enters on the ramp and crosses down to the audience.

The stage work lights die down. Lights isolate Rita Joe's father. Another light with prison bar shadows isolates Rita Joe in her area of the stage.

FATHER *(Looking down on Rita Joe):*   I see no way . . . no way . . . It's not clear like trees against snow . . . not clear at all . . .

To the audience.

But when I was fifteen years old, I leave the reserve to work on a threshing crew. They pay a dollar a day for a good man . . . an' I was a good strong man. The first time I got work there was a girl about as old as I . . . She'd come out in the yard an' watch the men working at the threshing machine. She had eyes that were the biggest I ever seen . . . like fifty-cent pieces . . . an' there was always a flock of geese around her. Whenever I see her I feel good. She used to stand an' watch me, an' the geese made a helluva lot of noise. One time I got off my rick an' went to get a drink of water . . . but I walked close to where she was watching me. She backed away, and then ran from me with the geese chasin' after her, their wings out an' their feet no longer touching the ground . . . They were white geese . . . The last time Rita Joe come home to see us . . . the last time she ever come home . . . I watched her leave . . . and I seen geese running after Rita Joe the same way . . . white geese . . . with their wings out an' their feet no longer touching the ground. And I remembered it all, an' my heart got so heavy I wanted to cry . . .

The light fades to darkness on the father, as he exits up the ramp and off. Rita Joe wakes from her dream, cold, shaking, desperate.

SINGER:

> The blue evening of the
> First warm day

Is the last evening.
There's not be another
Like it.

The priest enters from darkness with the policeman. He is dressed in a dark suit which needs pressing. He stops in half shadow outside Rita Joe's prison light.

The scene between them is played out in the manner of two country people meeting in a time of crisis. Their thoughts come slowly, incompletely. There is both fear and helplessness in both characters.

PRIEST: I came twice before they'd let me see you . . .

Rita Joe jumps to her feet. She smiles at him.

RITA: Oh, Father Andrew!
PRIEST: Even so, I had to wait an hour.

A long pause.

He clumsily takes out a package of cigarettes and matches from his pocket and hands them to her, aware that he is possibly breaking a prison regulation.

I'm sorry about this, Rita.

Rita Joe tears the package open greedily and lights a cigarette. She draws on it with animal satisfaction.

RITA: I don't know what's happening, Father Andrew.
PRIEST: They're not . . . hurting you here?
RITA: No.
PRIEST: I could make an appointment with the warden if there was something . . .
RITA: What's it like outside? . . . Is it a nice day outside? . . . I heard it raining last night . . . Was it raining?
PRIEST: It rains a lot here . . .
RITA: When I was a kid, there was leaves an' a river . . . Jaimie Paul told me once that maybe we never see those things again.

A long pause. The priest struggles with himself.

PRIEST: I've never been inside a jail before . . . They told me there was a chapel . . .

He points indefinitely back.

RITA: What's gonna happen to me? . . . That judge sure got sore . . .

She laughs.

PRIEST *(With disgust, yet unsure of himself):*   Prostitution this time?
RITA: I guess so . . .
PRIEST: You know how I feel . . . City is no place for you . . . nor for me . . . I've spent my life in the same surroundings as your father!
RITA: Sure . . . but you had God on your side!

She smiles mischievously. The priest angers.

PRIEST: Rita, try to understand . . . Our Lord Jesus once met a woman such as you beside the well . . . He forgave her!
RITA: I don't think God hears me here . . . Nobody hears me now, nobody except cops an' pimps an' bootleggers!
PRIEST: I'm here. I was there when you were born.
RITA: You've told me lots of times . . . I was thinkin' about my mother last night . . . She died young . . . I'm older than she was . . .
PRIEST: You mother was a good, hard-working woman. She was happy . . .

A pause between them.

RITA: There was frost on the street at five o'clock Tuesday morning when they arrested me . . . Last night, I remembered things flyin' an' kids runnin' past me trying to catch a chocolate wrapper that's blowin' in the wind . . .

She presses her hands against her bosom.

It hurts me here to think about them things!
PRIEST: I worry about you . . . Your father worries too . . . I baptized you . . . I watched you and Leenie grow into women!
RITA: Yes . . . I seen God in what you said . . . In your clothes! In your hair!
PRIEST: But you're not the woman I expected you to be . . . Your pride, Rita . . . your pride . . . may bar you from heaven.
RITA *(Mocking him):*   They got rules there too . . . in heaven?
PRIEST *(Angry):*   Rita! . . . I'm not blind . . . I can see! I'm not deaf . . . I know all about you! So does God!
RITA: My uncle was Dan Joe . . . He was dyin' and he said to me, "Long ago the white man come with Bibles to talk to my people, who had the land. They talk for hundred years . . . then we had all the Bibles, an' the white man had our land . . ."
PRIEST: Don't blame the Church! We are trying to help . . .
RITA *(With passion):*   How? I'm looking for the door . . .

PRIEST *(Tortured now):*   I . . . will hear your confession . . .

RITA: But I want to be free!

PRIEST *(Stiffly):*   We learn through suffering, Rita Joe . . . We will only be free if we become humble again.

Pause.

Will you confess, Rita Joe?

A long pause.

I'm going back on the four o'clock bus.

He begins walking away into the gloom.

I'll tell your father I saw you, and you looked well.

He is suddenly relieved.

RITA *(After him as he leaves):*   You go to hell!

The priest turns sharply.

Go tell your God . . . when you see him . . . Tell him about Rita Joe an' what they done to her! Tell him about yourself too! . . . That you were not good enough for me, but that didn't stop you tryin'! Tell him that!

The priest hurries away.

Guitar in. Rita Joe sits down, brooding.

SINGER:

> I will give you the wind and a sense of wonder
> As the child by the river, the reedy river.
> I will give you the sky wounded by thunder
> And a leaf on the river, the silver river.

A light comes up on the ramp where Jaimie Paul appears, smiling and waving to her.

JAIMIE *(Shouts):*   Rita Joe! I'm gonna take you dancing after work Friday . . . That job's gonna be alright!

Rita Joe springs to her feet, elated.

RITA: Put me back in jail so I can be free on Friday!

A sudden burst of dance music. The stage lights up and Jaimie Paul approaches her. They dance together, remaining close in the front centre stage.

SINGER:

> Round an' round the cenotaph,
> The clumsy seagulls play.
> Fed by funny men with hats
> Who watch them night and day.
>
> Sleepless hours, heavy nights,
> Dream your dreams so pretty.
> God was gonna have a laugh
> An' gave me a job in the city!

The music continues for the interlude.

Some young Indian men run onto the stage along the ramp and join Jaimie Paul and Rita Joe in their dance. The murderers enter and elbow into the group, their attention specifically menacing towards Jaimie Paul and Rita Joe. A street brawl begins as a policeman passes through on his beat. The murderers leave hastily.

> I woke up at six o'clock,
> Stumbled out of bed.
> Crash of steel and diesel trucks
> Damned near killed me dead
>
> Sleepless hours, heavy nights,
> Dream your dreams so pretty.
> God was gonna have a laugh
> An' gave me a job in the city!

Musical interlude.

Rita Joe and Jaimie Paul continue dancing languidly. The young Indian men exit.

> I've polished floors an' cut the trees,
> Fished and stooked the wheat.
> Now "Hallelujah, Praise the Lord,"
> I sing before I eat!
>
> Sleepless hours, heavy nights,
> Dream your dreams so pretty.
> God was gonna have a laugh
> An' gave me a job in the city!

Musical interlude.

The music dies as the young Indian men wheel in a brass bed, circle it around and exit.

The stage darkens except for a pool of light where Rita Joe and Jaimie Paul stand, embracing. Jaimie Paul takes her hand and leads her away.

JAIMIE: Come on, Rita Joe . . . you're slow.

RITA *(Happy in her memories, not wishing to forget too soon, hesitating):*   How much rent . . . for a place where you can keep babies?

JAIMIE: I don't know . . . maybe eighty dollars a month.

RITA: That's a lot of money.

JAIMIE: It costs a buck to go dancin' even . . .

They walk slowly along the apron to stage left, as if following a street to Jaimie Paul's rooming house.

It's a good place . . . I got a sink in the room. Costs seven bucks a week, that's all!

RITA: That's good . . . I only got a bed in my place . . .

JAIMIE: I seen Mickey an' Steve Laporte last night.

RITA: How are they?

JAIMIE: Good . . . We're goin' to a beer parlour Monday night when I get paid . . . the same beer parlour they threw Steve out of! Only now there's three of us goin' in!

They arrive at and enter his room.

A spot illuminates the bed near the wings of stage left. It is old, dilapidated.

Jaimie Paul and Rita Joe enter the area of light around the bed. He is aware that the room is more drab than he would wish it.

How do you like it . . . I like it!

RITA *(Examining room critically):*   It's . . . smaller than my place.

JAIMIE: Sit down.

She sits on edge of the bed and falls backward into a springless hollow.

He laughs nervously. He is awkward and confused. The ease they shared walking to his place is now constricted.

I was gonna get some grub today, but I was busy . . . Here . . .

He takes a chocolate bar out of his shirt pocket and offers it to her. She opens it, breaks off a small piece, and gives the remainder to him. He closes the wrapper and replaces the bar in his pocket. She eats ravenously. He walks around the bed nervously.

No fat d.p.'s gonna throw me or the boys out of that beer parlour or he's gonna get this!

He holds up a fist in a gesture that is both poignant and futile. She laughs and he glowers at her.

I'm tellin' you!

RITA: If they want to throw you out, they'll throw you out.

JAIMIE: Well, this is one Indian guy they're not pushing around no more!

RITA: God helps them who help themselves.

JAIMIE: That's right!

He laughs.

I was lookin' at the white shirts in Eaton's and this bugger comes an' says to me, you gonna buy or you gonna look all day?

RITA *(Looking around her)*:   It's a nice room for a guy, I guess . . .

JAIMIE: It's a lousy room!

Rita Joe lies back lengthwise in the bed. Jaimie Paul sits on the bed beside her.

RITA: You need a good job to have babies in the city . . . Clara Hill gave both her kids away they say . . .

JAIMIE: Where do kids like that go?

RITA: Foster homes, I guess.

JAIMIE: If somebody don't like the kid, back they go to another foster home?

RITA: I guess so . . . Clara Hill don't know where her kids are now.

Jaimie Paul twists sharply in his anger.

JAIMIE: Goddamn it!

RITA: My father says . . .

Jaimie Paul rises, crosses round the bed to the other side.

JAIMIE *(Harshly)*:   I don't want to hear what your father got to say! He's like . . . like the kind of Indian a white man likes! He's gonna look wise and wait forever . . . For what? For the kids they take away to come back?

RITA: He's scared . . . I'm scared . . . We're all scared, Jaimie Paul.

Jaimie Paul lies face down and mimes a gun through the bars.

JAIMIE: Sometimes I feel like takin' a gun and just . . .

He waves his hand as if to liquidate his environment and all that bedevils him. He turns over on his back and lies beside Rita Joe.

I don't know . . . Goddamnit, I don't know what to do. I get mad an' then I don't know what I'm doing or thinkin' . . . I get scared sometimes, Rita Joe.

RITA *(Tenderly)*:   We're scared . . . everybody . . .

JAIMIE: I'm scared of dyin' . . . in the city. They don't care for one another here . . . You got to be smart or have a good job to live like that.

RITA: Clara Hill's gonna have another baby . . .

JAIMIE: I can't live like that . . . A man don't count for much here . . . Women can do as much as a man . . . There's no difference between men and women. I can't live like that.

RITA: You got to stop worrying, Jaimie Paul. You're gonna get sick worryin'.

JAIMIE: You can't live like that, can you?

RITA: No.

JAIMIE: I can't figure out what the hell they want from us!

RITA *(Laughing)*:   Last time I was in trouble, the judge was asking me what I wanted from him! I could've told him, but I didn't!

They both laugh. Jaimie Paul becomes playful and happy.

JAIMIE: Last night I seen television in a store window. I seen a guy on television showing this knife that cuts everything it's so sharp . . . He was cutting up good shoes like they were potatoes . . . That was sure funny to see!

Again they laugh in merriment at the idea of such a demonstration. Jaimie Paul continues with his story, gesturing with his hands.

Chop . . . chop . . . chop . . . A potful of shoes in no time! What's a guy gonna do with a potful of shoes? Cook them?

They continue laughing and lie together again. Then Jaimie Paul sobers. He rises from the bed and walks around it. He offers his hand to Rita Joe, who also rises.

Drily.

Come on. This is a lousy room!

SINGER *(Reprise)*:

> God was gonna have a laugh,
> And gave me a job in the city!

The light goes down on Rita Joe and Jaimie Paul. The young Indian men clear the bed.

Cross fade the rear ramp of the stage. Rita Joe's father and the priest enter and cross the stage.

PRIEST: She got out yesterday, but she wouldn't let me see her. I stayed an extra day, but she wouldn't see me.

FATHER *(Sadly):*   I must go once more to the city . . . I must go to see them.
PRIEST: You're an old man . . . I wish I could persuade you not to go.
FATHER: You wouldn't say that if you had children, Andrew . . .

The lights go down on them.

The lights come up on centre stage front. Three young Indian men precede Mr. Homer, carrying a table between them. Mr. Homer follows with a hamper of clothes under his arm.

MR. HOMER: Yeh . . . right about there is fine, boys. Got to get the clutter out of the basement . . . There's mice coming in to beat hell.

Mr. Homer empties the clothes hamper on the table. The young Indian men step aside and converse in an undertone.

On the ramp, a young Indian man weaves his way from stage left and down to centre stage where the others have brought the table. He is followed by Jaimie Paul and Rita Joe, who mime his intoxicated progress.

Mr. Homer speaks to the audience . . .

The Society for Aid to the Indians sent a guy over to see if I could recommend someone who'd been . . . Well, through the mill, like they say . . . An' then smartened up an' taken rehabilitation. The guy said they just wanted a rehabilitated Indian to show up at their annual dinner. No speeches or fancy stuff . . . just be there.

The young Indian man lies down carefully to one side of Mr. Homer.

Hi, Louie. Not that I would cross the street for the Society . . . They're nothing but a pack of do-gooders out to get their name in the papers . . .

The young Indian man begins to sing a tuneless song, trailing off into silence.

Keep it down, eh, Louie? I couldn't think of anybody to suggest to this guy . . . so he went away pretty sore . . .

Rita Joe begins to rummage through the clothes on the table. She looks at sweaters and holds a red one thoughtfully in her hands.

Jaimie Paul is in conversation with the young Indian men to one side of the table.

Mr. Homer turns from audience to see Rita Joe holding the sweater.

Try it on, Rita Joe . . . That's what the stuff's there for.

Jaimie Paul turns. He is in a provocative mood, seething with rebellion that makes the humour he triggers both biting and deceptively innocent. The young Indian men respond to him with strong laughter. Jaimie Paul takes a play punch at one of them.

JAIMIE: Whoops! Scared you, eh?

He glances back at Mr. Homer, as if talking to him.

Can't take it, eh? The priest can't take it. Indian Department guys can't take it . . . Why listen to them? Listen to the radio if you want to hear something.

The young Indian men laugh.

Or listen to me! You think I'm smart?
YOUNG INDIAN MAN: You're a smart man, Jaimie Paul.
JAIMIE: Naw . . . I'm not smart . . .

He points to another young Indian man.

This guy here . . . calls himself squaw-humper . . . He's smart! . . . Him . . . he buys extra big shirts . . . more cloth for the same money . . . That's smart!

Laughter.

I'm not smart.

Seriously.

You figure we can start a business an' be our own boss?
YOUNG INDIAN MAN: I don't know about that . . .

Jaimie Paul leaves them and goes to lean over the young Indian man who is now asleep on the floor.

JAIMIE: Buy a taxi . . . Be our own boss . . .

He shakes the sleeping young Indian man, who immediately begins his tuneless song.

Aw, he's drunk . . .

Jaimie Paul goes over to the table and stares at the young Indian man beyond the table.

Soberly.

Buy everything we need . . . Don't be bums! Bums need grub an' clothes . . . Bums is bad for the country, right Mr. Homer?

MR. HOMER *(Nods):*   I guess so . . .

To Rita Joe who is now wearing the old sweater.

Red looks good on you, Rita Joe . . . Take it!

Jaimie Paul goes over and embraces Rita Joe, then pushes her gently away.

JAIMIE: She looks better in yellow. I never seen a red dandelion before.

He and the young Indian men laugh, but the laughter is hollow.

MR. HOMER: Come on, Jaimie! Leave the girl alone. That's what it's here for . . . Are you working?

JAIMIE *(Evasive, needling):*   Yeh! . . . No! . . . "Can you drive?" the guy says to me. "Sure, I can drive," I says to him. "Okay," he says, "then drive this broom until the warehouse is clean."

They all laugh.

MR. HOMER: That's a good one . . . Jaimie, you're a card . . . Well, time to get some food for you lot . . .

Mr. Homer leaves. Rita Joe feels better about the sweater. She looks to one of the young Indian men for approval. Jaimie Paul becomes grim-faced.

RITA: Do you like it?

YOUNG INDIAN MAN: Sure. It's a nice sweater . . . Take it.

JAIMIE: Take it where? Take it to hell . . . Be men!

He points after Mr. Homer.

He's got no kids . . . Guys like that get mean when they got no kids . . . We're his kids an' he means to keep it that way! Well, I'm a big boy now!

To Rita Joe.

I go to the employment office. I want work an' I want it now. "I'm not a goddamned cripple," I says to him. An' he says he can only take my name! If work comes he'll call me! "What the hell is this," I says to him. "I'll never get work like that . . . There's no telephone in the house where I got a room!''

Mr. Homer returns pushing a wheeled tray on which he has some food for sandwiches, a loaf of bread and a large cutting knife. He begins to make some sandwiches.

RITA *(Scolding Jaimie Paul):*   You won't get work talking that way, Jaimie Paul!

JAIMIE: Why not? I'm not scared. He gets mad at me an' I say to him . . . "You think I'm some stupid Indian you're talkin' to? Heh? You think that?''

Jaimie Paul struts and swaggers to demonstrate how he faced his opponent at the employment office.

MR. HOMER *(Cutting bread):*   You're a tough man to cross, Jaimie Paul.

JAIMIE *(Ignoring Mr. Homer, to the young Indian men):*   Boy, I showed that bastard who he was talkin' to!

RITA: Did you get the job?

JAIMIE *(Turns to her, laughing boyishly):*   No! He called the cops an' they threw me out!

They all laugh. The young Indian men go to the table now and rummage through the clothes.

MR. HOMER: Take whatever you want, boys . . . there's more clothes comin' tomorrow.

Jaimie Paul impulsively moves to the table where the young Indian men are fingering the clothes. He pushes them aside and shoves the clothes in a heap leaving a small corner of table clean. He takes out two coins from his pockets and spits in his hands.

JAIMIE: I got a new trick . . . Come on, Mister Homer . . . I'll show you! See this!

He shows the coins, then slams his hands palms down on the table.

   Which hand got the coins?

MR. HOMER: Why . . . one under each hand . . .

JAIMIE: Right!

He turns up his hands.

   Again?

He collects the coins and slaps his hands down again.

Where are the coins now? Come on, guess!

Mr. Homer is confident now and points to right hand with his cutting knife. Jaimie Paul laughs and lifts his hands.

The coins are under his left hand.

MR. HOMER: Son of a gun.
JAIMIE: You're a smart man.

He puts coins in his pockets and laughing, turns to Rita Joe, who stands uncertainly dressed in the red sweater. She likes the garment, but she is aware Jaimie Paul might resent her taking it. The young Indian men again move to the table, and Mr. Homer returns to making sandwiches.

MR. HOMER: There's a good pair of socks might come in handy for one of you guys!

A young Indian man pokes his thumbs through the holes in the socks, and laughs.

JAIMIE: Sure . . . Take the socks! Take the table!

He slaps the table with his hands and laughs.

Take Mister Homer cutting bread! Take everything!
MR. HOMER: Hey, Jaimie!
JAIMIE: Why not? There's more comin' tomorrow, you said!
RITA: Jaimie!
MR. HOMER: You're sure in a smart-assed mood today, aren't you?
JAIMIE (*Pointing to the young Indian man with the socks, but talking to Mr. Homer*):   Mister, friend Steve over there laughs lots . . . He figures . . . the way to get along an' live is to grab his guts an' laugh at anything anybody says. You see him laughing all the time. A dog barks at him an' he laughs . . .

Laughter from the young Indian man.

Laughs at a fence post fallin' . . .

Laughter.

Kids with funny eyes make him go haywire . . .

Laughter.

Can of meat an' no can opener . . .

Mr. Homer watches the young Indian men and grins at Jaimie Paul.

MR. HOMER: Yeh . . . He laughs quite a bit . . .
JAIMIE: He laughs at a rusty nail . . . Nice guy . . . laughs all the time.
MR. HOMER *(To Jaimie Paul, holding the knife):*   You wanted mustard on your
  bread or just plain?
JAIMIE: I seen him cut his hand and start laughin' . . . Isn't that funny?

The young Indian men laugh, but with less humour now.

MR. HOMER *(To Jaimie Paul):*   You want mustard? . . . I'm talkin' to you!
JAIMIE: I'm not hungry.

*The young Indian men stop laughing altogether. They become tense and suspicious of
Jaimie Paul, who is watching them severely.*

MR. HOMER: Suit yourself. Rita?

She shakes her head slowly, her gaze on Jaimie Paul's face.

RITA: I'm not hungry.

*Mr. Homer looks from Rita Joe to Jaimie Paul, then to the young Indian men. His
manner stiffens.*

MR. HOMER: I see . . .

*Jaimie Paul and Rita Joe touch hands and come forward to sit on the apron of the stage,
front. A pale light is on the two of them.*

*The stage lights behind them fade. A low light that is diffused and shadowy remains on
the table where Mr. Homer has prepared the food. The young Indian men move slowly
to the table and begin eating the sandwiches Mr. Homer offers to them. The light on
the table fades very low.*

Jaimie Paul hands a cigarette to Rita Joe and they smoke.

*Light comes up over the rear ramp. Rita Joe's father enters onto the ramp from the wings
of stage right. His step is resolute. The priest follows behind him a few paces. They have
been arguing. Both are dressed in work clothes of heavy trousers and windbreakers.*

JAIMIE: When I'm laughing, I got friends.
RITA: I know, Jaimie Paul . . .
PRIEST: That was the way I found her, that was the way I left her.
JAIMIE *(Bitterly):*   When I'm laughing, I'm a joker . . . A funny boy!

FATHER: If I was young . . . I wouldn't sleep. I would talk to people . . . let them all know!

JAIMIE: I'm not dangerous when I'm laughing . . .

PRIEST: You could lose the reserve and have nowhere to go!

FATHER: I have lost more than that! Young people die . . . young people don't believe me . . .

JAIMIE: That's alright . . . that's alright . . .

The light dies out on Jaimie Paul and Rita Joe. The light also dies out on Mr. Homer and young Indian men.

PRIEST: You think they believe that hot-headed . . . that troublemaker?

FATHER *(Turning to face the priest):*   Jaimie Paul is a good boy!

PRIEST: David Joe . . . you and I have lived through a lot. We need peace now, and time to consider what to do next.

FATHER: Eileen said to me last night . . . she wants to go to the city, I worry all night . . . What can I do?

PRIEST: I'll talk to her, if you wish.

FATHER *(Angry):*   And tell her what? . . . Of the animals there . . .

He gestures to the audience.

Who sleep with sore stomachs because . . . they eat too much?

PRIEST: We mustn't lose the reserve and the old life, David Joe . . . Would you . . . give up being chief on the reserve?

FATHER: Yes!

PRIEST: To Jaimie Paul?

FATHER: No . . . To someone who's been to school . . . Maybe university . . . who knows more.

PRIEST *(Relieved by this, but not reassured):*   The people here need your wisdom and stability, David Joe. There is no man here who knows as much about hunting and fishing and guiding. You can survive . . . What does a youngster who's been away to school know of this?

FATHER: *(Sadly):*   If we only fish an' hunt an' cut pulpwood . . . pick strawberries in the bush . . . for a hundred years more, we are dead. I know this, here . . .

He touches his breast.

The light dies on the ramp.

A light rises on stage front, on Jaimie Paul and Rita Joe sitting at the apron of the stage. Mr. Homer is still cutting bread for sandwiches. The three young Indian men have eaten and appear restless to leave. The fourth young Indian man is still asleep on the floor.

Rita Joe has taken off the red sweater, but continues to hold it in her hand.

JAIMIE *(To Mr. Homer):*   One time I was on a trapline five days without grub. I ate snow an' I walked until I got back. You think you can take it like me?

Mr. Homer approaches Jaimie Paul and holds out a sandwich to him.

MR. HOMER: Here . . . have a sandwich now.

Jaimie Paul ignores his hand.

RITA: Mister Homer don't know what happened, Jaimie Paul.

Mr. Homer shrugs and walks away to his sandwich table.

JAIMIE: Then he's got to learn . . . Sure he knows!

To Mr. Homer.

Sure he knows! He's feedin' sandwiches to Indian bums . . . He knows. He's the worst kind!

The young Indian men freeze and Mr. Homer stops.

MR. HOMER *(Coldly):*   I've never yet asked a man to leave this building.

Rita Joe and Jaimie Paul rise to their feet. Rita Joe goes to the clothes table and throws the red sweater back on the pile of clothes. Jaimie Paul laughs sardonically.

To Rita Joe.

Hey, not you, girl . . . You take it!

She shakes her head and moves to leave.

RITA: I think we better go, boys.

The sleeping young Indian man slowly raises his head, senses there is something wrong, and is about to be helped up, when . . .

JAIMIE: After five days without grub, the first meal I threw up . . . stomach couldn't take it . . . But after that it was alright . . .

To Mr. Homer, with intensity.

I don't believe nobody . . . No priest nor government . . . They don't know what it's like to . . . to want an' not have . . . to stand in line an' nobody sees you!

MR. HOMER: If you want food, eat! You need clothes, take them. That's all . . . But I'm running' this centre my way, and I mean it!

JAIMIE: I come to say no to you . . . That's all . . . that's all!

He throws out his arms in a gesture that is both defiant and childlike. The gesture disarms some of Mr. Homer's growing hostility.

MR. HOMER: You've got that right . . . No problems. There's others come through here day an' night . . . No problem.

JAIMIE: I don't want no others to come. I don't want them to eat here!

He indicates his friends.

If we got to take it from behind a store window, then we break the window an' wait for the cops. It's better than . . . than this!

He gestures with contempt at the food and the clothes on the table.

MR. HOMER: Rita Joe . . . where'd you pick up this . . . this loudmouth anyway?

RITA *(Slowly, firmly):*   I think . . . Jaimie Paul's . . . right.

Mr. Homer looks from face to face. The three young Indian men are passive, staring into the distance. The fourth is trying hard to clear his head. Jaimie Paul is cold, hostile. Rita Joe is determined.

MR. HOMER *(decisively):*   Alright! You've eaten . . . looked over the clothes . . . Now clear out so others get a chance to come in! Move!

He tries to herd everyone out and the four young Indian men begin to move away. Jaimie Paul mimics the gestures of Mr. Homer and steps in front of the young Indian men herding them back in.

JAIMIE: Run, boys, run! Or Mister Homer gonna beat us up!

Rita Joe takes Jaimie Paul's hand and tries to pull him away to leave.

RITA: Jaimie Paul . . . you said to me no trouble!

Jaimie Paul pulls his hand free and jumps back of the clothes table. Mr. Homer comes for him, unknowingly still carrying the slicing knife in his hand. An absurd chase begins around the table. One of the young Indian men laughs, and stepping forward, catches hold of Mr. Homer's hand with the knife in it.

YOUNG INDIAN MAN: Hey! Don't play with a knife, Mister Homer!

He gently takes the knife away from Mr. Homer and drops it on the food table behind. Mr. Homer looks at his hand, an expression of shock on his face.

Jaimie Paul gives him no time to think about the knife and what it must have appeared like to the young Indian men. He pulls a large brassiere from the clothes table and mockingly holds it over his breasts, which he sticks out enticingly at Mr. Homer. The young Indian men laugh. Mr. Homer is exasperated and furious. Rita Joe is frightened.

RITA: It's not funny, Jaimie!
JAIMIE: It's funny as hell, Rita Joe. Even funnier this way!

Jaimie Paul puts the brassiere over his head, with the cups down over his ears and the straps under his chin. The young Indian men are all laughing now and moving close to the table. Mr. Homer makes a futile attempt at driving them off.

Suddenly Jaimie Paul's expression turns to one of hatred. He throws the brassiere on the table and gripping its edge, throws the table and clothes over, scattering the clothes. He kicks at them. The young Indian men all jump in and, picking up the clothes, hurl them over the ramp.

Rita Joe runs in to try and stop them. She grips the table and tries lifting it up again.

MR. HOMER *(To Jaimie Paul):*   Cut that out, you sonofabitch!

Jaimie Paul stands watching him. Mr. Homer is in a fury. He sees Rita Joe struggling to right the table. He moves to her and pushes her hard.

You slut! . . . You breed whore!

Rita Joe recoils.

With a shriek of frustration, she attacks Mr. Homer, tearing at him. He backs away, then turns and runs.

Jaimie Paul overturns the table again. The others join in the melée with the clothes.

A policeman enters and grabs Jaimie Paul. Rita Joe and the four young Indian men exit, clearing away the tables and remaining clothes.

A sharp, tiny spotlight comes up on the face and upper torso of Jaimie Paul. He is wild with rebellion as the policeman forces him, in an arm lock, down towards the audience.

JAIMIE *(Screaming defiance at the audience):*   Not jus' a box of cornflakes! When I go in I want the whole store! That's right . . . the whole goddamned store!

Another sharp light on the magistrate standing on his podium looking down at Jaimie Paul.

MAGISTRATE: Thirty days!

JAIMIE *(Held by policeman):*   Sure, sure . . . Anything else you know?

MAGISTRATE: Thirty days!

JAIMIE: Gimme back my truth!

MAGISTRATE: We'll get larger prisons and more police in every town and city across the country!

JAIMIE: Teach me who I really am! You've taken that away! Give me back the real me so I can live like a man!

MAGISTRATE: There is room for dialogue. There is room for disagreement and there is room for social change . . . but within the framework of institutions and traditions in existence for that purpose!

JAIMIE *(Spits):*   Go to hell! . . . I can die an' you got nothing to tell me!

MAGISTRATE *(In a cold fury).*   Thirty days! And after that, it will be six months! And after that . . . God help you!

The magistrate marches off his platform and offstage.

Jaimie Paul is led off briskly in the other direction offstage.

The lights change.

Rita Joe enters, crossing the stage, exchanging a look with the singer.

SINGER:

> Sleepless hours, heavy nights,
> Dream your dreams so pretty.
> God was gonna have a laugh
> An' gave me a job in the city!

Rita Joe walks the street. She is smoking a cigarette. She is dispirited.

The light broadens across the stage.

Rita Joe's father and Jaimie Paul enter the stage from the wings of centre stage left.

They walk slowly towards where Rita Joe stands.

At the sight of her father, Rita Joe moans softly and hurriedly stamps out her cigarette. She visibly straightens and waits for the approaching men, her expression one of fear and joy.

FATHER: I got a ride on Miller's truck . . . took me two days . . .
JAIMIE: It's a long way, David Joe.

The father stops a pace short of Rita Joe and looks at her with great tenderness and concern.

FATHER *(Softly):*   I come . . . to get Rita Joe.
RITA: Oh . . . I don't know . . .

She looks to Jaimie Paul for help in deciding what to do, but he is sullen and uncommunicative.

FATHER: I come to take Rita Joe home . . . We got a house an' some work
    sometime . . .
JAIMIE: She's with me now, David Joe.
RITA *(Very torn):*   I don't know . . .
JAIMIE: You don't have to go back, Rita Joe.

Rita Joe looks away from her Father with humility. The father turns to Jaimie Paul.

He stands ancient and heroic.

FATHER: I live . . . an' I am afraid. Because . . . I have not done everything.
    When I have done everything . . . know that my children are safe . . .
    then . . . it will be alright. Not before.
JAIMIE *(To Rita):*   You don't have to go. This is an old man now . . . He has
    nothing to give . . . nothin' to say!

Rita Joe reacts to both men, her conflict deepening.

FATHER *(Turning away from Jaimie Paul to Rita Joe):*   For a long time . . . a very
    long time . . . she was in my hands . . . like that!

He cups his hands into shape of a bowl.

Sweet . . . tiny . . . lovin' all the time and wanting love . . .

He shakes his head sadly.

JAIMIE *(Angrily):*   Go tell it to the white men! They're lookin' for Indians that stay proud even when they hurt . . . just so long's they don't ask for their rights!

The father turns slowly, with great dignity, to Jaimie Paul. His gestures show Jaimie Paul to be wrong, the old man's spirit was never broken. Jaimie Paul understands and looks away.

FATHER: You're a good boy, Jaimie Paul . . . A good boy . . .

To Rita Joe, talking slowly, painfully.

I once seen a dragonfly breakin' its shell to get its wings . . . It floated on water an' crawled up on a log where I was sitting . . . It dug its feet into the log an' then it pulled until the shell bust over its neck. Then it pulled some more . . . an' slowly its wings slipped out of the shell . . . like that!

He shows with his hands how the dragonfly got his freedom.

JAIMIE *(Angered and deeply moved by the father):*   Where you gonna be when they start bustin' our heads open an' throwing us into jails right across the god-damned country?
FATHER: Such wings I never seen before . . . folded like an accordion so fine, like thin glass an' white in the morning sun . . .
JAIMIE: We're gonna have to fight to win . . . there's no other way! They're not listenin' to you, old man! Or to me.
FATHER: It spread its wings . . . so slowly . . . an' then the wings opened an' began to flutter . . . Just like that . . . see! Hesitant at first . . . then stronger . . . an' then the wings beatin' like that made the dragonfly's body quiver until the shell on its back falls off . . .
JAIMIE: Stop kiddin' yourself! We're gonna say no pretty soon to all the crap that makes us soft an' easy to push this way . . . that way!
FATHER: . . . An' the dragonfly . . . flew up . . . up . . . into the white sun . . . to the green sky . . . to the sun . . . faster an' faster . . . Higher . . . Higher!

The father reaches up with his hands, releasing the imaginary dragonfly into the sun, his final words torn out of his heart.

Rita Joe springs to her feet and rushes against Jaimie Paul, striking at him with her fists.

RITA *(Savagely):*   For Chris' sakes, I'm not goin' back! . . . Leave him alone . . . He's everything we got left now!

Jaimie Paul stands, frozen by his emotion which he can barely control. The father turns. Rita Joe goes to him.

The father speaks privately to Rita Joe in Indian dialect. They embrace.

He pauses for a long moment to embrace and forgive her everything. Then he goes slowly offstage into the wings of stage left without looking back.

FATHER: Goodbye, Rita Joe . . . Goodbye, Jaimie Paul . . .
RITA: Goodbye, Father.

Jaimie Paul watches Rita Joe who moves away from him to the front of the stage.

JAIMIE *(To her):*   You comin'?

She shakes her head to indicate no, she is staying.

Suddenly Jaimie Paul runs away from her diagonally across to the wings of rear stage left. As he nears the wings, the four young Indian men emerge, happily on their way to a party.

They stop him at his approach. He runs into them, directing them back, his voice breaking with feelings of love and hatred intermingling.

Shouting at them.

Next time . . . in a beer parlour or any place like that . . . I'll go myself or you guys take me home . . . No more white buggers pushin' us out the door or he gets this!

He raises his fist.

The group of young Indian men, elated by their newly-found determination, surround Jaimie Paul and exit into the wings of the stage. The light dies in back and at stage left.

The magistrate enters.

There is a light on Rita Joe where she stands. There is also a light around the magistrate. The magistrate's voice and purpose are leaden. He has given up on Rita Joe. He is merely performing the formality of condemning her and dismissing her from his conscience.

MAGISTRATE: I sentence you to thirty days in prison.
RITA *(Angry, defiant):*   Sure, sure . . . Anything else you know?
MAGISTRATE: I sentence you to thirty days in prison, with a recommenda-

tion you be examined medically and given all necessary treatment at the prison clinic. There is nothing . . . there is nothing I can do now.

RITA *(Stoically):*   Thank you. Is that right? To thank you?

MAGISTRATE: You'll be back . . . always be back . . . growing older, tougher . . . filthier . . . looking more like stone and prison bars . . . the lines in your face will tell everyone who sees you about prison windows and prison food.

RITA: No child on the road would remember you, mister!

The magistrate comes down to stand before her. He has the rambling confidence of detached authority.

MAGISTRATE: What do you expect? We provide schools for you and you won't attend them because they're out of the way and that little extra effort is too much for you! We came up as a civilization having to . . . yes, claw upwards at times . . . There's nothing wrong with that . . . We give you X-ray chest clinics . . .

He turns away from her and goes to the apron of the stage and speaks directly to the audience.

We give them X-ray chest clinics and three-quarters of them won't show up . . . Those that do frequently get medical attention at one of the hospitals . . .

RITA *(Interjecting):*   My mother died!

He does not hear her.

MAGISTRATE: But as soon as they're released they forget they're chronically ill and end up on a drinking party and a long walk home through the snow . . . Next thing . . . they're dead!

RITA *(Quietly):*   Oh, put me in jail an' then let me go.

MAGISTRATE *(Turning to her):*   Some of you get jobs . . . There are jobs, good jobs, if you'd only look around a bit . . . and stick with them when you get them. But no . . . you get a job and promise to stay with it and learn, and two weeks later you're gone for three, four days without explanation . . . Your reliability record is ruined and an employer has to regard you as lazy, undependable . . . What do you expect?

RITA: I'm not scared of you now, bastard!

MAGISTRATE: You have a mind . . . you have a heart. The cities are open to you to come and go as you wish, yet you gravitate to the slums and skid rows and the shanty-town fringes. You become a whore, drunkard, user of narcotics . . . At best, dying of illness or malnutrition . . . At worst, kicked or beaten to death by some angry white scum who finds in you something lower than himself to pound his frustrations out on! What's to be done? You Indians seem to be incapable of taking action to help yourselves. Someone must care for you . . . Who? For how long?

RITA: You don't know nothin'!

MAGISTRATE: I know . . . I know . . . It's a struggle just to stay alive. I know . . . I understand. That struggle is mine, as well as yours, Rita Joe! The jungle of the executive has as many savage teeth ready to go for the throat as the rundown hotel on the waterfront . . . Your days and hours are numbered, Rita Joe . . . I worry for the child I once saw . . . I have already forgotten the woman!

He turns away from her and exits into the wings of stage right.

The lights on Rita Joe fade.

Lights of cold, eerie blue wash the backdrop of the stage faintly.

Rita Joe stands in silhouette for a long moment.

Slowly, ominously, the three murderers appear on the ramp backstage, one coming from the wings of stage right; one from the wings of stage left; and one rising from the back of the ramp, climbing it. One of the murderers is whistling a soft nervous noise throughout their scene onstage.

Rita Joe whimpers in fear, and as the murderers loom above her, she runs along the apron to stage left.

Here she bumps into Jaimie Paul who enters. She screams in fear.

JAIMIE: Rita Joe!

RITA *(Terrorized)*:   Jaimie! They're comin'. I seen them comin'!

JAIMIE: Who's coming? What's the matter, Rita Joe?

RITA: Men I once dreamed about . . . I seen it all happen once before . . . an' it was like this . . .

Jaimie Paul laughs and pats her shoulders reassuringly. He takes her hand and tries to lead her forward to the apron of the stage, but Rita Joe is dead, her steps wooden.

JAIMIE: Don't worry . . . I can take care of myself!

A faint light on the two of them.

RITA: You been in jail now too, Jaimie Paul . . .

JAIMIE: So what? Guys in jail was saying that they got to put a man behind bars or the judge don't get paid for being in court to make the trial . . . Funny world, eh, Rita Joe?

RITA *(Nods)*:   Funny world

The light dies on them. They come forward slowly.

JAIMIE: I got a room with a hot plate . . . We can have a couple of eggs and
some tea before we go to the movie.
RITA: What was it like for you in jail?
JAIMIE: So so . . .

Jaimie Paul motions for Rita Joe to follow him and moves forward from her.

The distant sound of a train approaching is heard.

She is wooden, coming slowly after him.

RITA: It was different where the women were . . . It's different to be a
woman . . . Some women was wild . . . and they shouted they were riding
black horses into a fire I couldn't see . . . There was no fire there, Jaimie!
JAIMIE *(Turns to her, takes her arm):*   Don't worry . . . We're goin' to eat and
then see a movie . . . Come on, Rita Joe!

*She looks back and sees the murderers rise and slowly approach from the gloom. Her
speech becomes thick and unsteady as she follows Jaimie Paul to the front of the ramp.*

RITA: One time I couldn't find the street where I had a room to sleep
in . . . Forgot my handbag . . . had no money . . . An old man with a dog
said hello, but I couldn't say hello back because I was worried an' my
mouth was so sticky I couldn't speak to him . . .
JAIMIE: Are you comin'?
RITA: When you're tired an' sick, Jaimie, the city starts to dance . . .
JAIMIE *(Taking her hand, pulling her gently along):*   Come on, Rita Joe.
RITA: The street lights start rollin' like wheels an' cement walls feel like
they was made of blanket cloth . . .

*The sound of the train is closer now. The lights of its lamps flicker in back of the
stage.*

*Rita Joe turns to face the murderers, one of whom is whistling ominously. She whimpers
in fear and presses herself against Jaimie Paul.*

Jaimie Paul turns and sees the murderers hovering near them.

JAIMIE: Don't be scared . . . Nothing to be scared of, Rita Joe . . .

To the murderers.

What the hell do you want?

One of the murderers laughs. Jaimie Paul pushes Rita Joe back behind himself. He moves towards the murderers.

Taunting them.

You think I can't take care of myself?

With deceptive casualness, the murderers approach him. One of them makes a sudden lurch at Jaimie Paul as if to draw him into their circle. Jaimie Paul anticipates the trap and takes a flying kick at the murderer, knocking him down.

They close around Jaimie Paul with precision, then attack. Jaimie Paul leaps, but is caught mid-air by the other two. They bring him down and put the boots to him.

Rita Joe screams and runs to him. The train sound is loud and immediate now.

One of the murderers has grabbed Rita Joe. The remaining two raise Jaimie Paul to his feet and one knees him viciously in the groin. Jaimie Paul screams and doubles over.

The lights of the train are upon them. The murderers leap off the ramp leaving Jaimie Paul in the path of the approaching train.

Jaimie Paul's death cry becomes the sound of the train horn. As the train sound roars by, the murderers return to close in around Rita Joe.

One murderer springs forward and grabs Rita Joe. The other two help to hold her, with nervous fear and lust.

Rita Joe breaks free of them and runs to the front of the stage. The three murderers come after her, panting hard.

They close in on her leisurely now, playing with her, knowing that they have her trapped.

Recorded and overlapping voices . . .

CLERK: The court calls Rita Joe . . .
MAGISTRATE: Who is she? . . . Let her speak for herself . . .
RITA: In the summer it was hot, an' flies hummed . . .
TEACHER: A book of verse, a melting pot . . .
MAGISTRATE: Thirty days!
FATHER: Barkin' to beat hell . . . How! How!
JAIMIE *(Laughter, defiant, taunting):*   You go to hell!
PRIEST: A confession, Rita Joe . . .

Over the voices she hears, the murderers attack.

Dragging her down backwards, they pull her legs open and one murderer lowers himself on her.

RITA: Jaimie! Jaimie! Jaimie!

Rita Joe's head lolls over sideways. The murderers stare at her and pull back slightly.

MURDERER *(Thickly, rising off her twisted, broken body):*   Shit . . . She's dead . . . We hardly touched her.

He hesitates for a moment, then runs, joined by second murderer.

SECOND MURDERER: Let's get out of here!

They run up onto the ramp and watch as the third murderer piteously climbs onto the dead Rita Joe.

Sounds of a funeral chant. Mourners appear on riser backstage. Rita Joe's father enters from the wings of stage left, chanting an ancient Indian funeral chant, carrying the body of Jaimie Paul.

The murderer hesitates in his necrophillic rape and then runs away.

The young Indian men bring the body of Jaimie Paul over the ramp and approach. The body is placed down on the podium, beside Rita Joe's.

All the Indians, young and old, kneel around the two bodies. The father continues his death chant. The priest enters from the wings of stage right reciting a prayer. The teacher, singer, policeman and murderers come with him forming the outside perimeter around the Indian funeral.

PRIEST: Hail Mary, Mother of God . . . Pray for us sinners now and at the hour of our death . . .

Repeated until finally Eileen Joe slowly rises to her feet and turning to the priest and white mourners, says softly . . .

EILEEN *(Over the sounds of chanting and praying):*   No! . . . No! . . . No more!

The young Indian men rise one after another facing the outer circle defiantly and the cast freezes on stage, except for the singer.

SINGER:

> Oh, the singing bird
> Has found its wings
> And it's soaring!

My God, what a sight!
On the cold fresh wind of morning! . . .

During the song, Eileen Joe steps forward to the audience and as the song ends, says . . .

EILEEN: When Rita Joe first come to the city, she told me . . . The cement made her feet hurt.

(1970)

PART THREE

SHORT STORIES

Nathaniel Hawthorne

(1 8 0 4 – 1 8 6 4)

The first major American fiction writer, Nathaniel Hawthorne, was born in Salem, Massachusetts, the son of a Puritan sea captain who died on a voyage when Hawthorne was 4 years old. It was while convalescing from a leg wound, when he lived with his mother in a remote Maine village, that Hawthorne first developed his lifelong habits of reading and solitude. He graduated from Bowdoin College in Maine, where Longfellow was a classmate, then returned to Salem to lead a reclusive life of reading and writing. His first volume of stories, *Twice-Told Tales* (1837), brought him little fame. Hawthorne married in 1842 and lived for a few years in Concord, near Emerson and Thoreau. The publication of *The Scarlet Letter* (1850) established his reputation. From 1853 to 1857 Hawthorne served as consul in Liverpool, England; then he spent two years in Italy before returning to Concord, where he died in 1864.

Hawthorne writes within the "romance" genre. He imaginatively creates fictional projections of moral dilemmas, and his work tends toward the Gothic rather than toward the naturalistic. A pessimist in regard to social progress and reform (and thus at odds with the transcendentalist circle of Emerson and Thoreau), Hawthorne was fascinated, as Faulkner would be in the next century, by the specter of society in decline. Intellectually intrigued by the prospect of evil, his fiction is noted for its emphasis on moral responsibility and for its pessimistic reflection of a world dominated by Puritanism. His stories are allegorical and symbolic; he recognized a decadence inherent in Puritanism and the oppressing guilt and secrecy to which it inevitably led. But if his tone is gloomy and skeptical, there is also an element of faith and redemptive potential, which is found in integration within a community. Edgar Allan Poe called Hawthorne's style the "purest" of his time. As a storyteller, Hawthorne frequently intrudes into the text to guide the reader's response—as an author concerned with moral issues, he does not hesitate to tell as well as show. Hawthorne's themes of the presence of evil in a society built on the premise of infinite progress place him at the center of the American literary tradition and have made him a strong influence on writers such as Henry James and William Faulkner. His masterpiece, *The Scarlet Letter,* is one of the two or three major works of fiction written in nineteenth-century United States.

Hawthorne's novels include *The House of the Seven Gables* (1851), *The Blithedale Romance* (1852), and *The Marble Faun* (1860). His stories were collected in *Twice-Told Tales* (1837), *Mosses from an Old Manse* (1846), and *The Snow Image and Other Twice-Told Tales* (1851).

NATHANIEL HAWTHORNE

My Kinsman, Major Molineux

AFTER the kings of Great Britain had assumed the right of appointing the colonial governors, the measures of the latter seldom met with the ready and general approbation which had been paid to those of their predecessors, under the original charters. The people looked with most jealous scrutiny to the exercise of power which did not emanate from themselves, and they usually rewarded their rulers with slender gratitude for the compliances by which, in softening their instructions from beyond the sea, they had incurred the reprehension of those who gave them. The annals of Massachusetts Bay will inform us, that of six governors in the space of about forty years from the surrender of the old charter, under James II., two were imprisoned by a popular insurrection; a third, as Hutchinson[1] inclines to believe, was driven from the province by the whizzing of a musket-ball; a fourth, in the opinion of the same historian, was hastened to his grave by continual bickerings with the House of Representatives; and the remaining two, as well as their successors, till the Revolution, were favored with few and brief intervals of peaceful sway. The inferior members of the court party, in times of high political excitement, led scarcely a more desirable life. These remarks may serve as a preface to the following adventures, which chanced upon a summer night, not far from a hundred years ago. The reader, in order to avoid a long and dry detail of colonial affairs, is requested to dispense with an account of the train of circumstances that had caused much temporary inflammation of the popular mind.

It was near nine o'clock of a moonlight evening, when a boat crossed the ferry with a single passenger, who had obtained his conveyance at that unusual hour by the promise of an extra fare. While he stood on the landing-place, searching in either pocket for the means of fulfilling his agreement, the ferryman lifted a lantern, by the aid of which, and the newly risen moon, he took a very accurate survey of the stranger's figure. He was a youth of barely eighteen years, evidently country-bred, and now, as it should seem, upon his first visit to town. He was clad in a coarse gray coat, well worn, but in excellent repair; his under garments were durably constructed of leather, and fitted tight to a pair of serviceable and well-shaped limbs: his stockings of blue yarn were the incontrovertible work of a mother or a sister; and on his head was a three-cornered hat, which in its better days had perhaps

---

[1] Thomas Hutchinson (1711–80), colonial governor of Massachusetts from 1771 to 1774 and author of *History of the Colony and Province of Massachusetts Bay.*

sheltered the graver brow of the lad's father. Under his left arm was a heavy cudgel formed of an oak sapling, and retaining a part of the hardened root; and his equipment was completed by a wallet, not so abundantly stocked as to incommode the vigorous shoulders on which it hung. Brown, curly hair, well-shaped features, and bright, cheerful eyes were nature's gifts, and worth all that art could have done for his adornment.

The youth, one of whose names was Robin, finally drew from his pocket the half of a little province bill of five shillings, which, in the depreciation in that sort of currency, did not satisfy the ferryman's demand, with the surplus of a sexangular piece of parchment, valued at three pence. He then walked forward into the town, with as light a step as if his day's journey had not already exceeded thirty miles, and with as eager an eye as if he were entering London city, instead of the little metropolis of a New England colony. Before Robin had proceeded far, however, it occurred to him that he knew not whither to direct his steps; so he paused, and looked up and down the narrow street, scrutinizing the small and mean wooden buildings that were scattered on either side.

"This low hovel cannot be my kinsman's dwelling," thought he, "nor yonder old house, where the moonlight enters at the broken casement; and truly I see none hereabouts that might be worthy of him. It would have been wise to inquire my way of the ferryman, and doubtless he would have gone with me, and earned a shilling from the Major for his pains. But the next man I meet will do as well."

He resumed his walk, and was glad to perceive that the street now became wider, and the houses more respectable in their appearance. He soon discerned a figure moving on moderately in advance, and hastened his steps to overtake it. As Robin drew nigh, he saw that the passenger was a man in years, with a full periwig of gray hair, a wide-skirted coat of dark cloth, and silk stockings rolled above his knees. He carried a long and polished cane, which he struck down perpendicularly before him at every step; and at regular intervals he uttered two successive hems, of a peculiarly solemn and sepulchral intonation. Having made these observations, Robin laid hold of the skirt of the old man's coat, just when the light from the open door and windows of a barber's shop fell upon both their figures.

"Good evening to you, honored sir," said he, making a low bow, and still retaining his hold of the skirt. "I pray you tell me whereabouts is the dwelling of my kinsman, Major Molineux."

The youth's question was uttered very loudly; and one of the barbers, whose razor was descending on a well-soaped chin, and another who was dressing a Ramillies wig, left their occupations, and came to the door. The citizen, in the mean time, turned a long-favored countenance upon Robin, and answered him in a tone of excessive anger and annoyance. His two sepulchral hems, however, broke into the very centre of his rebuke, with most singular effect, like a thought of the cold grave obtruding among wrathful passions.

"Let go my garment, fellow! I tell you, I know not the man you speak of.

What! I have authority, I have—hem, hem—authority; and if this be the respect you show for your betters, your feet shall be brought acquainted with the stocks by daylight, tomorrow morning!"

Robin released the old man's skirt, and hastened away, pursued by an ill-mannered roar of laughter from the barber's shop. He was at first considerably surprised by the result of his question, but, being a shrewd youth, soon thought himself able to account for the mystery.

"This is some country representative," was his conclusion, "who has never seen the inside of my kinsman's door, and lacks the breeding to answer a stranger civilly. The man is old, or verily—I might be tempted to turn back and smite him on the nose. Ah, Robin, Robin! even the barber's boys laugh at you for choosing such a guide! You will be wiser in time, friend Robin."

He now became entangled in a succession of crooked and narrow streets, which crossed each other, and meandered at no great distance from the water-side. The smell of tar was obvious to his nostrils, the masts of vessels pierced the moonlight above the tops of the buildings, and the numerous signs, which Robin paused to read, informed him that he was near the centre of business. But the streets were empty, the shops were closed, and lights were visible only in the second stories of a few dwelling-houses. At length, on the corner of a narrow lane, through which he was passing, he beheld the broad countenance of a British hero swinging before the door of an inn, whence proceeded the voices of many guests. The casement of one of the lower windows was thrown back, and a very thin curtain permitted Robin to distinguish a party at supper, round a well-furnished table. The fragrance of the good cheer steamed forth into the outer air, and the youth could not fail to recollect that the last remnant of his travelling stock of provision had yielded to his morning appetite, and that noon had found and left him dinnerless.

"Oh, that a parchment three-penny might give me a right to sit down at yonder table!" said Robin, with a sigh. "But the Major will make me welcome to the best of his victuals; so I will even step boldly in, and inquire my way to his dwelling."

He entered the tavern, and was guided by the murmur of voices and the fumes of tobacco to the public-room. It was a long and low apartment, with oaken walls, grown dark in the continual smoke, and a floor which was thickly sanded, but of no immaculate purity. A number of persons—the larger part of whom appeared to be mariners, or in some way connected with the sea—occupied the wooden benches, or leather-bottomed chairs, conversing on various matters, and occasionally lending their attention to some topic of general interest. Three or four little groups were draining as many bowls of punch, which the West India trade had long since made a familiar drink in the colony. Others, who had the appearance of men who lived by regular and laborious handicraft, preferred the insulated bliss of an unshared potation, and became more taciturn under its influence. Nearly all, in short, evinced a predilection for the Good Creature in some of its various shapes, for this is a vice to which, as Fast Day[2] sermons of a hundred years ago will testify, we have a long hereditary claim. The only guests to whom Robin's sympathies inclined him were two or three sheepish countrymen, who were using the inn somewhat after the fashion of a Turkish caravansary; they had gotten themselves into the darkest corner of the room, and heedless of the Nicotian[3] atmosphere, were supping on the bread of their own ovens, and the bacon cured in their own chimney-smoke. But though Robin felt a sort of brotherhood with these strangers, his eyes were attracted from them to a person who stood near the door, holding whispered conversation with a group of ill-dressed associates. His features were separately striking almost to grotesqueness, and the whole face left a deep impression on the memory. The forehead bulged out into a double prominence, with a vale between; the nose came boldly forth in an irregular curve, and its bridge was of more than a finger's breadth; the eyebrows were deep and shaggy, and the eyes glowed beneath them like fire in a cave.

While Robin deliberated of whom to inquire respecting his kinsman's dwelling, he was accosted by the innkeeper, a little man in a stained white apron, who had come to pay his professional welcome to the stranger. Being in the second generation from a French Protestant, he seemed to have inherited the courtesy of his parent nation; but no variety of circumstances was ever known to change his voice from the one shrill note in which he now addressed Robin.

"From the country, I presume, sir?" said he, with a profound bow. "Beg leave to congratulate you on your arrival, and trust you intend a long stay with us. Fine town here, sir, beautiful buildings, and much that may interest a stranger. May I hope for the honor of your commands in respect to supper?"

"The man sees a family likeness! the rogue has guessed that I am related to the Major!" thought Robin, who had hitherto experienced little superfluous civility.

All eyes were now turned on the country lad, standing at the door, in his worn three-cornered hat, gray coat, leather breeches, and blue yarn stockings, leaning on an oaken cudgel, and bearing a wallet on his back.

Robin replied to the courteous innkeeper, with such an assumption of confidence as befitted the Major's relative. "My honest friend," he said, "I shall make it a point to patronize your house on some occasion, when"—here he could not help lowering his voice—"when I may have more than a parchment three-pence in my pocket. My present business," continued he, speaking with lofty confidence, "is merely to inquire my way to the dwelling of my kinsman, Major Molineux."

There was a sudden and general movement in the room, which Robin interpreted as expressing the eagerness of each individual to become his guide. But the innkeeper turned his eyes to a written paper on the wall,

[2] In New England, a day set apart, usually in March or April, for fasting and prayer.
[3] I.e., smoky.

which he read, or seemed to read, with occasional recurrences to the young man's figure.

"What have we here?" said he, breaking his speech into little dry fragments. " 'Left the house of the subscriber, bounden servant, Hezekiah Mudge,—had on, when he went away, gray coat, leather breeches, master's third-best hat. One pound currency reward to whosoever shall lodge him in any jail of the province.' Better trudge, boy; better trudge!"

Robin had begun to draw his hand towards the lighter end of the oak cudgel, but a strange hostility in every countenance induced him to relinquish his purpose of breaking the courteous innkeeper's head. As he turned to leave the room, he encountered a sneering glance from the bold-featured personage whom he had before noticed; and no sooner was he beyond the door, than he heard a general laugh, in which the innkeeper's voice might be distinguished, like the dropping of small stones into a kettle.

"Now, is it not strange," thought Robin, with his usual shrewdness,—"is it not strange that the confession of an empty pocket should outweigh the name of my kinsman, Major Molineux? Oh, if I had one of those grinning rascals in the woods, where I and my oak sapling grew up together, I would teach him that my arm is heavy though my purse be light!"

On turning the corner of the narrow lane, Robin found himself in a spacious street, with an unbroken line of lofty houses on each side, and a steepled building at the upper end, whence the ringing of a bell announced the hour of nine. The light of the moon, and the lamps from the numerous shop-windows, discovered people promenading on the pavement, and amongst them Robin hoped to recognize his hitherto inscrutable relative. The result of his former inquiries made him unwilling to hazard another, in a scene of such publicity, and he determined to walk slowly and silently up the street, thrusting his face close to that of every elderly gentleman, in search of the Major's lineaments. In his progress, Robin encountered many gay and gallant figures. Embroidered garments of showy colors, enormous periwigs, gold-laced hats, and silver-hilted swords glided past him and dazzled his optics. Travelled youths, imitators of the European fine gentlemen of the period, trod jauntily along, half dancing to the fashionable tunes which they hummed, and making poor Robin ashamed of his quiet and natural gait. At length, after many pauses to examine the gorgeous display of goods in the shop-windows, and after suffering some rebukes for the impertinence of his scrutiny into people's faces, the Major's kinsman found himself near the steepled building, still unsuccessful in his search. As yet, however, he had seen only one side of the thronged street; so Robin crossed, and continued the same sort of inquisition down the opposite pavement, with stronger hopes than the philosopher seeking an honest man, but with no better fortune. He had arrived about midway towards the lower end, from which his course began, when he overheard the approach of some one who struck down a cane on the flag-stones at every step, uttering, at regular intervals, two sepulchral hems.

"Mercy on us!" quoth Robin, recognizing the sound.

Turning a corner, which chanced to be close at his right hand, he hastened to pursue his researches in some other part of the town. His patience now was wearing low, and he seemed to feel more fatigue from his rambles since he crossed the ferry, than from his journey of several days on the other side. Hunger also pleaded loudly within him, and Robin began to balance the propriety of demanding, violently, and with lifted cudgel, the necessary guidance from the first solitary passenger whom he should meet. While a resolution to this effect was gaining strength, he entered a street of mean appearance, on either side of which a row of ill-built houses was straggling towards the harbor. The moonlight fell upon no passenger along the whole extent, but in the third domicile which Robin passed there was a half-opened door, and his keen glance detected a woman's garment within.

"My luck may be better here," said he to himself.

Accordingly, he approached the door, and beheld it shut closer as he did so; yet an open space remained, sufficing for the fair occupant to observe the stranger, without a corresponding display on her part. All that Robin could discern was a strip of scarlet petticoat, and the occasional sparkle of an eye, as if the moonbeams were trembling on some bright thing.

"Pretty mistress," for I may call her so with a good conscience, thought the shrewd youth, since I know nothing to the contrary,—"my sweet pretty mistress, will you be kind enough to tell me whereabouts I must seek the dwelling of my kinsman, Major Molineux?"

Robin's voice was plaintive and winning, and the female, seeing nothing to be shunned in the handsome country youth, thrust open the door, and came forth into the moonlight. She was a dainty little figure, with a white neck, round arms, and a slender waist, at the extremity of which her scarlet petticoat jutted out over a hoop, as if she were standing in a balloon. Moreover, her face was oval and pretty, her hair dark beneath the little cap, and her bright eyes possessed a sly freedom, which triumphed over those of Robin.

"Major Molineux dwells here," said this fair woman.

Now, her voice was the sweetest Robin had heard that night, the airy counterpart of a stream of melted silver; yet he could not help doubting whether that sweet voice spoke Gospel truth. He looked up and down the mean street, and then surveyed the house before which they stood. It was a small, dark edifice of two stories, the second of which projected over the lower floor, and the front apartment had the aspect of a shop for petty commodities.

"Now, truly, I am in luck," replied Robin, cunningly, "and so indeed is my kinsman, the Major, in having so pretty a housekeeper. But I prithee trouble him to step to the door; I will deliver him a message from his friends in the country, and then go back to my lodgings at the inn."

"Nay, the Major has been abed this hour or more," said the lady of the scarlet petticoat; "and it would be to little purpose to disturb him to-night, seeing his evening draught was of the strongest. But he is a kind-hearted man, and it would be as much as my life's worth to let a kinsman of his turn away from the door. You are the good old gentleman's very picture, and I could swear that was his rainy-weather hat. Also he has garments very much resembling those leather small-clothes. But come in, I pray, for I bid you hearty welcome in his name."

So saying, the fair and hospitable dame took our hero by the hand; and the touch was light, and the force was gentleness, and though Robin read in her eyes what he did not hear in her words, yet the slender-waisted woman in the scarlet petticoat proved stronger than the athletic country youth. She had drawn his half-willing footsteps nearly to the threshold, when the opening of a door in the neighborhood startled the Major's housekeeper, and, leaving the Major's kinsman, she vanished speedily into her own domicile. A heavy yawn preceded the appearance of a man, who, like the Moonshine of Pyramus and Thisbe, carried a lantern, needlessly aiding his sister luminary in the heavens. As he walked sleepily up the street, he turned his broad, dull face on Robin, and displayed a long staff, spiked at the end.

"Home, vagabond, home!" said the watchman, in accents that seemed to fall asleep as soon as they were uttered. "Home, or we'll set you in the stocks by peep of day!"

"This is the second hint of the kind," thought Robin. "I wish they would end my difficulties, by setting me there to-night."

Nevertheless, the youth felt an instinctive antipathy towards the guardian of midnight order, which at first prevented him from asking his usual question. But just when the man was about to vanish behind the corner, Robin resolved not to lose the opportunity, and shouted lustily after him,—

"I say, friend! will you guide me to the house of my kinsman, Major Molineux?"

The watchman made no reply, but turned the corner and was gone; yet Robin seemed to hear the sound of drowsy laughter stealing along the solitary street. At that moment, also, a pleasant titter saluted him from the open window above his head; he looked up, and caught the sparkle of a saucy eye; a round arm beckoned to him, and next he heard light footsteps descending the staircase within. But Robin, being of the household of a New England clergyman, was a good youth, as well as a shrewd one; so he resisted temptation, and fled away.

He now roamed desperately, and at random, through the town, almost ready to believe that a spell was on him, like that by which a wizard of his country had once kept three pursuers wandering, a whole winter night, within twenty paces of the cottage which they sought. The streets lay before him, strange and desolate, and the lights were extinguished in almost every house. Twice, however, little parties of men, among whom Robin distinguished individuals in outlandish attire, came hurrying along; but, though on both occasions they paused to address him, such intercourse did not at all enlighten his perplexity. They did but utter a few words in some language of which Robin knew nothing, and perceiving his inability to answer, bestowed a curse upon him in plain English and hastened away. Finally, the lad determined to knock at the door of every mansion that might appear worthy to be occupied by his kinsman, trusting that perseverance would overcome the fatality that had hitherto thwarted him. Firm in this resolve, he was passing beneath the walls of a church, which formed the corner of two streets, when, as he turned into the shade of its steeple, he encountered a bulky stranger, muffled in a cloak. The man was proceeding with the speed of earnest business, but Robin planted himself full before him, holding the oak cudgel with both hands across his body as a bar to further passage.

"Halt, honest man, and answer me a question," said he, very resolutely. "Tell me, this instant, whereabouts is the dwelling of my kinsman, Major Molineux!"

"Keep your tongue between your teeth, fool, and let me pass!" said a deep, gruff voice, which Robin partly remembered. "Let me pass, I say, or I'll strike you to the earth!"

"No, no, neighbor!" cried Robin, flourishing his cudgel, and then thrusting its larger end close to the man's muffled face. "No, no, I'm not the fool you take me for, nor do you pass till I have an answer to my question. Whereabouts is the dwelling of my kinsman, Major Molineux?"

The stranger, instead of attempting to force his passage, stepped back into the moonlight, unmuffled his face, and stared full into that of Robin.

"Watch here an hour, and Major Molineux will pass by," said he.

Robin gazed with dismay and astonishment on the unprecedented physiognomy of the speaker. The forehead with its double prominence, the broad hooked nose, the shaggy eyebrows, and fiery eyes were those which he had noticed at the inn, but the man's complexion had undergone a singular, or, more properly, a twofold change. One side of the face blazed an intense red, while the other was black as midnight, the division line being in the broad bridge of the nose; and a mouth which seemed to extend from ear to ear was black or red, in contrast to the color of the cheek. The effect was as if two individual devils, a fiend of fire and a fiend of darkness, had united themselves to form this infernal visage. The stranger grinned in Robin's face, muffled his party-colored features, and was out of sight in a moment.

"Strange things we travellers see!" ejaculated Robin.

He seated himself, however, upon the steps of the church-door, resolving to wait the appointed time for his kinsman. A few moments were consumed in philosophical speculations upon the species of man who had just left him; but having settled this point shrewdly, rationally, and satisfactorily, he was compelled to look elsewhere for his amusement. And first he threw his eyes along the street. It was of more respectable appearance than most of those into which he had wandered; and the moon, creating, like the imaginative power, a beautiful strangeness in familiar objects, gave something of romance to a scene that might not have possessed it in the light of day. The irregular and often quaint architecture of the houses, some of whose roofs were broken into numerous little peaks, while others ascended, steep and narrow, into a single point, and others again were square; the pure snow-white of some of their complexions, the aged darkness of others, and the thousand sparklings, reflected from bright substances in the walls of many; these matters engaged Robin's attention for a while, and then began to grow wearisome. Next he endeavored to define the forms of distant objects, starting away, with almost ghostly indistinctness, just as his eye appeared to grasp them; and finally he took a minute survey of an edifice which stood on the opposite side of the street, directly in front of the church-door, where he was stationed. It was a large, square mansion, distinguished from its neighbors by a balcony, which rested on tall pillars, and by an elaborate Gothic window, communicating therewith.

"Perhaps this is the very house I have been seeking," thought Robin.

Then he strove to speed away the time, by listening to a murmur which swept continually along the street, yet was scarcely audible, except to an unaccustomed ear like his; it was a low, dull, dreamy sound, compounded of many noises, each of which was at too great a distance to be separately heard. Robin marvelled at this snore of a sleeping town, and marvelled more whenever its continuity was broken by now and then a distant shout, apparently loud where it originated. But altogether it was a sleep-inspiring sound, and, to shake off its drowsy influence, Robin arose, and climbed a window-frame, that he might view the interior of the church. There the moonbeams came trembling in, and fell down upon the deserted pews, and extended along the quiet aisles. A fainter yet more awful radiance was hovering around the pulpit, and one solitary ray had dared to rest upon the open page of the great Bible. Had nature, in that deep hour, become a worshipper in the house which man had builded? Or was that heavenly light the visible sanctity of the place,—visible because no earthly and impure feet were within the walls? The scene made Robin's heart shiver with a sensation of loneliness stronger than he had ever felt in the remotest depths of his native woods; so he turned away and sat down again before the door. There were graves around the church, and now an uneasy thought obtruded into Robin's breast. What if the object of his search, which had been so often and so strangely thwarted, were all the time mouldering in his shroud? What if his kinsman should glide through yonder gate, and nod and smile to him in dimly passing by?

"Oh that any breathing thing were here with me!" said Robin.

Recalling his thoughts from this uncomfortable track, he sent them over forest, hill, and stream, and attempted to imagine how that evening of ambiguity and weariness had been spent by his father's household. He pictured them assembled at the door, beneath the tree, the great old tree, which had been spared for its huge twisted trunk and venerable shade, when a thousand leafy brethren fell. There, at the going down of the summer sun, it was his father's custom to perform domestic worship, that the neighbors might come and join with him like brothers of the family, and that the wayfaring man might pause to drink at that fountain, and keep his heart pure by freshening the memory of home. Robin distinguished the seat of every individual of the little audience; he saw the good man in the midst, holding the Scriptures in the golden light that fell from the western clouds; he beheld him close the book and all rise up to pray. He heard the old thanks-givings for daily mercies, the old supplications for their continuance, to which he had so often listened in weariness, but which were now among his dear remembrances. He perceived the slight inequality of his father's voice when he came to speak of the absent one; he noted how his mother turned her face to the broad and knotted trunk; how his elder brother scorned, because the beard was rough upon his upper lip, to permit his features to be moved; how the younger sister drew down a low hanging branch before her eyes; and how the little one of all, whose sports had hitherto broken the decorum of the scene, understood the prayer for her playmate, and burst into clamorous grief. Then he saw them go in at the door; and when Robin would have entered also, the latch tinkled into its place, and he was excluded from his home.

"Am I here, or there?" cried Robin, starting; for all at once, when his thoughts had become visible and audible in a dream, the long, wide, solitary street shone out before him.

He aroused himself, and endeavored to fix his attention steadily upon the large edifice which he had surveyed before. But still his mind kept vibrating between fancy and reality; by turns, the pillars of the balcony lengthened into the tall, bare stems of pines, dwindled down to human figures, settled again into their true shape and size, and then commenced a new succession of changes. For a single moment, when he deemed himself awake, he could have sworn that a visage—one which he seemed to remember, yet could not absolutely name as his kinsman's—was looking towards him from the Gothic window. A deeper sleep wrestled with and nearly overcame him, but fled at the sound of footsteps along the opposite pavement. Robin rubbed his eyes, discerned a man passing at the foot of the balcony, and addressed him in a loud, peevish, and lamentable cry.

"Hallo, friend! must I wait here all night for my kinsman, Major Moli-neux?"

The sleeping echoes awoke, and answered the voice; and the passenger, barely able to discern a figure sitting in the oblique shade of the steeple, traversed the street to obtain a nearer view. He was himself a gentleman in his prime, of open, intelligent, cheerful, and altogether prepossessing coun-tenance. Perceiving a country youth, apparently homeless and without friends, he accosted him in a tone of real kindness, which had become strange to Robin's ears.

"Well, my good lad, who are you sitting here?" inquired he. "Can I be of service to you in any way?"

"I am afraid not, sir," replied Robin, despondingly; "yet I shall take it kindly, if you'll answer me a single question. I've been searching, half the night, for one Major Molineux; now, sir, is there really such a person in these parts, or am I dreaming?"

"Major Molineux! The name is not altogether strange to me," said the gentleman, smiling. "Have you any objection to telling me the nature of your business with him?"

Then Robin briefly related that his father was a clergyman, settled on a small salary, at a long distance back in the country, and that he and Major Molineux were brothers' children. The Major, having inherited riches, and acquired civil and military rank, had visited his cousin, in great pomp, a year or two before; had manifested much interest in Robin and an elder brother, and, being childless himself, had thrown out hints respecting the future establishment of one of them in life. The elder brother was destined to succeed to the farm which his father cultivated in the interval of sacred duties; it was therefore determined that Robin should profit by his kinsman's generous intentions, especially as he seemed to be rather the favorite, and was thought to possess other necessary endowments.

"For I have the name of being a shrewd youth," observed Robin, in this part of his story.

"I doubt not you deserve it," replied his new friend, good-naturedly; "but pray proceed."

"Well, sir, being nearly eighteen years old, and well grown, as you see," continued Robin, drawing himself up to his full height, "I thought it high time to begin the world. So my mother and sister put me in handsome trim, and my father gave me half the remnant of his last year's salary, and five days ago I started for this place, to pay the Major a visit. But, would you believe it, sir! I crossed the ferry a little after dark, and have yet found nobody that would show me the way to his dwelling; only, an hour or two since, I was told to wait here, and Major Molineux would pass by."

"Can you describe the man who told you this?" inquired the gentleman.

"Oh, he was a very ill-favored fellow, sir," replied Robin, "with two great bumps on his forehead, a hook nose, fiery eyes; and, what struck me as the strangest, his face was of two different colors. Do you happen to know such a man, sir?"

"Not intimately," answered the stranger, "but I chanced to meet him a little time previous to your stopping me. I believe you may trust his word, and that the Major will very shortly pass through this street. In the mean time, as I have a singular curiosity to witness your meeting, I will sit down here upon the steps and bear you company."

He seated himself accordingly, and soon engaged his companion in animated discourse. It was but of brief continuance, however, for a noise of shouting, which had long been remotely audible, drew so much nearer that Robin inquired its cause.

"What may be the meaning of this uproar?" asked he. "Truly, if your town be always as noisy, I shall find little sleep while I am an inhabitant."

"Why, indeed, friend Robin, there do appear to be three or four riotous fellows abroad to-night," replied the gentleman. "You must not expect all the stillness of your native woods here in our streets. But the watch will shortly be at the heels of these lads and"—

"Ay, and set them in the stocks by peep of day," interrupted Robin, recollecting his own encounter with the drowsy lantern-bearer. "But, dear sir, if I may trust my ears, an army of watchmen would never make head against such a multitude of rioters. There were at least a thousand voices went up to make that one shout."

"May not a man have several voices, Robin, as well as two complexions?" said his friend.

"Perhaps a man may; but Heaven forbid that a woman should!" responded the shrewd youth, thinking of the seductive tones of the Major's housekeeper.

The sounds of a trumpet in some neighboring street now became so evident and continual, that Robin's curiosity was strongly excited. In addition to the shouts, he heard frequent bursts from many instruments of discord, and a wild and confused laughter filled up the intervals. Robin rose from the steps, and looked wistfully towards a point whither people seemed to be hastening.

"Surely some prodigious merry-making is going on," exclaimed he. "I have laughed very little since I left home, sir, and should be sorry to lose an opportunity. Shall we step round the corner by that darkish house, and take our share of the fun?"

"Sit down again, sit down, good Robin," replied the gentleman, laying his hand on the skirt of the gray coat. "You forget that we must wait here for your kinsman; and there is reason to believe that he will pass by, in the course of a very few moments."

The near approach of the uproar had now disturbed the neighborhood: windows flew open on all sides: and many heads, in the attire of the pillow, and confused by sleep suddenly broken, were protruded to the gaze of whoever had leisure to observe them. Eager voices hailed each other from house to house, all demanding the explanation, which not a soul could give. Half-dressed men hurried towards the unknown commotion, stumbling as they went over the stone steps that thrust themselves into the narrow footwalk. The shouts, the laughter, and the tuneless bray, the antipodes of music, came onwards with increasing din, till scattered individuals, and then denser bodies, began to appear round a corner at the distance of a hundred yards.

"Will you recognize your kinsman, if he passes in this crowd?" inquired the gentleman.

"Indeed, I can't warrant it, sir; but I'll take my stand here, and keep a bright lookout," answered Robin, descending to the outer edge of the pavement.

A mighty stream of people now emptied into the street, and came rolling slowly towards the church. A single horseman wheeled the corner in the midst of them, and close behind him came a band of fearful wind-instruments, sending forth a fresher discord now that no intervening buildings kept it from the ear. Then a redder light disturbed the moonbeams, and a dense multitude of torches shone along the street, concealing, by their glare, whatever object they illuminated. The single horseman, clad in a military dress, and bearing a drawn sword, rode onward as the leader, and by his fierce and variegated countenance, appeared like war personified; the red of one cheek was an emblem of fire and sword; the blackness of the other betokened the mourning that attends them. In his train were wild figures in the Indian dress, and many fantastic shapes without a model, giving the whole march a visionary air, as if a dream had broken forth from some feverish brain, and were sweeping visibly through the midnight streets. A mass of people, inactive, except as applauding spectators, hemmed the procession in; and several women ran along the sidewalk, piercing the confusion of heavier sounds with their shrill voices of mirth or terror.

"The double-faced fellow has his eye upon me," muttered Robin, with an indefinite but an uncomfortable idea that he was himself to bear a part in the pageantry.

The leader turned himself in the saddle, and fixed his glance full upon the country youth, as the steed went slowly by. When Robin had freed his eyes from those fiery ones, the musicians were passing before him, and the torches were close at hand; but the unsteady brightness of the latter formed a veil which he could not penetrate. The rattling of wheels over the stones sometimes found its way to his ear, and confused traces of a human form appeared at intervals, and then melted into the vivid light. A moment more, and the leader thundered a command to halt: the trumpets vomited a horrid breath, and then held their peace; the shouts and laughter of the people died away, and there remained only a universal hum, allied to silence. Right before Robin's eyes was an uncovered cart. There the torches blazed the brightest, there the moon shone out like day, and there, in tar-and-feathery dignity, sat his kinsman, Major Molineux!

He was an elderly man, of large and majestic person, and strong, square features, betokening a steady soul; but steady as it was, his enemies had found means to shake it. His face was pale as death, and far more ghastly; the broad forehead was contracted in his agony, so that his eyebrows formed one grizzled line; his eyes were red and wild, and the foam hung white upon his quivering lip. His whole frame was agitated by a quick and continual tremor, which his pride strove to quell, even in those circumstances of overwhelming humiliation. But perhaps the bitterest pang of all was when his eyes met those of Robin; for he evidently knew him on the instant, as the youth stood witnessing the foul disgrace of a head grown gray in honor. They stared at each other in silence, and Robin's knees shook, and his hair bristled, with a mixture of pity and terror. Soon, however, a bewildering excitement began to seize upon his mind; the preceding adventures of the night, the unexpected appearance of the crowd, the torches, the confused din and the hush that followed, the spectre of his kinsman reviled by that great multitude,—all this, and, more than all, a perception of tremendous ridicule in the whole scene, affected him with a sort of mental inebriety. At that moment a voice of sluggish merriment saluted Robin's ears; he turned instinctively, and just behind the corner of the church stood the lantern-bearer, rubbing his eyes, and drowsily enjoying the lad's amazement. Then he heard a peal of laughter like the ringing of silvery bells; a woman twitched his arm, a saucy eye met his, and he saw the lady of the scarlet petticoat. A sharp, dry cachinnation appealed to his memory, and, standing on tiptoe in the crowd, with his white apron over his head, he beheld the courteous little innkeeper. And lastly, there sailed over the heads of the multitude a great, broad laugh, broken in the midst by two sepulchral hems; thus, "Haw, haw, haw,—hem, hem,—haw, haw, haw, haw!"

The sound proceeded from the balcony of the opposite edifice, and thither Robin turned his eyes. In front of the Gothic window stood the old citizen, wrapped in a wide gown, his gray periwig exchanged for a nightcap, which was thrust back from his forehead, and his silk stockings hanging about his legs. He supported himself on his polished cane in a fit of convulsive merriment, which manifested itself on his solemn old features like a funny inscription on a tombstone. Then Robin seemed to hear the voices of the barbers, of the guests of the inn, and of all who had made sport of him that night. The contagion was spreading among the multitude, when all at once, it seized upon Robin, and he sent forth a shout of laughter that echoed through the street,—every man shook his sides, every man emptied his lungs, but Robin's shout was the loudest there. The cloud-spirits peeped from their silvery islands, as the congregated mirth went roaring up the sky! The Man in the Moon heard the far bellow. "Oho," quoth he, "the old earth is frolicsome to-night!"

When there was a momentary calm in that tempestuous sea of sound, the leader gave the sign, the procession resumed its march. On they went, like fiends that throng in mockery around some dead potentate, mighty no more, but majestic still in his agony. On they went, in counterfeited pomp, in senseless uproar, in frenzied merriment, trampling all on an old man's heart. On swept the tumult, and left a silent street behind.

"WELL, Robin, are you dreaming?" inquired the gentleman, laying his hand on the youth's shoulder.

Robin started, and withdrew his arm from the stone post to which he had instinctively clung, as the living stream rolled by him. His cheek was somewhat pale, and his eye not quite as lively as in the earlier part of the evening.

"Will you be kind enough to show me the way to the ferry?" said he, after a moment's pause.

"You have, then, adopted a new subject of inquiry?" observed his companion, with a smile.

"Why, yes, sir," replied Robin, rather dryly. "Thanks to you, and to my other friends, I have at last met my kinsman, and he will scarce desire to see my face again. I begin to grow weary of a town life, sir. Will you show me the way to the ferry?"

"No, my good friend Robin,—not to-night, at least," said the gentleman. "Some few days hence, if you wish it, I will speed you on your journey. Or, if you prefer to remain with us, perhaps, as you are a shrewd youth, you may rise in the world without the help of your kinsman, Major Molineux."

(1832)

Herman Melville

(1 8 1 9 – 1 8 9 1)

Melville was born in New York City, the son of well-educated, wealthy parents. In 1830 his father went bankrupt and died shortly afterward. After brief stints as a bank clerk, salesman, farmhand, and schoolteacher, Melville signed up as a cabin boy at age 18 on a ship bound for Liverpool. Infected with the adventure of the sea, he then took work aboard a whaler, the *Acushnet,* bound for the south seas. His adventures, which included being captured by cannibals, provided material for his first three novels and for *Moby Dick.* Initially successful as a novelist, Melville's later masterpieces were received with less enthusiasm. He eventually took work with the U.S. Custom House to support his family, a job that left little time for writing. When Melville died, his literary reputation was almost extinct.

In many ways Melville was the first modern novelist. His work is now universally recognized for its rich imagery, its superb incantatory prose, and its intricate exploration of human psychology, which Melville showed in the creation of gods and heroes and in the search for absolutes of truth and morality. *Moby Dick,* a masterpiece by turns lyrical, haunting, witty, mythical, religious, and naturalistic, utilizes the religions and commercial features of a particular region—nineteenth-century New England—as a complex metaphor for the individual's destructive quest for heroism, danger, and Faustian knowledge of the cosmos and the self. The finest of Melville's short stories —"Bartleby the Scrivener," "Benito Cereno," "The Encantadas"—investigate Melville's preoccupation with the evil seemingly inherent in nature itself. Melville uses the context of failed individual love and the ultimately isolated self. A posthumous novella, *Billy Budd,* is psychologically profound as it expores our ability to deceive ourselves (anticipating Conrad) and strikingly modern in its use of narrative strategies that duplicate the themes of the work.

Melville's early south sea novels were *Typee* (1846), *Omoo* (1847), and *Mardi* (1849). *Redburn* appeared in 1849, *White-Jacket* in 1850, and *Moby Dick* in 1851. Other major works include *Pierre* (1852), *The Piazza Tales* (1856), *The Confidence Man* (1857), and *Billy Budd,* which was first published in 1924.

HERMAN MELVILLE

Bartleby the Scrivener

I AM a rather elderly man. The nature of my avocations, for the last thirty years, has brought me into more than ordinary contact with what would seem an interesting and somewhat singular set of men, of whom, as yet, nothing, that I know of, has ever been written—I mean, the law-copyists, or scriveners. I have known very many of them, professionally and privately, and, if I pleased, could relate divers histories, at which good-natured gentlemen might smile, and sentimental souls might weep. But I waive the biographies of all other scriveners, for a few passages in the life of Bartleby, who was a scrivener, the strangest I ever saw, or heard of. While, of other law-copyists, I might write the complete life, of Bartleby nothing of that sort can be done. I believe that no materials exist, for a full and satisfactory biography of this man. It is an irreparable loss to literature. Bartleby was one of those beings of whom nothing is ascertainable, except from the original sources, and, in his case, those are very small. What my own astonished eyes saw of Bartleby, *that* is all I know of him, except, indeed, one vague report, which will appear in the sequel.

Ere introducing the scrivener, as he first appeared to me, it is fit I make some mention of myself, my employés, my business, my chambers, and general surroundings; because some such description is indispensable to an adequate understanding of the chief character about to be presented. Imprimis: I am a man who, from his youth upward, has been filled with a profound conviction that the easiest way of life is the best. Hence, though I belong to a profession proverbially energetic and nervous, even to turbulence, at times, yet nothing of that sort have I ever suffered to invade my peace. I am one of those unambitious lawyers who never addresses a jury, or in any way draws down public applause; but, in the cool tranquillity of a snug retreat, do a snug business among rich men's bonds, and mortgages, and title-deeds. All who know me, consider me an eminently *safe* man. The late John Jacob Astor, a personage little given to poetic enthusiasm, had no hesitation in pronouncing my first grand point to be prudence; my next, method. I do not speak it in vanity, but simply record the fact, that I was not unemployed in my profession by the late John Jacob Astor; a name which, I admit, I love to repeat; for it hath a rounded and orbicular sound to it, and rings like unto bullion. I will freely add, that I was not insensible to the late John Jacob Astor's good opinion.

Some time prior to the period at which this little history begins, my avocations had been largely increased. The good old office, now extinct in the State of New York, of a Master in Chancery, had been conferred upon me. It was not a very arduous office, but very pleasantly remunerative. I seldom lose my temper; much more seldom indulge in dangerous indignation at wrongs and outrages; but, I must be permitted to be rash here, and declare, that I consider the sudden and violent abrogation of the office of Master in Chancery, by the new Constitution, as a—premature act; inasmuch as I had counted upon a life-lease of the profits, whereas I only received those of a few short years. But this is by the way.

My chambers were upstairs, at No.———Wall Street. At one end, they looked upon the white wall of the interior of a spacious skylight shaft, penetrating the building from top to bottom.

This view might have been considered rather tame than otherwise, deficient in what landscape painters call 'life.' But, if so, the view from the other end of my chambers offered, at least, a contrast, if nothing more. In that direction, my windows commanded an unobstructed view of a lofty brick wall, black by age and everlasting shade; which wall required no spy-glass to bring out its lurking beauties, but, for the benefit of all near-sighted spectators, was pushed up to within ten feet of my window panes. Owing to the great height of the surrounding buildings, and my chambers being on the second floor, the interval between this wall and mine not a little resembled a huge square cistern.

At the period just preceding the advent of Bartleby, I had two persons as copyists in my employment, and a promising lad as an office-boy. First, Turkey; second, Nippers; third, Ginger Nut. These may seem names, the like of which are not usually found in the Directory. In truth, they were nicknames, mutually conferred upon each other by my three clerks, and were deemed expressive of their respective persons or characters. Turkey was a short, pursy Englishman, of about my own age—that is, somewhere not far from sixty. In the morning, one might say, his face was of a fine florid hue, but after twelve o'clock, meridian—his dinner hour—it blazed like a grate full of Christmas coals; and continued blazing—but, as it were, with a gradual wane—till six o'clock, P.M., or thereabouts; after which, I saw no more of the proprietor of the face, which, gaining its meridian with the sun, seemed to set with it, to rise, culminate, and decline the following day, with the like regularity and undiminished glory. There are many singular coincidences I have known in the course of my life, not the least among which was the fact, that, exactly when Turkey displayed his fullest beams from his red and radiant countenance, just then, too, at that critical moment, began the daily period when I considered his business capacities as seriously disturbed for the remainder of the twenty-four hours. Not that he was absolutely idle, or averse to business, then; far from it. The difficulty was, he was apt to be altogether too energetic. There was a strange, inflamed, flurried, flighty recklessness of activity about him. He would be incautious in dipping his pen into his inkstand. All his blots upon my documents were dropped there after twelve o'clock, meridian. Indeed, not only would he be reckless, and sadly given to making blots in the afternoon, but, some days, he went further, and was rather noisy. At such times, too, his face flamed with augmented blazonry, as if cannel coal had been heaped on anthracite. He made an unpleasant racket with his chair; spilled his sand-box; in mending his pens, impatiently split them all to pieces, and threw them on the floor in a sudden passion; stood up, and leaned over his table, boxing his papers about in a most indecorous manner, very sad to behold in an elderly man like him. Nevertheless, as he was in many ways a most valuable person to me, and all the time before twelve o'clock, meridian, was the quickest, steadiest creature, too, accomplishing a great deal of work in a style not easily to be matched—for these reasons, I was willing to overlook his eccentricities, though, indeed, occasionally, I remonstrated with him. I did this very gently, however, because, though the civilest, nay, the blandest and most reverential of men in the morning, yet, in the afternoon, he was disposed, upon provocation, to be slightly rash with his tongue—in fact, insolent. Now, valuing his morning services as I did, and resolved not to lose them—yet, at the same time, made uncomfortable by his inflamed ways after twelve o'clock—and being a man of peace, unwilling by my admonitions to call forth unseemly retorts from him, I took upon me, one Saturday noon (he was always worse on Saturdays) to hint to him, very kindly, that, perhaps, now that he was growing old, it might be well to abridge his labours; in short, he need not come to my chambers after twelve o'clock, but, dinner over, had best go home to his lodgings, and rest himself till tea-time. But no; he insisted upon his afternoon devotions. His countenance became intolerably fervid, as he oratorically assured me—gesticulating with a long ruler at the other end of the room—that if his services in the morning were useful, how indispensable, then, in the afternoon?

'With submission, sir,' said Turkey, on this occasion, 'I consider myself your right-hand man. In the morning I but marshal and deploy my columns; but in the afternoon I put myself at their head, and gallantly charge the foe, thus'—and he made a violent thrust with the ruler.

'But the blots, Turkey,' intimated I.

'True; but, with submission, sir, behold these hairs! I am getting old. Surely, sir, a blot or two of a warm afternoon is not to be severely urged against gray hairs. Old age—even if it blot the page—is honourable. With submission, sir, we *both* are getting old.'

This appeal to my fellow-feeling was hardly to be resisted. At all events, I saw that go he would not. So, I made up my mind to let him stay, resolving, nevertheless, to see to it that, during the afternoon, he had to do with my less important papers.

Nippers, the second on my list, was a whiskered, sallow, and, upon the whole, rather piratical-looking young man, of about five-and-twenty. I always deemed him the victim of two evil powers—ambition and indigestion. The ambition was evinced by a certain impatience of the duties of a mere copyist, an unwarrantable usurpation of strictly professional affairs, such as the original drawing up of legal documents. The indigestion seemed betokened in an occasional nervous testiness and grinning irritability, causing the teeth to audibly grind together over mistakes committed in copying; unnecessary maledictions, hissed, rather than spoken, in the heat of business; and especially by a continual discontent with the height of the table where he worked. Though of a very ingenious mechanical turn, Nippers could never get this table to suit him. He put chips under it, blocks of various sorts, bits of pasteboard, and at last went so far as to attempt an exquisite adjustment, by final pieces of folded blotting-paper. But no invention would answer. If, for the sake of easing his back, he brought the table lid at a sharp angle well up toward his chin, and wrote there like a man using the steep roof of a Dutch house for his desk, then he declared that it stopped the circulation in his arms. If now he lowered the table to his waistbands, and stooped over it in writing, then there was a sore aching in his back. In short, the truth of the matter was, Nippers knew not what he wanted. Or, if he wanted anything, it was to be rid of a scrivener's table altogether. Among the manifestations of his diseased ambition was a fondness he had for receiving visits from certain ambiguous-looking fellows in seedy coats, whom he called his clients. Indeed, I was aware that not only was he, at times, considerable of a ward-politician, but he occasionally did a little business at the Justices' courts, and was not unknown on the steps of the Tombs.[1] I have good reason to believe, however, that one individual who called upon him at my chambers, and who, with a grand air, he insisted was his client, was no other than a dun, and the alleged title-deed, a bill. But, with all his failings, and the annoyances he caused me, Nippers, like his compatriot Turkey, was a very useful man to me; wrote a neat, swift hand; and, when he chose, was not deficient in a gentlemanly sort of deportment. Added to this, he always dressed in a gentlemanly sort of way; and so, incidentally, reflected credit upon my chambers. Whereas, with respect to Turkey, I had much ado to keep him from being a reproach to me. His clothes were apt to look oily, and smell of eating-houses. He wore his pantaloons very loose and baggy in summer. His coats were execrable; his hat not to be handled. But while the hat was a thing of indifference to me, inasmuch as his natural civility and deference, as a dependent Englishman, always led him to doff it the moment he entered the room, yet his coat was another matter. Concerning his coats, I reasoned with him; but with no effect. The truth was, I suppose, that a man with so small an income could not afford to sport such a lustrous face and a lustrous coat at one and the same time. As Nippers once observed, Turkey's money went chiefly for red ink. One winter day, I presented Turkey with a highly respectable-looking coat of my own—a padded gray coat, of a most comfortable warmth, and which buttoned straight up from the knee to the neck. I thought Turkey would appreciate the favour, and abate his rashness and obstreperousness of afternoons. But no; I verily believe that buttoning himself up in so downy and blanket-like a coat had a pernicious effect upon him—upon the same

---

[1] A New York City prison.

principle that too much oats are bad for horses. In fact, precisely as a rash, restive horse is said to feel his oats, so Turkey felt his coat. It made him insolent. He was a man whom prosperity harmed.

Though, concerning the self-indulgent habits of Turkey, I had my own private surmises, yet, touching Nippers, I was well persuaded that, whatever might be his faults in other respects, he was, at least, a temperate young man. But, indeed, nature herself seemed to have been his vintner, and, at his birth, charged him so thoroughly with an irritable, brandy-like disposition, that all subsequent potations were needless. When I consider how, amid the stillness of my chambers, Nippers would sometimes impatiently rise from his seat, and stooping over his table, spread his arms wide apart, seize the whole desk, and move it, and jerk it, with a grim, grinding motion on the floor, as if the table were a perverse voluntary agent, intent on thwarting and vexing him, I plainly perceive that, for Nippers, brandy-and-water were altogether superfluous.

It was fortunate for me that, owing to its peculiar cause—indigestion—the irritability and consequent nervousness of Nippers were mainly observable in the morning, while in the afternoon he was comparatively mild. So that, Turkey's paroxysms only coming on about twelve o'clock, I never had to do with their eccentricities at one time. Their fits relieved each other, like guards. When Nippers's was on, Turkey's was off; and *vice versa.* This was a good natural arrangement, under the circumstances.

Ginger Nut, the third on my list, was a lad, some twelve years old. His father was a carman, ambitious of seeing his son on the bench instead of a cart, before he died. So he sent him to my office, as student at law, errand-boy, cleaner and sweeper, at the rate of one dollar a week. He had a little desk to himself, but he did not use it much. Upon inspection, the drawer exhibited a great array of the shells of various sorts of nuts. Indeed, to this quick-witted youth, the whole noble science of the law was contained in a nut-shell. Not the least among the employments of Ginger Nut, as well as one which he discharged with the most alacrity, was his duty as cake and apple purveyor for Turkey and Nippers. Copying law-papers being proverbially a dry, husky sort of business, my two scriveners were fain to moisten their mouths very often with Spitzenbergs, to be had at the numerous stalls nigh the Custom House and Post Office. Also, they sent Ginger Nut very frequently for that peculiar cake—small, flat, round, and very spicy—after which he had been named by them. Of a cold morning, when business was but dull, Turkey would gobble up scores of these cakes, as if they were mere wafers—indeed, they sell them at the rate of six or eight for a penny—the scrape of his pen blending with the crunching of the crisp particles in his mouth. Of all the fiery afternoon blunders and flurried rashnesses of Turkey, was his once moistening a ginger-cake between his lips, and clapping it on to a mortgage, for a seal. I came within an ace of dismissing him then. But he mollified me by making an oriental bow, and saying—'With submission, sir, it was generous of me to find you in stationery on my own account.'

Now my original business—that of a conveyancer and title-hunter, and drawer-up of recondite documents of all sorts—was considerably increased by receiving the master's office. There was now great work for scriveners. Not only must I push the clerks already with me, but I must have additional help.

In answer to my advertisement, a motionless young man one morning stood upon my office threshold, the door being open, for it was summer. I can see that figure now—pallidly neat, pitiably respectable, incurably forlorn! It was Bartleby.

After a few words touching his qualifications, I engaged him, glad to have among my corps of copyists a man of so singularly sedate an aspect, which I thought might operate beneficially upon the flighty temper of Turkey, and the fiery one of Nippers.

I should have stated before that ground-glass folding-doors divided my premises into two parts, one of which was occupied by my scriveners, the other by myself. According to my humour, I threw open these doors, or closed them. I resolved to assign Bartleby a corner by the folding-doors, but on my side of them, so as to have this quiet man within easy call, in case any trifling thing was to be done. I placed his desk close up to a small side-window in that part of the room, a window which originally had afforded a lateral view of certain grimy back-yards and bricks, but which, owing to subsequent erections, commanded at present no view at all, though it gave some light. Within three feet of the panes was a wall, and the light came down from far above, between two lofty buildings, as from a very small opening in a dome. Still further to a satisfactory arrangement, I procured a high green folding-screen, which might entirely isolate Bartleby from my sight, though not remove him from my voice. And thus, in a manner, privacy and society were conjoined.

At first, Bartleby did an extraordinary quantity of writing. As if long famishing for something to copy, he seemed to gorge himself on my documents. There was no pause for digestion. He ran a day and night line, copying by sun-light and by candle-light. I should have been quite delighted with his application, had he been cheerfully industrious. But he wrote on silently, palely, mechanically.

It is, of course, an indispensable part of a scrivener's business to verify the accuracy of his copy, word by word. Where there are two or more scriveners in an office, they assist each other in this examination, one reading from the copy, the other holding the original. It is a very dull, wearisome, and lethargic affair. I can readily imagine that, to some sanguine temperaments, it would be altogether intolerable. For example, I cannot credit that the mettlesome poet, Byron, would have contentedly sat down with Bartleby to examine a law document of, say, five hundred pages, closely written in a crimpy hand.

Now and then, in the haste of business, it had been my habit to assist in comparing some brief document myself, calling Turkey or Nippers for this purpose. One object I had, in placing Bartleby so handy to me behind the screen, was, to avail myself of his services on such trivial occasions. It was on the third day, I think, of his being with me, and before any necessity had arisen for having his own writing examined, that, being much hurried to complete a small affair I had in hand, I abruptly called to Bartleby. In my haste and natural expectancy of instant compliance, I sat with my head bent over the original on my desk, and my right hand sideways, and somewhat nervously extended with the copy, so that, immediately upon emerging from his retreat, Bartleby might snatch it and proceed to business without the least delay.

In this very attitude did I sit when I called to him, rapidly stating what it was I wanted him to do—namely, to examine a small paper with me. Imagine my surprise, nay, my consternation, when, without moving from his privacy, Bartleby, in a singularly mild, firm voice, replied, 'I would prefer not to.'

I sat a while in perfect silence, rallying my stunned faculties. Immediately it occurred to me that my ears had deceived me, or Bartleby had entirely misunderstood my meaning. I repeated my request in the clearest tone I could assume; but in quite as clear a one came the previous reply, 'I would prefer not to.'

'Prefer not to,' echoed I, rising in high excitement, and crossing the room with a stride. 'What do you mean? Are you moon-struck? I want you to help me compare this sheet here—take it,' and I thrust it toward him.

'I would prefer not to,' said he.

I looked at him steadfastly. His face was leanly composed; his gray eye dimly calm. Not a wrinkle of agitation rippled him. Had there been the least uneasiness, anger, impatience, or impertinence in his manner; in other words, had there been anything ordinarily human about him, doubtless I should have violently dismissed him from the premises. But as it was, I should have as soon thought of turning my pale plaster-of-paris bust of Cicero out of doors. I stood gazing at him a while, as he went on with his own writing, and then reseated myself at my desk. This is very strange, thought I. What had one best do? But my business hurried me. I concluded to forget the matter for the present, reserving it for my future leisure. So calling Nippers from the other room, the paper was speedily examined.

A few days after this, Bartleby concluded four lengthy documents, being quadruplicates of a week's testimony taken before me in my High Court of Chancery. It became necessary to examine them. It was an important suit, and great accuracy was imperative. Having all things arranged, I called Turkey, Nippers, and Ginger Nut, from the next room, meaning to place the four copies in the hands of my four clerks, while I should read from the original. Accordingly, Turkey, Nippers, and Ginger Nut had taken their seats in a row, each with his document in his hand, when I called to Bartleby to join this interesting group.

'Bartleby! quick, I am waiting.'

I heard a slow scrape of his chair legs on the uncarpeted floor, and soon he appeared standing at the entrance of his hermitage.

'What is wanted?' said he mildly.

'The copies, the copies,' said I hurriedly. 'We are going to examine them. There'—and I held toward him the fourth quadruplicate.

'I would prefer not to,' he said, and gently disappeared behind the screen.

For a few moments I was turned into a pillar of salt, standing at the head of my seated column of clerks. Recovering myself, I advanced toward the screen, and demanded the reason for such extraordinary conduct.

'*Why* do you refuse?'

'I would prefer not to.'

With any other man I should have flown outright into a dreadful passion, scorned all further words, and thrust him ignominiously from my presence. But there was something about Bartleby that not only strangely disarmed me, but, in a wonderful manner, touched and disconcerted me. I began to reason with him.

'These are your own copies we are about to examine. It is labour saving to you, because one examination will answer for your four papers. It is common usage. Every copyist is bound to help examine his copy. Is it not so? Will you not speak? Answer!'

'I prefer not to,' he replied in a flute-like tone. It seemed to me that, while I had been addressing him, he carefully revolved every statement that I made; fully comprehended the meaning; could not gainsay the irresistible conclusion; but, at the same time, some paramount consideration prevailed with him to reply as he did.

'You are decided, then, not to comply with my request—a request made according to common usage and common sense?'

He briefly gave me to understand, that on that point my judgment was sound. Yes: his decision was irreversible.

It is not seldom the case that, when a man is browbeaten in some unprecedented and violently unreasonable way, he begins to stagger in his own plainest faith. He begins, as it were, vaguely to surmise that, wonderful as it may be, all the justice and all the reason is on the other side. Accordingly, if any disinterested persons are present, he turns to them for some reinforcement for his own faltering mind.

'Turkey,' said I, 'what do you think of this? Am I not right?'

'With submission, sir,' said Turkey, in his blandest tone, 'I think that you are.'

'Nippers,' said I, 'what do *you* think of it?'

'I think I should kick him out of the office.'

(The reader, of nice perceptions, will here perceive that, it being morning, Turkey's answer is couched in polite and tranquil terms, but Nippers's replies in ill-tempered ones. Or, to repeat a previous sentence, Nippers's ugly mood was on duty, and Turkey's off.)

'Ginger Nut,' said I, willing to enlist the smallest suffrage in my behalf, 'what do *you* think of it?'

'I think, sir, he's a little *luny,*' replied Ginger Nut, with a grin.

'You hear what they say,' said I, turning toward the screen, 'come forth and do your duty.'

But he vouchsafed no reply. I pondered a moment in sore perplexity. But once more business hurried me. I determined again to postpone the consideration of this dilemma to my future leisure. With a little trouble we made out to examine the papers without Bartleby, though at every page or two Turkey deferentially dropped his opinion, that this proceeding was quite out of the common; while Nippers, twitching in his chair with a dyspeptic nervousness, ground out, between his set teeth, occasional hissing maledictions against the stubborn oaf behind the screen. And for his (Nippers's) part, this was the first and the last time he would do another man's business without pay.

Meanwhile Bartleby sat in his hermitage, oblivious to everything but his own peculiar business there.

Some days passed, the scrivener being employed upon another lengthy work. His late remarkable conduct led me to regard his ways narrowly. I observed that he never went to dinner; indeed, that he never went anywhere. As yet I had never, of my personal knowledge, known him to be outside of my office. He was a perpetual sentry in the corner. At about eleven o'clock though, in the morning, I noticed that Ginger Nut would advance toward the opening in Bartleby's screen, as if silently beckoned thither by a gesture invisible to me where I sat. The boy would then leave the office, jingling a few pence, and reappear with a handful of ginger-nuts, which he delivered in the hermitage, receiving two of the cakes for his trouble.

He lives, then, on ginger-nuts, thought I; never eats a dinner, properly speaking; he must be a vegetarian, then; but no; he never eats even vegetables, he eats nothing but ginger-nuts. My mind then ran on in reveries concerning the probable effects upon the human constitution of living entirely on ginger-nuts. Ginger-nuts are so called, because they contain ginger as one of their peculiar constituents, and the final flavouring one. Now, what was ginger? A hot, spicy thing. Was Bartleby hot and spicy? Not at all. Ginger, then, had no effect upon Bartleby. Probably he preferred it should have none.

Nothing so aggravates an earnest person as a passive resistance. If the individual so resisted be of a not inhumane temper, and the resisting one perfectly harmless in his passivity, then, in the better moods of the former, he will endeavour charitably to construe to his imagination what proves impossible to be solved by his judgment. Even so, for the most part, I regarded Bartleby and his ways. Poor fellow! thought I, he means no mischief; it is plain he intends no insolence; his aspect sufficiently evinces that his eccentricities are involuntary. He is useful to me. I can get along with him. If I turn him away, the chances are he will fall in with some less-indulgent employer, and then he will be rudely treated, and perhaps driven forth miserably to starve. Yes. Here I can cheaply purchase a delicious self-approval. To befriend Bartleby; to humour him in his strange wilfulness, will cost me little or nothing, while I lay up in my soul what will eventually prove a sweet morsel for my conscience. But this mood was not invariable with me. The passiveness of Bartleby sometimes irritated me. I felt strangely goaded on to encounter him in new opposition—to elicit some angry spark from him answerable to my own. But, indeed, I might as well have essayed to strike fire with my knuckles against a bit of Windsor soap. But one afternoon the evil impulse in me mastered me, and the following little scene ensued:—

'Bartleby,' said I, 'when those papers are all copied, I will compare them with you.'

'I would prefer not to.'

'How? Surely you do not mean to persist in that mulish vagary?'

No answer.

I threw open the folding-doors near by, and, turning upon Turkey and Nippers, exclaimed:

'Bartleby a second time says, he won't examine his papers. What do you think of it, Turkey?'

It was afternoon, be it remembered. Turkey sat glowing like a brass boiler; his bald head steaming; his hands reeling among his blotted papers.

'Think of it?' roared Turkey; 'I think I'll just step behind his screen, and black his eyes for him!'

So saying, Turkey rose to his feet and threw his arms into a pugilistic position. He was hurrying away to make good his promise, when I detained him, alarmed at the effect of incautiously rousing Turkey's combativeness after dinner.

'Sit down, Turkey,' said I, 'and hear what Nippers has to say. What do you think of it, Nippers? Would I not be justified in immediately dismissing Bartleby?'

'Excuse me, that is for you to decide, sir. I think his conduct quite unusual, and, indeed, unjust, as regards Turkey and myself. But it may only be a passing whim.'

'Ah,' exclaimed I, 'you have strangely changed your mind, then—you speak very gently of him now.'

'All beer,' cried Turkey; 'gentleness is effects of beer—Nippers and I dined together to-day. You see how gentle *I* am, sir. Shall I go and black his eyes?'

'You refer to Bartleby, I suppose. No, not to-day, Turkey,' I replied; 'pray, put up your fists.'

I closed the doors, and again advanced toward Bartleby. I felt additional incentives tempting me to my fate. I burned to be rebelled against again. I remembered that Bartleby never left the office.

'Bartleby,' said I, 'Ginger Nut is away; just step around to the Post Office, won't you? (it was but a three minutes' walk), and see if there is anything for me.'

'I would prefer not to.'

'You *will* not?'

'I *prefer* not.'

I staggered to my desk, and sat there in a deep study. My blind inveteracy returned. Was there any other thing in which I could procure myself to be ignominiously repulsed by this lean, penniless wight?—my hired clerk? What added thing is there, perfectly reasonable, that he will be sure to refuse to do?

'Bartleby!'

No answer.

'Bartleby,' in a louder tone.

No answer.

'Bartleby,' I roared.

Like a very ghost, agreeably to the laws of magical invocation, at the third summons, he appeared at the entrance of his hermitage.

'Go to the next room, and tell Nippers to come to me.'

'I prefer not to,' he respectfully and slowly said, and mildly disappeared.

'Very good, Bartleby,' said I, in a quiet sort of serenely-severe self-possessed tone, intimating the unalterable purpose of some terrible retribution very close at hand. At the moment I half intended something of the kind. But upon the whole, as it was drawing toward my dinner-hour, I thought it best to put on my hat and walk home for the day, suffering much from perplexity and distress of mind.

Shall I acknowledge it? The conclusion of this whole business was, that it soon became a fixed fact of my chambers, that a pale young scrivener, by the name of Bartleby, had a desk there; that he copied for me at the usual rate of four cents a folio (one hundred words); but he was permanently exempt from examining the work done by him, that duty being transferred to Turkey and Nippers, out of compliment, doubtless, to their superior acuteness; moreover, said Bartleby was never, on any account, to be dispatched on the most trivial errand of any sort; and that even if entreated to take upon him such a matter, it was generally understood that he would 'prefer not to'—in other words, that he would refuse point-blank.

As days passed on, I became considerably reconciled to Bartleby. His steadiness, his freedom from all dissipation, his incessant industry (except when he chose to throw himself into a standing revery behind his screen), his great stillness, his unalterableness of demeanour under all circumstances, made him a valuable acquisition. One prime thing was this—*he was always there*—first in the morning, continually through the day, and the last at night. I had a singular confidence in his honesty. I felt my most precious papers perfectly safe in his hands. Sometimes, to be sure, I could not, for the very soul of me, avoid falling into sudden spasmodic passions with him. For it was exceeding difficult to bear in mind all the time those strange peculiarities, privileges, and unheard-of exemptions, forming the tacit stipulations on Bartleby's part under which he remained in my office. Now and then, in the eagerness of dispatching pressing business, I would inadvertently summon Bartleby, in a short, rapid tone, to put his finger, say, on the incipient tie of a bit of red tape with which I was about compressing some papers. Of course, from behind the screen the usual answer, 'I prefer not to,' was sure to come; and then, how could a human creature, with the common infirmities of our nature, refrain from bitterly exclaiming upon such perverseness—such unreasonableness. However, every added repulse of this sort which I received only tended to lessen the probability of my repeating the inadvertence.

Here it must be said, that according to the custom of most legal gentle-men occupying chambers in densely populated law-buildings, there were several keys to my door. One was kept by a woman residing in the attic, which person weekly scrubbed and daily swept and dusted my apartments. Another was kept by Turkey for convenience sake. The third I sometimes carried in my own pocket. The fourth I knew not who had.

Now, one Sunday morning I happened to go to Trinity Church, to hear a celebrated preacher, and finding myself rather early on the ground I thought I would walk round to my chambers for a while. Luckily I had my key with me; but upon applying it to the lock, I found it resisted by some-thing inserted from the inside. Quite surprised, I called out; when to my consternation a key was turned from within; and thrusting his lean visage at me, and holding the door ajar, the apparition of Bartleby appeared, in his shirt-sleeves, and otherwise in a strangely tattered dishabille, saying quietly that he was sorry, but he was deeply engaged just then, and—preferred not admitting me at present. In a brief word or two, he moreover added, that perhaps I had better walk round the block two or three times, and by that time he would probably have concluded his affairs.

Now, the utterly unsurmised appearance of Bartleby, tenanting my law-chambers of a Sunday morning, with his cadaverously gentlemanly noncha-lance, yet withal firm and self-possessed, had such a strange effect upon me, that incontinently I slunk away from my own door, and did as desired. But not without sundry twinges of impotent rebellion against the mild effrontery of this unaccountable scrivener. Indeed, it was his wonderful mildness chiefly, which not only disarmed me, but unmanned me as it were. For I consider that one, for the time, is a sort of unmanned when he tranquilly permits his hired clerk to dictate to him, and order him away from his own premises. Furthermore, I was full of uneasiness as to what Bartleby could possibly be doing in my office in his shirt-sleeves, and in an otherwise dismantled condition of a Sunday morning. Was anything amiss going on? Nay, that was out of the question. It was not to be thought of for a moment that Bartleby was an immoral person. But what could he be doing there?—copying? Nay again, whatever might be his eccentricities, Bartleby was an eminently decorous person. He would be the last man to sit down to his desk in any state approaching to nudity. Besides, it was Sunday; and there was something about Bartleby that forbade the supposition that he would by any secular occupation violate the proprieties of the day.

Nevertheless, my mind was not pacified; and full of a restless curiosity, at last I returned to the door. Without hindrance I inserted my key, opened it, and entered. Bartleby was not to be seen. I looked round anxiously, peeped behind his screen; but it was very plain that he was gone. Upon more closely examining the place, I surmised that for an indefinite period Bartleby must have ate, dressed, and slept in my office, and that, too, without plate, mirror, or bed. The cushioned seat of a rickety old sofa in one corner bore the faint impress of a lean, reclining form. Rolled away under his desk, I found a blanket; under the empty grate a blacking box and brush; on a chair, a tin basin, with soap and a ragged towel; in a newspaper a few crumbs of ginger-nuts and a morsel of cheese. Yes, thought I, it is evident enough that Bartleby has been making his home here, keeping bachelor's hall all by himself. Immediately then the thought came sweeping across me, what miserable friendlessness and loneliness are here revealed! His poverty is great; but his solitude, how horrible! Think of it. Of a Sunday, Wall Street is deserted as Petra; and every night of every day it is an emptiness. This building, too, which of week-days hums with industry and life, at nightfall echoes with sheer vacancy, and all through Sunday is forlorn. And here Bartleby makes his home; sole spectator of a solitude which he has seen all-populous—a sort of innocent and transformed Marius brooding among the ruins of Carthage!

For the first time in my life a feeling of overpowering stinging melancholy seized me. Before, I had never experienced aught but a not unpleasing sadness. The bond of a common humanity now drew me irresistibly to gloom. A fraternal melancholy! For both I and Bartleby were sons of Adam. I remembered the bright silks and sparkling faces I had seen that day, in gala trim, swan-like sailing down the Mississippi of Broadway; and I contrasted them with the pallid copyist, and thought to myself, Ah, happiness courts the light, so we deem the world is gay; but misery hides aloof, so we deem that misery there is none. These sad fancyings—chimeras, doubtless, of a sick and silly brain—led on to other and more special thoughts, concerning the eccentricities of Bartleby. Presentiments of strange discoveries hovered round me. The scrivener's pale form appeared to me laid out, among uncaring strangers, in its shivering winding-sheet.

Suddenly I was attracted by Bartleby's closed desk, the key in open sight left in the lock.

I mean no mischief, seek the gratification of no heartless curiosity, thought I; besides, the desk is mine, and its contents, too, so I will make bold to look within. Everything was methodically arranged, the papers smoothly placed. The pigeon-holes were deep, and removing the files of documents, I groped into their recesses. Presently I felt something there, and dragged it out. It was an old bandanna handkerchief, heavy and knotted. I opened it, and saw it was a savings-bank.

I now recalled all the quiet mysteries which I had noted in the man. I remembered that he never spoke but to answer; that, though at intervals he had considerable time to himself, yet I had never seen him reading—no, not even a newspaper; that for long periods he would stand looking out, at his pale window behind the screen, upon the dead brick wall; I was quite sure he never visited any refectory or eating-house; while his pale face clearly indicated that he never drank beer like Turkey, or tea and coffee even, like other men; that he never went anywhere in particular that I could learn; never went out for a walk, unless, indeed, that was the case at present; that he had declined telling who he was, or whence he came, or whether he had any relatives in the world; that though so thin and pale, he never complained of ill health. And more than all, I remembered a certain unconscious air of pallid—how shall I call it?—of pallid haughtiness, say, or rather an austere reserve about him, which had positively awed me into my tame compliance with his eccentricities, when I had feared to ask him to do the slightest incidental thing for me, even though I might know, from his long-continued motionlessness, that behind his screen he must be standing in one of those dead-wall reveries of his.

Revolving all these things, and coupling them with the recently discovered fact, that he made my office his constant abiding-place and home, and not forgetful of his morbid moodiness; revolving all these things, a prudential feeling began to steal over me. My first emotions had been those of pure melancholy and sincerest pity; but just in proportion as the forlornness of Bartleby grew and grew to my imagination, did that same melancholy merge into fear, that pity into repulsion. So true it is, and so terrible, too, that up to a certain point the thought or sight of misery enlists our best affections; but, in certain special cases, beyond that point it does not. They err who would assert that invariably this is owing to the inherent selfishness of the human heart. It rather proceeds from a certain hopelessness of remedying excessive and organic ill. To a sensitive being, pity is not seldom pain. And when at last it is perceived that such pity cannot lead to effectual succour, commonsense bids the soul be rid of it. What I saw that morning persuaded me that the scrivener was the victim of innate and incurable disorder. I might give alms to his body; but his body did not pain him; it was his soul that suffered, and his soul I could not reach.

I did not accomplish the purpose of going to Trinity Church that morning. Somehow, the things I had seen disqualified me for the time from church-going. I walked homeward, thinking what I would do with Bartleby. Finally, I resolved upon this—I would put certain calm questions to him the next morning, touching his history, etc., and if he declined to answer them openly and unreservedly (and I supposed he would prefer not), then to give him a twenty-dollar bill over and above whatever I might owe him, and tell him his services were no longer required; but that if in any other way I could assist him, I would be happy to do so, especially if he desired to return to his native place, wherever that might be, I would willingly help to defray the expenses. Moreover, if, after reaching home, he found himself at any time in want of aid, a letter from him would be sure of a reply.

The next morning came.

'Bartleby,' said I, gently calling to him behind his screen.

No reply.

'Bartleby,' said I, in a still gentler tone, 'come here; I am not going to ask you to do anything you would prefer not to do—I simply wish to speak to you.'

Upon this he noiselessly slid into view.

'Will you tell me, Bartleby, where you were born?'

'I would prefer not to.'

'Will you tell me *anything* about yourself?'

'I would prefer not to.'

'But what reasonable objection can you have to speak to me? I feel friendly toward you.'

He did not look at me while I spoke, but kept his glance fixed upon my bust of Cicero, which, as I then sat, was directly behind me, some six inches above my head.

'What is your answer, Bartleby?' said I, after waiting a considerable time for a reply, during which his countenance remained immovable, only there was the faintest conceivable tremor of the white attenuated mouth.

'At present I prefer to give no answer,' he said, and retired into his hermitage.

It was rather weak in me, I confess, but his manner, on this occasion, nettled me. Not only did there seem to lurk in it a certain calm disdain, but his perverseness seemed ungrateful, considering the undeniable good usage and indulgence he had received from me.

Again I sat ruminating what I should do. Mortified as I was at his behaviour, and resolved as I had been to dismiss him when I entered my office, nevertheless I strangely felt something superstitious knocking at my heart, and forbidding me to carry out my purpose, and denouncing me for a villain if I dared to breathe one bitter word against this forlornest of mankind. At last, familiarly drawing my chair behind his screen, I sat down and said: 'Bartleby, never mind, then, about revealing your history; but let me entreat you, as a friend, to comply as far as may be with the usages of this office. Say now, you will help to examine papers to-morrow or next day: in short, say now, that in a day or two you will begin to be a little reasonable:—say so, Bartleby.'

'At present I would prefer not to be a little reasonable,' was his mildly cadaverous reply.

Just then the folding doors opened, and Nippers approached. He seemed suffering from an unusually bad night's rest, induced by severer indigestion than common. He overheard those final words of Bartleby.

'*Prefer not,* eh?' gritted Nippers—'I'd *prefer* him, if I were you, sir,' addressing me—'I'd *prefer* him; I'd give him preferences, the stubborn mule! What is it, sir, pray, that he *prefers* not to do now?'

Bartleby moved not a limb.

'Mr. Nippers,' said I, 'I'd prefer that you would withdraw for the present.'

Somehow, of late, I had got into the way of involuntarily using this word 'prefer' upon all sorts of not exactly suitable occasions. And I trembled to think that my contact with the scrivener had already and seriously affected me in a mental way. And what further and deeper aberration might it not yet produce? This apprehension had not been without efficacy in determining me to summary measures.

As Nippers, looking very sour and sulky, was departing, Turkey blandly and deferentially approached.

'With submission, sir,' said he, 'yesterday I was thinking about Bartleby here, and I think that if he would but prefer to take a quart of good ale every day, it would do much toward mending him, and enabling him to assist in examining his papers.'

'So you have got the word too,' said I, slightly excited.

'With submission, what word, sir,' asked Turkey, respectfully crowding himself into the contracted space behind the screen, and by so doing, making me jostle the scrivener. 'What word, sir?'

'I would prefer to be left alone here,' said Bartleby, as if offended at being mobbed in his privacy.

'*That's* the word, Turkey,' said I—'*that's* it.'

'Oh, *prefer?* oh yes—queer word. I never use it myself. But, sir, as I was saying, if he would but prefer—'

'Turkey,' interrupted I, 'you will please withdraw.'

'Oh certainly, sir, if you prefer that I should.'

As he opened the folding-door to retire, Nippers at his desk caught a glimpse of me, and asked whether I would prefer to have a certain paper copied on blue paper or white. He did not in the least roguishly accent the word prefer. It was plain that it involuntarily rolled from his tongue. I thought to myself, surely I must get rid of a demented man, who already has in some degree turned the tongues, if not the heads of myself and clerks. But I thought it prudent not to break the dismission at once.

The next day I noticed that Bartleby did nothing but stand at his window in his dead-wall revery. Upon asking him why he did not write, he said that he had decided upon doing no more writing.

'Why, how now? what next?' exclaimed I, 'do no more writing?'

'No more.'

'And what is the reason?'

'Do you not see the reason for yourself?' he indifferently replied.

I looked steadfastly at him, and perceived that his eyes looked dull and glazed. Instantly it occurred to me, that his unexampled diligence in copying by his dim window for the first few weeks of his stay with me might have temporarily impaired his vision.

I was touched. I said something in condolence with him. I hinted that of course he did wisely in abstaining from writing for a while; and urged him to embrace that opportunity of taking wholesome exercise in the open air. This, however, he did not do. A few days after this, my other clerks being absent, and being in a great hurry to dispatch certain letters by the mail, I thought that having nothing else earthly to do, Bartleby would surely be less inflexible than usual, and carry these letters to the Post Office. But he blankly declined. So, much to my inconvenience, I went myself.

Still added days went by. Whether Bartleby's eyes improved or not, I could not say. To all appearance, I thought they did. But when I asked him if they did, he vouchsafed no answer. At all events, he would do no copying. At last, in reply to my urgings, he informed me that he had permanently given up copying.

'What!' exclaimed I; 'suppose your eyes should get entirely well—better than ever before—would you not copy then?'

'I have given up copying,' he answered, and slid aside.

He remained as ever, a fixture in my chamber. Nay—if that were possible—he became still more of a fixture than before. What was to be done? He would do nothing in the office; why should he stay there? In plain fact, he had now become a millstone to me, not only useless as a necklace, but afflictive to bear. Yet I was sorry for him. I speak less than truth when I say that, on his own account, he occasioned me uneasiness. If he would but have named a single relative or friend, I would instantly have written, and urged their taking the poor fellow away to some convenient retreat. But he seemed alone, absolutely alone in the universe. A bit of wreck in the mid-Atlantic. At length, necessities connected with my business tyrannised over all other considerations. Decently as I could, I told Bartleby that in six days' time he must unconditionally leave the office. I warned him to take measures, in the interval, for procuring some other abode. I offered to assist him in this endeavour, if he himself would but take the first step toward a removal. 'And when you finally quit me, Bartleby,' added I, 'I shall see that you go not away entirely unprovided. Six days from this hour, remember.'

At the expiration of that period, I peeped behind the screen, and lo! Bartleby was there.

I buttoned up my coat, balanced myself; advanced slowly toward him, touched his shoulder, and said, 'The time has come; you must quit this place; I am sorry for you; here is money; but you must go.'

'I would prefer not,' he replied, with his back still toward me.

'You *must.*'

He remained silent.

Now I had an unbounded confidence in this man's common honesty. He had frequently restored to me sixpences and shillings carelessly dropped upon the floor, for I am apt to be very reckless in such shirt-button affairs. The proceeding, then, which followed will not be deemed extraordinary.

'Bartleby,' said I, 'I owe you twelve dollars on account; here are thirty-two; the odd twenty are yours—Will you take it?' and I handed the bills toward him.

But he made no motion.

'I will leave them here, then,' putting them under a weight on the table. Then taking my hat and cane and going to the door, I tranquilly turned and added—'After you have removed your things from these offices, Bartleby, you will of course lock the door—since everyone is now gone for the day but you—and if you please, slip your key underneath the mat, so that I may have it in the morning. I shall not see you again; so good-bye to you. If, hereafter, in your new place of abode, I can be of any service to you, do not fail to advise me by letter. Good-bye, Bartleby, and fare you well.'

But he answered not a word; like the last column of some ruined temple, he remained standing mute and solitary in the middle of the otherwise deserted room.

As I walked home in a pensive mood, my vanity got the better of my pity. I could not but highly plume myself on my masterly management in getting rid of Bartleby. Masterly I call it, and such it must appear to any dispassionate thinker. The beauty of my procedure seemed to consist in its perfect quietness. There was no vulgar bullying, no bravado of any sort, no choleric hectoring, and striding to and fro across the apartment, jerking out vehement commands for Bartleby to bundle himself off with his beggarly traps. Nothing of the kind. Without loudly bidding Bartleby depart—as an inferior genius might have done—I *assumed* the ground that depart he must; and upon that assumption built all I had to say. The more I thought over my procedure, the more I was charmed with it. Nevertheless, next morning, upon awakening, I had my doubts—I had somehow slept off the fumes of vanity. One of the coolest and wisest hours a man has, is just after he awakes in the morning. My procedure seemed as sagacious as ever—but only in theory. How it would prove in practice—there was the rub. It was truly a beautiful thought to have assumed Bartleby's departure; but, after all, that assumption was simply my own, and none of Bartleby's. The great point was, not whether I had assumed that he would quit me, but whether he would prefer so to do. He was more a man of preferences than assumptions.

After breakfast, I walked down town, arguing the probabilities *pro* and *con.* One moment I thought it would prove a miserable failure, and Bartleby would be found all alive at my office as usual; the next moment it seemed certain that I should find his chair empty. And so I kept veering about. At the corner of Broadway and Canal Street, I saw quite an excited group of people standing in earnest conversation.

'I'll take odds he doesn't,' said a voice as I passed.

'Doesn't go?—done!' said I; 'put up your money.'

I was instinctively putting my hand in my pocket to produce my own, when I remembered that this was an election day. The words I had overheard bore no reference to Bartleby, but to the success or non-success of some candidate for the mayoralty. In my intent frame of mind, I had, as it were, imagined that all Broadway shared in my excitement, and were debating the same question with me. I passed on, very thankful that the uproar of the street screened my momentary absent-mindedness.

As I had intended, I was earlier than usual at my office door. I stood listening for a moment. All was still. He must be gone. I tried the knob. The door was locked. Yes, my procedure had worked to a charm; he indeed must be vanished. Yet a certain melancholy mixed with this: I was almost sorry for my brilliant success. I was fumbling under the door-mat for the key, which Bartleby was to have left there for me, when accidentally my knee knocked against a panel, producing a summoning sound, and in response a voice came to me from within—'Not yet; I am occupied.'

It was Bartleby.

I was thunderstruck. For an instant I stood like the man who, pipe in mouth, was killed one cloudless afternoon long ago in Virginia, by summer lightning; at his own warm open window he was killed, and remained leaning out there upon the dreamy afternoon, till someone touched him, when he fell.

'Not gone!' I murmured at last. But again obeying that wondrous ascendency which the inscrutable scrivener had over me, and from which ascendency, for all my chafing, I could not completely escape, I slowly went downstairs and out into the street, and while walking round the block, considered what I should next do in this unheard-of perplexity. Turn the man out by an actual thrusting I could not; to drive him away by calling him hard names would not do; calling in the police was an unpleasant idea; and yet, permit him to enjoy his cadaverous triumph over me—this, too, I could not think of. What was to be done? or, if nothing could be done, was there anything further that I could *assume* in the matter? Yes, as before I had prospectively assumed that Bartleby would depart, so now I might retrospectively assume that departed he was. In the legitimate carrying out of this assumption, I might enter my office in a great hurry, and pretending not to see Bartleby at all, walk straight against him as if he were air. Such a proceeding would in a singular degree have the appearance of a home-thrust. It was hardly possible that Bartleby could withstand such an application of the doctrine of assumptions. But upon second thoughts the success of the plan seemed rather dubious. I resolved to argue the matter over with him again.

'Bartleby,' said I, entering the office, with a quietly severe expression, 'I am seriously displeased. I am pained, Bartleby. I had thought better of you. I had imagined you of such a gentlemanly organisation, that in any delicate dilemma a slight hint would suffice—in short, an assumption. But it appears I am deceived. Why,' I added, unaffectedly starting, 'you have not even touched that money yet,' pointing to it, just where I had left it the evening previous.

He answered nothing.

'Will you, or will you not, quit me?' I now demanded in a sudden passion, advancing close to him.

'I would prefer *not* to quit you,' he replied, gently emphasising the *not*.

'What earthly right have you to stay here? Do you pay any rent? Do you pay my taxes? Or is this property yours?'

He answered nothing.

'Are you ready to go on and write now? Are your eyes recovered? Could you copy a small paper for me this morning? or help examine a few lines? or step round to the Post Office? In a word, will you do anything at all, to give a colouring to your refusal to depart the premises?'

He silently retired into his hermitage.

I was now in such a state of nervous resentment that I thought it but prudent to check myself at present from further demonstrations. Bartleby and I were alone. I remembered the tragedy of the unfortunate Adams and the still more unfortunate Colt in the solitary office of the latter; and how poor Colt, being dreadfully incensed by Adams, and imprudently permitting himself to get wildly excited, was at unawares hurried into his fatal act—an act which certainly no man could possibly deplore more than the actor himself. Often it had occurred to me in my ponderings upon the subject, that had that altercation taken place in the public street, or at a private residence, it would not have terminated as it did. It was the circumstance of being alone in a solitary office, upstairs, of a building entirely unhallowed by humanising domestic associations—an uncarpeted office, doubtless, of a dusty, haggard sort of appearance—this it must have been, which greatly helped to enhance the irritable desperation of the hapless Colt.

But when this old Adam of resentment rose in me and tempted me concerning Bartleby, I grappled him and threw him. How? Why, simply by recalling the divine injunction: 'A new commandment give I unto you, that ye love one another.' Yes, this it was that saved me. Aside from higher considerations, charity often operates as a vastly wise and prudent principle— a great safeguard to its possessor. Men have committed murder for jealousy's sake, and anger's sake, and hatred's sake, and selfishness' sake, and spiritual pride's sake; but no man, that ever I heard of, ever committed a diabolical murder for sweet charity's sake. Mere self-interest, then, if no better motive can be enlisted, should, especially with high-tempered men, prompt all beings to charity and philanthropy. At any rate, upon the occasion in question, I strove to drown my exasperated feelings toward the scrivener by benevolently construing his conduct. Poor fellow, poor fellow! thought I, he don't mean anything; and besides, he has seen hard times, and ought to be indulged.

I endeavoured, also, immediately to occupy myself, and at the same time to comfort my despondency. I tried to fancy, that in the course of the morning, at such time as might prove agreeable to him, Bartleby, of his own free accord, would emerge from his heritage and take up some decided line of march in the direction of the door. But no. Half-past twelve o'clock came; Turkey began to glow in the face, overturn his inkstand, and become generally obstreperous; Nippers abated down into quietude and courtesy; Ginger Nut munched his noon apple; and Bartleby remained standing at his window in one of his profoundest deadwall reveries. Will it be credited? Ought I to acknowledge it? That afternoon I left the office without saying one further word to him.

Some days now passed, during which, at leisure intervals, I looked a little into 'Edwards on the Will,' and 'Priestley on Necessity.' Under the circumstances, those books induced a salutary feeling. Gradually I slid into the persuasion that these troubles of mine, touching the scrivener, had been all predestinated from eternity, and Bartleby was billeted upon me for some mysterious purpose of an all-wise Providence, which it was not for a mere mortal like me to fathom. Yes, Bartleby, stay there behind your screen, thought I; I shall persecute you no more; you are harmless and noiseless as any of these old chairs; in short, I never feel so private as when I know you are here. At last I see it, I feel it; I penetrate to the predestinated purpose of my life. I am content. Others may have loftier parts to enact; but my mission in this world, Bartleby, is to furnish you with office-room for such period as you may see fit to remain.

I believe that this wise and blessed frame of mind would have continued with me, had it not been for the unsolicited and uncharitable remarks obtruded upon me by my professional friends who visited the rooms. But thus it often is, that the constant friction of illiberal minds wears out at last the best resolves of the more generous. Though to be sure, when I reflected upon it, it was not strange that people entering my office should be struck by the peculiar aspect of the unaccountable Bartleby, and so be tempted to throw out some sinister observations concerning him. Sometimes an attorney, having business with me, and calling at my office, and finding no one but the scrivener there, would undertake to obtain some sort of precise information from him touching my whereabouts; but without heeding his idle talk, Bartleby would remain standing immovable in the middle of the room. So after contemplating him in that position for a time, the attorney would depart, no wiser than he came.

Also, when a reference was going on, and the room full of lawyers and witnesses, and business driving fast, some deeply occupied legal gentleman present, seeing Bartleby wholly unemployed, would request him to run round to his (the legal gentleman's) office and fetch some papers for him. Thereupon, Bartleby would tranquilly decline, and yet remain idle as before. Then the lawyer would give a great stare, and turn to me. And what could I say? At last I was made aware that all through the circle of my professional acquaintance, a whisper of wonder was running round, having reference to the strange creature I kept at my office. This worried me very much. And as the idea came upon me of his possibly turning out a long-lived man, and keep occupying my chambers, and denying my authority; and perplexing my visitors; and scandalising my professional reputation; and casting a general gloom over the premises; keeping soul and body together to the last upon his savings (for doubtless he spent but half a dime a day), and in the end perhaps outlive me, and claim possession of my office by right of his perpetual occupancy: as all these dark anticipations crowded upon me more and more, and my friends continually intruded their relentless remarks upon the apparition in my room; a great change was wrought in me. I resolved to gather all my faculties together, and forever rid me of this intolerable incubus.

Ere revolving any complicated project, however, adapted to this end, I first simply suggested to Bartleby the propriety of his permanent departure. In a calm and serious tone, I commended the idea to his careful and mature consideration. But, having taken three days to meditate upon it, he apprised me, that his original determination remained the same; in short, that he still preferred to abide with me.

What shall I do? I now said to myself, buttoning up my coat to the last button. What shall I do? what ought I to do? what does conscience say I *should* do with this man, or, rather, ghost. Rid myself of him, I must; go, he shall. But how? You will not thrust him, the poor, pale, passive mortal—you will not thrust such a helpless creature out of your door? you will not dishonour yourself by such cruelty? No, I will not, I cannot do that. Rather would I let him live and die here, and then mason up his remains in the wall. What, then, will you do? For all your coaxing, he will not budge. Bribes he leaves under your own paper weight on your table; in short, it is quite plain that he prefers to cling to you.

Then something severe, something unusual must be done. What! surely you will not have him collared by a constable, and commit his innocent pallor to the common jail? And upon what ground could you procure such a thing to be done?—a vagrant, is he? What! he a vagrant, a wanderer, who refuses to budge? It is because he will *not* be a vagrant, then, that you seek to count him *as* a vagrant. That is too absurd. No visible means of support; there I have him. Wrong again: for indubitably he *does* support himself, and that is the only unanswerable proof that any man can show of his possessing the means so to do. No more, then. Since he will not quit me, I must quit him. I will change my offices; I will move elsewhere, and give him fair notice, that if I find him on my new premises I will then proceed against him as a common trespasser.

Acting accordingly, next day I thus addressed him: 'I find these chambers too far from the City Hall; the air is unwholesome. In a word, I propose to remove my offices next week, and shall no longer require your services. I tell you this now, in order that you may seek another place.'

He made no reply, and nothing more was said.

On the appointed day I engaged carts and men, proceeded to my chambers, and, having but little furniture, everything was removed in a few hours. Throughout, the scrivener remained standing behind the screen, which I directed to be removed the last thing. It was withdrawn; and, being folded up like a huge folio, left him the motionless occupant of a naked room. I stood in the entry watching him a moment, while something from within me upbraided me.

I re-entered, with my hand in my pocket—and—and my heart in my mouth.

'Good-bye, Bartleby; I am going—good-bye, and God some way bless you; and take that,' slipping something in his hand. But it dropped upon the floor, and then—strange to say—I tore myself from him whom I had so longed to be rid of.

Established in my new quarters, for a day or two I kept the door locked, and started at every footfall in the passages. When I returned to my rooms, after any little absence, I would pause at the threshold for an instant, and attentively listen ere applying my key. But these fears were needless. Bartleby never came nigh me.

I thought all was going well, when a perturbed-looking stranger visited me, inquiring whether I was the person who had recently occupied rooms at No.————Wall Street.

Full of forebodings, I replied that I was.

'Then, sir,' said the stranger, who proved a lawyer, 'you are responsible for the man you left there. He refuses to do any copying; he refuses to do anything; he says he prefers not to; and he refuses to quit the premises.'

'I am very sorry, sir,' said I, with assumed tranquillity, but an inward tremor, 'but, really, the man you allude to is nothing to me—he is no relation or apprentice of mine, that you should hold me responsible for him.'

'In mercy's name, who is he?'

'I certainly cannot inform you. I know nothing about him. Formerly I employed him as a copyist; but he has done nothing for me now for some time past.'

'I shall settle him, then—good morning, sir.'

Several days passed, and I heard nothing more; and, though I often felt a charitable prompting to call at the place and see poor Bartleby, yet a certain squeamishness, of I know not what, withheld me.

All is over with him, by this time, thought I, at last, when, through another week, no further intelligence reached me. But, coming to my room the day after, I found several persons waiting at my door in a high state of nervous excitement.

'That's the man—here he comes,' cried the foremost one, whom I recognised as the lawyer who had previously called upon me alone.

'You must take him away, sir, at once,' cried a portly person among them, advancing upon me, and whom I knew to be the landlord of No.——Wall Street. 'These gentlemen, my tenants, cannot stand it any longer; Mr. B——,' pointing to the lawyer, 'has turned him out of his room, and he now persists in haunting the building generally, sitting upon the banisters of the stairs by day, and sleeping in the entry by night. Everybody is concerned; clients are leaving the offices; some fears are entertained of a mob; something you must do, and that without delay.'

Aghast at this torrent, I fell back before it, and would fain have locked myself in my new quarters. In vain I persisted that Bartleby was nothing to me—no more than to anyone else. In vain—I was the last person known to have anything to do with him, and they held me to the terrible account. Fearful, then, of being exposed in the papers (as one person present obscurely threatened), I considered the matter, and, at length, said, that if the lawyer would give me a confidential interview with the scrivener, in his (the lawyer's) own room, I would, that afternoon, strive my best to rid them of the nuisance they complained of.

Going upstairs to my old haunt, there was Bartleby silently sitting upon the banister at the landing.

'What are you doing here, Bartleby?' said I.

'Sitting upon the banister,' he mildly replied.

I motioned him into the lawyer's room, who then left us.

'Bartleby,' said I, 'are you aware that you are the cause of great tribulation to me, by persisting in occupying the entry after being dismissed from the office?'

No answer.

'Now one of two things must take place. Either you must do something, or something must be done to you. Now what sort of business would you like to engage in? Would you like to re-engage in copying for someone?'

'No; I would prefer not to make any change.'

'Would you like a clerkship in a dry-goods store?'

'There is too much confinement about that. No, I would not like a clerkship; but I am not particular.'

'Too much confinement,' I cried, 'why, you keep yourself confined all the time!'

'I would prefer not to take a clerkship,' he rejoined, as if to settle that little item at once.

'How would a bar-tender's business suit you? There is no trying of the eyesight in that.'

'I would not like it at all; though, as I said before, I am not particular.'

His unwonted wordiness inspirited me. I returned to the charge.

'Well, then, would you like to travel through the country collecting bills for the merchants? That would improve your health.'

'No, I would prefer to be doing something else.'

'How, then, would going as a companion to Europe, to entertain some young gentleman with your conversation—how would that suit you?'

'Not at all. It does not strike me that there is anything definite about that. I like to be stationary. But I am not particular.'

'Stationary you shall be, then,' I cried, now losing all patience, and, for the first time in all my exasperating connection with him, fairly flying into a passion. 'If you do not go away from these premises before night, I shall feel bound—indeed, I *am* bound—to—to quit the premises myself!' I rather absurdly concluded, knowing not with what possible threat to try to frighten his immobility into compliance. Despairing of all further efforts, I was precipitately leaving him, when a final thought occurred to me—one which had not been wholly unindulged before.

'Bartleby,' said I, in the kindest tone I could assume under such exciting circumstances, 'will you go home with me now—not to my office, but my dwelling—and remain there till we can conclude upon some convenient arrangement for you at our leisure? Come, let us start now, right away.'

'No; at present I would prefer not to make any change at all.'

I answered nothing; but, effectually dodging everyone by the suddenness and rapidity of my flight, rushed from the building, ran up Wall Street toward Broadway, and, jumping into the first omnibus, was soon removed from pursuit. As soon as tranquillity returned, I distinctly perceived that I had now done all that I possibly could, both in respect to the demands of the landlord and his tenants, and with regard to my own desire and sense of duty, to benefit Bartleby, and shield him from rude persecution. I now strove to be entirely carefree and quiescent; and my conscience justified me in the attempt; though, indeed, it was not so successful as I could have wished. So fearful was I of being again hunted out by the incensed landlord and his exasperated tenants, that, surrendering my business to Nippers, for a few days, I drove about the upper part of the town and through the suburbs, in my rockaway; crossed over to Jersey City and Hoboken, and paid fugitive visits to Manhattanville and Astoria. In fact, I almost lived in my rockaway for the time.

When again I entered my office, lo, a note from the landlord lay upon the desk. I opened it with trembling hands. It informed me that the writer had sent to the police, and had Bartleby removed to the Tombs as a vagrant. Moreover, since I knew more about him than anyone else, he wished me to appear at that place, and make a suitable statement of the facts. These tidings had a conflicting effect upon me. At first I was indignant; but, at last, almost approved. The landlord's energetic, summary disposition had led him to adopt a procedure which I do not think I would have decided upon myself; and yet, as a last resort, under such peculiar circumstances, it seemed the only plan.

As I afterward learned, the poor scrivener, when told that he must be conducted to the Tombs, offered not the slightest obstacle, but, in his pale, unmoving way, silently acquiesced.

Some of the compassionate and curious bystanders joined the party; and headed by one of the constables arm in arm with Bartleby, the silent procession filed its way through all the noise, and heat, and joy of the roaring thoroughfares at noon.

The same day I received the note, I went to the Tombs, or, to speak more properly, the Halls of Justice. Seeking the right officer, I stated the purpose of my call, and was informed that the individual I described was, indeed, within. I then assured the functionary that Bartleby was a perfectly honest man, and greatly to be compassionated, however unaccountably eccentric. I narrated all I knew, and closed by suggesting the idea of letting him remain in as indulgent confinement as possible, till something less harsh might be done—though, indeed, I hardly knew what. At all events, if nothing else could be decided upon, the almshouse must receive him. I then begged to have an interview.

Being under no disgraceful charge, and quite serene and harmless in all his ways, they had permitted him freely to wander about the prison, and, especially, in the enclosed grass-platted yards thereof. And so I found him there, standing all alone in the quietest of the yards, his face toward a high wall, while all around, from the narrow slits of the jail windows, I thought I saw peering out upon him the eyes of murderers and thieves.

'Bartleby!'

'I know you,' he said, without looking round—'and I want nothing to say to you.'

'It was not I that brought you here, Bartleby,' said I, keenly pained at his implied suspicion. 'And to you, this should not be so vile a place. Nothing reproachful attaches to you by being here. And see, it is not so sad a place as one might think. Look, there is the sky, and here is the grass.'

'I know where I am,' he replied, but would say nothing more, and so I left him.

As I entered the corridor again, a broad meat-like man, in an apron, accosted me, and, jerking his thumb over his shoulder, said, 'Is that your friend?'

'Yes.'

'Does he want to starve? If he does, let him live on the prison fare, that's all.'

'Who are you?' asked I, not knowing what to make of such an unofficially speaking person in such a place.

'I am the grub-man. Such gentlemen as have friends here, hire me to provide them with something good to eat.'

'Is this so?' said I, turning to the turnkey.

He said it was.

'Well, then,' said I, slipping some silver into the grub-man's hands (for so they called him), 'I want you to give particular attention to my friend there; let him have the best dinner you can get. And you must be as polite to him as possible.'

'Introduce me, will you?' said the grub-man, looking at me with an expression which seemed to say he was all impatience for an opportunity to give a specimen of his breeding.

Thinking it would prove of benefit to the scrivener, I acquiesced; and, asking the grub-man his name, went up with him to Bartleby.

'Bartleby, this is a friend; you will find him very useful to you.'

'Your sarvant, sir, your sarvant,' said the grub-man, making a low salutation behind his apron. 'Hope you find it pleasant here, sir; nice grounds—cool apartments—hope you'll stay with us some time—try to make it agreeable. What will you have for dinner to-day?'

'I prefer not to dine to-day,' said Bartleby, turning away. 'It would disagree with me; I am unused to dinners.' So saying, he slowly moved to the other side of the enclosure, and took up a position fronting the dead-wall.

'How's this?' said the grub-man, addressing me with a stare of astonishment. 'He's odd, ain't he?'

'I think he is a little deranged,' said I sadly.

'Deranged? deranged is it? Well, now, upon my word, I thought that friend of yourn was a gentleman forger; they are always pale and genteel-like, them forgers. I can't help pity 'em—can't help it, sir. Did you know Monroe Edwards?' he added touchingly, and paused. Then, laying his hand piteously on my shoulder, sighed, 'he died of consumption at Sing-Sing. So you weren't acquainted with Monroe?'

'No, I was never socially acquainted with any forgers. But I cannot stop longer. Look to my friend yonder. You will not lose by it. I will see you again.'

Some few days after this, I again obtained admission to the Tombs, and went through the corridors in quest of Bartleby; but without finding him.

'I saw him coming from his cell not long ago,' said a turnkey, 'maybe he's gone to loiter in the yards.'

So I went in that direction.

'Are you looking for the silent man?' said another turnkey, passing me. 'Yonder he lies—sleeping in the yard there. 'Tis not twenty minutes since I saw him lie down.'

The yard was entirely quiet. It was not accessible to the common prisoners. The surrounding walls, of amazing thickness, kept off all sounds behind them. The Egyptian character of the masonry weighed upon me with its gloom. But a soft imprisoned turf grew under foot. The heart of the eternal pyramids, it seemed, wherein, by some strange magic, through the clefts, grass-seed, dropped by birds, had sprung.

Strangely huddled at the base of the wall, his knees drawn up, and lying on his side, his head touching the cold stones, I saw the wasted Bartleby. But nothing stirred. I paused; then went close up to him; stooped over, and saw that his dim eyes were open; otherwise he seemed profoundly sleeping. Something prompted me to touch him. I felt his hand, when a tingling shiver ran up my arm and down my spine to my feet.

The round face of the grub-man peered upon me now. 'His dinner is ready. Won't he dine to-day, either? Or does he live without dining?'

'Lives without dining,' said I, and closed the eyes.

'Eh!—He's asleep, ain't he?'

'With kings and counsellors,' murmured I.

THERE would seem little need for proceeding further in this history. Imagination will readily supply the meagre recital of poor Bartleby's interment. But, ere parting with the reader, let me say, that if this little narrative has sufficiently interested him, to awaken curiosity as to who Bartleby was, and what manner of life he led prior to the present narrator's making his acquaintance, I can only reply, that in such curiosity I fully share, but am wholly unable to gratify it. Yet here I hardly know whether I should divulge one little item of rumour, which came to my ear a few months after the scrivener's decease. Upon what basis it rested I could never ascertain; and hence, how true it is I cannot now tell. But, inasmuch as this vague report has not been without a certain suggestive interest to me, however sad, it may prove the same with some others; and so I will briefly mention it. The report was this: that Bartleby had been a subordinate clerk in the Dead Letter Office at Washington, from which he had been suddenly removed by a change in the administration. When I think over this rumour, hardly can I express the emotions which seize me. Dead letters! does it not sound like dead men? Conceive a man by nature and misfortune prone to a pallid hopelessness, can any business seem more fitted to heighten it than that of continually handling these dead letters, and assorting them for the flames? For by the cartload they are annually burned. Sometimes from out the folded paper the pale clerk takes a ring—the finger it was meant for, perhaps, moulders in the grave; a bank-note sent in swiftest charity—he whom it would relieve, nor eats nor hungers any more; pardon for those who died despairing; hope for those who died unhoping; good tidings for those who died stifled by unrelieved calamities. On errands of life, these letters speed to death.

Ah, Bartleby! Ah, humanity!

(1853)

Henry James

(1 8 4 3 - 1 9 1 6)

Novelist, short-story writer, playwright, critic, essayist—Henry James's prolific career serves as a bridge between Victorian and modern fiction. He published major literary works as early as 1876, when George Eliot and Lord Tennyson were still writing, and as late as 1916, when James Joyce was writing *Ulysses* and Ezra Pound ruled literary London. Born in New York City of a wealthy family in 1843, James and his brother William, the famous philosopher and psychologist, were privately tutored in London, Geneva, Paris, and Bonn. James was given an opportunity to contrast American and European cultures. After a brief time at Harvard Law School, he turned his interests to literature. Shortly after the publication of his first collection of stories, *A Passionate Pilgrim* (1875), he settled permanently in London and eventually became a British citizen in 1915. James published a novel or volume of stories or essays almost every year for 40 years. He became increasingly famous, and was the undisputed dean of the London social circuit until he died of a stroke in 1916.

Influenced by French and Russian realists such as Flaubert and Turgenev, James is noted for his sensitive and realistically complex portrayal of character, his formally intricate and allusive style, and his subtle ambiguities of theme. He was devoted to developing a single, consistent point of view, and his late novels explored the problems of perspective and its role in perceiving others clearly. Uneasy with omniscient narration, James used a character as his narrator; and by a careful scenic progression, his narrative unfolded as it presented itself to the psyche of the narrator. His famous periodic sentences arose out of the necessity of modulating, focusing, and qualifying the intricate realities of that narrator's perceptions. James worked with one central theme: the contrast between American and European cultures. Despite excesses of style in his later works, and despite H. L. Mencken's valid observation that he "would have been vastly improved as a novelist by a few whiffs from the Chicago stockyards," James is a master of the formally structured, psychologically realistic novel.

James published some 64 volumes, including 20 novels and more than one hundred short stories, plays, essays, and books of travel. His major novels include *The American* (1877), *Daisy Miller* (1879), *The Portrait of a Lady* (1881), *What Maisie Knew* (1897), *The Turn of the Screw* (1898), *The Wings of the Dove* (1902), *The Ambassadors* (1903), and *The Golden Bowl* (1904).

HENRY JAMES

The Tree of Knowledge

I

IT was one of the secret opinions, such as we all have, of Peter Brench that his main success in life would have consisted in his never having committed himself about the work, as it was called, of his friend, Morgan Mallow. This was a subject on which it was, to the best of his belief, impossible, with veracity, to quote him, and it was nowhere on record that he had, in the connection, on any occasion and in any embarrassment, either lied or spoken the truth. Such a triumph had its honour even for a man of other triumphs—a man who had reached fifty, who had escaped marriage, who had lived within his means, who had been in love with Mrs Mallow for years without breathing it, and who, last not least, had judged himself once for all. He had so judged himself in fact that he felt an extreme and general humility to be his proper portion; yet there was nothing that made him think so well of his parts as the course he had steered so often through the shallows just mentioned. It became thus a real wonder that the friends in whom he had most confidence were just those with whom he had most reserves. He couldn't tell Mrs Mallow—or at least he supposed, excellent man, he couldn't—that she was the one beautiful reason he had never married; any more than he could tell her husband that the sight of the multiplied marbles in that gentleman's studio was an affliction of which even time had never blunted the edge. His victory, however, as I have intimated, in regard to these productions, was not simply in his not having let it out that he deplored them; it was, remarkably, in his not having kept it in by anything else.

The whole situation, among these good people, was verily a marvel, and there was probably not such another for a long way from the spot that engages us—the point at which the soft declivity of Hampstead began at that time to confess in broken accents to St John's Wood. He despised Mallow's statutes and adored Mallow's wife, and yet was distinctly fond of Mallow, to whom, in turn, he was equally dear. Mrs Mallow rejoiced in the statues—though she preferred, when pressed, the busts; and if she was visibly attached to Peter Brench it was because of his affection for Morgan. Each loved the other, moreover, for the love borne in each case to Lancelot, whom the Mallows respectively cherished as their only child and whom the friend of their fireside identified as the third—but decidedly the handsomest—of his godsons. Already in the old years it had come to that—that no one, for such a relation, could possibly have occurred to any of them, even to the baby itself, but Peter. There was luckily a certain independence, of the pecuniary sort, all round: the Master could never otherwise have spent his solemn *Wanderjahre*[1] in Florence and Rome and continued, by the Thames as well as by the Arno and the Tiber, to add unpurchased group to group and model, for what was too apt to prove in the event mere love, fancy-heads of celebrities either too busy or too buried—too much of the age or too little of it—to sit. Neither could Peter, lounging in almost daily, have found time to keep the whole complicated tradition so alive by his presence. He was massive, but mild, the depositary of these mysteries—large and loose and ruddy and curly, with deep tones, deep eyes, deep pockets, to say nothing of the habit of long pipes, soft hats and brownish, greyish, weather-faded clothes, apparently always the same.

He had "written," it was known, but had never spoken—never spoken, in particular, of that; and he had the air (since, as was believed, he continued to write) of keeping it up in order to have something more—as if he had not, at the worst, enough—to be silent about. Whatever his air, at any rate, Peter's occasional unmentioned prose and verse were quite truly the result of an impulse to maintain the purity of his taste by establishing still more firmly the right relation of fame to feebleness. The little green door of his domain was in a garden-wall on which the stucco was cracked and stained, and in the small detached villa behind it everything was old, the furniture, the servants, the books, the prints, the habits and the new improvements. The Mallows, at Carrara Lodge, were within ten minutes, and the studio there was on their little land, to which they had added, in their happy faith, to build it. This was the good fortune, if it was not the ill, of her having brought him, in marriage, a portion that put them in a manner at their ease and enabled them thus, on their side, to keep it up. And they did keep it up—they always had—the infatuated sculptor and his wife, for whom nature had refined on the impossible by relieving them of the sense of the difficult. Morgan had, at all events, everything of the sculptor but the spirit of Phidias—the brown velvet, the becoming *beretto,* the "plastic" presence, the fine fingers, the beautiful accent in Italian and the old Italian factotum. He seemed to make up for everything when he addressed Egidio with the "tu" and waved him to turn one of the rotary pedestals of which the place was full. They were tremendous Italians at Carrara Lodge, and the secret of the part played by this fact in Peter's life was, in a large degree, that it gave him, sturdy Briton that he was, just the amount of "going abroad" he could bear. The Mallows were all his Italy, but it was in a measure for Italy he liked them. His one worry was that Lance—to which they had shortened his godson—was, in spite of a public school, perhaps a shade too Italian. Morgan, meanwhile, looked like somebody's flattering idea of somebody's own person as expressed in the great room provided at the Uffizi museum for Portraits of Artists by Themselves. The Master's sole regret that he had not been born

---

[1] A year of travel before settling down to one's vocation.

rather to the brush than to the chisel sprang from his wish that he might have contributed to that collection.

It appeared, with time, at any rate, to be to the brush that Lance had been born; for Mrs Mallow, one day when the boy was turning twenty, broke it to their friend, who shared, to the last delicate morsel, their problems and pains, that it seemed as if nothing would really do but that he should embrace the career. It had been impossible longer to remain blind to the fact that he gained no glory at Cambridge, where Brench's own college had, for a year, tempered its tone to him as for Brench's own sake. Therefore why renew the vain form of preparing him for the impossible? The impossible—it had become clear—was that he should be anything but an artist.

"Oh dear, dear!" said poor Peter.

"Don't you believe in it?" asked Mrs Mallow, who still, at more than forty, had her violet velvet eyes, her creamy satin skin and her silken chestnut hair.

"Believe in what?"

"Why, in Lance's passion."

"I don't know what you mean by 'believing in it.' I've never been unaware, certainly, of his disposition, from his earliest time, to daub and draw; but I confess I've hoped it would burn out."

"But why should it," she sweetly smiled, "with his wonderful heredity? Passion is passion—though of course, indeed, you, dear Peter, know nothing of that. Has the Master's ever burned out?"

Peter looked off a little and, in his familiar, formless way, kept up for a moment a sound between a smothered whistle and a subdued hum. "Do you think he's going to be another Master?"

She seemed scarce prepared to go that length, yet she had, on the whole, a most marvellous trust. "I know what you mean by that. Will it be a career to incur the jealousies and provoke the machinations that have been at times almost too much for his father? Well—say it may be, since nothing but clap-trap, in these dreadful days, *can,* it would seem, make its way, and since, with the curse of refinement and distinction, one may easily find one's self begging one's bread. Put it at the worst—say he *has* the misfortune to wing his flight further than the vulgar taste of his stupid countrymen can follow. Think, all the same, of the happiness—the same that the Master has had. He'll *know.* "

Peter looked rueful. "Ah, but *what* will he know?"

"Quiet joy!" cried Mrs Mallow, quite impatient and turning away.

II

HE had of course, before long, to meet the boy himself on it and to hear that, practically, everything was settled. Lance was not to go up again, but to go instead to Paris where, since the die was cast, he would find the best advantages. Peter had always felt that he must be taken as he was, but had never perhaps found him so much as he was as on this occasion. "You chuck Cambridge then altogether? Doesn't that seem rather a pity?"

Lance would have been like his father, to his friend's sense, had he had less humour, and like his mother had he had more beauty. Yet it was a good middle way, for Peter, that, in the modern manner, he was, to the eye, rather the young stockbroker than the young artist. The youth reasoned that it was a question of time—there was such a mill to go through, such an awful lot to learn. He had talked with fellows and had judged. "One has got, to-day," he said, "don't you see? to know."

His interlocutor, at this, gave a groan. "Oh, hang it, *don't* know!"

Lance wondered. " 'Don't'? Then what's the use——?"

"The use of what?"

"Why, of anything. Don't you think I've talent?"

Peter smoked away, for a little, in silence; then went on: "It isn't knowledge, it's ignorance that—as we've been beautifully told—is bliss."

"Don't you think I've talent?" Lance repeated.

Peter, with his trick of queer, kind demonstrations, passed his arm round his godson and held him a moment. "How do I know?"

"Oh," said the boy, "if it's your own ignorance you're defending——!"

Again, for a pause, on the sofa, his godfather smoked. "It isn't. I've the misfortune to be omniscient."

"Oh, well," Lance laughed again, "if you know *too* much——!"

"That's what I do, and why I'm so wretched."

Lance's gaiety grew. "Wretched? Come, I say!"

"But I forgot," his companion went on—"you're not to know about that. It would indeed, for you too, make the too much. Only I'll tell you what I'll do." And Peter got up from the sofa. "If you'll go up again, I'll pay your way at Cambridge."

Lance stared, a little rueful in spite of being still more amused. "Oh, Peter! You disapprove so of Paris?"

"Well, I'm afraid of it."

"Ah, I see."

"No, you don't see—yet. But you will—that is you would. And you mustn't."

The young man thought more gravely. "But one's innocence, already——"

"Is considerably damaged? Ah, that won't matter," Peter persisted—"we'll patch it up here."

"Here? Then you want me to stay at home?"

Peter almost confessed to it. "Well, we're so right—we four together—just as we are. We're so safe. Come, don't spoil it."

The boy, who had turned to gravity, turned from this, on the real pressure in his friend's tone, to consternation. "Then what's a fellow to be?"

"My particular care. Come, old man"—and Peter now fairly pleaded—"*I'll* look out for you."

Lance, who had remained on the sofa with his legs out and his hands in his pockets, watched him with eyes that showed suspicion. Then he got up.

"You think there's something the matter with me—that I can't make a success."

"Well, what do you call a success?"

Lance thought again. "Why, the best sort, I suppose, is to please one's self. Isn't that the sort that, in spite of cabals and things, is—in his own peculiar line—the Master's?"

There were so much too many things in this question to be answered at once that they practically checked the discussion, which became particularly difficult in the light of such renewed proof that, though the young man's innocence might, in the course of his studies, as he contended, somewhat have shrunken, the finer essence of it still remained. That was indeed exactly what Peter had assumed and what, above all, he desired; yet, perversely enough, it gave him a chill. The boy believed in the cabals and things, believed in the peculiar line, believed, in short, in the Master. What happened a month or two later was not that he went up again at the expense of his godfather, but that a fortnight after he had got settled in Paris, this personage sent him fifty pounds.

He had meanwhile, at home, this personage, made up his mind to the worst; and what it might be had never yet grown quite so vivid to him as when, on his presenting himself one Sunday night, as he never failed to do, for supper, the mistress of Carrara Lodge met him with an appeal as to— of all things in the world—the wealth of the Canadians. She was earnest, she was even excited. "Are many of them *really* rich?"

He had to confess that he knew nothing about them, but he often thought afterwards of that evening. The room in which they sat was adorned with sundry specimens of the Master's genius, which had the merit of being, as Mrs Mallow herself frequently suggested, of an unusually convenient size. They were indeed of dimensions not customary in the products of the chisel and had the singularity that, if the objects and features intended to be small looked too large, the objects and features intended to be large looked too small. The Master's intention, whether in respect to this matter or to any other, had, in almost any case, even after years, remained undiscoverable to Peter Brench. The creations that so failed to reveal it stood about on pedestals and brackets, on tables and shelves, a little staring white population, heroic, idyllic, allegoric, mythic, symbolic, in which "scale" had so strayed and lost itself that the public square and the chimney-piece seemed to have changed places, the monumental being all diminutive and the diminutive all monumental; branches, at any rate, markedly, of a family in which stature was rather oddly irrespective of function, age and sex. They formed, like the Mallows themselves, poor Brench's own family—having at least, to such a degree, the note of familiarity. The occasion was one of those he had long ago learnt to know and to name—short flickers of the faint flame, soft gusts of a kinder air. Twice a year, regularly, the Master believed in his fortune, in addition to believing all the year round in his genius. This time it was to be made by a bereaved couple from Toronto, who had given him the handsomest order for a tomb to three lost children, each of whom they desired to be, in the composition, emblematically and characteristically represented.

Such was naturally the moral of Mrs Mallow's question: if their wealth was to be assumed, it was clear, from the nature of their admiration, as well as from mysterious hints thrown out (they were a little odd!) as to other possibilities of the same mortuary sort, that their further patronage might be; and not less evident that, should the Master become at all known in those climes, nothing would be more inevitable than a run of Canadian custom. Peter had been present before at runs of custom, colonial and domestic—present at each of those of which the aggregation had left so few gaps in the marble company round him; but it was his habit never, at these junctures, to prick the bubble in advance. The fond illusion, while it lasted, eased the wound of elections never won, the long ache of medals and diplomas carried off, on every chance, by every one but the Master; it lighted the lamp, moreover, that would glimmer through the next eclipse. They lived, however, after all—as it was always beautiful to see—at a height scarce susceptible of ups and downs. They strained a point, at times, charmingly, to admit that the public was, here and there, not too bad to buy; but they would have been nowhere without their attitude that the Master was always too good to sell. They were, at all events, deliciously formed, Peter often said to himself, for their fate; the Master had a vanity, his wife had a loyalty, of which success, depriving these things of innocence, would have diminished the merit and the grace. Any one could be charming under a charm, and, as he looked about him at a world of prosperity more void of proportion even than the Master's museum, he wondered if he knew another pair that so completely escaped vulgarity.

"What a pity Lance isn't with us to rejoice!" Mrs Mallow on this occasion sighed at supper.

"We'll drink to the health of the absent," her husband replied, filling his friend's glass and his own and giving a drop to their companion; "but we must hope that he's preparing himself for a happiness much less like this of ours this evening—excusable as I grant it to be!—than like the comfort we have always—whatever has happened or has not happened—been able to trust ourselves to enjoy. The comfort," the Master explained, leaning back in the pleasant lamplight and firelight, holding up his glass and looking round at his marble family, quartered more or less, a monstrous brood, in every room—"the comfort of art in itself!"

Peter looked a little shyly at his wine. "Well—I don't care what you may call it when a fellow doesn't—but Lance must learn to *sell,* you know. I drink to his acquisition of the secret of a base popularity!"

"Oh yes, *he* must sell," the boy's mother, who was still more, however, this seemed to give out, the Master's wife, rather artlessly conceded.

"Oh," the sculptor, after a moment, confidently pronounced, "Lance *will.* Don't be afraid. He will have learnt."

"Which is exactly what Peter," Mrs Mallow gaily returned—"why in the world were you so perverse, Peter?—wouldn't, when he told him, hear of."

Peter, when this lady looked at him with accusatory affection—a grace, on her part, not infrequent—could never find a word; but the Master, who was always all amenity and tact, helped him out now as he had often helped him before. "That's his old idea, you know—on which we've so often differed: his theory that the artist should be all impulse and instinct. *I* go in, of course, for a certain amount of school. Not too much—but a due proportion. There's where his protest came in," he continued to explain to his wife, "as against what *might,* don't you see? be in question for Lance."

"Ah, well"—and Mrs Mallow turned the violet eyes across the table at the subject of this discourse—"he's sure to have meant, of course, nothing but good; but that wouldn't have prevented him, if Lance *had* taken his advice, from being, in effect, horribly cruel."

They had a sociable way of talking of him to his face as if he had been in the clay or—at most—in the plaster, and the Master was unfailingly generous. He might have been waving Egidio to make him revolve. "Ah, but poor Peter was not so wrong as to what it may, after all, come to that he *will* learn."

"Oh, but nothing artistically bad," she urged—still, for poor Peter, arch and dewy.

"Why, just the little French tricks," said the Master: on which their friend had to pretend to admit, when pressed by Mrs Mallow, that these æsthetic vices had been the objects of his dread.

III

"I KNOW now," Lance said to him the next year, "why you were so much against it." He had come back, supposedly for a mere interval, and was looking about him at Carrara Lodge, where indeed he had already, on two or three occasions, since his expatriation, briefly appeared. This had the air of a longer holiday. "Something rather awful has happened to me. It *isn't* so very good to know."

"I'm bound to say high spirits don't show in your face," Peter was rather ruefully forced to confess. "Still, are you very sure you do know?"

"Well, I at least know about as much as I can bear." These remarks were exchanged in Peter's den, and the young man, smoking cigarettes, stood before the fire with his back against the mantel. Something of his bloom seemed really to have left him.

Poor Peter wondered. "You're clear then as to what in particular I wanted you not to go for?"

"In particular?" Lance thought. "It seems to me that, in particular, there can have been but one thing."

They stood for a little sounding each other. "Are you quite sure?"

"Quite sure I'm a beastly duffer? Quite—by this time."

"Oh!"—and Peter turned away as if almost with relief.

"It's *that* that isn't pleasant to find out."

"Oh, I don't care for 'that,' " said Peter, presently coming round again. "I mean I personally don't."

"Yet I hope you can understand a little that I myself should!"

"Well, what do you mean by it?" Peter sceptically asked.

And on this Lance had to explain—how the upshot of his studies in Paris had inexorably proved a mere deep doubt of his means. These studies had waked him up, and a new light was in his eyes; but what the new light did was really to show him too much. "Do you know what's the matter with me? I'm too horribly intelligent. Paris was really the last place for me. I've learnt what I can't do."

Poor Peter stared—it was a staggerer; but even after they had had, on the subject, a longish talk in which the boy brought out to the full the hard truth of his lesson, his friend betrayed less pleasure than usually breaks into a face to the happy tune of "I told you so!" Poor Peter himself made now indeed so little a point of having told him so that Lance broke ground in a different place a day or two after. "What was it then that—before I went—you were afraid I should find out?" This, however, Peter refused to tell him—on the ground that if he hadn't yet guessed perhaps he never would, and that nothing at all, for either of them, in any case, was to be gained by giving the thing a name. Lance eyed him, on this, an instant, with the bold curiosity of youth—with the air indeed of having in his mind two or three names, of which one or other would be right. Peter, nevertheless, turning his back again, offered no encouragement, and when they parted afresh it was with some show of impatience on the side of the boy. Accordingly, at their next encounter, Peter saw at a glance that he had now, in the interval, divined and that, to sound his note, he was only waiting till they should find themselves alone. This he had soon arranged, and he then broke straight out. "Do you know your conundrum has been keeping me awake? But in the watches of the night the answer came over me—so that, upon my honour, I quite laughed out. Had you been supposing I had to go to Paris to learn *that*?" Even now, to see him still so sublimely on his guard, Peter's young friend had to laugh afresh. "You won't give a sign till you're sure? Beautiful old Peter!" But Lance at last produced it. "Why, hang it, the truth about the Master."

It made between them, for some minutes, a lively passage, full of wonder, for each, at the wonder of the other. "Then how long have you understood——"

"The true value of his work? I understood it," Lance recalled, "as soon as I began to understand anything. But I didn't begin fully to do that, I admit, till I got *là-bas*."[2]

"Dear, dear!"—Peter gasped with retrospective dread.

"But for what have you taken me? I'm a hopeless muff—that I *had* to have rubbed in. But I'm not such a muff as the Master!" Lance declared.

"Then why did you never tell me——?"

"That I hadn't, after all"—the boy took him up—"remained such an idiot?

---

[2] Over there.

Just because I never dreamed *you* knew. But I beg your pardon. I only wanted to spare you. And what I don't now understand is how the deuce then, for so long, you've managed to keep bottled."

Peter produced his explanation, but only after some delay and with a gravity not void of embarrassment. "It was for your mother."

"Oh!" said Lance.

"And that's the great thing now—since the murder *is* out. I want a promise from you. I mean"—and Peter almost feverishly followed it up—"a vow from you, solemn and such as you owe me, here on the spot, that you'll sacrifice anything rather than let her ever guess——"

"That *I've* guessed?"—Lance took it in. "I see." He evidently, after a moment, had taken in much. "But what is it you have in mind that I may have a chance to sacrifice?"

"Oh, one has always something."

Lance looked at him hard. "Do you mean that *you've* had——?" The look he received back, however, so put the question by that he found soon enough another. "Are you really sure my mother doesn't know?"

Peter, after renewed reflection, was really sure. "If she does, she's too wonderful."

"But aren't we all too wonderful?"

"Yes," Peter granted—"but in different ways. The thing's so desperately important because your father's little public consists only, as you know then," Peter developed—"well, of how many?"

"First of all," the Master's son risked, "of himself. And last of all too. I don't quite see of whom else."

Peter had an approach to impatience. "Of your mother, I say—*always.*"

Lance cast it all up. "You absolutely feel that?"

"Absolutely."

"Well then, with yourself, that makes three."

"Oh, *me!*"—and Peter, with a wag of his kind old head, modestly excused himself. "The number is, at any rate, small enough for any individual dropping out to be too dreadfully missed. Therefore, to put it in a nutshell, take care, my boy—that's all—that *you're* not!"

"I've got to keep on humbugging?" Lance sighed.

"It's just to warn you of the danger of your failing of that that I've seized this opportunity."

"And what do you regard in particular," the young man asked, "as the danger?"

"Why, this certainty: that the moment your mother, who feels so strongly, should suspect your secret—well," said Peter desperately, "the fat would be on the fire."

Lance, for a moment, seemed to stare at the blaze. "She'd throw me over?"

"She'd throw *him* over."

"And come round to us?"

Peter, before he answered, turned away. "Come round to *you.*" But he had said enough to indicate—and, as he evidently trusted, to avert—the horrid contingency.

IV

WITHIN six months again, however, his fear was, on more occasions than one, all before him. Lance had returned to Paris, to another trial; then had reappeared at home and had had, with his father, for the first time in his life, one of the scenes that strike sparks. He described it with much expression to Peter, as to whom—since they had never done so before—it was a sign of a new reserve on the part of the pair at Carrara Lodge that they at present failed, on a matter of intimate interest, to open themselves—if not in joy, then in sorrow—to their good friend. This produced perhaps, practically, between the parties, a shade of alienation and a slight intermission of commerce—marked mainly indeed by the fact that, to talk at his ease with his old playmate, Lance had, in general, to come to see him. The closest, if not quite the gayest relation they had yet known together was thus ushered in. The difficulty for poor Lance was a tension at home, begotten by the fact that his father wished him to be, at least, the sort of success he himself had been. He hadn't "chucked" Paris—though nothing appeared more vivid to him than that Paris had chucked him; he would go back again because of the fascination in trying, in seeing, in sounding the depths—in learning one's lesson, in fine, even if the lesson were simply that of one's impotence in the presence of one's larger vision. But what did the Master, all aloft in his senseless fluency, know of impotence, and what vision—to be called such— had he, in all his blind life, ever had? Lance, heated and indignant, frankly appealed to his godparent on this score.

His father, it appeared, had come down on him for having, after so long, nothing to show, and hoped that, on his next return, this deficiency would be repaired. *The* thing, the Master complacently set forth was—for any artist, however inferior to himself—at least to "do" something. "What can you do? That's all I ask!" *He* had certainly done enough, and there was no mistake about what he had to show. Lance had tears in his eyes when it came thus to letting his old friend know how great the strain might be on the "sacrifice" asked of him. It wasn't so easy to continue humbugging—as from son to parent—after feeling one's self despised for not grovelling in mediocrity. Yet a noble duplicity was what, as they intimately faced the situation, Peter went on requiring; and it was still, for a time, what his young friend, bitter and sore, managed loyally to comfort him with. Fifty pounds, more than once again, it was true, rewarded, both in London and in Paris, the young friend's loyalty; none the less sensibly, doubtless, at the moment, that the money was a direct advance on a decent sum for which Peter had long since privately prearranged an ultimate function. Whether by these arts or others, at all events, Lance's just resentment was kept for a season—but only for a season—at bay. The day arrived when he warned his companion that he could hold out—or hold in—no longer. Carrara Lodge had had to listen to another lecture delivered from a great height—an infliction really heavier, at last, than, without striking back or in some way letting the Master have the truth, flesh and blood could bear.

"And what I don't see is," Lance observed with a certain irritated eye for what was, after all, if it came to that, due to himself too—"What I don't see is, upon my honour, how *you,* as things are going, can keep the game up."

"Oh, the game for me is only to hold my tongue," said placid Peter. "And I have my reason."

"Still my mother?"

Peter showed, as he had often shown it before—that is by turning it straight away—a queer face. "What will you have? I haven't ceased to like her."

"She's beautiful—she's a dear, of course," Lance granted; "but what is she to you, after all, and what is it to you that, as to anything whatever, she should or she shouldn't?"

Peter, who had turned red, hung fire a little. "Well—it's all, simply, what I make of it."

There was now, however, in his young friend, a strange, an adopted, insistence. "What are you, after all, to *her?*"

"Oh, nothing. But that's another matter."

"She cares only for my father," said Lance the Parisian.

"Naturally—and that's just why."

"Why you've wished to spare her?"

"Because she cares so tremendously much."

Lance took a turn about the room, but with his eyes still on his host. "How awfully—always—you must have liked her!"

"Awfully. Always," said Peter Brench.

The young man continued for a moment to muse—then stopped again in front of him. "Do you know how much she cares?" Their eyes met on it, but Peter, as if his own found something new in Lance's, appeared to hesitate, for the first time for so long, to say he did know. "*I've* only just found out," said Lance. "She came to my room last night, after being present, in silence and only with her eyes on me, at what I had had to take from him; she came—and she was with me an extraordinary hour."

He had paused again, and they had again for a while sounded each other. Then something—and it made him suddenly turn pale—came to Peter. "She *does* know?"

"She does know. She let it all out to me—so as to demand of me no more than that, as she said, of which she herself had been capable. She has always, always known," said Lance without pity.

Peter was silent a long time; during which his companion might have heard him gently breathe and, on touching him, might have felt within him the vibration of a long, low sound suppressed. By the time he spoke, at last, he had taken everything in. "Then I do see how tremendously much."

"Isn't it wonderful?" Lance asked.

"Wonderful," Peter mused.

"So that if your original effort to keep me from Paris was to keep me from knowledge—!" Lance exclaimed as if with a sufficient indication of this futility.

It might have been at the futility that Peter appeared for a little to gaze. "I think it must have been—without my quite at the time knowing it—to keep *me*!" he replied at last as he turned away.

(1900)

Sherwood Anderson

(1 8 7 6 – 1 9 4 1)

Sherwood Anderson was born in Camden, Ohio, a town settled only a generation earlier and still strongly imbued with the pioneer values that were to leave profound traces in Anderson's fiction. Largely self-educated, he was a farm laborer, factory worker, and copywriter. After serving in Cuba in the Spanish-American War, Anderson moved to Chicago, where he wrote for an advertising firm. He later became manager of a paint manufacturing firm in Elyria, Ohio. In 1912 he suffered a nervous breakdown and in 1913 he left his job and his family to pursue a career as a writer. He lived in Chicago, Paris, and New Orleans, where he met and encouraged William Faulkner. His first novel, *Windy McPherson's Son,* appeared in 1916. Eventually Anderson settled in Marion, Virginia. He died in Cristobal, in the Canal Zone, in 1941.

Anderson helped to make modern theories of fiction central to American writing. He was influenced by Gertrude Stein, D. H. Lawrence, and Theodore Dreiser, and in turn influenced the work of Ernest Hemingway, William Faulkner, F. Scott Fitzgerald, Thomas Wolfe, and John Steinbeck. He helped to advance the technique of the short story. Anderson dealt with the psychology of characters, and his themes depend on an emotional, almost poetic intensity rather than on the traditional development of plot through events. His work is highly autobiographical and reflects his own experiences in a naturalistic manner, charged with a semimythical twist. The typical Anderson plot depicts the hero wandering from city to city, his eventual success, then his disillusionment with the standard conceptions of that success in a world of corrupt industrialization. Anderson was one of the earliest fiction writers to explore sexuality and the subconscious in a realistic manner. His best work, *Winesburg, Ohio,* is a series of connected short stories that describe the constricted, thwarted lives of the local inhabitants. Anderson's work is uneven and most of his later fiction is considered weak.

Anderson's work includes *Windy McPherson's Son* (1916), *Winesburg, Ohio* (1919), *Poor White* (1920), *The Triumph of the Egg* (1921), *Horses and Men* (1923), *Dark Laughter* (1925), *Beyond Desire* (1932), and *Kit Brandon* (1936). He also wrote two volumes of autobiography that are almost as fictional as his novels: *A Story Teller's Story* (1924) and *Tar: A Midwest Childhood* (1926).

SHERWOOD ANDERSON

I Want to Know Why

WE got up at four in the morning, that first day in the east. On the evening before we had climbed off a freight train at the edge of town, and with the true instinct of Kentucky boys had found our way across town and to the race track and the stables at once. Then we knew we were all right. Hanley Turner right away found a nigger we knew. It was Bildad Johnson who in the winter works at Ed Becker's livery barn in our home town, Beckersville. Bildad is a good cook as almost all our niggers are and of course he, like everyone in our part of Kentucky who is anyone at all, likes the horses. In the spring Bildad begins to scratch around. A nigger from our country can flatter and wheedle anyone into letting him do most anything he wants. Bildad wheedles the stable men and trainers from the horse farms in our country around Lexington. The trainers come into town in the evening to stand around and talk and maybe get into a poker game. Bildad gets in with them. He is always doing little favors and telling about things to eat, chicken browned in a pan, and how is the best way to cook sweet potatoes and corn bread. It makes your mouth water to hear him.

When the racing season comes on and the horses go to the races and there is all the talk on the streets in the evenings about the new colts, and everyone says when they are going over to Lexington or to the spring meeting at Churchill Downs or to Latonia, and the horsemen that have been down to New Orleans or maybe at the winter meeting at Havana in Cuba come home to spend a week before they start out again, at such a time when everything talked about in Beckersville is just horses and nothing else and the outfits start out and horse racing is in every breath of air you breathe, Bildad shows up with a job as cook for some outfit. Often when I think about it, his always going all season to the races and working in the livery barn in the winter where horses are and where men like to come and talk about horses, I wish I was a nigger. It's a foolish thing to say, but that's the way I am about being around horses, just crazy. I can't help it.

Well, I must tell you about what we did and let you in on what I'm talking about. Four of us boys from Beckersville, all whites and sons of men who live in Beckersville regular, made up our minds we were going to the races, not just to Lexington or Louisville, I don't mean, but to the big eastern track we were always hearing our Beckersville men talk about, to Saratoga. We were all pretty young then. I was just turned fifteen and I was the oldest of the four. It was my scheme. I admit that and I talked the others into trying

779

it. There was Hanley Turner and Henry Rieback and Tom Tumberton and myself. I had thirty-seven dollars I had earned during the winter working nights and Saturdays in Enoch Myer's grocery. Henry Rieback had eleven dollars and the others, Hanley and Tom had only a dollar or two each. We fixed it all up and laid low until the Kentucky spring meetings were over and some of our men, the sportiest ones, the ones we envied the most, had cut out—then we cut out too.

I won't tell you the trouble we had beating our way on freights and all. We went through Cleveland and Buffalo and other cities and saw Niagara Falls. We bought things there, souvenirs and spoons and cards and shells with pictures of the falls on them for our sisters and mothers, but thought we had better not send any of the things home. We didn't want to put the folks on our trail and maybe be nabbed.

We got into Saratoga as I said at night and went to the track. Bildad fed us up. He showed us a place to sleep in hay over a shed and promised to keep still. Niggers are all right about things like that. They won't squeal on you. Often a white man you might meet, when you had run away from home like that, might appear to be all right and give you a quarter or a half dollar or something, and then go right and give you away. White men will do that, but not a nigger. You can trust them. They are squarer with kids. I don't know why.

At the Saratoga meeting that year there were a lot of men from home. Dave Williams and Arthur Mulford and Merry Myers and others. Then there was a lot from Louisville and Lexington Henry Rieback knew but I didn't. They were professional gamblers and Henry Rieback's father is one too. He is what is called a sheet writer and goes away most of the year to tracks. In the winter when he is home in Beckersville he don't stay there much but goes away to cities and deals faro. He is a nice man and generous, is always sending Henry presents, a bicycle and a gold watch and a boy scout suit of clothes and things like that.

My own father is a lawyer. He's all right, but don't make much money and can't buy me things and anyway I'm getting so old now I don't expect it. He never said nothing to me against Henry, but Hanley Turner and Tom Tumberton's fathers did. They said to their boys that money so come by is no good and they didn't want their boys brought up to hear gamblers' talk and be thinking about such things and maybe embrace them.

That's all right and I guess the men know what they are talking about, but I don't see what it's got to do with Henry or with horses either. That's what I'm writing this story about. I'm puzzled. I'm getting to be a man and want to think straight and be O.K., and there's something I saw at the race meeting at the eastern track I can't figure out.

I can't help it, I'm crazy about thoroughbred horses. I've always been that way. When I was ten years old and saw I was growing to be big and couldn't be a rider I was so sorry I nearly died. Harry Hellinfinger in Beckersville, whose father is Postmaster, is grown up and too lazy to work, but likes to stand around in the street and get up jokes on boys like sending them to

a hardware store for a gimlet to bore square holes and other jokes like that.
He played one on me. He told me that if I would eat a half a cigar I would
be stunted and not grow any more and maybe could be a rider. I did it. When
father wasn't looking I took a cigar out of his pocket and gagged it down
some way. It made me awful sick and the doctor had to be sent for, and then
it did no good. I kept right on growing. It was a joke. When I told what I
had done and why most fathers would have whipped me but mine didn't.

Well, I didn't get stunted and didn't die. It serves Harry Hellinfinger
right. Then I made up my mind I would like to be a stable boy, but had to
give that up too. Mostly niggers do that work and I knew father wouldn't
let me go into it. No use to ask him.

If you've never been crazy about thoroughbreds it's because you've never
been around where they are much and don't know any better. They're
beautiful. There isn't anything so lovely and clean and full of spunk and
honest and everything as some race horses. On the big horse farms that are
all around our town Beckersville there are tracks and the horses run in the
early morning. More than a thousand times I've got out of bed before
daylight and walked two or three miles to the tracks. Mother wouldn't of let
me go but father always says, "Let him alone," So I got some bread out of
the bread box and some butter and jam, gobbled it and lit out.

At the tracks you sit on the fence with men, whites and niggers, and they
chew tobacco and talk, and then the colts are brought out. It's early and the
grass is covered with shiny dew and in another field a man is plowing and
they are frying things in a shed where the track niggers sleep, and you know
how a nigger can giggle and laugh and say things that make you laugh. A
white man can't do it and some niggers can't but a track nigger can every
time.

And so the colts are brought out and some are just galloped by stable
boys, but almost every morning on a big track owned by a rich man who lives
maybe in New York, there are always, nearly every morning, a few colts and
some of the old race horses and geldings and mares that are cut loose.

It brings a lump up into my throat when a horse runs. I don't mean all
horses but some. I can pick them nearly every time. It's in my blood like in
the blood of race track niggers and trainers. Even when they just go slop-
jogging along with a little nigger on their backs I can tell a winner. If my
throat hurts and it's hard for me to swallow, that's him. He'll run like Sam
Hill when you let him out. If he don't win every time it'll be a wonder and
because they've got him in a pocket behind another or he was pulled or got
off bad at the post or something. If I wanted to be a gambler like Henry
Rieback's father I could get rich. I know I could and Henry says so too. All
I would have to do is to wait 'til that hurt comes when I see a horse and then
bet every cent. That's what I would do if I wanted to be a gambler, but I
don't.

When you're at the tracks in the morning—not the race tracks but the
training tracks around Beckersville—you don't see a horse, the kind I've
been talking about, very often, but it's nice anyway. Any thoroughbred, that

is sired right and out of a good mare and trained by a man that knows how, can run. If he couldn't what would he be there for and not pulling a plow?

Well, out of the stables they come and the boys are on their backs and it's lovely to be there. You hunch down on top of the fence and itch inside you. Over in the sheds the niggers giggle and sing. Bacon is being fried and coffee made. Everything smells lovely. Nothing smells better than coffee and manure and horses and niggers and bacon frying and pipes being smoked out of doors on a morning like that. It just gets you, that's what it does.

But about Saratoga. We was there six days and not a soul from home seen us and everything came off just as we wanted it to, fine weather and horses and races and all. We beat our way home and Bildad gave us a basket with fried chicken and bread and other eatables in, and I had eighteen dollars when we got back to Beckersville. Mother jawed and cried but Pop didn't say much. I told everything we done except one thing. I did and saw that alone. That's what I'm writing about. It got me upset. I think about it at night. Here it is.

At Saratoga we laid up nights in the hay in the shed Bildad had showed us and ate with the niggers early and at night when the race people had all gone away. The men from home stayed mostly in the grandstand and betting field, and didn't come out around the places where the horses are kept except to the paddocks just before a race when the horses are saddled. At Saratoga they don't have paddocks under an open shed as at Lexington and Churchill Downs and other tracks down in our country, but saddle the horses right out in an open place under trees on a lawn as smooth and nice as Banker Bohon's front yard here in Beckersville. It's lovely. The horses are sweaty and nervous and shine and the men come out and smoke cigars and look at them and the trainers are there and the owners, and your heart thumps so you can hardly breathe.

Then the bugle blows for post and the boys that ride come running out with their silk clothes on and you run to get a place by the fence with the niggers.

I always am wanting to be a trainer or owner, and at the risk of being seen and caught and sent home I went to the paddocks before every race. The other boys didn't but I did.

We got to Saratoga on a Friday and on Wednesday the next week the big Mullford Handicap was to be run. Middlestride was in it and Sunstreak. The weather was fine and the track fast. I couldn't sleep the night before.

What had happened was that both these horses are the kind it makes my throat hurt to see. Middlestride is long and looks awkward and is a gelding. He belongs to Joe Thompson, a little owner from home who only has a half dozen horses. The Mullford Handicap is for a mile and Middlestride can't untrack fast. He goes away slow and is always way back at the half, then he begins to run and if the race is a mile and a quarter he'll just eat up everything and get there.

Sunstreak is different. He is a stallion and nervous and belongs on the biggest farm we've got in our country, the Van Riddle place that belongs to Mr. Van Riddle of New York. Sunstreak is like a girl you think about sometimes but never see. He is hard all over and lovely too. When you look at his head you want to kiss him. He is trained by Jerry Tillford who knows me and has been good to me lots of times, lets me walk into a horse's stall to look at him close and other things. There isn't anything as sweet as that horse. He stands at the post quiet and not letting on, but he is just burning up inside. Then when the barrier goes up he is off like his name, Sunstreak. It makes you ache to see him. It hurts you. He just lays down and runs like a bird dog. There can't anything I ever see run like him except Middlestride when he gets untracked and stretches himself.

Gee! I ached to see that race and those two horses run, ached and dreaded it too. I didn't want to see either of our horses beaten. We had never sent a pair like that to the races before. Old men in Beckersville said so and the nigger said so. It was a fact.

Before the race I went over to the paddocks to see. I looked a last look at Middlestride, who isn't such a much standing in a paddock that way, then I went to see Sunstreak.

It was his day. I knew when I seen him. I forgot all about being seen myself and walked right up. All the men from Beckersville were there and no one noticed me except Jerry Tillford. He saw me and something happened. I'll tell you about that.

I was standing looking at that horse and aching. In some way, I can't tell how, I knew just how Sunstreak felt inside. He was quiet and letting the niggers rub his legs and Mr. Van Riddle himself put the saddle on, but he was just a raging torrent inside. He was like the water in the river at Niagara Falls just before it goes plunk down. That horse wasn't thinking about running. He don't have to think about that. He was just thinking about holding himself back 'til the time for the running came. I knew that. I could just in a way see right inside him. He was going to do some awful running and I knew it. He wasn't bragging or letting on much or prancing or making a fuss, but just waiting. I knew it and Jerry Tillford his trainer knew. I looked up and then that man and I looked into each other's eyes. Something happened to me. I guess I loved the man as much as I did the horse because he knew what I knew. Seemed to me there wasn't anything in the world but that man and the horse and me. I cried and Jerry Tillford had a shine in his eyes. Then I came away to the fence to wait for the race. The horse was better than me, more steadier, and now I know better than Jerry. He was the quietest and he had to do the running.

Sunstreak ran first of course and he busted the world's record for a mile. I've seen that if I never see anything more. Everything came out just as I expected. Middlestride got left at the post and I was way back and closed up to be second, just as I knew he would. He'll get a world's record too some day. They can't skin the Beckersville country on horses.

I watched the race calm because I knew what would happen. I was sure. Hanley Turner and Henry Rieback and Tom Tumberton were all more excited than me.

A funny thing had happened to me. I was thinking about Jerry Tillford the trainer and how happy he was all through the race. I liked him that afternoon even more than I ever liked my own father. I almost forget the horses thinking that way about him. It was because of what I had seen in his eyes as he stood in the paddocks beside Sunstreak before the race started. I knew he had been watching and working with Sunstreak since the horse was a baby colt, had taught him to run and be patient and when to let himself out and not to quit, never. I knew that for him it was like a mother seeing her child do something brave or wonderful. It was the first time I ever felt for a man like that.

After the race that night I cut out from Tom and Hanley and Henry. I wanted to be by myself and I wanted to be near Jerry Tillford if I could work it. Here is what happened.

The track in Saratoga is near the edge of town. It is all polished up and trees around, the evergreen kind, and grass and everything painted and nice. If you go past the track you get to a hard road made of asphalt for automobiles, and if you go along this for a few miles there is a road turns off to a little rummy-looking farm house set in a yard.

That night after the race I went along that road because I had seen Jerry and some other men go that way in an automobile. I didn't expect to find them. I walked for a ways and then sat down by a fence to think. It was the direction they went in. I wanted to be as near Jerry as I could. I felt close to him. Pretty soon I went up the side road—I don't know why—and came to the rummy farm house. I was just lonesome to see Jerry, like wanting to see your father at night when you are a young kid. Just then an automobile came along and turned in. Jerry was in it and Henry Rieback's father, and Arthur Bedford from home, and Dave Williams and two other men I didn't know. They got out of the car and went into the house, all but Henry Rieback's father who quarreled with them and said he wouldn't go. It was only about nine o'clock, but they were all drunk and the rummy looking farm house was a place for bad women to stay in. That's what it was. I crept up along a fence and looked through a window and saw.

It's what gave me the fantods. I can't make it out. The women in the house were all ugly mean-looking women, not nice to look at or be near. They were homely too, except one who was tall and looked a little like the gelding Middlestride, but not clean like him, but with a hard ugly mouth. She had red hair. I saw everything plain. I got up by an old rose bush by an open window and looked. The women had on loose dresses and sat around in chairs. The men came in and some sat on the women's laps. The place smelled rotten and there was rotten talk, the kind a kid hears around a livery stable in a town like Beckersville in the winter but don't ever expect to hear talked when there are women around. It was rotten. A nigger wouldn't go into such a place.

I looked at Jerry Tillford. I've told you how I had been feeling about him on account of his knowing what was going on inside of Sunstreak in the minute before he went to the post for the race in which he made a world's record.

Jerry bragged in that bad woman house as I know Sunstreak wouldn't never have bragged. He said that he made that horse, that it was him that won the race and made the record. He lied and bragged like a fool. I never heard such silly talk.

And then, what do you suppose he did! He looked at the woman in there, the one that was lean and hard-mouthed and looked a little like the gelding Middlestride, but not clean like him, and his eyes began to shine just as they did when he looked at me and at Sunstreak in the paddocks at the track in the afternoon. I stood there by the window—gee!—but I wished I hadn't gone away from the tracks, but had stayed with the boys and the niggers and the horses. The tall rotten looking woman was between us just as Sunstreak was in the paddocks in the afternoon.

Then, all of a sudden, I began to hate that man. I wanted to scream and rush in the room and kill him. I never had such a feeling before. I was so mad clean through that I cried and my fists were doubled up so my finger nails cut my hands.

And Jerry's eyes kept shining and he waved back and forth, and then he went and kissed that woman and I crept away and went back to the tracks and to bed and didn't sleep hardly any, and then next day I got the other kids to start home with me and never told them anything I seen.

I been thinking about it ever since. I can't make it out. Spring has come again and I'm nearly sixteen and go to the tracks mornings same as always, and I see Sunstreak and Middlestride and a new colt named Strident I'll bet will lay them all out, but no one thinks so but me and two or three niggers.

But things are different. At the tracks the air don't taste as good or smell as good. It's because a man like Jerry Tillford, who knows what he does, could see a horse like Sunstreak run, and kiss a woman like that the same day. I can't make it out. Darn him, what did he want to do like that for? I keep thinking about it and it spoils looking at horses and smelling things and hearing niggers laugh and everything. Sometimes I'm so mad about it I want to fight someone. It gives me the fantods. What did he do it for? I want to know why.

(1921)

James Joyce

(1 8 8 2 – 1 9 4 1)

An innovator in modern writing and one of the greatest novelists of any era, James Joyce was born in Dublin, the setting for his fictional universe. Joyce was the son of a talented but dissolute father, and his family moved from house to house as the father's fortunes declined. Joyce studied in Jesuit schools, then attended University College, Dublin, and dabbled briefly in medical studies in Paris. Since his midteens, Joyce had seen himself as a rebel who fought the narrow provincialism of Ireland and the Church. After his mother's death in 1902, Joyce left Dublin for the self-exile he felt was necessary for his art. He would never live in Ireland again, although he dwelt there in his imagination. Joyce and his common-law wife, Nora Barnacle (they married in 1931), lived in Trieste, where Joyce taught English; in Rome, where he worked in a bank; and in Zurich before settling in Paris in 1920, where they lived until World War II forced them to return to Zurich. After years of frustration, when his works were censored, Joyce made a breakthrough with the publication of *Dubliners* in 1914 and *Portrait of the Artist as a Young Man* in 1916, partly with Ezra Pound's help. The release of *Ulysses* made Joyce famous in literary circles throughout the world. The later years of his life were darkened by his daughter's insanity and by eye problems that left him in great pain and virtually blind.

Joyce wrote four major works of fiction: *Dubliners, A Portrait of the Artist as a Young Man, Ulysses,* and *Finnegans Wake.* They are distinct and original. *Dubliners* is a series of superbly crafted stories about the constriction and paralysis of life in Dublin. Each story is carefully realistic, yet the scenes form a dense, symbolic web that gives great resonance and universality to the themes. The stories are ordered to form the spiritual biography, from youth to middle age, of a "Dubliner," a character who is meant to be universal. *Portrait of the Artist* is finely honed and seems to be scrupulously objective. It tells the semiautobiographical story of Stephen Dedalus, Joyce's alter ego, through a series of anecdotes that depict the maturing artistic consciousness. *Ulysses* is a complex work that uses analogues with Homer's *Odyssey.* It tells the story of one day—June 16, 1904—in Dublin, and centers on the life of Leopold Bloom. It also includes the story of an increasingly disillusioned Dedalus, who is still mourning the death of his mother a year earlier. The novel is important for its human sympathy, for its brilliantly realized stream-of-consciousness technique, and for its encyclopedia of styles, which allow us to see the story from a multitude of perspectives. (It is Joyce who teaches us that perspective and style are inseparable.) The work blends mythical patterns and realistic, factual detail. Joyce spent the last 16 years of his life working on the obscure poetic "novel" *Finnegans Wake,* a work of great humor and beauty that is ultimately incomprehensible to those with less than a lifetime to devote to its riddles.

Joyce's works are *Chamber Music* (poetry, 1907); *Dubliners* (completed in 1907, published in 1914); *A Portrait of the Artist as a Young Man* (1916); *Exiles* (drama, 1918); *Ulysses* (1922); *Pomes Pennyeach* (poetry, 1927); and *Finnegans Wake* (1939). Part of an early version of *A Portrait of the Artist as a Young Man* was published as *Stephen Hero* in 1944.

JAMES JOYCE

Araby

NORTH RICHMOND STREET, being blind, was a quiet street except at the hour when the Christian Brothers' School set the boys free. An uninhabited house of two storeys stood at the blind end, detached from its neighbours in a square ground. The other houses of the street, conscious of decent lives within them, gazed at one another with brown imperturbable faces.

The former tenant of our house, a priest, had died in the back drawing-room. Air, musty from having been long enclosed, hung in all the rooms, and the waste room behind the kitchen was littered with old useless papers. Among these I found a few paper-covered books, the pages of which were curled and damp: *The Abbot,* by Walter Scott, *The Devout Communicant* and *The Memoirs of Vidocq.*[1] I liked the last best because its leaves were yellow. The wild garden behind the house contained a central apple-tree and a few straggling bushes under one of which I found the late tenant's rusty bicycle-pump. He had been a very charitable priest; in his will he had left all his money to institutions and the furniture of his house to his sister.

When the short days of winter came dusk fell before we had well eaten our dinners. When we met in the street the houses had grown sombre. The space of sky above us was the colour of ever-changing violet and towards it the lamps of the street lifted their feeble lanterns. The cold air stung us and we played till our bodies glowed. Our shouts echoed in the silent street. The career of our play brought us through the dark muddy lanes behind the houses where we ran the gantlet of the rough tribes from the cottages, to the back doors of the dark dripping gardens where odours arose from the ashpits, to the dark odorous stables where a coachman smoothed and combed the horse or shook music from the buckled harness. When we returned to the street light from the kitchen windows had filled the areas. If my uncle was seen turning the corner we hid in the shadow until we had seen him safely housed. Or if Mangan's sister came out on the doorstep to call her brother in to his tea we watched her from our shadow peer up and down the street. We waited to see whether she would remain or go in and, if she remained, we left our shadow and walked up to Mangan's steps resignedly. She was waiting for us, her figure defined by the light from the half-opened door. Her brother always teased her before he obeyed and I

---

[1] *The Devout Communicant* is a Catholic manual; *The Memoirs of Vidocq* concerns the career of Eugène François Vidocq, a French criminal who turned detective.

stood by the railings looking at her. Her dress swung as she moved her body and the soft rope of her hair tossed from side to side.

Every morning I lay on the floor in the front parlour watching her door. The blind was pulled down to within an inch of the sash so that I could not be seen. When she came out on the doorstep my heart leaped. I ran to the hall, seized my books and followed her. I kept her brown figure always in my eye and, when we came near the point at which our ways diverged, I quickened my pace and passed her. This happened morning after morning. I had never spoken to her, except for a few casual words, and yet her name was like a summons to all my foolish blood.

Her image accompanied me even in places the most hostile to romance. On Saturday evenings when my aunt went marketing I had to go to carry some of the parcels. We walked through the flaring streets, jostled by drunken men and bargaining women, amid the curses of labourers, the shrill litanies of shop-boys who stood on guard by the barrels of pigs' cheeks, the nasal chanting of street-singers, who sang a *come-all-you* about O'Donovan Rossa,[2] or a ballad about the troubles in our native land. These noises converged in a single sensation of life for me: I imagined that I bore my chalice safely through a throng of foes. Her name sprang to my lips at moments in strange prayers and praises which I myself did not understand. My eyes were often full of tears (I could not tell why) and at times a flood from my heart seemed to pour itself out into my bosom. I thought little of the future. I did not know whether I would ever speak to her or not or, if I spoke to her, how I could tell her of my confused adoration. But my body was like a harp and her words and gestures were like fingers running upon the wires.

One evening I went into the back drawing-room in which the priest had died. It was a dark rainy evening and there was no sound in the house. Through one of the broken panes I heard the rain impinge upon the earth, the fine incessant needles of water playing in the sodden beds. Some distant lamp or lighted window gleamed below me. I was thankful that I could see so little. All my senses seemed to desire to veil themselves and, feeling that I was about to slip from them, I pressed the palms of my hands together until they trembled, murmuring: *O love! O love!* many times.

At last she spoke to me. When she addressed the first words to me I was so confused that I did not know what to answer. She asked me was I going to *Araby.* I forget whether I answered yes or no. It would be a splendid bazaar, she said; she would love to go.

—And why can't you? I asked.

While she spoke she turned a silver bracelet round and round her wrist. She could not go, she said, because there would be a retreat that week in her convent. Her brother and two other boys were fighting for their caps and I was alone at the railings. She held one of the spikes, bowing her head

---

[2] Nickname of Jeremiah O'Donovan (1831–1915), known for his leadership in Ireland's move toward independence.

towards me. The light from the lamp opposite our door caught the white curve of her neck, lit up her hair that rested there and, falling, lit up the hand upon the railing. It fell over one side of her dress and caught the white border of a petticoat, just visible as she stood at ease.

—It's well for you, she said.

—If I go, I said, I will bring you something.

What innumerable follies laid waste my waking and sleeping thoughts after that evening! I wished to annihilate the tedious intervening days. I chafed against the work of school. At night in my bedroom and by day in the classroom her image came between me and the page I strove to read. The syllables of the word *Araby* were called to me through the silence in which my soul luxuriated and cast an Eastern enchantment over me. I asked for leave to go to the bazaar on Saturday night. My aunt was surprised and hoped it was not some Freemason affair. I answered few questions in class. I watched my master's face pass from amiability to sternness; he hoped I was not beginning to idle. I could not call my wandering thoughts together. I had hardly any patience with the serious work of life which, now that it stood between me and my desire, seemed to me child's play, ugly monotonous child's play.

On Saturday morning I reminded my uncle that I wished to go to the bazaar in the evening. He was fussing at the hall-stand, looking for the hat-brush, and answered me curtly:

—Yes, boy, I know.

As he was in the hall I could not go into the front parlour and lie at the window. I left the house in bad humour and walked slowly towards the school. The air was pitilessly raw and already my heart misgave me.

When I came home to dinner my uncle had not yet been home. Still it was early. I sat staring at the clock for some time and, when its ticking began to irritate me, I left the room. I mounted the staircase and gained the upper part of the house. The high cold empty gloomy rooms liberated me and I went from room to room singing. From the front window I saw my companions playing below in the street. Their cries reached me weakened and indistinct and, leaning my forehead against the cool glass, I looked over at the dark house where she lived. I may have stood there for an hour, seeing nothing but the brown-clad figure cast by my imagination, touched discreetly by the lamplight at the curved neck, at the hand upon the railings and at the border below the dress.

When I came downstairs again I found Mrs Mercer sitting at the fire. She was an old garrulous woman, a pawnbroker's widow, who collected used stamps for some pious purpose. I had to endure the gossip of the tea-table. The meal was prolonged beyond an hour and still my uncle did not come. Mrs Mercer stood up to go: she was sorry she couldn't wait any longer, but it was after eight o'clock and she did not like to be out late, as the night air was bad for her. When she had gone I began to walk up and down the room, clenching my fists. My aunt said:

—I'm afraid you may put off your bazaar for this night of Our Lord.

At nine o'clock I heard my uncle's latchkey in the halldoor. I heard him talking to himself and heard the hallstand rocking when it had received the weight of his overcoat. I could interpret these signs. When he was midway through his dinner I asked him to give me the money to go to the bazaar. He had forgotten.

—The people are in bed and after their first sleep now, he said.

I did not smile. My aunt said to him energetically:

—Can't you give him the money and let him go? You've kept him late enough as it is.

My uncle said he was very sorry he had forgotten. He said he believed in the old saying: *All work and no play makes Jack a dull boy.* He asked me where I was going and, when I had told him a second time he asked me did I know *The Arab's Farewell to His Steed.* [3] When I left the kitchen he was about to recite the opening lines of the piece to my aunt.

I held a florin tightly in my hand as I strode down Buckingham Street towards the station. The sight of the streets thronged with buyers and glaring with gas recalled to me the purpose of my journey. I took my seat in a third-class carriage of a deserted train. After an intolerable delay the train moved out of the station slowly. It crept onward among ruinous houses and over the twinkling river. At Westland Row Station a crowd of people pressed to the carriage doors; but the porters moved them back, saying that it was a special train for the bazaar. I remained alone in the bare carriage. In a few minutes the train drew up beside an improvised wooden platform. I passed out on to the road and saw by the lighted dial of a clock that it was ten minutes to ten. In front of me was a large building which displayed the magical name.

I could not find any sixpenny entrance and, fearing that the bazaar would be closed, I passed in quickly through a turnstile, handing a shilling to a weary-looking man. I found myself in a big hall girdled at half its height by a gallery. Nearly all the stalls were closed and the greater part of the hall was in darkness. I recognised a silence like that which pervades a church after a service. I walked into the centre of the bazaar timidly. A few people were gathered about the stalls which were still open. Before a curtain, over which the words *Café Chantant* were written in coloured lamps, two men were counting money on a salver. I listened to the fall of the coins.

Remembering with difficulty why I had come I went over to one of the stalls and examined porcelain vases and flowered tea-sets. At the door of the stall a young lady was talking and laughing with two young gentlemen. I remarked their English accents and listened vaguely to their conversation.

—O, I never said such a thing!

—O, but you did!

—O, but I didn't!

—Didn't she say that?

—Yes. I heard her.

[3] Sentimental poem by Caroline Norton (1808–77).

—O, there's a . . . fib!

Observing me the young lady came over and asked me did I wish to buy anything. The tone of her voice was not encouraging; she seemed to have spoken to me out of a sense of duty. I looked humbly at the great jars that stood like eastern guards at either side of the dark entrance to the stall and murmured:

—No, thank you.

The young lady changed the position of one of the vases and went back to the two young men. They began to talk of the same subject. Once or twice the young lady glanced at me over her shoulder.

I lingered before her stall, though I knew my stay was useless, to make my interest in her wares seem the more real. Then I turned away slowly and walked down the middle of the bazaar. I allowed the two pennies to fall against the sixpence in my pocket. I heard a voice call from one end of the gallery that the light was out. The upper part of the hall was now completely dark.

Gazing up into the darkness I saw myself as a creature driven and derided by vanity; and my eyes burned with anguish and anger.

(1914)

D. H. Lawrence

(1 8 8 5 - 1 9 3 0)

An important twentieth-century English novelist and a talented short-story writer and poet, David Herbert Lawrence was born in Eastwood, a village near Nottingham, England. He was the son of a coal miner. His mother was well-educated and dedicated herself to helping her children escape the working class. Lawrence was educated at University College, Nottingham, and taught school for a time. His first publication came in 1909, when Ford Madox Ford accepted some poems for the *English Review*. Disenchanted with industrial England and suffering from tuberculosis, Lawrence left teaching in 1911, the same year his first novel, *The White Peacock,* appeared. In 1912 Lawrence eloped with Frieda von Richthofen Weekley, who was already married. The couple traveled and lived in Germany, Austria, Italy, Sicily, England, France, Australia, Mexico, and New Mexico, where Lawrence dreamed of setting up a Utopian community. Lawrence meanwhile wrote a steady stream of novels, some of which were banned or condemned for their explicitness. Lawrence's first major novel was *Sons and Lovers* (1913). He died of tuberculosis in 1930.

Lawrence's novels are symbolic and dramatic narratives written in rich prose. They include charming descriptions of British rural life and fiery, apocalyptic evocations of cosmic longing and passionate, almost mystical sexuality. His novels demonstrate his antipathy toward the modern industrial society, which he thought oppressed and dehumanized workers like his father. Sexuality, a theme with which Lawrence is somewhat unjustifiably associated, serves in his fiction as an almost spiritual life force, one that combats the sterility of industrial society and genteel, sophisticated culture. In his later works, such as *Kangaroo, The Plumed Serpent,* and *Lady Chatterley's Lover,* Lawrence turns his attention to the role of power and dominance in human relationships and to the role of friendship ("blood brotherhood"), which complements sexuality. Lawrence was a profound psychological realist and an idealistic visionary. He has gained a permanent place in the literature of the modern era.

Lawrence wrote more than 40 volumes of poetry, fiction, essays, and drama. The major novels are *Sons and Lovers* (1913), *The Rainbow* (1915), *Women in Love* (1920), *Aaron's Rod* (1922), *Kangaroo* (1923), *The Plumed Serpent* (1926), and *Lady Chatterley's Lover* (1928). His collected poems were first published in 1928. Many of his finest short stories appeared in *The Prussian Officer* (1914) and *England, My England* (1922).

D. H. LAWRENCE

The Rocking-Horse Winner

THERE was a woman who was beautiful, who started with all the advantages, yet she had no luck. She married for love, and the love turned to dust. She had bonny children, yet she felt they had been thrust upon her, and she could not love them. They looked at her coldly, as if they were finding fault with her. And hurriedly she felt she must cover up some fault in herself. Yet what it was that she must cover up she never knew. Nevertheless, when her children were present, she always felt the centre of her heart go hard. This troubled her, and in her manner she was all the more gentle and anxious for her children, as if she loved them very much. Only she herself knew that at the centre of her heart was a hard little place that could not feel love, no, not for anybody. Everybody else said of her: "She is such a good mother. She adores her children." Only she herself, and her children themselves, knew it was not so. They read it in each other's eyes.

There were a boy and two little girls. They lived in a pleasant house, with a garden, and they had discreet servants, and felt themselves superior to anyone in the neighbourhood.

Although they lived in style, they felt always an anxiety in the house. There was never enough money. The mother had a small income, and the father had a small income, but not nearly enough for the social position which they had to keep up. The father went into town to some office. But though he had good prospects, these prospects never materialised. There was always the grinding sense of the shortage of money, though the style was always kept up.

At last the mother said: "I will see if I can't make something." But she did not know where to begin. She racked her brains, and tried this thing and the other, but could not find anything successful. The failure made deep lines come into her face. Her children were growing up, they would have to go to school. There must be more money, there must be more money. The father, who was always very handsome and expensive in his tastes, seemed as if he never *would* be able to do anything worth doing. And the mother, who had a great belief in herself, did not succeed any better, and her tastes were just as expensive.

And so the house came to be haunted by the unspoken phrase: *There must be more money! There must be more money!* The children could hear it all the time, though nobody said it aloud. They heard it at Christmas, when the expensive and splendid toys filled the nursery. Behind the shining modern rocking-horse, behind the smart doll's house, a voice would start whispering: "There *must* be more money! There *must* be more money!" And the children would stop playing, to listen for a moment. They would look into each other's eyes, to see if they had all heard. And each one saw in the eyes of the other two that they too had heard. "There *must* be more money! There *must* be more money!"

It came whispering from the springs of the still-swaying rocking-horse, and even the horse, bending his wooden, champing head, heard it. The big doll, sitting so pink and smirking in her new pram, could hear it quite plainly, and seemed to be smirking all the more self-consciously because of it. The foolish puppy, too, that took the place of the teddy-bear, he was looking so extraordinarily foolish for no other reason but that he heard the secret whisper all over the house: "There *must* be more money!"

Yet nobody ever said it aloud. The whisper was everywhere, and therefore no one spoke it. Just as no one ever says: "We are breathing!" in spite of the fact that breath is coming and going all the time.

"Mother," said the boy Paul one day, "why don't we keep a car of our own? Why do we always use uncle's, or else a taxi?"

"Because we're the poor members of the family," said the mother.

"But why *are* we, mother?"

"Well—I suppose," she said slowly and bitterly, "it's because your father has no luck."

The boy was silent for some time.

"Is luck money, mother?" he asked, rather timidly.

"No, Paul. Not quite. It's what causes you to have money."

"Oh!" said Paul vaguely. "I thought when Uncle Oscar said *filthy lucker*, it meant money."

"*Filthy lucre* does mean money," said the mother. "But it's lucre, not luck."

"Oh!" said the boy. "Then what *is* luck, mother?"

"It's what causes you to have money. If you're lucky you have money. That's why it's better to be born lucky than rich. If you're rich, you may lose your money. But if you're lucky, you will always get more money."

"Oh! Will you? And is father not lucky?"

"Very unlucky, I should say," she said bitterly.

The boy watched her with unsure eyes.

"Why?" he asked.

"I don't know. Nobody ever knows why one person is lucky and another unlucky."

"Don't they? Nobody at all? Does *nobody* know?"

"Perhaps God. But He never tells."

"He ought to, then. And aren't you lucky either, mother?"

"I can't be, if I married an unlucky husband."

"But by yourself, aren't you?"

"I used to think I was, before I married. Now I think I am very unlucky indeed."

"Why?"

"Well—never mind! Perhaps I'm not really," she said.

The child looked at her to see if she meant it. But he saw, by the lines of her mouth, that she was only trying to hide something from him.

"Well, anyhow," he said stoutly, "I'm a lucky person."

"Why?" said his mother, with a sudden laugh.

He stared at her. He didn't even know why he had said it.

"God told me," he asserted, brazening it out.

"I hope He did, dear!" she said, again with a laugh, but rather bitter.

"He did, mother!"

"Excellent!" said the mother, using one of her husband's exclamations.

The boy saw she did not believe him; or rather, that she paid no attention to his assertion. This angered him somewhere, and made him want to compel her attention.

He went off by himself, vaguely, in a childish way, seeking for the clue to 'luck'. Absorbed, taking no heed of other people, he went about with a sort of stealth, seeking inwardly for luck. He wanted luck, he wanted it, he wanted it. When the two girls were playing dolls in the nursery, he would sit on his big rocking-horse, charging madly into space, with a frenzy that made the little girls peer at him uneasily. Wildly the horse careered, the waving dark hair of the boy tossed, his eyes had a strange glare in them. The little girls dared not speak to him.

When he had ridden to the end of his mad little journey, he climbed down and stood in front of his rocking-horse, staring fixedly into its lowered face. Its red mouth was slightly open, its big eye was wide and glassy-bright.

"Now!" he would silently command the snorting steed. "Now, take me to where there is luck! Now take me!"

And he would slash the horse on the neck with the little whip he had asked Uncle Oscar for. He *knew* the horse could take him to where there was luck, if only he forced it. So he would mount again and start on his furious ride, hoping at last to get there. He knew he could get there.

"You'll break your horse, Paul!" said the nurse.

"He's always riding like that! I wish he'd leave off!" said his elder sister Joan.

But he only glared down on them in silence. Nurse gave him up. She could make nothing of him. Anyhow, he was growing beyond her.

One day his mother and his Uncle Oscar came in when he was on one of his furious rides. He did not speak to them.

"Hallo, you young jockey! Riding a winner?" said his uncle.

"Aren't you growing too big for a rocking-horse? You're not a very little boy any longer, you know," said his mother.

But Paul only gave a blue glare from his big, rather close-set eyes. He would speak to nobody when he was in full tilt. His mother watched him with an anxious expression on her face.

At last he suddenly stopped forcing his horse into the mechanical gallop and slid down.

"Well, I got there!" he announced fiercely, his blue eyes still flaring, and his sturdy long legs straddling apart.

"Where did you get to?" asked his mother.

"Where I wanted to go," he flared back at her.

"That's right, son!" said Uncle Oscar. "Don't you stop till you get there. What's the horse's name?"

"He doesn't have a name," said the boy.

"Gets on without all right?" asked the uncle.

"Well, he has different names. He was called Sansovino last week."

"Sansovino, eh? Won the Ascot.[1] How did you know this name?"

"He always talks about horse-races with Bassett," said Joan.

The uncle was delighted to find that his small nephew was posted with all the racing news. Bassett, the young gardener, who had been wounded in the left foot in the war and had got his present job through Oscar Cresswell, whose batman he had been, was a perfect blade of the 'turf'. He lived in the racing events, and the small boy lived with him.

Oscar Cresswell got it all from Bassett.

"Master Paul comes and asks me, so I can't do more than tell him, sir," said Bassett, his face terribly serious, as if he were speaking of religious matters.

"And does he ever put anything on a horse he fancies?"

"Well—I don't want to give him away—he's a young sport, a fine sport, sir. Would you mind asking him himself? He sort of takes a pleasure in it, and perhaps he'd feel I was giving him away, sir, if you don't mind."

Bassett was serious as a church.

The uncle went back to his nephew and took him off for a ride in the car.

"Say, Paul, old man, do you ever put anything on a horse?" the uncle asked.

The boy watched the handsome man closely.

"Why, do you think I oughtn't to?" he parried.

"Not a bit of it! I thought perhaps you might give me a tip for the Lincoln."

The car sped on into the country, going down to Uncle Oscar's place in Hampshire.

"Honour bright?" said the nephew.

"Honour bright, son!" said the uncle.

"Well, then, Daffodil."

"Daffodil! I doubt it, sonny. What about Mirza?"

"I only know the winner," said the boy. "That's Daffodil."

"Daffodil, eh?"

There was a pause. Daffodil was an obscure horse comparatively.

"Uncle!"

[1] The Ascot is a well-known British horse race, as are the Lincolnshire Handicap, the St. Leger Stakes, the Grand National run, the Lincolnshire run, and the Derby run, all of which are mentioned in the story.

"Yes, son?"

"You won't let it go any further, will you? I promised Bassett."

"Bassett be damned, old man! What's he got to do with it?"

"We're partners. We've been partners from the first. Uncle, he lent me my first five shillings, which I lost. I promised him, honour bright, it was only between me and him; only you gave me that ten-shilling note I started winning with, so I thought you were lucky. You won't let it go any further, will you?"

The boy gazed at his uncle from those big, hot, blue eyes, set rather close together. The uncle stirred and laughed uneasily.

"Right you are, son! I'll keep your tip private. Daffodil, eh? How much are you putting on him?"

"All except twenty pounds," said the boy. "I keep that in reserve."

The uncle thought it a good joke.

"You keep twenty pounds in reserve, do you, you young romancer? What are you betting, then?"

"I'm betting three hundred," said the boy gravely. "But it's between you and me, Uncle Oscar! Honour bright?"

The uncle burst into a roar of laughter.

"It's between you and me all right, you young Nat Gould,"[2] he said, laughing. "But where's your three hundred?"

"Bassett keeps it for me. We're partners."

"You are, are you! And what is Bassett putting on Daffodil?"

"He won't go quite as high as I do, I expect. Perhaps he'll go a hundred and fifty."

"What, pennies?" laughed the uncle.

"Pounds," said the child, with a surprised look at his uncle. "Bassett keeps a bigger reserve than I do."

Between wonder and amusement Uncle Oscar was silent. He pursued the matter no further, but he determined to take his nephew with him to the Lincoln races.

"Now, son," he said. "I'm putting twenty on Mirza, and I'll put five on for you on any horse you fancy. What's your pick?"

"Daffodil, uncle."

"No, not the fiver on Daffodil!"

"I should if it was my own fiver," said the child.

"Good! Good! Right you are! A fiver for me and a fiver for you on Daffodil."

The child had never been to a race-meeting before, and his eyes were blue fire. He pursed his mouth tight and watched. A Frenchman just in front had put his money on Lancelot. Wild with excitement, he flayed his arms up and down, yelling *"Lancelot! Lancelot!"* in his French accent.

Daffodil came in first, Lancelot second, Mirza third. The child, flushed and with eyes blazing, was curiously serene. His uncle brought him four five-pound notes, four to one.

---

[2] Nathaniel Gould (1857–1919), horse-racing journalist.

"What am I to do with these?" he cried, waving them before the boy's eyes.

"I suppose we'll talk to Bassett," said the boy. "I expect I have fifteen hundred now; and twenty in reserve; and this twenty."

His uncle studied him for some moments.

"Look here, son!" he said. "You're not serious about Bassett and that fifteen hundred, are you?"

"Yes, I am. But it's between you and me, uncle. Honour bright?"

"Honour bright all right, son! But I must talk to Bassett."

"If you'd like to be a partner, uncle, with Bassett and me, we could all be partners. Only, you'd have to promise, honour bright, uncle, not to let it go beyond us three. Bassett and I are lucky, and you must be lucky, because it was your ten shillings I started winning with. . . ."

Uncle Oscar took both Bassett and Paul into Richmond Park for an afternoon, and there they talked.

"It's like this, you see, sir," Bassett said. "Master Paul would get me talking about racing events, spinning yarns, you know, sir. And he was always keen on knowing if I'd made or if I'd lost. It's about a year since, now, that I put five shillings on Blush of Dawn for him: and we lost. Then the luck turned, with that ten shillings he had from you: that we put on Singhalese. And since that time, it's been pretty steady, all things considering. What do you say, Master Paul?"

"We're all right when we're sure," said Paul. "It's when we're not quite sure that we go down."

"Oh, but we're careful then," said Bassett.

"But when are you *sure?*" smiled Uncle Oscar.

"It's Master Paul, sir," said Bassett in a secret, religious voice. "It's as if he had it from heaven. Like Daffodil, now, for the Lincoln. That was as sure as eggs."

"Did you put anything on Daffodil?" asked Oscar Cresswell.

"Yes, sir. I made my bit."

"And my nephew?"

Bassett was obstinately silent, looking at Paul.

"I made twelve hundred, didn't I, Bassett? I told uncle I was putting three hundred on Daffodil."

"That's right," said Bassett, nodding.

"But where's the money?" asked the uncle.

"I keep it safe locked up, sir. Master Paul he can have it any minute he likes to ask for it."

"What, fifteen hundred pounds?"

"And twenty! And *forty,* that is, with the twenty he made on the course."

"It's amazing!" said the uncle.

"If Master Paul offers you to be partners, sir, I would, if I were you: if you'll excuse me," said Bassett.

Oscar Cresswell thought about it.

"I'll see the money," he said.

They drove home again, and, sure enough, Bassett came round to the garden-house with fifteen hundred pounds in notes. The twenty pounds reserve was left with Joe Glee, in the Turf Commission deposit.

"You see, it's all right, uncle, when I'm *sure!* Then we go strong, for all we're worth. Don't we, Bassett?"

"We do that, Master Paul."

"And when are you sure?" said the uncle, laughing.

"Oh, well, sometimes I'm *absolutely* sure, like about Daffodil," said the boy; "and sometimes I have an idea; and sometimes I haven't even an idea, have I, Bassett? Then we're careful, because we mostly go down."

"You do, do you! And when you're sure, like about Daffodil, what makes you sure, sonny?"

"Oh, well, I don't know," said the boy uneasily. "I'm sure, you know, uncle; that's all."

"It's as if he had it from heaven, sir," Bassett reiterated.

"I should say so!" said the uncle.

But he became a partner. And when the Leger was coming on Paul was 'sure' about Lively Spark, which was a quite inconsiderable horse. The boy insisted on putting a thousand on the horse, Bassett went for five hundred, and Oscar Cresswell two hundred. Lively Spark came in first, and the betting had been ten to one against him. Paul had made ten thousand.

"You see," he said, "I was absolutely sure of him."

Even Oscar Cresswell had cleared two thousand.

"Look here, son," he said, "this sort of thing makes me nervous."

"It needn't, uncle! Perhaps I shan't be sure again for a long time."

"But what are you going to do with your money?" asked the uncle.

"Of course," said the boy, "I started it for mother. She said she had no luck, because father is unlucky, so I thought if *I* was lucky, it might stop whispering."

"What might stop whispering?"

"Our house. I *hate* our house for whispering."

"What does it whisper?"

"Why—why"—the boy fidgeted—"why, I don't know. But it's always short of money, you know, uncle."

"I know it, son, I know it."

"You know people send mother writs,[3] don't you, uncle?"

"I'm afraid I do," said the uncle.

"And then the house whispers, like people laughing at you behind your back. It's awful, that is! I thought if I was lucky—"

"You might stop it," added the uncle.

The boy watched him with big blue eyes, that had an uncanny cold fire in them, and he said never a word.

"Well, then!" said the uncle. "What are we doing?"

"I shouldn't like mother to know I was lucky," said the boy.

"Why not, son?"

---

[3] Dunning letters from creditors.

"She'd stop me."

"I don't think she would."

"Oh!"—and the boy writhed in an odd way—"I *don't* want her to know, uncle."

"All right, son! We'll manage it without her knowing."

They managed it very easily. Paul, at the other's suggestion, handed over five thousand pounds to his uncle, who deposited it with the family lawyer, who was then to inform Paul's mother that a relative had put five thousand pounds into his hands, which sum was to be paid out a thousand pounds at a time, on the mother's birthday, for the next five years.

"So she'll have a birthday present of a thousand pounds for five successive years," said Uncle Oscar. "I hope it won't make it all the harder for her later."

Paul's mother had her birthday in November. The house had been 'whispering' worse than ever lately, and, even in spite of his luck, Paul could not bear up against it. He was very anxious to see the effect of the birthday letter, telling his mother about the thousand pounds.

When there were no visitors, Paul now took his meals with his parents, as he was beyond the nursery control. His mother went into town nearly every day. She had discovered that she had an odd knack of sketching furs and dress materials, so she worked secretly in the studio of a friend who was the chief 'artist' for the leading drapers. She drew the figures of ladies in furs and ladies in silk and sequins for the newspaper advertisements. This young woman artist earned several thousand pounds a year, but Paul's mother only made several hundreds, and she was again dissatisfied. She so wanted to be first in something, and she did not succeed, even in making sketches for drapery advertisements.

She was down to breakfast on the morning of her birthday. Paul watched her face as she read her letters. He knew the lawyer's letter. As his mother read it, her face hardened and became more expressionless. Then a cold, determined look came on her mouth. She hid the letter under the pile of others, and said not a word about it.

"Didn't you have anything nice in the post for your birthday, mother?" said Paul.

"Quite moderately nice," she said, her voice cold and absent.

She went away to town without saying more.

But in the afternoon Uncle Oscar appeared. He said Paul's mother had had a long interview with the lawyer, asking if the whole five thousand could not be advanced at once, as she was in debt.

"What do you think, uncle?" said the boy.

"I leave it to you, son."

"Oh, let her have it, then! We can get some more with the other," said the boy.

"A bird in the hand is worth two in the bush, laddie!" said Uncle Oscar.

"But I'm sure to *know* for the Grand National; or the Lincolnshire; or else the Derby. I'm sure to know for *one* of them," said Paul.

So Uncle Oscar signed the agreement, and Paul's mother touched the whole five thousand. Then something very curious happened. The voices in the house suddenly went mad, like a chorus of frogs on a spring evening. There were certain new furnishings, and Paul had a tutor. He was *really* going to Eton, his father's school, in the following autumn. There were flowers in the winter, and a blossoming of the luxury Paul's mother had been used to. And yet the voices in the house, behind the sprays of mimosa and almond-blossom, and from under the piles of iridescent cushions, simply trilled and screamed in a sort of ecstasy: "There *must* be more money! Oh-h-h; there *must* be more money. Oh, now, now-w! Now-w-w—there *must* be more money!—more than ever! More than ever!"

It frightened Paul terribly. He studied away at his Latin and Greek with his tutor. But his intense hours were spent with Bassett. The Grand National had gone by: he had not 'known', and had lost a hundred pounds. Summer was at hand. He was in agony for the Lincoln. But even for the Lincoln he didn't 'know', and he lost fifty pounds. He became wild-eyed and strange, as if something were going to explode in him.

"Let it alone, son! Don't you bother about it!" urged Uncle Oscar. But it was as if the boy couldn't really hear what his uncle was saying.

"I've got to know for the Derby! I've got to know for the Derby!" the child reiterated, his big blue eyes blazing with a sort of madness.

His mother noticed how overwrought he was.

"You'd better go to the seaside. Wouldn't you like to go now to the seaside, instead of waiting? I think you'd better," she said, looking down at him anxiously, her heart curiously heavy because of him.

But the child lifted his uncanny blue eyes.

"I couldn't possibly go before the Derby, mother!" he said. "I couldn't possibly!"

"Why not?" she said, her voice becoming heavy when she was opposed. "Why not? You can still go from the seaside to see the Derby with your Uncle Oscar, if that's what you wish. No need for you to wait here. Besides, I think you care too much about these races. It's a bad sign. My family has been a gambling family, and you won't know till you grow up how much damage it has done. But it has done damage. I shall have to send Bassett away, and ask Uncle Oscar not to talk racing to you, unless you promise to be reasonable about it: go away to the seaside and forget it. You're all nerves!"

"I'll do what you like, mother, so long as you don't send me away till after the Derby," the boy said.

"Send you away from where? Just from this house?"

"Yes," he said, gazing at her.

"Why, you curious child, what makes you care about this house so much, suddenly? I never knew you loved it."

He gazed at her without speaking. He had a secret within a secret, something he had not divulged, even to Bassett or to his Uncle Oscar.

But his mother, after standing undecided and a little bit sullen for some moments, said:

"Very well, then! Don't go to the seaside till after the Derby, if you don't wish it. But promise me you won't let your nerves go to pieces. Promise you won't think so much about horse-racing and *events,* as you call them!"

"Oh no," said the boy casually. "I won't think much about them, mother. You needn't worry. I wouldn't worry, mother, if I were you."

"If you were me and I were you," said his mother, "I wonder what we *should* do!"

"But you know you needn't worry, mother, don't you?" the boy repeated.

"I should be awfully glad to know it," she said wearily.

"Oh, well, you *can,* you know. I mean, you *ought* to know you needn't worry," he insisted.

"Ought I? Then I'll see about it," she said.

Paul's secret of secrets was his wooden horse, that which had no name. Since he was emancipated from a nurse and a nursery-governess, he had had his rocking-horse removed to his own bedroom at the top of the house.

"Surely you're too big for a rocking-horse!" his mother had remonstrated.

"Well, you see, mother, till I can have a *real* horse, I like to have *some* sort of animal about," had been his quaint answer.

"Do you feel he keeps you company?" she laughed.

"Oh yes! He's very good, he always keeps me company, when I'm there," said Paul.

So the horse, rather shabby, stood in an arrested prance in the boy's bedroom.

The Derby was drawing near, and the boy grew more and more tense. He hardly heard what was spoken to him, he was very frail, and his eyes were really uncanny. His mother had sudden strange seizures of uneasiness about him. Sometimes, for half an hour, she would feel a sudden anxiety about him that was almost anguish. She wanted to rush to him at once, and know he was safe.

Two nights before the Derby, she was at a big party in town, when one of her rushes of anxiety about her boy, her first-born, gripped her heart till she could hardly speak. She fought with the feeling, might and main, for she believed in common sense. But it was too strong. She had to leave the dance and go downstairs to telephone to the country. The children's nursery-governess was terribly surprised and startled at being rung up in the night.

"Are the children all right, Miss Wilmot?"

"Oh yes, they are quite all right."

"Master Paul? Is he all right?"

"He went to bed as right as a trivet. Shall I run up and look at him?"

"No," said Paul's mother reluctantly. "No! Don't trouble. It's all right. Don't sit up. We shall be home fairly soon." She did not want her son's privacy intruded upon.

"Very good," said the governess.

It was about one o'clock when Paul's mother and father drove up to their house. All was still. Paul's mother went to her room and slipped off her white fur cloak. She had told her maid not to wait up for her. She heard her husband downstairs, mixing a whisky and soda.

And then, because of the strange anxiety at her heart, she stole upstairs to her son's room. Noiselessly she went along the upper corridor. Was there a faint noise? What was it?

She stood, with arrested muscles, outside his door, listening. There was a strange, heavy, and yet not loud noise. Her heart stood still. It was a soundless noise, yet rushing and powerful. Something huge, in violent, hushed motion. What was it? What in God's name was it? She ought to know. She felt that she knew the noise. She knew what it was.

Yet she could not place it. She couldn't say what it was. And on and on it went, like a madness.

Softly, frozen with anxiety and fear, she turned the door-handle.

The room was dark. Yet in the space near the window, she heard and saw something plunging to and fro. She gazed in fear and amazement.

Then suddenly she switched on the light, and saw her son, in his green pyjamas, madly surging on the rocking-horse. The blaze of light suddenly lit him up, as he urged the wooden horse, and lit her up, as she stood, blonde, in her dress of pale green and crystal, in the doorway.

"Paul!" she cried. "Whatever are you doing?"

"It's Malabar!" he screamed in a powerful, strange voice. "It's Malabar!"

His eyes blazed at her for one strange and senseless second, as he ceased urging his wooden horse. Then he fell with a crash to the ground, and she, all her tormented motherhood flooding upon her, rushed to gather him up.

But he was unconscious, and unconscious he remained, with some brain-fever. He talked and tossed, and his mother sat stonily by his side.

"Malabar! It's Malabar! Bassett, Bassett, I *know!* It's Malabar!"

So the child cried, trying to get up and urge the rocking-horse that gave him his inspiration.

"What does he mean by Malabar?" asked the heart-frozen mother.

"I don't know," said the father stonily.

"What does he mean by Malabar?" she asked her brother Oscar.

"It's one of the horses running for the Derby," was the answer.

And, in spite of himself, Oscar Cresswell spoke to Bassett, and himself put a thousand on Malabar: at fourteen to one.

The third day of the illness was critical: they were waiting for a change. The boy, with his rather long, curly hair, was tossing ceaselessly on the pillow. He neither slept nor regained consciousness, and his eyes were like blue stones. His mother sat, feeling her heart had gone, turned actually into a stone.

In the evening, Oscar Cresswell did not come, but Bassett sent a message, saying could he come up for one moment, just one moment? Paul's mother was very angry at the intrusion, but on second thoughts she agreed. The boy was the same. Perhaps Bassett might bring him to consciousness.

The gardener, a shortish fellow with a little brown moustache and sharp little brown eyes, tiptoed into the room, touched his imaginary cap to Paul's mother, and stole to the bedside, staring with glittering, smallish eyes at the tossing, dying child.

"Master Paul!" he whispered. "Master Paul! Malabar came in first all right, a clean win. I did as you told me. You've made over seventy thousand pounds, you have; you've got over eighty thousand. Malabar came in all right, Master Paul."

"Malabar! Malabar! Did I say Malabar, mother? Did I say Malabar? Do you think I'm lucky, mother? I knew Malabar, didn't I? Over eighty thousand pounds! I call that lucky, don't you, mother? Over eighty thousand pounds! I knew, didn't I know I knew? Malabar came in all right. If I ride my horse till I'm sure, then I tell you, Bassett, you can go as high as you like. Did you go for all you were worth, Bassett?"

"I went a thousand on it, Master Paul."

"I never told you, mother, that if I can ride my horse, and *get there,* then I'm absolutely sure—oh, absolutely! Mother, did I ever tell you? I *am* lucky!"

"No, you never did," said his mother.

But the boy died in the night.

And even as he lay dead, his mother heard her brother's voice saying to her: "My God, Hester, you're eighty-odd thousand to the good, and a poor devil of a son to the bad. But, poor devil, poor devil, he's best gone out of a life where he rides his rocking-horse to find a winner."

(1932)

Katherine Mansfield

(1 8 8 8 – 1 9 2 3)

Katherine Mansfield, the daughter of Sir Harold Beauchamp, a prominent businessman, was born in Wellington, New Zealand. Mansfield chose to live in England, although most of her stories are set in her native country. After studying music at Queen's College, London, she returned to New Zealand in 1906. In that year she made a disastrous marriage, became pregnant by another man, and had a miscarriage. The short prose sketches written during this troubled period formed her first book, *In a German Pension*, published in 1911. Mansfield returned to London, where she met and eventually married critic John Middleton Murry. She began to write and publish steadily, in spite of increasingly poor health. Trips to France and Switzerland failed to cure her tuberculosis, and Mansfield died in January 1923. She was 35.

In her short stories, Mansfield expressed her themes with carefully chosen details rather than with explicit statements. She was a keen observer of the multitude of small details that make up the surfaces of her finely honed stories. (Her use of detail led many to compare her work with that of Chekhov.) Mansfield was also an innovator in her flawless use of temporal shifts, which allowed her to sketch large portions of her characters' histories without betraying either her tight economy of structure or her naturalistic textures. Although her career lasted only a decade, Mansfield was an influential writer.

Mansfield's major works are *In a German Pension* (1911), *Bliss and Other Stories* (1920), *The Garden Party and Other Stories* (1922), and *The Dove's Nest and Other Stories* (1923). A volume called *Collected Stories* appeared in 1945.

KATHERINE MANSFIELD

The Fly

"Y'ARE very snug in here," piped old Mr. Woodifield, and he peered out of the great, green leather armchair by his friend the boss's desk as a baby peers out of its pram. His talk was over; it was time for him to be off. But he did not want to go. Since he had retired, since his . . . stroke, the wife and the girls kept him boxed up in the house every day of the week except Tuesday. On Tuesday he was dressed up and brushed and allowed to cut back to the City for the day. Though what he did there the wife and girls couldn't imagine. Made a nuisance of himself to his friends, they supposed. . . . Well, perhaps so. All the same, we cling to our last pleasures as the tree clings to its last leaves. So there sat old Woodifield, smoking a cigar and staring almost greedily at the boss, who rolled in his office chair, stout, rosy, five years older than he, and still going strong, still at the helm. It did one good to see him.

Wistfully, admiringly, the old voice added, "It's snug in here, upon my word!"

"Yes, it's comfortable enough," agreed the boss, and he flipped the *Financial Times* with a paper-knife. As a matter of fact he was proud of his room; he liked to have it admired, especially by old Woodifield. It gave him a feeling of deep, solid satisfaction to be planted there in the midst of it in full view of that frail old figure in the muffler.

"I've had it done up lately," he explained, as he had explained for the past—how many?—weeks. "New carpet," and he pointed to the bright red carpet with a pattern of large white rings. "New furniture," and he nodded towards the massive bookcase and the table with legs like twisted treacle. "Electric heating!" He waved almost exultantly towards the five transparent, pearly sausages glowing so softly in the tilted copper pan.

But he did not draw old Woodifield's attention to the photograph over the table of a grave-looking boy in uniform standing in one of those spectral photographers' parks with photographers' storm-clouds behind him. It was not new. It had been there for over six years.

"There was something I wanted to tell you," said old Woodifield, and his eyes grew dim remembering. "Now what was it? I had it in my mind when I started out this morning." His hands began to tremble, and patches of red showed above his beard.

Poor old chap, he's on his last pins, thought the boss. And, feeling kindly, he winked at the old man, and said jokingly, "I tell you what. I've got a little drop of something here that'll do you good before you go out into the cold again. It's beautiful stuff. It wouldn't hurt a child." He took a key off his watch-chain, unlocked a cupboard below his desk, and drew forth a dark, squat bottle. "That's the medicine," said he. "And the man from whom I got it told me on the strict Q.T. it came from the cellars at Windsor Cassel."[1]

Old Woodifield's mouth fell open at the sight. He couldn't have looked more surprised if the boss had produced a rabbit.

"It's whisky, ain't it?" he piped, feebly.

The boss turned the bottle and lovingly showed him the label. Whisky it was.

"D'you know," said he, peering up at the boss wonderingly, "they won't let me touch it at home." And he looked as though he was going to cry.

"Ah, that's where we know a bit more than the ladies," cried the boss, swooping across for two tumblers that stood on the table with the water-bottle, and pouring a generous finger into each. "Drink it down. It'll do you good. And don't put any water with it. It's sacrilege to tamper with stuff like this. Ah!" He tossed off his, pulled out his handkerchief, hastily wiped his moustaches, and cocked an eye at old Woodifield, who was rolling his in his chaps.

The old man swallowed, was silent a moment, and then said faintly, "It's nutty!"

But it warmed him; it crept into his chill old brain—he remembered.

"That was it," he said, heaving himself out of his chair. "I thought you'd like to know. The girls were in Belgium last week having a look at poor Reggie's grave, and they happened to come across your boy's. They're quite near each other, it seems."

Old Woodifield paused, but the boss made no reply. Only a quiver in his eyelids showed that he heard.

"The girls were delighted with the way the place is kept," piped the old voice. "Beautifully looked after. Couldn't be better if they were at home. You've not been across, have yer?"

"No, no!" For various reasons the boss had not been across.

"There's miles of it," quavered old Woodifield, "and it's all as neat as a garden. Flowers growing on all the graves. Nice broad paths." It was plain from his voice how much he liked a nice broad path.

The pause came again. Then the old man brightened wonderfully.

"D'you know what the hotel made the girls pay for a pot of jam?" he piped. "Ten francs! Robbery, I call it. It was a little pot, so Gertrude says, no bigger than a half-crown. And she hadn't taken more than a spoonful when they charged her ten francs. Gertrude brought the pot away with her to teach 'em a lesson. Quite right, too; it's trading on our feelings. They think because we're over there having a look around we're ready to pay anything. That's what it is." And he turned towards the door.

---

[1] Windsor Castle, the official residence of the British royal family.

"Quite right, quite right!" cried the boss, though what was quite right he hadn't the least idea. He came round by his desk, followed the shuffling footsteps to the door, and saw the old fellow out. Woodifield was gone.

For a long moment the boss stayed, staring at nothing, while the grey-haired office messenger, watching him, dodged in and out of his cubbyhole like a dog that expects to be taken for a run. Then: "I'll see nobody for half an hour, Macey," said the boss. "Understand? Nobody at all."

"Very good, sir."

The door shut, the firm heavy steps recrossed the bright carpet, the fat body plumped down in the spring chair, and leaning forward, the boss covered his face with his hands. He wanted, he intended, he had arranged to weep. . . .

It had been a terrible shock to him when old Woodifield sprang that remark upon him about the boy's grave. It was exactly as though the earth had opened and he had seen the boy lying there with Woodifield's girls staring down at him. For it was strange. Although over six years had passed away, the boss never thought of the boy except as lying unchanged, unblemished in his uniform, asleep for ever. "My son!" groaned the boss. But no tears came yet. In the past, in the first months and even years after the boy's death, he had only to say those words to be overcome by such grief that nothing short of a violent fit of weeping could relieve him. Time, he had declared then, he had told everybody, could make no difference. Other men perhaps might recover, might live their loss down, but not he. How was it possible? His boy was an only son. Ever since his birth the boss had worked at building up this business for him; it had no other meaning if it was not for the boy. Life itself had come to have no other meaning. How on earth could he have slaved, denied himself, kept going all those years without the promise for ever before him of the boy's stepping into his shoes and carrying on where he left off?

And that promise had been so near being fulfilled. The boy had been in the office learning the ropes for a year before the war. Every morning they had started off together; they had come back by the same train. And what congratulations he had received as the boy's father! No wonder; he had taken to it marvellously. As to his popularity with the staff, every man jack of them down to old Macey couldn't make enough of the boy. And he wasn't in the least spoilt. No, he was just his bright, natural self, with the right word for everybody, with that boyish look and his habit of saying, "Simply splendid!"

But all that was over and done with as though it never had been. The day had come when Macey had handed him the telegram that brought the whole place crashing about his head. "Deeply regret to inform you . . ." And he had left the office a broken man, with his life in ruins.

Six years ago, six years . . . How quickly time passed! It might have happened yesterday. The boss took his hands from his face; he was puzzled.

Something seemed to be wrong with him. He wasn't feeling as he wanted to feel. He decided to get up and have a look at the boy's photograph. But it wasn't a favorite photograph of his; the expression was unnatural. It was cold, even stern-looking. The boy had never looked like that.

At that moment the boss noticed that a fly had fallen into his broad inkpot, and was trying feebly but desperately to clamber out again. Help! help! said those struggling legs. But the sides of the inkpot were wet and slippery; it fell back again and began to swim. The boss took up a pen, picked the fly out of the ink, and shook it on to a piece of blotting-paper. For a fraction of a second it lay still on the dark patch that oozed round it. Then the front legs waved, took hold, and, pulling its small sodden body up it began the immense task of cleaning the ink from its wings. Over and under, over and under, went a leg along a wing, as the stone goes over and under the scythe. Then there was a pause, while the fly, seeming to stand on the tips of its toes, tried to expand first one wing and then the other. It succeeded at last, and, sitting down, it began, like a minute cat, to clean its face. Now one could imagine that the little front legs rubbed against each other lightly, joyfully. The horrible danger was over; it had escaped; it was ready for life again.

But just then the boss had an idea. He plunged his pen back into the ink, leaned his thick wrist on the blotting paper, and as the fly tried its wings down came a great heavy blot. What would it make of that? What indeed! The little beggar seemed absolutely cowed, stunned, and afraid to move because of what would happen next. But then, as if painfully, it dragged itself forward. The front legs waved, caught hold, and, more slowly this time, the task began from the beginning.

He's a plucky little devil, thought the boss, and he felt a real admiration for the fly's courage. That was the way to tackle things; that was the right spirit. Never say die; it was only a question of . . . But the fly had again finished its laborious task, and the boss had just time to refill his pen, to shake fair and square on the new-cleaned body yet another dark drop. What about it this time? A painful moment of suspense followed. But behold, the front legs were again waving; the boss felt a rush of relief. He leaned over the fly and said to it tenderly, "You artful little b. . . ." And he actually had the brilliant notion of breathing on it to help the drying process. All the same, there was something timid and weak about its efforts now, and the boss decided that this time should be the last, as he dipped the pen into the inkpot.

It was. The last blot on the soaked blotting-paper, and the draggled fly lay in it and did not stir. The back legs were stuck to the body; the front legs were not to be seen.

"Come on," said the boss. "Look sharp!" And he stirred it with his pen—in vain. Nothing happened or was likely to happen. The fly was dead.

The boss lifted the corpse on the end of the paper-knife and flung it into the waste-paper basket. But such a grinding feeling of wretchedness seized him that he felt positively frightened. He started forward and pressed the bell for Macey.

"Bring me some fresh blotting-paper," he said, sternly, "and look sharp about it." And while the old dog padded away he fell to wondering what it was he had been thinking about before. What was it? It was . . . He took out his handkerchief and passed it inside his collar. For the life of him he could not remember.

(1922)

Katherine Anne Porter

(1 8 9 0 – 1 9 8 0)

Katherine Anne Porter was born in Indian Creek, Texas, in 1890, and was educated at home and in convent schools in Texas and Louisiana. She rebelled against family and regional values and traveled widely, working as a journalist and free-lance writer in New York, Dallas, Denver, Mexico, and Europe. In spite of her self-imposed exile, much of her best writing included her southern childhood. Porter's first volume of stories, *Flowering Judas*, did not appear until she was 40; after that, she built a considerable reputation. Porter gave lectures or readings at more than 200 universities in the United States and Europe and served as writer-in-residence at a number of American institutions. Her *Collected Stories* (1965) won the Pulitzer Prize for fiction. Porter died in 1980.

Porter, a very exacting writer, wanted to expose only her best work to the public. She destroyed work with which she was not satisfied. Not interested in representing life as alienating, she preferred to demonstrate the hope implicit in artistic creation, the ability to order an admittedly chaotic world. Given these values, it is not surprising that many critics have pointed to Henry James as her model; Porter herself professed a preference for Mansfield over Gertrude Stein. Porter is clearly a regional writer of the American South: like Faulkner, she used the metaphor of the fallen South to good advantage and wove its social texture into her work. But she is more detached in perspective than most regional writers. Her delicate symbolist technique and the acuity of her perception mark her as one of the finest short-story writers of her generation.

Porter's works include *Flowering Judas* (1930), *Hacienda* (1934), *Pale Horse Pale Rider* (1939), *The Leaning Tower* (1944), *Ship of Fools* (1962), and *The Collected Stories of Katherine Anne Porter* (1965). Her criticism, personal essays, and travel pieces were gathered in *The Days Before* (1967).

KATHERINE ANNE PORTER

The Grave

THE grandfather, dead for more than thirty years, had been twice disturbed in his long repose by the constancy and possessiveness of his widow. She removed his bones first to Louisiana and then to Texas as if she had set out to find her own burial place, knowing well she would never return to the places she had left. In Texas she set up a small cemetery in a corner of her first farm, and as the family connection grew, and oddments of relations came over from Kentucky to settle, it contained at last about twenty graves. After the grandmother's death, part of her land was to be sold for the benefit of certain of her children, and the cemetery happened to lie in the part set aside for sale. It was necessary to take up the bodies and bury them again in the family plot in the big new public cemetery, where the grandmother had been buried. At last her husband was to lie beside her for eternity, as she had planned.

The family cemetery had been a pleasant small neglected garden of tangled rose bushes and ragged cedar trees and cypress, the simple flat stones rising out of uncropped sweet-smelling wild grass. The graves were lying open and empty one burning day when Miranda and her brother Paul, who often went together to hunt rabbits and doves, propped their twenty-two Winchester rifles carefully against the rail fence, climbed over and explored among the graves. She was nine years old and he was twelve.

They peered into the pits all shaped alike with such purposeful accuracy, and looking at each other with pleased adventurous eyes, they said in solemn tones: "These were graves!" trying by words to shape a special, suitable emotion in their minds, but they felt nothing except an agreeable thrill of wonder: they were seeing a new sight, doing something they had not done before. In them both there was also a small disappointment at the entire commonplaceness of the actual spectacle. Even if it had once contained a coffin for years upon years, when the coffin was gone a grave was just a hole in the ground. Miranda leaped into the pit that had held her grandfather's bones. Scratching around aimlessly and pleasurably as any young animal, she scooped up a lump of earth and weighed it in her palm. It had a pleasantly sweet, corrupt smell, being mixed with cedar needles and small leaves, and as the crumbs fell apart, she saw a silver dove no larger than a hazel nut, with spread wings and a neat fan-shaped tail. The breast had a deep round hollow in it. Turning it up to the fierce sunlight, she saw that the inside of the hollow was cut in little whorls. She scrambled out, over the pile of loose earth that had fallen back into one end of the grave, calling to Paul that she had found something, he must guess what. . . . His head appeared smiling over the rim of another grave. He waved a closed hand at her. "I've got something too!" They ran to compare treasures, making a game of it, so many guesses each, all wrong, and a final showdown with opened palms. Paul had found a thin wide gold ring carved with intricate flowers and leaves. Miranda was smitten at sight of the ring and wished to have it. Paul seemed more impressed by the dove. They made a trade, with some little bickering. After he had got the dove in his hand, Paul said, "Don't you know what this is? This is a screw head for a *coffin!* . . . I'll bet nobody else in the world has one like this!"

Miranda glanced at it without covetousness. She had the gold ring on her thumb; it fitted perfectly. "Maybe we ought to go now," she said, "maybe one of the niggers 'll see us and tell somebody." They knew the land had been sold, the cemetery was no longer theirs, and they felt like trespassers. They climbed back over the fence, slung their rifles loosely under their arms—they had been shooting at targets with various kinds of firearms since they were seven years old—and set out to look for the rabbits and doves or whatever small game might happen along. On these expeditions Miranda always followed at Paul's heels along the path, obeying instructions about handling her gun when going through fences; learning how to stand it up properly so it would not slip and fire unexpectedly; how to wait her time for a shot and not just bang away in the air without looking, spoiling shots for Paul, who really could hit things if given a chance. Now and then, in her excitement at seeing birds whizz up suddenly before her face, or a rabbit leap across her very toes, she lost her head, and almost without sighting she flung her rifle up and pulled the trigger. She hardly ever hit any sort of mark. She had no proper sense of hunting at all. Her brother would be often completely disgusted with her. "You don't care whether you get your bird or not," he said. "That's no way to hunt." Miranda could not understand his indignation. She had seen him smash his hat and yell with fury when he had missed his aim. "What I like about shooting," said Miranda, with exasperating inconsequence, "is pulling the trigger and hearing the noise."

"Then, by golly," said Paul, "whyn't you go back to the range and shoot at bulls-eyes?"

"I'd just as soon," said Miranda, "only like this, we walk around more."

"Well, you just stay behind and stop spoiling my shots," said Paul, who, when he made a kill, wanted to be certain he had made it. Miranda, who alone brought down a bird once in twenty rounds, always claimed as her own any game they got when they fired at the same moment. It was tiresome and unfair and her brother was sick of it.

"Now, the first dove we see, or the first rabbit, is mine," he told her. "And the next will be yours. Remember that and don't get smarty."

"What about snakes?" asked Miranda idly. "Can I have the first snake?"

Waving her thumb gently and watching her gold ring glitter, Miranda lost interest in shooting. She was wearing her summer roughing outfit: dark blue overalls, a light blue shirt, a hired-man's straw hat, and thick brown sandals. Her brother had the same outfit except his was a sober hickory-nut color. Ordinarily Miranda preferred her overalls to any other dress, though it was making rather a scandal in the countryside, for the year was 1903, and in the back country the law of female decorum had teeth in it. Her father had been criticized for letting his girls dress like boys and go careering around astride barebacked horses. Big sister Maria, the really independent and fearless one, in spite of her rather affected ways, rode at a dead run with only a rope knotted around her horse's nose. It was said the motherless family was running down, with the Grandmother no longer there to hold it together. It was known that she had discriminated against her son Harry in her will, and that he was in straits about money. Some of his old neighbors reflected with vicious satisfaction that now he would probably not be so stiffnecked, nor have any more high-stepping horses either. Miranda knew this, though she could not say how. She had met along the road old women of the kind who smoked corn-cob pipes, who had treated her grandmother with most sincere respect. They slanted their gummy old eyes side-ways at the granddaughter and said, "Ain't you ashamed of yoself, Missy? It's against the Scriptures to dress like that. Whut yo Pappy thinkin about?" Miranda, with her powerful social sense, which was like a fine set of antennae radiating from every pore of her skin, would feel ashamed because she knew well it was rude and ill-bred to shock anybody, even bad-tempered old crones, though she had faith in her father's judgment and was perfectly comfortable in the clothes. Her father had said, "They're just what you need, and they'll save your dresses for school. . . ." This sounded quite simple and natural to her. She had been brought up in rigorous economy. Wastefulness was vulgar. It was also a sin. These were truths; she had heard them repeated many times and never once disputed.

Now the ring, shining with the serene purity of fine gold on her rather grubby thumb, turned her feelings against her overalls and sockless feet, toes sticking through the thick brown leather straps. She wanted to go back to the farmhouse, take a good cold bath, dust herself with plenty of Maria's violet talcum powder—provided Maria was not present to object, of course—put on the thinnest, most becoming dress she owned, with a big sash, and sit in a wicker chair under the trees. . . . These things were not all she wanted, of course; she had vague stirrings of desire for luxury and a grand way of living which could not take precise form in her imagination but were founded on family legend of past wealth and leisure. These immediate comforts were what she could have, and she wanted them at once. She lagged rather far behind Paul, and once she thought of just turning back without a word and going home. She stopped, thinking that Paul would never do that to her, and so she would have to tell him. When a rabbit leaped, she let Paul have it without dispute. He killed it with one shot.

When she came up with him, he was already kneeling, examining the wound, the rabbit trailing from his hands. "Right through the head," he said complacently, as if he had aimed for it. He took out his sharp, competent bowie knife and started to skin the body. He did it very cleanly and quickly. Uncle Jimbilly knew how to prepare the skins so that Miranda always had fur coats for her dolls, for though she never cared much for her dolls she liked seeing them in fur coats. The children knelt facing each other over the dead animal. Miranda watched admiringly while her brother stripped the skin away as if he were taking off a glove. The flayed flesh emerged dark scarlet, sleek, firm; Miranda with thumb and finger felt the long fine muscles with the silvery flat strips binding them to the joints. Brother lifted the oddly bloated belly. "Look," he said, in a low amazed voice. "It was going to have young ones."

Very carefully he slit the thin flesh from the center ribs to the flanks, and a scarlet bag appeared. He slit again and pulled the bag open, and there lay a bundle of tiny rabbits, each wrapped in a thin scarlet veil. The brother pulled these off and there they were, dark gray, their sleek wet down lying in minute even ripples, like a baby's head just washed, their unbelievably small delicate ears folded close, their little blind faces almost featureless.

Miranda said, "Oh, I want to *see*," under her breath. She looked and looked—excited but not frightened, for she was accustomed to the sight of animals killed in hunting—filled with pity and astonishment and a kind of shocked delight in the wonderful little creatures for their own sakes, they were so pretty. She touched one of them ever so carefully, "Ah, there's blood running over them," she said and began to tremble without knowing why. Yet she wanted most deeply to see and to know. Having seen, she felt at once as if she had known all along. The very memory of her former ignorance faded, she had always known just this. No one had ever told her anything outright, she had been rather unobservant of the animal life around her because she was so accustomed to animals. They seemed simply disorderly and unaccountably rude in their habits, but altogether natural and not very interesting. Her brother had spoken as if he had known about everything all along. He may have seen all this before. He had never said a word to her, but she knew now a part at least of what he knew. She understood a little of the secret, formless intuitions in her own mind and body, which had been clearing up, taking form, so gradually and so steadily she had not realized that she was learning what she had to know. Paul said cautiously, as if he were talking about something forbidden: "They were just about ready to be born." His voice dropped on the last word. "I know," said Miranda, "like kittens. I know, like babies." She was quietly and terribly agitated, standing again with her rifle under her arm, looking down at the bloody heap. "I don't want the skin," she said, "I won't have it." Paul buried the young rabbits again in their mother's body, wrapped the skin around her, carried her to a clump of sage bushes, and hid her away. He came out again at once and said to Miranda, with an eager friendliness, a confidential tone quite unusual in him, as if he were taking her into an important secret on equal terms; "Listen now. Now you listen to me, and don't ever forget. Don't you ever tell a living soul that you saw this. Don't tell a soul. Don't tell Dad because I'll get into trouble. He'll say I'm leading you into things you ought not to do. He's always saying that. So now don't you go and forget and blab out sometime the way you're always doing. . . . Now, that's a secret. Don't you tell."

Miranda never told, she did not even wish to tell anybody. She thought about the whole worrisome affair with confused unhappiness for a few days. Then it sank quietly into her mind and was heaped over by accumulated thousands of impressions, for nearly twenty years. One day she was picking her path among the puddles and crushed refuse of a market street in a strange city of a strange country, when without warning, plain and clear in its true colors as if she looked through a frame upon a scene that had not stirred nor changed since the moment it happened, the episode of that far-off day leaped from its burial place before her mind's eye. She was so reasonlessly horrified she halted suddenly staring, the scene before her eyes dimmed by the vision back of them. An Indian vendor had held up before her a tray of dyed sugar sweets, in the shapes of all kinds of small creatures: birds, baby chicks, baby rabbits, lambs, baby pigs. They were in gay colors and smelled of vanilla, maybe. . . . It was a very hot day and the smell in the market, with its piles of raw flesh and wilting flowers, was like the mingled sweetness and corruption she had smelled that other day in the empty cemetery at home: the day she had remembered always until now vaguely as the time she and her brother had found treasure in the opened graves. Instantly upon this thought the dreadful vision faded, and she saw clearly her brother, whose childhood face she had forgotten, standing again in the blazing sunshine, again twelve years old, a pleased sober smile in his eyes, turning the silver dove over and over in his hands.

(1944)

William Faulkner

(1 8 9 7 – 1 9 6 2)

William Faulkner was born in New Albany, Mississippi, and spent most of his life in nearby Oxford. In 1918 he was turned down by the U.S. Army and enlisted in the Canadian Royal Flying Corps. The war ended before he completed his training. He returned to Oxford and studied for two years at the University of Mississippi, then worked as a clerk and at other odd jobs so that he could write. His first book, a volume of lush, romantic poetry, called *The Marble Faun,* appeared in 1924. In 1925, while visiting New Orleans, Faulkner was encouraged by Sherwood Anderson and began to write his first novel. After a brief trip to Europe he returned to Mississippi; he also visited Hollywood occasionally. His first novel, *Soldiers' Pay,* launched his career in 1926. He began to create a fictional place, Yoknapatawpha County, in *Sartoris* (published in 1929). By the mid-thirties, Faulkner was recognized as a great writer. He worked for many years as a Hollywood screenwriter to supplement his income. Faulkner won two Pulitzer Prizes and the Nobel Prize in 1949. He died in Mississippi in 1962.

In his great novels—*The Sound and the Fury, As I Lay Dying, Light in August, Absalom, Absalom*—Faulkner combined sophisticated modern techniques with an epic sense; his narrative of the decline and fall of the great families of the South became the eternal story of all societies and all men and women. He was a powerful stylist and a profound psychologist. He used a stream-of-consciousness method, and James Joyce and Virginia Woolf are his only peers. His novels, particularly *Absalom, Absalom* and *The Sound and the Fury,* are intricately narrated from a variety of viewpoints. They have about them something of the stark, brutal simplicity of Greek tragedy, particularly the work of Aeschylus. A sense of original sin or of an inherent flaw fills the minds of Faulkner's characters and becomes a relentless, self-fulfilling psychosis. Faulkner sensed humanity's failure to achieve ideals— for example, the blindness to simple humanity in the South's treatment of blacks. He was fascinated by the fall of the great—of Sartoris, of Sutpen. But he found genuine virtue in the women and men who endure—the Dilseys, the Lena Groves. Faulkner's characters feel guilt and torment and suffering, endurance, loyalty, and love.

Faulkner's major novels include *Sartoris* (1929), *The Sound and the Fury* (1929), *As I Lay Dying* (1930), *Light in August* (1932), *Absalom, Absalom* (1936), *The Hamlet* (1940), *Go Down Moses* (1942), *Intruder in the Dust* (1948), *The Town* (1957), *The Mansion* (1959), and *The Reivers* (1962). Most of Faulkner's short stories were published in *Collected Stories* (1950).

WILLIAM FAULKNER

A Rose for Emily

I

WHEN Miss Emily Grierson died, our whole town went to her funeral: the men through a sort of respectful affection for a fallen monument, the women mostly out of curiosity to see the inside of her house, which no one save an old manservant—a combined gardener and cook—had seen in at least ten years.

It was a big, squarish frame house that had once been white, decorated with cupolas and spires and scrolled balconies in the heavily lightsome style of the seventies, set on what had once been our most select street. But garages and cotton gins had encroached and obliterated even the august names of that neighborhood; only Miss Emily's house was left, lifting its stubborn and coquettish decay above the cotton wagons and the gasoline pumps—an eyesore among eyesores. And now Miss Emily had gone to join the representatives of those august names where they lay in the cedar-bemused cemetery among the ranked and anonymous graves of Union and Confederate soldiers who fell at the battle of Jefferson.

Alive, Miss Emily had been a tradition, a duty, and a care; a sort of hereditary obligation upon the town, dating from that day in 1894 when Colonel Sartoris, the mayor—he who fathered the edict that no Negro woman should appear on the streets without an apron—remitted her taxes, the dispensation dating from the death of her father on into perpetuity. Not that Miss Emily would have accepted charity. Colonel Sartoris invented an involved tale to the effect that Miss Emily's father had loaned money to the town, which the town, as a matter of business, preferred this way of repaying. Only a man of Colonel Sartoris' generation and thought could have invented it, and only a woman could have believed it.

When the next generation, with its more modern ideas, became mayors and aldermen, this arrangement created some little dissatisfaction. On the first of the year they mailed her a tax notice. February came, and there was no reply. They wrote her a formal letter, asking her to call at the sheriff's office at her convenience. A week later the mayor wrote her himself, offering to call or to send his car for her, and received in reply a note on paper of an archaic shape, in a thin, flowing calligraphy in faded ink, to the effect that she no longer went out at all. The tax notice was also enclosed, without comment.

They called a special meeting of the Board of Aldermen. A deputation waited upon her, knocked at the door through which no visitor had passed since she ceased giving china-painting lessons eight or ten years earlier. They were admitted by the old Negro into a dim hall from which a stairway mounted into still more shadow. It smelled of dust and disuse—a close, dank smell. The Negro led them into the parlor. It was furnished in heavy, leather-covered furniture. When the Negro opened the blinds of one window, they could see that the leather was cracked; and when they sat down, a faint dust rose sluggishly about their thighs, spinning with slow motes in the single sun-ray. On a tarnished gilt easel before the fireplace stood a crayon portrait of Miss Emily's father.

They rose when she entered—a small, fat woman in black, with a thin gold chain descending to her waist and vanishing into her belt, leaning on an ebony cane with a tarnished gold head. Her skeleton was small and spare; perhaps that was why what would have been merely plumpness in another was obesity in her. She looked bloated, like a body long submerged in motionless water, and of that pallid hue. Her eyes, lost in the fatty ridges of her face, looked like two small pieces of coal pressed into a lump of dough as they moved from one face to another while the visitors stated their errand.

She did not ask them to sit. She just stood in the door and listened quietly until the spokesman came to a stumbling halt. Then they could hear the invisible watch ticking at the end of the gold chain.

Her voice was dry and cold. "I have no taxes in Jefferson. Colonel Sartoris explained it to me. Perhaps one of you can gain access to the city records and satisfy yourselves."

"But we have. We are the city authorities, Miss Emily. Didn't you get a notice from the sheriff, signed by him?"

"I received a paper, yes," Miss Emily said. "Perhaps he considers himself the sheriff . . . I have no taxes in Jefferson."

"But there is nothing on the books to show that, you see. We must go by the—"

"See Colonel Sartoris. I have no taxes in Jefferson."

"But, Miss Emily—"

"See Colonel Sartoris." (Colonel Sartoris had been dead almost ten years.) "I have no taxes in Jefferson. Tobe!" The Negro appeared. "Show these gentlemen out."

II

So SHE vanquished them, horse and foot, just as she had vanquished their fathers thirty years before about the smell. That was two years after her father's death and a short time after her sweetheart—the one we believed would marry her—had deserted her. After her father's death she went out very little; after her sweetheart went away, people hardly saw her at all. A few of the ladies had the temerity to call, but were not received, and the only sign of life about the place was the Negro man—a young man then—going in and out with a market basket.

"Just as if a man—any man—could keep a kitchen properly," the ladies said; so they were not surprised when the smell developed. It was another link between the gross, teeming world and the high and mighty Griersons.

A neighbor, a woman, complained to the mayor, Judge Stevens, eighty years old.

"But what will you have me do about it, madam?" he said.

"Why, send her word to stop it," the woman said. "Isn't there a law?"

"I'm sure that won't be necessary," Judge Stevens said. "It's probably just a snake or a rat that nigger of hers killed in the yard. I'll speak to him about it."

· The next day he received two more complaints, one from a man who came in diffident depreciation. "We really must do something about it, Judge. I'd be the last one in the world to bother Miss Emily, but we've got to do something." That night the Board of Aldermen met—three graybeards and one younger man, a member of the rising generation.

"It's simple enough," he said. "Send her word to have her place cleaned up. Give her a certain time to do it in, and if she don't . . ."

"Dammit, sir," Judge Stevens said, "will you accuse a lady to her face of smelling bad?"

So the next night, after midnight, four men crossed Miss Emily's lawn and slunk about the house like burglars, sniffing along the base of the brickwork and at the cellar openings while one of them performed a regular sowing motion with his hand out of a sack slung from his shoulder. They broke open the cellar door and sprinkled lime there, and in all the outbuildings. As they recrossed the lawn, a window that had been dark was lighted and Miss Emily sat in it, the light behind her, and her upright torso motionless as that of an idol. They crept quietly across the lawn and into the shadow of the locusts that lined the street. After a week or two the smell went away.

That was when people had begun to feel really sorry for her. People in our town, remembering how old lady Wyatt, her great-aunt, had gone completely crazy at last, believed that the Griersons held themselves a little too high for what they really were. None of the young men were quite good enough for Miss Emily and such. We had long thought of them as a tableau, Miss Emily a slender figure in white in the background, her father a spraddled silhouette in the foreground, his back to her and clutching a horsewhip, the two of them framed by the back-flung front door. So when she got to be thirty and was still single, we were not pleased exactly, but vindicated; even with insanity in the family she wouldn't have turned down all of her chances if they had really materialized.

When her father died, it got about that the house was all that was left to her; and in a way, people were glad. At last they could pity Miss Emily. Being left alone, and a pauper, she had become humanized. Now she too would know the old thrill and the old despair of a penny more or less.

The day after his death all the ladies prepared to call at the house and offer condolence and aid, as is our custom. Miss Emily met them at the door, dressed as usual and with no trace of grief on her face. She told them that her father was not dead. She did that for three days, with the ministers calling on her, and the doctors, trying to persuade her to let them dispose of the body. Just as they were about to resort to law and force, she broke down, and they buried her father quickly.

We did not say she was crazy then. We believed she had to do that. We remembered all the young men her father had driven away, and we knew that with nothing left, she would have to cling to that which had robbed her, as people will.

III

SHE was sick for a long time. When we saw her again, her hair was cut short, making her look like a girl, with a vague resemblance to those angels in colored church windows—sort of tragic and serene.

The town had just let the contracts for paving the sidewalks, and in the summer after her father's death they began the work. The construction company came with niggers and mules and machinery, and a foreman named Homer Barron, a Yankee—a big, dark, ready man, with a big voice and eyes lighter than his face. The little boys would follow in groups to hear him cuss the niggers, and the niggers singing in time to the rise and fall of picks. Pretty soon he knew everybody in town. Whenever you heard a lot of laughing anywhere about the square, Homer Barron would be in the center of the group. Presently we began to see him and Miss Emily on Sunday afternoons driving in the yellow-wheeled buggy and the matched team of bays from the livery stable.

At first we were glad that Miss Emily would have an interest, because the ladies all said, "Of course a Grierson would not think seriously of a Northerner, a day laborer." But there were still others, older people, who said that even grief could not cause a real lady to forget *noblesse oblige*—without calling it *noblesse oblige.* They just said, "Poor Emily. Her kinsfolk should come to her." She had some kin in Alabama; but years ago her father had fallen out with them over the estate of old lady Wyatt, the crazy woman, and there was no communication between the two families. They had not even been represented at the funeral.

And as soon as the old people said, "Poor Emily," the whispering began. "Do you suppose it's really so?" they said to one another. "Of course it is. What else could. . . ." This behind their hands; rustling of craned silk and satin behind jalousies closed upon the sun of Sunday afternoon as the thin, swift clop-clop-clop of the matched team passed: "Poor Emily."

She carried her head high enough—even when we believed that she was fallen. It was as if she demanded more than ever the recognition of her dignity as the last Grierson; as if it had wanted that touch of earthiness to reaffirm her imperviousness. Like when she bought the rat poison, the arsenic. That was over a year after they had begun to say "Poor Emily," and while the two female cousins were visiting her.

"I want some poison," she said to the druggist. She was over thirty then, still a slight woman, though thinner than usual, with cold, haughty black eyes in a face the flesh of which was strained across the temples and about the eye-sockets as you imagine a lighthouse-keeper's face ought to look. "I want some poison," she said.

"Yes, Miss Emily. What kind? For rats and such? I'd recom—"

"I want the best you have. I don't care what kind."

The druggist named several. "They'll kill anything up to an elephant. But what you want is—"

"Arsenic," Miss Emily said. "Is that a good one?"

"Is . . . arsenic? Yes, ma'am. But what you want—"

"I want arsenic."

The druggist looked down at her. She looked back at him, erect, her face like a strained flag. "Why, of course," the druggist said. "If that's what you want. But the law requires you to tell what you are going to use it for."

Miss Emily just stared at him, her head tilted back in order to look him eye for eye, until he looked away and went and got the arsenic and wrapped it up. The Negro delivery boy brought her the package; the druggist didn't come back. When she opened the package at home there was written on the box, under the skull and bones: "For rats."

IV

So THE next day we all said, "She will kill herself"; and we said it would be the best thing. When she had first begun to be seen with Homer Barron, we had said, "She will marry him." Then we said, "She will persuade him yet," because Homer himself had remarked—he liked men, and it was known that he drank with the younger men in the Elks' Club—that he was not a marrying man. Later we said, "Poor Emily" behind the jalousies as they passed on Sunday afternoon in the glittering buggy, Miss Emily with her head high and Homer Barron with his hat cocked and a cigar in his teeth, reins and whip in a yellow glove.

Then some of the ladies began to say that it was a disgrace to the town and a bad example to the young people. The men did not want to interfere, but at last the ladies forced the Baptist minister—Miss Emily's people were Episcopal—to call upon her. He would never divulge what happened during that interview, but he refused to go back again. The next Sunday they again drove about the streets, and the following day the minister's wife wrote to Miss Emily's relations in Alabama.

So she had blood-kin under her roof again and we sat back to watch developments. At first nothing happened. Then we were sure that they were to be married. We learned that Miss Emily had been to the jeweler's and ordered a man's toilet set in silver, with the letters H.B. on each piece. Two days later we learned that she had bought a complete outfit of men's cloth-ing, including a nightshirt, and we said, "They are married." We were really glad. We were glad because the two female cousins were even more Grier-son than Miss Emily had ever been.

So we were not surprised when Homer Barron—the streets had been finished some time since—was gone. We were a little disappointed that there was not a public blowing-off, but we believed that he had gone on to prepare for Miss Emily's coming, or to give her a chance to get rid of the cousins. (By that time it was a cabal, and we were all Miss Emily's allies to help circumvent the cousins.) Sure enough, after another week they de-parted. And, as we had expected all along, within three days Homer Barron was back in town. A neighbor saw the Negro man admit him at the kitchen door at dusk one evening.

And that was the last we saw of Homer Barron. And of Miss Emily for some time. The Negro man went in and out with the market basket, but the front door remained closed. Now and then we would see her at a window for a moment, as the men did that night when they sprinkled the lime, but for almost six months she did not appear on the streets. Then we knew that this was to be expected too; as if that quality of her father which had thwarted her woman's life so many times had been too virulent and too furious to die.

When we next saw Miss Emily, she had grown fat and her hair was turning gray. During the next few years it grew grayer and grayer until it attained an even pepper-and-salt iron-gray, when it ceased turning. Up to the day of her death at seventy-four it was still that vigorous iron-gray, like the hair of an active man.

From that time on her front door remained closed, save for a period of six or seven years, when she was about forty, during which she gave lessons in china-painting. She fitted up a studio in one of the downstairs rooms, where the daughters and granddaughters of Colonel Sartoris' contemporar-ies were sent to her with the same regularity and in the same spirit that they were sent to church on Sundays with a twenty-five-cent piece for the collec-tion plate. Meanwhile her taxes had been remitted.

Then the newer generation became the backbone and the spirit of the town, and the painting pupils grew up and fell away and did not send their children to her with boxes of color and tedious brushes and pictures cut from the ladies' magazines. The front door closed upon the last one and remained closed for good. When the town got free postal delivery, Miss Emily alone refused to let them fasten the metal numbers above her door and attach a mailbox to it. She would not listen to them.

Daily, monthly, yearly we watched the Negro grow grayer and more stooped, going in and out with the market basket. Each December we sent her a tax notice, which would be returned by the post office a week later, unclaimed. Now and then we would see her in one of the downstairs win-dows—she had evidently shut up the top floor of the house—like the carven torso of an idol in a niche, looking or not looking at us, we could never tell which. Thus she passed from generation to generation—dear, inescapable, impervious, tranquil, and perverse.

And so she died. Fell ill in the house filled with dust and shadows, with only a doddering Negro man to wait on her. We did not even know she was sick; we had long since given up trying to get any information from the Negro. He talked to no one, probably not even to her, for his voice had grown harsh and rusty, as if from disuse.

She died in one of the downstairs rooms, in a heavy walnut bed with a curtain, her gray head propped on a pillow yellow and moldy with age and lack of sunlight.

V

THE Negro met the first of the ladies at the front door and let them in, with their hushed, sibilant voices and their quick, curious glances, and then he disappeared. He walked right through the house and out the back and was not seen again.

The two female cousins came at once. They held the funeral on the second day, with the town coming to look at Miss Emily beneath a mass of bought flowers, with the crayon face of her father musing profoundly above the bier and the ladies sibilant and macabre; and the very old men—some in their brushed Confederate uniforms—on the porch and the lawn, talking of Miss Emily as if she had been a contemporary of theirs, believing that they had danced with her and courted her perhaps, confusing time with its mathematical progression, as the old do, to whom all the past is not a diminishing road but, instead, a huge meadow which no winter ever quite touches, divided from them now by the narrow bottle-neck of the most recent decade of years.

Already we knew that there was one room in that region above stairs which no one had seen in forty years, and which would have to be forced. They waited until Miss Emily was decently in the ground before they opened it.

The violence of breaking down the door seemed to fill this room with pervading dust. A thin, acrid pall as of the tomb seemed to lie everywhere upon this room decked and furnished as for a bridal: upon the valance curtains of faded rose color, upon the rose-shaded lights, upon the dressing table, upon the delicate array of crystal and the man's toilet things backed with tarnished silver, silver so tarnished that the monogram was obscured. Among them lay a collar and tie, as if they had just been removed, which, lifted, left upon the surface a pale crescent in the dust. Upon a chair hung the suit, carefully folded; beneath it the two mute shoes and the discarded socks.

The man himself lay in the bed.

For a long while we just stood there, looking down at the profound and fleshless grin. The body had apparently once lain in the attitude of an embrace, but now the long sleep that outlasts love, that conquers even the grimace of love, had cuckolded him. What was left of him, rotted beneath what was left of the nightshirt, had become inextricable from the bed in which he lay; and upon him and upon the pillow beside him lay that even coating of the patient and biding dust.

Then we noticed that in the second pillow was the indentation of a head. One of us lifted something from it, and leaning forward, that faint and invisible dust dry and acrid in the nostrils, we saw a long strand of iron-gray hair.

(1930)

Ernest Hemingway

(1 8 9 8 – 1 9 6 1)

A major American novelist, Ernest Hemingway was born in Oak Park, Illinois. He attended high school, then worked as a reporter for the Kansas City *Star*. He also wrote for the Toronto *Star* as a European correspondent in the early 1920s. His journalism experience contributed to his famous style: short, simple sentences and direct reporting of events with little adornment. During World War I, Hemingway served in Italy as a volunteer ambulance driver and was badly wounded in his legs. He was a war correspondent in China and in Europe and worked for the Republicans in the Spanish Civil War. He also lived on the Left Bank in Paris, where he met Ezra Pound, Gertrude Stein, and other American expatriates. In Paris, with his first wife, Hadley Richardson, Hemingway wrote *In Our Time* (a collection of short stories) and gathered the material for his first novel, *The Sun Also Rises.* He also lived for long periods in West Palm Beach and in Cuba. Hemingway was awarded the Nobel Prize in 1954, shortly after the publication of *The Old Man and the Sea.* He died in 1961.

Hemingway tried to describe reality as clearly as he could. It was his goal, he once wrote, to describe scenes so transparently that the reader soon forgot the words but still had the scenes themselves clearly in mind. The reality he depicted, however, was confined to the narrow boundaries of a violent and absurd world in which the old answers no longer applied. There was no new system to replace the old answers, and bare endurance and a cold, physical heroism were the only alternatives. Hemingway's self-consciously masculine heroes were characterized by self-control, stoicism, and grace under pressure. They held their own empirically derived code. Hemingway thought that an author should know the whole life story of a character, but need not describe much of the background in the text—it would be "felt" by the reader. The theory holds true in "Cat in the Rain," "Big Two-Hearted River," and "Hills Like White Elephants." Much of Hemingway's late work is inferior, but *In Our Time, The Sun Also Rises, A Farewell to Arms,* and *The Old Man and the Sea* are undeniably lasting.

Hemingway's major works are *In Our Time* (1925), *The Sun Also Rises* (1926), *Men Without Women* (stories, 1927), *A Farewell to Arms* (1929), *Death in the Afternoon* (1932), *For Whom the Bell Tolls* (1940), *The Old Man and the Sea* (1952), and *Islands in the Stream* (1970). His memoirs of the Paris years, *A Moveable Feast,* were published in 1964, after his death.

ERNEST HEMINGWAY

Hills Like White Elephants

THE hills across the valley of the Ebro were long and white. On this side there was no shade and no trees and the station was between two lines of rails in the sun. Close against the side of the station there was the warm shadow of the building and a curtain, made of strings of bamboo beads, hung across the open door into the bar, to keep out flies. The American and the girl with him sat at a table in the shade, outside the building. It was very hot and the express from Barcelona would come in forty minutes. It stopped at this junction for two minutes and went on to Madrid.

"What should we drink?" the girl asked. She had taken off her hat and put it on the table.

"It's pretty hot," the man said.

"Let's drink beer."

"Dos cervezas," the man said into the curtain.

"Big ones?" a woman asked from the doorway.

"Yes. Two big ones."

The woman brought two glasses of beer and two felt pads. She put the felt pads and the beer glasses on the table and looked at the man and the girl. The girl was looking off at the line of hills. They were white in the sun and the country was brown and dry.

"They look like white elephants," she said.

"I've never seen one," the man drank his beer.

"No, you wouldn't have."

"I might have," the man said. "Just because you say I wouldn't have doesn't prove anything."

The girl looked at the bead curtain. "They've painted something on it," she said. "What does it say?"

"Anis del Toro. It's a drink."

"Could we try it?"

The man called "Listen" through the curtain. The woman came out from the bar.

"Four reales."[1]

"We want two Anis del Toro."

"With water?"

"Do you want it with water?"

"I don't know," the girl said. "Is it good with water?"

[1] Spanish silver coins.

"It's all right."

"You want them with water?" asked the woman.

"Yes, with water."

"It tastes like licorice," the girl said and put the glass down.

"That's the way with everything."

"Yes," said the girl. "Everything tastes of licorice. Especially all the things you've waited so long for, like absinthe."

"Oh, cut it out."

"You started it," the girl said. "I was being amused. I was having a fine time."

"Well, let's try and have a fine time."

"All right. I was trying. I said the mountains looked like white elephants. Wasn't that bright?"

"That was bright."

"I wanted to try this new drink. That's all we do, isn't it—look at things and try new drinks?"

"I guess so."

The girl looked across at the hills.

"They're lovely hills," she said. "They don't really look like white elephants. I just meant the coloring of their skin through the trees."

"Should we have another drink?"

"All right."

The warm wind blew the bead curtain against the table.

"The beer's nice and cool," the man said.

"It's lovely," the girl said.

"It's really an awfully simple operation, Jig," the man said. "It's not really an operation at all."

The girl looked at the ground the table legs rested on.

"I know you wouldn't mind it, Jig. It's really not anything. It's just to let the air in."

The girl did not say anything.

"I'll go with you and I'll stay with you all the time. They just let the air in and then it's all perfectly natural."

"Then what will we do afterward?"

"We'll be fine afterward. Just like we were before."

"What makes you think so?"

"That's the only thing that bothers us. It's the only thing that's made us unhappy."

The girl looked at the bead curtain, put her hand out and took hold of two of the strings of beads.

"And you think then we'll be all right and be happy."

"I know we will. You don't have to be afraid. I've known lots of people that have done it."

"So have I," said the girl. "And afterward they were all so happy."

"Well," the man said, "if you don't want to you don't have to. I wouldn't have you do it if you didn't want to. But I know it's perfectly simple."

"And you really want to?"

"I think it's the best thing to do. But I don't want you to do it if you don't really want to."

"And if I do it you'll be happy and things will be like they were and you'll love me?"

"I love you now. You know I love you."

"I know. But if I do it, then it will be nice again if I say things are like white elephants, and you'll like it?"

"I'll love it. I love it now but I just can't think about it. You know how I get when I worry."

"If I do it you won't ever worry?"

"I won't worry about that because it's perfectly simple."

"Then I'll do it. Because I don't care about me."

"What do you mean?"

"I don't care about me."

"Well, I care about you."

"Oh, yes. But I don't care about me. And I'll do it and then everything will be fine."

"I don't want you to do it if you feel that way."

The girl stood up and walked to the end of the station. Across, on the other side, were fields of grain and trees along the banks of the Ebro. Far away, beyond the river, were mountains. The shadow of a cloud moved across the field of grain and she saw the river through the trees.

"And we could have all this," she said. "And we could have everything and every day we make it more impossible."

"What did you say?"

"I said we could have everything."

"We can have everything."

"No, we can't."

"We can have the whole world."

"No, we can't."

"We can go everywhere."

"No, we can't. It isn't ours any more."

"It's ours."

"No, it isn't. And once they take it away, you never get it back."

"But they haven't taken it away."

"We'll wait and see."

"Come on back in the shade," he said. "You mustn't feel that way."

"I don't feel any way," the girl said. "I just know things."

"I don't want you to do anything that you don't want to do——"

"Nor that isn't good for me," she said. "I know. Could we have another beer?"

"All right. But you've got to realize——"

"I realize," the girl said. "Can't we maybe stop talking?"

They sat down at the table and the girl looked across at the hills on the dry side of the valley and the man looked at her and at the table.

"You've got to realize," he said, "that I don't want you to do it if you don't want to. I'm perfectly willing to go through with it if it means anything to you."

"Doesn't it mean anything to you? We could get along."

"Of course it does. But I don't want anybody but you. I don't want any one else. And I know it's perfectly simple."

"Yes, you know it's perfectly simple."

"It's all right for you to say that, but I do know it."

"Would you do something for me now?"

"I'd do anything for you."

"Would you please please please please please please please stop talk-ing?"

He did not say anything but looked at the bags against the wall of the station. There were labels on them from all the hotels where they had spent nights.

"But I don't want you to," he said, "I don't care anything about it."

"I'll scream," the girl said.

The woman came out through the curtains with two glasses of beer and put them down on the damp felt pads. "The train comes in five minutes," she said.

"What did she say?" asked the girl.

"That the train is coming in five minutes."

The girl smiled brightly at the woman, to thank her.

"I'd better take the bags over to the other side of the station," the man said. She smiled at him.

"All right. Then come back and we'll finish the beer."

He picked up the two heavy bags and carried them around the station to the other tracks. He looked up the tracks but could not see the train. Coming back, he walked through the barroom, where people waiting for the train were drinking. He drank an Anis at the bar and looked at the people. They were all waiting reasonably for the train. He went out through the bead curtain. She was sitting at the table and smiled at him.

"Do you feel better?" he asked.

"I feel fine," she said. "There's nothing wrong with me. I feel fine."

(1927)

John Steinbeck

(1 9 0 2 – 1 9 6 8)

John Steinbeck was born in Salinas, California, and grew up near Monterey, the area that provided the setting for much of his fiction. He attended Stanford University, where he studied marine biology, then worked at a series of manual jobs and began to write. Frustrated in an attempt to break into the New York literary scene, he went back to California where he worked as a fruit picker and a caretaker. He lived in an isolated cottage and continued his writing. With the publication of *Tortilla Flat* in 1935, Steinbeck began to achieve popular and critical success, which climaxed four years later with the epic chronicle of the American Depression, *The Grapes of Wrath*. Steinbeck served as a correspondent in Europe during World War II. He was awarded the Pulitzer Prize in 1940 and the Nobel Prize in 1962.

Steinbeck was in many ways an anti-intellectual novelist: He responded to the unconscious "natural" forces that drive people and societies. He was influenced by biologist E. P. Ricketts, who taught the primacy of "what" or "how" over "why." The influence led to an intensely observed naturalism. Never an ideologue of the right or left, Steinbeck focused on character rather than on economic doctrine. *The Grapes of Wrath* is a masterful examination of American culture—a lyrical evocation of love, loss, and exile during the Depression—and a universal classic about human struggle. Steinbeck combines an objective, almost clinical, observation with a mythic belief in the power of the human individual. Other works—*Tortilla Flat, Of Mice and Men,* and many fine short stories—contribute to his place in American fiction.

Steinbeck's major works include *Tortilla Flat* (1935), *In Dubious Battle* (1936), *The Grapes of Wrath* (1939), *Of Mice and Men* (1937), *Cannery Row* (1945), and *East of Eden* (1952). Many of his best short stories are found in *The Long Valley* (1938).

JOHN STEINBECK

The Chrysanthemums

THE high grey-flannel fog of winter closed off the Salinas Valley from the sky and from all the rest of the world. On every side it sat like a lid on the mountains and made of the great valley a closed pot. On the broad, level land floor the gang plows bit deep and left the black earth shining like metal where the shares had cut. On the foothill ranches across the Salinas River, the yellow stubble fields seemed to be bathed in pale cold sunshine, but there was no sunshine in the valley now in December. The thick willow scrub along the river flamed with sharp and positive yellow leaves.

It was a time of quiet and of waiting. The air was cold and tender. A light wind blew up from the southwest so that the farmers were mildly hopeful of a good rain before long; but fog and rain do not go together.

Across the river, on Henry Allen's foothill ranch there was little work to be done, for the hay was cut and stored and the orchards were plowed up to receive the rain deeply when it should come. The cattle on the higher slopes were becoming shaggy and rough-coated.

Elisa Allen, working in her flower garden, looked down across the yard and saw Henry, her husband, talking to two men in business suits. The three of them stood by the tractor shed, each man with one foot on the side of the little Fordson. They smoked cigarettes and studied the machine as they talked.

Elisa watched them for a moment and then went back to her work. She was thirty-five. Her face was lean and strong and her eyes were as clear as water. Her figure looked blocked and heavy in her gardening costume, a man's black hat pulled low down over her eyes, clod-hopper shoes, a figured print dress almost completely covered by a big corduroy apron with four big pockets to hold the snips, the trowel and scratcher, the seeds and the knife she worked with. She wore heavy leather gloves to protect her hands while she worked.

She was cutting down the old year's chrysanthemum stalks with a pair of short and powerful scissors. She looked down toward the men by the tractor shed now and then. Her face was eager and mature and handsome; even her work with the scissors was over-eager, over-powerful. The chrysanthemum stems seemed too small and easy for her energy.

She brushed a cloud of hair out of her eyes with the back of her glove, and left a smudge of earth on her cheek in doing it. Behind her stood the neat white farm house with red geraniums close-banked around it as high as the windows. It was a hard-swept looking little house, with hard-polished windows, and a clean mud-mat on the front steps.

Elisa cast another glance toward the tractor shed. The strangers were getting into their Ford coupe. She took off a glove and put her strong fingers down into the forest of new green chrysanthemum sprouts that were growing around the old roots. She spread the leaves and looked down among the close-growing stems. No aphids were there, no sowbugs or snails or cutworms. Her terrier fingers destroyed such pests before they could get started.

Elisa started at the sound of her husband's voice. He had come near quietly, and he leaned over the wire fence that protected her flower garden from cattle and dogs and chickens.

"At it again," he said. "You've got a strong new crop coming."

Elisa straightened her back and pulled on the gardening glove again. "Yes. They'll be strong this coming year." In her tone and on her face there was a little smugness.

"You've got a gift with things," Henry observed. "Some of those yellow chrysanthemums you had this year were ten inches across. I wish you'd work out in the orchard and raise some apples that big."

Her eyes sharpened. "Maybe I could do it, too. I've a gift with things, all right. My mother had it. She could stick anything in the ground and make it grow. She said it was having planters' hands that knew how to do it."

"Well, it sure works with flowers," he said.

"Henry, who were those men you were talking to?"

"Why, sure, that's what I came to tell you. They were from the Western Meat Company. I sold those thirty head of three-year-old steers. Got nearly my own price, too."

"Good," she said. "Good for you."

"And I thought," he continued, "I thought how it's Saturday afternoon, and we might go into Salinas for dinner at a restaurant, and then to a picture show—to celebrate, you see."

"Good," she repeated. "Oh, yes. That will be good."

Henry put on his joking tone. "There's fights tonight. How'd you like to go to the fights?"

"Oh, no," she said breathlessly. "No, I wouldn't like fights."

"Just fooling, Elisa. We'll go to a movie. Let's see. It's two now. I'm going to take Scotty and bring down those steers from the hill. It'll take us maybe two hours. We'll go in town about five and have dinner at the Cominos Hotel. Like that?"

"Of course I'll like it. It's good to eat away from home."

"All right, then. I'll go get up a couple of horses."

She said, "I'll have plenty of time to transplant some of these sets, I guess."

She heard her husband calling Scotty down by the barn. And a little later she saw the two men ride up the pale yellow hillside in search of the steers.

There was a little square sandy bed kept for rooting the chrysanthemums.

With her trowel she turned the soil over and over, and smoothed it and patted it firm. Then she dug ten parallel trenches to receive the sets. Back at the chysanthemum bed she pulled out the little crisp shoots, trimmed off the leaves of each one with her scissors and laid it on a small orderly pile.

A squeak of wheels and plod of hoofs came from the road. Elisa looked up. The country road ran along the dense bank of willows and cottonwoods that bordered the river, and up this road came a curious vehicle, curiously drawn. It was an old spring-wagon, with a round canvas top on it like the cover of a prairie schooner. It was drawn by an old bay horse and a little grey-and-white burro. A big stubble-bearded man sat between the cover flaps and drove the crawling team. Underneath the wagon, between the hind wheels, a lean and rangy mongrel dog walked sedately. Words were painted on the canvas, in clumsy, crooked letters. "Pots, pans, knives, sisors, lawn morcs, Fixed." Two rows of articles, and the triumphantly definitive "Fixed" below. The black paint had run down in little sharp points beneath each letter.

Elisa, squatting on the ground, watched ω see the crazy, loose-jointed wagon pass by. But it didn't pass. It turned into the farm road in front of her house, crooked old wheels skirling and squeaking. The rangy dog darted from between the wheels and ran ahead. Instantly the two ranch shepherds flew out at him. Then all three stopped, and with stiff and quivering tails, with taut straight legs, with ambassadorial dignity, they slowly circled, sniffing daintily. The caravan pulled up to Elisa's wire fence and stopped. Now the newcomer dog, feeling out-numbered, lowered his tail and retired under the wagon with raised hackles and bared teeth.

The man on the wagon seat called out, "That's a bad dog in a fight when he gets started."

Elisa laughed. "I see he is. How soon does he generally get started?"

The man caught up her laughter and echoed it heartily. "Sometimes not for weeks and weeks," he said. He climbed stiffly down, over the wheel. The horse and the donkey drooped like unwatered flowers.

Elisa saw that he was a very big man. Although his hair and beard were greying, he did not look old. His worn black suit was wrinkled and spotted with grease. The laughter had disappeared from his face and eyes the moment his laughing voice ceased. His eyes were dark, and they were full of the brooding that gets in the eyes of teamsters and of sailors. The calloused hands he rested on the wire fence were cracked, and every crack was a black line. He took off his battered hat.

"I'm off my general road, ma'am," he said. "Does this dirt road cut over across the river to the Los Angeles highway?"

Elisa stood up and shoved the thick scissors in her apron pocket. "Well, yes, it does, but it winds around and then fords the river. I don't think your team could pull through the sand."

He replied with some asperity, "It might surprise you what them beasts can pull through."

"When they get started?" she asked.

He smiled for a second. "Yes. When they get started."

"Well," said Elisa, "I think you'll save time if you go back to the Salinas road and pick up the highway there."

He drew a big finger down the chicken wire and made it sing. "I ain't in any hurry, ma'am. I go from Seattle to San Diego and back every year. Takes all my time. About six months each way. I aim to follow nice weather."

Elisa took off her gloves and stuffed them in the apron pocket with the scissors. She touched the under edge of her man's hat, searching for fugitive hairs. "That sounds like a nice kind of a way to live," she said.

He leaned confidentially over the fence. "Maybe you noticed the writing on my wagon. I mend pots and sharpen knives and scissors. You got any of them things to do?"

"Oh, no," she said quickly. "Nothing like that." Her eyes hardened with resistance.

"Scissors is the worst thing," he explained. "Most people just ruin scissors trying to sharpen 'em, but I know how. I got a special tool. It's a little bobbit kind of thing, and patented. But it sure does the trick."

"No. My scissors are all sharp."

"All right, then. Take a pot," he continued earnestly, "a bent pot, or a pot with a hole. I can make it like new so you don't have to buy no new ones. That's a saving for you."

"No," she said shortly. "I tell you I have nothing like that for you to do."

His face fell to an exaggerated sadness. His voice took on a whining undertone. "I ain't had a thing to do today. Maybe I won't have no supper tonight. You see I'm off my regular road. I know folks on the highway clear from Seattle to San Diego. They save their things for me to sharpen up because they know I do it so good and save them money."

"I'm sorry," Elisa said irritably. "I haven't anything for you to do."

His eyes left her face and fell to searching the ground. They roamed about until they came to the chrysanthemum bed where she had been working. "What's them plants, ma'am?"

The irritation and resistance melted from Elisa's face. "Oh, those are chrysanthemums, giant whites and yellows. I raise them every year, bigger than anybody around here."

"Kind of a long-stemmed flower? Looks like a quick puff of colored smoke?" he asked.

"That's it. What a nice way to describe them."

"They smell kind of nasty till you get used to them," he said.

"It's a good bitter smell," she retorted, "not nasty at all."

He changed his tone quickly. "I like the smell myself."

"I had ten-inch blooms this year," she said.

The man leaned farther over the fence. "Look. I know a lady down the road a piece, has got the nicest garden you ever seen. Got nearly every kind of flower but no chrysanthemums. Last time I was mending a copper-bottom washtub for her (that's a hard job but I do it good), she said to me, 'If you ever run acrost some nice chrysanthemums I wish you'd try to get me a few seeds.' That's what she told me."

Elisa's eyes grew alert and eager. "She couldn't have known much about chrysanthemums. You can raise them from seed, but it's much easier to root the little sprouts you see there."

"Oh," he said. "I s'pose I can't take none to her, then."

"Why yes you can," Elisa cried. "I can put some in damp sand, and you can carry them right along with you. They'll take root in the pot if you keep them damp. And then she can transplant them."

"She'd sure like to have some, ma'am. You say they're nice ones?"

"Beautiful," she said. "Oh, beautiful." Her eyes shone. She tore off the battered hat and shook out her dark pretty hair. "I'll put them in a flower pot, and you can take them right with you. Come into the yard."

While the man came through the picket gate Elisa ran excitedly along the geranium-bordered path to the back of the house. And she returned carrying a big red flower pot. The gloves were forgotten now. She kneeled on the ground by the starting bed and dug up the sandy soil with her fingers and scooped it into the bright new flower pot. Then she picked up the little pile of shoots she had prepared. With her strong fingers she pressed them into the sand and tamped around them with her knuckles. The man stood over her. "I'll tell you what to do," she said. "You remember so you can tell the lady."

"Yes, I'll try to remember."

"Well, look. These will take root in about a month. Then she must set them out, about a foot apart in good rich earth like this, see?" She lifted a handful of dark soil for him to look at. "They'll grow fast and tall. Now remember this: In July tell her to cut them down, about eight inches from the ground."

"Before they bloom?" he asked.

"Yes, before they bloom." Her face was tight with eagerness. "They'll grow right up again. About the last of September the buds will start."

She stopped and seemed perplexed. "It's the budding that takes the most care," she said hesitantly. "I don't know how to tell you." She looked deep into his eyes, searchingly. Her mouth opened a little, and she seemed to be listening. "I'll try to tell you," she said. "Did you ever hear of planting hands?"

"Can't say I have, ma'am."

"Well, I can only tell you what it feels like. It's when you're picking off the buds you don't want. Everything goes right down into your fingertips. You watch your fingers work. They do it themselves. You can feel how it is. They pick and pick the buds. They never make a mistake. They're with the plant. Do you see? Your fingers and the plant. You can feel that, right up your arm. They know. They never make a mistake. You can feel it. When you're like that you can't do anything wrong. Do you see that? Can you understand that?"

She was kneeling on the ground looking up at him. Her breast swelled passionately.

The man's eyes narrowed. He looked away self-consciously. "Maybe I know," he said. "Sometimes in the night in the wagon there——"

Elisa's voice grew husky. She broke in on him, "I've never lived as you do, but I know what you mean. When the night is dark—why, the stars are sharp-pointed, and there's quiet. Why, you rise up and up! Every pointed star gets driven into your body. It's like that. Hot and sharp and—lovely."

Kneeling there, her hand went out toward his legs in the greasy black trousers. Her hesitant fingers almost touched the cloth. Then her hand dropped to the ground. She crouched low like a fawning dog.

He said, "It's nice, just like you say. Only when you don't have no dinner, it ain't."

She stood up then, very straight, and her face was ashamed. She held the flower pot out to him and placed it gently in his arms. "Here. Put it in your wagon, on the seat, where you can watch it. Maybe I can find something for you to do."

At the back of the house she dug in the can pile and found two old and battered aluminum saucepans. She carried them back and gave them to him. "Here, maybe you can fix these."

His manner changed. He became professional. "Good as new I can fix them." At the back of his wagon he set a little anvil, and out of an oily tool box dug a small machine hammer. Elisa came through the gate to watch him while he pounded out the dents in the kettles. His mouth grew sure and knowing. At a difficult part of the work he sucked his under-lip.

"You sleep right in the wagon?" Elisa asked.

"Right in the wagon, ma'am. Rain or shine I'm dry as a cow in there."

"It must be nice," she said. "It must be very nice. I wish women could do such things."

"It ain't the right kind of a life for a woman."

Her upper lip raised a little, showing her teeth. "How do you know? How can you tell?" she said.

"I don't know, ma'am," he protested. "Of course I don't know. Now here's your kettles, done. You don't have to buy no new ones."

"How much?"

"Oh, fifty cents'll do. I keep my prices down and my work good. That's why I have all them satisfied customers up and down the highway."

Elisa brought him a fifty-cent piece from the house and dropped it in his hand. "You might be surprised to have a rival some time. I can sharpen scissors, too. And I can beat the dents out of little pots. I could show you what a woman might do."

He put his hammer back in the oily box and shoved the little anvil out of sight. "It would be a lonely life for a woman, ma'am, and a scarey life, too, with animals creeping under the wagon all night." He climbed over the singletree, steadying himself with a hand on the burro's white rump. He settled himself in the seat, picked up the lines. "Thank you kindly, ma'am," he said. "I'll do like you told me; I'll go back and catch the Salinas road."

"Mind," she called, "if you're long in getting there, keep the sand damp."

"Sand, ma'am? . . . Sand? Oh, sure. You mean around the chrysantheums. Sure I will." He clucked his tongue. The beasts leaned luxuriously into their collars. The mongrel dog took his place between the back wheels. The wagon turned and crawled out the entrance road and back the way it had come, along the river.

Elisa stood in front of her wire fence watching the slow progress of the caravan. Her shoulders were straight, her head thrown back, her eyes half-closed, so that the scene came vaguely into them. Her lips moved silently, forming the words "Good-bye—good-bye." Then she whispered, "That's a bright direction. There's a glowing there." The sound of her whisper startled her. She shook herself free and looked about to see whether anyone had been listening. Only the dogs had heard. They lifted their heads toward her from their sleeping in the dust, and then stretched out their chins and settled asleep again. Elisa turned and ran hurriedly into the house.

In the kitchen she reached behind the stove and felt the water tank. It was full of hot water from the noonday cooking. In the bathroom she tore off her soiled clothes and flung them into the corner. And then she scrubbed herself with a little block of pumice, legs and thighs, loins and chest and arms, until her skin was scratched and red. When she had dried herself she stood in front of a mirror in her bedroom and looked at her body. She tightened her stomach and threw out her chest. She turned and looked over her shoulder at her back.

After a while she began to dress, slowly. She put on her newest underclothing and her nicest stockings and the dress which was the symbol of her prettiness. She worked carefully on her hair, penciled her eyebrows and rouged her lips.

Before she was finished she heard the little thunder of hoofs and the shouts of Henry and his helper as they drove the red steers into the corral. She heard the gate bang shut and set herself for Henry's arrival.

His step sounded on the porch. He entered the house calling, "Elisa, where are you?"

"In my room, dressing. I'm not ready. There's hot water for your bath. Hurry up. It's getting late."

When she heard him splashing in the tub, Elisa laid his dark suit on the bed, and shirt and socks and tie beside it. She stood his polished shoes on the floor beside the bed. Then she went to the porch and sat primly and stiffly down. She looked toward the river road where the willow-line was still yellow with frosted leaves so that under the high grey fog they seemed a thin band of sunshine. This was the only color in the grey afternoon. She sat unmoving for a long time. Her eyes blinked rarely.

Henry came banging out of the door, shoving his tie inside his vest as he came. Elisa stiffened and her face grew tight. Henry stopped short and looked at her. "Why—why, Elisa. You look so nice!"

"Nice? You think I look nice? What do you mean by 'nice'?"

Henry blundered on. "I don't know. I mean you look different, strong and happy."

"I am strong? Yes, strong. What do you mean 'strong'?"

He looked bewildered. "You're playing some kind of a game," he said helplessly. "It's a kind of a play. You look strong enough to break a calf over your knee, happy enough to eat it like a watermelon."

For a second she lost her rigidity. "Henry! Don't talk like that. You didn't know what you said." She grew complete again. "I'm strong," she boasted. "I never knew before how strong."

Henry looked down toward the tractor shed, and when he brought his eyes back to her, they were his own again. "I'll get out the car. You can put on your coat while I'm starting."

Elisa went into the house. She heard him drive to the gate and idle down his motor, and then she took a long time to put on her hat. She pulled it here and pressed it there. When Henry turned the motor off she slipped into her coat and went out.

The little roadster bounced along on the dirt road by the river, raising the birds and driving the rabbits into the brush. Two cranes flapped heavily over the willow-line and dropped into the river-bed.

Far ahead on the road Elisa saw a dark speck. She knew.

She tried not to look as they passed it, but her eyes would not obey. She whispered to herself sadly, "He might have thrown them off the road. That wouldn't have been much trouble, not very much. But he kept the pot," she explained. "He had to keep the pot. That's why he couldn't get them off the road."

The roadster turned a bend and she saw the caravan ahead. She swung full around toward her husband so she could not see the little covered wagon and the mismatched team as the car passed them.

In a moment it was over. The thing was done. She did not look back.

She said loudly, to be heard above the motor, "It will be good, tonight, a good dinner."

"Now you're changed again," Henry complained. He took one hand from the wheel and patted her knee. "I ought to take you in to dinner oftener. It would be good for both of us. We get so heavy out on the ranch."

"Henry," she asked, "could we have wine at dinner?"

"Sure we could. Say! That will be fine."

She was silent for a while; then she said, "Henry, at those prize fights, do the men hurt each other very much?"

"Sometimes a little, not often. Why?"

"Well, I've read how they break noses, and blood runs down their chests. I've read how the fighting gloves get heavy and soggy with blood."

He looked around at her. "What's the matter, Elisa? I didn't know you read things like that." He brought the car to a stop, then turned to the right over the Salinas River bridge.

"Do any women ever go to the fights?" she asked.

"Oh, sure, some. What's the matter, Elisa? Do you want to go? I don't think you'd like it, but I'll take you if you really want to go."

She relaxed limply in the seat. "Oh, no. No. I don't want to go. I'm sure I don't." Her face was turned away from him. "It will be enough if we can have wine. It will be plenty." She turned up her coat collar so he could not see that she was crying weakly—like an old woman.

(1937)

Eudora Welty

(b. 1 9 0 9)

Eudora Welty was born in Jackson, Mississippi, and studied at Mississippi State College for Women. She received her B.A. in 1929 from the University of Wisconsin and studied advertising in New York for a year before returning to Jackson. She published her first story in 1936 and her first collection of stories in 1941. Welty continues to live mainly in Mississippi, and she has taught and lectured at many American universities and at Cambridge, England. She has won many literary awards, including two O. Henry awards and the 1973 Pulitzer Prize for *The Optimist's Daughter.*

Welty is in many ways a regional writer, but she does not merely analyze the culture of the South. Her finest works are short stories. She is interested mainly in the psychology of the individual, particularly with something she calls "separateness" and with the possibility of reconciling separateness through love. Like Faulkner, Welty includes Gothic elements in her work; she also describes nostalgia for the declining southern aristocratic families. Her ability to evoke atmosphere and to recreate the tones, moods, and textures of the small-town and rural cultures of Mississippi is brilliant. Her characters include social outcasts—murderers, suicides, deaf-mutes, and the mentally handicapped. (This attraction is part of a southern tradition that includes William Faulkner and Flannery O'Connor.) Welty champions the family and community as forces that resist change and that preserve a sense of a collective memory in a modern, planned-obsolescence society.

Welty's works include *A Curtain of Green and Other Stories* (1941), *The Robber Bridegroom* (1947), *The Wide Net and Other Stories* (1943), *Delta Wedding* (1946), *The Golden Apples* (1949), *The Ponder Heart* (1954), *The Bride of Innisfallen* (1955), *Losing Battle* (1970), and *The Optimist's Daughter* (1972).

EUDORA WELTY

Why I Live at the P.O.

I WAS getting along fine with Mama, Papa-Daddy and Uncle Rondo until my sister Stella-Rondo just separated from her husband and came back home again. Mr. Whitaker! Of course I went with Mr. Whitaker first, when he first appeared here in China Grove, taking "Pose Yourself" photos, and Stella-Rondo broke us up. Told him I was one-sided. Bigger on one side than the other, which is a deliberate, calculated falsehood: I'm the same. Stella-Rondo is exactly twelve months to the day younger than I am and for that reason she's spoiled.

She's always had anything in the world she wanted and then she'd throw it away. Papa-Daddy gave her this gorgeous Add-a-Pearl necklace when she was eight years old and she threw it away playing baseball when she was nine, with only two pearls.

So as soon as she got married and moved away from home the first thing she did was separate! From Mr. Whitaker! This photographer with the popeyes she said she trusted. Came home from one of those towns up in Illinois and to our complete surprise brought this child of two.

Mama said she like to made her drop dead for a second. "Here you had this marvelous blonde child and never so much as wrote your mother a word about it," says Mama. "I'm thoroughly ashamed of you." But of course she wasn't.

Stella-Rondo just calmly takes off this *hat,* I wish you could see it. She says, "Why, Mama, Shirley-T.'s adopted, I can prove it."

"How?" says Mama, but all I says was, "H'm!" There I was over the hot stove, trying to stretch two chickens over five people and a completely unexpected child into the bargain, without one moment's notice.

"What do you mean—'H'm!'?" says Stella-Rondo, and Mama says, "I heard that, Sister."

I said that oh, I didn't mean a thing, only that whoever Shirley-T. was, she was the spit-image of Papa-Daddy if he'd cut off his beard, which of course he'd never do in the world. Papa-Daddy's Mama's papa and sulks.

Stella-Rondo got furious! She said, "Sister, I don't need to tell you you got a lot of nerve and always did have and I'll thank you to make no future reference to my adopted child whatsoever."

"Very well," I said. "Very well, very well. Of course I noticed at once she looks like Mr. Whitaker's side too. That frown. She looks like a cross between Mr. Whitaker and Papa-Daddy."

"Well, all I can say is she isn't."

"She looks exactly like Shirley Temple to me," says Mama, but Shirley-T. just ran away from her.

So the first thing Stella-Rondo did at the table was turn Papa-Daddy against me.

"Papa-Daddy," she says. He was trying to cut up his meat. "Papa-Daddy!" I was taken completely by surprise. Papa-Daddy is about a million years old and's got this long-long beard. "Papa-Daddy, Sister says she fails to understand why you don't cut off your beard."

So Papa-Daddy l-a-y-s down his knife and fork! He's real rich. Mama says he is, he says he isn't. So he says, "Have I heard correctly? You don't understand why I don't cut off my beard?"

"Why," I says, "Papa-Daddy, of course I understand, I did not say any such of a thing, the idea!"

He says, "Hussy!"

I says, "Papa-Daddy, you know I wouldn't any more want you to cut off your beard than the man in the moon. It was the farthest thing from my mind! Stella-Rondo sat there and made that up while she was eating breast of chicken."

But he says, "So the postmistress fails to understand why I don't cut off my beard. Which job I got you through my influence with the government. 'Bird's nest'—is that what you call it?"

Not that it isn't the next to smallest P.O. in the entire state of Mississippi.

I says, "Oh, Papa-Daddy," I says, "I didn't say any such of a thing, I never dreamed it was a bird's nest, I have always been grateful though this is the next to smallest P.O. in the state of Mississippi, and I do not enjoy being referred to as a hussy by my own grandfather."

But Stella-Rondo says, "Yes, you did say it too. Anybody in the world could of heard you, that had ears."

"Stop right there," says Mama, looking at *me.*

So I pulled my napkin straight back through the napkin ring and left the table.

As soon as I was out of the room Mama says, "Call her back, or she'll starve to death," but Papa-Daddy says, "This is the beard I started growing on the Coast when I was fifteen years old." He would of gone on till nightfall if Shirley-T. hadn't lost the Milky Way she ate in Cairo.

So Papa-Daddy says, "I am going out and lie in the hammock, and you can all sit here and remember my words: I'll never cut off my beard as long as I live, even one inch, and I don't appreciate it in you at all." Passed right by me in the hall and went straight out and got in the hammock.

It would be a holiday. It wasn't five minutes before Uncle Rondo suddenly appeared in the hall in one of Stella-Rondo's flesh-colored kimonos, all cut on the bias, like something Mr. Whitaker probably thought was gorgeous.

"Uncle Rondo!" I says. "I didn't know who that was! Where are you going?"

"Sister," he says, "get out of my way, I'm poisoned."

"If you're poisoned stay away from Papa-Daddy," I says. "Keep out of the hammock. Papa-Daddy will certainly beat you on the head if you come within forty miles of him. He thinks I deliberately said he ought to cut off his beard after he got me the P.O., and I've told him and told him and told him, and he acts like he just don't hear me. Papa-Daddy must of gone stone deaf."

"He picked a fine day to do it then," says Uncle Rondo, and before you could say "Jack Robinson" flew out in the yard.

What he'd really done, he'd drunk another bottle of that prescription. He does it every single Fourth of July as sure as shooting, and it's horribly expensive. Then he falls over in the hammock and snores. So he insisted on zigzagging right on out to the hammock, looking like a half-wit.

Papa-Daddy woke up with this horrible yell and right there without moving an inch he tried to turn Uncle Rondo against me. I heard every word he said. Oh, he told Uncle Rondo I didn't learn to read till I was eight years old and he didn't see how in the world I ever got the mail put up at the P.O., much less read it all, and he said if Uncle Rondo could only fathom the lengths he had gone to to get me that job! And he said on the other hand he thought Stella-Rondo had a brilliant mind and deserved credit for getting out of town. All the time he was just lying there swinging as pretty as you please and looping out his beard, and poor Uncle Rondo was *pleading* with him to slow down the hammock, it was making him as dizzy as a witch to watch it. But that's what Papa-Daddy likes about a hammock. So Uncle Rondo was too dizzy to get turned against me for the time being. He's Mama's only brother and is a good case of a one-track mind. Ask anybody. A certified pharmacist.

Just then I heard Stella-Rondo raising the upstairs window. While she was married she got this peculiar idea that it's cooler with the windows shut and locked. So she has to raise the window before she can make a soul hear her outdoors.

So she raises the window and says, *"Oh!"* You would have thought she was mortally wounded.

Uncle Rondo and Papa-Daddy didn't even look up, but kept right on with what they were doing. I had to laugh.

I flew up the stairs and threw the door open! I says, "What in the wide world's the matter, Stella-Rondo? You mortally wounded?"

"No," she says, "I am not mortally wounded but I wish you would do me the favor of looking out that window there and telling me what you see."

So I shade my eyes and look out the window.

"I see the front yard," I says.

"Don't you see any human beings?" she says.

"I see Uncle Rondo trying to run Papa-Daddy out of the hammock," I says. "Nothing more. Naturally, it's so suffocating-hot in the house, with all the windows shut and locked, everybody who cares to stay in their right mind will have to go out and get in the hammock before the Fourth of July is over."

"Don't you notice anything different about Uncle Rondo?" asks Stella-Rondo.

"Why, no, except he's got on some terrible-looking flesh-colored contraption I wouldn't be found dead in, is all I can see," I says.

"Never mind, you won't be found dead in it, because it happens to be part of my trousseau, and Mr. Whitaker took several dozen photographs of me in it," says Stella-Rondo. "What on earth could Uncle Rondo *mean* by wearing part of my trousseau out in the broad open daylight without saying so much as 'Kiss my foot,' *knowing* I only got home this morning after my separation and hung my negligee up on the bathroom door, just as nervous as I could be?"

"I'm sure I don't know, and what do you expect me to do about it?" I says. "Jump out the window?"

"No, I expect nothing of the kind. I simply declare that Uncle Rondo looks like a fool in it, that's all," she says. "It makes me sick to my stomach."

"Well, he looks as good as he can," I says. "As good as anybody in reason could." I stood up for Uncle Rondo, please remember. And I said to Stella-Rondo, "I think I would do well not to criticize so freely if I were you and came home with a two-year-old child I had never said a word about, and no explanation whatever about my separation."

"I asked you the instant I entered this house not to refer one more time to my adopted child, and you gave me your word of honor you would not," was all Stella-Rondo would say, and started pulling out every one of her eyebrows with some cheap Kress tweezers.

So I merely slammed the door behind me and went down and made some green-tomato pickle. Somebody had to do it. Of course Mama had turned both the niggers loose; she always said no earthly power could hold one anyway on the Fourth of July, so she wouldn't even try. It turned out that Jaypan fell in the lake and came within a very narrow limit of drowning.

So Mama trots in. Lifts up the lid and says, "H'm! Not very good for your Uncle Rondo in his precarious condition, I must say. Or poor little adopted Shirley-T. Shame on you!"

That made me tired. I says, "Well, Stella-Rondo had better thank her lucky stars it was her instead of me came trotting in with that very peculiar-looking child. Now if it had been me that trotted in from Illinois and brought a peculiar-looking child of two, I shudder to think of the reception I'd of got, much less controlled the diet of an entire family."

"But you must remember, Sister, that you were never married to Mr. Whitaker in the first place and didn't go up to Illinois to live," says Mama, shaking a spoon in my face. "If you had I would of been just as overjoyed to see you and your little adopted girl as I was to see Stella-Rondo, when you wound up with your separation and came on back home."

"You would not," I says.

"Don't contradict me, I would," says Mama.

But I said she couldn't convince me though she talked till she was blue in the face. Then I said, "Besides, you know as well as I do that that child is not adopted."

"She most certainly is adopted," says Mama, stiff as a poker.

I says, "Why, Mama, Stella-Rondo had her just as sure as anything in this world, and just too stuck up to admit it."

"Why, Sister," said Mama. "Here I thought we were going to have a pleasant Fourth of July, and you start right out not believing a word your own baby sister tells you!"

"Just like Cousin Annie Flo. Went to her grave denying the facts of life," I remind Mama.

"I told you if you ever mentioned Annie Flo's name I'd slap your face," says Mama, and slaps my face.

"All right, you wait and see," I says.

"I," says Mama, "*I* prefer to take my children's word for anything when it's humanly possible." You ought to see Mama, she weighs two hundred pounds and has real tiny feet.

Just then something perfectly horrible occurred to me.

"Mama," I says, "can that child talk?" I simply had to whisper! "Mama, I wonder if that child can be—you know—in any way? Do you realize," I says, "that she hasn't spoken one single, solitary word to a human being up to this minute? This is the way she looks," I says, and I looked like this.

Well, Mama and I just stood there and stared at each other. It was horrible!

"I remember well that Joe Whitaker frequently drank like a fish," says Mama. "I believed to my soul he drank *chemicals.*" And without another word she marches to the foot of the stairs and calls Stella-Rondo.

"Stella-Rondo? O-o-o-o-o! Stella-Rondo!"

"What?" says Stella-Rondo from upstairs. Not even the grace to get up off the bed.

"Can that child of yours talk?" asks Mama.

Stella-Rondo says, "Can she what?"

"Talk! Talk!" says Mama. "Burdyburdyburdyburdy!"

So Stella-Rondo yells back, "Who says she can't talk?"

"Sister says so," says Mama.

"You didn't have to tell me, I know whose word of honor don't mean a thing in this house," says Stella-Rondo.

And in a minute the loudest Yankee voice I ever heard in my life yells out, "OE'm Pop-OE the Sailor-r-r-r Ma-a-an!" and then somebody jumps up and down in the upstairs hall. In another second the house would of fallen down.

"Not only talks, she can tap-dance!" calls Stella-Rondo. "Which is more than some people I won't name can do."

"Why, the little precious darling thing!" Mama says, so surprised. "Just as smart as she can be!" Starts talking baby talk right there. Then she turns on me. "Sister, you ought to be thoroughly ashamed! Run upstairs this instant and apologize to Stella-Rondo and Shirley-T."

"Apologize for what?" I says. "I merely wondered if the child was normal, that's all. Now that she's proved she is, why, I have nothing further to say."

But Mama just turned on her heel and flew out, furious. She ran right upstairs and hugged the baby. She believed it was adopted. Stella-Rondo hadn't done a thing but turn her against me from upstairs while I stood there helpless over the hot stove. So that made Mama, Papa-Daddy and the baby all on Stella-Rondo's side.

Next, Uncle Rondo.

I must say that Uncle Rondo has been marvelous to me at various times in the past and I was completely unprepared to be made to jump out of my skin, the way it turned out. Once Stella-Rondo did something perfectly horrible to him—broke a chain letter from Flanders Field—and he took the radio back he had given her and gave it to me. Stella-Rondo was furious! For six months we all had to call her Stella instead of Stella-Rondo, or she wouldn't answer. I always thought Uncle Rondo had all the brains of the entire family. Another time he sent me to Mammoth Cave, with all expenses paid.

But this would be the day he was drinking that prescription, the Fourth of July.

So at supper Stella-Rondo speaks up and says she thinks Uncle Rondo ought to try to eat a little something. So finally Uncle Rondo said he would try a little cold biscuits and ketchup, but that was all. So *she* brought it to him.

"Do you think it wise to disport with ketchup in Stella-Rondo's flesh-colored kimono?" I says. Trying to be considerate! If Stella-Rondo couldn't watch out for her trousseau, somebody had to.

"Any objections?" asks Uncle Rondo, just about to pour out all the ketchup.

"Don't mind what she says, Uncle Rondo," says Stella-Rondo. "Sister has been devoting this solid afternoon to sneering out my bedroom window at the way you look."

"What's that?" says Uncle Rondo. Uncle Rondo has got the most terrible temper in the world. Anything is liable to make him tear the house down if it comes at the wrong time.

So Stella-Rondo says, "Sister says, 'Uncle Rondo certainly does look like a fool in that pink kimono!' "

Do you remember who it was really said that?

Uncle Rondo spills out all the ketchup and jumps out of his chair and tears off the kimono and throws it down on the dirty floor and puts his foot on it. It had to be sent all the way to Jackson to the cleaners and re-pleated.

"So that's your opinion of your Uncle Rondo, is it?" he says. "I look like a fool, do I? Well, that's the last straw. A whole day in this house with nothing to do, and then to hear you come out with a remark like that behind my back!"

"I didn't say any such of a thing, Uncle Rondo," I says, "and I'm not saying who did, either. Why, I think you look all right. Just try to take care of yourself and not talk and eat at the same time," I says. "I think you better go lie down."

"Lie down my foot," says Uncle Rondo. I ought to of known by that he was fixing to do something perfectly horrible.

So he didn't do anything that night in the precarious state he was in—just played Casino with Mama and Stella-Rondo and Shirley-T. and gave Shirley-T. a nickel with a head on both sides. It tickled her nearly to death, and she called him "Papa." But at 6:30 A.M. the next morning, he threw a whole five-cent package of some unsold one-inch firecrackers from the store as hard as he could into my bedroom and they every one went off. Not one bad one in the string. Anybody else, there'd be one that wouldn't go off.

Well, I'm just terribly susceptible to noise of any kind, the doctor has always told me I was the most sensitive person he had ever seen in his whole life, and I was simply prostrated. I couldn't eat! People tell me they heard it as far as the cemetery, and old Aunt Jep Patterson, that had been holding her own so good, thought it was Judgment Day and she was going to meet her whole family. It's usually so quiet here.

And I'll tell you it didn't take me any longer than a minute to make up my mind what to do. There I was with the whole entire house on Stella-Rondo's side and turned against me. If I have anything at all I have pride.

So I just decided I'd go straight down to the P.O. There's plenty of room there in the back, I says to myself.

Well! I made no bones about letting the family catch on to what I was up to. I didn't try to conceal it.

The first thing they knew, I marched in where they were all playing Old Maid and pulled the electric oscillating fan out by the plug, and everything got real hot. Next I snatched the pillow I'd done the needlepoint on right off the davenport from behind Papa-Daddy. He went "Ugh!" I beat Stella-Rondo up the stairs and finally found my charm bracelet in her bureau drawer under a picture of Nelson Eddy.

"So that's the way the land lies," says Uncle Rondo. There he was, piecing on the ham. "Well, Sister, I'll be glad to donate my army cot if you got any place to set it up, providing you'll leave right this minute and let me get some peace." Uncle Rondo was in France.

"Thank you kindly for the cot and 'peace' is hardly the word I would select if I had to resort to firecrackers at 6:30 A.M. in a young girl's bedroom," I says back to him. "And as to where I intend to go, you seem to forget my position as postmistress of China Grove, Mississippi," I says. "I've always got the P.O."

Well, that made them all sit up and take notice.

I went out front and started digging up some four-o'clocks to plant around the P.O.

"Ah-ah-ah!" says Mama, raising the window. "Those happen to be my four-o'clocks. Everything planted in that star is mine. I've never known you to make anything grow in your life."

"Very well," I says. "But I take the fern. Even you, Mama, can't stand there and deny that I'm the one watered that fern. And I happen to know where I can send in a box top and get a packet of one thousand mixed seeds, no two the same kind, free."

"Oh, where?" Mama wants to know.

But I says, "Too late. You 'tend to your house, and I'll 'tend to mine. You hear things like that all the time if you know how to listen to the radio. Perfectly marvelous offers. Get anything you want free."

So I hope to tell you I marched in and got that radio, and they could of all bit a nail in two, especially Stella-Rondo, that it used to belong to, and she well knew she couldn't get it back, I'd sue for it like a shot. And I very politely took the sewing-machine motor I helped pay the most on to give Mama for Christmas back in 1929, and a good big calendar, with the first-aid remedies on it. The thermometer and the Hawaiian ukulele certainly were rightfully mine, and I stood on the step-ladder and got all my watermelon-rind preserves and every fruit and vegetable I'd put up, every jar. Then I began to pull the tacks out of the bluebird wall vases on the archway to the dining room.

"Who told you you could have those, Miss Priss?" says Mama, fanning as hard as she could.

"I bought 'em and I'll keep track of 'em," I says. "I'll tack 'em up one on each side the post-office window, and you can see 'em when you come to ask me for your mail, if you're so dead to see 'em."

"Not I! I'll never darken the door to that post office again if I live to be a hundred," Mama says. "Ungrateful child! After all the money we spent on you at the Normal."

"Me either," says Stella-Rondo. "You can just let my mail lie there and *rot,* for all I care. I'll never come and relieve you of a single, solitary piece."

"I should worry," I says. "And who you think's going to sit down and write you all those big fat letters and postcards, by the way? Mr. Whitaker? Just because he was the only man ever dropped down in China Grove and you got him—unfairly—is he going to sit down and write you a lengthy correspondence after you come home giving no rhyme nor reason whatsoever for your separation and no explanation for the presence of that child? I may not have your brilliant mind, but I fail to see it."

So Mama says, "Sister, I've told you a thousand times that Stella-Rondo simply got homesick, and this child is far too big to be hers," and she says, "Now, why don't you all just sit down and play Casino?"

Then Shirley-T. sticks out her tongue at me in this perfectly horrible way. She has no more manners than the man in the moon. I told her she was going to cross her eyes like that some day and they'd stick.

"It's too late to stop me now," I says. "You should have tried that yesterday. I'm going to the P.O. and the only way you can possibly see me is to visit me there."

So Papa-Daddy says, "You'll never catch me setting foot in that post office, even if I should take a notion into my head to write a letter some place." He says, "I won't have you reachin' out of that little old window with a pair of shears and cuttin' off any beard of mine. I'm too smart for you!"

"We all are," says Stella-Rondo.

But I said, "If you're so smart, where's Mr. Whitaker?"

So then Uncle Rondo says, "I'll thank you from now on to stop reading all the orders I get on postcards and telling everybody in China Grove what you think is the matter with them," but I says, "I draw my own conclusions and will continue in the future to draw them." I says, "If people want to write their inmost secrets on penny postcards, there's nothing in the wide world you can do about it, Uncle Rondo."

"And if you think we'll ever *write* another postcard you're sadly mistaken," says Mama.

"Cutting off your nose to spite your face then," I says. "But if you're all determined to have no more to do with the U.S. mail, think of this: What will Stella-Rondo do now, if she wants to tell Mr. Whitaker to come after her?"

"Wah!" says Stella-Rondo. I knew she'd cry. She had a conniption fit right there in the kitchen.

"It will be interesting to see how long she holds out," I says. "And now—I am leaving."

"Good-bye," says Uncle Rondo.

"Oh, I declare," says Mama, "to think that a family of mine should quarrel on the Fourth of July, or the day after, over Stella-Rondo leaving old Mr. Whitaker and having the sweetest little adopted child! It looks like we'd all be glad!"

"Wah!" says Stella-Rondo, and has a fresh conniption fit.

"*He* left *her*—you mark my words," I says. "That's Mr. Whitaker. I know Mr. Whitaker. After all, I knew him first. I said from the beginning he'd up and leave her. I foretold every single thing that's happened."

"Where did he go?" asks Mama.

"Probably to the North Pole, if he knows what's good for him," I says.

But Stella-Rondo just bawled and wouldn't say another word. She flew to her room and slammed the door.

"Now look what you've gone and done, Sister," says Mama. "You go apologize."

"I haven't got time, I'm leaving," I says.

"Well, what are you waiting around for?" asks Uncle Rondo.

So I just picked up the kitchen clock and marched off, without saying "Kiss my foot" or anything, and never did tell Stella-Rondo good-bye.

There was a nigger girl going along on a little wagon right in front.

"Nigger girl," I says, "come help me haul these things down the hill, I'm going to live in the post office."

Took her nine trips in her express wagon. Uncle Rondo came out on the porch and threw her a nickel.

AND that's the last I've laid eyes on any of my family or my family laid eyes on me for five solid days and nights. Stella-Rondo may be telling the most horrible tales in the world about Mr. Whitaker, but I haven't heard them. As I tell everybody, I draw my own conclusions.

But oh, I like it here. It's ideal, as I've been saying. You see, I've got everything cater-cornered, the way I like it. Hear the radio? All the war news. Radio, sewing machine, book ends, ironing board and that great big piano lamp—peace, that's what I like. Butter-bean vines planted all along the front where the strings are.

Of course, there's not much mail. My family are naturally the main people in China Grove, and if they prefer to vanish from the face of the earth, for all the mail they get or the mail they write, why, I'm not going to open my mouth. Some of the folks here in town are taking up for me and some turned against me. I know which is which. There are always people who will quit buying stamps just to get on the right side of Papa-Daddy.

But here I am, and here I'll stay. I want the world to know I'm happy.

And if Stella-Rondo should come to me this minute, on bended knees, and *attempt* to explain the incidents of her life with Mr. Whitaker, I'd simply put my fingers in both my ears and refuse to listen.

(1941)

John Cheever

(1 9 1 2 – 1 9 8 2)

John Cheever, one of the best short-story writers of his generation, was born in Quincy, Massachusetts. Cheever's father went bankrupt in 1929. Also, in 1929, Cheever was expelled from Thayer Academy, an event that marked the end of his schooling and the beginning of his literary career. He moved to Boston to live with his brother. His first story, published in 1930 in *The New Republic,* dealt with being expelled. Many of his subsequent stories first appeared in the *New Yorker.* Except for four years during World War II, Cheever earned his living as a writer. He won the National Book award in 1957 and the Pulitzer Prize, for his collected stories, in 1978.

Cheever wrote formal, carefully structured short stories. Much of his work is nostalgic in tone. His stories describe the gradual disappearance of small-town and rural America and the encroachment of the superhighway, the supermarket, and the suburb. Cheever's satire grew increasingly biting as his career progressed. One novel, *Bullet Park,* shows the movement toward a darker, more grotesque humor. Cheever was a writer of manners; he closely studied the rituals and latent mythologies of suburban America and contrasted the carefully maintained decorum with the emotional turmoil and uncertainty that lay beneath. Many of his plots are episodic, and his narrative voice often intrudes to comment upon the action. But the lyric intensity of his style and his straightforward acknowledgment of the realities of modern, urban life situate him firmly as a chronicler of the contemporary world.

Cheever's works of short fiction include *The Way Some People Live* (1943), *The Housebreaker of Shady Hill* (1958), *The Brigadier and the Golf Widow* (1964), *The World of Apples* (1973), and *The Stories of John Cheever* (1978). His novels are *The Wapshot Chronicle* (1957), *The Wapshot Scandal* (1964), *Bullet Park* (1969), *Falconer* (1977), and *Oh What a Paradise It Seems* (1982).

JOHN CHEEVER

The Enormous Radio

JIM and Irene Westcott were the kind of people who seem to strike that satisfactory average of income, endeavor, and respectability that is reached by the statistical reports in college alumni bulletins. They were the parents of two young children, they had been married nine years, they lived on the twelfth floor of an apartment house near Sutton Place, they went to the theatre on an average of 10.3 times a year, and they hoped someday to live in Westchester. Irene Westcott was a pleasant, rather plain girl with soft brown hair and a wide, fine forehead upon which nothing at all had been written, and in the cold weather she wore a coat of fitch skins dyed to resemble mink. You could not say that Jim Westcott looked younger than he was, but you could at least say of him that he seemed to feel younger. He wore his graying hair cut very short, he dressed in the kind of clothes his class had worn at Andover, and his manner was earnest, vehement, and intentionally naïve. The Westcotts differed from their friends, their class-mates, and their neighbors only in an interest they shared in serious music. They went to a great many concerts—although they seldom mentioned this to anyone—and they spent a good deal of time listening to music on the radio.

Their radio was an old instrument, sensitive, unpredictable, and beyond repair. Neither of them understood the mechanics of radio—or of any of the other appliances that surrounded them—and when the instrument faltered, Jim would strike the side of the cabinet with his hand. This sometimes helped. One Sunday afternoon, in the middle of a Schubert quartet, the music faded away altogether. Jim struck the cabinet repeatedly, but there was no response; the Schubert was lost to them forever. He promised to buy Irene a new radio, and on Monday when he came home from work he told her that he had got one. He refused to describe it, and said it would be a surprise for her when it came.

The radio was delivered at the kitchen door the following afternoon, and with the assistance of her maid and the handyman Irene uncrated it and brought it into the living room. She was struck at once with the physical ugliness of the large gumwood cabinet. Irene was proud of her living room, she had chosen its furnishings and colors as carefully as she chose her clothes, and now it seemed to her that the new radio stood among her intimate possessions like an aggressive intruder. She was confounded by the number of dials and switches on the instrument panel, and she studied them thoroughly before she put the plug into a wall socket and turned the radio on. The dials flooded with a malevolent green light, and in the distance she heard the music of a piano quintet. The quintet was in the distance for only an instant; it bore down upon her with a speed greater than light and filled the apartment with the noise of music amplified so mightily that it knocked a china ornament from a table to the floor. She rushed to the instrument and reduced the volume. The violent forces that were snared in the ugly gumwood cabinet made her uneasy. Her children came home from school then, and she took them to the Park. It was not until later in the afternoon that she was able to return to the radio.

The maid had given the children their suppers and was supervising their baths when Irene turned on the radio, reduced the volume, and sat down to listen to a Mozart quintet that she knew and enjoyed. The music came through clearly. The new instrument had a much purer tone, she thought, than the old one. She decided that tone was most important and that she could conceal the cabinet behind a sofa. But as soon as she had made her peace with the radio, the interference began. A crackling sound like the noise of a burning powder fuse began to accompany the singing of the strings. Beyond the music, there was a rustling that reminded Irene unpleasantly of the sea, and as the quintet progressed, these noises were joined by many others. She tried all the dials and switches but nothing dimmed the interference, and she sat down, disappointed and bewildered, and tried to trace the flight of the melody. The elevator shaft in her building ran beside the living-room wall, and it was the noise of the elevator that gave her a clue to the character of the static. The rattling of the elevator cables and the opening and closing of the elevator doors were reproduced in her loudspeaker, and, realizing that the radio was sensitive to electrical currents of all sorts, she began to discern through the Mozart the ringing of telephone bells, the dialing of phones, and the lamentation of a vacuum cleaner. By listening more carefully, she was able to distinguish doorbells, elevator bells, electric razors, and Waring mixers, whose sounds had been picked up from the apartments that surrounded hers and transmitted through her loudspeaker. The powerful and ugly instrument, with its mistaken sensitivity to discord, was more than she could hope to master, so she turned the thing off and went into the nursery to see her children.

When Jim Westcott came home that night, he went to the radio confidently and worked the controls. He had the same sort of experience Irene had had. A man was speaking on the station Jim had chosen, and his voice swung instantly from the distance into a force so powerful that it shook the apartment. Jim turned the volume control and reduced the voice. Then, a minute or two later, the interference began. The ringing of telephones and doorbells set in, joined by the rasp of the elevator doors and the whir of cooking appliances. The character of the noise had changed since Irene had tried the radio earlier; the last of the electric razors was being unplugged, the vacuum cleaners had all been returned to their closets, and the static reflected that change in pace that overtakes the city after the sun goes down.

He fiddled with the knobs but couldn't get rid of the noises, so he turned the radio off and told Irene that in the morning he'd call the people who had sold it to him and give them hell.

The following afternoon, when Irene returned to the apartment from a luncheon date, the maid told her that a man had come and fixed the radio. Irene went into the living room before she took off her hat or her furs and tried the instrument. From the loudspeaker came a recording of the "Missouri Waltz." It reminded her of the thin, scratchy music from an old-fashioned phonograph that she sometimes heard across the lake where she spent her summers. She waited until the waltz had finished, expecting an explanation of the recording, but there was none. The music was followed by silence, and then the plaintive and scratchy record was repeated. She turned the dial and got a satisfactory burst of Caucasian music—the thump of bare feet in the dust and the rattle of coin jewelry—but in the background she could hear the ringing of bells and a confusion of voices. Her children came home from school then, and she turned off the radio and went to the nursery.

When Jim came home that night, he was tired, and he took a bath and changed his clothes. Then he joined Irene in the living room. He had just turned on the radio when the maid announced dinner, so he left it on, and he and Irene went to the table.

Jim was too tired to make even a pretense of sociability, and there was nothing about the dinner to hold Irene's interest, so her attention wandered from the food to the deposits of silver polish on the candlesticks and from there to the music in the other room. She listened for a few minutes to a Chopin prelude and then was surprised to hear a man's voice break in. "For Christ's sake, Kathy," he said, "do you always have to play the piano when I get home?" The music stopped abruptly. "It's the only chance I have," a woman said. "I'm at the office all day." "So am I," the man said. He added something obscene about an upright piano, and slammed a door. The passionate and melancholy music began again.

"Did you hear that?" Irene asked.

"What?" Jim was eating his dessert.

"The radio. A man said something while the music was still going on— something dirty."

"It's probably a play."

"I don't think it *is* a play," Irene said.

They left the table and took their coffee into the living room. Irene asked Jim to try another station. He turned the knob. "Have you seen my garters?" a man asked. "Button me up," a woman said. "Have you seen my garters?" the man said again. "Just button me up and I'll find your garters," the woman said. Jim shifted to another station. "I wish you wouldn't leave apple cores in the ashtrays," a man said. "I hate the smell."

"This is strange," Jim said.

"Isn't it?" Irene said.

Jim turned the knob again " "On the coast of Coromandel where the early pumpkins blow,' " a woman with a pronounced English accent said, " 'in the middle of the woods lived the Yonghy-Bonghy-Bò. Two old chairs, and half a candle, one old jug without a handle . . .' "

"My God!" Irene cried. "That's the Sweeneys' nurse."

" 'These were all his worldly goods,' " the British voice continued.

"Turn that thing off," Irene said. "Maybe they can hear *us.* " Jim switched the radio off. "That was Miss Armstrong, the Sweeneys' nurse," Irene said. "She must be reading to the little girl. They live in 17-B. I've talked with Miss Armstrong in the Park. I know her voice very well. We must be getting other people's apartments."

"That's impossible," Jim said.

"Well, that was the Sweeneys' nurse," Irene said hotly. "I know her voice. I know it very well. I'm wondering if they can hear us."

Jim turned the switch. First from a distance and then nearer, nearer, as if borne on the wind, came the pure accents of the Sweeneys' nurse again: " '*Lady Jingly! Lady Jingly!*' " she said, " '*sitting where the pumpkins blow, will you come and be my wife?* said the Yonghy-Bonghy-Bò . . .' "

Jim went over to the radio and said "Hello" loudly into the speaker.

" '*I am tired of living singly,*' " the nurse went on, " '*on this coast so wild and shingly, I'm a-weary of my life; if you'll come and be my wife, quite serene would be my life . . .* ' "

"I guess she can't hear us," Irene said. "Try something else."

Jim turned to another station, and the living room was filled with the uproar of a cocktail party that had overshot its mark. Someone was playing the piano and singing the "Whiffenpoof Song," and the voices that surrounded the piano were vehement and happy. "Eat some more sandwiches," a woman shrieked. There were screams of laughter and a dish of some sort crashed to the floor.

"Those must be the Fullers, in 11-E," Irene said. "I knew they were giving a party this afternoon. I saw her in the liquor store. Isn't this too divine? Try something else. See if you can get those people in 18-C."

The Westcotts overheard that evening a monologue on salmon fishing in Canada, a bridge game, running comments on home movies of what had apparently been a fortnight at Sea Island, and a bitter family quarrel about an overdraft at the bank. They turned off their radio at midnight and went to bed, weak with laughter. Sometime in the night, their son began to call for a glass of water and Irene got one and took it to his room. It was very early. All the lights in the neighborhood were extinguished, and from the boy's window she could see the empty street. She went into the living room and tried the radio. There was some faint coughing, a moan, and then a man spoke. "Are you all right, darling?" he asked. "Yes," a woman said wearily. "Yes, I'm all right, I guess," and then she added with great feeling, "But, you know, Charlie, I don't feel like myself any more. Sometimes there are about fifteen or twenty minutes in the week when I feel like myself. I don't like to go to another doctor, because the doctor's bills are so awful already, but I just don't feel like myself, Charlie. I just never feel like myself." They were not young, Irene thought. She guessed from the timbre of their voices that they were middle-aged. The restrained melancholy of the dialogue and the draft from the bedroom window made her shiver, and she went back to bed.

THE following morning, Irene cooked breakfast for the family—the maid didn't come up from her room in the basement until ten—braided her daughter's hair, and waited at the door until her children and her husband had been carried away in the elevator. Then she went into the living room and tried the radio. "I don't want to go to school," a child screamed. "I hate school. I won't go to school. I hate school." "You will go to school," an enraged woman said. "We paid eight hundred dollars to get you into that school and you'll go if it kills you." The next number on the dial produced the worn record of the "Missouri Waltz." Irene shifted the control and invaded the privacy of several breakfast tables. She overheard demonstrations of indigestion, carnal love, abysmal vanity, faith, and despair. Irene's life was nearly as simple and sheltered as it appeared to be, and the forthright and sometimes brutal language that came from the loudspeaker that morning astonished and troubled her. She continued to listen until her maid came in. Then she turned off the radio quickly, since this insight, she realized, was a furtive one.

Irene had a luncheon date with a friend that day, and she left her apartment at a little after twelve. There were a number of women in the elevator when it stopped at her floor. She stared at their handsome and impassive faces, their furs, and the cloth flowers in their hats. Which one of them had been to Sea Island? she wondered. Which one had overdrawn her bank account? The elevator stopped at the tenth floor and a woman with a pair of Skye terriers joined them. Her hair was rigged high on her head and she wore a mink cape. She was humming the "Missouri Waltz."

Irene had two Martinis at lunch, and she looked searchingly at her friend and wondered what her secrets were. They had intended to go shopping after lunch, but Irene excused herself and went home. She told the maid that she was not to be disturbed; then she went into the living room, closed the doors, and switched on the radio. She heard, in the course of the afternoon, the halting conversation of a woman entertaining her aunt, the hysterical conclusion of a luncheon party, and a hostess briefing her maid about some cocktail guests. "Don't give the best Scotch to anyone who hasn't white hair," the hostess said. "See if you can get rid of that liver paste before you pass those hot things, and could you lend me five dollars? I want to tip the elevator man."

As the afternoon waned, the conversations increased in intensity. From where Irene sat, she could see the open sky above the East River. There were hundreds of clouds in the sky, as though the south wind had broken the winter into pieces and were blowing it north, and on her radio she could hear the arrival of cocktail guests and the return of children and businessmen from their schools and offices. "I found a good-sized diamond on the bathroom floor this morning," a woman said. "It must have fallen out of that bracelet Mrs. Dunston was wearing last night." "We'll sell it," a man said. "Take it down to the jeweler on Madison Avenue and sell it. Mrs. Dunston won't know the difference, and we could use a couple of hundred bucks. . . ." " 'Oranges and lemons, say the bells of St. Clement's,' " the Sweeneys' nurse sang. " 'Halfpence and farthings, say the bells of St. Martin's. When will you pay me? say the bells at old Bailey. . . .' " "It's not a hat," a woman cried, and at her back roared a cocktail party. "It's not a hat, it's a love affair. That's what Walter Florell said. He said it's not a hat, it's a love affair," and then, in a lower voice, the same woman added, "Talk to somebody, for Christ's sake, honey, talk to somebody. If she catches you standing here not talking to anybody, she'll take us off her invitation list, and I love these parties."

The Westcotts were going out for dinner that night, and when Jim came home, Irene was dressing. She seemed sad and vague, and he brought her a drink. They were dining with friends in the neighborhood, and they walked to where they were going. The sky was broad and filled with light. It was one of those splendid spring evenings that excite memory and desire, and the air that touched their hands and faces felt very soft. A Salvation Army band was on the corner playing "Jesus Is Sweeter." Irene drew on her husband's arm and held him there for a minute, to hear the music. "They're really such nice people, aren't they?" she said. "They have such nice faces. Actually, they're so much nicer than a lot of the people we know." She took a bill from her purse and walked over and dropped it into the tambourine. There was in her face, when she returned to her husband, a look of radiant melancholy that he was not familiar with. And her conduct at the dinner party that night seemed strange to him, too. She interrupted her hostess rudely and stared at the people across the table from her with an intensity for which she would have punished her children.

It was still mild when they walked home from the party, and Irene looked up at the spring stars. " 'How far that little candle throws its beams,' " she exclaimed. " 'So shines a good deed in a naughty world.' " She waited that night until Jim had fallen asleep, and then went into the living room and turned on the radio.

JIM came home at about six the next night. Emma, the maid, let him in, and he had taken off his hat and was taking off his coat when Irene ran into the hall. Her face was shining with tears and her hair was disordered. "Go up to 16-C, Jim!" she screamed. "Don't take off your coat. Go up to 16-C. Mr. Osborn's beating his wife. They've been quarreling since four o'clock, and now he's hitting her. Go up there and stop him."

From the radio in the living room, Jim heard screams, obscenities, and thuds. "You know you don't have to listen to this sort of thing," he said. He strode into the living room and turned the switch. "It's indecent," he said. "It's like looking in windows. You know you don't have to listen to this sort of thing. You can turn it off."

"Oh, it's so horrible, it's so dreadful," Irene was sobbing. "I've been listening all day, and it's so depressing."

"Well, if it's so depressing, why do you listen to it? I bought this damned radio to give you some pleasure," he said. "I paid a great deal of money for it. I thought it might make you happy. I wanted to make you happy."

"Don't, don't, don't, don't quarrel with me," she moaned, and laid her head on his shoulder. "All the others have been quarreling all day. Everybody's been quarreling. They're all worried about money. Mrs. Hutchinson's mother is dying of cancer in Florida and they don't have enough money to send her to the Mayo Clinic. At least, Mr. Hutchinson says they don't have enough money. And some woman in this building is having an affair with the handyman—with that hideous handyman. It's too disgusting. And Mrs. Melville has heart trouble and Mr. Hendricks is going to lose his job in April and Mrs. Hendricks is horrid about the whole thing and that girl who plays the 'Missouri Waltz' is a whore, a common whore, and the elevator man has tuberculosis and Mr. Osborn has been beating Mrs. Osborn." She wailed, she trembled with grief and checked the stream of tears down her face with the heel of her palm.

"Well, why do you have to listen?" Jim asked again. "Why do you have to listen to this stuff if it makes you so miserable?"

"Oh, don't, don't, don't," she cried. "Life is too terrible, too sordid and awful. But we've never been like that, have we, darling? Have we? I mean, we've always been good and decent and loving to one another, haven't we? And we have two children, two beautiful children. Our lives aren't sordid, are they, darling? Are they?" She flung her arms around his neck and drew his face down to hers. "We're happy, aren't we, darling? We are happy, aren't we?"

"Of course we're happy," he said tiredly. He began to surrender his resentment. "Of course we're happy. I'll have that damned radio fixed or taken away tomorrow." He stroked her soft hair. "My poor girl," he said.

"You love me, don't you?" she asked. "And we're not hypercritical or worried about money or dishonest, are we?"

"No, darling," he said.

A MAN came in the morning and fixed the radio. Irene turned it on cautiously and was happy to hear a California-wine commercial and a recording of Beethoven's Ninth Symphony, including Schiller's "Ode to Joy." She kept the radio on all day and nothing untoward came from the speaker.

A Spanish suite was being played when Jim came home. "Is everything all right?" he asked. His face was pale, she thought. They had some cocktails and went in to dinner to the "Anvil Chorus" from *Il Trovatore*. This was followed by Debussy's "La Mer."

"I paid the bill for the radio today," Jim said. "It cost four hundred dollars. I hope you'll get some enjoyment out of it."

"Oh, I'm sure I will," Irene said.

"Four hundred dollars is a good deal more than I can afford," he went on. "I wanted to get something that you'd enjoy. It's the last extravagance we'll be able to indulge in this year. I see that you haven't paid your clothing bills yet. I saw them on your dressing table." He looked directly at her. "Why did you tell me you'd paid them? Why did you lie to me?"

"I just didn't want you to worry, Jim," she said. She drank some water. "I'll be able to pay my bills out of this month's allowance. There were the slipcovers last month, and that party."

"You've got to learn to handle the money I give you a little more intelligently, Irene," he said. "You've got to understand that we won't have as much money this year as we had last. I had a very sobering talk with Mitchell today. No one is buying anything. We're spending all our time promoting new issues, and you know how long that takes. I'm not getting any younger, you know. I'm thirty-seven. My hair will be gray next year. I haven't done as well as I'd hoped to do. And I don't suppose things will get any better."

"Yes, dear," she said.

"We've got to start cutting down," Jim said. "We've got to think of the children. To be perfectly frank with you, I worry about money a great deal. I'm not at all sure of the future. No one is. If anything should happen to me, there's the insurance, but that wouldn't go very far today. I've worked awfully hard to give you and the children a comfortable life," he said bitterly. "I don't like to see all of my energies, all of my youth, wasted in fur coats and radios and slipcovers and—"

"Please, Jim," she said. "Please. They'll hear us."

"*Who'll hear us?* Emma can't hear us."

"The radio."

"Oh, I'm sick!" he shouted. "I'm sick to death of your apprehensiveness. The radio can't hear us. Nobody can hear us. And what if they can hear us? Who cares?"

Irene got up from the table and went into the living room. Jim went to the door and shouted at her from there. "Why are you so Christly all of a sudden? What's turned you overnight into a convent girl? You stole your mother's jewelry before they probated her will. You never gave your sister a cent of that money that was intended for her—not even when she needed it. You made Grace Howland's life miserable, and where was all your piety and your virtue when you went to that abortionist? I'll never forget how cool you were. You packed your bag and went off to have that child murdered as if you were going to Nassau. If you'd had any reasons, if you'd had any good reasons—"

Irene stood for a minute before the hideous cabinet, disgraced and sickened, but she held her hand on the switch before she extinguished the music and the voices, hoping that the instrument might speak to her kindly, that she might hear the Sweeneys' nurse. Jim continued to shout at her from the door. The voice on the radio was suave and noncommittal. "An early-morning railroad disaster in Tokyo," the loudspeaker said, "killed twenty-nine people. A fire in a Catholic hospital near Buffalo for the care of blind children was extinguished early this morning by nuns. The temperature is forty-seven. The humidity is eighty-nine."

(1953)

Mavis Gallant

(b. 1 9 2 2)

Born Mavis de Trafford Young in Montreal, Gallant attended many schools
in Canada and the United States. She completed her education and returned
to Montreal, where she worked for the Montreal *Standard* and for the National Film Board. In 1950 she resigned her newspaper post and left Canada, determined to earn her living as a writer. She settled in Paris. One of
her earliest stories was published by the *New Yorker* in 1951; many of her
later stories first appeared there. Her first collection of stories, *The Other
Paris,* was published in 1956. She served as writer-in-residence at the University of Toronto in 1983–1984, but continues to live in Paris. Her volume
Home Truths: Selected Canadian Stories won the Governor-General's award in
1981.

Gallant's fictions have a complex, sophisticated structure that often in-
volves multiple narrative viewpoints. In her long short stories Gallant has
advanced the art of the miniature novel. Her themes are frequently social
in nature. As an expatriate writer, she is fascinated with the collisions of
different cultures and the wrenching personal adjustments individuals must
make when they move between alien social settings. Gallant also tackles this
theme in a historical way, describing the difficulties of societies in transition
between eras with fluctuating values. In *The Pegnitz Junction,* a collection of
stories, she focuses on the confrontation between modern German culture
and a past it feels impelled to remember yet desires desperately to forget.
Gallant's stories are often narrated from a detached perspective that is
shaded by delicate irony. This irony is perhaps both Gallant's strength and
weakness; it results in stories that are always meticulously clear in their
perceptions and impeccable in their diction, but occasionally so remote in
their sensibility that they evoke emotional sterility rather than the pathos
Gallant intends.

Gallant has published two novels, *Green Water, Green Sky* (1959) and *A
Fairly Good Time* (1970), and collections of shorter fiction including *The Other
Paris* (1956), *My Heart Is Broken* (1964), *The Pegnitz Junction* (1973), *From the
Fifteenth District* (1974), and *Home Truths* (1981).

His Mother

HIS mother had come of age in a war and then seemed to live a long grayness like a spun-out November. "Are you all right?" she used to ask him at breakfast. What she really meant was: Ask me how I am, but she was his mother and so he would not. He leaned two fists against his temples and read a book about photography, waiting for her to cut bread and put it on a plate for him. He seldom looked up, never truly saw her—a stately, careless widow with unbrushed red hair, wearing an old fur coat over her nightgown; her last dressing gown had been worn to ribbons and she said she had no money for another. It seemed that nothing could stop her from telling him how she felt or from pestering him with questions. She muttered and smoked and drank such a lot of strong coffee that it made her bilious, and then she would moan, "God, God, my liver! My poor head!" In those days in Budapest you had to know the black market to find the sort of coffee she drank, and of course she would not have any but the finest smuggled Virginia cigarettes. "Quality," she said to him—or to his profile, rather. "Remember after I have died that quality was important to me. I held out for the best."

She had known what it was to take excellence for granted. That was the difference between them. Out of her youth she could not recall a door slammed or a voice raised except in laughter. People had floated like golden dust; whole streets of people buoyed up by optimism, a feeling for life.

He sat reading, waiting for her to serve him. He was a stone out of a stony generation. Talking to him was like lifting a stone out of water. He never resisted, but if you let go for even a second he sank and came to rest on a dark sea floor. More than one of her soft-tempered lovers had tried to make a friend of him, but they had always given up, as they did with everything. How could she give up? She loved him. She felt shamed because it had not been in her to control armies, history, his stony watery world. From the moment he appeared in the kitchen doorway, passive, vacant, starting to live again only because this was morning, she began all over: "Don't you feel well?" "Are you all right?" "Why can't you smile?"—though the loudest sentence was in silence: Ask me how I am.

After he left Budapest (got his first passport, flew to Glasgow with a soccer team, never came back) she became another sort of person, an émigré's mother. She shed the last of her unimportant lovers and with the money her son was soon able to send she bought a white blouse, combs that would pin

864

her hair away from her face, and a blue kimono. She remembered long, tender conversations they had had together, and she got up early in the morning to see if a letter had come from him and then to write one of her own describing everything she thought and did. His letters to his mother said, Tell me about your headaches, are you still drinking too strong coffee, tell me the weather, the names of streets, if you still bake poppy-seed cakes.

She had never been any sort of a cook, but it seemed to her that, yes, she had baked for him, perhaps in their early years together, which she looked back upon as golden, and lighter than thistledown.

On Saturday afternoons she put on a hat and soft gray gloves and went to the Vörösmarty Café. It had once had a French name, Gerbeaud, and the circle of émigrés' mothers who met to exchange news and pictures of grandchildren still called it that. "Gerbeaud" was a sign of caste and the mark of a generation, too. Like herself, the women wore hats and sometimes scarves of fur, and each carried a stuffed handbag she would not have left behind on a tabletop for even a second. Their sons' letters looked overstamped, like those he sent her now. She had not been so certain of her rank before, or felt so quietly sure, so well thought of. A social order prevailed, as it does everywhere. The aristocrats were those whose children had never left Europe; the poorest of the poor were not likely ever to see their sons again, for they had gone to Chile and South Africa. Switzerland was superior to California. A city earned more points than a town. There was no mistaking her precedence here; she was a grand duchess. If Glasgow was unfamiliar, the very sound of it somehow rang with merit. She always had a new letter to show, which was another symbol of one's station, and they were warm messages, concerned about her health, praising her remembered skill with pies and cakes. Some mothers were condemned to a lowly status only because their children forgot to write. Others had to be satisfied with notes from foreign daughters-in-law, which were often sent from table to table before an adequate reading could be obtained. Here again she was in demand, for she read three foreign languages, which suggested a background of governesses and careful schools. She might have left it at that, but her trump credentials were in plain sight. These were the gifts he bestowed— the scarves and pastel sweaters, the earrings and gloves.

What she could not do was bring the émigré ritual to its final celebration; it required a passport, a plane ticket, and a visit to the absent son. She would never deliver into his hands the three immutable presents, which were family jewelry, family photographs, and a cake. Any mother travelling to within even a few miles of another woman's son was commissioned to take all three. The cake was a bother to carry, for the traveller usually had one of her own, but who could say no? They all knew the cake's true value. Look at the way her own son claimed his share of nourishment from a mother whose cooking had always been a joke.

No one had ever been close to Scotland, and if she had not applied for her own passport or looked up flight schedules it was for a good reason: her son had never suggested she come. And yet, denied even the bliss of sewing a garnet clip into a brassière to be smuggled to an unknown daughter-in-law, she still knew she was blessed. Other women were dismissed, forgotten. More than one had confided, "My son might as well be dead." She did not think of him as dead—how could she?—but as a coin that had dropped unheard, had rolled crazily, lay still. She knew the name of his car, of his street, she had seen pictures of them, but what did she know?

AFTER he disappeared, as soon as she had made certain he was safe and alive, she rented his room to a student, who stayed with her for three years in conditions of some discomfort, for she had refused, at first, to remove anything belonging to her son. His books were sacred. His records were not to be played. The records had been quite valuable at one time; they were early American rock slipped in by way of Vienna and sold at a murderous rate of exchange. These collected dust now, like his albums of pictures—like the tenant student's things too, for although she pinned her hair up with combs and wore a spotless blouse, she was still no better a housekeeper. Her tenant studied forestry. He was a bumpkin, and somewhat afraid of her. She could never have mistaken him for a son. He crept in and out and brought her flowers. One day she played a record for him, to which he listened with deference rather than interest, and she remembered herself, at eighteen, hearing with the same anxious boredom a warped scene from "Die Wal-küre," both singers now long dead. Having a student in the flat did not make her feel she was in touch with her son, or even with his generation. His room changed meanwhile; even its smell was no longer the same. She began to wonder what his voice had been like. She could see him, she dreamed of him often, but her dreams and memories were like films with the sound track removed.

The bumpkin departed, and she took in his place a future art historian—the regime produced these in awesome numbers now—who gave way, in turn, to the neurasthenic widow of a poet. The poet's widow was taken over in time by her children, and replaced by a couple of young librarians. And then came two persons not quite chosen by herself. She could have refused them, but thought it wiser not to. They were an old man and his pregnant granddaughter. They seemed to be brokenly poor; the granddaughter almost to the end of her term worked long hours in a plasma laboratory. And yet they appeared endowed with dark, important connections; no sooner were they installed than she was granted a telephone, which her tenants never used without asking, and only for laconic messages—the grandfather to state that his granddaughter was not yet at home, or the girl to take down the day and hour of a meeting somewhere. After the granddaughter had her baby they became four in a flat that had barely been comfortable for two. She cleared out the last of her son's records and his remaining books (the rest had long ago been sold or stolen), and she tried to establish a set of rules. For one, she made it a point to remain in the kitchen when her tenants took their meals. This was her home; it was not strictly a shared and still less a communal Russian apartment. But she could go only so far: it was at

Gerbeaud's that she ranked as a grand duchess. These people reckoned differently, and on their terms she was, if not at the foot of the ladder, then dangerously to one side of it; she had an émigré son, she received gifts and money from abroad, and she led in terms of the common good a parasitic existence. They were careful, even polite, but they were installed. She was inhabited by them, as by an illness one must learn to endure.

It was around this time—when her careless, undusted, but somehow pure rooms became a slum, festooned with washing, reeking of boiling milk, where she was seldom alone or quiet—that she began to drift away from an idea she had held about her age and time. Where, exactly, was the youth she recalled as happy? What had been its shape, its color? All that golden dust had not belonged to her—it had been part of her mother. It was her mother who had floated like thistledown, smiled, lived with three servants on call, stood with a false charming gaucherie, an arm behind her, an elbow grasped. That simulated awkwardness took suppleness and training; it required something her generation had not been granted, which was time. Her mother had let her coat fall on the floor because coats were replaceable then, not only because there had been someone to pick it up. She had carried a little curling iron in her handbag. When she quarrelled with her husband, she went to the station and climbed into a train marked "Budapest-Vienna-Rome," and her husband had thought it no more than amusing to have to fetch her back. Slowly, as "eighteen" came to mean an age much younger than her son's, as he grew older in Scotland, married, had a child, began slipping English words into his letters, went on about fictitious apple or poppy-seed cakes, she parted without pain from a soft, troubled memory, from an old gray film about porters wheeling steamer trunks, white fur wraps, bunches of violets, champagne. It was gone: it had never been. She and her son were both mistaken, and yet they had never been closer. Now that she had the telephone, he called her on Easter Sunday, and on Christmas Eve, and on her birthday. His wife had spoken to her in English:

"It's snowing here. Is it snowing in Budapest?"

"It quite often snows."

"I hope we can meet soon."

"That would be pleasant."

His wife's parents sent her Christmas greetings with stern Biblical messages, as if they judged her, by way of her son, to be frivolous, without a proper God. At least they knew now that she spoke correct English; on the other hand, perhaps they were simple souls unable to imagine that anything but English could ever be.

They were not out of touch; nor did he neglect her. No one could say that he had. He had never missed a monthly transfer of money, he was faithful about sending his overstamped letters and the colored snapshots of his wife, his child, their Christmas tree, and his wife's parents side by side upon a modern-looking sofa. One unposed picture had him up a ladder pasting sheets of plastic tiles on a kitchen wall. She could not understand the meaning of this photograph, in which he wore jeans and a sweater that might have been knitted by an untalented child. His hair had grown long, it strag-gled in brown mouse-tails over the collar of the lamentable pullover. He stood in profile, so that she could see just half of a new and abundant mustache. Also—and this might have been owing to the way he stood, because he had to sway to hold his balance—he looked as if he might have become, well, a trifle stout. This was a picture she never showed anyone at Vörösmarty Place, though she examined it often, by several kinds of light. What did it mean, what was its secret expression? She looked for the invisi-ble ink that might describe her son as a husband and father. He was twenty-eight, he had a mustache, he worked in his own home as a common laborer.

She said to herself, I never let him lift a finger. I waited on him from the time he opened his eyes.

In response to the ladder picture she employed a photographer, a former schoolfriend of her son's, to take a fiercely lighted portrait of her sitting on her divan-bed with a volume of Impressionist reproductions opened on her lap. She wore a string of garnets and turned her head proudly, without gaping or grinning. From the background wall she had removed a picture of clouds taken by her son, then a talented amateur, and hung in its stead a framed parchment that proved her mother's family had been ennobled. Actually a whole town had been ennobled at a stroke, but the parchment was legal and real. Normally it would not have been in her to display the skin of the dog, as these things were named, but perhaps her son's wife, looking at the new proud picture of his mother, might inquire, "What is that, there on the wall?"

She wrote him almost every morning—she had for years, now. At night her thoughts were morbid, unchecked, and she might have been likely to tell about her dreams or to describe the insignificant sadness of a lifetime, or to recall the mornings when he had eaten breakfast in silence, when talking to him had been like lifting a stone. Her letters held none of those things. She wrote wearing her blue, clean, now elderly kimono, sitting at the end of her kitchen table, while her tenants ate and quarrelled endlessly.

She had a long back-slanting hand she had once been told was the hand of a liar. Upside down the letter looked like a shower of rain. It was strange, mysterious, she wrote, to be here in the kitchen with the winter sun on the sparkling window (it was grimy, in fact; but she was seeing quite another window as she wrote) and the tenant granddaughter, whose name was Ilona, home late on a weekday. Ilona and the baby and the grandfather were all three going to a funeral this morning. It seemed a joyous sort of excursion because someone was fetching them by car; that in itself was an indication of their sombre connections. It explained, in shorthand, why she had not squarely refused to take them in. She wrote that the neighbors' radios could be heard faintly like the sounds of life breaking into a fever, and about Ilona preparing a boiled egg for the baby, drawing a face on the shell to make it interesting, and the baby opening his mouth, patting the table in a broken rhythm, patting crumbs with a spreadout hand. Here in the old kitchen she shared a wintry, secret, morning life with strangers.

Grandfather wore a hearing aid, but he had taken it apart, and it lay now on the table like parts of a doll's skull. Wearing it at breakfast kept him from enjoying his food. Spectacles bothered him, too. He made a noise eating, because he could not hear himself; nor did he see the mess around his cup and plate.

"Worse than an infant!" his granddaughter cried. She had a cross-looking little Tartar face. She tore squares of newspaper, one to go on the floor, another for underneath his plate. He scattered sugar and pipe ash and crusts and the pieces of his hearing aid. At the same time he was trying to attend to a crossword puzzle, which he looked at with a magnifying glass. But he still would not put his spectacles on, because they interfered with his food. Being deaf, he travelled alone in his memories and sometimes came out with just anything. His mind plodded back and forth. Looking up from the puzzle he said loudly, "My granddaughter has a diploma. Indeed she has. She worked in a hospital. Yes, she did. Some people think too much of themselves when they have a diploma. They begin to speak pure Hungarian. They try to speak like educated people. Not Ilona! You will never hear one word of good Hungarian from *her.*"

His granddaughter had just untied a towel she used as a bib for the child. She grimaced and buried her Tartar's grimace in the towel. Only her brown hair was seen, and her shaking shoulders. She might have been laughing. Her grandfather wore a benign and rather a foolish smile until she looked up and screamed, "I hate you." She reminded him of all that she had done to make him happy. She described the last place they'd lived in, the water gurgling in the pipes, the smell of bedbugs. She had found this splendid apartment; she was paying their rent. His little pension scarcely covered the coffee he drank. "You thought your son was too good for my mother," she said. "You made her miserable, too."

The old man could not hear any of this. His shaking freckled hands had been assembling the hearing aid. He adjusted it in time to hear Ilona say, "It is hard to be given lessons in correct speech by someone who eats like a pig."

He sighed and said only, "Children," as one might sound resigned to any natural enemy.

The émigré's mother, their landlady, had stopped writing. She looked up, not at them, but of course they believed they could be seen. They began to talk about their past family history, as they did when they became tense and excited, and it all went into the letter. Ilona had lost her father, her mother, and her little sister in a road accident when, with Grandfather, they had been on their way to a funeral in the suburbs in a bus.

Funerals seemed to be the only outing they ever enjoyed. The old man listened to Ilona telling it again, but presently he got up and left them, as if the death of his son allowed him no relief even so many years later. When he came back he had his hat and coat on. For some reason, he had misunderstood and thought they had to leave at once for the new excursion. He took his landlady's hand and pumped it up and down, saying, "From the bottom of my heart . . .," though all he was leading up to was "Goodbye." He did not let her hand go until he inadvertently brought it down hard on a thick cup.

"He has always embarrassed us in public," said Ilona, clearing away. "What could we do? He was my father's father."

That other time, said the old man—calmed now, sitting down in his overcoat—the day of the *fatal* funeral, there had been time to spare, out in a suburb, where they had to change from one bus to another. They had walked once around a frozen duckpond. He had been amazed, the old man remembered, at how many people were free on a working weekday. His son carried one of the children; little Ilona walked.

"Of course I walked! I was twelve!" she screamed from the sink.

He had been afraid that Ilona would never learn to speak, because her mother said everything for her. When Ilona pointed with her woolly fist, her mother crooned, "Skaters." Or else she announced, "You are cold," and pulled a scarf up over Ilona's apple cheeks.

"That was my sister," Ilona said. "I was twelve."

"Now, a governess might have made the child speak, say words correctly," said the old man. "Mothers are helpless. They can only say yes, yes, and try to repeat what the child seems to be thinking."

"He has always embarrassed us," Ilona said. "My mother hated going anywhere in his company."

Once around the duckpond, and then an old bus rattled up and they got in. The driver was late, and to make up for time he drove fast. At the bottom of a hill, on a wide sheet of black ice, the bus turned like a balky horse, rocked, steadied, and the driver threw himself over the wheel as if to protect it. An army lorry came down the hill, the first of two. Ilona's mother pulled the baby against her and pulled Ilona's head on her lap.

"Eight killed, including the two drivers," Ilona said.

Here was their folklore, their richness; how many persons have lost their families on a bus and survived to describe the holocaust? No wonder she and Grandfather were still together. If she had not married her child's father, it was because he had not wanted Grandfather to live with them. "You, yes," he had said to Ilona. "Relatives, no." Grandfather nodded, for he was used to hearing this. Her cold sacrifice always came on top of his disapproval.

Well, that was not quite the truth of it, the émigré's mother went on writing. The man who had interceded for them, whom she had felt it was wiser not to refuse, who might be the child's father, had been married for quite a long time.

The old man looked blank and strained. His eyes had become small. He looked Chinese. "Where we lived then was a good place to live with children," he said, perhaps speaking of a quarter fading like the edge of a watercolor into gray apartment blocks. Something had frightened him. He took out a clean pocket handkerchief and held it to his lips.

"Another army lorry took us to the hospital," said Ilona. "Do you know what you were saying?"

He remembered an ambulance. He and his grandchild had been wrapped in blankets, had lain on two stretchers, side by side, fingers locked together. That was what he remembered.

"You said, '*My mother, my mother,*'" she told him.

"I don't think I said that."

Now they are having their usual disagreement, she wrote her son. Lorry or ambulance?

"I heard," said Ilona. "I was conscious."

"I had no reason. If I said, 'My mother,' I was thinking, 'My children.'"

The rainstorm would cover pages more. Her letter had veered off and resembled her thoughts at night. She began to tell him she had trouble sleeping. She had been given a wonderful new drug, but unfortunately it was habit-forming and the doctor would not renew it. The drug gave her a deep sleep, from which she emerged fresh and enlivened, as if she had been swimming. During the sleep she was allowed exact and colored dreams in which she was a young girl again and men long dead came to visit. They sat amiably discussing their deaths. Her first fiancé, killed in 1943, opened his shirt to show the chest wound. He apologized for having died without warning. He did not know that less than a year later she had married another man. The dead had no knowledge of love beyond the span of their own lives. The next night, she found herself with her son's father. They were standing together buying tickets for a play when she realized he was dead. He stood in his postwar shabbiness, discreet, hidden mind, camouflaged face, and he had ceased to be with the living. Her grief was so cruel that, lest she perish in sleep from the shock of it, someone unseen but conciliating suggested that she trade any person she knew in order to keep him with her. He would never have the misery of knowing that he was dead.

What would her son say to all this? My mother is now at an age when women dream of dead men, he might tell himself; when they begin to choose quite carelessly between the dead and the living. Women are crafty even in their sleep. They know they will survive. Why weep? Why discuss? Why let things annoy you? For a long time she believed he had left because he could not look at her life. Perhaps his going had been as artless, as simple, as he still insisted: he had got his first passport, flown out with a football team, never come back. He was between the dead and the living, a voice on the telephone, an affectionate letter full of English words, a coin rolled and lying somewhere in secret. And she, she was the revered and respected mother of a generous, an attentive, a camouflaged stranger.

Tell me the weather, he still wrote. Tell me the names of streets. She began a new page: Vörösmarty Place, if you remember, is at the beginning of Váci Street, the oldest street in the Old City. In the middle of the Place stands a little park. Our great poet, for whom the Place is named, sits carved in marble. Sculptured figures look gratefully up to him. They are grateful because he is the author of the national anthem. There are plane trees full of sparrows, and there are bus stops, and even a little Métro, the oldest in Europe, perhaps old-fashioned, but practical—it goes to the Zoo, the Fine

Arts Museum, the Museum of Decorative Art, the Academy of Music, and the Opera. The old redoubt is there, too, at least one wall of it, backed up to a new building where you go to book seats for concerts. The real face of the redoubt has been in ruins since the end of the war. It used to be Moorish-romantic. The old part, which gave on the Danube, had in her day—no, in her mother's day—been a large concert hall, the reconstruction of which created grave problems because of modern acoustics. At Gerbeaud's the pastries are still the best in Europe, she wrote, and so are the prices. There are five or six little rooms, little marble tables, comfortable chairs. Between the stiff lace curtains and the windowpanes are quite valuable pieces of china. In summer one can sit on the pavement. There is enough space between the plane trees, and the ladies with their elegant hats are not in too much danger from the sparrows. If you come there, you will see younger people, too, and foreigners, and women who wait for foreigners, but most of the customers, yes, most, belong to the magic circle of mothers whose children have gone away. The café opens at ten and closes at nine. It is always crowded. "You can often find me there," she went on, "and without fail every Saturday," as if she might look up and see him draw near, transformed, amnesiac, not knowing her. I hope that I am not in your dreams, she said, because dreams are populated by the silent and the dead, and I still speak, I am alive. I wear a hat with a brim and soft gray gloves. I read their letters in three foreign languages. Thanks to you, I can order an endless succession of little cakes, I can even sip cognac. Will you still know me? I was your mother.

                                                                        (1979)

William H. Gass

(b. 1 9 2 4)

William H. Gass, short-story writer, novelist, and literary theorist, was born in Fargo, North Dakota. He was educated at Kenyon College, Ohio Wesleyan University, and Cornell University, where he earned a doctorate in 1954. During World War II, Gass served in China and Japan with the U.S. Navy. He has taught philosophy at the College of Wooster, Purdue University, and Washington University, in St. Louis. With the publication of *Omensetter's Luck* in 1966, Gass emerged as one of the most interesting new fiction writers of the 1960s. He received a Guggenheim Fellowship in 1969.

Gass is an experimental, philosophical fiction writer and his work is dense, intellectually challenging, and self-reflective, somewhat in the manner of Laurence Sterne. His themes, for example, time and history, are dealt with in an innovative and provocative manner. Multileveled and complex, Gass's fiction betrays his interest in philosophy and demonstrates a sensitive and penetrating narrative voice and a compelling insight into life in small-town central America. *Omensetter's Luck* deals with the effect a peaceful, simple man, in harmony with all around him, has on the lives of more "modern" people. Inevitably, as in Dostoevsky's *The Idiot,* the man's pure goodness arouses hatred, suspicion, and chaos, which can only be resolved through his departure. Gass's fiction has grown increasingly subservient to his logical-positivist philosophy; many critics think his work has grown increasingly empty.

Gass published a collection of stories, *In the Heart of the Heart of the Country* (1968), *Willy Masters' Lonesome Wife* (1968), and a "philosophical inquiry" called *On Being Blue* (1976). He has also published two volumes of essays.

WILLIAM H. GASS

In the Heart of the Heart of the Country

A PLACE

So I have sailed the seas and come . . .
to B . . .
a small town fastened to a field in Indiana. Twice there have been twelve
hundred people here to answer to the census. The town is outstandingly
neat and shady, and always puts its best side to the highway. On one lawn
there's even a wood or plastic iron deer.

You can reach us by crossing a creek. In the spring the lawns are green,
the forsythia is singing, and even the railroad that guts the town has straight
bright rails which hum when the train is coming, and the train itself has a
welcome horning sound.

Down the back streets the asphalt crumbles into gravel. There's Westbrook's with the geraniums, Horsefall's, Mott's. The sidewalk shatters.
Gravel dust rises like breath behind the wagons. And I am in retirement
from love.

WEATHER

In the Midwest, around the lower Lakes, the sky in the winter is heavy and
close, and it is a rare day, a day to remark on, when the sky lifts and allows
the heart up. I am keeping count, and as I write this page, it is eleven days
since I have seen the sun.

MY HOUSE

There's a row of headless maples behind my house, cut to free the passage
of electric wires. High stumps, ten feet tall, remain, and I climb these like
a boy to watch the country sail away from me. They are ordinary fields, a
little more uneven than they should be, since in the spring they puddle. The
topsoil's thin, but only moderately stony. Corn is grown one year, soybeans
another. At dusk starlings darken the single tree—a larch—which stands in
the middle. When the sky moves, fields move under it. I feel, on my perch,
that I've lost my years. It's as though I were living at last in my eyes, as I

have always dreamed of doing, and I think then I know why I've come here: to see, and so to go out against new things—oh god how easily—like air in a breeze. It's true there are moments—foolish moments, ecstasy on a tree stump—when I'm all but gone, scattered I like to think like seed, for I'm the sort now in the fool's position of having love left over which I'd like to lose; what good is it now to me, candy ungiven after Halloween?

A PERSON

There are vacant lots on either side of Billy Holsclaw's house. As the weather improves, they fill with hollyhocks. From spring through fall, Billy collects coal and wood and puts the lumps and pieces in piles near his door, for keeping warm is his one work. I see him most often on mild days sitting on his doorsill in the sun. I notice he's squinting a little, which is perhaps the reason he doesn't cackle as I pass. His house is the size of a single garage, and very old. It shed its paint with its youth, and its boards are a warped and weathered gray. So is Billy. He wears a short lumpy faded black coat when it's cold, otherwise he always goes about in the same loose, grease-spotted shirt and trousers. I suspect his galluses were yellow once, when they were new.

WIRES

These wires offend me. Three trees were maimed on their account, and now these wires deface the sky. They cross like a fence in front of me, enclosing the crows with the clouds. I can't reach in, but like a stick, I throw my feelings over. What is it that offends me? I am on my stump, I've built a platform there and the wires prevent my going out. The cut trees, the black wires, all the beyond birds therefore anger me. When I've wormed through a fence to reach a meadow, do I ever feel the same about the field?

THE CHURCH

The church has a steeple like the hat of a witch, and five birds, all doves, perch in its gutters.

MY HOUSE

Leaves move in the windows. I cannot tell you yet how beautiful it is, what it means. But they do move. They move in the glass.

POLITICS

. . . for all those not in love.

I've heard Batista described as a Mason. A farmer who'd seen him in Miami made this claim. He's as nice a fellow as you'd ever want to meet. Of Castro, of course, no one speaks.

For all those not in love there's law: to rule . . . to regulate . . . to rectify. I cannot write the poetry of such proposals, the poetry of politics, though sometimes—often—always now—I am in that uneasy peace of equal powers which makes a State; then I communicate by passing papers, proclamations, orders, through my bowels. Yet I was not a State with you, nor were we both together any Indiana. A squad of Pershing Rifles at the moment, I make myself Right Face! Legislation packs the screw of my intestines. Well, king of the classroom's king of the hill. You used to waddle when you walked because my sperm between your legs was draining to a towel. Teacher, poet, folded lover—like the politician, like those drunkards, ill, or those who faucet-off while pissing heartily to preach upon the force and fullness of that stream, or pause from vomiting to praise the purity and passion of their puke—I chant, I beg, I orate, I command, I sing—

> Come back to Indiana—not too late!
>   (Or will you be a ranger to the end?)
> Good-bye . . . Good-bye . . . oh, I shall always wait
>   You, Larry, traveler—
>   stranger,
>   son,
>   —my friend—

my little girl, my poem by heart, my self, my childhood.

But I've heard Batista described as a Mason. That dries up my pity, melts my hate. Back from the garage where I have overheard it, I slap the mended fender of my car to laugh, and listen to the metal stinging tartly in my hand.

PEOPLE

Their hair in curlers and their heads wrapped in loud scarves, young mothers, fattish in trousers, lounge about in the speedwash, smoking cigarettes, eating candy, drinking pop, thumbing magazines, and screaming at their children above the whir and rumble of the machines.

At the bank a young man freshly pressed is letting himself in with a key. Along the street, delicately teetering, many grandfathers move in a dream. During the murderous heat of summer, they perch on window ledges, their feet dangling just inside the narrow shelf of shade the store has made, staring steadily into the street. Where their consciousness has gone I can't say. It's not in the eyes. Perhaps it's diffuse, all temperature and skin, like an infant's, though more mild. Near the corner there are several large overalled men employed in standing. A truck turns to be weighed on the scales at the Feed and Grain. Images drift on the drugstore window. The wind has blown the smell of cattle into town. Our eyes have been driven in like the eyes of the old men. And there's no one to have mercy on us.

VITAL DATA

There are two restaurants here and a tearoom, two bars. one bank, three barbers, one with a green shade with which he blinds his window. two groceries. a dealer in Fords. one drug, one hardware, and one appliance store. several that sell feed, grain, and farm equipment. an antique shop. a poolroom. a laundromat. three doctors. a dentist. a plumber. a vet. a funeral home in elegant repair the color of a buttercup. numerous beauty parlors which open and shut like night-blooming plants. a tiny dime and department store of no width but several floors. a hutch, homemade, where you can order, after lying down or squirming in, furniture that's been fashioned from bent lengths of stainless tubing, glowing plastic, metallic thread, and clear shellac. an American Legion Post and a root beer stand. little agencies for this and that: cosmetics, brushes, insurance, greeting cards and garden produce—anything—sample shoes—which do their business out of hats and satchels, over coffee cups and dissolving sugar. a factory for making paper sacks and pasteboard boxes that's lodged in an old brick building bearing the legend OPERA HOUSE, still faintly golden, on its roof. a library given by Carnegie. a post office. a school. a railroad station. fire station. lumberyard. telephone company. welding shop. garage . . . and spotted through the town from one end to the other in a line along the highway, gas stations to the number five.

EDUCATION

In 1833, Colin Goodykoontz, an itinerant preacher with a name from a fairytale, summed up the situation in one Indiana town this way:

Ignorance and her squalid brood. A universal dearth of intellect. Total abstinence from literature is very generally practiced. . . . There is not a scholar in grammar or geography, or a *teacher capable* of *instructing* in them, to my knowledge. . . . Others are supplied a few months of the year with the most antiquated & unreasonable forms of teaching reading, writing & cyphering. . . . Need I stop to remind you of the host of loathsome reptiles such a stagnant pool is fitted to breed! Croaking jealousy; bloated bigotry; coiling suspicion; wormish blindness; crocodile malice!

Things have changed since then, but in none of the respects mentioned.

BUSINESS

One side section of street is blocked off with sawhorses. Hard, thin, bitter men in blue jeans, cowboy boots and hats, untruck a dinky carnival. The merchants are promoting themselves. There will be free rides, raucous music, parades and coneys, pop, popcorn, candy, cones, awards and drawings, with all you can endure of pinch, push, bawl, shove, shout, scream, shriek, and bellow. Children pedal past on decorated bicycles, their wheels a blur of color, streaming crinkled paper and excited dogs. A little later there's a pet show for a prize—dogs, cats, birds, sheep, ponies, goats—none of which wins. The whirlabouts whirl about. The Ferris wheel climbs dizzily into the sky as far as a tall man on tiptoe might be persuaded to reach, and the irritated operators measure the height and weight of every child with sour eyes to see if they are safe for the machines. An electrical megaphone repeatedly trumpets the names of the generous sponsors. The following day they do not allow the refuse to remain long in the street.

MY HOUSE, THIS PLACE AND BODY

I have met with some mischance, wings withering, as Plato says obscurely, and across the breadth of Ohio, like heaven on a table, I've fallen as far as the poet, to the sixth sort of body, this house in B, in Indiana, with its blue and gray bewitching windows, holy magical insides. Great thick evergreens protect its entry. And I live *in.*

Lost in the corn rows, I remember feeling just another stalk, and thus this country takes me over in the way I occupy myself when I am well . . . completely—to the edge of both my house and body. No one notices, when they walk by, that I am brimming in the doorways. My house, this place and body, I've come in mourning to be born in. To anybody else it's pretty silly: love. Why should I feel a loss? How am I bereft? She was never mine; she was a fiction, always a golden tomgirl, barefoot, with an adolescent's slouch and a boy's taste for sports and fishing, a figure out of Twain, or worse, in Riley. Age cannot be kind.

There's little hand-in-hand here . . . not in B. No one touches except in rage. Occasionally girls will twine their arms about each other and lurch along, school out, toward home and play. I dreamed my lips would drift down your back like a skiff on a river. I'd follow a vein with the point of my finger, hold your bare feet in my naked hands.

THE SAME PERSON

Billy Holsclaw lives alone—how alone it is impossible to fathom. In the post office he talks greedily to me about the weather. His head bobs on a wild flood of words, and I take this violence to be a measure of his eagerness for speech. He badly needs a shave, coal dust has layered his face, he spits when he speaks, and his fingers pick at his tatters. He wobbles out in the wind when I leave him, a paper sack mashed in the fold of his arm, the leaves blowing past him, and our encounter drives me sadly home to poetry— where there's no answer. Billy closes his door and carries coal or wood to his fire and closes his eyes, and there's simply no way of knowing how lonely and empty he is or whether he's as vacant and barren and loveless as the rest of us are—here in the heart of the country.

WEATHER

For we're always out of luck here. That's just how it is—for instance in the winter. The sides of the buildings, the roofs, the limbs of the trees are gray. Streets, sidewalks, faces, feelings—they are gray. Speech is gray, and the grass where it shows. Every flank and front, each top is gray. Everything is gray: hair, eyes, window glass, the hawkers' bills and touters' posters, lips, teeth, poles and metal signs—they're gray, quite gray. Cars are gray. Boots, shoes, suits, hats, gloves are gray. Horses, sheep, and cows, cats killed in the road, squirrels in the same way, sparrows, doves, and pigeons, all are gray, everything is gray, and everyone is out of luck who lives here.

A similar haze turns the summer sky milky, and the air muffles your head and shoulders like a sweater you've got caught in. In the summer light, too, the sky darkens a moment when you open your eyes. The heat is pure distraction. Steeped in our fluids, miserable in the folds of our bodies, we can scarcely think of anything but our sticky parts. Hot cyclonic winds and storms of dust crisscross the country. In many places, given an indifferent push, the wind will still coast for miles, gathering resource and edge as it goes, cunning and force. According to the season, paper, leaves, field litter, seeds, snow, fill up the fences. Sometimes I think the land is flat because the winds have leveled it, they blow so constantly. In any case, a gale can grow in a field of corn that's as hot as a draft from hell, and to receive it is one of the most dismaying experiences of this life, though the smart of the same wind in winter is more humiliating, and in that sense even worse. But in the spring it rains as well, and the trees fill with ice.

PLACE

Many small Midwestern towns are nothing more than rural slums, and this community could easily become one. Principally during the first decade of the century, though there were many earlier instances, well-to-do farmers moved to town and built fine homes to contain them in their retirement. Others desired a more social life, and so lived in, driving to their fields like storekeepers to their businesses. These houses are now dying like the bereaved who inhabit them; they are slowly losing their senses—deafness, blindness, forgetfulness, mumbling, an insecure gait, an uncontrollable trembling has overcome them. Some kind of Northern Snopes will occupy them next: large-familied, Catholic, Democratic, scrambling, vigorous, poor; and since the parents will work in larger, nearby towns, the children will be loosed upon themselves and upon the hapless neighbors much as the fabulous Khan loosed his legendary horde. These Snopes will undertake makeshift repairs with materials that other people have thrown away; paint halfway round their house, then quit; almost certainly maintain an ugly loud cantankerous dog and underfeed a pair of cats to keep the rodents down. They will collect piles of possibly useful junk in the back yard, park their cars in the front, live largely leaning over engines, give not a hoot for the land, the old community, the hallowed ways, the established clans. Weakening widow ladies have already begun to hire large rude youths from families such as these to rake and mow and tidy the grounds they will inherit.

PEOPLE

In the cinders at the station boys sit smoking steadily in darkened cars, their arms bent out the windows, white shirts glowing behind the glass. Nine o'clock is the best time. They sit in a line facing the highway—two or three or four of them—idling their engines. As you walk by a machine may growl at you or a pair of headlights flare up briefly. In a moment one will pull out, spinning cinders behind it, to stalk impatiently up and down the dark streets or roar half a mile into the country before returning to its place in line and pulling up.

MY HOUSE, MY CAT, MY COMPANY

I must organize myself. I must, as they say, pull myself together, dump this cat from my lap, stir—yes, resolve, move, do. But do what? My will is like the rosy dustlike light in this room: soft, diffuse, and gently comforting. It lets me do . . . anything . . . nothing. My ears hear what they happen to; I eat what's put before me; my eyes see what blunders into them; my thoughts are not thoughts, they are dreams. I'm empty or I'm full . . . depending; and I cannot choose. I sink my claws in Tick's fur and scratch the bones of his back until his rear rises amorously. Mr. Tick, I murmur, I must organize myself. I must pull myself together. And Mr. Tick rolls over on his belly, all ooze.

I spill Mr. Tick when I've rubbed his stomach. Shoo. He steps away slowly, his long tail rhyming with his paws. How beautifully he moves, I think; how beautifully, like you, he commands his loving, how beautifully he accepts. So I rise and wander from room to room, up and down, gazing through most of my forty-one windows. How well this house receives its loving too. Let out like Mr. Tick, my eyes sink in the shrubbery. I am not here; I've passed the glass, passed second-story spaces, flown by branches, brilliant berries, to the ground, grass high in seed and leafage every season; and it is the same as when I passed above you in my aged, ardent body; it's, in short, a kind of love; and I am learning to restore myself, my house, my body, by paying court to gardens, cats, and running water, and with neighbors keeping company.

Mrs. Desmond is my right-hand friend; she's eighty-five. A thin white mist of hair, fine and tangled, manifests the climate of her mind. She is habitually suspicious, fretful, nervous. Burglars break in at noon. Children trespass. Even now they are shaking the pear tree, stealing rhubarb, denting lawn. Flies caught in the screens and numbed by frost awake in the heat to buzz and scrape the metal cloth and frighten her, though she is deaf to me, and consequently cannot hear them. Boards creak, the wind whistles across the chimney mouth, drafts cruise like fish through the hollow rooms. It is herself she hears, her own flesh failing, for only death will preserve her from those daily chores she climbs like stairs, and all that anxious waiting. Is it now, she wonders. No? Then: is it now?

We do not converse. She visits me to talk. My task to murmur. She talks about her grandsons, her daughter who lives in Delphi, her sister or her husband—both gone—obscure friends—dead—obscurer aunts and uncles—lost—ancient neighbors, members of her church or of her clubs—passed or passing on; and in this way she brings the ends of her life together with a terrifying rush: she is a girl, a wife, a mother, widow, all at once. All at once—appalling—but I believe it; I wince in expectation of the clap. Her talk's a fence—a shade drawn, window fastened, door that's locked—for no one dies taking tea in a kitchen; and as her years compress and begin to jumble, I really believe in the brevity of life; I sweat in my wonder; death is the dog down the street, the angry gander, bedroom spider, goblin who's come to get her; and it occurs to me that in my listening posture I'm the boy who suffered the winds of my grandfather with an exactly similar politeness, that I am, right now, all my ages, out in elbows, as angular as badly stacked cards. Thus was I, when I loved you, every man I could be, youth and child—far from enough—and you, so strangely ambiguous a being, met me, heart for spade, play after play, the whole run of our suits.

Mr. Tick, you do me honor. You not only lie in my lap, but you remain alive there, coiled like a fetus. Through your deep nap, I feel you hum. You are, and are not, a machine. You are alive, alive exactly, and it means nothing to you—much to me. You are a cat—you cannot understand—you are a cat so easily. Your nature is not something you must rise to. You, not I, live in: in house, in skin, in shrubbery. Yes. I think I shall hat my head with a steeple; turn church; devour people. Mr. Tick, though, has a tail he can twitch, he need not fly his Fancy. Claws, not metrical schema, poetry his paws; while smoothing . . . smoothing . . . smoothing roughly, his tongue laps its neatness. O Mr. Tick, I know you; you are an electrical penis. Go on now, shoo. Mrs. Desmond doesn't like you. She thinks you will tangle yourself in her legs and she will fall. You murder her birds, she knows, and walk upon her roof with death in your jaws. I must gather myself together for a bound. What age is it I'm at right now, I wonder. The heart, don't they always say, keeps the true time. Mrs. Desmond is knocking. Faintly, you'd think, but she pounds. She's brought me a cucumber. I believe she believes I'm a woman. Come in, Mrs. Desmond, thank you, be my company, it looks lovely, and have tea. I'll slice it, crisp, with cream, for luncheon, each slice as thin as me.

POLITICS

O all ye isolate and separate powers, Sing! Sing, and sing in such a way that from a distance it will seem a harmony, a Strindberg play, a friendship ring . . . so happy—happy, happy, happy—as here we go hand in handling, up and down. Our union was a singing, though we were silent in the songs we sang like single notes are silent in a symphony. In no sense sober, we barbershopped together and never heard the discords in our music or saw ourselves as dirty, cheap, or silly. Yet cats have worn out better shoes than those thrown through our love songs at us. Hush. Be patient—prudent—politic. Still, Cleveland killed you, Mr. Crane. Were you not politic enough and fond of being beaten? Like a piece of sewage, the city shat you from its stern three hundred miles from history—beyond the loving reach of sailors. Well, I'm not a poet who puts Paris to his temple in his youth to blow himself from Idaho, or—fancy that—Missouri. My god, I said, this is my country, but must my country go so far as Terre Haute or Whiting, go so far as Gary?

When the Russians first announced the launching of their satellite, many people naturally refused to believe them. Later others were outraged that they had sent a dog around the earth. I wouldn't want to take that mutt from out that metal flying thing if he's still living when he lands, our own dog catcher said; anybody knows you shut a dog up by himself to toss around the first thing he'll be setting on to do you let him out is bite somebody.

This Midwest. A dissonance of parts and people, we are a consonance of Towns. Like a man grown fat in everything but heart, we overlabor; our outlook never really urban, never rural either, we enlarge and linger at the same time, as Alice both changed and remained in her story. You are blond. I put my hand upon your belly; feel it tremble from my trembling. We always drive large cars in my section of the country. How could you be a comfort to me now?

MORE VITAL DATA

The town is exactly fifty houses, trailers, stores, and miscellaneous buildings long, but in places no streets deep. It takes on width as you drive south, always adding to the east. Most of the dwellings are fairly spacious farm houses in the customary white, with wide wraparound porches and tall narrow windows, though there are many of the grander kind—fretted, scalloped, turreted, and decorated with clapboards set at angles or on end, with stained-glass windows at the stair landings and lots of wrought iron full of fancy curls—and a few of these look like castles in their rarer brick. Old stables serve as garages now, and the lots are large to contain them and the vegetable and flower gardens which, ultimately, widows plant and weed and then entirely disappear in. The shade is ample, the grass is good, the sky a glorious fall violet; the apple trees are heavy and red, the roads are calm and empty; corn has sifted from the chains of tractored wagons to speckle the streets with gold and with the russet fragments of the cob, and a man would be a fool who wanted, blessed with this, to live anywhere else in the world.

EDUCATION

Buses like great orange animals move through the early light to school. There the children will be taught to read and warned against Communism. By Miss Janet Jakes. That's not her name. Her name is Helen something—Scott or James. A teacher twenty years. She's now worn fine and smooth, and has a face, Wilfred says, like a mail-order ax. Her voice is hoarse, and she has a cough. For she screams abuse. The children stare, their faces blank. This is the thirteenth week. They are used to it. You will all, she shouts, you will all draw pictures of me. No. She is a Mrs.—someone's missus. And in silence they set to work while Miss Jakes jabs hairpins in her hair. Wilfred says an ax, but she has those rimless tinted glasses, graying hair, an almost dimpled chin. I must concentrate. I must stop making up things. I must give myself to life; let it mold me: that's what they say in *Wisdom's Monthly Digest* every day. Enough, enough—you've been at it long enough; and the children rise formally a row at a time to present their work to her desk. No, she wears rims; it's her chin that's dimpleless. Well, it will take more than a tablespoon of features to sweeten that face. So she grimly shuffles their sheets, examines her reflection crayoned on them. I would not dare . . . allow a child . . . to put a line around me. Though now and then she smiles like a nick in the blade, in the end these drawings depress her. I could not bear it—how can she ask?—that anyone . . . draw me. Her anger's lit. That's why she does it: flame. There go her eyes; the pink in her glasses brightens, dims. She is a pumpkin, and her rage is breathing like the candle in. No, she shouts, no—the cartoon trembling—no, John Mauck, John Stewart Mauck, this will not do. The picture flutters from her fingers. You've made me too muscular.

I work on my poetry. I remember my friends, associates, my students, by their names. Their names are Maypop, Dormouse, Upsydaisy. Their names are Gladiolus, Callow Bladder, Prince and Princess Oleo, Hieronymus, Cardinal Mummum, Mr. Fitchew, The Silken Howdah, Spot. Sometimes you're Tom Sawyer, Huckleberry Finn; it is perpetually summer; your buttocks are my pillow; we are adrift on a raft; your back is our river. Sometimes you are Major Barbara, sometimes a goddess who kills men in battle, sometimes you are soft like a shower of water; you are bread in my mouth.

I do not work on my poetry. I forget my friends, associates, my students, and their names: Gramophone, Blowgun, Pickle, Serenade . . . Marge the Barge, Arena, Uberhaupt . . . Doctor Dildoe, The Fog Machine. For I am now in B, in Indiana: out of job and out of patience, out of love and time and money, out of bread and out of body, in a temper, Mrs. Desmond, out of tea. So shut your fist up, bitch, you bag of death; go bang another door; go die, my dearie. Die, life-deaf old lady. Spill your breath. Fall over like a frozen board. Gray hair grows from the nose of your mind. You are a skull already—*memento mori*—the foreskin retracts from your teeth. Will your plastic gums last longer than your bones, and color their grinning? And is your twot still hazel-hairy, or are you bald as a ditch? . . . bitch . . . . . . bitch . . . . . . bitch. I wanted to be famous, but you bring me age—my emptiness. Was it *that* which I thought would balloon me above the rest? Love? where are you? . . . love me. I want to rise so high, I said, that when I shit I won't miss anybody.

BUSINESS

For most people, business is poor. Nearby cities have siphoned off all but a neighborhood trade. Except for feed and grain and farm supplies, you stand a chance to sell only what one runs out to buy. Chevrolet has quit, and Frigidaire. A locker plant has left its afterimage. The lumberyard has been, so far, six months about its going. Gas stations change hands clumsily, a restaurant becomes available, a grocery closes. One day they came and knocked the cornices from the watch repair and pasted campaign posters on the windows. Torn across, by now, by boys, they urge you still to vote for half an orange beblazoned man who as a whole one failed two years ago to win at his election. Everywhere, in this manner, the past speaks, and it mostly speaks of failure. The empty stores, the old signs and dusty fixtures, the debris in alleys, the flaking paint and rusty gutters, the heavy locks and sagging boards: they say the same disagreeable things. What do the sightless windows see, I wonder, when the sun throws a passerby against them? Here a stair unfolds toward the street—dark, rickety, and treacherous—and I always feel, as I pass it, that if I just went carefully up and turned the corner at the landing, I would find myself out of the world. But I've never had the courage.

THAT SAME PERSON

The weeds catch up with Billy. In pursuit of the holly-hocks, they rise in coarse clumps all around the front of his house. Billy has to stamp down a circle by his door like a dog or cat does turning round to nest up, they're so thick. What particularly troubles me is that winter will find the weeds still standing stiff and tindery to take the sparks which Billy's little mortarless chimney spouts. It's true that fires are fun here. The town whistle, which otherwise only blows for noon (and there's no noon on Sunday), signals the direction of the fire by the length and number of its blasts, the volunteer firemen rush past in their cars and trucks, houses empty their owners along the street every time like an illustration in a children's book. There are many bikes, too, and barking dogs, and sometimes—halleluiah—the fire's right here in town—a vacant lot of weeds and stubble flaming up. But I'd rather it weren't Billy or Billy's lot or house. Quite selfishly I want him to remain the way he is—counting his sticks and logs, sitting on his sill in the soft early sun—though I'm not sure what his presence means to me . . . or to anyone. Nevertheless, I keep wondering whether, given time, I might not someday find a figure in our language which would serve him faithfully, and furnish his poverty and loneliness richly out.

WIRES

Where sparrows sit like fists. Doves fly the steeple. In mist the wires change perspective, rise and twist. If they led to you, I would know what they were. Thoughts passing often, like the starlings who flock these fields at evening to sleep in the trees beyond, would form a family of paths like this; they'd foot down the natural height of air to just about a bird's perch. But they do not lead to you.

> Of whose beauty it was sung
> She shall make the old man young.

They fasten me.

If I walked straight on, in my present mood, I would reach the Wabash. It's not a mood in which I'd choose to conjure you. Similes dangle like baubles from me. This time of year the river is slow and shallow, the clay banks crack in the sun, weeds surprise the sandbars. The air is moist and I am sweating. It's impossible to rhyme in this dust. Everything—sky, the cornfield, stump, wild daisies, my old clothes and pressless feelings—seem fabricated for installment purchase. Yes. Christ. I am suffering a summer Christmas; and I cannot walk under the wires. The sparrows scatter like handfuls of gravel. Really, wires are voices in thin strips. They are words wound in cables. Bars of connection.

WEATHER

I would rather it were the weather that was to blame for what I am and what my friends and neighbors are—we who live here in the heart of the country. Better the weather, the wind, the pale dying snow . . . the snow—why not the snow? There's never much really, not around the lower Lakes anyway, not enough to boast about, not enough to be useful. My father tells how the snow in the Dakotas would sweep to the roofs of the barns in the old days, and he and his friends could sled on the crust that would form because the snow was so fiercely driven. In Bemidji trees have been known to explode. That would be something—if the trees in Davenport or Francisville or Carbondale or Niles were to go blam some winter—blam! blam! blam! all the way down the gray, cindery, snow-sick streets.

A cold fall rain is blackening the trees or the air is like lilac and full of parachuting seeds. Who cares to live in any season but his own? Still I suspect the secret's in this snow, the secret of our sickness, if we could only diagnose it, for we are all dying like the elms in Urbana. This snow—like our skin it covers the country. Later dust will do it. Right now—snow. Mud presently. But it is snow without any laughter in it, a pale gray pudding thinly spread on stiff toast, and if that seems a strange description, it's accurate all the same. Of course soot blackens everything, but apart from that, we are never sufficiently cold here. The flakes as they come, alive and burning, we cannot retain, for if our temperatures fall, they rise promptly again, just as, in the summer, they bob about in the same feckless way. Suppose though . . . suppose they were to rise some August, climb and rise, and then hang in the hundreds like a hawk through December, what a desert we could make of ourselves—from Chicago to Cairo, from Hammond to Columbus—what beautiful Death Valleys.

PLACE

I would rather it were the weather. It drives us in upon ourselves—an unlucky fate. Of course there is enough to stir our wonder anywhere; there's enough to love, anywhere, if one is strong enough, if one is diligent enough, if one is perceptive, patient, kind enough—whatever it takes; and surely it's better to live in the country, to live on a prairie by a drawing of rivers, in Iowa or Illinois or Indiana, say, than in any city, in any stinking fog of human beings, in any blooming orchard of machines. It ought to be. The cities are swollen and poisonous with people. It ought to be better. Man has never been a fit environment for man—for rats, maybe, rats do nicely, or for dogs or cats and the household beetle.

And how long the street is, nowadays. These endless walls are fallen to keep back the tides of earth. Brick could be beautiful but we have covered it gradually with gray industrial vomits. Age does not make concrete genial, and asphalt is always—like America—twenty-one, until it breaks up in crumbs like stale cake. The brick, the asphalt, the concrete, the dancing signs and garish posters, the feed and excrement of the automobile, the litter of its inhabitants: they compose, they decorate, they line our streets, and there is nowhere, nowadays, our streets can't reach.

A man in the city has no natural thing by which to measure himself. His parks are potted plants. Nothing can live and remain free where he resides but the pigeon, starling, sparrow, spider, cockroach, mouse, moth, fly and weed, and he laments the existence of even these and makes his plans to poison them. The zoo? There *is* the zoo. Through its bars the city man stares at the great cats and dully sucks his ice. Living, alas, among men and their marvels, the city man supposes that his happiness depends on establishing, somehow, a special kind of harmonious accord with others. The novelists of the city, of slums and crowds, they call it love—and break their pens.

Wordsworth feared the accumulation of men in cities. He foresaw their "degrading thirst after outrageous stimulation," and some of their hunger for love. Living in a city, among so many, dwelling in the heat and tumult of incessant movement, a man's affairs are touch and go—that's all. It's not surprising that the novelists of the slums, the cities, and the crowds, should find that sex is but a scratch to ease a tickle, that we're most human when we're sitting on the john, and that the justest image of our life is in full passage through the plumbing.

> That man, immur'd in cities, still retains
> His inborn inextinguishable thirst
> Of rural scenes, compensating his loss
> By supplemental shifts, the best he may.

Come into the country, then. The air nimbly and sweetly recommends itself unto our gentle senses. Here, growling tractors tear the earth. Dust roils up behind them. Drivers sit jouncing under bright umbrellas. They wear refrigerated hats and steer by looking at the tracks they've cut behind them, their transistors blaring. Close to the land, are they? good companions to the soil? Tell me: do they live in harmony with the alternating seasons?

It's a lie of old poetry. The modern husbandman uses chemicals from cylinders and sacks, spike-ball-and-claw machines, metal sheds, and cost accounting. Nature in the old sense does not matter. It does not exist. Our farmer's only mystical attachment is to parity. And if he does not realize that cows and corn are simply different kinds of chemical engine, he cannot expect to make a go of it.

It isn't necessary to suppose our cows have feelings; our neighbor hasn't as many as he used to have either; but think of it this way a moment, you can correct for the human imputations later: how would it feel to nurse those strange tentacled calves with their rubber, glass, and metal lips, their stainless eyes?

PEOPLE

Aunt Pet's still able to drive her car—a high square Ford—even though she walks with difficulty and a stout stick. She has a watery gaze, a smooth plump face despite her age, and jet black hair in a bun. She has the slowest smile of anyone I ever saw, but she hates dogs, and not very long ago cracked the back of one she cornered in her garden. To prove her vigor she will tell you this, her smile breaking gently while she raises the knob of her stick to the level of your eyes.

HOUSE, MY BREATH AND WINDOW

My window is a grave, and all that lies within it's dead. No snow is falling. There's no haze. It is not still, not silent. Its images are not an animal that waits, for movement is no demonstration. I have seen the sea slack, life bubble through a body without a trace, its spheres impervious as soda's. Downwound, the whore at wagtag clicks and clacks. Leaves wiggle. Grass sways. A bird chirps, pecks the ground. An auto wheel in penning circles keeps its rigid spokes. These images are stones; they are memorials. Beneath this sea lies sea: god rest it . . . rest the world beyond my window, me in front of my reflection, above this page, my shade. Death is not so still, so silent, since silence implies a falling quiet, stillness a stopping, containing, holding in; for death is time in a clock, like Mr. Tick, electric . . . like wind through a windup poet. And my blear floats out to visible against the glass, befog its country and bespill myself. The mist lifts slowly from the fields in the morning. No one now would say: the Earth throws back its covers; it is rising from sleep. Why is the feeling foolish? The image is too Greek. I used to gaze at you so wantonly your body blushed. Imagine: wonder: that my eyes could cause such flowering. Ah, my friend, your face is pale, the weather cloudy; a street has been felled through your chin, bare trees do nothing, houses take root in their rectangles, a steeple stands up in your head. You speak of loving; then give me a kiss. The pane is cold. On icy mornings the fog rises to greet me (as you always did); the barns and other buildings, rather than ghostly, seem all the more substantial for looming, as if they grew in themselves while I watched (as you always did). Oh my approach, I suppose, was like breath in a rubber monkey. Nevertheless, on the road along the Wabash in the morning, though the trees are sometimes obscured by fog, their reflection floats serenely on the river, reasoning the banks, the sycamores in French rows. Magically, the world tips. I'm led to think that only those who grow down live (which will scarcely win me twenty-five from *Wisdom's Monthly Digest*), but I find I write that only those who live down grow; and what I write, I hold, whatever I really know. My every word's inverted, or reversed—or I am. I held you, too, that way. You were so utterly provisional, subject to my change. I could inflate your bosom with a kiss, disperse your skin with gentleness, enter your vagina from within, and make my love emerge like a fresh sex. The pane is cold. Honesty is cold, my inside lover. The sun looks, through the mist, like a plum on the tree of heaven, or a bruise on the slope of your belly. Which? The grass crawls with frost. We meet on this window, the world and I, inelegantly, swimmers of the glass; and swung wrong way round to one another, the world seems in. The world—how grand, how monumental, grave and deadly, that word is: the world, my house and poetry. All poets have their inside lovers. Wee penis does not belong to me, or any of this foggery. It is *his* property which he's thrust through what's womanly of me to set down this. These wooden houses in their squares, gray streets and fallen sidewalks, standing trees, your name I've written sentimentally across my breath into the whitening air, pale birds: they exist in me now because of him. I gazed with what intensity . . . A bush in the excitement of its roses could not have bloomed so beautifully as you did then. It was a look I'd like to give this page. For that is poetry: to bring within about, to change.

POLITICS

Sports, politics, and religion are the three passions of the badly educated. They are the Midwest's open sores. Ugly to see, a source of constant discontent, they sap the body's strength. Appalling quantities of money, time, and energy are wasted on them. The rural mind is narrow, passionate, and reckless on these matters. Greed, however shortsighted and direct, will not alone account for it. I have known men, for instance, who for years have voted squarely against their interests. Nor have I ever noticed that their surly Christian views prevented them from urging forward the smithereening, say, of Russia, China, Cuba, or Korea. And they tend to back their country like they back their local team: they have a fanatical desire to win; yelling is their forte; and if things go badly, they are inclined to sack the coach. All in all, then, Birch is a good name. It stands for the bigot's stick, the wild-child-tamer's cane.

Forgetfulness—is that their object?

Oh, I was new, I thought. A fresh start: new cunt, new climate, and new country—there you were, and I was pioneer, and had no history. That language hurts me, too, my dear. You'll never hear it.

FINAL VITAL DATA

The Modern Homemakers' Demonstration Club. The Prairie Home Demonstration Club. The Night-outers' Home Demonstration Club. The IOOF, FFF, VFW, WCTU, WSCS, 4-H, 40 and 8, Psi Iota Chi, and PTA. The Boy and Girl Scouts, Rainbows, Masons, Indians and Rebekah Lodge. Also the Past Noble Grand Club of the Rebekah Lodge. As well as the Moose and the Ladies of the Moose. The Elks, the Eagles, the Jaynettes and the Eastern Star. The Women's Literary Club, the Hobby Club, the Art Club, the Sunshine Society, the Dorcas Society, the Pythian Sisters, the Pilgrim Youth Fellowship, the American Legion, the American Legion Auxiliary, the American Legion Junior Auxiliary, the Gardez Club, the Bridge for Fun

Club, the What-can-you-do? Club, the Get Together Club, the Coterie
Club, the Worthwhile Club, the Let's Help Our Town Club, the No Name
Club, the Forget-me-not Club, the Merry-go-round Club . . .

EDUCATION

Has a quarter disappeared from Paula Frosty's pocket book? Imagine the
landscape of that face: no crayon could engender it; soft wax is wrong; thin
wire in trifling snips might do the trick. Paula Frosty and Christopher Roger
accuse the pale and splotchy Cheryl Pipes. But Miss Jakes, I *saw* her. Miss
Jakes is so extremely vexed she snaps her pencil. What else is missing? I
appoint you a detective, John: search her desk. Gum, candy, paper, pencils,
marble, round eraser—whose? A thief. I can't watch her all the time, I'm
here to teach. Poor pale fossetted Cheryl, it's determined, can't return the
money because she took it home and spent it. Cindy, Janice, John, and
Pete—you four who sit around her—you will be detectives this whole term
to watch her. A thief. In all my time. Miss Jakes turns, unfists, and turns
again. I'll handle you, she cries. To think. A thief. In all my years. Then she
writes on the blackboard the name of Cheryl Pipes and beneath that the
figure twenty-five with a large sign for cents. Now Cheryl, she says, this won't
be taken off until you bring that money out of home, out of home straight
up to here, Miss Jakes says, tapping her desk.
   Which is three days.

ANOTHER PERSON

I was raking leaves when Uncle Halley introduced himself to me. He said
his name came from the comet, and that his mother had borne him prema-
turely in her fright of it. I thought of Hobbes, whom fear of the Spanish
Armada had hurried into birth, and so I believed Uncle Halley to honor the
philosopher, though Uncle Halley is a liar, and neither the one hundred
twenty-nine nor the fifty-three he ought to be. That fall the leaves had
burned themselves out on the trees, the leaf lobes had curled, and now they
flocked noisily down the street and were broken in the wires of my rake.
Uncle Halley was himself (like Mrs. Desmond and history generally) both
deaf and implacable, and he shooed me down his basement stairs to a room
set aside there for stacks of newspapers reaching to the ceiling, boxes of
leaflets and letters and programs, racks of photo albums, scrapbooks, bun-
dles of rolled-up posters and maps, flags and pennants and slanting piles
of dusty magazines devoted mostly to motoring and the Christian ethic. I
saw a bird cage, a tray of butterflies, a bugle, a stiff straw boater, and all kinds
of tassels tied to a coat tree. He still possessed and had on display the
steering lever from his first car, a linen duster, driving gloves and goggles,
photographs along the wall of himself, his friends, and his various machines,
a shell from the first war, a record of "Ramona" nailed through its hole to

a post, walking sticks and fanciful umbrellas, shoes of all sorts (his baby shoes, their counters broken, were held in sorrow beneath my nose—they had not been bronzed, but he might have them done someday before he died, he said), countless boxes of medals, pins, beads, trinkets, toys, and keys (I scarcely saw—they flowed like jewels from his palms), pictures of downtown when it was only a path by the railroad station, a brightly colored globe of the world with a dent in Poland, antique guns, belt buckles, buttons, souvenir plates and cups and saucers (I can't remember all of it—I won't), but I recall how shamefully, how rudely, how abruptly, I fled, a good story in my mouth but death in my nostrils; and how afterward I busily, righteously, burned my leaves as if I were purging the world of its years. I still wonder if this town—its life, and mine now—isn't really a record like the one of "Ramona" that I used to crank around on my grandmother's mahogany Victrola through lonely rainy days as a kid.

THE FIRST PERSON

Billy's like the coal he's found: spilled, mislaid, discarded. The sky's no comfort. His house and his body are dying together. His windows are boarded. And now he's reduced to his hands. I suspect he has glaucoma. At any rate he can scarcely see, and weeds his yard of rubble on his hands and knees. Perhaps he's a surgeon cleansing a wound or an ardent and tactile lover. I watch, I must say, apprehensively. Like mine-war detectors, his hands graze in circles ahead of him. Your nipples were the color of your eyes. Pebble. Snarl of paper. Length of twine. He leans down closely, picks up something silvery, holds it near his nose. Foil? cap? coin? He has within him—what, I wonder? Does he know more now because he fingers everything and has to sniff to see? It would be romantic cruelty to think so. He bends the down on your arms like a breeze. You wrote me: something is strange when we don't understand. I write in return: I think when I loved you I fell to my death.

Billy, I could read to you from Beddoes; he's your man perhaps; he held with dying, freed his blood of its arteries; and he said that there were many wretched love-ill fools like me lying alongside the last bone of their former selves, as full of spirit and speech, nonetheless, as Mrs. Desmond, Uncle Halley and the Ferris wheel, Aunt Pet, Miss Jakes, Ramona or the megaphone; yet I reverse him finally, Billy, on no evidence but braggadocio, and I declare that though my inner organs were devoured long ago, the worm which swallowed down my parts still throbs and glows like a crystal palace.

Yes, you were younger. I was Uncle Halley, the museum man and infrequent meteor. Here is my first piece of ass. They weren't so flat in those days, had more round, more juice. And over here's the sperm I've spilled, nicely jarred and clearly labeled. Look at this tape like lengths of intestine where I've stored my spew, the endless worm of words I've written, a hundred million emissions or more: oh I was quite a man right from the start; even when unconscious in my cradle, from crotch to cranium, I was erectile tissue; though mostly, after the manner approved by Plato, I had intercourse by eye. Never mind, old Holsclaw, you are blind. We pull down darkness when we go to bed; put out like Oedipus the actually offending organ, and train our touch to lies. All cats are gray, says Mr. Tick; so under cover of glaucoma you are sack gray too, and cannot be distinguished from a stallion.

I must pull myself together, get a grip, just as they say, but I feel spilled, bewildered, quite mislaid. I did not restore my house to its youth, but to its age. Hunting, you hitch through the hollyhocks. I'm inclined to say you aren't half the cripple I am, for there is nothing left of me but mouth. However, I resist the impulse. It is another lie of poetry. My organs are all there, though it's there where I fail—at the roots of my experience. Poet of the spiritual, Rilke, weren't you? yet that's what you said. Poetry, like love, is—in and out—a physical caress. I can't tolerate any more of my sophistries about spirit, mind, and breath. Body equals being, and if your weight goes down, you are the less.

HOUSEHOLD APPLES

I knew nothing about apples. Why should I? My country came in my childhood, and I dreamed of sitting among the blooms like the bees. I failed to spray the pear tree too. I doubled up under them at first, admiring the sturdy low branches I should have pruned, and later I acclaimed the blossoms. Shortly after the fruit formed there were falls—not many—apples the size of goodish stones which made me wobble on my ankles when I walked about the yard. Sometimes a piece crushed by a heel would cling on the shoe to track the house. I gathered a few and heaved them over the wires. A slingshot would have been splendid. Hard, an unattractive green, the worms had them. Before long I realized the worms had them all. Even as the apples reddened, lit their tree, they were being swallowed. The birds preferred the pears, which were small—sugar pears I think they're called—with thick skins of graying green that ripen on toward violet. So the fruit fell, and once I made some applesauce by quartering and paring hundreds; but mostly I did nothing, left them, until suddenly, overnight it seemed, in that ugly late September heat we often have in Indiana, my problem was upon me.

My childhood came in the country. I remember, now, the flies on our snowy luncheon table. As we cleared away they would settle, fastidiously scrub themselves and stroll to the crumbs to feed where I would kill them in crowds with a swatter. It was quite a game to catch them taking off. I struck heavily since I didn't mind a few stains; they'd wash. The swatter was a square of screen bound down in red cloth. It drove no air ahead of it to give them warning. They might have thought they'd flown headlong into a summered window. The faint pink dot where they had died did not rub out as I'd supposed, and after years of use our luncheon linen would faintly, pinkly, speckle.

The country became my childhood. Flies braided themselves on the flypaper in my grandmother's house. I can smell the bakery and the grocery and the stables and the dairy in that small Dakota town I knew as a kid; knew as I dreamed I'd know your body, as I've known nothing, before or since; knew as the flies knew, in the honest, unchaste sense: the burned house, hose-wet, which drew a mist of insects like the blue smoke of its smolder, and gangs of boys, moist-lipped, destructive as its burning. Flies have always impressed me; they are so persistently alive. Now they were coating the ground beneath my trees. Some were ordinary flies; there were the large blue-green ones; there were swarms of fruit flies too, and the red-spotted scavenger beetle; there were a few wasps, several sorts of bees and butterflies—checkers, sulphurs, monarchs, commas, question marks—and delicate dragonflies . . . but principally houseflies and horseflies and bottleflies, flies and more flies in clusters around the rotting fruit. They loved the pears. Inside, they fed. If you picked up a pear, they flew, and the pear became skin and stem. They were everywhere the fruit was: in the tree still—apples like a hive for them—or where the fruit littered the ground, squashing itself as you stepped . . . there was no help for it. The flies droned, feasting on the sweet juice. No one could go near the trees; I could not climb; so I determined at last to labor like Hercules. There were fruit baskets in the barn. Collecting them and kneeling under the branches, I began to gather remains. Deep in the strong rich smell of the fruit, I began to hum myself. The fruit caved in at the touch. Glistening red apples, my lifting disclosed, had families of beetles, flies, and bugs, devouring their rotten undersides. There were streams of flies; there were lakes and cataracts and rivers of flies, seas and oceans. The hum was heavier, higher, than the hum of the bees when they came to the blooms in the spring, though the bees were there, among the flies, ignoring me—ignoring everyone. As my work went on and juice covered my hands and arms, they would form a sleeve, black and moving, like knotty wool. No caress could have been more indifferently complete. Still I rose fearfully, ramming my head in the branches, apples bumping against me before falling, bursting with bugs. I'd snap my hand sharply but the flies would cling to the sweet. I could toss a whole cluster into a basket from several feet. As the pear or apple lit, they would explosively rise, like monads for a moment, windowless, certainly, with respect to one another, sugar their harmony. I had to admit, though, despite my distaste, that my arm had never been more alive, oftener or more gently kissed. Those hundreds of feet were light. In washing them off, I pretended the hose was a pump. What have I missed? Childhood is a lie of poetry.

THE CHURCH

Friday night. Girls in dark skirts and white blouses sit in ranks and scream in concert. They carry funnels loosely stuffed with orange and black paper which they shake wildly, and small megaphones through which, as drilled, they direct and magnify their shouting. Their leaders, barely pubescent girls, prance and shake and whirl their skirts above their bloomers. The young men, leaping, extend their arms and race through puddles of amber light, their bodies glistening. In a lull, though it rarely occurs, you can hear the squeak of tennis shoes against the floor. Then the yelling begins again, and then continues; fathers, mothers, neighbors joining in to form a single pulsing ululation—a cry of the whole community—for in this gymnasium each body becomes the bodies beside it, pressed as they are together, thigh to thigh, and the same shudder runs through all of them, and runs toward the same release. Only the ball moves serenely through this dazzling din. Obedient to law it scarcely speaks but caroms quietly and lives at peace.

BUSINESS

It is the week of Christmas and the stores, to accommodate the rush they hope for, are remaining open in the evening. You can see snow falling in the cones of the street lamps. The roads are filling—undisturbed. Strings of red and green lights droop over the principal highway, and the water tower wears a star. The windows of the stores have been bedizened. Shamelessly they beckon. But I am alone, leaning against a pole—no . . . there is no one in sight. They're all at home, perhaps by their instruments, tuning in on their evenings, and like Ramona, tirelessly playing and replaying themselves. There's a speaker perched in the tower, and through the boughs of falling snow and over the vacant streets, it drapes the twisted and metallic strains of a tune that can barely be distinguished—yes, I believe it's one of the jolly ones, it's "Joy to the World." There's no one to hear the music but myself, and though I'm listening, I'm no longer certain. Perhaps the record's playing something else.

(1968)

Flannery O'Connor

(1 9 2 5 – 1 9 6 4)

One of the most exciting fiction writers to emerge from the American South since William Faulkner, Flannery O'Connor was born in Savannah, Georgia. She studied at the Georgia State College for Women and at the University of Iowa, where she earned an M.F.A. in creative writing in 1947. She lived briefly in New York City and in Connecticut, then returned to the family farm in Georgia, where she resided for the next 14 years. O'Connor's fiction won extensive praise during her lifetime, and she won the O. Henry award in 1957. Her first novel, *Wise Blood,* appeared in 1952. The posthumous *Complete Short Stories* won the National Book Award in 1972. O'Connor died of tuberculosis in Georgia at the age of 39.

O'Connor is often identified as a southern Gothic writer and as a Catholic writer. The first label is accurate. The world she created in her fiction includes the grotesque excesses of sin and suffering she thought humanity capable of; it is a world filled with a wild and grimly demonic humor—for example, a crumbling cathedral ornamented with grinning gargoyles that cackle at the absurdity of life. To call O'Connor a Catholic writer is problematic. Undeniably, her world is a religious one, as were the worlds created by Melville, Faulkner, and Aeschylus. But her characters' struggles focus on an individual relationship with God, and it might be argued that O'Connor is, in essence, Protestant in temperament. The absurdity of the world can only be rendered meaningful by the redemption of Christ, but, like a "good man," that redemption is "hard to find," to borrow from the title of her first collection of stories. O'Connor expresses an acute sense of dislocation and isolation in her work.

O'Connor wrote two short novels, *Wise Blood* (1952) and *The Violent Bear It Away* (1960), and two fine collections of stories, *A Good Man Is Hard to Find* (1955) and *Everything That Rises Must Converge* (1965). Her stories were gathered in *The Complete Stories* (1972).

FLANNERY O'CONNOR

A Good Man Is Hard to Find

THE grandmother didn't want to go to Florida. She wanted to visit some of her connections in east Tennessee and she was seizing at every chance to change Bailey's mind. Bailey was the son she lived with, her only boy. He was sitting on the edge of his chair at the table, bent over the orange sports section of the *Journal.* "Now look here, Bailey," she said, "see here, read this," and she stood with one hand on her thin hip and the other rattling the newspaper at his bald head. "Here this fellow that calls himself The Misfit is aloose from the Federal Pen and headed toward Florida and you read here what it says he did to these people. Just you read it. I wouldn't take my children in any direction with a criminal like that aloose in it. I couldn't answer to my conscience if I did."

Bailey didn't look up from his reading so she wheeled around then and faced the children's mother, a young woman in slacks, whose face was as broad and innocent as a cabbage and was tied around with a green head-kerchief that had two points on the top like a rabbit's ears. She was sitting on the sofa, feeding the baby his apricots out of a jar. "The children have been to Florida before," the old lady said. "You all ought to take them somewhere else for a change so they would see different parts of the world and be broad. They never have been to east Tennessee."

The children's mother didn't seem to hear her but the eight-year-old boy, John Wesley, a stocky child with glasses, said, "If you don't want to go to Florida, why dontcha stay at home?" He and the little girl, June Star, were reading the funny papers on the floor.

"She wouldn't stay at home to be queen for a day," June Star said without raising her yellow head.

"Yes and what would you do if this fellow, The Misfit, caught you?" the grandmother asked.

"I'd smack his face," John Wesley said.

"She wouldn't stay at home for a million bucks," June Star said. "Afraid she'd miss something. She has to go everywhere we go."

"All right, Miss," the grandmother said. "Just remember that the next time you want me to curl your hair."

June Star said her hair was naturally curly.

The next morning the grandmother was the first one in the car, ready to go. She had her big black valise that looked like the head of a hippopotamus in one corner, and underneath it she was hiding a basket with Pitty Sing, the cat, in it. She didn't intend for the cat to be left alone in the house for three days because he would miss her too much and she was afraid he might brush against one of the gas burners and accidentally asphyxiate himself. Her son, Bailey, didn't like to arrive at a motel with a cat.

She sat in the middle of the back seat with John Wesley and June Star on either side of her. Bailey and the children's mother and the baby sat in front and they left Atlanta at eight forty-five with the mileage on the car at 55890. The grandmother wrote this down because she thought it would be interesting to say how many miles they had been when they got back. It took them twenty minutes to reach the outskirts of the city.

The old lady settled herself comfortably, removing her white cotton gloves and putting them up with her purse on the shelf in front of the back window. The children's mother still had on slacks and still had her head tied up in a green kerchief, but the grandmother had on a navy blue straw sailor hat with a bunch of white violets on the brim and a navy blue dress with a small white dot in the print. Her collars and cuffs were white organdy trimmed with lace and at her neckline she had pinned a purple spray of cloth violets containing a sachet. In case of an accident, anyone seeing her dead on the highway would know at once that she was a lady.

She said she thought it was going to be a good day for driving, neither too hot nor too cold, and she cautioned Bailey that the speed limit was fifty-five miles an hour and that the patrolmen hid themselves behind billboards and small clumps of trees and sped out after you before you had a chance to slow down. She pointed out interesting details of the scenery: Stone Mountain; the blue granite that in some places came up to both sides of the highway; the brilliant red clay banks slightly streaked with purple; and the various crops that made rows of green lace-work on the ground. The trees were full of silver-white sunlight and the meanest of them sparkled. The children were reading comic magazines and their mother had gone back to sleep.

"Let's go through Georgia fast so we won't have to look at it much," John Wesley said.

"If I were a little boy," said the grandmother, "I wouldn't talk about my native state that way. Tennessee has the mountains and Georgia has the hills."

"Tennessee is just a hillbilly dumping ground," John Wesley said, "and Georgia is a lousy state too."

"You said it," June Star said.

"In my time," said the grandmother, folding her thin veined fingers, "children were more respectful of their native states and their parents and everything else. People did right then. Oh look at the cute little pickaninny!" she said and pointed to a Negro child standing in the door of a shack. "Wouldn't that make a picture, now?" she asked and they all turned and looked at the little Negro out of the back window. He waved.

"He didn't have any britches on," June Star said.

"He probably didn't have any," the grandmother explained. "Little niggers in the country don't have things like we do. If I could paint, I'd paint that picture," she said.

The children exchanged comic books.

The grandmother offered to hold the baby and the children's mother passed him over the front seat to her. She set him on her knee and bounced him and told him about the things they were passing. She rolled her eyes and screwed up her mouth and stuck her leathery thin face into his smooth bland one. Occasionally he gave her a faraway smile. They passed a large cotton field with five or six graves fenced in the middle of it, like a small island. "Look at the graveyard!" the grandmother said, pointing it out. "That was the old family burying ground. That belonged to the plantation."

"Where's the plantation?" John Wesley asked.

"Gone With the Wind," said the grandmother. "Ha. Ha."

When the children finished all the comic books they had brought, they opened the lunch and ate it. The grandmother ate a peanut butter sandwich and an olive and would not let the children throw the box and the paper napkins out the window. When there was nothing else to do they played a game by choosing a cloud and making the other two guess what shape it suggested. John Wesley took one the shape of a cow and June Star guessed a cow and John Wesley said, no, an automobile, and June Star said he didn't play fair, and they began to slap each other over the grandmother.

The grandmother said she would tell them a story if they would keep quiet. When she told a story, she rolled her eyes and waved her head and was very dramatic. She said once when she was a maiden lady she had been courted by a Mr. Edgar Atkins Teagarden from Jasper, Georgia. She said he was a very good-looking man and a gentleman and that he brought her a watermelon every Saturday afternoon with his initials cut in it, E. A. T. Well, one Saturday, she said, Mr. Teagarden brought the watermelon and there was nobody at home and he left it on the front porch and returned in his buggy to Jasper, but she never got the watermelon, she said, because a nigger boy ate it when he saw the initials, E. A. T.! This story tickled John Wesley's funny bone and he giggled and giggled but June Star didn't think it was any good. She said she wouldn't marry a man that just brought her a watermelon on Saturday. The grandmother said she would have done well to marry Mr. Teagarden because he was a gentleman and had bought Coca-Cola stock when it first came out and that he had died only a few years ago, a very wealthy man.

They stopped at The Tower for barbecued sandwiches. The Tower was a part stucco and part wood filling station and dance hall set in a clearing outside of Timothy. A fat man named Red Sammy Butts ran it and there were signs stuck here and there on the building and for miles up and down the highway saying, TRY RED SAMMY'S FAMOUS BARBECUE. NONE LIKE FAMOUS RED SAMMY'S! RED SAM! THE FAT BOY WITH THE HAPPY LAUGH! A VETERAN! RED SAMMY'S YOUR MAN!

Red Sammy was lying on the bare ground outside The Tower with his head under a truck while a gray monkey about a foot high, chained to a small chinaberry tree, chattered nearby. The monkey sprang back into the tree and got on the highest limb as soon as he saw the children jump out of the car and run toward him.

Inside, The Tower was a long dark room with a counter at one end and tables at the other and dancing space in the middle. They all sat down at a board table next to the nickelodeon and Red Sam's wife, a tall burnt-brown woman with hair and eyes lighter than her skin, came and took their order. The children's mother put a dime in the machine and played "The Tennessee Waltz," and the grandmother said that tune always made her want to dance. She asked Bailey if he would like to dance but he only glared at her. He didn't have a naturally sunny disposition like she did and trips made him nervous. The grandmother's brown eyes were very bright. She swayed her head from side to side and pretended she was dancing in her chair. June Star said play something she could tap to so the children's mother put in another dime and played a fast number and June Star stepped out onto the dance floor and did her tap routine.

"Ain't she cute?" Red Sam's wife said, leaning over the counter. "Would you like to come be my little girl?"

"No I certainly wouldn't," June Star said. "I wouldn't live in a broken-down place like this for a million bucks!" and she ran back to the table.

"Ain't she cute?" the woman repeated, stretching her mouth politely.

"Aren't you ashamed?" hissed the grandmother.

Red Sam came in and told his wife to quit lounging on the counter and hurry up with these people's order. His khaki trousers reached just to his hip bones and his stomach hung over them like a sack of meal swaying under his shirt. He came over and sat down at a table nearby and let out a combination sigh and yodel. "You can't win," he said. "You can't win," and he wiped his sweating red face off with a gray handkerchief. "These days you don't know who to trust," he said. "Ain't that the truth?"

"People are certainly not nice like they used to be," said the grandmother.

"Two fellers come in here last week," Red Sammy said, "driving a Chrysler. It was a old beat-up car but it was a good one and these boys looked all right to me. Said they worked at the mill and you know I let them fellers charge the gas they bought? Now why did I do that?"

"Because you're a good man!" the grandmother said at once.

"Yes'm, I suppose so," Red Sam said as if he were struck with this answer.

His wife brought the orders, carrying the five plates all at once without a tray, two in each hand and one balanced on her arm. "It isn't a soul in this green world of God's that you can trust," she said. "And I don't count nobody out of that, not nobody," she repeated, looking at Red Sammy.

"Did you read about that criminal, The Misfit, that's escaped?" asked the grandmother.

"I wouldn't be a bit surprised if he didn't attack this place right here," said the woman. "If he hears about it being here, I wouldn't be none surprised to see him. If he hears it's two cent in the cash register, I wouldn't be a tall surprised if he . . ."

"That'll do," Red Sam said. "Go bring these people their Co'-Colas," and the woman went off to get the rest of the order.

"A good man is hard to find," Red Sammy said. "Everything is getting terrible. I remember the day you could go off and leave your screen door unlatched. Not no more."

He and the grandmother discussed better times. The old lady said that in her opinion Europe was entirely to blame for the way things were now. She said the way Europe acted you would think we were made of money and Red Sam said it was no use talking about it, she was exactly right. The children ran outside into the white sunlight and looked at the monkey in the lacy chinaberry tree. He was busy catching fleas on himself and biting each one carefully between his teeth as if it were a delicacy.

They drove off again into the hot afternoon. The grandmother took cat naps and woke up every few minutes with her own snoring. Outside of Toombsboro she woke up and recalled an old plantation that she had visited in this neighborhood once when she was a young lady. She said the house had six white columns across the front and that there was an avenue of oaks leading up to it and two little wooden trellis arbors on either side in front where you sat down with your suitor after a stroll in the garden. She recalled exactly which road to turn off to get to it. She knew that Bailey would not be willing to lose any time looking at an old house, but the more she talked about it, the more she wanted to see it once again and find out if the little twin arbors were still standing. "There was a secret panel in this house," she said craftily, not telling the truth but wishing that she were, "and the story went that all the family silver was hidden in it when Sherman came through but it was never found . . ."

"Hey!" John Wesley said. "Let's go see it! We'll find it! We'll poke all the woodwork and find it! Who lives there? Where do you turn off at? Hey Pop, can't we turn off there?"

"We never have seen a house with a secret panel!" June Star shrieked. "Let's go to the house with the secret panel! Hey Pop, can't we go see the house with the secret panel!"

"It's not far from here, I know," the grandmother said. "It wouldn't take over twenty minutes."

Bailey was looking straight ahead. His jaw was as rigid as a horseshoe. "No," he said.

The children began to yell and scream that they wanted to see the house with the secret panel. John Wesley kicked the back of the front seat and June Star hung over her mother's shoulder and whined desperately into her ear that they never had any fun even on their vacation, that they could never do what THEY wanted to do. The baby began to scream and John Wesley kicked the back of the seat so hard that his father could feel the blows in his kidney.

"All right!" he shouted and drew the car to a stop at the side of the road. "Will you all shut up? Will you all just shut up for one second? If you don't shut up, we won't go anywhere."

"It would be very educational for them," the grandmother murmured.

"All right," Bailey said, "but get this: this is the only time we're going to stop for anything like this. This is the one and only time."

"The dirt road that you have to turn down is about a mile back," the grandmother directed. "I marked it when we passed."

"A dirt road," Bailey groaned.

After they had turned around and were headed toward the dirt road, the grandmother recalled other points about the house, the beautiful glass over the front doorway and the candle-lamp in the hall. John Wesley said that the secret panel was probably in the fireplace.

"You can't go inside this house," Bailey said. "You don't know who lives there."

"While you all talk to the people in front, I'll run around behind and get in a window," John Wesley suggested.

"We'll all stay in the car," his mother said.

They turned onto the dirt road and the car raced roughly along in a swirl of pink dust. The grandmother recalled the times when there were no paved roads and thirty miles was a day's journey. The dirt road was hilly and there were sudden washes in it and sharp curves on dangerous embankments. All at once they would be on a hill, looking down over the blue tops of trees for miles around, then the next minute, they would be in a red depression with the dust-coated trees looking down on them.

"This place had better turn up in a minute," Bailey said, "or I'm going to turn around."

The road looked as if no one had traveled on it in months.

"It's not much farther," the grandmother said and just as she said it, a horrible thought came to her. The thought was so embarrassing that she turned red in the face and her eyes dilated and her feet jumped up, upsetting her valise in the corner. The instant the valise moved, the newspaper top she had over the basket under it rose with a snarl and Pitty Sing, the cat, sprang onto Bailey's shoulder.

The children were thrown to the floor and their mother, clutching the baby, was thrown out the door onto the ground; the old lady was thrown into the front seat. The car turned over once and landed right-side-up in a gulch off the side of the road. Bailey remained in the driver's seat with the cat—gray-striped with a broad white face and an orange nose—clinging to his neck like a caterpillar.

As soon as the children saw they could move their arms and legs, they scrambled out of the car, shouting, "We've had an ACCIDENT!" The grandmother was curled up under the dashboard, hoping she was injured so that Bailey's wrath would not come down on her all at once. The horrible thought she had had before the accident was that the house she had remembered so vividly was not in Georgia but in Tennessee.

Bailey removed the cat from his neck with both hands and flung it out the window against the side of a pine tree. Then he got out of the car and started looking for the children's mother. She was sitting against the side of the red gutted ditch, holding the screaming baby, but she only had a cut down her face and a broken shoulder. "We've had an ACCIDENT!" the children screamed in a frenzy of delight.

"But nobody's killed," June Star said with disappointment as the grandmother limped out of the car, her hat still pinned to her head but the broken front brim standing up at a jaunty angle and the violet spray hanging off the side. They all sat down in the ditch, except the children, to recover from the shock. They were all shaking.

"Maybe a car will come along," said the children's mother hoarsely.

"I believe I have injured an organ," said the grandmother, pressing her side, but no one answered her. Bailey's teeth were clattering. He had on a yellow sport shirt with bright blue parrots designed in it and his face was as yellow as the shirt. The grandmother decided that she would not mention that the house was in Tennessee.

The road was about ten feet above and they could see only the tops of the trees on the other side of it. Behind the ditch they were sitting in there were more woods, tall and dark and deep. In a few minutes they saw a car some distance away on top of a hill, coming slowly as if the occupants were watching them. The grandmother stood up and waved both arms dramatically to attract their attention. The car continued to come on slowly, disappeared around a bend and appeared again, moving even slower, on top of the hill they had gone over. It was a big black battered hearselike automobile. There were three men in it.

It came to a stop just over them and for some minutes, the driver looked down with a steady expressionless gaze to where they were sitting, and didn't speak. Then he turned his head and muttered something to the other two and they got out. One was a fat boy in black trousers and a red sweat shirt with a silver stallion embossed on the front of it. He moved around on the right side of them and stood staring, his mouth partly open in a kind of loose grin. The other had on khaki pants and a blue striped coat and a gray hat pulled down very low, hiding most of his face. He came around slowly on the left side. Neither spoke.

The driver got out of the car and stood by the side of it, looking down at them. He was an older man than the other two. His hair was just beginning to gray and he wore silver-rimmed spectacles that gave him a scholarly look. He had a long creased face and didn't have on any shirt or undershirt. He had on blue jeans that were too tight for him and was holding a black hat and a gun. The two boys also had guns.

"We've had an ACCIDENT!" the children screamed.

The grandmother had the peculiar feeling that the bespectacled man was someone she knew. His face was as familiar to her as if she had known him all her life but she could not recall who he was. He moved away from the car and began to come down the embankment, placing his feet carefully so that he wouldn't slip. He had on tan and white shoes and no socks, and his ankles were red and thin. "Good afternoon," he said. "I see you all had you a little spill."

"We turned over twice!" said the grandmother.

"Oncet," he corrected. "We seen it happen. Try their car and see will it run, Hiram," he said quietly to the boy with the gray hat.

"What you got that gun for?" John Wesley asked. "Whatcha gonna do with that gun?"

"Lady," the man said to the children's mother, "would you mind calling them children to sit down by you? Children make me nervous. I want all you all to sit down right together there where you're at."

"What are you telling US what to do for?" June Star asked.

Behind them the line of woods gaped like a dark open mouth. "Come here," said their mother.

"Look here now," Bailey began suddenly, "we're in a predicament! We're in . . ."

The grandmother shrieked. She scrambled to her feet and stood staring. "You're The Misfit!" she said. "I recognized you at once!"

"Yes'm," the man said, smiling slightly as if he were pleased in spite of himself to be known, "but it would have been better for all of you, lady, if you hadn't of reckernized me."

Bailey turned his head sharply and said something to his mother that shocked even the children. The old lady began to cry and The Misfit reddened.

"Lady," he said, "don't you get upset. Sometimes a man says things he don't mean. I don't reckon he meant to talk to you thataway."

"You wouldn't shoot a lady, would you?" the grandmother said and removed a clean handkerchief from her cuff and began to slap at her eyes with it.

The Misfit pointed the toe of his shoe into the ground and made a little hole and then covered it up again. "I would hate to have to," he said.

"Listen," the grandmother almost screamed, "I know you're a good man. You don't look a bit like you have common blood. I know you must come from nice people!"

"Yes mam," he said, "finest people in the world." When he smiled he showed a row of strong white teeth. "God never made a finer woman than my mother and my daddy's heart was pure gold," he said. The boy with the red sweat shirt had come around behind them and was standing with his gun at his hip. The Misfit squatted down on the ground. "Watch them children, Bobby Lee," he said. "You know they make me nervous." He looked at the six of them huddled together in front of him and he seemed to be embarrassed as if he couldn't think of anything to say. "Ain't a cloud in the sky," he remarked, looking up at it. "Don't see no sun but don't see no cloud neither."

"Yes, it's a beautiful day," said the grandmother. "Listen," she said, "you shouldn't call yourself The Misfit because I know you're a good man at heart. I can just look at you and tell."

"Hush!" Bailey yelled. "Hush! Everybody shut up and let me handle this!" He was squatting in the position of a runner about to sprint forward but he didn't move.

"I pre-chate that, lady," The Misfit said and drew a little circle in the ground with the butt of his gun.

"It'll take a half a hour to fix this here car," Hiram called, looking over the raised hood of it.

"Well, first you and Bobby Lee get him and that little boy to step over yonder with you," The Misfit said, pointing to Bailey and John Wesley. "The boys want to ast you something," he said to Bailey. "Would you mind stepping back in them woods there with them?"

"Listen," Bailey began, "we're in a terrible predicament! Nobody realizes what this is," and his voice cracked. His eyes were as blue and intense as the parrots in his shirt and he remained perfectly still.

The grandmother reached up to adjust her hat brim as if she were going to the woods with him but it came off in her hand. She stood staring at it and after a second she let it fall on the ground. Hiram pulled Bailey up by the arm as if he were assisting an old man. John Wesley caught hold of his father's hand and Bobby Lee followed. They went off toward the woods and just as they reached the dark edge, Bailey turned and supporting himself against a gray naked pine trunk, he shouted, "I'll be back in a minute, Mamma, wait on me!"

"Come back this instant!" his mother shrilled but they all disappeared into the woods.

"Bailey Boy!" the grandmother called in a tragic voice but she found she was looking at The Misfit squatting on the ground in front of her. "I just know you're a good man," she said desperately. "You're not a bit common!"

"Nome, I ain't a good man," The Misfit said after a second as if he had considered her statement carefully, "but I ain't the worst in the world neither. My daddy said I was a different breed of dog from my brothers and sisters. 'You know,' Daddy said, 'it's some that can live their whole life out without asking about it and it's others has to know why it is, and this boy is one of the latters. He's going to be into everything!'" He put on his black hat and looked up suddenly and then away deep into the woods as if he were embarrassed again. "Im sorry I don't have on a shirt before you ladies," he said, hunching his shoulders slightly. "We buried our clothes that we had on when we escaped and we're just making do until we can get better. We borrowed these from some folks we met," he explained.

"That's perfectly all right," the grandmother said. "Maybe Bailey has an extra shirt in his suitcase."

"I'll look and see terrectly," The Misfit said.

"Where are they taking him?" the children's mother screamed.

"Daddy was a card himself," The Misfit said. "You couldn't put anything over on him. He never got in trouble with the Authorities though. Just had the knack of handling them."

"You could be honest too if you'd only try," said the grandmother.

"Think how wonderful it would be to settle down and live a comfortable life and not have to think about somebody chasing you all the time."

The Misfit kept scratching in the ground with the butt of his gun as if he were thinking about it. "Yes'm, somebody is always after you," he murmured.

The grandmother noticed how thin his shoulder blades were just behind his hat because she was standing up looking down on him. "Do you ever pray?" she asked.

He shook his head. All she saw was the black hat wiggle between his shoulder blades. "Nome," he said.

There was a pistol shot from the woods, followed closely by another. Then silence. The old lady's head jerked around. She could hear the wind move through the tree tops like a long satisfied insuck of breath. "Bailey Boy!" she called.

"I was a gospel singer for a while," The Misfit said. "I been most everything. Been in the arm service, both land and sea, at home and abroad, been twict married, been an undertaker, been with the railroads, plowed Mother Earth, been in a tornado, seen a man burnt alive oncet," and looked up at the children's mother and the little girl who were sitting close together, their faces white and their eyes glassy; "I even seen a woman flogged," he said.

"Pray, pray," the grandmother began, "pray, pray . . ."

"I never was a bad boy that I remember of," The Misfit said in an almost dreamy voice, "but somewheres along the line I done something wrong and got sent to the penitentiary. I was buried alive," and he looked up and held her attention to him by a steady stare.

"That's when you should have started to pray," she said. "What did you do to get sent to the penitentiary that first time?"

"Turn to the right, it was a wall," The Misfit said, looking up again at the cloudless sky. "Turn to the left, it was a wall. Look up it was a ceiling, look down it was a floor. I forget what I done, lady. I set there and set there, trying to remember what it was I done and I ain't recalled it to this day. Oncet in a while, I would think it was coming to me, but it never come."

"Maybe they put you in by mistake," the old lady said vaguely.

"Nome," he said. "It wasn't no mistake. They had the papers on me."

"You must have stolen something," she said.

The Misfit sneered slightly. "Nobody had nothing I wanted," he said. "It was a head-doctor at the penitentiary said what I had done was kill my daddy but I known that for a lie. My daddy died in nineteen ought nineteen of the epidemic flu and I never had a thing to do with it. He was buried in the Mount Hopewell Baptist churchyard and you can go there and see for yourself."

"If you would pray," the old lady said, "Jesus would help you."

"That's right," The Misfit said.

"Well then, why don't you pray?" she asked trembling with delight suddenly.

"I don't want no hep," he said. "I'm doing all right by myself."

Bobby Lee and Hiram came ambling back from the woods. Bobby Lee was dragging a yellow shirt with bright blue parrots in it.

"Thow me that shirt, Bobby Lee," The Misfit said. The shirt came flying at him and landed on his shoulder and he put it on. The grandmother couldn't name what the shirt reminded her of. "No, lady," The Misfit said while he was buttoning it up, "I found out the crime don't matter. You can do one thing or you can do another, kill a man or take a tire off his car, because sooner or later you're going to forget what it was you done and just be punished for it."

The children's mother had begun to make heaving noises as if she couldn't get her breath. "Lady," he asked, "would you and that little girl like to step off yonder with Bobby Lee and Hiram and join your husband?"

"Yes, thank you," the mother said faintly. Her left arm dangled helplessly and she was holding the baby, who had gone to sleep, in the other. "Hep that lady up, Hiram," The Misfit said as she struggled to climb out of the ditch, "and Bobby Lee, you hold onto that little girl's hand."

"I don't want to hold hands with him," June Star said. "He reminds me of a pig."

The fat boy blushed and laughed and caught her by the arm and pulled her off into the woods after Hiram and her mother.

Alone with The Misfit, the grandmother found that she had lost her voice. There was not a cloud in the sky nor any sun. There was nothing around her but woods. She wanted to tell him that he must pray. She opened and closed her mouth several times before anything came out. Finally she found herself saying, "Jesus, Jesus," meaning, Jesus will help you, but the way she was saying it, it sounded as if she might be cursing.

"Yes'm," The Misfit said as if he agreed. "Jesus thrown everything off balance. It was the same case with Him as with me except He hadn't committed any crime and they could prove I had committed one because they had the papers on me. Of course," he said, "they never shown me my papers. That's why I sign myself now. I said long ago, you get you a signature and sign everything you do and keep a copy of it. Then you'll know what you done and you can hold up the crime to the punishment and see do they match and in the end you'll have something to prove you ain't been treated right. I call myself The Misfit," he said, "because I can't make what all I done wrong fit what all I gone through in punishment."

There was a piercing scream from the woods, followed closely by a pistol report. "Does it seem right to you, lady, that one is punished a heap and another ain't punished at all?"

"Jesus!" the old lady cried. "You've got good blood! I know you wouldn't shoot a lady! I know you come from nice people! Pray! Jesus, you ought not to shoot a lady. I'll give you all the money I've got!"

"Lady," The Misfit said, looking beyond her far into the woods, "there never was a body that give the undertaker a tip."

There were two more pistol reports and the grandmother raised her head like a parched old turkey hen crying for water and called, "Bailey Boy, Bailey Boy!" as if her heart would break.

"Jesus was the only One that ever raised the dead." The Misfit continued, "and He shouldn't have done it. He thrown everything off balance. If He did what He said, then it's nothing for you to do but throw away everything and follow Him, and if He didn't, then it's nothing for you to do but enjoy the few minutes you got left the best way you can—by killing somebody or burning down his house or doing some other meanness to him. No pleasure but meanness," he said and his voice had become almost a snarl.

"Maybe He didn't raise the dead," the old lady mumbled, not knowing what she was saying and feeling so dizzy that she sank down in the ditch with her legs twisted under her.

"I wasn't there so I can't say He didn't," The Misfit said. "I wisht I had of been there," he said, hitting the ground with his fist. "It ain't right I wasn't there because if I had of been there I would of known. Listen lady," he said in a high voice, "if I had of been there I would of known and I wouldn't be like I am now." His voice seemed about to crack and the grandmother's head cleared for an instant. She saw the man's face twisted close to her own as if he were going to cry and she murmured, "Why you're one of my babies. You're one of my own children!" She reached out and touched him on the shoulder. The Misfit sprang back as if a snake had bitten him and shot her three times through the chest. Then he put his gun down on the ground and took off his glasses and began to clean them.

Hiram and Bobby Lee returned from the woods and stood over the ditch, looking down at the grandmother who half sat and half lay in a puddle of blood with her legs crossed under her like a child's and her face smiling up at the cloudless sky.

Without his glasses, The Misfit's eyes were red-rimmed and pale and defenseless-looking. "Take her off and throw her where you thrown the others," he said, picking up the cat that was rubbing itself against his leg.

"She was a talker, wasn't she?" Bobby Lee said, sliding down the ditch with a yodel.

"She would of been a good woman," The Misfit said, "if it had been somebody there to shoot her every minute of her life."

"Some fun!" Bobby Lee said.

"Shut up, Bobby Lee," The Misfit said, "It's no real pleasure in life."

(1953)

Margaret Laurence

(b. 1 9 2 6)

Perhaps Canada's finest novelist, Margaret Laurence was born in the small prairie town of Neepawa, Manitoba. Her mother died when Laurence was 4, her father when she was 9. Laurence was raised in the strict Presbyterian household of her grandparents. In 1943 she won a scholarship to United College in Winnipeg. She married Jack Laurence, an engineer, and moved with him to England in 1949. They moved to Africa in 1950, where Laurence started to write. Her fiction began to appear in magazines in the early 1950s and her first novel, *This Side Jordan,* was published in 1960, three years after her return to Canada. In 1962 Laurence left Canada for England, where she wrote several of her finest novels and achieved recognition as Canada's leading novelist. She returned to Canada in 1969 to serve as writer-in-residence at the University of Toronto, then settled in the town of Lakefield, Ontario. She won the Governor-General's award in 1966 and in 1974.

In her fiction Laurence writes about human freedom and the shackles that hinder that freedom. Again and again, her characters search for a way to live independently, to reconcile themselves to the guilt and restrictions with which they have been burdened by society and by their loved ones. Laurence examines the way cultural and religious values serve as chains we must break and, paradoxically, as a necessary source of sanity and stability in a chaotic landscape. A master of subtle symbol and masked archetypes, Laurence has created an intellectually challenging and emotionally realistic fictional world. Her characters are the most fully rounded, the most completely *living,* in Canadian fiction. In the Manawaka tetralogy, she creates wise and sympathetic voices. The powerful emotional experience of her two masterpieces, *The Diviners* and *The Stone Angel,* marks her as a classic novelist.

Laurence's fictional works include *This Side Jordan* (1960), *The Tomorrow-Tamer* (1963), *The Stone Angel* (1964), *A Jest of God* (1966), *The Fire-Dwellers* (1969), *A Bird in the House* (1970), and *The Diviners* (1974). She has also written a collection of essays, *Heart of a Stranger* (1971), a children's book, a volume of translated and adapted African tales, and several books of travel and social history.

MARGARET LAURENCE

A Bird in the House

THE parade would be almost over by now, and I had not gone. My mother had said in a resigned voice, "All right, Vanessa, if that's the way you feel," making me suffer twice as many jabs of guilt as I would have done if she had lost her temper. She and Grandmother MacLeod had gone off, my mother pulling the low box-sleigh with Roddie all dolled up in his new red snowsuit, just the sort of little kid anyone would want people to see. I sat on the lowest branch of the birch tree in our yard, not minding the snowy wind, even welcoming its punishment. I went over my reasons for not going, trying to believe they were good and sufficient, but in my heart I felt I was betraying my father. This was the first time I had stayed away from the Remembrance Day parade. I wondered if he would notice that I was not there, standing on the sidewalk at the corner of River and Main while the parade passed, and then following to the Court House grounds where the service was held.

I could see the whole thing in my mind. It was the same every year. The Manawaka Civic Band always led the way. They had never been able to afford full uniforms, but they had peaked navy-blue caps and skyblue chest ribbons. They were joined on Remembrance Day by the Salvation Army band, whose uniforms seemed too ordinary for a parade, for they were the same ones the bandsmen wore every Saturday night when they played "Nearer My God to Thee" at the foot of River Street. The two bands never managed to practise quite enough together, so they did not keep in time too well. The Salvation Army band invariably played faster, and afterwards my father would say irritably, "They play those marches just like they do hymns, blast them, as though they wouldn't get to heaven if they didn't hustle up." And my mother, who had great respect for the Salvation Army because of the good work they did, would respond chidingly, "Now, now, Ewen—" I vowed I would never say "Now, now" to my husband or children, not that I ever intended having the latter, for I had been put off by my brother Roderick, who was now two years old with wavy hair, and everyone said what a beautiful child. I was twelve, and no one in their right mind would have said what a beautiful child, for I was big-boned like my Grandfather Connor and had straight lanky black hair like a Blackfoot or Cree.

After the bands would come the veterans. Even thinking of them at this distance, in the white and withdrawn quiet of the birch tree, gave me a sense of painful embarrassment. I might not have minded so much if my father had not been among them. How could he go? How could he not see how they all looked? It must have been a long time since they were soldiers, for they had forgotten how to march in step. They were old—that was the thing. My father was bad enough, being almost forty, but he wasn't a patch on Howard Tully from the drugstore, who was completely grey-haired and also fat, or Steward MacMurchie, who was bald at the back of his head. They looked to me like imposters, plump or spindly caricatures of past warriors. I almost hated them for walking in that limping column down Main. At the Court House, everyone would sing *Lord God of Hosts, be with us yet, lest we forget, lest we forget.* Will Masterson would pick up his old Army bugle and blow the Last Post. Then it would be over and everyone could start gabbling once more and go home.

I jumped down from the birch bough and ran to the house, yelling, making as much noise as I could.

> *I'm a poor lonesome cowboy*
> *An' a long way from home—*

I stepped inside the front hall and kicked off my snow boots. I slammed the door behind me, making the dark ruby and emerald glass shake in the small leaded panes. I slid purposely on the hall rug, causing it to bunch and crinkle on the slippery polished oak of the floor. I seized the newel post, round as a head, and spun myself to and fro on the bottom stair.

> *I ain't got no father*
> *To buy the clothes I wear.*
> *I'm a poor lonesome—*

At this moment my shoulders were firmly seized and shaken by a pair of hands, white and delicate and old, but strong as talons.

"Just what do you think you're doing, young lady?" Grandmother MacLeod enquired, in a voice like frost on a windowpane, infinitely cold and clearly etched.

I went limp and in a moment she took her hands away. If you struggled, she would always hold on longer.

"Gee, I never knew you were home yet."

"I would have thought that on a day like this you might have shown a little respect and consideration," Grandmother MacLeod said, "even if you couldn't make the effort to get cleaned up enough to go to the parade."

I realised with surprise that she imagined this to be my reason for not going. I did not try to correct her impression. My real reason would have been even less acceptable.

"I'm sorry," I said quickly.

In some families, *please* is described as the magic word. In our house, however, it was *sorry.*

"This isn't an easy day for any of us," she said.

Her younger son, my Uncle Roderick, had been killed in the Great War,

When my father marched, and when the hymn was sung, and when that unbearably lonely tune was sounded by the one bugle and everyone forced themselves to keep absolutely still, it would be that boy of whom she was thinking. I felt the enormity of my own offence.

"Grandmother—I'm sorry."

"So you said."

I could not tell her I had not really said it before at all. I went into the den and found my father there. He was sitting in the leather-cushioned armchair beside the fireplace. He was not doing anything, just sitting and smoking. I stood beside him, wanting to touch the light-brown hairs on his forearm, but thinking he might laugh at me or pull his arm away if I did.

"I'm sorry," I said, meaning it.

"What for, honey?"

"For not going."

"Oh—that. What was the matter?"

I did not want him to know, and yet I had to tell him, make him see.

"They look silly," I blurted. "Marching like that."

For a minute I thought he was going to be angry. It would have been a relief to me if he had been. Instead, he drew his eyes away from mine and fixed them above the mantelpiece where the sword hung, the handsome and evil-looking crescent in its carved bronze sheath that some ancestor had once brought from the Northern Frontier of India.

"Is that the way it looks to you?" he said.

I felt in his voice some hurt, something that was my fault. I wanted to make everything all right between us, to convince him that I understood, even if I did not. I prayed that Grandmother MacLeod would stay put in her room, and that my mother would take a long time in the kitchen, giving Roddie his lunch. I wanted my father to myself, so I could prove to him that I cared more about him than any of the others did. I wanted to speak in some way that would be more poignant and comprehending than anything of which my mother could possibly be capable. But I did not know how.

"You were right there when Uncle Roderick got killed, weren't you?" I began uncertainly.

"Yes."

"How old was he, Dad?"

"Eighteen," my father said.

Unexpectedly, that day came into intense being for me. He had had to watch his own brother die, not in the antiseptic calm of some hospital, but out in the open, the stretches of mud I had seen in his snapshots. He would not have known what to do. He would just have had to stand there and look at it, whatever that might mean. I looked at my father with a kind of horrified awe, and then I began to cry. I had forgotten about impressing him with my perception. Now I needed him to console me for this unwanted glimpse of the pain he had once known.

"Hey, cut it out, honey," he said, embarrassed. "It was bad, but it wasn't all as bad as that part. There were a few other things."

"Like what?" I said, not believing him.

"Oh—I don't know," he replied evasively. "Most of us were pretty young, you know, I and the boys I joined up with. None of us had ever been away from Manawaka before. Those of us who came back mostly came back here, or else went no further away from town than Winnipeg. So when we were overseas—that was the only time most of us were ever a long way from home."

"Did you want to be?" I asked, shocked.

"Oh well—" my father said uncomfortably. "It was kind of interesting to see a few other places for a change, that's all."

Grandmother MacLeod was standing in the doorway.

"Beth's called you twice for lunch, Ewen. Are you deaf, you and Vanessa?"

"Sorry," my father and I said simultaneously.

Then we went upstairs to wash our hands.

THAT winter my mother returned to her old job as nurse in my father's medical practice. She was able to do this only because of Noreen.

"Grandmother MacLeod says we're getting a maid," I said to my father, accusingly, one morning. "We're not, are we?"

"Believe you me, on what I'm going to be paying her," my father growled, "she couldn't be called anything as classy as a maid. Hired girl would be more like it."

"Now, now, Ewen," my mother put in, "it's not as if we were cheating her or anything. You know she wants to live in town, and I can certainly see why, stuck out there on the farm, and her father hardly ever letting her come in. What kind of life is that for a girl?"

"I don't like the idea of your going back to work, Beth," my father said. "I know you're fine now, but you're not exactly the robust type."

"You can't afford to hire a nurse any longer. It's all very well to say the Depression won't last forever—probably it won't, but what else can we do for now?"

"I'm damned if I know," my father admitted. "Beth—"

"Yes?"

They both seemed to have forgotten about me. It was at breakfast, which we always ate in the kitchen, and I sat rigidly on my chair, pretending to ignore and thus snub their withdrawal from me. I glared at the window, but it was so thickly plumed and scrolled with frost that I could not see out. I glanced back to my parents. My father had not replied, and my mother was looking at him in that anxious and half-frowning way she had recently developed.

"What is it, Ewen?" Her voice had the same nervous sharpness it bore sometimes when she would say to me, "For mercy's sake, Vanessa, what is it *now?*" as though whatever was the matter, it was bound to be the last straw.

My father spun his sterling silver serviette ring, engraved with his initials, slowly around on the table.

"I never thought things would turn out like this, did you?"

"Please—" my mother said in a low strained voice, "please, Ewen, let's not start all this again. I can't take it."

"All right," my father said. "Only—"

"The MacLeods used to have money and now they don't," my mother cried. "Well, they're not alone. Do you think all that matters to me, Ewen? What I can't bear is to see you forever reproaching yourself. As if it were your fault."

"I don't think it's the comedown," my father said. "If I were somewhere else, I don't suppose it would matter to me, either, except where you're concerned. But I suppose you'd work too hard wherever you were—it's bred into you. If you haven't got anything to slave away at, you'll sure as hell invent something."

"What do you think I should do, let the house go to wrack and ruin? That would go over well with your mother, wouldn't it?"

"That's just it," my father said. "It's the damned house all the time. I haven't only taken on my father's house, I've taken on everything that goes with it, apparently. Soemtimes I really wonder—"

"Well, it's a good thing I've inherited some practicality even if you haven't," my mother said. "I'll say that for the Connors—they aren't given to brooding, thank the Lord. Do you want your egg poached or scrambled?"

"Scrambled," my father said. "All I hope is that this Noreen doesn't get married straightaway, that's all."

"She won't," my mother said. "Who's she going to meet who could afford to marry?"

"I marvel at you, Beth," my father said. "You look as though a puff of wind would blow you away. But underneath, by God, you're all hardwood."

"Don't talk stupidly," my mother said. "All I hope is that she won't object to taking your mother's breakfast up on a tray."

"That's right," my father said angrily. "Rub it in."

"Oh Ewen, I'm sorry!" my mother cried, her face suddenly stricken. "I don't know why I say these things. I didn't mean to."

"I know," my father said. "Here, cut it out, honey. Just for God's sake please don't cry."

"I'm sorry," my mother repeated, blowing her nose.

"We're both sorry," my father said. "Not that that changes anything."

After my father had gone, I got down from my chair and went to my mother.

"I don't want you to go back to the office. I don't want a hired girl here. I'll hate her."

My mother sighed, making me feel that I was placing an intolerable burden on her, and yet making me resent having to feel this weight. She looked tired, as she often did these days. Her tiredness bored me, made me want to attack her for it.

"Catch me getting along with a dumb old hired girl," I threatened.

"Do what you like," my mother said abruptly. "What can I do about it?"

And then, of course, I felt bereft, not knowing which way to turn. . . .

My father need not have worried about Noreen getting married. She was, as it turned out, interested not in boys but in God. My mother was relieved about the boys but alarmed about God.

"It isn't natural," she said, "for a girl of seventeen. Do you think she's all right mentally, Ewen?"

When my parents, along with Grandmother MacLeod, went to the United Church every Sunday, I was made to go to Sunday school in the church basement, where there were small red chairs which humiliatingly resembled kindergarten furniture, and pictures of Jesus wearing a white sheet and surrounded by a whole lot of well-dressed kids whose mothers obviously had not suffered them to come unto Him until every face and ear was properly scrubbed. Our religious observances also included grace at meals, when my father would mumble "For what we are about to receive the Lord make us truly thankful Amen," running the words together as though they were one long word. My mother approved of these rituals, which seemed decent and moderate to her. Noreen's religion, however, was a different matter. Noreen belonged to the Tabernacle of the Risen and Reborn, and she had got up to testify no less than seven times in the past two years, she told us. My mother, who could not imagine anyone's voluntarily making a public spectacle of themselves, was profoundly shocked by this revelation.

"Don't worry," my father soothed her. "She's all right. She's just had kind of a dull life, that's all."

My mother shrugged and went on worrying and trying to help Noreen without hurting her feelings, by tactful remarks about the advisability of modulating one's voice when singing hymns, and the fact that there was plenty of hot water so Noreen really didn't need to hesitate about taking a bath. She even bought a razor and a packet of blades and whispered to Noreen that any girl who wore transparent blouses so much would probably like to shave under her arms. None of these suggestions had the slightest effect on Noreen. She did not cease belting out hymns at the top of her voice, she bathed once a fortnight, and the sorrel-coloured hair continued to bloom like a thicket of Indian paint-brush in her armpits.

Grandmother MacLeod refused to speak to Noreen. This caused Noreen a certain amount of bewilderment until she finally hit on an answer.

"Your poor grandma," she said. "She is deaf as a post. These things are sent to try us here on earth, Vanessa. But if she makes it into Heaven, I'll bet you anything she will hear clear as a bell."

Noreen and I talked about Heaven quite a lot, and also Hell. Noreen had an intimate and detailed knowledge of both places. She not only knew what they looked like—she even knew how big they were. Heaven was seventy-seven thousand miles square and it had four gates, each one made out of a different kind of precious jewel. The Pearl Gate, the Topaz Gate, the Amethyst Gate, the Ruby Gate—Noreen would reel them off, all the gates of Heaven. I told Noreen they sounded like poetry, but she was puzzled by my reaction and said I shouldn't talk that way. If you said poetry, it sounded like it was just made up and not really so, Noreen said.

Hell was larger than heaven, and when I asked why, thinking of it as something of a comedown for God, Noreen said naturally it had to be bigger because there were a darn sight more people there than in Heaven. Hell was one hundred and ninety million miles deep and was in perpetual darkness, like a cave or under the sea. Even the flames (this was the awful thing) *did not give off any light.*

I did not actually believe in Noreen's doctrines, but the images which they conjured up began to inhabit my imagination. Noreen's fund of exotic knowledge was not limited to religion, although in a way it all seemed related. She could do many things which had a spooky tinge to them. Once when she was making a cake, she found we had run out of eggs. She went outside and gathered a bowl of fresh snow and used it instead. The cake rose like a charm, and I stared at Noreen as though she were a sorceress. In fact, I began to think of her as a sorceress, someone not quite of this earth. There was nothing unearthly about her broad shoulders and hips and her forest of dark red hair, but even these features took on a slightly sinister significance to me. I no longer saw her through the eyes or the expressed opinions of my mother and father, as a girl who had quit school at grade eight and whose life on the farm had been endlessly drab. I knew the truth—Noreen's life had not been drab at all, for she dwelt in a world of violent splendours, a world filled with angels whose wings of delicate light bore real feathers, and saints shining like the dawn, and prophets who spoke in ancient tongues, and the ecstatic souls of the saved, as well as denizens of the lower regions—mean-eyed imps and crooked cloven-hoofed monsters and beasts with the bodies of swine and the human heads of murderers, and lovely depraved jezebels torn by dogs through all eternity. The middle layer of Creation, our earth, was equally full of grotesque presences, for Noreen believed strongly in the visitation of ghosts and the communication with spirits. She could prove this with her Ouija board. We would both place our fingers lightly on the indicator, and it would skim across the board and spell out answers to our questions. I did not believe wholeheartedly in the Ouija board, either, but I was cautious about the kind of question I asked, in case the answer would turn out unfavorable and I would be unable to forget it.

One day Noreen told me she could also make a table talk. We used the small table in my bedroom, and sure enough, it lifted very slightly under our fingertips and tapped once for *Yes,* twice for *No.* Noreen asked if her Aunt Ruthie would get better from the kidney operation, and the table replied *No.* I withdrew my hands.

"I don't want to do it any more."

"Gee, what's the matter, Vanessa?" Noreen's plain placid face creased in a frown. "We only just begun."

"I have to do my homework."

My heart lurched as I said this. I was certain Noreen would know I was lying, and that she would know not by any ordinary perception, either. But her attention had been caught by something else, and I was thankful, at least until I saw what it was.

My bedroom window was not opened in the coldest weather. The storm window, which was fitted outside as an extra wall against the winter, had three small circular holes in its frame so that some fresh air could seep into the house. The sparrow must have been floundering in the new snow on the roof, for it had crawled in through one of these holes and was now caught between the two layers of glass. I could not bear the panic of the trapped bird, and before I realised what I was doing, I had thrown open the bedroom window. I was not releasing the sparrow into any better a situation, I soon saw, for instead of remaining quiet and allowing us to catch it in order to free it, it began flying blindly around the room, hitting the lampshade, brushing against the walls, its wings seeming to spin faster and faster.

I was petrified. I thought I would pass out if those palpitating wings touched me. There was something in the bird's senseless movements that revolted me. I also thought it was going to damage itself, break one of those thin wing-bones, perhaps, and then it would be lying on the floor, dying, like the pimpled and horribly featherless baby birds we saw sometimes on the sidewalks in the spring when they had fallen out of their nests. I was not any longer worried about the sparrow. I wanted only to avoid the sight of it lying broken on the floor. Viciously, I thought that if Noreen said, *God sees the little sparrow fall,* I would kick her in the shins. She did not, however, say this.

"A bird in the house means a death in the house," Noreen remarked.

Shaken, I pulled my glance away from the whirling wings and looked at Noreen.

"What?"

"That's what I've heard said, anyhow."

The sparrow had exhausted itself. It lay on the floor, spent and trembling. I could not bring myself to touch it. Noreen bent and picked it up. She cradled it with great gentleness between her cupped hands. Then we took it downstairs, and when I had opened the back door, Noreen set the bird free.

"Poor little scrap," she said, and I felt struck to the heart, knowing she had been concerned all along about the sparrow, while I, perfidiously, in the chaos of the moment, had been concerned only about myself.

"Wanna do some with the Ouija board, Vanessa?" Noreen asked.

I shivered a little, perhaps only because of the blast of cold air which had come into the kitchen when the door was opened.

"No thanks, Noreen. Like I said, I got my homework to do. But thanks all the same."

"That's okay," Noreen said in her guileless voice. "Any time."

But whenever she mentioned the Ouija board or the talking table, after that, I always found some excuse not to consult these oracles.

"Do you want to come to church with me this evening, Vanessa?" my father asked.

"How come you're going to the evening service?" I enquired.

"Well, we didn't go this morning. We went snow-shoeing instead, re-member? I think your grandmother was a little bit put out about it. She went alone this morning. I guess it wouldn't hurt you and me, to go now."

We walked through the dark, along the white streets, the snow squeaking dryly under our feet. The streetlights were placed at long intervals along the sidewalks, and around each pole the circle of flimsy light created glistening points of blue and crystal on the crusted snow. I would have liked to take my father's hand, as I used to do, but I was too old for that now. I walked beside him, taking long steps so he would not have to walk more slowly on my account.

The sermon bored me, and I began leafing through the Hymnary for entertainment. I must have drowsed, for the next thing I knew, my father was prodding me and we were on our feet for the closing hymn.

> Near the Cross, near the Cross,
> Be my glory ever,
> Till my ransomed soul shall find
> Rest beyond the river.

I knew the tune well, so I sang loudly for the first verse. But the music to that hymn is sombre, and all at once the words themselves seemed too dreadful to be sung. I stopped singing, my throat knotted. I thought I was going to cry, but I did not know why, except that the song recalled to me my Grandmother Connor, who had been dead only a year now. I wondered why her soul needed to be ransomed. If God did not think she was good enough just as she was, then I did not have much use for His opinion. *Rest beyond the river*—was that what had happened to her? She had believed in Heaven, but I did not think that rest beyond the river was quite what she had in mind. To think of her in Noreen's flashy Heaven, though—that was even worse. Someplace where nobody ever got annoyed or had to be smoothed down and placated, someplace where there were never any family scenes—that would have suited my Grandmother Connor. Maybe she wouldn't have minded a certain amount of rest beyond the river, at that.

When we had the silent prayer, I looked at my father. He sat with his head bowed and his eyes closed. He was frowning deeply, and I could see the pulse in his temple. I wondered then what he believed. I did not have any real idea what it might be. When he raised his head, he did not look uplifted or anything like that. He merely looked tired. Then Reverend McKee pronounced the benediction, and we could go home.

"What do you think about all that stuff, Dad?" I asked hesitantly, as we walked.

"What stuff, honey?"

"Oh, Heaven and Hell, and like that."

My father laughed. "Have you been listening to Noreen too much? Well, I don't know. I don't think they're actual places. Maybe they stand for something that happens all the time here, or else doesn't happen. It's kind of hard to explain. I guess I'm not so good at explanations."

Nothing seemed to have been made any clearer to me. I reached out and took his hand, not caring that he might think this a babyish gesture.

"I hate that hymn!"

"Good Lord," my father said in astonishment. "Why, Vanessa?"

But I did not know and so could not tell him.

MANY people in Manawaka had flu that winter, so my father and Dr. Cates were kept extremely busy. I had flu myself, and spent a week in bed, vomiting only the first day and after that enjoying poor health, as my mother put it, with Noreen bringing me ginger ale and orange juice, and each evening my father putting a wooden tongue-depressor into my mouth and peering down my throat, then smiling and saying he thought I might live after all.

Then my father got sick himself, and had to stay at home and go to bed. This was such an unusual occurrence that it amused me.

"Doctors shouldn't get sick," I told him.

"You're right," he said. "That was pretty bad management."

"Run along now, dear," my mother said.

That night I woke and heard voices in the upstairs hall. When I went out, I found my mother and Grandmother MacLeod, both in their dressing-gowns. With them was Dr. Cates. I did not go immediately to my mother, as I would have done only a year before. I stood in the doorway of my room, squinting against the sudden light.

"Mother—what is it?"

She turned, and momentarily I saw the look on her face before she erased it and put on a contrived calm.

"It's all right," she said. "Dr. Cates has just come to have a look at Daddy. You go on back to sleep."

The wind was high that night, and I lay and listened to it rattling the storm windows and making the dry and winter-stiffened vines of the Virginia creeper scratch like small persistent claws against the red brick. In the morning, my mother told me that my father had developed pneumonia.

Dr. Cates did not think it would be safe to move my father to the hospital. My mother began sleeping in the spare bedroom, and after she had been there for a few nights, I asked if I could sleep in there too. I thought she would be bound to ask me why, and I did not know what I would say, but she did not ask. She nodded, and in some way her easy agreement upset me.

That night Dr. Cates came again, bringing with him one of the nurses from the hospital. My mother stayed upstairs with them. I sat with Grandmother MacLeod in the living room. That was the last place in the world I wanted to be, but I thought she would be offended if I went off. She sat as straight and rigid as a totem pole, and embroidered away at the needlepoint cushion cover she was doing. I perched on the edge of the chesterfield and kept my eyes fixed on *The White Company* by Conan Doyle, and from time to time I turned a page. I had already read it three times before, but luckily

Grandmother MacLeod did not know that. At nine o'clock she looked at her
gold brooch watch, which she always wore pinned to her dress, and told me
to go to bed, so I did that.

I wakened in darkness. At first, it seemed to me that I was in my own bed,
and everything was as usual, with my parents in their room, and Roddie
curled up in the crib in his room, and Grandmother MacLeod sleeping with
her mouth open in her enormous spool bed, surrounded by half a dozen
framed photos of Uncle Roderick and only one of my father, and Noreen
snoring fitfully in the room next to mine, with the dark flames of her hair
spreading out across the pillow, and the pink and silver motto cards from
the Tabernacle stuck with adhesive tape onto the wall beside her bed—*Lean
on Him, Emmanuel Is My Refuge, Rock of Ages Cleft for Me.*

Then in the total night around me, I heard a sound. It was my mother,
and she was crying, not loudly at all, but from somewhere very deep inside
her. I sat up in bed. Everything seemed to have stopped, not only time but
my own heart and blood as well. Then my mother noticed that I was awake.

I did not ask her, and she did not tell me anything. There was no need.
She held me in her arms, or I held her, I am not certain which. And after
a while the first mourning stopped, too, as everything does sooner or later,
for when the limits of endurance have been reached, then people must
sleep.

In the days following my father's death, I stayed close beside my mother,
and this was only partly for my own consoling. I also had the feeling that
she needed my protection. I did not know from what, nor what I could
possibly do, but something held me there. Reverend McKee called, and I
sat with my grandmother and my mother in the living room. My mother told
me I did not need to stay unless I wanted to, but I refused to go. What I
thought chiefly was that he would speak of the healing power of prayer, and
all that, and it would be bound to make my mother cry again. And in fact,
it happened in just that way, but when it actually came, I could not protect
her from this assault. I could only sit there and pray my own prayer, which
was that he would go away quickly.

My mother tried not to cry unless she was alone or with me. I also tried,
but neither of us was entirely successful. Grandmother MacLeod, on the
other hand, was never seen crying, not even the day of my father's funeral.
But that day, when we had returned to the house and she had taken off her
black velvet overshoes and her heavy sealskin coat with its black fur that was
the softest thing I had ever touched, she stood in the hallway and for the
first time she looked unsteady. When I reached out instinctively towards her,
she sighed.

"That's right," she said. "You might just take my arm while I go upstairs,
Vanessa."

That was the most my Grandmother MacLeod ever gave in, to anyone's
sight. I left her in her bedroom, sitting on the straight chair beside her bed
and looking at the picture of my father that had been taken when he gradua-

ted from medical college. Maybe she was sorry now that she had only the one photograph of him, but whatever she felt, she did not say.

I went down into the kitchen. I had scarcely spoken to Noreen since my father's death. This had not been done on purpose. I simply had not seen her. I had not really seen anyone except my mother. Looking at Noreen now, I suddenly recalled the sparrow. I felt physically sick, remembering the fearful darting and plunging of those wings, and the fact that it was I who had opened the window and let it in. Then an inexplicable fury took hold of me, some terrifying need to hurt, burn, destroy. Absolutely without warning, either to her or to myself, I hit Noreen as hard as I could. When she swung around, appalled, I hit out at her once more, my arms and legs flailing. Her hands snatched at my wrists, and she held me, but still I continued to struggle, fighting blindly, my eyes tightly closed, as though she were a prison all around me and I was battling to get out. Finally, too shocked at myself to go on, I went limp in her grasp and she let me drop to the floor.

"Vanessa! I never done one single solitary thing to you, and here you go hitting and scratching me like that! What in the world has got into you?"

I began to say I was sorry, which was certainly true, but I did not say it. I could not say anything.

"You're not yourself, what with your dad and everything," she excused me. "I been praying every night that your dad is with God, Vanessa. I know he wasn't actually saved in the regular way, but still and all—"

"Shut up," I said.

Something in my voice made her stop talking. I rose from the floor and stood in the kitchen doorway.

"He didn't need to be saved," I went on coldly, distinctly. "And he is not in Heaven, because there is no Heaven. And it doesn't matter, see? *It doesn't matter!*"

Noreen's face looked peculiarly vulnerable now, her high wide cheekbones and puzzled childish eyes, and the thick russet tangle of her hair. I had not hurt her much before, when I hit her. But I had hurt her now, hurt her in some inexcusable way. Yet I sensed, too, that already she was gaining some satisfaction out of feeling sorrowful about my disbelief.

I went upstairs to my room. Momentarily I felt a sense of calm, almost of acceptance. *Rest beyond the river.* I knew now what that meant. It meant Nothing. It meant only silence, forever.

Then I lay down on my bed and spent the last of my tears, or what seemed then to be the last. Because, despite what I had said to Noreen, it did matter. It mattered, but there was no help for it.

EVERYTHING changed after my father's death. The MacLeod house could not be kept up any longer. My mother sold it to a local merchant who subsequently covered the deep red of the brick over with yellow stucco. Something about the house had always made me uneasy—that tower room where Grandmother MacLeod's potted plants drooped in a lethargic and lime-green confusion, those long stairways and hidden places, the attic which I had always imagined to be dwelt in by the spirits of the family dead, that gigantic portrait of the Duke of Wellington at the top of the stairs. It was never an endearing house. And yet when it was no longer ours, and when the Virginia creeper had been torn down and the dark walls turned to a light marigold, I went out of my way to avoid walking past, for it seemed to me that the house had lost the stern dignity that was its very heart.

Noreen went back to the farm. My mother and brother and myself moved into Grandfather Connor's house. Grandmother MacLeod went to live with Aunt Morag in Winnipeg. It was harder for her than for anyone, because so much of her life was bound up with the MacLeod house. She was fond of Aunt Morag, but that hardly counted. Her men were gone, her husband and her sons, and a family whose men are gone is no family at all. The day she left, my mother and I did not know what to say. Grandmother MacLeod looked even smaller than usual in her fur coat and her black velvet toque. She became extremely agitated about trivialities, and fussed about the possibility of the taxi not arriving on time. She had forbidden us to accompany her to the station. About my father, or the house, or anything important, she did not say a word. Then, when the taxi had finally arrived, she turned to my mother.

"Roddie will have Ewen's seal ring, of course, with the MacLeod crest on it," she said. "But there is another seal as well, don't forget, the larger one with the crest and motto. It's meant to be worn on a watch chain. I keep it in my jewel-box. It was Roderick's. Roddie's to have that, too, when I die. Don't let Morag talk you out of it."

During the Second World War, when I was seventeen and in love with an airman who did not love me, and desperately anxious to get away from Manawaka and from my grandfather's house, I happened one day to be going through the old mahogany desk that had belonged to my father. It had a number of small drawers inside, and I accidentally pulled one of these all the way out. Behind it there was another drawer, one I had not known about. Curiously, I opened it. Inside there was a letter written on almost transparent paper in a cramped angular handwriting. It began—*Cher Monsieur Ewen*—That was all I could make out, for the writing was nearly impossible to read and my French was not good. It was dated 1919. With it, there was a picture of a girl, looking absurdly old-fashioned to my eyes, like the faces on long-discarded calendars or chocolate boxes. But beneath the dated quality of the photograph, she seemed neither expensive nor cheap. She looked like what she probably had been—an ordinary middle-class girl, but in another country. She wore her hair in long ringlets, and her mouth was shaped into a sweetly sad posed smile like Mary Pickford's. That was all. There was nothing else in the drawer.

I looked for a long time at the girl, and hoped she had meant some momentary and unexpected freedom. I remembered what he had said to me, after I hadn't gone to the Remembrance Day parade.

"What are you doing, Vanessa?" my mother called from the kitchen.

"Nothing," I replied.

I took the letter and picture outside and burned them. That was all I could do for him. Now that we might have talked together, it was many years too late. Perhaps it would not have been possible anyway. I did not know.

As I watched the smile of the girl turn into scorched paper, I grieved for my father as though he had just died now.

(1970)

Hugh Hood

(b. 1 9 2 8)

Born in Toronto, Hood was the son of an anglophone banker father and a francophone mother. He attended Roman Catholic schools, then entered St. Michael's College at the University of Toronto. He earned a Ph.D. in 1955 with a dissertation called "Theories of Imagination in English Thinkers, 1650–1790." He taught for some years at St. Joseph's College in Hartford, Connecticut, then accepted a position in the English department of the Université de Montréal, where he still works. Hood's first story appeared in the *Tamarack Review* in 1958; his first volume of stories was published in 1962. In 1969 he helped to form a performance group called the Montreal Story Tellers. (The group also included Clark Blaise and John Metcalf.) Since 1975 Hood has been working on an ambitious 12-novel sequence entitled *The New Age/Le nouveau siècle,* of which five novels have appeared.

Most readers know Hood as a short-story writer, and he launched his career with a volume of short fiction. (Since then many writers have followed his example, including Alice Munro, Clark Blaise, Mavis Gallant, and W. D. Valgardson.) Hood is unusual among modern Canadian writers in two ways. First, he is devoted to a documentary approach to the ideas, objects, and clichés of the historical periods he describes. In the *New Age* novels in particular, he includes factual, historical essays but does not integrate these discourses into the fictional texture of the story. Second, Hood is a consciously Catholic writer; he sees large symbolic patterns buried within apparently simple events. It is this consciousness, apparently, that has spurred Hood's ambitious desire to encapsulate the narrative of an entire era in the *New Age* cycle.

Hood has published six collections of stories, including *Flying a Red Kite* (1962), *Dark Glasses* (1976), and *None Genuine Without This Signature* (1980). His first novel, *White Figure, White Ground* (1964), was followed by *The Camera Always Lies* (1967), *A Game of Touch* (1970), *You Cant Get There from Here* (1972), and the *New Age* novels: *The Swing in the Garden* (1975), *A New Athens* (1977), *Reservoir Ravine* (1979), *Black and White Keys* (1982), and *The Scenic Art* (1984). A collection of Hood's essays, *Trusting the Tale,* was published in 1982. In 1984 Hood and Peter O'Brien co-edited a collection of new fiction from Montreal, *Fatal Recurrences*.

HUGH HOOD

New Country

THEY'D been staying in a borrowed apartment at the corner of Lawrence so the simplest thing to do was go straight up through Hogg's Hollow and get onto 401 going east from Yonge. Early Saturday afternoon, bright and cold in mid-March, with a rush of wind along the flanks of the car making it judder and fishtail at highway speeds, a light car, bouncy and jumpy and peppy. Lester didn't like to spend money on big cars, always drove a Nova or a Fairmont, changing them every October. He could always rely on his car.

He swung the six-months-old Nova across the service lanes, working his blinker lights and reading the rear-view mirrors expertly, and entered the eastbound through traffic at sixty-five. Molly never spoke while he was executing this manoeuvre. She liked to watch his face as his eyes flicked from the road to the mirror overhead, then to the left window, then across her to the right. He had had extra-large mirrors installed on every car they'd ever owned; you could see almost all the way around behind you if they were properly adjusted. Delivery of a new car each October meant an afternoon spent adjusting the mirrors for maximum visibility to the rear.

She waited for him to say something. When they first used to make this trip he would start to chat, on the way back to Stoverville, somewhere around Morningside Drive where the freeway drew away from the suburbs. These days he took longer to thaw. 401 spanned six full lanes of brisk traffic as far as Oshawa, and was being widened there, strewn with construction signs and warnings, and suddenly disappearing shoulders, arbitrary ramp-closings sprouting where wholly unlooked-for. Lester liked to hold his peace until the traffic thinned perceptibly, often saying little or nothing as far as Ajax or Whitby, then initiating a conversation only to lapse into glum silence as he negotiated the cramped outmoded underpasses of Oshawa.

"Ritson Road," he said suddenly, sighing. They were already almost forty miles along their way home. "Well, and how was she?"

"Brenda?"

"Just a minute till I get around this idiot."

She sat and waited; the seat-back punched powerfully at her shoulders; the blinker arrow came on; the car swayed.

"Brenda."

"Bad. She was bad, Lester. I think it was what we thought. She doesn't know. She didn't say anything about that; all she wanted to do was talk about her fibroids. I wanted to laugh, God forgive me. You know, Lester, I used to have this funny image of fibroids, like little pieces of candy. Like chocolates. I don't know why that was. Women talk about these things all the time and I don't suppose any of us has ever seen one. So you kind of make a picture in your mind of what they look like, and for years I've always imagined fibroids sitting in a row like fancy chocolates in a tray in an expensive candy store. In little crinkled brown paper pants. I think I've been seeing them as a lot of little Laura Secords. And I don't even know what a fibroid is."

"It must be made of fibre, judging by the word."

"I guess it is, but that doesn't tell me a thing. I believe they're little tumours of some kind. 'My fibroids were benign,' she kept saying, and she'd give me this awful grin. I think she suspects. I think it's what we thought. Way inside. I wish you could have seen her. I'd have liked to know what you thought. She had a poor colour, very very pale, very dry skin. And she used to have that lovely skin without a mark or a wrinkle on it. I wanted to cry, but I didn't dare show what I was thinking. All her clothes are two sizes too big for her and the worst thing is she suspects. I mean she sounded so beat-up and awful. She said her gynecologist was just awful to her, wouldn't call her by her first name on account of the feminists; it was Mrs. this, and Mrs. that. Never a friendly word, and the usual comic insults. 'We'll just take a little tuck in it to tighten you up,' he said, poking in her vaginal canal. It was so offensive. She said she felt she was the size of a motorman's glove inside, too big for fun. 'I'm all saggy in there,' she kept saying. 'I'm so ashamed, I'm so lapsed and saggy that Irving can't get any purchase. No wonder he never wants to do it anymore. It isn't that he's too small. I never felt he was too small. I've got a hole in me the size of a circus tent.' Then she started to cry buckets. 'Oh Molly,' she said, 'never let them do it to you. I don't know how I let that man talk me into it. I think he just does them for the money. The government pays, so why not? It's like tonsils; they used to do tonsils routinely but they don't anymore. Now it's hysterectomies. They see a woman fifty years old, and they want to gut her just because it's the in-thing to do. Don't let them try it on you, Molly. The cure is worse than the disease.' And she laughed. I don't know what disease she was thinking of, maybe pregnancy."

"At least they did have kids."

"They never see the kids now. Neither of the boys visited her in the hospital, and when Arlene came they had a shattering argument, according to Brenda. She said Arlene said she was faking it, can you imagine? I mean the day before, practically, they'd removed the poor woman's womb surgically, and her daughter accuses her of malingering. Maybe she expected to see it in a bottle on the bedside table, for proof. They've never got along, and the boys are off somewhere, and nobody knows where. Irving is worse than useless about it. He can't control them."

"I think Irving has his own problems."

"Yes, and poor Brenda has them to think about while she's lying there.

'They do this routinely,' she kept saying. 'They recommend it for everybody. It wasn't as if there was anything seriously wrong. Wait till I get up and around. I'm too thin. Everybody tells me I'm too thin.' Like that. Now tell me, was she just kidding me? Or herself?"

"I'd say she probably doesn't know for sure."

"Well nobody does."

Lester kept his eyes fixed on the big camper in front of him, a home-on-wheels with a high centre of gravity and a tendency to sway in a crosswind. He eased into the passing lane.

"Lester, did Irving say something to you?"

"Just a second."

He flipped the right blinker on.

"She's my sister. I've got a right to know if anybody does."

"Molly, when they got inside she was like fishnet. All they could do was sew her up and forget about it. I talked to Irving on Thursday night while you were at the hospital."

"My God! Where?"

"Oh everywhere. Liver, womb, ovaries."

"She's younger than I am."

"Yeah, what is it, about two years?"

"I don't think she's fifty yet, honey. I was born in May and she was born in early June. The fifth. The fifth of June. She'll be fifty next June the fifth."

Lester said nothing and Molly quavered, "The poor thing." They covered a short distance in heavy silence. Then the car mounted an elegant rising curve, five miles east of Oshawa along the shoulder of a knoll which over-looks the lake. At this point the shoreline curves in under the hillside, and motorists have a view of the water across a bay or inlet—technically perhaps a bight—which always seems calm. It is the last place on the highway to present a prospect of the water before Kingston, a hundred miles further down. Lester used to enjoy the sight of the lake; today he ignored it.

The car sped inland towards Bowmanville and the Flying Dutchman Motel.

"Sam didn't look any too good either," said Lester. "I don't think he's a well man. His hemorrhoids are a curse, he says, and you know, you can tell from the way he walks. He has this air cushion in the office. I used to think it was funny, but it isn't funny really. All he wants to talk about is his proctologist. I was forty-five before I knew what a proctologist did. Now it's all I hear about. He can't concentrate on the line. How can you talk to buyers when all the time you're afraid to sit down? It's undignified; it's painful; it's on your mind and you wonder if they'll have to cut you. He told me this horror story about some friend who had the operation for hemorrhoids, and was he ever sick? When he woke up he couldn't go to the toilet. Either way. After a couple of days they had to introduce a catheter; otherwise he'd have got kidney-poisoning or uremia or whatever. I'm no doctor. They shove this long tube up through your thing, you know, and it drains off the piss. It hurts like hell. Just from the shock of the operation, it's no picnic. I don't know

about Sammy. He hasn't been the same since Phil went. It was Phil who
created Style-Made Sportswear. Sam was always really more of the accountant than anything. He doesn't know how to talk to buyers, or dress a display
suite; he doesn't have the feel for it. He's anxious all the time and the
customers can sense it; they know they've got him over a barrel. He has to
do business so he can discount the orders and keep his cash flow in line. If
the paper isn't available the bank gets upset. Sam is an accountant; he can
judge to a second when the credit man from the bank is going to be on the
line. He's always had this line with the Commerce, oh, years and years. Now
they say that the industry is going to be phased out. They don't trust what
the government says about imports, and nobody knows what the hell is
happening. Getting goods into the stores is like a sport; you have to relax
and swing easy and not frighten them off by pushing. It's hard to go on
shipping to somebody who's in that frame of mind."

"Lester, he's your own brother."

"He's not the same. He hasn't been the same for two years, not since Phil
died. Imagine the shock! They were sitting in the office in the factory around
ten-thirty in the morning . . ."

"I don't want to hear this again."

". . . and Sammy hears the canteen wagon roll up. He says to Phil, 'What'll
I get you?' They used to take turns buying, I mean for thirty years. 'Get me
a coffee, no cream, and a roll of plain Tums,' says Phil. 'OK.' Sam goes out,
gets the stuff, a doughnut for him and the Tums for Phil, and he goes back
into the office and there he is, lying back in the chair with this look on his
face. Gone. Like somebody switched out the light, and Sam says he didn't
look peaceful. He looked like somebody hit him one hell of a smack on the
side of the head. Sammy's standing there with this roll of plain Tums and
the coffee getting cold in his hand. It stays in your mind."

Molly said, "It doesn't have to stay in your mind. It's not your affair."

"It's as much my affair as Brenda is your affair. He's my brother."

"You've never been as close as we were."

"He's a big account. Half our production goes to Style-Made. Almost half.
Thirty percent anyway. I should have seen it coming. I blame myself."

"What could you have done about it?"

"It was losing that cutter did it. Some people might think I just wanted
to unload every possible yard of goods on Style-Made, but it was never like
that. You can't be greedy. You've got to supply quality in a good selection
of widths; you've got to stay abreast of design trends. I admit it, I hate
polyester. It makes me feel cold all the time. But it has definite uses if you're
trying to produce sportswear at a price, so we have to be in a position to
supply cotton and poly at any time in nice colours and patterns, no matter
how I feel about it. I've given the trade maximum convenience and I've had
plenty of customers. Maybe I made a mistake by selling so much to Phil and
Sammy but they were always right there asking for our product. You don't
say to your brother, 'I can only let you have so much this season. I've got
you on a quota.' The effect of it is, I'm very tightly linked in with Style-Made,

in a tough marketing situation, and they've always got maximum yield from our fabrics. That old man was a wonder."

"Highlands of Hastings," said Molly.

"What?"

"You missed the sign. 'You are now entering the Highlands of Hastings regional vacation area.' "

"Already? We're making good time. We'll be home for dinner."

Molly shrugged her shoulders up and down vigorously, and wound her head on her neck. "It's around three," she said, "it won't be dark for hours and hours; the days are getting longer."

"Old Everett Stapleton. He was a wonder. He could cut more pieces from a length of goods than you'd believe. You never used to see their factory knee-deep in remnants. He could look at a length and see, right in the flat cloth, how many garments could be made up out of it, including sleeves and gussets, like some kind of a sculptor. The designers used to take instructions from him. If the design couldn't be cut economically from the goods, he'd show them how to re-work it. He'd re-do the sketches, right in the cutting room. Phil used to talk about him with tears in his eyes. Then he died, and they've never been able to replace him. After that, their ordering was less precise; they bought more, and I'll bet they produced fewer dozen garments from what they bought. A cutter like that . . . almost an artist, you'd have to say. I think it was losing him that brought on Phil's coronary. It isn't as though Phil was an old man. He was younger than Sam. I think Phil and I were about the same age. He always used to take good care of himself, then to go just like that."

Across the highway above the westbound lanes, a high ridge loomed up in a long gentle arc along the roadside, cutting off the view of the sky. They could see a long way ahead, perhaps two miles. Then the eastbound lanes banked down into a valley and were lost from view. The movement of the car and the presence of the high ridge beside them gave the impression that the car was floating idly and slowly towards a whirlpool.

"Highlands of Hastings," said Lester suddenly. "I wonder what the Highlands of Hastings are exactly? I wonder what they look like." He gave a sharp yank at the wheel. The car veered into the passing lane, then back to the right. Molly stared at him doubtfully.

"I've been going up and down the 401 for twenty years," he said discontentedly, "Stoverville to Toronto, Toronto to Stoverville. I've gotten to know this run too damn' well. Glen Miller Road, Wooler, Salmon River. I might as well be on tracks. I never see what's off to the side. I've never had a look at the Highlands of Hastings."

He stared fixedly at the high ground swelling up on the other side of the road.

Molly said, "Keep your eyes on the highway, Lester."

"I wonder what's happening in the Highlands of Hastings tonight. Is there really anybody there? Sometimes I get the impression that big ridge up there is nothing but a canvas drop. Here! Let's go and have a look at what's behind it." They passed a sign which said, *Hwy 30 North-South Brighton Next Exit Only 2 km.*

"Kilometres, kilometres, why couldn't they have left it miles? Messing around with everything. Can't keep their hands off anything." He put on the right blinker and turned onto the exit ramp. The car slowed abruptly, running down to the stop sign at the sideroad, deep in a cupped hollow to one side of 401. They sat at the stop sign, the car idling quietly in neutral, looking around them at the wholly foreign scene.

"Left," said Lester, "we'll go left; we'll have a look at the back country."

"It's past four o'clock."

"You said yourself, it won't be dark till late. It's almost spring—according to the calendar—and the fields seem clear. Come on, we've seen 401 too many times. We'll go up to Highway 7, and go home the back way. It'll be something to do for a change. It doesn't really matter if we get in tonight." He paused, then said as if amazed at the notion, "We could get a motel room; we could go the rest of the way tomorrow. After all, why not?"

A car drew up behind them and honked softly. Lester gave a slight start, then put the car in motion, turning left. The ground began to rise at once; they were climbing up a steep hill as they came out of the underpass on the other side of 401. The highway narrowed abruptly as they came up the hillside, and a tight curve around a spur of high ground concealed the freeway from sight behind them. The motor whined, and Lester shifted into second. He said, "I haven't done that in years." The car continued to climb for some moments.

"We're going up through that ridge," said Molly suddenly. "It isn't a piece of scenery, it's quite real." The road wound slowly upwards to the right for another mile and a half; they might have climbed three hundred and fifty feet. Then it emerged into a terrain which was utterly novel to them, perfectly unlike the open countryside around Toronto or the limestone ridges, the granite shelves and narrow beds of good soil north of Stoverville. This was a central Ontario landscape seen by fewer and fewer people. They felt transported back to the nineteen-thirties. Highway 30 had the grassy ditches and narrow shoulders and Queen's Highway markers, the cracked surfaces and sudden, poorly-marked curves and intersections of the thirties. Molly felt the pace and rhythm of the car slow and adapt itself to the altered driving conditions. She felt no apprehension. Lester was, if anything, a better driver at these speeds than at seventy. She began to enjoy the deliberate motion, staring out into the deserted fields—what she could see of them—with curiosity, and real surprise at their unfamiliar aspect. Shown them in a photograph, perhaps on a postcard, she would not have been able to identify them as any part of the province she knew. She had a vague impression that they resembled some part of France. Even the earth tones in the fields, where small snowbanks lingered in hedges and along the depressions of drainage ditches, seemed darker and more distant, oddly withdrawn. There was a slight peculiarity to the lie of the country which at first perplexed her.

An elderly International pickup, with a homemade stake body rattling loudly, came at them all at once around a curve, passing very near. Its front wheels had a pronounced shimmy. Lester took a quick look over his shoulder, disturbed by the narrow margin for passing. He dropped to forty. "Close enough," he said in a low voice, "maybe even too close. I wonder where we are exactly. Could you dig out the map? There's an Ontario road map in there somewhere."

She opened the glove compartment with an increasingly intense sense of *déjà vu*. When they had been an engaged couple, and for some short time after their marriage, Lester and Molly had made the usual weekend trips around their countryside along the back roads, on picnics and an occasional hayride. She always used to read the map for him, she remembered. She always had the customary comic trouble about re-folding the free road maps from the gas stations. They were no longer free, she reflected. Most stations couldn't be bothered to stock them, and those which did charged a dollar for a map.

"We're going north on Highway 30," she announced a moment later. "In a minute we'll be—no, here it is—we're going through Orland."

They passed a corner where a green arrow pointed eastwards. It said "Wooler."

"My gosh," said Lester, "so that's where Wooler is. I've never actually believed in the existence of Wooler. I wonder if there are five proofs for the existence of Wooler?"

"I'm enjoying this," said Molly. All the same she felt certain distinct qualms. She was not entirely happy with the prospect of the high, short fields. They were curiously broken and folded and they fell away out of view disturbingly, to reveal sudden deeps and shadows. It was still bright afternoon on the upper ground where the highway ran along between the small farms, but to either side the fields slanted away and down into obscurity. Here and there the entire rectangular outline of a field could be seen, a quarter-mile away from the road, lying athwart the pitch of neighbouring small hills, like a wet handkerchief draped on a radiator to dry. These fields had a convoluted up-and-down shape. Nearer the highway the enclosures seemed—and doubtless were—smaller, humped up beside the road. The fields were in work already, most of them, freshly-turned furrows awaiting the seed, perhaps already seeded and concealing new growth from her inexpert eye. There were no people visible in the fields, not so much as a tractor. It's late Saturday afternoon, she thought, and they've all gone into . . . into . . . she consulted the map. Where would they go on Saturday night? Codrington?

They went through Codrington as this question crossed her mind, and it was at once evident that Codrington was not where the crowds went on Saturday night; there was nobody in town. One or two farmhouse lights began to contest the late sunshine. Soon it would be time for dinner. She thought of Brenda and Sammy and Phil, briefly considered the prospect of reviving that conversation, rejected it, and waited for Lester to say something. He was concentrating on the road.

"My God, what country," he muttered. The car bounced and swerved. "We ought to be out of the high country pretty soon. Isn't Campbellford somewhere around here? I seem to remember . . ."

"Just a minute, just a minute." She rearranged the unhandy map. "There isn't room for this thing."

"It ought to be somewhere up ahead. We ought to look for a place to spend the night. I'll tell you, I wouldn't want to come up this way in the dark. I'm having to fight to hold the car steady."

"We go through a place called, just a minute till I get my glasses on, called Meyersberg, that's it. It can't be very big, so you'd better keep an eye open. After that we ought to be down out of these hills—which make me feel uncomfortable. Highlands of Hastings indeed! We ought to hit the Trent system somewhere up around Meyersberg, and after that it can't be more than a few miles to Campbellford. What makes you think of Campbellford particularly?"

"I just happen to remember it's around here. I saw a picture in some book. And there's your precious Meyersberg, look at that! It's a ghost town. I noticed in the paper the other day, last Saturday, an advertisement for a book called *Ghost Towns of Ontario.* It kind of made me think."

Molly folded the map carefully and put it away. She felt the car begin to descend. All at once, off to the right, a long stretch of water came in sight, broadening out as they approached, with huge shadows lying across it. As they came down the side of the hill—in second gear—they lost the sunlight, and the water looked flat and black and very cold.

"It isn't moving at all," Molly whispered.

"Is that a lake or the river?"

"I don't know what it is," she said, "and I'm not going to struggle with that damn' map again. There's no current in that water. Look! Not a ripple."

"We'll be into town in a few minutes," said Lester. "I can see lights ahead. Oh, somebody else I forgot to mention dropped dead in Toronto while we were there. Do you remember Lionel Breitbart?"

"No," she said, "I don't and I don't want to talk about it. What's the matter with you, Lester? Where did the middle of our lives go? When we used to take this trip what we talked about was who was getting engaged. Who was getting married . . . having a baby . . ."

"We'll find a place," he said through his teeth. He speeded up, heading into a blind curve.

(1980)

Stanley Elkin

(b. 1 9 3 0)

Stanley Elkin, born in New York City in 1930, was the son of a salesman. He attended the University of Illinois, where he received his B.A. in 1953 and his Ph.D. in 1961. In the early 1950s his short fiction began to appear in magazines; his first book was published in 1964. Elkin left the army in 1959 and joined the faculty of Washington University in St. Louis; he became a professor of English in 1969. He was a visiting lecturer at Smith College, the University of California, the University of Wisconsin, and Yale. He has received several awards and grants, including the *Paris Review* prize for humor in 1965 and a Guggenheim Fellowship in 1966.

Elkin is best known for his black humor and his satiric view of contemporary values and mores. His stories and novels are imaginative: His scenes continually take unexpected, often bizarre turns, and his characters, in their exuberant unconventionality, serve as perfect foils to the norms of staid society. Elkin's prose is an original headlong staccato filled with sudden, striking descriptions and startling but strangely apt images. Some critics have objected to the dominance of surface style in Elkin's work, but, in general, he is seen as a bleak absurdist. His works are leavened with wit and energy. A phrase from *The Dick Gibson Show,* a novel that was described as a radically new version of the "Great Gatsby" theme, sums up Elkin's persistent skewering of the myths people try to hold on to: "All there is . . . are the strange displacements of the ordinary."

Elkin's novels include *Boswell* (1964), *The Dick Gibson Show* (1971), *The Franchiser* (1976), *The Living End* (1979), and *George Mills* (1982). His volumes of short fiction are *Criers and Kibitzers, Kibitzers and Criers* (1965) and *The Making of Ashenden* (1972). *Searches and Seizures* (1973) is a collection of three novellas.

STANLEY ELKIN

A Poetics for Bullies

I'M Push the bully, and what I hate are new kids and sissies, dumb kids and smart, rich kids, poor kids, kids who wear glasses, talk funny, show off, patrol boys and wise guys and kids who pass pencils and water the plants—and cripples, *especially* cripples. I love nobody loved.

One time I was pushing this red-haired kid (I'm a pusher, no hitter, no belter; an aggressor of marginal violence, I hate *real* force) and his mother stuck her head out the window and shouted something I've never forgotten. *"Push,"* she yelled. *"You, Push.* You pick on him because you wish you had his red hair!" It's true; I *did* wish I had his red hair. I wish I were tall, or fat, or thin. I wish I had different eyes, different hands, a mother in the supermarket. I wish I were a man, a small boy, a girl in the choir. I'm a coveter, a Boston Blackie of the heart, casing the world. Endlessly I covet and case. (Do you know what makes me cry? The Declaration of Independence. "All men are created equal." That's beautiful.)

If you're a bully like me, you use your head. Toughness isn't enough. You beat them up, they report you. Then where are you? I'm not even particularly strong. (I used to be strong. I used to do exercise, work out, but strength implicates you, and often isn't an advantage anyway—read the judo ads. Besides, your big bullies aren't bullies at all—they're *athletes*. With them, beating guys up is a sport.) But what I lose in size and strength I make up in courage. I'm very brave. That's a lie about bullies being cowards underneath. If you're a coward, get out of the business.

I'm best at torment.

A kid has a toy bow, toy arrows. "Let Push look," I tell him.

He's suspicious, he knows me. "Go way, Push," he says, this mama-warned Push doubter.

"Come on," I say, "come on."

"No, Push. I can't. My mother said I can't."

I raise my arms, I spread them. I'm a bird—slow, powerful, easy, free. I move my head offering profile like something beaked. I'm the Thunderbird. "In the school where I go I have a teacher who teaches me magic," I say. "Arnold Salamancy, give Push your arrows. Give him one, he gives back two. Push is the God of the Neighborhood."

"Go way, Push," the kid says, uncertain.

"Right," Push says, himself again. "Right. I'll disappear. First the fingers." My fingers ball to fists. "My forearms next." They jackknife into

933

my upper arms. "The arms." Quick as bird-blink they snap behind my back, fit between the shoulder blades like a small knapsack. (I am double-jointed, protean.) "My head," I say.

"No, Push," the kid says, terrified. I shudder and everything comes back, falls into place from the stem of self like a shaken puppet.

"The arrow, the arrow. Two where was one." He hands me an arrow. *"Trouble, trouble, double rubble!"* I snap it and give back the pieces.

Well, sure. There *is* no magic. If there were I would learn it. I would find out the words, the slow turns and strange passes, drain the bloods and get the herbs, do the fires like a vestal. I would look for the main chants. *Then* I'd change things. *Push* would!

But there's only casuistical trick. Sleight-of-mouth, the bully's poetics. You know the formulas:

"Did you ever see a match burn twice?" you ask. Strike. Extinguish. Jab his flesh with the hot stub.

"Play 'Gestapo'?"

"How do you play?"

"What's your name?"

"It's Morton."

I slap him. "You're lying."

"Adam and Eve and Pinch Me Hard went down to the lake for a swim. Adam and Eve fell in. Who was left?"

"Pinch Me Hard."

I do.

Physical puns, conundrums. Push the punisher, the conundrummer!

But there has to be more than tricks in a bag of tricks.

I don't know what it is. Sometimes I think *I'm* the only new kid. In a room, the school, the playground, the neighborhood, I get the feeling I've just moved in, no one knows me. You know what I like? To stand in crowds. To wait with them at the airport to meet a plane. Someone asks what time it is. I'm the first to answer. Or at the ball park when the vendor comes. He passes the hot dog down the long row. I want *my* hands on it, too. On the dollar going up, the change coming down.

I am ingenious, I am patient.

A kid is going downtown on the elevated train. He's got his little suit on, his shoes are shined, he wears a cap. This is a kid going to the travel bureaus, the foreign tourist offices to get brochures, maps, pictures of the mountains for a unit at his school—a kid looking for extra credit. I follow him. He comes out of the Italian Tourist Information Center. His arms are full. I move from my place at the window. I follow for two blocks and bump into him as he steps from a curb. It's a *collision*—The pamphlets fall from his arms. Pretending confusion, I walk on his paper Florence. I grind my heel in his Riviera. I climb Vesuvius and sack his Rome and dance on the Isle of Capri.

The Industrial Museum is a good place to find children. I cut somebody's five- or six-year-old kid brother out of the herd of eleven- and twelve year olds he's come with. *"Quick,"* I say. I pull him along the corridors, up the stairs, through the halls, down to a mezzanine landing. Breathless, I pause for a minute. "I've got some gum. Do you want a stick?" He nods; I stick him. I rush him into an auditorium and abandon him. He'll be lost for hours.

I sidle up to a kid at the movies. "You smacked my brother," I tell him. "After the show—I'll be outside."

I break up games. I hold the ball above my head. "You want it? Take it."

I go into barber shops. There's a kid waiting. "I'm next," I tell him, "understand?"

One day Eugene Kraft rang my bell. Eugene is afraid of me, so he helps me. He's fifteen and there's something wrong with his saliva glands and he drools. His chin is always chapped. I tell him he has to drink a lot because he loses so much water.

"Push? Push," he says. He's wiping his chin with his tissues. "Push, there's this kid—"

"Better get a glass of water, Eugene."

"No, Push, no fooling, there's this new kid—he just moved in. You've got to see this kid."

"Eugene, get some water, please. You're drying up. I've never seen you so bad. There are deserts in you, Eugene."

"All right, Push, but then you've got to see—"

"Swallow, Eugene. You better swallow."

He gulps hard.

"Push, this is a kid and a half. Wait, you'll see."

"I'm very concerned about you, Eugene. You're dying of thirst, Eugene. Come into the kitchen with me."

I push him through the door. He's very excited. I've never seen him so excited. He talks at me over his shoulder, his mouth flooding, his teeth like the little stone pebbles at the bottom of a fishbowl. "He's got this sport coat, with a patch over the heart. Like a king, Push. No kidding."

"Be careful of the carpet, Eugene."

I turn on the taps in the sink. I mix in hot water. "Use your tissues, Eugene. Wipe your chin."

He wipes himself and puts the Kleenex in his pocket. All of Eugene's pockets bulge. He looks, with his bulging pockets, like a clumsy smuggler.

"Wipe, Eugene. Swallow, you're drowning."

"He's got this funny accent—you could die." Excited, he tamps at his mouth like a diner, a tubercular.

"Drink some water, Eugene."

"No, Push. I'm not thirsty—really."

"Don't be foolish, kid. That's because your mouth's so wet. Inside where it counts you're drying up. It stands to reason. Drink some water."

"He has this crazy haircut."

"Drink," I command. I shake him. *"Drink!"*

"Push, I've got no glass. Give me a glass at least."

"I can't do that, Eugene. You've got a terrible sickness. How could I let you use our drinking glasses? Lean under the tap and open your mouth."

He knows he'll have to do it, that I won't listen to him until he does. He bends into the sink.

"Push, it's *hot,*" he complains. The water splashes into his nose, it gets on his glasses and for a moment his eyes are magnified, enormous. He pulls away and scrapes his forehead on the faucet.

"Eugene, you touched it. Watch out, please. You're too close to the tap. Lean your head deeper into the sink."

"It's *hot,* Push."

"Warm water evaporates better. With your affliction you've got to evaporate fluids before they get into your glands."

He feeds again from the tap.

"Do you think that's enough?" I ask after a while.

"I do, Push, I really do," he says. He is breathless.

"Eugene," I say seriously, "I think you'd better get yourself a canteen."

"A canteen, Push?"

"That's right. Then you'll always have water when you need it. Get one of those Boy Scout models. The two-quart kind with a canvas strap."

"But you hate the Boy Scouts, Push."

"They make very good canteens, Eugene. *And wear it!* I never want to see you without it. Buy it today."

"All right, Push."

"Promise!"

"All right, Push."

"Say it out."

He made the formal promise that I like to hear.

"Well, then," I said, "let's go see this new kid of yours."

He took me to the schoolyard. "Wait," he said, "you'll see." He skipped ahead.

"Eugene," I said, calling him back. "Let's understand something. No matter what this new kid is like, nothing changes as far as you and I are concerned."

"Aw, Push," he said.

"Nothing, Eugene. I mean it. You don't get out from under me."

"Sure, Push, I know that."

There were some kids in the far corner of the yard, sitting on the ground, leaning up against the wire fence. Bats and gloves and balls lay scattered around them. (It was where they told dirty jokes. Sometimes I'd come by during the little kids' recess and tell them all about what their daddies do to their mommies.)

"There. See? Do you see him?" Eugene, despite himself, seemed hoarse.

"Be quiet," I said, checking him, freezing as a hunter might. I stared.

He was a *prince,* I tell you.

He was tall, tall, even sitting down. His long legs comfortable in expensive wool, the trousers of a boy who had been on ships, jets; who owned a horse, perhaps; who knew Latin—what *didn't* he know?—somebody made up, like a kid in a play with a beautiful mother and a handsome father; who took his breakfast from a sideboard, and picked, even at fourteen and fifteen and sixteen, his mail from a silver plate. He would have hobbies—stamps, stars, things lovely dead. He wore a sport coat, brown as wood, thick as heavy bark. The buttons were leather buds. His shoes seemed carved from horses' saddles, gunstocks. His clothes had once grown in nature. *What it must feel like inside those clothes,* I thought.

I looked at his face, his clear skin, and guessed at the bones, white as beached wood. His eyes had skies in them. His yellow hair swirled on his head like a crayoned sun.

"Look, look at him," Eugene said. "The sissy. Get him, Push."

He was talking to them and I moved closer to hear his voice. It was clear, beautiful, but faintly foreign—like herb-seasoned meat.

When he saw me he paused, smiling. He waved. The others didn't look at me.

"Hello there," he called. "Come over if you'd like. I've been telling the boys about tigers."

"Tigers," I said.

"Give him the 'match burn twice,' Push," Eugene whispered.

"Tigers, is it?" I said. "What do you know about tigers?" My voice was high.

"The 'match burn twice,' Push."

"Not so much as a Master *Tugjah.* I was telling the boys. In India there are men of high caste—*Tugjahs,* they're called. I was apprenticed to one once in the Southern Plains and might perhaps have earned my mastership, but the Red Chinese attacked the northern frontier and . . . well, let's just say I had to leave. At any rate, these *Tugjahs* are as intimate with the tiger as you are with dogs. I don't mean they keep them as pets. The relationship goes deeper. Your dog is a service animal, as is your elephant."

"Did you ever see a match burn twice?" I asked suddenly.

"Why no, can you do that? Is it a special match you use?"

"No," Eugene said, "it's an ordinary match. He uses an ordinary match."

"Can you do it with one of mine, do you think?"

He took a matchbook from his pocket and handed it to me. The cover was exactly the material of his jacket, and in the center was a patch with a coat-of-arms identical to the one he wore over his heart.

I held the matchbook for a moment and then gave it back to him. "I don't feel like it," I said.

"Then some other time, perhaps," he said.

Eugene whispered to me. "His accent, Push, his funny *accent.*"

"Some other time, perhaps," I said. I am a good mimic. I can duplicate a particular kid's lisp, his stutter, a thickness in his throat. There were two or three here whom I had brought close to tears by holding up my mirror to their voices. I can parody their limps, their waddles, their girlish runs, their clumsy jumps. I can throw as they throw, catch as they catch. I looked around. "Some other time, perhaps," I said again. No one would look at me.

"I'm *so* sorry," the new one said, "we don't know each other's names. You are?"

"I'm so sorry," I said. "You are?"

He seemed puzzled. Then he looked sad, disappointed. No one said anything.

"It don't sound the same," Eugene whispered.

It was true. I sounded nothing like him. I could imitate only defects, only flaws.

A kid giggled.

"Shh," the prince said. He put one finger to his lips.

"Look at that," Eugene said under his breath. "He's a sissy."

He had begun to talk to them again. I squatted, a few feet away. I ran gravel through my loose fists, one bowl in an hour-glass feeding another.

He spoke of jungles, of deserts. He told of ancient trade routes traveled by strange beasts. He described lost cities and a lake deeper than the deepest level of the sea. There was a story about a boy who had been captured by bandits. A woman in the story—it wasn't clear whether she was the boy's mother—had been tortured. His eyes clouded for a moment when he came to this part and he had to pause before continuing. Then he told how the boy escaped—it was cleverly done—and found help, mountain tribesmen riding elephants. The elephants charged the cave in which the mo—the *woman*—was still a prisoner. It might have collapsed and killed her, but one old bull rushed in and, shielding her with his body, took the weight of the crashing rocks. Your elephant is a service animal.

I let a piece of gravel rest on my thumb and flicked it in a high arc above his head. Some of the others who had seen me stared, but the boy kept on talking. Gradually I reduced the range, allowing the chunks of gravel to come closer to his head.

"You see?" Eugene said quietly. "He's afraid. He pretends not to notice."

The arcs continued to diminish. The gravel went faster, straighter. No one was listening to him now, but he kept talking.

"—of magic," he said, "what occidentals call 'a witch doctor.' There are spices that induce these effects. The *Bogdovii* was actually able to stimulate the growth of rocks with the powder. The Dutch traders were ready to go to war for the formula. Well, you can see what it could mean for the Low Countries. Without accessible quarries they've never been able to construct a permanent system of dikes. But with the *Bogdovii's* powder"—he reached out and casually caught the speeding chip as if it had been a ping-pong ball—"they could turn a grain of sand into a pebble, use the pebbles to grow stones, the stones to grow rocks. This little piece of gravel, for example, could be changed into a mountain." He dipped his thumb into his palm as I had and balanced the gravel on his nail. He flicked it; it rose from his nail like a missile and climbed an impossible arc. It disappeared. "The *Bogdovii* never revealed how it was done."

I stood up. Eugene tried to follow me.

"Listen," he said, "you'll get him."

"Swallow," I told him. "Swallow, you pig!"

I HAVE lived my life in pursuit of the vulnerable: Push the chink seeker, wheeler dealer in the flawed cement of the personality, a collapse maker. But what isn't vulnerable, *who* isn't? There is that which is unspeakable, so I speak it, that which is unthinkable, which I think. Me and the devil, we do God's dirty work, after all.

I went home after I left him. I turned once at the gate, and the boys were around him still. The useless Eugene had moved closer. *He* made room for him against the fence.

I ran into Frank the fat boy. He made a move to cross the street, but I had seen him and he went through a clumsy retractive motion. I could tell he thought I would get him for that, but I moved by, indifferent to a grossness in which I had once delighted. As I passed he seemed puzzled, a little hurt, a little—this was astonishing—guilty. *Sure* guilty. Why *not* guilty? The forgiven tire of their exemption. Nothing could ever be forgiven, and I forgave nothing. I held them to the mark. Who else cared about the fatties, about the dummies and slobs and clowns, about the gimps and squares and oafs and fools, the kids with a mouthful of mush, all those shut-ins of the mind and heart, all those losers? Frank the fat boy knew, and passed me shyly. His wide, fat body, stiffened, forced jokishly martial when he saw me, had already become flaccid as he moved by, had already made one more forgiven surrender. Who cared?

The streets were full of failure. Let them. Let them be. There was a paragon, a paragon loose. What could he be doing here, why had he come, what did he want? It was impossible that this hero from India and everywhere had made his home here; that he lived, as Frank the fat boy did, as Eugene did, as *I* did, in an apartment; that he shared our lives.

In the afternoon I looked for Eugene. He was in the park, in a tree. There was a book in his lap. He leaned against the thick trunk.

"Eugene," I called up to him.

"Push, they're closed. It's Sunday, Push. The stores are closed. I looked for the canteen. The stores are closed."

"Where is he?"

"Who, Push? What do you want, Push?"

"*Him.* Your pal. The prince. Where? Tell me, Eugene, or I'll shake you out of that tree. I'll burn you down. I swear it. Where is he?"

"No, Push. I was wrong about that guy. He's nice. He's really nice. Push, he told me about a doctor who could help me. Leave him alone, Push."

"Where, Eugene? *Where?* I count to three."

Eugene shrugged and came down the tree.

I found the name Eugene gave me—funny, foreign—over the bell in the outer hall. The buzzer sounded and I pushed open the door. I stood inside and looked up the carpeted stairs, the angled banisters.

"What is it?" She sounded old, worried.

"The new kid," I called, "the new kid."

"It's for you," I heard her say.

"Yes?" His voice, the one I couldn't mimic. I mounted the first stair. I leaned back against the wall and looked up through the high, boxy banister poles. It was like standing inside a pipe organ.

"Yes?"

From where I stood at the bottom of the stairs I could see only a boot. He was wearing boots.

"Yes? What is it, please?"

"*You*," I roared. "Glass of fashion, mold of form, it's me! It's Push the bully!"

I heard his soft, rapid footsteps coming down the stairs—a springy, spongy urgency. He jingled, the bastard. He had coins—I could see them: rough, golden, imperfectly round; raised, massively gowned goddesses, their heads fingered smooth, their arms gone—and keys to strange boxes, thick doors. I saw his boots. I backed away.

"I brought you down," I said.

"Be quiet, please. There's a woman who's ill. A boy who must study. There's a man with bad bones. An old man needs sleep."

"He'll get it," I said.

"We'll go outside," he said.

"No. Do you live here? What do you do? Will you be in our school? Were you telling the truth?"

"Shh. Please. You're very excited."

"Tell me your name," I said. It could be my campaign, I thought. His *name*. Scratched in new sidewalk, chalked onto walls, written on papers dropped in the street. To leave it behind like so many clues, to give him a fame, to take it away, to slash and cross out, to erase and to smear—my kid's witchcraft. "Tell me your name."

"It's John," he said softly.

"What?"

"It's John."

"John what? Come on now. I'm Push the bully."

"John Williams," he said.

"John Williams? John Williams? Only that? Only John Williams?"

He smiled.

"Who's that on the bell? The name on the box?"

"She needs me," he said.

"Cut it out."

"I help her," he said.

"You stop that."

"There's a man that's in pain. A woman who's old. A husband that's worried. A wife that despairs."

"You're the bully," I said. "Your John Williams is a service animal," I yelled in the hall.

He turned and began to climb the stairs. His calves bloomed in their leather sheathing.

"Lover," I whispered to him.

He turned to me at the landing. He shook his head sadly.

"We'll see," I said.

"We'll see what we'll see," he said.

That night I painted his name on the side of the gymnasium in enormous letters. In the morning it was still there, but it wasn't what I meant. There was nothing incantatory in the huge letters, no scream, no curse. I had never traveled with a gang, there had been no togetherness in my tearing, but this thing on the wall seemed the act of vandals, the low production of ruffians. When you looked at it you were surprised they had gotten the spelling right.

Astonishingly, it was allowed to remain. And each day there was something more celebrational in the giant name, something of increased hospitality, lavish welcome. John Williams might have been a football hero, or someone back from the kidnapers. Finally I had to take it off myself.

Something had changed.

Eugene was not wearing his canteen. Boys didn't break off their conversations when I came up to them. One afternoon a girl winked at me. (Push has never picked on girls. *Their* submissiveness is part of their nature. They are ornamental. Don't get me wrong, please. There is a way in which they function as part of the landscape, like flowers at a funeral. They have a strange cheerfulness. They are the organizers of pep rallies and dances. They put out the Year Book. They are *born* Gray Ladies. I can't bully them.)

John Williams was in the school, but except for brief glimpses in the hall I never saw him. Teachers would repeat the things he had said in their other classes. They read from his papers. In the gym the coach described plays he had made, set shots he had taken. Everyone talked about him, and girls made a reference to him a sort of love signal. If it was suggested that he had smiled at one of them, the girl referred to would blush or, what was worse, look aloofly mysterious. (*Then* I could have punished her, *then* I could.) Gradually his name began to appear on all their notebooks, in the margins of their texts. (It annoyed me to remember what *I* had done on the wall.) The big canvas books, with their careful, elaborate J's and W's, took on the appearance of ancient, illuminated fables. It was the unconscious embroidery of love, hope's bright doodle. Even the administration was aware of him. In Assembly the principal announced that John Williams had broken all existing records in the school's charity drives. She had never seen good citizenship like his before, she said.

It's one thing to live with a bully, another to live with a hero.

Everyone's hatred I understand, no one's love; everyone's grievance, no one's content.

I saw Mimmer. Mimmer should have graduated years ago. I saw Mimmer the dummy.

"Mimmer," I said, "you're in his class."

"He's very smart."

"Yes, but is it fair? You work harder. I've seen you study. You spend hours. Nothing comes. He was born knowing. You could have used just a little of what he's got so much of. It's not fair."

"He's very clever. It's wonderful," Mimmer says.

Slud is crippled. He wears a shoe with a built-up heel to balance himself. "Ah, Slud," I say, "I've seen him run."

"He has beaten the horses in the park. It's very beautiful," Slud says.

"He's handsome, isn't he, Club?" Club looks contagious, radioactive. He has severe acne. He is ugly *under* his acne.

"He gets the girls," Clob says.

He gets *everything*, I think. But I'm alone in my envy, awash in my lust. It's as if I were a prophet to the deaf. Schnooks, schnooks, I want to scream, dopes and settlers. What good does his smile do you, of what use is his good heart?

The other day I did something stupid. I went to the cafeteria and shoved a boy out of the way and took his place in the line. It was foolish, but their fear is almost all gone and I felt I had to show the flag. The boy only grinned and let me pass. Then someone called my name. It was *him.* I turned to face him. "Push," he said, "you forgot your silver." He handed it to a girl in front of him and she gave it to the boy in front of her and it came to me down the long line.

I plot, I scheme. Snares, I think; tricks and traps. I remember the old days when there were ways to snap fingers, crush toes, ways to pull noses, twist heads and punch arms—the old-timey Flinch Law I used to impose, the gone bully magic of deceit. But nothing works against him, I think. How does he know so much? He is bully-prepared, that one, not to be trusted.

It is worse and worse.

In the cafeteria he eats with Frank. "You don't want those potatoes," he tells him. "Not the ice cream, Frank. One sandwich, remember. You lost three pounds last week." The fat boy smiles his fat love at him. John Williams puts his arm around him. He seems to squeeze him thin.

He's helping Mimmer to study. He goes over his lessons and teaches him tricks, short cuts. "I want you up there with me on the Honor Roll, Mimmer."

I see him with Slud the cripple. They go to the gym. I watch from the balcony. "Let's develop those arms, my friend." They work out with weights. Slud's muscles grow, they bloom from his bones.

I lean over the rail. I shout down, "He can bend iron bars. Can he peddle a bike? Can he walk on rough ground? Can he climb up a hill? Can he wait on a line? Can he dance with a girl? Can he go up a ladder or jump from a chair?"

Beneath me the rapt Slud sits on a bench and raises a weight. He holds it at arm's length, level with his chest. He moves it high, higher. It rises above his shoulders, his throat, his head. He bends back his neck to see what he's done. If the weight should fall now it would crush his throat. I stare down into his smile.

I see Eugene in the halls. I stop him. "Eugene, what's he done for you?" I ask. He smiles—he never did this—and I see his mouth's flood. "High tide," I say with satisfaction.

Williams has introduced Club to a girl. They have double-dated.

A WEEK ago John Williams came to my house to see me! I wouldn't let him in.

"Please open the door, Push. I'd like to chat with you. Will you open the door? Push? I think we ought to talk. I think I can help you to be happier."

I was furious. I didn't know what to say to him. "I don't want to be happier. Go way." It was what little kids used to say to me.

"*Please* let me help you."

"*Please* let me—" I begin to echo. "Please let me alone."

"We ought to be friends, Push."

"No deals." I am choking, I am close to tears. What can I do? *What?* I want to kill him.

I double-lock the door and retreat to my room. He is still out there. I have tried to live my life so that I could keep always the lamb from my door.

He has gone too far this time; and I think sadly, I will have to fight him, I will have to fight him. Push pushed. I think sadly of the pain. Push pushed. I will have to fight him. Not to preserve honor but its opposite. Each time I see him I will have to fight him. And then I think   *of course!* And *I* smile. He has done *me* a favor. I know it at once. If he fights me he fails. He fails if he fights me. *Push pushed pushes!* It's physics! Natural law! I know he'll beat me, but I won't prepare, I won't train, I won't use the tricks I know. It's strength against strength, and my strength is as the strength of ten because my jaw is glass! *He doesn't know everything, not everything he doesn't.* And I think, I could go out now, he's still there, I could hit him in the hall, but I think, No, I want them to see, I want *them* to see!

The next day I am very excited. I look for Williams. He's not in the halls. I miss him in the cafeteria. Afterward I look for him in the schoolyard where I first saw him. (He has them organized now. He teaches them games of Tibet, games of Japan; he gets them to play lost sports of the dead.) He does not disappoint me. He is there in the yard, a circle around him, a ring of the loyal.

I join the ring. I shove in between two kids I have known. They try to change places; they murmur and fret.

Williams sees me and waves. His smile could grow flowers. "Boys," he says, "boys, make room for Push. Join hands, boys." They welcome me to the circle. One takes my hand, then another. I give to each calmly.

I wait. *He doesn't know everything.*

"Boys," he begins, "today we're going to learn a game that the knights of the lords and kings of old France used to play in another century. Now you may not realize it, boys, because today when we think of a knight we think, too, of his fine charger, but the fact is that a horse was a rare animal—not a domestic European animal at all, but Asian. In western Europe, for example, there was no such thing as a work horse until the eighth century. Your horse was just too expensive to be put to heavy labor in the fields. (This explains, incidentally, the prevalence of famine in western Europe, whereas famine is unrecorded in Asia until the ninth century, when Euro-Asian horse trading was at its height.) It wasn't only expensive to purchase a horse, it was expensive to keep one. A cheap fodder wasn't developed in Europe until the tenth century. Then, of course, when you consider the terrific risks that the warrior horse of a knight naturally had to run, you begin to appreciate how expensive it would have been for the lord—unless he was extremely rich—to provide all his knights with horses. He'd want to make pretty certain that the knights who got them knew how to handle a horse. (Only your knights errant—an elite, crack corps—ever had horses. We don't realize that most knights were *home* knights; *chevalier chez* they were called.)

"This game, then, was devised to let the lord, or king, see which of his knights had the skill and strength in his hands to control a horse. Without moving your feet, you must try to jerk the one next to you off balance. Each man has two opponents, so it's very difficult. If a man falls, or if his knee touches the ground, he's out. The circle is diminished but must close up again immediately. Now, once for practice only—"

"Just a minute," I interrupt.

"Yes, Push?"

I leave the circle and walk forward and hit him as hard as I can in the face.

He stumbles backward. The boys groan. He recovers. He rubs his jaw and smiles. I think he is going to let me hit him again. I am prepared for this. He knows what I'm up to and will use his passivity. Either way I win, but I am determined he shall hit me. I am ready to kick him, but as my foot comes up he grabs my ankle and turns it forcefully. I spin in the air. He lets go and I fall heavily on my back. I am surprised at how easy it was, but am content if they understand. I get up and am walking away, but there is an arm on my shoulder. He pulls me around roughly. He hits me.

"*Sic semper tyrannus,*" he exults.

"Where's your other cheek?" I ask, falling backward.

"One cheek for tyrants," he shouts. He pounces on me and raises his fist and I cringe. His anger is terrific. I do not want to be hit again.

"You see? You see?" I scream at the kids, but I have lost the train of my former reasoning. I have in no way beaten him. I can't remember now what I had intended.

He lowers his fist and gets off my chest and they cheer. "Hurrah," they yell. "Hurrah, hurrah." The word seems funny to me.

He offers his hand when I try to rise. It is so difficult to know what to do. Oh God, it is so difficult to know which gesture is the right one. I don't even know this. He knows everything, and I don't even know this. I am a fool on the ground, one hand behind me pushing up, the other not yet extended but itching in the palm where the need is. It is better to give than receive, surely. It is best not to need at all.

Appalled, guessing what I miss, I rise alone.

"Friends?" he asks. He offers to shake.

"Take it, Push." It's Eugene's voice.

"Go ahead, Push." Slud limps forward.

"Push, hatred's so ugly," Clob says, his face shining.

"You'll feel better, Push," Frank, thinner, taller, urges softly.

"Push, don't be foolish," Mimmer says.

I shake my head. I may be wrong. I am probably wrong. All I know at last is what feels good. "Nothing doing," I growl. "No deals." I begin to talk, to spray my hatred at them. They are not an easy target even now. "Only your knights errant—your crack corps—ever have horses. Slud may dance and Clob may kiss but they'll never be good at it. *Push is no service animal.* No. *No.* Can you hear that, Williams? There isn't any magic, but your no is still stronger than your yes, and distrust is where I put my faith." I turn to the boys. "What have you settled for? Only your knights errant ever have horses. *What have you settled for?* Will Mimmer do sums in his head? How do you like your lousy hunger, thin boy? Slud, you can break me but you can't catch me. And Clob will never shave without pain, and ugly, let me tell you, is *still* in the eye of the beholder!"

John Williams mourns for me. He grieves his gamy grief. No one has everything—not even John Williams. He doesn't have *me.* He'll never have me, I think. If my life were only to deny him that, it would almost be enough. I could do his voice now if I wanted. His corruption began when he lost me. "You," I shout, rubbing it in, "*indulger,* dispense me no dispensations. Push the bully hates your heart!"

"Shut him up, somebody," Eugene cries. His saliva spills from his mouth when he speaks.

"Swallow! *Pig, swallow!*"

He rushes toward me.

Suddenly I raise my arms and he stops. I feel a power in me. I am Push, Push the bully, God of the Neighborhood, its incarnation of envy and jealousy and need. I vie, strive, emulate, compete, a contender in every event there is. I didn't make myself. I probably can't save myself, but maybe that's the only need I don't have. I taste my lack and that's how I win—by having nothing to lose. It's not good enough! I want and I want and I will die wanting, but first I will have something. This time I will have something. I say it aloud. "This time I will have something." I step toward them. The power makes me dizzy. It is enormous. They feel it. They back away. They crouch in the shadow of my outstretched wings. It isn't deceit this time but the real magic at last, the genuine thing: the cabala of my hate, of my irreconcilableness.

Logic is nothing. Desire is stronger.

I move toward Eugene. *"I will have something,"* I roar.

"Stand back," he shrieks, "I'll spit in your eye."

"*I will have something.* I will have terror. I will have drought. I bring the dearth. Famine's contagious. Also is thirst. Privation, privation, barrenness, void. I dry up your glands, I poison your well."

He is choking, gasping, chewing furiously. He opens his mouth. It is dry. His throat is parched. There is sand on his tongue.

They moan. They are terrified, but they move up to see. We are thrown together. Slud, Frank, Clob, Mimmer, the others, John Williams, myself. I will not be reconciled, or halve my hate. *It's* what I have, all I can keep. My bully's sour solace. It's enough, I'll make do.

I can't stand them near me. I move against them. I shove them away. I force them off. I press them, thrust them aside. *I push through.*

(1965)

John Barth

(b. 1 9 3 0)

John Barth was born in Cambridge, Maryland, and was educated at Johns Hopkins University. He taught at Pennsylvania State University and the University of Buffalo, then returned to Johns Hopkins as professor of English in 1973. The academic world has provided the setting and subject for parody in Barth's fiction, particularly in his allegorical novel *Giles Goat-Boy,* in which an epic quest motif is played out entirely within the textual byways of scholarly pursuit. Barth's short fiction appeared in *Kenyon Review* and *Esquire* in the early 1950s, and his first novel, *The Floating Opera,* published in 1956, brought Barth widespread critical attention. A volume of short stories, *Chimera,* won the National Book award in 1972.

Barth writes epics of the absurd. He is a complex and witty parodist of the extravagant and the heroic. His works follow the tradition of Pope's *Dunciad* and *The Rape of the Lock.* In *The Sot-Weed Factor,* for example, the novel many critics consider to be his finest, Barth constructs a wild tale with a fanciful plot; the book describes the epic history of a Maryland tobacco farmer in the eighteenth century and is written in a style that mimics eighteenth-century prose. Barth's fiction is self-reflective and continually draws attention to itself as artifice. Especially in *Lost in the Funhouse* and *Chimera,* Barth examines the acts of writing and reading. The novels display a tendency toward ponderous and obvious structuring. But Barth often reaches through his self-reflective mirrors to achieve a truly profound analysis of the way people approach a chaotic but malleable universe. Barth's narrative experimentation, his erotic humor, and his use of myth have influenced younger American novelists.

Barth's novels are *The Floating Opera* (1956), *The End of the Road* (1958), *The Sot-Weed Factor* (1960), *Giles Goat-Boy* (1966), *Letters* (1979), and *Sabbatical* (1982). He has also published two volumes of shorter fiction, *Lost in the Funhouse* (1968) and *Chimera* (1972).

JOHN BARTH

Lost in the Funhouse

FOR whom is the funhouse fun? Perhaps for lovers. For Ambrose it is *a place of fear and confusion.* He has come to the seashore with his family for the holiday, *the occasion of their visit is Independence Day, the most important secular holiday of the United States of America.* A single straight underline is the manuscript mark for italic type, *which in turn* is the printed equivalent to oral emphasis of words and phrases as well as the customary type for titles of complete works, not to mention. Italics are also employed, in fiction stories especially, for "outside," intrusive, or artificial voices, such as radio announcements, the texts of telegrams and newspaper articles, et cetera. They should be used *sparingly.* If passages originally in roman type are italicized by someone repeating them, it's customary to acknowledge the fact. *Italics mine.*

Ambrose was "at that awkward age." His voice came out high-pitched as a child's if he let himself get carried away; to be on the safe side, therefore, he moved and spoke with *deliberate calm* and *adult gravity.* Talking soberly of unimportant or irrelevant matters and listening consciously to the sound of your own voice are useful habits for maintaining control in this difficult interval. *En route* to Ocean City he sat in the back seat of the family car with his brother Peter, age fifteen, and Magda G———, age fourteen, a pretty girl an exquisite young lady, who lived not far from them on B——— Street in the town of D———, Maryland. Initials, blanks, or both were often substituted for proper names in nineteenth-century fiction to enhance the illusion of reality. It is as if the author felt it necessary to delete the names for reasons of tact or legal liability. Interestingly, as with other aspects of realism, it is an *illusion* that is being enhanced, by purely artificial means. Is it likely, does it violate the principle of verisimilitude, that a thirteen-year-old boy could make such a sophisticated observation? A girl of fourteen is *the psychological coeval* of a boy of fifteen or sixteen; a thirteen-year-old boy, therefore, even one precocious in some other respects, might be three years *her emotional junior.*

Thrice a year—on Memorial, Independence, and Labor Days—the family visits Ocean City for the afternoon and evening. When Ambrose and Peter's father was their age, the excursion was made by train, as mentioned in the novel *The 42nd Parallel* by John Dos Passos. Many families from the same neighborhood used to travel together, with dependent relatives and often with Negro servants; schoolfuls of children swarmed through the railway cars; everyone shared everyone else's Maryland fried chicken, Virginia ham, deviled eggs, potato salad, beaten biscuits, iced tea. Nowadays (that is, in 19___, the year of our story) the journey is made by automobile—more comfortably and quickly though without the extra fun though without the *camaraderie* of a general excursion. It's all part of the deterioration of American life, their father declares; Uncle Karl supposes that when the boys take *their* families to Ocean City for the holidays they'll fly in Autogiros. Their mother, sitting in the middle of the front seat like Magda in the second, only with her arms on the seat-back behind the men's shoulders, wouldn't want the good old days back again, the steaming trains and stuffy long dresses; on the other hand she can do without Autogiros, too, if she has to become a grandmother to fly in them.

Description of physical appearance and mannerisms is one of several standard methods of characterization used by writers of fiction. It is also important to "keep the senses operating"; when a detail from one of the five senses, say visual, is "crossed" with a detail from another, say auditory, the reader's imagination is oriented to the scene, perhaps unconsciously. This procedure may be compared to the way surveyors and navigators determine their positions by two or more compass bearings, a process known as triangulation. The brown hair on Ambrose's mother's forearms gleamed in the sun like. Though right-handed, she took her left arm from the seat-back to press the dashboard cigar lighter for Uncle Karl. When the glass bead in its handle glowed red, the lighter was ready for use. The smell of Uncle Karl's cigar smoke reminded one of. The fragrance of the ocean came strong to the picnic ground where they always stopped for lunch, two miles inland from Ocean City. Having to pause for a full hour almost within sound of the breakers was difficult for Peter and Ambrose when they were younger; even at their present age it was not easy to keep their anticipation, *stimulated by the briny spume*, from turning into short temper. The Irish author James Joyce, in his unusual novel entitled *Ulysses*, now available in this country, uses the adjectives *snot-green* and *scrotum-tightening* to describe the sea. Visual, auditory, tactile, olfactory, gustatory. Peter and Ambrose's father, while steering their black 1936 LaSalle sedan with one hand, could with the other remove the first cigarette from a white pack of Lucky Strikes and, more remarkably, light it with a match forefingered from its book and thumbed against the flint paper without being detached. The matchbook cover merely advertised U.S. War Bonds and Stamps. A fine metaphor, simile, or other figure of speech, in addition to its obvious "first-order" relevance to the thing it describes, will be seen upon reflection to have a second order of significance: it may be drawn from the *milieu* of the action, for example, or be particularly appropriate to the sensibility of the narrator, even hinting to the reader things of which the narrator is unaware; or it may cast further and subtler lights upon the thing it describes, sometimes ironically qualifying the more evident sense of the comparison.

To say that Ambrose's and Peter's mother was *pretty* is to accomplish nothing; the reader may acknowledge the proposition, but his imagination is not engaged. Besides, Magda was also pretty, yet in an altogether different way. Although she lived on B—— Street she had very good manners and did better than average in school. Her figure was very well developed for her age. Her right hand lay casually on the plush upholstery of the seat, very near Ambrose's left leg, on which his own hand rested. The space between their legs, between her right and his left leg, was out of the line of sight of anyone sitting on the other side of Magda, as well as anyone glancing into the rearview mirror. Uncle Karl's face resembled Peter's—rather, vice versa. Both had dark hair and eyes, short husky statures, deep voices. Magda's left hand was probably in a similar position on her left side. The boy's father is difficult to describe; no particular feature of his appearance or manner stood out. He wore glasses and was principal of a T—— County grade school. Uncle Karl was a masonry contractor.

Although Peter must have known as well as Ambrose that the latter, because of his position in the car, would be the first to see the electrical towers of the power plant at V——, the halfway point of their trip, he leaned forward and slightly toward the center of the car and pretended to be looking for them through the flat pinewoods and tuckahoe creeks along the highway. For as long as the boys could remember, "looking for the Towers" had been a feature of the first half of their excursions to Ocean City, "looking for the standpipe" of the second. Though the game was childish, their mother preserved the tradition of rewarding the first to see the Towers with a candy-bar or piece of fruit. She insisted now that Magda play the game; the prize, she said, was "something hard to get nowadays." Ambrose decided not to join in; he sat far back in his seat. Magda, like Peter, leaned forward. Two sets of straps were discernible through the shoulders of her sun dress; the inside right one, a brassiere-strap, was fastened or shortened with a small safety pin. The right armpit of her dress, presumably the left as well, was damp with perspiration. The simple strategy for being first to espy the Towers, which Ambrose had understood by the age of four, was to sit on the right-hand side of the car. Whoever sat there, however, had also to put up with the worst of the sun, and so Ambrose, without mentioning the matter, chose sometimes the one and sometimes the other. Not impossibly Peter had never caught on to the trick, or thought that his brother hadn't simply because Ambrose on occasion preferred shade to a Baby Ruth or tangerine.

The shade-sun situation didn't apply to the front seat, owing to the windshield; if anything the driver got more sun, since the person on the passenger side not only was shaded below by the door and dashboard but might swing down his sunvisor all the way too.

"Is that them?" Magda asked. Ambrose's mother teased the boys for letting Magda win, insinuating that "somebody [had] a girlfriend." Peter and Ambrose's father reached a long thin arm across their mother to butt his cigarette in the dashboard ashtray, under the lighter. The prize this time for seeing the Towers first was a banana. Their mother bestowed it after chiding their father for wasting a half-smoked cigarette when everything was so scarce. Magda, to take the prize, moved her hand from so near Ambrose's that he could have touched it as though accidentally. She offered to share the prize, things like that were so hard to find; but everyone insisted it was hers alone. Ambrose's mother sang in iambic trimeter couplet from a popular song, femininely rhymed:

> *"What's good is in the Army;*
> *What's left will never harm me."*

Uncle Karl tapped his cigar ash out the ventilator window; some particles were sucked by the slipstream back into the car through the rear window on the passenger side. Magda demonstrated her ability to hold a banana in one hand and peel it with her teeth. She still sat forward; Ambrose pushed his glasses back onto the bridge of his nose with his left hand, which he then negligently let fall to the seat cushion immediately behind her. He even permitted the single hair, gold, on the second joint of his thumb to brush the fabric of her skirt. Should she have sat back at that instant, his hand would have been caught under her.

Plush upholstery prickles uncomfortably through gabardine slacks in the July sun. The function of the *beginning* of a story is to introduce the principal characters, establish their initial relationships, set the scene for the main action, expose the background of the situation if necessary, plant motifs and foreshadowings where appropriate, and initiate the first complication or whatever of the "rising action." Actually, if one imagines a story called "The Funhouse," or "Lost in the Funhouse," the details of the drive to Ocean City don't seem especially relevant. The *beginning* should recount the events between Ambrose's first sight of the funhouse early in the afternoon and his entering it with Magda and Peter in the evening. The *middle* would narrate all relevant events from the time he goes in to the time he loses his way; middles have the double and contradictory function of delaying the climax while at the same time preparing the reader for it and fetching him to it. Then the *ending* would tell what Ambrose does while he's lost, how he finally finds his way out, and what everybody makes of the experience. So far there's been no real dialogue, very little sensory detail, and nothing in the way of a *theme*. And a long time has gone by already without anything happening; it makes a person wonder. We haven't even reached Ocean City yet: we will never get out of the funhouse.

The more closely an author identifies with the narrator, literally or metaphorically, the less advisable it is, as a rule, to use the first-person narrative viewpoint. Once three years previously the young people *aforementioned* played Niggers and Masters in the backyard; when it was Ambrose's turn to be Master and theirs to be Niggers Peter had to go serve his evening papers; Ambrose was afraid to punish Magda alone, but she led him to the whitewashed Torture Chamber between the woodshed and the privy in the Slaves Quarters; there she knelt sweating among bamboo rakes and dusty Mason jars, pleadingly embraced his knees, and while bees droned in the lattice as if on an ordinary summer afternoon, purchased clemency at a surprising price set by herself. Doubtless she remembered nothing of this event; Ambrose on the other hand seemed unable to forget the least detail of his life. He even recalled how, standing beside himself with awed impersonality in the reeky heat, he'd stared the while at an empty cigar box in which Uncle Karl kept stone-cutting chisels: beneath the words *El Producto,* a laureled, loose-toga'd lady regarded the sea from a marble bench; beside her, forgotten or not yet turned to, was a five-stringed lyre. Her chin reposed on the back of her right hand; her left depended negligently from the bench-arm. The lower half of scene and lady was peeled away; the words EXAMINED BY ____ were inked there into the wood. Nowadays cigar boxes are made of pasteboard. Ambrose wondered what Magda would have done, Ambrose wondered what Magda would do when she sat back on his hand as he resolved she should. Be angry. Make a teasing joke of it. Give no sign at all. For a long time she leaned forward, playing cow-poker with Peter against Uncle Karl and Mother and watching for the first sign of Ocean City. At nearly the same instant, picnic ground and Ocean City standpipe hove into view; an Amoco filling station on their side of the road cost Mother and Uncle Karl fifty cows and the game; Magda bounced back, clapping her right hand on Mother's right arm; Ambrose moved clear "in the nick of time."

At this rate our hero, at this rate our protagonist will remain in the funhouse forever. Narrative ordinarily consists of alternating dramatization and summarization. One symptom of nervous tension, paradoxically, is repeated and violent yawning; neither Peter nor Magda nor Uncle Karl nor Mother reacted in this manner. Although they were no longer small children, Peter and Ambrose were each given a dollar to spend on boardwalk amusements in addition to what money of their own they'd brought along. Magda too, though she protested she had ample spending money. The boys' mother made a little scene out of distributing the bills; she pretended that her sons and Magda were small children and cautioned them not to spend the sum too quickly or in one place. Magda promised with a merry laugh and, having both hands free, took the bill with her left. Peter laughed also and pledged in a falsetto to be a good boy. His imitation of a child was not clever. The boys' father was tall and thin, balding, fair-complexioned. Assertions of that sort are not effective; the reader may acknowledge the proposition, but. We should be much farther along than we are; something has gone wrong; not much of this preliminary rambling seems relevant. Yet everyone begins in the same place; how is it that most go along without difficulty but a few lose their way?

"Stay out from under the boardwalk," Uncle Karl growled from the side of his mouth. The boys' mother pushed his shoulder *in mock annoyance.* They were all standing before Fat May the Laughing Lady who advertised the funhouse. Larger than life, Fat May mechanically shook, rocked on her heels, slapped her thighs while recorded laughter—uproarious, female— came amplified from a hidden loudspeaker. It chuckled, wheezed, wept; tried in vain to catch its breath; tittered, groaned, exploded raucous and anew. You couldn't hear it without laughing yourself, no matter how you felt. Father came back from talking to a Coast-Guardsman on duty and reported that the surf was spoiled with crude oil from tankers recently torpedoed offshore. Lumps of it, difficult to remove, made tarry tidelines on the beach and stuck on swimmers. Many bathed in the surf nevertheless and came out speckled; others paid to use a municipal pool and only sunbathed on the beach. We would do the latter. We would do the latter. We would do the latter.

Under the boardwalk, matchbook covers, grainy other things. What is the story's theme? Ambrose is ill. He perspires in the dark passages; candied apples-on-a-stick, delicious-looking, disappointing to eat. Funhouses need men's and ladies' room at intervals. Others perhaps have also vomited in corners and corridors; may even have had bowel movements liable to be stepped in in the dark. The word *fuck* suggests suction and/or and/or flatulence. Mother and Father; grandmothers and grandfathers on both sides; great-grandmothers and great-grandfathers on four sides, et cetera. Count a generation as thirty years: in approximately the year when Lord Baltimore was granted charter to the province of Maryland by Charles I, five hundred twelve women—English, Welsh, Bavarian, Swiss—of every class and character, received into themselves the penises the intromittent organs of five hundred twelve men, ditto, in every circumstance and posture, to conceive the five hundred twelve ancestors of the two hundred fifty-six ancestors of the et cetera et cetera et cetera et cetera et cetera et cetera et cetera et cetera of the author, of the narrator, of this story, *Lost in the Funhouse.* In alleyways, ditches, canopy beds, pinewoods, bridal suites, ship's cabins, coach and-fours, coaches-and-four, sultry toolsheds; on the cold sand under boardwalks, littered with *El Producto* cigar butts, treasured with Lucky Strike cigarette stubs, Coca-Cola caps, gritty turds, cardboard lollipop sticks, matchbook covers warning that A Slip of the Lip Can Sink a Ship. The shluppish whisper, continuous as seawash round the globe, tidelike falls and rises with the circuit of dawn and dusk.

Magda's teeth. She *was* left-handed. Perspiration. They've gone all the way, through, Magda and Peter, they've been waiting for hours with Mother and Uncle Karl while Father searches for his lost son; they draw french-fried potatoes from a paper cup and shake their heads. They've named the children they'll one day have and bring to Ocean City on holidays. Can spermatozoa properly be thought of as male animalcules when there are no female spermatozoa? They grope through hot, dark windings, past Love's Tunnel's fearsome obstacles. Some perhaps lose their way.

Peter suggested then and there that they do the funhouse; he had been through it before, so had Magda, Ambrose hadn't and suggested, his voice cracking on account of Fat May's laughter, that they swim first. All were chuckling, couldn't help it; Ambrose's father, Ambrose's and Peter's father came up grinning like a lunatic with two boxes of syrup-coated popcorn, one for Mother, one for Magda; the men were to help themselves. Ambrose walked on Magda's right; being by nature left-handed, she carried the box in her left hand. Up front the situation was reversed.

"What are you limping for?" Magda inquired of Ambrose. He supposed in a husky tone that his foot had gone to sleep in the car. Her teeth flashed. "Pins and needles?" It was the honeysuckle on the lattice of the former privy that drew the bees. Imagine being stung there. How long is this going to take?

The adults decided to forgo the pool; but Uncle Karl insisted they change into swimsuits and do the beach. "He wants to watch the pretty girls," Peter teased, and ducked behind Magda from Uncle Karl's pretended wrath. "You've got all the pretty girls you need right here," Magda declared, and Mother said: "Now that's the gospel truth." Magda scolded Peter, who reached over her shoulder to sneak some popcorn. "Your brother and father aren't getting any." Uncle Karl wondered if they were going to have fireworks that night, what with the shortages. It wasn't the shortages, Mr. M____ replied; Ocean City had fireworks from pre-war. But it was too risky on account of the enemy submarines, some people thought.

"Don't seem like Fourth of July without fireworks," said Uncle Karl. The inverted tag in dialogue writing is still considered permissible with proper names or epithets, but sounds old-fashioned with personal pronouns. "We'll have 'em again soon enough," predicted the boys' father. Their mother declared she could do without fireworks: they reminded her too much of the real thing. Their father said all the more reason to shoot off a few now and again. Uncle Karl asked *rhetorically* who needed reminding, just look at people's hair and skin.

"The oil, yes," said Mrs. M____.

Ambrose had a pain in his stomach and so didn't swim but enjoyed watching the others. He and his father burned red easily. Magda's figure was exceedingly well developed for her age. She too declined to swim, and got mad, and become angry when Peter attempted to drag her into the pool. She always swam, he insisted; what did she mean not swim? Why did a person come to Ocean City?

"Maybe I want to lay here with Ambrose," Magda teased.

Nobody likes a pedant.

"Aha," said Mother. Peter grabbed Magda by one ankle and ordered Ambrose to grab the other. She squealed and rolled over on the beach blanket. Ambrose pretended to help hold her back. Her tan was darker than even Mother's and Peter's. "Help out, Uncle Karl!" Peter cried. Uncle Karl went to seize the other ankle. Inside the top of her swimsuit, however, you could see the line where the sunburn ended and, when she hunched her shoulders and squealed again, one nipple's auburn edge. Mother made them behave themselves. "*You* should certainly know," she said to Uncle Karl. Archly. "That when a lady says she doesn't feel like swimming, a gentleman doesn't ask questions." Uncle Karl said excuse *him;* Mother winked at Magda; Ambrose blushed; stupid Peter kept saying "Phooey on *feel like!*" and tugging at Magda's ankle; then even he got the point, and cannonballed with a holler into the pool.

"I swear," Magda said, in mock *in feigned* exasperation.

The diving would make a suitable literary symbol. To go off the high board you had to wait in a line along the poolside and up the ladder. Fellows tickled girls and goosed one another and shouted to the ones at the top to hurry up, or razzed them for bellyfloppers. Once on the springboard some took a great while posing or clowning or deciding on a dive or getting up their nerve; others ran right off. Especially among the younger fellows the idea was to strike the funniest pose or do the craziest stunt as you fell, a thing that got harder to do as you kept on and kept on. But whether you hollered *Geronimo!* or *Sieg heil!*, [1] held your nose or "rode a bicycle," pretended to be shot or did a perfect jacknife or changed your mind halfway down and ended up with nothing, it was over in two seconds, after all that wait. Spring, pose, splash. Spring, neat-o, splash. Spring, aw fooey, splash.

The grown-ups had gone on; Ambrose wanted to converse with Magda; she was remarkably well developed for her age; it was said that that came from rubbing with a turkish towel, and there were other theories. Ambrose could think of nothing to say except how good a diver Peter was, who was showing off for her benefit. You could pretty well tell by looking at their bathing suits and arm muscles how far along the different fellows were. Ambrose was glad he hadn't gone in swimming, the cold water shrank you up so. Magda pretended to be uninterested in the diving; she probably weighed as much as he did. If you knew your way around in the funhouse like your own bedroom, you could wait until a girl came along and then slip away without ever getting caught, even if her boyfriend was right with her. She'd think *he* did it! It would be better to be the boyfriend, and act outraged, and tear the funhouse apart.

Not act; *be.*

"He's a master diver," Ambrose said. In feigned admiration. "You really have to slave away at it to get that good." What would it matter anyhow if he asked her right out whether she remembered, even teased her with it as Peter would have?

There's no point in going farther; this isn't getting anybody anywhere; they haven't even come to the funhouse yet. Ambrose is off the track, in some new or old part of the place that's not supposed to be used; he strayed into it by some one-in-a-million chance, like the time the roller-coaster car left the tracks in the nineteen-teens against all the laws of physics and sailed over the boardwalk in the dark. And they can't locate him because they don't know where to look. Even the designer and operator have forgotten this other part, that winds around on itself like a whelk shell. That winds around the right part like the snakes on Mercury's caduceus. Some people, perhaps, don't "hit their stride" until their twenties, when the growing-up business is over and women appreciate other things besides wisecracks and teasing and strutting. Peter didn't have one-tenth the imagination *he* had, not one-tenth. Peter did this naming-their-children thing as a joke, making up names

---

[1] *"Geronimo!"* is the traditional shout used by American paratroopers; *"Sieg heil!"* (Hail to victory!) was the traditional Nazi salute.

like Aloysius and Murgatroyd, but Ambrose knew *exactly* how it would feel
to be married and have children of your own, and be a loving husband and
father, and go comfortably to work in the mornings and to bed with your
wife at night, and wake up with her there. With a breeze coming through
the sash and birds and mockingbirds singing in the Chinese-cigar trees. His
eyes watered, there aren't enough ways to say that. He would be quite
famous in his line of work. Whether Magda was his wife or not, one evening
when he was wise-lined and gray at the temples he'd smile gravely, at a
fashionable dinner party, and remind her of his youthful passion. The time
they went with his family to Ocean City; the *erotic fantasies* he used to have
about her. How long ago it seemed, and childish! Yet tender, too, *n'est-ce
pas?*[2] Would she have imagined that the world-famous whatever remembered how many strings were on the lyre on the bench beside the girl on
the label of the cigar box he'd stared at in the toolshed at age ten while she,
age eleven. Even then he had felt *wise beyond his years;* he'd stroked her hair
and said in his deepest voice and correctest English, as to a dear child: "I
shall never forget this moment."

But though he had breathed heavily, groaned as if ecstatic, what he'd
really felt throughout was an odd detachment, as though someone else were
Master. Strive as he might to be transported, he heard his mind take notes
upon the scene: *This is what they call* passion. *I am experiencing it.* Many of the
digger machines were out of order in the penny arcades and could not be
repaired or replaced for the duration. Moreover the prizes, made now in
USA, were less interesting than formerly, pasteboard items for the most
part, and some of the machines wouldn't work on white pennies.[3] The gypsy
fortune-teller machine might have provided a foreshadowing of the climax
of this story if Ambrose had operated it. It was even dilapidateder than most:
the silver coating was worn off the brown metal handles, the glass windows
around the dummy were cracked and taped, her kerchiefs and silks long-
faded. If a man lived by himself, he could take a department-store manne-
quin with flexible joints and modify her in certain ways. *However:* by the time
he was that old he'd have a real woman. There was a machine that stamped
your name around a white-metal coin with a star in the middle: *A ____*. His
son would be the second, and when the lad reached thirteen or so he would
put a strong arm around his shoulder and tell him calmly: "It is perfectly
normal. We have all been through it. It will not last forever." Nobody knew
how to be what they were right. He'd smoke a pipe, teach his son how to
fish and softcrab, assure him he needn't worry about himself. Magda would
certainly give, Magda would certainly yield a great deal of milk, although
guilty of occasional solecisms. It don't taste so bad. Suppose the lights came
on now!

The day wore on. You think you're yourself, but there are other persons in

---

[2] Isn't it?

[3] The U.S. government minted zinc-coated steel pennies in an effort to conserve copper needed
for the World War II effort.

you. Ambrose gets hard when Ambrose doesn't want to, *and obversely.* Ambrose watches them disagree; Ambrose watches him watch. In the funhouse mirror-room you can't see yourself go on forever, because no matter how you stand, your head gets in the way. Even if you had a glass periscope, the image of your eye would cover up the thing you really wanted to see. The police will come; there'll be a story in the papers. That must be where it happened. Unless he can find a surprise exit, an unofficial backdoor or escape hatch opening on an alley, say, and then stroll up to the family in front of the funhouse and ask where everybody's been; *he's* been out of the place for ages. That's just where it happened, in that last lighted room: Peter and Magda found the right exit; he found one that you weren't supposed to find and strayed off into the works somewhere. In a perfect funhouse you'd be able to go only one way, like the divers off the highboard; getting lost would be impossible; the doors and halls would work like minnow traps or the valves in veins.

On account of German U-boats, Ocean City was "browned out": streetlights were shaded on the seaward side; shop-windows and boardwalk amusement places were kept dim, not to silhouette tankers and Liberty-ships for torpedoing. In a short story about Ocean City, Maryland, during World War II, the author could make use of the image of sailors on leave in the penny arcades and shooting galleries, sighting through the crosshairs of toy machine guns at swastika'd subs, while out in the black Atlantic a U-boat skipper squints through his periscope at real ships outlined by the glow of penny arcades. After dinner the family strolled back to the amusement end of the boardwalk. The boys' father had burnt red as always and was masked with Noxzema, a minstrel in reverse. The grownups stood at the end of the boardwalk where the Hurricane of '33 had cut an inlet from the ocean to Assawoman Bay.

"Pronounced with a long *o,*" Uncle Karl reminded Magda with a wink. His shirt sleeves were rolled up; Mother punched his brown biceps with the arrowed heart on it and said his mind was naughty. Fat May's laugh came suddenly from the funhouse, as if she'd just got the joke; the family laughed too at the coincidence. Ambrose went under the boardwalk to search for out-of-town matchbook covers with the aid of his pocket flashlight; he looked out from the edge of the North American continent and wondered how far their laughter carried over the water. Spies in rubber rafts; survivors in lifeboats. If the joke had been beyond his understanding, he could have said: *"The laughter was over his head."* And let the reader see the serious wordplay on second reading.

He turned the flashlight on and then off at once even before the woman whooped. He sprang away, heart athud, dropping the light. What had the man grunted? Perspiration drenched and chilled him by the time he scrambled up to the family. "See anything?" his father asked. His voice wouldn't come; he shrugged and violently brushed sand from his pants legs.

"Let's ride the old flying horses!" Magda cried. I'll never be an author. It's been forever already, everybody's gone home, Ocean City's deserted, the ghost-crabs are tickling across the beach and down the littered cold streets. And the empty halls of clapboard hotels and abandoned funhouses. A tidal wave; an enemy air raid; a monster-crab swelling like an island from the sea. *The inhabitants fled in terror.* Magda clung to his trouser leg; he alone knew the maze's secret. "He gave his life that we might live," said Uncle Karl with a scowl of pain, as he. The fellow's hands had been tattooed; the woman's legs, the woman's fat white legs had. *An astonishing coincidence.* He yearned to tell Peter. He wanted to throw up for excitement. They hadn't even chased him. He wished he were dead.

One possible ending would be to have Ambrose come across another lost person in the dark. They'd match their wits together against the funhouse, struggle like Ulysses past obstacle after obstacle, help and encourage each other. Or a girl. By the time they found the exit they'd be closest friends, sweethearts if it were a girl; they'd know each other's inmost souls, be bound together *by the cement of shared adventure;* then they'd emerge into the light and it would turn out that his friend was a Negro. A blind girl. President Roosevelt's son. Ambrose's former archenemy.

Shortly after the mirror room he'd groped along a musty corridor, his heart already misgiving him at the absence of phosphorescent arrows and other signs. He'd found a crack of light—not a door, it turned out, but a seam between the plyboard wall panels—and squinting up to it, espied a small old man, *in appearance not unlike* the photographs at home of Ambrose's late grandfather, nodding upon a stool beneath a bare, speckled bulb. A crude panel of toggle- and knife-switches hung beside the open fuse box near his head; elsewhere in the little room were wooden levers and ropes belayed to boat cleats. At the time, Ambrose wasn't lost enough to rap or call; later he couldn't find that crack. Now it seemed to him that he'd possibly dozed off for a few minutes somewhere along the way; certainly he was exhausted from the afternoon's sunshine and the evening's problems; he couldn't be sure he hadn't dreamed part or all of the sight. Had an old black wall fan droned like bees and shimmied two flypaper streamers? Had the funhouse operator—gentle, somewhat sad and tired-appearing, in expression not unlike the photographs at home of Ambrose's late Uncle Konrad—murmured in his sleep? Is there really such a person as Ambrose, or is he a figment of the author's imagination? Was it Assawoman Bay or Sinepuxent? Are there other errors of fact in this fiction? Was there another sound besides the little slap slap of thigh on ham, like water sucking at the chine-boards of a skiff?

When you're lost, the smartest thing to do is stay put till you're found, hollering if necessary. But to holler guarantees humiliation as well as rescue; keeping silent permits some saving of face—you can act surprised at the fuss when your rescuers find you and swear you weren't lost, if they do. What's more you might find your own way yet, *however belatedly.*

"Don't tell me your foot's still asleep!" Magda exclaimed as the three young people walked from the inlet to the area set aside for ferris wheels, carrousels, and other carnival rides, they having decided in favor of the vast and ancient merry-go-round instead of the funhouse. What a sentence, everything was wrong from the outset. People don't know what to make of him, he doesn't know what to make of himself, he's only thirteen, *athletically and socially inept,* not astonishingly bright, but there are antennae; he has . . . some sort of receivers in his head; things speak to him, he understands more than he should, the world winks at him through its objects, grabs grinning at his coat. Everybody else is in on some secret he doesn't know; they've forgotten to tell him. Through simple *procrastination* his mother put off his baptism until this year. Everyone else had it done as a baby; he'd assumed the same of himself, as had his mother, so she claimed, until it was time for him to join Grace Methodist-Protestant and the oversight came out. He was mortified, but pitched sleepless through his private catechizing, intimidated by the ancient mysteries, a thirteen year old would never say that, resolved to experience conversion like St. Augustine. When the water touched his brow and Adam's sin left him, he contrived by a strain like defecation to bring tears into his eyes—but felt nothing. There was some simple, radical difference about him; he hoped it was genius, feared it was madness, devoted himself to amiability and inconspicuousness. Alone on the seawall near his house he was seized by the terrifying transports he'd thought to find in toolshed, in Communion-cup. The grass was alive! The town, the river, himself, were not imaginary; time roared in his ears like wind; the world was *going on!* This part ought to be dramatized. The Irish author James Joyce once wrote. Ambrose M＿＿ is going to scream.

There is no *texture of rendered sensory detail,* for one thing. The faded distorting mirrors beside Fat May; the impossibility of choosing a mount when one had but a single ride on the great carrousel; the *vertigo attendant on his recognition* that Ocean City was worn out, the place of fathers and grandfathers, strawboatered men and parasoled ladies survived by their amusements. Money spent, the three paused at Peter's insistence beside Fat May to watch the girls get their skirts blown up. The object was to tease Magda, who said: "I swear, Peter M＿＿, you've got a one-track mind! Amby and me aren't *interested* in such things." In the tumbling-barrel, too, just inside the Devil's-mouth entrance to the funhouse, the girls were upended and their boyfriends and others could see up their dresses if they cared to. Which was the whole point, Ambrose realized. Of the entire funhouse! If you looked round, you noticed that almost all the people on the boardwalk were paired off into couples except the small children; in a way, that was the whole point of Ocean City! If you had X-ray eyes and could see everything going on at that instant under the boardwalk and in all the hotel rooms and cars and alleyways, you'd realize that all that normally *showed,* like restaurants and dance halls and clothing and test-your-strength machines, was merely preparation and intermission. Fat May screamed.

Because he watched the goings-on from the corner of his eye, it was Ambrose who spied the half-dollar on the boardwalk near the tumbling-barrel. Losers weepers. The first time he'd heard some people moving through a corridor not far away, just after he'd lost sight of the crack of light, he'd decided not to call to them, for fear they'd guess he was scared and poke fun; it sounded like roughnecks; he'd hoped they'd come by and he could follow in the dark without their knowing. Another time he'd heard just one person, unless he imagined it, bumping along as if on the other side of the plywood; perhaps Peter coming back for him, or Father, or Magda lost too. Or the owner and operator of the funhouse. He'd called out once, as though merrily: "Anybody know where the heck we are?" But the query was too stiff, his voice cracked, when the sounds stopped he was terrified: maybe it was a queer who waited for fellows to get lost, or a longhaired filthy monster that lived in some cranny of the funhouse. He stood rigid for hours it seemed like, scarcely respiring. His future was shockingly clear, in outline. He tried holding his breath to the point of unconsciousness. There ought to be a button you could push to end your life absolutely without pain; disappear in a flick, like turning out a light. He would push it instantly! He despised Uncle Karl. But he despised his father too, for not being what he was supposed to be. Perhaps his father hated *his* father, and so on, and his son would hate him, and so on. Instantly!

Naturally he didn't have nerve enough to ask Magda to go through the funhouse with him. With incredible nerve and to everyone's surprise he invited Magda, quietly and politely, to go through the funhouse with him. "I warn you, I've never been through it before," he added, *laughing easily;* "but I reckon we can manage somehow. The important thing to remember, after all, is that it's meant to be a *fun* house; that is, a place of amusement. If people really got lost or injured or too badly frightened in it, the owner'd go out of business. There'd even be lawsuits. No character in a work of fiction can make a speech this long without interruption or acknowledgment from the other characters."

Mother teased Uncle Karl: "Three's a crowd, I always heard." But actually Ambrose was relieved that Peter now had a quarter too. Nothing was what it looked like. Every instant, under the surface of the Atlantic Ocean, millions of living animals devoured one another. Pilots were falling in flames over Europe; women were being forcibly raped in the South Pacific. His father should have taken him aside and said: "There is a simple secret to getting through the funhouse, as simple as being first to see the Towers. Here it is. Peter does not know it; neither does your Uncle Karl. You and I are different. Not surprisingly, you've often wished you weren't. Don't think I haven't noticed how unhappy your childhood has been! But you'll understand, when I tell you, why it had to be kept secret until now. And you won't regret not being like your brother and your uncle. *On the contrary!*" If you knew all the stories behind all the people on the boardwalk, you'd see that *nothing* was what it looked like. Husbands and wives often hated each other; parents didn't necessarily love their children; et cetera. A child took things for granted because he had nothing to compare his life to and everybody acted as if things were as they should be. Therefore each saw himself as the hero of the story, when the truth might turn out to be that he's the villain, or the coward. And there wasn't one thing you could do about it!

Hunchbacks, fat ladies, fools—that no one chose what he was was unbearable. In the movies he'd meet a beautiful young girl in the funhouse; they'd have hairs-breadth escapes from real dangers; he'd do and say the right things; she also; in the end they'd be lovers; their dialogue lines would match up; he'd be perfectly at ease; she'd not only like him well enough, she'd think he was *marvelous;* she'd lie awake thinking about *him,* instead of vice versa—the way *his* face looked in different lights and how he stood and exactly what he'd said—and yet that would be only one small episode in his wonderful life, among many many others. Not a *turning point* at all. What had happened in the toolshed was nothing. He hated, he loathed his parents! One reason for not writing a lost-in-the-funhouse story is that either everybody's felt what Ambrose feels, in which case it goes without saying, or else no normal person feels such things, in which case Ambrose is a freak. "Is anything more tiresome, in fiction, than the problems of sensitive adolescents?" And it's all too long and rambling, as if the author. For all a person knows the first time through, the end could be just around any corner; perhaps, *not impossibly* it's been within reach any number of times. On the other hand he may be scarcely past the start, with everything yet to get through, an intolerable idea.

Fill in: His father's raised eyebrows when he announced his decision to do the funhouse with Magda. Ambrose understands now, but didn't then, that his father was wondering whether he knew what the funhouse was *for*—especially since he didn't object, as he should have, when Peter decided to come along too. The ticket-woman, witchlike, mortifying him when inadvertently he gave her his name-coin instead of the half-dollar, then unkindly calling Magda's attention to the birthmark on his temple: "Watch out for him, girlie, he's a marked man!" She wasn't even cruel, he understood, only vulgar and insensitive. Somewhere in the world there was a young woman with such splendid understanding that she'd see him entire, like a poem or story, and find his words so valuable after all that when he confessed his apprehensions she would explain why they were in fact the very things that made him precious to her . . . and to Western Civilization! There was no such girl, the simple truth being. Violent yawns as they approached the mouth. Whispered advice from an old-timer on a bench near the barrel: "Go crabwise and ye'll get an eyeful without upsetting!" Composure vanished at the first pitch: Peter hollered joyously, Magda tumbled, shrieked, clutched her skirt; Ambrose scrambled crabwise, tight-lipped with terror, was soon out, watched his dropped name-coin slide among the couples. Shame-faced he saw that to get through expeditiously was not the point; Peter feigned assistance in order to trip Magda up, shouted "I see Christmas!" when her legs went flying. The old man, his latest betrayer, cacked approval. A dim hall then of black-thread cobwebs and recorded gibber: he took Magda's elbow to steady her against revolving discs set in the slanted floor to throw your feet out from under, and explained to her in a calm, deep voice his theory that each phase of the funhouse was triggered either automatically, by a series of photoelectric devices, or else manually by operators stationed at peepholes. But he lost his voice thrice as the discs unbalanced him; Magda was anyhow squealing; but at one point she clutched him about the waist to keep from falling, and her right cheek pressed for a moment against his belt-buckle. Heroically he drew her up, it was his chance to clutch her close as if for support and say: "I love you." He even put an arm lightly about the small of her back before a sailor-and-girl pitched into them from behind, sorely treading his left big toe and knocking Magda asprawl with them. The sailor's girl was a string-haired hussy with a loud laugh and light blue drawers; Ambrose realized that he wouldn't have said "I love you" anyhow, and was smitten with self-contempt. How much better it would be to be that common sailor! A wiry little Seaman 3rd, the fellow squeezed a girl to each side and stumbled hilarious into the mirror room, closer to Magda in thirty seconds than Ambrose had got in thirteen years. She giggled at something the fellow said to Peter; she drew her hair from her eyes with a movement so womanly it struck Ambrose's heart; Peter's smacking her backside then seemed particularly coarse. But Magda made a pleased indignant face and cried, "All right for *you,* mister!" and pursued Peter into the maze without a backward glance. The sailor followed after, leisurely, drawing his girl against his hip; Ambrose understood not only that they were all so relieved to be rid of his burdensome company that they didn't even notice his absence, but that he himself shared their relief. Stepping from the treacherous passage at last into the mirror-maze, he saw once again, more clearly than ever, how readily he deceived himself into supposing he was a person. He even foresaw, wincing at his dreadful self-knowledge, that he would repeat the deception, at ever-rarer intervals, all his wretched life, so fearful were the alternatives. Fame, madness, suicide; perhaps all three. It's not believable that so young a boy could articulate that reflection, and in fiction the merely true must always yield to the plausible. Moreover, the symbolism is in places heavy-footed. Yet Ambrose M____ understood, as few adults do, that the famous loneliness of the great was no popular myth but a general truth—furthermore, that it was as much cause as effect.

All the preceding except the last few sentences is exposition that should've been done earlier or interspersed with the present action instead of lumped together. No reader would put up with so much with such *prolixity.* It's interesting that Ambrose's father, though presumably an intelligent man (as indicated by his role as grade-school principal), neither encouraged nor discouraged his sons at all in any way—as if he either didn't care about them or cared all right but didn't know how to act. If this fact should contribute to one of them's becoming a celebrated but wretchedly unhappy scientist, was it a good thing or not? He too might someday face the question; it would be useful to know whether it had tortured his father for years, for example, or never once crossed his mind.

In the maze two important things happened. First, our hero found a name-coin someone else had lost or discarded: *AMBROSE,* suggestive of the famous lightship[4] and of his late grandfather's favorite dessert, which his

[4] The Ambrose lightship, which protects the entrance to New York City harbor.

mother used to prepare on special occasions out of coconut, oranges, grapes, and what else. Second, as he wondered at the endless replication of his image in the mirrors, second, as he *lost himself in the reflection* that the necessity for an observer makes perfect observation impossible, better make him eighteen at least, yet that would render other things unlikely, he heard Peter and Magda chuckling somewhere together in the maze. "Here!" "No, here!" they shouted to each other; Peter said, "Where's Amby?" Magda murmured. "Amb?" Peter called. In a pleased, friendly voice. He didn't reply. The truth was, his brother was a *happy-go-lucky youngster* who'd've been better off with a regular brother of his own, but who seldom complained of his lot and was generally cordial, Ambrose's throat ached; there aren't enough different ways to say that. He stood quietly while the two young people giggled and thumped through the glittering maze, hurrah'd their discovery of its exit, cried out in joyful alarm at what next beset them. Then he set his mouth and followed after, as he supposed, took a wrong turn, strayed into the pass *wherein he lingers yet.*

The action of conventional dramatic narrative may be represented by a diagram called Freitag's Triangle:

or more accurately by a variant of that diagram:

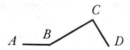

in which *AB* represents the exposition, *B* the introduction of conflict, *BC* the "rising action," complication, or development of the conflict, *C* the climax, or turn of the action, *CD* the dénouement, or resolution of the conflict. While there is no reason to regard this pattern as an absolute necessity, like many other conventions it became conventional because great numbers of people over many years learned by trial and error that it was effective; one ought not to forsake it, therefore, unless one wishes to forsake as well the effect of drama or has clear cause to feel that deliberate violation of the "normal" pattern can better can better effect that effect. This can't go on much longer; it can go on forever. He died telling stories to himself in the dark; years later, when that vast unsuspected area of the funhouse came to light, the first expedition found his skeleton in one of its labyrinthine corridors and mistook it for part of the entertainment. He died of starvation telling himself stories in the dark; but unbeknownst unbeknownst to him, an assistant operator of the funhouse, happening to overhear him, crouched just behind the plyboard partition and wrote down his every word. The operator's daughter, an exquisite young woman with a figure unusually well developed for her age, crouched just behind the partition and transcribed his every word. Though she had never laid eyes on him, she recognized that here was one of Western Culture's truly great imaginations, the eloquence of whose suffering would be an inspiration to unnumbered. And her heart was torn between her love for the misfortunate young man (yes, she loved him, though she had never laid though she knew him only—but how well! —through his words, and the deep, calm voice in which he spoke them) between her love et cetera and her womanly intuition that only in suffering and isolation could he give voice et cetera. Lone dark dying. Quietly she kissed the rough plyboard, and a tear fell upon the page. Where she had written in shorthand *Where she had written in shorthand* Where she had written in shorthand *Where she* et cetera. A long time ago we should have passed the apex of Freitag's Triangle and made brief work of the *dénouement;* the plot doesn't rise by meaningful steps but winds upon itself, digresses, retreats, hesitates, sighs, collapses, expires. The climax of the story must be its protagonist's discovery of a way to get through the funhouse. But he has found none, may have ceased to search.

What relevance does the war have to the story? Should there be fireworks outside or not?

Ambrose wandered, languished, dozed. Now and then he fell into his habit of rehearsing to himself the unadventurous story of his life, narrated from the third-person point of view, from his earliest memory parenthesis of maple leaves stirring in the summer breath of tidewater Maryland end of parenthesis to the present moment. Its principal events, on this telling, would appear to have been *A, B, C,* and *D.*

He imagined himself years hence, successful, married, at ease in the world, the trials of his adolescence far behind him. He has come to the seashore with his family for the holiday: how Ocean City has changed! But at one seldom at one ill-frequented end of the boardwalk a few derelict amusements survive from times gone by: the great carrousel from the turn of the century, with its monstrous griffins and mechanical concert band; the roller coaster rumored since 1916 to have been condemned; the mechanical shooting gallery in which only the image of our enemies changed. His own son laughs with Fat May and want; to know what a funhouse is; Ambrose hugs the sturdy lad close and smiles around his pipestem at his wife.

The family's going home. Mother sits between Father and Uncle Carl, who teases him good-naturedly who chuckles over the fact that the comrade with whom he'd fought his way shoulder to shoulder through the funhouse had turned out to be a blind Negro girl—to their mutual discomfort, as they'd opened their souls. But such are the walls of custom, which even. Whose arm is where? How must it feel. He dreams of a funhouse vaster by far than any yet constructed; but by then they may be out of fashion, like steamboats and excursion trains. Already quaint and seedy: the draperied ladies on the frieze of the carrousel are his father's father's mooncheeked dreams; if he thinks of it more he will vomit his apple-on-a-stick.

He wonders: will he become a regular person? Something has gone wrong; his vaccination didn't take; at the Boy-Scout initiation campfire he only pretended to be deeply moved, as he pretends to this hour that it is not so bad after all in the funhouse, and that he has a little limp. How long will it last? He envisions a truly astonishing funhouse, incredibly complex yet utterly controlled from a great central switchboard like the console of a pipe organ. Nobody had enough imagination. He could design such a place himself, wiring and all, and he's only thirteen years old. He would be its operator: panel lights would show what was up in every cranny of its cunning of its multifarious vastness; a switch-flick would ease this fellow's way, complicate that's, to balance things out; if anyone seemed lost or frightened, all the operator had to do was.

He wishes he had never entered the funhouse. But he has. Then he wishes he were dead. But he's not. Therefore he will construct funhouses for others and be their secret operator—though he would rather be among the lovers for whom funhouses are designed.

(1967)

Alice Munro

(b. 1 9 3 1)

Alice Munro was born and raised in Wingham, Ontario, a region of small towns and farmland that serves as the locale for much of her fiction. She attended the University of Western Ontario, in nearby London, from 1949 to 1951, then moved to British Columbia, where she lived for twenty years. Her early work was published in literary journals. Her first book, *Dance of the Happy Shades,* appeared in 1968, when Munro was 37; it won the Governor-General's award, and Munro gained immediate recognition as a major new writer. Most of Munro's stories appeared first in the *New Yorker* magazine. In 1972 Munro returned to western Ontario with her three daughters and now lives in Clinton, Ontario. Munro won a second Governor-General's award for *Who Do You Think You Are?* in 1978.

Munro often describes the subtle but devastating effects of social expectations on the lives of women in Canadian society, both rural and urban. She evokes moods and characters with great precision and control. Her sense of humor and the strength she gives her characters partly offset the lonely, alienating, and confining world in which they are often trapped. Recognized for her piercing realism and her keen understanding of human masks, Munro relates everyday dreams and dilemmas with sensitivity and compassion. She describes her subject as "the pain of human contact," the struggle of love and fear, paralysis, loss, and dependence. A regionalist writer in the best sense of that term, Munro meticulously creates the surfaces of the society her characters inhabit; she also suggests the unseen dangers and possibilities beneath that surface. Munro has remarked that, for her, writing is "more an attempt of recognition than understanding." Rarely has a writer recognized so much with such clarity. Munro is capable of moving her readers with shocks of recognition.

Munro's volumes of short fiction are *Dance of the Happy Shades* (1968), *Something I've Been Meaning to Tell You* (1974), and *The Moons of Jupiter* (1982). Two volumes include linked stories and lie somewhere between the genres of short story and novel: *Lives of Girls and Women* (1971) and *Who Do You Think You Are?* (1978).

ALICE MUNRO

Who Do You Think You Are?

THERE were some things Rose and her brother Brian could safely talk about, without running aground on principles or statements of position, and one of them was Milton Homer. They both remembered that when they had measles and there was a quarantine notice put up on the door—this was long ago, before their father died and before Brian went to school—Milton Homer came along the street and read it. They heard him coming over the bridge and as usual he was complaining loudly. His progress through town was not silent unless his mouth was full of candy; otherwise he would be yelling at dogs and bullying the trees and telephone poles, mulling over old grievances.

"And I did not and I did not and I did not!" he yelled, and hit the bridge railing.

Rose and Brian pulled back the quilt that was hung over the window to keep the light out, so they would not go blind.

"Milton Homer," said Brian appreciatively.

Milton Homer then saw the notice on the door. He turned and mounted the steps and read it. He could read. He would go along the main street reading all the signs out loud.

Rose and Brian remembered this and they agreed that it was the side door, where Flo later stuck on the glassed-in porch; before that there was only a slanting wooden platform, and they remembered Milton Homer standing on it. If the quarantine notice was there and not on the front door, which led into Flo's store, then the store must have been open; that seemed odd, and could only be explained by Flo's having bullied the Health Officer. Rose couldn't remember; she could only remember Milton Homer on the platform with his big head on one side and his fist raised to knock.

"Measles, huh?" said Milton Homer. He didn't knock, after all; he stuck his head close to the door and shouted, "Can't scare me!" Then he turned around but did not leave the yard. He walked over to the swing, sat down, took hold of the ropes and began moodily, then with mounting and ferocious glee, to give himself a ride.

"Milton Homer's on the swing, Milton Homer's on the swing!" Rose shouted. She had run from the window to the stairwell.

Flo came from wherever she was to look out the side window.

"He won't hurt it," said Flo surprisingly. Rose had thought she would chase him with the broom. Afterwards she wondered: could Flo have been frightened? Not likely. It would be a matter of Milton Homer's privileges.

"I can't sit on the seat after Milton Homer's sat on it!"

"You! You go on back to bed."

Rose went back into the dark smelly measles room and began to tell Brian a story she thought he wouldn't like.

"When you were a baby, Milton Homer came and picked you up."

"He did not."

"He came and held you and asked what your name was. I remember."

Brian went out to the stairwell.

"Did Milton Homer come and pick me up and ask what my name was? Did he? When I was a baby?"

"You tell Rose he did the same for her."

Rose knew that was likely, though she hadn't been going to mention it. She didn't really know if she remembered Milton Homer holding Brian, or had been told about it. Whenever there was a new baby in a house, in that recent past when babies were still being born at home, Milton Homer came as soon as possible and asked to see the baby, then asked its name, and delivered a set speech. The speech was to the effect that if the baby lived, it was to be hoped it would lead a Christian life, and if it died, it was to be hoped it would go straight to Heaven. The same idea as baptism, but Milton did not call on the Father or the Son or do any business with water. He did all this on his own authority. He seemed to be overcome by a stammer he did not have at other times, or else he stammered on purpose in order to give his pronouncements more weight. He opened his mouth wide and rocked back and forth, taking up each phrase with a deep grunt.

"And *if* the Baby—*if* the Baby—*if* the Baby—*lives*—"

Rose would do this years later, in her brother's living room, rocking back and forth, chanting, each *if* coming out like an explosion, leading up to the major explosion of *lives*.

"He will live a—good life—and he will—and he will—and he will—*not* sin. He will lead a *good life*—a *good life*—and he will *not sin*. He will *not sin!*"

"And if the baby—if the baby—if the baby—*dies*—"

"Now that's enough. That's enough, Rose," said Brian, but he laughed. He could put up with Rose's theatrics when they were about Hanratty.

"How can you remember?" said Brian's wife Phoebe, hoping to stop Rose before she went on too long and roused Brian's impatience. "Did you see him do it? That often?"

"Oh no," said Rose, with some surprise. "I didn't see him do it. What I saw was Ralph Gillespie *doing* Milton Homer. He was a boy in school. Ralph."

Milton Homer's other public function, as Rose and Brian remembered it, was to march in parades. There used to be plenty of parades in Hanratty. The Orange Walk, on the Twelfth of July; the High School Cadet Parade, in May; the schoolchildren's Empire Day Parade, the Legion's Church Parade, the Santa Claus Parade, the Lions Club Old-Timers' Parade. One of the most derogatory things that could be said about anyone in Hanratty was that he or she was fond of parading around, but almost every soul in town—in the town proper, not West Hanratty, that goes without saying—would get a chance to march in public in some organized and approved affair. The only thing was that you must never look as if you were enjoying it; you had to give the impression of being called forth out of preferred obscurity, ready to do your duty and gravely preoccupied with whatever notions the parade celebrated.

The Orange Walk was the most splendid of all the parades. King Billy at the head of it rode a horse as near pure white as could be found, and the Black Knights at the rear, the noblest rank of Orangemen—usually thin, and poor, and proud and fanatical old farmers—rode dark horses and wore the ancient father-to-son top hats and swallow-tail coats. The banners were all gorgeous silks and embroideries, blue and gold, orange and white, scenes of Protestant triumph, lilies and open Bibles, mottoes of godliness and honor and flaming bigotry. The ladies came beneath their sunshades, Orangemen's wives and daughters all wearing white for purity. Then the bands, the fifes and drums, and gifted step-dancers performing on a clean hay-wagon as a movable stage.

Also, there came Milton Homer. He could show up anywhere in the parade and he varied his place in it from time to time, stepping out behind King Billy or the Black Knights or the step-dancers or the shy orange-sashed children who carried the banners. Behind the Black Knights he would pull a dour face, and hold his head as if a top hat was riding on it; behind the ladies he wiggled his hips and diddled an imaginary sunshade. He was a mimic of ferocious gifts and terrible energy. He could take the step-dancers' tidy show and turn it into an idiot's prance, and still keep the beat.

The Orange Walk was his best opportunity, in parades, but he was conspicuous in all of them. Head in the air, arms whipping out, snootily in step, he marched behind the commanding officer of the Legion. On Empire Day he provided himself with a Red Ensign and a Union Jack, and kept them going like whirligigs above his head. In the Santa Claus parade he snatched candy meant for children; he did not do it for a joke.

You would think that somebody in authority in Hanratty would have put an end to this. Milton Homer's contribution to any parade was wholly negative; designed, if Milton Homer could have designed anything, just to make the parade look foolish. Why didn't the organizers and the paraders make an effort to keep him out? They must have decided that was easier said than done. Milton lived with his two old-maid aunts, his parents being dead, and nobody would have liked to ask the two old ladies to keep him home. It must have seemed as if they had enough on their hands already. How could they keep him in, once he had heard the band? They would have to lock him up, tie him down. And nobody wanted to haul him out and drag him away once things began. His protests would have ruined everything. There wasn't any doubt that he would protest. He had a strong, deep voice and he was a strong man, though not very tall. He was about the size of Napoleon. He had kicked through gates and fences when people tried to shut him out of their yards. Once he had smashed a child's wagon on the sidewalk, simply because it was in his way. Letting him participate must have seemed the best choice, under the circumstances.

Not that it was done as the best of bad choices. Nobody looked askance at Milton in a parade; everybody was used to him. Even the Commanding Officer would let himself be mocked, and the Black Knights with their old black grievances took no notice. People just said, "Oh, there's Milton," from the sidewalk. There wasn't much laughing at him, though strangers in town, city relatives invited to watch the parade, might point him out and laugh themselves silly, thinking he was there officially and for purposes of comic relief, like the clowns who were actually young businessmen, unsuccessfully turning cartwheels.

"Who is that?" the visitors said, and were answered with nonchalance and a particularly obscure sort of pride.

"That's just Milton Homer. It wouldn't be a parade without Milton Homer."

"THE village idiot," said Phoebe, trying to comprehend these things, with her inexhaustible unappreciated politeness, and both Rose and Brian said that they had never heard him described that way. They had never thought of Hanratty as a village. A village was a cluster of picturesque houses around a steepled church on a Christmas card. Villagers were the costumed chorus in the high school operetta. If it was necessary to describe Milton Homer to an outsider, people would say that he was "not all there." Rose had wondered, even at that time, what was the part that wasn't there? She still wondered. Brains, would be the easiest answer. Milton Homer must surely have had a low I.Q. Yes; but so did plenty of people, in Hanratty and out of it, and they did not distinguish themselves as he did. He could read without difficulty, as shown in the case of the quarantine sign; he knew how to count his change, as evidenced in many stories about how people had tried to cheat him. What was missing was a sense of precaution, Rose thought now. Social inhibition, though there was no such name for it at that time. Whatever it is that ordinary people lose when they are drunk, Milton Homer never had, or might have chosen not to have—and this is what interests Rose—at some point early in life. Even his expressions, his everyday looks, were those that drunks wear in theatrical extremity—goggling, leering, drooping looks that seemed boldly calculated, and at the same time helpless, involuntary; is such a thing possible?

The two ladies Milton Homer lived with were his mother's sisters. They were twins; their names were Hattie and Mattie Milton, and they were usually called Miss Hattie and Miss Mattie, perhaps to detract from any silly sound their names might have had otherwise. Milton had been named after his mother's family. That was a common practice, and there was probably no thought of linking together the names of two great poets. That coincidence was never mentioned and was perhaps not noticed. Rose did not notice it until one day in high school when the boy who sat behind her tapped her on the shoulder and showed her what he had written in his English book. He had stroked out the word *Chapman's* in the title of a poem and inked in the word *Milton,* so that the title now read: *On First Looking into Milton Homer.*

Any mention of Milton Homer was a joke, but this changed title was also a joke because it referred, rather weakly, to Milton Homer's more scandalous behavior. The story was that when he got behind somebody in a line-up at the Post Office or a movie theater, he would open his coat and present himself, then lunge and commence rubbing. Though of course he wouldn't get that far; the object of his passion would have ducked out of his way. Boys were said to dare each other to get him into position, and stay close ahead of him until the very last moment, then jump aside and reveal him in dire importunity.

It was in honor of this story—whether it was true or not, had happened once, under provocation, or kept happening all the time—that ladies crossed the street when they saw Milton coming, that children were warned to stay clear of him. *Just don't let him monkey around* was what Flo said. He was allowed into houses on those ritual occasions when there was a new baby—with hospital births getting commoner, those occasions diminished—but at other times the doors were locked against him. He would come and knock, and kick the door panels, and go away. But he was let have his way in yards, because he didn't take things, and could do so much damage if offended.

Of course, it was another story altogether when he appeared with one of his aunts. At those times he was hangdog-looking, well-behaved; his powers and his passions, whatever they were, all banked and hidden. He would be eating candy the aunt had bought him, out of a paper bag. He offered it when told to, though nobody but the most greedy person alive would touch what might have been touched by Milton Homer's fingers or blessed by his spittle. The aunts saw that he got his hair cut; they did their best to keep him presentable. They washed and ironed and mended his clothes, sent him out in his raincoat and rubbers, or knitted cap and muffler, as the weather indicated. Did they know how he conducted himself when out of their sight? They must have heard, and if they heard they must have suffered, being people of pride and Methodist morals. It was their grandfather who had started the flax mill in Hanratty and compelled all his employees to spend their Saturday nights at a Bible Class he himself conducted. The Homers, too, were decent people. Some of the Homers were supposed to be in favor of putting Milton away but the Milton ladies wouldn't do it. Nobody suggested they refused out of tender-heartedness.

"They won't put him in the Asylum, they're too proud."

Miss Hattie Milton taught at the high school. She had been teaching there longer than all the other teachers combined and was more important than the Principal. She taught English—the alteration in the poem was the more daring and satisfying because it occurred under her nose—and the thing she was famous for was keeping order. She did this without apparent effort, through the force of her large-bosomed, talcumed, spectacled, innocent and powerful presence, and her refusal to see that there was any difference between teen-agers (she did not use the word) and students in Grade Four. She assigned a lot of memory work. One day she wrote a long poem on the board and said that everyone was to copy it out, then learn it off by heart, and the next day recite it. This was when Rose was in her third or fourth year at high school and she did not believe these instructions were to be taken literally. She learned poetry with ease; it seemed reasonable to her to skip the first step. She read the poem and learned it, verse by verse, then said it over a couple of times in her head. While she was doing this Miss Hattie asked her why she wasn't copying.

Rose replied that she knew the poem already, though she was not perfectly sure that this was true.

"Do you really?" said Miss Hattie. "Stand up and face the back of the room."

Rose did so, trembling for her boast.

"Now recite the poem to the class."

Rose's confidence was not mistaken. She recited without a hitch. What did she expect to follow? Astonishment, and compliments, and unaccustomed respect?

"Well, you may know the poem," Miss Hattie said, "but that is no excuse for not doing what you were told. Sit down and write it in your book. I want you to write every line three times. If you don't get finished you can stay after four."

Rose did have to stay after four, of course, raging and writing while Miss Hattie got out her crocheting. When Rose took the copy to her desk Miss Hattie said mildly enough but with finality, "You can't go thinking you are better than other people just because you can learn poems. Who do you think you are?"

This was not the first time in her life Rose had been asked who she thought she was; in fact the question had often struck her like a monotonous gong and she paid no attention to it. But she understood, afterwards, that Miss Hattie was not a sadistic teacher; she had refrained from saying what she now said in front of the class. And she was not vindictive; she was not taking revenge because she had not believed Rose and had been proved wrong. The lesson she was trying to teach here was more important to her than any poem, and one she truly believed Rose needed. It seemed that many other people believed she needed it, too.

THE whole class was invited, at the end of the senior year, to a lantern slide show at the Miltons' house. The lantern slides were of China, where Miss Mattie, the stay-at-home twin, had been a missionary in her youth. Miss Mattie was very shy, and she stayed in the background, working the slides, while Miss Hattie commented. The lantern slides showed a yellow country, much as expected. Yellow hills and sky, yellow people, rickshaws, parasols, all dry and papery-looking, fragile, unlikely, with black zigzags where the paint had cracked, on the temples, the roads and faces. At this very time, the one and only time Rose sat in the Miltons' parlor, Mao was in power in China and the Korean War was underway, but Miss Hattie made no concessions to history, any more than she made concessions to the fact that the members of her audience were eighteen and nineteen years old.

"The Chinese are heathens," Miss Hattie said. "That is why they have beggars."

There was a beggar, kneeling in the street, arms outstretched to a rich lady in a rickshaw, who was not paying any attention to him.

"They do eat things we wouldn't touch," Miss Hattie said. Some Chinese were pictured poking sticks into bowls. "But they eat a better diet when they become Christians. The first generation of Christians is an inch and a half taller."

Christians of the first generation were standing in a row with their mouths open, possibly singing. They wore black and white clothes.

After the slides, plates of sandwiches, cookies, tarts were served. All were home-made and very good. A punch of grape juice and ginger-ale was poured into paper cups. Milton sat in a corner in his thick tweed suit, a white shirt and a tie, on which punch and crumbs had already been spilled.

"Some day it will just blow up in their faces," Flo had said darkly, meaning Milton. Could that be the reason people came, year after year, to see the lantern slides and drink the punch that all the jokes were about? To see Milton with his jowls and stomach swollen as if with bad intentions, ready to blow? All he did was stuff himself at an unbelievable rate. It seemed as if he downed date squares, hermits, Nanaimo bars and fruit drops, butter tarts and brownies, whole, the way a snake will swallow frogs. Milton was similarly distended.

METHODISTS were people whose power in Hanratty was passing, but slowly. The days of the compulsory Bible Class were over. Perhaps the Miltons didn't know that. Perhaps they knew it but put a heroic face on their decline. They behaved as if the requirements of piety hadn't changed and as if its connection with prosperity was unaltered. Their brick house, with its over-stuffed comfort, their coats with collars of snug dull fur, seemed proclaimed as a Methodist house, Methodist clothing, inelegant on purpose, heavy, satisfactory. Everything about them seemed to say that they had applied themselves to the world's work for God's sake, and God had not let them down. For God's sake the hall floor shone with wax around the runner, the lines were drawn perfectly with a straight pen in the account book, the begonias flourished, the money went into the bank.

But mistakes were made, nowadays. The mistake the Milton ladies made was in drawing up a petition to be sent to the Canadian Broadcasting Corporation, asking for the removal from the air of the programs that interfered with church-going on Sunday nights: Edgar Bergen and Charlie

McCarthy; Jack Benny; Fred Allen. They got the minister to speak about their petition in church—this was in the United Church, where Methodists had been outnumbered by Presbyterians and Congregationalists, and it was not a scene Rose witnessed, but had described to her by Flo—and afterwards they waited, Miss Hattie and Miss Mattie, one on each side of the outgoing stream, intending to deflect people and make them sign the petition, which was set up on a little table in the church vestibule. Behind the table Milton Homer was sitting. He had to be there; they never let him get out of going to church on Sunday. They had given him a job to keep him busy; he was to be in charge of the fountain pens, making sure they were full and handing them to signers.

That was the obvious part of the mistake. Milton had got the idea of drawing whiskers on himself, and had done so, without the help of a mirror. Whiskers curled out over his big sad cheeks, up towards his bloodshot foreboding eyes. He had put the pen in his mouth, too, so that ink had blotched his lips. In short, he had made himself so comical a sight that the petition which nobody really wanted could be treated as a comedy, too, and the power of the Milton sisters, the flax-mill Methodists, could be seen as a leftover dribble. People smiled and slid past; nothing could be done. Of course the Milton ladies didn't scold Milton or put on any show for the public, they just bundled him up with their petition and took him home.

"That was the end of them thinking they could run things," Flo said. It was hard to tell, as always, what particular defeat—was it that of religion or pretension?—she was so glad to see. The boy who showed Rose the poem in Miss Hattie's own English class in Hanratty high school was Ralph Gillespie, the same boy who specialized in Milton Homer imitations. As Rose remembered it, he hadn't started on the imitations at the time he showed her the poem. They came later, during the last few months he was in school. In most classes he sat ahead of Rose or behind her, due to the alphabetical closeness of their names. Beyond this alphabetical closeness they did have something like a family similarity, not in looks but in habits or tendencies. Instead of embarrassing them, as it would have done if they had really been brother and sister, this drew them together in helpful conspiracy. Both of them lost or mislaid, or never adequately provided themselves with, all the pencils, rulers, erasers, pen-nibs, ruled paper, graph paper, the compass, dividers, protractor, necessary for a successful school life; both of them were sloppy with ink, subject to spilling and blotting mishaps; both of them were negligent about doing homework but panicky about not having done it. So they did their best to help each other out, sharing whatever supplies they had, begging from their more provident neighbors, finding someone's homework to copy. They developed the comradeship of captives, of soldiers who have no heart for the campaign, wishing only to survive and avoid action.

That wasn't quite all. Their shoes and boots became well acquainted, scuffling and pushing in friendly and private encounter, sometimes resting together a moment in tentative encouragement; this mutual kindness particularly helped them through those moments when people were being se-lected to do mathematics problems on the blackboard.

Once Ralph came in after noon hour with his hair full of snow. He leaned back and shook the snow over Rose's desk, saying, "Do you have those dandruff blues?"

"No. Mine's white."

This seemed to Rose a moment of some intimacy, with its physical frank-ness, its remembered childhood joke. Another day at noon hour, before the bell rang, she came into the classroom and found him, in a ring of onlookers, doing his Milton Homer imitation. She was surprised and worried; surprised because his shyness in class had always equalled hers and had been one of the things that united them; worried that he might not be able to bring it off, might not make them laugh. But he was very good; his large, pale, good-natured face took on the lumpy desperation of Milton's his eyes gog-gled and his jowls shook and his words came out in a hoarse hypnotized singsong. He was so successful that Rose was amazed, and so was everybody else. From that time on Ralph began to do imitations; he had several, but Milton Homer was his trademark. Rose never quite got over a comradely sort of apprehension on his behalf. She had another feeling as well, not envy but a shaky sort of longing. She wanted to do the same. Not Milton Homer; she did not want to do Milton Homer. She wanted to fill up in that magical, releasing way, transform herself; she wanted the courage and the power.

Not long after he started publicly developing these talents he had, Ralph Gillespie dropped out of school. Rose missed his feet and his breathing and his finger tapping her shoulder. She met him sometimes on the street but he did not seem to be quite the same person. They never stopped to talk, just said hello and hurried past. They had been close and conspiring for years, it seemed, maintaining their spurious domesticity, but they had never talked outside of school, never gone beyond the most formal recognition of each other, and it seemed they could not, now. Rose never asked him why he had dropped out; she did not even know if he had found a job. They knew each other's necks and shoulders, heads and feet, but were not able to confront each other as full-length presences.

After a while Rose didn't see him on the street any more. She heard that he had joined the Navy. He must have been just waiting till he was old enough to do that. He had joined the Navy and gone to Halifax. The war was over, it was only the peacetime Navy. Just the same it was odd to think of Ralph Gillespie, in uniform, on the deck of a destroyer, maybe firing off guns. Rose was just beginning to understand that the boys she knew, how-ever incompetent they might seem, were going to turn into men, and be allowed to do things that you would think required a lot more talent and authority than they could have.

THERE was a time, after she gave up the store and before her arthritis became too crippling, during which Flo went out to Bingo games and sometimes played cards with her neighbors at the Legion Hall. When Rose was home on a visit conversation was difficult, so she would ask Flo about the people she saw at the Legion. She would ask for news of her own contemporaries, Horse Nicholson, Runt Chesterton, whom she could not really imagine as grown men; did Flo ever see them?

"There's one I see and he's around there all the time. Ralph Gillespie."

Rose said that she had thought Ralph Gillespie was in the Navy.

"He was too but he's back home now. He was in an accident."

"What kind of accident?"

"I don't know. It was in the Navy. He was in a Navy hospital three solid years. They had to rebuild him from scratch. He's all right now except he walks with a limp, he sort of drags the one leg."

"That's too bad."

"Well, yes. That's what I say. I don't hold any grudge against him but there's some up there at the Legion that do."

"Hold a grudge?"

"Because of the pension," said Flo, surprised and rather contemptuous of Rose for not taking into account so basic a fact of life, and so natural an attitude, in Hanratty. "They think, well, he's set for life. I say he must've suffered for it. Some people say he gets a lot but I don't believe it. He doesn't need much, he's all on his own. One thing, if he suffers pain he don't let on. Like me. I don't let on. Weep and you weep alone. He's a good darts player. He'll play anything that's going. And he can imitate people to the life."

"Does he still do Milton Homer? He used to do Milton Homer at school."

"He does him. Milton Homer. He's comical at that. He does some others too."

"Is Milton Homer still alive? Is he still marching in parades?"

"Sure he's still alive. He's quietened down a lot, though. He's out there at the County Home and you can see him on a sunny day down by the highway keeping an eye on the traffic and licking up an ice cream cone. Both the old ladies is dead."

"So he isn't in the parades any more?"

"There isn't the parades to be in. Parades have fallen off a lot. All the Orangemen are dying out and you wouldn't get the turnout, anyway, people'd rather stay home and watch their T.V."

On later visits Rose found that Flo had turned against the Legion.

"I don't want to be one of those old crackpots," she said.

"What old crackpots?"

"Sit around up there telling the same stupid yarns and drinking beer. They make me sick."

This was very much in Flo's usual pattern. People, paces, amusements, went abruptly in and out of favor. The turnabouts had become more drastic and frequent with age.

"Don't you like any of them any more? Is Ralph Gillespie still going there?"

"He still is. He likes it so well he tried to get himself a job there. He tried to get the part-time bar job. Some people say he got turned down because he already has got the pension but I think it was because of the way he carries on."

"How? Does he get drunk?"

"You couldn't tell if he was, he carries on just the same, imitating, and half the time he's imitating somebody that the newer people that's come to town, they don't know even who the person was, they just think it's Ralph being idiotic."

"Like Milton Homer?"

"That's right. How do they know it's supposed to be Milton Homer and what was Milton Homer like? They don't know. Ralph don't know when to stop. He Milton Homer'd himself right out of a job."

AFTER Rose had taken Flo to the County Home—she had not seen Milton Homer there, though she had seen other people she had long believed dead—and was staying to clean up the house and get it ready for sale, she herself was taken to the Legion by Flo's neighbors, who thought she must be lonely on a Saturday night. She did not know how to refuse, so she found herself sitting at a long table in the basement of the hall, where the bar was, just at the time the last sunlight was coming across the fields of beans and corn, across the gravel parking lot and through the high windows, staining the plywood walls. All around the walls were photographs, with names lettered by hand and taped to the frames. Rose got up to have a look at them. The Hundred and Sixth, just before embarkation, 1915. Various heroes of that war, whose names were carried on by sons and nephews, but whose existence had not been known to her before. When she came back to the table a card game had started. She wondered if it had been a disruptive thing to do, getting up to look at the pictures. Probably nobody ever looked at them; they were not for looking at; they were just there, like the plywood on the walls. Visitors, outsiders, are always looking at things, always taking an interest, asking who was this, when was that, trying to liven up the conversation. They put too much in; they want too much out. Also, it could have looked as if she was parading around the room, asking for attention.

A woman sat down and introduced herself. She was the wife of one of the men playing cards. "I've seen you on television," she said. Rose was always a bit apologetic when somebody said this; that is, she had to control what she recognized in herself as an absurd impulse to apologize. Here in Hanratty the impulse was stronger than usual. She was aware of having done things that must seem high-handed. She remembered her days as a television interviewer, her beguiling confidence and charm; here as nowhere else they must understand how that was a sham. Her acting was another matter. The things she was ashamed of were not what they must think she was ashamed of; not a flopping bare breast, but a failure she couldn't seize upon or explain.

This woman who was talking to her did not belong to Hanratty. She said she had come from Sarnia when she was married, fifteen years ago.

"I still find it hard to get used to. Frankly I do. After the city. You look better in person than you do in that series."

"I should hope so," said Rose, and told about how they made her up. People were interested in things like that and Rose was more comfortable, once the conversation got on to technical details.

"Well, here's old Ralph," the woman said. She moved over, making room for a thin, gray-haired man holding a mug of beer. This was Ralph Gillespie. If Rose had met him on the street she would not have recognized him, he would have been a stranger to her, but after she had looked at him for a moment he seemed quite unchanged to her, unchanged from himself at seventeen or fifteen, his gray hair which had been light brown still falling over his forehead, his face still pale and calm and rather large for his body, the same diffident, watchful, withholding look. But his body was thinner and his shoulders seemed to have shrunk together. He wore a short-sleeved sweater with a little collar and three ornamental buttons; it was light-blue with beige and yellow stripes. This sweater seemed to Rose to speak of aging jauntiness, a kind of petrified adolescence. She noticed that his arms were old and skinny and that his hands shook so badly that he used both of them to raise the glass of beer to his mouth.

"You're not staying around here long, are you?" said the woman who had come from Sarnia.

Rose said that she was going to Toronto tomorrow, Sunday, night.

"You must have a busy life," the woman said, with a large sigh, an honest envy that in itself would have declared out-of-town origins.

Rose was thinking that on Monday at noon she was to meet a man for lunch and to go to bed. This man was Tom Shepherd, whom she had known for a long time. At one time he had been in love with her, he had written love letters to her. The last time she had been with him, in Toronto, when they were sitting up in bed afterwards drinking gin and tonic—they always drank a good deal when they were together—Rose suddenly thought, or knew, that there was somebody now, some woman he was in love with and was courting from a distance, probably writing letters to, and that there must have been another woman he was robustly bedding, at the time he was writing letters to her. Also, and all the time, there was his wife. Rose wanted to ask him about this; the necessity, the difficulties, the satisfactions. Her interest was friendly and uncritical but she knew, she had just enough sense to know, that the question would not do.

The conversation in the Legion had turned on lottery tickets, Bingo games, winnings. The men playing cards—Flo's neighbor among them— were talking about a man who was supposed to have won ten thousand dollars, and never publicized the fact, because he had gone bankrupt a few years before and owed so many people money.

One of them said that if he had declared himself bankrupt, he didn't owe the money any more.

"Maybe he didn't owe it then," another said. "But he owes it now. The reason is, he's got it now."

This opinion was generally favored.

Rose and Ralph Gillespie looked at each other. There was the same silent joke, the same conspiracy, comfort; the same, the same.

"I hear you're quite a mimic," Rose said.

That was wrong; she shouldn't have said anything. He laughed and shook his head.

"Oh, come on. I hear you do a sensational Milton Homer."

"I don't know about that."

"Is he still around?"

"Far as I know he's out at the County Home."

"Remember Miss Hattie and Miss Mattie? They had the lantern slide show at their house."

"Sure."

"My mental picture of China is still pretty well based on those slides."

Rose went on talking like this, though she wished she could stop. She was talking in what elsewhere might have been considered an amusing, confidential, recognizably and meaninglessly flirtatious style. She did not get much response from Ralph Gillespie, though he seemed attentive, even welcoming. All the time she talked, she was wondering what he wanted her to say. He did want something. But he would not make any move to get it. Her first impression of him, as boyishly shy and ingratiating, had to change. That was his surface. Underneath he was self-sufficient, resigned to living in bafflement, perhaps proud. She wished that he would speak to her from that level, and she thought he wished it, too, but they were prevented.

But when Rose remembered this unsatisfactory conversation she seemed to recall a wave of kindness, of sympathy and forgiveness, though certainly no words of that kind had been spoken. That peculiar shame which she carried around with her seemed to have been eased. The thing she was ashamed of, in acting, was that she might have been paying attention to the wrong things, reporting antics, when there was always something further, a tone, a depth, a light, that she couldn't get and wouldn't get. And it wasn't just about acting she suspected this. Everything she had done could sometimes be seen as a mistake. She had never felt this more strongly than when she was talking to Ralph Gillespie, but when she thought about him afterwards her mistakes appeared unimportant. She was enough a child of her time to wonder if what she felt about him was simply sexual warmth, sexual curiosity; she did not think it was. There seemed to be feelings which could only be spoken of in translation; perhaps they could only be acted on in translation; not speaking of them and not acting on them is the right course to take because translation is dubious. Dangerous, as well.

For these reasons Rose did not explain anything further about Ralph Gillespie to Brian and Phoebe when she recalled Milton Homer's ceremony with babies or his expression of diabolical happiness on the swing. She did not even mention that he was dead. She knew he was dead because she still had a subscription to the Hanratty paper. Flo had given Rose a seven-year subscription on the last Christmas when she felt obliged to give Christmas presents; characteristically, Flo said that the paper was just for people to get their names in and hadn't anything in it worth reading. Usually Rose turned the pages quickly and put the paper in the firebox. But she did see the story about Ralph which was on the front page.

FORMER NAVY MAN DIES

Mr. Ralph Gillespie, Naval Petty Officer, retired, sustained fatal head injuries at the Legion Hall on Saturday night last. No other person was implicated in the fall and unfortunately several hours passed before Mr. Gillespie's body was discovered. It is thought that he mistook the basement door for the exit door and lost his balance, which was precarious due to an old injury suffered in his naval career which left him partly disabled.

The paper went on to give the names of Ralph's parents, who were apparently still alive, and of his married sister. The Legion was taking charge of the funeral services.

Rose didn't tell this to anybody, glad that there was one thing at least she wouldn't spoil by telling, though she knew it was lack of material as much as honorable restraint that kept her quiet. What could she say about herself and Ralph Gillespie, except that she felt his life, close, closer than the lives of men she'd loved, one slot over from her own?

(1978)

Mordecai Richler

(b. 1 9 3 1)

Mordecai Richler was born in Montreal in the Jewish working-class neighborhood of St. Urbain Street. He spent some time studying English at Sir George Williams College in Montreal, but dropped out to go to Europe. He spent two years there, living mainly in Paris. His first novel, *The Acrobats,* appeared in 1954, when Richler was back in Canada, working for the CBC. He moved to England, determined to make his living as a novelist. A few years later he published his first major work, *The Apprenticeship of Duddy Kravitz.* In 1972 he ended his long exile and returned to Montreal. He has won two Governor-General's awards, one for *Cocksure* and one for *St. Urbain's Horseman.*

Richler is a moralist and a satirist. In his fiction he discusses various moral options in a world with no moral norms. He satirizes the philistines of modern culture as he struggles with the ramifications of large-scale evil in the twentieth century. His exploration of the subject has been profound. Richler understands the desire of the post-Holocaust Jew to undertake heroic action to justify his survival and to purge his guilt for having survived; he also clearly sees the difficulty of such action in the modern world. He does not give in to this difficulty; instead, he acknowledges the inevitability of frustration and stresses the need to continue to strive, the need to refuse to abandon a personal mythology of unlimited potential. This facet of Richler's work is central to *St. Urbain's Horseman* and to *Joshua Then and Now;* it is present to some degree in most of his novels.

Richler's novels are *The Acrobats* (1954), *Son of a Smaller Hero* (1955), *A Choice of Enemies* (1957), *The Apprenticeship of Duddy Kravitz* (1959), *The Incomparable Atuk* (1963), *Cocksure* (1968), *St. Urbain's Horseman* (1971), and *Joshua Then and Now* (1980). Richler published a volume of autobiographical sketches, *The Street* (1969), and collections of journalism, a travel book, and a children's book.

MORDECAI RICHLER

Playing Ball on Hampstead Heath

DRIFTING through Soho one hot sticky evening in June, too early for the
theater, Jake stopped at the Nosh Bar for a sustaining salt beef sandwich.
He had only managed one squirting mouthful and a glance at the unit trust
quotations in the *Standard* (S & P Capital was steady, Pan-Australian was
down again) when he was distracted by an American couple. The bulging-
bellied man wore a seersucker suit and his wife clutched a *London A to Z* to
her bosom. The man opened a credit-card-filled wallet, briefly exposing an
international medical passport which listed his blood type, extracted a
pound note, and slapped it into the waiter's hand.

"I suppose," he said, winking, "I get twenty-four shillings change for
this?"

The waiter shot him a sour look.

"Tell your boss," the man continued, unperturbed, "that I'm a Gali-
cianer, just like him."

"Oh, Morty," his wife said, bubbling.

And the juicy salt beef on rye turned to leather in Jake's mouth. It's here
again, he realized, heart sinking—the season.

At the best of times, American and Canadian show business plenipotenti-
aries domiciled in London had many hardships to endure. The income-tax
tangle, scheming and incompetent workmen, uppity nannies, smog, choosing the right prep school for the kids, doing without real pastrami, and of
course keeping warm. But come the season, life was impossible. Come
summer, ocean liners and airplanes began to dump clamorous hordes of
relatives, friends of friends, long and better forgotten schoolmates and army
buddies, on London, thereby transmogrifying the telephone, charmingly
inefficient all winter, into an instrument of terror. Everyone who phoned,
no matter how remotely connected at home, exuded warmth and demanded
a night on the town. "Waddiya say to a pub crawl, old chap?" Or an invitation to dinner at home. "Well, Jakey, did you tell the Queen your Uncle
Moish was coming? Did she bake a cake?" You agreed, oh how many times
you agreed, the taxis were cute, the bobbies polite, and the pace slower than
New York or, in Jake's case, Montreal. "People still know how to enjoy life
here. I can see that." On the other hand, you've got to admit the bowler hats
are a scream, hotel service is from the stone ages, and the British have
snobby British accents. "Look at it this way, it isn't home."

Summer also meant, even if you had lived in London for years, though possibly paying your tax in Liechtenstein or Bermuda, being mistaken for a tourist everywhere. Suddenly truculent taxi drivers insisted on larger tips. Zoom went the price of antiques and pornography. The waiters in the Guinea were ruder and more condescending about wines, if possible. It required the sharpest of elbows to get close enough to put down a bet on the roulette table at the White Elephant. Summer was charged with menace, with *shnorrers*[1] and greenhorns from the New Country. So how sweet and soothing it was for the hard-core show biz expatriates to come together on a Sunday morning for a fun game of softball on Hampstead Heath, just as the Rajas of another dynasty had used to meet on the cricket pitch in Malabar.

Manny Gordon drove in all the way from Richmond, clapping a sporty tweed cap over his bald head and strapping himself and his starlet of the night before into his Aston-Martin at nine A.M. Bernard Levine started out from Ham Common, stowing a fielder's mitt and a thermos of martinis in the boot of his Jag, picking up Al Herman and Stan Cohen in Putney and Jimmy Grief and Myer Gross outside Mary Quant's on the King's Road. Moey Hanover had once startled the staff at the Connaught by tripping down the stairs on a Sunday morning, wearing a peak cap and a T shirt and carrying his personal Babe Ruth bat. A Bentley with driver, laid on by Columbia films, waited outside. Another Sunday Ziggy Alter had flown in from Rome, just for the tonic of a restorative nine innings. Frankie Demaine drove in from Marlow-on-Thames. Lou Caplan, Morty Calman, and Cy Levi usually brought their wives and children, while Monty Talman, ever mindful of his new twenty-one-year-old wife, always cycled to the Heath from St. John's Wood. Wearing a maroon track suit, he lapped the field eight or nine times before anyone else turned up.

Jake Hersh, a comparative novice, generally walked to the Heath from his flat in Swiss Cottage with Nancy and the kids, his tattered fielder's mitt, nappies, a baby's bottle, and three enervating bagels filled with chopped liver concealed under *The Observer* in his shopping bag.

Other players, irregulars, were drawn from the directors, actors, writers, producers, and agents who just happened to be in London working on a picture. The starting lineup on Sunday, July 25, 1965, was:

AL HERMAN'S TEAM	LOU CAPLAN'S BUNCH
Manny Gordon, ss.	Stan Cohen, 3b.
Bernard Levine, 2b.	Myer Gross, ss.
Jimmy Grief, 3b.	Frankie Demaine, lf.
Al Herman, cf.	Morty Calman, rf.
Ziggy Alter, lf.	Cy Levi, 2b.
Jack Monroe, rf.	Moey Hanover, c.
Monty Talman, 1b.	Johnny Roper, cf.

[1] Cheapskates.

Sean Fielding, c.   Jason Storm, 1b.
Alfie Roberts, p.   Lou Caplan, p.

Jake, an unusually inept player, was one of the subs. A utility fielder, he
sat on the bench with Lou Caplan's Bunch. It was a fine, all but cloudless
day, but looking around Jake anticipated friction, because some of the
players' first wives, or, as Ziggy Alter put it, the Alimony Gallery, was already
fulminating on the grass behind home plate.

First Al Herman's Team and then Lou Caplan's Bunch, both sides made
up of men mostly in their forties, trotted out, sunken bellies quaking, to take
a turn at fielding and batting practice. Last Sunday Frankie Demaine's ana-
lyst, walking the dog, had passed accidentally and lingered to watch the
game, his smile small but constant, and Frankie had gone 0 for 5; but today
Frankie looked his old lethal self. Morty Calman, on the other hand, was in
trouble. His first wife, Ethel, had come to watch and whenever Morty called
for a fly ball her sour piercing laughter cut across the field, undoing him.

Nate Sugarman, once a classy shortstop, but since his second coronary the
regular umpire, strode onto the field and called, "Play ball!"

First man up for Al Herman's Team was small, tricksy Manny Gordon, ss.
"Let's go, boychick!"

Manny, hunched catlike over the plate, was knotted with more than his
usual fill of anxiety. If he struck out, his starlet might glow for somebody
else; Lou Caplan, however, who was pitching for the first time since he had
signed his three-picture deal with 20th, would be grateful, and flattering
Lou was a good idea, especially since Manny had not been asked to direct
since *Chase. Strike one, called.*

"Atta boy, Lou. You've got a no-hitter going for you."

If, Manny thought, I hit a single I will be obliged to pass the time of day
with that stomach-turning queen, Jason Storm, 1b. *Ball one, inside.* He had
never hit a homer, so that was out, but if just this once *(Adonoi, Adonoi)* he
could manage a triple, he could have a word with—KNACK! *God damn it, it's
a hit! A double!* As the players on Al Herman's bench rose to a man, shouting
encouragement—

"Go, man! Go!"

—Manny, suffering under Lou Caplan's glare, scampered past first base
and took myopic, round-shouldered aim on second, wondering should he
say something rotten to Cy Levi, 2b., who was responsible for getting his
name on the blacklist years ago, or should he greet him warmly because after
all Cy had married Manny's first wife, the *putz,* [2] and so taken him off the
alimony hook. Decisions, decisions. Manny charged into second base, flat
feet flying, trying to catch Cy with a belt in the balls. He missed, but beat
the throw, grinned, and said, "Hi."

"You should come to visit the kid sometimes," Cy said. "He asks for you."

"I'd love to, but I'm too sensitive. If I see him I'll cry."

[2] Fool.

Bernard Levine struck out, which brought up Jimmy Grief, who was in a state. Jimmy had to hit but quickly, urgently, before bigmouth Cy Levi let it slip to Manny, who had not been invited, that the Griefs were giving a cocktail party on Friday. Jimmy swung at the first pitch, hitting it high and foul, and Moey Hanover, c., called for it and made the catch.

Which brought up big Al Herman, who homered, bringing in Manny Gordon ahead of him. Manny immediately sat down on the bench next to Grief. "Oh, Jimmy baby," he said, his smile ingenuous, "I was wondering, I mean if you and Estelle aren't busy on Friday, could you come to dinner at my place?"

"Have to check with Estelle. I'm not sure what we're doing on Friday yet."

Monty Talman scooped out the last of the Wholefood yogurt, stepped up to the plate, and immediately ground out to Gross, ss., retiring the side. Al Herman's Team, first inning: two hits, no errors, two runs.

LEADING off for Lou Caplan's Bunch, Stan Cohen singled to center and Myer Gross struck out, bringing up Frankie Demaine and sending all the outfielders back, back, back. Frankie whacked the third pitch long and high, an easy fly had Al Herman been playing him deep instead of outside right, where Manny Gordon's starlet was sprawled on the grass. Herman was the only man on either team who always played wearing shorts—shorts revealing an elastic bandage which began at his left kneecap and ran almost as low as the ankle.

"Oh, you poor darling," the starlet said, making a face at Al Herman's knee.

Herman, sucking in his stomach, replied, "Spain," as if he was tossing the girl a rare coin.

"Don't tell me. The beach at Torremolinos. Ugh!"

"No, no. The Civil War, for Christ's sake! Shrapnel. Defense of Madrid."

Demaine's fly fell for a homer, bringing in a panting Stan Cohen. Morty Calman popped to short and Cy Levi struck out, retiring the side.

Lou Caplan's Bunch, first inning: one hit, one error, two runs.

NEITHER side scored in the next two innings, which were noteworthy only because Moey Hanover's game began to deteriorate. In the second Moey muffed an easy pop fly and actually let Bernard Levine, still weak on his legs after his colonic irrigation and all but foodless week at Forest Mere Hydro, steal a base on him. The problem was Sean Fielding, the young Liverpoolnik whom Columbia had put under contract because Hy Silkin's son-in-law Jerry thought he looked like Peter O'Toole. The game had only just started when Lillian Hanover had sat down on the grass beside Fielding, which was making Moey nervy. Moey, however, had not burned his young manhood up at a yeshiva to no avail. Not only had he plundered the Old Testament for his *Bonanza* plots, but now his intensive Jewish education served him splendidly yet again. Moey remembered, *And it came to pass in the morning, that David wrote a letter to Joab, and sent it by the hand of Uriah. And he wrote in the letter, saying, Set Uriah in the forefront of the hottest battle, and retire ye from him, that he may be smitten, and die.* [3] Amen.

Lou Caplan yielded three successive hits in the third and Moey Hanover took off his catcher's mask, called for time, and strode to the mound.

"I'm all right," Caplan said. "Don't worry."

"It's not that. Tell me, love, when do you start shooting in Rome?"

"Three weeks tomorrow. You heard something bad?"

"No."

"You're a friend now. Remember. No secrets."

"I've had second thoughts about Sean Fielding. I think he's very exciting. He's got lots of appeal. Real magnetism. He'd be a natural to play Domingo."

Multicolored kites bounced in the skies over the Heath. Lovers strolled on the tow paths and locked together on the grass. Old people sat on benches sucking in the sun. Nannies passed, wheeling toddlers. The odd baffled Englishman stopped to watch the Americans at play.

"Are they air force chaps?"

"Film makers, actually. It's their version of rounders."

"Whatever is that enormous thing that woman is slicing?"

"Salami. Kosher."

"On the Heath?"

"Afraid so. One Sunday they actually set up a bloody folding table, right over there, with cold cuts and herrings and mounds of black bread and a whole bloody side of smoked salmon. *Scotch. Eight and six a quarter, don't you know?"*

"On the Heath?"

"Champagne. Mumm's. Out of paper cups. One of them had won a bloody award of some sort. *Look!"*

Alfie Roberts, the next man up, had connected on the first pitch. Only it wasn't a softball he hit, but a cherante melon, which splattered over the infield. A double, Nate Sugarman ruled.

GOING into the bottom of the fifth, Al Herman's Team led 6–3.

Cy Levi, first man up for Lou Caplan's Bunch, hit a triple, but heading for third he saw Jimmy Grief, 3b., waiting there with a mean expression on his face, and guessed that Jimmy knew Lou Caplan had hired him to rewrite Jimmy's script and so, instead of pulling up at third, Cy scooted for home and was caught in a rundown. Jimmy charged Cy, grinning, actually grinning, as he whacked the ball into his stomach, knocking him down. The two men rolled over in the dirt, where Cy managed to land Jimmy a good one in the nose with his shoe. "Sorry," he said.

Sorry? Nate Sugarman, the umpire, who had had nothing but heartache with the Jag he had bought from Cy Levi, waved him out of the game.

Which brought in Tom Hunt, a surly colored actor, to play second.

[3] II Samuel 12: 14–15

Next man up, Moey Hanover, lifted a lazy fly to left field, which Ziggy Alter trapped rolling over and over on the grass, until—just before getting up—he was in a position to peek under Natalia Calman's skirt. Something he saw there so unnerved him that he dropped the ball, turning pale and allowing Hanover to pull up safely at second.

Which brought up Johnny Roper, who crossed his eyes, dropped his bat, knocked his knees together, and did the twist, finally working a convulsed tearful Lou Caplan for a walk.

Which brought up Jason Storm to the delight of a pride of British queers who stood with their dogs on the first baseline, squealing and jumping. Jason hit a line drive to center and floated down the baseline to second, obliging the queers to move up a base.

With two out and the score tied 7–7 in the bottom of the sixth, Alfie Roberts was unwillingly retired for a new pitcher. It was Gordie Kaufman, a blacklisted writer for years, who now divided his labors between Rome and Madrid, asking $100,000 a spectacular. Gordie came in with the go-ahead run on third and Tom Hunt stepping up to the plate for the first time. Big black Tom Hunt figured that if he homered he would be put down for another buck nigger, good at games, but if he struck out, which would require rather more acting ability than was required of him on the set of *Othello X,* what then? He would enable a bunch of fat foxy Jews to feel big. Goysy. Screw them, Hunt thought.

Gordie Kaufman was perplexed, too. His stunning villa on Mallorca had ten bedrooms, his two boys were boarding at a reputable British public school, and Gordie himself was president, sole stockholder, and the only employee of a company that was merely a plaque in Liechtenstein. And yet—and yet—Gordie still subscribed to *The Nation;* and his spectaculars had content, that is to say, he filled his Roman slaves with antiapartheid dialogue and sagacious Talmudic sayings. If Hunt touches me for even a scratch single, he thought, I'll come off as a patronizing ofay. If he homers, I'm a shitty liberal. And so with the count 2 and 3 and a walk, the typical social democrat's compromise, seemingly the easiest way out for both men, Gordie, his proud Trotskyite past emerging, threw a burning fast ball right at Hunt, bouncing it off his head. Hunt threw away his bat and started for the mound, fists clenched, but not so hurried that players from both sides couldn't rush in to separate the two men, both of whom felt glowingly emancipated because they had triumphed over impersonal racial prejudice to recognize and hit each other as individuals on a fun Sunday on Hampstead Heath.

SOMETHING else of note happened in the sixth.

Going into the bottom of the inning the prime diversion had been Manny Gordon's toreador-trousered starlet. Again and again the men had meandered over, asking if she wanted to catch, a salami on an onion roll, or a drink. Then, in the bottom of the sixth, burly Alfie Roberts had been retired from the mound. He had been humiliated before his wife and children. He had been made to look a zero before hostile agents and producers and, he added to himself, dirtygoyhomosexual actors. Alfie, his last picture still riding in *Variety's* top money-making ten, walked to his Jag and returned to sit on the grass alongside the third baseline reading a book. A hardcover book. A hardcover book in a plain brown wrapper.

The word leaped from one bench to another, it electrified the field, making it spark with speculation. A hardcover book in a plain brown wrapper meant either Alfie only had an option on the property, and so it could possibly be wrested from him, or even more intriguing, the property was in the public domain. *My God, my God.* Woody Farber, the agent, strolled down the third baseline to where Alfie sat, his smile open, touchingly honest, only to have the suspicious bastard slam the book shut and sit on it. Next Phil Berger drifted over toward Alfie, forcing him to sit on the book again. Alfie slammed the book shut in Lou Caplan's face. Even Manny Gordon's starlet couldn't get anywhere.

Then, going into the crucial seventh inning, Alfie shook up the infield and was directly responsible for a failed double play, when he was seen to take out a pencil, lick it, and begin to make notes in the margin of his book. Enough is enough. Monty Talman called for time and walked over to confront Alfie. "Can't you work somewhere else?" he asked.

"Darling," Alfie said, "I didn't know you cared."

COME the crucial seventh, the Alimony Gallery grew restive and began to move in on the baselines and benches, demoralizing former husbands with their heckling. When Myer Gross, for instance, stepped up to the plate with a man on base and his teammates shouted, "Go, man. Go," one familiar grating voice floated out over the others, "Hit, Myer. Make your son proud of you just this once."

What a reproach the first wives were! How steadfast! How unchanging! Still Waiting for Lefty after all these years. Today maybe necks had gone pruney and stomachs had lowered and breasts had flattened, like yesterday's *latkas,*[4] but let no man say that these ladies had aged in spirit. Where once they had petitioned for the Scottsboro Boy, spit on their families over mixed marriages, packed their skinny scared boyfriends off to defend Madrid, split with old comrades over the Stalin-Hitler Pact, raised funds for Henry Wallace, demonstrated for the Rosenbergs, and never, never yielded to McCarthy, today they clapped hands at China Friendship Clubs, petitioned for others to Keep Hands Off Cuba and Vietnam, and made their sons chopped-egg sandwiches and sent them marching off to Aldermaston.

The sons. How well and honestly they had raised the sons. When George Gross, for instance, had returned from the hospital after his appendicitis operation and had tried, first morning home, to climb into bed with his mother, she had not rebuffed him with sweet old-fashioned lies. Instead she had said, "You must understand *why* you want to get into bed with me. It's

[4] Potato pancakes.

because you desire to make physical love to me. You wish to supplant your father.''

Davey Hanover did not have to sit through windy religious instruction at his private school. On the contrary, he had a note which entitled him to leave the classroom for the period and stand alone in the corridor, sometimes, it's true, wetting the floor. When nine-year-old Dickie Herman had put on lipstick and got into his older sister's dress for a hallowe'en party, he was told, no punches pulled, all about homosexuality. None of the children played with guns. Or watched violent shows on television. And when ten-year-old Judd Grief rebelled, he was taken to see a special screening of a concentration camp documentary so that he could understand clearly where gunplay led to.

Davey Hanover stammered. Dickie Herman suffered nightmares. Judd Grief wanted to grow up to be an SS Colonel. But all the children had been honestly brought up and knew there was no God and that all men were brothers and all wars bad.

The wives, nicely alimonied but bitterly alone, had known the early struggling years with their husbands, the rejections and the cold-water flats, but they had always remained loyal. They hadn't altered, their husbands had. Each marriage had shattered in the eye of its own self-made hurricane, but essentially the men felt, as Ziggy Alter had once put it so succinctly at the poker table, "Right, wrong, don't be *narish*, [5] it's really a question of who wants to grow old with Ana Pauker when there are so many juicy little bits we can now afford.''

So there they were, out on the grass chasing fly balls on a Sunday morning, short men, Jake thought fondly, overpaid men, tubby men, all well within the coronary and lung cancer belt, allowing themselves to look ridiculous in the hope of pleasing their new young girls. What appetites, Jake thought, what self-redeeming appetites they had. There was Ziggy Alter, who had once directed a play for the Group Theater. Here was Al Herman, who had used to throw marbles under horses' legs at demonstrations and now raced two horses of his own at Epsom. On the pitcher's mound stood Gordie Kaufman, who had once carried a banner that read *Non Passaran* [6] through the streets of Manhattan and now employed men specially to keep Spaniards off the beach at his villa on Mallorca. And sweating under a catcher's mask there was Moey Hanover, who had studied at a yeshiva, stood up to the committee, and was now on a sabbatical from Desilu.

Usually the husbands were able to avoid their used-up wives. They didn't see them in the gaming rooms at the White Elephant or in the Mirabelle or Les Ambassadeurs. But come Brecht to Shaftesbury Avenue and without looking up from the second row center they could feel them equating in their cotton bloomers in the second balcony, burning holes in their necks.

[5] Foolish.
[6] Spanish Republican battle cry during the Spanish Civil War meaning "They [the Fascists] shall not pass."

And count on them to turn up on a Sunday morning in summer on Hampstead Heath just to ruin a game of fun baseball. Even homering, as Al Herman did, was no answer.

"It's nice for him, I suppose," a voice on bench observed, "that on the playing field, with an audience, if you know what I mean, he actually appears virile."

IN the eighth inning Jack Monroe had to retire to his Mercedes-Benz for his insulin injection and Jake, until now an embarrassed sub, finally entered the game. Jake Hersh, thirty-four years old, one-time relief pitcher for Room 41, Fletcher's Field High, Montreal (1–4), trotted out to right field, mindful of his disc condition and hoping he would not be called on to make a tricksy catch. He assumed a loose-limbed stance on the grass, waving at his wife, grinning at his children, when without warning a sizzling drive came right at him. Jake, startled, did the only sensible thing; he ducked. And then outraged shouts from the bench reminded him where he was, in a softball game, that is, and he started after the ball.

"Fishfingers!"

"*Putz!*"

Runners on first and third broke for home as Jake, breathless, finally caught up with the ball. It had rolled to a stop under a bench where a nanny sat watching over an elegant perambulator. "Excuse me," Jake said.

"Americans," the nurse said.

"I'm a Canadian," Jake protested automatically, fishing the ball out from under the bench.

Three runs scored. Jake caught a glimpse of Nancy, unable to contain her laughter. The children weren't looking at him.

IN the ninth with the score tied 11–11, Sol Peters, another sub, stepped cautiously to the plate for Lou Caplan's Bunch. The go-ahead run was on second and there was only one out. Gordie Kaufman, trying to prevent a bunt, threw right at him and Sol, forgetting he was wearing contact lenses, held the bat in front of him to protect his glasses. The ball hit the bat and rebounded for a perfectly laid-down bunt.

"Run, you *shmuck.*"[7]

"Go, man."

Sol, astonished, ran, carrying the bat with him.

GOING into the bottom of the fourteenth, Al Herman's Team was leading 13–12. There were two out and a runner on third when Morty Calman stepped wearily up to the plate. If I hit, he thought, sending in the tying run, the game will go into yet another inning, and it will be too late for the pub. So Calman struck out, ending the game, and hollering, "I say, chaps, who's for a pinta?"

---

[7] Fool.

MONTY Talman phoned home.

"Who won?" his wife asked.

"We did, 13–12. But that's hardly the point. We had lots of fun."

"How many are you bringing back for lunch?"

"Eight."

"Eight?"

"I couldn't get out of inviting Johnny Roper. He knows Jack Monroe is coming."

"I see."

"A little warning. Don't, for Christ's sake, ask Cy how Marsha is. They're separating. And I'm afraid Manny Gordon is coming with a girl. I want you to be nice to her."

"Anything else?"

"If Gershon phones from Rome while the guys are there please remember I'm taking the call upstairs. And please don't start collecting glasses and emptying ashtrays at four o'clock, it's embarrassing—Bloody Jake Hersh is coming and it's just the sort of incident he'd pick on and joke about for months."

"I never—"

"All right, all right. Oh, Christ, something else. Tom Hunt is coming."

"The actor?"

"Yeah. Now listen, he's very touchy, so will you please put away Sheila's doll."

"Sheila's doll?"

"If she comes in carrying that bloody gollywog I'll die. Hide it. Burn it. Lock it up somewhere. Hunt gets script approval these days, you know."

"All right, dear."

"See you soon."

(1966)

John Updike

(b. 1 9 3 2)

John Updike was born in Shillington, Pennsylvania. His mother wrote fiction (none of it published) and his father taught school. Updike was educated at Harvard, where he was editor, writer, and illustrator for the *Harvard Lampoon,* and at the Ruskin School of Drawing and Fine Art in Oxford, England. Since 1955 he has worked for the *New Yorker* as a columnist and reviewer; he also has contributed poetry, fiction, and essays. His first book was a collection of witty lightweight verse and appeared in 1958. His first volume of fiction, a collection of *New Yorker* stories, was published in 1959. Updike has lived most of his adult life in Ipswich, Massachusetts, with his wife and four children. *Rabbit is Rich* (1981) earned Updike a Pulitzer Prize and the American Book Award.

Much of Updike's fiction has centered on small-town life in eastern United States, where he grew up. In his writing, he explores the ambitions and frustrations of that society. He is an observer of social habits and assumptions; in his own words, he seeks to be "faithful to the essential strangeness I feel in the mundane," to record the usual with great "precision and exhaustiveness." Updike's prose is always clear and energetic, albeit mannered. He has an eye for the subtle details of social change and its ramifications for personal experience. Updike's work is often clever and witty rather than sympathetic. His writing is enjoyed for its style and pacing, as well as its ability to demonstrate the strains of conflicting values in personal psychology.

Updike's fiction includes *The Poorhouse Fair* (1959), *Rabbit, Run* (1960), *Rabbit Redux* (1971), *Rabbit is Rich* (1981), *The Centaur* (1963), *Of the Farm* (1965), *Couples* (1968), *Bech: A Book* (1970), *Marry Me* (1979), and *The Witches of Eastwick* (1984). Updike has also published many volumes of short stories, five volumes of poetry, and some plays and essays.

JOHN UPDIKE

Commercial

IT comes on every night, somewhere in the eleven o'clock news. A CHILD runs down a STAIRCASE. A rotund ELDERLY WOMAN stands at the foot, picks up the CHILD, gives him a shake (friendly), and sets him down. There is MUSIC, containing the words "laughing child," "fur-lined rug," etc.

The STAIRCASE looks unexpectedly authentic, oaken and knobby and steep in the style of houses where we have childhoods. We know this STAIRCASE. Some treads creak, and at the top there is a branching many-cornered darkness wherein we are supposed to locate security and sleep. The wallpaper (baskets of flowers, at a guess, alternating with ivied medallions) would feel warm, if touched.

The CHILD darts offscreen. We have had time to register that it is a BOY, with long hair cut straight across his forehead. The camera stays with the ELDERLY WOMAN, whom by now we identify as the GRANDMOTHER. She gazes after the (supposedly) receding BOY so fondly we can imagine *"(gazes fondly)"* in the commercial's script.

The second drags; her beaming threatens to become blank. But now, with an electrifying touch of uncertainty, so that we do not know if it was the director's idea or the actress's, GRANDMOTHER slowly wags her head, as if to say, *My, oh my, what an incorrigible little rascal, what a lovable little man-child!* Her heart, we feel, so brims with love that her plump body, if a whit less healthy and compact, if a whit less compressed and contained by the demands and accoutrements of GRANDMOTHERLINESS, would burst. GRANDMOTHERLINESS massages her from all sides, like the brushes of a car wash.

And now (there is so much to see!) she relaxes her arms in front of her, the fingers of one hand gently gripping the wrist of the other. This gesture tells us that her ethnic type is Anglo-Saxon. An Italian mama, say, would have folded her arms across her bosom; and, also, wouldn't the coquetry of Mediterranean women forbid their wearing an apron out of the kitchen, beside what is clearly a front STAIRCASE? So, while still suspended high on currents of anticipation, we deduce that this is not a commercial for spaghetti.

Nor for rejuvenating skin crams or hair rinses, for the camera cuts from GRANDMOTHER to the BOY. He is hopping through a room. Not quite hopping, nor exactly skipping: a curious fey gait that bounces his cap of hair and evokes the tender dialectic of the child-director encounter. This CHILD, who, though a child actor acting the part of a child, is nevertheless also truly a

993

child, has been told to move across the fictional room in a childish way. He has obeyed, moving hobbled by self-consciousness yet with the elastic bounce that Nature has bestowed upon him and that no amount of adult direction can utterly squelch. Only time can squelch it.

We do not know how many "takes" were sifted through to get this second of movement. Though no child in reality (though billions of children have crossed millions of rooms) ever moved across a room in quite this way, an impression of CHILDHOOD pierces us. We get the message: GRANDMOTHER'S HOUSE (and the montage is so swift we cannot itemize the furniture, only concede that it appears fittingly fusty and congested) is cozy, safe—a place to be joyful in. Why? The question hangs.

We are in another room. A kitchen. A shining POT dominates the foreground. The BOY, out of focus, still bobbing in that unnatural, affecting way, enters at the background, comes forward into focus, becomes an alarmingly large face and a hand that lifts the lid of the POT. STEAM billows. The BOY blows the STEAM away, then stares at us with stagily popped eyes. Meaning? He has burned himself? There is a bad smell? The director, offscreen, has shouted at him? We do not know, and we are made additionally uncomfortable by the possibility that this is a spaghetti commercial after all.

Brief scene: GRANDMOTHER washing BOY's face. Bathroom fixtures behind. Theme of heat (cozy HOUSE, hot POT) subliminally emerges. Also: suppertime?

We do not witness supper. We are back at the STAIRCASE. New actors have arrived: a tall and vigorous YOUNG COUPLE, in stylish overcoats. Who? We scarcely have time to ask. The BOY leaps (flies, indeed; we do not see his feet launch him) upward into the arms of the MAN. These are his PARENTS. We ourselves, watching, welcome them; the depth of our welcome reveals to us a dread within ourselves, of something morbid and claustral in the old HOUSE, with its cunningly underlined snugness and its lonely household of benevolent crone and pampered, stagy brat. These other two radiate the brisk air of outdoors. To judge from their clothes, it is cold outside; this impression is not insignificant; our sense of subliminal coherence swells. We join in the BUSTLE of WELCOME, rejoicing with the YOUNG COUPLE in their sexual energy and safe return and great good fortune to be American and modern and solvent and fertile and to have such a picture-book GRANDMOTHER to babysit for them whenever they partake of some innocent infrequent SPREE.

But whose mother is GRANDMOTHER, the FATHER's or the MOTHER's?

All questions are answered. The actor playing the YOUNG FATHER ignores GRANDMOTHER with the insouciance of blood kinship, while the actress playing the YOUNG MOTHER hugs her, pulls back, reconsiders, then dips forward to bestow upon the beaming plump cheek a kiss GRANDMOTHER does not, evidently, expect. Her beaming wavers momentarily, like a candle flame when a distant door is opened. The DAUGHTER-IN-LAW again pulls back, as if coolly to contemplate the product of her affectionate inspiration. Whether her tense string of hesitations was spun artfully by an actress fulfilling a role or was visited upon the actress as she searched her role for nuances (we can imagine how vague the script might be: *Parents return. Greetings all around. Camera medium tight*), a ticklish closeness of maneuver, and towering outcroppings of good will, has been conveyed. The FAMILY is complete.

And now the underlying marvel is made manifest. The true HERO of the these thirty seconds unmasks. The FAMILY fades into a blue cartoon flame, and the MUSIC, no longer buried by visual stimuli, sings with clarion brilliance, "NATURAL GAS is a Beauti-ful Thing!"

A MAN, discovered in BED, beside his WIFE, suffers the remainder of the NEWS, then rises and turns off the TELEVISION SET. The screen palely exudes its last quanta of daily radiation. The room by default fills with the dim light of the MOON. Risen, the MAN, shuffling around the BED with a wary gait suggestive of inelasticity and an insincerely willed silence, makes his way into the bathroom, where he urinates. He does this, we sense, not from any urgent physical need but conscientiously, even Puritanically, from a basis of theory, to clear himself and his conscience for sleep.

His thoughts show, in vivid montage. As always when hovering above the dim oval of porcelain, he recalls the most intense vision of beauty his forty years have granted him. It was after a lunch in New York. The luncheon had been gay, prolonged, overstimulating, vinous. Now he was in a taxi, heading up the West Side Highway. At the 57th Street turnoff, the need to urinate was a feathery subliminal thought; by the Seventies (where Riverside Drive begins to rise like an airplane), it was a real pressure; by the Nineties (Soldiers' and Sailors' Monument crumbling, Riverside Park a green cliff looming), it had become a murderous imperative. Mastering shame, the MAN confessed his agony to the DRIVER, who, gradually suspending disbelief, swung off the highway at 158th Street and climbed a little cobblestone mountain and found there, evidently not for the first time, a dirty triangular garage. Mechanics, black or blackened, stared with white eyes as the strange MAN stumbled past them, back through the oily and junk-lined triangle to the apex: here, pinched between obscene frescoes, sat the most beautiful thing he ever saw. Or would ever see. It was a TOILET BOWL, a TOILET BOWL in its flawed whiteness, its partial wateriness, its total receptiveness: in the harmonious miracle of its infrangible and unvariable *ens*. The beautiful is, precisely, what you need at the time.

Quick cameo mug shots of Plato, Aquinas, Santayana, and other theorists of beauty, X'ed in rough strokes to indicate refutation.

Brief scene: MAN brushing teeth, rinsing mouth, spitting.

Cut to MOON, impassive.

Return to MAN. He stands before the bathroom cabinet, puzzling. He opens the door, which is also a mirror. Zoom to tiny red BOX. What is in the BOX? Something, we sense, that he resists because it does not conform to his ideal conception of healthy normality. He closes the door.

He sniffs. As he has been standing puzzling, the odor of his own body has risen to him, a potato-ish reproachful odor. When he was a child living, like the CHILD in the commercial, with adults, he imagined that adults emitted this odor on purpose, to chasten and discipline him. Now that it is his own odor, it does not seem chastening but merely nagging, like the pile of SLIT ENVELOPES that clutter the kitchen table every afternoon. Quick still of ENVELOPES. Reply of CHILD running down STAIRCASE to awaiting arms. We are, subliminally, affected.

Shuffling (in case he stubs his toe or steps on a pin), the MAN returns from the bathroom and proceeds around the BED. The TELEVISION SET is cold now. The MOON is cold, too. As if easing a read letter back into a slit envelope, he eases himself back into BED beside his WIFE. He sneaks his hand under her nightie and rubs her back; it is a ritual question. In ritual answer, the WIFE stirs in her sleep, awakens enough to realize that the room is cold, presses her body tight against that of the MAN, and falls again asleep. Asleep again. Again again. Asleep.

Now his half of the BED has been reduced to a third—a third, furthermore, crimped and indented by oblivious elbows and knees. The MAN's eyes close but his EARS open wide, terrible eyes from which lids have been scissored, vast deep wells hungry for the whispers and crackles of the WORLD. He buries his EARS alternately in the pillow, but cannot staunch both at once. He thinks of masturbating, but decides there is not enough room.

A radiator whistles: steam heat, oil-fired. Would natural gas be noiseless? A far car whirs. Surf, or wind, murmurs; or can it be a helicopter?

Now the CAT—a new actor!—mews a foot below the MAN's face. Svelte and insistent, the CAT wants to go out. The MAN, almost gratefully, rises. Better action than nothing, he thinks—in this a typical citizen of our fagged era. The CAT's whiskers, electric, shivering, tingle like frost on the MAN's bare ankles.

Together MAN and CAT go down a STAIRCASE. No oaken knobs here. The style is bare, modern. The MAN touches the wall: chill plaster.

The MAN opens the front door. GRASS, TREES, SKY, and STARS, abruptly framed, look colorless and flat as if, thus surprised, they had barely had time to get their outlines together. The STARS, especially, appear perfunctory: bullet holes in a hangar roof. The CAT darts offscreen.

We are back in the BED. The MAN turns the pillow over, to explore with his cheek its dark side. Delicately, yet borrowing insistent from the CAT's example, he pushes his WIFE's body toward her side of the BED, inch by inert inch. Minutes of patient nudging are undone when, surfacing toward consciousness, she slumps more confidingly into him. Does she wake, or sleep? Is her reclamation of two-thirds of the BED an instinctive territorial assertion of her insensate body, or is it the product, cerebral enough, of a calculation scribbled on the wavering marital ground between them? Here the MAN, our inadequate HERO, seems to arrive at one of those fumbling-points that usefully distract the brain with the motions of thinking while the body falls into thoughtless bliss. Hopeful pits and bubbles and soft, stretching aches develop within him, forerunners of merciful dissolution.

Abrupt cut. within a child's room, the HAMSTER, yielding to some sudden fantasy of speed and space, accelerates within his unoiled running-wheel. The clatter is epic; the HAMSTER twirls the world on a string.

We are back in the bathroom. The MAN imagines he must urinate again. The shadowy porcelain oval again reminds him of absolute beauty. A forlorn sense of surrender suffices the aroma of overripe potatoes. He is removing the little red BOX from the cabinet whose door is a mirror. He takes two small objects from this BOX. Zoom. They are little balls of WAX. Why? What on EARTH?

Back in the bedroom. The MOON in the window has shrunk in size. In contracting, it has gained heat; its pallor looks hot, almost solar.

The MAN inserts himself back into the BED. He inserts the wax EAR PLUGS into his ears. The sharp bright wires of noise etched on darkness dull down into gray threads, an indistinct blanket. He grows aware, sensate, of the tangible blanket, as a source of goodness, a SKY tangent to him. His WIFE mysteriously, voluntarily shifts her weight toward the wide horizon where all pressures meet in a dull wedge. A subterranean whistling noise dawns upon him as the sound of his own breathing. He has buried himself, his *ens.* The cave of his skull furs with nonsense. *Pan, fade, dissolve.* That is how it happens every night.

One question remains. What is being advertised?

(1) Ear plugs (2) Natural gas (3) Lucifer's fall (4) Nothing.

(1979)

Rudy Wiebe

(b. 1 9 3 4)

Rudy Wiebe was born on his family's farm in a tiny Mennonite village in northern Saskatchewan. His parents emigrated from the Soviet Union in 1930 and Wiebe grew up in a mixed ethnic environment where Low German was the primary language. He began to write when he was a student at the University of Alberta, where he received a B.A. in 1956 and an M.A. in 1960. He also studied for a year at Tübingen, in West Germany. In the early 1960s Wiebe taught at the Mennonite Brethren Bible College, edited the *Mennonite Brethren Herald,* published his first novel, *Peace Shall Destroy Many* (1962), and taught English at Goshen College, Indiana. Since 1967 he has been on the faculty of the University of Alberta, in Edmonton. Wiebe won the 1973 Governor-General's award for fiction for *The Temptations of Big Bear.*

Wiebe's fiction is, in many ways, symbolic of Canadian culture: it is epic in scope, yet concerned with a minority people, a fragment, and their struggle to integrate without losing their identity. His work has a moral vision inherited from the past, which must be translated—with struggles and doubts—into the terms of the modern world. Novels such as *The Temptations of Big Bear* and *The Scorched-Wood People* are experimental in their technique. They are both founded upon a Christian vision of radical unity. In the North American native peoples, Wiebe has found a parallel for the ambiguous situation of the Mennonite community in the contemporary world. Both groups are in danger of being polluted by middle-class values that erode their traditional distinctiveness; as functioning if diseased communities, both are better than no community at all. The depth of Wiebe's sensitivity, the ambitious scope of his fiction, and his ability to fuse history and myth make him one of the most interesting writers working today.

Wiebe's novels are *Peace Shall Destroy Many* (1962), *First and Vital Candle* (1966), *The Blue Mountains of China* (1970), *The Temptations of Big Bear* (1973), *The Scorched-Wood People* (1977), and *My Lovely Enemy* (1983). Wiebe's short stories are collected in *Where Is the Voice Coming From?* (1974).

RUDY WIEBE

Where Is the Voice Coming From?

THE problem is to make the story.

One difficulty of this making may have been excellently stated by Teilhard de Chardin: "We are continually inclined to isolate ourselves from the things and events which surround us . . . as though we were spectators, not elements, in what goes on." Arnold Toynbee does venture, "For all that we know, Reality is the undifferentiated unity of the mystical experience," but that need not here be considered. This story ended long ago; it is one of finite acts, of orders, of elemental feelings and reactions, of obvious legal restrictions and requirements.

Presumably all the parts of the story are themselves available. A difficulty is that they are, as always, available only in bits and pieces. Though the acts themselves seem quite clear, some written reports of the acts contradict each other. As if these acts were, at one time, too well known; as if the original nodule of each particular fact had from somewhere received non-factual accretions; or even more, as if, since the basic facts were so clear perhaps there were a larger number of facts than any one reporter, or several, or even any reporter had ever attempted to record. About facts that are still simply told by this mouth to that ear, of course, even less can be expected.

An affair seventy-five years old should acquire some of the shiny transparency of an old man's skin. It should.

Sometimes it would seem that it would be enough—perhaps more than enough—to hear the names only. The grandfather One Arrow; the mother Spotted Calf; the father Sounding Sky; the wife (wives rather, but only one of them seems to have a name, though their fathers are Napaise, Kapahoo, Old Dust, The Rump)—the one wife named, of all things, Pale Face; the cousin Going-Up-To-Sky; the brother-in-law (again, of all things) Dublin. The names of the police sound very much alike; they all begin with Constable or Corporal or Sergeant, but here and there an Inspector, then a Superintendent and eventually all the resonance of an Assistant Commissioner echoes down. More. Herself: Victoria, by the Grace of God etc., etc., QUEEN, defender of the Faith, etc., etc.; and witness "Our Right Trusty and Right Well-beloved Cousin and Councillor the Right Honorable Sir John Campbell Hamilton-Gordon, Earl of Aberdeen; Viscount Formartine, Baron Haddo, Methlic, Tarves and Kellie, in the Peerage of Scotland; Viscount Gordon of Aberdeen, County of Aberdeen, in the Peerage of the United Kingdom; Baronet of Nova Scotia, Knight Grand Cross of Our Most Distinguished Order of Saint Michael and Saint George, etc., Governor General of Canada." And of course himself: in the award proclamation named "Jean-Baptiste" but otherwise known only as Almighty Voice.

But hearing cannot be enough; not even hearing all the thunder of A Proclamation: "Now Hear Ye that a reward of FIVE HUNDRED DOLLARS will be paid to any person or persons who will give such information as will lead . . . (etc., etc.) this Twentieth day of April, in the year of Our Lord one thousand eight hundred and ninety-six, and the Fifty-ninth year of Our Reign . . ." etc. and etc.

Such hearing cannot be enough. The first item to be seen is the piece of white bone. It is almost triangular, slightly convex—concave actually as it is positioned at this moment with its corners slightly raised—graduating from perhaps a strong eighth to a weak quarter of an inch in thickness, its scattered pore structure varying between larger and smaller on its perhaps polished, certainly shiny surface. Precision is difficult since the glass showcase is at least thirteen inches deep and therefore an eye cannot be brought as close as the minute inspection of such a small, though certainly quite adequate, sample of skull would normally require. Also, because of the position it cannot be determined whether the several hairs, well over a foot long, are still in some manner attached or not.

The seven-pounder cannon can be seen standing almost shyly between the showcase and the interior wall. Officially it is known as a gun, not a cannon, and clearly its bore is not large enough to admit a large man's fist. Even if it can be believed that this gun was used in the 1885 Rebellion[1] and that on the evening of Saturday, May 29, 1897 (while the nine-pounder, now unidentified, was in the process of arriving with the police on the special train from Regina), seven shells (all that were available in Prince Albert at that time) from it were sent shrieking into the poplar bluffs as night fell, clearly such shelling could not and would not disembowel the whole earth. Its carriage is now nicely lacquered, the perhaps oak spokes of its petite wheels (little higher than a knee) have been recently scrapped, puttied and varnished; the brilliant burnish of its brass breeching testifies with what meticulous care charmen and women have used nationally-advertised cleaners and restorers.

Though it can also be seen, even a careless glance reveals that the same concern has not been expended on the one (of two) .44 calibre 1866 model Winchesters apparently found at the last in the pit with Almighty Voice. It also is preserved in a glass case; the number 1536735 is still, though barely, distinguishable on the brass cartridge section just below the brass saddle ring. However, perhaps because the case was imperfectly sealed at one time (though sealed enough not to warrant disturbance now), or because of simple neglect, the rifle is obviously spotted here and there with blotches of rust and the brass itself reveals discolorations almost like mildew. The rifle bore, the three long strands of hair themselves, actually bristle with

---

[1] A revolt of the Métis under the leadership of Louis Riel (1844–85) which was crushed after heavy fighting.

clots of dust. It may be that this museum cannot afford to be as concerned as the other; conversely, the disfiguration may be something inherent in the items themselves.

The small building which was the police guardroom at Duck Lake, Saskatchewan Territory, in 1895 may also be seen. It had subsequently been moved from its original place and used to house small animals, chickens perhaps, or pigs—such as a woman might be expected to have under her responsibility. It is, of course, now perfectly empty, and clean so that the public may enter with no more discomfort than a bend under the doorway and a heavy encounter with disinfectant. The door-jamb has obviously been replaced; the bar network at one window is, however, said to be original; smooth still, very smooth. The logs inside have been smeared again and again with whitewash, perhaps paint, to an insistent point of identity-defying characterlessness. Within the small rectangular box of these logs not a sound can be heard from the streets of the, probably dead, town.

> *Hey Injun you'll get hung for stealing that steer*
> *Hey Injun for killing that government cow you'll get three*
> *weeks on the woodpile Hey Injun*

The place named Kinistino seems to have disappeared from the map but the Minnechinass Hills have not. Whether they have ever been on a map is doubtful but they will, of course, not disappear from the landscape as long as the grass grows and the rivers run. Contrary to general report and belief, the Canadian prairies are rarely, if ever, flat and the Minnechinass (spelled five different ways and translated sometimes as "The Outside Hill," sometimes as "Beautiful Bare Hills") are dissimilar from any other of the numberless hills that everywhere block out the prairie horizon. They are bare; poplars lie tattered along their tops, almost black against the straw-pale grass and sharp green against the grey soil of the plowing laid in half-mile rectangular blocks upon their western slopes. Poles holding various wires stick out of the fields, back down the bend of the valley; what was once a farmhouse is weathering into the cultivated earth. The poplar bluff where Almighty Voice made his stand has, of course, disappeared.

The policemen he shot and killed (not the ones he wounded, of course) are easily located. Six miles east, thirty-nine miles north in Prince Alberta, the English Cemetery. Sergeant Colin Campbell Colebrook, North West Mounted Police Registration Number 605, lies presumably under a gravestone there. His name is seventeenth in a very long "list of non-commissioned officers and men who have died in the service since the inception of the force." The date is October 29, 1895, and the cause of death is anonymous: "Shot by escaping Indian prisoner near Prince Albert." At the foot of this grave are two others: Constable John R. Kerr, No. 3040, and Corporal C.H.S. Hockin, No. 3106. Their cause of death on May 28, 1897 is even more anonymous, but the place is relatively precise: "Shot by Indians at Min-etch-inass Hills, Prince Albert District."

The gravestone, if he has one, of the fourth man Almighty Voice killed is more difficult to locate. Mr. Ernest Grundy, postmaster at Duck Lake in 1897, apparently shut his window the afternoon of Friday, May 28, armed himself, rode east twenty miles, participated in the second charge into the bluff at about 6:30 p.m., and on the third sweep of that charge was shot dead at the edge of the pit. It would seem that he thereby contributed substantially not only to the Indians' bullet supply, but his clothing warmed them as well.

The burial place of Dublin and Going-Up-To-Sky is unknown, as is the grave of Almighty Voice. It is said that a Métis named Henry Smith lifted the latter's body from the pit in the bluff and gave it to Spotted Calf. The place of burial is not, of course, of ultimate significance. A gravestone is always less evidence than a triangular piece of skull, provided it is large enough.

Whatever further evidence there is to be gathered may rest on pictures. There are, presumably, almost numberless pictures of the policemen in the case, but the only one with direct bearing is one of Sergeant Colebrook who apparently insisted on advancing to complete an arrest after being warned three times that if he took another step he would be shot. The picture must have been taken before the joined the force; it reveals him a large-eared young man, hair brush-cut and ascot tie, his eyelids slightly drooping, almost hooded under thick brows. Unfortunately a picture of Constable R. C. Dickson, into whose charge Almighty Voice was apparently committed in that guardroom and who after Colebrook's death was convicted of negligence, sentenced to two months hard labour and discharged, does not seem to be available.

There are no pictures to be found of either Dublin (killed early by rifle fire) or Going-Up-To-Sky (killed in the pit), the two teenage boys who gave their ultimate fealty to Almighty Voice. There is, however, one said to be of Almighty Voice, Junior. He may have been born to Pale Face during the year, two hundred and twenty-one days that his father was a fugitive. In the picture he is kneeling before what could be a tent, he wears stripped denim overalls and displays twin babies whose sex cannot be determined from the double-laced dark bonnets they wear. In the supposed picture of Spotted Calf and Sounding Sky, Sounding Sky stands slightly before his wife; he wears a white shirt and a stripped blanket folded over his left shoulder in such a manner that the arm in which he cradles a long rifle cannot be seen. His head is thrown back; the rim of his hat appears as a black half-moon above eyes that are pressed shut in, as it were, profound concentration; above a mouth clenched thin in a downward curve. Spotted Calf wears a long dress, a sweater which could also be a man's dress coat, and a large fringed and embroidered shawl which would appear distinctly Dukhobour in origin if the scroll patterns on it were more irregular. Her head is small and turned slightly towards her husband so as to reveal her right ear. There is what can only be called a quizzical expression on her crumpled face; it may be she does not understand what is happening and that she would have asked a question, perhaps of her husband, perhaps of the photographers, perhaps even of anyone, anywhere in the world if such questioning were possible for an Indian lady.

There is one final picture. That is one of Almighty Voice himself. At least it is purported to be of Almighty Voice himself. In the Royal Canadian Mounted Police Museum on the Barracks Grounds just off Dewdney Avenue in Regina, Saskatchewan, it lies in the same showcase, as a matter of fact immediately beside, that triangular piece of skull. Both are unequivocally labelled, and it must be assumed that a police force with a world-wide reputation would not label *such* evidence incorrectly. But here emerges an ultimate problem in making the story.

There are two official descriptions of Almighty Voice. The first reads: "Height about five feet, ten inches, slight build, rather good looking, a sharp hooked nose with a remarkably flat point. Has a bullet scar on the left side of his face about 1 1/2 inches long running from near corner of mouth towards ear. The scar cannot be noticed when his face is painted but otherwise is plain. Skin fair for an Indian." The second description is on the Award Proclamation: "About twenty-two years old, five feet ten inches in height, weight about eleven stone, slightly erect, neat small feet and hands; complexion inclined to be fair, wavy dark hair to shoulders, large dark eyes, broad forehead, sharp features and parrot nose with flat tip, scar on left cheek running from mouth towards ear, feminine appearance."

So run the descriptions that were, presumably, to identify a well known fugitive in so precise a manner that an informant could collect five hundred dollars—a considerable sum when a police constable earned between one and two dollars a day. The nexus of the problems appears when these supposed official descriptions are compared to the supposed official picture. The man in the picture is standing on a small rug. The fingers of his left hand touch a curved Victorian settee, behind him a photographer's backdrop of scrolled patterns merges to vaguely paradisiacal trees and perhaps a sky. The moccasins he wears make it impossible to deduce whether his feet are "neat small." He may be five feet, ten inches tall, may weigh eleven stone, he certainly is "rather good looking" and, though it is a frontal view, it may be that the point of his long and flaring nose could be "remarkably flat." The photograph is slightly over-illuminated and so the unpainted complexion could be "inclined to be fair"; however, nothing can be seen of a scar, the hair is not wavy and shoulder-length but hangs almost to the waist in two thick straight braids worked through with beads, fur, ribbons and cords. The right hand that holds the corner of the blanket-like coat in position is large and, even in the high illumination, heavily veined. The neck is concealed under coiled beads and the forehead seems more low than "broad."

Perhaps, somehow, these picture details could be reconciled with the official description if the face as a whole were not so devastating.

On a cloth-backed sheet two feet by two and one-half feet in size, under the Great Seal of the Lion and the Unicorn, dignified by the names of the

Deputy of the Minister of Justice, the Secretary of State, the Queen herself and all the heaped detail of her "Right Trusty and Right Well Beloved Cousin," this description concludes: "feminine appearance." But the pictures: any face of history, any believed face that the world acknowledges as *man*—Socrates, Jesus, Attila, Genghis Khan, Mahatma Gandhi, Joseph Stalin —no believed face is more *man* than this face. The mouth, the nose, the clenched brows, the eyes—the eyes are large, yes, and dark, but even in this watered-down reproduction of unending reproductions of that original, a steady look into those eyes cannot be endured. It is a face like an axe.

IT IS now evident that the de Chardin statement quoted at the beginning has relevance only as it proves itself inadequate to explain what has happened. At the same time, the inadequacy of Aristotle's much more famous statement becomes evident: "The true difference [between the historian and the poet] is that one relates what *has* happened, the other what *may* happen." These statements cannot explain the storyteller's activity since, despite the most rigid application of impersonal investigation, the elements of the story have now run me aground. If ever I could, I can no longer pretend to objective, omnipotent disinterestedness. I am no longer *spectator* of what *has* happened or what *may* happen: I am become *element* in what is happening at this very moment.

For it is, of course, I myself who cannot endure the shadows on that paper which are those eyes. It is I who stand beside this broken veranda post where two corner shingles have been torn away, where barbed wire tangles the dead weeds on the edge of this field. The bluff that sheltered Almighty Voice and his two friends has not disappeared from the slope of the Minnechinass, no more than the sound of Constable Dickson's voice in that guardhouse is silent. The sound of his speaking is there even if it has never been recorded in an official report:

> *hey injun you'll get*
> *hung*
> *for stealing that steer*
> *hey injun for killing that government*
> *cow you'll get three*
> *weeks on the woodpile hey injun*

The unknown contradictory words about an unprovable act that move a boy to defiance, an implacable Cree warrior long after the three-hundred-and-fifty-year war is ended, a war already lost the day the Cree watch Cartier hoist his gun ashore at Hochelaga and they begin the long retreat west; these words of incomprehension, of threatened incomprehensible law are there to be heard just as the unmoving tableau of the three-day siege is there to be seen on the slopes of the Minnechinass. Sounding Sky is somewhere not there, under arrest, but Spotted Calf stands on a shoulder of the Hills a little to the left, her arms upraised to the setting sun. Her mouth is open.

A horse rears, riderless, above the scrub willow at the edge of the bluff, smoke puffs, screams tangle in rifle barrage, there are wounds, somewhere. The bluff is so green this spring, it will not burn and the ragged line of seven police and two civilians is staggering through, faces twisted in rage, terror, and rifles sputter. Nothing moves. There is no sound of frogs in the night; twenty-seven policeman and five civilians stand in cordon at thirty-yard intervals and a body also lies in the shelter of a gully. Only a voice rises from the bluff:

> *We have fought well*
> *You have died like braves*
> *I have worked hard and am hungry*
> *Give me food*

but nothing moves. The bluff lies, a bright green island on the grassy slope surrounded by men hunched forward rigid over their long rifles, men clumped out of rifle-range, thirty-five men dressed as for fall hunting on a sharp spring day, a small gun positioned on a ridge above. A crow is falling out of the sky into the bluff, its feathers sprayed as by an explosion. The first gun and the second gun are in position, the beginning and end of the bristling surround of thirty-five Prince Albert Volunteers, thirteen civilians and fifty-six policemen in position relative to the bluff and relative to the unnumbered whites astride their horses, standing up in their carts, staring and pointing across the valley, in position relative to the bluff and the unnumbered Indians squatting silent along the higher ridges of the Hills, motionless mounds, faceless against the Sunday morning sunlight edging between and over them down along the tree tips, down into the shadows of the bluff. Nothing moves. Beside the second gun the red-coated officer has flung a handful of grass into the motionless air, almost to the rim of the red sun.

And there is a voice. It is an incredible voice that rises from among the young poplars ripped of their spring bark, from among the dead somewhere lying there, out of the arm-deep pit shorter than a man; a voice rises over the exploding smoke and thunder of guns that reel back in their positions, worked over, serviced by the grimed motionless men in bright coats and glinting buttons, a voice so high and clear, so unbelievably high and strong in its unending wordless cry.

The voice of "Gitchie-Manitou Wayo"—interpreted as "voice of the Great Spirit"—that is, The Almighty Voice. His death chant no less incredible in its beauty than in its incomprehensible happiness.

I say "wordless cry" because that is the way it sounds to me. I could be more accurate if I had a reliable interpreter who would make a reliable interpretation. For I do not, of course, understand the Cree myself.

(1974)

Audrey Thomas

(b. 1 9 3 5)

Audrey Thomas was born in Binghamton, New York, and studied at Smith College and at St. Andrew's University in Scotland. She taught in England for a year before moving to Canada in 1959, where she received an M.A. and began a Ph.D. at the University of British Columbia. Many of her short stories are set in Ghana, where she and her husband lived in the mid-1960s. She returned to Vancouver in 1970 and had three daughters. After the breakdown of her marriage, in 1972, Thomas moved to Galiano Island, off the British Columbia coast. Her first volume of stories, *Ten Green Bottles,* was published in 1967.

In her short fiction, for which she is best known, Thomas is an energetic and original manipulator of narrative conventions and techniques. Her stories are narrated by a succession of voices, often a female persona at various stages of psychic development. Thomas also exploits the resources of postmodernist attitudes toward language: She indulges in etymological puns, multiple references of a given word, and extensive allusion, and she uses some of the spatial and typographical techniques associated with concrete poetry. Her themes include the painful edge of disintegration and the resulting pain, destructive sexuality, violence, and depression. Her fiction describes a cauldron of unsatisfactory human relationships, which often include a domineering and stereotypical male partner. The bleak psychic landscape of much of her fiction is a powerful evocation of the world of women who feel powerless, voiceless, fragmentary, and ridden by guilt in a society that is in many ways structured to frustrate their attempts to find wholeness.

Thomas's works of fiction are *Ten Green Bottles* (1967), *Mrs. Blood* (1970), *Munchmeyer and Prospero on the Island* (1971), *Songs My Mother Taught Me* (1973), *Blown Figures* (1974), *Ladies and Escorts* (1977), *Latakia* (1979), *Real Mothers* (1981), *Intertidal Lives* (1984), and *Goodbye Harold, Good Luck* (1986).

AUDREY THOMAS

Natural History

SOMETHING had run over her hand. Now she was wide awake and sitting up, the sleeping bag flung off, her heart pounding. What? The rat? No, don't be foolish—a mouse maybe, a vole, perhaps just the cat's tail swishing, as she came back to see if they were still persisting in this out-of-doors foolishness when there were all those comfortable beds and cushions inside. Clytie tried to get the cat to lie down at their feet, but it walked away.

"She probably thinks we're nuts," the mother said.

"Maybe she'll jump in the bathroom window and wait for us to come whining and begging to be let in."

"And she'll say, 'Well, my dears, now you know what it feels like when *I* want in'."

The cat was old, but very independent, except for wanting to sleep inside at night. They often spoke for her, having endowed her with the personality of a querulous, but rather imperious, old woman.

"Maybe she'll do us the favour of catching that rat," she added.

"You *know* that she won't," the child said. "She's afraid."

"She's not afraid; she's lazy."

But something would have to be done. No mouse could have gnawed a hole like that, right through the outside of the cottage and into the cupboard, under the sink, where the compost bucket was kept. A hole the size of a man's fist. They never saw the rat, but they heard it when they were lying in bed in the other room; and last night, it was on the roof, or rather, *in* the roof, directly over their heads. A determined *chewing* sound. They both woke up.

"I hope that it electrocutes itself on a wire."

"Do they really eat people?"

"No. Some of those old tales from Europe were probably based on fact. Maybe in times of famine—or when it was very cold. Maybe then. But these rats come off the fishboats; they're not starving. Rats are just big mice; there's no real biological difference." So she spoke to reassure her daughter, but nevertheless, they lay awake in the big double bed, holding hands, not liking the idea of a long, narrow, whiskered face suddenly appearing through the ceiling. Something would have to be done. She thought of rabies; she even thought of the plague. This morning, she had gone down to the store to see if they carried rat poison.

"Not any more," the storekeeper said. "We used to, but they won't let us any more. . . . Because we sell food," he added. "In case something spilled, I guess."

So, they'd have to take a trip to town and find a drugstore. Would they look at her strangely? She thought of Emma Bovary asking for arsenic. She said that she wanted to kill some rats that were keeping her awake. Cramming it into her mouth. Ugh. She would see if it were possible to get enough for only one rat. She came back up the path discouraged. She didn't want to go anywhere. She just wanted to stay here with her child and complete her recovery. Nice word that, re-cover. To cover yourself over again, something essential having been ripped away, like a deep rip in the upholstery. Then there had been the visitors to think about.

They were not sleeping outside because of the rat, but in spite of it. They were sleeping outside because of the full moon. They had talked about the moon for days. If it were fine ("And when wasn't it fine, over here, in July?" they asked each other), they would sleep out and watch the moon rise. And so, after supper, they carried out pillows and sleeping bags, a thermos of coffee and some cookies, in case they woke up early in the morning; and they made themselves a nest under the apple trees. The apples were still small and green, hardly distinguishable from the leaves. They were winter apples. There was a woven hammock that had been slung between two of the trees. She had rigged up a rope, thrown it over a stout branch and tied it, at the other end of the hammock, to a discarded wooden toy, so that one could lie in the hammock and reach up and gently rock oneself.

"The ultimate in laziness," she said. They took turns lying in the hammock, reading, the other one stretched out on an old blanket nearby.

But the moon had taken so long, so long that, first, the little girl had given a great sigh and turned over, backed up into the warmth of her mother, with her face away from the moon's rising, and slept; and then, the mother, too, slept.

But the mother was now wide awake, with the moon, high and white; and the moonlight falling over on the far side, hitting a white shed that lay beyond the house. Was it moving away from them or towards them? she wondered. Old wives' tales came back to her, about not letting the moonlight strike your face—and the memory of the blind girl that they had met that day, with her round, vacant, staring eyes. Ugh. Too many morbid thoughts.

She got up quietly and walked away a little bit to pee, squatting in the long grass. She had borrowed a scythe from a neighbour up the road, a real old-fashioned scythe, with a long wooden handle and a curved, vicious blade, and had found that, once she got the hang of it, she liked the rhythm of the thing, walking forward, moving her hips just so or the blade wouldn't cut clean, it simply hacked or flattened out the grass; but when they went to pick up the grass, they found that it was still fastened to the earth. She hadn't come around to this side yet with the scythe—perhaps tomorrow. The night was utterly still; even the owl, which they heard so often, but had never seen, was silent. And there was no breeze, except that, every so often, a ripple would pass through the firs, the alders, the pear tree and the apple trees which almost surrounded the house. It was as though the night itself were an animal, a huge dark cat which twitched and quivered from time to time in its sleep.

"I should sell this place by moonlight," she thought. "Then no one would notice the peeling paint or the cracked windowpanes or the impossible angle of the chimney."

"Describe this house," the blind girl had said, eagerly. "What does it look like?"

"It looks like a witch's house," Clytie said, without hesitation, "like something that a witch might live in." She was showing off—they had been reading Grimm's fairytales—but still, her mother was hurt.

"It's very beautiful," the blind girl's companion said. "The wall that you are leaning against is a lovely mustard-yellow and the couch that we are sitting on is purple."

"What sort of purple?"

"Very nearly the purple of that shawl you bought in Guadalajara."

So, she hadn't been blind long. Not long ago, she had seen and bought a purple shawl in a Mexican market. The girl—a young woman really—was terribly overweight and that, too, seemed recent. There was something about the way that she moved her body, or moved *in* her body, like a child all bundled up. Diabetes. Lifting the teapot, the mother's hand turned cold. The blindness, as well as the fatness, were merely signs that things inside had got out of control. What was the word? She had heard it often enough. "Stabilize." They hadn't, yet, been able to "stabilize" the disease. A seeing-eye dog, a magnificent golden Labrador, lay at the blind girl's feet. A plate of cookies was offered. They had been mixed and baked deliberately for their variety of texture: oatmeal cookies, chocolate chip, hermits. "If I'd only known," she thought. But it was interesting. Once again, the blind girl asked for visual description before she made her choice; indeed, she hardly touched the cookies at all.

Clytie watched every move, fascinated. The girl told them that she was writing poems. "Trying to get some of my anger out," she said with a little laugh. Perhaps she wanted to be asked to recite.

"We're sleeping outside tonight," Clytie said, "under the moon." The girl laughed again, the laugh too small for her large, awkward body. "Be careful not to look at a reflection of the moon in water," she said. "It's very dangerous to do that."

"Why?"

"I think that you're supposed to go mad."

Another old wives' tale.

And there was the moon now—silent, indifferent, unaware of all the myths and tales and proverbs which she had inspired! Words too, like lunatic, moony. The other day, she said to her daughter, "Stop mooning around and *do* something." As though the moon were aimless or haphazard when, in reality, she was so predictable, so orderly, that her passages could be predicted with extreme accuracy. "July 19th: Perigee moon occurs only six hours before full moon." Growing, brightening, reaching fullness; waning, dimming, beginning the whole thing over again. The old triple moon goddess, corresponding to the three phases of woman. Her little girl, Clytie, named not for the moon, but after the sunflower, was very orderly. She had drawn up a schedule at the beginning of the summer and taped it to the refrigerator door. They were going to have to work hard in the garden, yes. They were also going to have periods when each would wish to be alone, agreed; when one or the other would go out to the old shed and work on some private thing. They were going to start a study of intertidal creatures; they were going to paint the kitchen; they were going to learn the names of the constellations. There it all was, on the refrigerator door, all worked out—a calendar of orderly and edifying progression through the long summer, decorated in the corners with orange suns and purple starfish.

And there it remained, because things hadn't quite worked out like that. For one thing, it had been very hot; for another, they both seemed to have been overtaken with a kind of lethargy: the child, probably because she was growing so fast; the mother, perhaps because she was unwilling to really "come to" and think about the future.

They had worked hard during the winter, getting up at 6 a.m. and lighting fires, leaving time for a good breakfast before the yellow school bus came. And they went to bed early as well. If someone rang after 9 p.m., one or the other had to crawl out of bed in the dark to answer the phone.

She was writing a book and she worked all day while her daughter was away at school. She sat next to the wood stove, the cat asleep on a chair beside her. The simple life: it was what she craved and what she needed. On weekends, they did the wash in the old wringer-washer, shoving the clothes through the wringer with a wooden spoon; they baked bread and cookies, stacked wood, read books and listened to the radio.

"It seems so peaceful here!" the blind girl cried, as they sat in the front room, sipping tea and nibbling cookies. "It must be paradise to be here all year round."

Paradise: "a walled garden, an enclosure." Disaster: "a turning away from the stars."

The blind girl was from Los Angeles. Her companion, older, rather stern-faced until she smiled, was the of one of the earliest families on the island. "She wants so much to meet you," the woman said on the phone. "I have been reading your poems to her. It would mean a great deal to her."

She did not want to meet anyone, especially anyone who had suffered, who was perhaps suffering still, but she could think of no graceful way to get out of it. It hadn't been too bad, really. She wondered and worried about her daughter's reaction, but the child seemed more interested than alarmed.

"9 a.m.: exercises, bike-riding," the schedule announced, as they sat at the kitchen table in their nightgowns, eating scones and strawberry jam. "Two hours a day, intertidal life," it called down to them from where they dozed on the rocks, the green notebook—they were still on seaweed—neglected at the bottom of the towel. They painted each other's toes and fingernails impossible colours, and waved their hands and feet in the air to dry. They timed each other to see who could stay the longest in the icy water. The yellow paint for the kitchen remained in the shed while they lay on the hammock and the blanket and read *The Wind in the Willows* out loud.

"You can't help liking Toad," Clytie said. "I know that I shouldn't like him, but I do."

Strange little creatures done up in leggings and waistcoats, thinking our kinds of thoughts and feeling our emotions. "The English were particularly good at that," she thought. "And look at me, pretending the cat will pass moral judgment on our sleeping arrangements, and feeling that, any second now, I'll see her up in a tree, grinning."

But the rat was real. The rat would have to be dealt with. "The cat takes the rat," she thought, "but maybe only in the rhyme."

Sometimes, they drove down to the other end of the island to a sandy beach where the water was warmer, and they spent the afternoon and early evening there. Last week, there had been several young women sitting on the beach with their babies and watching their older children swim. She got into a discussion with a woman that she knew slightly, whom she hadn't seen in months. The woman was very beautiful, with curly dark hair and long dancer's legs. It turned out that her husband had left her and the children to go and live with a younger woman. "I'm better now," she said, "but I spent a month thinking up ways to kill him—to kill them both. Really."

"I believe you," she said. "Last winter, I chopped kindling every day. It wasn't kindling, of course, it was hands and fingers and lips; ears, eyes, private parts. Everything chopped up small and thrown into the stove. We were as warm as toast."

"I'm glad to hear somebody else admit to such feelings," the other woman said, laughing.

"What are all those operas about, those myths, those 'crimes of passion'? We just aren't open about it in these northern climates."

"He says that he can do so much for her," the other woman said.

(And the moon up there, female, shining always by reflected light, dependent on the sun, yet so much brighter, seemingly, against the darkness of the sky; so much more mysterious, changing her shape, controlling the waters, gathering it all in her net.)

It was dark when they drove back up the island and the eyes of the deer glowed yellow-gold in the headlights. Once or twice, they saw a raccoon with eyes like emeralds.

"Why don't our eyes do that at night?"

"I don't understand it completely," she said. "It's because those animals go out at night. They have something like a mirror, maybe like your bike reflector, at the back of the eye. This gives them a second chance to use whatever light there is. It hits the mirror and bounces back again. Then, what's left over shines out. 'Wasted light,' I think it's called. Your grandfather taught me all that stuff. He knew all about it, but he wasn't very good at explaining it, or at least not to me. Maybe he was just tired or maybe I wasn't very good at listening. I can still remember him trying to explain about the sun and moon, one Saturday morning, when I was about your age. I don't think that I *asked* him; I think that he just wanted to explain it! He had an orange, a grapefruit, a flashlight and a pencil. He stuck a pencil through the grapefruit for the earth on its axis, but I got terribly lost. I stood on one foot and then the other, and finally, I asked if I could go out and play. I think that he was terribly hurt."

The blind girl told stories about her dog. She made everything gay and light and witty. Once, she and another blind friend had taken their dogs into a posh Los Angeles restaurant. "It's against the law to keep us out," she explained. It was the friend's birthday, so they saved up their money to go out together and celebrate. The waiter was very helpful and they ordered a fancy meal. Their dogs lay quiet and well-behaved beneath the table. Everybody felt good.

"Then, Samson sort of sat up—I could feel him. He gave a sigh and did a huge shit, right by my chair. It was *so* awful. We could hear the people who were nearest to us, saying, 'Well, *really,*' and similar things. The smell was very powerful and we got hysterical. We were laughing our heads off at the whole idea. We could sort of 'feel' the maître d' hovering nearby, uncertain whether or not to kick these gross blind people out and maybe face some sort of lawsuit, or lose all his patrons; or just try to ignore the whole thing, pick up the poop and carry on."

"What happened?" At the mention of his name, the dog sat up, wagging his tail, as though he, too, were enjoying the story.

"Well, I carefully lowered my big, beautiful, starched dinner napkin, over where I thought the pile was—I didn't actually want to get my fingers in it—and then I called out: '*Waiter, waiter.* I'm afraid my dog has had a little accident.'"

"But we never went back there," she added when they stopped laughing. "Never."

"I would not have offered cookies," she thought, "if I had known. I would not have *tempted* her, especially with homemade cookies, offered by the young girl who had home-made them." The man who tried to teach her about the motions of the sun and moon and earth on its axis had been a diabetic too, or had become one, only much later in life than their visitor. He could not give up all the sweet rich foods that he loved. He was dead now; he did not even know that she had a child. "Just this once," he used to say, as he put sugar on his grapefruit, or ordered a dish of chocolate ice-cream. And her mother, joining in, would say, "Oh, it won't hurt him, just this once." He had been quite short-sighted and the thing that made her realize how dead he was, was, after the funeral, finding his bifocals in a drawer. How many cookies had the blind girl eaten? She couldn't remember.

"I don't really feel lonely any more," she said to her friend on the beach. "I used to. I used to think that I'd die from loneliness, as if it were a disease. I suppose that I'll want to be with someone again, but right now, I'm content. Only, some days—when the fucking clothesline breaks or I'm down to the wet wood, things like that—I wish that there were someone around. But then, I ask myself, 'Is it a husband that I want or a hired hand'?"

"A hired hand might be useful for other things as well."

"Or a hired finger." They giggled.

(He would have dealt with this rat, for instance. He would have got rid of it quick.)

One night, the cat caught a mouse and started munching it in the darkness of the room where she and Clytie were sleeping.

"Really," she said, waking up and recognizing what was going on.

And Clytie, laughing, got up in her long white nightdress and threw the cat outside.

She wasn't the least afraid of that. But she was terrified to be alone in the dark, as her mother had been terrified when she was a child, as perhaps all children were terrified of the dark. Which is why she sat here, now, wide awake and thoughtful, her half of the sleeping bag over her knees, rather than inside the house, sipping a cup of tea and reading until she became sleepy again.

They had done away with mousetraps because they couldn't stand that awful, final "click."

"Ugh," the child said, crawling back in bed, "that crunching sound was really *disgusting.*" And they both began to laugh.

"Shall we make her a mouse pie the next time she does that?"

"Would you? Would you really?"

"Why not?"

"It might smell terrible."

"Would you really make a mouse pie with a crust, like in *The Pie and the Pattypan?*"

"Oh God, I don't know. . . . Probably not."

They caught a rock cod near the government wharf and when they cleaned it and removed the stomach, there were three small crabs inside.

"I suppose that they have some sort of acid in their stomachs which dissolves the shell," she said.

"I guess everything just goes around eating everything else," her child said.

"Sometimes it seems that way."

The blind girl turned her head towards whomever was speaking; she turned towards the sound. The sunflower, Clytie, following her beloved Apollo as he crossed the sky. The moon, shining always with reflected light.

"Where are all the strong men," the woman on the beach said, "now that there are all these strong women?"

("I'm getting awfully symbolic out here, wide awake beneath the moon."

The absolute trust of her sleeping child moved her almost to tears. She would sit here all night, if necessary; it didn't matter.)

"I can't stay on this island forever," she thought. "I will end up like an old witch in a witch's cottage. I've got to give my life some serious attention. It's all very well to sit around reading fairytales and making a game of everything." She glanced at her daughter's long hair which was spread out on the pillow beside her. *"She'll* change; maybe she'll change first. She'll want more than this." Her namesake, turned into a sunflower, gazing blindly towards the sun. The moon (female), shining always by his light.

("Let her be strong," she thought. "Let her be strong and yet still loving." A few years ago, in the city, she had come home from school and announced, at dinner, that a policeman had come to the school and given a talk about "strangers." Her mother and father glanced quickly at one another. A little girl, her lunchbox beside her, had been found dead in a ditch.

"And what are strangers?" asked her father gently, curious as to what she had been told, yet wanting to keep the story light.

The child's reply was very serious.

"Strangers are usually men.")

"DIS-ASTER," they read in the dictionary: "a falling away from the stars." "Paradise," from the Persian: "a walled garden." *"Lunaticus"* f. L., "affected by the moon." And who had first made *that* connection? Galileo. He built his "optik glasse" and discovered that the moon (female, shining always with reflected light) was not the "luminous orb" of the poets, but rather, full of "vast protuberances, deep chasms and sinuosities."

Later, in England, men looked at a flea through a microscope and saw "the devil shut up in a glasse." Mankind was always wanting more, wanting to make far things nearer, small things larger; to know and understand it all. When the Americans stepped on the moon, one of her friends had written a long mock-heroic poem called "The Rape of Cynthia."

The trick was, of course, to try and get the right distance on everything; to stand in just the right relationship to it all. But how? Would her daughter be any better at it than she was? Another image came to mind, out of her childhood, a stereopticon belonging to her grandfather. She would sit with it, on a Sunday afternoon, sliding the crossbar up and down, until suddenly, "click," the two photographs taken at slightly different angles (St. Mark's, the Tower of London, Notre Dame) would become one picture, which would take on depth and a wonderful illusion of solidity. *That* was the trick. To slide it all—moon, blind girl, rat, the apple tree, her father's fingers tilting the pencil, her own solitude, the cat, the eyes of the deer, her daughter, this still moment, back/forth, back/forth, back/forth, until "click,"

until "click,"

until "click"—

there it was: wholeness, harmony, radiance; all of it making a wonderful kind of sense, as she sat there under the apple tree, beneath the moon.

And then, suddenly, because she *did* see, if only for an instant, she bent down and she shielded the child's body as the moonlight, finally, reached them.

"WHAT amazes me," Clytie said, just before she turned over and went to sleep, "is that we're just part of a system. We're all just floating around."

(1981)

John Metcalf

(b. 1 9 3 8)

John Metcalf was born in Carlisle, England, and educated at the University
of Bristol, where he received his B.A. in 1960 and a certificate of education
in 1961. He emigrated to Canada in 1962, where he taught high school in
Montreal and Alberta in the 1960s. In 1969 he took a post at Loyola College
in Montreal and published some stories in *New Canadian Writing, 1969.* In
1970 Metcalf's first collection of fiction was published; *The Lady Who Sold
Furniture* established him as one of Canada's finest short-story writers. Since
1971 Metcalf has taught and served as writer-in-residence at Concordia
University, the University of Ottawa, and the University of New Brunswick.

Metcalf writes finely honed, traditional short stories that often have sudden, vividly macabre shadows. He is an energetic and sometimes harsh critic
of the complacencies and incompetence of the Canadian literary establishment. As an anthologist, he co-edited the *Best Canadian Stories* series from
1977 to 1982 and is now co-editing *The New Press Anthology.* Metcalf's disci-
plined prose focuses on the immediate physical details of setting and event
and evokes the sights, sounds, smells, and textures that make his stories fully
imagined experiences for the reader. Many of the stories have a dark, even
grotesque, side to them, belying the apparently smooth surface of Metcalf's
fiction and, by implication, the smooth surfaces we lacquer onto our day-to-
day lives. Metcalf is also a novelist; his most successful novel is the witty but
black satire *General Ludd.*

Metcalf's short-story collections are *The Lady Who sold Furniture* (1970),
The Teeth of My Father (1975), and *Selected Stories* (1982). His novels are *Going
Down Slow* (1972) and *General Ludd* (1980). *Girl in Gingham* (1978) includes
two novellas. *Kicking Against the Pricks,* a collection of essays, appeared in
1982.

JOHN METCALF

Keys and Watercress

DAVID, with great concentration, worked the tip of his thumbnail under the fat scab on his knee. He carefully lifted the edges of the scab enjoying the tingling sensation as it tore free. His rod was propped against his other leg and he could just see the red blur of his float from the corner of his eye. He started to probe the centre of the crust.

"Had any luck?" a voice behind him said suddenly.

Startled, his thumbnail jumped, ripping the scab away. A bright bead of blood welled into the pit. The sun, breaking from behind the clouds, swept the meadow into a brighter green and made the bead of blood glisten like the bezel of a ring.

"Had any luck?" the old man said again. David twisted round to look at him. He wasn't in uniform and he wasn't wearing a badge and anyway he was far too old to be a bailiff. Unless he was a Club Member—and they could report you too. And break your fishing rod.

David glanced down the river towards the bridge and the forbidding white sign. "I'm only fishing for eels," he said. "With a seahook."

"Slippery fellows, eels," said the old man. "Difficult to catch."

"I haven't caught any yet," said David, hoping the old man wouldn't notice the grey eel-slime on the bank and the smeared fishing-bag.

The old man started to sit down. Wheezing harshly with the effort, he lowered himself until he was kneeling, and then, supporting himself on his hands, laboriously stretched out each leg like a dying insect in a jam jar. His anguished breathing eased slowly away into a throaty mutter. David felt more confident because he knew he could run nearly to the bridge by the time the old man had struggled to his feet.

Taking a blue silk handkerchief from the top pocket of his linen jacket, the old man dabbed at his forehead. "My word, yes!" he said. "Extremely slippery fellows." He took off his straw hat and rubbed his bald head with the blue handkerchief.

"They're a nuisance," said David. "The Club Members don't like catching them."

"And why is that?"

"Because they swallow the hook right down and you can't get it out," said David.

"You've hurt your knee," said the old man. The bead of blood had grown too large and toppled over, trickling down his knee to run into the top of his stocking.

"Oh, that's nothing," said David. "Only a scab."

"Yes," said the old man reflectively, "it's a pleasant day. A beautiful sky—beautiful afternoon clouds."

They sat silently staring across the flow of the river. Near the far bank in the shallows under the elderberry bushes the huge roach and chub basked in the sunshine, rising every now and then to nose soft circles in the water.

"Do you know the name of clouds like those?" asked the old man suddenly. "The *proper* name, I mean."

"No," said David.

"Well, the correct name is cumulus. Cumulus. You say it yourself."

"Cumulus," said David.

"Good! You won't forget, will you? Promise me you won't forget." There was a silence while the old man put on his spectacles from a tin case. Then, taking a fountain pen and a small black book from his inside pocket, he said, "But boys forget things. It's no use denying it—boys forget. So I'm going to write it down." He tore a page from the notebook and printed on it *"Cumulus* (clouds)."

As David tucked the paper into his shirt-pocket, he looked across at the old man who was staring into the water, a vague and absent look in his eyes. David watched him for a moment and then turned back to his float watching the current break and flow past it in a constant flurry. He tried to follow the invisible nylon line down into the depths where it ended in a ledger-weight and a turning, twisting worm.

"Every evening," said the old man, speaking slowly and more to himself than David, "when the light begins to fail, the cattle come down here to drink. Just as the night closes in."

"They've trampled the bank down further up-stream," said David.

"And I watch them coming across the fields," said the old man as though he hadn't heard. "I see them from my window."

The old man's voice died away into silence but suddenly, without warning, he belched loudly—long, rumbling, unforced belches of which he seemed quite unaware. David looked away. To cover his embarrassment, he started reeling in his line to check the bait and the clack of the ratchet seemed to arouse the old man. He groped inside his jacket and pulled out a large flat watch. With a click the lid sprang open. "Have you ever seen such a watch before?" he asked. "Such a beautiful watch?" He held it out on the palm of his hand.

"Do you know what watches like these are called?"

"No," said David. "I've never seen one before."

"They're called Hunters. And numbers like these are called roman numerals."

As the old man counted off the numbers on the watch-face, David stared at the old man's hand. The mottled flesh was puffy and gorged with fat blue veins which stood beneath the skin. He tried to take the watch without touching the hand which held it.

"What time does the watch say?" asked the old man.

"Half-past four," said David.

"Well then, it's time we had our tea," said the old man. "And you shall come and have tea with me."

"Thank you," said David, "but I've got to go home."

"But tea's prepared," said the old man and as he spoke he started to struggle to his feet. "Tea's prepared. In the house across the bridge—in the house with the big garden."

"But I really have to go," said David. "My mother'll be angry if I'm late."

"Nonsense!" said the old man loudly. "Quite untrue."

"Really. I do have to. . . ."

"We won't be long," said the old man. "You like my watch, don't you? You *do* like my watch."

"Oh, yes."

"Well, there you are then. What more proof do you need? *And,*" said the old man, "I have many treasures in my house." He stared at David angrily. "You would be a rude boy to refuse."

"Well . . . ," said David. "I really mustn't be long."

"Do you go to school?" the old man asked suddenly.

"Parkview Junior," said David.

"Yes," said the old man. "I went to school when I was a boy."

As David was sliding the rod-sections into the cloth case, the old man gripped his arm and said, "You may keep the watch in your pocket until we reach the bridge. Or you could hold it in your hand. Whichever you like." Then stopping David again he said, "And such a watch is called a . . . ?"

"A Hunter," said David.

The old man relaxed his hold on David's arm and said, "Excellent! Quite excellent! Always be attentive. Always accumulate *facts.*" He seemed very pleased and as they walked slowly along the river-path towards the bridge made little chuckling sounds inside his throat.

His breath labouring again after the incline from the bridge, the old man rested for a few moments with his hand on the garden gate. Then, pushing the gate open, he said, "Come along, boy. Come along. Raspberry canes everywhere, just as I told you."

David followed the old man along the path and into the cool hall. His eyes were bewildered at first after the strong sunlight, and he stumbled against the dark shape of the hall-stand.

"Just leave your things here," said the old man, "and we'll go straight in to tea."

David dropped his fishing-bag behind the door and stood his rod in the umbrella-stand. The old man went ahead down the passage and ushered him into the sitting room.

The room was long and, in spite of the French windows at the far end, rather dark. It was stuffy and smelled like his grandma.

In the centre of the room stood a table covered with green baize, but tea was laid out on a small cardtable at the far end of the room in front of the French windows.

Bookshelves lined the walls and books ran from ceiling to floor. The floor too was covered with piles of books and papers; old books with leather covers, musty and smelling of damp and dust, and perilous stacks of yellow *National Geographic* magazines.

A vast mirror, the biggest he'd ever seen, bigger even than the one in the barber's, stood above the fireplace, carved and golden with golden statues on each side.

David stared and stared about him, but his eyes kept returning to the lion which stood in front of the fireplace.

"Do you like it?" asked the old man. "It's stuffed."

"Oh, yes!" exclaimed David. "Can I touch it?"

"I've often wondered," said the old man, "if it's in good taste."

"Where did it come from?"

"Oh, Africa. Undoubtedly Africa. They all do, you know."

"I think it's terrific," said David.

"You may stay here, then, and I will go and put the kettle on," said the old man. As soon as the door had closed, David went and stuck his hand into the lion's snarling mouth and stroked the dusty orbs of its eyes with his fingertips. When he heard the old man's footsteps shuffling back down the passage, he moved away from the lion and pretended to be looking at a book.

"Do you take sugar?" asked the old man as they sat down at the cardtable in front of the French windows.

"No thank you," said David. "Just milk."

"No? Most interesting! *Most* interesting. In my experience, boys like sweet things. A deplorable taste, of course. Youth and inexperience."

He passed the teacup across the table and said sternly, "The palate must be educated." David didn't know what to say and because the old man was staring at him looked away and moved the teaspoon in his saucer. Putting down the silver teapot, the old man wrote in his notebook. "The love of sweetness is an uneducated love." Handing the note across the table he said, "Facts, eh? *Facts.*" He chuckled again inside his throat.

"And now," he continued—but then broke off again as he saw David staring out of the window into the orchard. "If you're quite ready? We have brown bread. Wholemeal. Thin-cut. And with Cornish butter." He ticked off each point on his fingers. "To be eaten with fresh watercress. Do you think that will please you?"

"Very nice, thank you," said David politely.

"But it's not simply a matter of taste, you see," said the old man fixing David with his eye. He shook his head slowly.

"Not simple at all."

"What isn't?" asked David.

"Not at all simple. Taste, yes, I grant you," said the old man, "but what about texture? Umm? Umm? What about vision?"

"What isn't simple?" David asked again.

The old man clicked his tongue in annoyance and said, "Come along, boy!" He glared across the table. "Your attention is lax. Always be attentive." He leaned across the cardtable and held up his finger. "Observe!" he said. "Observe the tablecloth. Cotton? Dear me, no! Irish linen. And *this.*" His fingertips rubbed slowly over the facets of the bowl. "Waterford glass —brilliant. Can you see the colours? The green of the cress and the drops of water like diamonds? Brilliant. A question of the lead-content, you see. You *do* see, don't you. You do understand what I'm telling you."

"Well . . . please," said David, "what's a texture?"

And once again the old man took out his notebook and his fountain pen.

When tea was finished, the old man wiped his lips with a linen napkin and said eagerly, "Well? Do you think you're ready? Shall you see them?"

"Please," said David, "I'd like to very much."

The old man pulled on the thick, tasselled rope which hung by the side of the window and slowly closed the red velvet curtains. "We don't want to be overlooked," he whispered.

"But there's no one there," said David. The old man was excitedly brushing the green baize and didn't seem to hear. With the red curtains closed, the room smelled even more stuffy, hot and stifling, as if the air itself were thick and red. And in the warm gloom the lion lost its colour and turned into a dark shape, a pinpoint of light glinting off its dusty eye. As David crossed over to the table he saw himself moving in the mysterious depths of the mirror.

"Come along, boy!" said the old man impatiently. "We'll start with the yellow box. There. Under the table."

The old man lifted the lid of the box and took out three small leather sacks. They were like the pictures in pirate books and as he laid them on the baize they chinked and jangled. Slowly, while David watched, very slowly, the old fingers trembled at the knots, and then suddenly the old man tipped the first sack spreading keys across the tabletop.

There were hundreds of keys; long rusted keys, flat keys, keys with little round numbers tied to them, keys bunched together on rings, here and there sparkling new Yale keys, keys to fit clocks and keys for clockwork toys. The old man's fingers played greedily among them, spreading them, separating large and small.

"Well?" he said, looking up suddenly.

"I've never seen so many," said David.

"Few people have," said the old man. "Few people have." His eyes turned back to the table, and he moved one or two of the keys as though they were not in their proper place. And then, as if remembering his manners, he said, "You may touch them. I don't mind if you do."

David picked up a few keys and looked at them. His hands became red with rust, and he dropped the keys back on the table, stirring them about idly with his fingertip.

"Not like that!" snapped the old man suddenly. "Do it properly! You have to heap them up and scatter them. If you're going to do it do it properly."

He pulled at the strings on the other bag and cascaded a stream of keys onto the table. The air swam with red rust. David sneezed loudly and the old man said, "Pay attention!"

He raked the keys together into a large heap and burrowed his hands deep into them. When they were quite buried, he stopped, his eyes gleaming with a tense excitement. His breathing was loud and shallow. He looked up at David, and his eyes widened. "Now!" he shouted, and heaved his hands into the air.

Keys rained and rattled about the room, clicking against the mirror, breaking a cup on the cardtable, slapping against the leather-covered books, and falling loudly on the floor-boards. A small key hit David on the forehead. The old man remained bent across the table as if the excitement had exhausted him. The silence deepened.

Suddenly, a key which had landed on the edge of the mantelpiece overbalanced and fell, rattling loudly on the tiles of the hearth. Still the old man did not move. David shifted his weight restlessly and said into the silence, "I think I'll have to be getting home now. My mother's expecting me."

The old man gave no sign that he had heard. David said again, "I'll have to be going now." His voice sounded flat and awkward in the silent room.

The old man pushed himself up from the table. Deep lines of irritation scored the side of his mouth. David began to blush under the fierceness of the old man's eyes. "I can't quite make up my mind about you," the old man said slowly. He did not take his eyes from David's face.

"Sometimes I think you're a polite boy and sometimes I think you're a rude boy." He paused. "It's unsettling." David looked down and fiddled with one of the buttons on his shirt.

"Lift up another box of keys," said the old man suddenly.

"But I have to go home," said David.

"Quite untrue," said the old man.

"Really I do."

"A lie!" shouted the old man. "You are lying. You are telling lies!" He pounded on the table with his fist so that the keys jumped. "I will not tolerate the telling of lies!"

"Please," said David, "can I open the curtains?"

"I'm beginning to suspect," said the old man slowly, "that you don't really like my keys. I'm beginning to think that I was mistaken in you."

"Please. Honest. I have to," said David, his voice high and tight with fear of the old man's anger.

"Very well," said the old man curtly. "But you are a rude boy with very little appreciation. I want you to know that." Reaching inside his jacket, leaving brown rust marks on the lapel, he took out his notebook and wrote in it. He passed the piece of paper across the table. David read, *You have very little appreciation.*

The old man turned away, presenting his silent and offended back. David didn't know what to do. Hesitantly he said, "I do like the keys. Really I do. And the lion. And thank you for the tea."

"So you're going now, are you?" asked the old man without turning around.

"Well I have to," said David.

"It's a great pity because I don't show it to many people," said the old man.

"Show what?"

"It would only take a moment," said the old man turning round, "but you're in too much of a hurry."

"What is it?"

"Can you really spare me two minutes? Could you bear to stay with me that long?" Suddenly he chuckled. "Of course you want to," he said. "Go and sit on the settee over there and I'll bring it to you."

"Can I open the curtains now?" asked David. "I don't . . . I mean, it's hot with them closed."

"Don't touch them! No. You mustn't!" said the old man. He was struggling to take something from one of the bookshelves. He came and stood over David and then stopped so that David could see the black leather case in his hands. It was so stuffy in the room that it was difficult to breathe properly, and when the old man was so close to him David became aware of a strong smell of urine. He tried to move away.

Almost reverently, the old man opened the leather case and lying on the red silk lining was a small grey ball. They looked at it in silence.

"There!" breathed the old man. "Do you know what it is?"

"No," said David.

"Go on! Go on!" urged the old man.

"I don't know," said David.

"Try."

"A marble?"

"A marble!" shouted the old man. "Why would I keep a marble in a leather case! Of course it isn't a marble! That's one of the most stupid remarks I've ever heard."

"I'm sorry," said David, frightened again by the anger in the old man's glaring face.

"You're an extremely silly boy. A brainless boy. A stupid boy." He slammed shut the leather case. "Stupid! Silly!" shouted the old man.

"I want to go home now," said David, beginning to get up from the settee. The old man pushed him back. "A marble!" he muttered.

"Please . . . ," said David.

"It's a bullet!" shouted the old man. "A rifle bullet."

"I didn't know," said David. He tried to get up again, but he was hemmed in by an occasional table and the crowding presence of the old man. The dim light in the room seemed to be failing into darkness. David's throat was dry and aching.

"This bullet," said the old man, "was cut out of my leg in 1899. December 1899. Next I suppose you'll tell me that you've never heard of the Boer War!"

David said nothing, and the old man's black shape loomed over him.

"*Have* you heard of the Boer War?"

David began to cry.

"*Have* you?"

"I want to go home," said David in a small and uncertain voice.

"Quite untrue," said the old man. "I will not tolerate liars. You told me you went to school, and yet you claim not to have heard of the Boer War." He gripped David by the shoulder. "Why? Why are you lying to me?"

"Please," said David. "I'm not telling lies. Please let me go."

"Oh, very well," said the old man. "Maybe you aren't. But stop crying. It irritates me. Here. You may touch the bullet." He opened and held out the leather case.

"There's no need to cry."

"I want to go home," snuffled David.

"I know!" said the old man. "I know what you'd like. I'll show you my leg. The bullet smashed the bone, you know. You *would* like that, wouldn't you?"

"No," said David.

"Of course you would."

The old man moved even nearer to the settee, and leaning forward over David, lifting with his hands, slowly raised his leg until his foot was resting on the cushion. The harsh wheezing of his breath seemed to fill the silent room. The smell of stale urine was strong on the still air. Slowly he began to tug at his trouser-leg, inching it upwards. The calf of his leg was white and hairless. The flesh sank deep, seamed and puckered, shiny, livid white and purple, towards a central pit.

"If you press hard," said the old man, "it sinks right in."

David shrank further away from the white leg. The old man reached down and grasped David's hand. "Give me your finger," he said.

David tore his hand free and, kicking over the coffee table, rolled off the settee. At first, in his panic, he wrenched the doorknob the wrong way. As he ran out of the darkened room, he heard the old man saying, "I've tried to teach you. I've tried to teach you. But you have *no appreciation.*"

(1970)

Jack Hodgins

(b. 1 9 3 8)

Jack Hodgins was born in the Comox Valley on Vancouver Island. His father was a logger; his grandparents were pioneers. After graduating from the University of British Columbia with a B.Ed. in 1961, he taught high school in Nanaimo until 1979 and then became writer-in-residence at the University of Ottawa for a year. At present, he lives on the west coast of Canada.

The "island mentality" permeates much of Hodgins's best work. Many of his stories are set on Vancouver Island, in Ireland, or in Japan, places that lie just off a large mainland, and are home to a wide variety of dramatic, sometimes bizarre, characters. Hodgins is also concerned with the invention of story and legend—with how stories are born, how they elaborate themselves, how they are adapted by different voices and then decline. In his novel *The Invention of the World* he explores, through a labyrinthine collection of documents and tall tales, the history of a pseudo-religious island community and its colorful scandals. The stories collected in *Spit Delaney's Island* discuss questions of faith and disjunction and describe the relationships between various imaginary worlds. Hodgins often weds invented myths to the myths of ancient Greece and Ireland to explore the sometimes vague distinction between fiction and reality.

Hodgins's short-story collections include *Spit Delaney's Island* (1976) and *The Barclay Family Theatre* (1981). His novels are *The Invention of the World* (1977) and *The Resurrection of Joseph Bourne* (1979), for which he won a Governor-General's award.

JACK HODGINS

The Trench Dwellers

MACKEN THIS, MACKEN THAT. Gerry Mack had had enough. Why should he waste his life riding ferries to weddings and family reunions? There were already too many things you were forced to do in this world whether you liked them or not. "And I've hated those family gatherings for as long as I can remember," he said. "Why else would I move away?"

The problem was that Gerry's Aunt Nora Macken really did believe family was important. She used to tell how the Mackens first settled on the north slope of the valley more than fifty years ago when Black Alex, her father, brought the whole dozen of his children onto the Island in his touring car and started hacking a farm out of what had for centuries been pure timber land. And would tell, too, that by now there was hardly a household left in all the valley that wasn't related to them in one way or another. What Aunt Nora called The Immediate Family had grown to include more than four hundred people, three-quarters of whom were named Smith or O'Brien or Laitenen though she called them all the Mackens.

There wasn't any real substitute for having a lot of relatives, she said. And the people who knew her best, this tall big-footed old maid living out on that useless farm, said that yes, she was right, there was no substitute for family.

And because Nora Macken lived on those three hundred acres of farmland which had gone back already in two generations to second-growth timber, she thought it her duty every time there was a wedding or a funeral to call a reunion of The Immediate Family the day after the ceremony. More than three hundred relatives gathered. The older people, her own generation, spent the day in the house telling each other stories about Black Alex, reassuring one another that he really was as mean and miserable as they remembered, but that it couldn't be denied he was a bit of a character, too, all the same.

The young adults drank beer outside in the grassy yard or on the verandah and talked about their jobs and their houses, and each of them tried to find out how much money the others were earning. The children chased each other between the dead orchard trees and climbed the rickety ladders to the barn mow and fought over the sticky slices of cake Nora Macken put outside on a folding card table in the sun.

As for someone like Gerry Mack, her nephew, who was the only member of The Immediate Family ever to move off Vancouver Island, these events were more than he could bear.

When Gerry was twenty years old he very nearly married Karen O'Brien, a pretty blonde he'd gone all the way through school with. They went to movies together on Saturday nights and sometimes to dances, and afterwards they parked up the gravel road to the city dump to kiss each other until their mouths were raw. But Karen was already a member of The Immediate Family and had half a dozen brothers eager to increase the population. Gerry balked at marriage. He was the son of one of Nora's older brothers and had wished since the time he was six years old that he'd been an orphan.

Soon after dumping Karen O'Brien he met a stoop-shouldered secretary named April Klamp, who was plain-looking and very dull and wore clothes that looked as if they were bought for someone else, perhaps her mother. But she was an only child and had no relatives at all, only a pair of doddering parents who didn't care very much what happened to her. Gerry asked her to marry him a week after their first meeting and of course she accepted. No one before had even given her so much as a second look.

Some member of The Immediate Family had a few words to say about it. It seemed odd, they said, that a young man as vibrant as Gerry couldn't find himself a wife who was more of a match. Aunt Nora, too, thought it was unusual, but she'd given Gerry up long ago as not a real Macken at heart. And besides, she said, it could have been worse. He could have married a churchgoer (something no Macken had ever done) or worse still remained a bachelor (something three of her brothers had done and become cranky old grouches as a result). "Just watch him," she said. "He'll cut off his nose to spite his face."

Gerry didn't particularly care what any of them thought. Before his wedding he took two letters off his name and became Gerry Mack. He got no argument from April, of course. She was quick to agree that having too much family was worse than having none at all. She didn't even mind that he insisted on getting married seventy miles down-island by a minister she'd never met so that it would be impossible to have a reception afterwards. And when he told her they would live on the mainland she merely nodded and said it was about time one of the Mackens showed a little spunk. Personally, she said, she'd always hated living on an island. She agreed with everything that Gerry Mack said and never took her eyes off his face while he spoke. It was clear to everyone that when Gerry married her what he got was not a separate person to live with but an extension of himself. Aunt Nora said he could have gone out and bought a wooden leg if that was all he wanted.

Though she added, "At least they won't ever get into a fight. An extra limb doesn't talk back."

Their intention was to move far inland, but Gerry hadn't driven a hundred miles up the Fraser Valley before he realized he couldn't stand to be away from the coast. They turned back and settled in a little town on the edge of the strait, facing across to the Island, directly across to the valley where he had grown up. They bought a house fifty feet from the beach, with huge plate-glass windows facing west, and began saving their money to buy a small boat of their own so they could fish in the evenings.

Because he was a young man with a good rich voice and many opinions, Gerry had no trouble getting a job as an open-line moderator for the new radio station. He spent the first week voicing as many outlandish ideas as he could think of and being as rude as he dared to people who phoned in, so it didn't take long for him to draw most listeners away from the competing station. Within a month he had a large and faithful following on both sides of the strait. People didn't say they listened to CLCB, they said they listened to Gerry Mack's station.

What pleased him most was knowing that whether they liked it or not, most of The Immediate Family would be listening to him every day. He could imagine them in their houses, cringing whenever he was rude to callers, and hoping no one else realized where he'd come from, and saying Thank goodness he'd had the sense to change his name. He made a habit of saying "So long, Nora" every day as a sign-off but didn't tell anyone what it meant. People in the mainland town guessed that Nora must be his wife's middle name or else the name of a grandmother who'd died when he was a little boy. None of them ever guessed, of course, that Aunt Nora Macken over on the Island sat by her radio every morning for the whole time he was on and went red in the face when he signed off, and told herself maybe he was the only real Macken in the lot after all, though she could spank him for his cheek.

And that, he thought, will show you that here's one Macken who has no need for family.

Though he did not know then, of course, that even the most weak-minded and agreeable wife could suddenly find a backbone and will in herself when she became pregnant. He was sitting in the living room with his feet up on the walnut coffee table looking for good controversial topics in the newspaper when she handed him the wedding invitation that had arrived in the mail that morning. "I think we should go," she said.

"The hell you say," he said, and read through the silver script. "We hardly know them. Who's this Peter O'Brien to us?"

"A cousin," she said. "But that doesn't matter. I think we should be there for the reunion the next day."

Gerry put down the newspaper and looked at his wife. She was rubbing a hand over her round swollen belly. "What for?" he said. "I've been to a million of them. They're all the same. I thought we moved over here to get away from all that."

She sat down beside him on the sofa and put her head against his shoulder. "It's been a year since we've even put a foot on the Island. Let's go just for the fun."

He looked down into her plain mousey hair, her white scalp. She had never asked for a thing before. "We'll go," he said, "but only on the condition that we leave the minute I can't stand any more."

They took the two-hour ferry ride across the strait, and though he sat with a book in his lap and tried to read, he found it hard to concentrate and spent a lot of time watching the Island get closer and bigger and more distinct. He hated sitting idle, he was a man who liked to be doing things, and right now he would have preferred to be at work in the radio station or digging in his garden.

Aunt Nora outdid herself. "Lord," she said. "This must be the best reunion ever. There are three hundred and fifty people here, at least, and listen to that racket! When the Mackens get together there's no such thing as a lull in the conversation, there's never a moment when tongues have ceased."

"They do seem to have the gift of the gab," April said.

"A Macken," Aunt Nora said, smiling, "is a sociable person. A Macken enjoys company and conversation."

Macken this Macken that, Gerry thought.

His cousin George Smith put a bottle of beer in his hand and steered him across the yard to lean up against someone's car. He said he couldn't understand why Gerry put up with all the bullshit he had to listen to on his show. He wanted to know why Gerry didn't just threaten to quit his job if people wouldn't smarten up.

Gerry noticed that the whole back yard and orchard were filled with parked cars, and that against nearly every car there was at least one pair leaning and drinking beer and talking. Only the old ones were inside. April was standing straighter than he'd ever seen her, laughing with a bunch of women gathered beside a new Buick. "It doesn't matter a damn to me what they say," he told George Smith. "It's just part of my job to listen. Sometimes I tell them to go take a flying leap, but what the hell? Who cares?"

George told him he'd cleared over fifteen hundred dollars last month, working in the pulp and paper mill, most of it from overtime. He said he couldn't understand why most of the rest of them worked in the logging camp or in stores in town where there was hardly any overtime at all. It was overtime, he said, that made it possible for him to buy this here little baby they were leaning on. He pushed down on the front fender of the sports car and rocked it gently and with great fondness. Then he asked Gerry if a person working for a radio station got paid a salary or a wage, and what kind of car was he driving anyways? Gerry pointed vaguely across the yard and said as far as he was concerned it was just a way of getting places. But George told him if he got enough overtime in in the next few months he intended to buy himself a truck and camper so he could take more weekends off to go fishing up in the lakes. "Everybody's got one," he said. "One time I went up to Gooseneck Lake with Jim and Harriet and there were sixteen truck-and-campers there already. Nine of them were Mackens. Even old Uncle Morris was there, driving a brand-new Chev, and he only makes the minimum wage at *his* job. I told him, I said How could you afford a thing like that? and he said It pays to have a son in the car-selling business. I said I bet you'll be paying for that thing for the rest of your life."

"And he said?" Gerry said.

"Nothing," George said. "He just told me I was jealous. Ha!"

April came across the yard and led Gerry away towards a large group of people sitting in lawn chairs in a circle and doing a lot of laughing. But Aunt Nora, tall Aunt Nora with all her dyed-black hair piled up on top of her head, intercepted them and took them inside so that Uncle Morgan, who had been sick in the hospital the whole time they were engaged, could meet April. "It won't do," she said, "to have strangers in the same family." She pushed them right into her cluttered little living room and made someone get up so April could have a comfortable chair. Gerry leaned against the door frame and wondered if old Black Alex realized when he was alive that the dozen kids he'd hauled onto the Island in his touring car would eventually become these aging wrinkled people.

And of course it was Black Alex they were talking about. Uncle Morris said "I mind the time he said to me Get off that roof boy or I'll stuff you down the chimney!" He laughed so hard at that he had to haul out a handkerchief to wipe the tears off his big red face.

Aunt Nora, too, shrieked. "Oh, that was his favourite! He was always threatening to stuff one of us down the chimney." Though she was careful to explain to April that never in his life did he do any such thing to any of them, that in fact the worst he ever did was apply the toe of his boot to their backsides. "He was a noisy man," she said, "But some of us learned how to handle him."

Then she drew everybody's attention to April and said, "As you can easily see, there's one more little Macken waiting to be born. Boy or girl we wish it luck."

"D'you know?" Uncle Morgan said. "Not one person in the family has ever named a child after Dad."

"No wonder!" Aunt Nora cried. "There could only be one Alex Macken. No one else would dare try to match him."

"Or want to," Aunt Katherine said. "Suppose they got his temper too, along with his name."

"One thing for sure," Aunt Nora said. "He'll have plenty of cousins to play with. He'll never run out of playmates or friends." Then, remembering, she added, "Of course, as long as they keep him isolated over there on the mainland I suppose he'll miss out on everything."

"It's terrible having no one to play with," April said. "Especially if you're too shy to go out making friends on your own. Just ask me, I know. At least with cousins you don't have to start from scratch. Nobody needs to be scared of a relative."

"Right!" Aunt Nora said, and looked right at Gerry. "Though there are some people who think loneliness is a prize to be sought after."

Gerry Mack knew, of course, that something had happened to the wife he thought was a sure bet to remain constant. It came as something of a surprise. After all, who expected an adult's foot to suddenly turn into a hand or start growing off in a new direction? He brooded about it all the way home on the ferry and wouldn't speak to her even while she got ready for bed. He sat in his living room until he was sure she'd gone to sleep, then he tiptoed in to the bedroom and undressed without turning on the light.

The next day he held off the phone calls that came into the station and kept the air waves to himself. From his little sound-booth he could look out across the strait. "From over here," he told his listeners, "from here on the mainland, Vancouver Island is just a pale blue chain of mountains stretched right across your whole range of vision. A jagged-backed wall between us and the open sea. Go have a look. Stop what you're doing for a minute and go to your window." He waited for a while, and thought not of the house-wives who were moving to the ocean side of their houses, but of the islanders who were over there listening and wondering what he was up to.

"There it is," he said. "Twenty miles away. I bet you hardly ever notice it there, like a fence that borders the back yard." He drank a mouthful of the coffee he kept with him throughout the show. "Now those of you who've been across on the ferry know that as you get closer those mountains begin to take on shapes and change from blue to green and show big chunks of logged-off sections and zig-zag logging roads like knife-scars up their sides. And closer still, of course, you see that along the edge of the Island, stretched out along the shelf of flatter land, is a chain of farms and fishing villages and towns and tourist resorts and bays full of log booms and penin-sulas dotted with summer cabins. All of it, ladies and gentlemen, facing over to us as if those people too think these mountains are nothing but a wall at their backs, holding off the Pacific."

He gulped coffee again and glanced at his watch. He thought of the mainlanders looking across. He thought of the islanders wondering what the hell he was talking about. Then he said, "But the funny thing is this: to those people over there on that island, this mainland they spend most of their lives facing is nothing but a blue chain of jagged mountains stretched across their vision like a wall separating them from the rest of North America. That continent behind us doesn't even exist to some of them. To them we look just the same as they do to us."

Then, just before opening the telephone lines to callers, he said, "What we live in is a trench. Do you suppose trench-dwellers think any different from the rest of the world?"

His line was busy for the rest of the morning. Most wanted to talk about why they liked living in a place like this, some asked him couldn't he think of a more pleasant comparison to make, and a few tried to change the subject to the recent tax increase. One long-distance call came in from the Island, an old man who told him he was jabbering nonsense and ought to be locked up, some place where all he could see would be bars and padded walls. "If you want to live in a trench," he said, "I'll dig you one. Six feet long by six feet deep." Gerry Mack hung up on his cackling laughter and vowed he would never cross that strait again.

But April told him that didn't mean *she* couldn't go across just whenever she felt like it.

So that when the next wedding invitation arrived he was ready for her announcement. Even if he didn't want to go, she said, she was heading across and taking Jimmy with her. He couldn't deprive her for ever of the pleasure of showing off her son to his family. And Jimmy, too, had a right to meet his cousins. She was pregnant again, and there was a new hard glint in her eye. Gerry Mack, when she talked like that to him, felt very old and wondered what life would have been like if he'd married Karen O'Brien. If that's what happened to women, he thought, you might as well marry your own sister.

When she came back she told him the reunion of course was a huge success and everybody asked where he was. She'd stayed right at Aunt Nora's, she said, and it was amazing how much room there was in that old farmhouse when everyone else had gone home. She'd felt right at home there. Jimmy had had a wonderful time, had made friends with dozens of cousins, and could hardly wait for the next time they went over. And oh yes, Aunt Nora sent him a message.

"What is it?" he said, weary.

"She says there's a wonderful new man on *their* radio station. She says she doesn't know of a single Macken who still listens to you. This new fellow plays softer music and isn't nearly so rude to his callers. She says people do appreciate good manners after all and she can't think of one good reason for you not to be at the next wedding."

"At the rate they're marrying," he said, "The Immediate Family will soon swallow up the whole Island."

"The Mackens believe in marriage," she said. "And in sticking together."

Mackens this Mackens that, Gerry Mack thought.

"Nora told me her father used to say being a Macken was like being part of a club. Or a religion."

"Do you know why they call him Black Alex?"

"Why?"

"When he was alive people used to call him Nigger Alex because his hair was so black and you never saw him without dirt on his hands and face. People over there never saw a real black man in those days. But the 'children' decided after his death that Black Alex was politer and what people would've called him if they'd only stopped to think."

"Well at least they called him something," she said. "It shows he was liked. It shows people noticed him. I never heard anyone call you anything but Gerry, an insipid name if I ever heard one. Pretty soon those people over there will forget you even exist."

"That's fine with me," Gerry Mack said, and went outside to sprinkle powder on his rose leaves.

But she followed him. "Sometimes I don't think it's family you're trying to get away from at all. I think it's humanity itself."

"Don't be ridiculous," he said. "If that was what I wanted I'd have become a hermit."

"What else are we?" She was on the verge of tears. "You don't let Jimmy play with anyone else's kids, none of them are good enough for you. And we've hardly any friends ourselves."

"Don't harp," he said. "Don't nag at me."

It passed through his mind to tell her she had no business going against his wishes when it came to bringing up the boy. But he was a strange kid anyway, and Gerry had always been uncomfortable with children. It was easier to let her do what she wanted with him.

When April went across to George Smith's wedding (his second) and took Jimmy and the baby with her, he knew she would not be coming back. He wasn't surprised when she didn't get off the Sunday evening ferry. He didn't even bother watching the ferries coming in during the next week. The only surprise was the sight of Aunt Nora getting out of a taxi the following weekend and throwing herself into the leather armchair in Gerry's living room.

"My God," she said. "It looks as if you could walk across in fifteen minutes but that damn ferry takes for ever."

"Where's April?" he said.

The wedding, she told him, was lovely. Because it was George's second the girl didn't try to make it into too much of a thing, but just as many people turned out for it as for his first. "He's got a real dandy this time," she said. "He's not going to want to spend so much time at his precious pulp mill when he's got this one waiting at home. She's got outdoor teeth of course, but still she is pretty!"

Gerry said George's first wife hadn't been much to look at, but then George was no prize himself.

Then, suddenly, Aunt Nora said, "I think she'll be asking you for a legal separation."

"Who?" he said, stupidly.

"I told her she could live with me. There's too much room in that old house for one person. I'll enjoy the company. I remember Dad saying if a Macken couldn't count on one of his own relatives in times of trouble, who could he count on? That little boy of yours is going to look just like him." She stood up and took off her coat and laid it over the back of her chair. Then she took a cigarette out of her purse and lit it and sat down again.

"If you want to come back with me and try to patch it up, that's all right."

"Patch what up?" he said. "We haven't even had a fight."

But she acted as if she hadn't heard. "I'll tell you something, Gerry, you've got spunk. Maybe you're the only real Macken in the whole kaboodle."

"Ha."

"And if you and April patch it up, if you want to live on the farm, that's all right with me too."

"Why should I want to live there?"

"It's the family homestead," she said, as if it was something he might have forgotten. "It's where your grandfather started out. Where the family began."

Gerry grunted and went to the refrigerator to get himself a bottle of beer.

"Well, somebody will have to take it over some day," she said. "You can see what's happened to the farm with just an old maid living on it. He never should have left it to me in the first place. Except, of course, it's the best place for holding family get-togethers and I know if it was left to anyone else they'd never get done."

"Look," he said. "You got her and my two kids. Three for one. That sounds like a pretty good trade to me."

"I just can't believe you don't care about those children," Aunt Nora said. "Those two little boys. No Macken has ever abandoned his own children. It doesn't seem natural."

"Natural," Gerry Mack said, and tilted up his bottle of beer. But when she caught the morning ferry home he did not go with her. In fact, he was to make only one more visit to the Island, and that would not be until two years later when he attended his son's funeral. Aunt Nora phoned him in the middle of the day to say the boy had drowned in a swimming accident. The Immediate Family was at the funeral, four hundred or so of them, standing all over the graveyard where Mackens were buried. He'd sat beside April in the chapel but when they got to the graveside she seemed to be surrounded by relatives and he was left alone, on the far side of the ugly hole where they were putting his son. Aunts and cousins were weeping openly, but April in their midst stared straight ahead with her jaw set like stone. She appeared then to have lost all of the slump that was once in her back. Even her mousey brown hair seemed to have taken on more life. When their eyes met she nodded in a way that might have been saying "Thank you" or might have been only a dismissal, or could perhaps have been simply acknowledging that she had noticed his, a stranger's, presence.

Aunt Nora, afterwards, cornered him in her little living room. She seemed smaller now, slightly stooped, getting old. There were deep lines in her face. "Now," she said. "Now do you see where your place is? Now do you see where you belong?"

He turned, tried to find someone to rescue him.

"This whole farm, Gerry, it's yours. Just move here, stay here where you belong."

And it was April who rescued him after all. She came into the room swiftly, her eyes darting with the quick concern of a hostess making sure everything was going well. "Oh Nora!" she said. "Uncle Morris was asking for you. I promised I'd take you to him."

When the old woman stood up to leave, April let her gaze flicker momentarily over him. Her complexion against the black dress looked nearly ivory. Beautiful skin. She would be a beautiful woman yet. "George Smith was wondering where you were," she said. "I told him I thought you'd already gone home."

For several years after that Aunt Nora visited the mainland every summer to report to Gerry on his wife and remaining son and to tell him all about the weddings and reunions he'd missed. April, she told him, had taken over the last reunion completely, did all the planning and most of the work. And some people on the Island were listening to him again she said, now that he was only reading the news, once a day.

But she stopped coming altogether years later when he sold the seaside house and moved in with a woman far up a gravel road behind town, in a junky unpainted house beside a swamp. She had nearly a dozen children from various fathers, some Scandinavian, two Indian, and one Chinese, and her name was Netty Conroy. Which meant, Aunt Nora Macken was soon able to discover after a little investigation, that she was related to more than half the people who lived in that mainland town, not to mention most who lived in the countryside around it. It was a strange thing, she told The Immediate Family, but she still felt closer to Gerry Mack than to any of the rest of them. Perhaps it was because she, too, had had a tendency to cut off her nose to spite her face. Everyone laughed at the notion because of course, they said, Aunt Nora had always had everything just the way she wanted it in this world.

(1976)

MARGARET ATWOOD*

Unearthing Suite

My parents have something to tell me: something apart from the ordinary course of conversation. I can guess this from the way they sit down first, both on the same chair, my mother on the arm, and turn their heads a little to one side, regarding me with their ultra-blue eyes.

As they have grown older their eyes have become lighter and lighter and more and more bright, as if time is leeching them of darkness, experience clarifying them until they have reached the transparency of stream water. Possibly this is an illusion caused by the whitening of their hair. In any case their eyes are now round and shiny, like the glass-bead eyes of stuffed animals. Not for the first time it occurs to me that I could not have been born, like other people, but must have been hatched out of an egg. My parents' occasional dismay over me was not like the dismay of other parents. It was less dismay than perplexity, the bewilderment of two birds who have found a human child in their nest and have no idea what to do with it.

My father takes a black leather folder from the desk. They both have an air of suppressed excitement, like children waiting for a grown-up friend to open a present they have wrapped; which will contain a joke.

"We went down and bought our urns today," my father says.

"You what?" I say, shocked. There is nothing wrong with my parents. They are in perfect health. I on the other hand have a cold.

"It's best to be prepared," my mother says. "We looked at plots but they're so expensive."

"They take up too much space," says my father, who has always been conscious of the uses to which the earth is wrongly in his opinion put. Conversation around the dinner table when I was growing up concerned itself more than once with how many weeks it would take a pair of fruit flies breeding unchecked to cover the earth to a depth of thirty-two feet. Not many, as I recall. He feels much the same about corpses.

"They give you a little niche too," says my mother.

"It's in here," says my father, indicating the folder as if I am supposed to remember about all this and deal with it at the right time. I am appalled: surely they aren't leaving something, finally, up to me?

"We wanted to be sprinkled," says my mother. "But they told us it's now illegal."

"That's ridiculous," I say. "Why can't you be sprinkled if you want to?"

*For biographical information, see page 448.

1036

"The funeral-parlour lobby," says my father, who has been known to be cynical about government decisions. My mother concedes that things might get a bit dusty if everyone were to be sprinkled.

"I'll sprinkle you," I say bravely. "Don't worry about a thing."

This is a rash decision and I've made it on the spur of the moment, as I make all my rash decisions. But I fully intend to carry it out; even though it will mean action, a thing I avoid when possible. Under pretense of a pious, visit I will steal my parents from their niche, substituting sand if necessary, and smuggle them away. The ashes part doesn't bother me; in fact I approve of it. Much better than waiting, like the Christians, for God to grow them once more instantaneously from the bone outward, sealed meanwhile rouged and waxed and wired, veins filled with formaldehyde, in cement and bronze vaults, a prey to mould and anaerobic bacteria. If God wants to make my parents again the molecules will do just as well to start with, same as before. It is not a question of matter, which turns over completely every seven years anyway, but of form.

We sit for a minute, considering implications. We are way beyond funerals and mourning, or possibly we have by-passed them. I am thinking about the chase, and being arrested, and how I will foil the authorities: already I am concocting fictions. My father is thinking about fertilizer, in the same tone in which other people think about union with the Infinite. My mother is thinking about the wind.

PHOTOGRAPHS have never done justice to my mother. This is because they stop time; to really reflect her they would have to show her as a blur. When I think of her she is often on skis. Her only discoverable ambition as a child was to be able to fly, and much of her subsequent life has been spent in various attempts to take off. Stories of her youth involve scenes in trees and on barn roofs, breakneck dashes on frothy-mouthed runaway horses, speed-skating races, and, when she was older, climbs out of windows onto forbidden fire escapes, done more for the height and adventure than for the end result, an after-hours college date with some young man or other who had been knocked over by her, perhaps literally. For my mother, despite her daunting athleticism and lack of interest in frilly skirts, was much sought after. Possibly men saw her as a challenge: it would be an accomplishment to get her to pause long enough to pay even a fleeting amount of attention to them.

My father first saw her sliding down a banister—I imagine, in the 1920s, that she would have done this side-saddle—and resolved then and there to marry her; though it took him a while to track her down, stalking her from tree to tree, crouching behind bushes, butterfly net at the ready. This is a metaphor but not unjustified.

One of their neighbours recently took me to task about her.

"Your poor mother," she said. "Married to your father."

"What?" I said.

"I see her dragging her groceries back from the supermarket," she said.

(True enough, my mother does this. She has a little cart with which she whizzes along the sidewalk, hair wisping out from her head, scarf streaming, exhausting anyone foolhardy enough to make the trip with her; by that I mean myself.) "Your father won't even drive her."

When I told her this story, my mother laughed.

My father said the unfortunate woman obviously didn't know that there was more to him than met the eye.

In recent years my mother has taken up a new winter exercise. Twice a week she goes dancing on figure skates: waltzes, tangos, foxtrots. On Tuesday and Thursday mornings she can be observed whirring around the local arena to the tune of "A Bicycle Built for Two" played over the scratchy sound system, speed undiminished, in mittens which do not match her skirt, keeping perfect time.

My father did what he did because it allows him to do what he does. There he goes now, in among the trees, battered grey felt hat—with or without a couple of trout flies stuck in the band, depending on what year we're talking about—on his head to keep things from falling into his hair, things that are invisible to others but which he knows all too well are lurking up there among the innocent-looking leaves, one or two or a clutch of children of any age tagging along after him, his own or his grandchildren or children attracted at random, as a parade attracts followers, as the sun attracts meteors, their eyes getting larger and larger as wonder after wonder is revealed to them: a sacred white larva that will pupate and fly only after seven years, a miraculous beetle that eats wood, a two-sexed worm, a fungus that crawls. No freak show can hold a candle to my father expounding Nature.

He leaves no stone unturned; but having turned it, to see what may be underneath—and at this point no squeals or expressions of disgust are permitted, on pain of his disfavour—he puts everything carefully back: the grub into its hollow, the woodborer beneath its rotting bark, the worm into its burrow, unless needed of course for fishing. He is not a sentimentalist.

Now he spreads a tarpaulin beneath a likely-looking tree, striped maple let us say, and taps the tree trunk with the pole of his axe. Heaven rewards him with a shower of green caterpillars, which he gathers tenderly in, to carry home with him and feed on leafy branches of the appropriate kind stuck into quart jars of water. These he will forget to replace, and soon the caterpillars will go crawling over our walls and ceiling in search of fodder, to drop as if on cue into the soup. My mother is used to this by now and thinks nothing of it.

Meanwhile the children follow him to the next tree: he is better than magicians, since he explains everything. This is indeed one of his purposes: to explain everything, when possible. He wants to see, he wants to know, only to see and know. I'm aware that it is this mentality, this curiosity, which is responsible for the hydrogen bomb and the imminent demise of civilization and that we would all be better off if we were still at the stone-worship-ping stage. Though surely it is not this affable inquisitiveness that should be blamed.

Look, my father has unearthed a marvel: a slug perhaps, a snake, a spider complete with her sack of eggs? Something educational at any rate. You can't see it from here: only the backs of the children's heads as they peer down into his cupped hands.

My parents do not have houses, like other people. Instead they have earths. These look like houses but are not thought of as houses, exactly. Instead they are more like stopping places, seasonal dens, watering holes on some caravan route which my nomadic parents are always following, or about to follow, or have just come back from following. Much of my mother's time is spent packing and unpacking.

Unlocking the door of one of their earths—and unlike foxes they get rid of bones, not by burial but by burning, the right thing to do unless you want skunks—I am greeted first by darkness, then by a profusion of objects heaped apparently at random but actually following some arcane scheme of order: stacks of lumber, cans of paint-brush cleaner with paintbrushes soaking in them, some of these dry and stiff or glued to the insides of the cans by the sticky residue left by evaporation, boxes of four-inch spikes, six-quart baskets filled with an assortment of screws, hinges, staples, and roofing-nails, rolls of roofing, axes, saws, brace-and-bits, levels, peevees, spoke-shaves, rasps, drills, post-hole diggers, shovels, mattocks, and crowbars. (Not all of these things are in the same place at the same time: this is a collective memory.) I know what each of these tools is for and may even at some time have used it, which may go part way towards explaining my adult slothfulness. The smell is the smell of my childhood: wood, canvas, tar, kerosene, soil.

This is my father's section of the house. In my mother's, things are arranged, on hooks and shelves, in inviolable order: cups, pots, plates, pans. This is not because my mother makes a fetish of housekeeping but because she doesn't want to waste time on it. All her favourite recipes begin with the word *quick*. Less is more, as far as she is concerned, and this means everything in its place. She has never been interested, luckily, in the house beautiful, but she does insist on the house convenient.

Her space is filled. She does not wish it altered. We used to give her cooking pots for Christmas until we realized that she would much rather have something else.

My father likes projects. My mother likes projects to be finished. Thus you see her, in heavy work gloves, carting cement blocks, one by one, or stacks of wood, from one location to another, dragging underbrush which my father has slashed, hauling buckets of gravel and dumping them out, all in aid of my father's constructionism.

Right now they are digging a large hole in the ground. This will eventually be another earth. My mother has already moved a load of cement blocks to the site, for lining it with; in the mornings she goes to see what animal tracks she can find on the fresh sand, and perhaps to rescue any toads and mice that may have tumbled in.

Although he is never finished, my father does finish things. Last summer a back step suddenly appeared on our log house up north. For twenty years my mother and I had been leaping into space whenever we wanted to reach the clothesline, using biceps and good luck to get ourselves back up and in. Now we descend normally. And there is a sink in the kitchen, so that dirty dishwater no longer has to be carried down the hill in an enamel pail, slopping over onto one's legs, and buried in the garden. It now goes down a drainhole in the approved manner. My mother has added her completing touch: a small printed sign Scotch-taped to the counter, which reads:

PUT NO FAT DOWN SINK.

A jar of dried bacteria stands nearby: one teaspoonful is poured down at intervals, so the stray tea leaves will be devoured. This prevents clogging.

Meanwhile my father is hard at work, erecting cedar logs into vertical walls for the new outhouse, which will contain a chemical toilet, unlike the old one. He is also building a fireplace out of selected pink granite boulders which my mother steps over and around as she sweeps the leaves off the floor.

Where will it all end? I cannot say. As a child I wrote small books which I began with the words *The End.* I needed to know the end was guaranteed.

My own house is divided in two: a room full of paper, constantly in flux, where process, organicism, and fermentation rule and dustballs breed; and another room, formal in design, rigid in content, which is spotlessly clean and to which nothing is ever added.

As for me, I will die no doubt of inertia. Though witness to my parents' exhausting vitality, I spent my childhood learning to equate goodness with immobility. Sitting in the bottoms of canoes that would tip if you lurched, crouching in tents that would leak if you touched them in rainstorms, used for ballast in motorboats stacked precariously high with lumber, I was told not to move, and I did not. I was thought of as being well-behaved.

At intervals my father would bundle the family and the necessary provisions into the current car—*Studebaker* is a name I remember—and make a pilgrimage of one kind or another, a thousand miles here, a thousand miles there. Sometimes we were in search of saw-flies; at other times, of grandparents. We would drive as long as possible along the almost empty post-war highways, through the melancholy small towns of Quebec or northern Ontario, sometimes down into the States, where there were more roadside billboards. Long after the minor-key sunsets late at night, when even the White Rose gasoline stations were closed, we would look for a motel; in those days, a string of homemade cottages beside a sign that read FOLDED WINGS, or, more somberly, VALHALLA, the tiny clapboard office festooned with Christmas-tree lights. Ever since then, *vacancy* has been a magic word for me: it means there is room. If we did not find a vacancy my father would simply pull over to the side of the road in some likely-looking spot and put up a tent. There were few campgrounds, no motorcycle gangs; there was more emptiness than there is now. Tents were not so portable then; they were heavy and canvas, and sleeping bags were dank and filled with kapok. Everything was grey or khaki.

During these trips my father would drive as fast as he could, hurling the car forward it seemed by strength of will, pursued by all the unpulled weeds in his gardens, all the caterpillars uncollected in his forests, all the nails that needed to be hammered in, all the loads of dirt that had to be shifted from one place to another. I, meanwhile, would lie on a carefully stowed pile of baggage in the back seat, wedged into a small place beneath the roof. I could see out of the window, and I would watch the landscape, which consisted of many dark trees and of the telephone poles and their curves of wire, which looked as if they were moving up and down. Perhaps it was then that I began the translation of the world into words. It was something you could do without moving.

Sometimes, when we were stationary, I held the ends of logs while my father sawed them, or pulled out designated weeds, but most of the time I lived a life of contemplation. In so far as was possible I sneaked off into the woods to read books and evade tasks, taking with me supplies filched from my mother's tin of cooking raisins and stash of crackers. In theory I can do almost anything; certainly I have been told how. In practice I do as little as possible. I pretend to myself that I would be quite happy in a hermit's cave, living on gruel, if someone else would make the gruel. Gruel, like so many other things, is beyond me.

WHAT is my mother's secret? For of course she must have one. No one can have a life so apparently cheerful, so seemingly lacking in avalanches and swamps, without having also a secret. By *secret* I mean the price she had to pay. What was the trade-off, what did she sign over to the Devil, for this limpid tranquillity?

She maintains that she once had a quick temper, but no one knows where it has gone. When she was forced to take piano lessons as part of a young lady's battery of accomplishments, she memorized the pieces and played them by rote while reading novels concealed on her lap. "More *feeling*," her teacher would say to her. Pictures of her at four show a shy-looking ringleted child bedecked in the lacey lampshade dresses inflicted on girls before the First World War, but in fact she was inquisitive, inventive, always getting into trouble. One of her first memories is of sliding down a red clay bank in her delicate white post-Victorian pantaloons. She remembers the punishment, true, but she remembers better the lovely feeling of the mud.

Her marriage was an escape from its alternatives. Instead of becoming the wife of some local small-town professional and settling down, in skirts and proper surroundings, to do charity work for the church as would have befitted her status, she married my father and took off down the St. John's river in a canoe, never having slept in a tent before; except once, just before the wedding, when she and her sisters spent a weekend practising. My father knew how to light fires in the rain and what to do about rapids, which alarmed my mother's friends. Some of them thought of her as having been kidnapped and dragged off to the wilderness, where she was imprisoned and forced to contend with no electricity, no indoor plumbing, and hordes of ravenning bears. She on the other hand must have felt that she had been rescued from a fate worse than death: antimacassars on the chairs.

Even when we lived in real houses it was something like camping out. There was an improvisational quality to my mother's cooking, as if the ingredients were not bought but scavenged: what we ate depended on what was at hand. She made things out of other things and never threw anything out. Although she did not like dirt, she could never take housecleaning seriously as an end in itself. She polished the hardwood floors by dragging her children over them on an old flannelette blanket. This sounds like fun until I reflect: they were too poor for floor polishers, maids, or babysitters.

After my birth she developed warts, all over both her hands. Her explanation was the ammonia: there were no disposable diapers then. In those days babies wore knitted woollen sweaters, woollen booties, woollen bonnets, and woollen soakers, in which they must have steamed like puddings. My parents did not own a wringer washer; my mother washed everything by hand. During this period she did not get out much to play. In the photographs, she is always posed with a sled or a carriage and one or two suspicious-looking infants. She is never alone.

Possibly she got the warts from being grounded; or more particularly, from me. It's a burden, this responsibility for the warts of one's mother, but since I missed out on the usual guilts this one will have to do. The warts point towards my mother's secret but do not reveal it. In any case they went away.

My mother lived for two years in the red-light district of Montreal without knowing what it was. She was informed only afterwards, by an older woman who told her she ought not to have done it. "I don't know why not," said my mother. That is her secret.

MY father studies history. He has been told by Poles that he knows more Polish history than most Poles, by Greeks that he knows more Greek history than most Greeks, by Spaniards that he knows more Spanish history than most Spaniards. Taking the sum total of worldwide *per capita* knowledge into consideration this is probably so. He alone, among my acquaintances, successfully predicted the war in Afghanistan, on the basis of past examples. Who else indeed was paying any attention?

It is his theory that both Hiroshima and the discovery of America were entomological events (the clue is the silkworm) and that fleas have been responsible for more massacres and population depletions than have religions (the clue is the bubonic plague). His overview is dire, though supported, he would hasten to point out, by the facts. Wastefulness, stupidity, arrogance, greed, and brutishness unroll themselves in technicolour panorama across our dinner table as my father genially carves the roast.

Should civilization as we know it destroy itself, he informs us, ladling the gravy—as is likely, he adds—it will never be able to rebuild itself in its present form, since all available surface metals have long since been exhausted and the extraction of deeper ones is dependent upon metal technologies, which, as you will remember, will have been demolished. There can never be another iron age, another bronze age; we will be stuck—if there is any *we,* which he doubts—with stone and bone, no good for aeroplanes and computers.

He has scant interest in surviving into the twenty-first century. He knows it will be awful. Any person of sense will agree with him (and lest you make the mistake of thinking him merely quaint, let me remind you that many do).

My mother, however, pouring out the tea and forgetting as usual who takes milk, says she wants to live as long as possible. She wants to see what happens.

My father finds this naïve of her, but lets it pass and goes on to discuss the situation in Poland. He recalls to our memories (paying his listeners the compliment, always, of pretending he is merely reminding them of something they have of course already known, long and well) the Second World War Polish cavalry charge against the German tanks: foolishness and bravery. But foolish. But brave. He helps himself to more mashed potato, shaking his head in wonder. Then, changing the subject, he delivers himself of one of those intricate and reprehensible puns he's so fond of.

How to reconcile his grim vision of life on earth with his undoubted enjoyment of it? Neither is a pose. Both are real. I can't remember—though my father could, without question, ferreting among his books to locate the exact reference—which saint it was who, when asked what he would do if the end of the world were due tomorrow, said he would continue to cultivate his garden. The proper study of mankind may be man, but the proper activity is digging.

My parents have three gardens: one in the city, which produces raspberries, eggplants, irises, and beans; another halfway up, which specializes in peas, potatoes, squash, onions, beets, carrots, broccoli, and cauliflower; and the one up north, small but lovingly cherished, developed from sand, compost, and rations of sheep and horse manure carefully doled out, which yields cabbages, spinach, lettuce, long-lasting rhubarb, and Swiss chard, cool-weather crops.

All spring and summer my parents ricochet from garden to garden, mulching, watering, pulling up the polyphiloprogenitive weeds, "until," my mother says, "I'm bent over like a coat hanger." In the fall they harvest, usually much more than they can possibly eat. They preserve, store, chill, and freeze. They give away the surplus, to friends and family, and to the occasional stranger whom my father has selected as worthy. These are sometimes women who work in bookstores and have demonstrated their discernment and intelligence by recognizing the titles of books my father asks for. On these he will occasionally bestow a cabbage of superior size and delightfulness, a choice clutch of tomatoes, or, if it is fall and he has been chopping and sawing, an elegant piece of wood.

In the winter my parents dutifully chew their way through the end products of their summer's labour, since it would be a shame to waste anything. In the spring, fortified with ever newer and more fertile and rust-resistant varieties from the Stokes Seed Catalogue, they begin again.

My back aches merely thinking about them as I creep out to some sinful junk-food outlet or phone up Pizza Pizza. But in truth the point of all this gardening is not vitaminization or self-sufficiency or the production of food, though these count for something. Gardening is not a rational act. What matters is the immersion of the hands in the earth, that ancient ceremony of which the Pope kissing the tarmac is merely a pallid vestigial remnant.

In the spring, at the end of the day, you should smell like dirt.

HERE is a fit subject for meditation: the dock. I myself use it, naturally, to lie down on. From it I can see the outlines of the shore, which function for me like a memory. At night I sit on it, in a darkness which is like no other, watching stars if there are any. At dusk there are bats; in the mornings, ducks. Underneath it there are leeches, minnows, and the occasional crayfish. This dock, like Nature, is permanently crumbling away and is always the same.

It is built on cribs of logs weighted down by granite boulders, which are much easier to move around underwater than they are on land. For this venture my father immersed himself in the lake, which he otherwise prefers to stay out of. No wonder; even on good days, at the height of summer, it is not what you would call warm. Scars go purple in it, toes go white, lips go blue. The lake is one of those countless pot-holes left by the retreating glaciers, which had previously scraped off all the topsoil and pushed it south. What remained is bedrock, and when you dip yourself into this lake you know that if you stay in it long enough or even very long at all you will soon get down to the essentials.

My father looks at this dock (his eyes narrowing in calculation, his fingers itching) and sees mainly that it needs to be repaired. The winter ice has been at it, the sun, the rain; it is patched and treacherous, threads of rot are spreading through it. Sometime soon he will take his crowbar to it, rip apart its punky and dangerous boards and the logs excavated by nesting yellow-jackets, and rebuild the whole thing new.

My mother sees it as a place from which to launch canoes, and as a handy repository for soap and towel when, about three in the afternoon, in the lull between the lunch dishes and reactivating the fire for supper, she goes swimming. Into the gelid, heart-stoppingly cold water she wades, over the blackened pine needles lying on the sand and the waterlogged branches, over the shells of clams and the carapaces of crayfish, splashing the tops of her arms, until she finally plunges in and speeds outward, on her back, her neck coming straight up out of the water like an otter's, her head in its white bathing cap encircled by an aureole of blackflies, kicking up a small wake behind her and uttering cries of:

Refreshing! Refreshing!

TODAY I pry myself loose from my own entropy and lead two children single-file through the woods. We are looking for anything. On the way we gather pieces of fallen birchbark, placing them in paper bags after first shaking them to get out the spiders. They will be useful for lighting the fire. We talk about fires and where they should not be lit. There are charcoal-sided trunks crumbling here and there in the forest, *mementi mori* of an ancient burnout.

The trail we follow is an old one, blazed by my brother during his trail-making phase thirty years ago and brushed out by him routinely since. The blazes are now weathered and grey; hardened tree blood stands out in welts around them. I teach the children to look on both sides of the trees, to turn once in a while and see where they have come from, so that they will learn how to find their way back, always. They stand under the huge trees in their raincoats, space echoing silently around them; a folklore motif, these children in the woods, potentially lost. They sense it and are hushed.

The Indians did that, I tell them, pointing to an old tree bent when young into knees and elbows. Which, like most history, may or may not be true.

Real ones? they want to know.

Real, I say.

Were they alive? they ask.

We go forward, clambering up a hill, over boulders, past a fallen log ripped open by a bear in search of grubs. They have more orders: they are to keep their eyes open for mushrooms, and especially for puffballs, which even they like to eat. Around here there is no such thing as just a walk. I feel genetics stealing over me: in a minute I will be turning over stones for them, and in fact I am soon on my hands and knees, grubbing a gigantic toad out from under a fallen cedar so old it is almost earth, burnt orange. We discuss the fact that toads will not give you warts but will pee on you when frightened. The toad does this, proving my reliability. For its own good I put it into my pocket and the expedition moves forward.

At right angles there's a smaller trail, a recent one, marked not by blazes but by snapped branches and pieces of fluorescent pink tape tied to bushes. It leads to a yellow birch blown down by the wind—you can tell by the roots, topsoil and leaf-mould still matted on them—now neatly sawn and stacked, ready for splitting. Another earthwork.

On the way back we circle the burn-heap, the garden, going as quietly as we can. The trick, I whisper, is to see things before they see you. Not for the first time I feel that this place is haunted, by the ghosts of those not yet dead, my own included.

NOTHING goes on forever. Sooner or later I will have to renounce my motionlessness, give up those habits of reverie, speculation, and lethargy by which I currently subsist. I will have to come to grips with the real world, which is composed, I know, not of words but of drainpipes, holes in the ground, furiously multiplying weeds, hunks of granite, stacks of more or less heavy matter which must be moved from one point to the other, usually uphill.

How will I handle it? Only time, which does not by any means tell everything, will tell.

THIS is another evening, later in the year. My parents have returned yet once again from the north. It is fall, the closing-down season. Like the sun my parents have their annual rhythms, which, come to think of it, are not unrelated to that simile. This is the time of the withering of the last bean plants, the faltering of the cabbages, when the final carrot must be prized from the earth, tough and whiskered and forked like a mandrake; when my parents make great altars of rubbish, old cardboard boxes, excess branches lopped from trees, egg cartons, who knows?—and ignite them to salute the fading sun.

But they have done all that and have made a safe journey. Now they have another revelation to make: something portentous, something momentous. Something has happened that does not happen every day.

"I was up on the roof, sweeping off the leaves—" says my mother.

"As she does every fall—" says my father.

It does not alarm me to picture my seventy-three-year-old mother clambering nimbly about on a roof, a roof with a pitch so steep that I myself would go gingerly, toes and fingers suctioned to the asphalt roofing like a tree-frog's adrenelin hazing the sky, through which I can see myself hurtling earthward after a moment of forgetfulness, a mis-step, one of those countless slips of the mind and therefore of the body about which I ought to have known better. My mother does these things all the time. She has never fallen off. She will never fall.

"Otherwise trees would grow on it," says my mother.

"And guess what she found?" says my father.

I try to guess, but I cannot. What would my mother have found on the roof? Not a pine cone, not a fungus, not a dead bird. It would not be what anyone else would find there.

In fact it turns out to be a dropping. Now I have to guess what kind of dropping.

"Flying squirrel," I hazard lamely.

No, no. Nothing so ordinary.

"It was about this big," says my father, indicating the length and the circumference. It is not an owl then.

"Brown?" I say, stalling for time.

"Black," says my father. They both regard me, heads a little on one side, eyes shining with the glee of playing this ancient game, the game of riddles, scarcely able to contain the right answer.

"And it had hair in it," says my father, as if now light will break upon me, I must surely guess.

But I am at a loss.

"Too big for a marten," says my father, hinting, waiting. Then he lowers his voice a little. "Fisher," he says.

"Really?" I say.

"Must be," says my father, and we all pause to savour the rarity of this event. There are not many fishers left, not many of those beautiful arboreal voracious predators, and we have never before found the signs of one in our area. For my father, this dropping is an interesting biological phenomenon. He has noted it and filed it, along with all the other scraps of fascinating data he notes and files.

For my mother however, this is something else. For her this dropping— this hand-long, two-fingers-thick, black, hairy dropping—not to put too fine a point on it, this deposit of animal shit—is a miraculous token, a sign of divine grace; as if their mundane, familiar, much-patched but at times still-leaking roof has been visited and made momentarily radiant by an unknown but by no means minor god.

(1983)

Acknowledgments

ANDERSON, SHERWOOD: Reprinted by permission of Harold Ober Associates Incorporated. Copyright © 1921 by B. W. Huebsch, Inc. Copyright renewed 1948 by Eleanor Copenhaver Anderson.

ATWOOD, MARGARET: "This Is a Photograph of Me" and "Progressive Insanities of a Pioneer" from *Selected Poems* © Margaret Atwood 1976. "You Begin" and "Burned Space" from *Two-Headed Poems* © Margaret Atwood 1978. "Interlunar" from *Interlunar* © Margaret Atwood 1984. Reprinted by permission of Oxford University Press Canada. "Unearthing Suite" from *Bluebeard's Egg* by Margaret Atwood. Reprinted by permission of McClelland and Stewart Limited.

AUDEN, W. H.: Reprinted by permission of Faber and Faber Limited from *Collected Poems* by W. H. Auden.

BARTH, JOHN: "Lost in the Funhouse" by John Barth, copyright © 1967 by The Atlantic Monthly Company. Reprinted from the book *Lost in the Funhouse* by permission of Doubleday & Company, Inc.

"BEOWULF": Translated by Michael Alexander (Penguin Classics, 1973). Copyright © Michael Alexander, 1973—pages 51–53 and 73–76. Reprinted by permission of Penguin Books Ltd.

BIRNEY, EARLE: "Vancouver Lights," "Bushed," "The Bear on the Delhi Road," and "Alaska Passage" from *Ghost in the Wheels* by Earle Birney. Reprinted by permission of McClelland and Stewart Limited.

BROWNING, ROBERT: "Soliloquy of the Spanish Cloister," "My Last Duchess," and "The Bishop Orders His Tomb at Saint Praxed's Church" from *Robert Browning: The Poems* (Volume One) by Robert Browning. Reprinted by permission of Yale University Press.

BURNS, ROBERT: From *Burns: Poems and Songs,* 1969. Reprinted by permission of Oxford University Press.

BYRON, GEORGE GORDON, LORD: From *The Poetical Works of Byron,* 1975, published by Houghton Mifflin Company.

"CAEDMON'S HYMN" and "THE WANDERER": Reprinted by permission of Faber and Faber Limited from *A Choice of Anglo-Saxon Verse* translated by Richard Hamer.

CAMPION, THOMAS: "My Sweetest Lesbia," "There Is a Garden in Her Face," and "Think'st Thou to Seduce Me Then" from *The Works of Thomas Campion,* edited by Walter R. Davis, published by Doubleday and Company.

CARMAN, BLISS: "Low Tide on Grand Pré" from *The Poems of Bliss Carman.* Reprinted by permission of McClelland and Stewart Limited.

CHAUCER, GEOFFREY: From *The Works of Geoffrey Chaucer,* second edition, edited by F. N. Robinson. Copyright © 1957 by The President and Fellows of Harvard College. Used with permission of Houghton Mifflin Company.

CHEEVER, JOHN: From *The Stories of John Cheever,* by John Cheever. Copyright © 1978 by John Cheever. Reprinted by permission of Alfred A. Knopf, Inc.

COLERIDGE, SAMUEL TAYLOR: From *Complete Poetical Works,* edited by Ernest Hartley Coleridge, 1912. Reprinted by permission of Oxford University Press.

CREELEY, ROBERT: From *The Collected Poems of Robert Creeley 1945–1975.* Reprinted by permission of the University of California Press.

CUMMINGS, E. E.: "in Just–," "O sweet spontaneous," and "Buffalo Bill's" reprinted from *Tulips & Chimneys* by E. E. Cummings by permission of Liveright Publishing Corporation. Copyright 1923, 1925 and renewed 1951, 1953 by E. E. Cummings. Copyright © 1973, 1976 by The Trustees for the E. E. Cummings Trust. Copyright © 1973, 1976 by George James Firmage. "next to of course god america i" and "since feeling is first" reprinted from *Is 5* poems by E. E. Cummings by permission of Liveright Publishing Corporation. Copyright 1926 by Horace Liveright. Copyright © 1954 by E. E. Cummings. Copyright © 1985 by George James Firmage.

DEWDNEY, CHRISTOPHER: "The Drawing Out of Colour," "In the Critical Half Light," and "The Song of Remote Control" from *Predators of The Adoration: Selected Poems 1972–82.* Reprinted by permission of McClelland and Stewart Limited.

DICKINSON, EMILY: Reprinted by permission of the publishers and the Trustees of Amherst College from *The Poems of Emily Dickinson,* edited by Thomas H. Johnson, Cambridge, Mass.: The Belknap Press of Harvard University Press, Copyright 1951, © 1955, 1979, 1983 by The President and Fellows of Harvard College.

DONNE, JOHN: From *The Complete English Poems,* edited by A. J. Smith, published by Penguin Books Ltd.

DRYDEN, JOHN: "Mac Flecknoe" from *The Works of John Dryden, Volume II, Poems 1681–1684,* edited by H. T. Swedenberg, Jr. Reprinted by permission of the University of California Press.

ELIOT, T. S.: Reprinted by permission of Faber and Faber Limited from *Collected Poems 1909–1962* by T. S. Eliot.

ELKIN, STANLEY: From *Criers and Kibitzers, Kibitzers and Criers,* by Stanley Elkin. Copyright © 1965 by Stanley Elkin. Reprinted by permission of Random House, Inc.

FAULKNER, WILLIAM: "A Rose for Emily" copyright 1930 and renewed 1958 by William Faulkner. Reprinted from *Collected Stories of William Faulkner* by permission of Alfred A. Knopf, Inc.

FERLINGHETTI, LAWRENCE: "In Goya's greatest scenes," "Sailing thru the straits of Demos," and "The world is a beautiful place" from *A Coney Island of the Mind.* Copyright © 1958 by Lawrence Ferlinghetti. Reprinted by permission of New Directions Publishing Corporation.

FROST, ROBERT: From *The Poetry of Robert Frost,* edited by Edward Connery Lathem. Reprinted by permission of the Estate of Robert Frost and Jonathan Cape Ltd.

GALLANT, MAVIS: Reprinted by permission of Georges Borchardt, Inc. and the author. Copyright © 1979 by Mavis Gallant.

GASS, WILLIAM: From *In the Heart of the Heart of the Country,* by William Gass. Copyright © 1958, 1961, 1962, 1967, 1968 by William Gass. Reprinted by permission of David R. Godine, Publisher, Boston.

GRAY, THOMAS: From *The Complete Poems of Thomas Gray,* 1966. Reprinted by permission of Oxford University Press.

HAWTHORNE, NATHANIEL: From *The House of the Seven Gables and the Snow Image and Other Twice-Told Tales,* 1883, published by Houghton Mifflin Company.

HEANEY, SEAMUS: "Death of a Naturalist" and "Churning Day" from *Death of a Naturalist.* "North" from *North.* "An Ulster Twilight" from *Station Island.* Reprinted by permission of Faber and Faber Limited.

HEMINGWAY, ERNEST: "Hills Like White Elephants" from *The Short Stories of Ernest Hemingway.* Copyright 1927 Charles Scribner's Sons; copyright renewed 1955 Ernest Hemingway. Reprinted by permission of Charles Scribner's Sons.

HERBERT, GEORGE: From *The Works of George Herbert,* 1941. Reprinted by permission of Oxford University Press.

HERRICK, ROBERT: From *The Poetical Works of Robert Herrick,* 1956. Reprinted by permission of Oxford University Press.

HODGINS, JACK: "The Trench Dwellers" from *Spit Delaney's Island* by Jack Hodgins. Reprinted by permission of Macmillan of Canada, A Division of Canada Publishing Corporation.

HOOD, HUGH: From *None Genuine Without This Signature.* Reprinted by permission of ECW Press.

HOUSMAN, A. E.: From *Collected Poems.* Reprinted by permission of The Society of Authors as the literary representative of the Estate of A. E. Housman and Jonathan Cape Ltd., publishers of A. E. Housman's *Collected Poems.*

HUGHES, TED: "View of a Pig" from *Lupercal.* "Examination at the Womb-Door" from *Crow.* Reprinted by permission of Faber and Faber Ltd.

JONSON, BEN: From *Ben Jonson: The Complete Poems.* Reprinted by permission of Yale University Press.

JOYCE, JAMES: From *Dubliners* by James Joyce. Copyright 1916 by B. W. Huebsch. Definitive text Copyright © 1967 by the Estate of James Joyce. Reprinted by permission of Viking Penguin Inc.

KEATS, JOHN: From *The Poetical Works of John Keats,* 1939. Reprinted by permission of Oxford University Press.

KLEIN, A. M.: "Portrait of the Poet as Landscape," "The Rocking Chair," and "Psalm XXVII" from *The Collected Poems of A. M. Klein.* Reprinted by permission of McGraw-Hill Ryerson Limited.

KROETSCH, ROBERT: "Stone Hammer Poem" and "Seed Catalogue, Section I" from *Field Notes* by Robert Kroetsch. Reprinted by permission of Stoddart Publishing, A Division of General Publishing Co. Limited, Toronto, Canada.

LAURENCE, MARGARET: "A Bird in the House" from *A Bird in the House.* Reprinted by permission of McClelland and Stewart Limited.

LAWRENCE, D. H.: From *The Collected Short Stories of D. H. Lawrence.* Reprinted by permission of Laurence Pollinger and the Estate of Mrs. Frieda Lawrence Ravagli.

LAYTON, IRVING: "Whatever Else Poetry Is Freedom," "A Tall Man Executes a Jig," "The Cold Green Element," and "Butterfly on Rock" from *The Darkening Fire: Selected Poems 1945–1968.* Reprinted by permission of McClelland and Stewart Limited.

LEVERTOV, DENISE: "O Taste and See" from *Poems 1960–1967.* Copyright © 1964 by Denise Levertov Goodman. Reprinted by permission of New Directions Publishing Corporation. "Prayer for Revolutionary Love" and "The Way It Is" from *The Freeing of the Dust.* Copyright © 1975 by Denise Levertov. Reprinted by permission of New Directions Publishing Corporation.

LIVESAY, DOROTHY: "Green Rain," "Autumn: 1939," and "The Three Emily's" from *Collected Poems: The Two Seasons.* Reprinted by permission of McGraw-Hill Ryerson Limited.

LOVELACE, RICHARD: From *The Poems of Richard Lovelace,* 1930. Reprinted by permission of Oxford University Press.

MAC PHERSON, JAY: "The Boatman," "Absence, Havoc," and "Words Failing" from *Poems Twice Told* by Jay MacPherson, © Oxford University Press Canada 1981.

MANSFIELD, KATHERINE: "The Fly" from *The Short Stories of Katherine Mansfield,* published by Alfred A. Knopf. Inc.

MARVELL, ANDREW: From *The Poems and Letters of Andrew Marvell,* 1952. Reprinted by permission of Oxford University Press.

MEDIEVAL BALLADS: From *The Oxford Book of Ballads,* edited by James Kinsley, 1969. Reprinted by permission of Oxford University Press.

MELVILLE, HERMAN: From *Selected Writings of Herman Melville,* published by Random House, Inc.

METCALF, JOHN: From *The Lady Who Sold Furniture.* Reprinted by permission of ECW Press.

MIDDLE ENGLISH LYRICS: From *The Oxford Book of Medieval English Verse,* edited by Celia and Kenneth Sisam, 1970. Reprinted by permission of Oxford University Press.

MILLER, ARTHUR: *Death of a Salesman* copyright 1949, renewed © 1977 by Arthur Miller. Reprinted by permission of Viking Penguin Inc. (See cautionary notice on page 653.)

MILTON, JOHN: Reprinted with permission of the publisher, Bobbs-Merrill Educational Publishing Company, Inc., from Milton, *Complete Poems and Major Prose,* edited by Merritt Y. Hughes © 1957, Odyssey Press (Bobbs-Merrill).

MUNRO, ALICE: "Who Do You Think You Are?" copyright © 1978 by Alice Munro. All rights reserved. Reprinted by permission of the author. The story is included in the collection entitled *Who Do You Think You Are?* (Macmillan of Canada) in Canada and in the collection entitled *The Beggar Maid* in the U.S. (Knopf or Penguin) and in the U.K. (Penguin).

O'CONNOR, FLANNERY: Copyright 1953 by Flannery O'Connor; renewed 1981 by Regina O'Connor. Reprinted from *A Good Man Is Hard to Find and Other Stories* by Flannery O'Connor by permission of Harcourt Brace Jovanovich, Inc.

ONDAATJE, MICHAEL: " 'The gate in his head,' " "King Kong meets Wallace Stevens," "White Dwarfs," and "Letters & Other Worlds" © Michael Ondaatje from *There's a Trick with a Knife I'm Learning to Do: Poems 1963–1978* (McClelland and Stewart) 1980, Toronto. Reprinted by permission of the author.

PLATH, SYLVIA: From *Ariel,* by Sylvia Plath, published by Faber and Faber, London, copyright Ted Hughes 1965. Reprinted by permission of Olwyn Hughes.

POPE, ALEXANDER: From *The Poems of Alexander Pope,* 1963. Reprinted by permission of Methuen & Co.

PORTER, KATHERINE ANNE: From *The Leaning Tower and Other Stories,* copyright 1944, 1972 by Katherine Anne Porter. Reprinted by permission of Harcourt Brace Jovanovich, Inc.

POUND, EZRA: "The Return" and "In a Station of the Metro" from *Personae.* Copyright 1926 by Ezra Pound. Reprinted by permission of New Directions Publishing Corporation. "Canto I" from *The Cantos of Ezra Pound.* Copyright 1934 by Ezra Pound. Reprinted by permission of New Directions Publishing Corporation.

PRATT, E. J.: Reprinted by permission of University of Toronto Press.

PURDY, AL: "The Country North of Belleville" and "Song of the Impermanent Husband" from *Being Alive.* "Piling Blood" from *Piling Blood.* Reprinted by permission of McClelland and Stewart Limited.

REANEY, JAMES: "Antichrist as a Child," "The Red Heart" and "The Alphabet" from *Poems* by James Reaney, copyright © 1972. Reprinted by permission of Press Porcépic Limited and the author.

RICHLER, MORDECAI: "Playing Ball on Hampstead Heath" from *St. Urbain's Horseman.* Reprinted by permission of McClelland and Stewart, The Canadian Publishers.

ROETHKE, THEODORE: "Old Florist" by Theodore Roethke, copyright 1946 by Harper & Bros.; "My Papa's Waltz" by Theodore Roethke, copyright 1942 by Hearst Magazines, Inc.; "I Knew a Woman" by Theodore Roethke, copyright 1954 by Theodore Roethke; "In a Dark Time" by Theodore Roethke, copyright © 1960 by Beatrice Roethke as Administratrix of the Estate of Theodore Roethke. Reprinted from *The Collected Poems of Theodore Roethke* by permission of Doubleday & Co., Inc.

RYGA, GEORGE: *The Ecstasy of Rita Joe* reprinted by permission of the author and Talon Books Ltd.

SCOTT, F. R.: "March Field," "Trans Canada," and "On the Terrace, Quebec" from *The Collected Poems of F. R. Scott.* Reprinted by permission of McClelland and Stewart Limited.

SEXTON, ANNE: "The Children," "Riding the Elevator into the Sky," and "The Rowing Endeth" from *The Awful Rowing Toward God* by Anne Sexton. Copyright © 1975 by Loring Conant, Jr., Executor of the Estate of Anne Sexton. Reprinted by permission of Houghton Mifflin Company.

SHAKESPEARE, WILLIAM: *Hamlet Prince of Denmark* from *The Pelican Shakespeare,* edited by Willard Farnham. Copyright © 1957, 1970 by Penguin Books Ltd. Reprinted by permission of Viking Penguin Inc. Selections from *The Sonnets* from *The Pelican Shakespeare,* edited by Douglas Bush and Alfred Harbage. Copyright © 1961, 1970 by Penguin Books Ltd. Reprinted by permission of Viking Penguin Inc.

SHELLEY, PERCY BYSSHE: From *The Complete Works of Percy Bysshe Shelley,* 1926–30. Reprinted by permission of Gordian Press.

SIDNEY, SIR PHILIP: From *The Poems of Sir Philip Sidney,* 1962. Reprinted by permission of Oxford University Press.

SMITH, A. J. M.: "The Lonely Land," "Swift Current," "News of the Phoenix," "Noctambule," "The Archer," and "The Wisdom of Old Jelly Roll" from *A. J. M. Smith Poems: New and Collected.* Reprinted by permission of McClelland and Stewart Limited.

SPENSER, EDMUND: Reprinted from *Edmund Spenser's Poetry,* A Norton Critical Edition, Selected and Edited by Hugh Maclean, by permission of W. W. Norton & Company, Inc. Copyright © 1982, 1968 by W. W. Norton & Company, Inc.

STEINBECK, JOHN: "The Chrysanthemums" from *The Long Valley,* by John Steinbeck. Copyright 1938, renewed © 1966 by John Steinbeck. Reprinted by permission of Viking Penguin Inc.

STEVENS, WALLACE: Copyright 1923 and renewed 1951 by Wallace Stevens. Reprinted from *The Collected Poems of Wallace Stevens,* by permission of Alfred A. Knopf, Inc.

TENNYSON, ALFRED, LORD: From *The Poems of Tennyson,* edited by Christopher Ricks. Reprinted by permission of Longman House.

THOMAS, AUDREY: "Natural History" from *Real Mothers,* by Audrey Thomas. Reprinted by permission of Talon Books Ltd.

THOMAS, DYLAN: From *Collected Poems.* Reprinted by permission of JM Dent.

UPDIKE, JOHN: Copyright © 1972 by John Updike. Reprinted from *Problems and Other Stories,* by John Updike, by permission of Alfred A. Knopf, Inc.

WEBB, PHYLLIS: "Marvell's Garden," "Breaking," and "A Question of Questions" from *The Vision Tree: Selected Poems,* by Phyllis Webb. Reprinted by permission of Talon Books Ltd.

WELTY, EUDORA: Copyright 1941, 1969 by Eudora Welty. Reprinted from her volume *A Curtain of Green and Other Stories* by permission of Harcourt Brace Jovanovich, Inc.

WHITMAN, WALT: "Song of Myself" (lines 1–81), "Out of the Cradle Endlessly Rocking," and "The Dalliance of the Eagles" from *Leaves of Grass,* by Walt Whitman. Reprinted by permission of New York University Press.

WIEBE, RUDY: "Where Is the Voice Coming From?" from *Where Is the Voice Coming From?* by Rudy Wiebe. Reprinted by permission of Rudy Wiebe and McClelland and Stewart Limited.

WILLIAMS, WILLIAM CARLOS: "Spring and All," "The Poor," "The Red Wheelbarrow," and "This Is Just to Say" from *Collected Earlier Poems.* Copyright 1938 by New Directions Publishing Corporation. Reprinted by permission of New Directions Publishing Corporation. "The Dance" from *Collected Later Poems.* Copyright 1944 by William Carlos Williams. Reprinted by permission of New Directions Publishing Corporation.

WORDSWORTH, WILLIAM: From *Poetical Works,* 1971. Reprinted by permission of Oxford University Press.

YEATS, W.B.: From *Collected Poems of W. B. Yeats.* Reprinted by permission of Michael B. Yeats and Macmillan London, Ltd.

Index of Authors, Titles, and First Lines